DETAIL FROM "MID DAY AT THE BELL INN" BY GEORGE MORLAND

MASTERS OF THE ART

Not only successful brewers, the Morlands also boasted an illustrious painter in the family. George Morland (1763-1804), became a noted painter of rustic Georgian English life. Indeed, he was a welcome and frequent guest at the family's pubs - often settling his bill with a masterly-drawn sketch. It was in tribute to him that the now familiar "sign of the artist" was originated, honouring both the painter's and the brewer's art.

DOG HOUSE HOTEL, FRILFORD HEATH, OXON

AN OUTSTANDING PORTFOLIO OF BEERS

From our flagship ale "Old Speckled Hen" to the distinctive "Morland Original Bitter," our fine family of beers are brewed with exceptional care and great enthusiasm by people proud to carry on the tradition begun so many years ago.

You'll find several Morland pubs in this Guide. Pay one a visit for a real taste of English history.

Egon Ronay's Guides
35 Tadema Road
London SW10 0PZ

Editorial Director **Andrew Eliel**
Publishing Director **Angela Nicholson**
Sales & Marketing Director **Stephen Prendergast**

Chairman **Roy Ackerman**
Leading Guides Ltd
Part of the Richbell Group of Companies

The contents of this book are believed correct at the time of printing. Nevertheless, the publisher can accept no responsibility for errors or omissions or changes in the details given.

ISBN 1 898718 80 6

Designed and typeset in Great Britain by Paul Fry, Bookman Projects Ltd.

First published 1995 by Bookman Projects Ltd.
Floor 22
1 Canada Square
Canary Wharf
London E14 5AP

Establishments are independently researched or inspected. Inspections are anonymous and carried out by Egon Ronay's Guides team of professional inspectors. They may reveal their identities at hotels in order to check all the rooms and other facilities. The Guide is independent in its editorial selection and does not accept advertising, payment or hospitality from listed establishments.

Egon Ronay's Guides Pub Awards

This year's award winners are presented here. Full details of the recipients can be found on the pages indicated.

14 Hoste Arms
Burnham Market
Pub of the Year

16 Olde Coach House
Ashby St Ledgers
Family Pub of the Year

18 Carrington Arms
Moulsoe
Pub Newcomer of the Year

20 The Pierhouse
Port Appin
Pub Hosts of the Year

22 Sun Inn
Winforton
Ploughman's of the Year

Full Contents: Page 4

CONTENTS

Introduction

Our gastronomic peregrinations sometimes seem endless as we wend our way through the ever-expanding minefield of pub food. Boil-in-the-bag ready-prepared dishes, bulk tubs of curry sauces, tasteless frozen puff pastry pie lids, exotic (and often excruciatingly horrible) dishes – convenience is the name of the game and we have to find where the corners are being cut. We don't expect home-baked bread, freshly-curled butter, daily fresh fish and spot-on service everywhere we go, but there *are* places that offer these standards and they stand head and shoulders above the crowd. The *Otter Inn* at Weston in Devon sums it up on its menu: 'We do not serve fast food. We serve food as fast as we can'.

Not a Restaurant Guide

This is not a Guide to pub restaurants. Last year we noted that more and more people were visiting pubs to eat; they were expecting restaurant-quality food at cheaper prices but were being disappointed by the lack of proper service, minimal 'trappings' and, in many cases, kitchens that simply could not cope at peak times. Complaints continue to pour in depicting stroppy landlords, amateur waitering, poor wine, cold food and so on; one reader wrote: 'the food was perfectly acceptable and the helpings were exceedingly generous but none of this could compensate for the appalling service and disagreeable atmosphere'.

We urge our readers to be wary of half-board terms offered by B&B pubs, inns and hotels where they might be steered into the dining-room at night for poorly-produced and over-priced meals that are badly served. Recommendations in this Guide are for bar food only unless specifically stated otherwise (ie we say 'also recommended in our *1996 Hotels and Restaurants Guide*'); we have removed all opening and closing times for restaurants to avoid confusion. When booking, ask if the pub offers two distinct menus in two distinct dining areas – many of the very best (and best-value) places in this Guide now offer one menu throughout (and not just at Sunday lunchtimes). For example, the *Pheasant* at Keyston in Cambridgeshire is a shining light, its inviting menu inscribed with this inducement: 'please feel free to eat as much or as little as you like'. A handful of places will not serve bar food in the evenings – once again, check before you arrive; similarly, if perhaps you are celebrating or doing business and want to eat in the more comfortable dining areas, some pubs do not open their smarter 'restaurants' at lunchtimes. Food is taken very seriously in 'dining pubs' and we try to highlight these types of establishment (like the *Old Barn* in Glooston, Leicestershire and the *Angel Inn* at Long Crendon in Buckinghamshire) in our stories.

Sunday Opening

The new licensing laws governing Sunday pub trading hours seem to have been greeted as a mixed blessing by many licensees we have spoken to during our research for this Guide. Most kitchens of the pubs listed in the Guide are already running at full speed and the thought of opening all day on Sunday is anathema to them; their kitchen staff deserve a break after a hectic Sunday lunch session. Other pubs – many recommended for atmosphere only – are taking every opportunity to increase their weekly bar takings (particularly in summer and in busy tourist areas) and have welcomed the longer licensing hours. The majority of pubs in this Guide have told us that they will not be opening all day on Sunday, although many had not yet made a final decision one way or the other; however, some will doubtless open for the odd extra hour here or there, perhaps at the end of a busy winter Sunday lunch when the fires are still glowing and the booze is still flowing, or on early summer evenings when the local cricket match has come to an early finish and sorrows need to be drowned! Sunday opening hours listed in the statistics at the end of each entry in the Guide should therefore be taken only as a rough guide.

Real Ales & Real Food

Our new beer symbol highlights those pubs where an unusual or above-average selection of real ales is offered. Micro breweries are currently a healthy area of expansion within the pub business and the list below details some pubs where the ales are actually brewed on the premises or nearby. If you're in Hereford & Worcester, why not pop into the *Moody Cow* for a pint of the appropriately named Raging Bull bitter?

Great Brew Pubs & Brewery Taps:

Cumbria, Cartmel Fell: *Masons Arms*
Cumbria, Hesket Newmarket: *Old Crown*
Devon, Hatherleigh: *Tally Ho*
Devon, Horsebridge: *Royal Inn*
Essex, Tillingham: *Cap & Feathers*
Greater Manchester, Manchester: *Lass O'Gowrie*
Hampshire, Cheriton: *Flower Pots*
Hereford & Worcester, Upton Bishop: *Moody Cow*
Hertfordshire, Barley: *Fox & Hounds*
Leicestershire, Somerby: *Old Brewery Inn* (Parish Brewery)
London SE5, Denmark Hill: *Phoenix & Firkin*
London SW1, Pimlico: *Orange Brewery*
West Midlands, Langley: *Brewery Inn* (Holt's Entire)
Norfolk, Woodbastwick: *Fur & Feather* (Woodforde's)
Staffordshire, Eccleshall: *St George Hotel* (Slater's Ales)
Suffolk, Southwold: *The Crown* (Adnams)
West Sussex, Oving: *Gribble Inn*
Borders (Scotland), Innerleithen: *Traquair Arms*
Jersey (Channel Islands), St Peter's Village: *Star & Tipsy Toad Brewery*

Many landlords go out of their way to source particularly interesting real ales and we have found real ales brewed using wheat, honey, ginger, coriander seeds, chocolate, raspberry, garlic, and even chili this year! Regularly-changing 'guest beers' are often where the real interest lies and many of the country's smallest brewers are well represented in this Guide. Look out for Teignworthy and Sharp's (see entries under Gunwalloe, Constantine and Lostwithiel) in the West Country (Devon and Cornwall); Goddard's on the Isle of Wight *(Seaview Hotel)*; Brewery-on-Sea in West Sussex (Brighton, *The Greys*); Stanway and Wickwar (both at the *Bakers Arms*, Broad Campden) plus Freeminer (Gwent, Lydart, *Gockett Inn*) in Gloucestershire; Hobson's in Shropshire (Much Wenlock, *Wenlock Edge Inn*); Weetwood (Tarporley, *Swan Hotel*) in Cheshire; Oakham in Leicestershire (Braunston, *Old Plough*); and lastly, Lastingham (Haltwhistle, *Milecastle Inn*) and Hexamshire (Hexham, *Dipton Mill Inn*) in Northumberland.

The *White Hart* in Ford, Wiltshire is a typical example of one of our recommended pubs where you'll find not only good food and good overnight accommodation but also a choice of up to 11 real ales – enough to make a weekend go with a swing! Similarly, the *Crown Inn* in Old Dalby, Leicestershire offers a choice of up to 14 real ales to sup while enjoying a game of pétanque or sampling their ambitious bar food.

London Renaissance

Pub premises are constantly being converted in the main towns and cities around the country; many are becoming popular bars for niche markets (sports, bare boards and music, students, women or Irish-themed). In London, however, a bevy of niche 'food' pubs have opened in the last year; they all aim to serve superior quality food, in the very successful fashion of *The Eagle* and *The Peasant*. These newcomers include *The Engineer* (which joins *The Lansdowne* in Primrose Hill); the *Chelsea Ram* and *Jim Thompson's* in Chelsea; and *The Westbourne, Prince Bonaparte* and *The Cow* in Westbourne Grove. Of this new breed, we found the *Chelsea Ram, The Westbourne* and *The Engineer* (probably the best of the new bunch) to be agreeably star-worthy; some, however, can be a bit of a bun fight for a seat where you can eat in comfort.

Family Friendly?

Applications by landlords for Children's Certificates have produced such varying responses from local magistrates that the certificate itself cannot yet be considered as an exclusive pointer to family-friendly pubs. Families *are* good business and publicans continue to invest in facilities that attract them – from wooden adventure playgrounds in the back garden to massive, pay-as-you-enter 'fun factories' being built by the big breweries who are investing heavily and expanding their family theme pub chains.

The family symbol ☺ in this Guide means that children are usually welcome inside the pub and that there are often a children's menu and other facilities indoors. Children are generally allowed in the bar to eat unless we specifically mention otherwise; a bar-less 'family room' is usually made available when there are restrictions in the dispensing bar itself; we have tried to distinguish pubs where families can enjoy a drink without feeling obliged to eat. Restrictions on children often apply in the evening in dining-rooms and restaurants. A solid section of pubs in this Guide do not welcome children (often the pubs are too small and run a very busy food operation) and have stated their case to us during our research; where their attitude is known we spell it out.

Our list of starred pubs will direct you to those pubs serving the very best bar food available in this country; should you find otherwise (or further pubs that are outstanding) then please write and tell us about your experiences using the Readers' Comments forms at the back of this Guide. If you do not receive satisfaction then, please, always complain at the time of your meal – this is the best way to allow the establishment to recompense you and to try to improve standards. In response to hundreds of letters that we receive every year, please note that we do *not* recommend the food in establishments with a B&B or A category only; where one of our wall plaques is displayed it clearly shows what our current recommendation is for.

Finally, we are delighted to welcome brewers Morland & Co as sponsors of this Guide with their 'famous Old Speckled Hen' – one of the country's leading cask-conditioned ales. Morland's involvement reflects the importance of real ale as a major attraction in the vast majority of pubs and inns that we recommend within these pages, and also the growing popularity of Old Speckled Hen as one of the most widely stocked guest beers. Look out for Old Speckled Hen – you'll find it regularly available at pubs in this Guide all around England (particularly near Morland's brewery in Abingdon, Oxfordshire) and even – as a guest beer – in Northern Ireland (*The Hillsdown Bar* in Hillsborough, Co Down) and Scotland (*Tweeddale Arms* in Gifford, Lothian).

Foreword

Congratulations on choosing Egon Ronay's "Old Speckled Hen" Guide, 1996 Pubs & Inns, the definitive guide to the best pubs and inns in Great Britain and Northern Ireland. While seeking out the pleasures and traditional qualities which are to be found in Britain's finest pubs, you will discover the delightful uniqueness of our country's heritage and hospitality.

What could be more fitting than to celebrate the best of British pubs with the help of one of the country's most celebrated ales? Morland's "Old Speckled Hen" is an established leader in its market, and is appreciated as a truly classic beer with a unique smoothness and subtle blend of flavours. Our advertising encourages drinkers to *hunt for perfection* in their choice of ale. When using Egon Ronay's "Old Speckled Hen" Guide, 1996 Pubs & Inns, you too will find perfection – pub perfection.

As the second oldest independent brewer in the country, Morland has spent 285 years producing fine traditional ales which provide pubs with an essential ingredient for the pub enthusiast – quality British beer. We are delighted to be associated with this year's Guide and to be supporting the best of Britain's pubs.

Happy hunting.

Mike Watts

Michael Watts,
Chief Executive
MORLAND PLC

The story behind "Old Speckled Hen."

"Old Speckled Hen" was destined to be associated with the best things Britain has to offer. The history of its name stretches back to 1927. In that year, MG produced a unique prototype saloon car. Canvas covered, painted gold and flecked with black, it was eventually used as a factory run-around vehicle – fondly called the "old speckled 'un" by locals in the town of Abingdon. Typical of names passed by word of mouth, this changed over time to the "old speckled hen".

As the 50th anniversary of the Abingdon factory approached, MG asked Morland, the established brewers in the town, to produce a special traditional ale to celebrate the occasion. Morland linked their ale to MG by naming it "Old Speckled Hen".

"Old Speckled Hen" is a pale ale which owes its distinctive character and dry taste to a unique strain of yeast, first used in 1896. The individual blend of flavours reflects skills developed over 285 years of independent brewing history.

Today "Old Speckled Hen" is an established premium traditional ale in Britain's beer market – an ale with a flavour as unique as the vintage car it is named after.

The brand is supported by a distinctive national advertising campaign. The advertisements are drawn in 19th century "Punch" magazine style, and feature a robust, yet very gentlemanly, fox – hunting for perfection!

For further information, phone the Morland Sales Office (01235) 540447.

"Old Speckled Hen"

How To Use This Guide

Order of Entries

London appears first and is in alphabetical order by establishment name. Listings outside London are in alphabetical order by location within divisions of England, Scotland, Wales, Channel Islands (inc the Isle of Man) and Northern Ireland. See contents page and the index for specific page numbers.

Map References

Map references alongside each pub entry are to the map section at the back of the Guide. Use this to select establishments in the area that you wish to visit.

Good Bar Food

We include establishments where our team of professional inspectors found good-quality **Bar Food**. Such pubs and inns are indicated by the symbol FOOD printed in the margin alongside the entry. No mention is made of a pub's separate restaurant operation unless one menu is served throughout the pub's dining areas or if the restaurant is also recommended in *Egon Ronay's Cellnet Guide 1996 Hotels & Restaurants*.

Dishes listed are meant to be typical of the pub's style and not a definitive menu description. We indicate when bar food is served and also any times when food is not available. Meal times in recommended restaurants may differ from bar food times. If there is an outdoor eating area we include this information in the statistics. Pubs serving outstanding bar food are indicated by a ★ alongside their name (see additional list of Starred Pubs on page 12).

Good Accommodation

We also inspect accommodation, and those pubs and inns recommended for an overnight stay are indicated by the symbol B&B in the margin alongside the entry. We list the number of bedrooms, the price for an en-suite double bedroom (with bath rather than shower where available) and a full cooked breakfast for two, and whether children are welcome overnight. Very occasionally the price of a cooked breakfast is not included but we have indicated where this is the case. 'Single' room prices do not always refer to single rooms as they may often refer to single occupancy of a double room.

We assume that it is possible to check-in all day; where this is not the case (and thus advisable to arrange a time when booking) we print check-in by arrangement. General accommodation closures around Christmas are not mentioned as these are so variable; however, if there is a regular period during the year that a pub is traditionally closed (say for staff holidays) then we list that information.

We have assigned a 'Sleep' symbol Zzz... to those pubs and inns that we consider offer particularly comfortable and/or quiet accommodation.

Pubs with Atmosphere

Pubs recommended for being particularly atmospheric, pleasant or interesting places in which to enjoy a drink (rather than the bar food or accommodation) are indicated by the symbol A alongside their entry. Interestingly-located pubs and those with particularly good real ales (micro-brewery pubs, for example) are also highlighted by the A symbol. All the pubs are clearly recommended for either Food FOOD, Accommodation B&B or Atmosphere A. Every year we get dozens of complaints about the food served in pubs where we do not recommend it; we urge readers to differentiate clearly between our recommendations.

Opening Hours

We have tried to ascertain from landlords their general opening hours; however, these should not be taken as firm times and readers should certainly assume that longer hours might apply in summer and shorter in winter. In particular, following the recent change in Sunday Licensing laws, Sunday opening hours may change from those times we have listed.

Beer
We indicate whether an establishment is a Free House (ie not owned by a brewery), and list the names of a number of regular real ales that were being offered when we last contacted the pub. These are often likely to change and should not be taken as permanent offers. Our new Beer symbol 🍺 indicates that an unusual or interesting range of beers is usually on offer – these may be micro-brewery pubs or 'brewery taps'.

Children Welcome
Entries indicate whether the pub has facilities suitable for families; those that offer a good combination of the facilities (perhaps where children are allowed in the bar to eat or where there's a special children's menu, a family room or an indoor/outdoor play area) are marked by the 'Family' symbol ☺. See also listings in the County Round-Up at the back of the Guide. If there is no mention of family facilities then readers should assume that the pub does not welcome children. Children may well be charged extra for breakfast if sharing their parents' bedroom free of charge overnight.

Credit Cards
We list credit cards accepted and also note those pubs which accept none. Occasionally, credit cards may only be accepted for accommodation and not for bar food.

Symbols

★	**Outstanding Bar Food**
ZZz...	**Particularly comfortable and/or quiet Accommodation**
🧀	**Good selection of British Cheeses**
☺	**Suitable for families**
🍺	**Particularly good or unusual range of real ales**
🍷	**Half a dozen or more wines served by the glass in the bar**

Starred Pubs 1996

London
EC1, Farringdon **The Eagle**
NW1, Clerkenwell **The Peasant**
NW1, Primrose Hill **The Engineer**
NW1, Primrose Hill **The Lansdowne**
SW10, Chelsea **Chelsea Ram**
W2, Westbourne Grove **The Westbourne**

England
Berkshire, West Ilsley **Harrow Inn**
Buckinghamshire, Long Crendon **The Angel**
Cambridgeshire, Keyston **Pheasant Inn**
Cambridgeshire, Madingley **Three Horseshoes**
Cambridgeshire, Wansford-in-England **The Haycock**
Cheshire, Higher Burwardsley **The Pheasant**
Cornwall, Gunwalloe **Halzephron Inn**
Cumbria, Cartmel Fell **Masons Arms**
Cumbria, Crosthwaite **Punch Bowl**
Cumbria, Ulverston **Bay Horse Inn**
Devon, Kingsteignton **Old Rydon Inn**
Devon, Rockbeare **Jack in the Green**
Devon, Trusham **Cridford Inn**
Dorset, Corscombe **Fox Inn**
Durham, Romaldkirk **Rose and Crown**
Essex, Horndon-on-the-Hill **Bell Inn**
Gloucestershire, Coln St Aldwyns **New Inn**
Gloucestershire, Great Rissington **The Lamb**
Hampshire, Winchester **Wykeham Arms**
Hereford & Worcester, Brimfield **The Roebuck**
Hereford & Worcester, Winforton **Sun Inn**
Kent, Ightham Common **Harrow Inn**
Kent, Ivy Hatch **The Plough**
Lancashire, Lydgate **White Hart**
Norfolk, Burnham Market **Hoste Arms**
Northumberland, Warenford **Warenford Lodge**
Oxfordshire, Bledington **King's Head Inn**
Oxfordshire, Cumnor **Bear & Ragged Staff**
Somerset, Batcombe **Batcombe Inn**
Somerset, Beckington **Woolpack Inn**
Somerset, Monksilver **Notley Arms**
Suffolk, Southwold **Crown**
Suffolk, Stoke-by-Nayland **Angel Inn**
Surrey, Grayswood **Wheatsheaf Inn**
West Sussex, Lower Beeding **Jeremy's at The Crabtree**
West Sussex, Midhurst **Angel Hotel**
North Yorkshire, Hetton **Angel Inn**
North Yorkshire, Saxton **Plough Inn**
North Yorkshire, Wass **Wombwell Arms**
West Yorkshire, Shelley **Three Acres**
Wiltshire, North Newnton **Woodbridge Inn**
Wiltshire, Rowde **George & Dragon**

Scotland
Fife, Kirkcaldy **Hoffmans**
Strathclyde, Kilberry **Kilberry Inn**

Channel Islands
Alderney, St Anne **Georgian House**

Wales
Gwent, Clydach **Drum & Monkey**
Powys, Llyswen **Griffin Inn**

Northern Ireland
Co Down, Hillsborough **Hillside Bar**

Pubs with starred bar food
Pubs with starred bar food and accommodation
SCOTLAND
Kirkcaldy
Kilberry
Warenford
ORTHERN
ELAND
illsborough
Romaldkirk
Crosthwaite
Cartmel Fell
Ulverston
Wass
Hetton
Saxton
Shelley
Lydgate
Higher Burwardsley
Burnham Market
ENGLAND
Wansford-in-England
Southwold
WALES
Brimfield
Keyston
Madingley
Winforton
Llyswen
Bledington
Stoke-by-Nayland
Great Rissington
Clydach
Coln St Aldwyns
Cumnor
Long Crendon
Horndon-on-the-Hill
West Ilsley
LONDON
Rowde
North Newnton
Ightham Common
Beckington
Ivy Hatch
Monksilver
Batcombe
Winchester
Grayswood
Lower Beeding
Midhurst
Corscombe
Rockbeare
Trusham
Kingsteignton
Gunwalloe
Alderney
Guernsey
St Anne
FRANCE
CHANNEL ISLANDS
Jersey
Leading Guides Ltd.

Awards

Pub of the Year

Hoste Arms

Burnham Market, Norfolk

Following a century of brewery ownership and 'systematic architectural abuse', five years' labour of love has enabled Paul Whittome to create his idea of a perfect country inn. The final touch has been the recent opening of six smart new bedrooms in a converted barn and the repainting of the exterior, giving a handsome cream finish to the facade of this 17th-century village inn. Continuous improvements and upgrading have seen high standards applied to all aspects of the Hoste's operations: the keen brigade of chefs in the open-to-view kitchen; the bedrooms that show flair in design and attention to housekeeping detail; and interesting real ales are served direct from the cask in the bar. Candle-light in the evenings, weekly live jazz and displays of entirely appropriate art give the pub a classy air. Whether it be a lunchtime snack sitting in the window seat of the front bar overlooking the green or in the extensive garden, afternoon tea in the airy conservatory or a pampered overnight stay in one of the comfortable four-poster beds, there is much to admire at the Hoste Arms.

Awards

Past Winners	
1995	**The Angel** Hetton, North Yorkshire
1994	**The Lamb** Great Rissington, Gloucestershire
1993	**Rose & Crown** Romaldkirk, Co Durham
1992	**The Roebuck** Brimfield, Hereford & Worcester

Awards

Family Pub of the Year

Old Coach House

Ashby St Ledgers, Northamptonshire

Built in 1894 as a cottage farmhouse in a tiny village, this friendly (and busy) little pub is run by Brian and Philippa McCabe; they have young children of their own and understand the needs of families well. Inside you will find all the accoutrements necessary for making dining out en famille a pleasant rather than tiresome experience. The children's menu offers ubiquitous family favourites (from spaghetti bolognaise on toast and fish fingers and fresh vegetables to toffee crunch cheesequake and chocolate bread-and-butter pudding) and should satisfy most young appetites; more demanding palates might appreciate main-menu items offered in half portions (until 8pm). Children eat free during 'happy hour' between 6pm and 7pm on Friday and Saturday. High-chairs, booster seats, puzzles, crayons and baby-changing facilities (in a disabled loo) are all provided. Outside in the walled garden the McCabes have recently had built a substantial multi-purpose wooden activity centre with twin towers, climbing nets, balancing walkways and a slide for youngsters. After a hectic run-around outside children can refresh themselves with milkshakes, Lucozade and Ribena or get tucked into a banana split! Free lollipops at the bar for those who ask (and good ales for Dad!). Good-value overnight accommodation for families is also offered. Convenient for J18 of M1.

"It's my independent view that family pubs are very Good News!"

Awards

Past Winners

1995	**Batcombe Inn** Batcombe, Somerset
1994	**Bridge Inn** Ratho, Lothian, Scotland
1993	**Star Inn** Harome, North Yorkshire
1992	**Double Locks** Alphington, Exeter, Devon

Pub Newcomer of the Year

Carrington Arms

Moulsoe, Buckinghamshire

Edwin and Trudy Cheeseman moved to this lovely Grade II listed building last year, providing them with a larger stage for their most original "cooking in view" concept. Their aim is to make eating out both serious and fun at the same time, removing some of the traditional barriers that have built up between kitchen and diner. Firstly they brought the ingredients to the fore by invitingly placing fresh fish and meat in display cabinets; secondly they installed an open-to-view cooking area with a flame grill (plus steamer and smoker) at one end of the pub's opened-out interior – enabling customers to be involved in the cooking process from beginning to end, inspired by both the sight of the food and the smell of it sizzling away. Edwin also entices diners with an oyster bar, authentic Thai dishes and homely puddings; for those who over-indulge there is budget bedroom accommodation in a single-storey building overlooking the orchard-like garden. It's a slick, unusual food operation in an unexpected setting – well worth the short detour from J14 of M1.

"Always on the lookout for a rising star!"

Awards

Past Winners

1995	**Cridford Inn,** Trusham, Devon
	Halzephron Inn, Gunwalloe, Cornwall
1994	**Five Arrows Hotel,** Waddesdon, Buckinghamshire
	Fox Inn, Lower Oddington, Gloucestershire
1993	**Fox & Hounds,** Starbotton, North Yorkshire
	Woodbridge Inn, North Newnton, Wiltshire

Pub Hosts of the Year

The Macleod Family

The Pierhouse & Seafood Restaurant

Port Appin, Strathclyde, Scotland

The setting is quite superb, the seafood as fresh as you will ever find and there's a warm Scottish welcome from Alan and Sheila Macleod and their family at this unusual inn right on the water's edge of Loch Linnhe. It's a real hands-on affair, with Sheila cooking confidently in the kitchen, Alan ensuring the overall operation runs smoothly, their daughter Julie managing the bar, and energetic son Callum and girlfriend Fiona providing happy food service with a smile, a mouth-trumpet tune and a sense of humour. Picture windows in the bar and at one end of the dining-room make the most of the sensational views and evolving weather scenes playing out over the towering Morvern Hills beyond the Isle of Lismore. When the weather closes in there are warming fires, bright, interesting artwork on the walls and an inviting menu – just watching one of the family collecting live shellfish from creels at the end of the concrete pier is a mouthwatering experience! The hospitality extends to comfortable bedrooms, long bar hours and an equally long line of malt whisky bottles from which one can savour a true taste of Scotland. The Macleods honed their innkeeping skills in Glasgow hotbeds but they have settled here amid the heavenly tranquillity and offer consummate cordiality.

"Hosts of the Year, eh? That deserves a few rounds!"

Awards

Past Winners

1995 **Robert & Sally Hughes**
Penhelig Arms Hotel
Aberdovey, Gwynedd, Wales

Awards

Ploughman's of the Year

Sun Inn

Winforton, Hereford & Worcester

If you're heading west from Hereford or Leominster towards Brecon make sure to stop off at Brian and Wendy Hibbard's cosy, welcoming roadside inn for lunch (except on Tuesdays, Nov-May). Wendy's passion for food is clearly evident in the tip-top (and good-value) ploughman's lunch made with a selection of up to eight British farmhouse cheeses. These are all listed and explained on blackboards and the choice might well include 'Hereford Hop' (hard, mild and buttery, coated in toasted hops), organic Shropshire Blue (creamy, blue-veined from Colston Basset Dairy), St Illtyd (Cheddar-type with white wine, garlic and herbs), White Stilton with apricots, Pencarreg (soft and full fat with a bloomy rind), smoked and mature Cheddar, plus a 'genuine' Caerphilly and Llanboidy (firm but creamy with a natural rind, made from milk of Red Poll cows). One's selection of cheeses is served with home-made coleslaw, red cabbage cooked with cider, apples and juniper berries, a pickled onion and a small salad garnish that might even feature cherry tomatoes from their own garden; brown and white rolls are from a local bakery and unsalted butter is served in a separate dish, as are two home-made chutneys (perhaps raw tomato or apple and marrow). One may also ask for a ploughman's lunch with smooth chicken liver paté (home-made with juniper berries, cream and brandy) or ham baked with cider and honey (if they are on the daily salad menu).

Awards

Specialist Cheesemakers Association

Past Winners

1995	**Nobody Inn** Doddiscombleigh, Devon
1994	**Shepherds Inn** Melmerby, Cumbria
1993	**Down Inn** Bridgnorth, Shropshire

THE ELUSIVE ALE AT LAST IN VIEW

(and thought of the heady pleasures that await spurs them on).

London

N1 The Albion FOOD

Tel 0171-607 7450 Map 16 C2
10 Thornhill Road Islington N1 1HW

In the middle of a quiet residential part of Islington, a Georgian pub that was once a coaching inn. The front is welcoming with creeping ivy, tables and benches outside and an old-fashioned illustrated sign of a coach. The front room has plenty of tables, settles and chairs around a large wooden bar. The top part of the bar and the walls are decorated with coaching and horse-related bric-a-brac. At the back, there is a dark-panelled bar and a homely pinkish non-smoking and non-dining lounge. The lovely paved garden (unusual for London) has a weeping willow, a trellis covered with creepers and plenty of tables and chairs. Food is served throughout the afternoon and, weather permitting in the summer, there is a barbecue as an alternative menu. Excellent quality cooking (available all day) covers a simple menu of old favourites like vegetable soup, steak and kidney pie with creamed potatoes, lamb chops and mint sauce, battered fried fish and mixed grill. *Open 11-11 (Sun 12-3, 7-10.30). **Bar Food** 12-9.30. **Beer** Theakston XB & Best, John Smith's. Garden, outdoor eating. Access, Amex, Diners, Visa.*

SW18 The Alma FOOD

Tel 0181-870 2537 **Fax 0181-874 9055** Map 17 B5
499 Old York Road Wandsworth SW18 1FT

Like the others in the Charles Gotto empire (*The Ship, The Castle* and *The Coopers Arms* – see entries) the Alma is a distinctive and atmospheric pub. Conveniently located across from Wandsworth station and close to Young's brewery (but more tricky if attempting to navigate the Wandsworth one-way system by car); once there, its bright green-tiled facade and hanging flower baskets immediately stand out. In the dark wood atmosphere of the airy central room, cast-iron tables and pinball and slot-machines range around an island bar counter. At the back, the dining-room has yellow-painted walls, framed cartoons, illustrations and beautiful pieces of antique kitchen and restaurant equipment. Daylight coming through the ceiling gives a soft and comfortable feel. The bar menu offers the likes of Toulouse sausage, eggs Benedict, mussels in cider, pasta du jour and sandwiches. Other dishes might include fresh mackerel fillets hollandaise and vegetable couscous. Besides the Young's on handpump, you'll find a superb selection of up to 27 international wines offered not only by bottle but, rather unusually, also by glass; their turnover allows such a good selection to be offered without any compromising of quality. Espresso and regular coffee are also available. *Open 11-11 (Sun 12-3, 7-10.30). **Bar Food** 12-3, 7-10.45. **Beer** Young's. Access, Amex, Diners, Visa.*

SE1 The Anchor A

Tel 0171-407 1577 **Fax 0171-407 0741** Map 17 D4
34 Park Street Bankside SE1 9DN

The original Anchor was burnt down ten years after the Great Fire but the present Georgian building is atmospheric with diverse split-level bars, intimate corners, old beams, panelling and leather seating. Located south-east of Southwark Bridge; the bankside terrace overlooks the City. Good selection of draught beers. *Open 11.30-11 (Sun 12-3, 7-10.30). **Beer** Courage, Ruddles, Adnams, Anchor Bitter, Morland Old Speckled Hen, guest beer. Riverview patio. Family room. Pub closed 25 & 26 Dec. Access, Amex, Diners, Visa.*

SW3 The Australian FOOD

Tel 0171-589 3114 Map 19 C5
29 Milner Street Chelsea SW3 2QD

Cricket fans will delight in this Nicholson's pub, the name and theme of which celebrate a very early game played by the first Australian touring team in nearby Lennox Gardens. The walls are covered with pictures of famous British and Australian players, and of an evening there tends ot be a young and lively clientele. During the daytime it's also useful to know that it's a short walk from Harrods and Peter Jones and that there are a few outside tables under the ivy-covered facade facing south and taking in the sun. The bar snack menu is straightforward, ranging from Antipodean egg and bacon pie and ploughman's lunches to deep-fried cod and chili con carne, plus daily specials and freshly-cut sandwiches (eg the Australian steak sandwich with "special secret sauce" and an enormous BLT). *Open 11-11 (Sun 12-3, 7-10.30). **Bar Food** 12-2.30. **Beer** Tetley, Adnams, Eldridge Pope Thomas Hardy, guest beer. Amex, access, Visa.*

W4 Bell & Crown A

Tel 0181-994 4164 Map 17 A5
Strand on the Green Chiswick W4 3PF

With a cane, furniture-filled conservatory and two levels of tables and benches outside overlooking the river, this Thamesside pub is in a delightfully tranquil spot on the towpath. There's a new food servery at the rear and separate conservatory/family room. Get there early for a table by the towpath. *Open 11-11 (Sun 12-3, 7-10.30).* ***Beer*** *Fuller's. Patio, outdoor eating. Access, Amex, Visa.*

EC4 Black Friar A

Tel 0171-236 5650 Map 17 D4
174 Queen Victoria Street Blackfriars EC4V 8DB

Built in 1875 on the site of the Black Friar monastery, this pub has a dazzlingly distinctive art nouveau interior dating back to 1905. Bas-relief bronze representations of monks in various stages of drunkenness adorn the outside walls; inside, they are represented going about their daily tasks and indulging their habits alongside astonishing marble arches, mirrors and extraordinary gold and coloured mosaics. It is difficult to tire of the busy decor, which constantly reveals unnoticed hints, inscriptions and monk figures. The pub closes early and can get busy with a mix of tourists and City clientele. Nicholson's.
Open 11.30-10 Mon-Wed (Thur & Fri to 11). ***Beer*** *Tetley, Wadworth 6X, Brakspear, Adnams. Pub closed Sat & Sun all day. Access, Visa.*

W8 The Britannia A

Tel 0171-937 1864 Map 19 A4
1 Allen Street Kensington W8 6UX

Half way down Allen Street (in spite of its number) this is a cheering and often surprisingly peaceful old pub just a few yards off Kensington High Street. At the front, public and saloon bars are divided by a partition, and share a horseshoe bar; wood-panelling, settles and other seats, some in the bow windows. At the back, beyond the narrow saloon, a spacious room has its own bar and food servery. *Open 11-11, Sun 12-3, 7-10.30.*
Beer *Young's, guest beer. Family room/conservatory. No credit cards.*

SW1 Buckingham Arms FOOD

Tel 0171-222 3386 Map 19 D4
62 Petty France St James's SW1H 9EU

The Buckingham Arms has an elegant feel, with chintzy curtains and etched mirrors behind the long bar. Within the spacious bar area is the dining-room and food counter. The menu may offer such home-made delights as the Buckingham burger, Stilton and celery tart, salmon puff pastry plat and chicken provençale. All dishes are prepared in the kitchen. One of the very few pubs in London where chips are deep-fried to order. 12 wines by the glass. Very busy at lunch time, it quietens down in the evening. *Open 11-11 (Sat 11-3 & 5.30-11, Sun 12-3 & 7-10.30).* ***Bar Food*** *12-2.30, 6-9 (no food Sun).*
Beer *Young's. Access, Amex, Diners, Visa.*

SW11 The Castle FOOD

Tel 0171-228 8181 Fax 0171-924 5887 Map 17 B5
115 Battersea High Street SW11 3JR

Run by Charles and Linda Gotto, who, as Young's tenants, also run *The Ship, The Alma* and *The Coopers Arms* (see entries). It's tucked away in Battersea, a little off the beaten track, with a simple frontage almost consumed now by the ivy planted a year ago. Inside is a successful combination of bare boards and rugs and an eclectic mix of furniture plus a large open fire. Three rooms are all served by one bar and include a little 24-seater bistro dining area, an open-plan main bar room and a high-ceilinged conservatory to the rear which opens on to a paved garden, also now well populated with plants. Food is taken seriously and the monthly-changing menu is supplemented by a specials blackboard heralding the day's fresh soup, pasta (fusilli with creamy leeks and courgettes) and fish dishes (pan-fried tiger prawns with garlic, lemon and parsley butter); fish cakes (served without vegetables) are always popular, as are a salad of warm duck breast marinated in

ginger and orange, beef Wellington, and sausages with ratatouille. Carve-your-own roasts are offered at Sunday lunchtime, but they must be pre-ordered by Thursday midday. Fine British cheeses from Neal's Yard Dairy served with fruit; ice cream cones or the likes of lemon brulée to finish. An espresso coffee machine is another little touch that distinguishes the Castle from so many of London's more mundane pubs. Friendly staff serve well-kept Young's ales and up to 32 wines by the glass. *Open 11-11 (Sun 12-3, 7-10.30).* ***Bar Food*** *12-3, 7-10 (no food Sun eve).* ***Beer*** *Young's. Paved Garden, outdoor eating, summer weekend barbecue. Access, Amex, Diners, Visa.*

SW10 Chelsea Ram ★ FOOD

Tel 0171-351 4008 Fax 0171-349 0885 Map 19 B6
32 Burnaby Street Chelsea SW10 0PL

Rather staid, backstreet Young's local recently transformed by new landlord Nick Elliot (former landlord of *The Fox* in Lower Oddington, Gloucestershire – see entry). The style is now more airy and more modern in style with rustic tables, a mix of tweed-covered chairs, shelves covered with everything from dried flowers to a sculpted foot and a token display of books. There's a strong emphasis on food, with a short menu supplemented by a handful of daily blackboard specials such as moules marinière, baked sardines or a special summer salad. More mainstream might be smoked haddock and horseradish pot, roasted vegetable salad with tomato salsa, gamey sausages, mash and onion gravy, tip-top salmon fishcakes with new potatoes, a tian of ratatouille and lemony dill and butter sauce, penne pasta with smoked salmon and dill, or a warm salad of chicken, bacon, avocado and mixed leaves. Adam's club sandwich or contrefilet Strinberg served with shoestring French fries, along with chocolate truffle torte, summer pudding with lemon sorbet, and a 'cheese of the moment' served with home-made oatcakes may complete the picture. The usual range of Young's ales is supplemented by a range of very drinkable wines (the landlord also trades in wines), champagne and Spanish cava by the glass. A few tables are set out on the pavement under awnings in summer. Upstairs is a small function room (sponsored by RCA records), seating 14. By the time this Guide is published phase two of the redevelopment should have been completed: the rear area of the pub is due to be opened out and a conservatory roof put in place, considerably expanding and brightening up the overall interior space. *Open 11-3, 5.30-11 (Sun 12-3, 7-10.30).* ***Bar Food*** *12-2.30, 7-10 (Sun 12-2, 7-9).* ***Beer*** *Young's. Access, Visa.*

W8 Churchill Arms FOOD

Tel 0171-727 4242 Map 18 A3
119 Kensington Church Street W8 4LN

Loquacious landlord Gerry O'Brien takes great pride in and is to a great degree responsible for the wonderful atmosphere, charm and originality which characterises this pub near Notting Hill tube station. Among many other things he is a collector par excellence; the walls of the attractive conservatory restaurant exhibit his impressive collection of 1600 butterflies and the ceiling of the bar is covered with chamber pots, brasses and copper ornaments. The food operation mixes standard pub fare like beef and Guinness pie, moussaka and plaice and chips with a popular Thai restaurant in the rear of the pub serving the likes of beef in green curry paste and coconut milk or fried rice with chicken, spring onions and Thai spices. Both chef and staff are Thai. Sandwiches and ploughman's lunches are also offered. *Open 11-11 (Sun 12-3, 7-10.30). Bar Food 12-3, 6-11.* ***Beer*** *Fuller's. Access, Visa.*

WC1 Cittie of Yorke FOOD

Tel 0171-242 7670 Map 16 C3
22 High Holborn WC1V 6BS

A recent redecoration included the installation of new lighting to accentuate the ornate ceilings in this fine piece of Victorian architecture. The back room is the most impressive, with high ceilings, lamps suspended from the rafters, a coal-burning stove and intimate little booths across the very long bar. The gantry above is stacked with thousand-gallon wine vats. The Vaulted Bar downstairs is a long room with low, vaulted ceilings and a cellar atmosphere. Food is available on both floors. Daily specials might include scampi, prawn and broccoli pie, nut cutlet provençale and braised lamb steak in red wine. Sandwiches are made to order. The Vaulted Bar tends to be quieter and the queue at its food counter is usually shorter. *Open 11.30-11 (Sat 11.30-3, 5-11). Pub closed Sun.* ***Bar Food*** *12-2.30, 5.30-10.* ***Beer*** *Sam Smith's Old Brewery Bitter & Museum Ale. Access, Amex, Visa.*

W4 City Barge A

Tel 0181-994 2148 Map 17 A5
27 Strand on the Green Chiswick W4 3PH

Riverside pub dating back to the 15th century; charming original, intimate bar at river level, plus a modern extension and warm, bright conservatory upstairs. Owned by the Scottish/Courage group (previously Scottish & Newcastle). *Open 11.30-11 (Sun 12-3, 7-10.30).* ***Beer*** *Wadworth 6X, Theakston Best & Old Peculier, John Smith's. Access, Visa.*

EC1 Cock Tavern FOOD

Tel 0171-248 2918 Map 16 D3
East Poultry Avenue Central Markets EC1A 9LH

Popular among food-hoovering meat traders, City folk and medics from Bart's this is a large basement restaurant hidden away in a pub at the very heart of Smithfield market. The animation and cheerful atmosphere start at 5.30am with a generous breakfast – choose from black pudding, kidneys, smoked haddock with poached egg, hash browns, bubble and squeak, eggs any way and so on ... The choice is extensive: seven set breakfasts, omelettes, rolls or sandwiches, all at competitive prices. The lunch menu concentrates on meat with 15 steak dishes including an 18oz T-bone steak with trimmings as standard plus occasional larger versions going up to 40oz (record eating time 13 minutes – and then he had a pudding!). It's not an establishment known for it's decor (although a re-paint was planned as we went to press) but nonetheless a fun place enlivened by the banter of serious trenchermen! *Open 6.30am-11pm.* ***Bar Food*** *5.30-10.30am, 12-3. Free House.* ***Beer*** *Courage Best, John Smith's, Young's. Pub closed at weekends & Bank Holidays. Access, Amex, Visa.*

SW3 Coopers Arms FOOD

Tel 0171-376 3120 **Fax 0171-352 9187** Map 19 B5
Flood Street Chelsea SW3 5TB

Under the same tenancy as *The Ship, The Alma* and *The Castle* (see entries) this is a small, lively Young's pub on two floors. The ground floor is a single room with a large, solid table on which newspapers are laid for perusal; the upstairs has waitress service and is useful if you want to get away from the hustle and bustle downstairs. It's the same blackboard menu throughout, though, offering a mix of traditional and more modern pub fare at lunch only; most dishes are well executed and you can help yourself to bread and butter. Choose from salmon fishcakes, potato watercress soup, stir-fried beef in oyster sauce and spinach bacon and avocado salad. Desserts might include apple and blackberry trifle and passion fruit sorbet. Particularly good range of wines served by the glass. *Open 11-11 (Sun 12-3, 7-10.30).* ***Bar Food*** *Lunch only 12.30-3.* ***Beer*** *Young's. Access, Amex, Visa.*

W2 The Cow FOOD

Tel 0171-221 0021 Map 18 A2
89 Westbourne Park Road W2 5QH

Tom Conran's newest venture specialises in oysters and Guinness, with Bloody Mary and Pimm's other favourite tipples in the bar. There are small, round, polished-wood tables for dining in the rear section of the long bar room that narrows towards the rear; diners may choose either from a mirrored-glass menu set high above the bar or from a short daily-changing list of specials. The latter might include Thai chicken with rice, chicken liver paté, seafood bisque, escabèche of sardines, while the regular menu could offer steaming earthenware bowls of moules marinière, Dublin Bay prawns, mussels gratinée, plus crab and lobster when available. Further choices might be wonderfully cheesy and creamy gnocchi delicately flavoured with nutmeg and basil, Italian peppered sausage and bean casserole or a vegetable soup like chilled spinach. On the first floor is a small dining-room with a short, more meatier menu; we are considerably less bullish about the food served here. *Open 12-3, 5.30-11 (Sat 12-11, Sun 12-3, 7-10.30).* ***Bar Food*** *12.30-2.30, 6-10.30 (Sat 12.30-10.30, Sun 12.30-2.30, 7.30-10). Pub closed Monday lunchtimes.* ***Beer*** *Fuller's London Pride, guest beer. No credit cards.*

NW8 Crockers Folly FOOD

Tel 0171-286 6608 Map 18 B1
24 Aberdeen Place Maida Vale NW8 8JR

Built in 1898, this was designed as a luxury hotel to accommodate passengers from Marylebone station which was eventually never built on the site. The Victorian design creates an extravagant atmosphere and the entrance hosts a beautiful two-tone marble counter and a large fireplace. High, arched doors open on to two rooms: one mainly used by drinkers and game-lovers (bar billiards and fruit machines), the second, characterised by etched windows and a high, baroque ceiling, for dining. There's a large selection of home-made pies, multifarious sausage dishes (lamb and rosemary, West Indian and beef and horseradish), a weird and wonderful mix-and-match of cheese platters and even vegetarian savoury crumbles. The traditional Sunday lunch offers a choice of two roasts. Nursery-style desserts. Just off Edgware Road, hog roast on Lord's match days. *Open 11-11 (Sun 12-3, 7-10.30).* ***Bar Food*** *12-2.30, 6.30-9.45 (hot), sandwiches served all day. Free House.* ***Beer*** *Shepherd Neame, Brakspear, Bass, Adnams, Theakston Best, guest beer. Access, Amex, Diners, Visa.*

W6 The Dove FOOD

Tel 0181-748 5405 Map 17 A4
19 Upper Mall Hammersmith W6 9TA

Rule Brittania was composed at this riverside pub, which dates from the 17th century and has cleverly escaped the blitz of modernization. It also boasts the world's smallest public bar but there's plenty of room elsewhere, including a cosy river terrace for fine weather. Lunchtimes see well-cooked traditional dishes; braised steak in Guinness, stuffed baked potatoes and various ploughman's platters. In the evenings (Sun to Thu only) Thai food is on offer, individually cooked to a standard which rivals many of London's better-known Thai restaurants. A selection of mixed starters, chicken satay, stir-fries of squid, beef or prawns (all including carefully-cooked egg fried rice). Both red, yellow and green curries are usually available, a green of beef with bamboo shoots being particularly delicious. Good Fuller's beers and friendly service. Not suitable for children under the age of 14. *Open 11-11 (Sun 12-3, 7-10.30). Bar Food 12-3, 6-10 (no food Fri & Sat evening).* ***Beer*** *Fuller's. Riverside patio/terrace, outdoor eating. No credit cards.*

EC1 The Eagle ★ FOOD

Tel 0171-837 1353 Map 16 C3
159 Farringdon Road EC1R 3AL

Pub, bar, restaurant? Who knows how to categorise a converted pub with pub drinking hours (except at weekends) that offers extraordinary, restaurant-quality food? As many people must come here for the food as for the busy bar atmosphere, but it's the total lack of restaurant service and facilities that keep The Eagle in the top league of London pubs. With a sanded hardwood floor, magnolia walls and a vibrant atmosphere this is still very much a pub, but the standard of the food raises it high above one's normal expectations. No bookings are taken but persevere, share a table, order your food at the top of your voice and enjoy the robust Mediterranean dishes cooked by co-owner David Eyre in an open-plan kitchen. At least eight options are marked up on a blackboard, often changing twice daily. There's always a cheese plate (Spanish Manchego with dulce de membrillo, or soft Italian with focaccia and rocket) and a simple dessert. One stalwart, *bife ana*, a marinated rump steak sandwich is a permanent fixture. Other recent choices have included Andalucian chickpea and mussel soup, Italian sausages with sweet roast onions and rocket, arista (Tuscan roast pork loin with garlic, fennel and parsley) and grilled swordfish steak with salmoriglio Egyptian potato salad. The food is decidedly above average, the prices are around £7-£9.50 for main courses and there's even an excellent range of wines by the glass. The first floor is an art gallery. *Open 12-11.* ***Bar Food*** *12.30-2.30, 6.30-10.30.* ***Beer*** *Charles Wells Eagle IPA & Bombardier, Ruddles County. Pub closed Sat & Sun, Bank Holidays, 2/3 weeks Christmas. No credit cards.*

N1 Eagle Tavern A

Tel 0171-253 4715 Map 16 D3
2 Shepherdess Walk off City Road N1 7LB

"Up and down the City Road, in and out the Eagle, that's the way the money goes, pop goes the weasel". Probably better known through the song than for the pub itself. Memories of the Royal Grecian theatre adorn the walls of the large comfortable bar, which has plenty of seating. The second bar has a simpler atmosphere with bare wooden floors and darkwood furniture. Background music and busy throughout the day. *Open 11-11. Pub closed all Sat and Sun eve.* ***Beer*** *Bass, Charles Wells Eagle IPA, up to six guest beers. Paved garden. Access, Visa.*

NW1 The Engineer ★ FOOD

Tel 0171-722 0950 **Fax 0171-483 0592** Map 16 C3
65 Gloucester Avenue NW1 8JH

Once upon a time this was a quiet, sleepy pub in a very residential part of Primrose Hill, where Princess Road joins Gloucester Avenue. It was built in 1846 by Isambard Kingdom Brunel, who is rather better known for his engineering feats of building more major projects such as railways, tunnels, bridges and steamships than for pubs. Standing on a corner site across from the London Filmmakers' Co-op its renaissance has created a new focal point for the area and now attracts a discerning dining crowd both from near and far. Run by Abigail Osborne and Tamsin Olivier, the place buzzes with activity. A walled, paved garden to the rear is extremely popular in fine weather and tables there are offered on a first-come, first-seated basis. The interior is brightly and very simply decorated in a fashionably rustic manner with a spacious, often crowded bar area and separate dining area (bookings essential) occupying the side and rear sections – a long narrow part and a couple of more intimate rooms, all set up for eating. Chef Robert Greenway, an Italian Philadelphian, produces food that is both imaginative and well prepared. The first-class menu changes fortnightly and an eclectic mix of dishes might include chilled yoghurt, cucumber and mint soup, tortellini in chicken broth and a Caesar salad or a delicious mix of braised fennel, roast peppers and warm goat's cheese. The short menu might continue with char-grilled organic rump steak with grilled vegetables, salad and 'baker' chips, or leg of spring lamb with minted new potatoes and rocket salad. Sunday brunch sees organic beefburgers with more 'baker' chips and a tomato and feta salad as well as the classic brunch offerings of eggs Benedict and eggs florentine. Cumberland sausages with Cheddar mash and red onion gravy, daily fresh egg pasta or fish dish (perhaps roast halibut with frisée, braised vegetables and plum tomato vinaigrette) and broccoli, pine nut and blue cheese tart are other typical dishes; try, also, their root vegetable crisps. There's a short, relatively inexpensive wine list with nine wines served by the glass and good-value house champagne. The Engineer has a very friendly, laid-back atmosphere and the staff were wonderful on our initial visits (the pub will have been open for less than a year when this Guide is published) – it's no wonder that the pub has proved to be such an instant success. Oh that every London neighbourhood could have a modern-style 'local' as good as this! *Open 12-11 (Tue 6-11 only), Sun 12-10.30.* ***Bar Food*** *12-3 (not Tue), 6-11 (Sun 12-3, 6-10.30). Closed Tuesday lunchtime.* ***Beer*** *Fuller's London Pride, guest beer. Garden, outside eating. Access, Visa.*

NW3 The Flask A

Tel 0171-435 4580 Map 16 B2
14 Flask Walk Hampstead NW3 1HE

Located in a pedestrian street off Hampstead High Street, the Flask is a favourite, friendly rendezvous for comedians, artists and drinkers alike. It has a proper public bar, separated from the saloon bar by the original Victorian panelling. The back room opens up on to a conservatory mainly used as a dining-room but also as a set up for charity events and music hall nights which the landlords frequently organise. Good selection of wines by the glass. *Open 11-11 (Sun 12-3, 7-10.30).* ***Beer*** *Young's. Conservatory. No credit cards.*

SE1 Founders Arms A

Tel 0171-928 1899 Map 17 D4
52 Hopton Street Bankside SE1 9JH

June 1996 should see the opening of the new Globe theatre just down the road from this large modern building (built in 1979) on the riverside. Located near Blackfriars Bridge and (for those prepared to wait until the year 2000!) the site of the new Tate Gallery. The bar is airy and bright with large picture windows looking out over the city and St Paul's Cathedral. The front terrace is large enough to cater for crowds of drinkers on busy, sunny days. Wonderful location, panoramic views. *Open 11-11 (Sun 12-3, 7-10.30).* ***Beer** Young's. Riverside terrace. Access, Amex, Visa.*

EC1 Fox & Anchor FOOD

Tel 0171-253 4838 Fax 0171-253 0696 Map 16 D3
115 Charterhouse Street EC1 6AA

Traditional Victorian London pub on the north side of Charterhouse Street (opposite Fox & Knot Street), with an atmosphere that can scarcely have changed in the last 100 years. Being across the road from Snmithfield meat market, a special charter allows breakfast to be washed down with strong liquid refreshment. Breakfast can be a gargantuan affair complete with black pudding or steak and kidneys if you so require, but smaller (and vegetarian) appetites are equally happily assuaged. Lunch brings sandwiches, steak and kidney pie (the house speciality), omelettes and a selection of good-quality steaks (although the chips are a bit of a let down). Deep-fried plaice and salads are offered for non-carnivores. Hardly gourmet fare, but an interesting pub (and there's certainly nothing wrong with the quality of the meat!). Over a dozen wines served by the glass. Booking advisable, particularly for breakfast – when you should expect to share a table. Upstairs is a private room seating 22. Nicholson's. *Open 7am-9pm (closed Sun & Bank Holidays).* ***Bar Food** 7-10.30am, (Sat from 8), 12-2.15.* ***Beer** Tetley Bitter, Nicholson's Best, Wadworth 6X, guest beers. Access, Amex, Diners, Visa.*

SW19 Fox & Grapes A

Tel 0181-946 5599 Map 17 B6
Camp Road Wimbledon SW19 4UN

Once a gin shop, converted with the next door stables into a pub in 1956, you'll find no TV or machines here, indeed, in their words: "no anything made after 1950". Strictly speaking that's not true – as we went to press the exterior (fronting Wimbledon Common) was receiving a facelift and the inside a redecoration – but it captures the atmosphere of this friendly, reliable, community pub perfectly. Lots of theme nights include celebrations of Burns Night, St George's Day, St Patrick's Day and so on. *Open 11-11 (Sun 12-3, 7-10.30).* ***Beer** Courage Best & Directors, Webster's, Marston's Pedigree, Wadworth 6X. Access, Amex, Visa.*

W1 French House FOOD

Tel 0171-437 2799 Map 18 D3
49 Dean Street Soho W1V 5HL

Formerly The York Minster (but known as 'Frenchie's' since having been the unofficial meeting place for the Free French during the war), this last of Soho's bohemian pubs only gained its present name about ten years ago. Long the haunt of actors, writers and artists, the walls of the single, small room are a photo montage of the more (and less) famous habitués both past and present, although room is also found in summer for a team list for the pub's next cricket match. Owners for some six years, Noel Botham (himself a writer) and his wife Lesley Lewis have happily kept things exactly as they have always been, without music, fruit machines or other modern intrusions. The bar is mainly for drinking rather than eating (especially at night when it gets pretty busy and it's then largely a case of drinking standing up), so bar food is limited to just two items: a sandwich made with home-made bread (perhaps cheese and salad) and something like duck liver paté with toast, both made by the folk who run the pub's first-floor restaurant (French House Dining Room – reservations on 0171-437 2477 – also recommended in *Egon Ronay's Cellnet Guide 1996 Hotels & Restaurants*); here, the short lunch and dinner menus (you can have just a single dish) offer main dishes like boiled ham with vegetables and parsley sauce, baked cod with potatoes and saffron, and roast pigeon, peas and lentils plus starters such as

sweet potato soup and kidneys and beetroot on toast, with steamed plum pudding and Welsh rarebit for afters. On the drinks front there is an unusually good range of over a dozen wines served by the glass, all at very realistic prices: try a petit Chablis, a Hugel pinot blanc (direct from the vineyard) or their house champagne. *Open 12-11 (Sun 12-3 & 7-10.30).* ***Bar Food*** *12.30-3, 6.30-10.30 (no food Sun). Restaurant 12.30-3, 6.30-11.30; closed Sun, Bank Holidays & 10 days Christmas/New Year. Access, Visa.*

SW3 Front Page FOOD

Tel 0171-352 2908 Fax 0171-352 8162 Map 19 B6
35 Old Church Street Chelsea SW3 5BS

In a quiet residential area of Chelsea, just off the hustle and bustle of Kings Road, stands the smart and stylish Front Page, on a prime corner site. Its white-painted exterior is decked with colourful hanging baskets and large, attractive gas lamps; inside is spacious, extremely light and airy, thanks to high ceilings and large windows which let in plenty of natural daylight. Rich navy blue curtains are matched by painted ceiling borders, and whirling ceiling fans help keep the room fresh. Part-panelled, it's furnished in informal rustic style with solid stripped wood tables, round-back chairs and long benches on well-worn floorboards; walls have minimal covering, save some Victorian-style nudes. At either end of the bar, two large blackboards display the day's food choice, which is interesting and light in a bistro style: regular favourites include snacks like Stilton and celery soup or BBQ chicken bites; as main courses, perhaps T-Bone steak, half-lobster thermidor or spicy chicken escalope in avocado and lemon salsa. Those traditionalists who crave a more solid English lunch are catered for with dishes like sausage and mash. Young, friendly and keen staff provide good service with a smile. This is a pub worth knowing about, just moments from the crush of the Kings Road and its array of busier, less welcoming places. *Open 11-3 (Sun from 12), 5.30-11 (Sat from 6, Sun 7-10.30).* ***Bar Food*** *12-2.30, 7-10 (Sun to 9.30).* ***Beer*** *Webster's Yorkshire Bitter, Boddingtons. Access, Visa.*

SE1 George Inn A

Tel 0171-407 2056 Fax 0171-403 6613 Map 17 D4
77 Borough High Street Southwark SE1 1NH

After almost 400 years of history this pub was rescued by the National Trust in the 1930s and is now run by Whitbread. It's London's only surviving original coaching inn, dating back to when London Bridge was the only way into the City. A large cobbled courtyard terrace overlooks the beautiful black and white frontage with its galleried section and hanging flower baskets. A series of bars is interlinked: the wine bar contains a food counter, the George Bar has low ceilings, dark beams, latticed windows and lantern lamps and the Old Bar has a dark, quiet atmosphere and an open fireplace. A popular pub with city types (until mid-evening), tourists and beer fans alike – a beer festival (with at least 12 real ales) is held during the third week of each month. *Open 11-11 (Sun 12-3, 7-10.30).* ***Beer*** *Boddingtons, Flowers, Fuller's London Pride, Greene King Abbot Ale, Whitbread Castle Eden. Family room. Access, Amex, Diners, Visa.*

E14 The Grapes A

Tel 0171-987 4396 Map 17 D4
76 Narrow Street Limehouse E14 8BP

Over 300 years old, the Grapes probably hasn't changed much since Dickens, a frequent visitor, used it as the model for the Six Jolly Fellowship Porters in 'Our Mutual Friend'. In this narrow riverside pub, squeezed in between buildings that used to house ships' chandlers, block and tackle makers, barge builders and the like, it's easy to imagine Thames watermen drinking in the downstairs bar, with its bare floorboards and boarded, nicotine-stained ceiling. Prime position for watching the passing traffic is from the new teak deck overlooking the river, whose murky water laps at the stilts of the building. Since the opening of the Limehouse tunnel there's no direct access from the Highway – as you approach the tunnel turn left up Butchers Row, right into Commercial Road, first right down Branch Road and keep your wheels in the left-hand gutter leading round to Narrow Street. *Open 12-11 (Sat 7-11 only, Sun usual hours).* ***Beer*** *Ind Coope Burton Ale, Tetley Bitter, Friary Meux, guest ale. Access, Amex, Diners, Visa.*

SW1 The Grenadier FOOD

Tel 0171-235 3074 Map 19 C4
18 Wilton Row Belgravia SW1 7NR

Not far from Hyde Park Corner, tucked away in the curve of cobbled Wilton Row mews, the bright red, white and blue frontage of this patriotic pub can't be missed. The intimate dark bar and restaurant were once used as a mess by the Duke of Wellington's Grenadiers and the place is full of historical atmosphere with even a few sabres, daggers and bugles hanging from the ceiling. The dark, panelled bar is small and customers spread outside on to the quiet cul-de-sac. Two candle-lit dining-rooms at the back are intimate with seats for just 21: try smoked Scottish salmon, Stilton puffs, beef Wellington. Both ingredients and cooking are of quality and this is traditional English food presented at its best including classics like fish'n'chips served with mushy peas. A set menu offers a traditional roast. Good snacks in the bar – from ploughman's lunches to sausage, beans and chips or scampi and chips. Sunday lunchtime is the perfect time for a Bloody Mary – don't forget to buy one for the ghost! Chef & Brewer. ***Bar Food** 12-2, 6-10 (Sun from 7). **Beer** Young's Special, Theakston Best & XB, guest beer. Pub closed 24 Dec eve-26 Dec, 31 Dec eve & 1 Jan. Access, Amex, Visa.*

W1 The Guinea FOOD

Tel 0171-409 1728 **Fax 0171-491 1442** Map 18 C3
30 Bruton Place off Berkeley Square W1X 7AA

Tucked away in a mews between Bruton Street and Berkeley Square, this Mayfair institution continues to gain acclaim for its charcoal-grilled Prime Scotch Highland steaks along with Rossmore oysters and Scottish smoked salmon in its rear restaurant (recommended in *Egon Ronay's Cellnet Guide 1996 Hotels and Restaurants* Tel 0171-499 1210). The bar menu offers a cheaper alternative to eating in the restaurant with enduring classics like their superior steak and kidney pie and grilled sausages at lunchtimes only. An interesting selection of hot ciabatta bread sandwiches is also out of the ordinary: try the Siciliano made with free-range chicken, smoked bacon, sun-dried tomatoes, mascarpone and chopped olives; or the Mirabeau with Aberdeen sirloin steak, lettuce, tarragon, anchovies, olives, tomatoes and mayonnaise; sandwiches are made to order (often at least a ten minute wait) and well worth the struggle through the Mayfair regulars who pack the small bar at lunchtime, when getting a seat is nigh on impossible. *Open 11-11 (Sat 6.30-11). Bar Food 12-3. **Beer** Young's. Pub closed lunch Sat & all Sun. Access, Amex, Diners, Visa.*

EC1 The Hope & Sir Loin FOOD

Tel 0171-253 8525 Map 16 D3
94 Cowcross Street Smithfield EC1M 6BH

Traditional Smithfield pub serving enormous breakfasts in the dining-rooms. Gourmands can start the day with the whole works: egg, bacon, sausage, black pudding, kidneys, liver, baked beans, tomatoes, mushrooms and toast. Less voracious appetites might settle for kippers or eggs-any-way. Grills and roasts are the lunchtime specialities, plus the likes of deep-fried scampi, veal in cream and mushrooms and steak & kidney pie. Reservations essential. ***Bar Food** 7.15am-9.30am, 12-2 (no food Sat or in evenings). **Beer** Courage, Webster's, Young's, Ruddles. Pub closed from 3.30pm Mon-Fri, all Sat, Sun, Bank Holidays & 25 Dec-5 Jan. Access, Amex, Visa.*

SE1 Horniman's FOOD

Tel 0171-407 3611 **Fax 0171-357 6449** Map 17 D4
Hay's Galleria Tooley Street London Bridge SE1 2HD

Right at the entrance of Hay's Galleria on the south bank overlooking the Thames by London Bridge, Horniman's is a modern interpretation of Victorian style in the premises of the family's tea-packing company. The tribute to Frederick John Horniman's travels is discreetly paid through a painted mural on top of the bar. It's part pub, part café and the tables on the gallerias have views of the river and the City in the background. The restaurant offers good hot and cold dishes (turkey pie, lamb chasseur casserole, broccoli and leek pie – all served with chips and vegetables) throughout the day. A popular pub with both tourists and businessmen. Families are welcome in a special area in the Pantry restaurant and children are offered special portions at special prices. *Open 11-11 (Sat to 4, Sun to 3). **Bar Food** 11-3. **Beer** Burton, Brakspear, Timothy Taylor's Landlord, Wadworth 6X, two guest beers. Pub closed weekend evenings. Access, Amex, Visa.*

SW6 Imperial Arms FOOD

Tel 0171-736 9179 Map 19 A6
577 Kings Road Chelsea SW6 2EH

At the back of the Imperial Arms, on Kings Road between World's End and Parsons Green is a paved terrace where tables and chairs are set out in summer. It's very much an eating pub, specialising in crustacea, shellfish and the barbecue. Rossmore oysters are served just as they are (rock or native) or cooked à la mornay, Rockefeller (on a bed of spinach with a dash of Pernod and cheese sauce) or Kilpatrick (an Aussie variant involving bacon strips and Worcester sauce). Cromer crabs and Scottish lobster also appear in their season, as does some truly wild Irish smoked salmon (in a platter or a sandwich). From the barbecue, overseen by larger-than-life landlord Cornelius O'Grady, come beefburgers, gammon steak, rump steak and wild boar sausages. In addtion there's a daily curry, seasonal stews and summer salads; all come at reasonable prices. Lighter snacks, too, like sandwiches and a good platter of cheeses, but the oysters are really the thing to shell out on. Opening times may be affected when Chelsea football team play at home. *Open 11-11, regular hours Sun.* ***Bar Food*** *breakfast from 10, 12-3, 7.30-11.* ***Beer*** *John Smith's, Morland Old Speckled Hen, Marston's Pedigree, Wadworth 6X. Patio, outdoor eating. Access, Amex, Visa.*

NW3 Jack Straw's Castle A

Tel 0171-435 8885 Fax 0171-794 4805 Map 16 B2
North End Way Hampstead NW3 7ES

The Inn was built in 1721 on the site of what used to be the hay wagon from which Jack Straw addressed the peasants during the 1381 revolt. Damaged during the Second World War, it was rebuilt in the early sixties. It has a clean country pub look and an agreeable courtyard with an arts and craft fair at weekends. Being one of the highest points in London, the second-floor restaurant has beautiful panoramic views over Hampstead Heath. *Open 11-11.* ***Beer*** *Bass, Fuller's London Pride, guest beer. Courtyard, outdoor eating area. Access, Amex, Diners, Visa.*

SW6 Jim Thompson's FOOD

Tel 0171-731 7636 Map 19 A6
617 Kings Road SW6 2EF

East meets West in a self-styled Oriental bar/restaurant and bazaar – Jim Thompson's is hardly your normal London pub! Named after the renowned American who opened up the Thai silk industry and then disappeared without trace in the Malaysian jungle, the pub bearing his name is themed to the hilt, with Oriental artefacts galore scattered around the pub's interior, each bearing its own (high) price tag. There are two food operations within: to the rear is a surprisingly spacious, high-ceilinged dining-room draped with floating silks, while to the front is a more usual bare brick-walled pub bar. In both, the menus offer a list of dishes that have been inspired by countries from the whole of IndoChina and the Spice Islands. Bar snacks on the one-plate Oriental Express menu might range from Malaysian satay, Singaporean dim sum and Thai salads to a Vietnamese stir-fry and Burmese noodles. Never the less, eating here is always interesting and diverting – particularly as it still operates very much as a pub. Sunday night see live jazz. JT's is on the bend of Kings Road where it joins New Kings Road – it's unusal and it's fun. A new JT's opened at 34 Surrey Street, Croydon (Tel 0181-256 0007) as we went to press. *Open 12-2.30, 7-11 (Sun to 10.30)* ***Bar Food*** *12-2.30, 5.30-7.30 (Sun 7-8.30). Restaurant until 11pm (Sun to 10.30).* ***Beer*** *Tetley, Marston's Pedigree. Access, Visa.*

W11 Ladbroke Arms A

Tel 0171-727 6648 Map 18 A3
54 Ladbroke Road Notting Hill Gate W11 3NW

Opposite Notting Hill police station, on the corner of Ladbroke Road and the charming Willby Mews. The front terrace welcomes you with open arms: built a few steps above street level, it is well stocked with tables, benches and parasols. Inside is a traditional mixture of mahogany panelling, yellow velvet-covered banquettes, large etched mirrors, a semi-circular bar with pillars and a split-level area at the back. There's a very civilised atmosphere with smiling faces and classical music softly playing in the background. *Open 12-11 (Sun 12-3, 7-10.30).* ***Beer*** *Courage Best & Directors, John Smith's, Shepherd Neame Spitfire Ale, Webster's Yorkshire, Wadworth 6X. Access, Visa.*

WC1 The Lamb FOOD

Tel 0171-405 0713 Map 16 C3
94 Lamb's Conduit Street off Theobalds Road WC1N 3LZ

Atmospheric Victorian pub which retains some original features like a beautiful U-shaped counter with gantry and snob screens. On the walls hang sepia photographs from the Holborn Empire, a Victorian music hall destroyed during the war. The pub gets very busy in the evenings with a jolly and friendly atmosphere. At lunchtime, home-cooked daily specials are worth a stop: beef stew in red wine, chicken in cider, meatloaf, pork and Guinness pie and well-prepared salads. There is a small dining area and a few tables are set outside on the rear patio. On Sundays, the Carvery restaurant is open on the first floor. *Open 11-11 (Sun 12-3, 7-10.30).* ***Bar Food*** *12-2.30 (evening salads only until 9pm).* ***Beer*** *Young's. Access, Visa.*

WC2 Lamb & Flag FOOD

Tel 0171-497 9504 Map 18 D3
33 Rose Street (off Garrick Street) Covent Garden WC2E 9EV

A busy Georgian pub steeped in history (Dryden was famously lynched here in 1679 and they still celebrate Dryden night) and retaining an atmosphere from Dickens' with low ceilings, dark-wood panelling and built-in benches on the ground floor. The two small, separate bars downstairs have limited seating areas and customers tend to spread out on to the paved area in front of the pub or in the quieter dining-room upstairs. The bar serves excellent ploughman's lunches made with French bread and Cheddar, Double Gloucester, Blue Shropshire or Stilton – all farmhouse cheeses – whilst upstairs is hot food like shepherd's pie, sausage and mash plus a roast beef every day. *Open 11-11 (Sun 12-3, 7-10.30). Bar Food 12-5 (restaurant to 2.30 only). No food evenings & all Sun.* ***Beer*** *Courage Best & Directors, John Smith's, Morland Old Speckled Hen, Wadworth 6X. No credit cards.*

EC3 Lamb Tavern FOOD

Tel 0171-626 2454 Map 17 D4
10-12 Leadenhall Market EC3V 1LR

In contrast to Richard Rodgers' ultra-modern Lloyds building next door is Leadenhall market, known for its Victorian cast iron and glass-covered cobbled lanes, as well as being home to the Lamb Tavern. A characterful place, with engraved glass windows, cast iron pillars, a tiled picture panel depicting Dick Whittington, and a spiral staircase leading up to a mezzanine floor. The pub was used as a location for the filming of Brannigan with John Wayne (as a photo of the 'Duke' together with landlady Linda Morris testifies) as well as a scene from the Winds of War with Robert Mitchum. Foodwise there's not a great deal of choice because they do just one thing and do it best – a succulent hot roast beef sandwich carved to order from the wing rib and served in lengths of real French bread. There are some other sandwiches for the adventurous (perhaps hot roast pork) but the beef is the best and by far the most popular. A delicious spin-off from all this beef-roasting is the dripping it generates, which can be had with a piece of French bread – a real treat. *Open 11-9.* ***Pub*** *closed Sat and Sun. Bar Food 11-2.30. Beer Young's. Access, Amex, Diners, Visa.*

NW1 The Lansdowne ★ FOOD

Tel 0171-483 0409 Map 16 C3
90 Gloucester Avenue Primrose Hill NW1 8HX

Old Victorian pub with real ales and yet something of a café feel following a conversion job a few years ago. Opened up and reduced to bare boards, there is a motley collection of tables and chairs, vases of fresh flowers and a few magazines piled up on an old chest. Amanda Pritchett can be seen at work in the small, spick and span kitchen where she cooks up the likes of minestrone soup, country terrine with relish and pickles, marinated chicken salad, sirloin steak with mash and peas and roast hake with aïoli and poached vegetables. The shortness of the menu – just five starters, five main courses and a few desserts written up on the blackboard daily – goes a long way to explain the excellence of the results. Not suitable for children under the age of 14. *Open 12-11 (Sun 12-3, 7-10.30, Mon 6-11 only).* ***Bar Food*** *12-2.30 (except Mon, Sun from 1), 7-10 (Sun 7.30-9.30).* ***Beer*** *Bass, guest beer. Six outside tables. Pub closed Mon lunch. No credit cards.*

N1 Marquess Tavern FOOD

Tel 0171-354 2975 Map 16 D3
32 Canonbury Street off Essex Road Islington N1 2TB

Tables set outside look out on to the green scenery of the canal running just yards away from this imposing Young's pub at the corner of Canonbury Street and Arran Walk. The bar inside is roomy and comfortable with elegant fireplaces and oil portraits. Food is served in the high-ceilinged dining-room at the back (unfortunately not as bright as the rest of the rooms). Lamb chops provençale, boiled bacon and parsley sauce or 'Marquess Red Pie' (corned beef, potato and onion) are examples of the typical daily specials that are prepared to order and come straight out of the kitchen. The selection of cold dishes is equally tempting: cheese- or paté-stuffed mushrooms, chips and salads and quiches are home-made. A daily roast and other pies, vegetarian dishes and regular pub favourites complete the picture. *Open 11-11 (Sun 12-3, 7-10.30).* ***Bar Food*** *11-9.30 (no food Sun).* ***Beer*** *Young's. Front patio, outdoor eating. No credit cards.*

W2 Monkey Puzzle A

Tel 0171-723 0143 Map 18 B2
30 Southwick Street off Sussex Gardens W2 1JQ

Situated on the ground floor of a modern building with a flowery outside terrace; the Monkey Puzzle has recently been acquired by Badger Inns and so one attraction is the selection of Hall & Woodhouse real ales which are hard to find in London. As we went to press new managers David and Penny Evans were busy making plans to cook up an all-new traditional pub fare menu and to spruce up the terrace. *Open 11-11 (Sun 12-10.30). Free House.* ***Beer*** *Hall & Woodhouse Badger Best, Hard Tackle & Tanglefoot, two guest beers. Terrace. Pub closed 25 Dec. Access, Amex, Diners, Visa.*

SW1 Morpeth Arms FOOD

Tel 0171-834 6442 Map 19 D5
58 Millbank SW1P 4RW

Located at the corner of Ponsonby Place and overlooking the river this is the perfect stop for Tate Gallery visitors. An impressive collection of law books graces the walls – the pub was purpose built for the Wardens of the old Millbank prison and an escaped prisoner still haunts it today. Home-made daily specials of cottage pie, lamb casserole and salads are available at the food counter for quick service. Braised oxtail with red wine and onion sauce, fresh deep-fried cod or haddock and special home-made burgers are prepared to order. Large selection of wines by the glass. A perfect stop for Tate Gallery visitors. *Open 11-11, Sun usual hours.* ***Bar Food*** *12-8.30.* ***Beer*** *Young's. Patio, outdoor eating. Access, Visa.*

SW1 Nag's Head FOOD

Tel 0171-235 1135 Map 19 C4
53 Kinnerton Street Belgravia SW1X 8ED

Probably the smallest pub in London but certainly not the least interesting. The front was built in 1780, when horses running around on Grosvenor Estate provided the inspiration for the name. The low-ceilinged, panelled bar and dining-room communicate through a narrow stairway. A 1930s' what-the-butler-saw machine and a fortune-telling machine taking old pennies are popular features, with takings going to Queen Charlotte's Hospital. Personal bric-a-brac and photographs give a homely and intimate feel. The home-made cooking brings steak and mushroom pie, beef curry and a ploughman's lunch with real-ale sausage back to life. Vegetarians are offered the likes of tomato and onion quiche plus macaroni cheese. Death by chocolate cake only for pudding in the summer; spotted dick and sponge puddings in the winter. A cover charge of £1 is made for meals served between 7 and 10pm. Kinnerton Street runs between Motcomb Street and Wilton Place (off Knightsbridge). *Open 11-11 (Sun 12-3, 7-10.30).* ***Bar Food*** *11.30-9.30 (Sun 12-3, 7-9). Free House.* ***Beer*** *Young's, Adnams, Tetley. No credit cards.*

W1 Newman Arms FOOD

Tel 0171-636 1127 Map 18 D2
23 Rathbone Street off Oxford Street W1P 1AG

Cosy, panelled bar set in a 260-year-old building on the site of an old ale house. The upstairs dining-room has a pleasant homely feel with red velvet curtains and wall seats, blue and white chequered tablecloths and a gas fire in winter. Pies, home-made with only the best ingredients, are a speciality. The selection includes steak and kidney, spicy shepherd's, fisherman's, vegetarian and chicken and broccoli, all baked to order. Rhubarb crumble, trifle and apple pie are some of the home-made desserts which change daily. *Open 11.30-11.30 (Sat 5.30-11 only). Pub closed Sun.* ***Bar Food*** *12-3.30.* ***Beer*** *Bass, Fuller's London Pride, Hancock's. Access, Visa.*

W1 O'Conor Don FOOD

Tel 0171-935 9311 Map 18 C2
88 Marylebone Lane W1

The O'Callaghans' family-run Irish pub offers a warm welcome and wholesome fare: "true Irish geniality in the heart of London's West End". Named after Don, Prince of Connacht, the chief of the Royal House of O'Conor out of which came 11 High Kings of Ireland and 26 successive Kings of Connacht. The building, on a corner site where Bentinck Street meets Marylebone Lane, has stained-glass windows on two sides. Within, the bar has bare floorboards and dark panelled walls decorated with polished Victorian mirrors and a series of Guinness advertisements. A collection of odd carver chairs and gate-legged tables add to the homely feel. Bar food shows that there is real enthusiasm (and more than a little skill) in the kitchen and includes excellent sandwiches, fresh Donegal oysters and daily specials from the upstairs dining-room such as lamb's liver, kidney and bacon with home-made chips, ham and colcannon with swede and mustard sauce, or excellent Irish stew with pearl barley. Seats fill up quickly, so get there early for food (particularly at lunchtime). Don't expect any real ale, but you can, of course, get a great pint of the dark stuff. If you're worried about which door to take for the conveniences then ladies should head for *fir* and gents for *mná*! The airy restaurant (Ard Ri Dining Room – meaning 'High King') has its own entrance and is recommended in our *1996 Hotels & Restaurants Guide*; its menu changes weekly (table d'hote £15 lunch, £18 dinner), but you can expect the likes of good soda bread, stuffed lamb's heart and red cabbage, roast stuffed suckling pig with spiced apple and celeriac purée or roast breast of goose with braised cabbage; Irish cheeses, treacle tart or baked apple with fresh custard might complete the culinary offerings. Charming, friendly service. *Open 11-3, 6-11 (Sun 12-3, 7-10.30).* ***Bar Food*** *12-9.30 (no food Sun, 1 week Christmas or Bank Holidays). Restaurant 12-2.30, 6-9.30 (closed Sat lunch & all Sun). Access, Visa.*

EC4 Old Bell Tavern A

Tel 0171-583 0070 Map 17 D4
95 Fleet Street EC4Y 1DH

The tavern was built by Sir Christopher Wren during the construction of St Bride's church nearby and features darkwood half-panelled walls with ochre sponge paint and cast-iron gas fireplaces. The bar is cosy and characterful. Solid wooden bar stools are set along the rear window with a selection of daily papers and more seating is available near the entrance. Food is limited to sandwiches made to order and there's an interesting selection of beers. Nicholson's. *Open 11-11.* ***Beer*** *Wadworth 6X, Tetley, Marston's Pedigree, Nicholson's, Brakspear, guest beer. Pub closed Sat & Sun. Access, Amex, Diners, Visa.*

EC2 Old Dr Butler's Head FOOD

Tel 0171-606 3504 **Fax 0171-606 4967** Map 16 D3
Mason's Avenue Coleman Street Moorgate EC2V 5BT

Built in 1610, it was destroyed during the Great Fire and rebuilt in 1666. Today, under the direction of Whitbread, it retains its beamed and panelled 17th-century atmosphere. Extremely busy at lunchtime, they prepare one of the City's best sandwiches, made with thick delicious crusty bread, filled with carved turkey, ham, roast beef, sausages or cheese. The same choice of meat and cheese is also available as a ploughman's lunch. The restaurant on the first floor has a full à la carte traditional menu offering roasts, seafood casserole, calf's liver with bacon and the like, however, as we went to press, there were

plans to move this to the second-floor restaurant and bring in a new modern English à la carte in its place. *Open 11-11.* ***Bar Food*** *Lunch only 11.30-2.30.* ***Beer*** *Boddingtons, Flowers, Marston's Pedigree, Fuller's London Pride, Brakspear, two guest beers. Closed Sat, Sun & Bank Holidays. Access, Amex, Diners, Visa.*

WC2 Opera Tavern A

Tel 0171-836 7321 Map 17 C4
23 Catherine Street WC2B 5JS

Friendly Victorian pub right across from the Drury Lane Theatre Royal. Original gas lamps remain above the bar and the walls are covered with theatre memorabilia. The small upstairs bar, cosily furnished with tables, chairs and a sofa, is used as the dining-room. Taylor Walker. *Open 12-11.* ***Bar Food*** *12-8.* ***Beer*** *Tetley, Burton, Young's. Pub closed Sun. Access, Amex, Diners, Visa.*

We only recommend food (Bar Food) in those establishments highlighted with the **FOOD** symbol.

SW1 Orange Brewery A

Tel 0171-730 5984 Map 19 C5
37 Pimlico Road SW1W 8NE

One of the few London pubs to brew their own beers: SW1 is a light bitter (3.8%), while SW2 (4.8%) and Pimlico Porter (4.5%) are richer and caramelised; in addition, seasonal ales and one-off beers are often brewed as guests or for special occasions. High ceilings, bare floors, tall stools around high tables and sofas – the bar is comfortable (and popular in the evenings). The Victorian gas wall lamps are still in working condition. A separate darkwood panelled dining-room has its own street entrance. Following a recent refurbishment there's also now a viewing area allowing the public to observe the brewing process in action. Part of the Scottish Courage group. *Open 11-11 (Sun 12-3, 7-10 30).* ***Beer*** *SW1, SW2, Pimlico Porter, seasonal guest ales. Access, Amex, Visa.*

EC1 The Peasant ★ FOOD

Tel 0171-336 7726 Map 16 C3
240 St John Street EC1V 4PH

Built in 1890, the former George & Dragon – a substantial Victorian gin palace – was transformed by Craig Schorn and Michael Kittos into a place where food is now very much its raison d'etre; booking is essential. The decor has been revamped but is still quite basic with plain wooden tables, darkwood bench seating and a mix of old-fashioned dining chairs. John Pountney is the chef here now and very good he is too. Some of the new-wave Italian influences have been lost from the regularly-changing menus and a more varied selection has been introduced. The food still comes with excellent crusty rustic bread, though, with extra virgin olive oil dip and many of the dishes are served in huge china bowls. Starters could be vine tomato, Jersey royal and rosemary soup, fried halloumi with a lemon and onion relish, Thai pork meatballs with a peanut and coriander sauce and fried polenta with marinated aubergines, mushrooms, olives and artichokes. For a main course the choice ranges from grilled skewers of monkfish with vine leaves and tabouleh to calf's liver with potatoes, artichokes and a lime and mint butter, skewered lamb with a vine tomato, cos, feta and mint salad and spaghettini with anchovies, tomato, chili and black olives. Equally desirable and well made are the desserts, which include lemon tart, water melon and passion fruit with Greek yoghurt, dark chocolate honey terrine with strawberry coulis and vanilla and caramel ice cream with biscotti. Also on offer is a prime British cheese served with oatcakes and celery. A short selection of wines is carefully chosen and all are available by the glass; three changing real ales show that The Peasant hasn't lost its pub identity. "12.5% service on all bills." Easy parking. ***Bar Food*** *12.30-2.30 & 6.30-10.45. Free House.* ***Beer*** *typically: Charles Wells Eagle & Bombardier, Ruddles County. Closed Sat lunch, all Sun, Bank Holidays, 10 days Christmas. Access, Visa.*

We do not accept free meals or hospitality – our inspectors pay their own bills and never book in the name of Egon Ronay's Guides.

SW3 Phene Arms FOOD

Tel 0171-352 3294 **Fax 0171-352 7026** Map 19 B6
9 Phene Street off Oakley Street Chelsea SW3 5NY

An unassuming neighbourhood pub tucked away in a quiet Chelsea cul-de-sac with the added attraction of having a terrace and quite a large garden for alfresco eating. There's a French chef here so the menu (see blackboard for daily specials) has a distinctly Continental style, right down to the sauces and generous use of garlic! The cheeseboard also leans towards France, though the puds are definitely British: treacle tart, various cheesecakes and summer pudding. Typical examples from the blackboard are starters such as grilled mussels with garlic butter smoked chicken and crab and avocado salads and king prawn Creole. For a main course, try pork medallions with a Dijon sauce, a rabbit casserole provençale, or sea bass in ginger and onion sauce. Bar food snacks are plainer: ordinary but decent sandwiches (not on Sunday) and 'things' with chips – the home-made beefburger is 100% pure beef. *Open 11-11 (Sun 12-3, 7-10.30).* ***Bar Food*** *12.30-2.30 (Sat & Sun to 4), 7.30-10.30 (Sat & Sun to 10). Children allowed to eat in restaurant only.* ***Beer*** *Adnams, Ruddles County & Best, Webster's Yorkshire. Garden, terrace, outdoor eating. Access, Amex, Diners, Visa.*

SE5 Phoenix & Firkin FOOD

Tel 0171-701 8282 Map 17 D5
5 Windsor Walk Denmark Hill SE5 8BB

Denmark Hill station was destroyed by a fire in 1980; the Phoenix & Firkin rose from its ashes thanks to Bruce's Brewery and public support. Now it's under the ownership of Taylor Walker (part of the Carlsberg-Tetley group), but the house-brewed beers (three permanent, three seasonal) are a major attraction. The interior structure of the station remains, with an extremely high ceiling allowing enough room for a comfortable mezzanine level. An enormous double-faced clock stands near the door. The decor is of brick, green paint and bare wood and there is live music on Monday nights (quite loud 'background' music at other times). The large food counter offers an appetising selection of varied salads, cold cuts, pies, samosas and onion bhajis; two daily hot dishes (mushroom and ham quiche with three salads, beef and ale) and a Sunday roast. Large baps with various fillings are served with salad. *Open 11-11, Sun 12-10.30.* ***Bar Food*** *12-8.30 (Sun to 7).* ***Beer*** *Own brews: Rail Ale, Phoenix, Dogbolter, two guest beers. No credit cards.*

W2 Prince Bonaparte FOOD

Tel 0171-229 5912 Map 18 A2
80 Chepstow Road W2 5BE

For many years this was a large Victorian public house indistinguishable from a myriad others scattered throughout the capital. Occupying a corner site with Talbot Road, it has recently undergone a mini metamorphosis and now offers well-prepared and imaginative food as well as a good selection of beers and wines. Where once there were three separate bars and an off-licence there is now just one very spacious, almost cavernous, L-shaped room with an extensive area towards the rear set out for diners. The decor is rather rough and ready (but then so might the clientele be at times) and the atmosphere is very laid-back and non-intimidating. Plain wooden tables and all manner of wooden chairs are set out facing the open-plan kitchen, itself an extension of the central, U-shaped bar counter. Philip Wright cooks and Beth Coventry helps prepare traditional offerings such as steak and kidney pie and fish cakes. Food orders are taken at the bar, having been chosen from the daily-changing blackboard menus slung high up on one wall. Tapas-style snacks are available from the bar: crostini with tapénade or taramasalata and slices of tortilla, for example. Typical dishes from a summer menu include Alentejo-style gazpacho (a thicker and chunkier Portuguese version of the perennial summertime favourite using oregano instead of basil), goat's cheese, sun-dried tomato and spinach tart, Morada bean (Spanish beans) chili with rice, guacamole and corn chips, salt-cured duck with a mushroom, cabbage and potato hash, red pepper and pesto spaghetti and grilled lamb steak with almond couscous and aubergine. There's little in the way of desserts – just some biscotti with a glass of dessert wine or a plate of Manchego cheese with quince jelly and bread. As well as real ales, the bar also offers natural elderflower cordial, Bass alcoholic lemonade and very good espresso coffee. Arrive early to ensure a table. *Open 11-11, (Sun 12-3, 7-10.30).* ***Bar Food*** *11-11 (Sun 12-3, 7-10.30).* ***Beer*** *Bass, Fuller's London Pride, guest beer. No credit cards.*

WC1 Princess Louise A

Tel 0171-405 8816 **Fax 0171-430 2544** Map 16 C3
208 High Holborn WC1V 7BW

A remarkable Victorian pub which has changed little this century and still boasts original mirrors surrounded by decorated floral tiles and ornate plasterwork. A minimum of eight traditional beers is gathered from around the country and is the major attraction, along with the impressive U-shaped bar that threads through the main room with its bare floorboards. The more comfortable upstairs lounge bar, whose bamboo plants and ceiling fans suggest a colonial feel, albeit with up-to-date, not-so-background music. Owned by Regent Inns. *Open 11-11 (Sat 12-3 & 6-11, Sun 12-2, 7-10.30). Free House.* ***Beer*** *Bass, Brakspear Bitter & Special, Gale's HSB, Greene King IPA, Adnams Best, Theakston, two guest ales. No credit cards.*

WC2 The Salisbury A

Tel 0171-836 5863 Map 18 D3
90 St Martin's Lane WC2N 4AP

A Victorian pub whose bronze nymph lamps dividing the semi-circle benches are a classic design. Original etched-glass partitions still remain but some walls have been plastered with theatre ads. One of London's oldest theatre pubs, it is still a popular meeting place for the theatrical fraternity. Taylor Walker. *Open 11-11 (Sun 12-3, 7-10.30).* ***Beer*** *Tetley, Burton Ale, Theakston. Family Room. Access, Amex, Diners, Visa.*

SW18 The Ship FOOD

Tel 0181-870 9667 Map 17 B5
41 Jews Row Wandsworth SW18 1TB

Directions to find the Ship don't sound promising: drive past Wandsworth bus garage and you'll see the pub beside a ready-mix concrete plant. Once there, though, things immediately begin to look up. A delightful terrace, complete with rose-covered rustic trellis, stretches all the way to the riverside and heaves with drinkers on fine days. The conservatory bar makes a pleasant, airy, most un-London-like venue, with its motley collection of old wooden tables, benches, chairs and pews; there's also a public bar, very much a locals' haunt. As we went to press, however, great changes were nearing completion here. Food was once obtained via a fair old scrum in an adjoining marquee, but that area has now become a new restaurant extension (housing 45 seats, bookings taken, waiter service). This area also now opens out on to a large, extended sunken garden. One menu is offered throughout and diners will now be able to eat in the original bar, conservatory or terrace. The new carte will include dishes such as rabbit terrine with sweet pepper and ginger pickles, mussel and squid stew, a plate of enchiladas with ham and peaches, and beef stifado with mash potato. Note that when weather permits the terrace barbecue will still be a focal point and many dishes on the indoor menu (eg chicken and fig kebabs and chargrilled lamb steak) will be barbecue-inspired, as before. The Ship is a Young's pub, under a joint tenancy with the nearby *Alma, Coopers Arms* in Chelsea and *The Castle* in Battersea (see entries). The beer is good and there's a superb selection of wines sold by the glass – nearly thirty at any one time. Children are welcome. *Open 11-11 (Sun 12-3, 7-10.30).* ***Bar Food*** *12.30-3, 7-10.* ***Beer*** *Young's. Riverside garden, outdoor eating, summer barbecue. Access, Amex, Visa.*

NW3 Spaniards Inn A

Tel 0181-455 3276 Map 16 B2
Spaniards Road Hampstead NW3 7JJ

Popular and comfortable weekend pub with a warm, friendly atmosphere; it has been both a toll house and the home of a Spanish ambassador in its long history. The ground-floor bar overlooks the garden and has lovely old settles, open fires and intimate corners, while upstairs (Turpin's Bar) is quieter. The vast garden is split in two by a narrow walkway covered with climbing ivy; one side has wooden tables and benches, the other white iron garden furniture with umbrellas. Budgies happily sing in the background aviary. Perfect stop for Hampstead hikers. Children are welcome. Parking for 42 cars. *Open 11-11 (Sun 12-3, 7-10.30).* ***Beer*** *Bass, Fuller's London Pride, Hancock's Traditional, up to three guest beers. Garden. Access, Visa.*

SW10 Sporting Page FOOD

Tel 0171-352 6465 **Fax 0171-352 8162** Map 19 B6
6 Camera Place Chelsea SW10 0BH

The former Red Anchor was remodelled and renamed five years ago with a young clientele -and therefore a wine bar atmosphere but with real ales and pub prices – in mind. There are dark blue walls above pale wood dado panelling, with decorative tiled panels depicting famous sporting events, the Boat Race among them, and sporting figures like W G Grace, while the seating is largely made up of upholstered benches around solid rosewood tables. Typical bar food dishes include hot chicken salad, croque monsieur and madame, and home-made salmon fishcakes with hollandaise. *Open 11-11 (Sun 12-3, 7-10.30). **Bar Food** 12-2.30, 7-10 (to 9.30 Sun). **Beer** Wadworth 6X, Webster's, Boddingtons. Patio, outdoor eating. Closed 25 & 26 Dec. Access, Visa.*

SW1 The Star A

Tel 0171-235 3019 Map 19 C4
6 Belgrave Mews West SW1

The delightfully different (for London) Star is tucked away in a cobbled mews between Halkin Place (itself off West Halkin Street) and Chesham Place, near Belgrave Square; the pub's exterior is resplendent with hanging baskets and flower tubs in summer. Visit when it's not packed (at weekday lunchtimes or early evening) and you'll find the atmosphere of a small, friendly local rather than that of a busy city pub. There are stools along the bar counter, stripped wood tables and chairs, cushioned settles and colonial ceiling fans; upstairs is a cosy bar, often used for private parties. Straightforward pub bar snacks (not at weekends) served by friendly staff. Opening hours are extended for the two weeks before Christmas. *Open 11-3, 5-11 (Fri 11.30-11, Sat 11.30-3, 7-11, Sun 12-3, 7-10.30). **Beer** Fuller's. Closed 25 & 26 Dec. No credit cards.*

W2 The Westbourne ★ FOOD

Tel 0171-221 1332 Map 18 A2
101 Westbourne Park Villas Notting Hill W2 5ED

🍷

The mish-mash of tables and chairs reflects the eclectice mix of clientele at this laid-back pub/restaurant. Opened in May 1995 by Oliver Daniaud and Sebastian Boyle, the converted pub was an immediate hit with the Notting Hillbillies. The pavement outside was a heaving throng of Notting Hill's Bohemian crowd in the heat of the summer, while in the evenings it may take a while to secure a table for eating. However, the wait is well worth while. The twice-daily-changing menu is chalked up on a board behind the bar along with the wines and beers available. The food choice is short, with only six or so dishes on offer at any one time, but the quality of the food is excellent. Typical from their opening summer menu was a large bowl of wonderfully spicy and well-chilled gazpacho served with chunky slices of country bread and extra virgin olive oil. Other dishes included tender, pink slices of roast leg of lamb served on a bed of puréed carrots and topped with a coarse and delicious salsa verde drizzled with more olive oil; spaghettini with chili, garlic, coriander and parmesan; a salad of mozzarella, vine tomatoes and avocado with a basil dressing, and cod baked with potatoes, tomatoes and thyme, accompanied by frisée lettuce and olives. Strawberries and cream or fresh greengages with yoghurt and honey might complete the picture for those going the whole hog. You order and pay for everything at the bar and the food is then delivered to the table by really cheerful staff. *Open 11-11 (Sun 12-10.30). Closed Monday lunchtime. **Bar Food** 1-3, 7-10. Free House. **Beer** Marston's Pedigree, Boddingtons. Credit card facilities applied for.*

EC1 Thomas Wethered A

Tel 0171-278 9983 Map 16 D3
33 Rosoman Street Farringdon EC1 0OH

Country-themed Whitbread pub which was the first in London to serve Wethered Bitter. The U-shape is laid out into different bars and lounges and the comfortable Directors Lounge at the back is used as a family room. *Open 11-11 (Sun 12-3, 7-10.30). **Beer** Brakspear, Boddingtons, four guest beers. Family room. Access, Amex, Visa.*

See the **County Round-Up** tinted pages for details of all establishments in county order.

SW6 White Horse FOOD

Tel 0171-736 2115 Fax 0171-610 6091 Map 17 B5
1-3 Parson's Green Fulham SW6 4UL

A substantial part-red sandstone Victorian pub standing at the northern end of Parsons Green, with a large, triangular walled patio to its front. The interior can only be described as hugely spacious – emphasising the decidedly pubby character of the place. On the periphery of the U-shaped room, the bar occupying the centre of the U, is a selection of leather chesterfield sofas and a few round tables with bentwood chairs. The food counter along one side of the bar has a series of booths, each seating six. Whether you're eating or just drinking, seating at peak times can be at a premium and this can rather detract from full and proper enjoyment of the food. A blackboard lists bar food such as home-made green pea and bacon chowder, leek quiche or broccoli au gratin. There are usually about three hot dishes at lunchtime and a few more in the evening: dishes like steak, mushroom and Adnams Extra pie, lamb's liver and Mackeson stout casserole, tagliatelle with squid, tomato and wine and spiced chicken cooked in cider, apricots and prunes. A dozen or so wines are promise by the glass, along with 15 Trappist beers (on a list of over 50 world classics) and the locally-brewed Freedom Pilsner lager. The long-serving landlady Sally Cruickshank has now retired and a new landlord has taken over, promising changes. *Open 11.30-3 (Sat 11-4, Sun 11-3), 5-11 (Sun 7-10.30). **Bar Food** 12-2.45 (Sat & Sun from 11), 5-10.30 (Sat 7-10.30 Sun 7-10). **Beer** Adnams Extra, Bass, M&B Highgate Mild, Harvey's Sussex Bitter, guest beer, seasonal specialities. Terrace, outdoor eating. Closed 24-27 Dec. Access, Amex, Visa.*

W8 Windsor Castle A

Tel 0171-727 8491 Map 19 A4
114 Campden Hill Road Kensington W8 7AR

A charming Georgian pub built in 1828 when (the entrance on Campden Hill Road being at the same height as the top of St Paul's Cathedral) one could see Windsor castle 20 miles away. The original panelling and built-in benches still remain and the three small bars have separate entrances. Traditional English cooking throughout the day; Sunday lunch roast beef. A shaded beer garden (one of London's busiest) at the rear is the main attraction in summer (and gets really packed), while a cosy country inn atmosphere prevails inside in winter. Both oysters and champagnes are sold at sensible prices. Not suitable for children inside. *Open 11-11 (Sun 12-4, 7-10.30). **Beer** Bass, Charrington IPA, Young's, Adnams Extra, Wadworth 6X, guest beer. Garden. Access, Amex, Visa.*

EC4 Witness Box FOOD

Tel 0171-353 6427 Map 17 D4
36 Tudor Street Temple EC4 0BH

Between the Embankment and Fleet Street, tucked away in the long basement of a modern office building. The decor is a mixture of traditional wood features, modern brick walls and painted murals of the Thames bank. Framed newspaper clippings of famous criminal events hang on the walls; there is even a special award for the best crime story of the year. Plenty of seating accommodates the busy crowd of regulars. The home-made cooking is only available at lunchtime and vanishes quite fast. The range covers sandwiches, salads, steak and kidney pie, lasagne and a few daily specials, possibly cheese, cauliflower and leek bake, lamb curry or braised lamb's liver and bacon. People come from miles around just for the proper home-made chips. Good selection of desserts, but not home-made. A more extensive blackboard menu is available (lunchtime only) in Chambers Wine Bar/restaurant at street level. 8-10 wines by the glass. Owned by Scottish/Courage group (previously Scottish & Newcastle). *Open 11-11. **Bar Food** 12-3.30. **Beer** Theakston Best, XB & Old Peculier, Courage Directors, Wadworth 6X. Pub closed Sat & Sun. Access, Amex, Diners, Visa.*

We endeavour to be as up-to-date as possible but inevitably some changes to landlords, chefs and other key staff occur after the Guide has gone to press.

EC4 Ye Olde Cheshire Cheese FOOD

Tel 0171-353 6170 **Fax 0171-353 0845** Map 17 D4
Wine Office Court 145 Fleet Street EC4A 2BU

A pub has stood here since 1538 but all we see today is that which has been re-built since 1667 – all, that is, except the great cellar vaults which survived the fire and all else since. The old bar and upper-floor dining-rooms still retain their 17th-century Chop house atmosphere, whilst new additions are more fashionably traditional. The Snug Bar, an extension in the front part of the building (entrance off Cheshire Court), is reserved for games with bar billiards, darts and satellite television. What used to be the courtyard is now the Courtyard Bar, with its original pavement floor. The Cheshire Room is a high-ceilinged rustic room that hosts hot and cold food counters offering the likes of fish and chips, roast beef and Yorkshire pudding, jam sponge pudding, bread-and-butter pudding and apple crumble. The Cellars Bar offers intimate corners and a pubby wine bar atmosphere; only snacks are available down here, with a speciality of hot Scotch roast beef sandwiches carved from the joint. To complete the picture, three floors of dining-rooms (The Chop Room seating 36, The Williams Room seating 35+25 in an annexe, The Johnson Room seating 32 and 25 in an annexe and top-floor Directors private room seating 16 – all available for private hire) offer a traditional à la carte menu. Sunday roast lunch is served in the bars only. No credit cards for bar meals. *Open 11.30-11 (Sun 12-3 only).* ***Bar Food*** *12-2.30 (restaurant à la carte only in the evening).* ***Beer*** *Sam Smith's Old Brewery & Museum Ale, up to four guest beers. Pub closed Sun eve, 24-26 Dec, New Year's Eve & Day and some Bank Holidays. Access, Amex, Diners, Visa.*

EC1 Ye Olde Mitre Tavern A

Tel 0171-405 4751 Map 16 D3
1 Ely Court Ely Place EC1N 6SJ

Located behind St Ethelreda's church and converted from the Bishop's house, Ye Olde Mitre dates back to the 18th century and is run for Taylor Walker by Don Sullivan. Access is between numbers 8 and 9 Hatton Garden or though a small passage in Ely Place. The Tavern's two small bars get extremely busy at lunchtime, bringing some life into the narrow Ely Court. Popular for their salmon, ham and cheese, and cheese and onion toasted sandwiches. The Bishops Room holds up to 30 for functions. *Open 11-11 Mon-Fri only.* ***Beer*** *Burton, Friary Meux, Tetley. Pub closed Sat, Sun & Bank Holidays. No credit cards.*

Many **B&B** establishments offer reduced rates for weekend and out-of-season bookings. Always ask about special deals for longer stays. Beware half-board terms in inns where we do not recommend **FOOD.**

England

ABBOTSBURY **Ilchester Arms** B&B

Tel 01305 871243 **Fax 01395 871225** Map 13 F3
Market Street Abbotsbury Dorset DT3 4JR

ZZz...

Abbotsbury is one of the prettiest villages in Dorset, its street lined with mellow-stone cottages and with the added attractions of the famous Swannery, the sub-tropical gardens, a medieval tithe barn and the ancient St Catherine's Chapel, it is an extremely popular destination. Also on the list of places to visit should be the Ilchester Arms, a rambling 16th-century coaching inn that dominates the heart of the village. Inside, a civilised and relaxed atmosphere prevails within the several heavily beamed, part-panelled and comfortably furnished rooms. Old tables, sofas in front of the inglenook, a wealth of old pictures – over 1000 – copper, brass, encased fish and numerous other old artefacts adorn the walls. The delightful en-suite bedrooms make this welcoming inn a most agreeable base from which to explore the area. All rooms are furnished to a high standard with dark wood reproduction furniture and decorated with quality wallpaper and matching fabrics – two rooms boasting canopied four-poster beds; one family room has a double and a sofa bed. Bathrooms are well equipped and other added comforts include TV, telephone and tea-making facilities. Two of the rooms are located in an adjacent converted stable block. Summer outdoor seating can be found on the sheltered patio, beyond the attractive and airy conservatory and on the lawn which affords splendid views towards St Catherine's Chapel on top of the neighbouring hill. Now a Premier Inn, part of Greenalls' Premier House group. *Family room. **Beer** Flowers Original, Bass, Wadworth 6X. Garden. **Accommodation** 10 bedrooms, all en suite, £48 (single £44). Children welcome overnight, cot available. Accommodation closed 24 & 25 Dec. Access, Visa.*

AINSTABLE **New Crown Inn** B&B

Tel 01768 896273 Map 4 C3
Ainstable nr Carlisle Cumbria CA4 9QQ

This recently reopened pub in a picturesque and remote village two miles above the Eden Valley has drawn instant praise from its early visitors. Totally reshaped and upgraded inside with not a hint of wasted space, the new bar, whose old flagstones and open hearth have been carefully restored, makes a fine setting for a fireside chat and the odd fishing story. Fittings and decor in the three bedrooms (one a single) have been kept just as simple with freestanding furniture, thick duvets and floral drapes. TVs and coffee-making facilities are all provided and each has its own neat, en-suite WC, bath and shower. Owned by Henry Lynch, whose family also run the *Duke's Head* in nearby Armathwaite (see entry). The bar snack menu holds promise. *Open 11-3, 6-11 (Sun 12-3, 7-10.30). Free House. **Beer** Tetley Best, three guest beers. Family room. **Accommodation** 3 bedrooms, all en suite, from £45 (single £25). Children welcome overnight, additional bed supplied (£10). Access, Visa.*

ALBURY HEATH **King William IV** A

Tel 01483 202685 Map 15a E4
Little London Albury Heath nr Guildford Surrey GU5 9DB

A surprisingly old-fashioned pub in a popular walking area (children and dogs welcome); cottagey little rooms with flagstone floor, enormous inglenook fireplace in main bar (off which, up a few stairs, is a separate dining area), rustic furnishings and attractive odd bits of bric-a-brac. Loos are outside and equally old-fashioned, but the small front garden can be a delightful, dingly dell-style, away-from-it-all place for a quiet pint in good weather – worth driving or walking your way round the lanes to find. Children welcome. *Open 11-3, 5.30-11, Sun 12-3, 7-10.30 (Sunday hours on Bank Holidays). Free House. **Beer** five regularly-changing real ales. Small front garden. Closed 25 Dec. No credit cards.*

ALCISTON **Rose Cottage** A

Tel 01323 870377 Map 11 B6
Alciston nr Polegate East Sussex BN27 6UW

Run by members of the Lewis family since 1959, this old-fashioned, wisteria-clad cottage pub nestles in the centre of a tiny hamlet on a dead-end lane near the base of the South Downs. Popular walkers' retreat and a venue for locals seeking a peaceful drink, either in the small front garden or in one of the rambling cosy rooms inside. Jasper, an African grey parrot, puts in regular lunchtime appearances before retiring upstairs in the afternoon to indulge in his predilection for watching war films. Each room is furnished with a good mix of sturdy tables and old, cushioned pews and adorned with a collection of harnesses, traps, farming memorabilia, stuffed birds or fishes in cases and other interesting bric-a-brac. Good

relaxed atmosphere. Rear paddock with chickens, geese, ducks and a pond. *Open 11.30-2.30, 6.30-11 (Sun 12-3, 7-10.30). Free House.* ***Beer*** *Harveys Best, guest beer. Garden, outdoor eating, tables in garden. Closed 25 Dec eve & all 26 Dec. No credit cards.*

ALDERMINSTER The Bell FOOD

Tel 01789 450414 Fax 01789 450998 Map 14 C1
Alderminster nr Stratford-on-Avon Warwickshire CV37 8NX

Devoted to the enjoyment of some quite serious food, the Bell now defines itself as a "Bistro and bar". It has, nonetheless, a more than adequate public real ale bar and Keith and Vanessa Brewer produce meals of a quality that is too good to ignore in a Guide devoted to good Pub food. As a dining venue it falls somewhere between the two, with food ordered from daily-changed blackboards at the bar and delivered with a fair amount of bustle in the bistro. The choice is extensive, from a carrot and orange soup, spinach mousse au gratin or water chestnuts with bacon and sweet and sour sauce to rogan josh, beef, orange and brandy casserole or steak, kidney and oyster pie – there are regularly up to 17 main-course choices! In addition, a long list of fresh fish and seafood dishes (Salcombe crab and lobster, coquilles St Jacques, Dover sole, sea bass) changes daily and is obviously a major attraction. The kitchen's dedication to all fresh ingredients plays its part, and there's hardly a chip in sight. Keep on to the end of the road and you'll be rewarded with luscious puddings such as tipsy sherry trifle, coffee and almond malakoff or sticky toffee pudding. A special two-course lunch (perhaps mild chicken curry and rice plus apple crumble and custard, £5.95) is offered from Mon-Fri. Special events, from "Symphony Suppers" to a Hallowe'en Pie Party play a regular part in the Bell's repertoire with complimentary year planners provided for diners to plan their next visit well ahead. Bookings advised for evenings. Free House. ***Bar Meals*** *12-2, (12-1.45 Sun), 7-9.45 (7-9 Sun).* ***Beer*** *Fuller's London Pride, Flowers IPA, Fuggles Imperial. Garden. Family room. Access, Visa.*

ALDWORTH Bell Inn A

Tel 01635 578272 Map 14a C3
Aldworth nr Reading Berkshire RG8 9SE

Especially popular with walkers on the Ridgeway Path, the Bell, of 14th-century origins, has been in the same family's hands for over 200 years. It has to be said that, externally, the pub's not particularly prettified and the old inn sign is decrepit, but its a Grade I listed building nonetheless and the interior has changed little either over the centuries. Five real ales, excellent Arkell's 3B for instance, are dispensed from a glass-panelled hatch which serves instead of any bar counter. Drinkers stand around in the hall or squeeze themselves into one of the candle-lit brick alcoves which give the place so much character. Food is restricted simply to hot, filled crusty rolls served up in wicker baskets: varieties range from cooked meats to smoked salmon with cream cheese or Cornish crab; home-made soup is served in winter. The pickled onions are extra! Worth a look nearby is the Norman village church famed for its massive stone effigies of the De La Beche family. *Open 11-3, 6-11 (Sun 12-3, 7-10.30).* ***Beer*** *Morells Mild & Oxford, Arkell's 3B & Kingsdown Ale, Hook Norton Best. Garden. Pub closed all Mon (except Bank Holidays). No credit cards.*

ALMONDSBURY Bowl Inn B&B

Tel 01454 612757 Fax 01454 619910 Map 13 F1
16 Church Road Lower Almondsbury nr Bristol Avon BS12 4DT

Zzz...

Just off the A38 and only two minutes' drive from the M5 (Junction 16), turn down Sunday's Hill to St Mary's Church in Lower Almondsbury; right next to it stands the Bowl, which in 1146 was a row of monks' cottages. Today's stone structure dates from the 16th century, though the just-completed bedroom conversions will wear well into the 21st! Uncovered wall niches, exposed roof timbers and original fireplaces all contribute to these rooms' unique charm, to which individual fabrics in bright colours and spotless fitted bathrooms have been added with flair and style. Beverage tray, colour TV, clock radio, trouser press and hairdryer comprise the comprehensive modern-day amenities. The single bar with its attendant two tiers of restaurant space is a buzzing, highly popular local venue with plenty of overspill to picnic tables by the roadside and an enclosed beer garden. ***Beer*** *Courage Best & Directors, John Smith's, guest beer. Patio and beer garden.* ***Accommodation*** *8 rooms, all en suite, £68.50, £39 at weekends (single £48.50, £20 at weekends). No dogs. Access, Amex, Diners, Visa.*

ALPHINGTON Double Locks FOOD

Tel 01392 56947 Map 13 D2
Alphington Exeter Devon EX2 6CT

The Double Locks – now under the ownership of the Bristol-based Smiles Brewery – isn't easy to find but it's well worth the effort. First find the Marsh Barton Trading Estate and drive through it to the council incinerator – don't worry, the pub is some way yet – until you reach the plank canal bridge, which is made for vehicles, although it may not appear to be. Once across, turn right, and a single-track road will bring you to the red-brick Georgian Double Locks in a splendid canalside location within sight of the Cathedral. Equally popular with business people and students, this is a fine summer pub: there are swans on the canal next to the lock, a large garden shaded by huge pine trees, and a barbecue both lunchtime and evening in summer, weather permitting. Inside is very informal. Several rooms have black- and white-tiled floors, draw-leaf domestic dining-room tables and lots of posters advertising local events – not far removed from a student bar at University. Chess, draughts, Monopoly, Scrabble and bar billiards are all keenly played. A huge blackboard displays the day's offerings, featuring almost as many options for vegetarians as for carnivores. Start, perhaps, with mushroom and coriander soup, garlic mushrooms and Stilton on toast or a selection of garlic breads with Cheddar, Stilton or goat's cheese topping, followed perhaps by turkey and mushroom pie, lasagne, baked potatoes, crepes and late breakfasts. Families welcome. *Open 11-11 (Sun 12-3, 7-10.30). **Bar Food** 11-10.30 (Mon-Sat),12-2, 7-10 (Sun). **Beer** Smiles Brewery Bitter, Best & Exhibition, Adnams Broadside, Greene King Abbot Ale, Wadworth 6x, Everards Old Original. Riverside garden, outdoor play area, outdoor eating, summer barbecue. Family room. Access, Visa.*

ALRESFORD Globe on the Lake FOOD

Tel 01962 732294 **Fax 01962 766008** Map 15 D3
The Soke Alresford Hampshire SO24 9DB

A superbly sited pub, only recently rejuvenated by new tenants, located at the bottom of Broad Street and on the banks of a reed-fringed lake – Alresford pond – complete with swans and dabbling ducks. The delightful waterside garden is a splendid summer spot for alfresco imbibing. Inside, the characterful main bar has been refurbished with new carpets, sturdy tables and chairs, and a deep, comfortable sofa in front of the open fire; local photographs and prints decorate the walls. The adjacent cosy restaurant has linen-clothed tables, candles and fresh flowers and includes an extension with seating that looks out over the lake. Chef-partner Terry McTurk's home-cooked, value-for-money bar snacks are listed on the ever-changing blackboard, which may include cauliflower cheese, cottage pie and vegetables, smoked salmon and prawn quiche, pork casseroled in cider, and ling (cod) baked with a cheese and bacon crust. Evening restaurant fare – also available in the bar – can be chosen from a board; examples include celery and walnut soup or duck rillettes with gooseberry conserve to start, followed by salmon poached on leeks with a watercress sauce, pork loin in a cider and cream sauce and duck breast 'sweet and sour'. Good, crisp vegetables. Raspberry mousse and peach and apple tart with kiwi sauce are typical puddings. A sign within reads "well-behaved children only". Park over the bridge on Broad Street. *Open 11-3. 6-11 (Sun 12-3, 7-10.30). **Bar Food** 12-2, 6.30-9.30 (Sun 7-9.30). **Beer** Wadworth 6X, Marston's Pedigree, John Smith's, Courage Best. Garden, outdoor eating. Access, Amex, Visa.*

ALSTONEFIELD George Inn A

Tel 01335 310205 Map 6 C3
The Green Alstonefield nr Ashborne Staffordshire DE6 2FX

The nearby Manifold Valley is a famous haunt for ramblers, and easy to get lost in. Drivers should follow the Deve valley road which connects Hulme End (B5054) with the A515. At the heart of this picturesque Derbyshire stone village, the Grandjean family warmly welcomes all comers, as long as muddy boots are left at the door. Service is from a tiny triangular stone-built bar; seating in three rooms in front of cosy fires, at picnic tables in the rear stable yard (with family camping available in the next field) or in front of the pub by the village green. The George gets pretty hectic at peak times and the crush can be quite convivial. *Open 11-2.30, 7-11 (Sun 12-3, 7-10.30); occasional all-day opening in Jul/Aug. **Beer** Burtonwood Bitter, James Forshaw's Bitter, Top Hat. Patio, outdoor eating. Family room. No credit cards.*

AMBERLEY Black Horse A

Tel 01453 872556 Map 14 B2
Amberley Gloucestershire GL5 5AD

Teetering on the very edge of the escarpment just below Minchinhampton Common, the pub's westerly aspect comes into its own on glorious summer evenings. Behind the bar itself is a picture window, and beyond it a prominent conservatory from which to soak in the panoramic views. Below are a tiered patio and garden, though parents should be mindful of a steep drop from the bottom wall to the meadow below. The upper garden has swings and picnic tables, and there's a separate games room with pool table and darts. A wide and regularly-changing range of real ales draws afficionados from far and wide. *Open 12-3, 6-11 (Sun 12-3, 7-10.30); 12-11 Sat in summer. Free House.* ***Beer*** *Smiles, Tetley & Archers Best, three guest beers. Garden. Access, Visa.*

AMPNEY CRUCIS Crown of Crucis B&B

Tel 01285 851806 Fax 01285 851735 Map 14a A2
Ampney Crucis Gloucestershire GL7 5RS

Zzz... 🍷

One of four Gloucestershire Ampneys, Crucis stands by the A417, 3 miles east of Cirencester. Established over 400 years, the refined, upmarket Crown has seen rapid growth in the last handful of years with the building of 25 hotel-style bedrooms, refurbishment of the oak-beamed bar and two-tiered restaurant and now a conservatory extension. Furnishings and decor in the bedrooms are uniform, as are up-to-date amenities and neat, fully-tiled bathrooms with over-bath showers. Fourteen ground-floor rooms are especially handy for those needing easy access; one room is specifically equipped for disabled guests; the clever courtyard lay-out affords most rooms a view over Ampney Brook, connected to the cricket ground opposite by a wooden footbridge. All-day room service shows that this is more inn than pub. Good selection of real ales and wines by the glass in the bar. *Open 11.45-10.* ***Beer*** *Theakston XB, Ruddles County, Archers Village. Stream-side garden.* ***Accommodation*** *25 bedrooms, all en suite, from £64 (from £49 single). Children welcome overnight (£17.50 if sharing parents' room, £25 in interconnecting room), additional bed & cot available. Accommodation closed 24-30 Dec. Access, Amex, Diners, Visa.*

ANSTY Ansty Arms B&B

Tel 01203 611817 Fax 01203 603115 Map 7 D4
Brinklow Road Ansty Coventry West Midlands CV7 9JP

Pub with accommodation lodge, two-tier eating, large conservatory and children's "Jungle Bungle" play area on high ground overlooking (and within earshot of) both motorways – a good spot and highly accessible – once you know the way! Take B4065 to Ansty from M6 at Junction 2 where it connects with the M69, and then follow B4029 signs to Rolls Royce PLC. A Premier Lodge, part of the Greenalls Group. ***Accommodation*** *28 rooms, all en suite. £39.50 midweek, £32.50 Fri-Sun. Children welcome overnight (high-chair, cot and an extra child's bed in parents' bedroom). Disabled access.* ***Beer*** *Tetley Best, Greenalls Strongarm, guest beer. Garden, outdoor eating. Access, Amex, Diners, Visa.*

APPLEBY-IN-WESTMORLAND Royal Oak Inn B&B

Tel 017683 51463 Fax 017683 52300 Map 5 D3
Bongate Appleby-in-Westmorland Cumbria CA16 6UN

Parts of the original building here are documented as being over 750 years old, and as it was once a coaching inn on the Penrith to Scarborough route, the Royal Oak can boast an unbroken history as a hostelry back to the 17th century. Both the snug and the Taproom are pristine examples of the traditional English pub. Oak panelling and stone walls, smoky-black beams and open smoky fires make a perfect environment in which to enjoy a particularly well-kept pint of real ale of which at least half a dozen brands plus guests and Bongate Special Pale (brewed by Hesket Newmarket Brewery) are always on tap. Bedrooms are necessarily small but nonetheless homely with leaded windows and creaky floors. A heavily-beamed attic is used as the family bedroom, and two rear rooms have doors opening directly on to the garden. There are also two stylish dining-rooms, one of them

reserved for non-smokers, and a first-floor residents' lounge looking out over the Bongate towards Appleby Castle. *Open 11-3, 6-11 (Sun 12-3, 7-10.30).* ***Beer*** *Bongate Special Ale, Yates Bitter & Premium, Theakston Best, Younger's Scotch, five guest beers. Family room.* ***Accommodation*** *9 rooms, 5 en suite, £59.50/£69.50 (single £27.50-£45.75). Children welcome overnight, extra bed and cot supplied (both £10). Closed 25 Dec (no accommodation 24/25 Dec). Access, Amex, Diners, Visa.*

ARMATHWAITE — Duke's Head Hotel — B&B

Tel 01697 4 72226 Map 4 C3
Armathwaite nr Carlisle Cumbria CA4 9PB

A long-standing favourite in the area, the Lynchs' pub stays firmly traditional, and retains an instant appeal for those with plenty of time to linger and reminisce. Its fishing connections are well documented in the Last Cast Lounge, from where it's only a few paces into a glorious garden with flower beds and beech trees disappearing down to the very banks of the river Eden below. The half-dozen bedrooms are traditionally furnished with TVs and beverage facilities throughout; most popular are the three with en-suite shower facilities, the remainder sharing two neatly-kept public bathrooms. "Well-behaved dogs are more than welcome." *Open 11-3, 6-11 (Sun 12-3, 7-10.30).* ***Beer*** *Boddingtons. Riverside garden.* ***Accommodation*** *6 bedrooms, 3 en suite, £45 (single £27.50). Closed 25 Dec. Access, Visa.*

ARNOLD — Burnt Stump — A

Tel 0115 963 1508 Map 7 D3
Burnt Stump Hill Arnold Nottingham Nottinghamshire NG5 8PA

It is the location, in 30 acres of country park on the fringe of Sherwood Forest, which makes the evocatively-named Burnt Stump such a popular spot. Four miles out of Nottingham, turn off the A60 Mansfield road a mile or so north of its junction with the A614. There's a wealth of open space for one or more of the family to exercise the dog, a cricket pitch below the terrace for others to watch Ravenshead cricket club at play, while children can act out their latest Robin Hood adventures in an extensive playground under the trees. In summertime there are bouncy castles and barbecues and a covered pop and crisps counter. Indoors, hungrier little outlaws have their own menu and non-alcoholic cocktail list, while at lunchtime the peckish in-laws are promised a "Hot Hoagie" in less than nine minutes. *Open 11-11 (Sun 12-3, 7-10.30).* ***Beer*** *Mansfield Riding Mild, Bitter & Old Baily. Garden, children's play area. Family room. Access, Amex, Visa.*

ASENBY — Crab & Lobster — FOOD

Tel 01845 577286 **Fax 01845 577109** Map 5 E4
Asenby nr Thirsk North Yorkshire YO7 3QL

As we went to press the thatch was being refreshed at this out-of-the-ordinary pub; it is hardly out of the way, though, being just off the A1. Very different in both concept and performance, the pub's popularity continues to grow. With an almost Bohemian interior of scatter rugs, jazz accompaniments (live every first Tuesday of the month) and liberally scattered junk in every nook and cranny, the *Crab & Lobster* is an unusual pub by any standards. A brasserie-type menu has a natural affinity towards fish, and the bar leaves plenty of room by day for pub-goers happy with a pint of Theakston's and a toasted BLT sandwich. Light lunches might include scallops with Gruyère and roast Piedmont peppers with anchovy, olives and parmesan or, more substantially, chicken confit with coconut and Basmati rice. By mid-evening, space is taken up with crudités and garlic sausage nibbles at the bar, where some congestion does occur in the wait for tables. Fish soup with aïoli and croutons and paella head the list of fish specialities with sea bass with ratatouille and parmesan and salmon with crab crust and lobster sauce further indications of the kitchen's vast and varied output. A new extension now matches the present thatched and listed building. Restaurant tables can be reserved separately by those wanting a little more elbow room and willing to pay a little extra. In summer, Sunday jazz barbecues make use of the marquee that has now become a permanent fixture. *Open 11-3, 6.30-11 (Sun 12-3 only).* ***Bar Food*** *11.30-3 (Sun from 12), 7-10 (except Sun eve). Free House.* ***Beer*** *Theakston Best & XB, Younger's Scotch & No 3. Garden. Pub closed Sun eve. Access, Amex, Visa.*

Ashby St Ledgers | Olde Coach House Inn | FOOD

Tel 01788 890349 **Fax 01788 891922** Map 15 D1 **B&B**
Ashby St Ledgers nr Rugby Warwickshire CV23 8UN

Zzz... 

Despite its Warwickshire address, Ashby St Ledgers is just across the county border in Northants, 3 miles from the M1, J18; alternatively, take the single track road signed off the A361, 4 miles north of Daventry. At the centre of this once-feudal village (population now 70) is Brian and Philippa McCabes' admirable pub where, from outside, you'd least expect to find one. Behind its ivy-covered facade is the cavernous, hollowed-out interior of a row of former cottages. Stone chimney breasts and cast-iron ranges still point to a certain antiquity. The printed menu is long, encompassing char-grills, "Old Favourites" (chilli, curry and lasagne), vegetarian options and a separate children's menu (puzzles, crayons, high-chairs, booster seats and baby-changing facilities are all provided). An additional blackboard menu adds an array of specials for the more adventurous: hot gunpowder chicken, spicy cottage pie, venison bourguignon and nut cutlets. Rather more predictable desserts are on display in a chill cabinet. There are half a dozen bedrooms, all ensuite, with TVs and tea trays, pine bedsteads and floral drapes plus abundant peace and quiet. Last year a multi-purpose children's adventure climbing frame was built in a protected, walled garden, allowing parents to get a break; once tired out, the children will hopefully sleep soundly in the main family bedroom, which offers a double and two single beds plus en-suite bathroom; two further rooms feature both double and sofa beds. With a happy mix of mid-week corporate customers, weekend function overnighters and those seeking out good pub food and exceptional real ales, the Olde Coach House Inn is a busy place. Even with all this, the pub still manages to win of our Family Pub of the Year award 1996! *Open 12-2.30, 6-11 (Sat 12-11, Sun 12-3, 7-10.30). Free House.* ***Bar Meals*** *12-2, 6-9.30 (7-9 Sun). Garden, outdoor eating.* ***Accommodation*** *6 bedrooms, all en suite £50 (single £42). Children welcome overnight (under-5s stay free), cot supplied.* ***Beer*** *St Ledger Ale (Chiltern Brewery), Flowers IPA & Original, Wadworth 6X, Boddingtons, Everards Old Original, Beechwood Bitter, guest beers. Access, Amex, Visa.*

Ashford-in-the-Water | Ashford Hotel | B&B

Tel 01629 812725 Map 6 C2
1 Church Street Ashford-in-the-Water nr Bakewell Derbyshire DE4 1QB

The former Devonshire Arms stands at the head of this picturesque Derbyshire village, just off the A6 and a mere stone's throw from the historic stone Sheepwash Bridge. Much original oak is retained in the beamed bar where log fires burn in winter; residents have use of their own cosy lounge, which opens on to a rear courtyard and enclosed garden. Each of the seven bedrooms (two with four posters) have been carefully remodelled in appropriately country style with floral-patterned wallpapers and bed linen; all are well equipped with direct-dial phones, TVs, clock radios and trouser presses. *Open 11-11 (Sun 12-10.30). Free House.* ***Beer*** *Mansfield Cask bitter, Riding & Old Baily. Garden.* ***Accommodation*** *7 bedrooms, all en suite (three with bath), £75 (four-poster £85, single £50). Children welcome overnight, additional bed (£10) and cot supplied. Access, Amex, Diners, Visa.*

Ashprington | Durant Arms | FOOD

Tel 01803 732240 Map 13 D3
Ashprington nr Totnes Devon TQ9 7UP

New landlords Graham and Eileen Ellis had just taken over at this neat and tidy, cream-painted 18th-century pub just as we went to press, however they have retained the same long-serving cook and kitchen staff who produce honest, home-cooked food. A flagged entrance hall leads into the main bar, with a bay window seat overlooking the village street, and into the spick-and-span dining room with neatly laid-out darkwood tables and chairs and a few settles. Plates adorn a high shelf around the walls and fresh flowers are an added touch on the tables. Lunchtime fare consists of hearty snacks listed on a daily-changing board and may include sweet and sour pork, beef curry, rabbit pie and the speciality 'big brown pot' – steak, kidney, vegetables and potatoes cooked in ale and topped with pastry. More imaginative dishes are featured on the evening blackboard which could offer creamy garlic mushroom pot or melon and raspberries for starters, followed by a choice of twelve main courses, for example pork tenderloin with orange and apple sauce, poached salmon with dill and cucumber sauce and monkfish in cream and garlic. Good home-made puddings. Only fresh local produce is used and only so many portions of each dish are available, so arrive early – especially at weekends – as the board may be wiped clean! One

bedroom (with en-suite shower) is now available (£40 double, £20 single); a self-contained cottage is also available for weekly let (£225 weekly, sleeps three in one bedroom plus a sofa bed, book well in advance); this accommodation has not yet been inspected. *Open 11-2.30, 6-11 (Sun 12-2.30, 7-10.30). **Bar Food** 12-2 & 6.30-9.30. Free House. **Beer** Marston's Pedigree, Brakspear Bitter. No credit cards.*

ASHPRINGTON — Waterman's Arms — FOOD

Tel & Fax 01803 732214 Map 13 D3 **B&B**

Bow Bridge Ashprington nr Totnes Devon TQ9 7EG

Delightfully situated on the banks of the River Harbourne, at the top of Bow Creek, the Waterman's is a favourite summer venue for alfresco riverside imbibing with resident ducks and – if you are lucky – kingfishers to keep you company. Bow Bridge is recorded in the Domesday Book and the inn until recently was a smithy and prior to that a brewery and a prison during the Napoleonic Wars. Enthusiastic owners Phoebe and Trevor Illingworth have transformed what was a small cottage into an efficiently-run and friendly inn with quality overnight accommodation. 'Tardis'-like inside, a series of neatly furnished rooms radiates away from the central servery, all filled with a mix of rustic furniture, old photographs, brass artefacts and other memorabilia. Home-cooked bar food caters for all tastes, from hearty snacks such as sandwiches, salads and platters to regular menu favourites including steak and kidney pie, rack of Devon lamb and steaks, all accompanied by good fresh vegetables, or (if desired) decent chips and salad. Fresh pasta dishes and an expanding range of exotic dishes (from the worldwide repertoire!) represent the unusual and a daily-changing blackboard might list a fresh soup, walnut and lentil bake or escalope of turkey 'annabella'. The mixed seafood salad platter is very popular and includes crab, prawns and fresh salmon. A separate pudding board may include home-made banoffee pie, bread-and-butter pudding and crème brulée. Ten beautifully fitted-out bedrooms have floral, cottagey fabrics and co-ordinating friezes around the walls, attractive dark-stained modern furniture and spotlessly-kept bathrooms with shower cubicles and efficient, thermostatically-controlled showers. Added comforts include telephone, cabinet-housed TV and tea-making facilities. Front rooms overlook the river and surrounding valley sides. The five newest rooms were sympathetically added last year; all have en-suite bathrooms and overlook the gardens; two family rooms have a double and a single bed plus room for a cot or further bed. Good breakfasts include a selection of fruits and a cooked menu choice that features smoked haddock and kippers. *Open 11-11 summer, 11-3, 6-11 winter, Sun 12-3 & 7-10.30). Free House. **Bar Food** 12-2.30 & 6.30-9.30 (Sun 7-9.30). **Beer** Dartmoor Best, Palmers IPA, Tetley Bitter, Bass. Garden, outdoor eating. Family Room. **Accommodation** 15 bedrooms, all en suite, £54-£70 (family room £58-£88, single £34-£42 according to season). Children welcome overnight (under-3s free, 3-5s £5, 6-10s £10, 11-14s £15), additional bed and cot supplied. Access, Visa.*

ASKERSWELL — Spyway Inn — A

Tel 01308 485250 Map 13 F2

Askerswell nr Bridport Dorset DT2 9EP

Tucked down a winding country lane a mile off the busy A35 Dorchester to Bridport road, this gloriously situated pub is the perfect spot in which to escape traffic tensions. Unwind in the traditional Spyway Bar where scrubbed pine tables, old settles, longcase clock and a timeless atmosphere pervades. A further bar and dining area are pine furnished and display an impressive assortment of farming memorabilia, brass artefacts and a collection of cups hanging from the beams. The garden is a delightful summer retreat, complete with shrubs, flowers, tiny stream and superb downland views. It is a popular tourist area; be early in summer. Around twenty wines are served by the glass; in addition, twenty-three George Gale country wines are on offer. *Open 11-3, 6-11 (Sun 12-3, 7-10.30). Free House. **Beer** Ruddles County, Ushers Best, Wadworth 6X. Garden. Amex.*

> Many **B&B** establishments offer reduced rates for weekend and out-of-season bookings. Always ask about special deals for longer stays. Beware half-board terms in inns where we do not recommend the **FOOD.**

ASKHAM — Punch Bowl Inn — FOOD

Tel 01931 712443 Map 4 C3
Askham nr Penrith Cumbria CA10 2PF

Four miles from junction 40 of the M6 this low, stone-built 18th-century inn, opposite the longest village green in Cumbria, is at the heart of the Earl of Lonsdale's Lowther Estate. Despite the cramped and often crowded bar which serves the front lounge, it is deceptively spacious beyond, with a family room, a second bar and a cosy dining-room to the rear. A vast menu which claims international status serves throughout. Alongside the 'Punch Bowl Specials' (Bampton chicken fritters; Dacre turkey bake) are French smokehouse quail, Chinese pork kebab, tagliatelle eglofski and a vegetarian Mexican bean pot. With plenty to please and amuse the youngsters, and the entire village green to play out on, the Punch Bowl's a popular family venue. *Open all day Mon-Sat during summer holiday season.* ***Bar Food*** *12-2 (Sun only), 7-9.* ***Beer*** *Whitbread Castle Eden, Timothy Taylor's Landlord, Morland Old Speckled Hen, guest beer. Patio, outdoor eating. Family room. Access, Visa.*

ASKRIGG — King's Arms Hotel — FOOD

Tel 01969 650258 **Fax 01969 650635** Map 5 D4 **B&B**
Market Place Askrigg in Wensleydale nr Leyburn North Yorkshire DL8 3HQ

Zzz...

Liz and Ray Hopwood's characterful, former coaching inn has an unbroken history dating back to 1760 when outbuildings, where the Back Parlour is now, housed John Pratt's racing stables. Turner is known to have stayed here while recording on canvas the tranquil Dales scenery of the early 1800s; today, the high-ceilinged main bar, complete with saddle hooks, oak settles and hunting prints, is universally recognised as The Drover's Arms as depicted on TV in James Herriot's All Creatures Great and Small. The smaller, low-beamed front bar retains a wig cupboard within its panelling; side snugs surround the green marble fireplace. The back bar is simply furnished and home to shove ha'penny and darts boards. Food outlets operate on two floors of this fascinating maze of interlocked cottages. A large blackboard menu complements the printed bar menu and evolves with the seasons. Typical of the 20 or so offerings are moules marinière with samphire, chicken liver parfait, smoked haddock and onion rings, toad in t'hole, Dales' lamb with Madeira sauce, 16oz plaice with lemon beurre noisette and home-made, homely puddings. Proper sandwiches and children's favourites are also offered. Upstairs, the elegant, panelled Clubroom Restaurant (30 seats, no children under 7, no smoking) serves fixed-price à la carte dinners and table d'hote lunch; the adjacent, 40-seater, no-smoking Silks Grill Room provides a balancing act between substantial Yorkshire breakfasts, simple steaks and fish, and sumptuous afternoon teas. All of the eleven bedrooms retain original features that are in keeping with the inn's manor-house style, the many oak beams and uneven floors complemented by antique furniture, one four-poster, half-tester and canopied brass beds, and quality colour co-ordinated fabrics; two suites attract the highest tariff. ***Bar Food*** *12-2, 7-9 (7-8.30 Sun). No children under 5 in the bar after 8pm. Free House.* ***Beer*** *Younger's No 3, Theakston Bitter, McEwan's 80/-, Dent Bitter, guest beer.* ***Accommodation*** *10 bedrooms, all en suite, £75, £85 & £105 (£50, £55 & £70 single); 2 suites (£95, £70 single). Children over 7 welcome overnight (7-16s free if sharing parents' room, own room 70% rate). Courtyard, family room. Access, Amex, Visa.*

ASTON — Flower Pot — FOOD

Tel 01491 574721 Map 15a D3 **B&B**
Ferry Lane Aston nr Henley-on-Thames Oxfordshire RG9 3DG

Zzz...

Situated off the A423 down a narrow lane in Aston. The 1890s' building is solid brick with plants attempting to climb the outside. Two small rooms provide a bar with banquette seating, rowing gear decorating the walls, and tables for 20 people. A large garden seats about 50. The pub is situated by a bridle path and, as it is 300 yards from the river towpath (where a sign advertises the pub's presence), walkers make up a large part of its trade. Landlady Pat Thathcer's food is simple and served in ample portions: home-made soup, beef and Guinness pie, fish and pasta bake, date and apple crumble; game features in winter. A traditional Sunday lunch is served in winter. Recent structural improvements have opened out what was a small bar into a larger bar space, with more comfortable seating for eating bar food. *Open 10.30-3, 6-11 (Sun 12-3, 7-10.30); open all day occasionally in summer, often at weekends.* ***Bar Food*** *12-2, 6.30-9 (not Sun eve).* ***Beer*** *Brakspear. Garden, outdoor eating.* ***Accommodation*** *3 bedrooms, 2 with en-suite showers, £49 (single £39). Children welcome overnight (under-10s stay free in parents' room) additional bed available. No dogs. Access, Diners, Visa.*

Aswarby Tally Ho Inn FOOD

Tel 01529 455205 Map 7 E3 **B&B**

Aswarby nr Sleaford Lincolnshire NG34 8SA

Just south of Sleaford before the turning off the A15 to Aswarby stands this fine mellow stone estate inn, which dates back some 200 years. The pleasant bar boasts exposed stone and brickwork aplenty, country prints, old settles, pews, open log fire and additional woodburner for cold winter days. More especially a good atmosphere prevails for relaxing diners tucking into the reliable home-cooked fare that is listed on a bar menu card and the regularly-changing blackboard menu. Satisfying choices may include Lincolnshire lamb casserole, oven-baked chop, spicy Tally Ho chicken, salmon, spinach and cheese pancakes and lighter bites such as bacon and mushrooms on toast and freshly-filled baguettes with ham, beef or prawns. Daily specials always feature a country soup and a hot dish. Good-value table d'hote Sunday lunch. To the rear is an attractive, pine-furnished restaurant. An adjacent stable block houses the six well-kept bedrooms, all of which have spotless, compact en-suite facilities (only two have a bath). Rooms are spacious, simply furnished, soothingly decorated and provide plenty of hanging and writing space. TVs and tea-makers are standard extras. *Open 12-3, 6-11 (Sun 12-3, 7-10.30). Free House.* ***Bar Food*** *12-2.30, 6.30-10 (Sun 12-2, 7-10).* ***Beer*** *Bateman XB, Bass, guest beer. Garden, children's play area.* ***Accommodation*** *6 bedrooms, all en suite, £45 (single £30). Children welcome overnight, extra bed supplied. Access, Visa.*

Aust Boar's Head A

Tel 01454 632278 Map 13 F1

Main Road Aust Avon BS12 3AX

A hidden, out-of-the-way spot, yet just a stone's throw from the M4 traffic thundering towards the Severn Bridge. The Aust lane is now a dead end. Standing by the church, the Boar's Head is a favoured local watering hole. Candles, lacy cloths and a succession of alcoves and inglenooks imbue an 18th-century feel to it all at night, and in winter a huge log fire flickers. To the rear there's a pretty stone-walled garden with a wishing well and beyond it a popular caravan site. *Open 11-3, 7-11 (Sun 12-3, 7-10.30).* ***Beer*** *Courage Best, Whitbread Best & three guest beers. Garden and patio. Access, Amex, Visa, Diners.*

Axbridge Lamb Inn B&B

Tel 01934 732253 Map 13 F1

The Square Axbridge Somerset TA6 2AP

Rambling, ancient town pub, romantically set opposite King John's hunting lodge, now an interesting museum. Open-plan bar area with bric-a-brac, beams and settles, as well as more modern intrusions. Overnight accommodation comprises a delightful large double room with older-style, freestanding furniture, Laura Ashley fabrics and a good-sized bathroom, and two further more basic and homely bedrooms that include a spacious family room. Attractive rear patio. *Open 12-2.30, 6.30-11 (Sun 12-3, 7-10.30), Sat hours may be longer. Free House.* ***Beer*** *Butcombe, Bass, Wadworth 6X, occasional guest beer. Garden/patio, outdoor eating.* ***Accommodation*** *3 bedrooms, 2 en suite (one with bath), £35-£45 (single £18-£25). Children welcome overnight, additional bed (£10) and cot (£5) available. Check-in by arrangement. Accommodation closed 24-26 Dec. Access, Visa.*

Axbridge Oak House Hotel B&B

Tel 01934 732444 **Fax 01934 733112** Map 13 F1

The Square Axbridge Somerset BS26 2AP

Less atmospheric than one would expect of an inn dating back to 1342 but it enjoys an enviable position overlooking the attractive village square, and is only a few yards from the parish church. There's now a bistro-style bar and the ten bedrooms, mostly en-suite, vary greatly in standard and style of decor and furnishings, some being kitted out with comfortable modern co-ordinating fabrics and pine furniture, while others are very modest. TVs, telephones, tea-makers and radios are standard. Three of the sparsely appointed bathrooms have shower/WC only. ***Beer*** *Wadworth 6X, Boddingtons. Family room.* ***Accommodation*** *9 bedrooms, £51 (single £38). Children welcome overnight, additional bed (£10) and cot (£5) available. Access, Amex, Visa.*

AXFORD **Red Lion Inn** FOOD

Tel 01672 520271 Map 14a A4 **B&B**

Axford nr Marlborough Wiltshire SN8 2HA

In a small hamlet three miles from Marlborough, this attractive 17th-century brick and flint inn offers clean and comfortable accommodation in a picturesque rural setting. Views across the lush Kennet Valley can be enjoyed from the modern, simply-furnished dining-room and bar and from the small grassy area with benches, adjacent to the car park. Local landscape paintings (many for sale) adorn the walls. A starter from the blackboard might be roulade of smoked salmon with smoked cheese and tarragon or chicken livers sautéed in Madeira and for main course, mixed pan-fried seafood, lamb rack served in orange and rosemary, or a more simple dish (chili con carne, lasagne or one of three vegetarian pastas) from the menu. Four compact and freshly decorated bedrooms are kept in very good order, each having TVs, beverage trays, hairdryers and newly fitted en-suite facilities with shower units. Two of the bedrooms are located in Pear Tree Cottage, reached by a path through the garden, where guests have use of a kitchen, sitting room and sunny patio with scenic views. Twelve or so wines by the glass. No smoking in the restaurant. *Open 11-3, 6-11 (Sun 12-3, 7-10.30). Bar Food 12-2.30, 6.30-10.30 (Sun 12-3, 7-10). Free House.* ***Beer*** *Wadworth 6X, Hook Norton, guest beer. Garden, children's play area.* ***Accommodation*** *4 bedrooms, all with en-suite shower, £45 (single £30). Children welcome overnight (under-4s stay free in parents' room). Check-in by arrangement. No dogs. Access, Visa.*

AYOT ST LAWRENCE **Brocket Arms** B&B

Tel 01438 820250 **Fax 01438 820068** Map 15a F2

Ayot St Lawrence Hertfordshire AL6 9BT

Splendid medieval pub – an unspoilt 14th-century gem – set within an equally splendid village close to Shaw's Corner, where George Bernard Shaw lived for forty years (now National Trust owned). Classic unadulterated three-roomed interior with a wealth of oak beams, an inglenook fireplace, a rustic mix of furniture and tasteful piped classical music. Those wishing to experience the historic charm further can stay upstairs in one of the four characterful bedrooms built into the timbered eaves. Furnished in traditional style – one with a four-poster bed – the rooms are simple and homely, and reputedly haunted by a monk from the local abbey. All share two adequate bathrooms. Those guests craving more modern creature comforts can book one of the three newer bedrooms housed in a converted old stable block across the courtyard. These are neatly carpeted and comfortably furnished in modern pine (one also boasts a four-poster bed), and (unlike main building rooms) they have central heating. Two have rather compact shower rooms, the third a clean en-suite bathroom, and all are equipped with tea-makers and clock radios. Pleasant walled garden for peaceful alfresco drinking. Families welcome. *Open 11-11 May-end Sept, 11-3, 6-11 winter (Sun 12-3, 7-10.30 all year). Free House.* ***Beer*** *Greene King Abbot & IPA, Wadworth 6X, Theakston Best, Dark Horse Sunrunner, guest beer. Garden.* ***Accommodation*** *7 bedrooms, 3 en suite, £55-£70 (single £40). Children welcome overnight, additional bed (£5) & cot supplied. No dogs. Access, Visa.*

BAGINTON **Old Mill Inn** B&B

Tel 01203 303588 **Fax 01203 307070** Map 6 C4

Mill Hill Baginton nr Coventry West Midlands CV8 2BS

A handy place to stay, close to the A45, A46 and five miles from the M6, yet tucked away peacefully in pine-studded grounds running down to the river Sowe. Public areas still retain many features of the 19th-century working mill, and outside a riverside patio is linked by a bridge to the garden. A well-designed modern block houses the bedrooms which have pine furniture, Laura Ashley designs and views of the river and weeping willows. Ample car parking. *Open 11-3, 5-11.30 (Sun 12-3, 7-10.30).* ***Beer*** *four real ales. Large garden, children's play area.* ***Accommodation*** *20 bedrooms, all en suite, £65 (single £60). Children welcome overnight, additional bed (£5) and cot available. No dogs. Access, Amex, Visa.*

We only recommend food (Bar Food) in those establishments highlighted with the **FOOD** symbol.

BAINBRIDGE — Rose & Crown Hotel — B&B

Tel 01969 650225 **Fax 01969 650735** Map 5 D4
Bainbridge Wensleydale North Yorkshire DL8 3EE

In the heart of the Wensleydale forest, Bainsbridge is a village of mellow stone houses set around the triangular green by which the old stocks stand. At its head, the 15th-century Rose & Crown still houses the Forest Horn, blown nightly from Holy Rood to Shrovetide as a guide to travellers towards its welcoming safety. Original beamed ceilings, open fires and antique furnishings give the small flagstoned bar its great character, though the adjacent games room is rather more utilitarian and less appealing. Bedrooms are cosy though not overly large. Three boast four-poster beds to complement their cottagey decor; all are equipped with TV, radio and hairdryers. Only four, however, have full bathrooms en suite, the remainder having WC and shower rooms only. ***Open*** *11-3, 6-11 (Sun 12-3, 7-10.30). Free House.* ***Beer*** *Webster's Yorkshire, Theakston's Best.* ***Accommodation*** *12 bedrooms, all en suite £54 (single £32). Children welcome overnight, extra bed (£10) and cot (£6) provided. Garden. Access, Visa.*

BALDWIN'S GATE — Slater's — B&B

Tel 01782 680052 **Fax 01782 680219** Map 6 B3
Marfield Gate Farm Baldwin's Gate nr Newcastle under Lyme Staffordshire ST5 5ED

Zzz...

Five miles from Junction 16 on the M6, this skilful conversion of former outbuildings on a working farm (they still have a 100-head milking herd) has created a stylish new accommodation pub with super facilities for youngsters. In addition to the family/function room (complete with nappy-changing facility in an adjacent ladies' loo) there's a safe, enclosed rear garden full of play equipment and a pair of ducks and geese to talk to. The grown-ups may make time for a game of bowls on the crown green lawn. Set around a cobbled courtyard behind the pub proper, three self-contained cottagey suites contain just about everything for short or long stays: en-suite bathrooms with over-bath showers, fitted kitchenettes and breakfast area, plus extra beds and cots at no extra charge. Breakfast in the dining-room if residents prefer: children's meals in pub or garden (all day on Sunday). Music on Tuesday and Sunday evenings. *Open 11-11 (Sun 11-10.30). Free House.* ***Beer*** *Marston's Bitter & Pedigree, Boddingtons. Garden, children's play area. Family room.* ***Accommodation*** *2 en suite rooms £47, 3 self-catering cottages (sleep up to 4, £45 + £6 breakfast per person). Children welcome overnight (free if sharing parents' room), additional bed and cot available. Access, Visa.*

BAMBURGH — Lord Crewe Arms — B&B

Tel 01668 214243 **Fax 01668 213273** Map 5 D1
Front Street Bamburgh Northumberland NE69 7BL

Friendly old inn in the middle of Bamburgh, a town dominated by its massive castle. Public areas include two rustic-style bars and two unpretentious lounges. Upstairs, bedrooms offer modest comforts with TVs and beverage trays but no telephones; five rooms do not have en-suite baths. Three rooms do not have en-suite facilities and are particularly good value for those wanting budget accommodation – £40, single £27.50. A new suite features a four-poster and one room has a bed-settee in addition to the double bed. No children under 5. The bar is only open at lunchtime in winter. *Open 11-3, 6-11 (Sun 12-3, 7-10.30). Free House.* ***Beer*** *Bass, Stones, guest beer.* ***Accommodation*** *24 rooms, 21 en suite, £68 (single £46). Closed Nov-end Mar. Access, Visa.*

BAMFORD — Yorkshire Bridge Inn — FOOD B&B

Tel 01433 651361 **Fax 01433 651812** Map 6 C2
Ashopton Road Bamford Derbyshire S30 2AB

Zzz... 

In the heart of the Derbyshire Peak District this inn dates from 1826 and is named after an old packhorse bridge on the river Derwent. Views from the central bar take in the peak of Win Hill – a beautiful setting in which to enjoy some good, reliable cooking. Bar food is split between a lunchtime and an evening menu. Lunchers may choose from hot or cold sandwiches, ploughman's, traditional hot dishes of the home-made steak and kidney pie variety, or from four vegetarian (cracked wheat and walnut casserole) or six salad (beef, ham, Cheddar) dishes; fresh fish is available from the blackboard on market days. In the evening similar fare is supplemented by a charcoal grill offering 'giant' T-bone steak and honey-glazed rack of lamb to the hungry crowd of walkers and sightseers. Accommodation

takes the form of an adjoining hotel converted from barns, now housing ten en-suite bedrooms, all with satellite TV, radios, telephones, and beverage-making facilities; for those wishing to escape the hurly-burly there is a peaceful lounge and a residents-only dining-room. Non-smokers have the pleasure of the conservatory and children are well catered for both on the menu (fish fingers, sausages or burgers) and outside where there is a slide and climbing frame. *Open 11-11 (Sun 12-3, 7-10.30).* ***Bar Food*** *12-2, 6-9 (Sat to 9.30, Sun from 7). Free House.* ***Beer*** *Stones, John Smith's Magnet, Bass, Boddingtons. Garden, outdoor eating, children's play area. Family room.* ***Accommodation*** *10 bedrooms, all en suite, £48 (single £35). Children welcome overnight (under-3s stay free in parents' room, 3-12s £5), additional bed and cot available. Access, Visa.*

BANBURY — Ye Olde Reine Deer Inn — FOOD

Tel 01295 264031 Map 14a B1

47 Parsons Street Banbury Oxfordshire OX16 8NB

With its inn sign hanging out over the middle of the road, this town-centre pub is the oldest building in Banbury (1570), where Oliver Cromwell once held court in a panelled back room (now used for functions). Landlord John Milligan of the Falkland Arms at nearby Great Tew (see entry) has renovated the building and introduced a policy of 'over-21s only'. Food, served only at lunchtimes, is limited to a selection of filled jacket potatoes, ploughman's and 'doorstep' sandwiches, plus a few dishes of the day such as salmon and broccoli quiche, lentil and tomato soup and ham and eggs with mashed potatoes and peas. Luxuriant hanging baskets of flowers decorate the front of the building and there is a small courtyard bar for summer drinking. A dozen country wines are dispensed from Victorian glass barrels behidn the bar. Parking for about 18 cars to the rear. *Open 11-2.30, 5-11 (Sat from 7). Bar Food 11.30-2.* ***Beer*** *Hook Norton, guest beer. Courtyard, outdoor eating. Pub closed all Sun, 25 Dec. No credit cards.*

BANTHAM — Sloop Inn — B&B

Tel 01548 560489 Map 13 D3

Bantham nr Kingsbridge Devon TQ7 3AJ

Set in an attractive coastal hamlet just 300 yards from the sea and one of the finest sandy beaches along this part of the coast, the 16th-century Sloop is a most peaceful inn in which to stay and explore the area. Associations with smuggling are deep for it was at one time owned by the notorious South Hams wrecker and smuggler John Whiddon. The atmospheric flagstoned interior has a strong nautical feel to it, with lots of sea-going memorabilia and the rear, plainly-furnished dining area is designed in the shape of a ship's cabin. In the main building there are five clean and neat en-suite bedrooms, generally of a good size, with modern furniture, clock/radio, TV and beverage-making kits. There are also self-catering flats available to the rear of the inn. *Open 11-2.30, 6-11 (Sun 12-3, 7-10.30). Free House.* ***Beer*** *Bass, Ushers Best Bitter, Blackawton Bitter.* ***Accommodation*** *5 bedrooms, all en suite, £54. No credit cards.*

BARDWELL — Six Bells Country Inn — FOOD

Tel 01359 250820 Map 10 C2 **B&B**

The Green Bardwell nr Bury St Edmunds Suffolk IP31 1AQ

Approached via a track (once the original coaching highway) off the village green, this rather plain, cream-painted 16th-century inn (Grade II listed) is surrounded by open countryside, views of which can be appreciated from both the warm and comfortable beamed bars and the converted stable-block bedrooms. Reliable bar food (around six starters and 18 main courses, on different lunch and dinner blackboards menus) encompasses 'magnificent mushroom soup, tiger prawn satay, tipsy lamb, Suffolk sausages with onion gravy and mashed potatoes at lunchtime; potted cheese, coarse pork terrine, rogan josh, Dover sole, steaks, steak and kidney pudding for dinner. Fresh fish and shellfish feature strongly on Fridays – try their deep-fried cod with hand-cut chips at lunch or lobster in the evening. More elaborate, restaurant-style fare (generally served in the simple country pine-furnished dining-room, where bookings are taken) can also be ordered in the bar. Puddings include luxury bread-and-butter pudding. The interesting, 30-bin list of wines from Adnams includes eleven half bottles. Peaceful and homely overnight accommodation is in converted barn and stable buildings; the eight en-suite bedrooms are furnished with modern pine and co-ordinating bedcovers and fabrics. All have clean, compact shower rooms, TVs, telephones and tea-makers and all are on the ground floor. Outside, a great deal of effort has gone into improving the patio and large garden over the last year; new floodlighting and paths have been installed and new window boxes, flower beds and trees planted. Children

are well catered for, with a Wendy House in the garden, high-chairs inside and a vanity unit for baby-changing in the Ladies. *Open 12-2.30, 7-11 (Sun to 10.30). Free House.* ***Beer*** *John Smith's Bitter, Adnams Southwold, guest beer.* ***Accommodation*** *8 bedrooms, all en suite £45-£55 (single £35-40). Children (and dogs) welcome overnight, extra bed £5 (for over-5s). Garden, outdoor eating, children's play area. Access, Visa.*

Barley — Fox & Hounds — FOOD

Tel 01763 848459 Map 15 F1
High Street Barley nr Royston Hertfordshire SG8 8HU

Pleasingly traditional white-painted 15th-century village local, with rambling, low-ceilinged rooms, splendid open fires, plus a separate dining area and conservatory. A beer drinker's favourite – the Fox & Hounds has served over 300 different real ales to date and 10 handpumps are constantly in use. A small bar menu offers lunchtime snack meals such as filled jacket potatoes or large granary baps, ploughman's and pork ribs. The longer main menu operates throughout the pub at lunchtime and in the evenings (bar and restaurant): whole plaice, whitebait, various steaks, home-made curries and pies (lamb and apricot). Vegetarians are well catered for with their own menu of at least eleven choices. Ice creams and sundaes are a speciality (9 varieties are on offer), as well as puddings such as strawberry pavlova, orange cheesecake and chocolate mousse. Traditional pub games are very popular with indoor and outdoor skittles, bar-billiards, shove-ha'penny, darts and dominoes; there's also a new boules pitch. The children's play area has a multi-purpose climbing frame with slide and swing; inside the pub there are baby-changing facilities and a children's menu is offered. *Open 12-2.30, 6-11 (Sun 12-3, 7-10.30).* ***Bar Food*** *12.30-2, 6.30-9.30 (Sun from 7). Free House.* ***Beer*** *home-brewed Nathaniel's Special (3.3%) & Flame Thrower (4.4%), Boddingtons Best & Mild, 6 guest beers. Garden, outdoor eating, children's play area, disabled facilities. Access, Visa.*

Barming — The Bull — A

Tel 01622 726468 Map 11 C5
5 Tonbridge Road Barming Maidstone Kent ME16 9HB

Neat exterior with pretty hanging baskets. Good choice of real ales. 15 tables set on the lawned garden. Bouncy castle for children. On the A26 Maidstone to Tonbridge road, 2½ miles from Maidstone; convenient for Junction 5 of the M20. Whitbread Wayside Inns. *Open 11-11 Mon-Sat, 12-10.30 Sun.* ***Beer*** *Boddingtons, Fremlins, 4 guest beers. Garden. Children's play area. Access, Visa.*

Barnard Gate — Boot Inn — FOOD

Tel 01865 881231 **Fax 01865 881834** Map 14a B2
Barnard Gate nr Witney Oxfordshire OX8 6AE

About 5 miles from Oxford, just off the Oxford-Cheltenham A40, the popular Boot Inn is run by George Dailey and his brother-in-law Steve Chick. The secret of its success is happy, young staff offering good food at extremely competitive prices. The result is an extremely busy pub at almost all times, so you would be well advised to book a table. A well-built extension complements the bar with apricot walls covered with prints and stone-flagged floors and has enabled the Boot to offer a larger menu with special dishes of the day on a blackboard next to the large open log fire. A terrace complete with fountain offers more tables outside; it's illuminated at night, creating the festive feeling of being abroad. The menu might include grilled king prawns, home-made soup, a variety of pasta dishes (penne with pepper tomato and chili sauce) or a vegetarian dish such as chargrilled Mediterranean vegetables topped with melted goat's cheese. Steaks are good and there is a selection of puddings (sticky toffee pudding, banoffi pie or crème brulée). *Open 11-11 (Sun 12-10.30).* ***Bar Food*** *12-2.30, 6.30-10 (Sun 12-9). Free House.* ***Beer*** *Morland Old Speckled Hen, Hook Norton, 2 guest beers. Terrace, outdoor eating. Access, Visa.*

Barnoldby-le-Beck — Ship Inn — A

Tel 01472 822308 Map 7 E2
Main Road Barnoldby-le-Beck Humberside DN37 OBG

17th-century village pub with a warming, real fire, separate restaurant and an award-winning garden. The landlord, Mr Gillis, is an avid supporter of Grimsby Town football team, who show an equal support for his ales. Recent interior refurbishment has brought a sparkle to the interior and a profusion of hanging baskets and tubs brings a seasonal splash of colour to the exterior. Six miles from the end of M180. Trent Taverns. *Open 11-3, 6.30-11 (Sun 12-3, 7-10.30).* ***Beer*** *Flowers Original, Theakston Best, Younger's No 3, Boddingtons. Paved beer garden. No credit cards.*

BARNSLEY — Village Pub — B&B

Tel 01285 740421 Map 14 C2
Barnsley Cirencester Gloucestershire GL7 5EF

Clearly once a row of roadside cottages next to the village school, the Village Pub is commendable for retaining both its unusual name and a cottage interior, quite in keeping with open fires, brass-hung beams and antique settles. The single bar dispenses to carpeted lounges and dining-room on one side and to drinkers on the summer patio through a quaint service window. So close is the main road that access to the pub is now sensibly to the rear, as are the bedrooms (thus well insulated from any traffic noise). Accommodation, as one might expect, is modest yet comfortable, with TVs available for those who tire of solitude. All but one have en-suite WC/shower rooms, the remaining single enjoying the benefit of its own, consequentially private, bathroom. On the B4425 Cirencester to Bibury road. *Open 12-3, 6-11 (Sun 12-3, 7-10.30). Free House.* ***Beer*** *Butcombe Bitter, Wadworth 6X, guest beers. Garden, patio.* ***Accommodation*** *5 bedrooms, all en suite, £44 (single £29). Children welcome overnight, additional bed available (under-5s free, over-5s £15). Check-in by arrangement. Pub and accommodation closed 25 Dec. Access, Amex, Visa.*

Many **B&B** establishments offer reduced rates for weekend and out-of-season bookings. Always ask about special deals for longer stays. Beware half-board terms in inns where we do not recommend the **FOOD.**

BARNSTON — Fox & Hounds — FOOD

Tel 0151 648 1323 Map 6 A2
Barnston Road Barnston Merseyside L61 1BW

Lunchtime snacking pub by hazardous bends on the A551; Barnston post office is 100 metres away. Alongside sandwiches and filled potatoes, the likes of quiche and Coronation chicken are reliably fresh. Cooking rises to chicken korma and grilled pork chop; vegetarian options of leek and mushroom crumble and cheese and spinach pancakes, perhaps. No chips, no music, no cigarette machine and no food Sunday lunch or any evening. Landlords Ralph and Helen Leech also own the *Jug & Bottle* (not yet inspected) in Heswall, ten minutes from Barnston. *Open 11.30-3, 5.30-11, (Fri & Sat in summer 11.30-11, Sun 12-3, 7-10.30).* ***Bar Food*** *12-2. Free House.* ***Beer*** *Courage Directors, Webster's Yorkshire, Ruddles County & Best, Marston's Pedigree. Garden. Family room. No credit cards.*

BARRINGTON — ·Royal Oak — FOOD

Tel 01223 870791 **Fax 01223 871845** Map 15 F1
31 West Green Barrington Cambridgeshire CB2 5R2

Dating from the 14th century, this striking half-timbered and thatched pub stands close to one of the largest village greens in the country. Colourful summer hanging baskets adorn its attractive facade which overlooks the splendid bench- and brolly-filled lawn – an ideal spot for fine weather imbibing. The rambling, beamed and low-ceilinged interior is divided into traditionally-furnished bars and filled with horse brasses, gleaming copper pans, antlers and tack. To the rear is a neat conservatory restaurant extension. Featured strongly on the printed menu are home-prepared vegetarian dishes, with at least 16 imaginative main courses from which to choose. Typical examples are vegetable and basil strudel with a lime glaze, Barrington loaf with a redcurrant glaze and pecan, mushroom and mango stroganoff. Meat eaters are not left out, with traditional steak and kidney pie, guinea fowl with a rosehip and peach glaze and rack of lamb making an appearance. Standard (but home-made) puddings. *Open 11.30-2.30, 6-11 (Sun 12-3, 7-10.30). Free House.* ***Bar Food*** *12-2, 6.30-10 (to 10.30 Fri/Sat, 7-10 Sun).* ***Beer*** *Greene King IPA & Abbot Ale, Adnams Southwold, Eldridge Pope Royal Oak. Garden, outdoor eating area. Family room. Access, Visa.*

We do not accept free meals or hospitality – our inspectors pay their own bills and **never** book in the name of Egon Ronay's Guides.

BASSENTHWAITE LAKE Pheasant Inn B&B

Tel 017687 76234 Fax 017687 76002 Map 4 C3
Bassenthwaite Lake nr Cockermouth Cumbria CA13 9YE

There remains a Dickensian feel to the splendid bar whose counter unusually comes to little above waist height. Here the tobacco-brown panelled ceiling, walls hung with Victorian prints and the low oak settles are a snug winter retreat. In summer a splendid spot for afternoon tea is the flower garden whose array of lupin, honeysuckle and rhododendron seemingly meander off into oblivion. *Open 11.30-2.30 (Sat 11-3), 5.30-10.30 (Fri to 11) (Sun 12-2.30, 7-10.30 – to 10 in winter). **Beer** Theakston Best, Bass. Garden. **Accommodation** 20 bedrooms, all en suite, from £64 (£68-£96 Sep/Oct, single £55). Children welcome overnight, additional bed (£20), cot supplied (charged). Access, Visa.*

BATCOMBE Batcombe Inn ★ FOOD

Tel 01749 850359 Fax 01749 850615 Map 13 F1
Batcombe nr Shepton Mallet Somerset BW4 6HE

Tucked away down a web of country lanes in the very rural Batcombe Vale, Derek and Claire Blezard's old honey-coloured stone coaching inn enjoys a peaceful position away from the main village, next to the church. The long and low-ceilinged main bar has exposed stripped beams and is warmly and tastefully decorated; terracotta sponged walls with ivy leaf stencilling are hung with several old paintings, creating a relaxed and homely atmosphere. A mix of individual chairs, deep window seats and darkwood furniture fronts a huge stone inglenook with log fire. Adjoining the bar is a high-ceilinged, no-smoking dining area in what used to be the old barn and toll-house. Bar food is reliably good with blackboards listing daily-changing specials such as home-made soups, Somerset Brie pasty, chicken piri piri, plaice fillets and vegetarian dishes. The printed menu is better than most, offering a range of hearty snacks, starters and main dishes, from smoked chicken and walnut salad and seafood crepes to Thai platter (chicken saté, Tiger prawns, spring rolls all in a chili dip). Accompanying salads are enormous and imaginative and main-dish vegetables are served separately and generously. Traditional Sunday lunch is always popular, as are non-alcoholic drinks such as elderflower pressé and a tasty ginger brew. Bookings are taken anywhere in the pub. A big welcome is made to families: children not only have their own 'Kiddies Corner' menu with a choice of nine items but they also have their own fully-equipped room complete with mini-trampoline, doll's house, drawing board, books, toys (including a Nintendo games console) and a video recorder with a good choice of films - enough to placate any child while relaxed parents enjoy their meal. Children's facilities extend to the rear garden play area for fine weather activity; there is also a changing and feeding area in an ante-room to the Ladies. A further car park extension, children's play areas and feature garden have recently been completed. Winner of our Family Pub of the Year Award in 1995. *Open 12-2.30, 7-11 (Sun 12-3, 7-10.30). **Bar Food** 12-1.45, 7-9.45 (to 9.30 Sun). Free House. **Beer** Butcombe Bitter, Wadworth 6X. Garden, patio, children's play area. Access, Visa.*

BATHAMPTON George Inn FOOD

Tel & Fax 01225 425079 Map 13 F1
Mill Lane Bathampton nr Bath Avon BA2 6TR

Hard by a stone-arched road bridge which crosses the Kennett and Avon canal (there's even a door into the pub from the tow-path), this is truly a picturesque spot. The Hall family have furnished it with hanging flower baskets every year for twenty years and the summer crowds regularly overflow on to the patio and into the garden. Diners order their food on pre-printed pads at a single bar and then wait at their chosen table. As ever, daily specials are probably the best bet: smoked chicken and broccoli pie or kidneys Turbigo, with crunchy chocolate fudge, perhaps, to follow. Children enjoy the creaky, spiral staircase which leads them to a beamed family room at eye level with the canal. Summer barbecues, with separate outside bar and food counters. *Open 11-2.30, 6-11 (Sun 12-2.30, 7-10.30) all day Sat in summer and Bank Holidays. **Beer** Courage, guest beer. Garden, patio and family room. No credit cards.*

BATHFORD The Crown FOOD

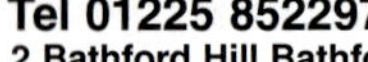

Tel 01225 852297 Map 14 B2
2 Bathford Hill Bathford nr Bath Avon BA1 7SL

Just off the A4, the Crown stands at the foot of Bathford Hill by a wide road junction which was once the eastern terminus for a train ride into nearby Bath. In its cavernous interior, which leads in turn to a delightful summer patio, everything is made easy for the visitor. Menus are available in French, German and Japanese. Those for the children are jokey and user-friendly. There's ample family seating and high-chairs in the no-smoking Garden Room and Simon the Magician appears on Sunday lunchtimes. The menu promotes itself as 'not fast food' and the selection is ambitious – some items may be suspended at peak times. Go, though, for the daily specials: reliable crusty pies, perhaps of duck and cherries or ham, leek and Stilton, cheese-topped seafood pancakes. Some exotic puddings with clotted cream (terrine of summer fruits) and good local cheeses. Tolerant staff provide high-chairs, books and small toys, but no chips! Nevertheless, jacket potatoes, French toast, hot dogs, small pizzas, small portions, Wall's ice creams, Salcombe Dairy ice cream tubs and kids' cocktails are on offer to keep junior appetites satisfied. *Open 12-2.30, 6.30-11 (Sun 12-3, 7-10.30). **Bar Food** 12-2, 6.30-9.30 (to 10 Fri & Sat, from 7 Sun). **Beer** Ushers Best, Wadworth 6X, 2 guest beers. Garden. Family Room and patio. Pub closed Mon lunchtime (except Bank Hols). Access, Amex, Diners, Visa.*

BEACONSFIELD Greyhound FOOD

Tel 01494 673823 Map 15a E3
Windsor End Beaconsfield Buckinghamshire HP9 2JN

The unassuming Greyhound pub enjoys its relatively undisturbed position on this tree-lined avenue, opposite the parish church at the peaceful 'Windsor End' of Beaconsfield. Its plain exterior appearance belies the characterful interior which dates back to the 15th century, and comprises three traditional, low-beamed bars with simple furnishings, open fires and a welcoming atmosphere. No music or intrusive games. Small rear dining-room with terracotta walls, cloth and candle-topped tables, quality watercolours and a relaxing ambience. Reliable home-cooked bar food is listed on a printed menu – home-made burgers flavoured with garlic, basil and tomato, seafood pie, steak and kidney pie, freshly-baked French bread sandwiches – and on twice-daily-changing blackboards, both available throughout the pub. Interesting specials may include mushroom soup and Greek salad as starters, followed by cod fillet in tomato sauce topped with parmesan or perhaps pork, apple and cider pie. Provençal vegetarian lasagne and a choice of fresh pasta dishes. Accompanying vegetables are crisp and plated separately. Round off your meal with a fresh berry mousse or maybe steamed apricot sponge. No children under 14 inside. *Open 11-3, 5.30-11 (Sun 12-3, 7-10.30). **Bar Food** 12-2.15, 7-10 (no **Bar Food** Sun eve). Free House. **Beer** Courage Best, Fuller's London Pride, Wadworth 6X, two guest beers. Garden, outdoor eating. Access, Amex, Visa.*

BEAUWORTH Milbury's A

Tel 01962 771248 Map 15 D3
Beauworth Cheriton nr Alresford Hampshire SO24 0PB

Set on a hill just to the south of the village, the site of some bronze age burial mounds or barrows, the pub's name is actually a corruption of Mill-Barrow, the name of the last remaining mound just 150 yards away. The South Down Way passes by the front door of this old tile-hung pub. The main bar boasts old brickwork, a flagstone floor and rough hewn three-legged tables, but the most fascinating feature is an enormous treadmill, within which a poor donkey once walked to raise water from a 300-foot well. For the price of a donation to the Guide Dogs for the Blind, you are invited to drop an ice-cube down the well and count the nearly eight seconds it takes to splash in the water far below. The former restaurant is now a further seating area. Children are made positively welcome, with their own small section on the menu and swings out in a large garden carved from one corner of a field. There is also a skittle alley, which must be booked. *Open 11-2.30 (Sat to 3), 6-11 (Sun 12-3, 7-10.30). Free House. **Beer** Milbury's (4.3%), Courage Directors, Tetley, Ansells, Hampshire Brewery King Alfred, Pendragon, several guest beers. Garden, outdoor eating, children's play area. Family room. Access, Amex, Visa.*

BECKINGTON Woolpack Inn ★ FOOD B&B

Tel 01373 831244 **Fax 01373 831223** Map 14 B3
Beckington nr Bath Somerset BA3 6SP

Zzz...

A splendidly restored former coaching inn that benefits greatly from a new section of the A36 trunk road that now bypasses Beckington. In the easy-going atmosphere within diners are encouraged to consume simply what they'd like just how and where they'd like it, and there is plenty of choice on the one menu that is served throughout. The bar boasts a revealed original fireplace, recreated window shuttering in lieu of curtains and re-laid traditional flagstone flooring. Behind it, the Garden Room was extended last year and now leads out on to a walled garden; this is the most popular dining area; the no-smoking Oak Room dining area seats a further twenty diners. Chef David Woolfall's menus are equally all-embracing with no obligation to order more than a starter-sized serving of, say, a Greek salad, smoked salmon or céviche of scallops with avocado, chili and lime (although all the starter dishes are dual-priced as starter or main course). There's every temptation to indulge further, though: particularly good daily fish specials, fresh tagliatelle with basil, pine nuts and parmesan, Bath sausages with onion gravy and coriander mash, home-made salmon fish cake with smoked salmon and chive sauce, or stir-fried vegetables and egg noodles in sesame oil with sambal and Indonesian sweet soya sauce. Prices are high, but so is the quality. Round off with walnut tart with honey and rum glaze and pistachio ice cream or a plate of interesting cheeses. Investment and attention to detail in the bedrooms are evident, with each room's individual design incorporating many original features supplemented by custom-built freestanding furniture and a comprehensive range of comforting amenities. The bathrooms are particularly well-appointed, with plenty of bright light, generous supplies of towels and toiletries and particularly powerful over-bath showers. Three larger 'Executive' rooms (one with four-poster) attract the higher tariff and two have direct access to the residents' rear garden. A new residents' lounge and a board room conference facility were created last year. *Open 11-3, 6-11 (Sun 12-3, 7-10.30).* ***Bar Meals*** *12-2, 7-10 (Sun to 9).* ***Beer*** *Bass, Wadworth Henry's IPA & 6X, guest beer. Walled garden, outdoor eating.* ***Accommodation*** *12 bedrooms, all en suite, £64.50-£84.50 (single £49.50-£59.50). Children welcome overnight, additional bed and cot available for sharing with parents in larger, Executive rooms only. Access, Visa.*

BECKLEY Abingdon Arms FOOD

Tel 01865 351311 Map 14a C2
High Street Beckley Oxfordshire OX3 9UU

A beautifully positioned, stone-built pub with inspiring views. The large, grassed garden is pretty, with a pleasant mix of trees, a summer house, a floodlit terrace and spacious seating. Within, the interior is plainly furnished with cloth-covered wall seats in the lounge and a separate public bar with a bar billiards table. Hugh and Mary Greatbatch have now been here for 25 years and Mary's cooking is still a great attraction. Her excellent food mirrors the seasons, with lots of delicious picnicky things in summer, cold poached salmon and smoked chicken amongst them, and warming bakes, curries with basmati rice and other hot dishes in winter (game pie with port sauce). Puddings like apple and almond tart and a mousse-like chocolate torte. In winter, regular special evenings are organised (on alternate Fridays) highlighting food from one particular country or region – booking is essential. Only children over 14 inside. Note late Sunday eve opening. The village is signposted off B4027. *Open 11.30-2.30, 6.30-11 (Sun 12-2.30, 8-10.30).* ***Bar Food*** *12.15-1.45, 7.15-9.15 (except Sun eves). Free House.* ***Beer*** *Tetley, Hook Norton, Wadworth 6X. Garden, outdoor eating. No credit cards.*

BEDFORD Embankment Hotel B&B

Tel 01234 261332 **Fax 01234 325085** Map 15 E1
Embankment Bedford Bedfordshire MK40 3PD

A small Tudor-style town-centre hotel sitting on the embankment of the River Ouse and providing comfortable accommodation that is popular with visiting businessmen. Twenty spacious upstairs bedrooms are furnished and decorated in uniform style with modern built-in furniture, good writing space and adequate en-suite shower rooms; TVs, tea-makers, radios and trouser presses are standard throughout. Last year's promised refurbishment of the facade and bar areas still has not been undertaken. *Open 11-2.30, 6-11 (Sun 12-3, 7-10.30).* ***Beer*** *Bass.* ***Accommodation*** *20 bedrooms, all en suite, £59.50 (single £49.50); weekend £49.95/£29.95. Children welcome overnight (under-2s stay free in parents' room), additional bed (£5) and cot supplied. Access, Amex, Diners, Visa.*

BEENHAM VILLAGE — Six Bells — FOOD B&B

Tel 01734 713368 Map 14a C4
Beenham Village nr Reading Berkshire RG7 5NX

Dating back some 200 years, this pub is a mixture of old and new. The bar is old, dimly lit, with mahogany counter and all the characteristics ofan old village pub. To the rear they have added an extension which has a large room suitable for parties and wedding receptions. All food is home-made: a large variety of omelettes, garlic mushrooms, soups (Stilton), stir-fried beef with black bean sauce, lemon chicken, poached fresh salmon, with a treacle and walnut tart or lemon meringue pudding to finish. A two-course roast meal is served on Sundays. Upstairs, there are four letting rooms, with tea/coffee-making facilities, radios and televisions. The bathrooms are adequate, the beds comfortable and all the rooms have lovely views over the neighbouring farmland. One single room has shower only. *Open 12-2.30, 6.15-11 (Sun 12-3, 7-10.30).* ***Bar Food*** *12-2.30, 7-10 (Sun 12-3, 7-10). Free House.* ***Beer*** *Flowers, Brakspear Bitter, occasional guest. Garden, outdoor eating.* ***Accommodation*** *4 bedrooms, all en suite, £49 (single £36). Children welcome overnight (rate depends on age), additional bed available. Access, Visa.*

BEER — Anchor Inn — FOOD B&B

Tel 01297 20386 Map 13 E2
Fore Street Beer nr Seaton Devon EX12 3ET

Zzz...

One of Britain's best-situated inns, the Anchor overlooks the stony beach whence the local crab boats set to sea in the early morning. Fish dominates the menu; dishes not only include local haddock and plaice, but also in the evenings medallions of monkfish in Dijon mustard sauce, baked whole red mullet with black olives, tomatoes and white wine, fresh scallops with bacon and mushrooms and supreme of salmon topped with prawns. They also cater well for meat-eaters and vegetarians in the spacious and comfortably furnished bars. Each of the eight bedrooms has private facilities (though not all are en suite and some have shower only); bright co-ordinated fabrics enliven them all, and some enjoy fine sea views. Entrance for residents is separate from the pub proper; there's a clubby TV lounge and the clifftop garden opposite is a spectacular location for an early evening drink. No pets. *Open 11-2.30, 5.30-11 (11-11 Mon-Sat in summer, Sun 12-2.30, 7-11).* ***Bar Food*** *12-2, 7-9.30. Free House.* ***Beer*** *Dartmoor Best, Otter Ale, Wadworth 6X. Garden, outdoor eating.* ***Accommodation*** *8 bedrooms, 5 en suite, £46-£56 (single £28-£42 seasonal). Children welcome overnight, additional bed & cot (price according to age) supplied. Access, Visa.*

BEETHAM — Wheatsheaf — B&B

Tel 01539 562123 Map 4 C4
Beetham Kilnthorpe Cumbria LA7 7AL

Just off the A6, a mile or so North of the Lancashire border, Mrs Shaw's homely hostelry has been in the same ownership now for over 25 years. Unsurprisingly, her many returning guests are welcomed as members of the extended family. Behind a facade of black-and-white gables and leaded windows are three interlinked bars which are very much the focal point of village life, while for more retiring residents there's a comfortable TV lounge available upstairs. The bedrooms are neat and attractively decorated, if on the whole rather small. There are TVs and tea makers, and spotlessly kept carpeted private bathrooms. The popular front rooms have views over the village and church grounds down towards the river Bela. *Open 11-3, 6-11 (Sun 12-3, 7-10.30). Free House.* ***Beer*** *Thwaites Bitter, Theakston Best, Boddingtons, Younger's Scotch Bitter.* ***Accommodation*** *6 bedrooms, all en suite, from £40 (single £30). Bar closed 25 & 26 Dec eve, accommodation closed 24-26 Dec. Access, Visa.*

BELFORD — Blue Bell Hotel — B&B

Tel 01668 213543 **Fax 01668 213787** Map 5 D1
Market Square Belford Northumberland NE70 7NE

Zzz... ☺

Creeper-clad, the Bell stands at the head of the village on a cobbled forecourt. In front are the old Market Place and stone cross (restored by English Heritage), and the Norman parish church stands on a hill behind. The pubbiest part is the Belford Tavern, licensed in old stables in the courtyard, where there's a games room, a children's menu and just one regularly-changing real ale on offer. The hotel's stone-flagged foyer leads to a stylish cocktail bar boasting a collection of miniature hand bells, and a restful residents' lounge. Bedrooms

are a mix, from those in the annexe (with shower/WCs only) to superior and de luxe rooms with full bathrooms and lovely views of the Blue Bell's 2-acre "garden of 10,000 blooms". One ground-floor room is equipped for disabled guests. *Open 11-3, 6-11 (Sun 12-3, 7-10.30). **Accommodation** 17 bedrooms, all en suite, £76-£88 seasonally (single £35-£42). Children welcome overnight (under-12s stay free in parents' room) additional bed and cot available. Dogs welcome by arrangement. Access, Amex, Visa.*

BELLINGDON Bull FOOD

Tel 01494 758163 Map 15a E2
Bellingdon Road Bellingdon Buckinghamshire HP5 2XU

Delightful little redbrick cottage on the north side of the village, enjoying a peaceful rural aspect as it's surrounded by fields. The attractive, low-beamed bar boasts a large inglenook, various display cases and every table is neatly laid out with place mats, for the Bull is now very much a dining pub. Bar food is reliable, with an interesting selection of dishes being listed on regularly-changing blackboard menus; there may be up to a dozen or so choices at each stage (including puddings). Choices may range from deep-fried Brie and prawn and asparagus brochette to Thai green chicken curry, chargrilled venison steak with Cumberland sauce, wild Tay salmon poached or grilled, seafood tagliatelle, pan-fried turbot with lemon and ginger 'gravy'. Fish is the thing here and the chef even brings the dressed crab back from Cromer himself. Sandwiches are not served, but a 'cold board' of home-cooked gammon with new potatoes and salad, jumbo sausages, home-made paté and hot peppered mackerel are popular as snackier dishes. *Open 12-3.30, 6-11 (Sun 12-3, 7-10.30). **Bar Meals** 12-3, 7-10 (no food Sun eve). **Beer** Ind Coope Burton Ale, Benskins Best, Tetley. Garden, outdoor eating, summer barbecue. Access, Amex, Visa.*

BENENDEN King William IV FOOD

Tel 01580 240636 Map 11 C6
The Street Benenden Kent TN17 5DJ

16th-century tile-hung village inn, up-market in style, reflecting its well-heeled location. Fresh flowers on plain wooden tables, a log fire in the huge inglenook, exposed beams and a relaxing lived-in air. By contrast, a splendidly traditional public bar with bare boards, TV, games machine and time-honoured pub games. Short daily-changing selection of good home-made dishes with fresh accompanying vegetables and little sign of chips – unless asked for. Choices may include smoked mackerel paté, fresh poached salmon, beef in red wine, leek and ham mornay and lasagne and salad. Peach melba torte and chocolate fudge cake may feature on the pudding board. *Open 11-3, 6-11 (Fri 5-11, Sat 11-11, Sun 12-3, 7-10.30). **Bar Food** 12-2.30, 7.30-9.30. No food Sun evening. **Beer** Shepherd Neame. Small side garden with benches. No credit cards.*

BENTWORTH Sun Inn FOOD

Tel 01420 562338 Map 15a D4
Sun Hill Bentworth Alton Hampshire GU34 5JT

Hidden down a tiny lane on the village edge, this pretty flower-bedecked and unspoilt rural pub dates from the 17th century when it was a pair of cottages. Little has changed inside over the years, where brick and board floors are laid with a rustic mix of old and new pine tables, benches and settles, original beams are hung with various horse brasses, walls are adorned with prints and plates and tasteful cosmetic touches – quality magazines, fresh and dried flowers – enhance the overall unblemished atmosphere. Two large inglenook fireplaces with open log fires warm the two main interlinking bars. To provide more seating space, a third adjoining room was added in a similar style, maintaining the unique traditional character of the pub. As well as the Sun's charm, real ale and a good selection of home-cooked dishes (listed on a hand-written menu and a regularly changing blackboard menu) are prime reasons for visiting. Reliable, uncomplicated dishes range from ploughman's and ham, egg and chips to seafood pasta, steak and kidney pie, sweet and sour chicken, lamb casserole and speciality giant Yorkshire puddings filled with beef and gravy. To finish, try the Bakewell tart or treacle tart. Outside to the front and side, among the flower tubs and baskets, there are several wooden tables for alfresco sipping. *Open 12-3, 6-11 (Sun 12-3, 7-10.30, pub closed Sun eve Nov-Mar). **Bar Food** 12-2, 7-9.30 (Sun to 9), no food on Sunday Nov-Mar. Free House. **Beer** Sun Special (from Hampshire Brewery in Andover), Wadworth 6X, Marston's Pedigree, Courage Best, Ruddles Best, Cheriton Pots Ale & Diggers Gold, Ringwood Best, several guest beers. Terrace, outdoor eating. Pub closed 25 Dec. No credit cards.*

BERWICK — Cricketers — A

Tel 01323 870469 Map 11 B6
Berwick nr Polegate East Sussex BN26 6SP

Unspoilt, 500-year-old brick and flint creeper-clad cottage located just off the A27 Lewes to Polegate road and a handy watering-hole for walkers from the South Downs Way. Inside, three charming rooms are delightfully unpretentious and traditional with half-panelled walls, open fires and simply furnished with scrubbed tables and wall benches on quarry-tiled floors. Popular locals' pub with a good chatty atmosphere and decent Harvey's ales tapped straight from the barrel in a rear room. Surrounded by a magnificent cottage garden – foxgloves, roses and flower-borders – it is an idyllic summer pub. No children inside. The landlord of the last nine years retired just after we went to press; let's hope the Cricketers remains unspoilt for the next nine and more. *Open 11-2.30 (Sat to 3), 6-11 (Sun 12-3, 7-10.30). **Beer** Harveys. Garden, lawn, outdoor eating, tables in garden. No credit cards.*

BIBURY — Catherine Wheel — FOOD

Tel 01285 740250 Map 14a A2 **B&B**
Bibury Gloucestershire GL7 5ND

Carol Ann Palmer's 500-year-old, mellow stone pub, recently re-roofed, carefully retains both the reputation and atmosphere of an unpretentious, unspoilt local. Its summer attractions include the colourful flower baskets, neatly tended lawns full of picnic tables and the baby black rabbits constantly in residence. In winter there's a chummy atmosphere at closely-set tables in front of warming wood-burning stoves. There's always a wealth of food on offer, with sandwiches, filled baked potatoes and children's choices by the dozen. Rather, though, look inside on the vast chalk boards for the fresh daily-changing fare of two or three soups, the likes of kidneys turbigo or Mexican-style chicken breast and most likely fresh grilled Bibury trout from the trout farm opposite – also well worth a visit. Busy as the tiny kitchen usually is, the food is consistently reliable and service is relaxed and friendly. A few steps across the car park the former outhouses have been re-roofed in Cotswold stone and now house four double bedrooms with en-suite bathrooms and up-to-date facilities; two are of family size with extra beds. *Open 11-11 (Sun 12-3, 7-10.30). **Bar Food** 11-11 (Sun 12-3, 7-10.30). Free House. **Beer** Archers Golden (or Village), Whitbread West Country Best, Tetley, Flowers Original, Boddingtons, Courage Best. Garden, outdoor eating. Family room. **Accommodation** 4 bedrooms, all en suite, £50. Children welcome overnight, additional bed and cot supplied. Access, Amex, Diners, Visa.*

BICKLEY MOSS — Cholmondeley Arms — FOOD

Tel 01829 720300 **Fax 01829 720123** Map 6 B3 **B&B**
Bickley Moss nr Malpas Cheshire SY14 8BT

Virtually opposite Cholmondeley Castle and gardens on the A49 and still part of the Viscount's estate is this redbrick former schoolhouse replete with family heirlooms, educational memorabilia, bell tower without and blackboards within. These last provide interesting reading with hollandaise sauce accompanying salmon fishcakes, chicken piri piri and pasta carbonara alongside traditional English steak and kidney or chicken and mushroom pie and a "school lunch" of spicy sausage and onion in a baguette. Finish, perhaps, with Caribbean hot fudged bananas or crepes laced with Grand Marnier. Overnight accommodation is across the car park in what must have been the head teacher's house. Four self-contained bedrooms (three doubles and a family room) are bright and cottagey with en-suite WC and shower rooms (not baths). All have telephones, television and clock radios, tea trays and hairdryers. It's back to school in the morning to report in for a slap-up breakfast. *Open 12-3, 7-11 (Sat from 6.30, Sun 12-3, 7-10.30). **Bar Food** 12-2.15 (Sun to 2), 7-10 (Sun to 9.30). Free House. **Beer** Boddingtons, Flowers IPA & Original, guest beer. Garden, outdoor eating. Family room. **Accommodation** 4 bedrooms, all en suite, £46 (single £34). Children welcome overnight (£6 when sharing parents' room), additional bed & cot available. Check-in by arrangement. Access, Visa.*

> We only recommend food (Bar Food) in those establishments highlighted with the **FOOD** symbol.

BIDDENDEN Three Chimneys FOOD

Tel 01580 291472 Map 11 C5
Biddenden nr Ashford Kent TN27 8HA

The Three Chimneys has every natural advantage of being a classic country pub, its original, small roomed layout and old-fashioned furnishings intact. Old settles, low beams, nice decor, warming open fires, absence of music and electronic games – glorious. Then there's the range of more than decent bar food including carrot and orange soup, kipper paté, veal and Madeira casserole and chicken breast in red wine, bacon and mushroom sauce. Basic bread and cheese – mature farmhouse cheddar or Stilton – comes with chunks of fresh granary bread and home-made chutney or pickled onions. Daily choice of four puddings – upside down marmalade pudding, date and walnut pudding. Good ales tapped direct from the casks behind the bar and a heady farm cider from Biddenden. The Garden Room is suitable for families and the shrub-filled garden is lovely for summer eating. Don't, incidentally, look for the three chimneys on the roof – the name comes from the pub's location at the meeting of three lanes, or Trois Chemins – 1 mile west of Biddenden on the A262 – as it was called by French prisoners of war kept near here in another century.
No children under 14 inside. *Open 11-2.30, 6-11 (Sun 12-2.30, 7-10.30).* ***Bar Food*** *12-2, 7-9.30. Free House.* ***Beer*** *Fremlins Best, Adnams Best, Brakspear Best, Marston's Pedigree, Morland Old Speckled Hen, Wadworth 6X, Harvey's Best (& Old Ale in winter). Lawned garden, outdoor eating area. Pub closed Christmas Day & Boxing Day. No credit cards.*

BIRCH VALE Sycamore Inn B&B

Tel 01663 742715 **Fax 01663 747382** Map 6 C2
Sycamore Road Birch Vale Hayfield Derbyshire DE55 6FG

Surrounded by woods of sycamore and silver birch, this quietly located pub at the fringe of the village (turn off the A6015 at Station Road) is built precariously into the side of a steep hill. In ten acres of grounds, the paddock slopes steeply down to the River Sett (although you can't see it), while beyond the lower car park there are a barbecue terrace, dovecotes, mini-aviary and a children's Tarzan trail playground. There are bars at two levels, the lower with regular entertainment and a clubby atmosphere while that above is given over largely to eating in neatly partitioned dining areas which include non-smoking and family rooms. With one exception, bedrooms look out across the valley; they're neatly appointed with whitewood furniture and patchwork quilts; all have en-suite facilities (four with baths), satellite TV, radios, beverage trays and trouser presses. For those with other pressing business, the only telephone provided is on the upper landing. *Open 11-11 (Sun 12-3. 7-10.30).* ***Beer*** *John Smith's, Marston's Pedigree, Courage Directors, guest beer. Garden, family room.* ***Accommodation*** *7 bedrooms, all en suite, £45 (single £29.50); family room sleeps four, £55. Children welcome overnight, additional bed (£10) and cot supplied. Access, Visa.*

BIRCHOVER Druid Inn FOOD

Tel 01629 650302 **Fax 01629 650599** Map 6 C2
Main Street Birchover Derbyshire DE4 2BL

Climb the long hill from the B5056 signposted Stanton Moor Stone Circle, and be sure not to miss a glimpse of Rowtor, high above the pub, where extraordinary fissures and passageways through the rock suggest very early occupation by man; hence the Druid's unusual name. From portal to chimney pot, the pub's entirely ivy-covered, with a terrace in front, and to one side, a partly no-smoking restaurant area on two floors, connected by a tiled passageway. Very much a dining pub, the menu fills four blackboards, including a vegetarian selection. A starter might be Szechuan-style spare ribs in garlic ginger soya sauce with salad or exotic prawn cocktail with brandy followed by a main course like trout topped with white wine sauce, prawns and mussels or honey-roast saddle of lamb with gooseberry and redcurrant sauce, and perhaps finish with a Bakewell pudding for dessert, all partnered by an above-average range of good-value wines by glass or bottle.
Booking advisable for weekends and evenings. Outside, the terrace overlooks fields.
Open 12-3, 7-11 (Sun 12-3, 7-10.30). ***Bar Food*** *12-2, 7-9.30 (to 9 in winter). Free House.* ***Beer*** *Mansfield Bitter, Morland Old Speckled Hen, Leather Breeches' Ashbourne Belter, guest beer. Patio/terrace. Family room. Access, Amex, Diners, Visa.*

BIRDLIP — Air Balloon — A

Tel 01452 862541 Map 14 B2
Crickley Hill Birdlip Gloucester Gloucestershire GL4 6JY

A prominent 17th-century inn adjacent to the A417/A436 junction, equidistant from Gloucester and Cheltenham, amusingly named to commemorate the exploits of a local balloonist. He took off from the top of nearby Crickley Hill on a maiden flight in 1802 and promptly vanished into thin air (or so the story goes). Today's tale is of a busy Whitbread Wayside Inn which packs in the families year-round. In winter are large log fires; on summer days hill-top gardens set out with play equipment and a bouncy castle. There are also picnic tables on the sheltered rear patio under a permanent awning. *Open 9am-11 (Sun 11-10.30). **Beer** Wadworth 6X, Flowers Original, Boddingtons, Greene King Abbot Ale, Morland Old Speckled Hen & Green Bullet, up to four guest beers. Access, Visa.*

BLACKAWTON — Normandy Arms — B&B

Tel 01803 712316 Map 13 D3
Chapel Street Blackawton nr Dartmouth Devon TQ9 7BN

Homely, 15th-century village inn with a welcoming atmosphere. Rustic pub furniture and various displays and memorabilia on the Normandy Landings theme adorn the much-modernised bars. Upstairs, comfortable accommodation is provided in five delightfully cottagey bedrooms, all with modern pine furniture, matching fabrics and spotlessly clean en-suite facilities with baths. TVs and beverage-making facilities are standard and hot-water bottles are thoughtfully provided for cooler nights. Front rooms enjoy good rural views. One family room sleeps three; £15 for an additional adult, £10 for a child; cot supplied. *Open 11.30-2.30, 6.30-11 (12-2, 7-11 in winter, Sun 12-3, 7-10.30). **Beer** Courage, Webster's Green Label, guest beer. Garden, outdoor eating. **Accommodation** 5 bedrooms, all en suite, £48 (single £30). Access, Visa.*

BLACKBOYS — Blackboys Inn — FOOD

Tel 01825 890283 Map 11 B6
Blackboys nr Uckfield East Sussex TN22 5LG

Following a nine-month closure after a serious fire, this splendid black-weatherboarded pub dates from 1389 and enjoys an attractive position set back from the B2192 west of Heathfield, overlooking an iris- and lily-covered pond. The delightfully old-fashioned interior has a series of interconnecting rooms featuring various pieces of antique furniture, interesting bric-a-brac and sought-after alcove window seats with views over the pond. Separate traditional public bar with bare boards, wooden furnishings, old juke box and pub games. A reliable range of bar food is listed on an extensive blackboard menu above the bar and may include a large bowl of home-made vegetable soup, seafood gratin and mushrooms baked in port and Stilton sauce for starters. Main course choices range from Celanese fish curry, steak and kidney pie and seafood pancake to gigot of lamb in a rich Catalan sauce with chick peas, Cajun chicken and calf's liver sautéed in butter. For dessert try the bread-and-butter pudding, crème brulée or treacle tart and custard. Ploughman's, filled jacket potatoes and salads for those wanting a lighter bite. Good alfresco seating beside the pond and the front green beneath the horse chestnut trees. *Open 11-3, 6-11 (Sun 12-3, 7-10.30). **Bar Food** 12-2.30, 6.30-10 (Sun 7-10). **Beer** Harveys. Garden, lawn and paved terrace, tables in garden. Access, Visa.*

BLACKBROOK — The Plough — FOOD

Tel 01306 886603 Map 15a F4
Blackbrook Road Blackbrook nr Dorking Surrey RH5 4DS

Popular, isolated rural inn located on a country lane south of Dorking, parallel with A24. Two spacious, comfortable and warmly welcoming bars with pleasant views through large windows and boasting a vast collection of over 500 ties and numerous old saws and farm tools. Fresh flowers top handsome copper-topped or old sewing machine tables. Well-stocked bar offering the full complement of King and Barnes ales, as well as 15 wines and seven vintage ports served by the glass. Choose one to accompany a reliable pub meal, especially a dish listed on the regularly-changing blackboard menu, such as a home-made soup, chicken liver paté with cockles, ginger and orange lamb, chicken hotpot with herb dumplings and Bajan vegetable and nut curry. The printed menu is more routine, with

regular pub favourites. Summer pudding, hot carrot pudding and Austrian chocolate cake may feature on the pudding list. Sheltered rear garden with chalet-style children's play house. No children under 14 inside. *Open 11-2.30, 6-11 (Sun 12-3, 7-10.30).* ***Beer*** *King & Barnes. Garden, children's play area. Pub closed 25, 26 & 1 Jan. No credit cards.*

BLACKO — Moorcock Inn — FOOD

Tel 01282 614186 Map 6 B1
Gisburn Road Blacko nr Nelson Lancashire BB9 6NF

Standing on its own alongside the A682 north of Blacko, the whitewashed Moorcock Inn is situated in wonderful rolling countryside near Pendle Hill and the Forest of Bowland. Inside is unassuming and unpretentious. Two adjoining rooms have plain painted walls, simple prints, brass plates and a collection of china plates; stone fireplaces are topped with ornaments and brassware. All the tables are laid for dining, surrounded by upholstered bench seating and simple wooden chairs, a style continued in the large adjoining dining-room. Large picture windows in both rooms offer lovely views over the surrounding landscape. Licensee Elizabeth Holt has built up an enviable reputation for good fresh food, and custom comes from far and wide. The menu is backed up by a daily-changing blackboard of specials (now the mainstay), where dishes could include a home-made game pie, salmon fillet with seafood sauce or medallions of fillet steak with red wine sauce. Beside these, the menu covers tried and trusted pub favourites like ham shank with light mustard sauce and a good selection of vegetarian dishes. Home-made, old-fashioned puddings. The cooking is perfectly competent, prices realistic, portions generous and the service both friendly and quick. Popular Sunday lunch. The Moorcock is a useful resting place after a bracing morning on the moors – the Pendle Walk almost passes the door – and in sunny weather the garden is lovely. *Open 12-2, 6.30-11.* ***Bar Food*** *12-2, 7-10 (Sun 12-10).* ***Beer*** *Thwaites. Garden. No credit cards.*

BLAKESLEY — Bartholomew Arms — B&B

Tel 01327 860292 Map 15 D1
High Street Blakesley Northamptonshire NN12 8RE

Charming, welcoming 17th-century inn with a collection of model ships and nautical artefacts in the public bar, plus guns and cricket memorabilia in the lounge. Simple, well-kept bedrooms at very reasonable prices. Pleasant garden with summer house. Particularly good choice of malt whiskies. *Open 11-3, 6.30-11 (Sun 12-3, 7-10.30). Free House.* ***Beer*** *Marston's Pedigree, Worthington. Garden.* ***Accommodation*** *4 bedrooms, 1 en suite with shower, £40 (single £18). Children welcome overnight (under-5s stay free in parents' room, 5-10s £5.50), additional bed and cot available. No credit cards.*

BLANCHLAND — Lord Crewe Arms — FOOD B&B

Tel 01434 675251 **Fax 01434 675337** Map 5 D2
Blanchland nr Consett Durham DH8 9SP

Zzz...

Wild and remote, and some 3 miles below Derwent Water in a deep valley. Blanchland Abbey can trace its origins back to 1165 – despite dissolution in 1576 the layout of its surrounding village remains unchanged to this day. At its heart is one of England's finest inns, containing relics of the abbey lodge and kitchens and set in a cloister garden which is now an ancient monument. Lord Crewe purchased the entire estate in 1704 from one Tom Foster, a Jacobite adventurer; the ghost of his sister Dorothy is claimed still to be in residence. A sense of history pervades the building's remarkably modernised yet largely unchanged interior, no more so than in the Crypt bar. The meals served here are substantial: bratwurst sausage with sauerkraut and warm potato salad, minced lamb kebab with Greek salad and wild boar and pheasant pie with salad do not constitute the average pub lunch. Evening options of baked salmon, minute steak or Brie and broccoli bake are rather more traditional. Ploughman's and filled brown rolls are lunchtime alternatives, while Sunday lunch features a hot and cold buffet. A three-course Sunday lunch is also served in the stylish first-floor restaurant overlooking the garden. Bedrooms, needless to say, are splendidly individual; suitably traditional in the old house with stone mullion windows and restored fireplaces and mantels, yet up-to-date with accessories from colour TVs to bespoke toiletries and thoughtful extras from mending kits to complimentary sherry. Altogether more contemporary are the style and furnishings of rooms in the adjacent Angel Inn – once a Wesleyan Temperance House – a mere newcomer dating from the 1750s. *Open 11-3, 6-11 (Sun 12-3, 7-10.30). Free House.* ***Beer*** *Vaux Samson.* ***Accommodation*** *18 rooms, £70-£98 (single £60-£75). Access, Amex, Diners, Visa.*

BLANDFORD FORUM Crown Hotel B&B

Tel 01258 456626 Fax 01258 451084 Map 14 B4
Blandford Forum Dorset DT11 7AJ

This fine Georgian coaching house has a civilised old-fashioned air and is busy in typical market-town style. Bars, lounges and reception area are more hotelly than pubby in atmosphere, all being heavily wood-panelled and furnished with comfortable deep leather chairs and settees, especially in the traditional lounges. Rambling corridors lead to 32 well-maintained bedrooms. Uniformly decorated in pale green, they all boast clean, fresh bathrooms, light modern furniture and are well equipped with satellite TV, telephones, radio alarms and beverage-making facilities. There is an attractive and secluded Victorian walled garden for residents' use and guests are welcome to fish – in season – on the banks of the River Stour, which flows through the hotel grounds. Badger Inns. ***Beer*** *Hall and Woodhouse Badger Best & Tanglefoot. Garden.* ***Accommodation*** *32 bedrooms, all en suite, £72 (4-poster £75, single £58). Children welcome overnight (under-2s stay free in parents' room), additional bed (£15) and cot (£10) available. Accommodation closed 24-28 Dec. Access, Amex, Diners, Visa.*

BLEDINGTON Kings Head Inn ★ FOOD

Tel 01608 658365 Fax 01608 658902 Map 14a A1 **B&B**
The Green Bledington nr Kingham Oxfordshire OX7 6HD

Zzz... 

A more delightful spot would surely be hard to find: facing the village green with its brook and border-patrolling ducks, this is surely the quintessential Cotswold pub. Dating back to the 15th century, the inn stands on the Gloucester border with its easterly wall resident in Oxfordshire. Inside, the low-ceilinged bar is full of ancient settles and simple wooden furniture and there's a separate lounge and dining-room – all equally agreeable settings in which to enjoy the Royces' imaginative pub food. Lunchtime 'bar fayre' offers a wide range, from unusual sandwiches (black pudding onion and mango) to aubergine gratin, chicken curry, a wide range of salads in summer (perhaps hot kipper and whisky or dressed crab), bowls of pasta with smoked salmon and dill or Parma ham and parmesan, and interesting specials like a fresh spinach and horseradish omelette or spiced vegetable risotto. These might be supplemented in winter by the likes of jugged hare, local rabbit and venison. Year-round, the sausage, mash and onion gravy and steak and wine pie remain top sellers. An à la carte evening menu sees plenty of variety without undue elaboration among the deftly-sauced main courses; a large roast rack of lamb is served with garlicky duchesse potatoes and bramble gravy and is considered a speciality. Sweets like chocolate biscuit cake and treacle tart are genuinely home-made. A set-price 'Snippets menu' is a monthly-changing, three-course table d'hote with alternative choices at each stage – particularly good value for residents (£9.95 as we went to press). There's an even wider choice of bedroom accommodation now, with a recently-opened rear extension of six additional bedrooms. Meticulous attention has been paid to their detail; the three ground-floor rooms are an added bonus for less mobile guests. The older, cottagey bedrooms (no-smoking) over the pub should not suffer by comparison (though they may be less suitable for an early night) although the floorboards may be a little creaky. Their appointments nonetheless are top class with direct-dial phones, TVs, clock radios and an array of extras. Residents here enjoy the use of a quiet smokers' lounge and a private patio. A changing mat and facilities are available on request in the Ladies. *Open 11-2.30, 6-11 (Sun 12-2.30, 7-10.30).*
Bar Meals *12-2, 7-9.30.* ***Beer*** *Hook Norton, Wadworth 6X, four guest beers. Garden, outdoor eating.* ***Accommodation*** *12 bedrooms, all with bath en suite, £60 (single £40). Children welcome overnight, additional bed (£5) & cot supplied. No dogs. Access, Visa.*

BLEDLOW Lions of Bledlow A

Tel 01844 343345 Map 15a D2
Church End Bledlow Buckinghamshire HP27 9PE

Tracks lead up into the Chiltern beechwoods from this unspoilt, low white-painted 16th-century former coaching inn, making it an ideal walking base. Summer visitors can imbibe in the attractive rear garden or on the edge of the village green, where benches enjoy a pleasant rural outlook. In winter, the charming, heavily-beamed and unadorned interior comes into its own. Ancient tiled floors, a huge inglenook with open fire, oak stalls with rustic tables, various brasses and copper pots and a chatty atmosphere characterise the four seating areas of this cosy, traditional country pub. *Open 11-3 & 6-11 (Sun 12-3 & 7-10.30). Free House.* ***Beer*** *Wadworth 6X, Ruddles County, four guest beers Garden. Access, Amex, Diners, Visa.*

BLEWBURY Blewbury Inn FOOD B&B

Tel 01235 850496 **Fax 01235 850691** Map 14a C3
London Road Blewbury nr Didcot Oxfordshire OX11 9PD

Modest but appealing, white-painted roadside dining pub whose two rooms (one is the no-smoking restaurant) feature pine boarding to dado height and wheelback chairs. Run by a keen young couple: Martine looks after front-of-house while chef Paul works away in the kitchen. A short yet always interesting menu serves both bar and restaurant with some four or five choices at each stage; there is usually an omelette at lunch but other than that there is no traditional snacky pub food offered. It's priced à la carte to encourage snacking but with a maximum price of £21.95 if all three courses are taken. Well-executed dishes such as red pepper mousse with basil sauce, baked goat's cheese with hazelnut dressing, braised lamb shank with tomato, olives and parsley sauce, chargrilled baby aubergine with pesto-flavoured ratatouille (there's always a vegetarian option) and ragout of seafood with tagliatelle demonstrate Paul's modern style. Equally good puds might include a hot plum soufflé or freshly-baked chocolate pithiviers. The lunch menu is slightly simpler and cheaper but is in a similar vein (pigeon or smoked trout salad, lemon sole with herb butter, herb omelette, trio of rabbit, redcurrant soup). A plated selection of cheeses (from a selection of around ten) is also offered. Three modest bedrooms (no phone, no remote-control for the TV and no dressing table/work space) are clean and well kept, each with its own en-suite shower room. *Open 12-2.30, 6-11 (Sun 12-3, 7-10.30). **Bar Meals** 12-2, 7-9.15. Free House. **Beer** Hook Norton, Brakspear, Arkell's 3B. **Accommodation** 3 rooms, all en suite, £50 (single £40). Check-in by arrangement. Pub closed Mon lunchtime. Access, Visa.*

BLICKLING Buckinghamshire Arms Hotel B&B

Tel 01263 732133 Map 10 C1
Blickling nr Aylsham Norfolk NR11 6NF

Zzz... 

Splendid Grade I listed 17th-century inn which stands deferentially at the gates of the even more magnificent Blickling Hall. Once the estate builders, house and later the servants' quarters to the fine National Trust property, it is an excellent place to stay with two of the three bedrooms having dramatic evening views across to the flood-lit hall. Attractively decorated, each room boasts original features, with "real" four-posters and sturdy old stripped pine and dark oak furnishings making this a most characterful and peaceful bed and breakfast stop. One room has an en-suite shower room, the others share a clean, good-sized bathroom with an old fashioned tub. Downstairs, the three charming and well-furnished bars have open fires and are typically National Trust in style of decor and taste. *Open 11-3, 6-11 (Sun 12-3, 7-10.30). Free House. **Beer** Adnams Bitter & Broadside, Woodforde's Wherry & Baldric, Sam Smith Old Brewery, two guest beers. **Accommodation** 3 bedrooms, one en suite with shower £60 (single £45). Check-in by arrangement. Children welcome overnight and anywhere. Garden, outdoor eating. Access, Visa.*

BLOCKLEY Crown Inn & Hotel FOOD B&B

Tel 01386 700245 **Fax 01386 700247** Map 14a A1
High Street Blockley nr Moreton-in-Marsh Gloucestershire GL56 9EX

At the heart of this most picturesque of Cotswold villages the Champion family's Crown is the jewel. Whilst retaining all the charm of a 16th-century coaching inn, it has been totally restored with loving care and considerable style. At street level the inn is fronted by a split-level bar decorated in muted tones and furnished with deep-cushioned sofas and leather club chairs. Here at any time, and at pavement tables in summertime, is a splendid spot to enjoy some simply executed yet consistently tasty bar snacks, which are supplemented daily by best-available produce from the fish markets. Honey-baked ham or beef with horseradish come in 1½-round sandwiches; winter may see a steak, Guinness and mushroom pie giving way in summer to Wye salmon salad or a fan of avocado and Stilton. In season are pristine fresh oysters, mackerel fillets with mustard vinaigrette and baked trout with prawns and mushrooms. For a treat, leave room for a good dessert like fresh raspberry roulade. Adjacent is the Crown's brasserie which extends the range of food choices. A relaxing residents' library is away from the bar's bustle. The Crown's bedrooms, already pretty smart but being refurbished as we went to press, have en-suite bath or shower rooms, TV, radio, hairdryer and beverage facilities. Exposed timberwork and original beams, the mellow stone walls and cast-iron bedroom fireplaces add to each room's individual appeal, while even more space is

to be found in the splendid four-poster rooms and suites. *Open 11-11 (Sun 12-3, 7-10.30).* ***Bar Food*** *12-2, 7-10. Free House.* ***Beer*** *Hook Norton, Donnington, four guest beers. Outdoor eating.* ***Accommodation*** *21 bedrooms, all en suite, £78-£114 (single £53). Access, Amex, Diners, Visa.*

BOLDRE — Red Lion — A

Tel 01590 673177 Map 14 C4
Boldre Lymington Hampshire SO41 8NE

Dating from around 1650 and mentioned as an alehouse in the Domesday Book, this most attractive New Forest pub has been run by the Bicknell family for over 20 years. Outside an old cart is strewn with flowers, and hanging baskets and troughs are a riot of colour in summer. Inside, a rambling series of four black-beamed rooms have their own country style, with real fires, a mix of old furnishings, hunting prints, farm tools, man-traps, tapestries and unusual collections of old bottles and chamber pots. Delightful secluded rear flower garden. No children under 14 allowed inside. *Open 11-3, 6-11 (Sun 12-3, 7-10.30).* ***Beer*** *Eldridge Pope. Garden. Pub closed 25 & 26 Dec. Access, Visa.*

BOLLINGTON — Church House Inn — FOOD

Tel 01625 574014 **Fax 01625 576424** Map 6 B2 **B&B**
Church Street Bollington Cheshire SK10 5PY

This quiet corner of Cheshire's largest village is where the discerning drop in for carefully-prepared lunchtime snacks and evening meals. The long menu offers filled baked potatoes and sandwiches through to chicken à la creme and steak Diane. There's an upper dining-room for evening use and private parties; to the rear, an enclosed garden for summer drinking. Daily specials complete the picture: perhaps dressed crab, vegetable moussaka, pork casserole or lamb and chutney stew, with lemon mousse pie or raspberry pavlova to finish. All the bedrooms (three singles, one twin and one double) are furnished in pine and have en-suite bathrooms, TVs and beverage-making facilities. *Open 12-2.30 (Sat to 3), 5.30-11 (Sun 12-3, 7-10.30).* ***Bar Food*** *12-2. 6.30-9.30 (Sun 7-9). Free House.* ***Beer*** *Theakston Best, Boddingtons, Jennings Bitter, Timothy Taylor's Landlord, Tetley Best. Garden. Family Room.* ***Accommodation*** *5 bedrooms, all en suite, £45 (family room £55, single £35; weekends: £37.50 double, £45 family, £27.50 single). No dogs. Access, Visa.*

BOLTER END — Peacock — FOOD

Tel 01494 881417 Map 15a D3
Lane End Bolter End Buckinghamshire HP14 3LU

Bolter End is a crossroads with a few houses and the pub is located opposite the Common. The only bar is divided into three sections and one menu applies throughout. Examples of menu dishes include chicken in fresh coriander, stincotto (whole gammon hock cooked in herbs) or Italian sausages with beans and hash browns; daily fresh fish such as creamy pollack with prawns and garlic; Aberdeen Angus steaks are also popular. Home-made puddings are the traditional kind – fruit crumbles, jam roly-poly, honey oat and lemon tart or sticky toffee pudding. No children under 14 inside. *Open 11.45-2.30, 6-11 (Sun 12-3, 7-10.30).* ***Bar Food*** *12-2, 7-10 (except Sun eve).* ***Beer*** *Ind Coope ABC, Tetley, two guest beers. Garden, outdoor eating. Access, Amex, Diners, Visa.*

BONCHURCH — Bonchurch Inn — A

Tel 01983 852611 Map 15 D4
The Shute Bonchurch Isle of Wight PO38 1NU

Italians Ulisse and Aline Besozzi give an invigorating Continental flavour to Bonchurch's village 'local', which has a good nautical atmosphere. There's a family room, a small saloon bar and the public bar is cut into the rocks of the Shute; a few tables are set in a cobbled, enclosed courtyard. Overnight accommodation (not inspected) is provided in three modest bedrooms (£34 double) and an extra bed or cot can be provided. From the main A3055 road (the one that goes round the whole of the south of the Island, Ryde-Freshwater), take the turning opposite the Leconfield Hotel down to Old Bonchurch. *Open 11-3, 6.30-11 (Sun 12-3, 7-10.30). Free House.* ***Beer*** *Courage Best & Directors, Marston's Pedigree. Courtyard. Family room. No credit cards.*

We endeavour to be as up-to-date as possible but inevitably some changes to landlords, chefs and other key staff occur after the Guide has gone to press.

BOOT — Burnmoor Inn — B&B

Tel 01946 723224 **Fax 01946 723337** Map 4 C3
Boot Eskdale Cumbria CA19 1TG

An attractive pebble-dashed old inn in a tiny hamlet, only three minutes' walk from the Eskdale railway terminus. Across the Esk by an old stone bridge are the restored Corn Mill and bridleways to Eel Tarn and Wasdale Head. The Fosters have run a friendly house here for a decade or more with a popular Austrian slant to much of Heidi's cooking. Residents enjoy the use of a neat, secluded dining and breakfast room – many come for the abundant peace and quiet. The bedrooms, four with bath and two with shower en suite (the other two sharing a toilet and bathroom), look out down the dale, or back up the hills towards Scafell; unencumbered by TVs or telephones, they are neat and simply furnished. *Open 11-2.45, 4.45-11 (Sun to 10.30). Free House.* ***Beer*** *Jennings Bitter & Cumberland Ale. Garden, children's play area.* ***Accommodation*** *8 bedrooms, 6 en suite with shower, £52 (single £23). Check-in by arrangement. Children over 4 welcome overnight, additional bed (£1 per year of age) available. No dogs. Access, Visa.*

BOTTLESFORD — Seven Stars — FOOD

Tel 01672 851325 **Fax 01672 851583** Map 14a A4
Bottlesford nr Woodborough Pewsey Wiltshire SH9 6LU

In this charming rural location, deep in the Vale of Pewsey with views across country to the White House, there's good news of the imminent addition of two en-suite bedrooms in the old brick barn for 1996. Make for Woodborough from the A345 at Pewsey (past the hospital), or from the mini roundabout at North Newnton to find the Seven Stars, almost lost down narrow lanes. The old, thatched building fronted by creepers and climbing roses has a splendid rambling interior of beams and black oak panelling and a central brick bar with quarry tile flooring. There's plenty of room to enjoy some masterfully produced bar food from the ever-enthusiastic, sometimes inspired Philippe Cheminade. Moules marinière, mousseline-sauced John Dory and the traditional cassoulet attest equally to his Gallic origins as to a broad range of skills, which also extend to fine presentation of the more traditional liver, bacon and onions, venison steak with garlic and mushrooms and seasonally available jugged hare. Regular fish deliveries satisfy the popular seafood platters (encompassing both lobster and winkles); both sandwiches and ploughman's lunches are also available. Two self-contained rooms at either end of the building double up for evening dining à la carte. The pub also boasts splendid gardens and grounds; a nine-acre tranche of land borders a shallow stream which winds down to the River Kennet; there are picnic tables here and hampers can be organised by arrangement. Meanwhile Fred and Max, the two pet rams, are not averse to giving rides to suitably small children. *Open 12-3, 6-11 (Sun 12-3, 7-10.30).* ***Bar Food*** *12-2.30, 6.30-9.30 (no food Sun eve). Free House.* ***Beer*** *Badger Best, Wadworth 6X, two guest beers. Garden, outdoor eating. Access, Visa.*

BOUGHTON ALUPH — Flying Horse Inn — FOOD — B&B

Tel 01233 620914 **Fax 01233 661010** Map 11 C5
Boughton Aluph nr Ashford Kent TN25 4HH

15th-century vine- and wisteria-clad inn occupying a charming spot overlooking the village green/cricket pitch, just off the A251 north of Ashford. Plenty of alfresco seating; ideal for lazy summer evenings watching the cricket. Single, beamed front bar with open log fire and adorned with hopbines and a collection of old ties. Small neat rear dining rom. Promising, daily-changing blackboard specials outshine the list of standard pub snacks available; four daily fish dishes are particularly popular. Choices may include paprika chicken, liver and bacon casserole, salmon steak with tarragon, Russian fish pie, steak and kidney pie and several fresh fish dishes, all accompanied by a selection of a least nine vegetables. Four neat and homely upstairs bedrooms have views across the green and surrounding countryside through unusual arched Gothic windows. Two have shower cubicles, all have washbasins and share two clean and spacious bathrooms. TVs and tea-makers are standard. *Open 11-3, 6-11 Mon-Wed, 11-11 Thu-Sat (winter: 11-3, 6-11, Mon-Sat), 12-3 & 7-10.30 Sun .* ***Bar Food*** *12-2, 6.30-9.30.* ***Beer*** *Wadworth 6X, Courage Best, Marston's Pedigree, Morland Speckled Hen, John Smith's, guest beer. Garden, outdoor eating.* ***Accommodation*** *4 bedrooms, 2 en suite (with shower). Check-in by arrangement. Access, Amex, Visa.*

Bowden Hill — Rising Sun — A

Tel 01249 730363 Map 14 B2
32 Bowden Hill Lacock Wiltshire SN15 2PP

It's the location and the friendly, chatty atmosphere that draws people to this tiny honey-coloured stone pub, set high on the hill above historic Lacock. The single rustic bar and adjoining room have a mix of old chairs, pine settles and kitchen tables laid out on flagstoned floors. A few old prints adorn the walls and in winter a good log fire warms the bar. The pub is owned by Roger Catté, head brewer of Mole's Brewery, so expect the full range of Mole's ales as well as guest beers, all kept in tip-top condition. On sunny, clear days space is at a premium on the two-level, flower tub- and bench-filled terrace, from where an unrivalled view of some 25 miles across the Avon Valley can be appreciated. On still summer evenings hot-air balloons can often be seen drifting across the sky. New landlord. *Open 11.30-2.30, 6-11 (Tue from 7), Sun 12-3, 7-10.30. Free House.* ***Beer** Mole's Ales: Tap Bitter, Best Bitter, Landlord's Choice & Brew 97, guest beers. Garden, outdoor eating, children's play area. Pub closed 25 Dec. No credit cards.*

Bowland Bridge — Hare & Hounds — B&B

Tel 015395 68333 Map 4 C4
Bowland Bridge nr Grange-over-Sands Cumbria LA11 6NN

Zzz... ☺

Truly rural, good-looking old inn owned by ex-international soccer player Peter Thompson and his wife Debbie. The bar successfully blends ancient and modern, with its rough stone walls, discreet farming bric-a-brac and simple wooden furniture; open fires spread warmth in winter weather. The dramatically high-ceilinged dining-room is for residents only; the residents' lounge is rather more chintzy. Bedrooms are immaculately kept, beamy, floral, and on the small side. Delightful garden. *Open 11-11 (Sun to 10.30). Free House.* ***Beer** Tetley. Garden, children's play area. **Accommodation** 16 bedrooms, 13 with en suite showers, £46 (single £33). Children welcome overnight (under-2s stay free in parents' room, 305s £5, 5 and over £10), additional bed and cot available. Access, Visa.*

Box — Bayly's — FOOD — B&B

Tel 01225 743622 Map 14 B2
High Street Box nr Corsham Wiltshire SN14 9NA

A busy and lively, solid-looking Bath stone inn, standing four-square on the A4 Bath to Chippenham road. It is named after the pub's first landlord in the early 1600s, Jacob Bayly, whose last will and testament hangs to this day behind the bar. Most noteworthy of its many period features is a magnificent open stone fireplace, and the circular pool table is quite a talking point. The greater part of the premises, however, is given over to eating, with speedy, informal service to its neatly-laid tables. From a daily-changing blackboard, lunch dishes may well include Wiltshire ham with egg and chips, chili con carne or a toasted club sandwich. The comprehensive fixed menu offers a wider selection of Stilton & pork paté, seafood platter, liver and bacon or beef stew and dumplings with, to follow, the Vicar's Tart (almond and fruit flan) and Wiltshire Whitepot (creamed bread-and-butter pudding). Landlady Jan Gynn's tireless output from the kitchen is highly popular and at peak times it can get very busy. For peace and quiet, and for weary travellers, Bayly's offers three bedrooms, all with neat en-suite WCs and showers, colour TV and beverage trays. *Open 12-2, 7-11 (Sun 12-2.30, 7-10.30). **Bar Food** 12-1.45, 7-9. Free House.* ***Beer** Wadworth 6X, Bass, guest beers in summer. **Accommodation** 3 bedrooms, all en suite with shower, £48 (single £30). Children welcome overnight (under-3s free if sharing parents' room), additional bed & cot available (£5). Small dogs only. No credit cards.*

We only recommend food (Bar Food) in those establishments highlighted with the **FOOD** symbol.

BRADLEY GREEN — Malt Shovel Inn — B&B

Tel 01278 653432 Map 13 E1
Blackmoor Lane Bradley Green nr Cannington Somerset TA5 2NE

Located beside a tiny lane just outside Cannington, this rambling 300-year-old pub enjoys a peaceful rural position surrounded by open farmland. Traditional homely interior with settles and sturdy elm tables and chairs in the main bar and a cosy snug bar with quarry-tiled floor. Bedrooms are clean and comfortable – one being a spacious family room – with modern furnishings, TVs, tea-makers and views across open fields to the Quantock Hills; their proximity making this a useful base from which to explore. Non en-suite rooms share adequate bathroom and toilet facilities. A new skittle alley/function room was added last year. Good, safe garden. *Open 11.30-3, 6.30-11 (Sun 12-3, 7-10.30). Free House.* ***Beer*** *Butcombe, John Smith's, guest beer. Garden. Family room.* ***Accommodation*** *4 bedrooms, 1 en suite with bath, £36 (single £21.50). Children welcome overnight (cot age stay free in parents' room, family room £42 for four, £39.50 for three). Accommodation closed 24-26 Dec. No credit cards.*

BRAMDEAN — Fox Inn — FOOD

Tel 01962 771363 Map 15 D3
Bramdean nr Alresford Hampshire SO24 0LP

Attractive 400-year-old white weatherboarded pub set back from the main road (A272). Inside is extensively modernised, and very much dining-orientated, well-kept and comfortable. Good lunchtime bar food is simple with such dishes as beef stroganoff and fresh cod. The evening menu is more restauranty with fillet steaks accompanied by a choice of sauces and fresh fish from Portsmouth (halibut fillet mornay; for dessert, home-made puddings like pavlova, crème brulée and treacle tart are offered. No children under 14 inside, but there's a large garden at the rear and patio in front. *Open 10.30-3, 6-11 (Sun 12-3, 7-10.30).* ***Bar Food*** *12-2, 7-9.* ***Beer*** *Marston's Pedigree & Bitter. Garden, outdoor eating, children's play area. Access, Amex, Visa.*

BRANSCOMBE — Masons Arms — FOOD B&B

Tel 01297 680300 **Fax 01297 680500** Map 13 E2
Branscombe nr Seaton Devon EX12 3DJ

Picturesque Branscombe lies in a steep valley, deep in National Trust land and only a ten minute walk away from the sea. Occupying most of the village centre is this delightful 14th-century, creeper-clad inn and its neighbouring terraces of cottages, which house most of the comfortable bedrooms. The proprietor of over 20 years' standing, Murray Inglis, has recently taken personal charge of the day-to-day running of the Arms whose motto is 'Now Ye Toil Not'. Beyond the pretty front terrace is a most charming bar with stone walls and floors, an assortment of old settles and a huge inglenook with open fire, which not only warms the bar but also cooks the beef or lamb spit-roasts offered on Thursdays (lunch and dinner at 1pm and 8pm), a simmering bourride (Provençal fish stew) at Friday lunchtimes (1pm), and monthly pig roasts (first Friday of the month from 8pm). Reliable bar food from the regular menu includes steamed steak and kidney pudding, chicken, Stilton and walnut strudel, deep-fried fillet of plaice with chips, and decent ploughman's lunches, sandwiches (try a toasted version with bacon and prune). On Sundays there's also a roast for lunch. There's also an attractive and tastefully-decorated restaurant (dinner only) with an old-world ambience. Exposed beams and the odd piece of antique furniture add to the charm of attractive bedrooms in the inn and old cottages opposite the pub; TVs, phones and clock/radios are standard throughout. Regular live music on Friday nights; beer festival at the end of July. No under-14s in the bar. Two miles off A3052, between Sidmouth and Colyford. *Open 11-2.30 (Sat to 3), 6-11 (Sun 12-3, 7-10.30).* ***Bar Food*** *12-2, 7-9.30. Free House.* ***Beer*** *Bass, Wadworth 6X, Dartmoor Best. Terrace, outdoor eating.* ***Accommodation*** *20 bedrooms, 19 en suite, £74 (hotel), £54-£64 (Cottages), £80 (The Linny) (single £28-£46). Children welcome overnight (2-10s £10), additional bed & cot supplied. Dogs welcome (£3 + food per night). Access, Visa.*

BRASSINGTON — Ye Olde Gate — A

Tel 01629 540448 Map 6 C3
Well Street Brassington Derbyshire DE4 4HJ

Revered by generations of pub-goers for its resolute resistance to change, two tiny rooms with a convivial atmosphere (accentuated by communal-sized tables) are hung everywhere with pewter tankards, copper pans and Toby jugs; big log fires in winter. They'll sell you

a filled baguette – a 'hero' or a 'submarine' – to keep hunger at bay. No under-10s indoors. Ramshackle ("rustic and in keeping with the pub's general style" might be a kinder description, says the landlord) rear garden. *Open 12-2.30 (Sat to 3), 6-11 (Sun 12-3, 7-10.30).* ***Beer*** *Marston's. Garden, outdoor eating, barbecues. Closed Monday lunchtime (except Bank Holidays). No credit cards.*

BRAUNSTON — Blue Ball Inn — FOOD

Tel 01572 722135 Map 7 E4
6 Cedar Street Braunston Oakham Leicestershire LE15 8QS

The Blue Ball of its title represents previous obfuscation of the inn sign of the 'Globe' pub, which has stood in Braunston since the early 1600s – surely one of the county's oldest pubs. Now reconverted to its former state, full of beams, inglenooks and crannies. Throughout the bars, a menu with the likes of of avocado Stilton, spare ribs and vegetable cannelloni are supplemented by blackboards proclaiming, perhaps, warm goat's cheese salad and grilled sea bass on a bed of fennel. A restaurant at the less frenetic end offers a three-course table d'hote menu. The food is undoubtedly good, and the atmosphere of a quaint thatched village pub has been carefully retained. Under the same ownership as *The Peacock* at Redmile in Nottinghamshire (see entry). *Open 11-2.30, 6.30-11 (Sun 12-3, 7-10.30).* ***Bar Food*** *12-2.30, 7-10 (Sun till 9.30). Free House.* ***Beer*** *Bass, Marston's Pedigree, Greene King Abbot Ale, Tetley, guest beer. Access, Diners, Visa.*

BRAUNSTON — Old Plough — FOOD

Tel 01572 722714 **Fax 01572 770382** Map 7 E4
Church Street Braunston Leicestershire LE15 8QY

Well-regarded local innkeepers Amanda and Andrew Reid have brought a wealth of experience also to their tastefully modernised inn on the fringe of the village. Healthy eating options and vegetarian alternatives (mushroom and walnut cannelloni) are well interspersed throughout a menu encompassing 'famous Plough crusties' (large granary filled rolls) through salads and steaks to chef Nick Quinn's specials. Ruddles beef pie, salmon and king prawn filo with saffron sauce or bacon-wrapped chicken breast with creamy leek sauce might arrive with chef's potatoes of the day and crisp, fresh vegetables. There is a separate ice cream menu but better options might be raspberry roulade or chocolate rum truffle tarte. With light lunches on the terrace and candle-lit dining in the picturesque conservatory a sense of occasion is easily engendered. Children are allowed in the bar to eat for lunch only. *Open 11-3, 6-11 (Sun 12-3, 7-10.30).* ***Bar Food*** *12-2, 7-10 (Sun till 9.30). Free House.* ***Beer*** *Theakston XB, Oakham Ales Old Tosspot, two guest beers. Garden, outdoor eating. Family Room. Access, Amex, Diners, Visa.*

BRENDON — Stag Hunters Hotel — FOOD — B&B

Tel 01598 741222 Map 13 D1
Brendon nr Lynton Devon EX35 1PS

Nestling beside the East Lyn River deep in the Doone Valley, this friendly, family-run hotel makes a good base for guests wishing to explore Exmoor. Adequate overnight accommodation is in 12 neatly-kept, en-suite rooms (eight with bath) kitted out with varying styles of furniture plus TVs and tea-makers. Comfortable residents' lounge. Homely, simply-furnished bars offering a short menu of home-cooked fare, such as steak and kidney pie, cottage pie, trout pan-fried with garlic and capers and good snacks like ploughman's and filled French sticks. Chicken in red wine with good vegetables or home-made pork pie with salad may feature on the specials board; game is popular in season. Popular riverside garden. *Open 11-11 (Sun 12-3, 7-10.30) Mar-Nov (shorter hours in winter).* ***Bar Food*** *12-9.30pm (Sun 12-2, 7-9.30). Free House.* ***Beer*** *St Austell Hicks Special, Tetley, Wadworth 6X. Garden, outdoor eating. Family room.* ***Accommodation*** *12 bedrooms, 11 en suite, £54 (single £27). Children welcome overnight (under-14s stay free in parents' room); additional bed and cot supplied. Access, Amex, Diners, Visa.*

Many **B&B** establishments offer reduced rates for weekend and out-of-season bookings. Always ask about special deals for longer stays. Beware half-board terms in inns where we do not recommend the **FOOD.**

BRERETON GREEN — Bears Head Hotel — FOOD B&B

Tel 01477 535251 **Fax 01477 535888** Map 6 B2
Brereton Green nr Sandbach Cheshire CW11 9RS

Fronted by the original half-timbered inn (which dates from 1615, if not earlier), this celebrated roadhouse alongside the A50 has expanded into a collection of buildings. Panels of wattle and daub, carefully preserved and displayed in the bar, are evidence of the building's longevity and, despite the many more recent extensions, its inglenook fireplaces and oak beams hung with horse brasses still have lots of old-fashioned charm. Today's pub, run by the Tarquini family for over 30 years, is divided into cosy alcoves by means of cleverly placed original timbers and panels, and is full of the fragrance of ubiquitous fresh flowers. Lunchtime and evening bar food is both stylish and substantial, ranging from open sandwiches with salad to satisfying hot dishes like lamb chops in rosemary and garlic butter with seasonal vegetables, or grilled fillet of plaice Caprice; daily specialities typically feature medallions of lamb in black bean sauce, a roast or cold poached salmon with salad. By night the restaurant evokes the stuff of dinner dates and anniversaries tinged with more than a hint of déjà-vu. Mammoth desserts arrive by trolley. And so to bed, where practical considerations for the business traveller generally take precedence over romance, with formica-topped, dual-purpose dressing tables and work spaces, television, radio, dial-out phones, hot beverage facilities and trouser presses. *Open 12-3, 6-11 (Sun 12-3, 7-10.30).* ***Bar Food*** *12-2, 7-10. Free House.* ***Beer*** *Bass, Burtonwood Best, Courage Directors, guest beer. Patio/terrace, outdoor eating.* ***Accommodation*** *24 bedrooms, all en suite (4 with bath), £56.50 (suite £65, single £42/£46); 20% tariff reduction at weekends. No dogs. Access, Amex, Visa.*

BRETFORTON — Fleece Inn — A

Tel 01386 831173 Map 14a A1
The Cross Bretforton nr Evesham Hereford & Worcester WR11 5JE

The stone, thatch and half-timbered Fleece has been owned by the National Trust since 1977, bequeathed by retiring landlady Lola Taplin on strict condition that the pub remained unaltered, and potato crisps weren't sold. It stands out today as a living, yet very lived-in, museum whose three interior rooms, the Brewhouse, the Dugout and the smoking-free Pewter Room (with unique pewter collection on an oak dresser), are now preserved for posterity. There's an array of antiquities and all the interior is original – grandfather clock, settles, rocking chair, inglenook fireplaces, beams, timbers, flagstone floors, cheese moulds et al. Children get a look in, except in the tiny bar, and are catered for superbly outside: there's a thatched heraldic barn, barbecue, extensive orchard garden and adventure playground. The wealth of hanging baskets and flower-filled stone tubs which adorn the central flagged and pebbled yard are an absolute picture in summer. It's always busy, so get there early at lunchtime to ensure a table. *Open 11-2.30, 6-11 (Sun 12-2.30, 7-10.30). Free House.* ***Beer*** *M&B Brew XI, up to four guest beers. Garden, outdoor eating area. No credit cards.*

BRIDPORT — Bull Hotel — B&B

Tel 01308 22878 Map 13 F2
34 East Street Bridport Dorset DT6 3LF

This white-painted 16th-century coaching inn stands in the historic town centre. A traditional relaxing interior includes a convivial bar and a comfortably furnished reception area and lounge. Across the pretty courtyard is a large function room and bar which attracts local bands and a good following at weekends. There are 22 bedrooms, 13 of which have full en-suite facilities. Rooms are light, clean and functional and decorated in soothing pastel shades and attractive fabrics. Modern cream-coloured units, TVs and beverage-making facilities are standard throughout. Snooker room. *Open 10-11 (Sun 12-2.30, 7-10.30).* ***Beer*** *Bass, Flowers IPA, Teignworthy Reel, guest beer.* ***Accommodation*** *22 bedrooms, 13 en suite, £49 (single £36). Children welcome overnight, additional bed (6-14yrs £10) and cot available. Access, Amex, Diners, Visa.*

BRIDPORT George Hotel FOOD

Tel 01308 423187 Map 13 F2 **B&B**
4 South Street Bridport Dorset DT6 3NQ

Zzz...

The George has been spruced up in the past year, yet it still retains the delightful eccentric air that makes it so popular. A handsome Georgian building located opposite the Town Hall, it opens its doors at 8.30am for continental breakfast – excellent coffee and croissants – served in the relaxing and informal main bar and tiny dining-room. Old-fashioned in style with Regency-style wallpaper, Victorian-style red painted bar and oil paintings on the walls, it is filled with soothing classical music during the day and often louder jazz and opera in the evenings. Reliable bar food is produced from the kitchen – on view – at one end of the bar. The regular menu lists excellent snacks such as croque monsieur, curry and rice, chicken breast in cream, mushroom and calvados sauce, home-made paté and a variety of omelettes. Daily specials feature fish fresh from West Bay – lemon sole stuffed with crab in a cream and vermouth sauce – and might also include soft herring roe on toast, home-made ham, chicken and mushroom pie and vegetarian stuffed pepper. Vegetables, salads and potatoes are charged separately. The full range of Palmers ales are dispensed on handpump – the brewery is only just down the road. Four modest bedrooms share a bathroom and toilet. ***Bar Food*** *12-2, 7-9.30 (No food Sun lunch, Bank Holidays, winter month evenings by arrangement).* ***Beer*** *Palmers. Family room.* ***Accommodation*** *4 bedrooms, £37 (single £18.50). Children welcome overnight, cot available. Access, Visa.*

BRIGHTON The Greys FOOD

Tel 01273 680734 Map 11 B6
105 Southover Street Brighton East Sussex BN2 2UA

Climb from the Old Steine towards Kemp Town to find this gem of a dining pub with just one bar and half a dozen tables laid for lunchtime eating. Piped classical music (at lunchtimes) and enthusiasm abound. A short, daily-changing menu is provided by Belgian chef Jean-Paul Salpetier, and evolves daily, changing entirely evry three weeks or so. Starters might include mushrooms with garlic and fresh herbs, whitebait with chili, fennel and garlic oil or cassolette of snails and mushrooms with a pastis sauce. Main courses are equally interesting: Mediterranean salad with king prawns and avocado, Oriental-style sirloin steak with crispy noodles or perfectly cooked pigeon breasts with a cranberry and vodka sauce. Good desserts (mainly from the deep freeze) such as iced soufflé with fresh cherries. Tuesday evening is Supper Club theme night, providing a table d'hote menu – each month a different area of the world is featured. Visitors are entertained with live jazz, blues or Latin music on Sunday lunchtimes and Monday evenings. A descriptive beer menu offers up to 13 Belgian beers, each served with their own glass. If Brewery-on-Sea's Spinnaker Buzz is the guest beer, try it – it's an unusual brew, made with honey. No children under 14. *Open 11-3, 5.30-11 (Sun 12.30-3, 7-10.30).* ***Bar Meals*** *12-2.30 (not Sun), 7.30-11 (Tue & Wed only, bookings only on Tue).* ***Beer*** *Flowers Original, Adnams, guest beers. Patio/terrace, outdoor eating. No credit cards.*

BRIGHTWELL BALDWIN Lord Nelson FOOD

Tel 01491 612497 Map 14a C3
Brightwell Baldwin nr Watlington Oxon OX9 5NP

Already a couple of hundred years old when it was named after Admiral Nelson – the pub's name was changed to Lord Nelson when England's most famous sailor was elevated to the peerage – some later additions to the original stone buildings include 18th-century gable ends and a quaint verandah at the front, where it faces the village church of a sleepy hamlet. The Old English Pub Company have recently bought the pub after a period of uncertainty; the beers and wine list have changed and the pub's now open on Sunday evenings. Inside, it's still immediately clear that this is a 'dining' pub; half is set up as a restaurant and raffia place mats on the remaining tables are ready to receive the bar snacks. Peter Neal is still the man behind the bar and Richard Britcliffe continues to toil away in the kitchen. The restaurant menu (also available in the bar) ranges from smoked salmon, garlic mushrooms with bacon and steak and kidney pie to pear belle Hélène and guinea fowl with a creamy cider and onion sauce. The more snacky bar menu might include Welsh rarebit, pasta dishes and ploughman's lunches. There's a patio with tables for summer eating and a pretty garden overhung by a large weeping willow. Not suitable for children under 8. *Open 12-3.30, 6.30-11 (Sun 12-3, 7-10.30).* ***Bar Food*** *12-2, 7-10 (Sun to 9.30).* ***Beer*** *Ruddles, John Smith's. Patio, outdoor eating. Access, Amex, Visa.*

BRIMFIELD The Roebuck ★ FOOD B&B

Tel 01584 711230 Fax 01584 711654 Map 14 A1
Poppies Restaurant Brimfield nr Ludlow Shropshire SY8 4NE

Zzz...

Carole Evans's pub and restaurant has been a leading light since 1983. It's a very individual pub and worthy of an exceptional detour just to savour the superb hospitality on offer. It takes so much effort to run a quality establishment at this level that Carole's energy simply has to be admired. There is certainly no finer pub restaurant (recommended in our 1996 Hotels & Restaurants Guide) round these parts than Poppies at the Roebuck. The public bar retains a pubby atmosphere, whereas the lounge bar – a characterful room with a 15th-century beamed ceiling and dark oak panels – could be the restaurant. It isn't – there's a separate dining-room which is a bright and cheery room with parquet floor and cane-back chairs in chintzy style, in keeping with the rest of the building. You can, however, book tables in the lounge bar, where Carole's food can be enjoyed at less than the restaurant prices. Her command of composition and subtle blends of colour and flavour are frankly bewildering. The long, exciting bar menu might encompass escabèche of trout dusted with poppy seeds, a crab pot with Melba toast, spinach and pine kernel pie with a fresh tomato and basil sauce, savoury bread-and-butter pudding with a watercress sauce, braised oxtail, and chicken in Dunkerton's cider pie. Both the daily soup and bread rolls are home-made, of course. There's a comprehensive list of hot and cold desserts to follow: caramel pyramid with spiced brown bread ice cream, raspberry terrine, lemon tart, open gooseberry tart with vanilla custard and burnt cream flavoured with cardamom and chocolate – leave room! Some fourteen cheeses are listed on a tip-top cheese menu, from Malvern (made with ewe's milk) to Long Clawson Blue Stilton. Ploughman's lunches are served with home-made pickles; a selection of cheeses is served with home-made oat cakes and walnut and sultana bread. The excellent wine list has a large selection of half bottles. There are three lovely cottage bedrooms (two doubles with showers and a twin with full bathroom) in which to stay overnight. Here, you'll find home-made biscuits, cake, cafetière coffee and quality teas – an example of the care you're likely to receive. A wonderful country breakfast, including Herefordshire apple juice, honey from the garden and Carole's home-made sausages, will set you up for the day and set the seal on a memorable stay. *Open 12-3, 7-11 (Sun 12-3, 7-10.30). **Bar Food** (no food Sun & Mon) 12-2, 7-10. Free House. **Beer** one regularly-changing real ale. Patio/terrace, outdoor eating. **Accommodation** 3 bedrooms, all en suite, £60 (single £45). Children welcome overnight. Check-in by arrangement. Pub and accommodation closed 25 & 26 Dec. Access, Amex, Visa.*

BRINKWORTH Three Crowns FOOD

Tel 01666 510366 Fax 01666 510694 Map 14 C2
Brinkworth nr Chippenham Wiltshire SN15 5AF

Set back from the road, close to the village church and green, Anthony and Allyson Windle's old stone pub draws a discerning clientele from miles around, who seek out the unusual and often adventurous dishes that are listed on the comprehensive blackboard menu. Diners can sit in the main bar, furnished with a variety of old and new pine and featuring two remarkable tables created from huge 18th-century bellows, or they can relax in the new light, airy and tastefully pine-furnished conservatory extension, which overlooks the tree- and shrub-bordered garden. Food is taken very seriously here, the selection of freshly-prepared dishes changing regularly, depending on the seasonal availability of produce. A giant blackboard proclaims the likes of rack of Welsh lamb topped with garlic breadcrumbs, wild boar steak, stuffed and baked whole sea bass, bacon-wrapped king scallops flamed in Benedictine, duck supreme with brandy and peppercorn sauce. All are elaborately described and accompanied by inventive sauces plus six crisply-cooked vegetables – portions are extremely generous and not for the faint-hearted. Results and presentation are consistently good. Those palates desiring plainer fare will not be disappointed: the menu may include hearty pies, such as beef and venison, steak and kidney, seafood or chicken tandoori, plus a range of steaks, salads and a couple of imaginative vegetarian dishes. Lighter 'big' bites are offered at lunchtime, including filled giant potatoes, ploughman's and a selection of filled double-decker rolls. Delicious home-made puddings may include Swiss chocolate terrine, honey and yoghurt cheesecake, banana pancake and a range of ice creams made on the premises. To accompany a meal there is a list of just under 50 sensibly-priced wines. *Open 10-3, 6-11 (Sun 12-3, 7-10.30). **Bar Food** 12-2, 6.30-9.30 (Sun 7-9.30). **Beer** Marston's Pedigree, Bass, Boddingtons, Wadworth 6X, guest beer. Garden, outdoor eating. Access, Amex, Diners, Visa.*

Brisley — Bell — FOOD

Tel 01362 668686 Map 10 C1
The Green Brisley Norfolk NR20 5DW

Enjoying a magnificent, isolated position set back from B1145 and just 200 yards from the village centre, this attractive, 16th-century warm brick-built pub overlooks the largest piece of common land in Norfolk, some 200 acres. Enthusiastic new manager Les Philip has made several improvements, most notably the development of a barbecue area outisde. Witin, there's a small, refurbished bar area with old beams, large brick fireplace and exposed brick walls, plus a separate, neatly laid-up dining-room. Emphasis on the extensive blackboard menus, especially the restaurant board, is on fresh fish hand-selected in Lowestoft. Choose wisely from the bar food board and printed list for a value-for-money, home-cooked meal. Freshly-cut chips are fine, but there is the option for potatoes and fresh vegetables. Dishes range from fresh asparagus, freshly-prepared mushroom soup and chicken liver paté to fresh salmon and hollandaise, crab mornay, lamb and vegetable lasagne and steak and kidney pie. Puddings include apple pie and summer pudding. Sunny front patio and benches by the pond for fine weather alfresco eating. Three en-suite rooms (£30 double) are now offered for overnight accommodation, but were not inspected in time for this Guide's publication. *Open 11-3, 6-11 (Sun 12-3, 7-10.30).* ***Bar Food*** *12-2.30 (to 3 Sat), 6-9.30.* ***Beer*** *Boddingtons, Flowers IPA. Beer Garden, outdoor eating area. Access, Visa.*

Bristol — Highbury Vaults — A

Tel 0117 973 3203 Map 13 F1
164 St Michael's Hill Kingsdown Bristol Avon BS2 8DE

A serious contender for Bristol's busiest pub, close to the University and Infirmary, thus popular with students and nurses. The tiny front snug bar and rear bar as well as the walled patio at the back are all often crowded with young people who seem to enjoy the odd libation or two. No children indoors (but allowed in patio garden until 9pm). No music or machines, either. *Open 12-11 Mon-Sat (Sun 12-3, 7-10.30).* ***Beer*** *Smiles Exhibition, Best & Brewery, Brains SA, three guest beers. Patio, summer barbecues. No credit cards.*

Broad Campden — Bakers Arms — FOOD

Tel 01386 840515 Map 14a A1
Broad Campden nr Chipping Campden Gloucestershire GL55 6UR

Mid-way by road between Chipping Campden and Blockley, the pub stands at a convenient junction for walkers following the Heart of England Way. Real ales, real fires and "real food" are the promised order of the day. Of the first, seven may be on tap at any one time, with guest ales prominently displayed. Log fires burn when required at each end of the single bar; space can be limited here in poor weather. Real enough, the food is varied and invariably prepared to order with consequent delays: be sure to take a table number when ordering if sitting outside. Most ambitious are the daily specials: pancake cannelloni, beef in beer casserole and chicken tikka masala. Less adventurously, perhaps, herby tomato soup, chili con carne and apple pie won't break the bank! Good vegetarian choice. Family weekends (July), folk music nights, beer festivals and a hot-air balloon meeting are annual events. ***Bar Food*** *12-2, 6-9.45 (Sun 7-8.45). Free House.* ***Beer*** *Stanway Stanney Bitter, Donnington BB, Wickwar Brand Oak Bitter, up to 4 guest beers. Garden, outdoor eating, children's play area. No credit cards.*

Broad Chalke — Queen's Head Inn — B&B

Tel 01722 780344 Map 14 C3
Broad Chalke nr Salisbury Wiltshire SP5 5EN

This homely, stone-built village inn, located close to a meandering chalk stream in the Ebble valley, was once a bakehouse and stables before becoming an alehouse and outlasting the three other inns that once existed in the parish. The main Village bar has stone walls, a beamed ceiling and a large inglenook, but the place to sit on fine days is in the sheltered rear courtyard, amid the honeysuckle and roses. With doors leading off the courtyard is the modern brick-built accommodation, which houses four light and spacious bedrooms, all of which are in good order offering en-suite facilities (all with bath), beverage-making kits, remote-control TVs and direct-dial telephones. One non-smoking bar. *Open 11-3, 7-11 (Sun 12-3, 7-10.30). Free House.* ***Beer*** *Wadworth 6X, Bass, Boddingtons, guest beer. Courtyard.* ***Accommodation*** *4 bedrooms, £45 (single £22.50). Children welcome overnight (£5), additional bed available. No dogs. Access, Visa.*

BROADHEATH Old Packet House FOOD B&B

Tel 0161 929 1331 Map 6 B2

Navigation Road Broadheath nr Altrincham Greater Manchester WA14 1ON

Hard by a canal bridge on the main A56, the distinctive Packet House stands dwarfed by newer development, its former purpose in life scarcely recalled by the old wharf behind it. Black and white outside, with its heavy leaded-light windows protected by ornamental wrought-iron, it's unexpectedly spacious within and lent a cottagey feel by open brick fireplaces, patterned curtains and button-back banquettes in the lounge and raised dining sections. The single chalk-board menu serves all comers: for lunchtime snacks choose perhaps from a daily soup, sweet herrings and salad, grilled Manx kippers, haddock and prawn gratin or cheese and mushroom pancakes. Monday to Saturday, full evening meals extend the range with typically substantial portions for hearty eaters; main dishes such as deep-fried king cod in tartare sauce or chicken breast in pepper sauce and treacle tart and chocolate fudge cake exemplify the range. Service is informal, verging on the jovial, diners replenishing their real ales and (draught) house wines direct from the bar. Of the five bedrooms, one double has bath/WC en suite, the three singles and remaining twin sharing two spacious bathrooms. TVs, trouser presses, fitted mahogany furniture and bright brass taps are generally smart and modern. Delightful beer garden. ***Bar Food** 12-2.30, 6.30-9.30 (except Sun). **Beer** Boddingtons, Webster's Yorkshire, Wilson's. Patio, outdoor eating. **Accommodation** 5 bedrooms, 1 en suite, £55 (single £35). Children welcome overnight (charge depends on age), additional beds available. No dogs. No credit cards.*

BROADHEMBURY Drewe Arms FOOD

Tel 01404 841267 Map 13 E2

Broadhembury Devon EX14 0NF

Dating back to the 15th century, the small, thatched, Drewe Arms has a charmingly rustic feel with dado-boarded walls, a pile of old magazines next to the inglenook fireplace (with real log fire), various rural artifacts and a warm, convivial atmosphere created by Nigel and Kerstin Burge. The blackboard bar snack menu majors on open sandwiches – 'prawns in a crowd', Stilton and sirloin steak, gravad lax with dill and mustard sauce – plus good, fresh seafood (sea bream with herb butter, dressed crab, griddled red mullet) and the likes of a potato and chive soup or hot chicken and bacon salad. There are also cheese ploughman's and puds like treacle tart and chocolate marquise. Everything is freshly cooked and served in generous portions in unfussy style. *Open 11-2.30, 6-11 (Sun 12-2.30, 7-10.30). **Bar Food** 12-2, 7-10 (except Sun eve). Free House. **Beer** Otter Bitter, Bright, Ale & Head. Garden, outdoor eating. No credit cards.*

BROCKHAMPTON Craven Arms FOOD

Tel 01242 820410 Map 14 C1

Brockhampton Gloucestershire GL54 5XQ

A deservedly popular pub hidden down winding lanes deep in the rolling Gloucestershire countryside: Brockhampton is 2 miles north of the A436 Cheltenham to Gloucester road. Approached under a stone lych gate, the garden extends to an enclosed paddock with a children's play area which includes a small summer house containing games for soggier days. Revealed within the Craven Arms are stone-flagged floors and a warren of rooms given over primarily to eating. Real ales are well represented in the bar, where the less adventurous may order broccoli and walnut quiche and steak sandwiches with chips. The daily blackboard menu, though, is the thing to go for, chicken in Stilton sauce, poached salmon with lemon and thyme or Dundee lamb representing both quality and value. Puddings are the old favourites – sticky toffee, banoffi pie or chocolate fudge cake with chocolate rum sauce. Dining tables are predominantly pine, their evening adornment of fresh carnations and candles quite in keeping with the pub's relaxed environment. *Open 11-2.30, 6-10.30 (Sun 12-2.30,7-10.30. **Bar Food** 12-2 (Sun from 12.30), 7-9.30. Free House. **Beer** Butcombe, Hook Norton, Wadworth 6X. Garden, outdoor eating, children's play area. Access, Visa.*

Many **B&B** establishments offer reduced rates for weekend and out-of-season bookings. Always ask about special deals for longer stays. Beware half-board terms in inns where we do not recommend the **FOOD.**

BROCKTON Feathers FOOD

Tel & Fax 01746 785202 Map 6 B4
Brockton nr Much Wenlock Shropshire TF13 6JR

The historic Feathers stands at a crossroads on the B4378 Much Wenlock to Craven Arms road, signed left to Bridgnorth and right to Church Stretton. Deceptively small outside, it's half-timbered at one end and stone-clad to the rear, where the entrance leads via a patio through the conservatory. Inside, it has been completely redecorated over the last year or so; the interior divides into an intimate wine bar with a black range and three interconnecting rooms on two levels devoted largely to eating. Martin and Andrea Hayward's upmarket dining pub is commendable for both the quality and diversity of the food served. The menu is mostly on a blackboard with an extensive range of specials: perhaps moules marinière, freshly-made pasta, fresh asparagus in season, rack of English spring lamb with garlic and rosemary, fillet steak served with popular sauté potatoes; starters are served as light snacks and ploughman's lunches are also offered. Salmon and crab meat in filo pastry and marinated duck breast in oyster and chili sauce might complete the picture along with traditional puddings like steamed toffee and date pudding with fudge sauce. Four tables on the patio may be reserved, otherwise bookings are only taken for parties of six and over. Beer-drinkers may enjoy a good pint of hand-pulled Banks's bitter, house wine comes by the bottle, glass or goblet, there are at least half a dozen each of named reds and whites by the bottle, and coffee arrives in a cafetière. Andrea's kitchen hand-bell announces when each cooked-to-order dish is ready, ensuring prompt delivery to tables; salad and garnishes are generous and Martin arrives equally promptly with the two-pint jug of home-made dressing. As we went to press there were two letting bedrooms (with showers, £40 double, families welcome) and three further rooms were due to come on line towards the end of 1995. Note: this Brockton (of which there are five in Shropshire) is five miles south-west of Much Wenlock. *Open 12-3 Sat & Sun only, 6.30-11 (Sun 7-10.30). **Bar Food** 12-2 (Sat & Sun only), 6.30-9.30 (Sun 7-9). Free House. **Beer** Banks's Bitter, Camerons Strongarm. Patio. Pub closed all Monday & L Tue-Fri. No credit cards.*

BROMHAM Greyhound Inn FOOD

Tel 01380 850241 Map 14 B3
Bromham nr Chippenham Wiltshire SN15 2HA

Just three miles from Devizes Locks (longest set of locks in Europe), this lively Wadworth's pub is run with enthusiasm and verve. Parts of it go back 300 years – in the more recent bar extension, an old well still remains in the middle of the room. The menu is often ingenious, featuring interesting Malaysian and Thai dishes, e.g. fiery pork. There are two dining-rooms seating 18 and 50 respectively but everyone eats everywhere in the Greyhound – beef in red wine, chicken in cream and vinegar and steak and kidney pie, with a summer fish menu featuring red snapper, Dover sole and whole crab salad, and on Sunday the roast lunch is available as just a main course. Tons of atmosphere, thanks largely to walls and ceilings festooned with bric-à-brac in both bars – over 500 advertising jugs in one! Intriguingly-named puddings: Mars Bar cheesecake, tiddly nickers and home-made ice creams such as banana and honey. Parents can get extra plates for informal children's portions. *Open 11-2.30, 6.30-11 (Sun 12-3, 7-10.30). **Bar Food** 12-2, 7-10.30 (Sun to 10). Free House. **Beer** Wadworth IPA and 6X. Garden, outdoor eating, children's play area. Access, Visa.*

BROOM Broom Tavern FOOD

Tel 01789 773656 **Fax 01789 772983** Map 14 C1
High Street Broom Warwickshire B50 5HL

Pretty, timbered village pub dating back to the 16th century with virginia creeper clinging to the outside and lots of black beams and brass within. The bar menu (mostly home-made although some puds and soups are not) offers plenty of choice from ploughman's, sandwiches and starters like duck paté and prawn cocktail to main dishes such as chicken chasseur, steak and kidney pie, lasagne verde and steaks plus omelettes and salad platters. Children are catered for with a special menu, a single high-chair and, on summer weekends and during school holidays, a 'bouncy castle' out in the garden. *Open 11-3, 6-11 (Sun 12-3, 7-10.30). **Beer** Theakston XB, Hook Norton Best Bitter, two guest beers. **Bar Food** 12-2, 7-9.30 (Sat 6.40-10, Sun 7-9). Garden. Access, Amex, Visa.*

BROOM — Cock Inn — A

Tel 01767 314411 Map 15a F1
23 High Street Broom Bedfordshire SG18 9NA

Stretching back from the only street of a village with no middle, no shops and a postage stamp-sized post office in the postmistress's front room, the Cock is a conversion of three interlinked Victorian cottages, its three panelled sitting areas furnished with bench seats and varnished table, and a games room complete with the locally popular chair-skittles table. Look inside the two front rooms and find a novel collection of metallised tobacco adverts and shelves of aged beer and medicine bottles. The bar, central to everything here, has remained unchanged for over a century, its cellar down four wooden steps, where the Greene King ale is drawn direct from the cask. New landlords as we went to press. *Open 12-3, 6-11 (Sun 12-3, 7-10.30).* ***Beer*** *Greene King. Garden. Family room. No credit cards.*

BUCKDEN — Buck Inn — FOOD B&B

Tel 01756 760228 **Fax 01756 760227** Map 5 D4
Buckden North Yorkshire BD23 5JA

Zzz...

Both the creeper-clad Georgian coaching inn and the village take their names from the fact that this was once the meeting place for local stag hunts; today it is tourists and walkers who are attracted to this fine old inn. The small bar with flagstone floor and old stone fireplace is in great contrast to the smart staff who offer swift, efficient service both in the extensive, carpeted bar-meal areas with their tapestry banquette seating or wheelback chairs, and in the pretty restaurant formed out of what was once the courtyard where local sheep auctions were held. The menu offers something for everybody from snacks like ploughman's, jacket potatoes and French stick sandwiches to full meals with such dishes as pan-fried liver with chipolatas and bacon, lasagne al forno, poached salmon, steaks and specials from the blackboard which could include beef and stout pie with gravy and tortellini pasta with tomato and pesto sauce. There are also vegetarian and children's sections, and a long list of home-made puddings. No chips or sandwiches in the evening. Pretty bedrooms with matching floral duvets and curtains are furnished in pine and all have TV, direct-dial telephone and tea- and coffee-making kit (although there is also room service available throughout the day and evening). Bathrooms, like the bedrooms, are smart and well-kept, mostly just with showers but five have bathtubs. *Open 11-11 Mon-Sat (Sun usual hours).* ***Bar Food*** *12-2.30 (Sun all day July & August), 6.30-9 (Fri & Sat to 9.30). Free House.* ***Beer*** *Theakston Old Peculier, Best & XB, Black Sheep Bitter & Special, guest beer. Patio, outdoor eating.* ***Accommodation*** *13 bedrooms, all en suite, £68 (single £34). Children welcome overnight (under-5s free, 5-10 ½ price, 11-14 two-thirds adult rate – if sharing parents' room), additional bed & cot (both £3) available. Access, Visa.*

BUCKLAND NEWTON — Gaggle of Geese — A

Tel 01300 345249 Map 13 F2
Buckland Newton Dorset DT2 7BS

Formerly the Royal Oak, The Gaggle of Geese is so named since a previous landlord bred geese as a hobby; the building dates back to 1834 when it started life as the village shop. Twice-yearly goose charity auctions still take place here. Located on the B3143, about halfway between Dorchester and Sherborne, this tranquil village pub has a civilised and attractive main bar and pretty garden complete with pond. Children are allowed in the skittle alley and dining-room. Certified caravan club location for up to five caravans. *Open 12-2.30, 6.30-11 (Sun 12-2.30, 7-10.30). Free House.* ***Beer*** *Hall & Woodhouse Badger Best, Bass, Wadworth 6X, Butcombe Bitter, two guest beers. Garden, children's play area. Family room. No credit cards.*

BUCKLER'S HARD — Master Builder's House Hotel — B&B

Tel 01590 616253 **Fax 01590 616297** Map 15 D4
Buckler's Hard nr Beaulieu Hampshire SO42 7XB

The grassy areas in front of this updated and extended 18th-century hotel run right down to the banks of the Beaulieu River, where many famous ships were once built for Nelson's fleet. The Yachtsman's Bar is popular with yachtsmen and tourists alike, and residents have their own homely lounge with easy chairs, period furniture and a large inglenook fireplace. Creaky floorboards and old-world charm make the six bedrooms in the main house

appealing (and quiet once the tourists have gone home); rooms in a purpose-built block are plainer but well equipped. *Open 11-3, 6-11 (11-11 Sat all year & Mon-Sat July & Aug), Sun 12-3, 7-10.30.* ***Beer*** *Burton, John Bull, Tetley.* ***Accommodation*** *23 bedrooms, £85 (4-poster £100, single £55-£65). Children welcome overnight (under 14s stay free in parents' room), additional bed and cot supplied. Garden. Access, Amex, Diners, Visa.*

BURCOT — Chequers — FOOD

Tel 01865 407771 Map 14a C3

Abingdon Road Burcot Oxfordshire OX14 3DP

Originally a staging post for River Thames barges and their crews, until what is now the A415 was built outside. Charming, part 16th-century beamed and thatched building with unspoilt quarry-tiled bars, open fires and a choice of books for customers to read. A daily-changing blackboard menu is the same for the bar and dining-room. Cook Mary Weeks offers simple home-made fare (including bread) – tomato apple and celery, chicken and tarragon and fish, cheese and broccoli pie, chicken and fennel lasagne and (genuine old fashioned suet) steak and kidney pudding – followed by melting meringues filled with peaches and cream and home-made brown bread ice-cream. Sunday lunch is served on the first Sunday of every month. Piano music on Friday and Saturday nights. *Open 11-2.30, 6-11 (Sun 12-3, 7-10.30).* ***Bar Food*** *12-2, 6.30-9 (no food Sun eve). Free House.* ***Beer*** *Ruddles County, Ushers Best, Archer's Village Bitter. Garden, outdoor eating. Access, Visa.*

BURFORD — The Angel — FOOD

Tel 01993 822438 Map 14a A2 **B&B**

Witney Street Burford Oxfordshire OX18 4SN

If the former Mason's Arms once fell from grace here, then today's newly-named, and redecorated, Angel Inn has taken off in full flight. Well worth seeking out just off the High Street, the Angel remains a pub and foregoes intrusive juke box and amusements in favour of two stylish cottage-style dining areas. The food is the better for it and diners reap the benefit. One menu is offered throughout and light meals and starters are interchangeable in the lunch hour: perhaps avocado stuffed with tuna and prawn mayonnaise or chicken liver paté, tagliatelle with cream and pesto, or pan-fried calf's liver with sage and butter; at night time there's no further compulsion to overspend. The daily fish specials are becoming increasingly popular, with a choice of at least five or so fish dishes on offer when overnight deliveries have come from Newlyn in Cornwall; skate, sea bass, lemon sole and monkfish all regularly feature – even dressed crab in season. To finish, there might be a very good summer pudding, caramelised lemon tart or mocha chocolate demitasse with cappuccino top. Summer dining terrace and gardens to the rear. Three en-suite letting bedrooms offer a cosy, restful night's sleep. Good breakfasts and exceptionally friendly service. *Open 11.30-2.30, 6.30-11 (Sun 12-3, 7-10.30).* ***Bar Food*** *12-2, 7-9.* ***Beer*** *Flowers IPA, Marston's Pedigree, two guest beers. Garden, outdoor eating.* ***Accommodation*** *3 rooms, all en suite, £49.50 (single £30-£35). Children welcome overnight, extra bed (£10) available. Check-in by arrangement. Pub closed Sun eve Nov-Mar. Access, Visa.*

BURFORD — Inn For All Seasons — FOOD

Tel 01451 844324 **Fax 01451 844375** Map 14a A2 **B&B**

The Barringtons Burford Oxfordshire OX18 4TN

Zzz...

Despite its Burford address, the inn's actually in Gloucestershire, alongside the A40 by the Barringtons turn. A passageway runs from the cellars to the old stone mines there, whence came the cutters for their regular sustenance. The stone was sent as far afield as Oxford and St Paul's Cathedral. From even further afield comes a regular clientele to enjoy the comforts of a small hotel whose interior has been meticulously restored to reflect 17th-century elegance. Leather wing chairs grace a flagstone bar adorned with rugby, motoring and flying memorabilia, much of the latter with local war-time connections. The nine bedrooms are models of comfort with TVs (not remote-controlled), tea-makers, trouser presses and hairdryers. All rooms have simple, neatly kept en-suite bathrooms (although the showers are pretty ineffective), and those in front are double-glazed against any intrusive noise from the busy road. Residents enjoy extensive use of their own lounge and the garden. The Inn is run by Matthew Sharp, whose menus might encompass tomato and basil soup, home-made taramasalata and hot toast, ploughman's lunches with granary bread, lamb and aubergine kebab with pilaf rice and a garlic and mint sauce or 10oz Scotch rump steak. Only bread and ice cream are bought in, all other fare is prepared on the premises; fresh fish and the meat is supplied by good local butchers. The three acres of garden are surrounded by

cypress trees and a dry stone wall. *Open 11-2.30, 6-11 (to 10.30 in winter), Sun 12-3, 7-10.30.* ***Bar Food*** *11.30-2 (from 12 Sun), 6.30-9.30 (7-9 Sun). Free House.* ***Beer*** *Hall & Woodhouse Badger Best, Wadworth 6X, Wychwood. Garden. Accommodation 10 bedrooms, all en suite, £75 (single £41.50). Children over 10 welcome, additional bed available (50% of single tariff). No dogs. Access, Amex, Visa.*

BURFORD — Lamb Inn — FOOD B&B

Tel 01993 823155 **Fax 01993 822228** Map 14a A2
Sheep Street Burford Oxfordshire OX18 4LR

It's difficult to exaggerate the mellow charm of the 14th-century Lamb Inn, tucked down a quiet side street off the High Street in this most attractive Cotswolds' town. Public rooms range from a rustic bar at one end of the building to a chintzy lounge at the other with in between a combination of the two featuring rugs on the flagstone floor, a collection of brass ornaments over the fireplace, a display of china figurines on a window shelf, fresh flowers and antique furniture – all polished and buffed to please the most exacting housekeeper. Warmed within by log fires for most of the year; there is also a very pretty walled garden to take advantage of the (hopefully) ever-improving English summers. Bar lunches, served throughout the ground floor, run from various ploughman's lunches, soup with granary bread and open prawn sandwich to steak and kidney pie, herb pancake with salmon and prawns and sautéed chicken livers. No bar snacks in the evening. What the bedrooms lack in extras, they make up for with cottagey appeal; all have antique furniture, pretty floral fabrics and many also have old beams and timbers in evidence. Remote-control TVs remind you it's the 20th century, but there are no telephones. One room features a four-poster bed. *Open 11-2.30, 6-11 (Sun 12-2.30, 7-10.30).* ***Bar Food*** *12-2. Free House.* ***Beer*** *Wadworth IPA & 6X. Family room.* ***Accommodation*** *16 bedrooms, all en suite, £85 Sun-Thu (£95 Fri & Sat, single £35/£37.50). Children welcome overnight, additional bed (£20) and cot (£6) available. Dogs by arrangement. Access, Visa.*

BURHAM — Golden Eagle — FOOD

Tel 01634 668975 Map 11 B5
80 Church Street Burham Kent ME1 3SD

Rather plain looking village local with a carpeted and simply furnished open-plan bar, original beams adorned with mugs and jugs and striking views across the Medway valley and the North Downs. Worthy of a visit for its unusual bar food, the changing blackboard menu consisting of some 30-odd Malaysian dishes: perhaps spicy nasi goreng, beef and black peppers in black bean sauce, Balinese pork, coconut beef, duck in plum sauce or king prawns and peppers in oyster sauce. In addition, at lunchtime you may find ploughman's lunches, jacket potatoes, sandwiches and gammon steak. *Open 11-2.30, 6.15-11 (Sun 12-3, 7-10.30).* ***Bar Food*** *12-2, 7-10. Free House.* ***Beer*** *Wadworth 6X, Marston's Pedigree, guest beer. Paved garden, outdoor eating. Pub closed 25 & 26 Dec. Access, Visa.*

BURITON — Five Bells — FOOD

Tel 01730 263584 Map 15 D3
Buriton High Street nr Petersfield Hampshire GU31 5RX

Dating back to the 16th century this well-refurbished brick and stone free house nestles in an attractive village at the base of the South Downs, a couple of minutes off the busy A3 (signposted heading south). Popular with South Downs Way walkers – 400 yards away – and a mixed local clientele, the pub offers a delightful rustic ambience within the series of rambling bars. Warmed by four large open fires and furnished with mainly sturdy pine on rug-strewn wood-block floors, it is a welcoming place in which to relax. The extensive menu – listed on beams and boards – is conveniently sectioned for ease of choice (spciy dishes, fish, vegetarian and so on) and the food is reliably good. The fish board may feature crab and sherry bake, whole trout with almonds or grilled lemon sole, while the main-course board could offer steak and kidney pie, wild rabbit in prunes and Calvados, liver and bacon casserole and more game dishes in winter. Other choices may include spicy Indonesian pork, mushroom and Brie flan and hearty lunchtime snacks – filled jacket potatoes, French sticks and ploughman's lunches to sustain hungry walkers. Interesting puddings such as apricot frangipane tart and gooseberry, honey and almond tart. Sunday lunch includes a vegetarian option. Good sheltered summer garden with vine-bearing trellis and fruit trees. Live monthly jazz and weekly Wednesday folk or country and western. In the last year barns have been converted for overnight bedroom accommodation; there were two rooms and self-catering cottages available as we went to press (but not yet inspected). If you stay overnight and see a small lady dressed in grey peasant clothes, don't worry – she's

been around for a long time! *Open 11-2.30 (to 3 Fri & Sat), 5.30-10.30 (to 11 Fri & Sat), Sun 12-3, 7-10.30. Free House.* ***Bar Food*** *12-2, 6.30-10 (12-2, 7-10 Sun).* ***Beer*** *Ballard's Best Bitter, Adnams Bitter, Ringwood Old Thumper, Friary Meux Best Bitter, Tetley, Ind Coope Burton Ale, guest beer. Garden, outdoor eating. Access, Amex, Visa.*

BURNHAM MARKET Hoste Arms ★ FOOD

Tel 01328 738257 **Fax 01328 730103** Map 10 C1 **B&B**
The Green Burnham Market Norfolk PE31 8HD

Zzz...   

A handsome, pale yellow-painted 17th-century inn (now much extended to the rear) occupying a prime position overlooking the green and parish church of this most picturesque village. Before Paul Whittome purchased the inn it had suffered more than a century of brewery ownership and subsequent architectural abuse. His relentless enthusiasm for the property (and the business) over the past five years has transformed the Hoste into one of the most popular inns along the Norfolk coast. It goes from strength to strength, with a new block of six elegant, extremely comfortable bedrooms completed since the last edition of this Guide. Two carefully-renovated front bars feature dark wood panelling, open brick fireplaces with winter log fires, rustic wooden floors and cushioned bow window seats with village views. Of note are the original paintings by wildlife artist Bruce Pearson illustrating a series of rural walks from the inn, Lord Decies' shell collection displayed in cabinets, and a permanent exhibition of Stephen Heffer's Norfolk coastal photographs. Live traditional jazz and R&B are popular Friday night events in the comfortably furnished piano bar. Above-average pub food draws on supplies of fresh local and seasonal produce (though Colman's mustard may be local it is not so seasonal!) from within a twenty mile radius and everything is prepared on the premises. Varied printed menu choices range from open sandwiches, local Burnham Norton oysters, country farmhouse paté with apricot chutney and toasted croute, generously-served honey-glazed ham hock with a sweet mustard sauce, and Norfolk chicken, leek and smoked bacon pie to half a dozen Asian dishes such as marinated monkfish with green chili and Singapore rice or salmon and Cromer crab fishcake with a coconut and curry sauce. Supplementary blackboards list daily specials. To finish, try the apple crumble, chocolate and hazelnut torte, a selection of three English cheeses or Prospero ice creams, made locally in Holt. Vegetarians might enjoy braised Cos lettuce with vegetarian oyster sauce and toasted sesame seeds. Sunday roasts. Cooking in the Norfolk Restaurant moves up a gear with a short, daily-changing dinner menu that is imaginative and offers good value; look out for local and beef from Wroxham Broads, mussels from Brancaster Staithe or sea bass and sea trout form Scolt Head Island. The global list of around 130 well-priced wines has sensible prices, useful notes and a selection of half bottles; well-kept ales are drawn straight from the cask. Upstairs, beyond the small gallery/lounge, are the majority of the charming bedrooms, four of which now boast four-posters. The rooms are all individually decorated, some with freestanding pine, others with antique pieces, designer fabrics and fittings. Spotless en-suite facilities (only four rooms have shower only) and TV, radio, tea-maker, telephone and hairdryer are all provided. The six newest rooms offer superb comfort and one can really look forward to a good night's sleep after exploring the Norfolk's north-coast salt marshes and sand dunes. First-rate breakfasts are served in the conservatory, which is also the venue for afternoon teas (free to residents). Year-round tariff reductions are offered for stays of two nights and over; the best deal is half price (Sun-Thu) from November to the end of March. Quite delightful garden with rustic benches and dry hop-filled conservatory. Winner of our 1996 Pub of the Year Award. *Open 11-11, Sun 12-10.30. Free House.* ***Bar Food*** *12-2.15, 7-9.30.* ***Beer*** *Ruddles County, Webster's Yorkshire Bitter, Woodforde's Wherry Bitter, guest beers. Garden, outside eating.* ***Accommodation*** *21 bedrooms, all en suite, £80-£100 (single £52). Children welcome overnight (under-4s free if sharing parents' room), additional bed and cot provided (£15). Access, Visa.*

Many **B&B** establishments offer reduced rates for weekend and out-of-season bookings. Always ask about special deals for longer stays. Beware half-board terms in inns where we do not recommend the **FOOD.**

BURNHAM THORPE **Lord Nelson** A

Tel 01328 738241 Map 10 C1

Walsingham Road Burnham Thorpe Norfolk P31 8HN

Unspoilt rural cottage located in a sleepy village close to Burnham Market and named after England's most famous seafarer, who was born in the nearby rectory. A narrow, worn brick-floored corridor leads to two rooms; a timeless, old-fashioned bar on the left boasting some magnificent high-backed settles and a few sturdy tables and plain chairs on a re-tiled floor. Nelson memorabilia in the form of prints and paintings adorn the walls. There is no bar; excellent Greene King ales are drawn straight from the cask in the adjacent cellar room and brought to the table. Also available is a popular rum concoction called "Nelson's Blood", which is made to a secret recipe by the previous long-serving landlord who still resides near the pub. A further warmly decorated and simply furnished room is ideal for families. Good-sized garden with bowling green, bat & ball, football net, basketball net, swing and slide for active youngsters to let off steam. *Open 11-3, 6-11 (12-3, 7-10.30 Sun), longer hours in summer. **Beer** Greene King. Garden, children's play area. No credit cards.*

BURNHAM-ON-CROUCH **Ye Olde White Harte Hotel** B&B

Tel & Fax 01621 782106 Map 11 C4

The Quay Burnham-on-Crouch Essex CM0 8AS

An old seaside inn where on sunny summer days you can take your drink to a lovely waterside terrace overlooking the busy yachting activity. Two characterful, wood-panelled bars have polished-oak furnishings, exposed beams, a good open fire and a nautical atmosphere; there's also a small, traditional residents' lounge. The best of the ninteen bedrooms (which vary in size and standard) are the eleven comfortable en-suite rooms with smart, modern decor, good fabrics and simple furniture. Five clean, tiled bathrooms have bath and shower. Original beams and brick fireplaces, and splendid estuary views are notable features. Eight rooms are self-styled as "basic". *Open 11-11 in summer, 11-3, 6-11 in winter (Sun 12-3, 7-10.30). Free House. **Beer** Adnams, Tolly Cobbold Bitter. Waterside Terrace. Family room. **Accommodation** 19 bedrooms, 11 en suite, £50/£60 (single £33/£37.40). Children welcome overnight (if sharing parents' room: under-5s £6.50, 6-12 yrs £8, over-12s £10), additional bed and cot available. Access, Visa.*

BURPHAM **George & Dragon** FOOD

Tel 01903 883131 Map 11 A6

Burpham nr Arundel West Sussex BN18 9RR

Burpham is signposted off the A27 near Arundel. At the end of three miles of a winding, climbing lane, one is rewarded with some fine views of the Arun valley, with Arundel Castle in the distance, and the pretty George & Dragon with its good food and real ales. Once the haunt of smugglers, the inn dates back to the mid 18th century; it is now divided into two very different halves: the bar with its exposed timbers, rustic tables and country chairs, and the smart dining-room with crisp white napery and elegant Regency-style chairs. The printed bar food lunch and supper menu covers the standard items – home-made soup, deep-fried mushrooms with garlic, grilled sirloin steak, jacket potatoes (with cheese and bacon), ploughman's and granary sandwiches – while a daily-changing blackboard menu lists around four fresh fish dishes, avocado crab, vegetarian chili, Irish stew and rosemary dumplings and chicken and leek crumble. Another blackboard lists a particularly good range of home-made puds, perhaps a rich dark chocolate mousse, a bright yellow mango cheesecake and a particularly good raspberry torte with coconut served with a hot raspberry coulis. The 100-year-old cricket club is next door (as is Mervyn Peake, author of Gormenghast, who is at rest in the village churchyard) Children (but not babies) are allowed in the bar to eat. No music or dogs allowed and "smoking is not encouraged". Now owned by Grosvenor Inns. *Open 11-2.30, 6-11 (Sun 12-3, 7-10.30). **Bar Food** 12-2, 7-9.45. **Beer** Courage Directors, Arundel Best, four guest beers. Terrace, outdoor eating. Bar closed Sun night mid Sept-Easter. Access, Amex, Visa.*

We only recommend food (Bar Food) in those establishments highlighted with the **FOOD** symbol.

BURSLEDON — Jolly Sailor — A

Tel 01703 405557 Map 15 D4
Lands End Road Old Bursledon Hampshire SO31 8DN

Three miles from M27 Junction 8, the Jolly Sailor overlooks the busy yachting marina activity on the River Hamble. Parking is restricted outside the pub but there is free parking at Old Bursledon railway station, which is a couple of minutes' walk up the lane; there are then 40 steps down (and back up!) to the pub entrance. Built as a shipbuilder's house in 1700 and later a vicarage, it became a pub in the early 1900s. It has its own jetty and yachtsmen have used this harbourside pub as a retreat ever since the days of Lord Nelson. More recently, it was featured in BBC TV's *Howard's Way*. The large terrace is a lovely spot to watch the nautical world go by and within the unspoilt interior the nautical front bar also has good views from sought-after bay window seats; the flagstoned back bar is old and characterful. Splendid alfresco seating on the bench-filled front terrace and along the jetty jutting out over the river. Try one of the fifteen fruity country wines on offer from Gales of Havant. Small, lawned garden area has a 100-year-old yew tree for shade. *Open 11-2.30, 6-11 (Sat 11-11, Sun 12-3, 7-10.30), maybe longer hours in summer.* ***Beer*** *Hall & Woodhouse Badger Best and Tanglefoot, Wadworth 6X, Gribble Ales' Jolly Sailor Bitter & Plucking Pheasant. Riverside garden. Access, Amex, Diners, Visa.*

BURTON — Old House at Home — FOOD

Tel 01454 218227 Map 14 B2
Burton nr Chippenham Wiltshire SN14 7LT

Somewhat up-market for a village local, the Old House at Home produces considerably more than the home cooking its name suggests. Full-time chefs produce such daily fare as lasagne, garlic steak, Murphy's lamb alongside 'Sally's steak and mushroom pie' and oriental chicken. Fresh fish is now a strong feature and might include salmon, monkfish, fillet of plaice, trout or fillet of red snapper. Granary sandwiches and ploughman's lunches at lunchtime only. A soft-stone building with a warm and welcoming timbered interior and log fires in winter. Music, food and wine from various countries are featured on a Monday theme evening once a month. Children allowed in bar to eat at lunchtime only. A new front patio was created last year out of Cotswold stone. *Open 12-2.30, 7-11 (Sun 12-3, 7-10.30). Pub closed Tuesday lunchtime.* ***Bar Food*** *12-2 (except Tue), 7-10 (Sun to 9.30). Free House.* ***Beer*** *Smiles, Bass, Wadworth 6X, Old Timer (winter). Garden, outdoor eating, children's play area. Access, Amex, Visa.*

BURY ST EDMUNDS — The Nutshell — A

Tel 01284 764867 Map 10 C2
The Traverse Bury St Edmunds Suffolk

Blink and you will miss this unique miniature pub tucked away between a newsagents and a building society on a pedestrianised zone just off the main market square. It claims to be the smallest pub in Britain, a title that is difficult to dispute as the single bar – measuring barely a hundred square feet – is positively crowded if eight people are inside drinking. Despite its size there are plenty of curios to interest the eye, notably collections of 'smallest' items, bank notes from around the world, military memorabilia and, unbelievably, a mummified cat and mouse hanging from the ceiling. Good, well-kept Greene King ales, a welcoming chatty atmosphere and the signing of the visitors book is obligatory. *Open 11-11 Mon-Sat (closed Sun).* ***Beer*** *Greene King. No credit cards.*

BUTTERLEIGH — Butterleigh Inn — A

Tel 01884 855407 Map 13 E2
Tiverton-Cullompton Road Butterleigh Devon EX15 1PN

Unspoilt farming pub in glorious countryside, just three miles from Junction 28 of the M5 motorway. The main bar is half lounge, half public end with simple wooden furnishings; a tiny snug takes just four intimate tables. Inglenook fireplace and old-fashioned pub games. No children indoors but there's a play area available in the garden. Black Hand cider (made on a local farm) is available in the summer. *Open 12-2.30, 6-11 (Sun 12-3, 7-10.30). Free House.* ***Beer*** *Cotleigh Tawny, Barn Owl and Old Buzzard, occasional guest beer. Garden, outdoor eating, children's play area. Access, Visa.*

BUTTERMERE **Bridge Hotel** B&B

Tel & Fax 017687 70252 Map 4 C3
Buttermere Cumbria CA13 9UZ

Zzz...

Looking across the valley to Red Pike and High Stile between which cascades Sourmilk Gill's waterfall, this is an idyllic spot, beloved of generations of fell-walkers. There are distinctly contrasting sides to the business, however. The Walker's bar is kept suitably rustic with rooms for rucksacks and boots permitted. A mere few paces distant, residents are treated to complimentary afternoon tea in the hotel lounge. Most of the bedrooms get a share of the majestic surrounding hills; the best of them have tiny wooden balconies teetering above the fast-rushing stream that bisects the property. Though general decor can be a little dark, all are enlivened by bright tiled bathrooms. No TVs or radios in the rooms, just P&Q. *Open 10.30-11. Free House.* ***Beer*** *Theakston Old Peculier, Black Sheep Best & Special Strong Bitter, one guest beer. Patio.* ***Accommodation*** *22 bedrooms, 21 en suite, £73, £106 half board (four-poster £85/£114 half board, single £36.50), seven apartments in grounds available on weekly terms. Children welcome overnight (under-4s stay free if sharing parents' room, 4-10s £17), additional bed and cot (£5) available. Access, Visa.*

BYTHORN **White Hart** FOOD

Tel 01832 710226 Map 7 E4
Bythorn nr Huntingdon Cambridgeshire PE18 0QM

17th-century coaching inn nestling in a peaceful village just off the A14 Huntingdon to Kettering road. Rambling interior comprising four relaxing and varied inter-connecting rooms featuring plenty of exposed brick, beams and boards, quarry tiles and colourful rugs topped with an interesting rustic assortment of furniture, including an old Chesterfield. Huge open fireplaces with log fires for winter days and tables strewn with books and magazines beckon those who intend settling down for a relaxed stay. Food emphasis in this welcoming establishment is rooted in the airy restaurant extension, although a short blackboard bar menu (except Saturday evenings) lists good lighter bites (no sandwiches) – perhaps spare ribs, pigeon pie, king prawns in batter, mussels in white wine and cream, spicy fish soup and roast loin of pork with orange sauce. However, those wishing to stay in front of the fire are welcome to choose from the more imaginative bistro fare. Starters range from quail's eggs and smoked salmon with Madeira sauce to chicken and sweetbreads in a puff pastry case, followed by half-guinea fowl with fresh limes or calf's liver with crispy bacon and onion gravy. Puddings include toasted fruit sabayon and fresh strawberry Romanoff. Four-course Sunday lunch. *Open 10-2, 6-11 (Sun 12-3 only). Pub closed all day Mon and Sun evening. Free House.* ***Bar Food*** *12-2, 6.30-10 (Sun 7-10, no* ***Bar Food*** *Sat eve).* ***Beer*** *Greene King. Paved patio, outdoor eating. Access, Visa.*

BYWORTH **Black Horse** FOOD

Tel 01798 342424 Map 11 A6
Byworth nr Petworth West Sussex GU28 0HO

Built on the site of a 15th-century friary in a sleepy village setting – just off the A283 Petworth to Pulborough road – the unusual three-storey Georgian facade of this friendly pub hides an ancient rustic interior. Beams, bare-boarded floors, scrubbed tables and padded wall seats characterise the three attractive interconnecting rooms and extraordinary upstairs Elizabethan dining-room. Bar food ranges from good standard pub snacks – grilled jacket potatoes, salads, steaks) – to more imaginative, daily-changing blackboard specials, such as a well presented breast of chicken with a tarragon cream sauce accompanied by a dish of well-cooked vegetables. Alternatives may include "real" French onion soup, 16oz steak and kidney pudding and halibut with Szechuan sauce. The home-made treacle tart is the best bet among the puds. Splendid summer alfresco imbibing on an old cobbled patio or among the flower borders and shrubs in the fine terraced garden with peaceful wooded valley views. *Open 11-3, 6-11 (Sun 12-3, 7-10.30).* ***Bar Food*** *11.30-1.45, 6-9.45 (12-1.45, 7-9.45 Sun). Garden, outdoor eating. Free House.* ***Beer*** *Young's Bitter, Ballard's Best, Gale's HSB, Fuller's London Pride. Access, Amex, Visa.*

We do not accept free meals or hospitality – our inspectors pay their own bills and **never** book in the name of Egon Ronay's Guides.

CADEBY Cadeby Inn A

Tel 01709 864009 Map 7 D2
Main Street Cadeby nr Doncaster South Yorkshire DN5 7SW

This atmospheric old inn was clearly once an elegant country farmhouse and stands today in a mature orchard garden full of flowering shrubs. There's plenty of space here for little ones to play safely, and the picnic tables are especially popular when there's a barbecue on. In poor weather, children are allowed in the snug only until 8pm. Original flagstones and fireplaces survive in the two bars whose counters are built in brick, while the walls are hung with horse collars, brasses and webbing. *Open 11.30-3, 5-11 (Sat 11-11, Sun 12-3, 7-10.30). Free House.* ***Beer*** *Tetley Best, Courage Directors, John Smith's Best & Magnet, Samuel Smith's Old Brewery. Garden, children's play area. Family room. Access, Visa.*

CADNAM White Hart FOOD

Tel 01703 812277 **Fax 01703 814632** Map 14 C4
Cadnam nr Lyndhurst Hampshire SO40 2NP

The Emberley family run this attractive and smartly-refurbished old coaching inn, located on the edge of the New Forest beside A31, near M27 Junction 1. A big welcome awaits families either in the extensive sheltered garden, complete with a paddock of animals, or in the spacious interior which boasts plenty of exposed brick, open fires and a comfortable mix of old and new furniture. The Emberleys' tried and tested bar food formula is very popular, with a broad spectrum of dishes catering for all tastes. Printed menu fare features the usual pub favourites – ploughman's, gammon steak and pineapple, haddock and chips – alongside more imaginative dishes like gigot of lamb with cherry and almond sauce. Blackboard specials improve matters further with game in season and fresh fish, perhaps dressed crab, sea bass or cod with caper sauce. Set 3-course Sunday roast lunch. Good selection of real ales and at least nine wines available by the glass. *Open 11-2.30, 6-11 (Sun 12-3, 7-10.30)* ***Bar Food*** *11-2, 6-9.30 (Sun 12-2, 7-9). Beer King & Barnes Sussex, Morland Old Speckled Hen, Flowers Original, Wadworth 6X. Garden, outdoor eating. Access, Visa.*

> We endeavour to be as up-to-date as possible but inevitably some changes to landlords, chefs and other key staff occur after the Guide has gone to press.

CALVER Chequers Inn FOOD B&B

Tel 01433 630231 Map 6 C2
Froggatt Edge Calver Derbyshire S30 1ZB

Originally four stone-built 18th century cottages, the Grade II listed Chequers stands alongside the B6054, a mile or so above Calver on the steep banks of Froggatt's Edge. Behind the pub, a landscaped beer garden gives way to some ten acres of steep, wild woodland. A daily-changing blackboard might offer marinated vegetables with a balsamic dressing, sweetbreads with a creamy mushroom sauce or a trio of sausages (lamb and mint, pork and apple and turkey and bacon) with apple chutney. The regular 'Innkeeper's Fare' sees a wide choice of interesting bar food , from scallops, steak and ouyster pie and a blacksmith's skillet with black pudding, bacon and mushrooms to crispy stir-fired duck, date and walnut strudel and a summer salad bowl. Hearty sandwiches include a dressed turkey hoagie, Cornish prawn with dressed crab mayonnaise, and beef with dill pickle on cheese and onions bread. To follow, a whole traditional Bakewell pudding is a challenge for two, sufficient even for four. The six bedrooms are furnished with pine bedsteads (one a four-poster) and pristine fabrics in muted tones. With plenty of space for armchairs, satellite TV and cosy bathrooms (with strong over-bath showers) these are truly comfortable rooms, with the promise of a restful night. *Open 11-3, 5-11 (Sun 12-3, 7-10.30). Free House.* ***Beer*** *Wards Best & Waggle Dance honey beer, Vaux Samson.* ***Bar Food*** *12-2 (Sun to 2.30), 6-9.30 (Sun from 7). Garden, outdoor eating.* ***Accommodation*** *6 bedrooms, all en suite, £49 (four-poster £59, single £39/£46). Children welcome overnight (under-3s stay free in parents' room), additional bed (£10) and cot available. Access, Visa.*

CAMBRIDGE The Eagle A

Tel & Fax 01223 301286 Map 15 F1
Bene't Street Cambridge Cambridgeshire CB2 3QN

Splendidly atmospheric city-centre pub situated close to the Corn Exchange and a stone's throw from King's College. Hidden behind the plain Georgian stone facade are five rooms of great architectural interest dating back to the 16th century. Sensitively restored in recent years, each relaxing room has a distinct, individual charm, boasting original features such as stripped pine panelling, mullioned windows, fine brick fireplaces and two medieval paintings. Tastefully adorned with sturdy wooden furnishing, William Morris fabrics and attractive prints, it is the haunt of students, dons and businessmen alike. Of particular interest is the red-painted ceiling in the Air Force Bar which preserves the hundreds of signatures of British and American airmen which were burnt on by candles and lighters during the Second World War. Cobbled and galleried courtyard with summer seating. Greene King. *Open 11-11 (Sun 12-3, 7-10.30). **Beer** Greene King. Courtyard. Access, Amex, Diners, Visa.*

CAMBRIDGE Free Press FOOD

Tel 01223 68337 Map 15 F1
Prospect Row Cambridge Cambridgeshire CB1 1QU

Tiny, totally non-smoking and highly atmospheric rowing-mad pub tucked away behind the police station, close to the city centre. Simply furnished, unspoilt interior, the snug is also used as the dining area, and rowing photographs are everywhere. It gets extremely busy; be early. Simple, hearty home-cooking is of the sort to defrost a cold-numbed oarsman – try the home-made soup (leek and potato or beef and vegetable), followed by port and ginger casserole, pasta, tuna and broccoli bake or game pie and finish with apricot or chocolate cake. In addition, there are usually hot and cold vegetarian dishes. *Open 12-2.30, 6-11 (Sun 12-3, 7-10.30). **Bar Food** 12-2, 6.30-8.30 (Sun 7-8.30). **Beer** Greene King IPA, Abbot. Garden, outdoor eating area. No credit cards.*

CAMBRIDGE Tram Depot A

Tel 01223 324553 Map 15 F1
Dover Street Cambridge Cambridgeshire CB1 1DY

Located half a mile east of the city centre, just off East Road, this lively and unusual pub occupies the brilliantly converted Cambridge Street Tramway Company stables. Designed in classic alehouse style with brick and flagstone floors topped with a rustic mix of old pine furniture, it has a good city atmosphere. Further seating in an upstairs gallery and out in the sheltered courtyard on warmer days. Piped classical music plays at lunchtime; jazz and blues in the evening. *Open 11.30-2.30, 5-11 (from 6 Sat, Sun 12-2.30, 7-10.30). **Beer** Everards Tiger Best & Old Original, Boddingtons, Theakston Old Peculier, three guest beers. Courtyard. No credit cards.*

CANTERBURY Falstaff Inn B&B

Tel 01227 462138 **Fax 01227 463525** Map 11 C5
8 St Dunstan's Street Canterbury Kent CT2 8AF

A centuries-old coaching inn by the outer walls of the city. Day rooms get character from original beams, leaded windows and polished oak tables; the inn has been completely refurbished throughout in the last year or so. Bedrooms are neat and pretty and the majority use solid modern furniture that suits the feel of the place perfectly; two room feature a four-poster bed (small supplement to the regular tariff). Within easy walking distance of the town centre, near the Westgate Tower. Pubby bar. Country Club (Whitbread) Hotels. *Open 11-11 (Sun 12-2.30, 7-10.30). **Beer** Marston's Pedigree, Fremlins Bitter, Boddingtons, guest beer. **Accommodation** 24 bedrooms, all en suite, £83. Children welcome overnight (under-16s stay free in parents' room), additional bed and cot available. Dogs by arrangement. Access, Amex, Diners, Visa.*

Many **B&B** establishments offer reduced rates for weekend and out-of-season bookings. Always ask about special deals for longer stays. Beware half-board terms in inns where we do not recommend the **FOOD.**

CAREY | Cottage of Content | B&B

Tel 01432 840242 **Fax 01432 840208** Map 14 B1
Carey nr Hereford Hereford & Worcester HR2 6NG

Zzz...

Follow prominent signs to Hoarwithy from the A49 or B4399 to find the only river crossing on this hidden stretch of the Wye. Deep in the valley, this aptly-named pub stands at the heart of a tiny village, fronted by a patio and porch; across the lane is a small stream and parking over a rickety wooden bridge. Within are flagstone floors and timbered alcoves with hops hanging from the beams and a central open staircase leading off the bar seemingly into the roof space. There are just four, suitably cottagey, bedrooms with sloping floors under their heavy roof timbers; three have en-suite bathrooms which are carpeted and neat, yet tiny. Oak furniture is on the sturdy side, while TVs and tea-makers appear almost incongruous in the setting. *Open 12-2.30, 7-11 (Sun 12-2.30, 7-10.30). Free House. **Beer** Hook Norton Best & Old Hooky, Bass. Garden. **Accommodation** 4 rooms, 3 en suite, £48 (single £30). Check-in by arrangement. Pub and accommodation closed 25 Dec. Access, Amex, Visa.*

CARLTON IN COVERDALE | Foresters Arms | FOOD

Tel & Fax 01969 640272 Map 5 D4 **B&B**
Carlton in Coverdale nr Leyburn North Yorkshire DL8 2BB

Chef Barrie Higginbotham is the licensee at this privately-owned free house at the heart of Coverdale. Look for signs off the A684 at West Witton. Internal refurbishment is now finished and it's very much a successful, upmarket dining pub. Indeed, the diversity of the blackboard menus suggests sufficient ambition to test any kitchen, yet the quality of ingredients and results are not seriously in doubt. From a simple soup and ham and eggs through to minute steaks, creamed leeks with smoked bacon and strips of beef fillet with a Dijon mustard sauce, a broad range of tastes can be pandered to. Best available produce from the fish markets is something of a speciality with good shellfish and, typically, whole roast sea bass. No sandwiches, but a Foresters platter with paté or cheese is offered at lunch only. Bread-and-butter or sticky toffee puddings individually cooked to order represent some classily turned-out puddings. The three en-suite bedrooms (with WC and showers rather than baths) have bright cottagey decor and crisp white duvets. In addition to TVs, radios, hairdryers and trouser presses, each room has its own plug for use of communal pay phone. Ask for the rear twin for one of the finest bedroom views in the Dales. *Open 12-3, 6.30-11 (Sun 12-3, 7-10.30). **Bar Food** 12-2, 7-9. Free House. **Beer** John Smith's, Theakston Best, three guest beers. **Accommodation** 3 bedrooms, £55 (single £30). Dogs welcome in one room only. Check-in by arrangement. Children welcome overnight, additional bed supplied. Outdoor eating area. Access, Visa.*

CARTERWAY HEADS | Manor House Inn | FOOD

Tel 01207 255268 Map 5 D3 **B&B**
Carterway Heads Shotley Bridge Northumberland DH8 9LX

The former Bolbec Manor House, standing high on the A68 (close to its junction with the B6278) was once part of an estate which traces its history back to the Norman Conquest. Almost a millennium later the Bolbec name has been revived in a dining-room converted from 200-year-old stables after renovations by the Pelley family. A wide choice of 'distinctly different' pub food is served throughout the pub's four rooms and is proclaimed on massive chalk boards. For starters, perhaps curried parsnip or Provençal fish soups, dill herrings with crème fraiche or grilled Craster kippers. Cumberland sausage with mash and mustard sauce and beef casserole with peppers and thyme are substantial main courses. Additional choices in the Bolbec Room might be rib of beef with béarnaise and turbot with leeks and shallots. Snackier items include French bread sandwiches, home-made paté and soup. There's a hand-picked selection of small grower's wines on show, racked for inspection. Four bedrooms are fitted out in pine and equipped with TVs, beverage trays and hairdryers. Planning restrictions, however, have left them all facing the main road; they share two bathrooms, are fully tiled and comprehensively equipped, and arguably enjoy the best view of any loos in the land. *Open 11-3, 6-11 (Sun 12-3, 7-10.30). **Bar Food** 12-2.30, 7-9.30 (7-9 Sun). Free House. **Beer** Butterknowle Bitter, Big Lamp ESB, two guest beers. **Accommodation** 4 bedrooms, £38.50 (single £22.50). Children welcome overnight, under-8s free, over-8s £10 if sharing parents' room, additional bed available. Check-in by arrangement. Garden, outdoor eating. Access, Visa.*

CARTHORPE Fox & Hounds FOOD

Tel 01845 567433 Map 5 E4
Carthorpe nr Bedale North Yorkshire DL8 2LG

The B6285, some 10 miles North of Ripon off the A1, leads to this sleepy Bedale village. If criticism there be of the former smithy which now houses the village pub, it must be of a lack of innate pubbiness which appears entirely due to Bernadette and Howard Fitzgerald's success in catering to a well-heeled clientele with some thoughtfully produced food. Served in both bar and restaurant of the L-shaped interior is a single menu of reliably home-cooked dishes updated daily; sandwiches and ploughman's lunches are also available to 'those who ask'. Strongly represented are the day's offerings from some careful shopping at the fish markets; whole dressed crab and mixed seafood hors d'oeuvre as curtain-raisers to whole Dover sole, filleted lemon sole rolled around smoked salmon and prawns and poached salmon hollandaise. Baby chicken cooked in Theakston's and rack of English lamb appease meat eaters and profiteroles with chocolate sauce or lemon cream pie to follow will assuage the heartiest appetites. All the puddings are home-made 'including the brandy snaps'. It is a good bet that from their varied list more wines are sold than the single real ale, though never on a Monday when the pub closes entirely. Children are welcome to eat in the dining-room. *Open 12-2, 7-11 (Sun 12-2.30, 7-10.30). Pub closed all day Monday. Free House.* ***Bar Food*** *12-2, 7-10.* ***Beer*** *John Smith's. Access, Visa.*

CARTMEL FELL Masons Arms ★ FOOD

Tel 01539 568486 **Fax 01539 568780** Map 4 C4
Strawberry Bank Cartmel Fell Cumbria LA11 6NW

The well-loved Masons Arms is a classic if ever there was one (although some readers report that the pub 'can get too busy for its own good'). The setting is glorious, perched on the hillside at Strawberry Bank with Lakeland views in all directions, and the interior is equally inspiring – a series of quaint, unspoilt little farmhouse rooms. In the main bar are polished old flagstones, a big open fire, sagging ceiling beams, simple country furniture and well-chosen pictures. Several cottagey anterooms offer old pews, odd bits of furniture, a sideboard, an old stove, and a curious little cupboard set into the wall. Tiny thickset windows frame pretty valley views; rough stone walls are freshly white-washed. Aside from excellent bar food, there's an array of drinks – including their own three home brews (named after local resident Arthur Ransome's books), and, in their comprehensive bottled beer list, well over 200 interesting international names. They make 'Knickerbocker Breaker' cider from their own apples as well as 'Damson Beer' – a cask fruit beer. The blackboard menu offers a pleasing variety of home-made dishes including half a dozen or so vegetarian choices. Simple country casseroles, like coachman's and damson and pork hotpots feature strongly on the list; pies are good, too (farmhouse courgette and sage Derby pie). Also on offer are hazelnut and lentil paté, French-style fish soup, leek, butterbean and Stilton strudel, nut roast layered with cranberries, Flemish beef carbonnade with bacon braised in trappist beer or chicken and pepper lasagne. Puddings, mostly of the good old-fashioned sort, are also not to be missed (peach melba crumble, toffee banoffi, Highland cream). Simple, well-cooked food tastes outstandingly fine in such splendid surroundings; be early for a seat on the terrace in summer. There's also a no-smoking dining-room upstairs. *Open 11.30-11 (Sun 12-3, 7-10.30).* ***Bar Food*** *12-2, 6-8.45 (Sun from 7). Free House.* ***Beer*** *Own Brews: Amazon, Great Northern, Big Six, Damson; Thwaites, guest beers. Garden, outdoor eating. Family room. Access, Amex, Visa.*

CASTERTON Pheasant Inn B&B

Tel 01524 271230 Map 4 C4
Casterton nr Kirkby Lonsdale Cumbria LA6 2RX

Melvin and May Mackie run this well-maintained, white pebbledash building at the heart of the village, enjoying some fine rear views over open country to the hills beyond. At the front, next to the A683, a colourful paved patio is furnished with rustic tables and bench seating. The Garden Room, a small summery lounge full of parlour plants, leads to the main bar, which is sectioned around a central servery; burgundy banquette seating, polished wood tables with fresh flowers, aerial photos of the pub and country pictures on the walls make for a pleasant, restful spot. While by no means luxurious, the bedrooms are both comfortable and well kept, with colour television, direct-dial phones, radios, beverage trays and neat, if rather small, bathrooms, all with showers recently added. There's one four-poster bed for the romantically inclined, and a twin-bedded ground-floor room suitable for

the disabled; most bedrooms have lovely countryside views. At least eight wines are served by the glass and there's an interesting collection of malt whiskies. *Open 11-3, 6-11 (Sun 12-3, 7-10.30). Free House.* ***Beer*** *Theakston Best & XB, Charles Wells Bombardier, Morland Old Speckled Hen. Garden, outdoor eating. Family room.* ***Accommodation*** *10 rooms, all en suite, £64 (single £37.50). Children welcome overnight (rate depends on age), additional bed and cot available (£5). Dogs by arrangement. Access, Visa.*

CASTLE ASHBY — Falcon Hotel — FOOD

Tel 01604 696200 Fax 01604 696673 Map 15 E1 **B&B**
Castle Ashby Northamptonshire NN7 1LF

Zzz...

Just six miles from Northampton (and easily found off the A428 Bedford road), Jo and Neville Watson's charming roadside establishment strikes a happy balance between historic country inn and well-appointed modern cottage hotel. Its founding in 1594 is commemorated in the small, atmospheric Cellar Bar that is approached by way of an original flagstone stairway. Bar meals (including sandwiches and ploughman's at lunchtime only) are served here on mahogany-topped, beer-barrel tables. More upmarket daily offerings might include carrot and coriander soup, cold poached salmon, steak and mushroom pie and vegetable chili; the bread is home-made. Lunch and dinner are also served in the rear dining extension which overlooks a delightful garden; fresh from it come the courgette flowers, artichokes and garden herbs which feature on seasonal menus. Whitewood furniture and gaily patterned fabrics imbue the main-house bedrooms with the country freshness their surroundings suggest; the bathrooms here are immaculately appointed. No less countrified, though rather plainer in decor, are the cottage bedrooms a stone's throw away at the heart of the village, just two minutes' walk away from the magnificent grounds and gardens of Castle Ashby House; two further rooms are in a cottage on the other side of the car park. Home-made jams and jellies are a memorable feature of the Falcon's hearty country breakfasts. No cheques or credit cards taken for under £20. Substantial tariff reductions in summer for two-night weekend stays (except during Castle Ashby House special events). *Open 12-3, 7-11 (Sun 12-2.30, 7-10.30).* ***Bar Food*** *12.15-2, 7.15-9. Free House.* ***Beer*** *Worthington, Fuller's London Pride, Adnams Extra, Webster's. Garden, outdoor eating.* ***Accommodation*** *16 bedrooms, all en suite, £75 (single £60). Access, Amex, Visa.*

CASTLE CARY — George Hotel — B&B

Tel 01963 350761 Fax 01963 350035 Map 13 F2
Market Place Castle Cary Somerset BA7 7AH

Stone from the original 13th-century castle was used to build this listed 15th-century, thatched coaching inn – one of the oldest pubs in the country. In part, it is even older – the elm beam over the inglenook fireplace in the front bar dates back a further 500 years and has been carbon dated to the 10th century. Each of the sixteen rooms is decorated in an individual, cottagey style using either pine or darkwood furniture. All rooms have TV, radio, telephone and tea or coffee-making facilities. Just before we went to press a new chef was appointed: Martin Barrett, who was previously at the *Walnut Tree* in West Camel (recommended in this Guide). *Open 10.30-3, 6-11 (Sun 12-3, 7-10.30). Free House.* ***Beer*** *Butcombe, Bass. Patio/terrace.* ***Accommodation*** *15 bedrooms, all en suite, £65/£70 (family room sleeping four £90, single £37-£45/£50). Children welcome overnight, additional bed (£12.50), cot available (£6). Access, Amex, Visa.*

CASTLE COMBE — Castle Inn — B&B

Tel 01249 783030 Fax 01249 782315 Map 14 B2
Castle Combe nr Chippenham Wiltshire SN14 7HN

Zzz...

At the centre of one of England's prettiest villages, right by the ancient monument stone cross, this famous hostelry can trace its own origins back to the 12th century. Now in the Hatton Hotels' group, it is arguably one of England's smartest inns. Attention to detail in exposing and retaining the intricate old stonework and centuries-old beams has been commendable, and nowhere is this better evidenced than in the conservatory that opens on to a private, enclosed patio; as a location for breakfasts served in several international guises, it is perhaps unparallelled. Each of the bedrooms has been modelled in individual style to a very high standard. Two 'Executive' rooms have en-suite whirlpool bathrooms and a third a Victorian-style slipper bath. Accessories which might elsewhere be thought of as luxuries are standard throughout, with remote-control TVs, radio-alarms with phones, trouser presses

and hairdryers. Here, the truly cossetting extras are complimentary fruit and mineral waters, boiled sweets, towelling robes, rubber ducks and resident teddy bears. *Open 11-11, Sun 12-3, 7-10.30. Free House.* ***Beer*** *Ruddles County, Wadworth 6X, guest beer.* ***Accommodation*** *7 rooms, all en suite, £80/£95 (single £60/£75). No dogs. Access, Amex, Diners, Visa.*

CASTLE COMBE — White Hart — A

Tel 01249 782295 Map 14 B2
Castle Combe nr Chippenham Wiltshire

Down and across the village square from the central stone cross stands the historic, cream-painted White Hart. It's down another step into the main bar, all leaded lights, stone alcoves and flagstone floors, which echo times past, warmed by the thigh-high dog grate that can throw an uncomfortable height of heat in winter. Convivial at the best of times, it can also be a crush. Across the passage, a carpeted lounge and family room have rather more space and less frenetic activity. To the rear, a glass-covered conservatory with flagstone floor leads through into a rear, cobbled beer garden. Parking is very limited in central Castle Combe; be warned that it's some 300 yards' walk down from the public car park. *Open 11-3, 5.30-11 (11-11 in summer, Sun 12-3, 7-10.30).* ***Beer*** *Wadworth IPA, 6X & Farmer's Glory, John Smith's, guest beer. Access, Visa.*

CASTLETON — Castle Hotel — B&B

Tel 01433 620578 **Fax 01433 621112** Map 6 C2
Castle Street Castleton Derbyshire S30 2WG

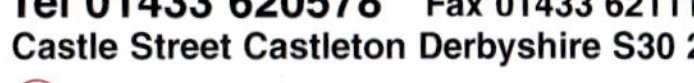

This pleasant old inn dating back in part to the 17th century features strongly for its accommodation. Comfortable bedrooms in the main house and stable-block annexe are all prettily decorated, with solid darkwood furnishings, including four-posters, and smartly tiled en-suite facilities (3 have whirlpool baths). Despite modernisation, the bars still offer plenty of old-world atmosphere – notably the Castle Bar with its flagstoned floors and low beamed ceilings. Bass Taverns. *Open 11-11 (Sun 12-2.30, 7-10.30).* ***Beer*** *Stones, two guest beers. Garden. Family room.* ***Accommodation*** *9 bedrooms, all en suite, £59-£79 (single £39.50, £59 Fri & Sat). Children welcome overnight (under-12s £12), additional bed and cot (no charge) available. Check-in by arrangement. Access, Amex, Diners, Visa.*

CASTLETON — Ye Olde Nags Head Hotel — FOOD B&B

Tel 01433 620248 **Fax 01433 621604** Map 6 C2
Castleton Derbyshire S30 2WH

17th-century coaching house in a tiny village at the head of Hope Valley, under the hilltop site of Peveril Castle. Bar meals are served both lunchtime and evening with cream of watercress soup, paté-filled mushrooms or plaice stuffed with prawns served in lobster sauce on offer; however, the emphasis is very much on the elegant two-tiered restaurant at night, where typical dishes could include poached sole rolled with asparagus, rösti fishcakes with parsley sauce, steak and kidney pie, smoked salmon and prawn croutons, or steak Roquefort, followed by chocolate and hazelnut meringue for dessert. Soup and sandwiches are also available. Bedrooms are also elegant, and furnished in a handsome period style, three with four-posters, all well-equipped. The most expensive offer spa baths; the cheapest shower and toilet only. A bright first-floor residents' lounge is done out in chintz and bamboo. *Open 11-11 (Sun 12-3, 7-10.30).* ***Bar Food*** *12-2.45, 6-10.45 (Sun 7-10). Free House.* ***Beer*** *Bass, Boddingtons.* ***Accommodation*** *8 bedrooms, all en suite, £60-£90 (single £42.50-£64.50). Children welcome overnight, additional bed (£12), cot available. Dogs by arrangement. Access, Amex, Diners, Visa.*

CAULDON — Yew Tree Inn — A

Tel 01538 308348 Map 6 C3
Cauldon Waterhouses nr Stoke-on-Trent Staffordshire ST10 3EJ

Alan East has acquired his vast collection of antiques and bric-a-brac over the last 34 years as landlord of this old-fashioned, stone-built pub. Persian rugs overlay original quarry-tiled floors and there are cast-iron copper-topped tables, a working pianola and giant Victorian music boxes which still operate for just 2p. Sleepy and undiscovered it is not, but worth a visit, nevertheless; go in the evening and hear the landlord performing on the pianola. Between A52 and A523, eight miles west of Ashbourne, five miles from Alton Towers. Children allowed in the 'Polyphon Room'. *Open 10-2.30 (Sat to 3), 6-11, Sun 12-3, 7-10.30. Free House.* ***Beer*** *Bass, Burton Bridge, M&B Mild. Family room. No credit cards.*

CAWTHORNE — Spencer Arms — A

Tel 01226 790228 Map 6 C2
21 Church Street Cawthorne Barnsley South Yorkshire S75 4HL

Smart Whitbread pub with two bar rooms and a separate restaurant area. Uniformed staff try hard to lift this pub above the run-of-the-mill chain standards. Close to 17th-century Cannon Hall and County Park. 4 miles west of Barnsley on the A635 Barnsley to Denby Dale road, just off the M1. New landlord as we went to press. Whitbread Wayside Inn. *Open 11-11, Sun 12-10.30.* ***Beer*** *Boddingtons, Flowers, Marston's Pedigree, guest beer. Garden. Access, Visa.*

CERNE ABBAS — New Inn — B&B

Tel 01300 341274 Map 13 F2
Cerne Abbas nr Dorchester Dorset DT2 7JF

'New' refers to 16th-century modernisation to an 11th-century structure – a red-brick arch and steep slate-stone roof – so no nasty architectural shocks here. It was originally used as a dormitory for the nearby Abbey, accommodating passing pilgrims, before becoming a coaching inn during the 16th century. Rooms are still available to passing travellers. Five modest bedrooms have sloping and creaking floors, attractive modern darkwood furniture, TVs and tea-making kits. All share just two clean and well-equipped bathrooms and a further toilet, as the listed status of the building prevents any alterations to incorporate en-suite facilities. Downstairs, there's a comfortably furnished bar adorned with farming memorabilia. There is an excellent selection of up to 14 wines by the glass, which are chosen from the wide-ranging list of 50 bottles. At the end of the courtyard is a large, peaceful walled garden with rose-beds and benches. The picturesque village is well worth a visit, as is the Bronze Age fertility symbol – the Cerne Abbas Giant – carved on the hillside above the village. *Open 11-3, 6-11 (Sun 12-3, 7-10.30).* ***Beer*** *Eldridge Pope, guest beer. Garden.* ***Accommodation*** *5 bedrooms, none en suite, £30 (single £25). Children welcome overnight, additional bed and cot available. Access, Amex, Visa.*

CERNE ABBAS — Red Lion — FOOD

Tel 01300 341441 Map 13 F2
Cerne Abbas Long Street nr Dorchester Dorset DT2 7JF

Unassuming, ancient Grade II listed pub with an unusual Victorian facade, thanks to a late 19th-century fire. The single carpeted bar is simply furnished and boasts a splendid 16th-century fireplace, crackling with logs in winter. Bar food ranges from a printed menu offering the usual favourites to a more interesting blackboard selection of hearty home-cooked dishes, which are the main emphasis of the kitchen. At least two choices of fish are featured – there's usually fresh trout – as well as a further five enjoyable dishes such as game pie in orange and port sauce, chicken sauté sauce, pan haggarty and pork escalope, all served with a crisp vegetable and a dish of new potatoes. There is always a freshly-prepared soup – mulligatawny, lemon and fennel or cucumber. Home-made desserts may include banana split and meringue nest. In summer months the delightful, well-tended and sheltered south-facing garden is a real oasis away from the busy village street. The ladies' loo is a real 5-star luxury specimen. *Open 11-11 (Sun 12-3, 7-10.30).* ***Bar Food*** *11.30-2.30, 6.30-11 (Sun 12-2.30, 7-10.30). Free House.* ***Beer*** *Wadworth 6X & IPA, guest beer. Garden, outdoor eating area. No credit cards.*

CHADLINGTON — Tite Inn — FOOD

Tel 01608 676475 Map 14a B1
Mill End Chadlington Oxfordshire OX7 3NY

This warm 16th-century Cotswold-stone pub is as pretty as a picture, complete with cottage roses clambering up the walls. Inside, the original rough stone walls remain, but otherwise it is almost too neat and tidy, with its modern carpeted floor and wheelback chairs. A table displaying newspapers and magazines is a nice touch, though, and there is also a garden room which features bunches of grapes hanging from a vine covering the roof. The origin of the unusual name is uncertain but is thought to refer to the nearby springs which used to feed a mill pond. Michael Willis behind the bar looks after the real ales (Dr Thirsty's Draught from the local Wychwood brewery is a regular guest beer), while Susan looks after the kitchen. Hearty home-made soups and succulent gammon sandwiches made with superior wholemeal bread are amongst the offerings listed on the regularly

changing blackboard menu, although bobotie (a sweet and spicy meat dish from South Africa) is, by popular demand, a permanent fixture, and there are always several vegetarian dishes available. One end of the bar is a restaurant with dishes ranging from chicken breast in cider and honey sauce to duck sausages with Cumberland sauce. A traditional roast is served on Sundays. Popular puddings include fruit crumble, hot sticky toffee pudding and chocolate and rum mousse. Children are made genuinely welcome and small portions are no problem. The huge garden with herbal and flower borders has tables laid out and children may play on the lawn. *Open 12-2.30, 6.30-11 (from 7 in winter, Sun 12-3, 7-10.30). Pub closed Mondays except Bank Holidays.* ***Bar Food*** *(No food Monday) 12-2 (Sun to 1.30), 6.30-9 (Sun 7-8.30). Free House.* ***Beer*** *Archers Village & Golden (or Best), two guest beers. Garden, outdoor eating. No credit cards.*

CHALE Clarendon Hotel & Wight Mouse Inn FOOD

Tel & Fax 01983 730431 Map 15 D4 
Chale Isle of Wight PO38 2HA

This 17th-century coaching inn (on the B3399) is a perennial favourite, for food, atmosphere, bed and breakfast and the genuine welcome to children: the Wight Mouse Inn was our 1990 Family Pub of the Year. Parents with children are treated like first-class citizens both inside and out. There are decent home-made bar meals too, featuring delicious local fish and seafood including mushrooms in garlic butter, local crab cocktail and breaded cod, and an astonishing 365 whiskies. The dining-room has a set five-course dinner menu for £17 which includes dishes such as chicken kebabs, carbonnade of beef, stuffed trout and chicken breast in cream sauce with grapes. Nice bedrooms in the Clarendon next door successfully blend period and modern comforts, excellent family facilities and pretty views of the sea. There are two family suites and the downstairs Clarendon suite has a waterbed. The rear garden overlooks Chalk Bay and the Needles. Apart from the playground and domestic animals (including Arthur the Shetland pony), nightly entertainment is provided all year round. *Open 11-midnight (Sun 12-3, 7-10.30).* ***Bar Food*** *11.30-10 (Sun 12-2.30, 7-9.30). Free House.* ***Beer*** *Marston's Pedigree, Wadworth 6X, Boddingtons, Whitbread Fuggles, Morrells Strong Country, Morland Old Speckled Hen. Garden, outdoor eating, children's play area. Family rooms.* ***Accommodation*** *13 bedrooms, 10 en suite (3 with bath), £65 (single £30, higher in season). Children welcome overnight (under-2s stay free in parents' room, 3-7 £7, 8-12 £20.50, 13-16 £22), additional bed and cot available. Dogs £3. Access, Visa.*

CHARING Royal Oak Inn B&B

Tel 01233 712612 Fax 01233 713355 Map 11 C5
High Street Charing Kent TN27 0HU

Homely inn located in the centre of an attractive medieval village at the base of the North Downs, just off the A20. Good pubby bar with bare boards and simple pine furniture and an upstairs function area in the old malting room. Neat, simply furnished accommodation in five en-suite bedrooms, the best rooms being located in the new rear extension. Good, clean bathrooms or compact shower rooms and TVs and tea-making facilities for added comfort. Handy overnight stop for the ferry ports or the Chunnel. *Open 11-11 (Sat & Sun 12-10.30). Free House.* ***Beer*** *Bass, Fuller's London Pride, Shepherd Neame, guest beer.* ***Accommodation*** *5 bedrooms, all en-suite, £42.50-£47.50 (single £30). Children welcome overnight (under-5s stay free in parents' room), additional bed and cot supplied. No dogs. Access, Visa.*

CHARLBURY Bell Hotel B&B

Tel 01608 810278 Fax 01608 811447 Map 14a B2
Church Street Charlbury Oxfordshire OX7 3PP

Zzz...

Historic Charlbury with its 7th-century St Mary's Church was royally chartered to hold cattle markets in 1256: the last one was held behind the Bell some 700 years later. With its own datestone of 1700, the mellow stone inn is full of character. The small flagstoned bar and sun-lounge makes guests feel much at home and in fair weather the patio looking down a long, sloping garden is a picturesque spot. Access to bedrooms is by steep staircases and narrow passageways yet the rooms themselves are spacious and neatly appointed with matching fabrics and up-to-date accessories which include hair-dryers, trouser presses and welcome clock-radios. The three smaller doubles have en-suite wc/showers only and one single is not en-suite, though its adjacent bathroom is private. Conference facilities in the

converted stable block accommodate up to 55. Children welcome (under 16s stay free in parents' room) cot and extra bed provided. *Open 11-3, 7-11 (Sun 12-3, 7-10.30). Free House.* ***Beer*** *Hook Norton Best, Wadworth 6X.* ***Accommodation*** *14 bedrooms, all en suite £75 (single £50). Children welcome overnight and allowed anywhere inside. Family room. Access, Amex, Diners, Visa.*

CHARLESTOWN — Pier House Hotel — B&B

Tel 01726 67955 **Fax 01726 69246** Map 12 B3
Charlestown St Austell Cornwall PL25 3NJ

Nearly all the rooms at this recently-expanded 18th-century hotel have either far-reaching sea views or they overlook the attractive harbour of this charming and popular little port. The fifteen-room bedroom extension was added only last year. Bedrooms vary in size and style; some feature attractive modern darkwood pieces of furniture, others are rather plain, but all are neat and clean with pretty floral fabrics, TVs, radio/alarms, telephone and tea-making facilities; good shower/bathrooms. Four family rooms have both a double and a single bed. Public areas include a small pubby bar with red barrel seats and wall benches and a rear dining area, which is open during the day for snacks and cream teas. *Open 11.30-2.30, 6.30-11 (11.30-11 in summer, Sun 12-2.30, 7-10.30). Free House.* ***Beer*** *Bass, guest beer.* ***Accommodation*** *27 bedrooms, all en suite (five with bath), £57-£62 (single £30/£37, family £78). Children welcome overnight. Access, Visa.*

CHARLESTOWN — Rashleigh Arms — B&B

Tel 01726 73635 Map 12 B3
Charlestown St Austell Cornwall PL25 3NJ

Under the same ownership as the Pier House Hotel on the quay, this much-extended and refurbished Georgian inn has an attractive flower-bedecked facade and a vast open-plan interior, furnished with blue velour padded wall bench seating and darkwood 'pub' furniture. The main interest of this inn is the five neat and comfortable first-floor bedrooms that are ideal for visiting St Austell businessmen and popular with holidaymakers not requiring the formalities and facilities of a hotel. All have modern pine furniture, floral duvets and curtains, bedside lamps and are light and airy with clean, compact shower rooms. *Open 11-11 (Sun 12-3, 7-10.30). Free House.* ***Beer*** *Wadworth 6X, Ruddles County, Bass, Tetley Bitter, Boddingtons, guest beer. Garden, outdoor eating area.* ***Accommodation*** *5 bedrooms, all en suite with showers, £48 (single £24). Access, Visa.*

CHARLTON — Horse & Groom — FOOD B&B

Tel 01666 823904 **Fax 01666 823390** Map 14 C2
Charlton nr Malmesbury Wiltshire SH16 9DL

Zzz...

The solidly elegant Cotswold stone house fronted by a tree-sheltered lawn stands in its own paddock well back from the B4040. Its history as a coaching inn dating back to the 16th century is well documented by the framed prints and drawings which hang in the rustic main bar which retains an evocative air of exposed stonework, woodblock flooring and assorted country farmhouse-style pine chairs and tables. The adjacent lounge and dining areas (where bookings are taken), recently revamped, are rather more intimately conducive to the enjoyment of the good bar food. Groomburgers, lasagne, and ham, egg and chips should satisfy traditionalists, while adventurous eaters can be tempted by starters of mushroom and nutmeg soup, armagnac paté, king prawns in filo pastry with curried mango or barbecued spare ribs; and no less by main courses like crispy duck and bacon salad with fruit and a plum sauce, marinated masala chicken, beef, stout and Stilton pie, pasta in Stilton and mushroom sauce or sesame seed-topped vegetarian filo parcels (with tomato, bean sprouts, and feta cheese). For a pub of apparently modest size and appointments, meanwhile, the three double bedrooms are a revelation: 32-channel satellite TV, hi-tech phones and complimentary fruit and mineral water are all provided. Gold-tapped, tiled bathrooms with towelling robes and his-and-hers toiletries provide hotel-style trappings. The task of co-ordinating operations (and fulfilling such high expectations) is undertaken by the two young licensees, Nichola King and chef Philip Gilder, who approach the challenge with great relish and good humour. *Open 12-3, 7-11 (Fri & Sat from 6, Sun 7-10.30).* ***Bar Food*** *12-2, 7-10 (Sun to 9.30). Free House.* ***Beer*** *Archers Village, Wadworth 6X, guest beer. Garden, outdoor eating, children's play area. Family room.* ***Accommodation*** *3 bedrooms, all en suite, £69.50 (single £55). Children over 8 welcome overnight. No dogs. Access, Visa.*

CHATTON Percy Arms B&B

Tel 01668 215244 Map 5 D1
Chatton nr Alnwick Northumberland WE66 5PS

"A romantic retreat, situated in a favourite neighbourhood, several miles of free fishing water in the Till. Half an hour's walk from Chillingham Castle, Park and wild cattle. Well-aired beds. Good stabling". Posted prominently at the bar, the words of John Fitzgerald, proprietor at the turn of the century, ring equally true today. Stabling – for residents – is as good as ever with beds as well-aired: one wonders what the former landlord would have made of en-suite WCs and showers, colour TVs and beverage trays, let alone the guests' private sauna. The sole village pub since 1874, today's black oak bar is many times bigger than that of yesteryear, with a childrens' and games room to the rear and a tiny garden in front. Children welcome overnight – one cot available free of charge. *Open 11-3, 6-11 (Sun 12-3, 7-10.30). Free House.* ***Beer*** *weekly-changing real ale.* ***Accommodation*** *7 bedrooms, 5 en suite (all with showers), £40 (single £20). Children welcome overnight (under-2s free and under-10s £10 in parents' room), additional bed and cot available. Garden. Access, Diners, Visa.*

CHENIES Red Lion FOOD

Tel 01923 282722 **Fax 01923 283797** Map 15a E2
Chenies Rickmansworth Hertfordshire WD3 6ED

Just up the lane from Chenies Manor, an unassuming, white-painted pub with a plain, simply-furnished main bar and a charming small dining area housed in the original 17th-century cottage to the rear with a tiled floor, old inglenook and rustic furniture. A varied selection of home-cooked bar food includes French bread sticks, wholemeal baps and jacket potatoes with unusual fillings and popular pies straight from the oven (Chenies lamb or venison and ale). A blackboard lists a few daily specials, including the vegetarian dish of the day. The pub is not suitable for children. *Open 11-2.30, 5.30-11 (Sun 12-3, 7-10.30).* ***Bar Food*** *12-2, 7-10 (to 9.30 Sun).* ***Beer*** *Benskins Best Bitter, Wadworth 6X, Morrells Bitter, guest beer. Access, Visa.*

CHERITON Flower Pots Inn FOOD B&B

Tel 01962 771318 Map 15 D3
Cheriton Alresford Hampshire SO24 0QQ

Originally built as a farmhouse in the 1840s by the head gardener of nearby Avington House, this unassuming and homely brick village pub is a popular place in which to enjoy simple, honest bar food, good home-brewed ales and comfortable overnight accommodation. Two traditional bars are delightfully music- and electronic game-free, the rustic public bar being furnished with pine tables and benches and the cosy saloon bar having a relaxing sofa among other chairs. Both have open winter fires and an added feature is a 27ft glass-topped well. A separate room has some easy chairs, numerous books and a television to keep children amused. A short value-for-money menu offers honest home-cooked snacks and features a range of jacket potatoes with decent fillings, generously-filled baps, chili, beef stew and a couple of daily specials such as sweet and sour chicken with egg fried rice, liver and bacon hotpot or chicken curry. Puddings are not available. These quick, filling snacks can be washed down by a choice of four real ales of varying strengths, brewed on the premises in the Cheriton Brewhouse. Also across the car park are five neat, pine-furnished bedrooms housed in a well-converted outbuilding. Downstairs rooms are compact, while the two attic rooms are light and airy with additional sofa beds; all have floral fabrics, TV, tea-makers, magazines and spotless, tiled shower rooms. *Free House.* ***Beer*** *Cheriton Brewhouse Pots Ale, Best Bitter & Diggers Gold. Garden, outdoor eating area.* ***Accommodation*** *5 bedrooms, all with en suite showers, £42 (single £25). No credit cards.*

Many **B&B** establishments offer reduced rates for weekend and out-of-season bookings. Always ask about special deals for longer stays. Beware half-board terms in inns where we do not recommend the **FOOD.**

CHERITON BISHOP **Old Thatch Inn** FOOD

Tel 01647 24204 Map 13 D2 **B&B**
Cheriton Bishop nr Exeter Devon EX6 6HJ

Attractive, white-painted and thatched roadside inn, located on the old A30 and a useful detour from the new dual carriageway for comfortable overnight accommodation and above-average bar food. A central fireplace is lit in winter and warms the rambling, carpeted and plainly furnished main bar; the smaller side room – Travellers Nook – is unusually decorated with Ordnance Survey maps. Bar food relies on an extensive printed menu that features standard favourites alongside a few more imaginative dishes that are well described; results on the plate should not disappoint. Starters or snacks include freshly-prepared soups (tomato, onion and herb), salad niçoise and sautéed kidneys, while main-course fare ranges from steak and kidney pudding and thatcher's pie to braised stuffed hearts, beef olives and daily pasta specials. One must ask about the daily paté, vegetarian dish, curry and puddings. Regular sweets include baked spiced bread pudding and thatch trifle. Homely, good-value accommodation is offered in three neat bedrooms with 'stag' furniture, TVs, tea-making kits, radio/alarms and clean en-suite facilities. No children under 14 on the premises. *Open 12-3 (Sat from 11.30), 7-11 (Sat from 6.30, Sun 12-3, 7-10.30).* ***Bar Food*** *12-1.45 (snacks until 2.15), 7-9.30 (Sun to 9). Free House.* ***Beer*** *Wadworth 6X, Cotleigh Tawny Bitter, Hall & Woodhouse Tanglefoot.* ***Accommodation*** *3 bedrooms with en suite baths, £44 (single £32.50). Check-in by arrangement. Access, Visa.*

CHESTER **Ye Olde King's Head** B&B

Tel 01244 324855 **Fax 01244 315693** Map 6 A2
48/50 Lower Bridge Street Chester Cheshire CH1 1RS

A striking black and white timber-framed building just a stone's throw from the Roman walls and river, yet handy for high street shopping. Residents find evening refuge from popular all-day bars in a first-floor lounge bar and Hudson's restaurant. Second-floor bedrooms house some remarkable features, the superb 16th-century roof trusses fortunately reinforced with forged steel pins. Dark hardwood fittings and co-ordinated fabrics stay in keeping, while comforts are plentiful with dial-out phones, TVs, tea trays and trouser presses: en-suite bathrooms are necessarily small, but are neatly appointed. Premier Inns, a division of Greenalls. ***Beer*** *Greenalls, guest beer.* ***Accommodation*** *8 bedrooms, all en suite, £48.40 (single £43.95). Children welcome overnight (£5, under-5s free), additional bed and cot available. Access, Amex, Diners, Visa.*

CHICKSGROVE **Compasses Inn** A

Tel & Fax 01722 714318 Map 14 C3
Chicksgrove Tisbury nr Salisbury Wiltshire SP3 6NB

A timeless air pervades this attractive, 16th-century thatched inn, set on a peaceful lane, deep in rolling Wiltshire countryside. An old cobbled path leads to the entrance of the charmingly unspoilt bar, which has a low-beamed ceiling, partly flagstoned floor and an assortment of traditional furniture arranged in many secluded alcoves. Various farming tools and tackle from bygone days adorn the bare walls and a 100-year-old set of table skittles maintain the old-world atmosphere. A small adjoining dining/children's room leads out to a sheltered rear garden with rural views – ideal (as is the front brolly- and bench-filled lawn) for a peaceful summer alfresco pint. Standards of housekeeping and general attention to detail in the previously recommended accommodation need to be considerably improved by the new owners. *Free House.* ***Beer*** *Tisbury Best Bitter, Bass, Wadworth 6X. Garden, children's play area. Family room. Pub closed Mondays. Access, Visa.*

CHIDDINGFOLD **Crown Inn** B&B

Tel 01428 682255 **Fax 01428 685736** Map 11 A5
The Green Petworth Road Chiddingfold Surrey GU8 4TX

Zzz...

Originally a guest house for pilgrims and Cistercian monks, the creeper-clad, medieval timber-framed Crown (built around 1258) is still offering hospitality to travellers. The soft furnishings in the main bar area have recently been refurbished and one's eye is taken by the massive old beams and huge inglenook fireplace. A panelled restaurant, of slightly later date, boasts an ornate plaster ceiling and examples of the stained glass for which Chiddingfold was famous during the 13th and 17th centuries. Creaking stairs and corridors lead to the bedrooms, some full of character with antique furniture (three with four-poster beds), and

others lighter and more modern in style. All have remote-control TV, direct-dial phone, beverage tray and trouser press. One of Hall and Woodhouse's Badger Inns. *Open 11-11 (Sun 12-3, 7-10.30).* ***Beer*** *Hall & Woodhouse Tanglefoot & Badger Best, Wadworth 6X, Charles Wells Eagle IPA. Terrace, courtyard,* ***Beer*** *garden.* ***Accommodation*** *8 bedrooms, all en suite, from £57 (4-poster £78, suite £90, single £47). Children welcome overnight, additional bed and cot available. Access, Amex, Diners, Visa.*

CHIDDINGSTONE — Castle Inn — A

Tel 01892 870247 **Fax 01892 870808** Map 11 B5
Chiddingstone Edenbridge Kent TN8 7AH

Located at the end of a unique, unspoilt row of Tudor timbered houses opposite the parish church, this historic tile-hung building dates from 1420 and boasts leaded casement windows and projecting upper gables. Like the rest of the village street, the pub is owned by the National Trust and remains delightfully unchanged with two traditional, atmospheric bars. Classic public bar with chequered quarry-tiled floor, beams, an old brick fireplace and rustic wall benches. Extra comfort can be found in the beamed lounge bar and alfresco summer eating in the pretty rear garden and courtyard. *Open 10.30-3, 6-11 (Sat 10.30-11, Sun 12-3, 7-10.30). Free House.* ***Beer*** *Harveys Sussex Bitter, Larkins Traditional, guest beer. Garden. Access, Amex, Diners, Visa.*

CHILGROVE — White Horse Inn — FOOD B&B

Tel 01243 535219 **Fax 01243 535301** Map 15 D3
Chilgrove nr Chichester West Sussex PO18 9HX

Wisteria-clad pub and restaurant (recommended in our *1996 Hotels & Restaurants Guide*) in a glorious Sussex Downs setting with not another building in sight. The bar is quite modest in appearance – red plastic banquettes and pink draylon chairs around simple wooden tables – and the only beer served comes from a small barrel sitting on the bar counter. The selection of wines is another matter, though, as landlord Barry Phillips (here for over 25 years) has created one of the best cellars in the country and from which around twenty or so wines (including champagne or a South African sparkler) are available by the glass at any one time. Bar meals, the responsibility of chef-partner Neil Rusbridger, are displayed on cards pinned up on a cork noticeboard. Typically the selection might include a gratin of Selsey Crab, gammon steak, roast Aylesbury Duck, coq au vin and steak au poivre along with ploughman's, sandwiches and salads. There are always a couple of vegetarian options and treacle tart and home-made ices. In the evenings there is also a short, three-course supper menu at £12.50 including coffee. No children indoors but there's plenty of room outdoors in good weather. Bedroom accommodation is now available in an adjacent cottage; five rooms (four doubles and one single: Tel 01243 535335) have en-suite bathrooms; four are approached up steep stairs, while a further couple are at ground-floor level and have facilities for the disabled. *Open 11-3, 6-11 (Sun 12-3 only). Pub closed all Monday and Sunday evening. Free House.* ***Bar Meals*** *12-2, 6-10 (not Mon or Sun eve).* ***Beer*** *Ballard's Best. Outdoor eating.* ***Accommodation*** *5 rooms, all en suite, £70 (single £50). No children under 14 overnight. Access, Amex, Diners, Visa.*

CHILHAM — White Horse — A

Tel 01227 730355 Map 11 C5
The Square Chilham Kent CT4 8BY

Probably the most photographed pub in the county, this attractive, white-painted and part-timbered pub nestles within what is arguably the prettiest village square in Kent. Sited next to the church and surrounded by medieval timbered houses, the White Horse dates from 1422 and offers weary tourists a welcome retreat within the three comfortably-furnished, interconnecting rooms, which are warmed by good winter log fires – one in a massive inglenook. An intriguing history includes the discovery in 1956 of two skeletons, possibly soldiers killed at the Battle of Chilham during the Wat Tyler rebellion of 1380 and now buried in the churchyard next door. Walled garden and front benches with village square views. No children inside. Whitbread Wayside Inn. *Open 11-11 (Sun 12-3, 7-10.30).* ***Beer*** *Fremlins Bitter, Flowers Original, Boddingtons, guest beer. Walled garden, outdoor eating area. Access, Visa.*

CHILHAM **Woolpack** B&B

Tel 01227 730208 **Fax 01227 731053** Map 11 C5
The Street Chilham Kent CT4 8DL

Dating from 1420, this pretty salmon pink-painted inn lies within 100 yards of Chilham's charming square. A historic place with a smartened-up exterior, refurbished olde-worlde bar, attractive dining-room and fourteen en-suite bedrooms. Rooms vary in size and location, the sole main building bedroom and one of the three wool store rooms boasting fine four-poster beds. Good overnight accommodation for families, one of the decent-sized family rooms having access to a sheltered garden with seating. The suite has three separate rooms: a double, single and twin plus a bathroom; priced up to £110 for 6 adults. Appealing floral fabrics, modern dark mahogany furniture, clean bath or shower rooms and TVs, tea-makers, telephones and clock-radios for added comfort. *Open 11-3, 6-11 (Sun 12-3, 7-10.30).* ***Beer*** *Shepherd Neame. Garden, courtyard, outdoor eating area.* ***Accommodation*** *13 bedrooms, all en suite, from £47.50 (family room with garden £65, four-poster £65, suite from £70, single £37.50). Children welcome overnight, cot supplied. Dogs by arrangement. Access, Amex, Visa.*

CHILLINGTON **Chillington Inn** FOOD B&B

Tel 01548 580244 Map 13 D3
Chillington nr Kingsbridge Devon TQ7 2JS

The front door of this white-painted 16th-century inn opens directly on to the main road through the village, with no pavement in between, so take care when leaving after a convivial evening. Inside, the unpretentiously snug bar has some unusual carved oak wall benches and tables, a warming open fire and two blackboards listing the monthly-changing selection of bar food. The highlight of the menu is the splendid range of up to nine home-made soups, which are a lunchtime favourite. Other good-value and hearty home-prepared snacks include French bread sandwiches, ploughman's lunches, chili with French bread, curries, Devon chicken casserole and various omelettes; you might even find local scallops served in the bar. The traditional Sunday roasts are very popular in winter. For more substantial meals the small attractive restaurant, boasting a fine stone fireplace, provides a short hand-written menu listing more elaborate fare. Main course emphasis is on West Country recipes such as chicken breast with cider, leeks and cream, herb-crusted rack of lamb with a blackcurrant sauce and a rich venison casserole; fresh fish is becoming increasingly popular. Good puddings – bread-and-butter pudding and spiced apple pancakes – come with thick clotted cream. Two charming bedrooms have matching wallpaper and fabrics in a pretty trellis pattern with bedhead drapes and ruffled blinds at the windows. Each room has a clean, good-sized bathroom across the corridor. There is also a new barn conversion family suite available (by prior arrangement) for daily B&B or weekly lets. Ava, a nine-year-old, "friendly" rotweiler keeps guard. No immediate off-street parking for residents, but you can park right outside on the road or 50 yards away. *Open 12-2 (Sat to 3), 6-11 (Sun 12-3, 7-10.30). Free House.* ***Bar Food*** *12-2 (Sat to 2.30) & 7-10.* ***Beer*** *Bass, Palmers IPA, occasional guest beer. Small garden, outdoor eating.* ***Accommodation*** *2 bedrooms, £39 (single £23.50). Children welcome overnight, additional bed supplied (£10), family suite by arrangement. Access, Diners, Visa.*

CHIPPING CAMPDEN **Eight Bells Inn** FOOD B&B

Tel 01386 840371 Map 14a A1
Church Street Chipping Campden Gloucestershire GL55 6JG

Originally built in the 14th century to house masons building the nearby church (and to store the bells), and over the years the pub is reputed to have played host to royalty and quite possibly William Shakespeare as well. A tiny, low Cotswold stone frontage hung with flower baskets reveals through its cobbled entranceway a single, cosily intimate bar and an enclosed courtyard with abundant greenery. Paul and Patrick Dare offer a blackboard menu that deserves serious consideration and they provide slick service. Green pea and mint soup, warm bacon and avocado salad, beefsteak and kidney pie, mixed seafood en croute, sirloin steaks peppered or plain; to follow, apricot and ginger crumble or a Colston Bassett Stilton with biscuits. French-stick sandwiches and ploughman's lunches are offered at lunchtime only. The additional tap bar is now available as an additional dining area. A barn has been converted into five double bedrooms (two with WC/shower only), one with a third bed, another with a pair of extra bunks. TVs and tea trays are already installed. *Open 11-3, 6-11*

See over

(Sun 12-3, 7-10.30). ***Bar Food*** *12-2.30, 6-9.30 (Sun from 7). Free House.* ***Beer*** *Tetley Bitter, Burton Ale, Wadworth 6X, Greene King Abbot. Garden, outdoor eating.* ***Accommodation*** *5 bedrooms, all en suite, £40. Children welcome overnight (under-2s stay free in parents' room, 2-10s £10). Check-in by arrangement. Additional bed available (£10). Dogs by arrangement. No credit cards.*

CHIPPING CAMPDEN — Noel Arms — B&B

Tel 01386 840317 **Fax 01386 841136** Map 14a A1
High Street Chipping Campden Gloucestershire GL55 6AT

Zzz...

Centuries-old traditions of hospitality live on at the inn where Charles II is said to have rested after his defeat at the battle of Worcester in 1651. In terms of atmosphere, however, the Noel Arms, right at the centre of this old wool-traders' town, has somehow lost a little of its former charm following its most recent extensions. The best and most authentic parts remain in the Dovers bar which opens direct on to the High Street through solid oaken doors. Lined in Cotswold stone and adorned with many genuine artefacts, the open double-sided fireplace and dog grate are of particular interest. From here, though, the pub opens out into the open-plan residents lounge and a newly-built (and rather unsympathetic) conservatory. Today's accommodation is a similar mixture of ancient and modern with the older bedrooms in the original building making up in character for what they lack in amenities, though by 17th-century standards the en-suite bathrooms, colour TV and dial-out phones are pretty civilized. Disabled guests will greatly appreciate the bedrooms (one room is fully equipped for those with limited mobility) in the rear extension that have access direct from the car park. Bar snacks are not available on Friday and Saturday nights. *Open 11-3 & 6-11 (Fri & Sat 11am-11pm, Sun 12-2.30 & 7-10.30).* ***Beer*** *Hook Norton Best, Bass, two guest beers.* ***Accommodation*** *26 rooms, all en suite, £80-£92 (single £60). Children welcome overnight (under-10s stay free in parents' room), additonal bed & cot supplied. Access, Amex, Diners, Visa.*

CHISLEHAMPTON — Coach & Horses — B&B

Tel 01865 890255 **Fax 01865 891995** Map 14a C2
Chislehampton nr Oxford Oxfordshire OX9 7UX

Though pretty much modernised over the years, the Coach & Horses still keeps some traces of its 16th-century beginnings. The bedrooms offer smartly kept, good practical accommodation with TVs and direct-dial phones. Showers are the norm, but a couple have bathtubs. The inn stands on the B480 south of Oxford. *Open 11-3, 6-11 (Sun 12-3, 7-10.30). Free House.* ***Beer*** *Hook Norton, Flowers, Boddingtons. Garden.* ***Accommodation*** *9 bedrooms, all en suite, £50 (weekend £45, single £45/£40). Children welcome overnight (under-12s stay free in parents' room), additional bed & cot available. Dogs by arrangement. Access, Amex, Diners, Visa.*

CHORLEYWOOD — Sportsman Hotel — B&B

Tel 01923 285155 **Fax 01923 285159** Map 15a E3
Station Approach Chorleywood Hertfordshire WD3 5NB

☺

The Sportsman was built on a hillside across the road from the underground station and dates from the late 19th century. Popular with visiting businessmen during the week, the 18 newly-refurbished bedrooms are a bit of a mix, but all are generally comfortable with modern darkwood furniture (some have modern pine) and brass light fittings; all are well equipped with TV, direct-dial telephones, radio-alarms, tea-making kits and trouser presses. En-suite bath/shower rooms are fully tiled. Light attractive decor extends to the public areas and the Garden Bar with its airy, plant-filled conservatory overlooking the spacious garden, terrace and children's play area. The hotel has a children's certificate; no-smoking areas and changing facilities are provided. *Open 11-11 (Sun 12-2.30, 7-10.30).* ***Beer*** *Bass.* ***Accommodation*** *18 bedrooms, all en suite, £52.50-£62.50 (£42.50-£52.50 single). Children welcome overnight, additional bed and cot supplied. Garden, children's play area. Family room. Access, Amex, Diners, Visa.*

See the **County Round-Up** tinted pages for details of all establishments in county order.

Church Enstone — Crown Inn — B&B

Tel 01608 677262 Map 14a B1
Mill Lane Church Enstone Oxfordshire OX7 4NN

Accommodation is a strong point at this 1760 Cotswold-stone, creeper-covered inn standing in a quiet village near the A34. Bedrooms – all kept in apple-pie order – have pretty fabrics and furnishings, very comfortable beds, private bathrooms, TVs and tea-makers. The bar has an inglenook fire place and is usually full of lively chat, serving well-kept real ale and decent wines. *Open 12-3, 7-11 (Sun 12-3, 7-10.30). Free House.* ***Beer*** *Boddingtons, Flowers Original, Marston's Pedigree, guest beer. Garden.* ***Accommodation*** *4 bedrooms, 3 en suite, £42 (single £30). Babies in own travel cot welcome overnight. No credit cards.*

Church Knowle — New Inn — A

Tel 01929 480357 Map 14 C4
Church Knowle nr Wareham Dorset BH20 5NQ

Overlooking the Purbeck Hills and located only 1½ miles from Corfe Castle, this attractive 16th-century inn is a favourite refreshment spot for both walkers and travellers enjoying an unspoilt corner of Dorset. Half-thatched and half-stone slated with deep porches, it is a picture in summer with carefully tended hanging baskets and tubs brimming with flowers, brightening up its ancient stone facade. The homely and welcoming interior was revamped last year, with a small lounge now knocked through into the original restaurant side to create a more open interior with warm green decor, dado rail, prints and sturdy tables and chairs all adding to the general charm of the building. The lounge has exposed stone walls and an open fire and the main bar is high-ceilinged. Hatchway service is available to those relaxing and admiring the splendid views from the delightful sheltered rear garden. Food was disappointing on our last visit. *Open 11-3, 6-11 (from 7 in winter), Sun 12-3, 7-10.30. Pub may be closed on Mondays – ring before travelling.* ***Beer*** *Flowers Original, Royal Wessex Bitter, guest beer. Access, Visa.*

Clanfield — The Plough at Clanfield — B&B

Tel 01367 810222 Fax 01367 810596 Map 14a B2
Bourton Road Clanfield Oxfordshire OX18 2RB

Zzz...

The Plough is a 16th-century Cotswold stone manor house that's more of an inn than a hotel, occupying a central position in pretty Clanfield village. The lack of a residents' lounge restricts guests to either their bedrooms – all of which are of a good size and comfortably equipped (four with whirlpool bath, the other two with just shower) – or the hotel bar, which is no real penalty as there's much original character in the form of old beams and a stone fireplace (but no real ale). The cosy bedrooms come with baby teddy bears to keep you company! Light lunches (snacks and sandwiches) are available. Hatton Hotels. *Open 11-11 (Sun 12-3, 7-10.30). Garden.* ***Accommodation*** *6 bedrooms, £85-£115 (single £65-£75). Children welcome overnight (under-7s stay free in parents' room), additional bed (£15) available. No dogs. Access, Amex, Diners, Visa.*

Clavering — Cricketers — FOOD

Tel 01799 550442 Fax 01799 550882 Map 10 B3
Clavering nr Saffron Walden Essex CB11 4QT

200 yards from the cricket green, this pub offers well-prepared home-made food on a menu that changes every 2-3 months. Start, perhaps, with prawn and smoked mackerel or walnut pastry tartlet, with half a roast guinea fowl, escalope of salmon or warm vegetable terrine to follow. The restaurant has seating for 70, the bar for 120 and 75 can eat outside. Dishes include 'mixed seafoods bound in a creamy cheese sauce with freshly-mae tagliatelle', chargrilled medallions of beef fillet with caramelised onions and a red wine sauce and supreme of chicken stuffed with mushrooms in puff pastry. The restaurant offers a 3-course Sunday lunch with choice of 10 starters and main courses for £16.50. Up to a dozen desserts are offered daily – try the treacle tart or lemon meringue pie. Wednesday night is 'Pudding Night' where the normal menu is supplemented with steak and kidney, Yorkshire and sweet steamed puds – all, of course, home-made. The next-door property was bought last year and six en-suite bedrooms have been created (double £55, single £45 excluding breakfast), two with four-poster beds; these have not yet been inspected. Ten minutes from Stansted Airport. *Open 12-2, 7-11 (Sun 12-3, 7-10.30).* ***Bar Food*** *12-2 (Sun to 2.30), 7-10 (Sun to 9.30). Free House.* ***Beer*** *Flowers IPA, Wethered, Boddingtons. Terrace, outdoor eating. Family room. Access, Amex, Visa.*

CLEARWELL — Wyndham Arms — FOOD — B&B

Tel 01594 833666 **Fax 01594 836450** Map 14 B2
Clearwell nr Coleford Gloucestershire GL16 8JT

Imperturbable hosts of the tranquil Wyndham John and Mary Stanford have now been joined by their son Robert, further enhancing the comprehensive service here. Traditional real ales, 17 wines served by the glass and a malt whisky collection (with over 25 from which to choose) are indicators of the public bar's civilised style, to which the menu is entirely apposite. A lunch still favoured by many is the 18-dish hors d'oeuvre trolley, the daily special might be fresh salmon and caper fish cakes, while open sandwiches of grilled bacon or chicken liver paté are practically meals in themselves. Accommodation is divided between original bedrooms in the evocative 600-year-old main building and a stone extension where room sizes, decor and comforts are altogether more modern. There's plenty of space for young children (cots, high-chairs and baby-listening are all readily available), and the less mobile appreciate use of 6 ground floor bedrooms with easy ramps into the pub. Early evening turn-down and dawn shoe-cleaning patrol aren't found in every pub: along with a hearty breakfast, it's all part, here, of the Wyndham service. Secure car-parking. *Open 11-11 (Sun 12-3, 7-10.30).* ***Bar Food*** *12-2, 7-9.30. Free House.* ***Beer*** *Flowers Original, Whitbread West Country Pale Ale. Garden, patio, outdoor eating.* ***Accommodation*** *17 bedrooms, all en suite, £61 (single £46.50). Children welcome overnight, additional bed and cot supplied. Access, Amex, Diners, Visa.*

CLEY-NEXT-THE-SEA — George & Dragon — B&B

Tel 01263 740652 **Fax 01263 741275** Map 10 C1
High Street Cley-next-the-Sea nr Holt Norfolk NR25 7RN

Standing head and shoulders above its neighbouring whitewashed cottage, this striking brick inn was rebuilt in 1897 in Edwardian style and enjoys an enviable position close to Cley's fine windmill overlooking an expanse of unspoilt salt marsh. For decades the inn has been a popular base for visiting naturalists, walkers and holidaymakers, and the good pubby bars have witnessed the forming of the Norfolk Naturalists Trust in 1926 and today daily bird observations are recorded in the "bird bible" – a large volume placed on a lectern in the main bar. Upstairs, most of the homely, simply furnished bedrooms, including the four-poster room, have far-reaching salt marsh views and six have clean, adequate en-suite facilities. TVs and tea-makers are standard. The residents lounge is the internal hide, complete with scrape-facing window and a pair of binoculars. Housekeeping is of a good standard. Good-sized garden across the lane with pétanque pitch. Being a well-visited coastal village, families are very welcome here and the provision of extra bed and cot in the family or larger rooms. There is no charge for babies and nominal charges for under and over 10s. Early evening meals can be provided from 6pm and young diners have their own menu and use of a high-chair. However, children must be carefully supervised in the garden. *Free House. Open 11-2.30, 6.30-11 (Sun 12-3, 7-10.30).* ***Accommodation*** *8 bedrooms, 6 en suite £50 (four-poster £65, single £30). Check-in by arrangement. Children welcome overnight (cot, high-chair and additional bed in parents' room available).* ***Beer*** *Greene King IPA & Abbot Ale, Tetley Bitter. No credit cards.*

CLIFFE — Black Bull — FOOD

Tel 01634 220893 **Fax 01634 221382** Map 11 B5
186 Church Street Cliffe Kent ME3 7QP

Late-Victorian pub on a historic tavern site. The three bars offer a constantly-changing line-up of real ales and at least eight wines by the glass. Eating may be in one of these or in the non-smoking, 40-seat, 18th-century cellar restaurant which is usually booked only once in an evening, so there's no hurry to leave, especially as they have an extended licence to serve up to midnight. The speciality is Far-Eastern – spring rolls and home-made prawn crackers are two of the starters; sotong sambal (squid with peppers and pineapple in spicy shrimp sauce) or hokkien braised pork are options for main courses which can be ordered with mee goreng (fried noodles with shrimps, meat and vegetables) or egg fried rice. There's also a set meal (two starters, four main dishes, rice and dessert) for two. The prices are lower in the bar where the main dish price includes vegetables and rice (chili chicken, sweet and sour) or beef stir fry. *Open 12-3, 7-11 (Sun 12-3, 7-10.30).* ***Bar Food*** *12-2, 7-10 (except Sun night). Free House.* ***Beer*** *two or three regularly-changing real ales. Access, Visa.*

CLIFTON Duke of Cumberland's Head FOOD

Tel 01869 338534 Map 14a C1 **B&B**
Clifton nr Deddington Oxfordshire OX5 4PE

A comfortable thatched pub on the B4031 with old beams, inglenook fireplace and wheelback chairs. Sam Harrison in the kitchen produces a strictly French menu for the small restaurant and more varied blackboard menu for the bar. A typical selection might include Stilton and onion soup, garlic mushrooms, salad niçoise sirloin steak, kleftiko, spaghetti bolognese, chili con carne, and grilled plaice. Puds like chocolate mousse, crème caramel and queen of puddings served with cream. Help yourself buffet on Sunday evenings. Upstairs, under the eves, three simple bedrooms have with en-suite shower rooms with WC, old pine furniture, TV and hot beverage kit but no telephones. Garden to the rear. *Open 12-3, 6.30-11 (Sun 12-3, 7-10.30). Free House.* ***Bar Food*** *12-2, 7-9.30.* ***Beer*** *Hook Norton Best, Wadworth 6X, Hampshire King Alfred's, Adnams Southwold Bitter, occasional guest. Garden, outdoor eating area.* ***Accommodation*** *3 bedrooms, all en suite, £45 (single £30). Check-in by arrangement. Access, Diners, Visa.*

CLIFTON HAMPDEN Plough Inn FOOD

Tel 01865 407811 **Fax 01865 407136** Map 14a C3 **B&B**
Clifton Hampden nr Abingdon Oxfordshire OX14 3EG

Zzz... ☺

A 16th-century thatched and timber-framed gem of a building, lovingly run by Turkish-born landlord Yuksel Bektas – always impeccably dressed, often in tail coat in the morning and dinner suit at night – and his family. It is now a delightful country pub that simply oozes charm and character. The cosy main bar, adjoining room and separate, less characterful, small dining-room are pristinely kept and feature low beams, deep red-painted walls, narrow wall benches; open fires at each end of the main bar give a welcoming feel immediately on entering. Characterful touches include Turkish coffee in the bar, pitta bread and toast with the particularly good breakfast and a fox's head resplendent with fez in the bar. The pub has an open-all-day policy, and food is served as long as the doors are open; the "no fried or frozen foods" policy is admirable. One can either eat informally in the bar rooms (or garden) or more formally in the dining-room up a few steps from the small bar. The former sees the usual traditional pub food (with a few, nice little twists), while the latter extends to smoked fish platter, pan-fried cod on a vegetable crostini with basil dressing, and chargrilled fillet of beef with a shallot and red wine jus. Up a few stairs off the bar, tucked beneath the thatch, is a spacious bedroom, tastefully decorated with four-poster bed, deep pink walls, attractive floral rose fabrics and matching Oriental bedside lamps; a basket of fruit, remote-control TV, copper kettle, two easy chairs and a splendid private bathroom (down a few steps) with a good, solid tub all add up to unusually good pub accommodation. Another spacious bedroom is up a few stairs at the other end of the building, also tucked under the thatch. Three further bedrooms, all as stylish as the original with four-posters, have been recently added in original, converted buildings just across the gravel yard. Enjoy a quiet pint in the garden (unless there's a wedding reception in a marquee) or take a stroll down the road to the baby river Thames. The Plough is one of a kind – no-smoking throughout, quality accommodation, good food and service, and Turkish hospitality (Mr Bektas will even drive you home if you've had a few too many, wash your car and shine your shoes overnight if you ask – nothing is too much trouble) – all in the heart of a pretty Oxfordshire village on the A415 Abingdon to Dorchester road. *Open 11am-11pm.* ***Bar Food*** *11am-11pm.* ***Beer*** *Webster's Yorkshire Bitter, Ruddles County, Courage Best. Accommodation 5 en-suite rooms, £55 (single £39.50). Children welcome overnight, additional bed and cot provided. Garden. No dogs. Access, Visa.*

> Many **B&B** establishments offer reduced rates for weekend and out-of-season bookings. Always ask about special deals for longer stays. Beware half-board terms in inns where we do not recommend the **FOOD.**

Cockwood Anchor Inn FOOD

Tel 01626 890203 Map 13 E3
Cockwood nr Dawlish Devon EX6 8RA

The small vine-covered verandah of this 400-year-old fisherman's cottage pub is a super spot in which to sit and watch the colourful fishing boats and wildlife in the tiny harbour across the lane and the Exe estuary beyond. Inside, although extended over the years, the rustic main bar remains unspoilt, with black panelling, low ceilings and lots of intimate little alcoves in the three snug areas, one of which has a welcoming coal fire. Local seafood, especially shellfish, is the main attraction here, especially the impressive range of sauces for mussels and oysters, which are delivered daily from local beds along the River Exe. Also worth investigating is the fresh fish board – red mullet in lemon butter, halibut in tarragon sauce – and the daily specials such as home-made soup, seafood grill and honey-roast lamb. The main printed menu offers a fairly routine choice of pub favourites, but the choice of real ale is anything but mundane. Parking can be difficult, especially on busy summer days. *Open 11-11 (Sun 12-2.30, 7-10.30). **Bar Food** 12-2.30 (Sun to 2), 6.30-10 (Sun 7-9.30). **Beer** Bass, Boddingtons, Eldridge Pope Royal Oak, Marston's Pedigree, Flowers, three guest beers. Paved Beer garden, outdoor eating. Access, Visa.*

> We only recommend food (Bar Food) in those establishments highlighted with the **FOOD** symbol.

Cockwood Ship Inn FOOD

Tel 01626 890373 Map 13 E3
Cockwood nr Dawlish Devon EX6 8PA

Originally an old victualler's house, dating from 1640, this homely, cream-painted inn overlooks the old harbour inlet and reedbeds. Carefully modernised inside, it is a popular place in which to appreciate a bar food menu that favours the fishy. A brasserie-style menu with a French accent lists traditional fare and good local fish. Sandwiches and other light bites are also offered, while non fish-fanciers can tuck into steaks, cold meat salads and a vegetarian selection. Outdoor eating and drinking can be enjoyed from a high-level garden, which affords splendid open views across the Exe estuary to Exmouth. No children under 14 in the bar area. *Open 11-3, 5.30-11 (Sat 11-11, Sun 12-3, 7-10.30). **Bar Food** 12-2 (Sun to 2.30), 6.30-10 (Mon-Fri winter 7-9, Sun 7-9.30). Family room. **Beer** Ushers Best, Founder's Ale & Four Seasons (seasonal ales), John Smith's. Garden, outdoor eating. Access, Amex, Visa.*

Colchester Foresters Arms FOOD

Tel 01206 42646 Map 10 C3
Castle Road Colchester Essex CO1 1UW

No-frills local situated near the castle and Roman wall. Built originally as two cottages and converted to a pub in the 1920s, it has two tiny, often bustling, interconnecting bars with simple furnishings, bar billiards, piped jazz music and, rather surprisingly, an above-average, daily-changing menu of home-cooked food. Beyond an extensive list of sandwiches with unusual fillings one might find deep-fried Brie in filo with raspberry sauce, chicken breast in basil and tomato, beef and mushroom pie and half a dozen vegetarian choices, followed by sticky toffee pudding or vol-au-vent filled with fresh raspberries and cream. Front patio with benches. Sunday roast. Pretty basic, but unusual for a bit of a back-street boozer! Whitbread. *Open 11.30-3, 5.30-11 (Fri, Sat & during school hols 11-11, Sun 12-3, 7-10.30). **Bar Food** 12-2.30, 7-9.30. No food Sun evening. **Beer** Flowers IPA, Boddingtons. Access, Visa.*

Colchester Rose and Crown Hotel B&B

Tel 01206 866677 **Fax 01206 866616** Map 10 C3
East Street Colchester Essex CO1 2TZ

Magnificent ancient black-and-white timbered inn that has stood on the corner of the old Ipswich and Harwich roads since the 15th century. Once an old posting house, it is now a well-appointed inn having been carefully extended and refurbished over the past few years. A pubby bar attracts a busy local trade and is full of character with open fires, heavy

beams and antique, cushioned pews and settles. Old-world charm extends upstairs into the main-building bedrooms – three of which boast sturdy four-poster beds – with leaded windows, wall timbers and uneven floors. Newer extension bedrooms are uniform in size, decor and furnishings, all being very comfortable and well equipped with older-style darkwood furniture and quality co-ordinating fabrics. Fully-tiled bathrooms have overhead showers. Full complement of added comforts from remote-controlled TVs (with satellite channels) to trouser presses. *Open 11-11.30 (Sun 12-10.30). Free House.* ***Beer*** *Tetley Bitter.* ***Accommodation*** *30 bedrooms, all en suite, £58-£119 (single £58). Children welcome overnight (under-5s stay free in parents' room, 5-12s half price), additional bed and cot available. No dogs. Closed 27-29 Dec. Access, Amex, Diners, Visa.*

COLEFORD — New Inn — FOOD

Tel 01363 84242 **Fax 01363 85044** Map 13 D2 **B&B**

Coleford Devon EX17 5BZ

Pretty, 13th-century thatched cottage inn set beside the River Cole in an equally attractive village, deep in the heart of unspoilt Devon countryside. 'Captain', the chatty resident parrot, welcomes folk into the characterful rambling interior, with the charming ancient bar blending successfully with dining-room extension into the old barns: fitted red carpets, fresh white walls, heavy beams, simple wooden furniture and settles and a discreet variety of attractive brass and bric-a-brac. Bar food is reliable and home-cooked, relying on fresh local produce: Brixham fish, West Country cheeses, eggs and cream from a nearby farm. The comprehensive blackboard menu has an international flavour, featuring Greek salad, seafood provençale and a hearty lentil soup as a snack or starter, with main course options that include Mediterranean lamb, Mexican pasta, beef stifado and bobotie. Local estate game appears regularly on the winter menu. Good puddings range from chocolate mousse to apple sultana puff. A decent list of over 50 wines is supplied by Christopher Piper wines. Comfortable and peaceful overnight accommodation is guaranteed in the three spacious, light and airy en-suite bedrooms; newly refurbished, with quality floral fabrics and antique furniture plus TV and tea-making facilities as added comforts. Good breakfasts. There's a stream-side patio for quiet alfresco summer drinking. *Open 11.30-2.30, 6-11 (Sun 12-3, 7-10.30). Free House.* ***Beer*** *Otter Ale, Hall & Woodhouse Badger Best, Wadworth 6X, guest beer. Garden, outdoor eating area.* ***Accommodation*** *3 bedrooms, all en suite, £49.50 (single £32). Access, Amex, Diners, Visa.*

COLLYWESTON — Cavalier Inn — B&B

Tel 01780 444288 Map 7 E4

Collyweston nr Stamford Lincolnshire DE9 3PQ

Previously the Slaters Arms, the pub changed its name when the slate mine closed and the work force moved away. The inn itself is a terrace of small 19th-century cottages, yet a glass window let into the bar floor reveals a much earlier stone spiral stairway to a tiny cellar. All the rooms are on the first floor, away from the bar, quiet and have white, freestanding furniture; TVs and beverage facilities are provided (but no phones). Rooms have views of the church and across the valley. Breakfast includes Lincolnshire sausages, of course. Four miles from Stamford on the A43. *Open 11-2.30, 6.30-11 (Sun 12-3, 7-10.30). Free House.* ***Beer*** *Ruddles Best & County, John Smith's. Garden. Family room.* ***Accommodation*** *6 bedrooms, all en suite, £32 (single £25). Children welcome overnight. No dogs. Check-in by arrangement. Access, Amex, Diners, Visa.*

COLN ST ALDWYNS — New Inn — ★ — FOOD

Tel 01285 750651 **Fax 01285 750657** Map 14a A2 **B&B**

Coln St Aldwyns nr Cirencester Gloucestershire GL7 5AN

Since Brian and Sandra-Anne Evans came to this sleepy Cotswolds village in 1992, they have transformed the New Inn into a delightfully romantic, creeper-covered inn. Behind its picture postcard frontage of flower baskets and ivy, interior conversion has created a succession of little rooms as adaptable to the demands of diners as are the menus to satisfy them. The Courtyard bar menu – ideal for lighter lunches in the long bar with its dried hops, bare Cotswolds stone walls, quarry-tiled floor and inglenook fire – offers a wide choice, from minute steak toasted sandwich and poughman's lunches (with a selection of four cheeses, chutney and pickles) to smoked haddock gratin with leeks and chives, smoked chicken, sun-dried tomato and macaroni bake, lamb's liver with bacon, mash and mustard sauce, and egg custard tart with home-made nutmeg ice-cream. "Ask at the bar for

children's meals." In the evening one can push the boat out and enjoy new chef Tony Robson-Burrell's fixed-price à la carte menu in the restaurant, perhaps commencing with grilled goat's cheese with endive, air-dried tomatoes and crostini or Oriental duck spring roll with aromatice Chinese spices, followed by fillets of plaice with fondant potatoes, leeks and thyme, rack of Cornish lamb with Provençal vegetables, rosemary and garlic or breast of chicken with pesto mash and beetroot sauce. Particularly good dishes enjoyed last year were fillets of red mullet provençale with crisp vegetables, breast of guinea fowl with caramelised onions, smoked baon and leeks, and prune and armagnac clafoutis with orange ice cream – just three of many star-worthy dishes! Leave room for rhubarb muffins with custard sauce and rhubarb coulis, apricot crème brulée with dentelle or banana and rum omelette with clotted cream – obviously chef has an inventive sweet tooth! The selection of British and French cheeses is also very good. Configuration of the bedrooms, utilising virtually every angle of the roof space, is for each resident to discover and all to wonder at – here a romantic four-poster room, there the sunken bath in a former stair-well – and epitomise the delights in store for those who come to stay; self-styled as "a private castle of comfort", it isn't far off! There are carefully-chosen floral prints on the walls and chintz drapes at the windows; direct-dial phones, remote-controlled TVs and tea- and coffee-making facilities are all provided. Tip-top food in both bar and restaurant, stylish overnight accommodation and warm hospitality. *Open 11.30-2.30, 5.30-11 (Sat all day 11-11, Sun 12-3, 7-10.30).* ***Bar Food*** *12-2 (Fri & Sat to 2.15), 7-9.30 (Sat to 10). Free House.* ***Beer*** *Hook Norton Best, Wadworth 6X, Morland Original, guest beer. Terrace, outdoor eating.* ***Accommodation*** *11 bedrooms, all en suite, £75 (suite/family room £90, single £50) inc. Children welcome overnight (under-4s stay free in parents' room), additional bed (£15) and cot (£5) available. No dogs in rooms. Access, Amex, Visa.*

COLSTON BASSETT — Martins Arms — FOOD

Tel 01949 81361 Map 7 D3

School Lane Colston Bassett Nottinghamshire NG12 3FD

Formerly the Squire's residence, set among horse chestnuts in an estate garden, the pub exudes quiet country-house charm (scatter cushions, window drapes, hunting prints) to which the bar itself seems almost an intrusion; however, you will find some top-notch Bateman XB and impeccable wines from Lay & Wheeler. Food is offered on different menus in both the antique-furnished dining-room complete with its own lounge and in the bar, which opens on to a lawn. Particularly good bar snacks cover the range from sandwiches and baguettes to light appetisers like grilled goat's cheese, savoury pancakes, Welsh rarebit and smoked salmon cornets; main courses might be chargrilled steaks, sautéed salmon with fresh tagliatelle and a lemon, tarragon and cream sauce or four vegetarian choices. Freshly-made desserts – like beer pudding with banana toffe sauce ro white chocolate quenelles with dark amaretto sauce – and a selection of six cheeses (including Colston Bassett Stilton, of course) to follow. Children under 14 are not permitted inside. Landlords Lynne Bryan and Salvatore Inguantas also run the Crown Inn at Old Dalby (see entry). *Open 12-3, 6-11 (Sun 12-3, 7-10.30).* ***Bar Food*** *12-2, 6-10 (no food Sun eve). Free House.* ***Beer*** *Marston's Best & Pedigree, Bateman XB & XXXB, two guest beers. Garden. No credit cards.*

COMBE HAY — Wheatsheaf — FOOD

Tel 01225 833504 Map 13 F1

Combe Hay nr Bath Avon BA2 7EG

Perched on a hillside looking across a small valley, the Wheatsheaf dates back to the 17th century and is as pretty as a picture, its black and white facade smothered in flowers and pierced with the entrances to dovecotes, built into the walls and still inhabited. Narrow, twisting lanes lead to this charming village, hidden away in a fold of hills to the south of Bath. Well-spaced rustic tables and benches in the large sloping garden make the best of the views, an ideal spot for summer eating and drinking. Inside there are rough stone walls, massive solid wooden tables, and also a huge blackboard menu: food is important here. Typical dishes from the bar menu are game terrine, pan-fried chicken livers with mustard, white wine and cream sauce, deep-fried mushrooms filled with Brie and home-made enchiladas, while the specials board may feature pan-fried medallions of venison with a red wine, oyster and mushroom sauce or king prawns in garlic butter and whisky. Home-made puddings include chocolate nut crunch, summer pudding and home-made cheesecakes. Real ales are drawn direct from the barrel. Large selection of fruit wines. *Open 11-2.30 (Sat to 3), 6.30-11 (from 5.30 in summer, Sun 12-3, 7-10.30).* ***Bar Food*** *12-2, 6.30-9.30 (Sun 7-9).* ***Beer*** *Courage Best, Wadworth 6X, John Smith's Smooth, guest beer. Garden, outdoor eating. No credit cards.*

COMPTON Coach & Horses FOOD

Tel 01705 631228 Map 15 D3

The Square Compton nr Chichester West Sussex PO18 9NA

Located in the village square and beside the B2146 Chichester to Petersfield road, this white-painted 15th-century coaching inn caters for all desires within its homely Village Bar and separate beamed lounge and restaurant. Mellow pine characterises the lively locals' bar where one can enjoy a good hearty bar snack, such as chicken and mushroom pie, breast of chicken with mustard sauce, Selsey dressed crab as well as soup, ploughman's platters and sandwiches, all of which are listed on a blackboard menu. Home-made lasagne has featured for ten years! Those seeking a more convivial dining atmosphere could venture next door into the charming lounge and adjacent restaurant, both boasting open log fires. A further board features more imaginative and pricier fare to suit the surroundings. Puddings include icky sticky toffee pudding and home-made brown bread ice cream. Good range of six well-kept real ales and a short list of 15 good value wines to choose from. A small secluded garden lies beyond the skittle alley. *Open 11-2.30, 6-11 (Sun 12-2.30, 7-10.30). Free House. **Bar Food** 12-2, 6-9.30 (Sun from 7). **Beer** Fuller's ESB, McEwans Export, four guest beers. Garden, outdoor eating. Children allowed anywhere. Access, Visa.*

CONGRESBURY White Hart FOOD

Tel 01934 833303 Map 13 F1

Wrington Road Congresbury Avon BS19 5AR

Combined quaint village pub and dining venue hidden down a long lane off the A370 (follow the Wrington Road). A conventional line in snacks and salads is supplemented by some more promising home-cooked fare: steak and Guinness pie, chicken curry through to haddock and broccoli gratin, bobotie and poached salmon steak served with a choice of potatoes and vegetables or salad. An increasing attraction is Sunday lunch, especially with families, who have use of a neat conservatory looking across the large pub garden and away towards the Mendips; no children are allowed in the bars. With plastic bottles of pop from the bar youngsters can amuse themselves in full view on the play equipment. There's also an aviary by the terrace. *Open 11-2.30, 6-11 (Sun 12-3, 7-10.30). **Bar Food** 12-2, 6-9.30 (Sun 7-9). **Beer** Hall & Woodhouse. Garden. Patio, children's play area. Family room. Access, Visa.*

CONSTANTINE Trengilly Wartha Inn FOOD B&B

Tel & Fax 01326 340332 Map 12 B4

Nancenoy Constantine nr Helston Cornwall TR11 5RP

Zzz... 

One mile due south of Constantine down country lanes, the Inn sits in a beautiful wooded valley looking down towards Polpenwith Creek on the Helford River. The unpretentious main bar is happily unmodernised with games machines and pool table relegated to a separate room and another tapestry upholstered 'lounge' area where families are welcome; there's a small children's section on the menu too. For summer there are tables on the vine-covered patio and in the garden beyond. A further alfresco area is around a lake in the valley bottom. There is a long list of 'Trengilly Classics' on the bar food mneu but the most interesting options appear on the blackboard. This features fresh fish from Newlyn like lobster, sea bass and skate wings; in addition there might be fish soup, grilled goat's cheese, pork fillet with cider and apricots served on fine buttered noodles, and homely puddings. You might also find crab open sandwiches and ploughman's lunches. Last orders for 'should I, shouldn't I?' sweets are taken at 2.30pm and 10pm – go on, try a local farm ice cream or a sampler of desserts in miniature (a great idea taken from much fancier restaurants). The separate restaurant offers a two- or three-course dinner. Good range of wines by the glass selected from a list of 160, regularly-changing real ales and three strong scrumpy ciders. Six cosy bedrooms are light and pretty with good, modern carpeted bathrooms and up-to-date conveniences such as remote-control TV and direct-dial telephones. Well maintained and comfortable accommodation. *Open 11-2.30, 6-11 (Sun 12-3, to 2.30 in winter, 7-10.30). **Bar Food** 12-2.15 (Sun to 2), 6.30-9.30 (Sun from 7.15). Family room, conservatory. Free House. **Beer** Sharp's, Furgusons Dartmoor Best, St Austell XXXX Mild, up to four guest beers. Garden, outdoor eating. **Accommodation** 6 bedrooms, 5 en suite, £56-£60 (single £40). Children welcome overnight, additional bed (£8) and cot (£2) provided in one larger room. Access, Amex, Diners, Visa.*

Cookham Dean — Inn on the Green — FOOD

Tel 01628 482638 Map 15a E3
The Green Cookham Dean nr Marlow Berkshire SL6 9NZ

Tucked away in one corner of the large village green, this interesting pub has four dining areas but only a small bar. Two small drinking rooms (with just seven tables) lead through to a Swiss chalet-style dining-room, off which the high-ceilinged Lamp Room restaurant and a small conservatory lead. The short bar menu (and daily blackboard specials) is the best bet; the range might cover smoked mackerel mousse, steak in a baguette with chips, sausage and mash, bacon and three cheese salad, warm goat's cheese salad and monkfish with peppers and sherry. Outside, there's a small patch of grass to the front (plus the enormous green a little further away), a large walled courtyard barbecue area (lit by wall lights and heated by tall gas burners, Apr-Oct) and an acre of paddock behind the car park. It's a wonderful summer pub for families with youngsters: the rear grassed area features picnic tables, a tree house, a chalet-style 'Nut House', double slide, climbing frame and rubber tyre swings; however, in winter and in the evenigns the inside is too intimate for anything less than very well-behaved juniors. Casual food service, but generous portions – stick to the simpler dishes. Two cottagey bedrooms (with en-suite showers) were being converted as we went to press. Easy parking. *Open 12-3, 6-11 (Sun 12-3, 7-10.30). **Bar Food** 12-2, (Sun to 2.30), 6.30-10 (no food Sun eve in winter). Free House. **Beer** Brakspear, Boddingtons, Fuller's London Pride, guest beer. Garden, terrace, outdoor eating, children's play area. Pub closed 25, 26 Dec and 1 Jan eve. Access, Amex, Visa.*

Cookham Dean — Jolly Farmer — FOOD

Tel 01628 482905 Map 15a E3
Cookham Dean nr Marlow Berkshire SL6 9PD

Homely and traditional village pub located opposite the parish church and close to the vast village green. Two simply furnished interconnecting bars with open fires, and a separate small and cosy dining-room in which to enjoy wholesome, home-cooked pub food. Blackboard choices may range from Stilton and cider soup and warm goat's cheese on beef tomato salad to chicken and mushroom pie, pork and vegetable curry and haddock and egg crumble at lunchtimes, with more imaginative evening options like pork medallions with a sherry and mustard sauce. Sandwiches and ploughman's at lunchtime only. Apple pie and crème brulée are typical pudding options. Good summer garden with children's play area. Well-behaved children only inside. *Open 11.30-3, 5.30-11 (Sat from 6), Sun 12-3, 7-10.30. **Bar Food** 12-2.30, 7.30-9.30. No food Sun evening. Free House. **Beer** Courage Best, Gales HSB, guest beer. Garden, outdoor eating, children's play area. Access, Visa.*

Corbridge — Angel Inn — FOOD — B&B

Tel 01434 632119 Map 5 D2
Main Street Corbridge nr Hexham Northumberland NE45 5LA

Zzz..

Saxon Corbridge, just off both the A68 and A69 trunk routes, stands above the 17th-century stone bridge across the Tyne where the former Head inn was once the town's posting inn. Its latest guardian angel, Mandy McIntosh Reid, has certainly dusted the place with a little of her own magic. The Angel today is smartly carpeted throughout (except in the locals' Tap Room) and an upmarket approach is reinforced by the food: here you will find reliable Northumbrian cooking of a style and value which has achieved regular local approval. Daily-changing bar/lounge menus encompass the likes of fennel and orange soup, braised halibut with crabmeat, stir-fried chicken with ginger and Cumberland sausage with onion gravy. In the foyer lounge, nonetheless, space is found for morning coffees, a lunchtime sandwich and afternoon teas. The five recently completed bedrooms haven't been skimped over either. There are satellite TVs, roomy bathrooms with a certain feminine touch (cotton buds and bath foam) quality free-standing pine furniture and bold colour schemes. The three twins (families welcome) are roomier than the doubles: views are either from the front down to the river or to the rear overlooking a pretty walled garden. *Free House. **Beer** Theakston Best & XB, Younger's No 3, McEwan's 80/-, guest beer. Open 11-3, 5-11 (12-3, 7-10.30 Sun). **Bar Food** 12-2.15, 6-9.15 (7-9.15pm Sun). **Accommodation** 5 rooms, all en suite, £54 (£39 single). Additional bed and cot available. Access, Amex, Diners, Visa.*

CORFE CASTLE — The Fox — A

Tel 01929 480449 Map 14 D4

West Street Corfe Castle Dorset BH20 5HD

Unspoilt 16th-century inn, with a very snug little front bar and slightly less enchanting larger lounge. Recent renovations uncovered a doorway which has been turned into an alcove, a 13th-century fireplace and a well that is now lit and glass-covered. Its mature, pretty garden with views of the famous ruin make the Fox especially appealing in summer. Children under 14 are not allowed indoors. *Open 11-3 (to 2.30 in winter), 6-11 (from 6.30 in winter), Sun 12-3, 7-10.30. Free House.* ***Beer*** *Gibbs Mew Bishop's Tipple, Wadworth 6X, Greene King Abbot Ale, Ind Coope Burton Ale, Eldridge Pope Royal Oak. Garden. No credit cards.*

CORNWORTHY — Hunters Lodge Inn — FOOD

Tel 01803 732204 Map 13 D3

Cornworthy Totnes Devon TQ9 7ES

Unspoilt, simply-furnished country local with a low-ceilinged bar and a cosy dining-room with an old stone fireplace and attractive blue table linen. Vast, little-changing blackboard menus hide some good home-cooked dishes among the deep-fried choices with chips and the bought-in puddings. The lunchtime-only board will offer good home-made soups, cottage pie, courgette and tomato bake, fresh Brixham plaice and a splendid steak and kidney pie served with huge portions of four crisp vegetables and a bowl of potatoes; sandwiches and ploughman's at lunch also. On the long menu (available in bar and restaurant) more elaborate dishes might include lamb in redcurrant and red wine, Greek-style lamb with rice and feta cheese salad and halibut in lime and wine with prawns and crab claws. Fish specialities are the special mixed grill (a mix of fish and meat), whole cracked crab and half a grilled lobster in herb butter. A three-course Sunday lunch is a popular event and it is advisable to book in the evenings and at weekends. No children under 14 in the restaurant (except Sun) but they are very welcome in the bar where there are games, toys and a high-chair available. Cider lovers should sample the 'Pig's Squeal'. ***Bar Food*** *12-2.30 & 7-10. Free House.* ***Beer*** *Blackawton 44, Ushers Best, guest beer. Garden, outdoor eating, children's play area. No credit cards.*

CORSCOMBE — Fox Inn — ★ — FOOD

Tel 01935 891330 Map 13 F2

Corscombe Dorset DT2 0NS

"Real Ale, Country Cooking. No Chips or Microwaves" it says on the postcard, showing Martyn Lee's pretty little thatched pub of stone and cob, built in 1620 and located down a web of narrow lanes deep in unspoilt Dorset countryside (the village is signposted off the A356 Crewkerne to Dorchester, then follow signs to the pub – it's not easy to find). All is equally appealing inside, and the small entrance lobby is decorated with a wild flower and ivy mural painted directly on to the walls. Beyond are two bars, one, with its hunting prints, old pine furniture and band of chatty locals, the other prettily furnished with blue gingham curtains, tablecloths, banquette seat covers – even the fabric covering the bar stools. A huge old stone fireplace boasts a real log fire in winter, while behind the bar a collection of plates, copper and pewter ware is displayed and real ale and farm cider is dispensed straight from the cask. All is overseen by an array of stuffed owls in glass cases. It's still very much a locals' pub, complete with local cricket team, but more and more discerning diners are beginning to find their way to this rural backwater for chef Will Longman's imaginative choice of bar food. Quality produce from good local suppliers, including fresh fish from Bridport and game in season from local estates help create the interesting daily-changing blackboard menu. Choices may include grilled goat's cheese salad and fine beans with Parma ham and garlic to start, followed by breast of guinea fowl with tarragon and cream, fillet of turbot with cider sauce and whole John Dory baked with garlic and herbs; good accompanying vegetables. Other dishes include beef casserole, fish soup and Fox's Favourite chicken in a cream sauce. Sunday usually sees a choice of roasts. Puddings range from blackberry fool and caramelised apple tart to an excellent cheeseboard featuring, among others, local Denhay Cheddar, Somerset goat's and Shropshire Blue. Alfresco eating across the lane by the brook or at the sturdy, long wooden table in the attractive conservatory; it seats 20 and is ideal for parties. There is also a private room available for hire, seating up to 10. *Open 12-3, 7-11 (may be open all day Sat, Sun 12-2.30, 7-10.30).* ***Bar Food*** *12-2, 7-9. Free House.* ***Beer*** *Smiles, Palmers BB, Fuller's London Pride, Exmoor. Garden, outdoor eating. Family room. No credit cards.*

Corsham — Methuen Arms — B&B

Tel 01249 714867 **Fax 01249 712004** Map 14 B2
2 High Street Corsham Wiltshire SN13 0HB

Housed around the remains of a 14th-century nunnery, and converted into a brewery and coaching inn around 1608, there's abundant history here. Among notable features in public areas are the 100ft Long Bar containing its own skittle alley, and outstanding examples of stonemasonry through the ages to be found in the Winter's Court restaurant. Bedrooms in the main, Georgian, house overlooking a fairly constant stream of traffic, are on the utilitarian side (several with WC/shower rooms only). To the rear, and set around a courtyard facing the serene garden, the newer bedrooms have a touch more elegance, enhanced in the honeymoon suites by four-poster and half-tester beds. New owners took over here early in 1995. *Open 10-2.30, 6-11 (Sun 12-3, 7-10.30). Free House.* ***Beer*** *Bass, Tetley, Gibbs Mew Salisbury Best.* ***Accommodation*** *25 bedrooms, all en suite £55 (single £38). Children welcome overnight, additional bed (£15) and cot (£8.50) available. Lounge for residents. Family room. Garden. No dogs. Access, Visa.*

Coventry — William IV — FOOD

Tel 01203 686394 Map 6 C4
1059 Foleshill Road Coventry West Midlands CV6 6ER

There's a sign to Bedworth (B4113) from the M6, Junction 3, and the pub is about equidistant from this point and the city centre in Foleshill. What was arguably Britain's first authentically Indian pub remains unusual as the Himalayan Balti cooking favoured here is now much copied using convenience preparations. Perminder and Jatinder Bains offer a range of "Pele's" curries that runs to one hundred or more variations including Balti meat or chicken Rogan Josh, both meat and vegetarian thalis and the speciality chicken saagwla. Eating here is quite an experience and shows up the majority of British pub curries for the sham that they are. M&B mild is served on electric pump. Bass Taverns. *Open 11-2.30 (Fri & Sat to 3), 6-11 (Fri & Sat from 5), Sun 12-3, 7-10.30.* ***Bar Food*** *12-2.30, 6-10.30 (Fri/Sat 5-10.45, Sun 7-10). Access, Amex, Visa.*

Coxwold — Fauconberg Arms — FOOD B&B

Tel 01347 868214 Map 5 E4
Main Street Coxwold North Yorkshire YO6 4AD

This is a charmingly civilised, if invariably busy place, with handsome old furnishings and an open fire, located near Shandy Hall and Byland Abbey. Landlady Nicky Jaques produces adventurous and varied bar food: cream of celeriac and coconut soup, smoked salmon and watercress mousse, pan-fried lamb with apple, mint and rosemary gravy; sandwiches and ploughman's lunches at lunchtime only. The restaurant offers a 3-course table d'hote menu at Sunday lunch, and in the evenings one menu applies throughout the pub, offering choices such as hickory-smoked chicken and melon with avocado dip, envelopes of puff pastry with Stilton and celery paté and spiced peach mayonnaise; boned half duckling with Bramley apple purée with cherry and Kirsch gravy or filo pastry pouches of fresh fish served with champagne sauce. At least eight wines are available by the glass. Bedrooms have long been popular here too, and still look like good value. The setting is delightful, in a peaceful, straggling village, and the church across the road is worth a look; Lawrence Sterne is buried there. *Open 11-3, 6.30-11 (Sat from 6, Sun 12-3, 7-10.30).* ***Bar Food*** *12-2, 7-9. Free House.* ***Beer*** *Tetley, Theakston Best, John Smith's. Patio, outdoor eating.* ***Accommodation*** *4 bedrooms, one with shower en suite, £40 (single £24). Children welcome overnight, additional bed (£10) available. Access, Visa.*

Cranborne — Fleur de Lys — B&B

Tel 01725 517282 **Fax 01725 517631** Map 14 C4
5 Wimborne Street Cranborne Dorset BH21 5PP

Historical connections are many at this ivy-clad inn set in the heart of the village; Thomas Hardy visited when writing *Tess of the D'Urbervilles* in 1891, Rupert Brooke wrote a poem on the premises, and Hanging Judge Jeffreys also once stayed the night. The pub itself is modernised and pleasant, with period features remaining. Good-sized en-suite bedrooms are clean and comfortable, and decorated in country style with pretty floral fabrics and modern darkwood furniture. Equipped with central heating, TVs and tea-makers, they make an ideal base from which to explore this unspoilt part of Dorset, especially Cranborne Chase. *Open 10.30-3, 6-11 (Sun 12-3, 7-10.30).* ***Beer*** *Hall & Woodhouse. Garden.* ***Accommodation*** *8 bedrooms, all en suite (four with bath), £42-£55 (£29-£35). Children welcome overnight (under-5s free if sharing parents' room, 5-12s ½-price), additional bed & cot available. Access, Amex, Visa.*

CRANMORE — Strode Arms — A

Tel 01749 880450 Map 13 F1
Cranmore nr Shepton Mallett Somerset BA4 4QT

13th- and 14th-century coaching inn, formerly a farmhouse, opposite the village pond. Delightfully rustic within and full of memorabilia from the East Somerset Railway (otherwise known as the Strawberry Line) which is 500 yards away. Particularly welcoming features are the provision of daily papers and a huge fireplace in the main lounge. Vintage cars meet outside on the first Tuesday of the month. Terrace overlooking the village pond and a beer garden to the rear. No children under 14 in the bars; plenty of room outside in good weather. *Open 11.30-2.30, 6.30-11 (Sun 12-3, 7-10.30). Pub closed Sun eve in winter (Oct-Mar inc). Free House.* ***Beer*** *Flowers IPA, Marston's Pedigree, Wadworth 6X & guest beer. Garden. Access, Visa.*

CRASTER — Jolly Fisherman — A

Tel 01665 576461 Map 5 E1
Haven Hill Craster nr Alnwick Northumberland NE66 3TR

The village's only pub perches on a craggy hill above the quay, home of the local lifeboatmen and a summer haunt for visiting landlubbers. Its best aspects are from a raised lounge bar revealing massive seascapes through picture windows on two sides, and from a lower garden and patio, a little above high water, with pathways down by the harbour wall to the rocky shoreline. With boats in the harbour and the local fishery opposite, seafood sandwiches are their stock-in-trade: crab, prawn and salmon. *Open 11-3, 6-11 (12-3, 7-10.30 Sun).* ***Beer*** *Wards Thorne Best Bitter. Gardens. Family room. Quayside. No credit cards.*

CRAWLEY — Fox & Hounds — FOOD B&B

Tel & Fax 01962 776285 Map 15 D3
Crawley nr Winchester Hampshire SO21 2PR

Zzz...

A splendid redbrick pub built (like the rest of the picturesque village) at the turn of the century and converted to look much older than it is, with a fine overhanging timber facade and bow windows. The open-plan interior is comfortably furnished with a mix of padded benches and seats, arranged around a variety of tables, and lots of china plates decorate the walls of both bar and adjacent dining-room. The regularly-changing blackboard menu features game in season and good-value fresh fish – delivered twice a week from Poole and Cornwall – in dishes such as Spanish fish soup, seafood pancakes and fresh whole lemon sole meunière. Other popular speciality dishes include home-made pies – steak, venison and kidney – and a hearty spicy cheese and lentil loaf. Sandwiches and ploughman's lunches at lunchtimes (except Sunday). Crème caramel with fresh oranges and Grand Marnier or a chocolate shell filled with ice cream and fruits complete a meal. Upstairs are three pristinely-kept, en-suite bedrooms, all attractively decorated in pastel shades of peach and apricot with tasteful co-ordinating fabrics. Individual pieces of pine and antique furniture furnish the rooms and landing. Extra touches include two well-equipped, large bathrooms, good TVs, magazines and china crockery on each beverage tray. Bookings taken throughout for food. *Open 11.45-2:30, 6-11 (Sun 12-3, 7-10.30).* ***Bar Food*** *12-2, 7-9.30 (Sun to 9). Free House.* ***Beer*** *Wadworth 6X, Gales BB. Garden, patio, outdoor eating area.* ***Accommodation*** *3 bedrooms, all en suite, £55 & £60 (single £40 & £45). Children welcome overnight. Additional bed (£10) available. Dogs by arrangement. Access, Visa.*

CRAY — White Lion Inn — A

Tel 01756 760262 Map 5 D4
Cray Buckden Skipton North Yorkshire BD23 5JB

Titular headquarters of the Wharfdale Head Gun Club, the Lion nestles in a deep valley on the road (B6160) between Wharfdale and Bishopsdale at the foot of Buckden Pike. For droves of fell walkers and families it's a sure shot in all weathers. Flagstoned within by a huge open range, the bar is a chummy place to dry off over a welcome pint of Moorhouse's (leaving muddy boots outside, please!). A sun-soaked front patio comes into its own in summer; parents can relax while across the road children in their dozens splash in and around the Beck, seemingly oblivious of the true purpose of its aged stepping stones. Children and well-behaved dogs are welcome indoors. *Open 11-3, 6-11 (12-3, 7-10.30 Sun). Free House.* ***Beer*** *Tetley Best, Moorhouse's Premier & Pendle Witches Brew, guest beer. Family room. Access, Visa.*

CRAZIES HILL — The Horns — FOOD

Tel 01734 401416 Map 15a D3
Crazies Hill Wargrave Berkshire RG10 8LY

Recently renovated (but not too much) by Brakspear's brewery, the Horns started life in Tudor times as a hunting lodge to which a barn (now converted as part of the pub) was added some 200 years later. Very much the unspoilt country pub in style, it has no fruit machines and no piped music, just country furniture, traditional pub games – darts, shove ha'penny – and conversation. Not primarily a foody place but lunchtimes from Tuesday to Saturday there are various filled rolls, ploughman's, a late breakfast and about half-a-dozen blackboard specials like split pea and bacon soup, liver and bacon, Cumberland sausage and mash and chili. On Friday and Saturday evenings a more brasserie-style menu is in operation (served in the barn dining area, booking essential). *Open 11-3, (Mon-Thu to 2.30), 5.30-11 (Sun 12-3, 7-10.30). **Bar Food** 12-2 (not Sun or Mon). **Beer** Brakspear. Garden, outdoor eating, disabled facilities. Pub closed 1 Jan. No credit cards.*

CRESSWELL — Izaak Walton Inn — FOOD

Tel 01782 392265 Map 6 B3
Cresswell Stoke-on-Trent Staffordshire ST11 9RE

A good place to know in this area, despite being somewhat wedged between the busy A50 and the Stoke-Nottingham railway: turn off to the village from the old A522 at Draycott-in-the-Moors. Carpeted throughout with smartly varnished tables and chairs, yet very much a 'pub serving food', it is popular enough these days to render weekend booking virtually essential. Once tables are allocated, order at the bar from a lengthy, all-embracing menu supplemented by snacks and sandwiches at lunchtime (not Sunday) and chef's specials on a strategically placed blackboard: watercress and potato soup; lamb and apricot curry, or choose your own chicken supreme filling from blue cheese Stilton, crab meat or apples and cider sauce; and perhaps a gooey banana split to finish. Happy Eating Hour from 6-7. No smoking in eating areas. *Open 12-2.30, 6-11 (Sun 12-10.30). **Bar Food** 12-2, 6-10. Free House. **Beer** Marston's Pedigree. Garden, outdoor eating. Pub closed 25 & 26 Dec. Access, Visa.*

CROSCOMBE — Bull Terrier — B&B

Tel 01749 343658 Map 13 F1
Croscombe nr Wells Somerset BA5 3QJ

This lovely old pub was originally a priory where the abbots of Glastonbury used to live and was first licensed in 1612. Three bars: the Inglenook with red carpet, cushioned wall seats and original Jacobean beams, the Snug and the Common bar plus a family/dining-room. The attractive, elevated walled garden which backs on to the church (floodlit at night) overlooks the surrounding countryside. Simple overnight accommodation comprises three neat and homely upstairs bedrooms. Two sport compact en-suite facilities (one with tub, one with shower only) while the third shares with the landlord's family. All have TVs, radio-alarms and tea- and coffee-making facilities. No children or dogs overnight. *Free House. **Beer** regularly-changing selection of real ales. Garden. Family room. **Accommodation** 3 bedrooms, 2 en suite, £46 (single £30). No dogs. Pub closed all Monday Oct-Mar. Access, Visa.*

CROSTHWAITE — Punch Bowl Inn  — FOOD

Tel 01539 568237 **Fax 01539 568875** Map 4 C4
Crosthwaite nr Kendal Cumbria LA8 8HR

Next to the village church, the Punch Bowl Inn dates back to the 16th century and incorporates an old barn conversion in which you'll find the galleried entrance with its pitched roof. The interior, with rough-plaster walls and black gloss-painted timbers, somehow fails to give the impression of this having long been a hostelry. One area is permanently set up for eating and at busy times all but a few tables are occupied by diners; food is clearly important here (and very good it is, too). Chef-landlord Steven Doherty's menu is full of tempting dishes like a deliciously light and flavoursome soufflé suissesse (an upside-down cheese soufflé), gravad lax with blinis and a dill and sweet mustard sauce, lentil and bacon soup, aubergine and polenta with fennel, topped with mozzarella, basil and balsamic vinegar, cod florentine, chicken schnitzel, braised oxtail, and rump steak bordelaise. Don't forget to leave room for such puds as chocolate tart with vanilla sauce, apple feuilleté and floating islands. At lunchtime there are also sandwiches; otherwise, it's the same menu lunch and evening (for snacks as well as full meals), except for Sunday lunch which is

a two- or three-course fixed-price affair that always includes a traditional roast among the options. There's a shortish wine list with about half the bottles under £10, but listed vintages cannot be relied upon. Steven and Marjorie Doherty, previously at the *Brown Horse* in Winster (recommended in this Guide last year), took over here early in 1995 and had not yet made any improvements to the basic bedrooms when we inspected. *Open 11.30-3 & 5.30-11 (Sun 12-3, 7-10.30). Closed 25 Dec.* ***Bar Food*** *12-2 & 6-9. Free House.* ***Beer*** *Theakston Best Bitter, guest beers. Patio. Access, Visa.*

CULLOMPTON — Manor House Hotel — B&B

Tel 01884 32281 **Fax 01884 38344** Map 13 E2
2/4 Fore Street Cullompton Devon EX15 1JL

Built as the town house for a rich wool merchant, this hotel-cum-inn dates in part to 1603, and fine old casement windows jut out from the freshly-painted black and white facade. Inside has an attractive mix of styles, the knotty pine bar Victorian in feel but with a distinct, pubby atmopshere. The appealing bedrooms are all individually decorated, with stylishly co-ordinated fabrics, nicely framed botanical prints, plenty of pieces of china and plates on the walls and good freestanding furniture in mahogany or an orangey pine finish. All the usual modern comforts: TV (with satellite), radio, telephone, tea/coffee-making facilities and a trouser press. Carpeted bathrooms have wooden toilet seats, good thermostatically-controlled showers over the baths, and nice touches like cotton wool, pot-pourri and decent toiletries. Most rooms are at the front of the building facing the main road (double-glazing helps to reduce the traffic noise) and one of the two quieter rooms to the rear has a pair of bunk beds for families. Excellent-value overnight accommodation. *Open 11-11 (Sun 12-3, 7-10.30). Free House.* ***Beer*** *Boddingtons, Flowers. Patio/terrace. Family room.* ***Accommodation*** *10 bedrooms, all en suite, £50 (family room sleeps 4 £65, single £41.50). Children welcome overnight, additional bed (£7.50) and cot supplied. No dogs (guide dogs only). Access, Amex, Visa.*

CUMNOR — Bear & Ragged Staff ★ — FOOD

Tel 01865 862329 **Fax 01865 865366** Map 14a B2
Appleton Road Cumnor nr Oxford Oxfordshire OX2 9QH

Bruce Buchan, formerly chef/proprietor of *The Fish* at Sutton Courtenay (and also gaining a star there in last year's Guide) a few miles south of Cumnor, took over here in May 1995 after a period of uncertainty for the pub. It's always been a busy location for pub lunches but now quality cooking has come to the fore in both the comfortable, flagstoned bar with its bare stone walls, beams and open fires and in the dining-room. The former might see good vegetarian options like warm onion and gruyère tart or grilled polenta with ratatouille and basil, five or so fishy dishes – from potted Arbroath smokies with tomato and cream to kedgeree and gambas pil pil – salads and a handful of interesting, very upmarket sandwiches (prawn, cucumber and mayonnaise, steak and onion baguette, toasted ciabatta and Welsh rarebit). The restaurant menu is very much in a modern English mode with the likes of timbale of Brixham scallops and leeks, crispy duck and five spice salad, smoked salmon chowder among the daily selection of around four starters; the main courses always feature particularly good fresh fish: on an opening menu we found a tranche of salmon with creamy potatoes and chanterelles, rissoles of monkfish with courgette chutney, whole roast baby sea bass with chick peas and tomatoes, and charred tuna fish with niçoise salad. Combine this superb fish selection with a choice of meat cuts such as roast rump of new-season lamb with herb crumble, duck breast with rösti, cracked pepper and caramel onions, fillet of Angus beef with foie gras and supreme of chicken with asparagus and you've got a very interesting menu that would not disgrace even the most modern of London restaurants. A selection of British farmhouse cheeses, terrine of English summer pudding, marinated figs with apple fritters and honey parfait, plus white chocolate quenelles with a dark chocolate sauce complete the culinary picture for the starry-eyed. The infant wine list was already showing distinct signs of maturity and multi-cultural influences. To find the ivy-clad pub, follow signs to Cumnor from the A420, continue along the one-way system into the village, then bear left into the High Street and Appleton Road is on the left. *Open 11-3, 5-11 (Sun 12-3 & 7-10.30).* ***Bar Food*** *12-2.15, 7-10 (Sun to 9.30).* ***Beer*** *Bass, Morrells Oxford Bitter, Varsity & Mild. Garden. Access, Amex, Diners, Visa.*

We do not accept free meals or hospitality – our inspectors pay their own bills and **never** book in the name of Egon Ronay's Guides.

DALWOOD — Tuckers Arms — FOOD — B&B

Tel 01404 881342 **Fax 01404 881802** Map 13 E2
Dalwood nr Axminster Devon EX13 7EG

Picture-book-pretty, thatched pub in a delightful Axe Valley village, signposted off the A35 west of Axminster. Parts of the bar date back 700 years to when the building was a manor house; it later became an important coaching inn on the old London-Exeter road. The main low-ceilinged bar complete with inglenook, beams and rustic furnishings is the setting in which to sample some reliable bar food. Beyond the routine snack menu (with French-stick sandwiches and ploughman's lunches) is a further menu listing popular dishes like 'Tuckers Tiddies' – a light puff pastry pillow filled with either mixed seafood or chicken in cider – supreme of chicken with fresh tarragon, rack of lamb and kidneys in red wine. Extra blackboard dishes favour fresh fish: salmon, local trout, freshwater pike and crab, as well as maybe cauliflower and Stilton soup, rare roast beef and hash browns or maybe Cumberland sausage with redcurrant jelly and onion sauce. A rear extension houses the five clean and functional bedrooms with floral curtains and matching bed covers. All have TVs, tea-makers and well-fitted, fully tiled en-suite bathrooms with showers. In summer months the exterior is festooned with colourful flower tubs and baskets. *Open 12-3, 6.30-11 (7-10.30 Sun).* ***Bar Food*** *12-2, 7-10 (to 9.15 Sun). Free House.* ***Beer*** *Wadworth 6X, Boddingtons Bitter, Flowers Original, Otter Ale. Garden, outdoor eating.* ***Accommodation*** *5 bedrooms, all en suite with showers, from £40 (single £25). Access, Amex, Visa.*

DAMERHAM — Compasses Inn — B&B

Tel 01725 518231 Map 14 C3
Damerham nr Fordingbridge Hampshire SP6 3HQ

Zzz... ☺

Attractive 16th-century coaching inn located in the heart of the village next to the cricket green. Enthusiastic owners have smartly refurbished the carpeted open-plan lounge bar with new pine furniture, central woodburner, decent prints and pretty wallpaper. Separate spartan public bar with traditional games. Overnight accommodation in six bedrooms; these are light and airy with small print wallpapers, co-ordinating fabrics, comfortable furnishings and tiled en-suite facilities plus TVs and tea-makers. Good summer garden with children's play things. *Open 11-2.30, 6-11 (Sat 11-11, Sun 12-3, 7-10.30). Free House.* ***Beer*** *Wadworth 6X, Flowers Original, Ringwood Best, Hampshire Brewery Compasses Ale, guest beer. Garden, children's play area.* ***Accommodation*** *6 bedrooms, all en suite (two with bath), £50 (four-poster with bath £60, family room sleeping 2 + 2 under-12s £75, single £29.50). Children weclome overnight (under-12s half-price). Access, Visa.*

DANBY — Duke of Wellington — B&B

Tel 01287 660351 Map 5 E3
Danby nr Whitby North Yorkshire YO21 2LY

Just two miles from the A171 and approached across a windswept moor, the ivy-clad stone pub stands at the head of Danby village; Esk Dale's activity centre is just a half-mile walk away. Despite its somewhat ramshackle exterior, there's a warm welcome within from the Howat family. Bedrooms, now nine in number (four more than last year), have pine furniture, appealing decor, colour TVs and tea-making equipment; all but one have their own en-suite facilities, the remaining room having an adjoining private bathroom. There's a cosy, private residents' lounge for those wishing to escape with a good book, while in the revamped bar an agreeable mixture of tourists, fell-walkers and locals soon strike up acquaintances over a pint or two of the Duke's well-kept real ales. *Open 11-3, 7-11 (Sun 12-3, 7-10.30). Free House.* ***Beer*** *John Smith's Magnet & Extra Smooth, Ruddles Best, Marston's Pedigree, Cameron Strong Arm.* ***Accommodation*** *8 bedrooms, 7 en suite, £44 (single £22). Children welcome overnight, under-5s stay free in parents' room, cot available. Access, Visa.*

DARTINGTON — Cott Inn — FOOD — B&B

Tel 01803 863777 **Fax 01803 866629** Map 13 D3
Dartington nr Totnes Devon TQ9 6HE

Zzz...

A delightful 14th-century stone- and cob-built inn, continuously licensed since 1320, with a wonderful, 183ft thatched roof. Landlords David and Susan Grey keep both the bar and tiny restaurant neat, with lots of blackened beams, open fires, a mixture of antique and older pieces of furniture and plenty of gleaming brass bits and pieces. Lunch is an impressive hot

and cold buffet affair offering home-made quiches, various meats, Dart salmon and an array of freshly-prepared salads. Evening fare is more imaginative with blackboards in the bar listing such dishes as sauté of chicken with cream, tarragon and peppers, carbonnade of beef, seafood grill (gurnard, salmon, monkfish, mussels, king prawns), rack of lamb with bramble jelly, tournedos of beef with paté and red wine and tenderloin of pork stuffed with black olives in Madeira sauce; vegetarian options. There's usually a choice of three roasts for Sunday lunch. Overnight accommodation comprises six compact bedrooms tucked beneath the heavy thatch. All are neat and tidy with modern pine furnishings, pretty floral fabrics; four have compact bathrooms with overhead showers. TVs, tea-makers and telephones are standard throughout. *Open 11-2.30, 5.30-11 (Sun 12-3, 7-10.30).* ***Bar Food*** *12-2.15 (to 2.30 Sat & Sun), 6.30-9.30 (Sun from 7). Garden, outdoor eating.* ***Accommodation*** *6 bedrooms, all en suite, £50 (single £45). Children over 5 welcome overnight, additional bed (£10) supplied. Pub closed 25 Dec eve. Accommodation closed 25 Dec. Access, Amex, Visa.*

DARTMOUTH — Cherub — FOOD

Tel 01803 832571 Map 13 D3

13 Higher Street Dartmouth Devon TQ6 9BB

This magnificent example of a medieval timbered house (Dartmoor's oldest building, dating from 1380) was at one time a wealthy wool merchant's house. Famous for its overhanging beamed facade and the unusual first-floor windows, it takes its name from the type of boat built on the Dart for the wool export trade. Inside, the busy table-crammed tiny bar is full of atmosphere with original oak timbers and inglenook fireplace, plus a narrow, twisting staircase leading up into the small restaurant. Bar food might include beef and ale stew, Cherub smokie and smoked chicken baked with cheese sauce, broccoli and ham; all are served with salad or granary bread; sandwiches and ploughman's lunches are also available all day. Fresh fish dishes are featured on the little-changing blackboard menu – John Dory in Pernod and chive sauce and sole roulade with tarragon or for vegetarians, mushroom stroganoff. These also appear on the more elaborate evening restaurant menu as does a selection of meat dishes, for example guinea fowl in a rosemary sauce and steaks, both served with six fresh vegetables. No children in the bar but children over four are allowed in the restaurant before 9pm. Choice of 50 malt whiskies. *Open 11-11 (Sun 12-3, 7-10.30).* ***Bar Food*** *12-2.30 & 6.30-10. Free House.* ***Beer*** *Wadworth 6X, Morland Old Speckled Hen, Flowers Original, guest beer. Access, Visa.*

DARTMOUTH — Royal Castle Hotel — B&B

Tel 01803 833033 **Fax 01803 835445** Map 13 D3

11 The Quay Dartmouth Devon TQ6 9PS

Zzz...

Commanding the best site overlooking the small harbour and the Dart estuary beyond, this handsome, established inn/hotel is a most welcoming and comfortable place to stay. Originally four Tudor houses built on either side of a narrow lane, which now forms the lofty and attractive hallway, it boasts some oil paintings, antique furniture and the magnificent Bell Board, full of room-call bells, each one pitched at a different note. Of the two bars, the Harbour Bar is distinctly pubby and lively throughout the day, whereas the more refined and spacious Galleon Bar is a popular coffee stop and sports a weaponry display. All the 25 bedrooms are beautifully decorated, each in its own individual style with quality wallpapers and matching fabrics. Some rooms have four-posters, others antique brass beds and most are furnished with tasteful pieces of furniture. Several more expensive rooms enjoy river views and are light and airy with huge bathrooms, two with jacuzzi baths, some with showers only. Added touches include tissues, cotton wool balls and Woods of Windsor toiletries. TVs, telephones and tea-makers are standard throughout. If up early, linger over a good breakfast at one of the three sought-after window seats, overlooking the harbour and river. Twelve wines by the glass. Private garage facilities available. *Open 11-11, Sun 12-3, 7-10.30. Free House.* ***Beer*** *Boddingtons, Ruddles, Flowers IPA, Bass. Garden.* ***Accommodation*** *25 bedrooms, all en suite, £80 (£114 with river view, single £50). Children welcome overnight (under-16s stay free in parents' room). Access, Visa.*

Many **B&B** establishments offer reduced rates for weekend and out-of-season bookings. Always ask about special deals for longer stays. Beware half-board terms in inns where we do not recommend the **FOOD.**

DEDHAM Marlborough Head Hotel FOOD B&B

Tel 01206 323250 Map 10 C3
Mill Lane Dedham Essex CO7 6DH

Dedham is a charming village surrounded by picturesque Constable country, and the Marlborough Head, which occupies that most traditional of sites directly opposite the church, has been dispensing hospitality for over 550 years. Woodcarving is a speciality here, outside on the black and white timbered upper storey of the building, inside above a massive old fireplace in the entrance lobby, as well as a particularly fine carved oak fireplace, original to the inn and now found in the family/coach party room. Several other rooms and bars, one featuring a heavily beamed ceiling, are furnished with good eating-height tables and the odd copper or brass ornament. Food orders are made at a leather-topped desk, quoting the number painted on a little stone on your table, from a long menu that runs the gamut from sandwiches or a simple jacket potato to the likes of paupiettes of haddock with prawn sauce and fresh breast of chicken with mushroom sauce. Not to be missed is the Marlborough soup made with vegetables and a proper beef stock. Try to leave room for pudding, too, perhaps a hazelnut tart or a rhubarb crumble. Spacious bedrooms, two doubles and two singles, are modestly but pleasantly furnished with a variety of pieces from the antique-ish and old pine to more modern bedside tables. Each has a few old timbers and sloping floors, and candlewick bedspreads add a homely touch. All except one have compact, lino-floored en-suite shower rooms with toilets; one of the doubles has a proper bathroom. *Open 10-11 (Sun 12-3, 7-10.30).* ***Bar Food*** *12-2.30 (Sun to 2.45), 7-9.30 (Sat to 10). Morning coffee, afternoon and high teas also served.* ***Beer*** *Worthington, Burton Bitter. Garden, patio, outdoor eating. Family room.* ***Accommodation*** *4 bedrooms, all en suite, £50 (single £32.50). No dogs. Pub closed 25 Dec. Access, Amex, Diners, Visa.*

DENT Sun Inn A

Tel 01539 625208 Map 5 D4
Main Street Dent Cumbria LA10 5QL

Right on the cobbled main street and looking out over the parish church towards the Dale's surrounding hills, the Sun is picture postcard pretty outside and postage stamp size within, a shining example of a sadly-dying breed of village local. Dent beers, brewed nearby since 1990, prove a big draw here, and the setting of original timbers, winter log fires and a gravelled beer garden "out back" are all conducive to its enjoyment. Modest accommodation in three bedrooms, all sharing a bathroom. *Open 11-2.30, 7-11 (Fri from 6.15, Sat & school holiday periods 11-11, Sun 12-3, 7-10.30). Free House.* ***Beer*** *Younger's Scotch, Dent Bitter, Ramsbottom Strong Ale & T'Owd Tup stout. Gravelled Beer garden. Access, Visa.*

DERBY Abbey Inn A

Tel 01332 558297 Map 6 C3
Darley Street Darley Abbey Derby Derbyshire DE22 1DX

Probably used for guest accommodation by the monks of the Abbey of St Mary of Darley in the 12th century, this medieval hall-house fell into gradual decay following the monasteries' dissolution in 1538. Fully 440 years elapsed before its restoration again saw the doors open for all to enjoy the Abbey's hospitality. High, exposed roof trusses and hammer beams are a feature of the upper bar whose leaded lights and church pew seating are quite in keeping. Approached by spiral stairs, the cavernous Under Croft Bar plays host to gregarious night-time activity, with folk evenings every other Sunday. The toilets here, though, remain appropriately primitive. *Open 11.30-2.30, 6-11 (Sat 12-2.30, 6-11, Sun 12-3, 7-10.30).* ***Bar Food*** *12-2.30 (except Sun).* ***Beer*** *Sam Smith's Old Brewery & Museum ale. No credit cards.*

DERBY Ye Olde Dolphin Inn A

Tel 01332 349115 Map 6 C3
6/7 Queen Street Derby Derbyshire DE5 1NR

The oldest pub in Derby, dating from the 16th century, in a conveniently central spot in the city centre. No juke box or machines and real open fire. There are four rooms: snug, bar, lounge and the Offilers Bar which is devoted to the former brewery of that name with memorabilia adorning the walls. *Open 10.30-11 (Sun 12-3, 7-10.30).* ***Beer*** *M&B Highgate Mild, Bass, Stones, Worthington, Marston's Pedigree, two guest beers. Patio. Access, Visa.*

DEVIZES — Bear Hotel — FOOD B&B

Tel 01380 722444 Fax 01380 722450 Map 14 C3
The Market Place Devizes Wiltshire SN10 1HS

This famous old town-centre coaching inn has been welcoming guests for over 400 years, including George III accompanied by Queen Charlotte and more recently Harold Macmillan when he was Prime Minister. It is still a comfortable place to visit and stay, for it retains that old-fashioned air within its beamed and panelled lounges and dining-rooms. The main bar, furnished with winged wall settles and plush chairs around a large open fire, opens early, as it is a popular coffee stop for shoppers. Devizes is the home of the Wadworth brewery, so where better to sup a pint or two? Later, at lunchtime, it fills again with people seeking out the popular bar snacks, such as home-made soup, giant Yorkshire pudding with Cheddar, sausage, turkey, Stilton or ham and a range of ploughman's and freshly-cut sandwiches. A further selection of hot and cold dishes – which can also be eaten in the bar – is available in the traditional, oak-panelled Lawrence Room restaurant at lunchtime. More imaginative and substantial meals are served in the Lawrence Room on weekend evenings and at both lunchtime and evening in the more elegant Master Lambton Restaurant. Rambling staircases and a labyrinth of sloping corridors lead to the comfortable and spacious en-suite bedrooms, all of which are equipped, furnished and maintained to a very high standard, as one would expect from a hotel of this standing. Several rooms have four-posters and residents have their own lounge with deep armchairs, sofas and open fires.
Bar open 11-3, 6-11 (Thu-Sat 11-11, Sun 12-3, 7-10.30). ***Bar Food*** *10-2.30, 7-9.30.*
Beer *Wadworth 6X & IPA, guest beer. Patio, outdoor eating. Family room.*
Accommodation *24 bedrooms, all en suite, £70 (single £45). Children welcome overnight (under-5s stay free in parents' room), additional bed (£15) and cot available.*
Pub and accommodation closed 25 & 26 Dec. Access, Visa.

DIGGLE — Diggle Hotel — B&B

Tel 01457 872741 Map 6 C2
Station House Diggle Greater Manchester OL3 5JZ

If approaching from the north on the A670, you'll need to pass the turn-off to the village of Diggle and use the turning circle as left turns are prohibited. Once through the village, watch out for signs for the Diggle Hotel (by the school). The hotel itself, a dark stone building by the railway line, dates back to 1789, and is close to the (disused) longest canal tunnel in Britain, some three and a quarter miles long. Inside, the building is neat and unpretentious. The main room (and adjoining small room where children can sit) is full of polished brass and copperware, and the plain walls decorated with a number of country pictures. One wall has a display of bank notes and coins, both past and present – it's interesting to see how the notes have shrunk (in size and value!) over the years. Over the bar itself there's a collection of photos of the locals. Upstairs there are three neat, unfussy double bedrooms, two of them quite compact, the largest with views towards the village. Modern fitted furniture is used in all rooms, as are duvets with pretty floral covers, and washbasins. The shared and carpeted bathroom also has a separate shower unit. A homely residents' lounge has fawn upholstered seating, books and games. The Mitchell family are friendly and charming hosts, and their staff are equally pleasant. *Open 11-3, 5-11 (Sun 12-3, 7-10.30). Free House.* ***Beer*** *Timothy Taylor's Golden Best & Landlord, Boddingtons OB Mild & Bitter, guest beer. Garden. Family room.* ***Accommodation*** *3 bedrooms, sharing bathroom, £35 (single £25). Children welcome overnight (free if sharing parents' room), additional bed and cot available. No dogs. Access, Amex, Visa.*

DODDISCOMBLEIGH — Nobody Inn — FOOD B&B

Tel 01647 252394 Map 13 D3
Doddiscombleigh nr Exeter Devon EX6 7PS

Zzz...

Difficult to find, but this delightful old village inn is worth the hazardous drive through narrow lanes off the A38 at Haldon Racecourse, 3 miles west of Exeter. According to legend, a previous owner closed and locked the door against the knocking of weary travellers, pretending that there was nobody in, and it has remained the 'Nobody Inn' ever since. The mood is set by a wealth of old beams, ancient settles and a motley collection of antique tables; horse brasses and copper pots and pans decorate the inglenook fireplace, and a real fire burns in winter. The varied and value-for-money bar menu might include sandwiches made with locally-baked malted wheatmeal bread, a home-made coarse duck liver paté with port and herbs and the special Nobody soup made with chicken stock, vegetables and fruit. More substantial dishes appear on the daily-changing blackboard, such

as chicken and apricot pie, Arabian lamb, beef Provençal and for vegetarians stuffed aubergine and vegetable pasta. But ensure you leave room for possibly the best collection of West Country cheeses to be found anywhere. Six different cheeses can be chosen from a selection of up to forty, including cow's, goat's and ewe's milk cheeses, many of them unpasteurised. Their own vegetable garden supplies all the herbs for the kitchen plus globe artichokes and, next year (hopefully!), their first crop of asparagus. The globe-trotting wine list is impressive, featuring over 700 bins. Twenty wines are also offered by the glass and there at least 250 whiskies from which to choose. Four of the modestly comfortably bedrooms are in the inn itself, two with en-suite shower and toilet, plus tea-makers and a drinks tray bearing full bottles of brandy, gin and sherry – charged up by consumption at bar prices. Soundproofing against the noise from the bar is very poor, so those seeking some peace and quiet should book one of the three larger en-suite rooms located in a small, early 17th-century manor house about 150 yards away, next to the church. These are comfortably and traditionally furnished and a ready-to-serve Continental breakfast is provided in the fridge; alternatively, stroll up to the inn for a cooked breakfast. No children under 14. B&B for horses 150yds down the road! *Open 12-2.30 (to 3 Sun), 6-11 (Sun 7-10.30). **Bar Food** 12-2, 7-10. Free House. **Beer** Bass, RCH PG Steam, Branscombe Vale Nobody's, guest beer. Garden, outdoor eating. **Accommodation** 7 bedrooms, 6 en suite (one with bath), £59 (single £23-£35). Children over 14 welcome overnight. Pub & accommodation closed 25 Dec eve. No dogs. Access, Amex, Visa.*

DONINGTON-ON-BAIN — Black Horse — B&B

Tel 01507 343640 Map 7 E2
Main Road Donington-on-Bain Lincolnshire LN11 9TJ

Zzz... ☺

Attractively set in a delightful Wolds village and on the Viking Way walk, this much extended and modernised inn is a popular destination locally and also with visitors seeking comfortable overnight accommodation. Inside, a rambling series of rooms radiate out from the original 18th-century core or snug back bar with its low ceiling (beware of the perilously low central beam) and brick fireplace with log fire. A central inner room is decorated with Viking murals, while numerous horsebrasses and farming implements adorn the simply furnished main area. Rather gloomy dining area and lively public bar and games room. Light and spacious bedrooms are housed in the adjacent "motel-style" block and feature modern pine furnishings, wicker chairs, pretty fabrics and extras like remote-controlled TV and tea-makers. Spotless, compact en-suite facilities with efficient showers. Wheelchair access. The Black Horse is also a favourite with families as children are made very welcome in the mural room and adjacent dining-room, where they can order from their own menu and enjoy an early evening meal if staying overnight. Two high-chairs and a changing shelf in the Ladies may make life easier for parents. Summer days can be enjoyed in the safe rear garden where youngsters can let off steam on the swings, slide and climbing frame. *Open 11.30-3, 7-11. Free House. **Beer** Courage Directors, Ruddles Best Bitter, John Smith's Bitter, guest beers. Garden, children's play area. Family room. **Accommodation** 8 bedrooms, all en suite with showers, £40 (single £25). Children welcome overnight (price varies depending on age), additional bed and cot available. Access, Visa.*

DORCHESTER — Kings Arms — B&B

Tel 01305 265353 **Fax 01305 260269** Map 13 F2
30 High East Street Dorchester Dorset DT1 1HF

A substantial Georgian inn dominating the busy main street of this attractive county town, famous for its associations with the author Thomas Hardy, who resided in the nearby village of Lower Bockhampton. Locals fill the comfortable, low-ceilinged bar, while good-value overnight accommodation is proving popular among businessmen, families on the move (each room sleeps two adults and two children under 16) and tourists following the Hardy trail. Bedrooms are uniformly decorated in restful pastel colours and floral fabrics, with easy chairs and well-equipped bathrooms (all with bath/shower) enhancing a relaxing stay, although bow-fronted rooms overlooking the High Street could suffer from traffic noise. Tea-makers, satellite TV, trouser press, hairdryer and telephone are standard extras. Residents' lounge. Premier Lodge (part of Greenall's). *Open 11-3, 6-11, Fri & Sat 11-11, Sun 12-3, 7-10.30. **Beer** Wadworth 6X, Marston's Pedigree, Boddingtons, Flowers Original, Bass, Courage Directors. **Accommodation** 31 rooms, all en suite, £39.95 excluding breakfast (Fri-Sun £32.50) Children welcome overnight, under-12s share parents' room free (two family rooms), cot available. No dogs. Access, Amex, Visa.*

Dorchester-on-Thames — George Hotel — B&B

Tel 01865 340404 **Fax 01865 341620** Map 14a C3
High Street Dorchester-on-Thames Oxfordshire OX10 7HH

With a history spanning more than 500 years, the George is one of the oldest inns in the land. Focal point of the public area is a fine beamed bar. Bedrooms in the main building have a solid, old-fashioned feel, some cosy and snug under oak beams, two with solid four-posters. Other rooms have less character but are still very adequate. *Open 11-3, 6-11 (Sun 12-3, 7-10.30). Free House.* ***Beer*** *Brakspear Bitter, guest beer. Garden.* ***Accommodation*** *17 bedrooms, all en suite, £70 (single £55). Children welcome overnight, additional bed (£10) and cot (£5) available. Access, Amex, Diners, Visa.*

Dorstone — Pandy Inn — FOOD

Tel 01981 550273 Map 9 D5
Dorstone Golden Valley Hereford & Worcester HR3 6AN

The Pandy (located off the B4348) is the oldest inn in Herefordshire. It was built in 1185 by Richard De Brito, a Norman knight, to house his workers while building Dorstone Church as atonement for his part in the murder of Thomas Becket. Vegetarians are well catered for with a variety of dishes to choose from including cheesy vegetable bake and spinach and mushroom lasagne. Sandwiches and ploughman's platters are offered at lunchtime only. Fresh fish from Cornwall features on Fridays – plaice, scampi, king prawns, sewin. Among the 'Light Bites & Starters' on the menu are crispy whitebait and deep-fried Camembert. Follow with one of the 'House Specialities' – perhaps garlic chicken, wild rabbit pie or the 'greedy gammon, with as many eggs as you can eat'. Finally, choose one of the dozen or so desserts (mostly home-made) on the 'Puddings & Treats' menu which includes locally-made sheep's milk ice cream in some unusual flavours. Lawned garden with swing for children. ***Bar Food*** *12-2, 7-10. Free House.* ***Beer*** *Bass, Felinfoel Double Dragon, Smiles Best Bitter, Hook Norton, Wye Valley Dorothy Goodbody seasonal ales. Garden, outdoor eating. Pub closed Mon lunchtime and all day Tue Nov-Easter. No credit cards.*

Downham — Assheton Arms — FOOD

Tel 01200 441227 Map 6 B1
Downham nr Clitheroe Lancashire BB7 4BJ

The pub's unusual name commemorates the Assheton family, Earls of Clitheroe and landlords of the entire village since 1558. Standing at its head by the church and surrounded by picturesque stone cottages, the village local retains a cheerfully warm, traditional air. Single bar and sectioned rooms house an array of solid oak tables, wing-back settees and window seats. There's no mystery, either, attached to the food, ordered at a separate counter where the kitchen is in full view. Predictable starters run through ham and vegetable broth, and Stilton paté. Grills of plaice or steaks and treacle sponge and custard follow familiar lines. Sandwiches and ploughman's platters are available all day. Herring pieces in dill and beef Madras extend the snack range on a specials board whose main courses have a generally fishy emphasis: poached salmon with prawn and cucumber sauce or a crab thermidor show the kitchen at its best. *Open 12-3, 7-11 (Sun 12-3, 7-10.30).* ***Bar Food*** *12-2, 7-10.* ***Beer*** *Boddingtons, Castle Eden Best, Flowers Original. Patio, outdoor eating. Family room. Access, Amex, Visa.*

Drakeholes — Griff Inn — FOOD — B&B

Tel 01777 817206 Map 7 D2
Drakeholes near Bawtry Nottinghamshire

Less a hamlet than a multiple road junction, where the A631 meets the B6045, Drakeholes marks a right-angle turn on the Chesterfield canal where it tunnels for 150 yards under the road system. Standing above the basin, fronted by a large patio and canalside picnic tables, the Griff (once known as the White Swan) is built in the same distinctive red brick which characterises the estate village (both shopless and publess) of nearby Wiseton Hall. The 18th-century inn's interior echoes the grand style of an earlier age, with its marble-floored entrance foyer and bar, and intimate oak-panelled cocktail lounge. Grand eating is not, however, de rigueur, the extensive bar menu encompassing old-fashioned pies like chicken and mushroom, sandwiches, ploughman's platters, lasagne and a seafood platter. There is a carvery every day at lunchtime and from 5.30-8pm. The restaurant combines table d'hote and a Sunday lunch with an ambitious à la carte. The Griff is certainly useful to know for a quiet country stay in the Idle valley. Bedrooms are neatly appointed in pastel shades and varnished pine, which create a cottagey effect without frill or particular luxury. There are

televisions but no phones. En-suite bathrooms are spacious and airy with good, powerful showers for early morning invigoration prior to a substantial country breakfast. *Open 11.30-3, 5.30-11 (Sun 12-3, 7-10.30). **Bar Food** 11.30-2.15, 5.30-10 (Sun 12-2.30, 7-9.30). Free House. **Beer** Castle Eden, Boddingtons, Flowers IPA. Garden, outdoor eating. **Accommodation** 3 bedrooms, all en suite, £50 (single £35). Children welcome overnight (£7.50 if sharing parents' room), additional bed and cot available. Check-in by arrangement. No dogs. Pub closed in winter all Mon and Sun eve. Access, Visa.*

DRAYTON The Roebuck FOOD B&B

Tel 01295 730542 Map 14a B1
Drayton nr Banbury Oxfordshire OX15 6EN

Standing next to the A422 about a mile from Banbury is an attractive 16th-century stone pub which has built up a strong local following for its excellent food. The low-beamed bars with their rough, painted walls and solid wooden tables provide a cosily atmospheric setting for everything from the 'Roebuck Special' (fresh cold ham off the bone) to deep-fried Brie wedges with salad, grilled lemon sole in butter, scampi provençale and cracked wheat casserole. The specials board, where you might find a home-made soup, a daily pasta dish or curry, also does good business. Sandwiches and ploughman's platters also available. There are two neat bedrooms with up-to-date furniture, one with exposed beams and a sloping ceiling. They share a functional shower room and are both equipped with remote-control TVs, tea-makers and magazines. No dogs. *Open 11-3, 6-11 (Sun 12-3, 7-10.30). **Bar Food** 11.30-2 (Sun from 12), 7-9.45 (no food Sun eve). Free House. **Beer** Hook Norton, Boddingtons, Fuller's London Pride, Tetley, guest beer. Patio. **Accommodation** 2 bedrooms with shared shower room, £35 (£25 single). **Accommodation** closed last 3 weeks in December. Access, Visa.*

DRIFFIELD Bell Hotel B&B

Tel 01377 256661 Fax 01377 253228 Map 7 E1
Market Place Driffield Humberside YO25 7AP

Period charm and modern amenities combine in a coaching inn that's more than 250 years old, but now very much a hotel. Conference and function facilities are in the restored Old Town Hall, and further conversion houses a leisure complex. Day rooms include the 18th-century wood-panelled Oak Room, the flagstoned Old Corn Exchange buffet/bar and a residents' lounge. Bedrooms boast antique furniture and up-to-date comforts. No children under 12. The 20 acres of gardens (800yds away from the hotel) have been developed over the last year, providing both formal gardens and mixed wetland; deer may be introduced and there is trout fishing on Driffield Beck. *Open 11-2, 6-11 (Sun 12-3, 7-10.30). Free House. **Beer** four regularly-changing real ales. Garden, indoor swimming pool, spa bath, steam room, sauna, solarium, squash. **Accommodation** 14 bedrooms, all en suite, £75 (single £55). Children over 12 welcome overnight. No dogs. Access, Amex, Diners, Visa.*

DRONFIELD Old Sidings FOOD

Tel 01246 410023 Map 6 C2
91 Chesterfield Road Dronfield Derbyshire S18 6XE

Tucked roadside by a bridge on the main Sheffield railway line, there's nothing particularly pretty about the Old Sidings, although extensive refurbishments have spruced up the interior with the installation of wood panelling and even more railway paraphernalia.
Vast menus signal the galley's intentions, with plenty of goods on which to stoke up.
Once aboard, the special Shunters menu and Buffet Car dining are just the ticket. Sunday lunch is popular (half price for children). Eight wines served by the glass. *Open 12-11 (Sun 12-3, 7-10.30). **Bar Food** 12-2.30 (Sun to 2), 6-8.30 (Sun from 7). Free House. **Beer** Stones, Worthington, Highgate Dark, Hancock's HB, Bass. Patio. Access, Diners, Visa.*

DUDDINGTON Royal Oak Hotel B&B

Tel 01780 444267 Map 7 E4
Duddington nr Stamford Lincolnshire PE9 3QE

Zzz...

Popular, small family-run hotel set beside the A43 Stamford to Corby road at the end of this charming village. The bar is modern, but by no means without character, due in part to plush banquette seating, lots of greenery and well-lit prints of Victorian scenes. Comfortable overnight accommodation in six decent-sized rooms, attractively done out in pastel shades and floral wallpapers, have antique-style reproduction pieces, Victorian prints and good beds

with brass bedsteads. TVs, phones and tea-makers are standard and the clean, carpeted shower rooms (one with bath) are fully tiled. Handy stopover point for weary travellers heading north or south. *Open 10.30-3, 6-11 (Sun 12-2, 7-10.30). Free House.* ***Beer*** *Ruddles County, John Smith's, Webster's Yorkshire. Garden.* ***Accommodation*** *6 bedrooms, all en suite (five with shower), £40/£45 (single £28.50). Children welcome overnight, additional bed (£8) available. Dogs by arrangement. Access, Amex, Visa.*

DUMMER — The Queen — FOOD

Tel 01256 397367 Map 14a C4

Dummer nr Basingstoke Hampshire RG22 2AD

Handy for M3 travellers, this attractive whitewashed inn is set in an equally pretty and up-market village, less than a mile from Junction 7. The neat, low-ceilinged and softly-lit bar area is open-plan in style, with several brick and wall partitions creating cosy alcoves and a small, intimate dining area. A printed bar menu highlights some good favourites, ranging from pasta dishes, hearty burgers, steaks and omelettes to gigantic freshly-made sandwiches served with salad and crisps. More imaginative fare features on the daily-changing blackboard: poached Scotch salmon with asparagus, lamb cutlets in rosemary sauce, cod in beer batter with chips, or the ever-popular home-made steak and kidney pudding, all served with a generous selection of vegetables. A good-value 4-course lunch is available on Sundays. The rear sun-trap terrace and lawn with benches is ideal for summer eating. Live music Sunday eves. *Open 11-3, 5.30-11 (Sun 12-3, 7-10.30).* ***Bar Food*** *12-2.30, 6-10 (Sun 12-2.30, 7-10).* ***Beer*** *Courage Best & Directors, two guest beers. Garden, outdoor eating. Access, Amex, Diners, Visa.*

DUNBRIDGE — Mill Arms Inn — FOOD

Tel 01794 340401 Map 14 C3

Dunbridge nr Romsey Hampshire SO51 0LF

🍷

Cream- and green-painted village pub opposite the Mottisfont (Dunbridge) railway station. Dark blue banquettes and lots of greenery share the bar with fruit and quiz machines and there are tables outside in the garden when the weather is kind. A skittle alley to the rear (for pre-booked groups only) has a new pine bar and country-style decor with red gingham table cloths and curtains. A nicely varied blackboard bar menu ranges from sandwiches, steak and kidney pie and soup of the day to moules marinière and an individual Bailey's Irish Cream cheesecake that popular demand has made a permanent feature. Over a dozen wines are available by the glass. The separate restaurant is included in our *1996 Hotels & Restaurants Guide. Open 11-3, 6-11 (Sun 12-3, 7-10.30).* ***Bar Food*** *12-2.15 (Sun to 2.30), 7-10 (Fri & Sat to 10.30). Free House.* ***Beer*** *Ruddles County, Hampshire Brewery King Alfred's & Lionheart, John Smith's. Garden, outdoor eating. Access, Amex, Diners, Visa.*

DUNSTAN — Cottage Inn — B&B

Tel 01665 576658 Map 5 D1

Dunstan nr Alnwick Northumberland WE66 3SZ

Purchased as a row of derelict cottages by Lawrence & Shirley Jobling in 1975, reconstruction into quite a modest guest house preceeded their finally opening the Cottage Inn as a pub in 1988. Central to the entire conversion, and fully visible in the bar, is the three-foot thick orchard wall of Craster Tower, which stands on the fringe of the pub's 8-acre wooded garden. In front, facing Dunstan's only street, are several self-contained apartments (available for weekly lets) while to the rear the wing of ground-floor bedrooms faces a garden of pine and poplar, with dovecote and abundant wild-life. Fully equipped with baths and showers, all are equipped with TVs, room phones and coffee-making equipment. In between are the clubby bar, games room and a wealth of memorabilia in the Harry Hotspur Room. Both children and wheelchair users are particularly well-catered for. Hearty breakfasts are served in the bright, flower-filled conservatory. *Open 11-3, 6-11 (Sun 12-3, 7-10.30). Free House.* ***Beer*** *Ruddles Best, Theakston Best. Garden. Family room.* ***Accommodation*** *10 rooms, all en suite, £57 (single £35). Access, Visa.*

Many **B&B** establishments offer reduced rates for weekend and out-of-season bookings. Always ask about special deals for longer stays. Beware half-board terms in inns where we do not recommend the **FOOD.**

DUNWICH **Ship Inn** FOOD

Tel 01728 648219 **Fax 01728 648675** Map 10 D2 
St James Street Dunwich Suffolk IP17 3DT

Well-loved old smugglers' inn overlooking the salt marshes and sea in a peaceful coastal hamlet – 2½ miles off B1125 at Westleton – and popular with walkers and birdwatchers from the nearby RSPB Minsmere reserve. The delightful unspoilt public bar offers nautical bric-a-brac, a wood-burning stove in a huge brick fireplace, flagged floors and simple wooden furnishings. There's also a plain carpeted dining-room and a conservatory room for families. The welcoming and enthusiastic owners – Stephen and Ann Marshlain – have been at the helm here for over 10 years now and offer good, simple food; the restaurant menu applies throughout the pub in the evenings; bar meals at lunchtime only. For lunch, choose home-made soup, chicken and mushroom pie or prawn ploughman's from the galley chilled servery and in the evenings maybe sardines marinaded in a citrus dressing, the locally renowned Dunwich fish'n'chips (always available) or Ship's seafood pancake from the printed menu. Finish off with home-made desserts, such as boozy bread-and-butter pudding, apple crumble and apple and cider flan. Beyond the bars a fine Victorian staircase leads to simple cottagey bedrooms, which are light and clean with pretty fabrics, period features and splendid views from leaded pane windows. Summer imbibing on a sheltered paved yard (resplendent in summer with hanging baskets and flowering tubs) and in the very secure garden surrounded by a hedge. No children in the bar. *Open 11-3, 6-11 (Sun 12-3, 7-10.30). Free House.* ***Bar Meals*** *12-2, 7.30-9.30. Family Room.* ***Beer*** *Adnams Southwold & Broadside, Greene King Abbot Ale. Garden, outdoor eating.* ***Accommodation*** *5 bedrooms, 1 en suite, £54 (not en suite £44, single £22). Children welcome overnight, additional bed (£10) and cot supplied. Check-in by arrangement. Access, Visa.*

DUXFORD **John Barleycorn** FOOD

Tel 01223 832699 Map 10 B3
Moorfield Road Duxford Cambridge CB2 4PP

Tucked at the far end of the village, a mile from the A1301, this well-kept, 17th-century thatched pub is resplendant with hanging baskets, tubs and borders in high summer. Delightful, single low-beamed and softly-lit bar with a rustic mix of country furniture, large brick fireplace and neatly decorated with plates, horse harnesses and tasteful prints. A comfortable, relaxing and uncluttered bar and an ideal venue in which to enjoy a hearty home-cooked meal from a short list of dishes. Good favourites – ploughman's, salads, grills served with mange tout or salad and new potatoes – plus substantial choices like roast guinea fowl, Irish stew or venison pie and smoked haddock with poached eggs. Interesting open sandwiches – hot black pudding with gooseberries. Summer alfresco eating on the rear patio with additional seating in the converted barn. No under-14s in the bar. *Open 12-2.30, 6.30-11 (Sun 12-2.30, 7-10.30).* ***Bar Food*** *12-2, 6.30-10 (Sun 7-10).* ***Beer*** *Greene King. Garden, outdoor eating. Access, Visa.*

EASINGTON **Mole & Chicken** FOOD

Tel 01844 208387 Map 15a D2
Easington Aylesbury Buckinghamshire HP18 9EY

Between Junction 7 of the M40 and Aylesbury; take the B4011 from Thame past Long Crendon (2 miles), following the Chilton road outside the village and turn left at the top of Carters Lane (opposite the Chandos Arms), then straight on for half a mile. This pretty pub boasts truly magnificent views of the Oxfordshire/Buckinghamshire countryside. Inside, the rag-washed walls are hung with hunting prints and candle lighting; a low, beamed ceiling and hand-painted floor in the Tuscany style are complemented by two roaring log fires. There's seating for 60 people at oak and pine tables, and half a ton of French oak on bricks forms the attractive bar. Good, home-cooked food such as baked sweet pepper with mixed cheeses, fusilli pasta with a choice of sauces, interesting warm salads (monkfish and bacon with a walnut pesto dressing), half a Norfolk duckling with "undoubtedly the best orange sauce in the world", Thai prawn curry, ham with two fried eggs and shoestring chips, chargrilled steaks and fresh fish – an eclectic selection if ever there was one. Hot and cold desserts are home-made. *Open 11-3.30, 6-12 (Sun 12-3, 7-10.30).* ***Bar Food*** *12-2, 6.30-10 (Sun 12-9.30). Free House.* ***Beer*** *Hook Norton, Morland IPA & Old Speckled Hen. Garden, outdoor eating. Access, Amex, Visa.*

EAST CHALDON — Sailors Return — FOOD

Tel 01305 853847 Map 14 B4

East Chaldon Dorchester Dorset DT2 8DN

Two good reasons for tracking down this isolated and charming pub: to enjoy the glorious peaceful views across the village and beyond to the Purbeck Hills and to try the good range of home-cooked bar food on offer. Originally an 18th-century thatched cottage, it has been well extended at either end, providing a comfortable dining area and a larger bar area, complete with barn-type roof, old timbers, ropes, floats and lobster pots – not a fruit machine in sight!. Old flagstones maintain the character of the rustic core, which comprises two low-ceilinged interconnecting rooms, furnished with scrubbed pine tables. Also sited here is the large blackboard menu listing the wide range of good-value bar food. The home-cooked daily specials – fresh fish, pies and casseroles – are the best bet. These may include pork, celery and apricot casserole, Lancashire hot-pot, steak and Guinness pie and a freshly prepared soup. Fish choices such as black bream, cod fillet and whole plaice are served with chips, although a selection of vegetables can be requested. Steaks ranging from 8oz to 24oz are very popular here. Alfresco diners are spoilt for choice with a front bench-filled terrace with uninterrupted views and a sheltered rear garden to choose from.
Open 11-2.30, 6.30-11 (Sun 12-2.30, 7-10.30). ***Bar Food*** *12-2, 7-9 (Fri & Sat to 9.30). Free House.* ***Beer*** *Wadworth 6X, Whitbread Strong Country, Hook Norton Old Hooky, guest beers. Garden, terraced area, outdoor eating. No credit cards.*

> We only recommend food (Bar Food) in those establishments highlighted with the **FOOD** symbol.

EAST DEREHAM — Kings Head Hotel — B&B

Tel 01362 693842 **Fax 01362 693776** Map 10 C1

Norwich Road East Dereham Norfolk NR19 1AD

Now under its second set of owners within the last two years, this modest 17th-century coaching inn is near the town centre. A cosy red-carpeted bar, busy with locals, looks out past the patio to an attractive, lawned family garden set with tables and chairs. Spotless bedrooms have tasteful, darkwood furniture and pretty fabrics. Five rooms are located in the light and airy converted stable block; the remainder are in the main building. All offer TV, clock-radio, direct-dial telephones and tea-making kits and twelve have neat en-suite facilities. Two large rooms have an extra bed and further beds and cots are available at a small charge. A grass tennis court is available for residents and locals (booking required).
Open 11-3, 6-11 (12-3, 7-10.30 Sun). Free House. ***Beer*** *John Smith's, Adnams, guest beer. Garden, outdoor eating.* ***Accommodation*** *17 bedrooms, 12 en suite, £40-£50 (single £25-£40). Children welcome overnight (high-chair and cot available). Access, Amex, Diners, Visa.*

EAST GARSTON — Queens Arms Hotel — B&B

Tel 01488 648757 Map 14a B4

Newbury Road East Garston nr Newbury Berkshire RG16 7ET

Set in the heart of horse-country and frequented by an assortment of stable lads, well known jockeys and prominent trainers, this modernised and extended rural inn is a good base from which to explore the scenic Lambourn valley, or for those keen race goers attending the Newbury meeting. It is also a convenient stopover for M4 travellers, with J14 only 3½ miles distant. Bedrooms are clean and comfortable with simple limed fitted furniture, modern co-ordinating fabrics and an attractive pastel decor. Well-fitted, tiled bathrooms or compact shower rooms. All boast TVs, telephones, trouser presses and tea-makers for added comfort. Relaxing, wood-panelled bar and adjoining restaurant.
Open 11-11 (Sun 12-3, 7-10.30). No real ales. Garden, children's play area. ***Accommodation*** *13 bedrooms, all en suite (four with bath), £42.50-£47.50 (single £27.50-£35). Children welcome overnight (under-3s stay free in parents' room), additional bed and cot available. No dogs. Access, Visa.*

> We do not accept free meals or hospitality – our inspectors pay their own bills and **never** book in the name of Egon Ronay's Guides.

EAST HADDON — Red Lion Hotel — FOOD B&B

Tel 01604 770223 **Fax 01604 770767** Map 15 D1
East Haddon Northamptonshire NN6 8BU

Thatch-roofed little hotel built of golden stone in a country location seven miles from Junction 18 of the M1. Pleasant, relaxing lounge bar with a mix of furnishings, china and pewter, smaller, plainer public bar. Recommended for its cottagey, well-kept bedrooms (two twins, two doubles and a single; all en suite with shower plus two bathrooms available to share); TVs, phones and beverage facilities are all provided. Sunday lunch (£13.95) offers a good choice, as does the long, handwritten list of bar food: home-made stockpot soup, sandwiches, grilled sardines, home-made paté, fishcakes, individual cottage pie, Lincolnshire sausages and mash with onion gravy, cold meat platter with bubble and squeak (or chips) and pickles – "everything is home-made except the mayonnaise". Leave plenty of room for homely puddings like bread-and butter pudding, sherry trifle and chocolate roulade. No dogs in rooms, but kennels are provided. *Open 11-2.30, 6-11 (Sun 12-2.30, 7-10.30). **Bar Food** 12.15-2, 7-9.30. No **Bar Food** Sun eve. **Beer** Charles Wells Eagle & Bombardier & up to five guest beers. Garden. **Accommodation** 5 bedrooms, £59 (single £42). Children welcome overnight (under-4s stay free in parent's room, 5-12s ½-price), additional bed and cot available. Check-in by arrangement. No dogs. Access, Amex, Diners, Visa.*

EAST ILSLEY — The Swan — B&B

Tel 01635 281238 **Fax 01635 281791** Map 14a C3
East Ilsley nr Newbury Berkshire RG16 0LF

A well-run, friendly family pub at the heart of an attractive Berkshire village: turn off the A34 just 3 miles north of the M4, Junction 13. The Swan is operated by Morlands, the brewers from nearby West Ilsley, and by the bar is posted a record of their landlords, unbroken since 1865. The pub, however, was a coaching inn in the early 1700s and despite today's open-plan interior many original features remain within its many rooms and alcoves, alongside collections of brewery artefacts, cartoons, local photographs and miniature bottles which have been accumulated over the years. Residents overnight enjoy the best of the old building's charm in carefully modernised bedrooms, now all en suite and neatly equipped with beverage trays, colour TVs and direct-dial phones – two are non-smoking. In summer, the trellised rear patio is a picturesque spot where parents can sit while the children let off steam in the adjacent garden. *Open 10.30-2.30, 6-11 (Sun 12-3, 7-10.30). **Beer** Morland, guest beer. Family room, patio, garden and play area. **Accommodation** 10 rooms, all en suite (three with bath), £45 (single £32.50/£36). Children welcome overnight, additional bed (£5). Check-in by arrangement. Access, Visa.*

EAST MEON — Ye Olde George Inn — FOOD B&B

Tel & Fax 01730 823481 Map 15 D3
East Meon Hampshire GU32 1NH

Originally two cottages, the oldest part of the Olde George dates back to the 15th century. Situated close to the church and beside the River Meon in the village centre, it has been welcoming customers for over 300 years. Four inglenooks, a wealth of heavy beams, bare brick walls and an assortment of sturdy scrubbed tables characterise the rambling bar and attractive adjacent restaurant. The unusual horseshoe-shaped bar dispenses well-conditioned ales and a selection of country wines, while the kitchen produces an interesting range of home-cooked bar food. The printed menu items include home-baked ham, egg and chips, vegetarian enchilada, sardines in garlic butter, fisherman's pie and the usual sandwiches and filled jacket potatoes. Daily specials listed on a board might feature up to four freshly-made soups, chicken and bacon pie, seafood lasagne, salmon and tarragon quiche and wild mushrooms in filo pastry with a tomato and coriander coulis. Good puddings. Cream teas are served all week in summer and at weekends in winter. Upstairs, five simply-furnished, good-sized rooms are clean, light and airy with the usual comforts of TV, tea-making kits and standard en-suite facilities. *Open 11-11 (Sun 12-3, 7-10.30). **Bar Food** 12-2.30, 7-10. Free House. **Beer** Greene King Abbot, Flowers Original, Bass. Patio, outdoor eating. **Accommodation** 5 bedrooms, all en suite, £50, single £27.50. Children welcome overnight (under-3s free in parents' room, 3-14s half-price), additional bed available. Access, Amex, Visa.*

EAST WITTON Blue Lion FOOD

Tel 01969 624273 **Fax 01969 624189** Map 5 D4 **B&B**
East Witton nr Leyburn North Yorkshire DL8 4SN

Zzz...

At the gateway to Coverdale and Wensleydale, East Witton stands on the A6108 just a mile from the Cover Bridge. The rather stern-looking, stone-built Blue Lion, originally a coaching inn in the 19th century, has recently been sympathetically restored to former glories, yet retaining its truly evocative mood. The single bar faces a huge stone fireplace where a log fire burns year-round. Here the blackboards might offer duck and pork terrine, confit of duck on potato and black pudding galette or scorched king scallops with sun-dried tomato butter to start, following with main courses of baked fillet of halibut with spicy crab topping, roast fillet of salmon with caramelised onions, tomato and ginger butter sauce, a warm salad of duck confit, ham shank and Toulouse sausage or confit of lamb shoulder baked in filo pastry with a pearl barley, tomato and onion gravy. Sandwiches and ploughman's platter may be available at lunchtime, but, in general, this is serious, upmarket pub dining. For residents, the dining-room at night is candle-lit and intimate. Bedrooms are all individually furnished, with a mixture of period furniture and state-of-the-art additions such as remote-control TVs. En-suite bathrooms are more than adequate, while comfort and commensurate privacy are ensured by the lack of any telephones. *Open 11am-11pm (Sun 12-3, 7-10.30). **Bar Food** 12-2, 7-9.30. Free House. **Beer** Theakston Best & Old Peculier, Boddingtons, guest beer. Garden, outdoor eating. **Accommodation** 9 bedrooms, all en suite, £70 (£39.50 single). Children welcome overnight, additional bed (£5) and cot (£5) available. Access, Visa.*

EASTGATE Ratcatchers Inn FOOD

Tel 01603 871430 Map 10 C1
Eastgate nr Cawston Norfolk NR10 4HA

A pleasantly old-fashioned free house, dating from 1861, standing in a rural spot just off the B1149 one mile south of Cawston. A warm and friendly atmosphere pervades the neatly furnished bar and restaurant areas which are both laid up for diners, for food is very much the thing here. The appeal is the extensive range of home-cooked meals listed in a veritable tome of a menu, a 14-page epic of jokily-named dishes. Nevertheless, additional imaginative daily specials and a packed pub – it is advisable to book – instills confidence in the enthusiastic kitchen. Use of fresh local produce is clearly evident – fish from Lowestoft, shellfish direct from the North Norfolk coast, produce from local smokehouses and naturally-aged cuts of meat from a nearby butcher. The 'home-made' policy extends to freshly-baked bread, herb oils, chutneys, stocks and pickled samphire plus the use of fresh herbs from the garden. Fish comes in a variety of forms (monkfish in beer batter deep-fried with a caper and gherkin sauce, Dover sole) and dipping into the menu might reveal steak and kidney pie served with either a short-crust or puff-pastry top, moussaka, salads, doorstep sandwiches, at least 15 vegetarian, vegan or diabetic options, plus grills named after film stars. Specials may include thick ham and lentil soup, crab pancake and peppered chicken. Home-made puddings have Dickensian titles like Faversham's Favourite (summer pudding). Separate cheese menu listing twelve varieties, six of them British. An interesting list of wines has at least a dozen available by the glass. *Open 11.45-2.30, 5.45-11 (Sun 12-3, 7-10.30). Free House. **Bar Food** 11.45-2, 6-10.15 (Sun 12-2, 7-9.45). **Beer** Hancock's Best Bitter, Bass, Adnams Extra. Garden, outdoor eating. No credit cards.*

EASTLING Carpenter's Arms FOOD

Tel 01795 890234 **Fax 01795 890654** Map 11 C5 **B&B**
The Street Eastling nr Faversham Kent ME13 0AZ

The mellow redbrick Carpenter's Arms dates back to the 14th-century and can be found on the edge of a sleepy village, eight miles southwest of Faversham on the backslope of the North Downs. Character interior with two inglenook fireplaces – one in the charming bar and another in the cosy, brick-floored restaurant which has an old baking oven; corn dollies decorate the old timbers and beams, and a host of flowers and pot plants add a homely touch. The short and simple bar menu lists a hearty home-made soup, steak and kidney pie with vegetables and lamb casserole, and a few standard snacks such as burgers, carpenter's lunch and countryman's lunch (ploughman's with ½lb spicy Kent sausage). Popular for fish'n'chips on Fridays. Next door in a typically Kentish white clapperboard house, reached via its own old brick path, are three peaceful bedrooms, two of them rather on the small side with shower cabinets and toilets en suite. The best room is much more spacious with

a full en-suite bathroom. All have the same floral curtains, which contrast rather oddly with abstract patterned duvets, as well as TVs and radio alarms. Good breakfasts are served in the restaurant. Children over 7 are welcome in the restaurant only. *Open 11-4, 6-11 (Sun 12-3, 7-10.30), all day in summer.* ***Bar Food*** *11.30-2.30 (Sun to 1.30), 6.30-10.30. No* ***Bar Food*** *Sunday eve. No under-14s allowed in bar.* ***Beer*** *Shepherd Neame. Lawned garden, outdoor eating area, summer barbecue.* ***Accommodation*** *3 bedrooms, all en suite, £45 (single £35). Children over 12 welcome overnight (no extra bed supplied). No dogs. Access, Amex, Visa.*

EASTON-ON-THE-HILL Exeter Arms FOOD

Tel 01780 57503 Map 7 E4
Stamford Road Easton-on-the-Hill nr Stamford Northamptonshire PE9 3NS

Weather-worn, white-painted old inn set beside the A43, two miles south-west of Stamford. Charming open-plan interior, the single, knocked-through bar being tastefully decorated in deep terracotta and green with a good mix of wooden furnishings, quality watercolours and prints, plenty of greenery and light classical music enhancing the relaxed atmosphere. Chef/proprietor David Waycott says that he has gone up a gear since our most recent visit and now claims to be more of a restaurant than a dining pub. One menu is served throughout, but the regularly-changing chalkboard offers the likes of eight or nine choices of fish and other seafood. These are proving the most popular and might include Cromer crab, lemon sole, sea bass or seafood pasta. *Open 12-3, 7-10 (Sun 12-3, 7-10.30).* ***Bar Food*** *12-2.* ***Beer*** *Courage Directors. Access, Visa.*

EBBESBOURNE WAKE Horseshoes Inn FOOD B&B

Tel 01722 780474 Map 14 B3
Ebbesbourne Wake nr Salisbury Wiltshire SP5 5JF

Zzz...

The Ebble valley and more especially the village of Ebbesbourne Wake seem to have escaped the hustle and bustle of modern day life, as it nestles among the folds in the Downs, close to the infant River Ebble. This peaceful unspoilt rural charm is reflected in the village inn that has been run "as a proper country pub" by the Bath family for over 20 years. Its 17th-century brick facade is adorned with climbing roses and honeysuckle, while inside the traditional layout of two bars around a central servery still survives. The main bar is festooned with an array of old farming implements and country bygones and a mix of simple furniture fronts the open log fire. Well-kept real ales are served straight from the cask and both local farm cider and free-range eggs are also sold across the bar. Bar food is good value and homely, the best choice being the freshly-prepared dishes that are chalked up on the blackboard menu, featuring chicken and ham pie served with plenty of crisp vegetables, home-made ham quiche, venison sausage casserole and steak and kidney pie. The standard printed menu highlights the range of sandwiches, ploughman's and other hot dishes. The set 3-course Sunday lunch is superb value for money, extremely popular and served throughout (booking necessary). The flower- and shrub-filled garden is perfect for summer alfresco eating and safe for children, who also have access to view the four goats and pot-bellied pig in the pets area. Those wanting to explore this tranquil area further can stay overnight in one of the two modest bedrooms at either end of the inn; both are decorated in a cottagey style with pretty fabrics and wallpaper and have TVs, tea-making kits and their own private facilities. A peaceful night's sleep is guaranteed. *Open 11.30-3, 6.30-11, (Sun 12-3, 7-10.30).* ***Bar Food*** *12-2, 7-9 (Sat to 9.30). Free House.* ***Beer*** *Adnams Broadside, Wadworth 6X, Ringwood Best, guest beer. Garden, outdoor eating, pet area.* ***Accommodation*** *2 bedrooms, both en suite (one with bath), £40 (single £25). Children welcome overnight, (under-2s stay free in parents' room, 3-12s by arrangement), additional bed and cot available. No credit cards.*

ECCLESHALL St George Hotel B&B

Tel 01785 850300 **Fax 01785 861452** Map 6 B3
Castle Street Eccleshall Staffordshire ST21 6DF

A carefully restored 250-year-old coaching inn which enjoys a central crossroad position in Eccleshall. The oak-beamed bar, which is open all day, has an opaque glass 'smoke room' panel and red-brick inglenook, and there is also a relaxing little lounge. Cottage-style bedrooms, many with open fires, exposed beams with vaulted ceilings and canopied or four-poster beds, are thoughtfully equipped and all have private facilities. A micro brewery was set up in May 1995 and they now brew their own Slater's Ales: bitter (3.6%), original (4%) and premium (4.4%). *Bar open 11-11, Sun 12-3, 7-10.30. Free House.* ***Beer*** *Slater's Ales, two guest beers.* ***Accommodation*** *10 bedrooms, all en suite, £65, (single £45), weekend reductions (£25 per person Fri-Sun). Children welcome overnight (under-8s share parents' room free), additional bed and cot available. Access, Amex, Diners, Visa.*

EDBURTON — Tottington Manor — FOOD B&B

Tel 01903 815757 **Fax 01903 879331** Map 11 B6
Edburton nr Henfield West Sussex BN5 9JL

Zzz...

A 17th-century Grade II listed inn-cum-hotel in its own grounds at the foot of the South Downs, with lovely views. The bar is simple and properly pubby with country furniture and an open fire and an adjacent comfortably furnished lounge is used for pre-dinner drinks and by residents. Good lunchtime bar food includes an imaginative choice of sandwiches and ploughman's platters, spinach, ricotta and wild mushroom cannelloni, dim sum and regularly-changing specials like six Rossmore oysters, beef and Guinness pie, pan-fried pork loin steak with rosemary and a daily fish board selection, perhaps fresh squid Thai-style or a whole sea bass. Emphasis in the evenings is on more elaborate restaurant fare, but residents can take advantage of the 3-course table d'hote menu that includes a half bottle of wine. Traditional Sunday roast is served in the Downs Room. Bedrooms are pretty, with soothing colours and good sturdy furniture. All are neat and tidy with added touches like magazines, biscuits, mineral water and a box of tissues in each room. Good summer garden. No children under 5 allowed in the bar or restaurant. *Open 11-3, 6-11 (Sun 12-3 only). Bar closed Sun eve.* ***Bar Food*** *12-2.15 (no snacks in eve). Free House.* ***Beer*** *Fuller's London Pride, guest beer.* ***Accommodation*** *6 rooms, all en suite (three with baths), £60-£67.50 (single £37.50). Children welcome overnight (under-3s stay free in parents' room, 4-12s £10). Access, Amex, Diners, Visa.*

EGLOSHAYLE — Earl of St Vincent — A

Tel 01208 814807 Map 12 B3
Egloshayle Wadebridge Cornwall PL27 6HT

Originally built as a boarding house for the masons who constructed the church and named after one of Nelson's admirals, the Earl is a most extraordinary pub hidden away in the old part of a rambling village. Lovingly rescued from being a run-down local, it is now a splendid, welcoming hostelry filled to the brim with Edward Connolly's personal antique collection. The relaxing atmospheric bar has heavy beams, some wood panelling, an open fire fronted by two comfortable armchairs, various sturdy tables and chairs, old paintings and prints and most noticeable of all an amazing collection of antique clocks – from grandfather clocks to unusual ball-bearing clocks – that fill every available surface. Unbelievably, all are in perfect working order and 'time' is called by a cacophony of chimes, bongs and cuckoos. A tiny intimate snug bar resounds with ticking clocks. Those with time on their hands can while away an hour or two in the award-winning garden, ablaze with flowers in summer. *Open 11-3, 6.30-11 (Sun 12-3, 7-10.30).* ***Beer*** *St Austell. Garden. No credit cards.*

ELKESLEY — Robin Hood Inn — FOOD

Tel 01777 838259 Map 7 D2
High Street Elkesley Nottinghamshire DW22 8AJ

☺

The lounge bar and tiny dining-room of this comparatively modest Whitbread pub are the setting for pub food that's better than one might expect. Landlord Alan Draper is an enthusiastic cook and serves one menu throughout; typically, this might offer avocado and bacon salad, cod chowder or smoked duck breast salad with ratatouille chutney to start, following with roast cod on stewed forest mushrooms,, baked salmon fillet with herb mayonnaise, whole grilled lemon sole, pan-fried pork fillet with grain mustard and cream sauce or steaks. Baguette sandwiches and ploughman's platters are served at both lunch and dinner. Note: only light snacks are served on Monday evenings. *Open 11.30-3, 6.30-11 (Sat 11.30-11, Sun 12-3, 7-10.30).* ***Bar Food*** *12-2, 7-9 (Sat till 10, no food Sun eve).* ***Beer*** *Whitbread, Castle Eden, Boddingtons, guest beer. Family Room. Garden, children's play area. Access, Visa.*

> Many **B&B** establishments offer reduced rates for weekend and out-of-season bookings. Always ask about special deals for longer stays. Beware half-board terms in inns where we do not recommend the **FOOD.**

ELLERBY Ellerby Hotel FOOD B&B

Tel 01947 840342 Fax 01947 841221 Map 5 E3
Ellerby Saltburn-by-Sea Cleveland TS13 5LP

Zzz... ☺

David & Janet Alderson have transformed a run-down village pub into a country inn. The much-extended main bar and attendant dining-room provide plenty of space in which to enjoy a wide range of substantial fare, of which a large proportion is changed daily and posted on prominent blackboards. From starters encompassing onion bhajis and sesame chicken, progress to chargrilled smoked gammon, roast duck breast with black cherry sauce or perhaps a cheese-topped vegetarian pancake; accompanying vegetables are fresh and plentiful. Monthly Chinese banquets have proved highly popular. Nine bedrooms are furnished to a commendably high standard with varnished pine furniture and bright floral drapes; all have TVs, dial-out phones, trouser presses and hairdryers. Bathrooms are fully tiled and carpeted, with large baths and separate shower stalls (two have WC and shower only). *Open 11-3, 6.30-11.* ***Bar Food*** *12-2, 7-9.30 (Sat & Sun 11-11 in Summer). Free House.* ***Beer*** *John Smith's, Tetley Bitter. Garden, outdoor eating area.* ***Accommodation*** *9 bedrooms, all en suite (two with shower only), £50 (single £33). Children under six stay free in parents' room. Access, Visa.*

ELLISFIELD The Fox FOOD

Tel 01256 381210 Map 14a C4
Green Lane Ellisfield nr Basingstoke Hampshire RG25 2QW

Four miles from the M3, Junction 6, tucked down a leafy lane in unspoilt countryside, this homely village pub is a popular lunchtime venue for business people from Basingstoke. Its appeal (apart from its location) is the excellent selection of up to seven well-kept real ales and the honest, unpretentious home-cooked food that are served in the two comfortable, pine-furnished and music-free bars. Exposed brick walls, light-oak wood panelling and an open log fire provide a convivial eating atmosphere. The regularly-changing blackboard menu lists a short selection of dishes, ranging from a 20oz T-bone steak, and steak and kidney pie to a hot chili served with garlic bread, and a hearty lamb and mint casserole, accompanied by new potatoes and fresh vegetables. Sandwiches and ploughman's platters are always available. *Open 11.30-2.30 (Sat to 3), 6.30-11 (Sun 12-3, 7-10.30).* ***Bar Food*** *12-2, 7-9.30 (except Mon eve, Sun to 9). Free House.* ***Beer*** *Gales HSB, Marston's Pedigree, Wadworth 6X, Hall & Woodhouse Tanglefoot, Theakston Old Peculier, Hampshire Brewery King Alfred's. Garden, outdoor eating. Access, Visa.*

ELSENHAM The Crown FOOD

Tel 01279 812827 Map 10 B3
High Street Elsenham nr Bishop's Stortford Hertfordshire CM22 6DG

Once a row of three 300-year-old character cottages, this attractive, flower-decked and well-cared-for village inn has a traditional carpeted and low-ceilinged interior complete with brasses, beams, open fires and a relaxing atmosphere. Separate lively public bar offering a variety of games. Bar food relies primarily on an extensive and varied printed menu (lasagne, steak and kidney pie), featuring good pub favourites, as well as interesting home-cooked dishes like freshly-made Crownburgers (for lunch only) served with home-made whisky relish, crab and prawn or asparagus and blue cheese pastry tartlet, rack of lamb with a port sauce, scrumpy chicken, chicken with avocado and mint, Provençal mussels or pork T-bone with tarragon and French mustard sauce. To accompany, there are well-cooked vegetables or choose a selection of fresh salads from the self-service salad bar. Large brown granary baps and ploughman's platters are served at lunchtime only. Home-made puddings include the tireless landlady Barbara Good's unusual ice creams such as almond and amaretto, brown bread or fresh coconut and white chocolate – up to 14 at any one time; rhubarb crumble with proper custard, summer pudding, fresh fruit trifle Barbara also hand-makes the pub's chips and crisps every day! South-facing front patio with benches and a beer garden to the rear (with children's play area). Not only a pub but also the headquarters of the Elsenham Cricket Club. The pub is actually in Essex, albeit with a Herts postal address. *Open 11-3, 6-11, Sun 12-2.30, 7-10.30.* ***Bar Food*** *12-2, 7.30-9.30. No food Sun evening. Children welcome in bar to eat.* ***Beer*** *Crouch Vale Brewery Bitter, guest beers. Garden, children's play area. Access, Amex, Diners, Visa.*

ELSLACK — Tempest Arms — B&B

Tel 01282 842450 **Fax 01282 843331** Map 6 B1
Elslack nr Skipton North Yorkshire BD23 3AY

Just off the A56 near its junction with the A59 and only three miles from Skipton, the pub nestles in a verdant hollow with its own stream winding picturesquely round the garden. To the rear of the pub proper, and with its own secure entrance, a purpose-built block houses well-appointed bedrooms that are fully equipped for the '90s with TVs, telephones and plenty of well-lit workspace for the business guest. En-suite bathrooms are a little small, but being fully tiled with strong over-bath showers they are more than adequate. Two rooms have three beds. Double-glazed and well back from the road, accommodation here promises less Tempest than Midsummer Night's Dream. *Open 11-3, 6.30-11 (from Easter-end Sept: 11-11 Sat, 12-10.30 Sun). Free House.* ***Beer*** *Tetley, Theakston Best, Thwaites Best & Craftsman. Garden, outdoor eating area.* ***Accommodation*** *10 bedrooms, all en suite £52 (family rooms sleeping 3/4 £62/£72, single £46). Access, Amex, Diners, Visa.*

> We only recommend food (Bar Food) in those establishments highlighted with the **FOOD** symbol.

ELSTEAD — Woolpack — FOOD

Tel 01252 703106 Map 15a E4
The Green Elstead Surrey GU8 6HD

On an old wool trading route, the tile-hung Woolpack was in fact originally built as a wool-bale store in the 18th century, and only later developed into a hostelry. Now comfortably countrified, various artefacts dotted about the place still hint at the pub's previous use: bobbins and spindles of yarn, a lamb's fleece, an ancient pair of scales and a partly woven rug. Today folk flock here to enjoy the famously-generous portions of home-cooked dishes chosen from a long blackboard menu which might encompass Thai fish cakes, baked goat's cheese on toast with garlic and mango sauce, monkfish in Pernod fennel and cream sauce (or perhaps merlin in lime and coriander butter) and a range of pies (steak and kidney, cod and prawn and chicken and ham). No sandwiches, but ploughman's platters are popular. Genuinely home-made puddings might include Mrs. Swayne's pudding (layers of a mix of cake and breadcrumbs, chocolate chips and cream) or apple strudel. Busy Sunday lunches. Children can have smaller portions at smaller prices, or opt for baked beans and tinned spaghetti on toast. A family room has nursery rhyme murals and bunches of flowers hung up to dry from the ceiling; there's also a slide, swing and climbing frame in the pretty garden. *Open 11-2.30, 6-11 (Sun 12-3, 7-10.30).* ***Bar Food*** *12-2, 7-9.45 (Sun 7.15-9).* ***Beer*** *Two regularly-changing real ales. Garden, outdoor eating, children's play area. Family room. Access, Visa.*

ELSTED — Three Horseshoes — A

Tel 01730 825746 Map 15 D3
Elsted nr Midhurst West Sussex GU29 0JX

Bowed walls, terracotta-tiled floors, gnarled beams, mellow stained plasterwork and a good open fire in the vast inglenook all create an atmosphere of genuinely unspoilt charm in this popular 16th-century inn, originally built as a drovers, ale house. Evening candlelight enhances the romantic old-world atmosphere. Good range of real ales dispensed straight from the cask. Well-tended garden with rustic tables and benches and lovely views over the South Downs. *Open 11-2.30, 6-11 (Sun 12-3, 7-10.30). Free House.* ***Beer*** *Ballard's Best Bitter, Cheriton Brewhouse Pots Ale, Fuller's London Pride, Otter Ale. Garden, lawn, outside eating area, tables in garden. Access, Visa.*

> We do not accept free meals or hospitality – our inspectors pay their own bills and **never** book in the name of Egon Ronay's Guides.

ELSTED MARSH Elsted Inn FOOD

Tel 01730 813662 Map 15 D3
Elsted Marsh nr Midhurst West Sussex GU29 0JT

Unprepossessing Victorian roadside pub built to serve the railway in the steam age (when there was a station here), but later left stranded by Dr Beeching's 'axe' in the 1960s. This explains the old railway photographs that adorn the thankfully unmodernised and unpretentious bars, in what is very much a local community pub, free of background music and electronic games but with plenty of traditional pub pastimes like shove ha'penny, darts, cards, dominoes and even conversation. There are two small bars with lots of original wood in evidence, original shutters and open fires. A small dining-room, candle-lit in the evening, boasts an old pine dresser and colourful cloths on a few dining tables surrounded by a motley collection of old chairs. Tweazle Jones and her partner Barry Horton produce varied menus with dishes that are always home-made and based on good local produce. The likes of jumbo sausage, fresh trout, king prawns in garlic or lemon butter, home-cooked ham salad, as well as door-stop sandwiches, baked potatoes and ploughman's are available as bar snacks, whilst more elaborate fare on the daily menu might be bacon pudding, beef and beer pie, venison stew or rabbit casserole. Children can have half portions at half price, and there's a car tyre hanging from a plum tree in the shady garden to keep them amused, plus pétanque for the adults. Dogs are welcome or at least tolerated by the house hounds, Truffle and Sam, and an area of the garden is fenced off to keep dogs and children apart. Steak nights and curry nights are a popular regular feature here. B&B is available – £30 for a double, no children under 12; there is one double room and a bunk room for adults. Plans are afoot to convert a coach house and provide four more en-suite double rooms. *Open 11-3, 5.30-11 (Sat from 6, Sun 12-3, 7-10.30). **Bar Food** 12-2.30, 7-9.30 (Sat to 10, Sun to 9). Free House. **Beer** Ballard's, Fuller's London Pride, guest beer. Garden, outdoor eating, boules, children's play area. Access, Visa.*

ELTERWATER Britannia Inn B&B

Tel 01539 437210 **Fax 01539 437311** Map 4 C3
Elterwater nr Ambleside Cumbria LA22 9HP

Zzz...

Next to the tiny village green dominated by a magnificent maple tree, fronted by its own colourful window boxes, the black-and-white-painted Britannia is a summer picture. Ever-popular with the walkers who throng to Langdale valley are the garden chairs and slate-topped tables on the pub's front terrace as both front and rear bars are tiny. Residents have their own chintzy lounge with oak beams, antiques and an open log fire. Within the pub, six of the bedrooms have entirely adequate en-suite facilities while a seventh has its own private bathroom across the corridor. All have individually controlled central heating, colour TVs, telephones, hairdryers and beverage-making facilities. Alternative accommodation across the green at Maple Tree Corner is especially handy for family use and generously priced at a lower rate, which nevertheless includes a hearty Lakeland breakfast served back at the inn. *Open 11-11 (Sun usual hours). Free House. **Beer** Jennings Bitter & Mild, Boddingtons, guest beer. Garden. **Accommodation** 13 bedrooms, 7 en suite, £62 (single £23.50). Children welcome overnight. Accommodation closed 25 Dec. Access, Visa.*

EMERY DOWN New Forest Inn FOOD B&B

Tel 01703 282329 Map 14 C4
Emery Down nr Lyndhurst Hampshire SO43 7DY

Prettily set in woodland, the building of the inn was the result of the first successful establishment of squatters' rights on Crown land in the early 18th-century. The original caravan that used to sell ale forms part of the front lounge porchway. Much extended since, it has a big, busy open-plan bar and fairly modern seating and style, with effective country touches and real fires. The reliable bar food available here aims to please all tastes, and the regular printed menu features old favourites and chips, as well as some interesting home-cooked dishes. A daily-changing specials board increases the choice of freshly-prepared meals such as sauté of lamb with raspberries, rabbit in mustard sauce and venison in pear and cinnamon, all accompanied by fresh vegetables. Home-made puddings like toasted lemon brulée, treacle and walnut tart and fruit Pavlova round off the meal. Bedrooms are clean, comfortable and homely, three having en-suite facilities (two with bath), the fourth having its own private, but not en-suite, bathroom; TVs are now provided. The room above the

kitchen can be unbearably hot and airless in summer. The three-level rear garden is a super summer spot for alfresco imbibing with benches and tables among the well-tended flower borders and mature shrubs and trees. Whitbread Wayside Inn. *Open 11-11 (Sun 12-3, 7-10.30).* ***Bar Food*** *12-9.30 (Sun 12-9).* ***Beer*** *Flowers Original, Strong Country Bitter, Greene King Abbot Ales, Gale's HSB, two guest beers. Garden, outdoor eating.* ***Accommodation*** *4 bedrooms, 3 en suite, £50 (single £25). Children welcome overnight (under-3s stay free in parents' room), additional bed (£10) and cot supplied. Access, Visa.*

EMPINGHAM — White Horse — FOOD

Tel 01780 460221 **Fax 01780 960521** Map 7 E3 **B&B**

2 Main Street Empingham nr Oakham Leicestershire LE15 8PR

Zzz... ☺

A stone's throw from serene Rutland Water, Roger Bourne's civilised pub (including newly refurbished bar area) is the centre of village life, a meeting-place for walkers and birdwatchers and convenient for access from the A1 at Stamford and the market town of Oakham. In attempting to be all things to most callers its day stretches from morning coffee and croissants through lunches and cream teas to late evening suppers. Central to the three eating areas, which include a family room, is the food counter displaying cold meats and home-made sweets backed by a blackboard of daily dishes offering the likes of liver and onions, hot pots, pies, fresh Rutland trout with almonds, surf'n'turf, perhaps, plus quiche, self-served salads and junior pizzas. Home-made hoagies, savoury fish pancakes, Glastonbury lamb and home-made Yorkshire puddings with a filling of your choice constitute substantial bar meals. The best bedrooms, all recently refurbished, are in the stables, kitted out in varnished pine and each with its own well-appointed bathroom. In the main building, rooms are bright and neat though more modest, with shared bathing facilities. One room has a four-poster. *Open 10.30-11 (Sun 12-3, 7-10.30).* ***Bar Food*** *12-2 (Sat & Sun to 2.15), 7-10 (Sun to 9.30).* ***Beer*** *John Smith's, Courage Directors, Ruddles, Wadworth 6X. Garden, outdoor eating, disabled WC. Family room.* ***Accommodation*** *14 rooms, 9 en suite, £55 (four-poster £60, single £42). Children welcome overnight (under-2s stay free in parents' room, 2-8s half-price), extra bed and cot available. Access, Amex, Diners, Visa.*

ESKDALE GREEN — Bower House Inn — FOOD

Tel 019467 23244 **Fax 019467 23308** Map 4 C3 **B&B**

Eskdale Green Holmbrook Cumbria CA19 1TD

Zzz... ☺

Despite its out-of-the-way location, the Connors' informal, friendly inn continues to find favour with a faithful and returning clientele. Headquarters of the Eskdale cricket team, the bar has a distinctly clubby feel and opens on to an enchanting, enclosed garden of pine and shrub, with a tiny wooden bridge traversing the village stream. Children can play safely here. Bar menus more reflect the public demand for steak and kidney pie and scampi than show off the kitchen's prowess; however, choices from the specials board may include devilled whitebait and pork loin in apple and Calvados. Dinner, served at smartly polished mahogany tables, is the preferred choice of residents and might consist of cock-a-leekie soup, escalope of veal with Gruyère and tiramisu. This is a delightful place to stay for peace and quiet in the Eskdale valley; bedrooms are divided between the main house, where they are abundant in character, the converted stables and garden cottages, subtly extended and thoughtfully equipped to meet modern-day demands. There are three large rooms suitable for family occupation. After a restful night, it's traditional to tuck into a hearty Lakeland breakfast. *Open 11-11 (Sun 12-3, 6.30-10.30).* ***Bar Food*** *12-2, 6.30-9.30 (Sun from 7). Free House.* ***Beer*** *Theakston Best, Hartleys XB, Courage Directors, Younger's Scotch Bitter. Riverside garden, outdoor eating.* ***Accommodation*** *24 rooms, all en suite, £56 (single £45). Children welcome overnight, extra bed and cot supplied (£8). No dogs. Access, Amex, Visa.*

We do not accept free meals or hospitality – our inspectors pay their own bills and **never** book in the name of Egon Ronay's Guides.

ETTINGTON **Houndshill** B&B

Tel 01789 740267 Map 14 C1
Banbury Road Ettington nr Stratford-on-Avon Warwickshire CV37 7NS

A friendly, family-operated roadhouse which includes children's play areas and a licensed campsite in its extensive grounds. The clean, tidy decor of the lounge bar and adjoining dining-room is repeated in the pine-clad bedrooms and compact bathrooms with over-bath showers. Up-to-date direct-dial phones and remote-control TVs ensure a degree of comfort commensurate with the price range. Very useful to know, as it's beside the A422 Banbury road, four miles south of Stratford. *Open 12-2.30, 6-11 (Sun 12-3, 7-10.30). Free House.* ***Beer*** *Theakston Best, XB. Garden, outdoor eating, children's play area. Family room.* ***Accommodation*** *8 bedrooms, all en suite, £45 (family rooms sleeping up to 4 £55/£60, single £28). Children welcome overnight, additional bed (from £5) and cot (£5) supplied. Dogs by arrangement. Access, Visa.*

EWEN **Wild Duck Inn** B&B

Tel & Fax 01285 770310 Map 14 C2
Drakes Island Ewen nr Cirencester Gloucestershire GL7 6BY

ZZz...

Lovely Cotswold village pub near the Water Park. The dimly-lit Post Horn bar is nicely poised between traditional and smartened up; the restaurant has red walls, candles in bottles, and simple pine furniture. The bedrooms (particularly the two with four-poster beds in the oldest part of the building) are decent, though the extension-housed remainder might seem surprisingly modern in style. The latest addition is a bridal suite with four-poster.
The Grouse Room residents' lounge, a haven of peace overlooking the pretty gardens, is also open to diners. *Open 11-11 (Sun 12-3, 7-10.30). Free House.* ***Beer*** *Duck Pond Bitter, Theakston Best & Old Peculier, Deakins Red Admiral, Wadworth 6X, guest beer. Garden.* ***Accommodation*** *10 bedrooms, all en suite, £65 (4-poster £75, single £48). Children welcome overnight (under-4s free if sharing parents' room, 4-10s £10), additional bed and cot available. Access, Amex, Visa.*

EXFORD **Crown Hotel** FOOD B&B

Tel 01643 831554 **Fax 01643 831665** Map 13 D1
Exford Somerset TA24 7PP

ZZz...

Long a favourite among the huntin', shootin' and fishin' set, the 17th-century Crown stands by the green in a lovely village. After a few troubled years the hotel has recently undergone major refurbishment under new owners and now offers country pursuit followers a touch of luxury in the heart of Exmoor. Seventeen, very comfortable en-suite bedrooms have been tastefully furnished with quality pieces and equipped with TVs, telephones and hairdryers; room service is provided for refreshments. Lots of traditional charm in the lounge and rustic pubby bar, in which some above-average bar food can now be enjoyed. Good snacks or starters might include spicy crab soup, coarse pork terrine, lightly baked tomatoes filled with creamed goat's cheese and marinated Scottish salmon, with main-course options include fresh fish and shellfish from Brixham and many more seasonal dishes (like game) than before. To finish, try the chocolate mousse or pears gently simmered in a spicy red wine syrup served with caramel ice cream. Stabling available for those wishing to bring their own horses. *Open 11-3, 6-11 (Sun 12-3, 7-10.30).* ***Bar Food*** *12-2, 6.30-9.30 (Sun from 7). Free House.* ***Beer*** *Brakspear Bitter, Flowers Original, Boddingtons. Garden, outdoor eating. Family room.* ***Accommodation*** *17 rooms, all en suite, £68-£80 (single £34-£55). Children welcome overnight (under-10s stay free in parents' room), additional bed and cot supplied. Access, Amex, Visa.*

EYAM **Miner's Arms** FOOD B&B

Tel 01433 630853 Map 6 C2
Water Lane Eyam Derbyshire S30 1RG

Sideways on to the village square, the pub is a row of white-painted cottages fronted by a butcher's shop; drive gently up Water Lane to find residents' parking at the rear. A tiny triangle of garden gives access from the High Street, the croft adjoining having been a burial ground at the time of Eyam's plague in 1665/6; no wonder the place claims to be haunted. A balanced selection of bar lunches might include carrot and lentil soup, haddock mornay, lamb and mint sausages with onion gravy and a cauliflower and Stilton quiche; to follow, Bakewell tart and sherry trifle. The evening à la carte extends to the level of wild red

venison in Madeira sauce and English-style roast duckling; this is careful cooking, neatly presented, with service supervised by the caring Nick Cook. The seven bedrooms extend through into the adjoining cottages; they are clean and bright with adequate en-suite facilities (one single has WC/shower only). Welcoming touches include mineral water and a selection of books; more practical are remote-control TVs, clock radios and a hot beverage tray. Monday night is village darts night. *Open Tue-Sat 12-3, Mon-Sat 7-11 (Sun 12-3 only).* ***Bar Food*** *12-2 (except Sun – restaurant only). Free House.* ***Beer*** *Boddingtons, guest beer. Patio, outdoor eating (lunchtime only).* ***Accommodation*** *7 bedrooms, all en suite (two with bath), £45 (single £25). Children welcome overnight, additional bed and cot available (£5). Check-in by arrangement. No dogs. Pub closed Sun nights and Monday lunchtime, accommodation closed 1st 2 weeks Jan. Access, Visa.*

EYNSHAM — Newlands Inn — FOOD

Tel 01865 881486 **Fax 01865 883672** Map 14a B2
Newland Street Eynsham nr Whitney Oxfordshire OX8 1LD

A lost corner of the 16th century hides just off the A40 – devoid of street lamps at night the setting can be magical. Unperturbed by the two resident ghosts, Nick Godden charcoal grills one of the best steaks around, and his barbecued hickory-flavoured spare ribs and Cajun catfish have their fans also. The flagstone floors, candle-lit dining-room (where bookings are taken) and roaring log fires create the draw in winter; on summer evenings the rear patio with its canvas awning is a pleasant spot for a snack and occasionally there will be a barbecue in progress. Among the blackboard specials look for toad in the hole with gravy or smoked haddock au gratin and pan-fried king prawns in garlic butter. Phone beforehand on Sundays for a roast cooked to order, in winter booking is also advisable on Fridays and Saturdays. No food on winter evenings. Children welcome. *Open 11-2 (Sat to 3), 5.30-11 (Sat from 6), Sun 12-3, 7-10.30.* ***Bar Food*** *12-2, 7-9.30 (no food Sun eve) or eve from end Mar-end Oct only.* ***Beer*** *Greene King IPA, Bass, Worthington Best. Garden, outdoor eating, patio. Access, Visa.*

FACCOMBE — Jack Russell Inn — B&B

Tel 01264 737315 Map 14a B4
Faccombe nr Andover Hampshire SP11 0DS

Zzz...

Faccombe is a tiny, out-of-the-way village signposted off the A343 north of Hurstbourne Tarrant. The present simple redbrick Jack Russell Inn is located opposite the pond and was rebuilt in 1983 after the previous building fell down while being renovated. It is quickly being mellowed by a spreading Virginia creeper and hanging baskets of flowers. New landlord David Hill (who also cooks) has completetly redecorated and refurbished since taking over; adjacent to the small bar is a light and airy conservatory that gives access to the large, totally secure garden with a children's play area. Three simple bedrooms, just one with en-suite bathroom (the other two rooms share a bath), offer good, clean accommodation with televisions, but no telephones. *Open 12-3, 7-11 (Sun 12-3, 7-10.30). Free House.* ***Beer*** *Theakston Best, two guest beers. Garden, children's play area.* ***Accommodation*** *3 bedrooms, 1 en suite, £40 (single £25). Children welcome overnight (under-5s stay free in parents' room). Access, Amex, Visa.*

FARNHAM — Museum Hotel — FOOD

Tel 01725 516261 Map 14 C3 **B&B**
Farnham nr Blandford Forum Dorset DT11 8DE

The Museum Hotel owes its name and its present existence to General Pitt Rivers who took over a Gypsy School nearby and housed one of his Museums in it, the most famous of which still exists in Oxford. The present 'curator' (and chef) is John Barnes. The main bar – Coopers Bar – dates from Cromwellian times and occupies the original long and low cottage. It boasts a large inglenook fireplace, light oak and pine tables, tasteful green fabrics, local paintings and soothing classical music – a civilised dining atmosphere. A small, intimate dining-room is in an airy conservatory extension. In complete contrast, the Woodlands Bar attached to the far side of the building, is simply furnished and houses an assortment of pub games. Bar food can be extremely variable, with the main menu featuring firm favourites like steak and kidney and oyster pudding, chicken curry and a choice of grills, as well as unusual salads and starters, sandwiches and ploughman's platters. Weekly-changing specials

enhance proceedings at both lunchtime and in the evening. Stable block accommodation comprises four rather compact bedrooms with modern pine, matching fabrics and spacious, well equipped and sparkling clean en-suite bathrooms. The usual added comforts are here, plus a stocked mini-fridge. Sun-trap patio and sheltered walled garden. *Open 11-3, 6-11 (Sun 12-3, 7-10.30).* ***Bar Food*** *12-1.45, 7.9.30. Free House.* ***Beer*** *Wadworth 6X, Brakspear Bitter, two guest beers. Garden, patio, outdoor eating, children's play area.* ***Accommodation*** *4 bedrooms, all en suite, £50 (four-poster £65, single £35). Check-in by arrangement. No dogs. Access, Visa.*

FAUGH — String of Horses Inn — FOOD

Tel 01228 70297 **Fax 01228 70675** Map 4 C2 **B&B**
Faugh Heads Nook nr Carlisle Cumbria CA4 9EG

Zzz...

Take the turning signed to Heads Nook from A69 at Corby Hill, four miles from M6 Junction 43; a mile past the village stores and post office is the sharp left turn to Faugh (pronounced locally as "Faff"). Built in the late 17th century as a packhorse inn, nowadays there are open fires and oak beams and an interior packed with antiques and prints, copper and brassware. There's usually plenty of home cooking to be enjoyed, the daily specials boards promising the likes of salmon shanty with asparagus, ever-popular curries, porc au poivre, sandwiches, ploughman's platters and home-made puddings. Each bedroom is individually designed, their contrasting styles incorporating hand-painted furniture and bold-patterned fabrics, crowned canopies, brass bedsteads and four-posters. Ostentatious gold-tapped bathrooms include round and double hand-made Bonsack baths, several with built-in jacuzzis. Additional facilities include the mini-leisure centre with a sauna, solarium, whirlpool and ergometer, and a heated open-air pool and sunbathing patio. *Open 11.30-3, 5.30-11, Sun 12-3, 7-10.30.* ***Bar Food*** *12-2.30, 7-10. No real ales. Outdoor eating.* ***Accommodation*** *14 bedrooms, all en-suite, £68-£98 (single £58-£80). Children welcome overnight (under-12s stay free in parents' room), additional bed and cot supplied. Pub closed 25 & 26 Dec. Access, Diners, Visa.*

FEN DRAYTON — Three Tuns — A

Tel 01954 230242 Map 15 F1
High Street Fen Drayton Cambridgeshire CB4 5SJ

Characterful timbered old pub, originally housing the local trade or guild hall of Fen Drayton. The present bar is outside the original building, but brims with atmosphere: heavy moulded beams from the 15th century, inglenook fireplaces, oak furnishings, and lots of quality bric-a-brac. It can get extremely busy, particularly on Wednesdya nights when the local league play on the new pétanque piste. *Open 11-2.30, 6.30-11 (Sun 12-2.30, 7-10.30).* ***Beer*** *Greene King. Garden, children's play area. Access, Visa.*

FENSTANTON — King William IV — FOOD

Tel 01480 462467 Map 15 F1
High Street Fenstanton Cambridgeshire PE18 9JF

Look out for the old clock tower as this attractive white-painted inn is next door. Once three separate cottages, it is very much the hub of village life with a lively bar area and a comfortably furnished dining area, including a rear, plant-festooned Garden Room. Food is reliable with home-cooked dishes appearing on the bi-monthly changing printed menu and the constantly varying blackboard list. Choose, perhaps, from sandwiches, ploughman's platters (these at lunch and Sun evening only) or stuffed mushrooms, fresh grilled sardines and home-made soup to start, followed by a traditional steak and kidney pudding, fillet of pork or fricassee of monkfish with lemon and ginger. Good, separately plated vegetables. Vegetarians will always find two options on the board. Popular Sunday roast and a selection of six puddings, notably hot chocolate sponge and treacle and walnut pie. Capability Brown is buried in the village churchyard. *Open 11-3.30, 6-11 (Sun 12-3, 7-10.30).* ***Bar Food*** *11-2.15, 7-10 (Sun 12-2.15, 7-9).* ***Beer*** *Greene King. Access, Amex, Visa.*

Many **B&B** establishments offer reduced rates for weekend and out-of-season bookings. Always ask about special deals for longer stays. Beware half-board terms in inns where we do not recommend the **FOOD.**

FINGEST Chequers Inn A

Tel 01491 638335 Map 15a D3

Fingest nr Henley-on-Thames Buckinghamshire RG9 6QD

Charming 15th-century brick-and-flint pub located opposite a unique Norman church in a tiny hamlet set deep in the Chiltern Hills. Unspoilt and traditionally furnished interior – free from intrusive music and electronic games – boasting ceiling beams, an 18th-century settle, open fires and tastefully adorned with prints, horsebrasses, decorative plates, and a few guns and pistols. Sunny lounge area with French windows opening out on to a delightful sun-trap garden with colourful flower borders and rural views. Good walking country. Fingest is signposted off B480 Marlow to Stokenchurch road. *Open 11-3, 6-11 (Sun 12-3, 7-10.30).* ***Beer*** *Brakspear. Garden. Access, Amex, Diners, Visa.*

FIR TREE Duke of York FOOD

Tel 01388 762848 Map 5 D3 **B&B**

Fir Tree nr Crook Co Durham DL15 8DG

From whitewashed stone pub to extended and comfortable roadside inn (standing by the A68 one mile from Crook town), the grand old Duke – in landlord Roy Suggett's family for several generations now – continues to march along. Mr Suggett, here since 1988, provides more-than-adequate ale and refreshment for a perceptibly discerning market. Voluminous blackboards offer lasagne, steak and kidney pie, fresh fish and chips, chicken chasseur, pork Zaccheroff and lamb fillet in hot pepper sauce with, perhaps, a salmon terrine to start and banana split or chocolate orange log to follow. Alongside are snacks like home-made soup, open sandwiches, hot beef in a bun, ploughman's platters and grilled steaks from an all-encompassing menu offered both in the lounge bar and dining-room. Four en-suite bedrooms are individually decorated in a "luxurious but olde worlde" style; they are named after Co Durham castles and furnished with stained solid pine furniture, remote-controlled TVs, direct-dial telephones and beverage facilities. Incidentally, all the bar fittings, tables and light fittings are by 'Mouseman' Thompson (look out for his carved trademark) and date from 1967. *Open 11-11 (12-3, 7-10.30).* ***Bar Food*** *12-2.30, 6-10 (Sun 12-2.30, 7-10). Free House.* ***Beer*** *Bass, Worthington, guest beer.* ***Accommodation*** *4 bedrooms, all en suite (two with bath), £59 (single £48). Children over 10 welcome overnight, additional bed (£11) provided. Garden, outdoor eating. Access, Visa.*

FIRLE Ram Inn FOOD

Tel 01273 858222 Map 11 B6 **B&B**

Firle West Firle nr Lewes East Sussex BN8 6NS

The road runs out once it eventually reaches Firle village at the foot of the Downs. It's a quiet backwater now, but this (almost unbelievably) was once a main stage-coach route and the Ram an important staging post. Built of brick and flint and partly tile-hung, the inn displays a fascinating mixture of periods. The Georgian part was once the local courthouse. Other parts are older, and the kitchen dates back nearly 500 years. The main bar is a simple, unpretentious affair with a motley collection of tables and chairs and old photos.

A no-smoking snug bar is similarly modest. A daily-changing blackboard menu lists the selection of home-made food which makes use of good local produce. Choose from an excellent range of ploughman's lunches, a deep bowl of vegetable soup, smoked bacon roly-poly, steak and kidney pie and a short choice of freshly baked pizzas. Puddings include banana and toffee pie and apple, pear and other fruits crumble. Vegetarians are well catered for. Simple bedrooms are bright and fresh, with a variety of antique furniture. The largest and best en-suite room enjoys downland views and features a shower cabinet and en-suite toilet; the other three rooms share a rather basic shower room. The fourth bedroom is up two flights of stairs in the attic, with a very high elevation and views over the garden; it shares facilities and does not have a hand basin. All rooms have tea and coffee-making kits but, as a matter of policy, no televisions or radios. Splendid flint-walled garden for peaceful summer drinking. *Open 11.30-3, 7-11 (Sun 12-3, 7-10.30).* ***Bar Food*** *12-2, 7-9. Free House.* ***Beer*** *Harveys Sussex Bitter, Otter Bitter, Hop Back Summer Lightning, Harveys Old Ale in winter. Garden, outdoor eating, tables in garden.* ***Accommodation*** *4 bedrooms, 1 en suite, £60 (£50 not en suite, single £35). No children under 14 overnight. Check-in by arrangement. Pub closed Christmas Day evening. Accommodation closed Christmas Eve and Christmas Day. Dogs welcome. Access, Visa.*

FITTLEWORTH **The Swan** B&B

Tel 01798 865429 **Fax 01798 865546** Map 11 A6
Lower Street Fittleworth nr Pulborough West Sussex RH20 1EN

One can luxuriate in the peaceful beauty of the lovely award-winning garden of flowers and herbs of this 14th-century tile-hung inn, and see where the River Arun meets the Rother by taking a peaceful river walk. Inside, fresh flowers adorn the hallway and reception and the dark panelled picture lounge boasts a fine collection of early 19th-century paintings embedded in the upper panels. The main bar displays policeman's truncheons above the vast inglenook, and brass and copper trinkets hang from the beams. Villagers enjoy darts in the small public bar. Spotless Laura Ashley-style bedrooms are comfortable and well appointed – TVs, tea-makers, trouser presses, telephones, hairdryers – and feature modern pine furniture, although two rooms have fine mahogany 4-poster beds. Good en-suite facilities, with three of the bedrooms sharing two smart bathrooms. A warm welcome awaits families. Children can eat with parents anywhere in the bar, choose from their own menu or request smaller portions of adult dishes and eat at any time of the day. A wooden climbing frame in the safe garden will keep the more active offspring amused on fine days. Under-2s are accommodated free overnight; older children are charged a nominal £6 if sharing a parents' room. Cots available. New landlords were due to arrive at this superior Whitbread Wayside Inn as we went to press. *Open 11-11 (Sun 12-10.30).* ***Beer*** *King & Barnes Sussex, Boddingtons, Wadworth 6X. Garden, outdoor eating, children's play area.* ***Accommodation*** *10 bedrooms, 7 en suite, £55 (single £25). Children welcome overnight (cot, high-chair and extra child's bed if sharing). Access, Diners, Visa.*

FLETCHING **Griffin Inn** FOOD B&B

Tel 01825 722890 **Fax 01825 722810** Map 11 B6
Fletching East Sussex TN22 3NS

Zzz...

Simon de Montfort's army camped outside Fletching church prior to the Battle of Lewes in 1256. These days visitors with a more peaceful intent are made more than welcome at the 16th-century Griffin Inn, which is at the heart of Saxon Fletching's picturesque main street, and is everything a village local should be. The main bar has old beams and wainscot walls, a copper-hooded brick fireplace and a motley collection of old pews and wheelback chairs; the public bar provides a pool table and fruit machine for the amusement of the local youth and there's a pretty restaurant. Good home-made food is a major attraction, with a varied blackboard menu available in the bar and a short, more imaginative daily-changing à la carte menu on offer in the restaurant (more extensive Fri and Sat evenings). An eclectic choice in the bar might range from Nico's terrine of veal, bacon and herbs, chicken liver parfait, salmon and spring onion fishcakes, whole roast red mullet and herbs, lamb stew and sausage, mash and onion gravy. Imaginative accompanying salads. There are also chargrills, homely puddings and generous ploughman's platters. Excellent wine list. There are four charming, bedrooms, three with four-poster beds purpose-built to counteract the sloping floors and to ensure a level night's rest. Tea- and coffee-making kits and TVs are provided and the substantial breakfast is worth getting up for. In summer, the rear garden offers outstanding views across rolling Sussex countryside. *Open 12-3, 6-11 (Sun to 10.30).* ***Bar Food*** *12-2.30, 7-9.30. Free House.* ***Beer*** *Harveys Sussex Bitter, Hall & Woodhouse Tanglefoot, Fuller's London Pride, Badger Best Bitter, guest beer. Garden, 2 large lawns and patio, outdoor eating, summer barbecue.* ***Accommodation*** *4 rooms, all en suite, £65 (weekends £75, single £40). Children welcome overnight (free on sofa bed in parents' room), cot available. Check-in by arrangement. Pub closed Christmas Day. Accommodation closed 24 & 25 Dec. No dogs in bedrooms. Access, Amex, Visa.*

FONTHILL GIFFORD **Beckford Arms** B&B

Tel 01747 870385 **Fax 01747 870496** Map 14 B3
Fonthill Gifford nr Salisbury Tisbury Wiltshire SP3 6PX

Peacefully situated on a minor road (follow signposts to Fonthill Bishop from the A303), opposite Fonthill Estate and adjoining its vineyard, this 18th-century stone-built inn is a good base from which to explore the estate footpaths and the unspoilt scenery of the Nadder Valley. The modernised, yet attractive lounge bar with open fire and the airy Garden Room lead out on to a sun-trap patio and a delightful raised, flower- and shrub-filled garden – ideal for summer alfresco imbibing. The seven compact and comfortable

en-suite bedrooms are upstairs and two of them feature four-poster beds. All rooms are spacious, neat, clean and refreshingly decorated with matching floral wallpaper and fabrics; they are also well equipped with TV, clock-radio, tea-making kit, hairdryer and good toiletries. Long-stay guests may find some of the rooms rather too cramped, with little luggage space. *Open 11-3, 6-11 (Sun 12-3, 7-10.30). Free House.* ***Beer*** *Courage Best, Wadworth 6X, guest beer. Garden, outdoor eating. Family room.* ***Accommodation*** *8 bedrooms, all en suite, £49.50 (four-poster £54.50, single £29.50 with shower). Children welcome overnight (under-5s stay free in parents' room, 5-16s £9.50) additional bed and cot available. Small dogs by arrangement. Access, Amex, Visa.*

FORD — Dinton Hermit — FOOD

Tel 01296 748379 Map 15a D2
Ford nr Aylesbury Buckinghamshire HP17 8XH

In an isolated hamlet and set back from the lane, this 15th-century stone cottage pub is named after John Briggs, clerk to one of the judges who condemned Charles I to death. Two small and homely bars are well maintained, each having part exposed stone walls, brick fireplaces and a mix of rustic furniture. Popular locally, both bars fill quickly with customers seeking out the hearty, home-cooked food – asparagus pancakes, steak and mushroom pie, chicken curry, chili, vegetarian hotpot and decent sandwiches and salads. Additional, more elaborate dishes like duck in orange and ginger and medallions of lamb with white wine and caper sauce appear on the evening menu. Good vegetables, generously served. Large, pretty garden with rural views – ideal for sunny days. *Open 11-2.30, 6-11 (Sun 12-2, 7-10.30).* ***Bar Food*** *12-2 & 7-9.30 (no food Sun or Mon).* ***Beer*** *ABC Bitter, Tetley, Wadworth 6X. Pub closed 2 weeks at Christmas, 2 weeks in July. No credit cards.*

FORD — Plough Inn — FOOD B&B

Tel 01386 584215 Map 14a A1
Temple Gutting Ford Gloucestershire GL54 5RU

A gregarious pub in something of an agrarian setting on a bend in the B4077. There's an old well in the walled garden and a mixture of abandoned filling station and farmyard behind. The simply furnished bars recall the pub's past days as a farmhouse with flagstone floors, pine tables and high-backed settles, and diners move easily through to a neatly-laid dining-room which is cosily candle-lit at night. Food starts at 9am for breakfast and is available all day, the best of the day's choices prominently displayed on blackboards. There's chilled gazpacho or Stilton and celery soup followed by grilled Donnington trout or steak, mushroom and Guinness casserole to make a meal of, while all-in-one snacks might include dill-cured gravad lax or cauliflower cheese with tomatoes and Stilton; freshly-cut sandwiches are served at lunch only, ploughman's platters available all day. In increasing numbers regulars are leaving room for the generously portioned, home-made, banoffi or pecan pies and seasonal summer pudding. Four simple bedrooms: three in a converted courtyard barn with en-suite showers, and one within the main pub building with en-suite bathroom; all have remote-controlled TVs and hot beverage facilities. *Open 11am-11pm (Sun 12-3 & 7-10.30).* ***Bar Food*** *12-2.30, 6.30-9.30 (Fri & Sat to 10, no food Sun eve).* ***Beer*** *Donnington BB & SBA. Garden, outdoor eating.* ***Accommodation*** *4 bedrooms, all en suite, £40 & £50 (single £25). Children welcome overnight (accommodated free in parents' room), additional bed supplied. Pub closed 25 Dec. Access, Visa.*

FORD — White Hart — FOOD B&B

Tel 01249 782213 **Fax 01249 783075** Map 14 B2
Ford nr Chippenham Wiltshire SN14 8RP

Idyllically situated beside a babbling trout stream in the Wyvern Valley, this rambling, mellow-stone, 16th-century coaching inn offers both character and charm in its low-ceilinged bar and in the adjacent dining areas. The inn is well run by its owners, Chris and Jenny Phillips, who cater for all requirements, providing good ale, consistently reliable food and a high standard of accommodation. Subsequently the White Hart is a very popular and busy inn. The cosy, unspoilt half-panelled bar throngs with drinkers, many of whom are attracted by the continually varying selection of up to eleven real ales that are drawn from the cellar. Discerning diners, seeking out imaginative and well-cooked food head next door into one of the two attractive dining areas where antiques, various rugs, an array of furniture and numerous paintings help create a convivial atmosphere. Choosing from a sensibly short, weekly-changing menu one might start with melon and a fresh fruit coulis

or salad of smoked salmon with sour cream dressing, following with a good choice of meat dishes (perhaps rack of English lamb (served pink) with a mixed fruit compote and a mint and redcurrant sauce), three fish (fillet of monkfish with a julienne of vegetables and a wholegrain mustard and tarragon sauce) and two vegetarian options. Puddings range from banoffi pie to gooseberry crumble and custard. Lighter snacks like chicken and vegetable pie, ploughman's platters and a range of sandwiches are available at lunchtimes only. The final ingredient to this successful inn is the comfortable en-suite accommodation, most of the rooms being located across the lane in the converted stables. All are attractively decorated and furnished (some with four-posters) and equipped with TV, beverage tray, radio, telephone and trouser press. Residents have use of an outdoor swimming pool (heated in summer). Five miles from Junction 17 of the M4. *Open 11-2.30 (Sat to 2.45), 5.30-11 (Sun 12-2.45, 7-10.30).* ***Bar Food*** *12-2, 7-9.30 (Sun to 9). Free House.* ***Beer*** *Flowers IPA, Smiles Best, Shepherd Neame Spitfire, Wadworth 6X, Hall & Woodhouse Tanglefoot, Boddingtons, Theakston Old Peculier, Bass, Marston's Pedigree. Patio, outdoor eating. Family room.* ***Accommodation*** *11 bedrooms, all en suite, £59 (single £43). Children welcome overnight, (under-12s £10 plus meals as taken) additional bed and cot available (both £10). Access, Amex, Diners, Visa.*

FORDCOMBE — Chafford Arms — FOOD

Tel 01892 740267 Map 11 B5
Fordcombe nr Tunbridge Wells Kent TN3 0SA

A blackboard outside this imposing rather than beautiful village tile-hung pub announces crabs (perhaps dressed with prawns) and Dover soles. Both are regular features on the menu and are served alongside a longish home-cooked menu which also offers more usual pub food – lamb chops Dijon, steak and kidney pie and vegetarian quiche. Service is particularly friendly and good-humoured and there is a sense of dedication and commitment in the cooking, even when the pub is exceptionally busy. Pleasant and somewhat wild garden with pub tables. *Open 11-3, 6-11 (Sun 12-3, 7-10.30).* ***Bar Food*** *12.30-2, 7.30-9.45 (no food Sun eve).* ***Beer*** *Strong of Romsey, Wadworth 6X, King & Barnes. Garden. Access, Visa.*

FOREST ROW — Brambletye Hotel — B&B

Tel 01342 824144 **Fax 01342 824833** Map 11 B6
Forest Row East Sussex RH18 5EZ

Recently refurbished hotel located beside the busy A22 in the village centre and close to the Ashdown Forest. The attractive building houses a good locals bar, Black Peter's, dispensing eal ales, and comfortable overnight accommodation in 25 en-suite bedrooms. Most rooms occupy a rear extension that surrounds a pleasant courtyard, and all are neatly furnished in modern style with light oak furniture and good fabrics. Main-building rooms have more charm and character, but all have TVs, telephones and tea-makers for added comfort. *Open 11-3 & 5.30-11 (Sun 12-3 & 7-10.30). Free House.* ***Beer*** *Harveys Best Better, Courage Diretors. Paved courtyard.* ***Accommodation*** *25 bedrooms, all en suite, £69.50 (weekend £55, family room sleeping four £85, single £54, weekend £45). Children welcome overnight, additional bed £10, cot £3. Access, Amex, Visa.*

FORTY GREEN — Royal Standard of England — A

Tel 01494 673382 **Fax 01494 523332** Map 15a E3
Forty Green nr Beaconsfield Buckinghamshire HP9 1XT

Granted its title and coat-of-arms in 1651 by Charles II who sheltered here after the Battle of Worcester, this splendid pub is one of our oldest free houses with a history dating back over 900 years. Tremendous interior with many of the magnificent oak beams having nautical origins, including the massive carved transom from an Elizabethan ship, which now forms part of the entrance hall. Amid a superb array of collectors' items and artefacts this is a truly atmospheric setting for a drink, but unfortunately the food on offer is a cheap and cheerful buffet-style operation. Hamlet signposted off the B474 north of Beaconsfield. *Open 11-3, 5.30-11 (Sun 12-3, 7-10.30). Free House.* ***Beer*** *Marston's Pedigree & Owd Roger, Morland Old Speckled Hen, guest beers. Garden. Pub closed 25 Dec eve. Access, Visa.*

FOTHERINGHAY — Falcon Inn — FOOD

Tel 01832 226254 Map 7 E4
Fotheringhay nr Oundle Northamptonshire PE8 5HZ

By night, the imposing, illuminated church serves as a golden beacon, visible for miles. Standing almost beside it in the main street of this historic village, the Falcon is in many respects the perfect village pub – busy, with a lively friendly crowd and charming staff.

Their reputation for offering good value food for lunch and dinner has spread far and wide, so booking is advisable to avoid disappointment. Prices are marginally cheaper at lunchtime though the choice remains the same – changing daily. Some dishes such as roast duckling with apple and rosemary or chicken in burgundy wine sauce with mushrooms can run out – they only make a batch of 8 or so for each sitting, helping to ensure the freshness of their produce. The menu encompasses everything from a ploughman's lunch or supper and baked spiced grapefruit to venison cutlets in port and orange sauce and fresh Scotch salmon fishcakes. The food is generally simple and unfussy, reflecting the delightful informality of this inn. Afternoon teas are served 3-5pm in summer "when the local hall isn't doing them". In 1587 Mary Stuart, Queen of Scots was beheaded at nearby Fotheringhay Castle, now mere ruins. *Open 10-3, 6-11 (Sun 12-3, 7-10.30).* ***Bar Food*** *12.15-2, 6.45-9.30 (Sun 7-9), no Bar Food Monday. Free House.* ***Beer*** *Adnams Southwold & Broadside, Elgood's Cambridge, Ruddles County, Nethergate IPA, Bass. Garden, outdoor eating. Access, Visa.*

FOWEY — King of Prussia — B&B

Tel 01726 832450 Map 12 C3
Quayside Fowey Cornwall

Zzz...

Pride of place on the tiny quay goes to this most unusual three-storey pink-washed building, which overlooks the perpetually busy quayside and river estuary and across to Pont Pill creek, a sheltered inlet filled with sailing craft. It was built by and named after the notorious smuggler John Carter, who operated from Prussia Cove. A clergyman by day and smuggler by night, his ill-gotten gains built the pub and his dual role in life is reflected in the unusual double-sided inn sign. Beyond the lively main bar, complete with juke box and a young crowd, are six delightful en-suite bedrooms, all of which have splendid river views. Neatly refurbished with co-ordinating colours, fabrics and friezes and furnished with modern pine, they are fresh, clean and very comfortable. Usual facilities include TVs and tea-makers, plus in summer months your own colourful window-box of flowers which spill into the room. Bathrooms are compact, well fitted-out and spotless. Breakfast is taken in the tiny pine-furnished restaurant. *Open 11-11 (Sun 12-3, 7-10.30).* ***Beer*** *St Austell.* ***Accommodation*** *6 bedrooms, all en suite, £46 (single £23). Access, Amex, Visa.*

FOWEY — Ship Inn — B&B

Tel 01726 833751 Map 12 C3
Fowey Cornwall PL23 1AZ

Tucked away among the narrow streets and only 200 yards from the quay, the Ship dates from the 16th-century and is one of the oldest buildings in an attractive little fishing town. Local fishermen congregate in the main bar, which has exposed stone walls, comfortable wall bench seating and various nautical items. Of the six bedrooms, the most popular is the one located in what remains of the original building, which boasts an ornamental ceiling, fine panelled walls and a carved chimney-piece with the date 1570. Other rooms are modern in style with pastel walls and fabrics and simply furnished with new pine. Two overlook the town church. One room has en-suite facilities (and both double and single beds), the others wash basins in the room and all share two sparkling, spacious and fully-tiled bathrooms; one further room (not en suite) also sleeps three. Large residents' lounge. *Open 11-3, 6-11 (Sun 12-3, 7-10.30).* ***Beer*** *St Austell.* ***Accommodation*** *6 bedrooms, 1 en suite, £37-£41 (single £18.50). Children welcome overnight, additional bed and cot supplied. Accommodation closed 25 & 26 Dec. Access, Visa.*

FOWLMERE — Chequers Inn — FOOD

Tel 01763 208369 Map 15 F1
High Street Fowlmere Cambridgeshire SG8 7SR

When Samuel Peyps spent a night here in 1659, the inn was already a popular travellers' rest. Its period charm largely survives and it still goes into many diaries as a good place for refreshment. Beyond the most appealing white-painted facade a civilised, up-market ambience pervades the comfortably furnished and carpeted split-level bar area and the adjacent galleried restaurant. The convivial atmosphere is an ideal one in which to enjoy some good, reliable bar food. Choices are listed on a daily-changing blackboard menu and may feature white onion soup, Stilton and walnut paté – both served with excellent warm French bread – pork and smoked sausage cassoulet, mussels in white wine, cream and garlic and trout fillet in orange sauce. Accompanying vegetables are crisp and salads imaginative. Vegetarian offerings include bean and vegetable crumble. Good cheeseboard, served with

walnut bread. Good global wine list with at least seven wines served by the glass. Rear conservatory extension and delightful rear lawn with flower beds and shrub borders. *Open 12-2.30, 6-11 (Sun 12-3,, 7-10.30). Free House.* ***Bar Food*** *12-2 (Sun to 2.30), 7-10 (Sun to 9.30).* ***Beer*** *Tolly Original, Burton Ale. Garden, outdoor eating. Access, Amex, Diners, Visa.*

FOWNHOPE — Green Man — B&B

Tel 01432 860243 **Fax 01432 860207** Map 14 B1
Fownhope Hereford & Worcester HR1 4PE

A fine old black-and-white, half-timbered inn at the heart of the village and less than a 10-minute walk from the banks of the River Wye, the 'Naked Boy' as it was once called, dates back possibly to the year of Henry VII's accession in 1485. Its historical associations continue through the Civil War to the 18th and 19th centuries when the Green Man became a petty sessional court and coaching inn on the Hereford to Gloucester route (now called the B4224). There is still plenty of timber and stonework extant in the succession of interconnecting rooms which surround the central bar servery. Residents perhaps get the pick in a comfortable lounge with armchairs set around an open log fire, and choice of dining areas including one for non-smokers. Accommodation is of a varying, though commendably high standard, divided between the inn and some smaller annexe rooms, with pride of place going to the old four-posters and former 'Judge's Room', well equipped for family use, which overlooks an enclosed rear courtyard. Here there is also the Stable Room, ideal for residents who prefer to be on the ground floor. Appointments, which run from TV and telephones to tea-trays, hairdryers and trouser presses, are standard throughout. *Open 11-3, 6-11 (Sun 12-3, to 2.30 in winter, 7-10.30). Free House.* ***Beer*** *Samuel Smith Old Brewery, Marston's Pedigree, Hook Norton Best, Courage Best, John Smith's. Garden. Family room.* ***Accommodation*** *20 bedrooms, all en suite, £50 (single £31). Children welcome overnight (under 5 yrs £2.50, 5-12 yrs £7.50), additional bed and cot available. Access, Amex, Visa.*

FRAMPTON MANSELL — Crown Hotel — B&B

Tel 01285 760601 **Fax 01285 760681** Map 14 B2
Frampton Mansell nr Stroud Gloucestershire GL6 8JB

Zzz...

Of 16th-century origin, the Crown stands at the heart of the village just off the A419 and just within the Cotswold district; its extensive acreage of ground falls steeply away through mature woods and orchard to the Thames/Severn canal far below. While the bar areas are typically quaint, the pub opens out into larger rear extensions. The largest of these houses a dozen spacious bedrooms uniformly fitted out with mahogany furniture, gold-tapped avocado bathrooms and close carpeting. The four ground-floor rooms, with direct access from the car park, are especially convenient for the less mobile, while it's the abundant peace and quiet amid restful panoramic views which proves to be one of the pub's greatest assets (the food is still not one of them). *Open 11-2.30, 6.30-11 (Fri & Sat from 6, Sun 12-3, 7-10.30). Free House.* ***Beer*** *Oakhill Best, Wadworth 6X. Garden. Family room.* ***Accommodation*** *12 bedrooms, all en suite, £45 (family room sleeping up to 4 £55, single £25). Children welcome overnight (under-8s stay free in parents' room), additional bed (£5) and cot supplied. Pub closed 25 Dec eve. Accommodation closed 25 Dec. Access, Visa.*

FREELAND — Shepherds Hall Inn — B&B

Tel 01993 881256 Map 14a B2
Witney Road Freeland Oxfordshire OX8 8HQ

Once known as the 'Shepherds All' and originally a 13th-century shelter for shepherds and drovers, the green-shuttered inn today offers plain and practical accommodation. The exterior of the pub is resplendent with colourful flower boxes in summer and there's a dovecote in the car park. Within the pub, the bar is filled with antique furniture, copper and brass and wheelback chairs, and a collection of plates adorns the walls. Five bedrooms (three of which are in an annexe) are clean, comfortable and modern in style, and include TVs, radios, telephones and tea-making facilities. The annexe rooms have neat, tiled shower rooms, and the pub rooms have private bathrooms. The patio and lawned garden with flowerbeds is safe for children, who also have their own purpose-built play area. On the

A4095 half-way between Woodstock and Witney. *Open 10-2.30, 6-11 (Sun 12-3, 7-10.30). Free House.* ***Beer*** *Wadworth 6X, Flowers IPA. Garden, children's play area. Family room.* ***Accommodation*** *5 bedrooms, all en suite (two with bath), £40 (single £25). Children welcome overnight (under-2s stay free in parents' room), additional bed (£5) and cot supplied. Access, Visa.*

FRILFORD HEATH — Dog House Hotel — B&B

Tel 01865 390830 Fax 01865 390860 Map 14a C3
Frilford Heath Marcham nr Abingdon Oxfordshire OX13 6QJ

A ten-minute drive from Oxford, this pleasant 300-year-old tile-hung inn commands a lovely view over the Vale of the White Horse. The bar is spacious, and incorporates a central stone fireplace with a real winter fire. Eight bedrooms are non-smoking, all have en-suite facilities, TVs with satellite channels, telephones, hairdryers and pine furniture. Top of the range is the four-poster bridal suite (the inn is a popular venue for summer weddings); two family rooms sleep three. Note the considerably reduced tariff at weekends. *Open 11-11 (Sun 12-3, 7-10.30).* ***Beer*** *Morland. Garden, children's play area.* ***Accommodation*** *19 bedrooms, all en suite, £69 (Fri & Sat £44, family rooms £79 – weekends £58, four-poster £80, single £65). Children welcome overnight, additional cot (£5) available. Access, Amex, Diners, Visa.*

FRILSHAM — Pot Kiln — A

Tel 01635 201366 Map 14a C4
Frilsham nr Hermitage Berkshire RG16 0XX

A remote country pub on the Yattendon to Bucklebury lane, delightful in summer in the pretty sheltered garden with its soothing outlook across open fields to woodland. The name derives from this being the site of old brick kilns (abandoned after the war) and the building is, appropriately, of attractive redbrick construction. Inside is distinctively old-fashioned, with three simply-furnished bars leading off a small lobby bar. Bare boards, sturdy wooden tables, cushioned wall bench seating and warming open fires characterise the good, relaxing atmosphere, with a successful mix of chatty locals and passing ramblers filling the unspoilt bars. Impromptu folk music some Sunday evenings. Well-behaved children who don't leave an "appalling mess" are welcome indoors. *Open 12-2.30, 6.30-11 (Sun 12-3, 7-10.30). Free House.* ***Beer*** *Arkell's Best, Morland Original & Old Speckled Hen, Morrells Mild. Garden. Family room. No credit cards.*

FRITHELSTOCK — Clinton Arms — FOOD B&B

Tel 01805 623279 Fax 01805 624006 Map 12 C2
Frithelstock Torrington Devon EX38 8JH

Lively landlords Robert and Amanda Andrews have reversed the fortunes of this homely and unpretentious pub which nestles in a sleepy, affluent village two miles west of Torrington off the A386. Home-cooked bar meals and evening restaurant fare (also available in the bar) are attracting folk from far and wide, notably for the exotic ingredients – African desert locusts, bison, crocodile, kangaroo, ostrich and aligator – that have become "very popular" in the last year. Lighter bites are well-cooked pub favourites like fisherman's pie, gammon steak, omelettes, jacket potatoes and ploughman's platters. There are 116 items on the menu – you can even try a 'Clinton Combination' of wild boar with juniper and bison sausages served with chips or crusty bread. Upstairs, accommodation comprises three spacious and pleasantly decorated bedrooms with equally good-sized en-suite facilities. One room overlooks the small village green and three more bedrooms were due to come on stream around Easter of 1996. Delightful walled garden with tables and chairs plus numerous playthings to keep children amused. *Open 12-2.30, 5.30-11 (Sun 12-3, 7-10.30).* ***Bar Food*** *12-2, 7-10 (Sun to 9.30). Free House.* ***Beer*** *Bass, guest beer. Garden, outdoor eating. Family room.* ***Accommodation*** *3 rooms, all en suite, £46 (single £25). Children welcome overnight, additional bed and cot supplied. Check-in by arrangement. Access, Visa.*

We only recommend food (Bar Food) in those establishments highlighted with the **FOOD** symbol.

FULKING Shepherd & Dog FOOD

Tel 01273 857382 Map 11 B6
Fulking nr Henfield West Sussex BN5 9LU

In a truly glorious setting nestling at the base of the South Downs in a picturesque village, this 14th-century pub is named after the shepherds who farmed the surrounding downs and once served the travelling shepherds on their way to nearby Findon fair. It boasts inglenook fireplaces, polished oak tables, a low beamed ceiling and is decorated with numerous old artefacts, including a collection of shepherds crooks. A varied selection of bar meals ranges from tomato and orange soup or marinated feta cheeses and olive salad to start, followed by beef and Guinness pie, rack of lamb with rosemary sauce and pollack topped with a pesto crust. Lighter lunchtime snacks include a range of ploughman's, granary sandwiches and salads. Rhubarb and apple crumble, chocolate and coconut tart and Bakewell tart are among the home-made puddings. Idyllic terraced summer garden with stream and play area. No children under 14 inside. *Open 11-3 (to 2.30 in winter), 6-11 (Sun 12-3, 7-10.30).* ***Bar Food*** *12-2 (to 2.15 in winter), 7-9.30 (Sun 12-2.30, 7.30-9.30). Free House.* ***Beer*** *Courage Best & Directors, Harveys Best Bitter, Webster's Yorkshire Bitter. Garden, outdoor eating area. Access, Amex, Visa.*

FULLERS MOOR Copper Mine FOOD

Tel 01829 782293 Map 6 A3
Nantwich Road Fullers Moor nr Broxton Cheshire CH3 9JH

Geoff and Linda Aldridge's carpeted and pine-clad dining pub is interestingly adorned with mining memorabilia inside, while outside there's a spacious summer garden and barbecue. Last year a 30-seater, no-smoking conservatory was added, as was more variety to the food. Wholemeal sandwiches, open or closed, speciality batches with hot fillings and baked jacket potatoes (perhaps topped with creamy blue cheese, coleslaw and peppers or prawns in seafood sauce) are always on offer on the snack menu. More substantially, look for the daily specials like Cheddar cheese soup with croutons and fresh chives, scrambled eggs with prawns on a toasted muffin, Maltese chicken (in a cream and Pernod sauce) with avocado, grilled Dover sole or turkey, sausage, onion and pineapple kebabs. A variety of steaks and sauces is also offered in the evening, as is a selection of five or so vegetarian dishes. Sunday lunches see a choice of roasts alongside five or so further hot selections; children's favourites (or a small portion of the roast) come with a free 'goody' bag. 'Traditional puddings, tempting desserts and luxury ice creams' complete the picture. Walkers should ask landlady Linda about details of the Sandstone Trail (along the sandstone Central Cheshire Ridge) and of local castles. *Open 12-3, 7-11 (Sun 12-3, 7-10.30).* ***Bar Food*** *12-2.30, 7-9.30.* ***Beer*** *Burtonwood, Bass. Garden, outdoor eating. Patio. Access, Amex, Diners, Visa.*

FYFIELD White Hart A

Tel 01865 390585 Map 14a B2
Main Road Fyfield nr Abingdon Oxfordshire OX13 5LN

John and Sherry Howard's 500-year-old former chantry house (abolished in 1548) has been a pub since 1580 when St John's College in Oxford, large local landowners, leased it to tenants but reserved the right to 'occupy it if driven from Oxford in pestilence' – so far this has not been invoked! At some time in its history the large hall was divided into two floors, but in 1963 this was removed, thereby restoring the main hall's original proportions and exposing the 15th-century arch-braced roof to view. There's still a splendid 30-foot-high minstrel's gallery overlooking the main bar and the interior features original oak beams and flagstone floors. To one side, a more intimate bar features an inglenook fireplace; other rooms are generally used for dining and some of them are no-smoking. The long bar menu runs the whole gamut of traditional pub food and includes vegetarian options; families are bound to find something to share. The very large, rambling lawned garden includes a children's play area. Just off A420, seven miles from Abingdon and eight miles from Oxford. *Open 11-3, 6-11 (Sun 12-3, 7-10.30). Free House.* ***Beer*** *Boddingtons, Hook Norton, Wadworth 6X, Theakston Old Peculier, two guest beers. Garden. Family room. Pub closed 25 & 26 Dec. Access, Amex, Visa.*

We only recommend food (Bar Food) in those establishments highlighted with the **FOOD** symbol.

GEDNEY DYKE — The Chequers — FOOD

Tel & Fax 01406 362666 Map 7 F3
Main Street Gedney Dyke Lincolnshire PE12 0AJ

Gedney Dyke lies off the A17, 3 miles east of Holbeach, isolated amid vast open fenland. One can find this unassuming white-painted pub in the heart of the village, but you will not be alone for this humble establishment attracts diners from miles around, as well as having a loyal local clientele. The homely carpeted bar has a chatty atmosphere, an open fire and is simply furnished, a trend which continues into the adjacent, unfussy dining area. Space is at a premium, especially during busy times. The blackboard bar snack menu above the bar is rather run-of-the-mill (sandwiches lunchtimes only), but home-cooked options like bobotie and leek and Stilton bake stand out. Most, however, order from the more imaginative restaurant menu and daily-changing specials board – also available in the bar – which features some interesting dishes, for example, Cajun chicken, sautéed pigeon breast served on a pocket of onion marmalade with a mustard sauce, baked sea bass with fennel, sea bream with Provençal sauce and guinea fowl with avocado and papaya salsa. A separate pudding board may highlight English walnut tart or St Emilion au chocolat. Fresh fish is delivered from Grimsby. Well-chosen global list of wines from Adnams at sensible prices. *Open 12-3, 7-11 (Sun 12-3, 7-10.30). **Bar Food** 12-2, 7-9 (Thur-Sat 7-9.30). Free House. **Beer** Adnams Best, Bateman XXXB, Greene King Abbot Ale, Bass, Morland Old Speckled Hen. Garden, outside eating. Access, Amex, Diners, Visa.*

GLEMSFORD — Black Lion — FOOD

Tel 01787 280684 **Fax 01787 280817** Map 10 C3
Lion Road Glemsford Suffolk CO10 7RF

On entering the Lion, it turns out to have a treasure of a Tudor interior complete with half-timbered walls and rehabilitated timbers, which today serve to frame and support the bar. With this noble lineage is a mixed decor of distinctly Edwardian feel; quarry-tiled floors, country prints, leather armchairs and bay-window seats, all of which is at once both uncluttered and charming. Licensee Anne White concentrates on producing good home cooking: lasagne and chicken or beef and Guinness pie are good examples on the bar food menu. There's a wider choice of dishes in the dining-room but the cooking remains uncomplicated: garlic mushrooms, mackerel and dill paté, steak and kidney pie in Abbot Ale, grilled salmon. Their fruit pies and toffee apple tart are also home-made. There are four or five vegetarian dishes on both menus and, for those who favour a roast, a three-course traditional Sunday lunch is offered. *Open 11-3, 6-11 (Sun 12-3, 7-10.30). **Bar Food** 12-2.30, 6.30-9.30 (no food Sun eve). **Beer** Greene King. Garden, outdoor eating, children's play area. No credit cards.*

GLOOSTON — Old Barn — FOOD

Tel 01858 545215 Map 7 D4 **B&B**
Main Street Glooston Leicestershire LE16 7ST

On the route of the Old Roman road called the Gartree, the Old Barn stands at the centre of a tiny hamlet and just across the road from a picture postcard row of stone terraced cottages; the pub's 16th-century frontage of tiny leaded windows framed by flowering boxes and hanging baskets also makes a summer picture. Within, the premises have now been knocked through so that the small upper bar now leads down into the larger cellar bar where a log fire burns in winter; bookings are taken in the upper, no-smoking restaurant part only. Prominently displayed blackboard menus run, typically, from home-made fish soup, smoked trout in home-made horseradish and spiced chicken wings to seafood risotto, ham hock with English mustard sauce, dressed crab, sautéed fillet of pork with a gooseberry glaze. The handful of puddings are all home-made: perhaps banoffi pie, chocolate mousse, summer pudding or a plate of cheese. Fixed-price, three-course Sunday lunches offer exceptional value. The bedrooms – two doubles and a twin, are well fitted out, with duvets, trouser press and hairdryer, small televisions and bedside radio. Owing to lack of space, the modular fitted shower rooms are a cramped, if practical, solution. Hosts Charles and Claire Edmondson-Jones and chef/partner Stewart Sturge offer good food, good service and genuine friendliness; the Old Barn is simply one of those pubs to which people keep going back. *Open 12-2.30 (Sat to 3 Sun), 7-11. Pub closed Mon-Fri lunch & Sun eve. **Bar Food** 12-1.45 (Sat snacks only, Sun blackboard and fixed-price lunch), 7-9.30. Free House. **Beer** Theakston Best & XB, two guest beers. Garden, outdoor eating. **Accommodation** 3 bedrooms, all en suite with shower, £49.50 (single £37.50). Children welcome overnight, cot available. Check-in by arrangement. Access, Amex, Visa.*

GOATHLAND — Mallyan Spout Hotel — FOOD B&B

Tel 01947 896486 **Fax 01947 896327** Map 5 F3
Goathland nr Whitby North Yorkshire YO22 5AN

Zzz... 

Goathland village is tucked into a fold in the moors two miles off the A159 and some 9 miles from Whitby. The unusual name of Peter and Judith Heslop's inn derives from the waterfall which cascades down the wooded valley just yards from the pub garden; hugging the valley's contours runs the North Yorkshire Moors Railway. Lunchtime in the Spout Bar can be a busy occasion with customers regularly overflowing into the Hunt Bar and hotel lounge next door. Ever-popular are the Mallayan home-cured beef, deep-fried monkfish and chips, pork and chicken pie, alongside sandwiches and ploughman's. Puddings to follow are of the sticky toffee and summer fruits varieties. Evenings see the hotel restaurant move up a gear, with bar food restricted to the Spout public bar only. Incidentally, the hoppy and malty Double Chance bitter served here is named after the Grand National winner and is brewed in the former stable block in Malton where the horse was once kept. Bedrooms, indubitably upmarket in a purely pubby context, are housed to the rear and the side of the Jacobean-style, ivy-covered hotel; of the four small and cottagey rooms in the coach house, two are on the ground floor for those with mobility problems; second-floor rooms in the main hotelhave cottage-style, low ceilings. Four large bedrooms (no dogs or children in these) have splendid views of the valley – two rooms have balconies; some rooms have half-tester or Laura Ashley coronet-draped beds. En-suite bathrooms are generally on the small side, except in the four newest rooms. Negotiate, if you can, a larger room if arriving with a family; no reduction for children's meals in the restaurant at dinner (when children under 6 are not welcome); high-tea served from 6-7pm. *Open 11-11 (Sun 12-3, 7-10.30).* ***Bar Food*** *12-2, 7-9 (from 7 Sun). Free House.* ***Beer*** *Malton Double Chance. Garden, patio. Family room.* ***Accommodation*** *26 bedrooms, all en suite, £65-£145 (£45-£60 single). Children welcome overnight (under-2s stay free in parents' room), additional bed (£10) and cot available. Hotel closed 4-21 Jan. Access, Amex, Diners, Visa.*

GODSTOW — Trout Inn — A

Tel 01865 54485 Map 14a C2
195 Godstow Road Lower Wolvercote nr Oxford Oxfordshire OX2 8PN

This famous medieval pub situated on the River Thames at Godstow on the outskirts of Wolvercote still attracts thousands of visitors every year. In summer, the cobbled terrace beside the fast-running river with its weir makes a restful place for a quiet pint while watching the peacocks wandering round the terrace and catching a glimpse of the chub in the clear water. The bridge across to the private island is now sadly falling apart but it is still possible to see across to the island with its famous stone lion, and on to the now-ruined Godstow Nunnery where the fair Rosamund (Henry II's mistress) was imprisoned. Inside the pub you'll find flagstone floors, beamed ceilings and bare floorboards, with welcoming open fires in winter. Be warned, the Trout can get very busy in the summer. *Open 11-11 (Sun 12-10.30).* ***Beer*** *Bass, Charrington IPA, guest beer. Riverside garden. Family room. Access, Amex, Diners, Visa.*

GOOSNARGH — Bushells Arms — FOOD

Tel 01772 865235 **Fax 01772 861837** Map 6 B1
Church Lane Goosnargh Lancashire PR3 2BH

Just 4 miles from Junction 32 of the M6, this modernised Georgian building offers a splendid alternative to the expensive plastic food of the motorway service areas. To reach the pub, follow the A6 North and turn on to the B5269; once in the village, take the left turn opposite the post office, and you'll find the Bushells Arms about a quarter of a mile along on the right. It's run by the experienced David and Glynis Best, who have written a book on the business side of pub catering, using much of their own experience. Certainly the food at the Bushells is first-rate; cooking is in the hands of Glynis, who produces a long, wide and cosmopolitan selection of specials, blackboard-listed behind the food counter, as well as those on the distinguished printed menu. A truly international menu includes spring rolls and falafel for starters with Greek stifado, chicken Kiev or chili con carne to follow. British dishes aren't forgotten either: a steak, kidney and Murphy's pie is admirably handled. There are fine accompaniments, too, like O'Brien potatoes, a delicious mix of diced potato with cream, peppers, spices, garlic and Parmesan cheese. No sandwuches, but ploughman's platters available all day. The interior of the pub itself is cleverly divided into a number of alcoves by using effective wooden screens and exposed sandstone columns and walls. There's also lots of greenery, not all of it real. Seating is

mainly on plush red button banquettes and stools, arranged around unfussy wooden tables, and a couple of the areas are non-smoking. Brasses and watercolours in a real mix of styles hang on the walls, and there's piped music. To the rear is a well-maintained garden with white plastic patio furniture, useful in summer when the pub can get extremely busy. Staff are noticeably welcoming and friendly. The village, incidentally, is pronounced 'Goozner'. *Open 12-3, 6-11 (Sun 12-3, 7-10.30). Occasional bar closures on Mondays.* ***Bar Food*** *12-2.15, 7-10.* ***Beer*** *Tetleys, Boddingtons. Garden, outdoor eating. No credit cards.*

Gosfield — Green Man — FOOD

Tel 01787 472746 Map 10 C3
The Street Gosfield Essex CO9 1TT

A rust-brick roadside pub on the A1017, 2 miles off the A131. The bar and eating areas are more or less one and the same, presided over by two tropical fish tanks. The day's dishes are displayed on the blackboard: mostly English as in perhaps tomato soup, beef casserole with dumplings, salmon cutlet, or liver and bacon, all accompanied by two vegetables and a choice of potatoes. Lighter snacks, including Welsh rarebit, soft roes on toast with bacon and sandwiches, are also available. The centrepiece, however, is the cold lunchtime buffet, laden with home-cooked ham on the bone, roast turkey, pork, beef and lamb joints, a whole salmon and a colourful selection of salads. Equally inviting are the delights on the sweet trolley, a rarity in pubs, with temptations such as Paris Brest, apricot and ginger charlotte, profiteroles, chocolate gateau, pear tart – most certainly none of your bought-in puds here! Landlord John Arnold keeps an eye on diners, making sure their needs are satisfied; the charming waitresses are efficiency personified. *Open 11-3, 6.30-11 (Sun 12-3, 7-10.30).* ***Bar Food*** *11-2.30, 6.30-10.* ***Beer*** *Greene King. Access, Amex, Visa.*

Goudhurst — Star & Eagle — B&B

Tel 01580 211512 **Fax 01580 211416** Map 11 B5
High Street Goudhurst Kent TN17 1AL

Behind the splendid timbered and gabled facade vintage charm and modern comfort blend harmoniously in a fine 14th-century hostelry owned by Whitbread. Beams, bricks, vaulted stonework and inglenooks make great appeal in the public rooms, while creaking floors and odd angles are the order of the day in the bedrooms. These vary in size and shape and the majority are furnished in pine, though the four-poster room has some antiques. In the public areas, period appeal survives in exposed beams, open brick fireplaces and old settles. *Open 11-11 Mon-Sat (Sun 12-3, 7-10.30).* ***Beer*** *Flowers Original, Fremlins. Garden. Family room, children's playroom.* ***Accommodation*** *11 bedrooms, 9 en suite, £45 (Sun-Thur), £48 Fri & Sat (four-poster £50 – £65 Fri & Sat, single £32.50). Children welcome overnight (under-5s free if sharing parents' room, 3-16s £15), additional bed and cot available. Dogs by arrangement only. Access, Amex, Visa.*

Grange Moor — Kaye Arms — FOOD

Tel 01924 848385 Map 6 C1
29 Wakefield Road Grange Moor West Yorkshire WF4 4BG

True family involvement has raised both expectations and results since the Coldwell family bought the Kaye Arms from Tetley's Brewery, and it goes from strength to strength. Arrive early for the table of your choice (there are no reservations) and lunch at leisure from a legion of choices. Top sellers include the cheese soufflé with Waldorf salad and smoked chicken; sandwiches like marinated chicken or chargrilled salmon with grilled peppers are always popular, as are ploughman's platters – all served with home-made bread (24 loaves are baked daily). More substantial lunch and evening fare brings into play the likes of chicken in filo pastry, salmon fillets with lime butter and some first-class char grilled steaks. To the uninitiated (and the brewery, perhaps), the complaint might be that this is no pub, as crisps and real ales are totally overlooked; yet carefully chosen wines by the glass remain, in this context, a better complement. A policy of three pounds added to the cost price of any bottle (rather than a triple multiplication of it) provides plenty of choice and value at a price which the average pub-goer should appreciate. *Open 11.30-3, 7-11 (Sat 6.30-11).* ***Bar Food*** *(no food Mon lunch) 12-2, 7.30-10 (Sat from 6.30, Sun to 9.30). No real ales. Pub closed Monday lunchtime. Access, Visa.*

GRANTCHESTER **Rupert Brooke** A

Tel 01223 840295 Map 15 F1
2 The Broadway Grantchester nr Cambridge

Named after the poet who immortalised this beautiful village of thatched and lime-washed cottages in his poem "The Vicarage, Grantchester". Brooke lived nearby and used the pub as his local before the First World War. An interesting collection of memorabilia relating to the poet adorns the walls of the comfortably refurbished interior which boasts plenty of exposed brick, beams, standing timbers and some cosy seating areas. The village can be reached from Cambridge via a delightful footpath across Grantchester Meadows. Copious seating at picnic tables in the garden. Whitbread Wayside Inns. *Open 11-11 (Sun 12-3, 7-10.30). **Beer** Flowers IPA, Boddingtons, Wadworth 6X guest beer. Garden. Access, Visa.*

GRAYSWOOD **Wheatsheaf Inn** ★ FOOD

Tel 01428 644440 Map 11 A6 **B&B**
Grayswood nr Haslemere Surrey GU27 2DE

Having run three successful pubs in West Sussex over the past decade the Colman family have ventured into Surrey to this Victorian village inn, located beside the busy A286 near the parish church, cricket pitch and green (where there's a children's playground), for their next challenge. There's a neat and comfortable bar area with older-style furniture, quality prints and fabrics, with the adjacent spacious L-shaped restaurant sporting artistic plants, marble-topped tables, a terracotta-tiled floor and cushioned rattan chairs, creating a relaxing 'Italian-style' ambience. Quality of cooking and food presentation matches the stylish surroundings, with both the regularly-changing lunch and dinner menus listing imaginative pub fare; one menu is served throughout. Typical dishes might incude warm salad of mushrooms with pancetta ham and chili oil, smoked salmon and scrambled eggs, mushroom and red pepper risotto. fusilli pasta with Provençal sauce, pan-seared tuna with a lime sauce, as well as a range of sandwiches, a mixed-cheese ploughman's and salads. Specials might encompass steak and kidney pie, peppered medallions of monkfish on a tomato compote with a chive cream sauce, and roast rack of lamb with chargrilled vegetables, tomato and basil sauce. Round off the meal with a home-madepudding: perhaps lemon tart with raspberry and mango coulis or a chocolate truffle slice. Short, global list of keenly-priced wines. Seven comfortable en-suite bedrooms are housed in a newish rear brick extension. Uniformly modern in decor and furnishings they have clean marble-floored bathrooms, as well as TVs, telephones and tea-makers for added comfort. Conference facilities. *Open 11-3, 6-11 (Sun 12-3, 7-10.30). **Bar Food** 12-2, 6.30-10. Free House. **Beer** Ballard's Bitter, Wadworth 6X, Wheatsheaf Bitter, Hall & Woodhouse Badger Best. Garden, outdoor eating. **Accommodation** 7 bedrooms, all en suite, £55 (single £40). Children welcome overnight (under-5s stay free in parents' room), additional bed (£5) and cot available. Check-in by arrangement. No dogs. Access, Visa.*

GREAT CHESTERFORD **Plough** A

Tel 01799 530283 Map 10 B3
High Street Great Chesterford Essex CB10 1PL

Delightful 18th-century village pub with a traditional, unspoilt and well-cared-for interior, despite the addition of a more modern rear extension which houses the bar. Original cottagey bars feature exposed standing timbers and ceiling beams, two warming winter fires in inglenooks and neatly arranged tables. The airy extension leads out on to an attractive patio and lawn for summer alfresco drinking. Children can enjoy the large adventure playground with its aerial runway, wooden climbing frames and swings. *Open 11-3, 6-11 (Sun 12-3, 7-10.30 or all day). **Beer** Greene King. Garden, children's play area. Family room. Access, Visa.*

GREAT KIMBLE **Bernard Arms** FOOD

Tel 01844 346172 **Fax 01844 346173** Map 15a D2 **B&B**
Great Kimble nr Aylesbury Buckinghamshire HP27 0XS

On the A4010 about 3 miles north of Princes Risborough. The original early 19th-century core of a coaching inn has been much modernised and extended to include a homely Victorian-style bar decorated with plates and prints of birds and sea scenes on the walls, currency from around the world covering the bar shelves and three unusual old chimney pots containing plants. Blackboard bar menus change seasonally with all the inventive dishes

being home-made using fresh herbs from their own herb garden; warm goat's cheese salad, Nile perch, loin of pork with sage sauce, grilled chicken fillet with garlic and herbs, Bakewell tart or summer pudding served with custard, ice cream or cream. An excellent leek puff with Dijon mustard was recently enjoyed. A separate restaurant offers two table d'hote menus. A 3-course traditional Sunday lunch is also served. Results on the plate are good, each dish served with fresh, crisp vegetables; service is efficient and friendly. Lovely garden in which to escape the noisy road. Five bedrooms with basins and showers share two toilets; TV, tea-makers and telephones are standard. Choice of 26 malt whiskies at the bar. *Open 11-3, 6-11 (12-3, 7-10.30).* ***Bar Food*** *12-2.30, 7-10.* ***Beer*** *Benskins Best, Tetley Bitter, Burton Ale, Wadworth 6X. Garden, games room.* ***Accommodation*** *5 bedrooms, £45 (single £35, triple £55). Children welcome overnight, additional cot available. Access, Visa.*

GREAT MISSENDEN — The George — A

Tel 01494 862084 **Fax 01494 865622** Map 15a E2
94 High Street Great Missenden Buckinghamshire HP16 0BG

A Grade II listed ancient monument, the George still has its 15th-century timbers intact; there are a dozen foot-thick beams on the bar parlour ceiling alone. There are two intimate rooms for the main bar and a wood-burning fire, while a further room is also warmed by a fire. Six smart, en-suite bedrooms have TV, radio, hairdryer, telephone and tea/coffee-making facilities; four have en-suite bathrooms, the other two just a shower. A grass and shingle patio/garden at the back is safe for children. *Open 11-11 (Sun 12-3, 7-10.30).* ***Beer*** *Wadworth 6X, Adnams Southwold, two guest beers. Patio/garden.* ***Accommodation*** *6 bedrooms, all en suite, £49.95. Access, Amex, Visa.*

GREAT RISSINGTON — The Lamb — ★ — FOOD — B&B

Tel 01451 820388 **Fax 01451 820724** Map 14a A2
Great Rissington Cheltenham Gloucestershire GL54 2LP

Zzz... 🍷

Dating back nearly 300 years, the oldest part of the Lamb was originally a stone Cotswold farmhouse. Over the last 50 years one of its more celebrated claims to fame lies in the memory of a ditched wartime bomber which crashed in the garden, its propeller still preserved above the stove in the bar. For 16 years now the Lamb has been home to the Cleverlys whose extensions and improvements are a tribute to the family name; there is master craftsmanship everywhere here, to the extent that joins between the original and much newer parts are virtually indistinguishable. Kate Cleverly's labours in the kitchen are evident and home cooking remains the key: you'll find the likes of cold poached salmon, fresh lemon sole or haddock with a spinach and cheese topping, salads and pasta dishes, steak and kidney pie, liver and bacon and filled jacket potatoes (lunchtimes) served in the bar. The restaurant offerings are more serious but prices are still fairly kind; among the choices might be grilled sardines, avocado and smoked bacon salad, half a roast duckling with an orange sauce, vegetarian lasagne, and local trout stuffed with an apricot and almond stuffing. The Lamb remains essentially a chatty, informal village local whose same informality draws returning guests for an overnight stay to enjoy the Lamb's great tranquillity. Richard and Kate's skills have combined in the creation of charming bedrooms which include built-in wardrobes made with salvaged timbers, and two four-poster beds. Kate's contribution is the pretty decor, each room highly individual in style, with co-ordinating fabrics and wall coverings. Most of the furniture is antique and all but two rooms, which share a shower room, have en-suite bathrooms (five with showers rather than baths). They make a virtue out of not having television or radios in most of the rooms but addicts will find a television (and a log fire) in the cosy residents' lounge, as well as in the four top-of-the-range suites. There's a heated indoor swimming pool (May-Oct) in the delightful garden for residents and a separate beer garden to one side of the pub. Several high-chairs are provided and children are welcome. Dogs (£1.50 per night, not including food) are only permitted in the bedrooms; over thirteen years visitors to the Lamb have contributed over £25,000 to a Guide Dog fund, providing 26 dogs. *Open 11.30-2.30, 6.30-11 (Sun 12-2.30, 7-10.30).* ***Bar Food*** *12-1.45, 7-9 (Fri & Sat to 9.30). Free House.* ***Beer*** *Morland Old Speckled Hen, guest beer. Garden, outdoor eating.* ***Accommodation*** *12 bedrooms, all en suite, £52 (four-poster £60, suite £65-£75, single from £30). Children welcome overnight (under-2s free if sharing parents' room), additional bed (£10), cot available (£3.50). Accommodation closed 25 & 26 Dec. Access, Amex, Visa.*

GREAT RYBURGH **Boar Inn** B&B

Tel 01328 829212 Map 10 C1
Great Ryburgh nr Fakenham Norfolk NR21 0DX

Zzz...

If you are looking for peaceful and quiet accommodation within handy reach of the Norfolk coastline, the Boar Inn, a white-washed pub nestling near the river Wensum in a sleepy village, is the place to go. On chilly nights a log fire crackles in the huge inglenook fireplace of the low-beamed bar and there are more beams upstairs in the cottagey bedrooms. Each room has a wash basin, TV and tea-making facilities and they share facilities. *Open 11-2.30, 6.30-11 (Sun 12-3, 7-10.30). Free House.* ***Beer*** *Greene King IPA, Wensum Bitter, Adnams Bitter, guest beer. Garden.* ***Accommodation*** *3 bedrooms with shared facilities, £32 (single £22). Children welcome overnight (charge depends on age), cot available. Dogs by arrangement. Access, Visa.*

GREAT TEW **Falkland Arms** FOOD

Tel 01608 683653 **Fax 01608 683656** Map 14a B1
Great Tew Oxfordshire OX7 4DB

Great Tew has the inestimable advantage of being a bit out of the way and not on the main tourist trail. It must be one of the prettiest of Cotswold villages. Despite the ambition implied by its name, it's actually rather a small place, with barely a score of mostly thatched cottages, a small general store and, naturally, in its rightful place opposite the church, the village inn. Dating back to the 16th century, the creeper-clad Falkland Arms must be close to everybody's ideal country pub, with high-backed settles, a flagstone floor and a prized collection of hundreds of jugs and mugs hanging from the old beams. A pretty garden shaded by a large hornbeam tree is complete with dovecote, whose occupants seem to spend most of the day perched on the pub's stone-tiled roof cooing to each other. 50 malt whiskies and 14 country wines are available, as are snuff and even clay pipes ready-filled with tobacco. Food is served at lunchtimes only from a short but varied blackboard menu that changes daily but always includes a vegetarian dish, along with ploughman's and filled baps. Everything is home-made, from a cod and prawn crumble, pork and Stilton hot pot, or duck and apricot pie to sponges and crumbles. Four cottagey bedrooms, two with four-poster beds and two with old iron bedsteads, are furnished with antiques and decorated with pretty co-ordinating fabrics and wall coverings. The largest, under the eaves, has a pitched ceiling, exposed timbers and its own en-suite bathroom. Others have showers and, all but one, their own toilets. Televisions and tea/coffee facilities are standard, and you can help yourself to fresh milk from the kitchen. Breakfast is at 9 o'clock prompt (9.30 on Sundays) and they like the rooms vacated by 10.30 on the day of departure. Bookings must be confirmed in writing with a 50% deposit. *Open 11.30-2.30, 6-11 (Sun 12-2, 7-10.30).* ***Bar Food*** *12-2 (except Sun & Mon). Free House.* ***Beer*** *Donnington Best, Hook Norton Best, Wadworth 6X, Hall & Woodhouse Tanglefoot, five guest beers. Garden, outdoor eating, children's play area.* ***Accommodation*** *4 bedrooms, 3 en suite (one with bath), £50 (single £30). Children welcome overnight (under-5s free if staying in parents' room). No dogs. Check-in by arrangement. Pub closed lunchtime Monday (except Bank Holidays). No credit cards.*

GRETA BRIDGE **Morritt Arms Hotel** B&B

Tel 018336 627232 **Fax 018336 627392** Map 5 D3
Greta Bridge Rokeby nr Barnard Castle Co Durham DL12 9SE

New owners are in the process of restoring the traditional charm to this 17th-century former coaching inn just off the A66 (three miles from Barnard Castle); it stands right by the old stone bridge that is now safely by-passed by today's more modern highway. Sue Atkinson and Barbara-Anne Johnson aim to recreate the warmth and style of days gone by. The atmosphere of the public rooms is characterised by polished block floors laid with Chinese carpets and the deeply-comfortable, loose-covered armchairs arranged in small groups in the cosy lounge with its open log fire. The main Dickens Bar has a mural painted in 1946 by John Gilroy, who took well-known local figures and created a Dickensian theme around them; the Sir Walter Scott Bar has more of a 'local' atmosphere. The bedrooms are simple and homely, each with a trouser press, hairdryer, mineral water and remote-controlled TV. *Open 11-3, 6-11.* ***Bar Food*** *12-2, 6-9 (12-2, 7-8.45 Sun).* ***Beer*** *Timothy Taylor Landlord, Butterknowle Conciliation Ale.* ***Accommodation*** *17 bedrooms, all en suite, £70-£95 (single £55). Children welcome overnight, additional bed (£15) and cot (£5) available. Garden, croquet, bowls, children's play area. Access, Amex, Diners, Visa.*

Gretna — Gretna Chase Hotel — B&B

Tel 01461 337517 **Fax 01461 337766** Map 4 C2
Gretna nr Carlisle Cumbria DG16 5JB

Patrons of the first marriage house over the Scottish border used the nearby Gretna Chase for stabling their horses. That function has long since ceased, but today's honeymooners can install themselves in a splendid four-poster suite. All rooms (with TVs and direct-dial phones) feature quality furniture and fabrics, and most overlook the award-winning garden of 2 ½ acres. There is a spacious Victorian reception hall, plenty of bar space and a little lounge. *Open 11-11 (Sun 12-3, 7-10.30).* ***Beer*** *Theakston Best. Garden.* ***Accommodation*** *8 bedrooms, 6 en suite, £60 (four-poster £80, single from £38). Children welcome overnight (under-4s stay free in parents' room, 4-12 £10), additional bed & cot available. Dogs by arrangement. Pub closed 2 weeks January. Access, Amex, Visa.*

Gretton — Royal Oak — FOOD

Tel 01242 602477 Map 14 C1
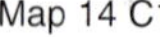
Gretton nr Winchombe Gloucestershire GL54 5EP

Extensive gardens and playing areas (including a tennis court for rent) and regular summer visits by the steam train from Winchcombe all contribute to the irresistible summer attractions of the Royal Oak. Low hop-hung beams adorned with pewter mugs and chamber pots and open log fires, whose glow is reflected in polished flagstones, make it equally appealing in winter. Add to this a good range of real ales and a vast blackboard menu and you have unravelled the secrets of this Cotswold pub's popular success. Sizzling potato skins with garlic mayonnaise and crab and mushroom pot can be either snacks or starters. Main courses run from Normandy chicken with apples and cider and baked ham with cauliflower cheese to popular omelettes Arnold Bennet (with smoked haddock or spinach and cheese). No sandwiches, but ploughman's platters are served all day. Finish off, perhaps, with lemon cream torte or triple chocolate cake (not home-made). The old building does have a certain charm, its mellow stone and rickety porch seemingly held together by the creepers which flourish in the old oak's shadow. *Open 11-3, 6-11 (Sun 12-3, 7-10.30).* ***Bar Food*** *12-2, 7-9.30. Free House.* ***Beer*** *Smiles Best, John Smith's, Wadworth 6X, Ruddles County, Morland Old Speckled Hen, Marston's Pedigree. Garden, outdoor eating. Access, Amex, Visa.*

Grindleford — Maynard Arms Hotel — FOOD B&B

Tel 01433 630321 **Fax 01433 630445** Map 6 C2
Main Road Grindleford Derbyshire S30 1HP

A solid-stone roadside inn located in the Peak National Park, on a hillside outside the village. There's a spacious and attractive public bar, and the Longshaw cocktail bar exudes a stylish and comfortable ambience for the enjoyment of some simply conceived and reliably produced bar food. Pasta bows in a four-cheese sauce and pan-fried black pudding with English mustard, original Yorkshire puddings with fillings or vegetable and mushroom Wellington are virtually meals in themselves. More adventurous choices may include flying fish in curried oil and sizzling chili beef with tagliatelle and stir-fried vegetables. All comers are invited also to leave room for the traditional Bakewell pudding served hot with cream. As befits an old coaching inn, the grand style, large, airy bedrooms overlook the Derwent Valley through elegant stone mullion windows. Suitably up-to-date accessories include direct-dial phones, remote-control TVs and trouser presses. A meeting room next to the first-floor residents' lounge has recently been added. *Open 11-3, 6-11, Sun 12-3, 7-10.30.* ***Bar Food*** *12-2 (Sun to 2.30), 6-9.30 (Sun from 7). Free House.* ***Beer*** *Whitbread Eden, Boddingtons. Garden, outdoor eating. Family room.* ***Accommodation*** *11 bedrooms, all en suite, £59.50 & £69.50 (w/end £79.50, single £44.50 & £49.50, £54 at w/end). Children welcome overnight, additional bed (£10) and cot available. Access, Amex, Visa.*

We only recommend food (Bar Food) in those establishments highlighted with the **FOOD** symbol.

GUITING POWER — Ye Olde Inne — FOOD

Tel 01451 850392 Map 14a A1

Winchcombe Rd Guiting Power nr Stow-on-the-Wold Gloucestershire GL54 5UX

The far end of the single lane running through this picturesque Cotswold village goes by the unlikely name of Th'Ollow Bottom. Here the Olde Inne nestles – a low, listed, 17th-century stone pub and a little hollowed out itself inside. Best of the three tiny rooms is the flagstone-floored dining-room with its sandblasted ceiling timbers and a recently-exposed inglenook. Enthusiastic landlord Bill Tu oversees the kitchen. Old favourites, including asparagus gratinée, frikadeller (Danish pork rissoles) and curried nut roast predominate on the printed menu, with the more adventurous pigeon in red wine and fillet steak with salsa verde chalked up on the bar canopy. Look out, though, for some of Bill's native Burmese favourites like fish koftas or coconut chicken with noodles which make regular guest appearances to spice things up. However, filled granary cobs, ploughman's platters, lasagne and steak and kidney pie show that traditional pub fare is not overlooked. Hearty, home-made puddings. Sunday lunches in winter and junior portions of Golden Tiddlers for toddlers ensure that there is something of good quality and value for all comers. *Open 11.30-2.30, 6-11 (Fri from 5.30, Sun 12-3, 7-10.30). **Bar Food** 12-2, 6.30-9.30 (Sun from 7). Free House. **Beer** Theakston Best, Hook Norton Best, guest beer. Garden, patio, outdoor eating. Access, Visa.*

> Many **B&B** establishments offer reduced rates for weekend and out-of-season bookings. Always ask about special deals for longer stays. Beware half-board terms in inns where we do not recommend the **FOOD.**

GUNWALLOE — Halzephron Inn ★ — FOOD — B&B

Tel 01326 240406 Map 12 A4

Gunwalloe nr Helston Cornwall TR12 7QB

Zzz...

Situated four miles south of Helston on the west coast of the Lizard peninsula, the Halzephron Inn commands an enviable position perched high up above Gunwalloe Fishing Cove, with spectacular views across Mount's Bay to Penzance and the Land's End peninsula (in fine weather). Its rugged stone exterior feels the full force of 2,000 miles of wild Atlantic weather, but inside there is a genuine warm welcome from amiable hosts Angela and Harry Davy Thomas. They have rejuvenated this 500-year-old smugglers' inn (a shaft still exists leading to a tunnel to the beach); the latest addition is a new family room, complete with blackboard, toys and games (and a children's menu), created from an outside stone and slate store. The two spick-and-span, low-ceilinged inter-connecting bars have been simply, yet tastefully refurbished, featuring attractive checked fabrics, scatter cushions on padded wall benches, warming winter fires, general fishing memorabilia, shining copper and brass and original watercolours of Cornish scenes. The intimate 'Captain's Table' cottage dining-room has a head-cracking low ceiling, stone walls, blue and white checked tablecloths topped with antique candlesticks and a cosy atmosphere, plus a charming sea view. Both lunch and evening printed menus offer a varied selection of dishes to please all tastes, from pub favourites to good steaks and home-cooked fare. However, the real emphasis is on the twice daily-changing blackboard menu which lists more imaginative fare using the best of local ingredients. Here everything is home-made, from carrot and coriander soup, smoked fish paté, kedgeree and hot baked crab to lemon sole stuffed with salmon mousse, chicken marengo and pork fillet with caramelised apples. Vegetarians will not be disappointed with cheese and herb soufflé or creamy leek croustade. Puddings like fresh fruit pavloa, hazelnit and chocolate meringue and crème caramel. High standards extend upstairs to the two delightful bedrooms which have been kitted out with flair; they enjoy rolling country views. Notable features include old stripped-pine furniture, Laura Ashley fabrics and wallpapers, colourful cushioned director's chairs, hand-made quilts, original watercolours and nice added touches like fresh fruit, biscuits, mineral water and various books and magazines. Most enjoyable breakfasts. An excellent base from which to explore this unspoilt corner of Cornwall. No children under 14 overnight. *Open 11.30-3, 6.30-11 (Sun 12-3, 7-10.30). **Bar Food** 12-2, 7-9.30. Free House. **Beer** Fergusons Dartmoor Best Bitter & Legend, Sharp's Doombar. Garden, outdoor eating. **Accommodation** 2 rooms, both en suite (one with bath), £50 (single £35). Check-in by arrangement. Access, Visa.*

HAILEY — Bird in Hand — FOOD B&B

Tel 01993 868321 **Fax 01993 868702** Map 14a B2
Whiteoak Green Hailey nr Witney Oxfordshire OX8 5XP

Zzz...

A delightful 'residential country inn' in a rural setting, one mile north of Hailey on B4022. The neat, low-walled roadside garden gives an indication of the standards aimed for inside and the large car park shows its popularity as a dining pub. Inside, four stone-walled bar rooms include one with a long bar, sofa, pews and old tables, plus another with an inglenook where a wood fire burns during winter; the rooms are candle-lit at night. New head chef Ivan Reid was previously at the *New Inn* at Coln St Aldwyns and the Angel at Long Crendon (both still well recommended in this Guide). Here, his menu offers a long list of dishes that might include poppy seed pastry with herring roes and curry buter sauce, crab and fresh coconut salad with orange and grapefruit, three or so pasta dishes, steak and kidney pudding, charcoal grilled steaks and honey-glazed duck breast with saffron apples. These are supplemented by a blackboard of daily fresh fish and other specials like tomato and thyme soup, panaché of local game with Savoy cabbage and bacon or grilled monkfish with red onions and sweet pepper sauce. The snack card offers the likes of ploughman's, sandwiches, scampi, home-cooked cold ham and children's favourites. Sixteen spacious and comfortable, cottagey rooms are in a U-shaped, two-storey building with wooden balconies overlooking a central grassed courtyard. Two ground-floor twin rooms for the disabled; two large, family rooms have a double and a single bed plus a sofa bed and room for a cot. Pine furnishings, thoughtful touches and good housekeeping bring all rooms up to an above-average pub standard. Room-only prices are quoted, but the prices we quote here include cooked breakfasts (as for all the entries in this Guide). *Open 11-11 (Sun 12-3, 7-10.30).* ***Bar Food*** *12-2, 7-9.45 (Sun 7.15-9.30). Free House.* ***Beer*** *Boddingtons, Bass, guest beer. Patio, outdoor eating.* ***Accommodation*** *16 rooms, all en suite, £51 Sun-Thu, £60 Fri & Sat (single £44, £50 Fri & Sat, family room +£12 per person). Children welcome overnight, cot supplied. Check-in by arrangement on Sun afternoon. Dogs by arrangement. Closed three days at Christmas. Access, Visa.*

HALLATON — Bewicke Arms — FOOD

Tel 01858 555217 Map 7 D4
1 Eastgate Hallaton Leicestershire LE16 8UB

Leicestershire countryside. Hallaton itself is locally renowned for the parish church's Norman tower, the conical butter cross on the village green – right across the road from the pub – and the tiny village museum which offers a unique insight into its rural past. The pub is a cracking good local and a predictable printed menu lists the usual steaks and grills, ploughman's and sandwiches – look to the specials board for more adventurous options. Starters typically include garlic mushrooms, deep-fried Camembert, and paté maison, while top-sellers among the main courses include Somerset beef in dry cider and chicken Boursin. Vegetarians get a good look in, too, with risotto, lasagne and a cauliflower, courgette and mushroom bake topped with Stilton crumble, and there's a fair choice of home-made puddings of the cheesecake, pavlova and treacle sponge and custard genre. The pub is consistently busy and the more recently added Bottom Room, stone clad with a bow window, Austrian blinds and an effective library theme, opens when demand dictates. At weekends it's almost certain to be full, so better book. *Open 12-2.30, 7-11 (Sun 12-3, 7-10.30).* ***Bar Food*** *12-2, 7-9.45. Free House.* ***Beer*** *Marston's Pedigree, Ruddles Best & County, Webster's Yorkshire Bitter. Garden, outdoor eating. Access, Visa.*

HALTWHISTLE — Milecastle Inn — FOOD

Tel 01434 320682 Map 5 D2
Military Road Haltwhistle Northumberland NE49 9NN

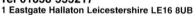

A mere 500 yards from the 42nd milecastle of Hadrian's Wall, the Paynes' neatly-kept inn stands on the B6318, 1½ miles out of town. Probably once a small farm with attendant drover's cottages, it would seem to have a long history of hospitality. Today's cosy, stone-lined interior is hung with a vast collection of brass ornaments and artefacts. The bar nonetheless runs to no more than a half dozen tables. Daily menus are thus kept sensibly short with an emphasis on the hearty pies much favoured by a regular passing trade of wall-walkers. Of these, hot beef & venison or wild duck and boar, perhaps, may be preceeded by leek and potato soup and followed by the popular banoffi pie. There's a front patio and

large, safe garden (now walled-in, with new hard standing for tables, and a dovecote) for leisurely enjoyment of the good real ales. Walkers in muddy boots (and children under 5) are not allowed in the bar. *Open 12-3, 6.30-11 (Sun 12-2.30, 7-10.30).* ***Bar Food*** *12-2, 7-9 (Sun 7-9, to 8.45 in winter). Children over 5 years allowed in the bar to eat. Free House.* ***Beer*** *Tetley, Richardson Four Seasons, Black Sheep Bitter, Lastingham Curate's Downfall. Garden, outdoor eating. Access, Amex, Diners, Visa.*

HAMPSTEAD MARSHALL White Hart Inn FOOD

Tel 01488 658201 **Fax 01488 657192** Map 14a B4
Hampstead Marshall nr Newbury Berkshire RG15 0HW

The splendid herbaceous borders around the neat lawn at the front of this 16th-century inn are very English, and the pride and joy of Dorothy Aromando, but inside the Latin influence of husband Nicola predominates in the White Hart's Italian menu. A few old beams, mingling with some newer ones, give clues to the age of the building, but the decor is basically simple: red plush in the bar, red cloths on the tables of the restaurant leading off it. The same handwritten menu serves for both bar and restaurant. Nicola makes his own pasta and consequently there's a selection of pasta dishes alongside meat dishes. Two favourites are quadroni (ravioli) with wild mushrooms and spinach fettuccine with small lamb meatballs stuffed with mozzarella cheese in a wine, mushroom and cream sauce. Otherwise the menu offers soup of the day, goat's cheese grilled with garlic and yoghurt, Dover sole, chicken breast with ham and asparagus and spinach and ricotta pancake. Amongst the home-made puddings, the crème caramel is outstanding, freshly cooked and with the topping caramelised to just the right degree; tiramisu and cassata might also appear alongside sticky toffee pudding. An old barn to the rear of the pub has been converted into six uncluttered bedrooms with pine furniture and good cotton bedding. All have neat en-suite bathrooms with showers over their bathtubs. Get one of the two large rooms under the eaves, if you can, which have sloping ceilings and exposed timbers, as well as an extra bed for family use. The two single rooms are very compact. Good, freshly-cooked breakfasts set you up for the day ahead. *Open 11.30-2.30, 6-11 (Pub closed Sunday).* ***Bar Food*** *12-2, 6.30-10 (restaurant to 9.30). Free House.* ***Beer*** *Hall & Woodhouse Badger Best, Wadworth 6X. Garden, outdoor eating.* ***Accommodation*** *6 bedrooms, all en suite, £60 (family room sleeping three £65, single £40). Children welcome overnight, additional bed available (£5). No dogs. Check-in by arrangement. Pub closed all Sunday and two weeks in summer. Access, Amex, Visa.*

HARBERTON Church House Inn A

Tel 01803 863707 Map 13 D3
Church House Inn Harberton nr Totnes Devon TQ9 7SF

Tucked away by the church in a sleepy village amid steep narrow lanes off the A381 Totnes to Kingsbridge road, this fine building was originally a chantry house for monks, one of whom is said to be still lurking on the premises, and the Church House didn't pass out of clerical hands until 1950. The carefully removed plaster of centuries has revealed ancient fluted oak beams, a magnificent medieval oak screen, a Tudor window frame and 13th-century glass. The open-plan bar area was once the great chamber, and is now furnished with old pews and settles. *Open 12-3, 6-11 (Sat 11.30-3, 6-11, Sun 12-3, 7-10.30). Free House.* ***Beer*** *Bass, Courage Best, guest beers. Pub closed 25 & 26 Dec eve, 1 Jan eve. No credit cards.*

HARE HATCH Queen Victoria FOOD

Tel 01734 402477 Map 15a D3
Blakes Lane Hare Hatch Berkshire RG10 9TA

This convivial, low-ceilinged 17th-century two-roomed local can be found just off the A4 and is a popular refreshment spot between Reading and Maidenhead. Simply furnished interior which still has some of the original straw and dung walling, a collection of miniature jugs hanging from the ceiling rafters, a real fire and a fruit machine. Blackboards list a reliable selection of bar meals along with the usual favourites. Choices may include hot fresh crab meat with brandy and Parmesan, sautéed chicken livers with bacon and granary toast, and main dishes like beef korma with wild rice, lamb and rosemary casserole and herb and vegetable pasta with anchovy bread. Well-cooked accompanying vegetables. Colourful alfresco patio seating amid overflowing flower baskets and tubs. *Open 11-3, 5.30-11 (Sun 12-3, 7-10.30).* ***Bar Food*** *11.30-2.45, 6.30-10.45 (Sun 12-2.45, 7-10.15).* ***Beer*** *Brakspear. Garden, outdoor eating. No credit cards.*

HAREWOOD Harewood Arms B&B

Tel 0113 288 6566 **Fax 0113 288 6064** Map 6 C1
Harrogate Road Harewood nr Leeds West Yorkshire LS17 9LH

Zzz...

A fashionable address opposite the gates of Harewood House and convenient location on the A61 halfway between Leeds and Harrogate ensure particular mention for this elegant inn. Formerly a coaching house, with a history dating back to 1815, it has been meticulously restored by Sam Smith, the brewers of Tadcaster. Though fully carpeted and rather studiously appointed, the three lounge bars retain an essentially pubby feel and are much frequented by a business, golfing and race-going fraternity. Nonetheless, temptation to over-price their best-selling Old Brewery Bitter (£1.22 per pint in Sept 1995) has been commendably resisted. Traditional oak bed frames and freestanding furniture have been used as a unifying theme in individually designed bedrooms, the majority of which are in the former coach-house wing overlooking the terrace, formal rose garden and rolling Yorkshire countryside. Four are conveniently located on the ground floor. A full range of room accessories – from remote-control TVs and trouser presses to bidets and over-bath showers – is impressive, a factor reflected in their rather higher-than-average room prices. *Open 11-11 (Sun 12-3, 7-10.30).* ***Beer*** *Sam Smith's Old Brewery Bitter. Family Room. Garden, terrace.* ***Accommodation*** *24 rooms, all en suite, £78 (reduced weekend tariff, single £65). Children welcome overnight, additional bed and cot (both £12) available. Access, Amex, Diners, Visa.*

HAROME Star Inn FOOD

Tel 01439 770397 Map 5 E4
Main Street Harome nr Helmsley North Yorkshire YO6 5JE

The Star exhibits an ageless charm with its thick, thatched roof and evocative, low-beamed interior. Field sports and motoring magazines abound alongside the national dailies, and daily specials are headlined on the bar blackboard, in conjunction with a larger "carte" which has more notions of being a restaurant (as the adjacent larger dining-room effectively is). Bar food covers the range of steak and kidney pie, lasagne with chips, baked potatoes and perhaps scallops with mushrooms and bacon, chicken livers with cream and brandy or rack of lamb with Grand Marnier cream and oranges. To follow, huge nursery puddings (rhubarb crumble or blackberry and apple tart) are liberally sauced with custard. *Open 12-3, 6.30-11 (winter from 7), Sun 12-3, 7-10.30 (pub closed all Monday & L Tue). Free House.* ***Bar Food*** *12-2, 6.30-9.30 (no food all day Monday & L Tue).* ***Beer*** *Theakston Best & Old Peculier, Timothy Taylor Landlord, Tetley. Garden, outdoor eating area. Pub closed Mon & Tues. Access, Visa.*

HASCOMBE White Horse FOOD

Tel 01483 208258 Map 11 A5
Hascombe nr Godalming Surrey GU8 4JA

Grade II listed, 16th-century pub nestling in a beautiful corner of Surrey close to Winkworth Arboretum (NT). Charming and immaculate interior comprising a rambling series of unspoilt, beamed rooms, all tastefully decorated with Laura Ashley wallpapers and kitted out with attractive pine in cosy alcoves, decent prints and open fires. Neat restaurant area with linen-clothed tables and separate hop and farming memorabilia-adorned public bar. Reliable bar food choices are chalked up on a daily-changing blackboard and may include home-made steakburger, steak and kidney pie, Coronation chicken, lamb and mint kebabs and grilled calf's liver. Also on offer are imaginative door-step sandwiches (bacon and avocado) and a selection of salads, such as dressed crab. Colourful summer terrace and pretty, extensive garden, ideal for fine weather imbibing. *Open 11-3, 5.30-11 (Sat from 6), Sun 12-3, 7-10.30.* ***Bar Food*** *12-2.20, 7-10.* ***Beer*** *Wadworth 6X, King & Barnes Sussex, guest beer. Family room. Access, Amex, Visa.*

We only recommend food (Bar Food) in those establishments highlighted with the **FOOD** symbol.

HASELBURY PLUCKNETT Haselbury Inn FOOD

Tel & Fax 01460 72488 Map 13 F2
Haselbury Plucknett nr Crewkerne Somerset TA18 7RJ

The distinct dining bias is an increasing draw at the Pooleys' spacious village inn just off the A30 (Crewkerne 3 miles). Comprehensive menus are on show for both the Country Bar and Stables restaurant, candle-lit by night and set with lacy cloths and fresh flowers. Specials boards supplement the bar offerings (making a total of some 70 dishes): beef stroganoff, chicken kiev and vegetable and cashew nut tikka. Regular features are a daily lunch brunch – except on Sunday when roasts are substituted – and a celebrated barbecue selection offered nightly. Fish, flesh and fowl all appear in voluminous guises on the restaurant menu, a noticeably Spanish influence in some of the food being reflected by much of the piped music. While there is a clear reliance on the fryers, vegetables at least are fresh and plentiful. Up to 25 gooey, creamy desserts are something of a high point, with toffee pecan cheesecake with butterscotch sauce being ever-popular. To end, there are plenty of liqueur coffees and particularly good espresso. *Open 12-3, 7-11 (Sun 12-3, 7-10.30).* ***Bar Food*** *12-2, 7-10 (not Mon).* ***Beer*** *Hickelbury, Butcombe Best, Wadworth 6X, Charles Wells Bombardier, Teignworthy Beachcomber & Reel Ale. Garden, children's play area. Access, Amex, Visa.*

HASTINGWOOD COMMON Rainbow & Dove A

Tel 01279 415419 Map 11 B4
Hastingwood Common Essex CM17 9JX

Charming old rose-covered pub dating from the 16th-century, its name a reference to Noah's Ark (and it gets almost as crowded inside). Despite its close proximity to the busy M11 (a quarter of a mile from J7), the garden is a popular attraction on summer days with its adjacent 18-hole putting course and paddock. Escape the incessant traffic noise inside, within the three characterful and cosy, low-beamed rooms with open fires, rustic furnishings and collections of horse brasses and a few golf clubs. *Open 11.30-3, 5.30-11 (Sun 12-3, 7-10.30).* ***Beer*** *Ansells Best Bitter, Bass, Friary Meux. Garden. Access, Visa.*

HATHERLEIGH George Hotel B&B

Tel 01837 810454 **Fax 01837 810901** Map 13 D2
Market Street Hatherleigh nr Okehampton Devon EX20 3JN

Zzz... 

Dating from 1450, this ancient cob-and-thatch town-centre inn was once a rest house and sanctuary for the monks of Tavistock. In later years it became a brewery, tavern, a law court and a coaching inn before developing into what is now a most comfortable and historic small hotel. Off the central cobbled courtyard in the converted brewhouse and coachman's loft is the main bar and family area extension, while the original inn's bar oozes charm and antiquity with old beams, an oak-panelled wall, an enormous fireplace and an assortment of cushioned seats and sofas. It is now largely confined to residents or waiting diners, as the attractive restaurant is next door. The Farmers Bar across the courtyard is like a small bistro and locals' bar and opens on Thu-Sat nights only. Sloping floors and low 'head-cracking' doorways lead to eleven individually furnished bedrooms with pretty chintz fabrics, pieces of old or antique furniture and generally good clean en-suite facilities. Three rooms have elegant four-poster beds. TVs, telephones and tea-making facilities are the added comforts and residents also have the use of a charming lounge and the outdoor swimming pool. Eight/ten wines available by the glass. *Open 11-3.30, 6-11 (Sun 12-3, 7-10.30). Free House.* ***Beer*** *Bass, Boddingtons, two guest beers.* ***Accommodation*** *11 bedrooms, 9 en suite, £69.50, four-poster £82, single £48-£55. Children welcome overnight, additional bed (£6), cot supplied. Access, Amex, Visa.*

HATHERLEIGH Tally Ho B&B

Tel 01837 810306 Map 13 D2
14 Market Street Hatherleigh Devon EX20 3JN

The exterior appearance of this market town-centre building belies the true age of this 15th-century inn which has recently undergone a change of ownership. Jason and Megan Tidy, both new to the pub business, are continuing the tradition of brewing on site an interesting range of real ales for the pub. The bar is charmingly rustic with a heavily beamed

ceiling, part woodblock and part exposed brick floor; sturdy old furnishings and two upholstered easy chairs flank one of the two stone fireplaces, both with warming woodburners. Various plates and attractive paintings decorate the walls and the convivial atmosphere is enhanced by the classical music that fills this game-free bar. Superior overnight accommodation is still good value and provided in three well-designed and comfortable bedrooms. All are furnished with old pine and decorated with attractive fabrics and quality prints, with added comforts including TV, telephone, clock/radios and a complimentary miniature sherry and a welcoming hand-written note from the proprietor on arrival. Bathrooms are fresh and clean with expensive sanitaryware. Continental breakfast is served with an extra charge for cooked items. Dogs are not allowed in the rooms but they can be housed in a kennel in the garden. *Open 11-3, 6-11, Sun 12-3, 7-10.30. Free House.* ***Beer*** *Own brews: Potboiler's Brew, Tarka's Tipple, Nutters, Thurgia. Garden, aviary, outdoor eating area with thatched barbecue.* ***Accommodation*** *3 bedrooms, all en suite (one with bath), £50 (single £30). Access, Amex, Visa.*

HATHERSAGE — Hathersage Inn — B&B

Tel 01433 650259 **Fax 01433 651199** Map 6 C2
Hathersage Derbyshire S30 1BB

The ivy-clad, stone-built inn stands by Hathersage's steep main street in the heart of the Peak District National Park; pub to the front where the recently refurbished Cricketers' Bar (bar snacks available at lunch and dinner) is full of local memorabilia and quietly residential to the rear with a lounge bar and cosy dining-room. Bedrooms are neatly kept, with plenty of extras from TV and radio-alarm to drinks tray and fresh fruit. There are six Executive rooms, four-posters and a honeymoon suite. Children are not encouraged. *Open 11-3, 6-11 (SUn 12-3, 7-10.30). Free House.* ***Beer*** *John Smith's, Webster's Yorkshire Bitter, Courage Directors.* ***Accommodation*** *15 bedrooms, all en suite, £62 (four-poster & Executives £72, single £47-£52). Access, Amex, Diners, Visa.*

THE HAVEN — Blue Ship — A

Tel 01403 822709 Map 11 A6
The Haven nr Billingshurst West Sussex RH14 9BS

Hidden in the depths of the Sussex countryside along a tiny lane off the A29 north of Billingshurst, this splendid rural gem is well worth tracking down. An unassuming Victorian brick and tile-hung exterior – festooned with a rampant climbing clematis – hides a charming 15th-century core, characterised by the classic main bar, which features a worn red-brick floor, low heavy beams, a large inglenook and scrubbed pine tables and sturdy wooden benches. Well-kept King & Barnes ales tapped straight from the cask are dispensed via a small hatch servery. A flagstoned passageway leads to two further rooms added in later years, a games room full of traditional pub games – no music or electronic machines here – and access to the peaceful cottage garden, a delight on warm summer days. *Open 11-3, 6-11 (Sun 12-3,7-10.30).* ***Beer*** *King & Barnes Sussex Bitter, Broadwood & seasonal ales. Garden, lawn, patio. Family room. No credit cards.*

HAWKSHEAD — Drunken Duck Inn — FOOD / B&B

Tel 01539 436347 **Fax 01539 436781** Map 4 C3
Barngates Hawkshead nr Ambleside Cumbria LA22 0NG

Zzz...

Take the Tarn Hows turning at Outgate off the B5286 to find the Drunken Duck, formerly the Barngate Inn, standing high in the hills with spectacular views across distant Lake Windermere to its backdrop of craggy hills. There's a healthy range of well-kept real ales to accompany an impressive array of bar meals. A hard-working kitchen produces volumes of vegetarian fare from Brie and asparagus or garlic mushroom paté to ricotta tortellini in tomato and herb sauce and vegetable chili with lentils and rice. In addition to voluminous rolls and ploughman's at lunchtimes comes lamb with spinach and apricots, Moroccan lamb tageen, perhaps, and Cumberland sausage casserole. Treacle tart and jam roly poly are traditionally filling walkers' puds. Overnight guests are housed in stylish, individually designed bedrooms, some in stripped pine others with carefully chosen antique pieces. Fabrics feature soft restful shades, while the well-lit bathrooms have good over-bath showers, good towelling and quality toiletries. TVs, telephones and tea trays are all provided. *Open 11.30-3, 6-11 (Sun 12-3, 7-10.30).* ***Bar Food*** *12-2, 6.30-9 (Sun from 7). Free House.* ***Beer*** *Yates Bitter & Drunken Duck Ale, Mitchell's Lancaster Bomber,*

See over

Jennings Bitter, Theakston Old Peculier, Boddingtons. Garden, outdoor eating. ***Accommodation*** *10 bedrooms, all en suite, £69 (single £50). Children welcome overnight, additional bed (£12) and cot (£5) available. Accommodation closed 25 Dec. Access, Amex, Visa.*

HAWKSHEAD Queen's Head Hotel FOOD

Tel 01539 436271 **Fax 01539 436781** Map 4 C3 **B&B**

Hawkshead Cumbria LA22 0NS

The Queen's Head here is that of Elizabeth I; at the heart of this traffic-free village the black and white painted 16th-century frontage hides a cavernous pub within, full of period character and camaraderie. Food from the varied menus can be taken anywhere at lunch in the panelled bar areas and dining-room, although at busy times it's certainly advisable to find a free table first! Main courses are typified by chicken biryani, devilled lamb's kidneys and a vegetarian crespela Italiana. Sandwiches are served at lunchtime only, ploughman's and filled jacket potatoes are generally available on the bar/lounge menu. Residents and others wishing to eat in the dining-room at night or for Sunday lunch (served all day) are advised to book in advance. Ten bedrooms within the pub have low beams, modest furnishings and compact en-suite bathrooms; two have old-fashioned four-posters and there are a couple of family rooms sleeping three. The balance of the accommodation is in two adjacent cottages which are only yards away, and could conceivably be a good deal quieter. *Open 11-11 (Sun 12-3, 7-10.30).* ***Bar Food*** *12-2.30, 6.15-9.30.* ***Beer*** *Hartleys XB & Mild, Robinson's Bitter. Outdoor eating.* ***Accommodation*** *13 bedrooms, 11 en suite, £59.50 (4-poster £70, single £45). Children welcome overnight (under-10s £12.50, 10-16 £17.50). Access, Diners, Visa.*

HAWORTH Old White Lion Hotel B&B

Tel 01535 642313 **Fax 01535 646222** Map 6 C1

Main Street Haworth West Yorkshire BD22 8DU

This Brontë village hotel goes back three hundred years. Formerly a coaching inn, part of the old building was a meeting room for masonics. An ongoing programme of refurbishment is now complete in the fourteen bedrooms, each having been individually decorated. They have en-suite bathrooms and are equipped with televisions, radio/alarms, telephones and tea/coffee-making facilities. Three single rooms have en-suite showers and two family rooms sleep three and four. Guests can relax in the oak-panelled residents' lounge. The restaurant was created from three weaver's cottages. *Open 11-3, 6-11 (Sun 12-3, 7-10.30). Free House.* ***Beer*** *Webster's Yorkshire, John Smith's, Wilson's Original. Family room.* ***Accommodation*** *14 bedrooms, all en suite, £46-£60 (single £38-£43). Children welcome overnight, additional bed and cot (£11) available. No dogs. Access, Amex, Diners, Visa.*

HAY-ON-WYE Old Black Lion FOOD

Tel 01497 820841 Map 9 D5 **B&B**

26 Lion Street Hay-on-Wye Hereford & Worcester HR3 5AD

Owners John and Joan Collins run this ever-popular old coaching inn. On the bar menu dishes range from a home-made, daily soup, devilled whitebait and a selection of ploughman's lunches (try the Continental with salami, soft cheese and garlic sausage) to seafood vol-au-vent, smoked cod and tomato bake Welsh lamb and lemon stew, and vegetarian options (black bean curry with brown rice or saffron and vegetable risotto). The daily specials board might extend the range further to include warm pigeon salad with walnut dressing, oysters, baked Cornish hake with a squid provençale sauce or herb-encrusted rack of lamb, finishing with rhubarb cobbler or chocolate, date and walnut meringue cake. In the evening the Cromwell restaurant menu is available throughout the dining areas, so you can indulge further with the likes of laverbread cakes with cockles, venison bourguignon or a lion mixed grill. An separate bar menu is devoted solely to steaks, sauced or plain. Bedrooms within the main building, of 17th-century origins, render the Black Lion justifiably famous. Refurbishment has generally enhanced the building's character and comforts of high degree that include direct-dial phones, TVs, radios, beverage trays and bright duvets (traditional bedding provided on request). Rooms in the annexe are more modern, though no less comfortable; all rooms (with the exception of one single with a private bathroom) have entirely acceptable en-suite facilities. Families particularly enjoy the Cromwell Room with its gallery and two additional beds. Speciality breakfasts include a salmon fisherman's version with smoked eel and aquavit plus one for romantics: scrambled

egg with caviar and a quarter bottle of champagne (for two). The whole pub is candle-lit at night and there's no smoking in the restaurant. Not suitable for children under 5 (over-8s in the restaurant only). *Open 11-3, 6-11 (Sun 12-3, 7-10.30). **Bar Food** 12-2.30, 7-9.30 (in winter to 9, Sun 12-2.15, 7-9). Free House. **Beer** Flowers Original, Bass. Small patio, outdoor eating. **Accommodation** 10 bedrooms, 9 en suite, £43.90 (family room sleeping 4 £63.90, single £19.95/£25). Children over 5 welcome overnight (5-12s £10, over-12s £14), additional bed (£10) and cot available. Access, Amex, Visa.*

HAYDON BRIDGE — General Havelock Inn — FOOD

Tel 01434 684376 Map 5 D2
Ratcliffe Road Haydon Bridge Northumberland NE47 6ER

cottages. It was named after Sunderland-born General Henry Havelock, who relieved the Indian town of Lucknow in the late 1880s. The interior of the pub is also dark green. In the front bar area there are wrought-iron-legged tables, stripped wood and padded benches, and some brilliant wildlife photographs taken by a local photographer. The pub's main draw, though, is its dining-room in the converted stables to the rear, a high-ceilinged room with exposed beams, natural stone walls, ready-set polished tables and watercolours of local scenes. The cooking is in the accomplished hands of self-taught chef Angela Clyde, who prides herself on using only fresh produce: meat comes from a local butcher in Hexham, and fish is delivered twice a week from North Shields. The short lunchtime menu includes soup like Stilton and onion or a terrine amongst the starters, followed by a daily roast and a fish dish. Sandwiches and ploughman's platters are available at lunchtime only. In the evenings a set price four-course menu has a more upmarket feel. Cooking is of a high standard, and the puddings are also first-class: Danish chocolate bar and a splendid apricot tart are typical. Service is friendly and casual but efficient. To the rear of the dining-room is a paved patio which runs down to a lawn and the River Tyne. Though the pub has its regulars who use the bar for a drink, this is really more of a dining pub, and people travel some distance to eat here. Weekends (including a popular Sunday lunch) can be very busy, so booking is advised. *Open Wed-Sat 11.30-2.30, 7-11, Sun 12-2, 8-10.30. **Bar Food** 12-2.30. Free House. **Beer** Tetley. Riverside garden, outdoor eating. Closed all Mon and all Tue, first 2 weeks Sept & 2 weeks Jan. No credit cards.*

HAYTOR VALE — Rock Inn — FOOD

Tel 01364 661305 **Fax 01364 661242** Map 13 D3 **B&B**
Haytor Vale nr Newton Abbot Devon TQ13 9XP

Zzz...

Dating back 200 years, this sturdy pub stands in a tiny Dartmoor village below Haytor, the best known of the Dartmoor tors. A characterful, traditional interior has sturdy old furnishings, plenty of antique tables, settles, prints, a grandfather clock and various pieces of china over the two fireplaces. Both the main bar and the attractive adjoining rooms are popular settings in which to appreciate the reliably good bar food, with a particularly strong list of light meals and good hearty snacks, and the promise of fresh vegetables. After a day on the moor healthy appetites can be satisfied with beef and venison pie, Dartmoor rabbit cooked in whole grain mustard sauce and good steaks. Lighter snacks range from salads and sandwiches to filled jacket potatoes and omelettes. Fresh fish from Brixham includes poached Devon salmon and monkfish with a tomato and garlic sauce. To finish there may be tangy treacle and lemon tart with clotted cream and lemon meringue pie; Sunday roast is popular and there are six good West Country cheeses on the board. The ten bedrooms are attractively decorated. Four de luxe rooms and the Georgian four-poster room are individually fitted out with quality fabrics, easy chairs and some period pieces of furniture, with prices to match. All rooms are spacious with clean en-suite facilities, and well appointed, with TVs, tea-making kits, mineral water, fruit juices, radios and telephones. Sheltered courtyard to the side and lawned area across the lane. *Open 11-11 (Sun 12-3, 7-10.30). **Bar Food** 11-2.30, 6.30-9.30. Free House. **Beer** Eldridge Pope Hardy Ale & Royal Oak, Dartmoor Bitter, Bass, guest beer. Garden, Family room. **Accommodation** 10 bedrooms, 8 en suite, £65 (four-poster £91, single £39.95). Children welcome overnight (under-5s stay free in parents' room, 5-14s £8.55). Access, Amex, Visa.*

We only recommend food (Bar Food) in those establishments highlighted with the **FOOD** symbol.

HEATH King's Arms A

Tel 01924 377527 Map 6 C1

Heath Common Heath nr Wakefield West Yorkshire WF1 5SL

Built in the early 1700s and converted to pub use in 1841, the King's Arms has been operated by Clark's Brewery of nearby Wakefield since 1989. It stands by the green in 100 acres of common grassland. Genuinely unaltered and commendably unspoilt. Gas mantles still burn in the three tiny flagstone bars which are lined with unique carved oak panelling. Don't expect miracles from the bar food; rather, just soak in the unique atmosphere. Clark's Festival Ale is the added bonus for beer drinkers. A conservatory is suitable for families and has access to the garden. *Open 11.30-3, 5.30-11 (Sun 12-3, 7-10.30).* ***Beer*** *Clark's Traditional Bitter & Festival Ale, Tetley Traditional, Timothy Taylor Landlord. Garden. Family room. Access, Visa.*

HEATHTON Old Gate A

Tel 01746 710431 Map 6 B4

Heathton Claverley Shropshire WV5 7EB

A much-extended 17th-century inn down country lanes some five miles from Bridgworth on the Staffordshire border. There's plenty to amuse antiquarians in the parlour: hanging from the beams are decorative Toby and water jugs, from the walls and lintels framed watercolours, old prints and brass flat irons. Bar food encompasses both the traditional (toasties, children's favourites, ploughman's) and more interesting specials like Greek-style lamb in filo pastry with a rosemary sauce. The Old Stable snug contains more suitable seating for families when the weather precludes use of the garden's picnic tables and play area. Eight miles from Junction 2 of the M5 and near Halfpenny Green Airport. *Open 12-2.30, 6.30-11 (Sun 12-3, 7-10.30).* ***Beer*** *Tetley Bitter, Holts (HP&D) Entire, Enville Ale, guest beer. Family room. Garden, children's play area. Access, Amex, Diners, Visa.*

HELFORD Shipwrights Arms A

Tel 01326 231235 Map 12 B4

Helford nr Helston Cornwall TR12 6JX

Stunningly located on the banks of the Helford estuary, its approach road is so narrow that in summer months it's restricted to pedestrian use only. The picturesque walk through the village is well worth it for this pretty thatched pub has a magical terraced garden, complete with colourful flowers, palms and picnic benches on the water's edge. The interior is quite special too, staunchly traditional, with rustic simple furnishings, plenty of nautical bits and pieces and lots of yachting types swapping unlikely stories. The pub and terraces can get extremely busy in the summer. *Open 11-2.30, 6-11 (Sun 12-2.30, 7-10.30).* ***Beer*** *Castle Eden, Flowers, IPA. Garden. Access, Visa.*

HELMSLEY Feathers B&B

Tel 01439 770275 **Fax 01439 771101** Map 5 E4

Market Place Helmsley North Yorkshire YO6 5BH

"Elmslac", a Saxon village on the river Rye settled in 600 AD was listed in Domesday, and as Helmsley, renowned for its Norman castle, had a well-documented history throughout the Middle Ages. Feathers was once a merchant's house with the highest rent in town, later it was split into two cottages and is now re-unified by the friendly Feather family. There are, of course, two entrances, two bars – with a unifying theme of the local "Mouse Man" furniture – two dining-rooms and two stair-wells. Two floors of bedrooms provide accommodation that is more practical than luxurious; TVs and tea trays are provided, alarm clocks and hairdryers available on request. Family rooms (sleeping up to 4) with en-suite bathrooms offer good value, with under-12s accommodated free (meals charged as taken). Several smaller rooms have en-suite WC/shower rooms only, and the three remaining unconverted singles share adequate facilities. *Open 11-11 (Sun 12-3, 7-10.30). Free House.* ***Beer*** *John Smith's, Theakston Best & Old Peculier, guest beer. Garden, family room.* ***Accommodation*** *17 bedrooms, 13 en suite, £60 (single £25/£35). Children welcome overnight (under-12s stay free in parents' room), additional cot available. Accommodation closed Christmas week. Access, Amex, Diners, Visa.*

HENTON Peacock Hotel B&B

Tel 01844 353519 **Fax 01844 353891** Map 15a D2
Henton nr Chinnor Oxfordshire OX9 4AH

This very pretty 600-year-old thatched, black and white timbered inn is in a sleepy village just off the B4009. The bar is comfortable and immaculately kept. 17 bedrooms are in the extension, which also houses the residents' lounge. There are now 20 in total and all are smart and well equipped. *Free House.* ***Beer*** *Brakspear. Patio.* ***Accommodation*** *20 bedrooms, all en suite, £62-£84 (single £45-£52), weekend tariff reductions. Children welcome overnight (rate depends on age), additional bed available. Dogs by arrangement only. Access, Amex, Diners, Visa.*

HERMITAGE Sussex Brewery A

Tel 01243 371533 **Fax 01243 379684** Map 15 D4
36 Main Road Hermitage nr Emsworth West Sussex PO10 8AU

A fresh carpet of sawdust is laid daily at this Grade II listed pub, and open fires are continually alight from October to Easter. No food recommendation here, but the remarkable selection of 48 different types of sausage (usually served with mash, beans, fried onions and gravy) on the bar menu deserves a mention. There's no jukebox or fruit machine, not even a cigarette machine. *Open 11-11 (Sun 12-3, 7-10.30). Free House.* ***Beer*** *Badger Best, Wadworth 6X, Hall & Woodhouse Tanglefoot, Hard Tackle & Hermitage Best, Charles Wells Bombardier, guest beers. Garden, children's play area. Family room. Amex.*

HESKET NEWMARKET Old Crown A

Tel 016974 78288 Map 4 C3
Hesket Newmarket nr Caldbeck Cumbria CA7 8JG

Opened by Chris Bonnington by telex from Katmandu in 1988, the Old Crown's on-site brewhouse (run by co-owner Jim Fearnley) produces six unusually-named beers, for example the award-winning 'Doris's 90th Birthday Ale'. Brewery tours take place on Tue, Wed and Thu evenings, followed by supper in the tiny dining-room (where there are now once-monthly curry suppers). The new owners have plans to landscape the rear garden, through which the brewery is approached. *Open 11-3 (Mon-Thu only), 5.30-11 (Sun 12-3, 7-10.30). Free House.* ***Beer*** *own brewery: Great Cockup Porter, Skiddaw Special, Doris's 90th, Blancathra Bitter, Old Carrock Strong Ale.* ***Beer*** *garden. Pub closed Mon-Thu lunchtimes. No credit cards.*

HETTON Angel Inn ★ FOOD

Tel 01756 730263 **Fax 01756 730363** Map 6 C1
Hetton nr Skipton North Yorkshire BD23 6LT

Deservedly popular for its tip-top bar food, the Angel promotes a brasserie image with its smart attendants in ankle-length aprons. A dozen or more wines deserving of appreciation by the glass and tall bottles of chili dressing at every table help temper the traditionally pubby feel. Yet the country pub does remain in its central bar and progressive dining-rooms – from no-smoking snug to smart restaurant; the food has a modern British accent with many Mediterranean overtones. The superb bar menu might see rustic fish soup, pressing of York ham and foie gras, AWT (open sandwich with smoked salmon, cream cheese, smoked bacon and home-made chutney), confit of duck, rump steak with Caesar salad and pommes lyonnaise alongside a selection of daily fresh fish specials (perhaps queen scallops with garlic and Gruyère or roast cod with tomato fondue and soft herb crust and a grain mustard sauce) – this is serious food, but the prices are still surprisingly reasonable (even though the Angel won our Pub of the Year award last year for its outstanding pub food). The menu proclaims: "We are not a fast food outlet! There are many specialists in this field. We cook everything with great care. When we are busy this will cause delay, even though our kitchen is working flat out. We hope that any wait will be worthwhile." It certainly is – dishes score highly for flavour, presentation and value. Ever-popular sticky toffee pudding with caramel sauce, crème brulée, and hot, steamed sponge pudding with fresh raspberry sauce and home-made custard are among the enticements for the sweet-toothed. Printed

placemats in the bar areas invite customers to sample their fixed-price dinners (£22.95), but little further inducement appears to be needed as reservations at night for the restaurant (recommended in our *1996 Hotels & Restaurants Guide*) remain a virtual necessity; here you will find superior touches like a choice of four home-baked breads. Three-course Sunday lunches (£17) offer both an interesting choice and excellent value, given the quality. Over two dozen malt whiskies at the bar and, usually, and interesting trio of pudding wines by the glass (perhaps a Hungarian Tokaji Aszu 5 Puttonyos, a South African Zonnebloem late-harvest or a riesling from Washington State). Customers are requested to respect residents' considerations when parking. *Open 12-3, 6-11 (Sun 12-3, 6-10.30).* ***Bar Food*** *12-2, 6-10. Restaurant Meals Sun 12-2, Mon-Sat 7-9.30 (closed L Mon-Sat, D Sun). Free House.* ***Beer*** *Black Sheep Best & Special, Boddingtons, King & Barnes Twelve Bore Bitter, guest beer. Patio, outdoor eating. Pub closed one week in Jan. Access, Amex, Visa.*

HEXHAM — Dipton Mill Inn — FOOD

Tel 01434 606577 Map 5 D2
Dipton Mill Road Hexham Northumberland NE46 1YA

Less than a 10-minute drive out of town (follow Whitley Chapel signs off the B6531 past Hexham Racecourse), Geoff and Janet Brooker's inn nestles by the stone road bridge in a deep hollow. Within its tiny interior there's a single warm and intimate bar with welcoming, open fires. If everything within is on a small scale, the daily lunch menus are no less accidental in concept. Home cooking of manageable proportions is limited on the blackboard to soup, three or four daily hot dishes like steak and kidney or beef and Guinness pies with fresh vegetables, commendable nursery puddings (perhaps bread-and-butter or apple and almond pie with cream or custard) and locally-produced ice creams. In addition to sandwiches there are five or six cheeses for ploughman's lunches, and vegetarians can tuck into a cheese and broccoli flan. Sheer size restricts children from the bar; there's a tiny rear games room for when it's cold or wet; the fine-weather benefit is a spacious, walled garden complete with its own wooden bridge over the old mill stream – a splendid spot. *Open 12-12.30, 6-11 (12-3, 7-10.30 Sun). Free House.* ***Beer*** *Hexhamshire Shire Bitter, Devil's Water & Whapweasel, Theakston Best, guest beers.* ***Bar Food*** *12-2.30, 6-8.30. Garden. No credit cards.*

HIGH RODING — Black Lion — A

Tel 01371 872847 Map 11 B4
High Roding nr Great Dunmow Essex CM6 1NT

Attractive black-and-white timbered Tudor roadside pub in a charming Essex village, full of character buildings. Landlord Osvaldo Ricci has made it his home for the past 23 years and the spick-and-span, intimate bar is full of old beams, standing timbers, a rustic collection of wooden furniture and a brick-built bar counter. Cosy atmosphere enhanced by piped light opera and classical music, and fresh flowers on each table. Small, separate dining-room. *Open 11-3, 6-11 (Sun 12-3, 7-10.30).* ***Beer*** *Ridleys. Garden. Access, Visa.*

HIGHCLERE — Yew Tree — FOOD — B&B

Tel 01635 253360 **Fax 01635 254977** Map 14a C4
Andover Road Hollington Cross Highclere Berkshire RG15 9SE

Jenny Wratten's 'restaurant with rooms' hasn't changed the original character of the 'traditional inn' from which it was created. Huge logs smoulder in the inglenook fireplace while old scrubbed pine tables and the odd sofa sit beneath ancient beams. Several interconnecting rooms comprise the more formal restaurant but the same restaurant-style menu is served throughout. Seasonally-changing choices (plus dishes of the day) might include chilled gazpacho, salmon fishcakes with creamy tomato sauce, gammon steak, field mushroom risotto with Roquefort cheese, pork tenderloin with mustard sauce, and rabbit in white wine, smoked bacon and cream sauce. Finish, perhaps, with a savoury (Welsh rarebit or herring roes on toasted muffins), Jenny's rhubarb fool, baked egg custard tart or farmhouse cheeses served with apple, celery, water biscuits and their own walnut bread. Tuesday is the best day for seafood and shellfish. Jenny's brother Simon runs front-of-house. Eight wines are offered by the glass. Six cottagey bedrooms offer overnight accommodation with direct-dial telephones, remote-control TVs, beverage trays and little extras like books and magazines; all have en-suite bathrooms, half with shower and WC only. Just south of the village, on the A343. ***Bar Food*** *12-2.30 (Sun to 3), 6.30-9.30 (Fri & Sat to 10, Sun 7-9). Free House.* ***Beer*** *Brakspear, Wadworth 6X, Flowers Original. Garden, outdoor patio eating.* ***Accommodation*** *6 bedrooms, all en suite, £55 (single £40). Children welcome overnight (under 5s stay free in parents' room), additional bed available. Dogs by arrangement. Access, Visa.*

HIGHER BURWARDSLEY Pheasant Inn ★ FOOD

Tel 01829 770434 **Fax 01829 771097** Map 6 A3 **B&B**
Higher Burwardsley nr Tattenhall Cheshire CH3 9PF

Zzz... 

The Pheasant is best located by following signs to the candle factory from the A534. It is tucked into the hillside amongst the Peckforton hills, and on arrival, it's plain to see that the place was once a farm, and the more surprising, therefore, to find that there has been a pub here since the 17th century. The oldest part, a half-timbered sandstone farmhouse, is the venue for the bar, which claims to house the largest log fire in Cheshire. The adjacent Highland Room generally known as the Bistro, was once the kitchen and retains the old cast-iron range. The most recent addition is an imposing conservatory that looks over a tiered patio and, beyond this, right across the Cheshire plain towards North Wales. Bar snacks encompass a broad range that might commence with deep-fried whitebait with paprika or sautéed mushrooms in garlic and herb butter, moving on, perhaps, to home-made curry with poppadom and mango chutney, fresh fish (a speciality) and cold platters (ploughman's, salads). A selection of ten sandwiches is listed and children are offered the usual list of favourites. Daily specials extend the kitchen's repertoire to the likes of seafood in a puff pastry case, halibut steak with tomato and prawn sauce, darne of Scottish salmon with grapes and breast of duck with port and blackberries – the style is conventional but the execution is above-average. Sunday lunch is always popular as it's such good value. Space is limited – booking is advised. Landlord David Greenhaugh has an unusual and passionate interest, namely his prize-winning herd of pedigree Highland cattle that graze nearby. The friendly bunch of staff go out of their way to be pleasant and helpful. The old barn has been skilfully converted into six very comfortable bedrooms, equipped to the highest pub standards, with televisions, clock radios, hairdryers, mini-bars and roomy bathrooms. Stonework interiors are eye-catching, and nights tranquil. Two further bedrooms, housed in the pub proper, boast original beams and brighter bathrooms, as well as memorable views. Credit cards taken for amounts of £20 and over only. *Open 11.30-3, 7-11 (Sun 12-3, 7-10.30).* ***Bar Food*** *12-2, 7-9.30 (Sat to 10). Free House.* ***Beer*** *Bass. Garden, outdoor eating. Family room.* ***Accommodation*** *10 bedrooms, all en suite, £70 & £80 (single £45). Children welcome overnight (0-10 yrs free, over 10 yrs £10), additional bed & cot available. Dogs by arrangement. Access, Amex, Visa.*

HIMLEY Crooked House A

Tel 01384 238583 Map 6 B4
Coppice Mill Himley nr Dudley West Midlands DY3 4DA

This is not a particularly attractive setting; turning off B4176 between Womborne and Dudley, the long lane runs down through woods past urban forest, landfill and quarry. Yet the sight at the lane's end is simply extraordinary. Once the Glynne Arms, the 250-year-old building was a victim of subsidence in Victorian times and teeters alarmingly from right to left. One bar door opens out at an oblique angle and instills an uneasy feeling of collapsing through it – and this is on the way in! Meanwhile, in the upper bar, (for a charitable donation) customers can watch a ball-bearing apparently roll upwards along the dado. Despite some recent levelling of the floor, many's the customer who appears all at sea with his legs. A more recent extension houses a family-friendly conservatory overlooking a small adventure playground. Saturday barbecues. No children under 14 in the bars. *Open 11-11 Mon-Sat Apr-end Aug, 11.30-2.30, 6.30-11 Sept-end Mar, Sun 12-3, 7-10.30 all year round.* ***Beer*** *Banks's Mild & Bitter, Marston's Pedigree, guest beer. Patio, children's play area. No credit cards.*

HINDON Lamb at Hindon FOOD

Tel 01747 820573 **Fax 01747 820605** Map 14 B3 **B&B**
Hindon Salisbury Wiltshire SP3 6DP

Wisteria clings to one corner of this mellow 17th-century coaching inn. At its height, 300 post horses were kept here to supply the great number of coaches going to and from London and the West Country. Prime Minister William Pitt was apparently most put out to find no fresh horses available when he stopped off in 1786. But there have also been less reputable visitors: Silas White, a notorious smuggler said to be leader of the Wiltshire Moonrakers, used the Lamb as the centre of his nefarious activities. Inside, the long bar is divided into several areas and is furnished with some sturdy period tables, chairs and settles. A splendid old stone fireplace with log fire creates a warm, homely atmosphere, which is also enhanced by an ever-changing collection of paintings by local artists both here and in

the smarter restaurant. The blackboard bar menu is sensibly not over-long, but still manages to offer a reasonable choice – smoked trout salad, pork chop and mustard sauce, cream of broccoli and potato soup, and for pudding chocolate Drambuie pie and fresh pineapple crumble. Granary sandwiches, ploughman's platters and salads are always available. The emphasis is fishy on Tuesdays and Fridays, and in winter there's also plenty of game, from the estate of the local landowner who bought the inn a few years ago. No-smoking restaurant. Upstairs, there are thirteen en-suite bedrooms, which are furnished and decorated to varying styles and standards. *Open 11-11, Sun 12-3, 7-10.30.* ***Bar Food*** *12-2, 7-10.* ***Beer*** *Wadworth 6X, Boddingtons, Oakhill Best, Ringwood. Garden, outdoor eating.* ***Accommodation*** *13 bedrooms, all en suite, £55 (four-poster £65, single £38). Children welcome overnight, (under-3s stay free in parents' room), additional bed (£10) and cot (£10) available. Access, Amex, Visa.*

HOLKHAM — Victoria Hotel — B&B

Tel 01328 710469 Map 10 C1
Park Road Holkham Norfolk

An imposing large brick building situated at one of the entrances (on A149) to Holkham Hall, one of Britain's most majestic stately homes, the estate owned Victoria makes a good base from which to explore local walks, nature reserves and coastal villages. Built in the early 1800s to house the entourage to visiting aristocracy, it still offers overnight accommodation in five comfortable, yet simply furnished en-suite bedrooms. All are light and spacious with pretty fabrics, TVs, beverage-making facilities and most have delightful rural outlooks. The homely ambience is maintained downstairs in the large lounge/dining area which is warmly decorated in green and furnished in modern pine, with relaxing settees and easy chairs fronting a good winter log fire. Pleasing views across the well tended garden and lush coastal pastures. The traditional spartan tap-room is popular with walkers. Holkham beach is only a short stroll away. *Open 11-3, 7-11 (12-3, 7-11 Sun). Free House.* ***Beer*** *Adnams Mild & Southwold, Greene King IPA, Marston's Pedigree, guest ale.* ***Accommodation*** *7 bedrooms, all en suite, £50 (single £27.50). Dogs by arrangement. Garden, outside eating. Children welcome overnight. Access, Amex, Diners, Visa.*

HOLNE — Church House Inn — B&B

Tel 01364 631208 Map 13 D3
Holne nr Ashburton Devon TQ13 7SJ

Situated in an attractive Dartmoor village on the southern flanks of the moor, this welcoming inn was built in 1329 as either a dwelling house for the workers on the church, or as a resting place for visiting clergy and worshippers in the church. It is still a popular meeting place for locals, Dartmoor ramblers and car tourers alike. Pleasantly rustic bars, furnished with a huge carved settle and an assortment of simple tables and chairs are appealing. The six modest bedrooms upstairs have superb rural views. All are neat and comfortable and simply furnished, with four rooms having small clean bathrooms with showers; two rooms share a bathroom. Added comforts of TV and tea-making kits are standard and residents have the use of a cosy, antique-filled lounge. *Open 11.30-3, 6.30-11 (Sun 12-3, 7-10.30). Free House.* ***Beer*** *Dartmoor Best Bitter, Wadworth 6X, Palmers IPA, guest beer.* ***Accommodation*** *6 bedrooms, 4 en suite, £50 (not en suite £39, single £27.50). Children welcome overnight (under-2s stay free in parents' room, 3-5s £5, 5+ £10), additional bed available. Check-in by arrangement. Access, Visa.*

HOLT — Old Ham Tree — FOOD

Tel 01225 782581 Map 14 B3 **B&B**
Holt nr Trowbridge Wiltshire BA14 6PY

Two miles north of Trowbridge, a cleanly modernised, beamed and pleasant 18th-century inn near the village green. Reliably good, simple food in the form of steak and Guinness pie, fresh bream Provençal-style, monkfish salad with smoked bacon on a bed of mixed leaves, chicken casserole or halibut steak with prawn sauce. Sandwiches, ploughman's platters and vegetarian options are also offered. Puddings are homely (and home-made): apple pie and lemon meringue pie. Bedrooms are centrally-heated, clean and airy, white-painted with matching furniture, pretty floral fabrics, and share a modern bathroom. Residents' television lounge above the bar. *Open 11.15-3, 6.30-11 (Sun 12-3, 7-10.30).* ***Bar Food*** *11.30-2.30, 6.30-10 (Sun from 7). Free House.* ***Beer*** *Wadworth 6X, Marston's Pedigree, Robinson's Best, guest beer. Garden, outdoor eating.* ***Accommodation*** *4 bedrooms, £32 (single £22.50). Children welcome overnight, additional bed available. Dogs welcome by arrangement. Access, Amex, Diners, Visa.*

HOLYWELL — Old Ferry Boat — B&B

Tel 01480 463227 Map 10 B2
Holywell St Ives Cambridgeshire PE17 3TG

A thousand years of history are behind this delightful thatched and wisteria-draped riverside inn, originally a monastic ferry house. Situated by the River Great Ouse where there is ample mooring, the Old Ferry boat has a particularly charming panelled alcove off the main bar, and good views from the sun terrace. It is haunted by Juliet, a young victim of unrequited love, so don't go on March 17th unless you want to join the ghost hunters! The seven neatly refurbished bedrooms are individually decorated with quality wallpapers and fabrics, but vary in size – minute to small – and standard of facilities. Two boast space for old pine four-posters and good-sized bathrooms, others are compact (to say the least) with beds against the wall and tiny shower rooms. Despite these drawbacks, two have delightful views over the river and a serene rural scene. *Open 11-3, 6-11 (Sun 12-3, 7-10.30). Free House.* ***Beer*** *Bass, Courage Directors, Charrington IPA, Nethergate Old Growler, Webster's Yorkshire.* ***Accommodation*** *7 bedrooms, all en suite £49.50-£68 (single £39.50). Check-in by arrangement. Garden, outdoor eating. Access, Visa.*

HOLYWELL GREEN — Rock Inn Hotel — B&B

Tel 01422 379721 **Fax 01422 379110** Map 6 C1
Holywell Green Nr Halifax West Yorkshire HX4 9BS

Zzz...

In a quiet village just a couple of minutes' drive from Junction 24 of the M62 (ask directions when booking), this inn began life as a row of 17th-century stone cottages. Over the last 14 years or so it has been considerably extended and revamped by landlord Robert Vinson to incorporate function rooms (they specialise in weddings) as well as the bedrooms. The bar is most comfortable in modern, designer-Victorian style with red leather chesterfields, frilly glass lampshades and a new conservatory extension. Bedrooms are not large but manage to squeeze in everything from trouser press and hairdryer to satellite TV, beverage kit and drinks tray with a couple of beers and miniature spirits. All rooms are very similar, with dark-stained pine ceilings, rich Victorian colour schemes and compact bathrooms that all have showers over unusually deep, round tubs. Also unusual are the three 'four-posters' that do not actually have posts but mirrored canopies fixed to the ceiling. One room has a couple of bunk beds for children and another family room sleeps three. A notably friendly place. *Open 11.30-11 (Sun 12-3, 7-10.30). Free House.* ***Beer*** *Theakston Best, Tetley, Scottish & Newcastle No. 3, Black Sheep, guest beer. Terrace. Family room.* ***Accommodation*** *18 bedrooms (3 with four-posters), all en suite, £79/£69 weekends (single £59/£38 weekends). Children welcome overnight (under-3s stay free in parents' room), additional bed (£10), cot supplied. Access, Amex, Diners, Visa.*

> We do not accept free meals or hospitality – our inspectors pay their own bills and **never** book in the name of Egon Ronay's Guides.

HOPE — Poacher's Arms — B&B

Tel 01433 620380 Map 6 C2
Castelton Road Hope Derybshire S30 2RD

Gladys Bushell's much-extended roadside pub (on the A625) is as popular as ever with walkers, cyclists and visitors to the Peak's National Park. With eating and seating areas which include a family room, rear conservatory and two dining-rooms there's just one central bar servery to cope with the crush. Amid the modern beamed decor there's a limited degree of elegance and comfort; there are wider seats, button-backed banquettes and copper-topped bar tables, some of which are rather too small for comfortable eating. Bedrooms are rather more generously sized, sporting a mixture of floral papers, curtains and bedspreads. Freestanding pine or mahogany furniture, remote control TV, clock radio, phone, hairdryer and hot drinks tray all combine to fulfil the basic requirements of a comfortable and restful stay. Patterned carpeting runs through to the en-suite bathrooms whose fittings and decor are just a little basic. *Open 12-3, 6-11.* ***Beer*** *Courage Directors, John Smith's, Marston's Pedigree.* ***Accommodation*** *6 bedrooms, all en suite, £52 (single £39). Children welcome overnight (under-4s stay free in parents' room), additional bed (£10) & cot supplied. Access, Amex, Visa.*

HOPESGATE Stables Inn FOOD

Tel 01743 891344 Map 8 D3
Drury Lane Hopesgate nr Minsterley Shropshire SY5 0EP

Debbie and Denis Harding's tiny, secluded inn (from which there are wonderful views over to Long Mountain and up to The Stiperstones) is set in glorious countryside above the Hope valley and signposted down country lanes from the A488, four miles south of Minsterley. Originally built in the 1680s as a pub for drovers between Montgomery and Shrewsbury, it's a distinctly traditional pub, whose attraction, in addition to the good food and beer, is an atmosphere in which good company can be enjoyed in the absence of intruding gaming machines or juke boxes. The bar is L-shaped, its blackened oak beams hung with pottery mugs, and the imposing open stone fireplace burns logs in winter. The mood is intimate and friendly and the fairly limited food-serving hours reflect the landlords' understanding of the need for a country pub to continue to play its important part in local life as a social gathering centre rather than being overwhelmed by diners all week. Lunchtime choices, posted on the blackboard, range from home-made celery and Stilton soup and hot local sausages with salad and crispy rolls, to potted shrimps, beef, Guinness and walnut casserole, creamy haddock pancake, country rabbit pie and lamb's liver and bacon. Evening eating (Wed to Sat only) is a mite more serious. Booking is strongly advised as there are only four tables in the tiny dining-room (so diners usually overflow into the adjacent snug). Debbie's cooking is always satisfying and might offer a choice of around six dishes at each stage: avocado and tomato salad, hot garlic mushrooms, lamb's kidneys hot pot, fresh sea bream fillets marinated in Cajun spices, and half a roast guinea fowl with bacon, walnuts, prunes and cider give the picture. They're substantial eaters in these parts, so there's no shortage of takers for puddings: steamed chocolate fudge pud, treacle sponge with custard, the landlady Debbie's now celebrated bread-and-butter pudding, or spiced plum crumble served with local farm ice cream. ***Bar Food*** *12-1.30 (no food Mon), dinner Wed-Sat only 7-8.30. Free House.* ***Beer*** *Wood's Special, Felinfoel Double Dragon, guest beers. Patio/terrace. Pub closed Mondays. No credit cards.*

HOPTON WAFERS Crown Inn FOOD B&B

Tel 01299 270372 **Fax 01299 271127** Map 6 B4
Hopton Wafers nr Cleobury Mortimer Shropshire DY14 0NB

The creeper-clad Crown in the Norman hamlet of Hopton Wafers is set in its own garden which slopes down to one of the many streams (crossed here by the A4117) that flow down to the Teme valley. Bounded on three sides by terraces of tables with their colourful summer parasols, it's a splendid spot for alfresco eating. Inside, the Rent Room, where once local villagers came to pay their rents, houses an atmospheric and intimate bar. Snacks and bar meals have a strongly fishy emphasis, but meat-eaters and vegetarians are not forgotten, with perhaps beef in stout pie, escalope of venison, celery and cashew risotto or tagliatelle in Stilton cream sauce. Home-made puddings might include treacle tart, Bakewell tart or a banana and rum trifle. Behind a central stone chimney, in which huge log fires burn on both sides in winter, is the Hopton Poacher restaurant. The decor and character of the bedrooms are commendable. Unsuspecting overnighters are in for a treat of exposed rafters, sloping corridors and creaky floorboards – with which the automatic trouser press and bathroom telephone extensions seem faintly at odds. Three bedrooms are family rooms, there's one high-chair and the garden is large, with trees, stream and pond. *Open 12-3, 6-11 (Sun 12-3, 7-10.30).* ***Bar Food*** *12-2.30, 6.30-9.30 (Sat to 10, Sun from 7). Free House.* ***Beer*** *Wadworth 6X, Boddingtons, Marston's Pedigree, guest beer. Riverside garden, outdoor eating.* ***Accommodation*** *8 bedrooms, all en suite, £65 (single £39.50). Children welcome overnight, additional bed (£10) and cot (£5) available. No dogs. Access, Visa.*

HORAM Gun Inn FOOD

Tel 01825 872361 Map 11 B6
Gun Hill Horam Heathfield East Sussex TN21 0JU

Extended 16th-century tiled and timbered pub enjoying a peaceful rural location just off the A22 northwest of Hailsham. Neat open-plan interior with a series of comfortably furnished alcove seating areas, several open fires, an old kitchen Aga, fresh flowers and various prints, copper and brass artefacts. Head for the blackboard menu for the daily-changing selection of

home-cooked dishes, which supplements a standard printed menu of pub favourites. Good reliable choices may include decent pies – Sussex fidget, chicken, ham and leek and lamb, apricot and rosemary – fresh salmon and asparagus pancakes, lasagne of smoked haddock, mussels and spinach and Sussex smokie in white wine and mustard sauce. Fresh fish comes from Newhaven. Keen to cater for all tastes there is the choice of fresh vegetables, chips, jacket potatoes or a selection of fresh, imaginative salads from the regularly replenished salad bar. Three vegetarian options might include broccoli bake or ricotta and spinach pancakes. For a home-made pudding try the treacle tart, apple crumble or summer pudding. Cream teas are available each afternoon between April and October. Overnight accommodation comprises three homely, simply furnished bedrooms with TVs, tea-makers and rural views. One has en-suite facilities, the others share a clean bathroom and two toilets. Continental breakfasts are served in the room. Good summer lawn. *Open summer 11-11, winter 11-3, 6-11, Sun 12-3, 7-10.30.* ***Bar Food*** *Apr-Oct 12-10, winter 12-2, 6-10, Sun 12-2, 7-10. Free House.* ***Beer*** *Larkins Sovereign, Harveys Sussex Bitter, Flowers original, guest beer. Garden, lawn, outside eating, children's play area. No credit cards.*

HORNDON — Elephant's Nest — FOOD

Tel 01822 810273 Map 12 C3
Horndon Mary Tavy nr Tavistock Horndon Devon PL19 9NQ

Isolated 16th-century inn located on the flanks of Dartmoor and reached via narrow, high-hedged lanes from the A386 Tavistock to Okehampton road at Mary Tavy (signposted). Named after a portly landlord with a bushy beard it is a character pub for wild winter weather with its window seats, rustic furnishings, old rugs, flagstones, heavy beams and open fires. The large garden has open views across the moor and picnic tables for summer days; rabbits, ducks, goats, geese and chickens in pens should keep the children interested. It is a busy dining pub with an extensive blackboard menu listing popular pub favourites as well as a range of home-cooked daily dishes – perhaps huntsman casserole, liver and orange casserole, Tavy trout, steak and kidney pie, peanut and lentil roulade (all about £5) – served with a choice of chips and salad or vegetables. 'Pete's Puds' include treacle and walnut tart and steamed apple and date sponge. *Open 11.30-2.30, 6.30-11 (Sun 12-2.30, 7-10.30).* ***Bar Food*** *11.30-2, 6.30-10 (Sun to 9.30). Family room. Free House.* ***Beer*** *St Austell's HSD, Palmers IPA, Boddingtons, guest beers. Garden, outdoor eating. No credit cards.*

HORNDON-ON-THE-HILL — Bell Inn & Hill House ★ — FOOD B&B

Tel 01375 673154 Fax 01375 361611 Map 11 B4
High Road Horndon-on-the-Hill Essex SS17 8LD

Zzz...

Located in the village centre a few doors from one another, John and Christine Vereker's 500-year-old Bell Inn offers a blackboard menu and a friendly rustic, pubby ambience including beams, unpolished wood tables and flagstone floors; Hill House next door has more formal dining in a pretty pastel-coloured room. A hot cross bun is nailed to a ceiling beam at the Bell every Good Friday, and the collection of shrunken, fossilised old buns is now pretty spectacular. The Bell menu features both simple and more unusual dishes: perhaps mussel soup, chicken livers with black pudding or red mullet with orange salad for starters, followed by chargrilled sirloin steak with tarragon béarnaise, beef stew with pimentos, lamb steak with tarragon, braised lamb's liver casserole or poached salmon. A 'taffy' (affectionately named after a Welsh regular who liked his ploughman's with hot bread) is a ploughman's platter with a choice of ham or cheese and good, locally-baked bread; further traditional fare like steak and kidney pie and chili are also available as bar snacks. The Bell Restaurant, to the rear of the bar, is a relaxed, informal setting. In Hill House the restaurant is more formal and a fixed-price menu does away with the simpler, more pubby items. Chef Sean Kelly's cooking is imaginative, skilfully executed and produces very enjoyable results on the plate; a dish of seafood sausage with cream and leek sauce, and his personal favourite, lamb cutlets stuffed with haggis and baked in pastry. Chocolate pudding with vanilla custard, baby pineapple with lemon sorbet and lemon soufflé with almond biscuits among the bar menu desserts. Above and also to the rear of Hill House are pretty, cottagey en-suite bedrooms, each thoughtfully equipped and neatly maintained; four rooms are upstairs in the Bell. A sporty, friendly community pub, free from music, gaming machines and pool tables. Booking essential in the restaurants (both of which are recommended in our *1996 Hotels & Restaurants Guide*). Large courtyard with seating in summer. *Open 11-2.30, 6-11 (Sat 11-3, 6-11, Sun 12-3, 7-10.30).* ***Bar Food*** *12.15-2, 6.15-10. Free House.* ***Beer*** *Bass, Charrington IPA, Fuller's London Pride, guest beers.* ***Accommodation*** *14 rooms, all en suite, £45/£55. Accommodation closed 24-30 Dec. Access, Amex, Visa.*

HORNINGSEA **Plough & Fleece** FOOD

Tel 01223 860795 Map 10 B3

High Street Horningsea Cambridgeshire CB5 9JG

A Grade II listed building, built in the Dutch style so popular in the East Anglia of the late 18th century when Dutch engineers came to advise on the draining of the Fenlands. The generally very busy Plough & Fleece owes its great popularity to old-fashioned regional cooking, which is often given a modern interpretation. Come here for homely, comforting hot-pots, cottage pie and hot cockles with garlic butter, as well as more contemporary treatments of dinner-partyish food, like honey-roast guinea fowl, or a perfect poached salmon. Puddings are suitably gorgeous and cream-laden; the Northamptonshire chocolate pudding in particular has an informal international fan club but there are at least seven others to choose from. Sandwiches and ploughman's platters are offered at lunchtime, when there's a busy business trade. All this means the pub can get crowded but the dining-room extension provides a welcome haven for non-smokers. In addition to the traditional roast on the reduced Sunday menu, Romany rabbit proves equally as popular. The atmosphere is homely and traditional in feel, especially so in the unspoilt public bar, with its ancient settles, tiled floor, elm tables and custard-coloured walls. The lounge is comfortable rather than characterful and invariably packed with bar meal diners. Arrive early at lunchtime to beat the scrum. Children (minimum age 5) allowed in dining-room only. *Open 11.30-2,30, 7-11 (Sun 12-3, 7-10.30).* ***Bar Food*** *12-2 (Sun to 1.30), 7-9.30 (except Sun/Mon eve).* ***Beer*** *Greene King. Garden, outdoor eating. Access, Amex, Visa.*

HORRINGER **Beehive** FOOD

Tel 01284 735260 Map 10 C3

The Street Horringer Suffolk IP29 5SD

Genuine home-made food is served throughout the bar areas here, and tables can be booked: the ratio of reservations to casual droppers-in is usually about 50/50. A printed menu is much more imaginative than most, and a specials board with delicious fresh fish makes the choice even more difficult. The fish may be cooked simply – grilled with butter and wine. Other choices are a sauté of prawns with sesame seeds, spring onions and soy sauce, honey-roast duck salad with crispy bacon and raisins, lightly poached smoked haddock topped with an egg and a rich cheese sauce, linguine with creamy mushroom sauce, and ploughman's lunch. Where better than to enjoy a plate of Suffolk ham carved from the bone and served with pickles and a salad bowl? End your meal with a selection from their home-made puddings – perhaps banoffi pie, Beehive tart (sponge, butter and raisins) or treacle tart – or with a hot chocolate and whipped cream. Rambling, traditionally furnished little rooms radiate off a central servery, warmed by a wood-burning stove. The terrace has five or so tables and there are picnic tables on the lawn. *Open 11.30-2.30, 7-11 (Sun 12-3, 7-10.30).* ***Bar Food*** *12-2, 7-9.30 (except Sun eve).* ***Beer*** *Greene King. Garden, outdoor eating. Access, Visa.*

HORSEBRIDGE **Royal Inn** FOOD

Tel 01822 870214 Map 12 C3

Horsebridge Tavistock Devon PL19 8PJ

Three excellent reasons for a detour to Terry and Julie Wood's informal and relaxing 15th-century pub, once a nunnery: to look at the ancient Tamar Bridge, to sample their own home-brewed ales (of which it is reported that no-one has been able to drink more than five pints!) and to try the landlady's cooking. Filled rolls, ploughman's, pot meals and imaginative salads are all typical fare, along with the likes of seafood pancakes, sherried kidneys, venison in wine, beef in ale, and chicken, Stilton and mushroom slice; "no chips or fried food". Meringue roulade and apricots in brandy to tempt the sweet-toothed. No children under 14 inside. *Open 12-2.30, 7-11 (Sun 12-2.30, 7-10.30).* ***Bar Food*** *12-2, 7.15-9 (Sat to 9.30, no food Sun). Free House.* ***Beer*** *Sharp's Own Cornish, Bass, plus own home brews: Heller, Horsebridge Best, Tamar, Right Royal. Patio, outdoor eating. No credit cards.*

HORTON-IN-RIBBLESDALE Crown Hotel FOOD B&B

Tel 01729 860209 **Fax 01729 860444** Map 5 D4
Horton-in-Ribblesdale nr Settle North Yorkshire BD24 0HF

Sandwiched between two road bridges on the B6479 where Bransgyll runs into the Ribble, the Crown is centrally located amid the Three Peaks at the heart of the Ribble Valley. At the pub, three generations now come into play. Landlady Norma Hargreaves moved here over 30 years ago with her parents; now, daughter Helen is in charge of the kitchen. She makes home-made pies and puddings, plus an extended range that might include Provençal baked halibut, turkey breast with mushroom and smoked bacon sauce and apricot and courgette gratin. Freshly-baked 'crusties' (small baguettes, lunchtime only) and ploughman's are also offered. In terms of accommodation, to term the bedrooms modest is not to decry them, as an absence of TVs and phones remains intentional. Internal dimensions of this unaltered 17th-century inn dictate, though, against much modernisation and there are but two rooms with en-suite bathrooms and a further five with added shower stalls. Two adjacent cottages offer self-contained private accommodation for larger parties. Being an altogether family-run affair there's also a special promise that "parents with children are welcome here to do exactly what other normal people like to do". Longer opening hours in summer. *Open 11-3, 6-11, Sat 11-11, Sun 12-3, 7-10.30.* ***Bar Food** 12-2, 6-9. Garden. **Beer** Theakston XB. Family room. **Accommodation** 9 bedrooms, two en suite, £34-£42 midweek, £38-£47 Fri, Sat & BH (single £17.25). No credit cards.*

HOUGHTON CONQUEST Knife & Cleaver B&B

Tel 01234 740387 **Fax 01234 740900** Map 15a E1
Houghton Conquest nr Ampthill Bedfordshire MK45 3LA

Three miles from Ampthill and equidistant from Junctions 12 and 13 of the M10, opposite the medieval parish church in a sleepy village, the Knife & Cleaver is more an inn than a pub. The accommodation is especially pleasing, in spacious brick-built garden rooms standing alongside a mature orchard. In addition to TVs, telephones, radio-alarm clocks and beverage facilities, the mini-fridge in each room is thoughtfully stored each day with fresh milk. The less mobile are especially well catered for, with wide, paved bedroom access and ramps into the pub proper where there's a Jacobean oak-panelled bar and a Victorian-style conservatory restaurant behind. *Open 12-2.30, 7-11 (Sun 12-3, closed Sun eve). Free House. **Beer** Batemans XB, Adnams Extra. Garden. Family room. **Accommodation** 9 bedrooms, all en suite, £59/£66, £45 single. Children welcome overnight (under-5yrs free in parents' room), extra bed and cot supplied. Access, Amex, Diners, Visa.*

HOVINGHAM Worsley Arms Hotel B&B

Tel 01653 628234 **Fax 01653 628130** Map 5 E4
Hovingham North Yorkshire YO6 4LA

Zzz...

Built in 1841 as an adjunct to the unsuccessful development of Hovingham as a spa, the inn has remained in the hands of the Worsley family from that day to this. Described as "late-Georgian" in style, it overlooks the green of this most unspoilt of North Riding villages. The Cricketers Bar, appropriately named as it's the headquarters of the local team, is hung with a unique photographic collection of the county's greatest in action, many of whom played at the Hovingham Hall ground. It's generally lively here, with some good Double Chance from the nearby Malton brewery and bistro-style bar food (soup, baked oysters, fancy sandwiches, fishcakes, warm salads). The inn itself has a more refined feel in its elegant lounges with deep armchairs and abundant reading matter. Sunday lunches and table d'hote dinners are served in the sedate dining-room, heavy with fine 18th-century portraits. Spacious bedrooms echo the Georgian feel with large windows and sumptuous drapes and co-ordinated fabrics. Bathrooms with large bathsheets and abundant toiletries are best described as traditional. *Open 11-3, 6-11 (Sun 12-3, 7-10.30). Free House. **Beer** Malton Double Chance, John Smith's, Theakston Old Peculier. Garden, outdoor eating, patio. Tennis, squash. Family room. **Accommodation** 22 rooms, all en suite, £98 (single £62). Children welcome, extra bed (£15) and cot (£5) provided. Access, Amex, Visa.*

HOXNE — The Swan — FOOD

Tel 01379 668275 Map 10 C2
Low Street Hoxne Suffolk IP21 5AS

A Grade II listed 15th-century inn built by the Bishop of Norwich as the guest quarters to his now defunct summer palace. It's been a hostelry since at least 1619 and the interior, which features high ceilings and fluted oak joists, is suitably evocative of centuries gone by. Some good bar food includes sandwiches and omelettes (fillings to order), mixed cheese ploughman's, scampi and lamb cutlets on the hand-written menu; courgette and rosemary soup, spinach and garlic terrine, pork fillet in brandy cream sauce and cod and prawn gratinée might feature as daily specials, along with spinach, chick pea and cumin parcels in tomato sauce for vegetarians and chocolate pot or orange mousse for sweet. Only a cold buffet at summer Sunday lunchtime; three-course Sunday lunch menu in winter. No bar meals on Saturday evenings (only restaurant). Outside, there's a large, tree-bordered garden where you can play croquet. The village is pronounced Hoxon (in case you want to feel like a local). *Open 12-2.30, 5.30-11, Sat 12-3, 5.30-11, Sun 12-3, 7-10.30.* ***Bar Food*** *12-2, 7-9 (except Sat D & Sun L).* ***Beer*** *Adnams Bitter (and Old & Tally Ho in winter), Greene King Abbot. Garden, outdoor eating. Pub closed 25 Dec. Access, Visa.*

HURLEY — Dew Drop Inn — A

Tel 01628 824327 Map 15a D3
Near Hurley Berkshire SL6 6RB

Signposted off the A43, this is a tucked-away, well-loved and genuinely unpretentious cottage pub. The garden which backs on to National Trust woodland is delightful in summer. It's a real hideaway of a place in winter, when the twin log fires in the main bar are crackling. Miles of local walks make this rural retreat very popular with walkers and dog owners. *Open 11.15-2.30, 6.15-11 (Sun 12-2.30, 7-10.30).* ***Beer*** *Brakspear Ordinary & Old. Garden, children's play area. No credit cards.*

HURTMORE — The Squirrel — A

Tel 01483 860223 **Fax 01483 860592** Map 15a E4
Hurtmore nr Godalming Surrey GU7 2RN

☺

A convenient stopping point on the London-Portsmouth A3 road (which runs by rather unobtrusively behind the hedge at the top of the garden), just south of Guildford. New landlord Jordi Vazquez has already made a few changes: the main bar area has been opened out (but the low tables and comfortable sofas retained) and the airy conservatory brasserie turned into a restaurant; outside, the gently terraced garden – complete with picnic tables, swings, slide and wooden play house – is now fenced and safer for families. The covered patio is a pleasant spot for a drink on a sunny day. Improvements have been promised in both the bar food and the accommodation; the former is rather undistinguished (stick to the simplest of fare), while the latter is in thirteen small, pine-furnished rooms (one is a family room with bunk beds) in cottages across the car park. Hurtmore pay-as-you-play golf course is close by. *Open 11-3, 5.30-11 (Sun 12-2.30, 7-10.30). Free House.* ***Beer*** *Ruddles County, Courage Best, Theakston Best. Garden, children's play area. Access, Amex, Diners, Visa.*

IBSTONE — The Fox — B&B

Tel 01491 638289 **Fax 01491 638873** Map 15a D3
Ibstone nr High Wycombe Buckinghamshire HP14 3GG

Zzz... ☺

Much modernised and extended 300-year-old inn located on the Chiltern ridgeway opposite Ibstone Common, and close to acres of beechwood rambles. With the M40 (J5) only a mile away, this rural inn is a handy overnight stop for travellers, for the nine en-suite rooms are comfortable and well equipped. All rooms feature co-ordinating fabrics, modern pine furniture, clean fully tiled shower rooms and a full complement of added comforts – tea-makers, TVs, direct-dial telephones, clock-radios, trouser presses and hairdryers. Rear rooms have soothing views across fields and woodland. Relaxing, simply furnished bars and a delightful sunny front terrace and well-tended garden. *Open 11-3, 6-11, Sun 12-3, 7-10.30.* ***Beer*** *Greene King Abbot Ale, Brakspear Bitter, Fuller's London Pride, guest beer. Garden. Family room.* ***Accommodation*** *9 bedrooms, all en suite with shower, £58-£76 per night (single £41-£58). Children welcome overnight, additional bed supplied. Dogs by arrangement. Access, Amex, Diners, Visa.*

Icklingham — Red Lion — FOOD

Tel 01638 717802 **Fax 01638 515702** Map 10 C2
High Street Icklingham Suffolk IP28 6PS

Fine 16th-century village inn set back from the A1101 with a neat front lawn and raised rear terrace overlooking fields. Sympathetically restored and well refurbished two-bar interior featuring low "smoke" brown ceilings with heavy, black-painted beams, an exposed brick fireplace and an assortment of antique and sturdy tables, benches, pews and chairs arranged on rug-strewn wooden floors. Relaxing ambience enhanced by piped classical music, various newspapers and magazines to read and evening candlelight. A reliable range of interesting home-cooked bar food is offered. Blackboard lists may feature fresh asparagus soup, Newmarket sausages and mash, lamb cutlets with redcurrant sauce, chicken and mushroom pie and a huge wooden bowl of warm fillet of chicken and crispy pasta salad. Good accompanying vegetables – definitely no chips! Granary sandwiches and ploughman's platters are available all day. Fresh fish from Lowestoft may top 15 varieties on Thursday evenings, including fillet of codling, lemon sole and grilled plaice, along with more unusual choices. Round the meal off with sticky treacle tart, raspberry fool or ginger pudding with lemon sauce. Well-kept Greene King ales and a good range of wines, including country fruit wines. Children welcome. The licensees also run the *Pykkerell Inn* at Ixworth (see entry). *Open 12-3, 6-11, Sun 12-3, 7-10.30. **Bar Food** 12-2.30, 6-10 (Sun 7-9). **Beer** Greene King. Garden, outdoor eating. Access, Visa.*

Ightham Common — Harrow Inn — ★ — FOOD

Tel 01732 885912 Map 11 B5
Common Road Ightham Common nr Borough Green Kent TN15 9ER

Coloured lights around the door offer a welcome at this unusual Virginia creeper-hung stone inn on a country lane full of pretty grand houses. In the small front bar a couple of stuffed birds in glass cases and old motor racing photos are mounted above dado pine panelling, and there's a pair of old leather armchairs and a pool table in the room next door; the whole effect wobbles on the very fine line between characterful and seedy, but boxes of board games and newspapers laid out on a side table are a nice touch, and the landlord and his friendly staff soon dispel any doubts. Gerard Costelloe has an impressive catering background, and the cooking is excellent. Well-balanced soups arrive in large tureens, from which one helps oneself, along with a whole freshly baked rye loaf on its own bread board. There are always a couple of pasta dishes, at least one of them vegetarian, as well as the likes of pies, baked red snapper and venison sausages. It's worth saving a little space for dessert, like bread-and-butter pudding or a classic summer pudding, properly made, its bread thoroughly soaked in the juice of soft fruits. The bars are not really suitable for chidren but they are welcome (particularly for Sunday lunch) in the cottagey restaurant, its conservatory extension complete with grape vine. The menu here tends to be somewhat more adventurous. Given the rather tacky walls, the sloping flagstoned floors and the very smoky and poorly-ventilated atmosphere in the bar, this is not the sort of place one expects to find such good food, served by friendly staff and sold at equally friendly prices – unusual and eccentric, yes, but worthy in its own special way. *Open 12-3, 6.30-11, Sun 12-3, 7-10.30. **Bar Food** 12-2, 7-9.30. Free House. **Beer** Marston's Pedigree, Greene King IPA & Abbot. Garden, outdoor eating. Family room. Access, Amex, Visa.*

Ilmington — Howard Arms — FOOD — B&B

Tel & Fax 01608 682226 Map 14a A1
Lower Green Ilmington nr Shipston-on-Stour Warwickshire CV36 4LN

Zzz...

For its location by the village green and setting in a mature orchard garden, the yellow-stone Howard Arms falls into the 'irresistible' category, a picture by day, romantically lit at night. Centuries-old connections with one of England's most illustrious families adds a touch of history to draw the crowds to its flagstoned bar and open-plan restaurant. Menus change daily, a single blackboard offering the same choices throughout, and all food orders are taken at the bar. Sandwiches and ploughman's platters, using freshly-baked crusty rolls, are offered at lunchtimes (not Sun). More substantially, seasonal asparagus is a popular starter or there's a home-made soup, perhaps; follow fishily with a seafood croissant or lemon sole with almonds; for meatier choices the likes of lamb and rosemary pie, chicken tarragon, rib-eye steak with bacon and red wine sauce; for vegetarians there's canneloni with ricotta and spinach and, to follow, lime crème brulée and Irish whiskey tart. One menu is served throughout, but bookings are taken in the restaurant where the service is more formal; a traditional Sunday lunch is also offered here. Just two bedrooms are let, a large twin with quite enough space for a family to stay, and the king-sized double for the more romantically

inclined; en-suite facilities include both bath and shower, and there are no phones to impinge on the peace. *Open 11-2.30, 6-11, Sun 12-3, 7-10.30.* ***Bar Food*** *12-2, 7-9 (Sun eve summer only Apr-Sept, Fri & Sat to 9.30). Free House.* ***Beer*** *Boddingtons, Everards Tiger, guest beer. Garden, outdoor eating.* ***Accommodation*** *2 bedrooms, both en suite, £50 (single £30). Children welcome overnight, additional bed and cot available (£5). Check-in by arrangement. No dogs. Access, Amex, Visa.*

Ivy Hatch — The Plough ★ FOOD

Tel 01732 810268 Map 11 B5
Coach Road Ivy Hatch Kent TN15 0NL

Quite apart from its outstandingly good cooking, the Plough is the kind of pub just about everyone would love to have as their local. A large mid 18th-century roadside inn dominating this little hamlet, it's just enough off the beaten track, although well signposted. Within, it's peaceful and genuinely unspoilt, with dark pitch mahogany in the light of a crackling log fire, and candlelight by night. By way of contrast, the conservatory dining extension is light and fresh, with its soft pink linens, cane furniture and decorative greenery. The chef-manager, Daniel Humbert, offers one menu throughout the pub and he continues to produce excellent food: choose an excellently flavoured soup (cream of wild celeriac and Stilton), stir-fried monkfish and scallops provençale or grilled goat's cheese and sweet pepper salad, then perhaps an unusual venison casserole with cider, coriander and wild mushrooms, steamed sea char, pan-fried Cajun-style duo of John Dory and tuna, grilled rump steak bordelaise or lamb's liver and bacon. Finish with a classic, tangy tarte au citron, a delicate crème brulée, bread-and-butter pudding, sticky toffee pudding or strawberry tuile – all show a lightness of touch and substantial skill. Bastille Day, July 14, is celebrated in suitably Gallic style – book well in advance for frogs' legs, cassoulet, braised snails in red wine and shallots, cote de boeuf and a magnificent dish of Brittany-style seafood. Tables can be booked throughout (including the conservatory). Air-conditioned. *Open 12-3, 6-11 (Sun 7-10.30).* ***Bar Food*** *12-2, 7-9.30. No bar food D Sun. Free House.* ***Beer*** *Brakspear Bitter, Marston's Pedigree, guest beers. Garden, outdoor eating. Access, Visa.*

Ixworth — Pykkerell Inn FOOD

Tel 01359 230398 Map 10 C2
High Street Ixworth Suffolk IP31 2HH

Don't be fooled by the unassuming brick exterior for it belies the true age of this rambling old coaching inn. Its medieval 15th-century charm has been carefully revealed throughout the series of rooms which ooze antiquity and atmosphere. Stripped ancient panelling, heavily carved beams, bare-boarded floors strewn with colourful Persian rugs, a library and a delightful mix of antique tables and chairs characterise this most civilised place. Added welcome touches include brass candle-holders on tables, soothing classical music and newspapers to browse. Food matches the ambience and decor in quality and style, with imaginative home-cooked dishes – using fresh local ingredients – in both bar and à la carte restaurant drawing a generally upmarket clientele from far and wide. Various blackboards list the day's fare, notably fresh fish from Lowestoft such as fillet of codling. Further choices range from asparagus soup, Tiger Bay prawns in garlic butter and Newmarket sausages and mash to pork chops with apple and cider sauce, warm fillet of chicken and crispy pasta salad and delicious home-cooked Suffolk ham with Shrewsbury sauce, served with crisp fresh vegetables. More adventurous restaurant fare can also be ordered in the bar. Leave room for an excellent pudding like luxury bread-and-butter pudding and ginger pudding with lemon sauce. Good range of wines, including over 15 country fruit wines. Rear courtyard seating for warmer days overlooks a fine timber-framed Elizabethan barn. Licensees also run the *Red Lion* at Icklingham (see entry). *Open 12-2.30, 6-11, Sun 12-3, 7-10.30.* ***Bar Food*** *12-2.30, 6-10 (Sun 7-9).* ***Beer*** *Greene King. Garden, outdoor eating. Access, Visa.*

Kegworth — Cap and Stocking FOOD

Tel 01509 674814 Map 7 D3
20 Borough Street Kegworth Leicestershire DE74 2FF

Far from being either Leicestershire's oldest or most fashionable pub, today's high-flying 'Cap' is as evocative as its name, remarkable not least for its pétanque piste in the old walled garden and the ancient tradition of Bass-served-in-the-jug. The kitchen crew produces customer-inspired dishes from meat and provisions bought in daily. As well as filled cob rolls, ploughman's platters and pizzas, the clamour is for ever-spicier curries, '*chicken tak-a-tan*', wider vegetarian options and even more custard with the popular puddings like hot treacle. Parking very limited. Convenient for M1 J24. *Open 11.30-3, 6-11 (Sun 12-3, 7-10.30).* ***Bar Food*** *12-2.30, 6.30-9 (Sun from 7).* ***Beer*** *Bass, M&B Mild, two guest beers. Garden, outdoor eating, pétanque. Family room. No credit cards.*

KELSTON — Old Crown — A

Tel 01225 423032 Map 13 F1
Bath Road Kelston nr Bath Avon BA1 9AQ

Standing alongside the old coaching route from Bristol to Bath (now the A431), with its car park across the busy road, the Old Crown is a gem of a place which has the carefully cultivated air of being by-passed by time. By day and by night flickering candles along the bar and mantleshelves, constantly highlighting strings of hops above the bar, are reflected in the glass of the pub's collection of framed prints and montages. The front rooms have shining, uneven flagstone floors, polished tables and carved oak settles. Beyond are two dining-rooms, prettily appointed, where most of the serious eating goes on. Real-ale buffs though, can enthuse over the authentic bank of four unaltered 1930s' beer engines which still dispense some fine Bass, Butcombe and regular guest brews. No children under 14 inside; however, there are picnic tables at the back, prettily laid out in a mature orchard. *Open 11.30-2.30, 5-11 (Sun 12-3, 7-10.30). Free House.* ***Beer*** *Bass, Butcombe, Wadworth 6X & Old Timer (winter) & Farmer's Glory (summer), Smiles Best. Garden. Access, Visa.*

KEMPSEY — Walter de Cantelupe Inn — FOOD

Tel 01905 820572 Map 14 B1
Kempsey nr Worcester Hereford & Worcester WR5 3NA

In a modest former cider house on the A38 one and a half miles south of Worcester's city boundary, Martin Lloyd Morris has been plying his trade since late 1991. He provides a welcoming atmosphere, well-kept real ales and purposefully fresh food selections kept sensibly simple; the menu changes with the seasons. Beside a lunch menu offering the likes of granary bread sandwiches, steak and kidney pie, noodles with smoked ham and tomato and moist omelettes, there are daily lunch blackboard specials. As evenings draw a hungrier crowd, the range then might run to cream of barley, bacon and beer soup, skewered king prawns and mushrooms with a basil vinaigrette, hot soft roes, butterflied beef fillet with jammed shallots and a rich gravy, salmon and potato cakes with dill butter sauce, pistachio-filled chicken supreme with a curried cream, poached salmon salad with mint mayonnaise, hot mullet with peppers and new potatoes, baked pears in filo pastry with a redcurrant sauce, locally-made ice creams and British farmhouse cheeses. Because chef Chris Bennett uses only fresh produce dishes are limited by supply, so first come, first served. *Open 12-2.30, 5.30-11 (winter from 6, Sun 12-3, 7-10.30).* ***Bar Food*** *12-2.30, 6-9 (to 9.30 Fri & Sat). No bar food Sun eve (except Sun before Bank Holiday Mondays). Free House.* ***Beer*** *Timothy Taylor's Landlord, Marston's Best, guest beer. Outdoor eating area. Access, Visa.*

KEYSOE — Chequers Inn — A

Tel 01234 708678 Map 15 E1
Pertenhall Road Keysoe Bedfordshire MK44 2HR

Dating back to 1520, the Chequers' one bar is divided into two by an unusual pillared fireplace; log fires in cold weather. The separate lounge opens on to a large, lawned garden complete with a Wendy House, playtree and swing. *Open 12-2.30, 6.30-11 (Sun 12-3, 7-10.30). Free House.* ***Beer*** *Hook Norton Best Bitter, guest beer. Garden, children's play area. Pub closed all Tue. Access, Visa.*

KEYSTON — Pheasant Inn ★ — FOOD

Tel 01832 710241 **Fax 01832 710340** Map 7 E4
Village Loop Road Keyston nr Bythorn Cambridgeshire PE18 ORE

Peacefully located near the church in this upmarket village and only a couple of miles from the busy A14 Huntingdon to Kettering road (if ever there was a pub worthy of a special detour then this is it), this long, low, whitewashed pub/restaurant with low, thatched roof and original timbers promises much in character and atmosphere, and the food lives up to it all in admirable fashion. Inside, you'll find heavy, dark oak beams and walls hung with old hunting photos, the odd stuffed pheasant and even a fox, too. One menu is served throughout the rambling, neatly-furnished bars and in the more formal Red Room (where the only difference is larger tables, linen napkins and no smoking); it changes twice-weekly,

offering a comprehensive range of around a dozen starters (also suitable as a light snack - "please feel free to eat as much or as little as you like"), such as leek and Parma ham risotto with parmesan cheese, haricot bean and truffle soup, seared chicken with daikon and teriyaki sauce or spicy salmon and tuna fishcakes with peanuct and cucumber dressing. An equal number of imaginative main dishes may feature curried lamb's kidneys with a timbale of rice and pickled chilis, steamed fillet of brill with roasted red peppers and a potato and chive salad, spinach and ricotta tart with roasted Mediterranean vegetables or breast and thigh of pheasant with red cabbage and roast potatoes. Finish with one of the dozen puddings – perhaps baked rum and raisin cheesecake, spotted Dick and custard, hot pancakes with coconut ice cream and maple syrup – or a selection of Neal's Yard British cheeses served with apple and celery. Traditional Sunday roast is always offered along with nine other options. Fresh fish is delivered daily from either Dorset or London, but most of the fine ingredients used here come from local suppliers less than two miles distant. The Pheasant remains at heart a well-kept friendly village pub, as deservedly popular for its range of cask-conditioned ales as for its superb list of wines (unusually arranged by flavour not area), of which an even dozen may be ordered by the glass; five or so dessert wines are also offered by the glass. The helpful wines notes are worth following. *Open 11-3, 6-11 (Sun 12-2, 7-10.30). **Bar Meals** 12-2, 6.30-10 (Sun 7.15-9.45). Free House. **Beer** Fuller's London Pride, Adnams Best, Courage, Directors, two guest beers. Garden, outdoor eating. Family room. Closed 25, 26 Dec & 1 Jan eve. Access, Amex, Diners, Visa.*

KILVE — Hood Arms — FOOD

Tel 01278 741210 Map 13 E1 **B&B**

Kilve nr Bridgwater Somerset TA5 1EA

Zzz...

Pristine 17th-century white village coaching inn at the front of the Quantock Hills, a mile from the sea, with log fires, a large collection of horse brasses and a complete set of a show harness above the fireplace. Modernised, comfortable interior, with wood-burning stove in the carpeted main bar, which is bistro-like in the evenings. The menu varies from prawn cocktail, chicken and broccoli mornay and National Trust pie to Dover sole, chicken Kiev or spinach and garlic lasagne. Puddings are the old favourites – treacle tart, sherry trifle, rum tipsy cake. Also smaller, cosy lounge. Friendly, welcoming service. Bedrooms, all with baths en suite, have TV, beverage facilities, trouser press and hairdryer; two rooms at the rear are the quietest and overlook the pleasant garden. *Open 11-2.30, 6-11 (Sun 12-2, 7-10.30). **Bar Food** 12-2 (12-1.30 Sun), 6.30-10 (7.15-9.30 Sun). Free House. **Beer** Boddingtons, Flowers Original. Garden, outdoor eating. **Accommodation** 5 bedrooms, all en suite, £62 (single £38). Children welcome overnight (minimum age 8). Access, Visa.*

KING'S LYNN — Tudor Rose — B&B

Tel 01553 762824 Fax 01553 764894 Map 10 B1

St Nicholas Street off Tuesday Market Place King's Lynn Norfolk PE30 1LR

Located just off the main Market Place, this medieval timber-framed merchant's house was built around 1500 with a brick townhouse extension added in the 1640s. Beyond the medieval oak studded door lies a good panelled pubby bar, a charming 15th-century beamed restaurant and twelve neat and tidy bedrooms, some of which have views of St Nicholas's Chapel. At present, accommodation is modest with modern furniture, clean en-suite facilities and most of the added comforts – TV, clock-radio, tea-makers, telephones and hairdryers. Plans however are still afoot, with the enthusiastic new owners planning to gradually upgrade and refurbish each bedroom. *Open 11-11 (Sun 12-3, 7-10.30). Free House. **Beer** Boddingtons, Bass, Woodforde's Wherry, guest beer. Garden, outdoor eating access. **Accommodation** 13 bedrooms, 11 en suite (two with private bath not en suite), £50 (single £38.50). Children welcome overnight (under-10s free), additional bed (£10) and cot supplied. Access, Amex, Visa.*

KINGSAND — Halfway House Inn — FOOD

Tel 01752 822279 Map 12 C3 **B&B**

Kingsand nr Torpoint Cornwall PL10 1NA

Attractive pink-washed inn tucked among the narrow lanes and houses of this quaint fishing village, and only a few yards from the seafront. Comfortably refurbished over the past two years by David and Sarah Riggs it has become a popular place in which to dine and more recently to stay. Relaxing, carpeted and stone walled bar furnished with a mix of old pine and small copper-topped tables and warmed by a good woodburning stove. A routine bar

menu (sandwiches, granary rolls, ploughman's platters, jacket potatoes, all-day breakfast) is enhanced by an imaginative blackboard selection of dishes that are served in both the bar and the small cosy restaurant. As one might expect, it is very fish orientated. Start, perhaps, with delicious crab puffs in a pool of pesto sauce, a selection of smoked fish or a freshly made tomato soup, followed by cassoulet of brill, scallops and crab, ragout of turbot and scallops with cream and basil, roast garlic monkfish with peppers or chicken Basque with tomato, garlic and basil and lamb noisettes with chasseur sauce. Chocolate marquise with coffee bean sauce and passion fruit mousse may feature on the pudding board. Co-ordinating Laura Ashley fabrics, wall friezes and wallpapers grace the well kitted out, fresh and clean en-suite bedrooms which are furnished with modern pine pieces, cane chairs, and attractive prints with a seashore theme adorn the walls. Each window has its own colourful and overflowing box of flowers in the summer. A family bedroom has bunk beds. Value-for-money overnight accommodation. *Open 11-3, 6-11 (longer hours in summer, Sun 12-3, 7-10.30).* ***Bar Food*** *12-2, 7-9.45. Free House.* ***Beer*** *Bass, Boddingtons, Flowers Original, guest beer.* ***Accommodation*** *5 bedrooms, all with shower en suite, £39 (family room £60, single £19.50). Children welcome overnight (under-7s stay free in parents' room, 7-12s half price), additional bed & cot available. Access, Amex, Diners, Visa.*

KINGSCOTE — Hunters Hall — FOOD

Tel 01453 860393 **Fax 01453 860707** Map 14 B2 **B&B**

Kingscote nr Tetbury Gloucestershire GL8 8XZ

Five miles from Tetbury on the A4135 Hunters Hall is an ideal spot for a family day out. It sports a lovely tree-lined garden with extensive play areas and assault course, while on wet days parents and little ones use the gallery room, almost hidden above the pub's interlinked beamed and flagstoned bars. Bar food is a safe bet with dishes like lamb and red wine casserole, grilled pork loin with smoked bacon and Brie, smoked chicken and mayonnaise salad, and rainbow trout with almonds changing daily; steak and kidney pie is a speciality. A lunchtime buffet in the dining-room remains ever-popular. Good selection of wines by the glass. Standing separately, a Cotswold stone block of recent construction houses the bedrooms, residents' lounge and a conference facility. With roomy en-suite bathrooms, remote-control TV and dial-out phone, neither space nor comfort is stinted: two ground-floor rooms incorporate facilities for the disabled, and a large suite has two double bedrooms. *Open 11-3, 6-11 (Sun 12-3, 7-10.30).* ***Bar Food*** *12-2 (cold buffet to 2.30), 6.30-9.45. Free House.* ***Beer*** *Bass, Hook Norton Best, Marston's Pedigree, Uley Old Spot. Garden, outdoor play area. Family room.* ***Accommodation*** *12 bedrooms, all en suite, £58 (four-poster £65, single £44). Children welcome overnight (family room for 3 – £68, for 4 – £80). Additional bed (£10) and cot (£4) available. Access, Amex, Diners, Visa.*

KINGSKERSWELL — Barn Owl Inn — FOOD

Tel 01803 872130 Map 13 D3 **B&B**

Kingkerswell nr Newton Abbot Devon TQ12 5AN

Zzz...

Look out for a sign on the A380 to the Barn Owl Inn, which offers decent food, good bedrooms and a friendly welcome. Lovingly restored by the Warners, the original 16th-century farmhouse has a neat if unremarkable exterior which makes its characterful interior even more of a surprise. Old beams, rough stone walls and flagstoned floors have been uncovered, and real log fires warm each of the three bars in winter. One room features an inglenook fireplace, another an ancient black-leaded range, while in the largest bar (now more intimate), oak panelling and an ornate plasterwork ceiling are rather grander than might be expected of a modest farmhouse. Fresh flowers on all the tables add to the general charm of the surroundings. A printed bar menu offers a standard choice of pub meals, from cold platters and filled jacket potatoes to steaks. Home-cooked daily specials listed on the blackboard improve matters significantly with such dishes as lamb en croute, steak and kidney pie, pork goulash, fisherman's casserole and pheasant and chicken with Cumberland sauce, all accompanied by a decent selection of vegetables. Remember to bring your appetite; portions are generous. Six bedrooms within the original farmhouse combine considerable charm with conveniences like television and direct-dial telephones. Extensive sound-proofing effectively eliminates any noise from the bars below. Rooms are cottagey in style with black beams, white plaster walls, dark-stained pine furniture locally made in solid country style and their own individual floral fabrics. The 'signature' design is also used above dados in the bathrooms and in panels on the doors, the outsides of which are covered with old floorboards, thus cunningly concealing the modern fireproof doors within. Bowls of fruit, fresh flowers and mineral water add the final homely touch to the pristinely kept

rooms. No children under 14 are permitted in either bars or bedrooms, but they are welcome in the small walled garden. *Open 11.30-2.30, 6.30-11 (Sun 12-3, 7-10.30).* ***Bar Food*** *11.45-2 (Sun from 12), 6.30-10 (Sun from 7). Free House.* ***Beer*** *Fergusons Dartmoor, Ind Coope Burton Ale, Wadworth 6X. Garden, outdoor eating.* ***Accommodation*** *6 bedrooms, all en suite, £60 (single £40). Pub & accommodation closed 3 days after Christmas. No dogs. Access, Amex, Diners, Visa.*

KINGSTEIGNTON — Old Rydon Inn ★ — FOOD

Tel 01626 54626 **Fax 01626 56980** Map 13 D3
Old Rydon Road Kingsteignton Newton Abbot Devon TQ12 3QG

Hermann Hruby (pronounced Ruby) continues to maintain his high standards in producing some of the best pub food in the South West, and in that respect little has changed since the Hrubys bought the Old Rydon in 1978 except for the building of a splendid, and large, heated conservatory, leafy with vines, jasmine, bougainvillaea and other plants. It's a Grade II listed former farmhouse, converted in the 1960s with an original old cider loft forming an attractive part of the bar, previously the farm stables. Underneath the plank and beam ceiling adorned with pewter mugs is a raised log fire; the whitewashed stone walls are hung with antlers and horns. Tables here are drinking style, too small and cramped for relaxed dining, and many of the seats are converted barrels. The place to dine is in the comfortable conservatory, or on warm sunny days at a table on the patio or in the sheltered walled garden – an ideal summer venue for lunch. Separate from the bar, a relaxing diners' lounge leads through to the charming little restaurant, in the oldest part of the building. Most visitors come for the delicious and interesting food (including sandwiches and ploughman's platters) which, in the bar, is listed on twice daily-changing blackboards and might include mushroom, bacon and parsley soup, pork, chicken and herb terrine, vegetable, lentil and coriander leaf curry with cumin and ginger, Mexican turkey hotpot with vegetables in a spicy tomato and chili sauce, stir-fried vegetable chow mein and a memorable Italian-style seafood tagliatelle with cod, prawns, mushrooms, fresh spinach leaves and pesto sauce, topped with cheese. Excellent puddings range from Swiss nut fudge and fruit frangipane to scrumpy bread pudding. Service is polite and very efficient. Children are welcome in the conservatory or upstairs. The pub is awkward to locate as it now hides within a modern housing estate, but it is best approached along Longford Lane off the A381, then take Rydon Road which lies on your left. *Open 11-2.30, 6-11 (Sun 12-3, 7-10.30).* ***Bar Food*** *12-2, 7-10. Free House.* ***Beer*** *Wadworth 6X, Bass, guest beer. Garden, outdoor eating. Pub closed 25 Dec. Access, Amex, Diners, Visa.*

KINGSTON — The Juggs — FOOD

Tel 01273 472523 **Fax 01273 476150** Map 11 B6
The Street Kingston nr Lewes East Sussex BN7 3NT

Just off the A27, a short distance from Brighton, you will find this picturesque little 15th-century inn made from two tiny cottages. The name 'Juggs' originates from the leather jugs the women used to carry on their heads to collect fish from the market. The main bar is particularly characterful with its low ceilings, rough black timbers, rustic benches and yellowing walls; there's also a small no-smoking dining area (same menu in both, bookings taken). The home-made steak and kidney puddings have a reputation for being enormous and good value, the Sussex bangers are made by a local butcher and served with chips, and puddings, all home-made, are considered a speciality: perhaps chocolate nutcake and butterscotch toffee with maple sauce. Open sandwiches and ploughman's platters are also offered. Off the family room is a large picture window that now overlooks a Japanese garden. *Open 11-3, 6-11 (Sun 12-3, 7-10.30), July-Sept 11-11.* ***Bar Food*** *12-2 (Sun to 2.15), 6-9.30 (Sun from 7). Free House.* ***Beer*** *Harveys Best, King & Barnes Broadwood Festive, guest beer. Garden, outdoor eating, children's play area. Family room. Pub closed 26 Dec & 1 Jan. Access, Amex, Visa.*

KINTBURY — Dundas Arms — FOOD — B&B

Tel 01488 658263 **Fax 01488 658568** Map 14a B4
53 Station Road Kintbury nr Newbury Berkshire RG15 0UT

Reached via Halfway, past the Kintbury turnoff from the Hungerford-bound A4, this well-loved, reliable old-fashioned waterside inn, by the Kennet and Avon canal, has been run by the Dalzell-Pipers since the 1960s. The civilised bar has a striking display of blue patterned

plates entirely covering one wall. The riverside patio is very popular on summer lunchtimes. The comfortable dining-room with canal views is the stage for owner David's cooking. Fresh local ingredients are prepared with skill, confidence and a notable lack of fuss. These talents show up well in dishes like paté-stuffed quail with peppered red jelly and grilled red mullet with a lively citrus sauce which appear on the 3-course lunch menu; ploughman's lunches and further light lunches dishes (rough country paté, potted shrimps, grilled rump steak with chips, leek and gruyère pie with salad and children's meals) appear on a short lunchtime bar menu. Dinner is à la carte: perhaps warm ratatouille with grilled Italian bread, home-cured gravad lax with mustard and dill sauce, duck breast with lemon sauce, baked cod with a herb crust or casseroled beef with kumquats. The Dalzell-Pipers are particularly proud of their outstanding wine list which features genuinely cheap prices for some classy wines. Food is also served in the small 'Cocktail' bar. Pleasant bedrooms are in a converted livery and stable block, with French windows opening on to a quiet private terrace, where garden furniture is provided for each room. Also recommended in our *1996 Hotels & Restaurants Guide. Open 11-2.30, 6-11 (Sun 12-2.30, 7-10.30).* ***Bar Food*** *(No food all Sun, Mon eve) 12-2, 7-9.15.* ***Beer*** *Morland Original, Charles Wells Bombardier, Shepherd Neame Spitfire. Canalside patio/terrace, outdoor eating.* ***Accommodation*** *5 bedrooms, all en suite, £65 (single £55). Children welcome overnight (under-4s stay free in parents' room, 5-10s £6), additional bed available. Check-in by arrangement. Dogs by arrangement. Closed Christmas-New Year. Access, Amex, Visa.*

Many B&B establishments offer reduced rates for weekend and out-of-season bookings. Always ask about special deals for longer stays. Beware half-board terms in inns where we do not recommend the FOOD.

KIRKBY LONSDALE Snooty Fox Tavern FOOD

Tel 01524 271308 Fax 01524 272642 Map 4 C4 **B&B**
Main Street Kirkby Lonsdale Cumbria LA6 2AH

Zzz...

Former Jacobean coaching inn near the town square. Inside, the various bars and eating areas sport all sorts of interesting bits and pieces from a collection of period clothing to numerous stuffed animals and birds in glass cases. Chef-manager Gordon Cartwright, who runs things with wife Joanna, operates a long menu with a wide range of around 40 dishes, from scampi and chips (with home-made tartare sauce), soup (with apricot and walnut bread) and steak and kidney pudding to deep-fried gruyère fritters on peach purée, poached Shetland salmon with sauce vin blanc, haunch of venison simmered in claret, and supreme of corn-fed guinea fowl with haggis on tagliatelle with apricot brandy sauce; not forgetting jacket potatoes, salads, spotted dick and much else besides. With such a long menu it's not surprising that quality can sometimes be a little variable, but everything is home-made and enjoyable. Bookings are suggested for Sunday lunches. Around eight wines are available by the glass. There is a small walled beer garden to the rear across a cobbled courtyard. Children are made welcome with small portions and high-chairs. Bedrooms, of which there are now nine (and all no-smoking), have all been completely refurbished in the last year with a variety of furniture (sometimes antique) and pretty duvet covers with co-ordinating curtains. Many have characterful exposed timbers and all are now en suite; just one has a bath, the others fully-tiled shower rooms. No telephones in the bedrooms. Breakfasts show that Gordon Cartwright's experience in the kitchens at Sharrow Bay in Ullswater has paid dividends: choose from pan-fried apple rings, sautéed mushrooms, hash browns and Berry black pudding to go with the more usual egg, smoked bacon, local pork sausage, roasted tomoato and fried bread – all served on elegant Villeroy & Boch plates. Own parking for ten cars. *Open 11-11 (Sun 12-3, 7-10.30).* ***Bar Food*** *12-2.30 & 6.30-10 (Sun 7-9.30). Free House.* ***Beer*** *Hartleys XB, Theakston Best, Timothy Taylor's Landlord. Garden. Family room.* ***Accommodation*** *9 rooms, all en suite (one with bath), £46-£49.50 (single £26). Children welcome overnight, additional beds for under-10s (£10) and cots (£5) are available. Dogs by arrangement only. Accommodation closed 24-26 Dec. Access, Amex, Diners, Visa.*

We only recommend food (Bar Food) in those establishments highlighted with the **FOOD** symbol.

Kirkbymoorside — George & Dragon Hotel — FOOD B&B

Tel & Fax 01751 433334 Map 5 E4
Market Place Kirkbymoorside North Yorkshire YO6 6AA

Zzz...

Agreeably fulfilling its dual role of town-centre hostelry and quiet country inn, Stephen and Frances Colling's George and Dragon stands imposingly by the cobbled square of picturesque Kirkbymoorside. There's a single bar in front, with sporting prints and paraphernalia, where bar food is listed on large blackboards and every available beam above the servery. Choices here start with chicken liver, Stilton and walnut or smoked salmon patés, progressing to seafood hotpot, cheese and spinach roulade and venison casserole, with voluminous puddings (like treacle tart and custard) to follow. Ever-popular, however, remain the steak and kidney pie with red wine onion and rabbit pie, and two-course Sunday roast. Sandwiches and ploughman's platters at lunchtimes only. Housed in two detached rear buildings, one a former brewhouse, the bedrooms overlook an enclosed wall garden. A reduction in the number of rooms has made much more space in those remaining, and artistic interior designs have greatly enhanced their individual appeal. Features include remote-control TVs, dial-out phones and hairdryers; revamped bathrooms have smart over-bath showers and complimentary toiletries. Residents enjoy exclusive use of the garden lounge. Children under 16 accommodated free in parent's room. *Open 11-3, 6-11 (Sun 12-3, 7-10.30).* ***Bar Food*** *12-2.15, 6.30-9.15. Free House.* ***Beer*** *John Smith's, Timothy Taylor's Landlord, Theakston XB. Garden, patio, outdoor eating. Family room.* ***Accommodation*** *19 bedrooms, all en suite, £69 (£45 single). Children welcome overnight, additional bed and cot available. Access, Visa.*

Knapp — Rising Sun — FOOD

Tel 01823 490436 Map 13 E2
Knapp North Curry nr Taunton Somerset TA3 6BG

Directions here are hard to give and just as hard to follow. Meander down the lanes from the hamlet of Ham (six miles west of Junction 25 on the M5), right on the lip of the Somerset levels, and then keep a lookout for the arrows. Built as a Longhouse in 1480 and 'rediscovered' since the arrival of Tony Atkinson in 1989, the Sun attracts its fill of worshippers of fine, fresh fish these days, and diners should mark out their spot especially early at weekends. Separated by a lounge bar with deep sofas in front of a cast-iron stove, two cottage dining areas are now given over to some serious eating with top billing given to fresh fish from Brixham and elsewhere – Tony self-styles the Rising Sun as a 'restaurant with a bar', although there are no table cloths and the service is not formal. Chef Wendy Repton's prodigious output from the kitchen might include chunky bouillabaisse, smoked trout or gravlax to start, following with brill, skate, bream, gurnard, Dover sole or bass served with careful saucing; so popular are the megrims (Torbay sole), lobsters and langoustines that availability cannot be promised to later arrivals. A typical daily special might be grilled black tilapia with a Madeira and oyster sauce; meat eaters may prefer a steak or roast mallard duck with orange and brandy sauce. More traditional, pubby lunchtime snacks (open sandwiches, ploughman's platters, ham, egg and chips) are also available; in the evening the place steps up a gear and the snackier items are not served. Half portions for children, popular Sunday lunch with roast rib of beef, Yorkshire pudding and hot fishy bits on the bar and flowery summer patios are all added draws. *Open 11.30-2.30, 6.30-11 (Sun 12-3, 7-10.30).* ***Bar Meals*** *12-2, 7-9.30.* ***Beer*** *Boddingtons, Bass, Exmoor Ale. Patio. Family Room. Access, Visa.*

Knightwick — Talbot Hotel — FOOD B&B

Tel 01886 821235 **Fax 01886 821060** Map 14 B1
Knightwick nr Worcester Hereford & Worcester WR6 5PH

On the banks of the river Tewe, on which it has fishing rights, the Talbot stands by a disused road bridge and conveniently back from the new crossing on the busy A44. Dating in parts from the 14th Century, it retains an evocative interior of oak beams and blackened brick, the bar's finest feature being the back-to-back open fire and cast-iron, wood-burning stove which share a central chimney. There's a whizz in the kitchen, producing commendably varied home-cooking on a daily menu that services both bar and dining-room. For a snack, try the blue cheese pancake, salmon quiche or substantial Hungarian bean pot, while diners may satiate themselves on a three-course meal of hot and sour fish

soup, sweet and sour pork, or medallions of venison with, to follow, a summer pudding or treacle 'hollygog' – "pastry rolled with golden syrup and baked in milk until it goes all caramelly". Fish (monkfish in pastry, skate, sardines) is becoming increasingly popular and game features in season – perhaps rabbit casserole or pigeon breast with chocolate ravioli containing pine nuts, sultanas and cream cheese. The bedrooms' up-to-date amenities include colour TVs, tea trays and dial-out telephones with little other obeisance to ostentation or modernity. Furnishings and decor are generally modest and comfortable in a cottagey style – best employed in the newer bedroom extension. Above the bars, three bedrooms are larger and more characterful but share their bathing and toilet facilities. Over 20 wines available by the glass. *Open 11-11 (Sun 12-3, 7-10.30). **Bar Food** 12-2, 6.30-9.30 (Sun 7.30-9). Free House. **Beer** Bass, Worthington Best, Hobson's Bitter. Patio/terrace, outdoor eating. Family room. **Accommodation** 10 bedrooms, 7 en suite, £42-£56.50 (single £24-£31). Children welcome overnight (charged according to age), additional bed (£10) and cot (£5) available. Access, Visa.*

KNOWL HILL — Bird in Hand — B&B

Tel 01628 826622 Fax 01628 826784 Map 15a D3
Bath Road Knowl Hill Twyford Berkshire RG10 9UP

Zzz...

Set well back from the A4, the inn that exists today bears little resemblance to the hostelry bestowed with a Royal Charter by King George III in the late 1700s. Today's extensions to the lounge bar and patio, with umbilical connections to a new 15-bedroom wing have incorporated much of the old stonework on the inside. In places it's a seamless join, elsewhere the stitch lines are visible. Leather armchairs, wood panelling and a huge canopied open fireplace are the major features of the sturdy oak lounge. The new wing is centred round a brick courtyard facing a secluded and mature garden. Though light on decor, with blush walls and lined fitted units, the bedrooms are fully equipped for today's executive market (and priced accordingly, although rates are reduced at weekends). Trouser presses and hairdryers are added to the usual accoutrements of direct-dial phones and remote-control TVs. Bright bathrooms are three-quarter tiled with strong over-bath showers. Double glazing throughout keeps noise from the busy road fully at bay. *Open 11-3, 6-11 (Sun 12-3, 7-10.30). Free House. **Beer** Fuller's London Pride, Brakspear, Flowers Original. Garden, disabled facilities. Family room. **Accommodation** 15 bedrooms, all en suite, £90 (weekend double/twin £70, single £70 weekend £55). Children welcome overnight (under-5s stay free in parents' room, 6-12s £10), additional bed and cot available. Accommodation closed 7 days at Christmas. Access, Amex, Diners, Visa.*

KNOWSTONE — Masons Arms — FOOD

Tel 01398 341231 Map 13 D2
Knowstone South Molton Devon EX36 4RY

Thatched, 13th-century inn tucked away in a tranquil hamlet in the foothills of Exmoor, in the sort of spot where dogs fall asleep in the middle of the road. Grade II listed with a charming unspoilt interior characterised by heavy black beams, sturdy old furniture, huge inglenook with roaring winter log fire and a delightful chatty atmosphere. Super spot to while away an hour or two with a pint and play a traditional pub game. Those tempted to linger for something to eat will find that the home-cooked food complements the surroundings: rustic, hearty and value-for-money. Light snacks or starters include freshly-made soups, excellent patés such as cheese and walnut or smoked mackerel – and salads. More substantial, daily-changing specials might range from salmon kedgeree and liver and bacon hotpot to poussin in orange sauce, good curries – Thursday night is 'curry night' - and filling pies like cheese and onion or venison. Puddings like home-made treacle tart served with clotted cream, apricot and almond flan or mascarpone and yoghurt terrine with a fresh strawberry coulis, plus West Country cheeses. The tiny, beamed restaurant is no-smoking. To accompany the food there is a good list of wines and real ales dispensed straight from the cask. Standard of accommodation ranges from basic to homely, the most acceptable room being en suite and in the adjacent cottage. Peaceful rear patio and garden with rolling rural views towards Exmoor. 1½ miles north of the A361 midway between Tiverton and South Molton. *Open 12-3, 6-11 (from 7 in winter), Sun 12-3, 7-10.30. **Bar Food** 12-2, 7-9.30 (to 9 Sun). Free House. **Beer** Cotleigh Tawny Ale, Hall & Woodhouse Badger Best. Garden, outdoor eating. Family room. Pub closed 25 & 26 Dec eve. No credit cards.*

LACOCK George Inn FOOD

Tel 01249 730263 Map 14 B2
4 West Street Lacock nr Chippenham Wiltshire SN15 2LH

The virtual epitome of the traditional village pub. The George could scarcely be in a more ideal spot than the National Trust village of Lacock. Starting life in 1361 as the Black Boy with its own brewery in farm buildings to the rear, its many modernisations have preserved and re-utilised many of the original timbers. Central to the bar is a unique mounted dog-wheel built into the open fireplace and used for spit-roasting in the 16th-century (the dog was not roasted, but trained to rotate the wheel). Today's pub lives well alongside such idiosyncrasy with its close-packed tables on odd levels set beneath a wealth of old pictures at many an odd angle. From a menu of firm favourites, traditional steak and kidney pie is always popular alongside fresh chicken breast in white wine, cream and garlic, 14oz T-bone steak, plaice stuffed with prawns and mushrooms and a vegetarian cheese, onion and potato pie. "You can have anything from a bowl of chips to a Dover sole", says the landlord. Desserts include apple and blackberry pie and sticky toffee pudding. The large garden stretches out on both sides of the rear car park; beyond it is a safe play area for youngsters, close by an old stocks to restrain the most troublesome. True to its long-standing identity as a family concern, the licensees' family not only provides overnight farmhouse accommodation nearby but also lays on complimentary transport to and from the pub. Enquiries should be addressed to the pub. *Open 10-3, 5-11 (11-11 Fri & Sat in summer), Sun 12-3, 7-10.30.* ***Bar Food*** *12-2.30, 6-10 (Sun from 7).* ***Beer*** *Wadworth. Garden, outdoor eating, children's play area. Access, Visa.*

LAMARSH Red Lion A

Tel 01787 227918 Map 10 C3
Lamarsh Essex CO8 5EP

Enjoying a peaceful location overlooking the gently-rolling landscape bordering the River Stour valley, this charming little tiled Essex pub dates from the 14th century. It's a wonderful place to frequent on a sunny summer's evening when the perfectly-positioned front benches make the most of the view. Beams abound in the comfortable modernised interior with its rather ecclesiastical, carved and inscribed bar counter and welcoming winter log fire. The 16th-century barn holds a games room and is popular with locals. *Open 11-3, 6-11 (Sat 11-11), Sun 12-3, 7-10.30. Free House.* ***Beer*** *Greene King IPA, Nethergate Sidewinder, Porter's Suffolk Bite. Garden, children's play area. Family room. Access, Visa.*

LANGDALE Three Shires Inn B&B

Tel 01539 437215 Map 4 C3
Little Langdale nr Ambleside Cumbria LA22 9NZ

Zzz...

Little Langdale stands at a point in the Cumbrian mountains where the former three shires of Cumberland, Westmorland and Lancashire once came together. Built in 1872 entirely in Lakeland slate, the inn sustained those crossing the nearby Wrynose and Hardknott passes to and from the coast. Still a travellers' haven today, the Three Shires is notable for its tranquillity amid restful scenery whose only early morning intrusions are the birds and nearby brook. The slate bar and streamside patio are nonetheless very popular with walkers throughout the day, and the standard fare served up is decidedly for the heartier appetite. Residents enjoy use of their own lounge and flower-laden verandah from which to soak up the views and relax. Bedrooms are bright and spotless with generally floral-patterned decor. Though four of the rooms are on the small side, and only three are family-size, their perennial popularity is due in no small measure to an absence of TVs (they are now in some rooms) and telephones: as ever was, solitude here is king. Although a rather 'adult' pub, families are well catered for; there's a terraced garden to one side of the pub through which a stream runs, and the restaurant and one of the bars are designated non-smoking. *Open Feb-end Nov 11-11 (Dec & Jan 11-3, 6.30-11), Sun 12-3, 7-10.30.* ***Beer*** *Webster's Yorkshire, guest beers. Garden. High tea from 5.* ***Accommodation*** *10 rooms, all en suite, £68 (single £34). Children welcome overnight, additional bed and cot available. Accommodation closed Mon-Thu Dec & Jan. No dogs. No credit cards.*

LANGLEY — Brewery Inn — A

Tel 0121 5446467 Map 6 C4
91 Station Road Langley Birmingham West Midlands B69 4LW

Turn off the M5 at Junction 2 and head directly into the industrial estate (originally named Junction 2 Industrial Estate); just less than a mile later, Station Road bears left past Albright and Wilson. Though it can't be seen now, there's a Thomas Telford bridge over the canal, known here as "The Crow", which is the highest navigable waterway in Europe. By the bridge, brewers Holt, Plant and Deakin's pub is a modern, yet authentic restoration of the Telford era; the Victorian 'snob windows' which separate the lounge bar servery from the 'public' may be one of only two sets left in existence. A larger window, picture-size, allows tipplers a view of the brew house where Holt's ever-popular Entire is brewed. Legions of real ale afficionados accompany it with a 'Dibble Donker' – a doorstop sandwich with three layers of thick, crusty locally-baked bread filled with cheese, onion and black pudding! Landlord Tony Stanton feels, he says, more like a curator than a publican, as there's such a wealth of history here and many gallons of pure enjoyment – in fact, it's a barrel of laughs. Classical music or big band jazz plays. *Open 11-2.30, 6-11 (Sun 12-2.30, 7-10.30).* ***Beer** Holts Entire, guest beer. No credit cards.*

LANGLEY MARSH — Three Horseshoes — FOOD

Tel 01984 623763 Map 12 E2
Langley Marsh Wiveliscombe Somerset TA4 2UL

Handsome 300-year-old red sandstone village inn with a homely old fashioned interior that is full of curiosities, from collections of banknotes and beermats to model aeroplanes and pictures of vintage cars – the landlord's spare-time passion. Lively 'locals' front room with traditional games and a comfortable back bar with piano, stone fireplace, a rustic mix of sturdy furniture and perhaps piped jazz music. Further attractions are the numerous real ales and Perry's farmhouse cider – all tapped straight from the cask – and the reliably delicious food which is all home-cooked. You will not find chips or fried food on the constantly-changing handwritten menu (nor on the children's menu), just hearty, freshly-prepared dishes with interesting vegetarian options. Choices may include Somerset fish pie, beef hot-pot, pigeon breasts in cider and cream, courgette and mushroom bake, mangetout and tomato au gratin and haricot beans in Galliano. Filling snacks include warming soups, filled rolls and jacket potatoes; pizzas – in two sizes, normal and enormous – are something of a speciality and cooked in the aga. If there's room, finish with mincemeat, apple and brandy pancakes or raspberry and almond cream. Alfresco seating on the verandah or in the garden for warmer days. No under-14s in the bar, only in the family games room. *Open 12-2.30, 7-11 (Sun 12-2.30, 7-10.30). **Bar Food** 12-2 7-9.30 (Sun to 9). Free House. **Beer** Ringwood Best, Wadworth 6X, Young's, Butcombe, Palmers IPA, guest beers. Garden, outdoor eating, children's play area. No credit cards.*

LANGSTONE — Royal Oak — A

Tel 01705 483125 Map 15 D4
19 Langstone High Street Langstone Havant Hampshire PO9 1RY

Historic 16th-century pub with stunning views over Chichester Harbour. Right on the water's edge, the water reaches the front door when the tide's exceptionally high! Originally a row of cottages used in conjunction with the adjacent old mill, they later traded under a "tidal licence" before the bridge to Hayling Island was built, allowing travellers a drink while waiting for the ebb tide. An individual rustic charm characterises the unspoilt interior. The neatly kept bars boast flagstone and polished pine floors, exposed beams, open fires and old wooden furnishings; a cosy haven on wild winter days. Warmer sunny days can be enjoyed with a drink on the front benches or in the secluded rear garden, which is a safe refuge for families and where a pet's corner runs the gamut from budgies to goats and a pot-bellied pig. *Open 11-11. **Beer** Flowers, Gale's HSB, Boddingtons, Marston's Pedigree, guest beer. Garden, outdoor eating, beside water's edge. Family Room, children welcome inside. Access, Visa.*

LAVENHAM Angel Inn FOOD

Tel 01787 247388 Fax 01787 248344 Map 10 C3 **B&B**
Market Place Lavenham Suffolk CO10 9QZ

Zzz... ☺

First licensed in 1420, the Angel looks on to the market place of one of the best preserved medieval towns in England. Inside, the bar has been opened up without losing any of its original charm, with half set up for eating and the other half well supplied with board games, playing cards and shelves of books. There are quiz and bridge nights and on Friday evenings Roy Whitworth (one of the partners) entertains with classical music at the piano. Carrot and coriander soup, fresh grilled sardines, lamb in paprika and cream, duck breast in juniper sauce and steak and kidney pie are typical offerings from the daily-changing evening menu; lunchtime brings similar dishes (at slightly lower prices) plus some more snacky items like ploughman's and cauliflower cheese. Good puds include excellent fruit pies served with custard in a separate jug. Bedrooms are all en suite (four with shower, four with bath) and full of character with old beams, sloping floors and traditional freestanding furniture. All have TV, direct-dial phone and tea- and coffee-making kit. Children are made welcome with a couple of high-chairs, free cots and "put-u-up" beds; ask for small menu portions. For summer there are tables in a secluded garden plus permanent tables. *Open 11-11 (Sun 12-3, 7-10.30). **Bar Food** 12-2.15, 6.30-9.15. **Beer** Nethergate, Adnams Southwold, Mauldons White Adder, guest beer. **Accommodation** 8 bedrooms, all en suite, £50 (weekends £60, single £37.50). Children welcome overnight, additional bed and cot available. Garden, patio, outdoor eating. Family room. Closed 25 & 26 Dec. Access, Amex, Visa.*

LEDBURY Feathers Hotel FOOD

Tel 01531 635266 Fax 01531 632001 Map 14 B1 **B&B**
High Street Ledbury Hereford & Worcester HR8 1DS

Right in the town centre, a classic timber-framed former coaching inn and corn exchange dating from 1564 with oddly-shaped, en-suite, double-glazed bedrooms (including one with a lovely four-poster), original Elizabethan wall paintings, uneven, creaky floors and drunken staircases. Remote-control TV, bedside tea-tray and hairdryers are standard. Good lunchtime snacks in the hop-bedecked Fuggles bar: Fuggles home-made soup, Thai-style prawns in hot garlic sauce, tarte provençale, salmon and cumin seed fishcakes with a tomato suace and French fries, home-made hamburger, grilled steaks, venison casserole with smoked bacon, red wine and chestnuts. For dessert you might find rhubarb compote in a ginger basket and a rose-scented cream, treacle and pecan nut tart, or Drambuie and raspberry flummery. Annual real ale and cider festival on August bank holiday, music weekly on Tuesdays and small rear patio available in good weather. Four miles from the M50 Junction 2. ***Bar Food** 12-2, 7-10 (Sun to 9.30). **Beer** Bass, Directors. **Accommodation** 11 rooms, all en suite £85. Access, Amex, Diners, Visa.*

LEDBURY Ye Olde Talbot Hotel B&B

Tel 01531 632963 Map 14 B1
New Street Ledbury Hereford & Worcester HR8 2DX

Now under new ownership, the historic Talbot is a Grade II listed building and dates back to 1596; it was the scene of a well-documented skirmish between the Cavaliers and Roundheads in 1745. The classic Oak Room panelling is complete to this day with the bullet holes to prove it; here also there are magnificent Jacobean carvings and overmantel. Past a vast carved oak door guests have their own use of a tiny first-floor lounge in a bow-fronted cantilever room which overhangs the street above the front door. Bedrooms, complete with exposed beams and creaking, uneven floors, are much in character. Three only have room for en-suite WC/shower rooms, the remainder sharing loos and a bathroom: all offer TV, beverage tray and clock radio. Two beamed, copper-hung bars, warmed by open winter fires, are intimate and convivial, and there's also a rear courtyard for summer drinking and occasional barbecues. The bedroom tariff is also quoted without breakfast (£34.50/£29.50). *Open 11.30-3, 5-11 (Sun 12-3, 7-10.30). Free House. **Beer** Bass, Hancock's HB, Ansells Bitter. Courtyard. **Accommodation** 7 bedrooms, 3 en suite, £46 (single £35). Children welcome overnight (under-12s stay free in parents' room), additional bed and cot available. Access, Amex, Visa.*

LEDSHAM **Chequers Inn** A

Tel 01977 683135 Map 7 D1
Claypit Lane Ledsham nr South Milford West Yorkshire LS25 5LP

Deep in the Don valley at the heart of a hidden village stands the old ivy-covered Chequers, complete with a low, roadside, bow-fronted window that lends the pub an almost Dickensian air. The entrance to the bar and first-floor restaurant is round to the rear, and the servery has its back to the village street. Tiered above a pebbled walkway are the colourful flower-filled patios which form the beer garden, so well frequented in summer. It's a popular, thriving local. *Open 11-3, 5.30-11, Sat 11-11. Pub closed Sundays.* ***Beer*** *Younger's Scotch, No 3 & Best, Theakston Best. Patio. Family Room. Access, Visa.*

LEEDS **Whitelocks** A

Tel 0113 245 3950 Map 6 C1
Turks Head Yard Briggate Leeds West Yorkshire LS1 6HB

Lauded by the poet laureate, John Betjeman, as "the very heart of Leeds", this was the city's first-ever Luncheon Bar. Owned for nigh on a century up to 1944 by the Whitelock family (who were builders and piano tuners), it's virtually unchanged since its last facelift (it coincided with the arrival in Leeds of electricity). The bar top is copper and the sandwich servery marble; the whole bar is fronted by hand-finished ceramic tiles. The well-heeled may lunch in a panelled rear dining-room while the more down-to-earth may encroach on the many park benches which stretch the length of Turks Head Yard. Today's Luncheon Bar offers little beyond sandwiches, a pie or two and the famed Yorkshire puddings served with mince and onion gravy. Over a decent pint of Younger's ale customers hark back to the pre-war prices (Pie 2d; Cheese and Biscuits 1d) etched on the old servery mirrors – evocative reminders of the Whitelock's heyday. No children indoors. No adjacent parking. Look for the pub sign high above Briggate (a pedestrianised shopping street opposite Debenham's); the entrance to the yard is now a tunnel and can be easily missed. *Open 11-11 (Sun 12-3, 7-10.30).* ***Beer*** *Younger's IPA, Scotch Bitter, IPA, 80/- & No 3, Theakston Best. Terrace. Access, Amex, Visa.*

LEICESTER **Welford Place** FOOD

Tel 0116 247 0758 **Fax 0116 247 1843** Map 7 D4
9 Welford Place Leicester Leicestershire LE1 6ZH

Follow signs for the Phoenix Arts Centre (whose car park is almost directly opposite) to find this striking Victorian building, a former Victorian gentlemen's club adjoining the Leicester magistrates' courts. Welford Place, built in 1876 and restored in 1991 still retains an aura of grandeur. Michael and Valerie Hope (who also run the *Wig & Mitre* in Lincoln) have created a spacious bar and restaurant, self-styled as a "Restaurant Pub of Rare Quality" (and they're not far off). The former is a striking semi-circular room with high windows overlooking Welford Place itself and furnished with leather armchairs and glass-topped tables, while the latter, a quietly civilised room has two great chandeliers suspended from its lofty ceiling. The menus operate throughout the day all year and any item is available at any time, but the restaurant is reserved for full meals. There are two set menus as well as the à la carte, both in a style of cooking that is modern while retaining traditional elements. Typical starters might include Stilton soup with blue cheese sablé, galantine of free-range chicken with apple and ginger chutney or a warm salad of prawns and butter beans. Main dishes could be fillet of sea bass with salmon mousseline, spinach and hollandaise sauce, roast quail with lemon and coriander stuffing on couscous, roast rack of lamb with minted pea purée and pan-fried breast of Gressingham duck with pears. The selection of cheeses is always interesting, generally with a mix of British and French. Enjoyable cooking with friendly service. On-street parking during the evenings and on Sundays. *Open 11-11 (breakfast 8am-12), drinks with meals only on Sun (to 10.30).* ***Bar Food*** *all day (to 10.30 Sun), breakfast and snack menu served 8-12 & 3-6. Free House.* ***Beer*** *Ruddles Best & County. Access, Amex, Diners, Visa.*

We only recommend food (Bar Food) in those establishments highlighted with the **FOOD** symbol.

LENHAM — Dog & Bear Hotel — B&B

Tel 01622 858219 **Fax 01622 859415** Map 11 C5
The Square Lenham Maidstone Kent ME17 2PG

This attractive coaching inn dates from 1602 and overlooks the pretty village square. Splendid oak beams combine with new up-to-date decor and comfortable seating in the bar, and there is a welcoming little foyer-lounge. Centrally-heated bedrooms with darkwood furniture and bright contemporary fabrics all have direct-dial telephones, TVs, tea-making facilities and neatly-kept, en-suite bathrooms. Main building rooms have more charm and character, with the newer rooms beyond the rear courtyard offering more space. 10 minutes from Leeds Castle. Invicta Country Inns (Shepherd Neame). *Open 11-11 (Sun 12-3, 7-10.30).* ***Beer*** *Shepherd Neame. Garden, paved courtyard.* ***Accommodation*** *24 bedrooms, all en suite, £49.50 (family room sleeping four £60, four-poster £55, single £37.50). Children welcome overnight, additional bed and cot available. Access, Visa.*

LEOMINSTER — Royal Oak Hotel — B&B

Tel 01568 612610 **Fax 01568 612710** Map 14 A1
South Street Leominster Hereford & Worcester HR6 8JA

Modest accommodation in an early-18th-century coaching house on the corner of Etnam Street and South Street. Historic relics of its earlier glories are to be found in the Regency Room, complete with chandeliers and minstrel's gallery, and the brick-lined cellar bar which is a cosy spot in the evenings. The main Oak Bar boasts two enormous log fires and serves good real ales and guest beers (Woods Parish Best, perhaps). Bedrooms come in a mixture of sizes and styles with one or two smallish singles, six spacious family rooms and a fine four-poster suite. All have carpeted bathrooms, while room comforts run through TV and intercom (for baby listening and wake-up calls) to tea and coffee makers and electric blankets. *Open 10-11, Sun 12-3, 7-10.30.* ***Beer*** *Wood's Special, guest beer. Small patio.* ***Accommodation*** *18 bedrooms, all en suite, £45 (4-poster £55, single £31.50). Children welcome overnight (under-12s stay free in family rooms), additional bed and cot available. Dogs welcome by arrangement. Access, Amex, Diners, Visa.*

LIFTON — Arundell Arms — FOOD B&B

Tel 01566 784666 **Fax 01566 784494** Map 12 C2
Lifton Devon PL16 0AA

Set in a valley of five rivers, close to the uplands of Dartmoor, Anne Voss-Bark's upmarket, creeper-clad old Devon inn is a favourite destination for those who enjoy the country pursuits of shooting, riding, walking, birdwatching and in particular fishing – the River Tamar flows past the bottom of the garden and the inn has 20 miles of fishing rights along its length. A truly civilised air pervades throughout its smart interior, from the elegant lounge with deep comfortable sofas and armchairs, antique furnishings, tasteful fabrics and hunting prints, to the refined hotel-like bar where good-quality bar snacks are served. The short printed menu may feature a salad of baked goat's cheese with hazelnut dressing or a soup with home-baked bread to start, followed by interesting salads (perhaps Tamar salmon with sorrel mayonnaise or smoked duck breasts with roasted garlic, lemon grass, French beans amd olives) and light, imaginative hot dishes such as a 'casserole of sea fishes' with creamed leeks and saffron rice, pan-fried lamb's liver, kidneys and bacon or a creamy omelette with smoked haddock and Gruyère cheese. Various sandwiches (egg and anchovy, croque monsieur) and a ploughman's platter with three mixed local cheeses, salad, pickle and home-made bread are also available, as is the daily dessert choice. The attached and independently-run Courthouse Bar is a very pubby locals' bar serving real ale and basic bar snacks. Expensive decor and furnishings extend upstairs to the 29 bedrooms, although some have plainer wall-fitted units; road-facing rooms are double-glazed to quell traffic noise. Bathrooms are well appointed with good toiletries and, as one can expect at this level, all the usual comforts grace each room. Choice of seventeen wines by the glass, restaurant non-smoking. The hotel and handsome restaurant (Set L £13-£27, Set D £23-£27) are also recommended in our *1996 Hotels & Restaurants Guide. Open 11-11 (Sun 12-3, 7-10.30). Free House.* ***Beer*** *up to four real ales in the Courthouse Bar. Garden, outdoor eating area, skittle alley.* ***Accommodation*** *29 bedrooms all en suite, £78-£97 (single £39-£61). Children welcome overnight (under-17s stay free in parents' room), additional bed and cot available. Accommodation closed 25 & 26 Dec. Access, Amex, Diners, Visa.*

LINCOLN Wig & Mitre FOOD

Tel 01522 535190 **Fax 01522 532402** Map 7 E2
29 Steep Hill Lincoln Lincolnshire LN2 1LU

The Hope family's trendy city-centre pub is not the historic ale-house it purports to be, but is nonetheless a classic. Its really rather ordinary exterior, a glass shop front under a flower-laden cast-iron balcony, stands between the Lincoln Vintner and Chantilly's bridal shop; Lincoln cathedral is just a stone's throw away across cobbled streets where once the Roman via principalis ran, and its echoing hourly chimes are almost deafening. The pub's interior – which also has a rear access from Drury Lane – is meticulously restored with genuine Tudor timbers, between which sections of 13th-century daub and wattle walls are still visible. Connected by three staircases, there's a warren of rooms in which to eat, two bars and a tiny rear patio, as well as a table from which you can pick up the day's papers for a browse. The menu encourages all comers to eat as little or as much as they'd like at any time throughout the premises, thus encompassing every taste and pleasing all pockets, and the catering is ambitious: breakfast starts at 8am with the papers and food is served through to 11pm. There are two daily blackboard menus, one taking over from the other at around 5.30pm. More serious offerings might include warm salad of goat's cheese on a garlic crouton with grapes and pine kernels, creamy tagliatelle with fresh salmon and artichokes, a daily fresh fish dish, duck breast with fresh ginger and spring onion couscous, and rack of lamb with a herb and garlic crumb crust served with ratatouille and a slow-cooked tomato sauce. Snacks range from smoked salmon with scrambled eggs to crumpets, Lincolnshire plum bread, prawn and curried mayonnaise sandwiches, good cheeses (both French and British), banoffi pie and a rich almond tart with crème anglaise. Good choice of wines by the glass. *Open 11-12.* ***Bar Food*** *8am-11 (snack menu 8am-12 & 3-6). Free House.* ***Beer*** *Sam Smith's Old Brewery & Museum Ale. Patio/terrace, outdoor eating. Closed 25 Dec. Access, Amex, Diners, Visa.*

LINTON Fountaine Inn FOOD

Tel 01756 752210 Map 6 C1
Linton nr Skipton North Yorkshire BD23 JHJ

An idyllic village green complete with stone bridge over a little stream is the setting for this charming mid-17th century inn which was recently restored in sympathetic style by Francis Mackwood. Several interconnecting rooms (one for non-smokers and one where children are made welcome) feature old beams (plus some false ones but its hard to tell the difference) and built-in settles. On a short printed menu there are various open sandwiches, cold platters such as home-roast ham, tuna and chicken plus the likes of gammon and eggs, lamb cutlets and fresh local trout, not forgetting the Linton Yorker – a giant Yorkshire pudding filled with gravy, sausage or the casserole of the day. For the sweet-toothed there are some good home-made puds, while for those with more savoury tastes there's the local Wensleydale cheese which comes either blue, smoked or in the traditional white style. For children there are "turkey aeroplanes", farmhouse sausages or "golden fishes" plus a single high-chair. The village green is well used in summer although the publican is not allowed to put out any tables or chairs. *Open 12-3, 7-11 (to 10.30 Sun).* ***Bar Food*** *12-2.15 (to 2.30 Sun), 7-9.15. Free House.* ***Beer*** *Black Sheep Best Bitter & Special, Jennings Bitter. Family room. No credit cards.*

LINWOOD High Corner Inn B&B

Tel 01425 473973 **Fax 01425 480015** Map 14 C4
Linwood Ringwood Hampshire BH24 3QY

Much extended and modernised, early 18th-century inn set in seven acres of the New Forest and located along a quarter-mile gravel track off the narrow lane linking Lyndhurst and the A338 near Ringwood. A quiet hideaway in winter, mobbed in high summer, it is a popular retreat for families with numerous bar-free rooms, a Lego/Duplo room, an outdoor adventure playground and miles of Forest walks. Overnight accommodation comprises eight well-equipped bedrooms offering teletext TV, telephone, trouser press, hairdryer, tea-makers and en-suite facilities. *Open 11-3, 7-10.30 (winter), 11-3, 6-11 (summer), 11-4, 6-11 Sat (winter), 11-11 Sat (summer), Sun 12-3, 7-10.30.* ***Beer*** *Wadworth 6X, Boddingtons, Hampshire Bitter. Garden, outdoor play area. Family room (three rooms), indoor play room.* ***Accommodation*** *8 bedrooms, all en suite, £63 (single £47), weekend £69. Squash court, DIY stabling. Children welcome overnight, additional bed and cot available. Check-in by arrangement. Access, Amex, Diners, Visa.*

LITTLE BRAXTED Green Man FOOD

Tel 01621 891659 Map 11 C4
Kelvedon Road Little Braxted Essex CM8 3LB

Tucked away in a long, straggling little hamlet signposted off B1389 near the A12 Witham bypass. Keep going down the lane past St Nicholas's church, back into open countryside, past a couple of farms, take a right branch of the road and eventually you'll come to the Green Man. This unspoilt little brick-and-tiled pub has a comfortable lounge decorated with a large collection of horse brasses and a traditional, tiled public bar off which is a games room. Good, wholesome home-cooked and value-for-money food attracts a loyal clientele to this secluded country destination. A printed snack (sandwiches and jacket potatoes – "robust" is an understatement, portions are generous) menu is supplemented by a sensibly-short, daily-changing blackboard list of dishes that might encompass pasta, prawn and basil pot served with salad and hot French bread, melon balls with prawns, garlic mayonnaise and salad, hot crab pot with freshly-baked brown bread, quiches, individual cottage pies, smoked mackerel salad, beef in wine or Oriental-style pork. Vegetarian options may include baked stuffed aubergine and cheese and vegetable loaf. Finish off with fresh strawberries and cream in summer, a tangy home-made lemon soufflé or steamed date and coffee pudding. Expect to wait, this is no fast food operation. No children under 14 in the bar. Tree-shaded summer garden to the rear. *Open 11.30-3, 6-11, Sun 12-3, 7-10.30.* ***Bar Food*** *12-2.15, 7-9.30 (Sun 12-2, 7-9).* ***Beer*** *Ridleys. Garden. No credit cards.*

LITTLE CANFIELD Lion & Lamb A

Tel 01279 870257 Map 10 B3
Little Canfield nr Great Dunmow Essex CM6 1SR

On the A120 Colchester to Puckeridge road, three miles from Junction 8 of the M11 (3 miles west of Great Dunmow), this large family-dining pub is 200 years old in parts with more modern extensions. Open brickwork, exposed pine and artefacts inside while the fenced garden is ideal for children (bouncy castle on long weekends and an old boat has been turned into a play area). Children may eat in the restaurant and choose from their own menu. *Open 11-2.30, 6-11 (Sun 12-3, 7-10.30).* ***Beer*** *Ridleys. Garden, children's play area, disabled WC. Family room. Access, Visa.*

LITTLE COMPTON Red Lion Inn FOOD B&B

Tel 01608 674397 **Fax 01608 674521** Map 14a B1
Little Compton nr Moreton-in-Marsh Gloucestershire GL56 0RT

David and Sarah Smith run their charming 16th-century village inn with warmth and pride, offering good plain cooking to match the simple surroundings of exposed stone walls, beams and sturdy wooden furnishings. Follow thick, spicy mulligatawny soup or mushrooms in garlic butter with a huge helping of chicken chasseur, roast duck with black cherry, peach and orange curacao, home-made lasagne or rump steak cut from the joint to your own specification. Ploughman's platters and filled granary rolls make lighter bites and there are puddings like whisky trifle, raspberry meringue or pina colada ice cream. Upstairs, the three bedrooms overlook the attractive garden and share a spacious carpeted bathroom, and each has its own washbasin and tea-making facilities. Two rooms feature original beams and two have open stone walls. *Open 11-2.30, 6-11 (Sun 12-3, 7-10.30).* ***Bar Food*** *12-2 (Sun to 1.30), 7-8.45 (Sat to 9.30).* ***Beer*** *Donnington BB and SBA. Garden, outdoor eating, children's play area.* ***Accommodation*** *3 bedrooms, share bathroom, £36 (single £24). Children welcome overnight (minimum age 8), additional bed (£10). Check-in by arrangement. No dogs. No smoking in bedrooms. Access, Visa.*

LITTLE COWARNE Three Horseshoes FOOD B&B

Tel 01885 400276 Map 14 B1
Little Cowarne nr Bromyard Hereford & Worcester HR7 4RQ

Zzz... 

Though not immediately obvious, one can still make out the remains of a tiny two-roomed pub that once stood on this site: the newest brick is an uneven match with the old and dormers have been added to the frontage. The Shoes' interior is now a spacious dining pub, with considerable thought given equally to the needs of children and the elderly or disabled. The success of Norman and Janet Whittall in attracting both in equal measure is to be commended. Kitchen production is also prodigious from light bar snacks of haddock and prawn smokies or very popular devilled kidneys on toast (or with rice) through to a carvery

Sunday lunch. Seasonally-changing main courses offer near endless variety, many flavoured with fresh herbs from the garden: rabbit with lovage in cider and cutlets of salmon in chive sauce. The sauté potatoes are particularly good and a local baker makes crusty bloomers and granary loaves for the sandwiches and ploughman's platters (perhaps served with home-made pickled pears, spiced damsons or apple and ginger chutney). Among the home-made desserts apple pie and sticky toffee cake are perennially popular, and the home-made ice creams are outstanding: brown bread or loganberry, and one made with damsons – fresh from trees in the paddock, naturally. A pair of quiet country bedrooms (one double, one a twin) are done in an appropriate country style with a lovely rural aspect. Free from intrusive telephones, they're otherwise bang up-to-date with colour TVs, clock radios, tea-making facilities and small but effective WC/shower rooms. *Open 11-3, 6.30-11 (Sun 12-3, 7-10.30). **Bar Food** 12-2.30 (Sun 12-2), 6.30-10 (Sun 7-9.30). **Beer** Webster's Yorkshire, John Smith's, Ruddles County. Garden/patio, outdoor eating, barbecue. **Accommodation** 2 bedrooms, both en suite, £33 (single £16.50). Children welcome overnight (under-5s free, otherwise half-price), additional bed and cot available. Check-in by arrangement. Access, Visa.*

LITTLE HAMPDEN — Rising Sun — FOOD

Tel & Fax 01494 488393 Map 15a E2

Little Hampden nr Great Missenden Buckinghamshire HP16 9PS

Nestling among beech trees at the end of a sleepy village lane, this smart brick-built pub has become a popular dining venue in this peaceful part of the Chilterns. A central bar serves three neat and simply-furnished interconnecting rooms, warmed by an open fire and a woodburner during the winter. A few prints and some interesting indentures decorate the plain walls. A short inventive selection of dishes (rather than the standard range of pub fare) is listed on both the printed menu and on the weekly-changing blackboards. For starters or a light snack one might, typically, choose from deep-fried filo parcel with spinach, Brie and Stilton, minute steak in a baguette, hot croissant filled with prawns and asparagus or chicken livers with bacon and raspberry vinaigrette. Varied main courses may feature grilled fillet of sea bass, home-smoked roast pork with pineapple and barbecue sauce, salmon coulibiac, plus specials like rack of lamb with a rosemary and herb sauce, all served with fresh vegetables. The Woodman's lunch is a particularly good value and hearty lunch – soup, roll, paté, Stilton, Cheddar, Brie, pickles and salad. Walnut toffee tart or peach crème brulée might be found among the eight or so listed on the pudding board. Walkers are welcomed, but their muddy boots aren't in the bar. *Open Tue-Sat 11.30-2.30, 6.30-11 (Sun 12-3 only, closed eve). **Bar Food** 12.30-2, 7-9 (not Sun). Free House. **Beer** Marston's Pedigree, Brakspear, Adnams Southwold, Morland Old Speckled Hen. Garden. Pub closed Sun eve & all Mon except Bank Holiday lunchtimes. Access, Visa.*

We do not accept free meals or hospitality – our inspectors pay their own bills and **never** book in the name of Egon Ronay's Guides.

LITTLE LONGSTONE — Packhorse Inn — A

Tel 01629 640471 Map 6 C2

Little Longstone nr Bakewell Derbyshire DE45 1NN

18th-century village cottage tavern in the Peak Distric National Park, full of old-fashioned charm. Popular with walkers doing the Monsal Trail which runs between Bakewell and Millers Dale. Real fires and no music inside; outside, there's a steep little garden with a fish pond, rabbits and goats. Children welcome inside only if eating. *Open 11-3, 5-11 (Sat from 6), Sun 12-3, 7-10.30. **Beer** Marston's Pedigree and Best Bitter. Garden. No credit cards.*

LITTLE ODELL — Mad Dog — A

Tel 01234 720221 Map 15 E1

212 High Street Little Odell Bedfordshire MK43 7AR

A one-bar-only thatched pub close to the Harrold-Odell country park. Real fire (and a ghost) in the inglenook, no music, and a roundabout for the children in the garden. The name comes from a supposed cure for the bite of mad dogs which 18th-century landlords took in payment of a debt. Children not allowed indoors (the pub is too small), so it's only suitable as a family pub in summer. New tenants took over early last year, but little has changed apart from new garden seating. *Open 11-2.30, 6-11 (Sun 12-3, 7-10.30). **Beer** Greene King IPA, Abbot Ale and Rayments. Garden, children's play area. Access, Visa.*

LITTLE STRETTON **Ragleth Inn** A

Tel & Fax 01694 722711 Map 6 A4
Ludlow Road Little Stretton Shropshire SY6 6RB

Laying claim to be one on the oldest brick-built pubs in the land, the Ragleth is tucked at the foot of Long Mynd (National Trust), a haven for walkers. Boots, dry dogs and well-behaved children are allowed in the walkers bar. The lounge is a more sedate setting for a quiet pint, the enclosed rear garden offering a summer alternative. Two letting rooms, sharing a bathroom and shower, are offered for B&B (not inspected). *Open 12-2.30, 6-11 (Sun 12-3, 7-10.30). Free House.* ***Beer*** *Marston's Bitter & Pedigree, Morland Old Speckled Hen. Garden. Family room. No credit cards.*

LITTLEBURY **Queen's Head** FOOD

Tel 01799 522251 **Fax 01799 513522** Map 10 B3 **B&B**
Littlebury nr Saffron Walden Essex CB11 4TD

Occupying a corner site in the village centre, this attractive yellow-painted inn dates from the early 15th-century and welcomes visitors into its carefully refurbished bar and dining-room, which preserve low beamed ceilings, some standing timbers, a rustic red-and-black tiled floor and two cosy snug areas, one with easy chairs and open fire, the other furnished with sturdy wooden tables and chairs and sporting attractive wall stencilling. Reliable home-cooked food is a popular attraction here, the short daily-changing blackboard menu featuring an imaginative choice of dishes that draw on fresh herbs, vegetables and fruit grown in their extensive kitchen garden. A typical menu may list cream of fish soup, chicken liver parfait and baked avocado with Stilton butter among the starters, followed by fresh fish specialities – ling with orange and basil, haddock with mushroom sauce, herring in garlic – plus Oxford lamb steak with raspberries, shepherd's pie and pork chop with greengages. Extra evening dishes generally include game options like roast pheasant brigerade. Home-made raspberry flan. Regular lunch special of soup and light main course, set 2-course roast lunch and fish and chip supper on Sundays. Frequently rotating choice of six real ales and a short list of 14 wines available by the bottle or glass. Accommodation comprises six uniformly decorated and furnished bedrooms with clean, tiled en-suite bathrooms. Two family rooms and a rather compact single room with tiny shower room. All – except the quiet rear room – face the main road and with no secondary glazing they could well be noisy. TVs, telephones, clock/radios and tea-makers are standard. Continental breakfasts only (the price below, along with all the B&B prices in this guide, includes cooked breakfast – £6). Sheltered walled garden with play equipment geared for younger children. *Open 12-11 (Sun 12-3, 7-10.30).* ***Bar Food*** *12-2, 7-9 (no food Sun except residents may eat Sun eve). Free House.* ***Beer*** *Worthington Best, Timothy Taylor's Landlord, Marston's Pedigree, Bass, Innkeeper's Bitter. Garden, outdoor eating, children's play area.* ***Accommodation*** *6 bedrooms, all en suite, £57 (single £36). Children welcome overnight, £5 extra, additional cot available. Access, Diners, Visa.*

LITTON **Red Lion Inn** A

Tel 01298 871458 Map 6 C2
Litton nr Tideswell Derbyshire SK17 8QH

The Hodgson family have run their pub in their inimitable way since the 1950s. The less the Red Lion changes all these years on the more special it becomes as there are so very few left like it. One secret is to find the pub open and pop in for a "Boddy" or a pint, for instance, of a guest beer from a firkin racked up on top of the bar. Yet to eat here remains an evening, or weekend lunch, to be planned well in advance, especially in view of the Red Lion's restricted opening hours (which we list below), and its total resistance to change (which, hopefully, will continue). *Open 12-2 Sat & Sun only, 7-11 Tue to Sat. Free House.* ***Beer*** *Boddingtons, guest beer. Pub closed all Mon, L Tue to Fri, Sun eve, 10 days end of September. Access, Visa.*

LIVERPOOL **Philharmonic Dining Rooms** A

Tel 0151 709 1163 Map 6 A2
36 Hope Street Liverpool Merseyside L1 9BX

An extraordinary cathedral of Victorian confidence and excess. Built in 1896 as a gentlemen's club, this Grade A listed building has glorious tiling, carving, panelling and etched glass. The woodwork was handcrafted by the shipbuilders at the time. It's a social museum piece but with modern intrusions like a juke box and fruit machine. Remarkable Victorian toilets (ornate with marble and tiles – the throne room)! *Open 11.30-11, Sun 12-3, 7-10.30.* ***Beer*** *Jennings, Burton, Walker Best Bitter, Tetley Bitter & Imperial. No credit cards.*

LLANYMYNECH — Bradford Arms — FOOD

Tel 01691 830582 Map 8 D3

Llanymynech Oswestry Shropshire SY22 6EJ

Village pub (the building is in England, but entry is via Wales through the front door!) with above-average food in its spotless, comfortably traditional bar. It's an old coaching inn that's been Victorianised. The bar menu ranges from a daily, home-made soup such as leek and potato, warm venison loaf with plum and apple chutney or gravadlax with mustard and dill to smoked duck and apple with Cumberland sauce, fillet steak kebab withbarbecue sauce or Swedish lamb casserole with coffee sauce. A blackboard might proclaim daily specials like fillet of sea bass poached in dry vermouth. The à la carte restaurant menu (evenings only) may offer king prawns with asparagus with garlic butter, baked eggs in chive and sour cream sauce, loin of lamb with almonds and port sauce and salmon with white wine and prawn sauce. Very good puddings – rum and walnut gateau, American peach pie or a most unusual red wine bread pudding with candied peel, almonds and sultanas. 12 tip-top "real" British cheeses are helpfully described on the menu and served with good, crusty bread (or biscuits), celery and apple. The 80-strong wine list offers a good spread. *Open 12-2, 7-11 (Sun 12-2.30, 7-10.30). **Bar Food** 12-2 (Sun to 1.45), 7-10 (Sun to 9.30). Free House. **Beer** one changing real ale. Patio, outdoor eating. Pub closed Mondays (except Bank Holidays). No credit cards.*

LODERS — Loders Arms — FOOD

Tel 01308 422431 Map 13 F2

Loders nr Bridport Dorset DT6 3SA

When Roger and Helen Flint took over this unassuming stone pub it was just another struggling village local trying to survive on little custom. Nowadays, their honest home-cooking is both imaginative and good value for money. Its popularity is so great now that it is advisable to book for both lunch and dinner in the tiny, 24-seat dining-room. Those popping in for just a bar snack will not be disappointed with the choice of six hearty, hot dishes that are generally available such as lasagne, chicken and parmesan bake, mushroom and broccoli quiche, a freshly-prepared soup (perhaps leek and Stilton) plus generously-filled French baguettes. More imaginative fare can be appreciated in the simply-furnished dining-room, where a short yet varied list of interesting dishes is chalked up on a blackboard.

The menu changes regularly with seasonal availability of produce and when new ideas and recipes are introduced, although some firm favourites remain faithfully on the board. To start, there may be fresh, marinated anchovies with tomato and basil salad, black pudding with home-made chutney, smoked chicken and mango salad, fresh crab and coriander parcel or chilled watercress and almond soup, followed by a choice of at least 8 well-presented main courses, for example devilled kidneys, scallops on a bed of fennel with oyster mushrooms, venison steak flambéed in gin with juniper berries or whole baby guinea fowl with Dijon mustard and rosemary sauce. As well as new potatoes, each dish is accompanied by four or five crisply-cooked vegetables. Summer diners can wait for their table in the small rear garden which enjoys rural hillside views. *Open 11.30-3, 6-11 (Sun 12-3, 7-10.30). **Bar Food** 12.30-2, 7.30-9 (no food Sun eves in winter). **Beer** Palmers IPA, Bridport Bitter, Tally Ho (winter) & 200 (summer). Garden, outdoor eating. Access, Visa.*

LODSWORTH — Halfway Bridge — FOOD

Tel 01798 861281 Map 11 A6

Lodsworth nr Petworth West Sussex GU28 9BP

On the A272 midway between Petworth and Midhurst, the mellow, red-brick Halfway Bridge was originally built as a coaching inn in 1740. Today, efficiently run by the friendly Hawkins family, it's still catering to travellers with real ales and real food from an extensive blackboard menu that may range from home-made soup, garlic stuffed mussels and mushrooms in cream and tarragon to steak, kidney and Guinness pie, lamb's liver and bacon, lamb in red wine and rosemary, and fish stew. Large open sandwiches are served with salad and sauté potatoes at lunchtimes only. If you're really hungry go for the half roast duck and honey or the quails with orange and Pernod sauce, both served with fresh vegetables. Those with room for a pudding could try the walnut and treacle tart or the banana toffee pie. The same menu operates in both the neat country-style dining-room and throughout the series of cosy, tastefully furnished interconnecting rooms that form the bar. Real fires (one room features an old kitchen range) offer a warm welcome in winter; for the summer there are tables out on the lawn and on the sheltered rear patio. For a celebration, try a bottle of the local Gospel Green méthode champenoise cider. *Open 11-3, 6-11 (Sun 12-3, 7-10.30). Free House. **Bar Food** 12-2 (Sun to 2.30), 7-10. **Beer** Gale's HSB, Flowers Original, two guest beers. Garden, outdoor eating. Access, Visa.*

LONG CRENDON — The Angel Inn ★ — FOOD B&B

Tel 01844 208268 Map 15a D2
Bicester Road Long Crendon Buckinghamshire HP18 9EE

Zzz...

Restaurant or pub? The distinction becomes rather blurred here, and really doesn't matter anyway – the fact is that the food here is indisputably good. Whether having just a bowl of soup or a full meal one can eat either in the bar area with its old sofas and wooden settles or in one of the several eating rooms – one showing some of the original wattle and daub construction, another a Lloyd Loom-furnished conservatory – with soft floral cloths on the tables. The same menu appears on blackboards above the bar and on handwritten sheets – if eating 'restaurant-style' – with everything from freshly-baked baguette sandwiches, pasta dishes like bacon and pesto or marinated Italian seafood, Lancashire black pudding with noodles and mustard sauce, bangers 'n' mash, steak frites and ploughman's to Provençal fish soup with rouille, rack of lamb with glazed shallots and a honey and rosemary glaze, confit of duck with beans and steak au poivre. With deliveries direct from Billingsgate a couple of times a week it's worth checking out the day's fish dishes (rightly considered their speciality) too: perhaps roast cod with scallops and spinach, chargrilled squid with chili and tapénade or baked hake with mussel risotto. Of the four appealing, en-suite bedrooms (two with shower/WC only) two are particularly characterful with old black beams. Furniture varies from old pine to some more modern pieces and all rooms have TV, direct-dial phones and tea/coffee-making facilities. *Open 12-2.30, 6.30-10 (Sun 12-3, closed Sun eve & all Sun in summer May-Aug).* ***Bar Meals*** *12-2.30, 6.30-10 (not Sun eve). Free House.* ***Beer*** *Brakspear Bitter, guest beer.* ***Accommodation*** *4 bedrooms, all en suite, £50 (single £35). Access, Visa.*

LONG MELFORD — Bull Hotel — B&B

Tel 01787 378494 **Fax 01787 880307** Map 10 C3
Hall Street Long Melford Sudbury Suffolk CO10 9JG

Situated in the heart of this attractive old wool town, a magnificent half-timbered inn, originally built for a rich wool merchant in 1450. It became an inn over a century later and boasts a wealth of impressively carved and moulded oak beams throughout its elegantly refurbished interior. Beyond the entrance hall are two relaxing and tastefully-furnished lounges with huge inglenooks and a separate pubby bar serving real ale. Weary travellers will find that the civilised ambience and high standards extend upstairs to the comfortable and well-appointed bedrooms; added extras include TVs, clock-radios and telephones. Ten bedrooms are designated non-smoking and three are suitable for families. Splendid courtyard with wrought-iron furniture beneath the old weavers gallery. Room service from 7am to 11pm. A Forte hotel. *Bar open 11.30-2, 7-11 (Sun 12-3, 7-10.30).* ***Beer*** *Greene King IPA, Courage Directors.* ***Accommodation*** *25 bedrooms, all en suite, £85 & £95 (superior & family rooms), mini suite £100, suite £110 (single £65): room-only prices (cooked breakfast £8.50 per person). Children welcome overnight (under-16s free if sharing parents' room). Access, Amex, Diners, Visa.*

LONGFRAMLINGTON — Granby Inn — FOOD B&B

Tel 01665 570228 **Fax 01665 570736** Map 5 D2
Longframlington Northumberland NE65 8DP

On the A697, cosy, attractively modernised little 18th-century inn with colourful window boxes and a busy dining business. Food is served in the restaurant as well as the bar-and-lounge. For the latter, food is ordered at the bar and from then on, tables are waitress served. The menu is extensive (from moules marinière to lobster, and mushrooms on toast to steak chasseur) and helpings very generous, served on enormous oval plates; vegetarian options like mushroom stroganoff or broccoli and cream cheese pie are also offered. Sandwiches and ploughman's platters are always available. Good puddings might include deep-filled home-made apple pie or a homely and boozy sherry trifle (complete with fresh strawberries in season). Main-building bedrooms are small, neat and modern. Three garden chalets (mobile homes) incorporate a small sitting area, fridge and bathroom, and standards of housekeeping are reliably high everywhere. Good breakfasts: try the kippers. *Open 11-3, 6-11 (Sun 12-3, 7-10.30).* ***Bar Food*** *11-2 (Sun 12-1.30), 6-9.30 (Sun 7-9.30). Children over 8 allowed (if eating) in lounge at lunchtime. Free House.* ***Beer*** *Worthington Best Bitter.* ***Accommodation*** *5 bedrooms, all en suite, £50 (single £28.50). Children welcome overnight (chalets sleep three, from £45) No dogs. Access, Visa.*

LONGSTOCK Peat Spade FOOD

Tel & Fax 01264 810612 Map 14 C3
Longstock nr Stockbridge Hampshire SO20 6DR

Unusual paned windows overlook the peaceful village lane and idyllic heavily thatched cottages at this striking, red-brick and gabled Victorian 'pub' that nestles in the heart of the Test Valley, only 100 yards from the famous trout stream. The uncluttered and neatly furnished bar/dining-room is delightfully music-free and is more akin to a smart restaurant, with individual tables sensibly arranged around a central magazine- and book-laden table. Combined with tasteful fabrics, effective subtle lighting and a warm welcome, a relaxed convivial atmosphere ensues in which to appreciate some quality pub food. There is no room for an array of microwaves, freezers and fridges here, so landlady and cook Julie Tuckett prepares to order all the simply described dishes – listed on the two short blackboard menus and on the value-for-money set dinner menu. Chicken, lamb and pork will not be featured here so expect a well-thought-out choice of dishes that rely on game – especially hare, rabbit and venison in winter – fresh fish and imaginative salad. The seasonally-changing menu may include shellfish soup, salade 'Maison' (perhaps mixed leaves, melon and avocado, topped with warm and smooth Sussex goat's cheese and a light oil dressing), breast of guinea fowl or goose, roast fillet of salmon with samphire, and tarte 'Maison' (aubergine, tomato and feta tarte served with salad). The short, set 3-course dinner menu offers a choice of two dishes per course. Puddings may offer a very light bread-and-butter with clotted cream, apricot brioche, chocolate and walnut cheesecake, sherry trifle or tiramisu. To accompany your meal (and perhaps while away the time should there be any delay – this is not a place where things happen in a rush) there is an impressive choice of at least sixteen wines available by the glass (in two sizes and including two pudding wines) from the comprehensive wine list. Outdoor summer eating can be enjoyed in the large and secluded rear garden. *Open 12-3, 7-11 (Sun 12-3, closed eve)* ***Bar Food*** *12-2, 7-10.30 (except Sun eve). Free House.* ***Beer*** *two changing real ales. Garden, outdoor eating. Pub closed Sun eve, 25 & 26 Dec. Amex, Diners.*

LONGWORTH Blue Boar FOOD

Tel 01865 820494 Map 14a B2
Tucks Lane Longworth Oxfordshire OX13 5ET

Pretty thatched pub covered with wisteria in the centre of a small village. Inside are two log fires and quarry tiles on the floors – lots of atmosphere with old wooden skis hanging from the ceiling. Good-value food: typical dishes include home-made soup, Thai vegetable curry, beef and Guinness pie, smoked goat's cheese with walnuts and artichoke hearts and good steaks. Follow this with ubiquitous sticky toffee pudding or apple and blueberry crumble served with cream or ice cream. The rear garden, complete with weeping willow and roses, has picnic tables for outdoor eating, as well as a vegetable patch which supplies the kitchen. A annual pig roast takes place on Whitsun May Bank Holiday. *Open 11.30-2.30, 6-11 (Sun 12-3, 7-10.30).* ***Bar Food*** *12-2, 7-10 (Sun to 9.45).* ***Beer*** *Morrells, guest beer. Garden, outdoor eating. Access, Amex, Visa.*

LOSTWITHIEL Royal Oak FOOD

Tel 01208 872552 Map 12 C3 **B&B**
Duke Street Lostwithiel Cornwall PL22 1AH

Popular, 13th-century inn just off the main road in the original capital of Cornwall and supposedly linked to nearby Restormel Castle by a smuggling or escape tunnel. Catering for all tastes, the lively, slate flagstoned public bar (complete with juke box, modern and traditional games) attracts a good local following. In contrast, the comfortably furnished and carpeted lounge bar has tables with red and white checked cloths and is very much geared to a dining clientele. Close inspection of a fairly standard printed menu and of the additional blackboard selection of meals will reveal some good home-cooked dishes, such as Fowey salmon with dill and cucumber sauce, Mrs Hine's 'famous' cow pie, fresh local plaice, Dover sole, Barbary duckling with orange and ginger sauce and an authentic curry choice. Chips may arrive with the lasagne, but most main courses have the option of a full salad or an excellent selection of four well-cooked vegetables that usually includes dauphinoise potatoes. Plainer pub fare (no sandwiches or ploughman's platters in the evening) – Angus beef steaks, grilled trout and salads – is unlikely to disappoint in either quality or presentation. To finish, clotted cream is served with a deliciously gooey treacle tart. Those

wishing to explore the area will find one of the upstairs bedrooms a most comfortable base. Spacious, well-decorated and furnished with a mix of period and pine furniture, they all have TV, radio/alarms, and beverage-making facilities, with two of the rooms boasting clean, en-suite bathrooms. *Open 11-11 (Sun 12-3, 7-10.30).* ***Bar Food*** *12-2, 6.30-10 (Sun 7-9.30). Free House.* ***Beer*** *Flowers Original, Bass, Fuller's London Pride, Marston's Pedigree, Sharp's, two guest beers. Outdoor eating area.* ***Accommodation*** *6 bedrooms, 4 en suite, £51.50 (single £29.50). Access, Amex, Diners, Visa.*

LOUTH — Masons Arms — B&B

Tel 01507 609525 Map 7 F2
Cornmarket Louth Lincolnshire LN11 9PY

Useful to know in an area not highly blessed with accommodation pubs is the Masons, a former posting inn dating from the 18th century. Right in the centre of the Cornmarket, the inn is run by resident proprietors Mike and Margaret Harrison, who offer five bedrooms complete with well-equipped, en-suite facilities. Two further double bedrooms share a restored Victorian bathroom and separate WC. Bars are open all day, with fastidiously-tended real ales on handpump and six wines available by the glass. A welcoming, friendly inn. *Open 11-11 (Sun and Bank Holidays 12-3, 7-10.30), Mon-Sat in summer from 10am for coffee. Free House.* ***Beer*** *Bateman's Dark Mild, XB, XXXB & Salem Porter, Marston's Pedigree, Bass, guest beer.* ***Accommodation*** *10 rooms, 5 en suite (3 with bath), £45 (single £20). Children welcome overnight, additional bed (£5) and cot available. No dogs. Accommodation closed 24-26 Dec. Access, Visa.*

LOW CATTON — Gold Cup Inn — A

Tel 01759 371354 Map 7 D1
Low Catton Humberside YO4 1EA

Five miles east of York, south of Stamford Bridge on the A166; can also be approached from east of Kexby, off A1078. Modernised but pleasant, relaxing and unpretentious pub run by Ray and Pat Hales; there are two welcoming, real fires and high-backed wooden pews in the rambling three-room lounge in contrast to a noisier back games room. The beer garden/paddock at the rear of the building features ponies, goats and geese to delight children and has access to the river bank. *Open 12-2.30 (closed Mon L), 6-11 (Sat 12-11, Sun 12-10.30). Free House.* ***Beer*** *Tetley, John Smith's. Garden, children's play area. Pub closed Monday lunchtime (except Bank Holidays). Family room. No credit cards.*

LOW NEWTON BY THE SEA — The Ship — A

Tel 01665 576262 Map 5 D1
Low Newton by the Sea nr Alnwick Northumberland NE66 3EL

The 'village green' is just a grassy area enclosed on three sides by fishermen's cottages, one of which is the pub, and on the fourth side by the beach itself. As with so many coastal villages, public parking is restricted to an area just away from the beach, leaving you a short walk to the sand, green or pub – indeed popular with holidaymakers and locals alike. The Ship is quite charming, largely as a result of the Hoppers, who run it in a very friendly fashion. Outside, there are picnic tables on the grass, while inside it has the air of somewhere from the early part of the century – creels hang over the bar to remind you of the seaside location. *Open Easter-end Oct 11-11 (Sun 12-3, 7-10.30), winter 11-3, 7-11. Free House.* ***Beer*** *Ruddles Bitter, guest beer. Garden. Family room. No credit cards.*

LOWER ASHTON — Manor Inn — FOOD

Tel 01647 252304 Map 13 D3
Lower Ashton nr Christow Devon EX6 7QL

Small, traditional Teign Valley local with garden in front overlooking fields and Valley. The welcome is friendly within the two homely and simply furnished bars which are warmed in winter by open fires. Good, unfussy, honest and home-cooked food prepared by landlady Clare Mann using fresh ingredients sees such hearty dishes as beef and apricot casserole, lamb curry, pork, leek and prune pie, ragout of lamb and vegetarian choices – perhaps mushroom provençale, vegetable bake – on the daily specials board. This is a chip-free zone! Fish from Brixham is becoming increasingly important and a daily fish board might offer grilled salmon, trout or lemon sole plus seafood and pasta mornay with garlic bread or

caulifower and prawn au gratin. Sandwiches are made using locally-baked malted loaves and jacket potatoes and ploughman's platters are always available. Real-ale lovers have four brews to choose from plus regularly changing guest beers (over 700 different ales have been offered since 1981); 25 ales at the annual beer festival in September. *Open Tue-Sat 12-2.30, 6-11 (Sat from 7, Sun 12-2.30, 7-10.30).* ***Bar Food*** *12-1.30, 7-9.30 (Sun to 9). Free House.* ***Beer*** *Wadworth 6X, Theakston XB, Bass, Teignworthy, guest beer. Garden, outdoor eating. Pub closed Mon (except Bank Holidays). No credit cards.*

Lower Beeding Jeremy's at The Crabtree ★ FOOD

Tel 01403 891257 Fax 01403 891606 Map 11 B6
Brighton Road Lower Beeding West Sussex RH13 6PT

Jeremy Ashpool relocated home three years ago (from The King's Head, Cuckfield) to the cream-painted Crabtree public house, which stands immediately alongside the A281 just south of Lower Beeding. The front of the building is Georgian and the rear section dates back to 1579 when it was a haunt for smugglers. Mentioned briefly in Hilaire Belloc's The Four Men, the pub is now tied to King and Barnes and features a good range of their beers including their new range of seasonal draughts. The bar is very simply furnished with just a few round tables and stools. One has to book to ensure a table in one of the restaurant's two rooms. The dining-room is non-smoking or there's the characterful Smugglers, an ancient beamed room at the rear with an inglenook. In the evening the emphasis is very much on a more upmarket, three-course à la carte (but fixed-price) menu and there's also a good-value, set, three-course menu midweek; the latter might feature a creamy mushroom and leek soup followed by baked cod with lemon and herb crust and end with strawberries and raspberries in cream. There is also a daily-changing, short à la carte lunch menu with dishes such as creamy fish soup with fresh haddock, roasted Barbary duck salad with beetroot and orange mascarpone and asparagus tart with tomato dressing; more substantial dishes might be ham and vegetable pie, wild rabbit with mustard sauce or grilled cod with mussels. Delicious puddings to finish include an irresistible warm toffee pudding with butterscotch sauce. Otherwise, there are simple sandwiches (prawn, smoked salmon) and ploughman's with cheddar, Stilton, Tornegus or Shropshire blue for lunch only. *Open 11-3, 5.30-11 (Sun 12-3, 7-10.30).* ***Bar Food*** *12.30-2 (reduced bar menu Sun or fixed-price roast lunch menu), 7.30-9.45 (no eve bar menu, Monday gourmet nights, Tue-Thur set menu & 3-course, fixed-price à la carte). No food Sun eve.* ***Beer*** *King & Barnes. Garden. Access, Visa.*

Lower Brailes George Hotel FOOD

Tel 01608 685223 Map 14a B1 **B&B**
Lower Brailes nr Banbury Oxfordshire OX15 5HN

On the B4035 four miles from Shipston on the Banbury road, the old George was a near-derelict property a mere two years ago. Things have changed rapidly under the Browns' experienced hands. Pine tables in the bright public bar and polished mahogany in the panelled lounge (opening through a French window into the picturesque flower garden) vie with one another as prime locations for a bar snack. Home cooking lies at the heart of everything, from the cream of celery and lentil soup, rump steak and onion sandwich and Thai chicken curry to steak and kidney pie cooked in Old Hooky. The former pool room and bottle store have been knocked through, the oak beams and splendid inglenook exposed and an intimate and romantic atmosphere created in the new dining-room, though it's equally acceptable to have a less formal meal in the bar or lounge. Either way the prominent blackboards keep abreast of Peter Brown's latest shopping for bargains in Birmingham market. Typical results might be grilled darne of salmon served with warm basil dressing and escalopes of veal with white wine, mushrooms and cream, appearing with generous portions of freshly-cooked vegetables, while Jane Brown lends her hand to the home production of such treats as jam sponge with custard and strawberry Bakewell tart. Bedroom accommodation offers a high degree of comfort, style and amenities, including en-suite facilities with bath and shower, remote-control TVs, direct-dial phones, hairdryers and trouser presses. ***Bar Food*** *12-2, 6.30-9.30.* ***Beer*** *Hook Norton Mild, Best & Old Hooky. Garden, outdoor eating. Family room.* ***Accommodation*** *6 bedrooms, all en suite, £48 (£35 single). Children welcome overnight (under-5s stay free in parents' room). Check-in by arrangement. No dogs. No credit cards.*

LOWER FROYLE — Prince of Wales — FOOD

Tel 01420 23102 Map 15a D4
Lower Froyle Hampshire GU34 4LJ

A rather modern and ordinary looking Edwardian-style village pub, built in the 1930s after the original thatched pub had burnt down. The modest open-plan bar and dining-room is often busy with a dining clientele seeking out the reliably good home-cooked food.
A regularly-changing blackboard menu highlights the old favourites – chili, lasagne, grilled rainbow trout – and a few imaginative choices such as duck breast in soya sauce and honey and a fresh fish list (mainly Thur-Sun) which may include roast monkfish with tarragon or sea bass cooked with fresh ginger and spring onions; scallops, lobster and crab are also very popular. In the evenings, a separate printed menu accompanies the blackboard and features beef Wellington, veal cordon bleu, chicken supreme with a Stilton and celery sauce, plus further fish dishes. A traditional 3-course Sunday lunch is good value. Very few of the puddings are home-made, but the bread-and-butter and Queen of puddings are. *Open 12-3, 6-11 (Sun 12-3, 7-10.30).* ***Bar Food*** *12-2, 7-10 (except Sun eve). Free House.* ***Beer*** *Fuller's ESB & London Pride, Timothy Taylor's Landlord, two guest beers. Garden, outdoor eating. Pub closed 25 Dec. Access, Visa.*

LOWER ODDINGTON — The Fox — FOOD

Tel 01451 870888 **Fax 01451 870666** Map 14a A1
Lower Oddington nr Stow-on-the-Wold Gloucestershire GL56 0UR

Tucked off the A436 just outside old Stow, this Cotswold hamlet is famed for its 11th-century church of St. Nicholas. Outside, the Fox is faced in yellow stone, while within it is fitted internally with the style and flair. Its balance between country brasserie/bistro and village pub has been carefully thought out in a succession of plainly furnished rooms with graduated colour schemes – from fresh, summery lemon, through magnolia to the rag-washed bar with 'designer nicotine overtones'. Food asserts its prominence in imaginative and colourful dishes that exhibit an equal attention to both flavour and balance. From Brie and broccoli soup or spinach soufflé with anchovy sauce, progress to the likes of moussaka, fish pie, garganelle pasta with wild mushrooms, crème fraiche and fresh Parmesan, kidneys in mustard sauce or the popular salmon and potato fish cakes with parsley sauce. There are peppered sirloin steaks, a Sunday sirloin roast served rare and simpler snacks like French bread sandwiches with prawn mayonnaise or honey-roast ham and salad. Among the desserts, the lemon crunch, treacle tart and 'Fox's chocolate challenge' are all home-made, too. Outside is half an acre of walled garden. *Open 12-3, 6.30-11 (Sun 12-3, 7-10.30).* ***Bar Food*** *12-2, 7-10 (Sun to 9.30). Free House.* ***Beer*** *Hook Norton, Marston's Pedigree, guest beer. Garden, terrace, outdoor eating. Family room. Access, Visa.*

LOWER PEOVER — Bells of Peover — A

Tel 01565 722269 Map 6 B2
The Cobbles Lower Peover nr Knutsford Cheshire WA16 9PZ

Recommended primarily for its atmosphere (although it's a popular local dining pub): originally a home for monks, a lovely, creeper-covered old pub by the church, at the end of a cobbled lane off the B5081. Toby jugs of all sizes and styles make amusing company in the snug, where the bar counter is to be found; the barless main room has a collection of copper and brass and decorative blue plates. No children under 14 in the bar area. *Open 11.30-3, 5.30-11 (Sun 12-3, 7-10.30).* ***Beer*** *Greenalls. Patio/terrace. Access, Visa.*

LOWER WIELD — Yew Tree Inn — FOOD

Tel 01256 389224 Map 14a C4
Lower Wield nr Alresford Hampshire SO24 9RX

Isolated beside a narrow country lane off the B3046 Alresford-Basingstoke road, the Yew Tree acquires its name from the 300-year-old tree by which it stands. The local cricket pitch lies opposite and the sport is taken very seriously in these parts, the main, simply furnished, bar being particularly busy on summer Sundays. At other times, this welcoming rural retreat is a popular dining venue; the tables in the cosy, beamed restaurant are neatly laid with place mats, fresh flowers, linen napkins and are candlelit in the evenings.
The attraction here is the reliable range of home-cooked food, from decent bar snacks like generously filled baguettes, baked potatoes, ploughman's, ham salad and steak and kidney pie to a blackboard menu listing more inventive and ambitious dishes. To start, there may

be rosette of avocado and fresh Cornish crab, jacket potato with escargots, followed by baked whole megrim with olive oil, lemon and herbs, fillet of Angus beef with red wine and horseradish crust and roast breast of duckling with honey and peppercorns, all served with a separate dish of fresh crunchy vegetables. To finish, try the steamed dark pudding or creme brulée. The simpler bar snacks are not available Friday or Saturday evenings. Traditional Sunday lunch features a choice of three roasts; children are charged half price. Large peaceful garden with rural outlook. *Open 12-3, 6-11 (Sun 12-3, 7-10.30).* ***Bar Food*** *12-2.15, 7-9.45 (Tue-Sat only). Free House.* ***Beer*** *Cheriton Brewhouse Pots Ale & Diggers Gold. Garden, patio, children's play area. Pub closed Mon eve. Access, Visa.*

LOWESWATER — Kirkstile Inn — B&B

Tel 01900 85219 Map 4 C3

Loweswater nr Cockermouth Cumbria CA13 0RV

Stretching as far as the eye can see, the woods, fells and lakes are as much a draw today as they must have been in the inn's infancy some 400 years ago. The beck below meanders under a stone bridge, oak trees fringing its banks with mighty Melbreak towering above. The pub's interior retains the warm cosiness of interlinked rooms with an enclosed verandah, a TV lounge reserved for residents and the Little Barn housing a games room for wet days. Consistent with Lakeland tradition, lunches and afternoon teas are kept rather basic, with residents returning for table d'hote dinner (reservations only, although our recommendation here is for B&B only). The oldest, and smallest bedrooms in the original cottage share bathroom and toilets, while those in the extension have more space and en suite facilities. All have background heating, quilts and beverage facilities; communal laundry and drying rooms are readily available for the droves of walkers who return nightly to make Kirkstile their home. *Open 11-11 (Sun 12-3, 7-10.30).* ***Beer*** *Jennings Bitter, Cockerhoop & Cumberland Ale. Garden. Family Room.* ***Accommodation*** *10 bedrooms, 8 en suite, £55 (single £45). Children welcome overnight, additional bed (£12), and cot (£7) available. Bar closed 25 Dec eve (except for residents). Access, Visa.*

LOWSONFORD — Fleur De Lys — A

Tel & Fax 01564 782431 Map 14 C1

Lowsonford nr Henley-in-Arden Warwickshire B95 5HJ

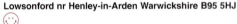

A long, low Whitbread pub with crooked chimneys and wrinkly roof whose canalside position and outdoor tuck shop deservedly attract a family clientele. A score or more picnic tables spread out along the bank, from where parents can watch the longboats while the under-12s master the climbing frames. The garden-side ketchup station of plastic disposable packets suggests quite a lot about the food inside; there are plenty of children's meals and a galleried family room, complete with rocking horses and high-chairs indoors. New landlord. *Open 11-11 (Sun 12-3, 7-10.30).* ***Bar Food*** *12-9.30 (closed 3-6 in winter).* ***Beer*** *Boddingtons, Flowers Best & Original, two guest beers. Garden, children's play area. Family room. Access, Visa.*

LUDGVAN — White Hart — A

Tel 01736 740574 Map 12 A4

Ludgvan nr Penzance Cornwall TR20 8EY

Dating from the 14th century and possibly older than the adjacent church, this stone village local is well worth a trip inland, away from the busy coast. The atmospheric interior has been carefully created in old-fashioned style and is a most welcoming and relaxing place in which to enjoy a drink, free from modern-day intrusions of piped music and games machines that seem to feature in many of the pubs in this touristy area. Ochre coloured walls, low beams, a rug-strewn wooden floor and a motley assortment of rustic tables and chairs characterise the main bar, and various jugs, mugs, books, prints and bric-a-brac fill every nook and cranny around the room. An adjacent small dimly-lit room boasts an old black kitchen range, a collection of plates and two intimate boxed seating areas, one ideal for two people, the other for a small private gathering. Real ale is tapped straight from the cask and if visiting on a Monday evening you may find the local male voice choir in full song. *Open 11-2.30, 6-11 (Sun 12-3, 7-10.30).* ***Beer*** *Flowers IPA, Cornish Original, Marston's Pedigree. Garden. No credit cards.*

LUDLOW — Church Inn — B&B

Tel 01584 872174 Map 6 A4
Church Street Buttercross Ludlow Shropshire SY8 1AW

One of the oldest sites in Ludlow, going back at least seven centuries, the former 'Wine Taverne by the Cross' stands wedged between the old Buttercross and St Laurence's church. A compact and convivial all-day bar opens on to pedestrian Church Street; regularly-changing guest ales, landlord Stuart Copland's particular pride and joy, are a feature here. Above, the bedrooms offer practical comforts, pastel-coloured duvets, remote-control TVs and beverage facilites. All are en suite, though three have shower/WC only, and there's one spacious family suite sleeping three. Parking may appear difficult but ask about on-street parking around the corner. *Open 11-11 (Sun 12-3, 7-10.30). Free House.* ***Beer*** *Ruddles County, Webster's Yorkshire, Courage Directors, guest beers.* ***Accommodation*** *9 bedrooms, all en suite (3 with shower), £40 (single £28, Fri & Sat £40). Children welcome overnight, additional bed and cot available. Access, Visa.*

LUDLOW — Unicorn Inn — FOOD B&B

Tel 01584 873555 Map 6 A4
Lower Corve Street Ludlow Shropshire SY8 1DU

☺

At the end of a row of 17th-century farmers' cottages stands this tiny half-timbered pub backing on to the river Corve, which flows into the Teme at Ludlow. Though dating from 1635, unbelievably only three years ago it housed a disco; today, under the impeccable guidance of Alan and Elisabeth Ditchburn, it's a jewel of a pub. The bar is all linenfold panels and original timbers in front of a vast stone-lined fire grate. Through to the rear, dining tables are neatly laid and cosily candle-lit at night. An eat-anywhere policy is sensibly applied to the main meals, chalked up daily on strategically-hung boards. Typically, dishes might include a home-made soup, mussels in pesto batter, wild boar in English wine and mushroom sauce and three daily fish dishes (perhaps tuna mornay or salmon with lemon and cucumber); to follow, try toffee pecan pie or lemon syllabub. For those of lesser appetite are bar snacks of open sandwiches, jacket potatoes and ploughman's platters, Evesham rarebit, chicken tikka masala and fresh asparagus gratinée. Additionally, a comprehensive vegetarian menu, regularly amended, offers the likes of Moroccan orange salad, mushroom tikka, savoury roast and jambalaya for vegans. Not only is the food good, but the welcome is genuine and the service informal and friendly. Bedrooms are limited by space – and listed building constraints – from undergoing unsuitable alterations. Exposed roof trusses are certainly original and the creaking floors wholly in character. There are TVs available for those who can't endure the abundant peace and quiet. One bedroom only has a full en-suite bathroom – and it's tiny; two more have showers/WC only, while the remaining two bedrooms share adequate adjacent facilities. *Open 12-2.30, 6-11 (Sun 12-3, 7-10.30).* ***Bar Food*** *12-2.15, 6-9.45 (Sun 7-9). Free House.* ***Beer*** *Bass, Worthington. Riverside terrace.* ***Accommodation*** *5 bedrooms, 3 en suite, £40 (single £20). Children welcome overnight, additional bed and cot available. Access, Amex, Visa.*

LURGASHALL — Noah's Ark — A

Tel 01428 707346 Map 11 A6
Lurgashall nr Petworth West Sussex GU28 9ET

450-year-old pub in a classic village green setting by the church and overlooking the cricket pitch; longer Sunday opening hours could at last assuage the afternoon thirsts of the cricketers and allow them to celebrate successes or drown their sorrows. Perhaps best in summer when the tile-hung frontage is bedecked with flowers in hanging baskets and tables are set outside on the front grassed area; cosy in winter. *Open 11.30-2.30, 6.30-11 (Sun 12-3, 7-10.30).* ***Beer*** *Greene King IPA, Abbot Ale & Rayments Special Bitter. Family room. Garden. Access, Visa.*

> Many **B&B** establishments offer reduced rates for weekend and out-of-season bookings. Always ask about special deals for longer stays. Beware half-board terms in inns where we do not recommend the **FOOD.**

LUXBOROUGH Royal Oak FOOD B&B

Tel 01984 640319 Map 13 E1
Luxborough nr Dunster Exmoor National Park Somerset TA23 0SH

Nestling by a stream at the bottom of a steep-sided valley, deep in Exmoor's Brendon Hills, the thatched Royal Oak is a truly rural 14th-century inn. No piped music, no fruit machines and no posh fixtures and fittings have intruded here. In short, no attempt whatsoever to tart the place up for the holidaymakers, which is perhaps why so many flock here during the summer months. The several rooms have flagstoned or cobbled floors, low beams, old kitchen tables and hardly a pair of matching chairs. Besides uncontrived charm, another good reason for a visit here is the splendid choice of well-kept real ales. An extensive, all-day menu ranges widely, from sandwiches and jacket potatoes to home-made soups partnered by great wedges of crusty bread, and substantial main dishes like venison casserole or duck breast in red wine, rosemary and cranberry sauce. Game features in season – perhaps rabbit, pigeon, pheasant or partridge; there's always a vegetarian dish, and the ubiquitous fish fingers are offered to children. Steaks and fish and a few other extras appear for the additional evening menu. It's still very much a locals' pub: Tuesday night is quiz night, and every Friday a folk club takes over the back room, which has a pool table (in winter only). Two bedrooms are available for overnight guests but, being above the bars, are probably not suitable for families with children or others with an early bedtime. Rooms are perfectly clean and respectable but this is not luxury accommodation (and the tariff is suitably restrained). The large, shared bathroom is in good order. *Open 11-2.30, 6-11 (Sun 12-3, 7-10.30; 6.30-11 Easter-Nov). **Bar Food** 12-2, 7-10 (Sun to 9.30). Free House. **Beer** Flowers IPA, Cotleigh Tawny, Exmoor Gold, Bateman's XXXB, up to three guest beers. Garden, outdoor eating. **Accommodation** 2 bedrooms, £30 (single £20). No children overnight. Check-in by arrangement. No dogs. Pub closed 25 Dec eve. No credit cards.*

LYDDINGTON Old White Hart FOOD

Tel 01572 821703 **Fax 01572 821965** Map 7 E4
51 Main Street Lyddington nr Uppingham Leicestershire LE15 9LF

Truly a traditional local, standing by the village green with its honey-coloured cottages and backdrop of the picturesque Welland valley. Gatherings of the pétanque club are a regular feature of summer evenings when the flower-filled beer garden is at its best. Menus throughout the bars and restaurant are firmly British and equally traditional. For lunch are the Anglesey eggs (baked in a ramekin with leeks, bacon and cheese), Essex devilled whitebait or mushrooms Lyddington and the farmhouse recipe 'Hen on her nest' (chicken, mushroom and herbs on a bed of sautéed potatoes). More elaborate evening fare adds 'Trout the Welsh way' (wrapped in bacon with leek and Caerphilly sauce) and fillet of lamb with apricot and thyme stuffing. There's plenty of choice for vegetarians on request and home-made desserts show a bias towards fruit and cream. ***Bar Food** 12-2, 7-10 (no food Sunday evening). Free House. **Beer** Greene King IPA, Rayments Bitter, Abbot. Garden, outdoor eating. Ten flood-lit pétanque areas. Access, Visa.*

LYDFORD Castle Inn FOOD B&B

Tel 01822 820242 **Fax 01822 820454** Map 12 C3
Lydford nr Okehampton Devon EX20 4BH

Just a stone's throw from open moors, the pink-washed, wisteria-entangled Castle is certainly a pretty little pub, but it's not until you go inside that you realise how old it is. Much is 12th-century, with various later additions, and it just oozes atmosphere, with its slate floor and low sagging ceilings turned a deep amber colour by time and smoke. The place is literally crammed with bits and pieces collected by landlords over the years, including several marvellous old high-backed settles (some with little roofs), dozens of decorative plates, numerous old photos and handbills and a fine collection of Hogarth prints (not a fruit machine or juke box in sight). Seven of only 31 remaining Lydford pennies minted by Ethelred the Unready in the 10th century are on display, the rest being held by the British Museum. The Castle's reputation for good food and a friendly welcome is safe in the hands of owners Mo and Clive Walker. Mo controls proceedings in the kitchen, producing an eclectic range of dishes listed on a daily-changing blackboard in the bar. Favourites are the Oriental-style dishes – chicken curry, beef rendang, Malaysian vegetable

stew – and well-cooked traditional dishes and home-made soups – ham and lentil, Stilton and asparagus – Dartmoor pie (with venison and apricots), jugged hare, salmon and trout fishcakes and pork and apple cobbler, all served with fresh vegetables. At lunchtime (when there are no sandwiches, but there is a very good Devon cheese platter), this menu applies throughout the inn, but at night it's limited to the smaller bar and snug, when the main bar becomes a restaurant (bookings taken) offering a three-course table d'hote menu and an à la carte choice. Bookings are also taken for dining on the covered patio outside, where five tables are a lovely spot for summer alfresco eating. Six of the modestly comfortable bedrooms are en suite while the other two share a perfectly acceptable bathroom; antique furniture features in all rooms, the Castle Room sporting a four-poster bed. Immediately next door to the inn is the castle with its rather gruesome history; local folklore has it that even to this day the birds, sensing its evil, will not go near the place. Rather more welcoming, the local church boasts some fine wood carving on no less than 69 pew ends, and a very fine rood screen. Just a short walk away is the picturesque Lydford Gorge and its woodland walks. *Open 11.30-3, 6-11 (Sun 12-3, 7-10.30).* ***Bar Food*** *12-2.30, 6.30-9.30 (Sun 7-9). Free House.* ***Beer*** *Blackawton Bitter, Wadworth 6X, two guest beers. Garden, outdoor eating. Family room.* ***Accommodation*** *8 bedrooms, 6 en suite, £52.50 (four-poster £57.50, single £38.75). Children welcome overnight (under-5s stay free in parents' room), additional bed (£4-£15) & cot (£5) available. Access, Amex, Diners, Visa.*

LYDGATE — White Hart ★ FOOD

Tel 01457 872566 Map 6 C2
51 Stockport Road Lydgate nr Oldham Lancashire OL4 4JJ

Local boy Charles Brierley had his first beer at this typical blackened-stone, 200-year-old Lancashire pub. He must have liked it (the pub, that is, as well as the beer), because – moving on a few years – he returned and bought it. It was then in an almost derelict state, but a year of refurbishment has turned the White Hart into a smart and comfortable hostelry. A couple of areas are reserved for drinkers but the rest is set up for eating from a Brasserie menu that ranges well beyond the usual pub fare: omelette Arnold Bennett, open sandwich of smoked salmon, bacon and cream cheese, parfait of chicken livers with port wine jelly, tian of wild mushrooms, spinach and pine nuts, tempura of cod with tartare sauce, confit of duck with peppered livers. There are also steaks, a roast ham sandwich (with home-made chutney) and afters like sticky toffee pudding, rhubarb crème brulée and a selection of British farmhouse cheeses. The quality and sophistication of the food is down to head chef John Rudden (formerly at *The Angel,* Hetton – our 1995 Pub of the Year) whose kitchen also serves a separate, first-floor restaurant. At Sunday lunchtimes there is a set, two- or three-course lunch, with roast sirloin of beef offered in addition to the regular menu. The bar wines, with about ten served by the glass, are just a sample from the main restaurant list that is available on request. The village of Lydgate is located about three miles north-east of Oldham on the A669 – neither the village nor the road number are marked on most road maps; head for Grasscroft and you'll be on the right track! *Open 12-3 & 5-11 (Sun 12-3, 7-10.30). Closed Mon lunchtime (except Bank Holidays).* ***Bar Food*** *12-3 & 5.30-8.30 (Sun 7-9). Free House.* ***Beer*** *JW Lees, Coach House Brewing Co, Boddingtons, Webster's Green Label Best, guest beers. Outdoor eating. Access, Visa.*

LYMPSHAM — Batch Farm Country Hotel B&B

Tel 01934 750371 **Fax 01934 750501** Map 13 E1
Lympsham nr Weston-super-Mare Somerset BS24 0EX

Mr and Mrs Brown's hotel, with its 50-acre grounds, stands in open farmland through which the river Axe flows. Origins of the former farmhouse are evident in the beams which adorn the bar and residents' lounges, while the neat, practical bedrooms enjoy views of either the Mendip or Quantock hills. The adjoining Somerset Suite is a popular venue for functions up to 70. Lympsham is about 3 miles from Junction 22 of the M5.
Free House. Garden, coarse fishing. ***Accommodation*** *8 bedrooms, all en-suite, £54 (single £33). Children welcome overnight (rate depends on age), additional bed and cot available. No dogs. Closed 1 week Christmas. Access, Amex, Diners, Visa.*

We do not accept free meals or hospitality – our inspectors pay their own bills and **never** book in the name of Egon Ronay's Guides.

LYNMOUTH — Rising Sun Hotel — B&B

Tel 01598 753223 **Fax 01598 753480** Map 13 D1
Harbourside Lynmouth Devon EX35 6EQ

Zzz...

Hugo Jeune has spent a great deal of money in lovingly restoring his 14th-century thatched pub and adjacent cottages which climb steeply up the slope from the Lynmouth breakwater. The bedrooms boast individual decor, stylish fabrics, pine furniture, colour TV, direct-dial phones and spotless bathrooms; the top cottage, where the poet Shelley spent his honeymoon in 1812, has been decked out for modern newly-weds, complete with four-poster bed, sitting room and a private garden. Romance is in the air; Shelley wrote of his stay: 'the climate is so mild that myrtles of immense size twine up our cottage and roses bloom in the open air in winter'. There's another literary connection: R.D. Blackmore wrote part of *Lorna Doone* here. The inn owns a stretch of river for salmon fishing. Bar snacks range from filled soft-grain rolls, home-made soup and ploughman's, baked potatoes, a seafood platter, local trout, grilled plaice and steak, mushroom and Guinness pie. *Free House.* ***Beer*** *Whitbread Royal Wessex Bitter & Pompey Royal (Gale's). Garden.* ***Accommodation*** *16 bedrooms, all en suite, from £79 (cottage £118, single £44.50). No children under 5, 5-12s half price if sharing, additional bed (£10) and cot (£5) available. Dogs by arrangement. Access, Amex, Diners, Visa.*

MACCLESFIELD — Sutton Hall — FOOD — B&B

Tel 01260 253211 **Fax 01260 252538** Map 6 B2
Bullocks Lane Sutton Macclesfield Cheshire SK11 0HE

Zzz...

Central to the building, a wood- and stone-built 16th-century mansion in use as a nunnery until just 30 years ago, is the pub itself, which has a stunning interior. The black oak beams, gnarled and knotted, that frame the bar are certainly of much older origin than the rest of the structure (there having been a manor house on this site since 1093), and a unique atmosphere is created by the combination of oak panelling, exposed stonework, leaded windows and two large log-burning fireplaces, one of them guarded by a medieval knight in armour. The bar menu is fiercely traditional. Starters and snacks are of the deep-fried button mushrooms stuffed with cream cheese, home-made vegetable soup and home-made cannelloni variety, while the main dishes – goujons of lemon sole, grilled sirloin steak, spinach pancakes with ratatouille filling and sour cream dressing and perhaps lasagne – are good value for money. The adjacent restaurant, kitted out in flock wallpaper with polished yew tables, takes itself a little more seriously. Bedroom conversion has seen the installation of bathrooms throughout, plus modern-day amenities like remote-control televisions, direct-dial phones, trouser presses and hairdryers. The antique flavour, however, is well preserved in lace-covered four-poster beds and deep leather easy chairs, although (a penalty of antiquity) there's a distinct shortage of natural daylight through their leaded Gothic windows, further dimmed by heavily overhanging eaves. The Hall's immediate environs, backing on to a working farm at the rear, appear so close to ramshackle as to cause some initial concern, but the warmth of the interior and the casual tomfoolery between landlords Robert and Phyllida Bradshaw, staff and regulars suggest that such imperfection and incompleteness are not, perhaps, entirely accidental. *Open 11-11 (Sun 12-3,7-10.30).* ***Bar Food*** *12-2.30 (Sun to 3), 7-9.45. Free House.* ***Beer*** *Bass, Stones, Marston's, guest beer. Large garden, outdoor eating. Family room (weekend lunch).* ***Accommodation*** *10 bedrooms, all en suite, £85 (single £68.95). Children welcome overnight (rate depends on age), cot available. Check-in by arrangement. Access, Amex, Visa.*

MADINGLEY — Three Horseshoes ★ — FOOD

Tel 01954 210221 **Fax 01954 212043** Map 15 F1
High Street Madingley Cambridgeshire CB3 8AB

Built in the early 1900s, this neat white-painted, thatched pub with tables outside and a pretty garden is all about eating. Young chef/manager Richard Stokes's modern Mediterranean style of cooking is reflected on the imaginative and comprehensive three-weekly-changing menu, which is available throughout the relaxed bar and slightly more formal restaurant (also recommended in our *1996 Hotels & Restaurants Guide*). Begin with duck confit with red & yellow peppers, black olives and fried basil, a minestrone soup with pesto and parmesan or a salad of sun-dried tomatoes, olives, artichokes, parmesan, Parma ham and capers. Main-course options may range from roast monkfish with a ragout of wild

mushrooms and vegetables and a red wine, grain mustard and butter sauce or daube of boeuf bourguignon to tandoori chicken with spiced couscous, and stuffed rabbit leg with onion, parsley, Parma ham, mashed potato, sautéed spinach and mustard sauce; all demonstrate how far this is from standard pub fare. Puddings are more familiar – crème brulée, sticky toffee pudding, lemon tart – and there are some splendid unpasteurised British cheeses from Neal's Yard Dairy. About 20 wines by the glass (if one includes the dessert wines and a couple of vintage ports) chosen from a commendable list of good-value wines. *Open 11.30-2.30, 6-11 (Sun 12-2.30, 7-10.30).* ***Bar Food*** *11.30-2 (Sun 12-2), 6.30-10 (Sun 7-9.30). Free House.* ***Beer*** *Adnams Southwold, guest beers. Garden. Access, Amex, Diners, Visa.*

MAIDENSGROVE Five Horseshoes FOOD

Tel 01491 641282 Fax 01491 641086 Map 15a D3
Maidensgrove nr Stonor Henley-on-Thames Oxfordshire RG9 6EY

Well established as an eating house, this old brick pub stands alongside the lane which winds past Russell's Water, off the B481. Paper money from around the world frames the bar where food is ordered, and there's little enough available, for two, for less than a crisp bill or two. From a comprehensive list, where blackboard chalk has been replaced by paint, are the likes of a prawn-filled baked potato, great Five Horseshoes hors d'oeuvre and chicken or vegetable stir-fry. Daily dishes are nonetheless prominent, with main courses of chicken breast stuffed with crab mousse or crab thermidor being typical. Follow with home-made ice creams, crème brulée or nutty treacle pie. Barbecues in fine weather (Thursday evening, Sunday lunch and evening) feature steaks and lamb, chicken and seafood kebabs and there's patio seating under a swaying octagonal awning. Hidden away to the pub's rear, the Café Shoes attempts a little more adventure with main courses in much the same price range. Individual tables, or a whole room for 20, are bookable in advance. No children under 14 permitted in the bar, or in the restaurant in the evenings. *Open 11-2.30, 6.30-11 (Sun 12-3, 7-10.30).* ***Bar Food*** *12-1.45, 7-9.30.* ***Beer*** *Brakspear. Family Room. Barbecue patio and garden. Access, Visa.*

MANCHESTER Lass O'Gowrie A

Tel & Fax 0161 273 6932 Map 6 B2
36 Charles Street Manchester M1 7DB

A short walk from the city centre, right by the BBC, Lass O'Gowrie is a must as much for Manchester's students of architecture as for enthusiasts of real ale and micro-brewing. The building's facade is fully tiled in brightly-glazed browns and greens, quite literally shining as a credit to the city's clean air. Inside, the cavernous neo-Victorian recreation (somewhat gentrified for today's consumers) comes complete with gas mantles, sanded floorboards and mock-antique signboards. Above the bar are lined up some fine examples of the ancient art of cooperage, while the lining of the pub's upper walls and ceiling consists entirely of stretched hopsacks whose former contents have doubtless featured in many a brew. Central to the main bar is a glassed-in canopy through which the curious can gaze down into the cellar to see the vats. Lighter LOG 35 (ABV 3.6%) and maltier LOG 42 (ABV 4%) – the names indicative of their respective strengths – are the home brews hand-pulled up to the single servery and dispensed in staggering quantities. To temper a heavy lunchtime session cut sandwiches and the likes of bacon baps are on offer at very reasonable prices. Whitbread. *Open 11.30-11 (Sun 12-3, 7-10.30).* ***Beer*** *LOG 35 & LOG 42, guest beers. Visa.*

MANCHESTER Mark Addy FOOD

Tel 0161 832 4080 Map 6 B2
Stanley Street Salford Manchester M3 5EJ

Head for New Bailey Street where the old Albert Bridge crosses the River Irwell into Salford; on the Manchester bank opposite is the Pump House People's History museum. Once a jetty and waiting room for the river ferry, this is an imaginative and truly different pub that takes its name from the only civilian to be presented the Royal Albert Medal (VC) by Queen Victoria. Born on the banks of the Irwell, Mark Addy received this award for rescuing fifty drowning passengers from the river. Behind a waterside courtyard the single bar still sports the old flagstone floor and sandstone, barrel-vaulted brick ceiling encased behind full-length picture windows. Such is the range of cheeses on offer that it's best to visit in a sizeable party. Platefuls of tangy white Cheshire, Windsor Red and Sage Derby constitute a colourful display and are accompanied by baskets of freshly-baked granary bread. Shopping is meticulous: the blue Stilton comes only from Long Clawson Dairy in

Melton Mowbray and the full-blooded Cricketer from Cricket Malherbie farm in Somerset. As there are also several Belgian patés (including vegetarian varieties) to add to the feast it's unsurprising – though undeniably generous – that take-away bags are also provided. *Open 11.30-11 (Sun 12-3, 7-10.30). Closed 25 & 26 Dec.* ***Bar Food*** *11.30-8, Sun 12-3. Free House.* ***Beer*** *Boddingtons, Marston's Best, guest beer. Terrace. Outdoor eating. No credit cards.*

MANCHESTER — New Ellesmere — B&B

Tel 0161 728 2791 Fax 0161 794 8222 Map 6 B2
East Lancs Road Swinton Manchester M27 3AA

Very handy (and decently-priced) accommodation – especially for families – midway between the city centre and M62 (Junction 14) on the East Lancashire Road. 'Per room' prices apply, including weekend discounts, with all the ground-floor doubles including fold-out sofa beds. While remaining furniture and fittings are a mite utilitarian, up-to-date amenities include free satellite TV and radio channels, direct-dial phones, hairdryers and trouser presses. Full en-suite facilities include heated towel rails and over-bath showers. Breakfasts, currently priced at £4.45, include a full grill. Children welcomed, with high-chairs, changing facilities, indoor play area, garden and play area all provided. Part of Greenalls' chain of Premier Lodges. *Open 11-11 (Sun 12-3, 7-10, 3-7 with food only).* ***Beer*** *Greenalls Original, Tetley, guest beer. Garden. Family room.* ***Accommodation*** *27 bedrooms, all en suite, £39.50 (per room, weekends £32.50), breakfast extra. Children welcome overnight, additional bed and cot available. Access, Amex, Visa.*

MARKET OVERTON — Black Bull — FOOD

Tel 01572 767677 Map 7 E3
Market Overton Leicestershire LE15 7PW

Having bought a semi-derelict, part-thatched ale-house in 1985, John and Valerie Owen have single-mindedly created a relaxed local pub with good-value dining. The bar's agreeable interior of red banquettes, polished tables, poker-back chairs and background popular music (there are speakers everywhere, even in the loos!) creates a chatty, relaxed atmosphere in which to engage in banter and enjoy the beer. Across a central area of original flagstone floor is the dining-room, converted from a garage, which offers the likes of sizzling chicken with a Cantonese sauce, half a roast Barbary duck, home-made soups, seafood tagliatelle and Rutland chicken with wild mushroom sauce on the blackboard menu, plus daily specials like stuffed loin of pork. Sandwiches available lunchtime only. Upstairs, one en-suite double and a twin bedroom (not inspected) are equipped with televisions. *Open 11-2.30, 6-11 (Sun 12-3, 7-10.30).* ***Bar Food*** *12-2, 7-10.* ***Beer*** *Ruddles Best & County, Theakston Best & XB, Younger's Best, guest beer. Patio, outdoor eating. Access, Visa.*

> We endeavour to be as up-to-date as possible but inevitably some changes to landlords, chefs and other key staff occur after the Guide has gone to press.

MARSH GIBBON — The Greyhound — FOOD

Tel 01869 277365 Map 14a C1
Marsh Gibbon nr Bicester Buckinghamshire OH6 0HA

A listed, traditional old pub with 17th-century brickwork without and an unusually modern food offering within. Thai snacks (satay, wun tuns, spring rolls, spare ribs) and main courses – try the special fried noodles, 'never sober' beef, roast duck curry or one of seven ways with vegetables – are served to diners at sewing-machine tables in the beamed main bar with its bare stone walls. A £10 minimum food charge applies in the restaurant where there are also £16 set menus for four or more people. Picnic tables are set on the attractive front garden; to the rear is another garden, this time with trees and a swing and climbing frame for children. A friendly society of bell-ringers (and up to 1000 friends!) has met here for around 200 years on the nearest Saturday to May 29th. The Greyhound is south-east of Marsh Gibbon, best approached via Blackthorn on the Bicester-Aylesbury A41. *Open 12-3, 6-11. Free House.* ***Beer*** *Fuller's London Pride, Greene King Abbot & IPA, Hook Norton Best, McEwan's 80/-. Garden, children's play area. Access, Amex, Diners, Visa.*

MARSHSIDE Gate Inn FOOD

Tel 01227 860498 Map 11 C5
Boyden Gate Marshside nr Canterbury Kent CT3 4EB

Delightfully set beside a lane in a tiny hamlet – 2 miles from A28 Canterbury to Margate road at Upstreet – and surrounded by farmland and marshes, this unpretentious rural retreat prides itself on still being "a talkers' pub", in tandem with a thriving bar meal trade. Two welcoming and rustic interconnecting rooms have quarry-tiled floors, a central brick fireplace with winter log fire and a selection of sturdy pine tables, chairs and old pews. Fresh, local produce is used to produce homely, honest English fare (like a spicy sausage hotpot), and perhaps a home-made vegetable flan or hot bacon and mushroom torpedo, along with home-made burgers and a famous black pudding sandwich served with mango chutney. Well-kept Shepherd Neame ales are dispensed direct from the barrel and free-range eggs and local vegetables are also sold over the bar. Splendid summer garden with cottage flowers, stream and duck pond with resident ducks and geese – a constant amusement to children. Quiz night is Thursday night. *Open 11-2.30 (Sat to 3), 6-11 (Sun 12-3, 7-10.30).* ***Bar Food*** *12-2 (Sat 11.30-2.30) 6-9.30 (Sun 12-2.30, 7-9).* ***Beer*** *Shepherd Neame. Garden, outdoor eating area, summer barbecue. Family room. No credit cards.*

MAYFIELD Rose & Crown Inn FOOD B&B

Tel 01435 872200 **Fax 01435 872200** Map 11 B6
Fletching Street Mayfield East Sussex TN20 6TE

Zzz... 

Delightful 16th-century pub in a historic village, alongside what was the original London-Brighton road, now a quiet village lane. Unspoilt bars, particularly the two small front ones, have ochre walls, beams, inglenook fireplace, two log fires, and an atmosphere in which shove ha'penny and cribbage are still keenly played. One comprehensive menu features reliable home-cooked dishes and applies both in the bar and cosy restaurant where there's an extensive global wine list. Start, perhaps, with crab cakes with ginger and spring onion chutney, or layered aubergine, leek, feta and walnut terrine, moving on to Corsican chicken breast wrapped in smoked bacon and served with a garlicky sauce of shallots, olives and sun-dried tomatoes, a veal, wild boar, gammon and apple pie or Moroccan lamb tageen with minted couscous, followed by one of the home-made puddings, perhaps treacle and walnut tart, exotic mixed fruit crumble, American baked apple cheesecake or lemon brulée. Separate vegetarian and fresh fish menus. Upstairs are four quaint, beamed bedrooms, each with antique pine furniture – one with a fine brass bed – and a comfortable easy chair; they are equipped with beverage-making facilities, TVs clock/radios, hairdryers and trouser presses. Spotless en-suite bathrooms, all with bath and shower. Breakfast is charged extra. Landscaped front terrace with village views. Now owned by The Magic Pub Company, but the same team remains in the kitchen. *Open 11-3, 5-11 (Sat 11-11, Sun 12-3, 7-10.30).* ***Bar Food*** *11.30-2.30, 6.30-9.30 (Fri & Sat 10, Sun 7-9.30). Free House.* ***Beer*** *Harveys Sussex Bitter, Flowers IPA and Original, Hall & Woodhouse Tanglefoot, Bass, guest beer. Garden, paved terrace, outdoor eating.* ***Accommodation*** *4 bedrooms, all en suite, from £48 (single £38), breakfast £13.90 for 2 extra. Children welcome overnight, additional bed (£10) available. Check-in by arrangement. Small dogs welcome by arrangement. Access, Visa.*

MELKSHAM King's Arms Hotel B&B

Tel 01225 707272 **Fax 01225 702085** Map 14 B3
Market Place Melksham Wiltshire SW12 6EX

Across from Melksham's Market Place, the Bath-stone former coaching inn with its cobbled forecourt and abundant flower displays is the old town's summer centrepiece. Residents here are well catered for with a quiet, cosy lounge leading through to an intimate dining-room. By contrast, the lounge bar is functional and less private. Bedrooms vary between a period, beamed style and the bright and more spacious, arched doubles probably favoured by those with work to do. Ten bedrooms have bathrooms en suite, while four smaller singles share two barely adequate public bathrooms, a fact reflected in their lower tariff. *Open 11-2.30, 5-11 (Sun 12-3, 7-10.30).* ***Beer*** *Wadworth 6X & Henry's IPA, Bass.* ***Accommodation*** *14 rooms, 10 en suite, £49 (single £45). Children welcome overnight (under-10s stay free in parents' room), additional bed and cot available. Access, Amex, Diners, Visa.*

MELLOR — Devonshire Arms — FOOD

Tel 0161 427 2563 Map 6 C2
Longhurst Lane Mellor nr Stockport Greater Manchester SK6 5PP

A regular Devonshire drinker claims to have lived in Derbyshire, Cheshire and Greater Manchester without ever having moved house, so close is the pub to this area's ever-changing boundaries. When Brian and Joan Harrison moved in here, on to the menu came tiger prawns in filo pastry, mussel chowder and Kung-Po chicken with sherry sauce, thus extending the boundaries of good pub food. Authentic curries, however, remain Brian's abiding passion, with fresh spices and nan regularly ferried in from cosmopolitan Stockport. Kashmiri lamb; Raseda Jingha with prawns, ginger and yoghurt, buttered chicken masala and 'malaida unday' (the last word in curried eggs) are a representative sample. While the full menu is currently served only at lunchtime, the rear lounge, opening on to the rear patio and garden, is available for evening 'entertaining', supplemented by jazz on Thursday nights. *Open 11.30-3, 5.30-11 (Sun 12-3, 7-10.30). Closed 25 Dec.* ***Bar Food*** *12-2.30, evening meals Mon only 7-9.30.* ***Beer*** *Robinson's Best, Hartley's. Garden, outdoor eating. No credit cards.*

MELLOR — Millstone Hotel — FOOD

Tel 01254 813333 **Fax 01254 812628** Map 6 B1 **B&B**
Church Lane Mellor Blackburn Lancashire BB2 7JR

Zzz...

Daniel Thwaites, the Blackburn brewers, operate the Shire Inns chain; its original flagship, the Millstone remains true to its roots and is closest to the brewery. Pub first and foremost, it has a thriving local trade and is consistently busy for their Miller's bar food which offers the likes of Caesar salad with charred chicken, baked Loch Fyne Queen scallops with Gruyère cheese and cream, roasted tomato and crab salad, smoked Scottish salmon are offered as starters; main courses might extend the choice to chicken tikka, sweet and sour pork with prawns, poached Scottish salmon, beef balti or a cheese ploughman's lunch. By comparison, the à la carte restaurant and en-suite bedrooms are decidedly 'hotel' and priced accordingly. Smart bedrooms come in both standard and executive grades (including three suites), with satellite TV, direct-dial telephones, trouser presses and hairdryers throughout. Executive rooms receive rather more space, towelling bathrobes and top-drawer toiletries in the en-suite bathrooms. Of great benefit to the less active is the wing of five ground-floor bedrooms (there is no lift) which are also appreciated by parents of very little ones.
Open 11-11 (Sun 12-3, 7-10.30). ***Bar Food*** *12-2, 7-8.45.* ***Beer*** *Thwaites Mild and Bitter, guest beer. Patio.* ***Accommodation*** *18 bedrooms, all en suite, £88/108 (single £69/89), weekends £58 (single £49). Children welcome overnight (under-14s free if staying in parents' room), additional bed and cot available. Access, Amex, Visa.*

MELMERBY — Shepherds Inn — FOOD

Tel 01768 881217 Map 4 C3
Melmerby nr Penrith Cumbria CA10 1HF

Martin and Christine Baucutt have built up a fine reputation here. At the heart of their operation is Christine's cooking and it's no exaggeration that regulars cross and re-cross the Pennines simply to sample the variety on offer. On any one day, creamed mushroom soup, Stilton and walnut pasta bake, cheese, onion and courgette quiche and lamb's liver lyonnaise may be just the 'specials'; regular favourites still include bowls of chili, lamb rogan josh, chestnut and leek pie, and a traditional Sunday roast. Up to a dozen sweets displayed on the counter come with lashings of 'Jersey' cream, while cheese enthusiasts can choose from some twenty or more on offer, including interesting North Country varieties. A sensible, no-nonsense attitude towards the young enables grown-up meals as they'd like. No fish fingers here, but chips possible and scrambled egg, even, on request; high-chairs, too.
A twenty-one bin wine list can be supplemented by 'tastings' from Martin's private cellar; less exotically, English country fruit wines are available by the glass and there is a selection of at least 50 malt whiskies. *Open 10.30, 6-11 (Sun 12-3, 7-10.30). Closed 25 Dec.*
Bar Food *11-2.30, 6-9.45. Free House.* ***Beer*** *Jennings Cumberland Ale and Sneck Lifter, Boddingtons, guest beers. Family room. No-smoking area and cobbled patio. Access, Amex, Diners, Visa.*

MELTHAM Will's O'Nat's FOOD

Tel 01484 850078 Map 6 C2

Blackmoorfoot Road Meltham Huddersfield West Yorkshire HD7 3PS

The unusual name – meaning "William's (place), son of Nathaniel" – might also be topographically described as "Reservoir's (side) O'Meltham". Avoiding the village altogether, it's easiest to find off the A62 just south of Slaithwaite, passing Blackmoorfoot reservoir, from where the pub's in full view. By the same simple terms, the Schofields' food might be described as populist, yet it's evidently fathered from a long-standing pedigree. Regular instances of top-selling specials running out is, as ever, indicative of a dedicated kitchen, and the constantly-updated blackboards demonstrate a downright determination to feed all comers. A plethora of sandwiches runs from egg mayonnaise and rare roast beef to bacon and black pudding; snacks and salads galore include green-lip mussels, Greek feta and olive salad and smoked salmon. Some plentiful home cooking produces the likes of lamb, potato and courgette bake, chicken pieces in leek and Stilton sauce and admirable home-cooked tongue with mustard sauce. In addition, there's daily fresh fish and an interesting range of English cheeses. The majority of diners choose the upper eating area, away from the central bar servery, where views are of the moorland and surrounding hills. They're well served by friendly, hard-working youngsters who wear their tabards proudly and make light at peak periods of inevitable delays. *Open 11.30-3 (Sat to 3.30), 6-11 (Sat from 6.30, Sun 12-3, 7-10.30).* ***Bar Food*** *11.30-2, 6-10 (Sat from 6.30, Sun 12-2, 7-10).* ***Beer*** *Tetley, Old Mill Bitter. Patio. Access, Amex, Visa.*

METAL BRIDGE Metal Bridge Inn B&B

Tel & Fax 01228 74206 Map 4 C2

Floriston Metal Bridge Cumbria CA6 4HG

Pretty bed and breakfasting hostelry in a picturesque hamlet setting on the Esk estuary. The exterior and bedrooms have experienced complete refurbishment this year but the old bar (formerly a fisherman's house) is still decorated with beamed bars, nets and rods. The five bedrooms, four of which are en suite, are agreeably rustic with pine furniture and nice views, and all have TVs; one is a single with a separate (but private) bathroom. No smoking in the conservatory. *Open 11-3, 5.30-11 (Sun 12-3, 7-10.30).* ***Beer*** *Scottish & Newcastle Scotch, McEwan's Export, Theakston Traditional Ale. Riverside garden. Family room.* ***Accommodation*** *5 bedrooms, 4 en suite, £45 (single £25/35). Children welcome overnight (children stay free if sharing parents' room, family room £50), additional bed & cot available. Access, Amex, Diners, Visa.*

MICHELDEVER Dever Arms FOOD

Tel 01962 774339 Map 15 D3

Winchester Road Micheldever Hampshire SO21 3DG

Enthusiastic owners Michael and Violet Penny run this well-maintained pub set in the heart of a charming, thatched and timbered village. Three neatly furnished and carpeted interconnecting rooms sport a village local atmosphere, with a sensibly-placed bar billiards table and darts board at one end. For diners, there's a comfortable eating area close to the inglenook fireplace plus a smart little adjacent dining-room. Popularity stems from the interesting selection of freshly-prepared bar meals. A printed 'hearty snack' menu is supplemented by daily-changing blackboard menus, displayed around the fireplace, which may include hot croissant with smoked turkey and melted Brie, fresh wild mushrooms in white wine and tarragon or roulade of smoked salmon and cream cheese. Main courses range from Dever game pie and chicken breast with port and cumin to baked swordfish on a red pepper sauce. A well-stocked bar boasts a good range of locally-brewed real ales, all of which can be sampled on summer days on the quiet patio to the rear of the pub. *Open 11.30-3, 6-11 (Sun 12-3, 7-10.30).* ***Bar Food*** *12-2 (Sun to 1.45), 7-10 (not Sun eve). Free House.* ***Beer*** *Hop Back Summer Lightning, Cheriton Brewhouse Pots Ale, guest beers. Garden, outdoor eating area. Family room. Access, Amex, Visa.*

We do not accept free meals or hospitality – our inspectors pay their own bills and **never** book in the name of Egon Ronay's Guides.

MICKLEHAM King William IV FOOD

Tel 01372 372590 Map 15a F4
Byttom Hill Mickleham Surrey RH5 6EL

It's neither particularly easy to find nor to park at this old alehouse originally built for Lord Beaverbrook's estate staff; parts of the pub date back to 1790. Up a track above the Frascati restaurant (before the sign to Mickleham) on the main A24 heading south, north of Dorking; park at the foot of the hill and it's a short walk up to the pub. Since the pub is on a steep slope it's rather rambly but the terraced garden is lovely, with splendid views across the Mole Valley, arbours, rambling roses and terracotta planters as a centrepiece; and there's even a serving hatch to the garden – handy for walkers with muddy boots. On a typical blackboard menu you might find a particularly good selection of vegetarian dishes (perhaps up to six), ploughman's lunches, seafood pie, jacket potatoes, breast of chicken with brandy and mushroom sauce, jumbo sausage in French bread or cold poached salmon with salad and new potatoes. Sandwiches are not served at weekends and Bank Holidays, and there's not a chip in sight. Homely puds may include brown Betty, seasonal fruit crumble (rhubarb and apple) or treacle tart. Sunday roast lunches. No children under 14 in main bar area. Only suitable for families in summer. *Open 11-3, 6-11, Sun 12-3, 7-10.30.* ***Bar Food*** *12-2, 7-9.45 (no food Mon evening). Free House.* ***Beer*** *Boddingtons, Adnams Best, Hall & Woodhouse Badger Best, Hogs Back Traditional English Ale, guest beer. Garden. Access, Visa.*

MIDDLEHAM Black Swan B&B

Tel 01969 622221 Map 5 D4
Market Place Middleham North Yorkshire DL8 4NP

The stones that built this town-centre inn came from Middleham Castle at the time when Cromwell was punishing it for being on the Royalist side in the Civil War. Today Middleham is a rather more peaceful and quite pretty little market town – the smallest in Yorkshire apparently. The comfortable bar comes complete with old beams and cushioned high-backed settles but it is the bedroom accommodation that we recommend here. The four rooms at the front are the most characterful (and the largest), with exposed ceiling beams; however, all are equally prettily decorated in co-ordinating floral fabrics and wall coverings and most have French-style, sometimes fitted, furniture. All have neat, carpeted bathrooms (the small single has shower and WC only) with showers over tubs; all rooms have TV, direct-dial phones and tea- and coffee-making kits. The resident ghosts are reputedly quite friendly. *Open 11-11 (Sun 12-3, 7-10.30). Free House.* ***Beer*** *John Smith's, Theakston Best, Mild, XB & Old Peculier. Garden, outdoor eating. Family room.* ***Accommodation*** *7 bedrooms, all en suite, £42/57 (single £25/28). Children welcome overnight (under-12s £12), additional bed & cot available (£5). Check-in by arrangement. Accommodation closed 24, 25 & 26 Dec. Access, Visa.*

MIDDLETON Ye Olde Boar's Head A

Tel 0161 643 3520 Map 6 B2
Long Street Middleton Greater Manchester M24 3UE

Established as a hostelry in 1632 and first licensed in 1753, this striking, timbered set of buildings is Elizabethan in appearance but arguably has even earlier origins; some remarkable remains of its original construction were unearthed and carefully preserved during restoration work by JW Lees's brewery in 1989. A small snug commemorates Middleton's favourite 19th-century son, the poet and radical Samuel Bamford. Elsewhere within a splendid building still divided by original timbers and oak partitions, the Fisherman's and Sessions room (the latter now given over to TV and darts) are careful recreations of former times. Tuesday evening discos. No-smoking room at lunchtime (12-2). *Open 11-3, 5-11 (Sat from 7, Sun 12-3, 7-10.30).* ***Beer*** *Lees. Paved rear patio. Amex.*

MIDDLETON STONEY Jersey Arms B&B

Tel 01869 343234 **Fax 01869 343565** Map 14a C1
Middleton Stoney nr Bicester Oxfordshire OX6 8SE

Zzz...

Small, family-owned and -managed, 17th-century Cotswold-stone inn, now a hotel and restaurant. Alongside the B430 (between Junctions 9 & 10 of the M40), it is well placed for Woodstock, Blenheim Palace and Oxford (even Silverstone race circuit). The unpretentious and cosy bars have a traditional feel. Cottagey bedrooms are divided between the main house (where wooden beams and creaking floors abound) and the courtyard where they are a little more up to date; the Langtry Suite has a four-poster bed and sitting room.

Rooms are equipped with colour teletext TVs, direct-dial telephones, hairdryers and en-suite bathrooms (bath and shower). Room service is also offered. Day rooms include a low-ceilinged bar warmed by an open fire and a new lounge with half panelling and comfortable seating. *Open 11-11 (Sun 12-3, 7-10.30). Free House.* ***Beer*** *Younger's Scotch and Theakston Best. Garden.* ***Accommodation*** *16 bedrooms, all en suite, £79.50/£95/£125 (single £65/£85). Children welcome overnight, children under 11 free if sharing parents' room, additional bed and cot available. No dogs. Access, Amex, Diners, Visa.*

MIDDLETON-IN-TEESDALE Teesdale Hotel FOOD

Tel 01833 640264 **Fax 01833 640651** Map 5 D3 **B&B**
Market Place Middleton-in-Teeside nr Barnard Castle Co Durham DL12 029

At the centre of this rather austere, stone-built village deep in the High Pennines the Streit family have been practising their own brand of hospitality for nearly twenty years. Over the years the dayrooms have been carefully modernised throughout, tastefully furnished and immaculately kept. Audrey and her daughter handle the kitchen in a style which brings new respectability to the term "home cooking" while in the front-of-house former chef Dieter, in his own words, "helps to take the strain". Commendably varied bar menus (including an entire vegetarian section) run from baked egg and asparagus gratinée for a snack through to Hungarian goulash with noodles or poached salmon. A tapas-style menu – tuna fish salad, meatballs in a spicy chili tomato sauce – is served all day in the Rally Bar, which leads out on to a large summer terrace. Individually-decorated bedrooms are for the most part full of colour and natural light, those on the first floor having neatly-kept, if rather basic, en-suite bathrooms. At the top level, three new fully-tiled en-suite shower rooms have been carefully incorporated; the remaining rooms here, one of family size, share end-of-corridor facilities. In keeping with their own philosophy the Streits have resisted the provision of so-called "hospitality trays" (and room phones, too) in favour of a cheerily delivered early morning tea tray. *Open 7.45am-11pm (Sun 7.45-10.30).* ***Bar Food*** *12-2, 7-9 (tapas menu 11-10).Free House.* ***Beer*** *Tetley, Ind Coope Burton Ale. Terrace. Outdoor eating.* ***Accommodation*** *12 bedrooms, 9 en suite, £60.50 (single £38-£50). Children welcome overnight (under-8s stay free if sharing parents' room, 8-14s £7.50), cot available. Access, Visa.*

MIDHURST Angel Hotel ★ FOOD

Tel 01730 812421 **Fax 01730 815928** Map 11 A6 **B&B**
North Street Midhurst West Sussex GU29 9DN

Zzz...

Once a coaching inn dating back to the 16th century, the Angel is virtually plumb in the town centre. The plain white-painted Georgian facade gives no real indication of the warmth and welcome waiting within. Public rooms are largely centred around the two bars and restaurants with a relatively quiet residents' open lounge area at the front. Furnishings throughout are a mixture of well-maintained polished antiques, deep relaxing armchairs and settees with paintings and prints on the walls – the usual traditional trappings that befit a well-cared-for establishment such as this. Bedrooms, all on upper floors, are of a good size and comfortably appointed, offering all expected extras. Bathrooms are up-to-date and kept in good order, with all, except one, having showers over tubs. Four rear rooms, including newer suites overlook the ruins of Cowdray Castle in the distance. Diners have a choice of two eating places, both offering the same food: the brasserie area, adjacent to the bar, is rustic in style and less informal in character, while the dining-room, in contrast, is spacious and classically elegant with large, well-spaced tables. Prices are cheaper in the brasserie. Chef Andrew Stevenson, working in conjunction with owner Peter Crawford-Rolt, produces dishes as diverse as galantine of duck with a loganberry compote, a salad with lobster, avocado and mango, grilled Cornish monkfish with forest mushrooms and marinated chicken breast with polenta and aubergine relish. The fish is particularly good here, the style of cooking is eclectic and the execution of the dishes first-rate. Victorian walled garden. *Open 11-2.30, 6-11 (Sun 12-3, 7-10.30).* ***Bar Food*** *12-2.30, 6-10 (Sun to 9.30). Free House.* ***Beer*** *Gale's, guest beer. Garden.* ***Accommodation*** *21 bedrooms, all en suite, £75-150 (single from £69). Children welcome overnight, additional bed (£20) and cot (£10) available. No dogs. Access, Amex, Diners, Visa.*

We endeavour to be as up-to-date as possible but inevitably some changes to landlords, chefs and other key staff occur after the Guide has gone to press.

MILL GREEN — Viper — A

Tel 01277 352010 Map 11 B4
Mill Green nr Ingatestone Essex CM4 0PS

Surrounded by woodland and common land a few miles north of Ingatestone and the A12, the Viper is a popular, idyllically set little country pub (formerly two cottages), best enjoyed after a wander through the surrounding countryside. The charm of the environment is enhanced by a peaceful, large garden full of shrubs and flowers and the traditional, simply-furnished interior of the two small bars. A further draw is the choice of well-kept real ales. Simple snacks available lunchtime only. No children inside. *Open 11-2.30 (Sat 3), 6-11 (Sun 12-3, 7-10.30). Free House.* ***Beer*** *regularly-changing real ales. Garden. No credit cards.*

MILTON — Jolly Brewers — A

Tel 01223 860585 Map 10 B3
5 Fen Road Milton Cambridgeshire CB4 6AD

Painted cream and dark green, with a picket fence around the front garden, and with its roses and hanging baskets, from a distance the Jolly Brewers resembles a cottage. Located 1½ miles from the A45, in the old part of the village, it's appealingly unpretentious, with low-beamed ceilings, pine and darkwood tables, and jugs of fresh flowers in the two bars. The back garden has a slide and a swing. Children allowed in the bar to eat at weekend lunchtimes. The pub is said to "host a ghost". *Open 11.30-2.30 (Sat from 12), 6-11 (Sat from 7, Sun 12-3, 7-10.30).* ***Beer*** *Flowers IPA, Tetley, Bass. Garden, outdoor play area. No credit cards.*

MILTON ABBAS — Hambro Arms — FOOD

Tel 01258 880233 Map 14 B4 **B&B**
Milton Abbas nr Blandford Forum Dorset DT11 0BP

Crowning the top of this idyllic 'showpiece' village street lined with uniform thatched cottages and lawns is the attractive, long thatch of the 18th-century Hambro Arms. Most days, especially in summer, the attractively-furnished lounge and dining-room of this friendly inn are busy with people seeking refreshment after a visit to Milton Abbey or after climbing the long village street. Those who arrive early can appreciate, on fine days, the picturesque village view from one of the well-sited picnic benches to the front of the pub. Inside the lounge bar there is a comfortable collection of tables and chairs and two open fireplaces, one with woodburner, while the separate, livelier and rather spartan public bar houses a juke box and pool table. The choice of food runs from standard snacks to more substantial dishes such as their speciality pies – perhaps steak and mushroom or beef and oyster – a range of steaks and a selection of four vegetarian meals. More elaborate dishes are featured on the daily-changing blackboard, which regularly lists fresh fish from Weymouth and well-sauced meat dishes like pigeon breast en croute in a redcurrant and cognac sauce. Three-course Sunday lunch carvery. Upstairs, overlooking the village street, are two pretty, individually-decorated bedrooms. Floral, chintzy fabrics abound with matching curtains and bedcovers and as well as the usual comforts of TVs, clock-radios and tea-makers there are thoughtful extras like a stocked mini-fridge, fresh flowers, pot pourri and biscuits. En-suite bathrooms are well equipped with showers, baths and good toiletries. A further two en-suite rooms are available in a village house a few miles away. No children in accommodation or pub. Greenalls. *Open 11-3, 6.30-11 (Sun 12-3, 7-10.30).* ***Bar Food*** *12-2, 7-9.30 (Sat to 10, Sun to 8.30).* ***Beer*** *Flowers Original, Boddingtons. Patio, outdoor eating area.* ***Accommodation*** *2 bedrooms, both en suite, £50 (single £30). No children overnight. Check-in by arrangement. No dogs. Access, Visa.*

MITHIAN — Miners Arms — FOOD

Tel 01872 552375 Map 12 B3
Mithian nr St Agnes Cornwall TR5 0QU

Ancient inn located in a picturesque village and only a mile or so from the bustling beaches of the north coast. Built in 1577, the inn is delightfully unspoilt and typically Cornish in character for it retains its traditional layout, featuring low ceilings, wonky walls, woodblock floors and an open fire in the main bar. A cosy lounge displays a genuine Elizabethan ceiling frieze, half wood-panelled walls and shelves full of books, bottles and interesting ornaments. Also of note is the fascinating wall painting of Elizabeth I and the penance cupboard which

at one time had a beautifully carved mahogany seat. The cellar bar is ideal for families and leads out into the sheltered garden. Bar food choices are limited to a short printed menu and a few daily specials, but what is on offer is good and mostly home-made. Local crab is used in preparing the crab bake which is served with walnut and dill bread, and soups are freshly prepared. Main-course dishes include a chunky steak and kidney pie accompanied by fresh vegetables or salad, beef curry and good ploughman's lunches. Specials may range from green-lipped mussels to lamb and apricot casserole. Attractive front cobbled terrace with picnic benches. *Open 12-3, 6.30-11 (Sun 12-3, 7-10.30).* ***Bar Food*** *12-3, 6.45-9.30.* ***Beer*** *Marston's Pedigree, Boddingtons. Garden, outdoor eating area. No credit cards.*

MOLESWORTH — Cross Keys — B&B

Tel 01832 710283 Map 7 E4
Molesworth nr Huntingdon Cambridgeshire PE18 0QF

Skittles, darts and pool are all enjoyed by the locals at this unpretentious, 200-year-old pub which has a relaxed and friendly atmosphere. The bedrooms are warm, quiet and comfortable. All rooms offer en-suite bathrooms (bath and shower), TVs, direct-dial phones and tea-makers. An adventure playground is under construction. *Open 11-3, 6-11 (Sun 12-3, 7-10.30). Free House.* ***Beer*** *Bateman's XB, Flowers Best, McEwan's Export, guest beer. Garden.* ***Accommodation*** *10 bedrooms, all en suite, £36.50 (single £23.25). Children welcome overnight (rate depends on age), additional bed and cot available. Access, Visa.*

MONKSILVER — Notley Arms — ★ — FOOD

Tel 01984 656217 Map 13 E2
Monksilver Taunton Somerset TA4 4JB

☺

Sarah and Alistair Cade run their white-painted roadside village pub with inimitable flair and have built up a formidably good reputation. The interior is charmingly simple: an L-shaped bar with plain wooden furniture, black and white timbered walls, candles at night, and twin wood-burning stoves; a small but bright and cheery family room leads off, and there's a stream at the bottom of the trim, cottagey garden. The big attraction here, though, is the bar food, which roughly divides into three categories – the traditional, the Eastern or exotic, and the vegetarian – all given equal thought, using the finest fresh ingredients and cooked with sure-handed skill. Old favourites and four or five daily hot specials are chalked up on the blackboard: start with an excellent home-made soup, like a well-balanced, tasty tomato and fresh plum or carrot and caraway soup (served with French-flour bread).
For a light but satisfying lunch, choose one of the delicious pitta bread sandwiches with garlic butter, tender meats and good crispy salad. Chinese red roast pork features well-marinated cubes of meat in a soy, five spice and hoi sin sauce, with stir-fried pimento and courgette. The fresh salmon and spinach strudel, old-fashioned lamb casserole with onion dumplings, home-made fresh pasta dishes, bacon, leek and cider suet pudding and spicy courgette kofta are equally fine, as are puddings, with light pastry and good local cream. Try the lemon and cottage cheese cheesecake, apricot bread-and-butter pudding or treacle tart, or a locally-made ice cream. A few more restaurant dishes like steaks and trout are added to the evening menu. Despite the crowds at peak times, all runs effortlessly smoothly and with good humour. *Open 11.30-2.30, 6.30-11 (Sun 12-2.30, 7-10.30). Closed 2 weeks end Jan-early Feb.* ***Bar Food*** *12-2 (Sun to 1.45), 7-9.30 (Sun to 9). Free House.* ***Beer*** *Exmoor Ale, Morland Old Speckled Hen, Ushers Best, Wadworth 6X. Riverside garden, outdoor eating. Family room. No credit cards.*

MONTACUTE — King's Arms Inn — FOOD — B&B

Tel 01935 822513 **Fax 01935 826549** Map 13 F2
Montacute Somerset TA15 6UU

Zzz...

A 16th-century hamstone inn that was once an ale-house owned by the abbey situated in a very picturesque and unspoilt village. Today's comfortable little inn, now run by enthusiastic new licensees, has a relaxing lounge (Windsor Room) with deep sofas and the popular Pickwick Bar. The latter features a log fire in winter, real ales and has a much sought-after window seat with village views. Both the bar and adjacent new seating area fill up quickly at lunchtimes with Montacute House (NT) visitors in search a good bar meal. Beyond the help-yourself buffet and filled baguettes (lunch only), new chef Graham Page prepares a reliable and varied range of dishes that are listed on a seasonally-changing menu: fish soup, grilled sardines with a herb butter, smoked salmon and cream cheese omelette and trout and watercress fishcakes with a tomato sauce. Blackboard specials highlight fresh fish.

Characterful and comfortable accommodation is in thirteen en-suite (bath and shower) bedrooms, especially in the well-appointed executive rooms which have dark mahogany furnishings and attractive fabrics; one room boasts an elegant four-poster. Follow a peaceful night with a walk on the National Trust's wooded St Michael's Hill behind the hotel. *Open 11.30-2.30, 6-11 (Sun 12-3, 7-10.30). **Bar Food** 12-2, 7-9.30. Free House. **Beer** Bass, Wadworth 6X. Garden. **Accommodation** 13 bedrooms, all en suite, £69/£75 (single (£49/£55). Children welcome overnight, additional bed (£7) and cot available. No dogs. Access, Amex, Visa.*

MORETON-IN-MARSH Redesdale Arms B&B

Tel 01608 650308 Fax 01608 651843 Map 14a A1
High Street Moreton-in-Marsh Gloucestershire GL56 0AW

Flagstone floors, some old pine panelling and exposed stonework and a real log fire in winter give character to the bars at this brewery-owned former coaching inn on the main street of town. There's also a small rattan-furnished conservatory to the rear. Bedrooms offer all the usual amenities plus carpeted, en-suite bathrooms, all with shower over the tub. Part of Greenalls' Premier House group. *Open 11-11 (Sun 12-3, 7-10.30). **Beer** Bass, Boddingtons, guest beer. Family Room. **Accommodation** 17 bedrooms, all en suite, £39.50 (family £69), breakfast charged extra. Children welcome overnight (under-10s stay free in parents' room), cot available. Access, Amex, Diners, Visa.*

MORETONHAMPSTEAD White Hart Hotel B&B

Tel 01647 440406 Fax 01647 440565 Map 13 D2
The Square Moretonhampstead Devon TQ13 8NF

A fine, traditional 400-year-old inn, formerly a Georgian posting house, set in the heart of a village on the edge of Dartmoor. The oak-beamed bar, where an open fire adds its cheery glow, houses all sorts of copper and brass bric-a-brac, and there is a comfortable lounge. TVs, radios and phones are provided in the spotless bedrooms, which are comfortably furnished in old-fashioned style; all of the rooms have private facilities that include power showers. There are 15 golf courses within 30 miles, plus fishing on the Teign and marvellous walks in Dartmoor National Park. Unfortunately, the likeable long-serving landlord, Peter Morgan, who made this one of the friendliest inns in the area, was planning to retire from the business as we went to press. *Open 11-11 (Sun 12-3, 7-10.30). Free House. **Beer** Boddingtons, Bass, Smiles. Family room. **Accommodation** 20 bedrooms, all en suite, £63 (single £43). No children under 10. Garden. Access, Amex, Diners, Visa.*

MORWENSTOW Bush Inn A

Tel 01288 331242 Map 12 C2
Morwenstow nr Bude Cornwall EX23 9SR

Set in an isolated cliff-top hamlet close to bracing coastal path walks, the simple, traditional and very unspoilt Bush makes an ideal resting place. Once a monastic resting house on the pilgrim route between Spain and Wales, it is reputed to be one of the oldest pubs in Britain with parts dating back to 950 when it was a hermit's cell. Further evidence of its antiquity is the Celtic piscina carved from serpentine stone and set into one wall of the bar. Flagged floors, ancient built-in settles, old stone fireplaces and rustic furnishings characterise the charming interior that is thankfully devoid of intrusive games and music. No children indoors. No dogs. Signposted off A39 at Crimp. *Open 12-3, 7-11 (Sun 12-3, 7-10.30). Closed Mon Oct-Apr (except Bank Hols). **Beer** St Austell HSD. No credit cards.*

MOTCOMBE Coppleridge Inn FOOD

Tel 01747 851980 Fax 01747 851858 Map 14 B3 **B&B**
Motcombe Shaftesbury Dorset SP7 9HW

Zzz...

The Coppleridge Inn is a splendid example of how to convert an 18th-century farmhouse and its adjoining farm buildings into a successful all-round inn. Set in 15 acres of meadow, woodland and gardens it enjoys a lofty position with far-reaching views across the Blackmore Vale. The old farmhouse forms the nucleus of the operation, comprising a welcoming bar with stripped pine tables, attractive prints and a small gallery with seating. There's a comfortable lounge with flagstoned floor and inglenook fireplace and a delightful light and airy restaurant with open country views. In the bar a comprehensive blackboard menu lists the daily selection of reliable home-cooked dishes that are on offer. Begin with a good choice of soups – perhaps carrot and coriander or celery and Stilton – or artichoke with lemon mayonnaise and smoked trout paté, followed by an interesting and varied range

of main courses, such as John Dory in Cambozola sauce, lamb rogan josh, venison and wild mushrooms in red wine, or haddock and mushroom gratin. Home-made pizzas are a speciality on Tuesday and Friday nights. Across the lawned courtyard are ten well-appointed, en-suite bedrooms, all superbly incorporated into the single-storey old barns. Tasteful, attractive fabrics, pine furniture, mini-bar, TV, telephone, radio, sparkling clean bathrooms with bidet and rural views characterise these comfortable rooms. Also part of the complex is a hair salon and a magnificent barn that has been converted into a conference and function room. *Open 11-11 (Sun 12-3, 7-10.30).* ***Bar Food*** *12-2.30, 6-10.30 (Sun 12.2.30, 7-10). Free House.* ***Beer*** *Butcombe Bitter, Brakspear Best, guest beer. Garden, outdoor eating area. Children's play area.* ***Accommodation*** *10 bedrooms, all en suite, £70 (single £40). Access, Amex, Diners, Visa.*

MOULSOE Carrington Arms FOOD

Tel 01908 218050 **Fax 01908 217850** Map 15a E1 **B&B**

Cranfield Road Moulsoe nr Newport Pagnell Buckinghamshire MK16 0HB

Edwin and Trudy Cheeseman previously ran *The Black Horse* in nearby Woburn (recommended in this Guide last year, but no longer so) until the end of 1994, when they sold up and moved to this lovely old Grade II listed building with leaded windows, bringing their most original 'cooking in view'concept with them. They opened up the interior, transferred the front door to the back and installed a custom-made chef's grill and refrigerated food display cabinet at one end. Very much an informal dining pub (no bookings except for business lunches), the open-to-view food concept is definitely the main attraction: plain or marinated Aberdeen Angus steaks and fresh seafood – perhaps sea bass, tilapia, salmon, parrot fish, red mullet, halibut and tiger prawns – are all invitingly laid out for you to make your choice; live lobsters and duck breasts marinated in gin and chili might also be on offer. Both fish and meat are sold by the ounce, so you can choose your cut and portion size as well as style of cooking, which is either flame-grilling, steaming or smoking (hot-smoked salmon is worth waiting for). Jacket potatoes or gooey, garlicky potatoes and a small salad are the only accompaniments, although an excellent dish of wild mushrooms cooked with bacon and garlic can be shared between diners. The oyster bar – Edwin will tempt you with just one oyster if you've never sampled them – is a most unusual pub attraction, admirably complemented by a selection of chilled vodkas (try a shot of Absolut pepper vodka with your bivalves!). Caramelised onion soup topped with Gruyère cheese, authentic Thai 'po thak' fisherman's stewpot, red beef and green chicken Thai curries, dressed Cromer crab salad, Brie and apple omelette, hot Scotch kipper fillet roll with orange chutney and ploughman's lunches complete the savoury picture, with the likes of excellent individual caramelised rice pudding, bread-and-butter with orange pudding, and Bakewell tart with custard to finish. To the rear of building is a block of eight small bedrooms decorated in straightforward, cottagey style with pine fittings and en-suite bathrooms. The bedrooms lead directly out on to the orchard-like back garden – possibly bad news on busy summer evenings but a boon for parents who can sit in a deck chair outside their bedroom door with a pint in hand while the offspring head off to the Land of Nod inside. The fact that this is no ordinary pub is exemplified by the interesting New World house wines and the tiny Gents, where a carpet graces the floor and where both stencilling and Thelwell prints adorn the walls. Now this is what we call a welcome motorway break: really good, proper food and budget-priced, modest accommodation in a quiet, straggling village setting, just one mile from Junction 14 of M1 via A509. Winner of our 1996 Newcomer of the Year Award. *Open 11-2.30, 6-11, Sun 12-3, 7-10.30.* ***Bar Food*** *12-2, 6-10, Sun 12-2.30, 7-9.30. Free House.* ***Beer*** *Charles Wells Eagle IPA, three guest beers. Garden.* ***Accommodation*** *8 rooms, all en suite, £35 (double or single). Children welcome overnight, extra bed and cot provided. Check-in by arrangement. No dogs. Access, Amex, Diners, Visa.*

MOULTON Black Bull Inn FOOD

Tel 01325 377289 Map 5 E3

Moulton nr Richmond North Yorkshire DL10 6QJ

A mile south of Scotch Corner, this usually very busy retreat from the A1 is as popular as ever for its bar food. The lunchtime meals venue is the characterful, relaxing bar, warmed by a roaring fire in winter. Light meals include Welsh rarebit and bacon, various sandwiches, home-made soup, seafood pancake and spare ribs. The attractive Conservatory (complete with huge grapevine) and one of the original Pullman carriages, vintage 1932, from the Brighton Belle and the adjacent Seafood Bar open for the evening trade, when the pub becomes a fish and seafood restaurant proper, serving shellfish from the west coast of Scotland and seafood from the east coast of England. The Black Bull pub and restaurant's reputation, nurtured by the Pagendam family for over 30 years, extends far beyond North Yorkshire and is also recommended in our *1996 Hotels & Restaurants Guide*. Not suitable

for children under 7. *Open 12-2.30, 6-11 (Sun 12-3). Closed Sun eve.* ***Bar Food*** *12-2 (except Sun). Free House.* ***Beer*** *Theakston Best, Tetley. Patio/terrace, outdoor eating. Access, Amex, Visa.*

MOUSEHOLE — Ship Inn — B&B

Tel 01736 731234 Map 12 A4
Mousehole Penzance Cornwall TR19 6QX

Delightfully unassuming little fishing pub, set by the harbour in this beautiful coastal village of pretty fisherman's cottages and attractive narrow alleyways. The plain stone facade shields a most characterful interior, which retains much of its original rustic charm with heavy black beams and panelling, granite floors, built-in wooden wall benches and, as one might expect, a nautical theme pervades the bars. Busy harbour scenes and the panorama over Mount's Bay can be appreciated by residents from two of the three homely bedrooms. Simply furnished and decorated with pastel shades and matching floral fabrics, all have en-suite shower rooms, TV, hairdryer and tea-making facilities. The relaxing window seats and views make up for the basic facilities in the room. A small sun-trap terrace overlooks the village rooftops. *Open 10.30-11 (Sun 12-3, 7-10.30).* ***Beer*** *St Austell. Terrace, outdoor eating. Family room.* ***Accommodation*** *3 bedrooms, all en suite, £40 (single £20). No credit cards.*

MUCH WENLOCK — Wenlock Edge Inn — FOOD — B&B

Tel 01746 785403 Map 6 B4
Hilltop nr Much Wenlock Shropshire TF3 6DJ

Zzz...

The somewhat austere look of this stone roadside pub on the B4371 belies the warmth of welcome you'll find inside. To find it, follow the road a good four miles up the edge from Much Wenlock and into the National Trust Park; from the large car park opposite is a pathway to the spectacular observation point at Ippikins Rock. Home to the Warnig family for over ten years now, its reputation as one of the area's friendliest hostelries is well deserved – and that's not as tall a story as some of those told at the monthly 'story-telling-Monday' gatherings. The menu, like the landlord, is on the chatty side with winter's popular 'wedgie pie', 'oink and apple' or locally-farmed venison casserole giving way to such summery delights as tomato and red pepper soup, fresh salmon and leek flan and smoked chicken and broccoli gratin. Stephen Warnig plays host from the bar, breaking the ice between diners who are virtually rubbing shoulders at closely-packed tables and insistently urging follow-up portions of treacle tart and chocolate chimney, or perhaps the hot tipsy bananas. Demand for overnight accommodation is constant from talkers and walkers, conservationists and conversationalists who, when the babble dies down, are assured of a quiet night's sleep. All three bedrooms are smart and comfortable, with pine furniture and plenty of thick winter bedding; they have en-suite WCs and pressure showers supplied from the pub's own spring. Detached from the pub proper, the cottage room is the most spacious, with a convenient hallway to house walkers' boots and canine companions. A hearty breakfast here is de rigueur. *Open 11.30-2.30, 6.30-11 (Sun 12-2.30, 7-10.30). Closed Mon lunchtime (except Bank Holidays).* ***Bar Food*** *12-2, 7-9 (no food Monday). Free House.* ***Beer*** *Hobsons Best & Town Crier, Webster's Yorkshire. Garden, outdoor eating.* ***Accommodation*** *4 bedrooms, all en suite, £55 (single £40). No children under 8 overnight. No dogs. Access, Visa.*

MYLOR BRIDGE — Pandora Inn — FOOD

Tel 01326 372678 Map 12 B3
Restronguet Creek Mylor Bridge nr Falmouth Cornwall TR11 5ST

Yachtsmen are welcome to moor their craft at the end of the 140ft pontoon that extends out into the creek from this superbly sited and most attractive thatched 13th-century building – one of Cornwall's best-known inns. Although a boat is by far the easiest way to approach this creek-side inn, it lies at the end of a series of narrow lanes off the A39 (from which it is signposted) and it is advisable to arrive early as the car park soon fills to capacity on fine days. Named after the naval ship sent to Tahiti to capture the mutineers of Captain Bligh's Bounty, the Pandora retains its unspoilt traditional layout and boasts low wooden ceilings, wall panelling, flagged floors, a good winter log fire, a black-painted kitchen range and many maritime mementoes. It is not only the pub's position, patio and pontoon that attract folk here; the range of bar food is unlikely to disappoint. Good fresh seafood and local fish is the main emphasis, with dishes like shell-on prawns, seafood platter,

Restronguet fish pie, moules marinière and local crab Thermidor. Puddings include home-made treacle tart, lemon meringue pie or apricot and almond Bakewell. Very popular are the hearty sandwiches, in particular the Pandora Club and chocolate spread (with chips!) for chocoholic children! Daily specials might be peppered steak in red wine casserole or ham, leek and pineapple au gratin. The Andrew Miller restaurant upstairs serves more imaginative dishes, especially fish, and enjoys peaceful river views. During the summer Cornish cream teas are served every afternoon in the bar or on sunny days out on the pontoon. Over a dozen wines served by the glass. *Open 11-11 (Sun 12-10.30) in summer, 12-2.30, 7-11 (Sun 12-3, 7-10.30) in winter. **Bar Food** 12-2.30 (to 2 in winter), 6.30-9.30 (Sun and in winter from 7). **Beer** St Austell. Creekside terrace, pontoon, outdoor eating. Access, Amex, Visa.*

Nassington — Black Horse Inn — FOOD

Tel 01780 782324 Map 7 E4
2 Fotheringhay Road Nassington Northamptonshire PE8 6QB

The white-painted Black Horse is a rather restaurant-style pub with a couple of dining-rooms, but drinkers can sit on stools at the bar counter (constructed from old oak doors reclaimed from Rufford Abbey) or in the pink, plush, beamed lounge area in front of an old stone fireplace; the latter may once have warmed Mary Queen of Scots as it was originally part of nearby Fotheringhay Castle. One can eat in any part of the pub from any part of the extensive menu that covers snacks (steak sandwich, home-made lasagne), appetisers (Camembert fritters, coquilles St Jacques), house specialities (magret of duck Montmorency, chicken zingara), fish dishes (lemon sole Normandie), vegetarian dishes (vegetable and cream cheese crumble, aubergine Margarita), steaks from the grill and puddings like a chocolate cup and sticky toffee pudding. Despite the large menu, supplemented by a blackboard of dishes of the day, everything is home-cooked by hard-working chef Darrell Belliveau, who must look forward to Sunday lunchtimes when the menu is limited to a traditional three-course roast lunch. There's a very pretty walled garden for summer eating and drinking. Watch out for the frequent theme nights and events. Now owned by the Old English Pub Company, but the kitchen output remains the same. *Open 12-2.30, 7-11 (Sun 12-3, 7-10.30). **Bar Food** 12-1.45, 7-9.45 (Sun to 9). Free House. **Beer** Bass, Tetley, guest beers. Garden, outdoor eating. Access, Visa.*

Needingworth — Pike & Eel — B&B

Tel 01480 463336 Map 10 B2
Needingworth nr St Ives Cambridgeshire PE17 3YW

Located at the end of a long and narrow country lane right on the banks of the River Great Ouse, adjacent to a marina, the Pike and Eel dates back to the 17th century. The present owner, John Stafferton, has been here over 20 years and in that time has gradually upgraded and enlarged the property. The whole place has a very homely, traditional atmosphere with polished, beaten copper tables in the huge, oak-beamed bar. Next door is a much smaller, quieter residents' lounge where there's a warming coal fire in the open fireplace in winter. Upstairs, there's a further residents' lounge. They are all decorated in an attractive and pretty style, some with old-fashioned pieces of furniture, all well co-ordinated. TVs and tea and coffee facilities are provided. Carpeted bathrooms are neat, modern and of a good size. *Open 11-11 (Sun 12-3, 7-10.30). Free House. **Beer** Bass, Greene King IPA, Young's Special, Ruddles County. Riverside garden. Family room. **Accommodation** 6 bedrooms, all en suite £55 (single £40). Children free under 2 years, additional bed (£15), cot available. Access, Amex, Visa.*

Nettlebed — White Hart — FOOD

Tel 01491 641245 **Fax 01491 641423** Map 15a D3
Nettlebed Oxfordshire RG9 5OD

The Worsdells have revived this 16th-century coaching inn on the A423. The red-brick exterior belies its age but once inside, old timbers, low beams and the creaking floor boards of the bedrooms tell of its history. In more recent times, the White Hart was the unofficial 'Mess' for nearby RAF Benson, with Douglas Bader a frequent visitor; scenes from the film of his wartime exploits, *Reach for the Sky*, were filmed here. Today, food is a major attraction with a seasonally-changing menu listing favourites like steak and kidney pudding, and a lunchtime snack menu offering club sandwiches, ploughman's lunches and omelettes. A blackboard highlights imaginative daily specials like smoked chicken and bacon on a creamy sauce served on a bed of pasta verde to start, followed by pan-fried breast of chicken with scallops and oyster mushrooms in a creamy curry sauce, or maybe lemon sole and prawn roulade. Separate, more sophisticated restaurant menu. Afternoon teas come with home-made scones and a beautifully moist fruit cake. Six characterful bedrooms offer good

cotton bedding, feather pillows and carpeted en-suite bath/shower rooms with large, soft bath-sheets. All rooms have remote-controlled TV and direct-dial phones plus extras like fresh fruit and a welcoming glass of sherry. Five of the six rooms face the road so some traffic noise is unavoidable despite the secondary glazing. A neat garden and patio to the rear make a good spot for summer drinking and eating. *Open 11-11, (Sun 12-10.30).* ***Bar Food** 12-2.30, 2-6 (afternoon tea), 6-10 (Sun 7-9.30).* ***Beer** Brakspear. Garden, outdoor eating. Family room.* ***Accommodation** 6 bedrooms, all en suite, from £69.50 (4-poster £79.50, single £49.50). Children welcome overnight, additional bed available by prior arrangement. No dogs. Access, Visa.*

NETTLECOMBE — Marquis of Lorne — FOOD

Tel 01308 485236 **Fax 01308 485666** Map 13 F2  **B&B**

Nettlecombe nr Bridport Dorset DT6 3SY

Since taking over this modernised and extended 16th-century inn – set in an isolated rural position at the base of Eggardon Hill – Ian and Anne Barrett have successfully reversed the inn's fortunes after a period of closure. Comfortably refurbished bar areas, named after local hills, have access to the extensive and well-maintained garden (with children's play area) and enjoy beautiful valley views across Powerstock village. Reliable, unpretentious home-cooked pub food can be found on the regularly-changing blackboard menu that serves the whole pub. Wintertime favourites include decent pies – beef, Guinness and Stilton, lamb and apricot – and game casserole, while summer salads accompany fresh crab, smoked platter and vegetable and asparagus slice. Other notable dishes include freshly-battered cod and chips and the Marquis mixed grill. Good soups, crisp vegetables and home-made puddings. Improvements extend upstairs into the six comfortable, light and airy bedrooms, all of which have spotless shower rooms. Newly-refurbished rooms feature smart, modern pine furnishings, while others are kitted out, at present, with more functional furniture; all have remote-controlled TVs, telephones, hairdryers and beverage-making facilities. Most enjoy splendid views across unspoilt Dorset countryside. Best reached from the A3066 north of Bridport (5 miles), by following signs for West Milton and Powerstock along narrow country lanes. *Open 11-2.30, 6-11 (winter from 6.30, Sun 12-3, 7-10.30).* ***Bar Food** 12-2, 7-9.30.* ***Beer** Palmers BB, IPA, 200 Ale & Tally Ho! Garden, children's play area. Family room.* ***Accommodation** 6 bedrooms, all en suite, £55 (single £30). Access, Visa.*

> We do not accept free meals or hospitality – our inspectors pay their own bills and never book in the name of Egon Ronay's Guides.

NEW YORK — Shiremoor House Farm — FOOD

Tel 0191-257 6302 Map 5 E2

Middle Engine Lane New York Newcastle-on-Tyne Tyne & Wear NE29 8D2

The Fitzgerald group discovered and restored this former set of derelict farmhouse buildings to which they felt they could attract a discerning clientele of pub-goers. Shiremoor remains unique, its circular gin-gang (a kind of horse-powered threshing machine) forming the back drop to a bar from which radiates a succession of eating areas, carefully broken up by upturned barrels, easy chairs and an assortment of Britannia and scrubbed pine tables.

To a degree, out-and-out quality is subordinated to the demands of sheer volume, but there remains no doubt as to the value for money. A daily "sizzle dish", perhaps julienne of beef with hoi sin sauce, beef stroganoff and rice and cod with tarragon and lemon sauce amply illustrate the point. For vegetarians, Oriental mushrooms and rice, and for children small portions of virtually anything (in addition to fish fingers on request) cover almost any family's options. Outdoors are picnic tables on the patios, a wooden pill-box seat for the hardy on windy days, and plenty of safe space, albeit without play equipment, for roaming about in. *Open 11-11 (Sun 12-10.30)* ***Bar Food** 12-2.30, 6-9 (Sat 12-9, Sun 12-9). Free House.* ***Beer** Theakston Best & Old Peculiar, Stones Best, Black Sheep Special, Mordue Workie Ticket, Jennings Cumberland, various guest beers. Outdoor eating on the terrace. Family Room. Access, Amex, Visa.*

NEWCASTLE-ON-TYNE Cooperage A

Tel 0191 232 8286 Map 5 E2

32 The Close Quayside Newcastle-on-Tyne Tyne and Wear NE1 3RF

Arguably the oldest pub in town, the timber-framed former brewery teeters roadside by the "Long Stairs" on Newcastle's famed waterfront, where a succession of high-and lower-level bridges criss-cross the Tyne. For real ale buffs a single bar merits attention, resting on halved wooden kilderkins and bedecked with pewter and pottery mugs. Up to seven beers and two draught ciders are on tap at any one time. 5 miles from A194. *Open 11-11 (12-3, 7-10.30 Sun). Free House. **Beer** Tetley Best, Burton Ale, Marston's Owd Roger, Cooperage Best, weekly-changing guest beers. Access, Visa.*

NEWNHAM George Inn FOOD

Tel 01795 890237 Map 11 C5

Newnham nr Faversham Kent ME9 0LL

Fine rugs on polished wood floors, exposed beams, open fires, evening candlelight, tasteful prints, pretty flowers and a piano are a sample of the civilised ingredients at this lovingly cared for 16th-century tile-hung village pub. The food is always imaginative and varied, and takes over the whole interior at mealtimes, as there's no separate dining or restaurant area. All needs are satisfied with the regular menu listing popular lunchtime favourites from ploughman's lunches and sandwiches to interesting salads, decent pies – steak and kidney – and pasta dishes. More substantial choices include a range of steaks, rack of lamb with rosemary and salmon fillet bonne femme. Beyond this is a short, hand-written list of impressive daily-changing specials. Inventive dishes using game according to season, and fresh local produce may include warm salad of duck breast with walnut oil dressing and leek and goat's cheese tartlet to start, followed by pot-roast shoulder of lamb with apricot stuffing, local rabbit in filo, pan-fried pork fillet with cream and asparagus and fish brochette with piquant sauce. Good accompanying vegetables. Unusual vegetarian choices range from aduki bean and chestnut loaf to almond and aubergine fritters with creamy mint sauce. Puddings include rhubarb crumble, pecan and maple syrup pie and chocolate roulade. Large, peaceful garden backing on to sheep pastures. A new chef has recently taken over; the style of cooking is expected to remain the same and, hopefully, so will the quality. *Open 10.30-3, 6-11 (Sun 12-3, 7-10.30). **Bar Food** 12-2, 7.30-10 (No bar food D Sun and all day Mon). **Beer** Shepherd Neame. Garden, outdoor eating area. No credit cards.*

NEWTON Queen's Head FOOD

Tel 01223 870436 Map 15 F1

Newton nr Cambridge Cambridgeshire CB2 5PG

For over thirty years now the Short family have owned and operated their tiny "fossilised" village pub which to this day resists change. Simple home-made soup served in earthenware mugs and sandwiches (good roast beef and smoked salmon) cut and filled to order in the tiny bar servery have achieved near cult status over the years, while the bitter, served direct from the cask, is a flat yet flavourful beer. Village tradition, preserved by skittles table and a dilapidated dart board, is echoed by pine settles, rickety chairs and old school benches. *Open 11.30-2.30, 6-11 (Sun 12-2, 7-10.30). **Bar Food** 12-2.15 (Sun to 1.30), 6.30-10 (Sun from 7). Free House. **Beer** Adnams Best, Broadside, Extra and Old Ale (winter). Outdoor eating. Family room. No credit cards.*

NEWTON Red Lion FOOD

Tel 01529 497256 Map 7 E3

Newton nr Sleaford Lincolnshire NG31 0EE

In a quiet hamlet tucked away off the A52, this is a civilised, neatly-kept pub with shaded rear garden and play area. Popular unchanging formula is the cold carvery/buffet of fish and carefully-cooked cold meats, from pink beef ribs on the bone to Lincolnshire sausages. Price depends on size of plate and the number of meats chosen; help yourself from a dozen or more accompanying salads. Popular hot roast carvery every Saturday evening and Sunday lunchtime, with home-cooked hot dishes, such as fisherman's hotpot, Newton hotpot (lamb casserole cooked in beer) and liver and onions featuring on the menu during the winter months. Limited choice of starters (soup, home-made paté, prawn cocktail) and an

ever-changing array of home-made desserts. Children's prices and eating areas; informal, easy-going atmosphere. *Open 11.30-3, 6-11 (Mon from 7, Sun 12-3, 7-10.30). Closed 25 Dec.* ***Bar Food*** *12-2, 7-10 (Sun to 9). Free House.* ***Beer*** *Bass, Bateman's XXXB, John Smith's. Garden, outdoor eating, children's play area. Family room. No credit cards.*

NEWTON-ON-OUSE Dawnay Arms A

Tel 01347 848345 Map 7 D1

Newton-on-Ouse nr York North Yorkshire YO6 2BR

Turn off the A19, 5 miles north of York, for this pretty village with its famous National Trust property at Beningbrough Hall and impressive black-and-white Grade II listed pub. Fronting a sloping garden down to the Ouse it comes into its own in summer with moorings for boating enthusiasts and large tiered patios for alfresco refreshment. Especially family-friendly, there's play equipment in the garden, cartoon children's menus for colouring, birthday parties and barbecues. *Open 11.30-3, 6.30-11 (12-3, 7-10.30 Sun). Free House.* ***Beer*** *John Smith's, Tetley, Theakston Best XB & Old Peculier. Garden, outdoor eating area. Family Room. Access, Visa.*

NEWTON ON THE MOOR Cook & Barker Inn FOOD B&B

Tel 01665 575234 Map 5 D2

Newton on the Moor Felton Morpeth Northumberland

Lynn & Phil Farmer's stone pub with a burgeoning reputation for food stands just off (and literally overlooking) the A1, 10 miles North of Morpeth. From its elevated position superb views of the Northumbrian coast are an added attraction for those who come to stay. Those who do not book for lunch had best come early, as ordering at the bar and finding an agreeable spot in the maze of rooms can create a log-jam. Nevertheless the kitchen copes manfully, working to a menu of gargantuan proportions that includes sandwiches and ploughman's lunches and is supplemented by the daily labour of blackboard specials. Adventurous flavourings are the kitchen's hallmark: vegetable soup with five spice, stir-fry beef with ginger and spring onions, cauliflower, broccoli and mushroom pepper pot, turkey casserole with black beans and wild rice and Oriental chicken with cashew nuts. Barring a small selection on the blackboard in the snug, meals at night go up a gear in price and complexity; all of which is classy enough to suggest that an overnight stay could be special. With its spa bath and romantic setting, the best of four new bedrooms certainly will not disappoint, and the rest aren't far behind with their en-suite baths and showers, TVs, beverage trays and trouser presses. *Open 11-3, 6-11 (Sun 12-3, 7-10.30).* ***Bar Food*** *12-2, 6-9. Free House.* ***Beer*** *Theakston Best, Younger's No 3, Boddingtons, Newcastle Exhibition, guest beer(s). Garden, outdoor eating. Family Room.* ***Accommodation*** *4 rooms, all en suite £65 (single £30). Children welcome overnight (free under 10). Cot and bedding available. Access, Amex, Visa.*

NEWTON ST CYRES Crown & Sceptre FOOD

Tel 01392 851278 Map 13 D2

Newton St Cyres nr Exeter Devon EX5 5DA

Alongside the A377 about two miles from Exeter, this simple roadside pub has in the past few years enjoyed a good local reputation for its food due to the presence of capable landlords Graham and Carolyn Wilson. The blackboard scripted menu lists generously-filled sandwiches like an Oak Special with ham and Cheddar cheese or Brunch – toasted wholemeal bread filled with herby sausages and a fried egg on top – as well as more substantial dishes such as cheesy aubergine bake, beef and stout stew or fresh fish from Brixham (perhaps grilled plaice with a herb sauce). Puddings might include an apple and honey crumble or a treacle and walnut tart served with clotted cream. Roast Sunday lunch. One bar, more for the locals, includes a pool table, and the garden (over a footbridge across a fenced-off, safe stream) has a tree house, swings, slides and climbing frame. *Open 11.30-2.30, 6-11 (Sun 12-3, 7-10.30).* ***Bar Food*** *12-2,7-9.* ***Beer*** *Bass, Boddingtons. Garden, riverside patio, outdoor eating, children's play area. Family room. No credit cards.*

We endeavour to be as up-to-date as possible but inevitably some changes to landlords, chefs and other key staff occur after the Guide has gone to press.

North Dalton — Star Inn — B&B

Tel 01377 217688 Map 7 E1

Warter Road North Dalton Humberside YO25 9UX

The Georgian Star sits right next to the village pond where the coach horses were watered at a stopping-off point on the old Minster Way. Inside, it has largely been remodelled in recent years with rough white plaster walls and exposed brick features in the cosy, welcoming bar and the creation of seven smart, comfortable bedrooms. All are of a good standard but vary a little; a couple have pine-boarded ceilings, one a splendid old brass bedstead; all have good solid wood furniture, neat, fully-tiled bathrooms – one with shower and WC only – direct-dial phone, remote-control TV and tea/coffee-making kit. *Open 11-3, 6-11 (Sun 12-3, 7-10.30). Free House.* ***Beer*** *John Smith's, guest beer. Garden, outdoor eating. Family room.* ***Accommodation*** *7 bedrooms, all en suite, £39.50 (single £29.50). No dogs. Access, Visa.*

North Newnton — Woodbridge Inn — ★ — FOOD — B&B

Tel & Fax 01980 630266 Map 14a A4

North Newnton nr Pewsey Wiltshire SN9 6JZ

Akin to a 20th-century staging post, with a warm welcome to every weary traveller extended all day, every day by landlords Lou and Terri Vertessy. As well as the abundant enthusiasm that has contributed so much to the rejuvenation of this pub, their commitment and imagination has brought to these parts some truly unusual pub food. Terry's worldwide experience in the kitchen leans towards the American Deep South for her fish Creole; Mexican food has become a hot favourite, represented by sizzling beef fajitas and spicy chicken chimichangas; from the Far East comes hoi sin yong yoke (Cantonese-style stir-fry lamb and vegetables in a hoi sin sauce with chili) and keong choong (ginger and peanut stir-fry beef). European offerings include Provençal pasta, Bretagne pork and Stilton chicken. Simpler bar food – sandwiches, steak and ale pie, woody vegetable pie, American-style burgers, Mexican burritos – are served all day, with the more serious restaurant fare (available throughout the pub) being served from 7pm. Daily blackboard specials may list navarin of lamb and broccoli and basil soup. Prospective weekend diners are advised to book; a self-contained back room is available for parties up to ten. The comfortable and well-cared-for bar has a polished wooden floor, an assortment of furniture and is decorated with decent prints, plates and pieces of china. The Vertessys have converted three neat and tidy bedrooms for guests' use, all with cottagey wallpapers and fabrics, freestanding darkwood or pine furniture and fresh flowers. One has en-suite facilities, the others share an acceptable bathroom. Situated by the A345 bridge over the Avon, one and a half miles north of Upavon, it has a huge, colourful riverside meadow garden, part of which is fenced off to create an eating area where children can also play. Four pétanque pistes; trout fishing can be organised on the River Avon. "Well-behaved children are always welcome" – but not dogs. *Open 11-11 (Sun 12-3, 7-10.30).* ***Bar Food*** *11-10.30 (Sun 12-2.30, 7-10).* ***Beer*** *Wadworth, guest beer. Garden, children's play area.* ***Accommodation*** *3 bedrooms, 1 en suite, £35 (single £30), not en suite £30 (single £25). Children welcome overnight (under-5s free if sharing parents' room), additional bed (£10), cot available.* ***Accommodation*** *closed 25 Dec. No dogs. Access, Amex, Diners, Visa.*

North Wootton — Crossways Inn — B&B

Tel 01749 890237 **Fax 01749 890476** Map 13 F1

North Wootton nr Shepton Mallet Somerset BA4 4EU

The Crossways Inn overlooks Glastonbury Tor across the historic Vale of Avalon. It is a modernised hotel enjoying a peaceful setting amidst lovely unspoilt countryside. Well-kept bedrooms are pleasantly decorated with floral fabrics and all have good thick carpets and duvets as well as hairdryers, trouser presses, TVs and tea-makers. Compact, modern en-suite (most with showers) facilities throughout. There is a small lounge for residents' use. Families are welcome, but there's no garden. *Open 11-3, 6-11 (Sun 12-3, 7-10.30). Free House.* ***Beer*** *Wadworth 6X, Bass, Toby, Boddingtons. Patio.* ***Accommodation*** *17 bedrooms, all en suite, £35 (single £25). Children welcome overnight (rate depends on age). Dogs by arrangement only. Access, Visa.*

North Wootton — Three Elms — B&B

Tel 01935 812881 Map 13 F2
North Wootton nr Sherborne Dorset DT9 5JW

Simple, old-fashioned local set beside the A3030 between Sherborne and Bishop's Caundle, and whose L-shaped bar was extended several years ago, creating a country coffee shop feel in one area and more pubby in the other. The focal point is landlord Howard Manning's collection of over 1000 die-cast model cars, gathered over the years. Added attractions include the range of nine real ales (local breweries are favoured) and the far-reaching views towards Bulbarrow Hill from the neat, lawned rear garden, complete with small play area. Three neat and tidy, cottagey bedrooms sport pretty wallpapers and fabrics, older-style pine furniture (including a four-poster bed) and numerous books and ornaments. All share an attractive bathroom, but, with the thoughtful addition of bathrobes behind each door, a midnight trip will not be an embarrassing exercise. "All well-behaved children welcome." *Open 11-2.30, 6.30-11 (Fri & Sat from 6, Sun 12-3, 7-10.30). Free House.* ***Beer*** *Fuller's London Pride, Boddingtons, Hop Back Summer Lightning, Butcombe, Shepherd Neame Spitfire, Smiles, guest beers. Garden, children's play area.* ***Accommodation*** *3 bedrooms, £35 (single £20). Children welcome overnight (under-3s stay free in parents' room), additional bed and cot available. Check-in by arrangement. Access, Visa.*

Northleach — Wheatsheaf Hotel — FOOD — B&B

Tel 01451 860244 **Fax 01451 861037** Map 14a A2
West End Northleach Gloucestershire GL54 3E2

Zzz...

Quietly situated in the celebrated Wood Town (just off the A429) is the Langs' people-friendly period coaching inn. Being family-run, it's family-orientated as well, with plenty of minor diversions for the young-at-heart in the bar while meals are ordered from a daily-changing, all-embracing menu. Sandwiches, salads, cheese ploughman's lunches, a handful of vegetarian options, hot croissant with smoked chicken and cream sauce, fresh cod in a light beer batter, baked Bibury trout with parsley and butter sauce show the style. As a base for walkers and Cotswold explorers, the Wheatsheaf offers bedrooms all individually furnished to a high standard; two have king-size beds, and while four of the en-suite bathrooms have wc/showers only, all the rooms have TV, beverage trays and dial-out phones. *Open 12-2.30, 6-11 (Sun 12-2.30, 7-10.30).* ***Bar Food*** *12-2, 6-8.45 (Sun 7-8.30). Free House.* ***Beer*** *Marston's Best & Pedigree.* ***Accommodation*** *10 rooms, all en suite £49/£52 (midweek) £52/£55 (weekends) (single £39 midweek only). No dogs. Garden. Access, Visa.*

Norton — Hundred House Hotel — FOOD — B&B

Tel 01952 730353 **Fax 01952 730355** Map 6 B4
Bridgnorth Road Norton nr Shifnal Shrophire TF11 9EE

In the old 'hundred' of Brimstree, alongside what is today the busy A442, there's an unbroken history of there being a hostelry at Norton since the 14th century. The thatched barn which separates the car park from the road was once the local court and remains of the old stocks and whipping post are still to be found there. The main, creeper-clad redbrick inn, of Georgian origin, stands in its own mature orchard and garden in which all-comers are invited to wander at their leisure, and from which come the hand-dried flowers which hang from virtually every beam within the pub. All this is indicative of the personality Hundred House gains from the inimitable input of Henry and Sylvia Phillips and family (here since 1986). There's a particularly warm and intimate feel in the muted tones of the mellow-brick, tiled floors, stained-glass windows, colourful patchwork leather upholstery and festooned beams of the bar and dining areas, a setting to which the food has little trouble doing justice. Griddled black pudding and apple sauce and bruschetta with tapénade, dried tomatoes and basil typify the range of culinary skills and sources, while main courses may encompass salmon fish cakes with tomato and cumin sauce, spiced chicken and bacon salad with mint vinaigrette, sausage, mash and onion gravy, cassoulet of lamb and chorizo sausage and a savoury pancake of red peppers, mushrooms and coriander. To supplement both bar and à la carte menus, daily specials might include a ham and broccoli soup, ravioli of crayfish with coriander, roast saddle of hare with a summer fruits sauce and, to follow, perhaps a blueberry pie or iced prune and armagnac terrine from the usually excellent desserts – the "ultimate dessert" brings a selection all on one dish with fresh fruit and home-made ice

cream. Those seeking a lighter snack can order a ploughman's platter at lunchtime or in the evening. Both names and colour schemes in the enchanting bedrooms return to the garden for their inspiration, incorporating pastel shades, brass bedsteads with patchwork covers, cane rocking chairs and even padded swing seats suspended invitingly from the rafters. From fresh flowers and pot-pourri to cotton buds and heart-shaped pin cushions, virtually every conceivable extra is contrived to make guests feel fully at home in cosy and cossetting surroundings; two superior rooms are very large. Well-equipped en-suite facilities, all with bath, most with overhead showers. Throughout the day and evening there is room service of drinks and light snacks. *Open 11-3, 6-11 (Sun 12-3, 7-10.30).* ***Bar Food*** *12-2.30, 6-10 (7-9 Sun). Free House.* ***Beer*** *Phillips Heritage and Ailrics Old Ale, Ansells Dark Mild, Flowers Original, guest beer. Garden, outdoor eating.* ***Accommodation*** *10 bedrooms, all en suite, £69/£79/£88 (single £59-£69). Children welcome overnight, additional bed and cot available (children share parents' room free). Dogs by arrangement only. Access, Amex, Visa.*

NORTON ST PHILIP — George Inn — FOOD

Tel & Fax 01373 834224 Map 13 F1
Norton St Philip nr Bath Somerset BA3 6LH

Certainly one of the oldest licensed premises in the land, the George has been around since before liquor licenses were introduced! A Carthusian guest house since its first building in the 13th century, it has retained its present architectural features for over 700 years now. Surviving to this day are the massive Gothic doorway, sloping cobbled courtyard and unique timbered galleries. On 12th June 1668 Samuel Pepys and party dined here, while in June 1685 the Duke of Monmouth occupied the whole village for a week prior to his defeat at Sedgemoor. In this unique atmosphere, wonderfully steeped in history, landlords Andrew and Juliette Grubb have created a popular destination in which to sample good home-cooked meals listed on the reliable and varied bar menus. Dishes extend from good pub favourites, including filled baguettes (lunch only) and ploughman's lunches, to blackboard specials, for example smoked fish terrine, wild boar paté, smoked fish and prawn pancakes, vegetable quiche, pan-fried duck breast with plum sauce and smoked pork loin cutlets in a mango sauce, with main courses accompanied by a huge dish of fresh and crisp vegetables. Puddings include chocolate mousse, treacle tart and a light and dark chocolate terrine. *Open 11-3, 5.30-11 (Sun 12-3, 7-10.30).* ***Bar Food*** *12-2.30, 6.30-9.45 (Sun 7-9.30).* ***Beer*** *Bass, Wadworth 6X, Henry's IPA & Old Timer. Outdoor eating. Family Room. Access, Visa.*

NORWICH — Adam & Eve — A

Tel 01603 667423 Map 10 C1
Bishopsgate Norwich Norfolk NR3 2RZ

Historic old tavern – the oldest in the city – located along Palace Street close to the cathedral. Part 13th-century, it was built as a brewhouse to serve bread and ale to the workmen who built the cathedral, and later extended in the 14th and 15th centuries, with the addition of the Dutch gables which give this popular ale house a most unusual appearance. Reputedly haunted by the ghost of Lord Sheffield who was hacked to death here in 1549, the two bars and tiny snug feature ancient carved benches and high-backed settles built into part-panelled walls and old tiled floors. The lower bar is thought to be over 700 years old. Good summer drinking patio and a handy pay and display car park next door. *Open 11-11 (Sun 12-3, 7-10.30).* ***Beer*** *Morland Old Speckled Hen, Ruddles County, Wadworth 6X, John Smith's Bitter, Adnams Southwold, guest beer. Patio, outdoor eating area. Family room. No credit cards.*

NOSTERFIELD — Freemasons Arms — FOOD

Tel 01677 470548 Map 5 E4
Nosterfield Bedale North Yorkshire DL8 2QP

The low, white-painted row of cottages and barn sparkles within, adorned in front of a blazing log fire with a mish-mash of pub-associated artefacts from pewter pots to miners' lamps and horse-tack. To this was added a warmth of welcome and a confidence which suggests these young publicans know that they are going places. The food on offer here is very popular – booking advisable – its success based not on trying to be a restaurant but nebvertheless serving good food from fresh ingredients of a quality that would not go amiss in one. Alongside baked salmon with prawns and herb butter sauce and Thai beef with oyster sauce and egg fried rice diners will find the Freemasons mixed grill, steak pies and tagliatelle provençale. Herbs from the pub garden contribute to the freshly-made soups and

all the desserts and gateaux are home-made. A hand-picked list of wines is that, too, of an enthusiast, while both Theakston's and the irresistible Black Sheep Bitter are kept in fine condition in the rebuilt beer cellar. A new chef took over as we went to press. *Open 12-2, 6-11 (Mon 7-11 only) (Sun 12-2, 7-10.30). Free House.* ***Bar Food*** *12-2.30, 7-9 (no food Mon).* ***Beer*** *Theakston Best, Tetley, Black Sheep Bitter, guest beer. Access, Visa.*

NOTTINGHAM — Lincolnshire Poacher — A

Tel 0115 941 1584 Map 7 D3

161-163 Mansfield Road Nottingham Nottinghamshire NG1 3FR

A true pub-goer's "paraphernalia pub" is perhaps the best way to describe the former Old Gray Nag's Head, now leased by the Tynemill Group from brewers Bateman's. A large obituary to the hundreds (they say) of independents swallowed up by one major brewer is displayed above the bar, whilst an eminently more sensible arrangement with their current landlords enables a wide range of popular and little-known guest ales always to be on offer. Yet anyone out for a tasting needn't stop there, as nigh on six dozen whiskies and single malts (as well as a range of Continental bottled beers) are an open invitation to the connoisseur. *Open 11-3, 5-11 (Fri & Sat 11-11) (Sun 12-3, 7-10.30).* ***Beer*** *Bateman's Dark Mild, XB, Salem Porter, XXXB & Victory Ale, Bass, Marston's Pedigree, guest beers. Patio. No credit cards.*

NOTTINGHAM — Ye Olde Trip to Jerusalem — A

Tel 0115 947 3171 Map 7 D3

Brewhouse Yard Castle Road Nottingham Nottinghamshire NG1 6AD

Built into the caves at the foot of Nottingham Castle's wall and formerly its brewhouse, Ye Olde Trip to Jerusalem (known as the Pilgrim in the 18th century) has been a pub for 800 years – "the oldest inn in England", a habitual resting place for crusading knights on their way to outwit the heathen overseas. The present building is mainly 17th-century; the unique rock-face walls are most apparent in the spooky upstairs bar, which is opened only when the pub is busy. Downstairs has panelled walls, built-in cushioned settles, and exposed-rock alcoves; visitors' banknotes and coins litter the beams. In fine weather there are patios to the side and back, and extra seating in the cobbled yard opposite; souvenirs are available at the bar. No under-18s in the bar. *Open 11-11 (Sun 12-3, 7-10.30).* ***Beer*** *Hardys & Hansons Kimberley Best Bitter, Classic & Best Mild, Marston's Pedigree. Patio/terrace. Access, Amex, Visa.*

NUFFIELD — Crown — FOOD

Tel 01491 641335 Map 15a D3

Nuffield nr Henley-on-Thames Oxfordshire RG9 5SJ

Pleasantly refurbished pub with beams and inglenook, now a popular dining pub. Ann and Gerry Bean run it in a quietly civilised fashion and offer food that covers a range from mushroom and cashew nut paté to fine steak and kidney pie on their bi-monthly changing menu. Daily blackboard specials may include lime peppered chicken kebabs and Creole crab for starters, followed by grilled salmon fillet with black pepper and capers or couscous-filled aubergines with a yoghurt and coriander dressing. Lighter snacks like sandwiches and ploughman's lunches are always availabe. Good choice of homely puddings. Value-for-money house wines. No children in the evenings. *Open 11-2.30 (Sat to 3), 6-11, (Sun 12-3, 7-10.30).* ***Bar Food*** *12-2, 6.45-9.45 (Sun to 9.30).* ***Beer*** *Brakspear Bitter & Special, Boddingtons. Garden. Family room. No credit cards.*

NUNNEY — George at Nunney — B&B

Tel 01373 836458 **Fax 01373 836565** Map 13 F1

11 Church Street Nunney Somerset BA11 4LW

White-painted, street-fronting coaching inn, its sign stretched right over the road, opposite a brook and the 13th-century castle ruin in the centre of this picturesque village. Rambling and much modernised open-plan interior with winter log fire. Bedrooms of various shapes are modestly furnished, apart from the comfortable four-poster room. Some overlook the pretty walled garden, some the castle; all have private bath or shower, telephones, satellite TV, tea-makers and trouser presses. Functional overnight accommodation. *Open 12-3, 5-11 (winter from 6.30) (Sun 12-3, 7-10.30). Free House.* ***Beer*** *John Smith's, Exmoor Ale, Bass, Wadworth 6X. Garden, outdoor eating. Family room.* ***Accommodation*** *9 bedrooms, all en suite, £58 (single £42). Children welcome overnight, additional bed (£5) and cot (£2.50) available. Access, Visa.*

NUNNINGTON — Royal Oak — FOOD

Tel 01439 748271 Map 5 E4
Nunnington nr York North Yorkshire YO6 5US

A laid-back and friendly local with a food bias at the heart of the village, just up from a foot-bridge over the river Rye and hence a short walk from the National Trust's Nunnington Hall. Stone jugs and assorted farm implements hang from the beams while behind Tony's one-man bar are suspended the blackboards of best-bet specials which emanate from Bo Simpson's highly productive kitchen. Herb dumplings with steak and kidney and tasty garlic bread with a crumb-topped fisherman's pot are well-conceived variations on familiar themes; similarly chicken breasts are served with cheese and mustard sauce, and sweet and sour vegetables come in a crispy batter. Bright and crunchy accompanying salads can be enlivened to taste from the preferred relish tray. To follow are a good choice of puddings from rhubarb crumble to lemon mousse and tiramisu. A quiet dining-room extension is available for reserved tables (and families), though the same menus hold good throughout. Light classical favourites provide a popular and relaxing background to the general hubbub of appreciative diners. No children under 8 in the bar. *Open 11.45-2.30, 6.30-11 (Sun 12-3, 7-10.30). **Bar Food** 12-1.45, 6.30-9 (7-9 Sun). Free House. **Beer** Tetley, Burton Ale, Theakston Old Peculier. Access, Visa.*

NUNTON — Radnor Arms — FOOD

Tel 01722 329722 Map 14 C3
Nunton nr Salisbury Wiltshire SP5 4HS

This welcoming ivy-clad village pub dates from the 17th century and part of it once served as the village stores and post office. Locals come now for the well-kept ale and for the honest home-cooked selection of meals that are served in its low-ceilinged and simply-furnished main bar and neat, opened-out dining areas. Traditional lunchtime favourites, including ploughman's and sandwiches (also available in the evenings), can be found on the printed menu, while the changing blackboard menu advertises the lunch specials and evening choices. Fresh fish dishes and rib-eye steak are regulars on the board, which may also include smoked trout, herrings in Madeira, pork fillet with Stilton and mushrooms, and red bream fillet with a prawn and Pernod sauce. Treacle and walnut tart and home-made bread-and-butter pudding are popular puddings. The large rear garden has fine rural views, plenty of picnic benches and much to amuse energetic children. *Open 11-3, 6-11 (Sun 12-3, 7-10.30). **Bar Food** 12-2, 7-9.30. **Beer** Hall & Woodhouse Tanglefoot & Badger Best, Charles Wells Eagle IPA. Garden, outdoor eating, children's play area, disabled facilities. Family room. No credit cards.*

NUTHURST — Black Horse — A

Tel 01403 891272 Map 11 A6A
Nuthurst Street Nuthurst Horsham West Sussex RH13 6LH

Occupying an attractive row of 17th-century brick cottages, this charming pub was, unbelievably, a coaching inn on the old Brighton to Horsham road, now a quiet backwater off the A281 southeast of Horsham. Beyond the raised front terrace, hanging baskets and stripped pine doors lies a classic main bar featuring an old flagstoned floor, a huge inglenook with winter log fire, heavy beams and rustic pine furnishings. Character extends into the wooden floored snug bar and beamed dining-room with horse brasses, hunting prints and old photographs of local characters and village scenes. Good alfresco seating on the peaceful front terrace and in the sheltered rear garden complete with stream, shrubs and trees. Interesting local walks. *Open 11-3, 6-11 (Sun 12-3, 7-10.30). Free House. **Beer** Eldridge Pope Hardy Country, Adnams Southwold, King & Barnes Sussex, Wadworth 6X. Garden, front terrace and lawn, outdoor eating, tables in garden. Access, Visa.*

ODDINGTON — Horse & Groom Inn — B&B

Tel 01451 830584 Map 14a A1
Upper Oddington nr Moreton-in-Marsh Gloucestershire GL56 OXH

Zzz...

A typically picturesque Cotswold inn with a flagstoned interior, aglow in winter with real log fires and ablaze with summer colour in a sloping garden complete with ornamental pond and play area. Neatly-kept bedrooms give a taste of village life, unencumbered by intrusive phones. Of four in the eaves above the bar, one has a full bathroom; two bright bedrooms, with WC/showers only, are in former stables across the yard. New owners. *Open 11.30-2.30, 6-11 (Sun 12-3, 7-10.30). Free House. **Beer** Hook Norton Best, Wadworth*

6X, Courage Directors, John Smith's, guest beer. Garden, play area. Family room. ***Accommodation*** *7 bedrooms, all en suite, £50 (single £32.50). Children welcome overnight, (under 1s £5, 1-2s £10, 2-10s £15), additional bed and cot available. Check-in by arrangement. No dogs. Access, Visa.*

ODELL Bell FOOD

Tel 01234 720254 Map 15 E1
Horesfair Lane Odell Bedfordshire MK43 7AG

There's great virtue in being content with serving the very simplest of pub food when the circumstances demand it, and at the tiny Bell Inn they've got it just about right. From the front, it's a mellow-stone, thatched house, and the original two front rooms, connected by a single bar servery, can still be clearly seen. Round the back, a brick extension has brought a succession of little rooms at varying levels, their low tables and stools adding to the almost miniature feel of the place. Old beams and original mantels, framing a cast-iron range at one end, are hung with a collection of old brass beer taps; less traditional but rather more hygienic stainless steel engines are in active service now. Doreen Scott's stock-in-trade, in circumstances where the pub never appears less than full, is her single-dish flans of bacon vegetables or pissaladière and pizza, and omelettes which come with salad or chips or both, and appear designed to be eaten with fork only, in a confined space – which they are. Otherwise, there are cold platters, toasties and sandwiches (with commendable hand-sliced bread) and ploughman's lunches. Added to these is a section honestly labelled "deep-fried" for lovers of scampi and other such things, and a routine dessert list with boozy chocolate mousse, rhubarb fool and yokel pie. A blackboard menu also materialises, offering turkey and mushroom pie, seafood pasta or mango chicken casserole – positively prodigious output from space so confined. It gets extremely busy, overflowing on summer days on to the sunny patio and into the garden under trees down on the banks of the Great Ouse. *Open 11-2.30, 6-11 (Sun 12-3, 7-10.30).* ***Bar Food*** *12-2, 7-9.30 (Sun 7-9 in summer only).* ***Beer*** *Greene King, guest beer. Garden, outdoor eating. Family room. No credit cards.*

Many **B&B** establishments offer reduced rates for weekend and out-of-season bookings. Always ask about special deals for longer stays. Beware half-board terms in inns where we do not recommend the **FOOD.**

ODIHAM George Hotel B&B

Tel 01256 702081 **Fax 01256 704213** Map 15a D4
High Street Odiham nr Basingstoke Hampshire RG25 1LP

First granted a licence in 1540, the privately-owned George is one mile from M3 (J5). Main-house bedrooms (including two four-posters) have creaking floors and low beams, while rooms in the converted coach house and former barn are modern behind original exteriors. Accessories throughout are thoroughly modern, and all rooms have private bath/shower facilities. Farming artefacts decorate the flagstoned bar, while the residents' lounge features exposed stonework. *Open 11-11 (Sun 12-3, 7-10.30). Free House.* ***Beer*** *Courage Best & Directors, Wadworth 6X. Garden.* ***Accommodation*** *18 bedrooms, all en suite, £75/£90, (single £65) weekend reductions. Children welcome overnight (babies free in parents' room, otherwise under-14s £15), additional bed & cot available. Access, Amex, Diners, Visa.*

OLD AMERSHAM King's Arms A

Tel 01494 726333 **Fax 01494 433480** Map 15a E3
30 High Street Old Amersham Buckinghamshire HP7 0DJ

The jetty gables of the ancient black-and-white timbered King's Arms overlook the broad high street of this attractive old market town. Dating back to the 15th century it is one of the oldest pubs in England and a mellow atmosphere fills the main bar that retains much of its original character. A wealth of beams, standing timbers, tiny alcoves, two huge inglenook fireplaces and an assortment of settles and old furniture make it a fascinating pub to visit. There is a flower-filled courtyard and a sheltered lawn with seating. Cream teas are served from 3-5pm on summer Sundays. *Open 11am-11pm (Sun 12-3, 7-10.30). Free House.* ***Beer*** *Tetley, Benskins Bitter, Ind Coope Burton Ale, two guest beers. Garden. No credit cards.*

OLD DALBY — Crown Inn — FOOD

Tel 01664 823134 Map 7 D3
Debdale Hill Old Dalby nr Melton Mowbray Leicestershire LE14 3LF

Tucked away down a lane in the village centre, this 300-year-old converted farmhouse is today the home of some enjoyable, often ambitious cooking. Cosy, antique-furnished bars are the setting for the sampling of such home-made dishes as beef and oyster pie, duck breast with a mango and passion fruit and red wine jus, sweet and sour monkfish, salmon and asparagus ragout or ratatouille crumble, all of which may appear on the quarterly-changing menus. Local Colston Bassett Stilton features amongst a good choice of cheeses. Simpler snacks like sandwiches and ploughman's platters are available at both lunchtime and evening. Eat in either the restaurant or in the bar where there is a constantly-changing selection of draught bitters (up to 14) always available. A large, pleasant and secluded garden provides a haven for children and offers a terraced area for outdoor eating from which guests can watch regular games of pétanque organised by local enthusiasts. *Open 12-3, 6-11 (Sun 12-3, 7.10.30). **Bar Food** 12-2, 6-10 (except Sun eve). Free House. **Beer** up to 14 guest beers: Adnams, Marston's Pedigree, Hardys & Hansons Kimberley, Morland Old Speckled Hen, Greene King Abbot Ale, Bateman's XB & XXXB. Garden, outdoor eating. Family room. No credit cards.*

OLDBURY-ON-SEVERN — Anchor Inn — FOOD

Tel 01454 413331 Map 13 F1
Church Road Oldbury-on-Severn Avon BS12 1QA

The hamlet of Oldbury lies deep in the flatlands of the Severn estuary two miles west of Thornbury and just half a mile from the water's edge. Michael Dowdeswell's old pub has a flower-decked stone frontage, a brick-lined pine-furnished rear dining-room and extensive streamside garden where a game of boules in the orchard is known locally as "Petanchors". An extensive bar food menu, typed up each day, relies on fresh local produce and regular favourites include grilled Gloucestershire 'snorkers' sausages, an Oldbury 'Flat 'At' filled with roast beef and onion gravy, and sticky toffee pudding. The same menu serves in all locations with orders taken at the bar: note here the Bass and Theakston Old Peculier drawn from the cask as well as the traditional hand-pulled ales. Severn salmon baked with white wine sauce, or cold with salad, leads the more substantial main meals alongside chargrilled sirloin and spiced butterfly chicken breasts, and there are both vegetarian and meat curries, as well as a choice of ploughman's lunches. Good choice of at least 75 whiskies and plenty of wines, including ten served by the glass. Book for the dining-room. *Open 11.30-2.30, 6.30-11 (Sat from 6, Sun 12-3, 7-10.30). **Bar Food** 11.30-2 (Sun from 12), 6.30-9.30 (Sun from 7). Free House. **Beer** Bass, Butcombe, Marston's Pedigree, Fuller's London Pride, Worthington Best, Theakston's Best & Old Peculier. Garden, outdoor eating. Access, Visa.*

OMBERSLEY — King's Arms — FOOD

Tel 01905 620315 **Fax 01905 620145** Map 14 B1
Ombersley nr Droitwich Hereford & Worcester WR9 0EW

This wonderful, crooked-looking, black-and-white timbered inn sports thick, blackened oak beams hung with agricultural implements, gleaming brasses and polished copper pans that reflect the huge open fires in winter within its characterful bars. The Charles II and Devonshire lounges are predominantly designated for eating, with prompt service to your chosen table. From a single menu, the choice is wide, though more tried and trusted than bristling with novelty: home-made soup – tomato and basil – ploughman's lunches and sandwiches (lunch only, except Sunday), deep-fried Brie in sesame seeds, grilled green-lipped mussels; steak and kidney pie, turkey pasta bake and sirloin steaks; vegetarian options – three-cheese macaroni – and a reasonable line of home-made puddings, such as chocolate mousse and bread-and-butter pudding. Owing to its popularity, the pub is unsuitable for children under 8, and 8-16s are admitted for full meals only until 8.30. There is, however, a sheltered rear patio to accommodate the unsuspecting and the hardy. Just off the A449 between Worcester and Kidderminster. *Open 11-2.30, 5.30-11 (Sun 12-10.30). **Bar Food** 12.15-2.15 (Sun 12-10), 6-10. Free House. **Beer** Bass, Marston's Pedigree, Boddingtons. Terrace, outdoor eating. Access, Amex, Visa.*

ONECOTE — Jervis Arms — FOOD

Tel 01538 304206 **Fax 01538 304514** Map 6 C3
Onecote nr Leek Staffordshire ST13 7RU

On B5053 (off A523) and positioned just at the edge of the Peak National Park, the pub stands on one bank of the Hamps river – park on the opposite bank and cross a footbridge into the garden. While the picnic tables, play area and ducks are super, parents should be mindful of the littlest ones by this fast-flowing stream. Vegetarian and children's meals both feature prominently on the printed menu (curried nut, fruit and vegetable pie; egg, chips and beans) alongside pretty standard pub grub. A little more adventure emanates from the blackboard: peppered pork, chicken masala and beef Madras help spice things up a little. Adjacent to the pub is holiday accommodation in a converted barn. *Open 12-2.30 (Sat to 3), 7-11 (Sat from 6, Sun 12-10.30).* ***Bar Food*** *12-2, 7-10 (Sat from 6, Sun 12-10). Free House.* ***Beer*** *Theakston XB & Old Peculier, Bass, Marston's Pedigree, Ruddles County, Worthington Best, Tetley Mild. Riverside garden, children's play area. Closed 25 & 26 Dec. Family rooms. No credit cards.*

OSMOTHERLEY — Three Tuns — FOOD

Tel 01609 883301 Map 5 E3 **B&B**
Osmotherley nr Northallerton North Yorkshire DL6 3BN

The Dysons' deserved reputation for good food has resulted in the Three Tuns being referred to as "the Fish Pub". Choice is as diverse as the market allows: tempting platefuls of langoustines, moules or king scallops; reliably cooked sea bass and Dover soles, both plain or with classic sauces, served with crisp fresh vegetables and a personal bread board. Behind the single, oak-framed bar a quietly elegant dining-room is the popular place to enjoy the likes of non-aquatic alternatives such as Pig-in-a-Poke and roast glazed half-shoulder of lamb with Shrewsbury sauce. Customers in the bar needn't be the poorer cousins: smoked salmon and scrambled eggs and seafood Thermidor can be enjoyed as a snack and the equally popular doorstep sandwiches are knife-and-fork affairs. Home-made puddings range from lemon mousse and praline meringue to strawberry and whisky trifle and local Yorkshire cheeses. Service here may, however, be suspended as the dining-room fills up: booking essential at weekends. Upstairs under the eaves are three stylish, if compact, bedrooms; with en-suite facilities (two with showers only), teletext TVs, dial-out phones and stylish towelling bathrobes they have gained overnight popularity with a discerning business clientele. *Open 11-45-3, 6.45-11 (Sun 12-3, 7-10.30).* ***Bar Food*** *12-2.30, 7-9.30 (Sun 12-2 only). Free House.* ***Beer*** *Theakston Best, XB & Old Peculier, Younger's No 3, McEwan's Best. Garden, outdoor eating area.* ***Accommodation*** *3 bedrooms, all en suite, £55 (single £40). Children welcome overnight (extra bed available if sharing with parents). Access, Visa.*

OVER HADDON — Lathkil Hotel — FOOD

Tel 01629 812501 Map 6 C2 **B&B**
Over Haddon nr Bakewell Derbyshire DE45 1JE

The Lathkil scores with its unparalleled views of the Peak National Park and spectacular Lathkil Dale several hundred feet below. Signposted from the B5055 White Peak scenic route, just two miles from Bakewell, it's been a pub since 1813 or earlier and extensions in the 1930s created a Victorian-style bar whose use of miniature-sized tables and chairs gives an illusion of space; there's also a post-war dining-room extension with huge picture windows for making the most of the view. Lunch is served buffet-style from a hot and cold counter to the rear, with standard bar food including soup, paté, filled cob rolls, steak and kidney pie and quiche. Dinner à la carte (for residents only on Sunday evening) produces melon with prawns and Marie Rose sauce, fish soup, chicken stuffed with leek in Stilton sauce, or spinach and ricotta canneloni. Puddings are home-made and frequently change at peak times, cheesecake and treacle tart perhaps giving way to fruit crumble, Bakewell pudding or lemon meringue pie. Four bedrooms with en-suite bathrooms (one a single with shower only) may be limited in space but are comprehensive in facilities: all have TV, clock radio and a personal bar and fridge. The best two, at the front, look across the dale to Youlgrave and the original village of Nether Haddon, now part of the Haddon estate. *Open 11.30-3, 6.30-11 (Sun 12-3, 7-10.30).* ***Bar Food*** *12-2, Mon-Thur 7-9 (Fri & Sat restaurant only). Free House.* ***Beer*** *Wards Best, Thorne Best & Mild. Patio, outdoor eating. Family room (lunchtimes only).* ***Accommodation*** *4 bedrooms, all en suite, £60 (single £32.50). Children welcome overnight (rate depends on age). Check-in by arrangement. Access, Visa.*

OVER PEOVER — The Dog — FOOD

Tel & Fax 01625 861421 Map 6 B2 **B&B**

Well Bank Lane Over Peover nr Knutsford Cheshire WA16 8UP

Frances and Jim Cunningham promote The Dog as a pub serving food, and so popular has it proved that these days table reservations are the norm. A well-tried formula invites choice of snacks – sandwiches and ploughman's lunches – starters and main courses from the daily-updated blackboard that offers a range of soups (perhaps curried apple and parsnip), duck and orange paté and black pudding with mustard ahead of an equally wide range of main courses. Substantial dishes with vegetables and choice of potatoes are all well priced; rabbit pie, smoked haddock and prawn au gratin, smoked salmon and prawn pancake and rack of lamb with apricot and ginger exemplify the range. Home-made desserts are selected from a groaning sideboard and cold cabinet replete with fruit pies, bread-and-butter pudding, pavlovas and gateaux. The Dog's identity as village local is retained in the Tap Room, while there's plenty of space for casual drinking on the front patio or in a rear garden, where a more limited snack service operates. In terms of its food, the pub could write North-Western appetites into folklore, the term 'volume' being applicable equally to the portions as to the numbers who tuck into them. The individually-decorated bedrooms are equally popular, their cottage appeal enhanced by the practical addition of spacious, carpeted bath/shower rooms, TVs, trouser presses and beverage trays – they attract a clientele quite capable of providing their own telephones! *Open 11-3, 5.30-11 (Sun 12-3, 7-10.30).* ***Bar Food*** *12-2.30 (bookings essential Sun), 7-9. Free House.* ***Beer*** *Jennings Mild, Greenalls Original, Flowers IPA, Tetley, guest beer. Garden, outdoor eating.* ***Accommodation*** *3 bedrooms, all en suite, £59.50, weekend £49.50 (single £39.50). Children welcome overnight (charge depends on age), additional bed available. Dogs by arrangement. Access, Visa.*

OVER STRATTON — Royal Oak — FOOD

Tel 01460 240906 Map 13 F2

Over Stratton nr South Petherton Somerset TA13 5LQ

This row of three 400-year-old thatched cottages merges with its neighbours in the main street of the village and, but for the pub sign, it would be easy to miss altogether; at the South Petherton roundabout (A303) take the old Ilminster town-centre road. Cottage atmosphere is still the secret of an interior with a real sense of style. Original features like old beams, hamstone and flag floors (as well as a couple of stone pillars that look to have been there for ever but were actually salvaged from the cellars of a nearby house a few of years ago) blend successfully with dark rag-rolled walls, scrubbed wooden tables, a polished granite bar counter and extensive displays of dried flowers, hops and strings of garlic. The extensive menu lists sandwiches and ploughman's lunches plus deep-fried Brie and crab Mexicana among the starters, followed by various steaks, salmon steak in a dill and green peppercorn sauce or Barbary duck in a grape and white wine sauce. Home-made puddings may include poached hot pear with butterscotch sauce. A Booty Box is on the children's menu, full of goodies including a wholemeal sandwich, cheese, fruit, crisps and a crunchy bar – all served in a special box that children can take away with them. Weather permitting, grills are cooked to order on the weekend barbecue outside, beyond which there are swings, a junior assault course and trampolines to keep the kids amused. New managers, but the same kitchen team remains. *Open 11-3, 6-11 (Sun 12-3, 7-10.30).* ***Bar Food*** *12-2.15, 7-10 (Sun 9.30).* ***Beer*** *Hall & Woodhouse Tanglefoot & Badger Best, Wadworth 6X. Garden, outdoor eating, children's play area. Access, Visa.*

OVING — Gribble Inn — A

Tel 01243 786893 Map 11 A6

Gribble Lane Oving nr Chichester West Sussex PO90 6BP

Set on the edge of a peaceful village three miles east of Chichester, this attractive, 16th-century thatched cottage is named after one long-term occupant, Rose Gribble. A pub since 1980, it retains much of its original charm with a low, heavily-beamed bar, a big log fire in a raised hearth and a good mix of country furnishings. Large, comfortably-furnished, no-smoking family room and adjacent skittle alley. Popular attractions here are the excellent range of home-brewed ales and the splendid cottage garden with climbing roses and rustic wooden tables and benches beneath apple trees; an ideal venue for summer alfresco imbibing. *Open 11-2.30, 6-11 (Sun 12-3, 7-10.30), Sat in summer 11-11.* ***Beer*** *Hall & Woodhouse Badger Best, own brews: Gribble Ale, Reg's Tipple, Blackadder, Pig's Ear, Plucking Pheasant, Ewe Brew. Garden, lawn, outside eating. Family room. Access, Visa.*

OVINGTON **Bush Inn** FOOD

Tel 01962 732764 Map 15 D3
Ovington nr Alresford Hampshire SO24 0RE

Located just off the A31 on a peaceful lane, this unspoilt 17th-century rose-covered cottage enjoys an enviable picturesque setting, close to one of Hampshire's famous chalk trout streams – the River Itchen. Scenic riverside walks are very popular, as are the rustic bars and bench-filled garden of the Bush, both of which are often crammed with people replenishing their energy after a stroll, especially on fine summer weekends. Three intimate, softly-lit bars boast dark-painted walls, an assortment of sturdy tables, chairs and high-backed settles and a wealth of old artefacts, prints and stuffed fish. On cold winter nights the place to sit with a pint of traditional ale is in front of the roaring log fire. On the eating side, food varies from routine bar meals listed on a printed menu that includes ploughman's lunches and sandwiches to a daily specials board highlighting a short, but rather more interesting choice of dishes: perhaps home-made spicy chicken royale soup, grilled local trout, chili con carne, and warm Thai beef salad. The tiny bar boasts a changing selection of at least five real ales, over eight wines served by the glass and numerous country wines. *Open 11-2.30, 6-11 (Sun 12-3, 7-10.30).* ***Bar Food*** *12-2, 6.30-9.30 (Sun from 7). Free House.* ***Beer*** *Gales HSB, Wadworth 6X, Morrells Strong Country Bitter, Flowers Original, guest beer. Riverside terrace, outdoor eating. Access, Visa.*

OXFORD **The Bear** A

Tel 01865 721783 Map 14a C2
Alfred Street Oxford Oxfordshire OX1 4FH

Just a step back from the High Street and claiming to be Oxford's oldest pub (dating from 1242) the Bear is easily identified in summer by its impressive display of hanging baskets. There's precious little sign today of antiquity inside, bar its dimensions themselves – most of the walls are modestly panelled and the beams and ceilings encased in nicotine-enhanced ragwashed plasterboard. A medium-sized coach load (not an uncommon occurrence) will virtually fill the bar. The Bear's tie collection is nonetheless legendary: over 8,000 university, regimental and sports club ties are displayed in glass cases on virtually every wall and most of the ceiling. Though the beer is plentiful and consistently good, be prepared to wait your turn at the tiny servery. Thankfully in fine weather there's space to spread out into the paved beer garden under the beech trees. Don't go looking for the pub by car, though, as parking is impossible. *Open 12 noon-11 (Sun 12-3, 7-10.30).* ***Beer*** *Tetley Best, Burton Ale, Eldridge Pope Royal Oak & Thomas Hardy Country Bitter, guest beer. Patio. No credit cards.*

PADSTOW **Old Custom House** B&B

Tel 01841 532359 **Fax 01841 533372** Map 12 B3
South Quay Padstow Cornwall PL28 8ED

Proudly set on the quayside with picturesque views across the bustling harbour with its colourful boats and beyond over the Camel estuary, the Old Custom House began life as the Customs and Excise building in the 1800s. St Austell Brewery refurbished the inn, creating in spacious, well-decorated and neatly furnished public areas that display a good collection of prints. A light and airy conservatory at the front of the building has a quarry-tiled floor and cushioned cane furniture – a popular spot from which to watch harbour life. Of the 27 tastefully furnished and well-equipped bedrooms, over half enjoy harbour and estuary views. Modern in style with fresh, co-ordinating fabrics and wallpapers, they all have spacious and sparkling bathrooms with good fixtures and fittings, fluffy towels and a hairdryer. The honeymoon suite has an elegant four-poster, a double shower and a large, deep jacuzzi set in the floor. Telephone, beverage-making facility and satellite TV are standard throughout. *Open 11-11, (Sun 12-3, 7-10.30). Cream teas 3-5 in summer.* ***Beer*** *St Austell XXXX Mild, Tinners Ale.* ***Accommodation*** *27 bedrooms, all en suite, £80 (single £61). Children welcome overnight (under-3s free, 3-12 half price), additional bed and cot available. Access, Amex, Diners, Visa.*

PELYNT — Jubilee Inn — B&B

Tel 01503 220312 **Fax 01503 220920** Map 12 C3
Pelynt nr Looe Cornwall Pl3 2JZ

Originally called the Axe Inn, this attractive, pink-washed, 16th-century inn patriotically changed its name in 1887 to celebrate the first fifty years of Queen Victoria's reign. Ornate crowns top the front pillars and various prints and portraits of the Queen and pieces of Victorian china decorate the characterful lounge bar. Also furnishing the smart public areas are a delightful collection of antique tables and chairs which front the fine fireplace with its gleaming copper hood. There is also a simple, flagstone-floored public bar. Ten good-sized bedrooms vary greatly in style and quality of furniture. All are individually furnished, some pleasantly furnished in period-style with good antiques – one with a four-poster, another with half-tester and matching chest of drawers – while others are simply furnished in modern style. All have en-suite facilities (nine with shower-trays), and telephone, TV, radio/alarm and beverage-making facilities are standard. A homely lounge is available for residents' use. Outdoor imbibing can be appreciated on the rear patio and in the extensive garden with an adjacent terrace and barbecue area. *Open 11-3, 6-11 (Sat 11-11, Sun 12-10.30). Free House.* ***Beer*** *Furgusons Dartmoor Legend, St Austell XXXX Mild. Garden, outdoor eating area, children's play area.* ***Accommodation*** *10 bedrooms, all en suite, £60 (single £33). Children welcome overnight (0-3 free, 4-13 half price), additional bed and cot available. Access, Visa.*

PEMBRIDGE — New Inn — FOOD

Tel 01544 388427 Map 14 A1
Market Square Pembridge Hereford & Worcester HR6 9DZ

There is nothing new about this exceedingly old inn, one of England's finest, standing at the heart of a picturesque medieval village of stone and half-timbered houses. Opposite the old covered market (all of six by twelve metres in dimension) and the 14th-century Church Approach. This is where peace was reportedly signed following the battle of Mortimer's Cross in 1461. The inn itself probably pre-dates this by some 150 years and is a treasure trove of massive oak timbers, sloping flagstone floors and bulging walls: of two tiny bars the 'public', containing a huge Open fire and massive settle, is probably the pick. Menus are sensibly scaled down to complement the limited space available, though portions are hearty enough for today's trenchermen. Warm seafood salad, cheesy leek and potato bake and lamb cutlets in damson and redcurrant wine can be preceded by mushrooms and bacon in garlic and cream or followed by the likes of baked bananas (or apricot cheesecake). Ploughman's platters and sandwiches are always available for those calling in for a light snack. *Open 11-3, 6-11 (Sun 12-3 7-10.30).* ***Bar Food*** *12-2, 7-9.30 (Sat to 10). Free House.* ***Beer*** *Ruddles County & Best, John Smith's, guest beer. Patio/terrace, outdoor eating. No credit cards.*

PENELEWEY — Punch Bowl & Ladle — A

Tel 01872 862237 Map 12 B3
Penelewey nr Feock Cornwall

The idyllic exterior of rose-covered walls, heavy thatched porches and roof belie the true size of this much-extended, 15th-century cottage, set sideways on to the road. Tacked on to the back is a vast dining area, but the main interest here is the warren of unspoilt rooms housed in the original cottage. Once used as a courthouse and a meet for Customs and Excise men, the charming series of interconnecting, low-beamed rooms have a relaxing ambience in which to enjoy a pint and read some of the tourist literature and daily papers provided. There is much to catch the eye, from collections of rural bygones, plates, books, photographs and old tins to an array of rustic pine tables, sofas, easy chairs and some antique pieces of furniture. A handy stop for Trelissick Gardens (NT) and the King Harry Ferry across the River Fal. Sunday afternoon teas. *Open 11-11 (Sun 12-10.30).* ***Beer*** *Boddingtons, Flowers Original, Bass, Courage Directors, guest beers. Patio. Access, Visa.*

PENISTONE — Cubley Hall — FOOD

Tel 01226 766086 Map 6 C2
Mortimer Road Penistone South Yorkshire S30 6AW

The interior of this unusual conversion from Edwardian country house to what is almost a 'stately pub' is resplendent with oak panelling, mosaic floors and ornate ceilings. It echoes a bit when empty but hums along busily when full and, with sizeable parties accommodated in the conservatory, there can be a scrum for tables to eat at. Food follows generally

predictable lines from ploughman's platters, sandwiches and beefburger and onions through to the steak and grill range, but the daily specials come to the rescue: smoked salmon and scrambled eggs, Cubley game pie, beef Mexican in spicy sauce and a choice of fresh fish dishes are better indicators of a capable kitchen which also produces weightier weekend fare for the adjacent Workhouse Carvery (check opening times). The extensive gardens and grounds with play areas (even with the occasional bouncy castle) and drinking patios are a major draw for families through the summer. No smoking in the 'Green Room'. *Open 11-3, 6-11 (Sun 12-3, 7-10.30).* ***Bar Food*** *12-2, 6-9 (Sat to 10). Free House.* ***Beer*** *Bentley's Yorkshire Bitter, Marston's Pedigree, Flowers Original, three guest beers. Large garden and patio, outdoor eating, children's play area. Family room. Access, Amex, Diners, Visa.*

PENN STREET — Hit & Miss — FOOD

Tel 01494 713109 Map 15a E3
Penn Street nr Amersham Buckinghamshire HP7 0PX

200-year-old brick-built village pub with an attractive wisteria-clad facade and located opposite its own cricket pitch. Unpretentious and comfortably modernised interior with two neat yet simply furnished bars, an Open fire, a separate restaurant and a relaxing music, and game-free atmosphere. Extensive menus listed on four blackboards should suit all tastes, with standard favourites plus a selection of reliable, home-cooked dishes and daily fresh fish specials. Typical bar fare ranges from filled jacket potatoes, ploughman's platters, sandwiches, cold meat salads, steak and kidney pie, stuffed plaice, half a dozen fresh oysters and tagliatelle carbonara. The restaurant à la carte menu can be ordered in the bar and offers more imaginative fare. Roast Sunday lunch is a popular affair. Under the same ownership as *The Dove* (see entry) in Hammersmith, London W6. *Open 11-3, 6-11 (Sun 12-3, 7-10.30).* ***Bar Food*** *11-3 (Sun from 12), 6-11 (Sun 7-10.30). Free House.* ***Beer*** *Brakspear Bitter, Fuller's London Pride, Hook Norton Old Hooky, guest beer. Garden, outdoor eating. Access, Amex, Diners, Visa.*

PERRANUTHNOE — Victoria Inn — B&B

Tel & Fax 01736 710309 Map 12 A4
Perranuthnoe nr Penzance Cornwall TR20 9NP

Pretty pink-washed village inn originally built to accommodate the masons who extended the church in the 15th century, and officially described as a safe house for the clergy. With the sea and a safe beach just down the road the comfortable, typically Cornish stone-walled bar, adorned with various seafaring and fishing memorabilia, and the sheltered sun-trap rear terrace fill up early with visitors. A warm welcome is offered to families, who make use of the spacious games room. Two homely bedrooms are simply furnished and decorated and have their own WC, shower and washbasin; a TV is provided in the adjacent lounge. A small kitchen complete with fully-stocked fridge is available for those early risers catching the dawn ferry from Penzance to the Scilly Isles, the Victoria being a most convenient overnight halt. Breakfast will also be cooked for you on request. *Open 11.30-3 (winter from 12), 6-11 (winter from 6.30), Sun 12-3, 7-10.30.* ***Beer*** *John Smith's Bitter, Ushers Best & Founders Ale. Garden.* ***Accommodation*** *2 bedrooms, both with shower en suite, £25 (single £20). Children welcome overnight by arrangement (under-3s stay free in parents' room). Check-in by arrangement. No dogs. No credit cards.*

PETWORTH — Welldiggers Arms — FOOD

Tel 01798 342287 Map 11 A6
Pulborough Road Petworth West Sussex GU28 0GH

Once occupied by welldiggers as its name suggests, this 300-year-old roadside cottage can be located along the A283 Pulborough road, 2 miles east of Petworth. Two low-ceilinged bars furnished with a rustic collection of sturdy oak tables and benches are generally bustling with diners as this is very much a dining-orientated pub. Popular with enthusiasts of racing (Goodwood), shooting and polo (Cowdray Park), it is a useful rendezvous or stopping-off point in which to enjoy some reliable bar food. Excellent seafood – fish soup, mango and king prawn salad, whole sea bass, fresh lobster, whole Dover sole, seafood platter – and properly hung steaks. Alternatives on the blackboard menu may include Greek salad, calf's liver and onion, braised oxtail, courgette cheesebake and local game in season. For pudding, try the home-made treacle tart or banoffee pie. Sunday roasts. Alfresco eating on the rear patio with views towards the South Downs. *Open 11-3, 6-11 (Sun 12-3, closed evening).* ***Bar Food*** *12-2, 6-10. Free House.* ***Beer*** *Young's Best Bitter & Special. Garden, outdoor eating. Access, Diners, Visa.*

PHILLEIGH Roseland Inn FOOD

Tel 01872 580254 Map 12 B3
Philleigh Cornwall TR2 5NB

17th-century cob-built Cornish treasure peacefully positioned beside the parish church in an out-of-the-way village, two miles from the King Harry Ferry that crosses the River Fal. The front terrace is delightfully floral with colourful climbing roses, while indoors there are old-fashioned seats, lovely old settles, worn slate floors, fresh flowers, low beams and a welcoming fire. Spotlessly kept and run with enthusiastic panache by Graham and Jacqui Hill, the Roseland is a popular rural destination for reliable pub food. The menu and blackboard specials cover a range from decent sandwiches and ploughman's platters, local goat's cheese salad, leek and smoked bacon bake or seafood tagliatelle to whole lemon sole, local mussels in white wine and green peppercorn salmon. Fish is delivered from a local trawler. The garden is closed off from the road and has a rocking horse and slides for children. Afternoon teas are served during July and August. *Open 11.30-3, 6.30-11 (July & August 11.30-11), Sun 12-3, 7-10.30. **Bar Food** 12-2.15, 6.30-9. **Beer** Marston's Pedigree, Greenalls Bitter, Bass. Garden. No credit cards.*

PICKERING White Swan FOOD B&B

Tel & Fax 01751 472288 Map 5 E4
The Market Place Pickering North Yorkshire YO18 7AA

Zzz...

In the eleven years since coming here, Dierdre Buchanan has become The White Swan, and this charming town-centre inn becomes her, too. For her regulars and the casual drinker there's the traditional pubbiness of the oak-panelled bar and snug which overlook Pickering's sloping main street. Residents both new and oft-returning enjoy privileged use of a quietly elegant lounge and a warm welcome from both Mrs Buchanan and her loyal staff which helps make them feel well at home. Bar food strays little from tried and tested favourites, but of a quality which suggests a quietly competent kitchen. Lamb's liver and onions, grilled Pickering trout and mushroom stroganoff are typical of daily-updated offerings; for Sunday lunch as many as three roasts are available in the bar. Desserts are generous and nicely presented (fruit Pavlova, bread-and-butter pudding and chocolate truffle torte) or there's a Yorkshire cheeseboard available. Lighter snacks like ploughman's platters and sandwiches only appear on the lunchtime menu. Gradual upgrading of the thirteen en-suite (bath and shower) bedrooms continues, with most featuring quality pine furniture and personally selected antique pieces. Rich floral borders and matching duvet covers add a touch of class and much-needed brightness and colour to the decor. *Open 11-3, 6-11 (Mon & Sat 11-11), Sun 12-3, 7-10.30. **Bar Food** 12-2, 6.30-8 (Fri & Sat no bar suppers/restaurant only). Free House. **Beer** Theakston Best, Cameron Lion Bitter. Garden, outdoor eating area. **Accommodation** 13 bedrooms, all en suite, £76 (single £55). Dogs welcome in rooms. Children welcome overnight, additional child's bed in shared room (£10) and cot available. Access, Amex, Visa.*

PICKHILL Nag's Head FOOD B&B

Tel 01845 567391 **Fax 01845 567212** Map 5 E4
Pickhill nr Thirsk North Yorkshire YO7 4JG

Ever-youthful and enthusiastic publicans Raymond and Edward Boynton will shortly celebrate their Jubilee at the pub which has become synonymous with Yorkshire hospitality at its best. Immaculately-kept real ales, monthly wine selections (offered also by the glass) and an array of 40-odd malt whiskies are the domain of one brother, against which his sibling's kitchen output measures up admirably. Menu boards here do not so much proclaim daily specials as spell out the kitchen's entire repertoire. For starters, go perhaps for crispy mussels with a shrimp and prawn sauce or mushrooms stuffed with Stilton and York ham. For a bar snack try seafood pancake mornay, tandoori chicken or a choice of sandwiches and ploughman's platters. Main meals extend to pan-fried fillet of venison in bramble and port sauce and grey mullet with black bean sauce, plus traditional puddings such as Brown Betty, sticky toffee pudding and squidgy chocolate roulade to follow. Similar fare, plus a few select extras are served in the restaurant. As a place to stay, the Nag's Head is similarly above reproach. Well signed just off the A1, it was one of many 17th-century coaching inns which serviced the London to Edinburgh route; it is the best one to boast a genuine Yorkshire 'weather-stone' which remains essential reading for the meteorologically

credulous. Bedrooms are divided between the pub and next-door house standing in a neatly tended garden, and a self-contained cottage which can be let in its entirety. Remote-control TV, dial-out phone and beverage tray are standard appointments in the rooms, the majority of which have plenty of desk space. Carpeted bathrooms are neat and well appointed, though four have WC/shower rooms only. Large family room and plenty of space in several rooms have space for an additional bed or cot, with children charged according to age and what they eat. Yorkshire breakfast in the morning could prove irresistible. *Open 11-11 (Sun 12-3, 7-10.30).* ***Bar Food*** *12-2, 6-10. Free House.* ***Beer*** *Hambleton Bitter, Theakston Best, XB & Old Peculier, John Smiths, guest beer. Garden, outdoor eating.* ***Accommodation*** *15 bedroom, all en suite, £48 (single £34). Children welcome overnight. Access, Amex, Visa.*

PICKLESCOTT — Bottle & Glass Inn — FOOD B&B

Tel 01694 751345 Map 6 A4
Picklescott nr Church Stretton Shropshire SY6 6NR

Zzz...

Follow well-signed lanes from the A49 at Dorrington, or the scenic route over Long Mynd from the Strettons to happen on this epitome of locals, complete with palm-reading gypsy (for ladies only!). Rear extensions to the original two-roomed stone-built pub have been sympathetically handled, the dining area leading to a barbecue terrace and rear garden. Food throughout stays with the safe options: home-baked ham, grills of steak and fish supplemented by daily specials (Stilton soup, lasagne, curries) and lunchtime salads, sandwiches and savoury-filled baked potatoes. Sunday carvery with eight fresh vegetables; booking essential. Families are very welcome; there are picnic tables on a sun-trap front patio and safe playing by the village stream opposite. Comfortable, character bedrooms have been expertly created in the roof space with brass bedsteads, co-ordinated fabrics and gold-tapped bathrooms with over-bath showers. The temptation of telephones has been resisted in favour of TVs, tea trays and trouser presses. Well-balanced youngsters may be accommodated overnight strictly by prior arrangement. *Open 11-3, 7-11 (Sun 12-3, 7-10.30).* ***Bar Food*** *12-2, 7-10. Free House.* ***Beer*** *Bass, Worthington Best. Garden, patio. Family room.* ***Accommodation*** *3 bedrooms, all en suite, £50 (single £25). Children welcome overnight by arrangement only. Check-in by arrangement. No dogs. No credit cards.*

PIDDLEHINTON — Thimble Inn — A

Tel 01300 348270 Map 13 F2
Piddlehinton nr Dorchester Dorset DT2 7TD

The Thimble is no longer thimble-sized nor is it the quaint, creeper-clad village local that we once knew. The traditional two-bar layout has disappeared and a splendid thatched extension has been built. This curves along the tiny River Piddle with small bridges linking it to the attractive, summer flower-filled garden, which enjoys rolling country views. Internally, it is very smart with tasteful decor, good prints and subdued lighting; the open-plan bars are furnished with an assortment of pub tables and chairs. A feature of the bar is the 27ft glass-topped well. *Open 12-2, 7-11 (Sun 12-3, 7-10.30). Free House.* ***Beer*** *Ringwood Best & Old Thumper, Hardy Country, Hall & Woodhouse Hard Tackle. Garden, outdoor eating. No credit cards.*

PILLEY — Fleur de Lys — FOOD

Tel 01590 672158 Map 14 C4
Pilley nr Lymington Hampshire SO41 5QG

☺

This attractive, thatched pub nestles in a tiny village right on the edge of the New Forest. Originally it was a pair of foresters' cottages and the tree roots and fireplace opening (an old New Forest Rights tradition) can still be seen in the stone-flagged entrance passage. Beyond, three interconnecting rooms are neat and tidy, boasting beams, a huge inglenook, a comfortable mix of tables and chairs and various bric-a-brac. Bar food still caters for all tastes by offering the old favourites – ploughman's platters, barbecue spare ribs and salad – plus grilled mussels with garlic and parmesan, nut roast and ginger prawns with rice on the printed scroll menu. Daily specials enhance the choice of dishes with fresh local fish featuring strongly: ling, herring, hake, mackerel, whole lemon sole and lobster thermidor. Further blackboard-listed meals include home-made soup – celery and Stilton – Moroccan beef, pork in ginger and beef in Guinness, apricots and prunes. A new chef has recently been appointed but the style (and, hopefully, the quality) is expected to remain the same. Good sheltered garden with marquee and weekend summer barbecues. Afternoon teas

in high season. *Open 11-3, 6-11 (Sat and mid-summer 11-11), Sun 12-10.30.* ***Bar Food*** *11.30-2.30, 6-9.30 (Sun 12-2, 7-9).* ***Beer*** *Ringwood Best, Boddingtons, Flowers Original, Marston's Pedigree, guest beer. Garden, outdoor eating. Access, Visa.*

PIMPERNE — Anvil Hotel — B&B

Tel 01258 453431 **Fax 01258 480182** Map 14 B4
Pimperne nr Blandford Forum Dorset

Set back from the busy A345 Salisbury to Blandford road, this pretty, thatched cottage dates from 1535. Low ceilings, thick walls, old black beams and an inglenook fireplace characterise the tile-floored restaurant, while more modern plush wall-bench seating features in the neat and relaxing lounge bar and in the newly-extended Forge Bar. Up a narrow, steep staircase and tucked beneath the thatch are nine clean and comfortable bedrooms. All are attractively decorated and furnished with modern telephones and tea-making facilities. Compact en-suite facilities, all with bath and shower, are spotlessly clean. Delightful flower-filled front garden with a shady spot beneath a huge weeping willow tree. *Open 12-2.30, 6-11 (Sun 12-3, 7-10.30). Free House.* ***Beer*** *Wadworth 6X, Bass. Garden, outdoor eating area.* ***Accommodation*** *10 bedrooms, all en suite, £70 (single £45). Children welcome overnight, additional bed and cot available. Access, Amex, Diners, Visa.*

PIN MILL — Butt & Oyster — A

Tel 01473 780764 Map 10 C3
Pin Mill Chelmondiston nr Ipswich Suffolk 1RP 1JW

Classic riverside pub set in a tiny hamlet off the B1456 at Chelmondiston, south-west of Ipswich. Dating from the 17th century, this old bargeman's retreat is still frequented by sailors and fishermen and on busy summer days it is chock full of tourists, all enjoying the simple charm of its old settles, tiled floors and fine views across Buttermans Bay, part of the River Orwell. Nautical artefacts and photographs adorn the wood-panelled walls of the main bar and the 'smoke room' features a collection of model ships. Both bars are free of intrusive music and electronic games. Be early for the sought-after waterside window seats, or one of the sturdy benches adjacent to the slipway; it's an ideal spot to watch the setting sun on fine summer evenings. Traditional winter pub games are popular when the crowds have gone home. *Open 11-3, 7-11 (winter Sat 11-11, summer 11-11), Sun 12-3, 7-10.30.* ***Beer*** *Tolly Cobbold Original, Bitter and Mild, Bass, guest beer. Garden, outdoor eating. Family Room. No credit cards.*

PITTON — Silver Plough — FOOD

Tel 01722 712266 Map 14 C3
Pitton nr Salisbury Wiltshire SP5 1DZ

The Silver Plough was a farmhouse until after the Second World War. Everything about the attractive, long building is neat and well kept: the lawns at the front, full of white plastic tables and chairs for summer drinking, and the tastefully-furnished main bar with its dust-free jugs, bottles and curios hanging from the ceiling timbers. Sturdy antique oak settles, various tables and quality paintings and prints characterise this bar and the snug bar with its neighbouring skittle alley – both popular with locals. It's very much a dining pub offering a good range of home-cooked bar meals using fresh local produce from reliable local suppliers, including Pitton's smokery. Menu choices include an above-average bar snack menu featuring freshly-cut sandwiches and unusual cheese ploughman's lunches, French-style casserole, home-made fishcakes, hearty soups – perhaps leek and bacon – and various pasta dishes. More inventive fare such as a salad of goat's cheese with roast baby beetroot, char-grilled lamb steak with a pear and rosemary sauce, and salmon baked with a crust of Cajun spices and topped with lime butter highlight the evening-only restaurant à la carte (also served in the bar), which, like the bar menu, changes every six weeks. Variety is enhanced by daily blackboard specials. Popular 3-course Sunday lunch. The global wine list is strong on New Zealand wines (with no less than ten offered by the glass) and a raft of country wines. *Open 11-3, 6-11 (Sun 12-3, 7-10.30).* ***Bar Food*** *12-2.30, 7-9.30. Free House.* ***Beer*** *John Smith's, Courage Directors, Eldridge Pope Hardy Ale, Wadworth 6X. Garden, outdoor eating. Family room. Access, Amex, Diners, Visa.*

> We do not accept free meals or hospitality – our inspectors pay their own bills and never book in the name of Egon Ronay's Guides.

PLUCKLEY — Dering Arms — FOOD

Tel 01233 840371 Fax 01233 840498 Map 11 C5
Pluckley nr Ashford Kent TN27 0RR

Located a mile from the village beside Pluckley Station, this impressive manorial building was once the Dering Estate hunting lodge and boasts curving Dutch gables, rounded triple lancet 'Dering' windows, and a rather spooky grandeur. Splendid interior to match, with high ceilings, wood or stone floors, a tall, exposed brick fireplace, stripped-pine doors, various sturdy wooden tables, long Victorian benches and some old leather easy chairs. A relaxing atmosphere pervades in which to enjoy the good bar food listed on two short blackboard menus. Favourite snacks – sandwiches and ploughman's platters with home-made chutney – can be found on one; a range of interesting home-cooked dishes on the other. A typical choice may include gazpacho soup, soft herring roes with crispy bacon, mackerel grilled with capers, grilled plaice, and lamb, apricot and coriander pie with a decent shortcrust pastry top. Fresh fish from Hythe dominates the imaginative daily-changing restaurant menu (also available in the bar), for example red snapper with sorrel sauce, whole crab salad and fillet of sea bream meunière. Good local Goacher's ales and a Biddenden farm cider are favoured here; wine drinkers can choose from an interesting list of 82 wines. Regular gourmet evenings, summer barbecues and live jazz or classical music in the sheltered garden. *Open 11-3, 6-11 (Sun 12-3, 7-10.30). Closed 26 & 27 Dec.* ***Bar Food** 12-2 & 7-9.30 (Sat to 10). No food Sun evening. Free House.* ***Beer** Goacher's Maidstone Ale, Dering Ale & Dark Ale. Garden, outdoor eating. Family room. Access, Amex, Visa.*

PLUSH — Brace of Pheasants — FOOD

Tel 01300 348357 Map 13 F2
Plush Dorchester Dorset DT2 7RQ

Originally two cottages and a forge, dating from the 16th century, this attractive collection of thatched, brick and flint buildings became an inn in the mid-1930s and must surely be one of the prettiest in Dorset. The location is idyllic, nestling in a peaceful rural hamlet, surrounded by rolling downland. A brace of glass-encased stuffed pheasants hangs above the main cottage door that leads into the charmingly unspoilt bar, complete with a huge inglenook (used for seating), a further log fire and an assortment of traditional furniture. Guns, prints and harnesses decorate the walls and the separate, cosy restaurant has tables neatly laid with linen cloths. The attraction here, other than its setting, is the consistently good bar food. Separate blackboards for both lunch and evening fare list the weekly-changing specials which supplement an extensive printed menu selection. Lunch features the usual ploughman's platters and salads, plus an excellent range of lighter bites, including chicken liver paté, crab savoury and soft herring roes. Substantial home-cooked lunch dishes may include steak, kidney and mushroom pie, liver, bacon and onions and fresh grilled plaice. Evening fare is more adventurous: fillet steak with a port and Stilton sauce, venison in a mushroom and Madeira sauce and, of course, pheasant Rob Roy. Well-cooked vegetables accompany each dish. Puddings, listed on a board, range from raspberry pavlova to apple and plum crumble. There is a delightful garden with mature trees and shrubs and a continental-style vine-covered pergola with seating beneath. *Open 12-2.30, 7-11 (Sun 12-3, 7-10.30).* ***Bar Food** 12-1.45, 7-9.45. Free House.* ***Beer** Smiles Best, Wadworth 6X, guest beer. Garden, children's play area. Family room. Access, Visa.*

PLYMOUTH — The China House — A

Tel 01752 260930 Map 12 C3
Marrowbone Slip Sutton Harbour Plymouth Devon PL4 ODW

The China House has had many uses since being built as a quayside warehouse in the mid-1600s: King's bakehouse, hospital for seamen, porcelain factory (from which period it takes its name) and prison, amongst other uses. Now cleverly rebuilt inside to reflect its warehouse days with great bulks of timber, cast-iron pillars and sets of mock cargo, it makes a most unusual hostelry. There is a no-smoking area and a narrow verandah jutting out over the water of Sutton Harbour. Regular jazz and blues nights. *Open 11-11.30, Sun 12-10.30.* ***Beer** Wadworth 6X, Dartmoor Best & Strong, guest beer. Terrace. Access, Amex, Visa.*

Polkerris **Rashleigh Inn** A

Tel 01726 813991 Map 12 B3
Polkerris Fowey Cornwall PL25 3NJ

Literally on the beach in a tiny isolated cove and known locally as the 'Inn on the Beach', the Rashleigh is well worth seeking out for its magnificent setting. Once the old lifeboat station, until becoming a pub in 1924, it is a popular refreshment spot for coast path walkers and for families using the beach in the summer. Summer alfresco drinking is unrivalled in this area, for the table-filled terrace is a splendid place from which to watch the sun set across St Austell Bay. On cooler days the sea views can still be admired from the warmth of the main bar, especially from the bay-window seats. Parents enjoying a drink on the terrace can keep an eagle eye on their children playing on the beach. *Open 11-3, 6-11 (Sun 12-3, 7-10.30). Free House.* ***Beer*** *St Austell HSD, Dartmoor Best, Burton Ale, Bass. Outdoor eating area. Access, Visa.*

Port Gaverne **Port Gaverne Hotel** B&B

Tel 01208 880244 **Fax 01208 880151** Map 12 B3
Port Gaverne Port Isaac Cornwall PL29 3SQ

Zzz...

Set in a sheltered cove 50 yards from the beach is this charming 17th-century inn; run by Midge Ross for the last 26 years. The ship-shape, character pubby bar has a polished slate floor and the tiny snug bar features a collection of china, old local photographs, a genuine ship's table and carved chest, and an interesting diorama of the port years ago. Upstairs, along the warren of corridors lined with attractive paintings and watercolours lie nineteen cheerful, individually decorated bedrooms which boast pretty fabrics and wallpapers and attractive en-suite bathrooms. Antique furniture grace the older rooms in the main building, but all have thoughtful homely touches like pieces of china and ornaments, plus tissues, TV, hairdryer and telephone for added comfort. Fresh, clean and comfortable accommodation, the best room affording a sea view. Self-catering cottages are also available. Children welcome in the Green Door bar opposite *(Open all day in summer) and in the small 'Cabin' bar in winter. Open 11-2.30, 6-11 (summer 11-11, Sun 12-3, 7-10.30). Free House.* ***Beer*** *Sharp's Doombar Bitter, Flowers IPA, Bass. Garden.* ***Accommodation*** *19 bedrooms, all en suite, £98 (single £47). Children welcome overnight (under-3s stay free in parents' room, 3-12s half price), additional bed & cot available. Hotel closed early Jan-mid Feb. Access, Amex, Diners, Visa.*

Porthleven **Harbour Inn** B&B

Tel 01326 573876 Map 12 A4
Porthleven nr Helston Cornwall TR13 9JB

Situated in an unspoilt fishing village, this old fisherman's pub enjoys good views across the colourful collection of fishing boats and dinghies that fill the picturesque little harbour twenty yards away. Inside, there is a comfortable lounge area and a much larger and livelier public bar area, while upstairs Accommodation is offered in ten en-suite bedrooms, six of which have harbour views. Cottagey in style with pretty floral fabrics, wallpaper and matching duvet covers, they are neatly furnished with modern pine and the large, adequately equipped bathrooms have good overhead showers. Added comforts include TV, telephone, hairdryer and beverage-making facilities. The rooms have recently been refurbished. *Open 11-11, (Sun 12-3, 7-10.30).* ***Beer*** *St Austell HSD, Bosun's Bitter. Family Room.* ***Accommodation*** *10 bedrooms, 8 en suite, £56 (single £31, family suite £80), additional bed available. No dogs. Access, Amex, Visa.*

Porthleven **Ship** A

Tel 01326 572841 Map 12 A4
Porthleven nr Helston Cornwall TR13 9JS

Set in the cliffside and perched on the harbour wall, this old fisherman's pub enjoys a magnificent position looking out across the quaint working harbour and out to sea. The view is best appreciated in summer from the series of terraced lawns that rise up the cliff behind the pub. On wild winter days, climb the flight of stone steps and savour the view from the warmth of a window seat in the nautical bric-a-brac adorned bar, complete with good log fires. The family room – the 'Smithy' – adjoins the garden, while the ground-floor cellar bar is used only in the summer. The tiny harbour is attractively lit by fairy lights at night. *Open 11-2.30, 7-11 (11.30-11 in summer, Sun 12-3, 7-10.30).* ***Beer*** *Ushers Best & Founder's Ale, Courage Best. Family Room. No credit cards.*

Powerstock — Three Horseshoes Inn — FOOD — B&B

Tel 01308 485328 Map 13 F2
Powerstock Bridport Dorset DT6 3TF

'The Shoes' (as it is affectionately known locally) is a Victorian stone inn set in a sleepy village amid narrow, winding lanes and best reached from the A3066 north of Bridport. Rebuilt in 1906 after a devastating fire, but solidly old-fashioned in style with simple country furnishings in both the bustling bar and in the two pine-panelled dining-rooms. People come from miles around to this reliable old favourite for the chef/licensee Pat Ferguson and Jason Williams's food; it's not cheap, certainly, but it is fresh and delicious, specialising in fish from local boats, Dorset lamb and seasonal game. The extensive, daily-changing blackboard list of home-cooked dishes serves both bar and restaurant. Begin perhaps with salad of pigeon breasts with lardons and croutons, fish soup or char-grilled squid marinaded in oil with garlic and chili, and fish fanciers can then continue with baked sea bream with garden herbs, bourride or turbot fillet seasoned with crushed black pepper. Meat and game dishes like garlic-studded rack of Dorset lamb and escalopes of venison marinated in red wine with garlic and herbs are all served with well-cooked vegetables. Lighter bites include interesting fresh pasta dishes, salads and freshly-baked baguettes. Traditional puddings include summer berry tart, sticky toffee pudding and sunken chocolate soufflé. Must book for busy Sunday lunches. Good Palmers ales and a choice of eight wines by the glass. Delightful terraced garden and rear patio with village and valley views for summer eating. Four simple, centrally-heated bedrooms with traditional older-style furniture, TV and tea-maker provide homely overnight accommodation. Two are spacious and comfortable with clean, en-suite bathrooms, the others are rather too compact and share a bathroom. *Open 11-2.30, 6-11 (Sun 12-3, 7-10.30).* ***Bar Food*** *12-2, 7-10.* ***Beer*** *Palmers BB & IPA. Garden, outdoor eating, children's play area.* ***Accommodation*** *4 bedrooms, 2 en suite, £40/£45 (single £30). Children welcome overnight, additional bed and cot available. Check-in by arrangement. Access, Amex, Visa.*

Priors Dean — White Horse — FOOD

Tel 01420 588387 Map 15 D3
Priors Dean nr Petersfield Hampshire GU32 1DA

Also called the *Pub with No Name*; there is no sign. Fiendish to get to: leave Petersfield on the A272 Winchester-bound, turn right towards Steep, then after about 5 miles, take the East Tisted road at the crossroads, then immediate right down the second gravel track. It's worth the effort, for this is a quite wonderful 17th-century farmhouse pub of utterly simple (uncomfortable, some would say) charm, genuinely unspoilt by modernity and surrounded by 13 acres of fields belonging to the pub. The bar menu includes various dishes like beef and ale pie, deep-pan lasagne, farmhouse cottage pie, spinach and mushroom lasagne, and in winter ("when the Aga is lit, as it is not the same on an electric stove") thick country soup. First World War poet Edward Thomas wrote his first published work, *Up in the Wind*, about the pub; it's 750 feet up on the top of the Downs, with peaceful views on every side. There are 20 country wines and up to nine real ales on handpump. No children indoors but play area in garden. *Open 11-2.30 (Sat to 3), 6-11 (Sun 12-3, 7-10.30).* ***Bar Food*** *12-2.* ***Beer*** *Ballard's Best Bitter, No Name Best & Strong, Ringwood Fortyniner, Gale's BB, HSB & Festival Mild. Garden, outdoor eating, children's play area. No credit cards.*

Raby — Wheatsheaf Inn — A

Tel 0151 336 3416 Map 6 A2
The Green Raby Merseyside L63 4JH

Wedged amid a row of old farm buildings, the 'Thatch', as it is known, dates from around 1611 and is today just about the Wirral's last surviving rural pub. Notable within is a genuine snug, opposite the single bar, which is constructed from aged settles around a brick-lined inglenook fronted by a massive oak lintel. The wide choice of well-kept real ales and over 100 whiskies are the main attractions, although lunchtime snacks are popular (no food Sunday lunch or any evening). Strictly no under-18s admitted. *Open 11-3, 5.30-10.30 (Sun 12-2, 7-10.30). Free House.* ***Beer*** *Thwaites Bitter, Courage Directors, Jennings Bitter, Theakston Best, XB & Old Peculier, Tetley, Burtonwood, Younger's Bitter. No credit cards.*

RADWELL Swan Inn FOOD

Tel 01234 781351 Map 15a E1
Felmersham Road Radwell Bedfordshire MK43 7HS

Quaint 17th-century thatched country pub located near the River Ouse within a delightful village. Rustic charm characterises the homely, simply-furnished and tiny two-bar interior, and the continued enthusiasm of the landlords, Alan and Carol Clarke, has proved successful over the past year for this friendly dining pub. An extensive and varied menu lists a few favourites, including ploughman's platters and sandwiches, but predominantly features home-cooked fare using fresh local ingredients, especially fish and game, and is supplemented by good daily blackboard specials. Choices range from chili-braised mushrooms on a bed of noodles for starters to venison in red wine, medallions of pork in calvados and cream and unusual Oriental dishes like teriyaki beef and stir-fry chicken with bamboo shoots, water chestnuts and orange and green ginger sauce. Vegetarian options. Puddings include St Clement's sponge and apple pie. Plans for the large garden include a pets' corner and children's play area. *Open 12-2.30, (Sat to 3), 5-11 (Sun 12-3, 7-10.30).* ***Bar Food*** *12-2, 7-9.30 (no food Sun eve).* ***Beer*** *Charles Wells Eagle & Bombardier, guest beer. Garden, outdoor eating. Access, Amex, Visa.*

RAMSBURY Bell at Ramsbury FOOD

Tel 01672 520230 Map 14a A4
The Market Square Ramsbury nr Marlborough Wiltshire SN8 2PE

The Bell's stock-in-trade remains the provision of good-quality, carefully-prepared bar food at affordable prices. Sensibly short and to the point, both the printed and daily-changing blackboard menus give equal billing to ploughman's platters, and sandwiches (lunch only), home-made soups and patés and single-course snacks such as medallions of beef fillet in green peppercorn sauce, paté-stuffed chicken breast wrapped in bacon with a Stilton sauce, and duck breast roasted pink with a cassis sauce, while fresh fish (monkfish, bream, lemon sole) and steaks, sauced or plain, are accompanied by plainly-cooked fresh vegetables; Sunday roast. To follow are plenty of traditional nursery puddings from spotted Dick to rhubarb crumble and home-made ices and sorbets. Twenty malt whiskies. No-smoking area. *Open 12-3, 6-11 (Sun 12-3, 7-10.30).* ***Bar Meals*** *12-2 (Sat and Sun to 2.30), 7-9 (Fri & Sat to 9.45, Sun to 9.30). Free House.* ***Beer*** *Wadworth 6X, Henry's IPA, Hook Norton Best, two guest beers. Garden, outdoor eating. Family room. Access, Amex, Visa.*

RAVENSTONEDALE Black Swan Inn B&B

Tel 01539 623204 **Fax 01539 623604** Map 5 D3
Ravenstonedale nr Kirkby Stephen Cumbria CA17 4NG

Zzz...

A ten-minute drive from J38 of M6 via A685 brings you into a peaceful village nestling on the edge of the Howgill fells. The Black Swan is a quiet little turn-of-the-century Lakeland stone hotel run since 1988 by Gordon and Norma Stuart. One of the stone-walled bar rooms is very much a locals' bar, while the other has a refined pub air with highly-polished, copper-topped tables and interesting guest beers. Thomas the black cat (whose portrait hangs proudly on the wall) may already have the best seat! Three spacious, ground-floor bedrooms have particularly good disabled facilities (and ramp access into the bars), while the rest – "above stairs" – are comfortably furnished in traditional style with floral decor. On the first floor is a homely sitting room. Across the road is a delightful, sheltered garden with a small footbridge across the local beck. The local tennis court is available to residents and lake fishing is within a two-mile walk; their own river fishing requires the use of a car to reach it. *Open 12-3, 6-11 (Sun 12-3, 7-10.30), all day in summer (not Sun). Free House.* ***Beer*** *Theakston Best, Younger's Scotch, Jennings Cumberland, three guest beers. Garden, lake and river fishing, tennis.* ***Accommodation*** *16 bedrooms, £70 (single £48.50). Children welcome overnight, additional bed (£10) and cot (no charge) available. Access, Amex, Diners, Visa.*

RAVENSTONEDALE Fat Lamb B&B

Tel 01539 623242 Map 5 D3
Crossbank nr Ravenstonedale Kirkby Stephen Cumbria CA17 4LL

Dramatic panoramic views soak in every changing mood of the surrounding fells and moorland at this remote but popular walking and touring base on A683. Originally built in the 17th century as a farmhouse, Paul and Helen Bonsall's inn offers a warmth inside that contrasts vividly with its rather bleak open-countryside setting. The small, cosy main bar room leads through to a lounge that overlooks a rear patio and lawned garden edged by

large ash trees; at the bottom of the lower field is a wetland nature reserve. Several bedrooms are conveniently on the ground floor, in former outhouses, with wheelchair access; all have neat, if compact, bathrooms and tea-making facilities but no TVs. Rooms in the original building have the best views; four family rooms sleep up to four. Nine miles from M6 J37 via Sedbergh, or take the A685 to Ravenstonedale (turn right at Newbiggin-on-Lune) from J38 and continue down the narrow, dry-stone-walled country lanes for two miles until the junction with A683. *Open 11-3, 6-11 (Sun 12-3, 6-11), also for coffees and teas.* ***Beer*** *Mitchell's. Patio, garden, children's sand pit.* ***Accommodation*** *12 bedrooms, all en suite, £56 (single £32). Children welcome overnight (under-6s stay free if sharing parents' room, 6-12s £6), additional bed and cot provided. No credit cards.*

REDMILE — Peacock Inn — FOOD

Tel 01949 842554 **Fax 01949 843746** Map 7 D3
Church Corner Redmile Nottinghamshire NG13 0GA

Turn off the A52 at the signs to Belvoir Castle to find Redmile deep in the flatlands. Its pub, the Peacock, was rescued from dereliction some seven years ago. The interior is a tribute to the skills of landlord Colin Crawford whose restoration of its old fireplaces and former ships' timbers is commendable, as is his work in enclosing the rear flagstoned patio to create a skylit Garden Room replete with wrought-iron tables and fanciful murals. Frank Garbez supervises a busy kitchen: from the daily-changing blackboard wild mushrooms in puff pastry and grilled sardines could precede such main courses as pan-fried salmon or rack of lamb with pistou sauce with a fromage frais cheesecake or chocolate and orange millefeuille to follow. A la carte dishes – perhaps seafood brochette, fillet steak with Colston Bassett Stilton heart wrapped in bacon with port sauce, and aniseed iced mousse in chocolate shell with fresh fruit – come in less-than-authentic French translations. Fixed-price menus are also offered. A lighter snack menu features, among others, fresh pasta dishes and filled baguettes. The atmosphere, however, remains one of the Crawfords' village local, for they were brought up here: their 'locals' in turn have much to be grateful for. Booking advisable for both bar and restaurant. The Crawfords also run the *Blue Ball* in Braunston, Leicestershire (see entry). *Open 11-11 (Sun 12-3, 7-10.30).* ***Bar Food*** *12-2 (Sun to 3), 6.30-10 (Sun from 7). Free House.* ***Beer*** *Greene King Abbot Ale, Bass, Tetley, Marston's Pedigree, guest beer. Garden, outdoor eating. Family room. Access, Diners, Visa.*

REETH — Buck Hotel — B&B

Tel 01748 884210 **Fax 01748 884802** Map 5 D3
Reeth Richmond North Yorkshire DL11 6SW

☺

Newly painted in brilliant white, the Buck is an imposing building standing at the head of this prettiest of Dales villages; the fascinating Swaledale Folk House inn is a short walk away across the green. Nigel Fawcett's friendly pub scores highly with families for its separate games room, safe back garden, children's menus and choices of family accommodation. All ten bedrooms have TVs, tea trays and en-suite facilities (two with shower only); the best have fabulous views of the surrounding hills. Afternoon teas. *Open 11-3, 6-11 (Sat to 12, Sun 12-10.30).* ***Beer*** *Theakston Best & XB. Garden.* ***Accommodation*** *10 bedrooms, all en suite £49 (single £25). Children welcome overnight (under-8s stay free in parents' room), cot, high-chair and child's bed available. Access, Visa.*

REMENHAM — Little Angel — FOOD

Tel 01491 574165 **Fax 01491 411879** Map 15a D3
Remenham nr Henley-on-Thames Oxfordshire RG9 2LS

🍷

Just over the bridge from Henley-on-Thames, on the Berkshire side of the river, the 17th-century Little Angel in Remenham (not to be confused with The Angel public house on the Henley side of the bridge) is very much an eating pub. At present the same extensive menu operates in the pubby bar with its dark red ceilings, throughout the further neat dining-rooms and in the recently-built conservatory restaurant with its crisply-clothed tables. However, when refurbishment is complete, there are plans to introduce a separate grill menu in the restaurant. Eat outside and on summer weekends you get the added attraction of being able to watch the local cricketers, whose pitch is right next door. As it stands, dishes may include deep-fried Brie parcels on a bed of lettuce with a hot cranberry sauce, salad of the day, perhaps rare beef, baked cod with garlic and herb crust with saffron and parsley sauce, sausage and mash, beef stroganoff and chicken and Stilton, with the addition of sandwiches and ploughman's platters served in the bar area. There is a choice of

eight wines by the glass. Smart young uniformed men and women provide efficient service. *Open 11-3, 6-11 (Sun 12-3, 7-10.30).* ***Bar Food*** *12-2.30, 7-10.* ***Beer*** *Brakspear Bitter & Special, guest beer. Terrace, outdoor eating. Access, Amex, Diners, Visa.*

RENNINGTON — Masons Arms — B&B

Tel 01665 577275 Fax 01665 577894 Map 5 D1
Rennington nr Alnwick Northumberland WE66 3RX

ZZZ...

Just one and a half miles from the A1, the "Stamford Cot" (as it's known locally) stands in open country well back from the Northumbrian coastal resorts. There's a genuinely warm welcome here from Frank and Dee Sloan to their skilfully converted single-room bar, with open fires at each end, and cosy dining-room. Guests should be aware, however, that the pub does get very busy with quite an up-market crowd, so that some participation in the convivial atmosphere thus engendered is practically de rigueur. Main-house Accommodation comprises one large suite with a double and single room, plus a lounge and en-suite bathroom. Four smart and fully equipped en-suite (bath only) bedrooms are housed in former stables to the rear of the inn. A hearty Northumbrian breakfast is guaranteed, firmly setting up guests for a day's exploring. No children under 14 overnight or in the bar. no infants in the dining-room in the evening. *Open 12.30-2.30 6.30-11 (Sun 12.30-2.30, 7-10.30). Free House.* ***Beer*** *Courage Directors, Ruddles Best, Boddingtons. Patio. Family Room.* ***Accommodation*** *5 bedrooms, all en suite, £47 (single £35). Access, Visa.*

RICKLING GREEN — Cricketers Arms — B&B

Tel 01799 543210 Fax 01799 543512 Map 10 B3
Rickling Green nr Saffron Walden Essex CB11 3YE

Victorian redbrick-built pub enjoying a peaceful position overlooking the village green and cricket pitch. Inside there is a homely bar and lounge, a newly-refurbished dining-room and a small and cosy side room which has access to the delightful front terrace – a popular spot in which to relax and watch an innings or two. People needing an overnight stop close to Stansted aiport (ten minutes' drive away) will find the five comfortable bedrooms, housed in a modern rear extension, most convenient and acceptable. All are uniformly equipped with reproduction darkwood furniture, decent fabrics and have clean, tiled en-suite shower rooms. Added comforts include TVs, radio alarms, telephones, trouser presses, hairdryers and tea-makers. Two family rooms with additional beds. *Open 11-3, 6-11 (Sun 12-3, 7-10.30). Free House.* ***Beer*** *Flowers IPA & guest beers. Patio garden. Family room.* ***Accommodation*** *7 bedrooms, all en suite, from £60 (single £50), family room £75 (sleeps 3-5), weekend reductions. Children welcome overnight (under-4s stay free in parents' room), additional bed (£10) & cot (£5). Dogs by arrangement. Access, Amex, Diners, Visa.*

RINGLESTONE — Ringlestone Inn — FOOD

Tel 01622 859900 Fax 01622 859966 Map 11 C5
Ringlestone Harrietsham Wormshill Kent ME17 1NX

Splendidly atmospheric 16th-century inn, remotely tucked away beside the Pilgrim's Way on top of the North Downs between Harrietsham and Wormshill. An ale house since 1615, its three charming inter-connecting bars boast brick-and-flint walls and floors, low-beamed ceilings, a huge inglenook with winter woodburner and a good assortment of rustic furniture, including carved settles and a magnificent 17th-century oak dresser with the inscription 'A Ryght Joyouse and welcome greetynge to ye all' etched into it. This still rings true today with visitors attracted by the range of ales drawn straight from the cask, local scrumpy ciders, the selection of 24 strong country wines served by the glass and the reliable bar food on offer. Lunchtime fare is help-yourself buffet-style with a choice of casseroles, curries and pies, or a range of salads, ploughman's platters and sandwiches. Arrive early for the best of the food and to avoid the queues that form around the cramped servery! Evening fare is more formal within the candle-lit bars and adjacent dining-room with the home-made pies – ham, leek and parsnip wine, chicken and bacon in cowslip wine, beef in blackberry and raisin wine – being the highlight of the printed menu. Puddings include brandy bread pudding and treacle and nut tart. Delightfully peaceful summer patio and garden. *Open 12-3, 6-11 (winter from 6.30, Sun 12-3, 7-10.30).* ***Bar Food*** *12-2, 7-9.30. Free House.* ***Beer*** *Harveys Sussex, Tetley, Shepherd Neame Spitfire, Fuller's London Pride, Theakston Best & Old Peculier, Young's Bitter, regular guest beers. Garden, outdoor eating area. No food 25 Dec. Access, Amex, Diners, Visa.*

RIPLEY — Boar's Head Hotel — FOOD

Tel 01423 771888 **Fax 01423 771509** Map 6 C1 **B&B**

Ripley nr Harrogate North Yorkshire H53 3AY

Zzz..

Dating back to 1830 when the Lord of the Manor rebuilt the village next to his castle (Open to the public during the summer), this former coaching inn in the cobbled village square was refurbished by the present Lord (Sir Thomas Ingilby) some four years ago and turned into a hotel. Oil paintings and furniture from the castle help to create the country-house feel in tranquil drawing and morning rooms and the individually decorated bedrooms, which favour plain walls and stylish matching fabrics. Antique furniture features in rooms in the main building and in the larger rooms in another house across the cobbled square, while those in the former stable block are furnished with white-painted wicker pieces. A warm red, 38-seater dining-room in one wing is a further outlet for chef David Box's accomplished cooking. The excellent wine list has exceedingly kind prices. In another wing there is a pubby bar/bistro with snacks for the discerning: home-made soup (tomato and basil), sandwiches, filled jacket potatoes, broccoli, mushroom and Stilton quiche, vegetable strudel, calf's liver and bacon, fresh pasta dishes, pecan pie and crème brulée are representative of the range on offer. Tea is served from 3 to 5pm in the two lounges – home-made sponges, fruit cakes, scones and sandwiches. Outdoor eating in the courtyard next to the bar. *Open 11-3, 6-11 (summer 11-11, Sun 12-3, 7-10.30).* ***Bar Food*** *12-2.30, 6.30-9.30 (Sun from 7). Free House.* ***Beer*** *Theakston Best & Old Peculier, guest beer.* ***Accommodation*** *25 rooms, all en suite, £90/£105 (single £75/£95) Children welcome overnight (under-12s free, over-12s £20 if sharing parents' room, half full rate if in own room), additional bed and cot available. Garden, tennis, coarse fishing. Access, Amex, Diners, Visa.*

RIPPONDEN — Old Bridge Inn — A

Tel 01422 822595 **Fax 01422 824810** Map 6 C1

Priest Lane Ripponden nr Sowerby Bridge West Yorkshire HX6 4DF

Ancient pub (dating back to 1313) with medieval character, enormously thick stone walls and some nice old furniture in its three connecting bars. Probably originally a 14th-century monastic guest house. The modern world intrudes little into the finished interior; no machines, music or pool table, and pump clips are only tolerated for guest beers. There isn't even an inn sign. Children not allowed indoors. No garden, but tables and chairs are set on the cobbled frontage. *Open 11-4, 5.30-11 (Sat 11-11, Sun 12-3, 7-10.30). Free House.* ***Beer*** *Black Sheep Special, Timothy Taylor's Best & Golden Best, Ryburn Bitter, guest beer. Access, Visa.*

ROCHDALE — Egerton Arms — A

Tel 01706 46183 **Fax 01706 715343** Map 6 B1

Ashworthy Road Bamford Rochdale Lancashire OL11 5UP

This reputedly haunted pub, known locally as the Chapel House, stands next to St James's chapel high on the moor above Rochdale. Turn on the Ashworth road off the Bury and Heywood Road (A680) by the Ashworth reservoir. Family dining forms an integral part of the set-up and food is served all day on Sundays. *Open 12-3, 6-11 (Sat 11-11, Sun 12-10.30). Free House.* ***Beer*** *Ruddles Best & County, Webster's Yorkshire, guest beer. Patio. Pub closed 1st week Jan. Access, Visa.*

ROCKBEARE — Jack in the Green ★ — FOOD

Tel 01404 822240 Map 13 E2

Rockbeare nr Exeter Devon

A few years ago even the most weary of A30 travellers would not have given this roadside inn a second glance. Nowadays, rather than accelerating away, the brake should be applied, ready for the turning into the car park of what has become a most welcoming refreshment stop. Enthusiastic owners Paul Parnell and Charles Manktelow (and now credit must also go to new chef Matthew Mason, ex-*Gidleigh Park* hotel) run this white-painted roadside pub, one of the best eating establishments along this popular route to and from Devon. The smart exterior is bedecked with attractive flower tubs and baskets, while inside the open-

plan bar and dining areas have neatly arranged darkwood furniture, church pews and a carved oak dresser. Tasteful hunting theme paintings and prints decorate the walls and an Open fire warms the main dining area, while a few easy chairs and comfortable wooden-armed sofas are conveniently placed for waiting restaurant diners. Choosing from the excellent-value set (but regularly-changing) menu, an imaginative and well-presented meal may begin with trio of smoked fish with tarragon viniagrette or pan-fried pigeon breasts with basil and potato purée, followed by home-made quail pasties truffled with mushrooms and roast breast of duck with lime, ginger, chili and potato rösti. Those travellers popping in for a quick, lighter bite will not be disappointed by the interesting range of generously-served bar meals. Blackboards list the choice, including a whole menu board of ploughman's platters alone, while other daily chalked-up menus offer soups – broccoli and almond – and main courses like fresh pasta with beans, mushrooms and basil, home-made chicken and tarragon pie, or Cumberland sausage with bubble and squeak and mustard sauce, all with a selection of seasonal vegetables. Delicious desserts like sticky toffee pudding and fresh gooseberry and apple tart. Good-value set Sunday lunch. A carefully-chosen selection of over 80 wines includes wines of the month, a range of half-bottles and a menu of twelve wines served by the glass. Alfresco imbibers wishing to escape the traffic noise can relax in the sheltered rear courtyard or retreat to the splendid orchard garden and its Open rural views. Five miles from Junction 29 of the M5. Disabled WC. *Open 11-2.30 (Fri & Sat to 3), 6-11 (Fri from 5.30, Sun 12-3, 7-10.30).* ***Bar Food*** *11.30-2 (Sat to 2.30, Sun 12-2.30), 6.30-9.30 (Fri & Sat to 10, Sun from 7). Free House.* ***Beer*** *John Smith's Bitter, Bass, Wadworth 6X, guest beer. Closed 25 & 26 Dec. Garden. Access, Visa.*

ROCKBOURNE Rose & Thistle FOOD

Tel 01725 518236 Map 14 C3
Rockbourne nr Fordingbridge Hampshire SP6 3NL

Originally two 17th-century thatched cottages, this delightful, long and low whitewashed pub enjoys a most tranquil location within one of Hampshire's most picturesque and affluent downland villages. It is a splendid village inn decorated and furnished to a high standard. Country-style fabrics, dried flowers and magazines are tasteful touches in the charming, beamed bars which boast a collection of polished-oak tables, carved settles and benches and two huge fireplaces with winter log fires. Quality pub food, served in the civilised, music-free lounge/dining area, is light and simple at lunchtimes, including a daily home-made soup (served with fresh granary bread and a dish of butter), soft herring roes on toast, elegant Welsh rarebit served with bacon and tomato, scrambled eggs with smoked salmon and prawns, and ploughman's platters. Evening fare is more elaborate: a monthly-changing menu and a daily specials board that might feature fresh Portuguese sardines, home-made chicken liver paté laced with wild mushrooms to start, followed by imaginative and well-presented main dishes like leg of lamb steak with a warm mint and orange sauce, pan-fried lemon sole fillet, duck breast on spinach with an apricot and brandy sauce, or monkfish wrapped in bacon with a creamy prawn sauce. Interesting, al dente vegetables accompany each dish. Mainly home-made puddings. Traditional roast and many other options at Sunday lunchtime (booking advised). To round off a good meal, cafetière coffee comes with petits fours. A well-stocked bar dispenses four real ales of varying strengths and offers some six wines by the glass, from a worldwide list of 50 well-priced and carefully-chosen wines. Children allowed only in the 30-seater dining-room. *Open 11-3, 6-11 (Sun 12-3, 7-10.30).* ***Bar Food*** *12-2.30, 7-9.30. Free House.* ***Beer*** *Courage Best, Adnams Broadside, two guest beers. Garden. Access, Visa.*

ROKE Home Sweet Home Inn FOOD

Tel 01491 838249 Map 14a C3
Roke nr Benson Oxfordshire OX9 6JD

A row of low, stone white-painted former cottages (just off the B4009) well befits its homely title and image as a gentrified country pub. The pretty, walled garden in front has picnic tables and a pantiled wishing well. Popular lunchtime snacks are most notable for their number, with a vast selection of 30 sandwiches offered – from roast beef to smoked salmon club-style – and 40 more variations on salad and baked potato themes. Cooked lunches selected from the blackboards may well include salmon fish cakes, guinea fowl with mushroom sauce or beef medallions with brandy, cream and mushrooms. A more extended menu selection in the evening, served in either the bar or a prettily-appointed dining-room, engages further flights of fancy based around grilled steaks and exotic fish dishes. *Open 11-3, 5.30-11 (Sun 12-3, 7-10.30).* ***Bar Food*** *12-2, 5.30-10 (Sun 7-9.30). Free House.* ***Beer*** *Brakspear Bitter, Eldridge Pope Royal Oak. Garden. Access, Visa.*

ROMALDKIRK Rose & Crown ★ FOOD B&B

Tel 01833 650213 **Fax 01833 650828** Map 5 D3
Romaldkirk nr Barnard Castle Co Durham DL12 9EB

ZZz... 

The Rose and Crown continues to go from strength to strength; Christopher Davy's cooking is a model of consistency, with his restaurant at the Rose and Crown now firmly established as an entry in our *1996 Hotels and Restaurants Guide*. Both at lunchtime and in the evenings meals served in the elegant lounge bar and Crown Room are not, however, overlooked to any degree. Traditional favourites, from port sausages with black pudding and onion confit to smoked Loch Fyne salmon with scrambled eggs are always cooked with flair; colourful presentation, with coleslaw and marinated mushrooms, turns a humble brown bread bap into a memorable repast: chicken, pineapple, celery and walnuts constitute a typical filling. Best value of all, though, are the daily lunch specials which are rightly used as the showcase for a kitchen which is never slow to experiment and always actively evolving new dishes. Home-cured gravlax is a perfect curtain raiser to a hot confit of duck leg with lentils and salad or the locally-renowned Whitby Woof topped with prawns and nut-brown butter. Exemplary puds, typified by sticky toffee pudding and baked apple filo parcels, and perfectly-selected local cheeses (Cotherstone, Blue Wensleydale) make for a difficult choice of 'afters'. Creaking floorboards, beams, stripped stone walls, well-chosen antique furniture and contemporary fabrics feature in the en-suite bedrooms (all, except one, having bath and showers) and duvets can be swapped for sheets and blankets.
Front views overlook the village green. Five further rooms, in an outside annexe, are more uniform in size and design, with modern furniture and fittings. *Open 11-30-3, 5.30-11 (Sun 12-3, 7-10.30). **Bar Food** 12-1.30, 6.30-9.30 (7-9 Sun). Free House. **Beer** Theakston Best & Old Peculier, Marston's Pedigree. **Accommodation** 12 bedrooms, all en suite, £75 (single £54). Children welcome overnight (under-5s free if sharing), additional bed (£12) available. Access, Visa.*

ROSEDALE ABBEY Milburn Arms FOOD B&B

Tel & Fax 01751 417312 Map 5 E3
Rosedale Abbey nr Pickering North Yorkshire YO18 8RA

ZZz...

Tranquil surroundings in the beautiful North Yorkshire moors are the big attraction of Terry and Joan Bentley's delightful country hotel which has parts dating back to the 1700s. Their brochure states 'we're also the village pub' and, indeed, the spacious bar with its low beams does have a pubby atmosphere and comes complete with dart board and a couple of games machines. But it's the extensive range of bar meals that is the big attraction; tiger tail prawns in garlic and ginger, home-made Yorkshire pudding with rich onion gravy, grilled Farndale goat's cheese with salad, oak-smoked salmon and fresh asparagus tagliatelle, venison casserole with green ginger wine and juniper, Provençal fish stew and an excellent treacle tart demonstrate the range. Bedrooms are individually decorated in a variety of styles – rich reds and blues, pale pink and yellow, pastel seersucker fabric – and furnished with a mixture of pine, freestanding darkwood and hotel unit-style furniture. All have good bathrooms (with showers over tubs) plus TV, direct-dial phone and beverage kit. A good spot in summer is the peaceful garden, opposite the village green, with tables set out under a splendid 150-year-old cedar tree. *Open 11.30-3, 6-30-11 (Sun 12-3, 7-10.30). **Bar Food** 12-2 (Sat & Sun to 2.15), 7-9.30. Free House. **Beer** Bass, Stones, Theakston XB & Old Peculier, guest beer. Garden, outdoor eating. **Accommodation** 12 bedrooms, all en suite, £74 (single £44). Children welcome overnight (under-5s £6.50, 5-12s £10, over-12s £15 if sharing parents' room) additional bed and cot available. Dogs welcome in ground-floor annexe rooms only. Accommodation closed 23-25 Dec. Access, Diners, Visa.*

ROSEDALE ABBEY White Horse Farm Hotel FOOD B&B

Tel 01751 417239 **Fax 01751 417781** Map 5 E3
Rosedale Abbey nr Pickering North Yorkshire YO18 8SE

ZZz...

The White Horse was a farm when Rosedale Abbey was a thriving mining village with a population ten times greater than it is now. As was then the practice, one end of the farmhouse was turned into a 'taps room' for the miners and its transformation into today's hotel had begun. The bar is full of interest with a couple of rough-hewn tree trunks acting as poles holding up the ceiling beams, stuffed birds, a fish in a glass case, horse harness and much more besides decorating the walls, some of which are of rough, exposed stone.

Yorkshire fare features strongly on the bar menu: Yorkshire pudding with roast beef and onion gravy, Rosedale rarebit made with Theakston bitter, Whitby haddock pots, roast pheasant with an orange and ginger sauce; along with supreme of chicken with Stilton sauce and creamy tagliatelle with wild mushrooms. There are also various sandwiches, filled baguettes ploughman's platters and a short list of puds. Bedrooms, including two de luxe rooms with separate sitting areas, are prettily decorated with matching floral bedcovers (no duvets here), curtains and dado band around the woodchip walls. Even the en-suite bathrooms, half with showers and half with tubs, co-ordinate with their respective bedrooms. All rooms have TV and tea- and coffee-making equipment and some have wonderful views across Rosedale. 30 whiskies available at the bar. No children in the bar areas after 8.30pm. Take the A170 out of Pickering going north; after approximately three miles turn right – follow signs to Rosedale for seven miles and the pub is clearly signposted from the village. *Open 12-2.30, 6.30-11 (Sat 12-11, Sun 12-3, 7-10.30).* ***Bar Food*** *12-2 6.30-9.30 (Sun from 7). Free House.* ***Beer*** *Tetley Traditional, Theakston Best, XB & Old Peculier, guest beer. Garden, outdoor eating. Family room.* ***Accommodation*** *15 bedrooms, all en suite, £60 (single £35) – winter reductions. Children welcome overnight (under-5s £5, 5-14s half price) additional bed and cot available. Dogs by arrangement. Accommodation closed 25 Dec. Access, Amex, Diners, Visa.*

ROWDE — George & Dragon ★ FOOD

Tel 01380 723053 **Fax 01380 724738** Map 14 B3
High Street Rowde Wiltshire SN10 2PN

Inspired, inventive and realistically-priced cooking emanates from the kitchen of Tim and Helen Withers' village pub leased from Wadworth's brewery. A single bar has half a dozen Britannia tables and there are two dozen assorted bentwood chairs in the dining-room set at plain, unclothed tables. Everywhere are blackboards proclaiming what's on offer, the emphasis firmly being on fresh fish from Cornwall. Dishes run from imaginative ploughman's platters, or a chard and saffron tart to well-presented main-course dishes such as grilled guinea fowl with lime, fillet of turbot steamed with garlic, ragout of John Dory, mullet and prawn, and monkfish with green peppercorns, brandy and cream. A typical set lunch menu offers alternatives only at each course, perhaps crostini or brandade salad, then salmon fishcakes with hollandaise or chicken and lobster sausage, ending with chocolate torte and coffee bean sauce or rhubarb and ginger crumble. Out of 60 names on the wine list a commendable 14 are available by the glass. Booking is always advised, at least one week in advance for tables at weekends. Tables in the walled garden during good weather. The pub's 'English-only' policy is extended to the mineral water and cheeses, of which Stilton, Allerdale, Sharpham and Cotherstone are a typical selection. *Open 12-3 (not Mon), 7-11 (Mon from 7.30, 12-3, 7-10.30). Closed Mon lunch, 25, 26 Dec & 1 Jan.* ***Bar Food*** *Tue-Sat only 12-2, 7-10.* ***Beer*** *Wadworth 6X & IPA. Garden, outdoor eating. Access, Visa.*

RUCKHALL — Ancient Camp Inn B&B

Tel 01981 250449 **Fax 01981 251581** Map 14 A1
Ruckhall nr Eaton Bishop Hereford & Worcester HR2 9QX

Zzz...

The route from the A465 at Belmont Abbey to Ruckhall turns into a twist of narrow lanes. Once there, look carefully for signs to the Ancient Camp, so named because the site was once an Iron Age fort. Certainly, it must have been impregnable from the northern side, as the pub stands atop an escarpment overlooking a wide bend in the river Wye. In fair weather, there's a fine view across the fertile river valley from a front patio bordered by roses, the backdrop of the inn fronted by window boxes and hanging baskets. The interior decor of the pub retains the original stonework and flagstone floors, which results in an intimate atmosphere to which dried flowers and huge log fires add a special glow in winter. At the rear are three neat bedrooms with en-suite showers; to the front, two superb bedrooms, one with a private sitting room, the other's en-suite bath elevated to maximise its river view. All are centrally heated, with telephone, television and bedside clock radio. No children under 8 in pub or accommodation. New owner (and chef) since the last edition of this Guide. *Open 12-3, 7-11. CLosed all day Monday. Free House.* ***Beer*** *Wood's Parish, Whitbread West Country Pale Ale. Riverside garden, outdoor eating. Family room.* ***Accommodation*** *5 bedrooms, all en suite, £58/£48 (single £45/£35). Children welcome overnight, additional bed available (£15). No dogs. Access, Visa.*

Rudge — Full Moon — B&B

Tel 01373 830936 **Fax 01373 831366** Map 14 B3
Rudge nr Frome Somerset BA11 2QF

Conveniently located two miles from the A36 at its junction with the A361 (and equally close to the Woodland Park) is the sleepy hamlet of Rudge. Its white-painted village inn is of 16th-century origins and its interior has been meticulously restored; there's a wealth of interior stonework, old fireplaces and uneven flagstone floors in a succession of intimate nooks and alcoves whose focal point is a friendly locals' bar. All manner of local history and memorabilia provides the starting point for a tall story or two. An extension which threatens to dwarf the original has its ground floor given over to a function room. Above are the five en-suite bedrooms (four with shower only), purpose-built and a little cottagey in style. All are neatly equipped with TV, direct-dial phone, radio-alarm and tea- and coffee-making facility: there's one decent-sized family room. To the pub's rear the walled garden is neatly kept and has some swings; from here, as from the bedrooms, there are lovely rural views down to Broker's Wood. *Open 12-3, 6-11 (Sun 12-3, 7-10.30). Free House.* ***Beer*** *Bass, Wadworth 6X, Butcombe. Garden, children's play area. Family room.* ***Accommodation*** *5 bedrooms, all en suite, £45 (£30 single, £60 family room). Children welcome overnight (free if sharing parents' room), additional bed and cot available. Access, Amex, Visa.*

Running Waters — Three Horseshoes Inn — B&B

Tel 01913 720286 Map 5 E3
Sherburn House Running Waters nr Durham Co Durham DH1 2SR

With fine views over open country and north-west towards Durham (4 miles), the 'Shoes' stands by the busy A181, fronted by old ploughshares and farming implements; the Running Waters of its location reflects olden times when water was carried from its underground stream by the monks of nearby Sherborne House. While none of the refashioned bedrooms are particularly spacious, they all have en-suite facilities (two with shower-trays only), TV, tea-maker and radio-alarm, and are decorated in a bright, cottagey style. There's a small residents' lounge area and a fenced-in rear garden; front double-glazing ensures that the morning traffic will not become intrusive. *Open 11-3, 6-11 (Sun 12-3, 7-10.30). Free House.* ***Beer*** *Ruddles Best, Marston's Pedigree, guest beer. Garden.* ***Accommodation*** *6 bedrooms, all en suite £46 (single £30, family room £55). Children welcome overnight (under-6s stay free in parents' room), additional bed and cot available. Check-in by arrangement. Access, Diners, Visa.*

Rusper — Star Inn — A

Tel 01293 871264 Map 11 A5
High Street Rusper West Sussex RH12 4RA

4 miles west of Crawley, close to the A24. Just south of the Sussex/Surrey border, close (but not particularly convenient for) Gatwick Airport. A heavily-beamed, traditional old coaching inn dating back to 1460. The menu stays sensibly short and game dishes feature in season. Landlord Derek Welton has been running the Star in his own inimitable style for 12 years. Whitbread Wayside Inns. *Open 11-11 (Sun 12-3, 7-10.30).* ***Beer*** *Fremlins, Brakspear, Marston's Pedigree, Boddingtons. Garden. Family Room, Access, Visa.*

Saddleworth — Green Ash Hotel — B&B

Tel 01457 871035 **Fax 01457 871414** Map 6 C2
Denshaw Road Delph Saddleworth Greater Manchester OL3 5TS

Zzz...

Just a decade ago, one man saw this burned-out Co-Op warehouse and barn as an unrivalled investment opportunity; today, Terry Ogden's civilised country inn is the realisation of that dream. Rebuilt and extended entirely in handsome Derbyshire stone, it stands proud on the A640 above Delph village enfolded by the woody moors. Each of the bedrooms enjoys a share of the view; they possess in common a high degree of comfort and practical up-to-date accoutrements with satellite TV, radio alarms, direct-dial phones and trouser presses. Included in executive standard rooms are mini-bars; all bathrooms are bright, fully-tiled and have over-bath showers. This is decidedly more inn than pub; there's Tetley bitter on hand pump to enjoy in the bar or on the scenic, sun-trapped patio. Small well-trained" dogs in rooms only. Nearest motorway Junctions: 21 & 22 of M62. *Open 12-2, 5-11 (Sun 12-3, 7-10.30). Free House.* ***Beer*** *Tetley, three guest beers. Garden.* ***Accommodation*** *15 bedrooms, all en suite, £52/62 (single £39.50). Children welcome overnight (under-2s stay free in parents' room, 3-9s £5), additional bed (£5) and cot available. Access, Amex, Visa.*

Saffron Walden — Eight Bells — FOOD

Tel 01799 522790 Map 10 B3
18 Bridge Street Saffron Walden Essex CB10 1BU

A newly refurbished, solidly traditional pub whose bar is partitioned by ancient wall timbers into two smaller rooms, complete with old furniture and exposed timbers and brick. The old barn restaurant has been extended to include a central gallery and the walls are hung with tapestries and flags. The bar and restaurant menus offer reliably good food: ploughman's, home-made soup, fresh Cromer crab, roast duckling with orange sauce, home-made lasagne plus a large selection of fresh fish – prawn thermidor, whole grilled plaice with parsley butter, with hot toffee-apple fudge cake, or Morello cherry cheesecake for pudding. Food is served all day Sunday from noon to 9.30. *Open 11-3, 6-11 (Sun 12-10.30). **Bar Food** 12-2.30, 6.00-9.30 (Sat to 10, Sun 12-9.30). Free House. **Beer** Adnams Bitter, Burton, Friary Meux, Tetley, guest beer. Garden, outdoor eating. Family room. Access, Amex, Visa.*

Saffron Walden — Saffron Hotel — FOOD

Tel 01799 522676 Fax 01799 513979 Map 10 B3
High Street Saffron Walden Essex CB10 1AY

Formerly a coaching inn with origins in the 16th century, the Saffron Hotel is more hotel than pub today but the green plush bar still welcomes all and offers real ale and bar snacks. The printed bar menu includes steak and kidney pie, minute steak with Stilton, skate wing with caper, prawn and nut butter as well as baked potatoes with different fillings. The blackboard menu changes daily – Lincolnshire sausage casserole, lamb's liver and bacon. Bedrooms come in all shapes and sizes, some with head-threatening beams. The best and largest have been refurbished with stylish fabrics and smart new veneered furniture, the worst are cramped singles that share a shower room. All have telephone and TV. *Open 11-11 (Sun 12-3, 7-10.30). **Bar Food** 12-2, 7-9 (Fri & Sat to 9.30). Free House. **Beer** Flowers, Adnams. Terrace. **Accommodation** 17 bedrooms, all en suite, £65 (4-poster £85, single £45/£50). Children welcome overnight (0-3 yrs free if sharing parents' room), additional bed (£10) and cot available. Access, Amex, Diners, Visa.*

St Agnes — Driftwood Spars Hotel — B&B

Tel & Fax 01872 552428 Map 12 B3
Trevaunance Cove St Agnes Cornwall TR5 0RT

Constructed in the 17th century of huge ship's timbers and spars (hence the name), with stone and slate, the hotel – once a marine chandlery and tin miners trading post – is located just 100 yards from one of Cornwall's best beaches, making it an ideal family destination for a holiday. Accommodation comprises nine neat and tidy en-suite rooms – one family room with bunk beds – featuring attractive co-ordinating fabrics, and a mix of furnishings that ranges from comfortable new pine to modern-style white furniture. Rooms are well equipped and two afford peaceful sea views. Guests are treated to the sound of waves on the beach and live music on Fridays and Saturdays. *Open 11-11 (Sun 12-3, 7-10.30). Free House. **Beer** St Austell HSD, Sharp's, guest beer. Family room. **Accommodation** 9 bedrooms, all en suite, £58 (single £29). Children welcome overnight (under-4s stay free, over-4s half price in parents' room), cot available. Accommodation closed 25 Dec. Access, Amex, Diners, Visa.*

St Albans — Garibaldi — FOOD

Tel 01727 855046 Map 15a F2
61 Albert Street St Albans Hertfordshire AL1 1RT

Popular old town-centre pub located down a narrow back street not far from St Albans Abbey. Pleasant Victorian style interior with a central servery, a few alcove seating hidey-holes and a piney, café-style conservatory dining-room leading to a narrow patio with tables and chairs. Food servery displaying salads, plus a sandwich, ploughman's platters and filled jacket potato list and a blackboard listing home-cooked hot specials, such as curried apple soup, spicy vegetable couscous, steak and ESB pie and chicken in a mulled wine sauce. This is a chip-free zone so expect fresh vegetables or salads. Mexican dishes and three-course Sunday roast. Puddings are mainly of the bought-in variety. Snacks and salads only served between 2 and 6 pm. *Open 11-11 (Sun 12-3, 7-10.30). **Bar Food** 12-9 (no food Sun eve). **Beer** Fuller's, guest beer. Garden, outdoor eating. No credit cards.*

St Albans — Rose & Crown — A

Tel 01727 851903 Map 15a F2
St Michael's Street St Albans Hertfordshire AL3 4SG

This is a pleasingly simple, woody and traditional 300-year-old pub located in the upmarket St Michael's 'village' suburb of the town, close to Verulamium Park and the Roman Museum. Classic public bar with heavy beams, huge fireplace, sturdy furnishings and a chatty atmosphere free from intrusive music and games. Simple, unadorned and comfortable lounge bar and flower-decked side patio for fine weather imbibing. Renowned locally for its imaginative and unusual range of American-style 'gourmet' sandwiches available at lunchtimes. Regular live folk and blues music, barbershop singing and quiz nights. *Open 11.30-3, 5.30-11 (Sat from 6, Sun 12-3, 7-10.30).* ***Beer*** *Adnams, Tetley, Wadworth 6X, guest beer. Garden. No credit cards.*

St Austell — White Hart — B&B

Tel 01726 72100 **Fax 01726 74705** Map 12 B3
Church Street St Austell Cornwall PL25 4AT

Attractive and comfortable accommodation is offered in this three-storey town-centre hotel, dating from the 16th century and located opposite the church. All the well-looked-after bedrooms have smart darkwood furniture, quality floral fabrics, pink and plum decor and the usual comforts of satellite TV, telephones, tea-making facilities and hairdryers. Modern carpeted bathrooms (two with shower only) are spacious, fully-tiled and clean. Public areas include the well-furnished Admirals Bar and the more pubby Captains Bar, complete with pool tables, darts and other games. Decent prints decorate the walls throughout the inn. Note: nearby parking is difficult. *Open 11-11 (Sun 12-3, 7-10.30). Afternoon teas served.* ***Beer*** *St Austell.* ***Accommodation*** *18 bedrooms, all en suite £63 (single £40). Children welcome overnight (under-12s stay free in parents' room), cot available. Access, Amex, Diners, Visa.*

We endeavour to be as up-to-date as possible but inevitably some changes to landlords, chefs and other key staff occur after the Guide has gone to press.

St Briavels — George Inn — B&B

Tel 01594 530228 **Fax 01594 530260** Map 14 B2
High Street St Briavels nr Lydney Gloucestershire GL15 6SP

A moody old part-medieval pub whose sombre stonework and blackened beams yet create intimate nooks and crannies warmed by real log fires in winter, with one of the bars featuring a fascinating 10th-century Celtic coffin lid. In full view of the ruined medieval St Briavels castle, rooks and royalty joust on an inlaid patio chessboard. Modest yet comfortable accommodation provided in three en-suite bedrooms (two with WC/showers only) is housed under the eaves with an outlook either up the village street or down over the castle, which like the inn is reputed to be haunted. Choice of 25 malt whiskies at the bar. No smoking dining-room. *Open 11-3, 6.30-11 (Sun 12-3, 7-10.30). Free House.* ***Beer*** *Wadworth 6X, Marston's Pedigree, Courage Directors, Boddingtons, guest beer. Patio, outdoor eating. Family room.* ***Accommodation*** *3 bedrooms, all en suite £40 (single £25). Children welcome overnight, additional bed (£20). Visa.*

St Kew — St Kew Inn — A

Tel 01208 841259 Map 12 B3
St Kew nr Wadebridge Cornwall PL30 3HB

Well off the beaten track, amid tiny lanes in a small hamlet in a splendid wooded valley, the 16th-century St Kew Inn is a peaceful spot in which to savour a relaxing summer drink in the large attractive garden, which looks towards the parish church. Inside, the atmospheric main bar has a slate floor laid with high-backed settles and Windsor chairs; a popular window seat overlooks the cobbled courtyard, resplendent with summer flower tubs and baskets. A fine black-painted kitchen range burns logs and warms this bar in winter, old meat hooks hang from the ceiling and generally a good chatty atmosphere prevails. There is a further stone-walled bar and a small dining-room. Local ales are served in the traditional way, straight from the barrel. *Open 11-2.30, 6-11 (Sun 12-2.30, 7-10.30).* ***Beer*** *St Austell. Garden, outdoor eating area. Access, Visa.*

St Mawes — Rising Sun — FOOD B&B

Tel 01326 270233 Map 12 B4
The Square St Mawes Cornwall TR2 5DJ

Zzz...

Popular and lively little hotel that occupies a splendid position overlooking the quaint harbour and its 19th-century quay. The busy, simply furnished 'locals' bar has a good pubby atmosphere, and is a favourite among the gig rowers. More refined is the small cane-furnished conservatory which houses the lounge bar and has access to the harbour-view terrace that attracts the crowds when the sun shines. Bedrooms are smart with attractive wallpapers and fabrics, modern pine furniture, TVs, tea-makers, telephones and all bar one have immaculate en-suite bathrooms. Front rooms enjoy peaceful harbour and headland vistas. As we went to press the hotel was closing for a complete refurbishment; hopefully, it can only get better! *Open 11-11 in summer (wunter 11-2.30, 6-11, Sun all year 12-3, 7-10.30). **Beer** St Austell. Terrace, outdoor eating. **Accommodation** 11 rooms, 10 en suite, £64/£79 (single £32/£39.50). Children welcome overnight (under-10s stay free in parents' room), additional bed and cot available. Access, Amex, Visa.*

St Mawgan — Falcon Inn — A

Tel 01637 860225 Map 12 B3
St Mawgan Newquay Cornwall TR8 4EP

In the heart of the holiday land where good unspoilt traditional pubs are an endangered breed, the Falcon survives and is a haven for the discerning pub-goer. Nestling in a most attractive village, deep in the Vale of Lanherne and a stone's throw from its tiny stream, this 16th-century wisteria-clad inn is a popular summer destination with those escaping the bucket-and-spade brigade on the beach. Inside, the main bar is neatly arranged and decorated with pine farmhouse tables and chairs, trellis wallpaper and decent prints and is thankfully music and game-free. The adjacent dining-room has a rug-strewn flagged floor, a pine dresser and French windows leading out into the bench-filled cobbled courtyard. Beyond a rose-covered arch there is a splendid terraced garden, ideal for enjoying some summer refreshment. *Open 11-3, 6-11 (Sun 12-3, 7-10.30). **Beer** St Austell. Garden, outdoor eating area. Access, Diners, Visa.*

St Neots — Chequers Inn — FOOD

Tel 01480 472116 Map 15 E1
St Mary's Street Eynesbury nr St Neots Cambridgeshire PE19 2TA

A lovely old English country pub, where you can sit in the main bar with its roaring winter fires and highly-polished dark furniture or at tables with green tablecloths for bar food, or in the dining area for more substantial meals. The changing blackboard bar menu offers home-cooking by landlord David Taylor: cauliflower and broccoli soup, steak and mushroom pie or steak and ale pie, a substantial ploughman's lunch, mushrooms with garlic butter and croutons, pasta with chicken and vegetarian options like hazelnut roast and pasta and courgette provençale. Puddings include home-made bread-and-butter pudding and fruit crumbles. Set Sunday lunch £12. Children are kept amused in the outdoor play area in the fenced-off garden. *Open 10.30-3, 7-11 (Sun 12-2, 7-10.30). **Bar Food** 12-2, 7-9.45 (Sun to 9). Free House. **Beer** Webster's Yorkshire, Boddingtons, Wadworth 6X. Garden, outdoor eating, children's play area. Access, Amex, Diners, Visa.*

St Neots — Eaton Oak — B&B

Tel 01480 219555 **Fax 01480 407520** Map 15 E1
Crosshall Road Eaton Ford St Neots Cambridgeshire PE19 4AG

The completely renovated Charles Wells brewery's Eaton Oak is located at the junction of the A1 and A45 but the bedrooms are happily undisturbed by traffic – you can expect a comfortable overnight stay. The rooms in the motel extension are large and warm, with fitted units, colour TVs, tea-makers, direct-dial telephones and well-fitted bath/shower rooms. In the main building (once a farmhouse) the bar has been extended along with the restaurant and a conservatory added which leads on to the garden. Families are well looked after (even a free kiddies menu) and an outdoor play area is provided. *Open 11-2.30, 6-11 (Sun 12-3, 7-10.30). **Beer** Charles Wells, guest beer. **Accommodation** 9 bedrooms, all en suite, £50 (single £40). Children welcome overnight (rate depends on age), additional bed available. Check-in by arrangement. Access, Amex, Visa.*

SALISBURY Haunch of Venison A

Tel 01722 322024 Map 14 C3
1-5 Minster Street Salisbury Wiltshire SP1 1TB

Antiquity and charm ooze from this ancient and tiny city-centre pub, which dates from 1320 when it was built as a church house for nearby St Thomas's Church. Three rooms, usually busy with tourists, radiate from the minuscule pewter-topped bar and are affectionately known as the 'horsebox', a tiny snug off the entrance lobby; the 'House of Commons', which features a chequered stone floor and plenty of wooden panels, beams and carved oak benches; and the upper room or 'House of Lords', boasting a 600-year-old fireplace with a small side window displaying a mummified hand holding a pack of 18th-century playing cards, which was discovered here in 1903. 160 malt whiskies. Children allowed upstairs only. *Open 11-11 (Sun 12-3, 7-10.30).* ***Beer*** *Courage Best & Directors. Access, Amex, Diners, Visa.*

SALISBURY King's Arms Hotel B&B

Tel 01722 327629 Fax 01722 414246 Map 14 C3
7a-11 St John's Street Salisbury Wiltshire SP1 2SB

The half-timbered, wattle and daub facade of this historic city inn, located opposite the Cathedral Close, dates from the early 1600s, while the main core of the inn was built at least ninety years before the first foundations were laid for the magnificent cathedral. Oak panelling and beams abound in the log fire-warmed bars and in the clean and comfortable en-suite bedrooms, two of which have four-posters, and reached by a winding staircase plus a series of sloping-floored corridors. The converted stable across the courtyard houses three bedrooms decorated in a light, modern style. A high standard of comfort is guaranteed with all rooms having TVs, telephones, tea-making kits and trouser presses. Residents' lounge. *Open 11-3, 6-11 (Sun 12-10.30). Free House.* ***Beer*** *Flowers Original, Wadworth 6X, Boddingtons. Courtyard.* ***Accommodation*** *15 bedrooms, all en suite, £68/£78/£88 (single £45/£55, family Room £98). Children welcome overnight (under-2s stay free in parents' room, 3-12s £12), additional bed and cot available. Access, Amex, Diners, Visa.*

SATWELL Lamb Inn A

Tel 01491 628482 Fax 01491 628900 Map 15a D3
Satwell nr Shepherds Green Henley-on-Thames Oxfordshire RG9 4QZ

An untypically tiny Thames Valley inn, tucked away off the B841, two miles south of Nettlebed. Beneath a weird agglomeration of unevenly pitched roofs, it contains only two small rooms within; floors are quarry tile and the tables are assorted. Every nook and cranny seems taken up with collectables: old beer bottles (glass and earthenware) dating back to the last century; an old dog grate, butter churn and mangle. There's extra room to spread out in the garden, while very little ones can frolic on a swing or a slide. Young tenant licensees, less than sartorially elegant in appearance, seem otherwise eager to please. Minimum of six wines by the glass. *Open 12-3, 6-11 (Sat 11-11, Sun 12-3, 7-10.30).* ***Beer*** *Brakspear. Garden, children's play area. Family room. No credit cards.*

SAUNDERTON Rose & Crown Inn B&B

Tel 01844 345299 Fax 01844 343140 Map 15a D2
Wycombe Road Saunderton Princes Risborough Buckinghamshire HP27 9NP

Located beside the A4010, this large pub dates back to 1840 and has a spacious, neatly-furnished bar and lounge area. Business-orientated accommodation comprises modest, functional bedrooms with built-in units and compact en-suite facilities (six with showers only). Two superior bedrooms are furnished and decorated to a good standard. TVs, tea-makers, telephones and radio-alarms are standard. Double-glazing helps to reduce traffic noise on road-facing rooms. Attractive sun-trap terrace reached through French doors leading off the no-smoking Beechwood Restaurant. *Open 11-3 & 5.30-11 (Sun 12-3 & 7-10.30). Free House.* ***Beer*** *Brakspear Bitter, Morrells Varsity, Morland Bitter. Garden.* ***Accommodation*** *17 bedrooms, 14 en suite £64.95/£67.95 (single £39.95/£54.95/£59.95). Children welcome overnight, additional bed and cot available (£5-£10). Accommodation closed 25-27 December. Garden. Access, Amex, Diners, Visa.*

We do not accept free meals or hospitality – our inspectors pay their own bills and never book in the name of Egon Ronay's Guides.

Sawley — Sawley Arms — FOOD

Tel 01765 620642 Map 6 C1
Sawley Fountains Abbey Ripon North Yorkshire HG4 3EQ

A fine old-fashioned dining pub whose immaculate upkeep and enduring popularity are a tribute to the devotion of June Hawes, who has been in control here for some 26 years. The garden, her pride and joy, is a recent Britain in Bloom winner, while the pub inside is flower-filled and homely. In a succession of alcoves and tiny rooms (two being non-smoking), legions of regulars find their chosen spots and order at the bar from a varied menu amply supplemented by truly tempting daily specials. Pride is taken equally in June's range of freshly-cut sandwiches, delicious soups which on any one day might be celery, apple and tomato or leek and apricot; pancakes, another popular item, may be filled with salmon and herbs, or peaches with curried prawns, with home-made bread and butter pudding for dessert. The range of food is further extended by night when one end of the pub becomes rather more restauranty and choices will include steak pie with buttercrust pastry and half a duckling with Curaçao sauce. Further puddings include apple pie and amaretti schokoladen torte or there's a plate of English cheeses. Capable, friendly service in a warm atmosphere. No children under 8 indoors. *Open 11.30-3, 6.30-11 (Sun 12-3, 7-10.30). **Bar Food** 12-2, 7-9 (no food Sun eve & all day Mon). Free House. **Beer** Theakston Best, Younger's Scotch. Garden, outdoor eating. Access, Visa (only over £10).*

Saxton — Plough Inn ★ FOOD

Tel 01937 557242 Map 7 D1
Headwell Lane Saxton nr Tadcaster North Yorkshire IS24 9PB

Once a farmhouse, this white-stone Victorian building in the main street of the village is officially a pub, although now more of a restaurant. However, you can still have just a drink in the carpeted bar with its pew seating, armchairs and sewing-machine tables. At lunchtime only one can enjoy chef/landlord Simon Treanor's bar snacks, either one of the lunchtime specials (minute steak with mushrooms, breast of chicken with curried butter), a sandwich (hot rare beef, prawn mayonnaise, ploughman's lunch) or something from the restaurant's blackboard menu. The latter might include starters like chicken and game terrine, warm pigeon salad and home-made soup and main dishes such as rump of beef with garlic mash, fillet of sole with onion marmalade and red wine jus, and guinea fowl with sweet potatoes and smoked bacon. Good puds like sticky toffee pudding, strawberry pavlova and almond tart with cinnamon-flavoured clotted cream. About half a dozen wines are available by the glass. In summer there a few tables out on the roadside lawn. Between Tadcaster and Sherburn in Elmet off A162, not far from A1 (via B1217). *Open 12-3 & 6-11. Closed D Sun, all Mon & 3 days Christmas. **Bar Meals** 12-2 (Tue-Sat), Restaurant 12-2, 6.30-10 (not Sun eve). Free House. **Beer** Theakston's Best Bitter, guest beer. Garden, outdoor eating. Access, Visa.*

Scales — White Horse — FOOD

Tel 017687 7924 Map 4 C3
Scales nr Threlkeld Cumbria CA12 4SY

Set back from the A66 between Keswick and Penrith and 1000 feet above sea level, the whitewashed White Horse is surrounded by stunning Cumbrian countryside and is within easy reach of splendid walking country. Immaculately kept, the interior has uneven whitewashed walls, a low beamed ceiling, a slate fireplace (customers put coins between the gaps and the money is later collected for charity) and well-polished copper pans and lots of plants add to the rustic atmosphere. In the past year new Cumbrian-born owners Bruce and Pauline Jackson have maintained the pub's reputation for honest home-cooking using fresh local ingredients, with produce supplied by a trout-farming uncle from Borrowdale, a farming brother, local butchers and game from a nearby estate. Lunchtime choices are listed on a blackboard menu and may feature Wabberthwaite sausage with mushrooms and salad, ploughman's platters with a choice of Northern cheeses, a hearty home-made soup, various salads and lamb cobbler with vegetables. Evenings bring candlelight and a more restauranty menu. Dishes on the printed list – Borrowdale trout with almonds, pork fillet with shallots, mushrooms, cream and brandy – are supplemented by daily specials like cauliflower an watercress soup, Greystoke pie (local estate game pie) and grilled Wabberthwaite ham with eggs and home-made pickles, mustards and chutneys. For dessert try the chocolate terrine, or may be Totty's gingerbread served hot with rum butter. *Open 12-2.30, 6.30-11 (Sun 12-3, 7-10.30). Closed Mon Nov-Easter. **Bar Food** 12-1.45, 6.30-9 (Sun from 7). **Beer** Jennings Best, Yates, Hesket Newmarket Blencathra. Patio, outdoor eating. Family room. Access, Visa.*

SCOLE | Scole Inn | B&B

Tel 01379 740481 **Fax 01379 740762** Map 10 C2
Ipswich Road Scole nr Diss Scole Norfolk IP22 4DR

Built in 1655 by a wool merchant, this grand-looking red brick inn is Grade 1 listed for its architectural interest. Splendid brick gables front and rear show a Dutch influence. Bedrooms in the Georgian stable block are quieter and more modern than those in the main building, which face a busy lorry route. These rooms, though, are full of character, many having carved oak doors, old timbers and fireplaces plus four-poster or half-tester beds. All bedrooms have well-equipped bath/shower rooms. The beamed, pubby bar is also full of atmosphere with a vast brick fireplace, dark oak furniture and an 'old English Inn' ambience. Lyric Hotels. *Open 11-11 (Sun 12-3, 7-10.30).* ***Beer*** *Adnams Southwold & Broadside, guest beer.* ***Accommodation*** *23 bedrooms, all en suite £66/£76 (single £52). Children welcome overnight (under 12 free). Garden. Access, Amex, Diners, Visa.*

SEAHOUSES | Olde Ship | FOOD

Tel 01665 720200 **Fax 01665 721383** Map 5 D1 **B&B**
9 Main Street Seahouses Northumberland NE68 7RD

Zzz...

Perched above the small harbour with splendid sea views out to the Farne Islands, the Olde Ship began life as a farmhouse in 1745 and was first licensed in 1812. It has been in present licensees Alan and Jean Glen's family since 1910. Behind the grey stone exterior there lies a real treasure trove of nautical paraphernalia collected over 85 years. The saloon bar is full of objects hanging from ceiling, walls and bar; a ship's figurehead, oars, diving helmet, brass lamps, ship's wheel, baskets, model boats, pictures, barrels, fishing gear and more besides. The smaller cabin bar has panelling, royal blue upholstered seating and even more collectibles, while a small area to the rear (where children can sit) features stuffed seabirds in cases. Good bar food is generously priced and ranges from rich crab soup and generously-filled sandwiches to wonderful, old-fashioned English desserts (raspberry pie, golden sponge, gooseberry crumble, Brown Betty, sticky toffee meringue gateau). Main courses might include lamb korma, beef stovies, beef in stout, liver and onions or a roast rib of beef with Yorkshire pudding. In the restaurant, generally open weekends only unless very busy, the menu offers a good choice of courses; booking advised. Upstairs, the nautical theme continues, with a fine collection of large model boats in one of the first-floor hallways. The bedrooms, including three in outside annexes, are clean, neat and unfussy, with plain painted walls and cottagey bedspreads; furniture varies from modern fitted units to more traditional freestanding pieces; two rooms have four-poster beds. Direct-dial telephone, television (with satellite) and mineral water are standard, and every room is en suite, though half have shower only, and some are on the small side. The pub also has its own lawn and summerhouse overlooking the harbour and enjoying fabulous views. In the evenings, the bars fill with the locals and fishermen who mix well with visitors. *Open 11-3, 6-11 (Sun 12-3, 7-10.30).* ***Bar Food*** *12-2.30, 7-8.30. Free House.* ***Beer*** *Theakston Best & XB, Longstone, Marston's Pedigree, Morland Old Speckled Hen, Newcastle Exhibition, McEwan's Scotch. Garden, putting, outdoor play area. Family room.* ***Accommodation*** *16 bedrooms, all en suite, £68 (single £34), winter reductions. Children welcome overnight (minimum age 10). Check-in after 2pm. No dogs. Closed Dec & Jan. Access, Visa.*

SEAVIEW | Seaview Hotel | FOOD

Tel 01983 612711 **Fax 01983 613729** Map 15 D4 **B&B**
High Street Seaview Isle of Wight PO34 5EX

A small early Victorian hotel, charmingly and efficiently run by Nicholas and Nicola Hayward; the hotel's two pubby bars are at the very heart of this small seaside town's life and the bar meals are always popular. Just yards from the seafront with its pebble beach and pretty assortment of sailing dinghies bobbing in the Solent, the hotel has enormous charm, starting with the small front patio complete with flagpole, and the little rear courtyard which heaves in season with youngsters. Both bars have a nautical theme, one with small round tables and a myriad of photos of old ships on the walls, the other more rustic in style with bare floorboards, dado pine panelling and, more unusually, part of an old ship's mast. Try a pint of the particularly good Goddard's, brewed on the Island. The bar menu is served both inside and outside on the terrace: hot crab ramekin, plaice and chips or local lobster usually feature and crab (when available) and shell-on prawns are also always popular. Traditional Sunday lunch served 12.30-1.30 (ring to check availability). Pretty bedrooms – blues and yellows are the favoured colours – are most appealing, with lots of pictures, books

and objets d'art. The best, and largest, rooms feature antique furniture; others have simple white-painted built-in units, and most en-suite facilities feature baths and showers. Two of the rooms have small patios (unfortunately overlooking the small rear car park) and on the top floor there's also a family suite, its two bedrooms separated by a sitting room. Two cosy lounges (one on the first floor is non-smoking, the other to the rear of the back bar is cosy and dimly lit) are reserved for residents and restaurant diners. Recommended in our *1996 Hotels & Restaurants Guide. Open 11-3, 6-11 (Sun 12-3, 7-10.30).* ***Bar Food*** *12-2 (Sun to 1.45), 7-9.30. Free House.* ***Beer*** *Flowers IPA, Goddard's Special. Patio/terrace, outdoor eating.* ***Accommodation*** *16 bedrooms, all en suite, from £60/£92 (single from £40/£70). Children welcome overnight (ring for prices – high season exceptions), additional bed and cot (£2.50) available. Access, Amex, Diners, Visa.*

SEDGEFIELD — Dun Cow Inn — B&B

Tel 01740 620894 Map 5 E3

43 Front Street Sedgefield Stockton-on-Tees Cleveland TS21 3AT

Zzz...

A splendid old inn – in this village of near a dozen pubs – which received Civic Trust awards for its bedroom conversions in 1974. Roof beams and black and white timber-framed walls have been exposed and restored, skilfully set off by the tapestry-weave fabrics used for the bed-heads, counterpanes and curtains. There are no en-suite bathrooms, though the three which are shared (including one fully tiled with a modern pulse shower) do enter into the spirit with splendidly evocative, yet up-to-date, bathroom fittings. Teletext TVs, fresh fruit and bedside boiled sweets greet the overnight visitor – breakfast orders placed the night before are cheerfully served at guests' chosen hour next morning. Plans are afoot to make three of the bedrooms en suite by the end of 1995. *Open 11-3, 6-11 (Sun 12-3, 7-10.30). Free House.* ***Beer*** *Theakston Best & XB, Newcastle Exhibition, McEwan's Scotch. several weekly-changing guest beers.* ***Accommodation*** *6 rooms, not en suite £45 (single £36.50). Children welcome overnight, additional bed and cot available. Access, Amex, Diners, Visa.*

SELLACK — Loughpool Inn — FOOD

Tel 01989 730236 Map 14 B1

Sellack nr Ross-on-Wye Hereford & Worcester HR9 6LX

A popular dining pub and an equally pleasant spot for summer drinking around picnic tables under the weeping willows. The generally unspoilt interior features flagstones, log fires and two dining-rooms whose cloths and candles create a rather more sedate dining ambience. New owners Malcolm and Janet Hall have maintained the blackboard menus yet have increased the range of specials and vegetarian dishes on offer in the bar. Regular favourites include Cumberland sausage, steak and kidney pie, salmon steak and ploughman's platters, with home-made daily dishes, such as Stilton paté, wild boar casserole in cider and apples, pork in brandy and Portuguese-style sardines, enhancing the choice. For pudding try the treacle nut flan or oranges in Grand Marnier. *Open 11-30-3, 6.30-11 (Sun 12-3, 7-10.30).* ***Bar Food*** *12-2, 7-9.30. Free House.* ***Beer*** *Bass, Hereford Supreme, John Smith's. Garden. Family room. Access, Visa.*

SELLING — White Lion — FOOD

Tel 01227 752211 Map 11 C5

The Street Selling nr Faversham Kent ME13 9RQ

Surrounded by tubs of flowers, this charming 300-year-old village pub is decorated inside in traditional Kentish-style with swags of hops. Half set up for eating and half for drinking there are wheelback chairs, an inglenook fireplace, dressers loaded with plates and tureens and lots of fresh flowers and plants. The menu always includes a traditional beef suet pudding and steak and kidney pie plus steaks, freshly-cut sandwiches and ploughman's lunches (three cheeses with apple) along with the likes of potted crab in butter, mushrooms provençale and a few more exotic items such as spicy Indian samosas with a tamarind dip and black-eyed bean curry. For those with particularly spicy tastes Monday night is curry night. A good selection of puds of which about half are brought-in. 48 malt whiskies at the bar. Live jazz Monday evenings. *Open 11-3, 6.30-11 (Sun 12-3, 7-10.30).* ***Bar Food*** *12-3 (Sun to 2), 7-9.30 (Sat to 10, Sun to 9).* ***Beer*** *Shepherd Neame. Garden, outdoor eating. Family room. Access, Visa.*

SEMINGTON — Lamb on the Strand — FOOD

Tel 01380 870263 Map 14 B3
99 The Strand Semington nr Trowbridge Wiltshire BA14 6LL

A carefully refurbished old ivy-clad farmhouse, set beside the A361 between Devizes and Trowbridge and run in civilised-style by the hard-working Flaherty family. Original features and fireplaces have been revealed and a tasteful collection of old darkwood furniture, farmhouse high-back chairs, a carved oak corner cupboard, quality fabrics and prints have created a relaxed and upmarket air in both the neat bar and small intimate dining-room. The latter, painted dark green and candle-lit, is particularly popular in the evenings and the soothing tones of light classical music enhance the overall atmosphere of this charming country pub. Quality bar food is the main emphasis at the Lamb, the daily-changing blackboard menu offering a pleasing variety of home-made dishes, all of which make use of fresh local produce. Start with herrings in a Madeira sauce, smoked chicken and mango, mushroom in a Stilton sauce, followed by well-presented main-course dishes such as lamb casserole with apricot, noisettes of lamb, breast of Barbary duck with marsala sauce and crusty chicken. Fresh fish – salmon with a wine and cream sauce, monkfish provencale – and good vegetarian dishes – chick pea hotpot, hazelnut and vegetable loaf – feature on the menu. To round off a meal, inviting puddings may include bread pudding in whisky sauce, kissel with ice cream and chocolate truffle cake. A competitively priced wine list includes at least eight house wines served by the glass. To the side of the pub is a delightful garden with shrubs, trees and wrought-iron tables and chairs, from which there are fine views over open countryside. The whole pub is completely no-smoking at weekends, with only a couple of tables allocated for smokers at other times. *Open 12-3, 6.30-11 (Sun 12-3, closed Sun eve). **Bar Food** 12-2, 6.30-9 (Sat to 9.30). Free House. **Beer** Eldridge Pope Hardy Country, Dorchester Bitter. Garden, outdoor eating. Access, Visa.*

We do not accept free meals or hospitality – our inspectors pay their own bills and **never** book in the name of Egon Ronay's Guides.

SEMLEY — Benett Arms — FOOD

Tel 01747 830221 **Fax 01747 830152** Map 14 B3
Semley nr Shaftesbury Dorset SP7 9AS

This unusually tall, white-painted building enjoys an enviable rural location on the edge of the village, opposite the green and overlooking the isolated church. Inside, a warm welcome is ensured in the rustic, split-level and simply furnished bar, which is warmed in winter by an open fire. The printed bar menu covers the standard items – various sandwiches, ploughman's platters, steak and kidney pie, lasagne and Wiltshire ham, egg and chips – while a daily-changing blackboard menu displays the more interesting and unusual dishes that are on offer. Fresh fish from Poole features well and may include poached salmon in Normandy butter, moules marinière and grilled cod fillet served with vegetables. The unusual comes in the form of chorizos served with sauerkraut and game features well in season, notably pheasant casseole and jugged hare. Home-made puddings usually include the popular treacle and walnut tart and lemon crunch. On Sunday a traditional roast lunch is served. An above-average selection (about 15) of worldwide house wines is served, by both bottle and glass. *Open 11-2.30, 6-11 (Sun 12-3, 7-10.30). **Bar Food** 12-2, 7-10. **Beer** Gibbs Mew. Garden, outdoor eating, children's play area. Family room. Access, Amex, Diners, Visa.*

SENNEN COVE — Old Success Inn — B&B

Tel 01736 871232 **Fax 01736 871457** Map 12 A4
Sennen Cove by Whitesands Bay Cornwall TR19 7DG

Zzz...

Located off the A30, next to the huge expanse of Whitesands Bay and only a mile north of Land's End, the 17th-century inn has been well refurbished to provide accommodation in twelve comfortable bedrooms that have impressive sea views. Especially popular are the rooms that capture the famous sunset sinking into the sea, the most attractive being the spacious honeymoon suite with its four-poster bed. All rooms have pretty floral curtains and print wallpaper, solid modern pine furnishings and good clean en-suite facilities. Added

comforts include satellite TV and tea-makers and residents have use of a stylish lounge complete with picture window and sea view. The pubby 'Charlies Bar' is modern and open-plan in layout with a mix of pub furniture, stools and high-backed benches and various local seafaring photographs of bygone days decorate the walls. *Open 11.30-2.30, 6.30-11 (Sun 12-3, 7-10.30). Free House.* ***Beer*** *Bass, St Austell Tinners Ale & XXXX Mild, Outdoor eating area.* ***Accommodation*** *12 bedrooms, 10 en suite, £52/£68/£80 (single £26/£30). Children welcome overnight (0-2s £5 for cot, 2-5s 25% of tariff, 6-11s 50%, 12-14s 75%). Access, Visa.*

SEVENOAKS — Royal Oak — FOOD

Tel 01732 451109 Fax 01732 740187 Map 11 B5 **B&B**
High Street Sevenoaks Kent TN13 1HY

A former coaching inn with abundant atmosphere and character. Rich, bold colours perfectly complement the fabric of the building. Traditional or antique furniture is used in the bedrooms, which are decorated in individual, often striking style. Neat, bright bathrooms. Among the day rooms are a cosy pub-like bar/bistro with candle-topped scrubbed pine tables and comfortable, well-upholstered seats, a beautifully furnished drawing room and a conservatory. The informal bistro menu may list warm chicken and bacon salad, poached salmon, asparagus and avocado pear with diced Stilton and olive oil dressing and daily choices like pan-fried lamb's liver and bacon. The charming and comfortable restaurant comprises several rooms that are partially panelled and cleverly lit, creating a relaxing atmosphere. Chef James Butterfill manages to include something for everyone on his à la carte, and the three-course fixed-price menus offer particularly good value. Outdoor eating in good weather on a creeper-clad patio. Wine list features eight house wines available by the large glass. *Open 11-3, 6-11 (Sun 12-3, 7-10.30).* ***Bar Food*** *12-2.30, 7-10 (Sun to 9.30). Patio, outdoor eating, tennis. Free House.* ***Beer*** *Ruddles Best, Morland Old Speckled Hen.* ***Accommodation*** *37 rooms, all en suite, £70 (single £60). Children welcome overnight (under-10s stay free in parents' room), additional bed (£15) and cot (£10) available. Access, Amex, Diners, Visa.*

SHALDON — Ness House Hotel — B&B

Tel 01626 873480 Fax 01626 873486 Map 13 D3
Marine Drive Shaldon Devon TQ14 0HP

The Ness House Hotel overlooks the Teign estuary and across to the town of Teignmouth. Built in 1810, it has retained its Regency exterior and is set in 22 acres of parkland. The twelve rooms (1 bridal suite, five apartments, 2 family suites, 3 doubles and 1 single) all have en-suite facilities and are equipped with modern facilities. Room service is available. There is a spacious open-plan bar with a no-smoking area and, at the back, a small, simple lounge. *Open 11-11 (Sun 12-3, 7-10.30). Free House.* ***Beer*** *Eldridge Pope Royal Oak, Palmers IPA, Tetley, Fergusons Dartmoor Legend, guest beer. Garden, outdoor eating.* ***Accommodation*** *14 bedrooms, all en suite, £65/£80 (single £40/£55). Children welcome overnight (under-5s stay free in parents' room 5-14s £15), additional bed (£15) and cot available (no charge). Access, Amex, Visa.*

SHAMLEY GREEN — Red Lion Inn — FOOD

Tel & Fax 01483 892202 Map 15a E4 **B&B**
Shamley Green Surrey GU5 0UB

Listed, 300-year-old building overlooking the village green and cricket pitch, with a smart and well-cared-for interior boasting three open fireplaces, a pleasant mix of modern pine and antique furnishings, tasteful prints and fresh flowers and candles on tables. Reliably good, homely food listed on the blackboard in the bar – tagliatelle with seafood and mushrooms, Dijon peppered chicken breast, steak and mushroom pie, artichoke and green olive crepes – with printed restaurant menu fare (also served in the bar) offering more substantial main courses such as wild salmon steak with prawn and dill sauce and calf's liver Marsala with grapes and bacon. Fresh and al dente accompanying vegetables. Popular puddings include deep lemon pie and sticky toffee pudding. Those popping in for just a snack will find filled baguettes and jacket potatoes among the lighter bite options. Fresh, chintzy, antique-furnished bedrooms upstairs – one has a four-poster – all with en-suite facilities (three with shower only). *Open 11-11, Sun 12-3, 7-11.* ***Bar Food*** *12-3, 5.30-10 (Sun 7-9.30)* ***Beer*** *Greene King Abbot Ale, Friary Meux, Tetley, guest beer. Garden, outdoor eating.* ***Accommodation*** *4 bedrooms, all en suite, £45 (single £35). Children welcome overnight (family room from £55), additional bed and cot available. Access, Amex, Diners, Visa.*

SHARDLOW Old Crown FOOD

Tel 01332 792392 Map 7 D3
Cavendish Bridge Shardlow Derbyshire DE72 2HL

Signed just of the A6, Cavendish Bridge was the old road crossing of the Trent into Derbyshire, now mercifully a dead end, where the old bridge collapsed, some thirty feet above the river. The Old Crown, recently rescued from a possibly similar fate, now breathes new and vibrant life within stone walls hung with old tobacco and brewery posters and beams hung at every conceivable point with pottery water jugs. A high turnover of real ales draws the locals and high-piled plates of food almost everyone else. Landlord Peter Morton-Harrison operates his own inimitable food-ordering system on his note pad (cometh the man, cometh the menu) while the best food bets on the specials board are equally idiosyncratic. Upside-down fish pie has reached Mark II phase (laced with Pernod), while the beef and chicken hotties are generously fired up with tabasco. Less potent options may include Mediterranean chicken and pork Wellington, along with a variety of sandwiches and ploughman's platters. The balance of a conservative menu places volume, perhaps, above variety though no one seems to care that much. Good ale and a genial atmosphere more than paper over the cracks. *Open 11-3, 5-11 (Sun 12-3, 7-10.30).* ***Bar Food** 12-2. Free House. **Beer** Marston's Pedigree, Bass, 6 guest beers. Garden, outdoor eating. No credit cards.*

SHAVE CROSS Shave Cross Inn A

Tel 01308 868358 Map 13 F2
Marshwood Vale Shave Cross Dorset DT6 6HW

Once a busy resting place for pilgrims on their way to Whitchurch Canonicorum, as well as monastic visitors, who frequently had their tonsures trimmed while staying, hence the name. Delightfully situated off-the-beaten track in the beautiful Marshwood Vale, 5 miles from Bridport, this charming 14th-century thatched cob-and-flint inn has a stone floor, inglenook fireplace, beamed ceiling, rustic furnishings, and a delightful flower-filed suntrap garden. Through the skittle alley, there's a children's play area. Local scrumpy cider. *Open 12-2.30 (Sat to 3), 7-11 (Sun 12-3, 7-10.30). Closed Mon except Bank Holidays. Free House. **Beer** Bass, Eldridge Pope Royal Oak, Hall & Woodhouse Badger Best. Garden, children's play area. Family room. No credit cards.*

SHEFFORD WOODLANDS Pheasant Inn FOOD

Tel 01488 648284 Map 14a B4
Baydon Rd Shefford Woodlands nr Hungerford Berkshire RG16 7AA

Zzz...

On the lip of Lambourn Downs, just a quarter of a mile from the M4 Junction 14 (turn on to the B4000), the Pheasant stands in view of the motorway. A new brick wall, sporting colourful flower troughs, enhances the white-tiled frontage, and in view of the traffic noise the double-glazed conservatory porch is a welcome addition. Despite an unaltered public bar and somewhat primitive toilets in a lean-to, the body of the pub has been made over to dining, with prodigious choices chalked up on ubiquitous blackboards; kitchen output is dependable rather than inspired. Beyond a choice of sandwiches and ploughman's platters, one will find good home-made tomato soup and prawn and celery cocktail among the typical starters, followed by seafood pie and venison and black cherry casserole for a one-course lunch, with chicken breast with garlic and herb sauce, salmon with lemon butter, rich beef casserole and peppered fillet steak constituting more substantial dinners. Hot and cold sweets are home-made and gooey, such as treacle tart or banana split. Set 3-course Sunday lunch. There are picnic tables in the garden for fine weather and regular summer barbecues. *The Royal Oak* in Wootton Rivers (see entry) is under the same ownership. *Open 11-3, 5.30-11 (Sun 12-3, 7-10.30). **Bar Food** 12-2.15, 6.30-9.30 (Sun 12-2, 7-9). Free House. **Beer** Wadworth 6X, Brakspear Bitter, guest beers. Garden, outdoor eating, Access, Visa.*

Many **B&B** establishments offer reduced rates for weekend and out-of-season bookings. Always ask about special deals for longer stays. Beware half-board terms in inns where we do not recommend the **FOOD.**

SHELF — Duke of York — B&B

Tel 01422 202056 **Fax 01422 206618** Map 6 C1
West Street Stone Chair Shelf Halifax West Yorkshire HX3 7LN

The 17th-century former coaching inn, right by the A644, is pub in front and flooring factory to the rear. Local foundries have contributed over the years to the collection of brassware and blow-torches which adorn the interior, alongside the whisky jugs, chamber pots and jam pans which hang from its blackened oak beams. Bedrooms, meanwhile, attract a mid-week business clientele in an area not over-blessed with comparable competition. In addition to five en-suite bedrooms in the pub, there are seven self-contained rooms in a row of weavers' cottages across the road. These retain the old stone walls and fireplaces, and on the ground floor, it's plain to see that the bathrooms (with shower/WC only) were once the kitchens. *Open 11-11 (Sun 12-3, 7-10.30). Free House.* ***Beer*** *Boddingtons Mild & Best, Trophy Bitter, Castle Eden, Timothy Taylor's Best & Landlord, Flowers Original. Patio.* ***Accommodation*** *12 bedrooms, all en suite (most with shower/WC only), £50 (single £35), weekend reductions. No dogs. Access, Amex, Diners, Visa.*

SHELLEY — Three Acres Inn ★ — FOOD — B&B

Tel 01484 602606 **Fax 01484 608411** Map 6 C1
Roydhouse Shelley nr Huddersfield West Yorkshire HD8 8LR

Set high in the Pennines above Huddersfield, the Emley Moor television mast (red-lit at night) provides a useful landmark for finding the unassuming, greystone Three Acres, which is on the Emley road, off B6116 at Shelley village. Central to the inn is a long bar counter framed in darkwood panelling beneath solid oak beams, lent further character at night by candle-lit tables and lively accompaniment from the grand piano. With over 26 years' consistent performance at the top level, Neil Truelove and Brian Orme still attract the crowds for bar food which is commendable for its unswerving quality and simplicity. Among the comprehensive range of unusually good sandwiches (available lunch and evening), a BLT of crispy bacon, firm, ripe tomatoes and home-made mayonnaise typifies attention to every detail in this department; a pan-fried sirloin steak version, served on crusty bread with onions and chipped potatoes that are genuinely home-made, becomes a meal in itself. For a full meal, main courses ranging from pork and duck rilettes with a tomato and onion chutney to salmon fishcakes with hollandaise sauce and grilled yellow-finned tuna with niçoise oil and devilled anchovies vie for prominence alongside roasts of the day, shortcrust-topped steak, kidney and mushroom pie and Whitby haddock (served with traditional mushy peas). From the specials blackboard, a croustade of chorizo with sun-dried tomatoes and parmesan laid over baby spinach leaves was rated by one inspector as "outstanding". To follow are the justifiably memorable desserts such as panacotta with poached vanilla fruits and millefeuille of orange sable biscuit with white chocolate mousse. At either end of the bar are two more formal dining-rooms offering an evening à la carte and traditional 3-course Sunday lunch. Booking here is essential. The quality, however, of this dedicated team's food is beyond question, and anyone looking for such adventurous flavours – and not a little conviviality of atmosphere – will surely not be disappointed. The Three Acres bridges the gap between small hotel and country inn with a choice of quality accommodation. Bedrooms in the main building are spacious and airy, and furnished in traditional-style natural pine with colour co-ordinated fabrics. Much smiliar decor has been used in the newer annexe, housed in much older stone cottages across the lane, where the rooms are that good bit smaller and single rooms are equipped with WC and showers only; those businessman with work to do may find these last a little cramped. Three rooms are large enough for families and one pair connect. All are nonetheless immaculately kept and equipped with TVs, direct-dial phones, trouser presses and plenty of toiletries. *Open 12-11 (Sat 7-11.30 only, Sun 12-3, 7-10.30), closed Sat lunchtime.* ***Bar Food*** *12-2 (not Sat), 7-10. Free House.* ***Beer*** *Mansfield Riding Traditional Bitter, Dark Mild & Old Baily, Timothy Taylor's Landlord, guest beer.* ***Accommodation*** *20 bedrooms, all en suite, £57.50 (single £47.50), weekend reductions. Children welcome overnight, additional bed and cot available. Access, Amex, Visa.*

SHENINGTON — Bell Inn — FOOD

Tel 01295 670274 Map 14a B1
Shenington nr Banbury Oxfordshire OX15 6NQ

Just five miles west of Banbury (turn off the A422) Shenington is a comfortable, sleepy village boasting a celebrated Norman church. By the three-acre green, the Bell is very much at the heart of village life. Don't miss the locals' bar down one side of the pub if you're in search of a fine pint of Hook Norton – the originating brewery is only six miles away. To the front, the two dining-rooms with attendant log fires are cosy and intimate.

Here Stephen Dixon supervises food ordering (with sweets chalked up on Scotty, the itinerant cut-out dog) while Jennifer is the genius behind a regularly-evolving range of seasonal food, as well as preparing freshly-cut sandwiches and popular ploughman's platters. A typical starter would be mushrooms in cream and paprika, followed by lamb and lime casserole, cod in celery sauce or an almond celery and cashew bake. Super puddings follow the lines of raspberry crumble and banoffi pie. The Bell has four bedrooms, two of them en suite (£15 per person), which are offered on a strictly casual basis. *Open 12-3, 7-11 (Sun 12-3, 7-10.30). Closed Sun eve Oct-Mar.* ***Bar Food*** *12-3, 7-9. Free House.* ***Beer*** *Boddingtons, Hook Norton Best. Garden. Family Room. Access, Visa.*

SHEPPERTON — Anchor Hotel — B&B

Tel 01932 221618 Fax 01932 252235 Map 15a F4
Church Square Shepperton Middlesex TW17 9JZ

A favourite haunt of Charles Dickens, the historic Anchor has dominated Shepperton's tiny square for over 400 years. Despite serious fire damage some years ago, the Disraeli Room retains original linenfold oak panelling, and the evocative Anchor Bar has been meticulously restored. Bedrooms, of which only 7 are doubles and all but one have shower/WCs only, all offer TVs, tea-makers and direct dial telephones. The best front doubles overlook the tiny square where once illegal prizefighters stood toe to toe; when the Bow Street runners were spied approaching, they would escape across the Thames to open country. *Open 11-2.30, 5.30-11 (Sun 12-3, 7-10.30). Free House.* ***Beer*** *Eldridge Pope Royal Oak & Hardy Country Ale.* ***Accommodation*** *29 bedrooms, all en suite, £75 (single from £49), weekend reductions. Children welcome overnight (under-12s stay free in parents' room), additional bed and cot available. Patio. Access, Amex, Diners, Visa.*

SHEPPERTON — King's Head — A

Tel 01932 221910 Map 15a F4
Church Square Shepperton Middlesex TW17 9JY

Across the square from the Anchor, the name of Nell Gwynne is most commonly associated with the King's Head. Although the two front bars have recently been made one, the traditional feel of its interior remains unchanged; floors are flagstoned, connecting doorways and alcoves are tiny and in winter log fires burn in an impressive inglenook. To the rear, a summer gazebo and enclosed patio are conducive to sociable drinking, though just as many may meander down from the square, glasses in hand, to take in a view of the river. *Open Mon & Tues 11-3, 5-11 & Wed-Sat 11-11 (Sun 12-3, 7-10.30). Free House.* ***Beer*** *Courage Best & Directors, John Smith's. Patio/terrace. Family room. No credit cards.*

SHEPPERTON — Warren Lodge — B&B

Tel 01932 242972 Fax 01932 253883 Map 15a F4
Church Square Shepperton Middlesex TW17 9JZ

Arguably the least pubby of Shepperton's hostelries, it nonetheless enjoys the choicest location. Riverside terrace and garden are shaded by a handsome old walnut tree, and there's comfortable seating both in the spacious beamed bar and panelled reception lounge. Most bedrooms, both in the main 18th-century house and two wings of later additions, share serene river views: all have TVs, tea-makers and hairdryers. On-going refurbishment will result in baths replacing most of the remaining en suite shower facilities. *Open 11-3, 6-11 (Sun 12-3, 7-10.30). No real ales. Garden.* ***Accommodation*** *48 bedrooms, all en suite, £85 (single £65), tariff reductions at weekends. Children welcome overnight (under-16s stay free if sharing parents' room), additional bed and cot available. Accommodation closed 5 days at Christmas. No dogs. Access, Amex, Diners, Visa.*

SHERFIELD ENGLISH — Hatchet Inn — FOOD

Tel 01794 322487 Map 14 C3
Sherfield English Romsey Hampshire SO51 6FP

Set back from the main road, this homely 17th-century pub is a popular stopping-off point for A27 travellers between Salisbury and Romsey. Refreshment is provided in two simply furnished and carpeted bars, the larger lounge/dining-room housing the blackboard menu which lists the daily-changing bar snacks and the twice-weekly-changing choice of more substantial main meals. Food is freshly prepared, generously served – a chicken and ham pie filled with chunks of tender meat in a creamy sauce and served with a selection of vegetables – and good value. Other lighter meals include steak and kidney pie, curry, home-cooked ham, egg and chips and a range of ploughman's platters, sandwiches and salads. Main courses feature up to six fresh fish dishes – fillet of sea bream with cream and dill sauce, lemon sole – as well as rack of lamb with a rosemary and redcurrant sauce and

supreme of chicken with a leek and Stilton sauce. Sunday is a busy day here: the traditional roast draws a full house, booking essential. *Open 11.30-3.30, 6-11 (Sun 12-3, 7-10.30).* ***Bar Food*** *12-2, 7-9. Free House.* ***Beer*** *Courage Best, Wadworth 6X, Bass. Garden, outdoor eating. Family room. Access, Amex, Visa.*

SHERSTON — Rattlebone Inn — A

Tel & Fax 01666 840871 Map 14 B2
Church Street Sherston Wiltshire SN16 0LR

Only 6 miles from the M4 this busy old Cotswold-stone pub still has its original stone roof intact, and lots more exposed stone, oak beams and open fires inside. Boules competitions in the fenced garden. Choice of over 60 malt whiskies. *Open 11.30-3, 5.30-11 (Sat and bank holidays 11-11, Sun 12-3, 7-10.30). Free House.* ***Beer*** *Smiles Best, Bass, Wadworth 6X, Rattlebone Pale Ale, guest beers. Garden. Access, Amex, Diners, Visa.*

SHIFNAL — Oddfellows — FOOD B&B

Tel 01952 461517 Fax 01952 463855 Map 6 B4
Market Place Shifnal nr Telford Shropshire TF11 9AH

What was once the Star Hotel close to the railway station is now part-pub, part-brasserie in a novel ground-floor conversion which utilises wood-block flooring and a pine-clad bar canopy to balance the trendy installation of assorted pine and cast-iron tables, sofas, banquettes and pews which form the tiered quartet of eating areas. An assorted age group seems as at home with a mixture of 1960s' and 70s' pop classics as they are with menu concepts as diverse as club sandwiches of sirloin steak, asparagus, mange tout and bean salad, spicy chicken and almond curry and pork brochettes with peanut sauce. Some of the better fare appears towards the top of this wide price range: grilled sea bass with leeks, scallop, prawn and monkfish salad or duck breast with plums and coriander. Accompany your meal with one of the 25 wines served by the glass, including champagne. There is still overnight accommodation available in four pine-furnished en-suite (showers only) bedrooms above; but it appears to be on a rather random basis with Continental breakfast obtainable from a communal kitchen. The best we can suggest is that one phones ahead for clarification. Live jazz on Sundays. *Open Mon-Thur 12-3, 6-11, Fri & Sat 11-11 (Sun 12-3, 7-10.30).* ***Bar Food*** *12-2.30, 6-10 (Sun from 7). Free House.* ***Beer*** *Boddingtons, Timothy Taylor's Landlord, guest beer. Patio.* ***Accommodation*** *4 bedrooms, all en suite, £35 (single £25). Check-in by arrangement. Access, Amex, Visa.*

SHIPTON-UNDER-WYCHWOOD — Lamb Inn — FOOD B&B

Tel 01993 830465 Fax 01993 832025 Map 14a B2
High Street Shipton-under-Wychwood Oxfordshire OX7 6DQ

Tucked away down a quiet side road, the Lamb is a typical 17th-century Cotswold building, complete with honey-coloured stone walls and stone tiled roof, and its neat little patio with parasol-shaded tables makes an ideal spot in summer. Inside, all is equally immaculate. The beamed bar has a polished woodblock floor and mostly antique furniture: a settle here, a pew there, and attractive old oak tables. At lunchtimes, the cold buffet displayed in the bar offers cold cuts like salmon, ham and beef for salads, sandwiches and ploughman's, a vegetarian tart, hot dishes of the day and just a roast on Sundays. In the evening an extensive blackboard menu offers the choice of a full three-course meal or perhaps just a light snack. Main dishes like venison in port wine, fillet of pork with calvados or several fresh fish choices come in generous portions with good simply-cooked fresh vegetables; as a bonus, someone in the kitchen has the cool, light hand needed to produce a melt-in-the-mouth pastry for the home-made fruit pies. For more formal dining there is a cosy low-beamed restaurant with similar fare on a set price (3-course, £21) dinner menu. The owner's interest in wine is evident from a well-chosen wine list, ten of which are available by the glass. The Lamb's five bedrooms are all as neat as a new pin, with cream-coloured melamine furniture and spotless modern bathrooms, all with bath and shower. Three of the rooms boast some old beams and these help lend a little extra character. Televisions, radio-alarms, direct-dial phones and tea and coffee making kit are standard, with mineral water and bowls of fruit as welcoming extras. The convivial hubbub from the bar below is quite audible in some rooms, which might be a problem if you want an early night. Good hearty cooked breakfasts are worth getting up for. No under-14s overnight. *Open 11-3, 6-11 (Sun 12-3, 7-10.30.* ***Bar Food*** *12-2, 7-10. Free House.* ***Beer*** *Hook Norton Best, Wadworth 6X, Wychwood Fiddlers Elbow. Patio/terrace, outdoor eating.* ***Accommodation*** *5 bedrooms, all en suite, £75 weekends £85 (single £58). Access, Amex, Visa.*

SHIPTON-UNDER-WYCHWOOD Shaven Crown Hotel FOOD B&B

Tel & Fax 01993 830330 Map 14a B2

High Street Shipton-under-Wychwood Oxfordshire OX7 6BA

Originally a 14th-century hospice to Bruern Abbey, this is a charming medieval building constructed around a delightful courtyard garden (complete with goldfish pond), where you can eat in good weather. In addition to lunch and dinner, visitors are offered breakfast, morning coffee and afternoon tea. Choices on the Buttery Bar's blackboard menu include Toronto-style potato skins, smoked turkey and avocado, hot croissant stuffed with ham, leek and mushroom sauce, curried prawns and salmon, cod and dill fishcakes. Vegetarian specials may include nut and Stilton roast. Delicious desserts feature chocolate mousse Basque, bread and butter pudding and home-made ice-creams. A 2/3-course Sunday lunch is served in the no-smoking restaurant where a more elaborate table d'hote dinner menu operates in the evenings. Charming service. The newly-refurbished bedrooms vary in size, some smaller than one might expect for the price. En suite facilities include three with shower-trays only. *Open 12-2.30, 7-11 (Sun 12-3, 7-10.30).* ***Bar Food*** *12-2, 7-9.30 (Sun to 9). Free House.* ***Beer*** *Hook Norton Best, guest beers. Garden, outdoor eating.* ***Accommodation*** *9 bedrooms, 8 en suite, from £66/£82 (single £33). Children welcome overnight (charge depends on age). Check-in by arrangement. Guide dogs only. Access, Visa.*

SHOBDON Bateman Arms FOOD

Tel 01568 708374 Map 14 A1

Shobdon nr Leominster Hereford & Worcester HR6 9LX

The Williams family have returned to take over the running of an historic pub which they've actually owned for some years: the black and white timbered former farmhouse stands on the B4362 at the heart of the village. They've smartened it up greatly, moving the bar to a more central position, extending the dining area to the lower-level former function room and carpeting throughout to create a more conducive ambience for eating. Young Gary Williams looks after the bar and the business of eating while Tracy keeps a watchful eye on the kitchen. The once long printed menu has given way to a blackboard list featuring favourites like sandwiches and ploughmans platters, grills, plus vegetarian selections (broccoli and courgette strudel), all supplemented by some varied and imaginative daily specials. Steak and kidney pudding, Cajun chicken with tarragon cream sauce and chunky Mediterranean fish casserole are indicative of the choices. Up to four daily choices on the fresh fish board, the top seller being "Elegant fish and chips": cod in beer batter with chips served up in pages of the Financial Times. New no-smoking dining area. *Open 12-2.30, 7-11 (Sun 12-3, 7-10.30).* ***Bar Food*** *12-2, 7-9.45. Free House.* ***Beer*** *Bass, Woods Parish. Garden. Access, Visa.*

SHROTON Cricketers FOOD

Tel 01258 860421 Map 14 B4

Shroton nr Blandford Forum Dorset DT11 8QD

Homely village local, situated opposite the village green and close to the unique sloping cricket pitch, which is superbly sited beneath Hambledon Hill. Thirsty cricketers (this pub is their HQ), walkers refreshing themselves along the Wessex Way and local drinkers fill the simply-furnished bar that includes, to one side, a pool table and various cricketing memorabilia. Diners complete the cross-section of people that frequent this humble establishment. They seek out the honest home-cooked food, especially the often unusual fresh fish selection – sea bream, pollock, grouper – that are on the menus here. A no-frills bar snack menu, which includes filled baguettes, is supplemented by freshly-prepared daily blackboard specials such as pasta with courgettes and mushroom sauce, chicken and ham pie, sirloin steak and gammon steak. Well-maintained and sheltered rear garden with flower beds and a trellis of climbing roses is ideal for outdoor eating. It is worth noting that Shroton is still referred to as Iwerne Courtney on some maps. New chef since our most recent visit, but the style (and, hopefully, the quality) is promised to remain the same. *Open 11.30-2.30, 6.30-11 (Mon-Thur in winter from 7, Sun 12-3, 7-10.30).* ***Bar Food*** *12-2, 7-9.45 (Sun to 9.15). Free House.* ***Beer*** *Flowers Original, Bass, Smiles, Fuller's London Pride, Ringwood Best, Butcombe, guest beer. Garden, outdoor eating. Access, Visa.*

We endeavour to be as up-to-date as possible but inevitably some changes to landlords, chefs and other key staff occur after the Guide has gone to press.

SIBFORD GOWER **Wykham Arms** FOOD

Tel 01295 780351 Map 14a B1

Sibford Gower Banbury Oxfordshire OX15 5RX

Yellow stone, mature thatch and a blaze of flowers and hanging baskets are picture-postcard material here in summer at this attractive 17th-century village pub. In winter the interior is warmed by real fires and the tiny dining-room with low beams and exposed stone walls takes on an altogether more cosy air. The renovated bars are fully carpeted and quite sedate, their best feature being an old stone well, now glass-covered to form an unusual bay-window table. The Hook Norton ales are nicely kept and bar food can be relied upon. Main menu items include filled baguettes and ploughman's platters, while the half-dozen home-cooked specials may feature parsnip and potato soup, tandoori chicken, cheese-topped cottage pie, various warms salads and spinach and mushroom lasagne. Sunday roasts. Children are made very welcome and there are swings under the trees and a play area in a pretty back garden. *Open 12-3, 6.30-11 (Sun 13-3, 7-10.30). **Bar Food** 12-2.30, 7-9.30 (Sun to 9, possibilty of no food Mon in winter). Free House. **Beer** Hook Norton Best, Wadworth 6X, Morland Old Speckled Hen, guest beer. Garden. Patio. Access, Visa.*

> We do not accept free meals or hospitality – our inspectors pay their own bills and never book in the name of Egon Ronay's Guides.

SKIDBY **Half Moon Inn** FOOD

Tel 01482 843403 Map 7 E1

16 Main Street Skidby Humberside HU16 5TG

Chips with everything is not the stuff of the Half Moon; its speciality is home-made Yorkshire puddings – eight different combinations including one with vegetarian gravy. They are almost big enough to obscure the waitress. The half-acre garden has its own 'Sproggies Bar' for children, together with the only huge suspended spiral climbing frame in the country. The pub itself is not without idiosyncrasies, having four little bars and wooden pillar supports. Alongside snacks like ploughman's lunches and sandwiches are home-made pies, soups, chilis, curries and burgers. New owners since our last edition, but the same kitchen team. *Open 11-11 (Sun 12-3, 7-10.30). **Bar Food** 12-10 (Sun 12-2.30, 7-10). **Beer** John Smith's, Marston's Pedigree. Garden, outdoor eating, children's play area. Access, Visa.*

SKIRMETT **Old Crown** FOOD

Tel 01491 638435 Map 15a D3

Skirmett nr Henley-on-Thames Oxfordshire RG9 6TD

Set by the village lane overlooking open fields, this charming, 350-year-old pub has an unspoilt and restful atmosphere that pervades throughout its two cottagey rooms and adjacent old-fashioned tap room. Beams, quarry-tiled and flagstone floors, an inglenook fireplace and an assortment of rustic sturdy furniture – from pine pews to trestle tables – characterise the traditional interior. A vast collection of bric-a-brac clutters every available space. There is no music, no games machines and no counter; the well-conditioned Brakspear ales are dispensed straight from the cask in the old still-room beyond the tiny serving hatch. Bar food is reliable and home-cooked and although the varied menu rarely changes – except for the occasional extra starter or the addition of fresh crab – the tried and tested formula is a successful if not a cheap one. To start, perhaps a freshly-prepared soup such as tomato and basil, a rich home-made paté like Stilton and walnut, or creamy garlic mushrooms, followed by well-presented pub favourites: steak, kidney and mushroom pie, lasagne (the latter served with chips or salad) and more inventive main dishes like Dutch calf's liver pan-fried in butter, medallions of pork with apricots and cream and poached salmon with dill and prawn sauce, all served with good vegetables. To finish, there are various ice creams, cheesecakes or toffee pudding. Those popping in for just a snack will find ploughman's platters (lunch only) and a range of filled jacket potatoes. Splendid secret summer garden with benched areas surrounded by mature shrubs, willows and flower-beds. No children under 10 either inside or out in the mature cottage garden; no draught lager, either, for that matter. 5 miles north of Henley. *Open 11-2.30, 6-11 (Sun 12-2.30, 7-10.30), pub closed all Mon (except Bank Holiday lunchtimes. **Bar Food** 12-2, 7-9 (Sun to 8.30) possibly closed for food Sun eve Nov-Feb. **Beer** Brakspear. Garden. No credit cards.*

SMALLBURGH **The Crown** FOOD

Tel 01692 536314 Map 10 D1 **B&B**
Smallburgh Norwich NR12 9AD

Thatched, beamed 15th-century village inn set beside the busy A149 Great Yarmouth to Cromer road with a peaceful, well-tended rear beer garden, complete with flower borders and picnic benches. Homely, simply-furnished bar areas with barrel furniture, a large open fire and blackboard menus listing reliable, home-cooked daily specials. Choices may include a well-flavoured soup – watercress and lettuce – served with a warm roll, Cromer crab and salad, steak and mushroom pie with horseradish pastry, chicken breast with Stilton and mustard and baked cod fillet with tomato, onion and garlic sauce, all served with fresh vegetables. Routine printed bar menu listing various sandwiches and ploughman's platters. Sunday roasts. Upstairs in the roof space are two freshly painted, clean and tidy bedrooms with attractive fabrics, sturdy furniture and dormer windows in the sloping roof. TVs, radios and tea-makers are standard. Both share an adequate, good-sized bathroom. No children under 14 in the bar, over 7s only in the restaurant. *Open 12-3, 5.30-11 (Sat 12-4, 7-11, Sun 12-3, 7-10.30). Closed Sun eve in winter.* ***Bar Food*** *12-2, 6-9 (Sat eve 7-9.30, no food Sun eve).* ***Beer*** *Greene King Abbot Ale, Boddingtons, Tetley, Flowers IPA, guest beer. Garden, outdoor eating.* ***Accommodation*** *2 bedrooms, neither en suite £35 (single £20). Children over 7 welcome overnight (7-12s £9, over 12s £15), additional bed available. Check-in by arrangement. Access, Visa.*

SMARDEN **The Bell** FOOD

Tel 01233 770283 Map 11 C5
Bell Lane Smarden Kent TN26 8PW

Tiled and rose-covered medieval Kentish inn in peaceful countryside (take the road between the church and Chequers pub, then left at the junction). Rambling and rustic interior full of character with low, hop-festooned oak beams, inglenook fireplaces and a motley mix of old wooden furnishings in three flagstoned bars that are candelit in the evenings. Adjacent games/family room with pool table. Bar food is reliable, especially the hearty range of home-made daily specials such as fish pie, Kentish liver and bacon casserole, coq au vin and beef stroganoff. Ploughman's platters and sandwiches available lunch and evening. Well-stocked bar dispensing nine real ales on hand pump, the heady Biddenden scrumpy cider and eight wines by the glass. No under-14s in the Cellar Bar or Monk's Bar. Good summer garden. *Open 12-3, 7-11 (Sun 12-3, 7-10.30).* ***Bar Food*** *12-2 (Sun to 2.30), 6.30-10 (Sat to 10.30, Sun 7-10). Free House.* ***Beer*** *Fremlins, Flowers Original, Fuller's London Pride, Shepherd Neame Master Brew, Goacher's Best, Ringwood Old Thumper, guest beer. Garden, outdoor eating. Family room. Access, Amex, Diners, Visa.*

SMARDEN **Chequers Inn** FOOD

Tel 01233 770217 **Fax 01233 770623** Map 11 C5 **B&B**
1 The Street Smarden Kent TN27 8QA

14th-century weatherboarded pub located close to the church in the heart of this most attractive village. Charming Chequers Bar with light oak woodblock floor, sturdy wooden tables and chairs and an exposed brick fireplace. Separate, neatly furnished lounge bar and dining area with open fire. No intrusive games or music. Decent bar food listed on a regularly changing menu runs from the simplest snack – sandwiches, ploughman's platters – to more restaurant-style dishes that might include cream of cauliflower soup, navarin of lamb and up to five fresh fish dishes, such as salmon and spinach en croute, monkfish in red pepper sauce and wing of skate in black butter. Separate dish of good, well-cooked fresh vegetables. Five homely and cottagey bedrooms upstairs feature exposed beams and wall timbers, simple decor with Laura Ashley fabrics and a few older pieces of darkwood furniture. Recent upgrading has created en suite facilities in three of the rooms, the other sharing a spacious and clean bathroom. Good choice for breakfast. *Open 10-3.30, 6-11 (Sun 12-3, 7-10.30).* ***Bar Food*** *11-3 (Sun from 12), 6.30-10 (Sun 7-10). Free House.* ***Beer*** *Bass, Charrington IPA, Young's Special, Morland Old Speckled Hen, guest beer. Garden, outdoor eating.* ***Accommodation*** *5 bedrooms, 3 en suite, £45 (single £20). Children welcome overnight (under-5s stay free if sharing parents' room), additional bed (£5) and cot available. Accommodation closed 24 & 25 Dec. Access, Visa.*

SMARTS HILL — Bottle House Inn — FOOD

Tel 01892 870306 **Fax 01892 871094** Map 11 B5
Smarts Hill Penshurst Kent

Well-modernised 15th-century pub remotely situated on a country lane 2 miles south-west of Penshurst off B2188. Low beams, a good inglenook fireplace and sturdy pub furniture characterise the friendly and welcoming bar and attractive dining-room. The varied bar menu is the main attraction here and it can get very busy early on with eager diners. Beyond a fairly standard selection of starters or lighter meals, including ploughman's platters, an extensive, daily-changing main course menu hides some interesting and reliable dishes such as chicken supreme, rack of lamb, tagliatelle carbonara, a decent steak and kidney pie and chicken breast in cream, brandy and mustard sauce. Portions are generous and accompanying vegetables well cooked. Peaceful front lawn and patio with country views. *Open 11-3, 6-11 (Sun 12-3, 7-10.30). **Bar Food** 12-2, 7-10. Free House. **Beer** Larkins Bitter, Harveys Sussex, Ruddles Best, Ind Coope Burton Ale. Garden, outdoor eating. Access, Amex, Visa.*

SNAPE — Golden Key — FOOD

Tel 01728 688510 Map 10 D3
Priory Road Snape Suffolk IP17 1SQ

A delightful and tasteful 15th-century, cottage-style pub close to Snape Maltings concert hall, with a colourful summer hanging-basket festooned facade and alfresco front patio. Inside the main bar has a quarry-tiled old fashioned public end and a carpeted lounge end, with neatly arranged scrubbed pine tables and some fine old settles fronting one of the two open fires. The blackboard menu holds few surprises, but the food is carefully prepared and home-cooked. Choose from sound favourites such as home-made samosas with a yoghurt and mint dip and a decent soup – mixed bean – followed by sausage, egg and onion pie, smoked haddock quiche, whole lemon sole, sea bass, fresh lobster and a steak selection. There's freshly-filled rolls, ploughman's platters, roast beef on Sundays and several wines are served by the glass. Puddings are popular, including the home-made chocolate brandy cake and hot lemon cake. At the time of going to press the landlords had just finished two en-suite bedrooms, handy B&B for Snape Maltings activities. *Open 11-3, 6-11 (Sun 12-3, 7-10.30). **Bar Food** 12-2.30, 6-9.30 (7-9.30 Sun). **Beer** Adnams, guest beers. Patio, outdoor eating. No credit cards.*

SNETTISHAM — Rose & Crown — B&B

Tel 01485 541382 **Fax 01485 543172** Map 10 B1
Old Church Road Snettisham nr King's Lynn Norfolk PE31 7LX

New landlords Anthony and Jeanette Goodrich took over here recently and have already made improvements that include a promising new menu, interesting-sounding daily specials (Cromer crab, Norfolk asparagus in season, but not yet inspected) and an improved wine list (from Adnams, all available by the glass). Tucked away in the village centre this splendid white-painted 14th-century inn was originally built to house the craftsmen who built the beautiful local church. Beyond the attractive flower-decked facade lie a warren of three bars linked by a twisting, tile-floored corridor. Heavy oak beams, old uneven red-tiled floors, inglenook fireplaces and comfortable settles characterise the traditional front bar and locals' bar. A collection of old farm implements decorates the charming front bar. Overnight guests are accommodated in three recently refurbished upstairs bedrooms, reached via a very steep staircase. Rooms are light, spacious, prettily decorated and all have TV and tea-makers. Beware of the head-cracking low doorways! A cottage 30 yards down the road is also available for B&B. The pub can become very crowded when busy. Families are welcome here with open arms and the delightful extension, children's room and garden can be brimming with contented children. After feasting on the under-12s' menu – toddlers have the use of high-chairs – youngsters can escape into the safe walled garden and clamber around the improved play area which boasts a slide, a play house, two wooden forts, monkey bars and a connecting walkway, with a soft wood-chip floor. Less active children may find the cages with guinea pigs and parakeets more entertaining. There is a mothers' baby-changing unit in the Ladies. Regular live music (mainly jazz) in the Garden Room. *Open 11-3, 5-11 (summer all day), Sat 11-11, Sun 12-2.30, 7-10.30. Free House. **Beer** Bass, Adnams Bitter & Broadside, two guest beers. Garden, outdoor eating, children's play area. **Accommodation** 3 rooms, all en suite, £50 (single £35). Children welcome overnight, additional bed available (£10). Check-in by arrangement. No dogs. Access, Visa.*

SOMERBY Old Brewery Inn A

Tel 01664 454866 Map 7 D3
High Street Somerby Leicestershire LE14 2PZ

Those to whom the quaffing of fine ale is akin to the staff of life will rejoice at the life the Old Brewery Inn has restored to the quiet village of Somerby. Closed and derelict a mere seven years ago, it now houses landlord and brewer Barrie's commendable Parish brewery whose products already have a burgeoning reputation. In the bar, by the 40-foot well (to be used one day, it is hoped, in further beer production) samples of Parish Special (still £1 per pint), Somerby Premium and Poachers Ale hold more than their own alongside ever-changing guest brews – 16 hand pumps in total. For those in bolder mood, Baz's Bonce Blower, at 10% ABV, is probably the country's strongest ale. Food ranging from beefburgers to steaks ensures that there are plenty of foundations to lay under a sampling session. Increasingly popular are the brewery tours, for twelve or more, at a price inclusive of food and all you can drink (£18). For those who may find the experience totally overwhelming, there's bedroom accommodation in the old stables where three twin rooms share the necessary ablutions. Monthly Monday jazz nights. *Open 11.30-2.30, 6-10.30 (Sun 12-3, 7-10.30). Free House.* ***Beer*** *Parish Special Bitter, Somerby Premium, Parish Farm Gold, Mild, Porter, Poachers Ale, Baz's Bonce Blower, guest beers. Garden, outdoor eating, occasional BBQs. Children's play area.* ***Accommodation*** *3 double bedrooms, £25 (single £15). Children welcome overnight (under-5s stay free in parents' room). Check-in by arrangement. Access, Visa.*

> Many **B&B** establishments offer reduced rates for weekend and out-of-season bookings. Always ask about special deals for longer stays. Beware half-board terms in inns where we do not recommend the **FOOD.**

SONNING The Bull A

Tel 01734 693901 **Fax 01734 691057** Map 15a D4
High Street Sonning Berkshire RG4 0UP

Quintessentially southern English traditional pub, its ancient black and white exterior covered with plants and flowers – you can sit outside and admire them and the view across the peaceful parish churchyard opposite – while in its two linked rooms there are sturdy old beams, gleaming brass, quarry tiles, barrel chairs and an inglenook fireplace, alive with logs in winter, ablaze with flowers in summer. Unusually, the brewery leases this fine village pub from the church who own the building. *Open 11-3, 5.30-11 (Sat from 6, Sun 12-3, 7-10.30).* ***Beer*** *Gale's, guest beer. Patio/terrace. Access, Visa.*

SOUTH HARTING Ship Inn FOOD

Tel 01730 825302 Map 15 D3
South Harting West Sussex GU31 5PZ

This white-painted mid-17th-century inn in the centre of the village is adorned with hanging flower baskets and a wisteria is getting established. Mind your head once through the door, as the beams are rather low. The interior furnishings are a mixture of varnished rustic tables, banquettes and wheelback chairs with hunting prints on the walls. The main bar is largely given over to eating, with an extensive menu of mostly home-made dishes; soup is popular, perhaps celeriac and apple, and the steak and kidney pie combines chunks of lean beef with a crisp pastry lid. Fresh seafood is a speciality and fish starters feature strongly on the menu – crevettes provençale, gravad lax, marinated herrings or potted shrimps whilst the comprehensive list of main dishes offers plenty of variety: salmon fishcakes, game pie, rack of lamb, lemon sole (price by weight) and fish pie. Leave room for splendidly traditional puddings like treacle tart to round things off. It's usually wise to book for meals but at lunchtime and all afternoon snacks are also offered, like sandwiches and jacket potatoes. Diverse, carefully chosen wine list. A small public bar has a dartboard and fruit machine. Children under 14 years are not allowed inside, but in fine weather are welcome in the small garden, which boasts an aviary with cockatiel and quail amongst other birds. *Open 11-11 (Sun 12-3, 7-10.30).* ***Bar Food*** *12-2.30, 7-9.30 (snacks all day, Sun to 9, no food Sun eve Oct-Mar). Free House.* ***Beer*** *Palmers IPA & '200' Ale, Fuller's London Pride, guest beers. Garden, outdoor eating. Access, Amex, Diners, Visa.*

South Harting — White Hart — FOOD

Tel 01730 825355 Map 15 D3
High Street South Harting West Sussex GU31 5QB

Pleasant village pub with three beamed bars, wooden tables, polished wood floors, log fires and a decent choice of good, fresh food. Known for their traditional country recipes, the licensees display their menu on a blackboard where specials appear daily – lamb baked in rosemary, tuna bake, beef stroganoff and steak and kidney pie are typical choices. Separate simple bar snack menu includes sandwiches and ploughman's platters. On Thursday, Friday and Saturday evenings the restaurant, formerly an old scullery, with flagstone floors and open inglenook fireplace, serves an à la carte menu. Vegetarians may wish to try the corn and avocado bake or chestnut and red wine patties. Desserts are the old favourites: bread-and-butter pudding, treacle tart or fresh fruit puddings. In fine weather, families may wish to venture into the beautiful garden overlooking the South Downs where children can safely play around the pond and waterfall. *Open 11-2.30 (Sat to 3), 6-11 (Sun 12-3, 7-10.30). **Bar Food** 11-2 (Sun from 12), 7-9.30 (except Mon eve, Sat & Sun to 10). Free House. **Beer** Ind Coope Burton Ale, Friary Meux Best, Tetley, guest beers. Garden, outdoor eating, children's play area. Family room (with toy box). No credit cards.*

South Leigh — Mason Arms — A

Tel 01993 702485 Map 14a B2
South Leigh nr Witney Oxfordshire OX8 6XN

A short distance from the A40 (East Witney turn-off), families and alfresco diners can enjoy the spacious garden with peacocks of this large thatched pub in the centre of a small village. Flagstoned bar with a multitude of coppers and brasses. Sowlye (the old name for South Leigh) is specially brewed for the pub. Generous Sunday roasts. *Open 11.30-2.30, 6.30-11 (Sun 12-3, 7-10.30). Closed Mon. Free House. **Beer** Sowlye Bitter, guest beer. Garden. Access, Visa.*

South Pool — Millbrook Inn — FOOD

Tel 01548 531581 Map 13 D3
South Pool nr Kingsbridge Devon TQ7 2RW

Opening hours at this white-painted, 400-year-old pub vary somewhat according to the state of the tide in the creek that extends into the heart of the pretty village, bringing a number of the Millbrook's customers by boat. Inside, it is small and cosy with tapestry cushions on the wheelback chairs and ceiling beams decorated with old clay pipes, horse brasses, old bank notes and hundreds of visiting cards. To the rear, a tiny terrace overlooks a small stream which is home to a family of ducks. Home-cooked fare appears on the twice daily-changing blackboard menu; lunchtime favourites range from poached salmon or fresh crab sandwiches and filled seafood bagels to fisherman's pie and cheesy leek and potato bake, with evening extras like seafood pasta, goulash, sirloin steak and a choice of fresh fish dishes. Puds such as Devon apple cider cake and treacle tart provide a sweet conclusion. New owners since the last edition of this Guide. *Open 11-2.30, 5.30-11 (winter from 6.30, Sun 12-3, 7-10.30). **Bar Food** 12-2, 6.30-9 (Sun from 7). Free House. **Beer** Bass, Ruddles Best, Wadworth 6X, guest beer. Covered forecourt & streamside terrace, outdoor eating. Family room. No credit cards.*

South Zeal — Oxenham Arms — B&B

Tel 01837 840244 **Fax 01837 840791** Map 13 D2
South Zeal Devon EX20 2JT

Just off the A30, 17 miles west of Exeter this ancient, romantically fronted, creeper-covered inn is in the centre of rural South Zeal. Genuinely unspoilt inside too, with worn flag floors, vast open fires, original beams, rough plaster walls, spooky passageways, solidly traditional drinking areas, and a relaxing clubbish lounge. Isolated garden overlooking Dartmoor at the back. Nice, old-fashioned bedrooms (one with four-poster) offer discreet modern comforts; delightful place to stay. *Open 11-2.30, 6-11 (Sun 12-2.30, 7-10.30). Free House. **Beer** Furgusons Dartmoor Best, Princetown Jail Ale, guest beer. Garden. Family room. **Accommodation** 8 bedrooms, 7 en suite, £50 (single £40). Children welcome overnight, additional cot (£3) and bed (£5.50 inc. breakfast) provided if sharing parents' room. Access, Amex, Diners, Visa.*

SOUTHWOLD — The Crown ★ FOOD B&B

Tel 01502 722275 **Fax 01502 727223** Map 10 D2
High Street Southwold Suffolk IP18 6DP

Zzz...  

Next-door brewers, Adnams, take the credit for the stylish restoration of Southwold's central Georgian inn. While not without fault in attempting to be most things to all comers, the Crown is to be applauded for its success in bringing straightforward food, prime-condition beers and excellent wines to the average spender. The nautically themed rear bar is complete with binnacle and navigation lamps; the bar's curved and glassed-in rear panel gives the entirely fitting impression of being the flagship's bridge. To the front, facing the High Street, the Parlour serves as lounge and coffee shop; the front bar and attendant restaurant, decked out with green-grained panelling and Georgian-style brass lamps, has a refined air, yet is totally without pretension or stuffiness. The weekly-changing bar menu (plus four extra daily dishes) highlights excellent local fish such as terrine of white fish on a bed of watercress and parsley salad, baked fillet of cod with a lemon and chili crust, and seafood chowder with coriander and ginger. Other options range from aubergine and garlic soup and stir-fried pork fillet with sweet oyster sauce to roast guinea fowl with spiced lentils. Most meals are served in both starter and main-course sizes at good-value prices. Finish off with hot apple and black cherry crumble, lemon and lime tart or a selection of Neal's Yard cheeses. In addition to the fine wine list chosen by Simon Loftus there's a splendid supplementary, monthly-changing list of 20 or so wines, available by both glass and bottle. The non-smoking restaurant has interesting fixed-price menus. Traditional roast beef and Yorkshire pudding is served in the restaurant on Sundays. Bedrooms are well equipped, with antique or decent reproduction pieces and bright fabrics and furnishings: all have private bathrooms though three are not strictly en suite (the bathroom is across a corridor); one family room has a double and two single beds. Pleasant staff offer a warm welcome and good but informal service. A light breakfast is served promptly in the bedroom along with the morning paper. *Open 10.30-3, 6-11 (Sun 12-3, 7-10.30). Pub and accommodation closed 1 week Jan.* ***Bar Food*** *12.15-1.45, 7.15-9.45.* ***Beer*** *Adnams. Patio, outdoor eating.* ***Accommodation*** *12 bedrooms, 9 en suite, £61 (family room £89, single £40). Children welcome overnight, additional bed (£10) and cot (£5) available. Check-in from 1pm onwards. No dogs. Access, Amex, Diners, Visa.*

SOWERBY BRIDGE — The Hobbit B&B

Tel 01422 832202 **Fax 01422 835381** Map 6 C1
Hob Lane Sowerby Bridge West Yorkshire HX6 3QL

Standing on the very lip of the moor (follow directions, below, carefully), the Hobbit enjoys panoramic views over the Pennines and Sowerby Bridge far below. A relaxed and welcoming place, it's a haven for families, with Bilbo's bistro open all day, every day: youngsters receive a fun pad on arrival. Connecting bedrooms are available for families, with special weekend rates, while a thoughtful array of accessories appeals equally to the mid-week business traveller. Satellite TVs, for instance, include a video channel and fresh milk is conveniently kept in a corridor fridge. A cottage annexe across the road contains a pair of splendidly-furnished executive bedrooms which also benefit from the finest views down the valley. No-smoking areas in bistro and restaurant. Watch out for the many and varied theme nights, notably the murder and mystery evenings, and special children's events. Take the A58 to Sowerby Bridge by the Railway Viaduct, turn onto Station Road, then right at the police station, left at the T-Junction, continue up the hill and then right at the crossroads. *Open 11.45-11 (up to 2am with meals, Sun 12-11).* ***Beer*** *John Smith's, Courage Directors, Ruddles Best. Garden, two patios.* ***Accommodation*** *22 rooms, all en suite (14 with shower/WC only), £63 (single £42/£49) weekend reductions. Children welcome overnight (under-6s stay free in parents' room, 6-12s £11), cot available. No dogs. Access, Amex, Visa.*

Many **B&B** establishments offer reduced rates for weekend and out-of-season bookings. Always ask about special deals for longer stays. Beware half-board terms in inns where we do not recommend the **FOOD.**

SPARSHOLT — The Plough — FOOD

Tel 01962 776353 Map 15 D3
Sparsholt nr Winchester Hampshire SO21 2NW

A delightful flower- and shrub-filled garden complete with children's playhouses, wooden garden chalet, chickens and donkeys is a popular summer feature at this much-extended 200-year-old cottage, located on the edge of the village. The smartly refurbished bar area, recently incorporating the original cottage front rooms, feature pine tables, a dresser and comfortable cushioned chairs, with plenty of attractive prints brightening up the walls and an open fireplace for cooler days. Reliable and often imaginative bar food is attracting a loyal dining clientele, for beyond a good sandwich board one will find a monthly-changing snack menu offering the likes of salad niçoise, spiced Greek meat loaf, tuna and leek bake, and a daily-changing board listing chilled cucumber and mint soup, smoked trout and feta cheese au gratin, followed by wild boar casserole, mélange of red mullet, cod and salmon with aïoli sauce and stuffed aubergines with tabbouleh, all served with fresh vegetables. Short list of home-made puddings. Well-kept Wadworth ales and at least six acceptable wines available by the glass. *Open 11-3, 6.30-11 (Sun 12-3, 7-10.30).* ***Bar Food*** *12-2, 7-9 (Fri & Sat to 9.30).* ***Beer*** *Wadworth 6X & Henry's IPA, guest beer. Garden, children's play area. No credit cards.*

SPELDHURST HILL — George & Dragon — FOOD

Tel 01892 863125 **Fax 01892 871094** Map 11 B5
Speldhurst Hill nr Tunbridge Wells Kent TN3 0NN

Set back from the village lane, this magnificent black and white timbered inn is thought to be one of the oldest pubs in southern England, dating as it does from 1212. Inside, a wealth of ancient features exist, from an enormous inglenook, heavy carved ceiling beams, vast flagstones, antique cushioned settles and wall panelling in the main bar to the huge original roof timbers in the charming Oak Room restaurant. A good range of real ales, local Chiddingstone cider and an impressive global list of wines all complement the extensive range of home-cooked bar food on offer. Highlights of the daily printed menu and the interesting specials board may include broccoli and almond soup, fishcakes with lobster sauce, beef stroganoff, spicy Moroccan lamb with apricots and almonds and lamb steak with green pepper sauce. Chips and salad accompany pub favourites and good fresh vegetables are generously served with main dishes. Both sandwiches and ploughman's platters are available lunch and evening. Standard selection of puddings. Separate à la carte menu can be enjoyed in the character restaurant, where monthly Friday night jazz suppers can be enjoyed. Front lawn and patio for fine weather imbibing. *Open 11-11 (Sun 12-10.30).* ***Bar Food*** *12-2, 7-10 (no food Sun eve). Free House.* ***Beer*** *Harveys Best & Sussex, Young's Special, Fuller's London Pride. Garden, outdoor eating. Access, Amex, Visa.*

SPREYTON — Tom Cobley Tavern — B&B

Tel 01647 231314 Map 13 D2
Spreyton Devon EX17 5AL

This peaceful white-washed village local draws plenty of visitors in the summer months due to its name and associations with 'Widecombe Fair'. It was in 1802 that Tom Cobley and all left the village for Widecombe and his cottage still stands opposite the pub. The unspoilt main bar has an open fire, cushioned settles and dispenses some good Devon ale straight from the cask. Those on the historical trail can be accommodated in one of the four homely and comfortably furnished bedrooms which have attractive fabrics and bedcovers. None are en suite, but the adjacent bathroom facilities are spotlessly clean. Summer alfresco drinking can be enjoyed on the pretty flower-bedecked gravel terrace or in the rear garden with its far-reaching views. *Open 12-2.30, 6-11 (Sun 12-3, 7-10.30), closed Monday lunchtime. Free House.* ***Beer*** *Cotleigh Tawny, Exe Valley Dob's Bitter, Hall and Woodhouse Tanglefoot.* ***Accommodation*** *4 bedrooms, not en suite, £36 (single £18). Children welcome overnight (under 6 months stay free in parents' room, under-2s £6, 2-6 £12), additional cot available (£6). Check-in by arrangement. Garden, outdoor eating area. No credit cards.*

We endeavour to be as up-to-date as possible but inevitably some changes to landlords, chefs and other key staff occur after the Guide has gone to press.

SPRINGTHORPE New Inn FOOD

Tel 01427 838254 Map 7 E2
16 Hill Road Springthorpe Lincolnshire DN21 5PY

Created from a row of brick cottages over 100 years ago, this homely off-the-beaten-track village local enjoys a peaceful position close to the parish church and overlooking the small green. An unpretentious and welcoming atmosphere awaits visitors in the comfortable carpeted lounge and in the separate, spartan locals bar. Along the corridor is a neat and cottagey dining-room, which bustles with set Sunday lunch diners (bookings only). A short and simple printed bar menu features mainly standard dishes, but standing out from the rest are the landlady's traditional home-cooked specials, such as a hearty soup – cheese and broccoli – served with warm rolls, sausage, bacon and liver casserole, steamed steak and kidney pudding, smoked haddock fishcakes or fresh cod and plaice. Puddings include bread and butter pudding and syrup and sultana sponge. *Open 12-2, 7-11 (Sun 12-2, 7-10.30). Closed Monday evening.* ***Bar Food*** *12-2, 7-10. Free House.* ***Beer*** *Bateman XXXB, Marston's Pedigree, Garden. Access, Visa.*

STAMFORD Bull & Swan B&B

Tel 01780 63558 Map 7 E3
High Street St Martins Stamford Lincolnshire PE9 2LJ

Opposite the former house of Lady Wingfield, who in 1643 persuaded Cromwell not to raze the town, today's Bull and Swan is wonderfully preserved; its inheritors should be truly grateful to their erstwhile neighbour for its survival. Its stone facade and mullion windows house an intimate pub within, its plain two-tiered timbered bar hung with horsebrasses and bric-a-brac. Bedroom accommodation is modest with five of the simply furnished rooms sporting en-suite showers (only one has a bath), some of which are very cramped indeed. The best and biggest room takes character from its sloping floor, angled ceiling and the bright duvets and light paintwork. Other rooms are looking rather dated and in need of some investment. All have TV, clock-radio and tea-makers. *Open 11.30-2.30, 6-11 (Sun 12-3, 7-10.30).* ***Beer*** *Bass, Tetley. Garden.* ***Accommodation*** *7 bedrooms, 5 en suite £45 (single £35). Check-in by arrangement. Children welcome overnight (charge depends on age. No dogs. Access, Visa.*

> We do not accept free meals or hospitality – our inspectors pay their own bills and never book in the name of Egon Ronay's Guides.

STAMFORD George of Stamford FOOD

Tel 01780 55171 **Fax 01780 57070** Map 7 E3 **B&B**
71 St Martins Stamford Lincolnshire PE9 2LB

Zzz...

Arguably the finest and grandest of England's old coaching inns, the George is a fully modernised hotel (recommended in our *1996 Hotels & Restaurants Guide*) that retains some wonderful period atmosphere. It's believed that there's been a hostelry of sorts here since the Norman period, originally as a stopping place for pilgrims on their way to the Holy Land, and a crypt under what is now the cocktail bar is certainly medieval, while much of the present building, which dates from 1597, remains in the veritable warren of rooms that make up the public areas. Facing the High Street, the oak-panelled London Suite and York Bar were once waiting rooms for the "twenty up and twenty down" stages which passed this way, but for the modern pub-goer this bar is probably the least attractive, being solidly masculine in its appearance. The Garden Lounge, however, which is exotically bedecked in orchids, palms and orange trees, provides a fine setting for informal eating throughout the day (7am-11pm): lunch includes a fine cold buffet, with which, incidentally, up to 20 wines are offered by the glass. Next door, and by far the most picturesque spot, is the enclosed courtyard. Surrounded by the ivy-covered hotel buildings, hung with vast flowering baskets and illuminated by old street lamps, it makes an ideal venue for morning coffee and afternoon tea, as well as barbecues on mid-summer evenings. Restaurant dining, in an elegant, chandeliered hall sporting silver urns, duck presses, and domed carving wagons (daily roast joints) and serving trolleys (smoked salmon, cheese, desserts) still in daily use, runs along traditional (and comparatively pricey) lines with adventurous touches; gentlemen are 'respectfully' requested to wear a jacket and tie. The super wine list is keenly priced, expertly compiled and simple to use. Accommodation at the George is strictly hotel, which is fine if you're prepared to pay. A liveried porter shows you to the room and there's a full, cosseting night service. The comfort of plushly-draped bedrooms, close-carpeted

through to the bathrooms fitted out with bespoke toiletries, generous towels and rather wonky telephone showers is all wonderfully 'British'. A morning tray of tea (with folded daily paper – no, it's not ironed!) appears at the appointed time, and a traditional English breakfast is served down in the Garden Lounge. *Open 11-11.* ***Bar Food*** *12-11. Free House.* ***Beer*** *Adnams Broadside.* ***Accommodation*** *47 bedrooms, all en suite (3 single rooms with shower only), £105-£160 (single £78/£88). Children welcome overnight, additional bed (£12) and cot available. Garden, outdoor eating, beautician, hair salon. Access, Amex, Diners, Visa.*

STANFORD DINGLEY — Bull Country Inn — FOOD

Tel 01734 744409 Map 14a C4
Stanford Dingley nr Reading Berkshire RG7 6LS

The pretty redbrick Bull has its origins genuinely in the 15th century and its sturdy oak pillars mid-bar are certainly load-bearing. They divide the beamed lounge bar into two intimate areas which are primarily made over to eating, and their refined air is augmented by light classical background music. With only half a dozen or so tables to service, and a tiny kitchen from which to work, menus are kept sensibly short while the service shines by being so friendly and obliging. For a snack are filled baked potatoes and ploughman's platters; home-cooked daily specials are typified by leek, cheese and potato pie, creamed chicken with avocado, an authentic curry and chocolate roulade. More substantial dinners might start with a creamy Stilton soup or garlic, bacon and mushrooms on toast, with turkey almond and grilled steaks to follow; those in the know will go for the excellent 'pommes Dauphinoise'. There's a fairly-priced choice of wines by the bottle and both the Bass and Brakspear ales are kept in fine condition. Children are allowed in the saloon bar up to 8.30pm (except Saturday evenings). Six miles from Junction 12 of the M4 – follow the A4 west to the second roundabout, turn right on the A340 towards Pangbourne, take the first left to Bradfield, then left again after which you will find Stanford Dingley signposted on the right. *Open 12-3, 7-11 (Sun 12-3, 7-10.30). Closed Mon lunchtime except Bank Holidays.* ***Bar Food*** *12-2.30, 7.30-10. Free House.* ***Beer*** *Bass, Archers Village, Brakspear. Garden. Family room. No credit cards.*

STANNERSBURN — Pheasant Inn — FOOD — B&B

Tel & Fax 01434 240382 Map 5 D2
Stannersburn Falstone nr Hexhan Northumberland NE48 1DD

Zzz...

Just a mile from Kielder Water in the Northumberland National Park stands the four centuries old farmhouse which now houses the Pheasant. The Kershaw family's conversion of the former Crown Inn has been painstaking and purposeful. The carpeted Lounge Bar is in muted tones and in the warm mellow pine dining-room traditional pub food is served from a kitchen reliably run by Irene and son Robin. Always available are the likes of ploughman's platters and sandwiches (lunch only) lasagne, haddock fillets and steak and kidney pie: daily specials encompass sweet pickled herrings, Northumbrian lamb with rosemary and redcurrant and baked trout stuffed with prawns. Follow with sticky toffee pudding or meringue nests filled with ice cream and summer berries. There are no chips here; rather, the kitchen's reputation rests firmly on freshly-cooked vegetables and roast prime sirloin for a commendable Sunday lunch. In the Barn and Hemmel, bedroom conversion is, for now, complete; furnishings are colourful and TV, hairdryers and beverage trays the standard fittings. Fully en suite, the family room and three larger twins have full-size bathtubs with showers; remaining doubles have WC and showers only. All are smartly tiled and brightly lit. All bedrooms and the dining-room are non-smoking areas. *Open 11-3, 6-11 (Sun 12-3, 7-10.30). May close Mon in winter.* ***Bar Food*** *12-2.30, 7-9. Free House.* ***Beer*** *Tetley, Ind Coope Burton Ale.* ***Accommodation*** *8 bedrooms, all en suite, £52 (£30 single). Children welcome overnight (under 5s stay free in parents' room), additional bed available. Family room. Access, Visa.*

STANTON ST JOHN — Star Inn — FOOD

Tel & Fax 01865 351277 Map 14a C2
Stanton St John nr Oxford Oxfordshire OX9 1EX

A former 18th-century butcher's shop and abattoir (now owned by Wadworth) with lots of period feel in the two original little bars, both low-beamed, one brick-floored, the other carpeted and furniture-crammed. Families can eat in a separate no-smoking room and

children can use the outside play area. Reliably good food is offered on a simple menu – carrot and orange soup, salmon and spinach pie, lamb and apricots, fisherman's platter, various sandwiches and ploughman's platters and such puddings as raspberry pavlova or bread-and-butter pudding served with clotted cream. A separate vegetarian menu with a choice of six dishes is always available. Landlords the Tuckers also own the *Sparkford Inn* in Somerset (Tel 0963 440218). *Open 11-2.30, 6.30-11 (Sun 12-3, 7-10.30).* ***Bar Food** 12-2, 7-10 (7-9.30 Sun).* ***Beer** Wadworth Henry's IPA, 6X, Old Timer (in winter) & Farmer's Glory, Hall and Woodhouse Tanglefoot. Garden, outdoor eating, children's play area. Access, Visa.*

STANTON WICK — Carpenters Arms — FOOD

Tel 01761 490202 Fax 01761 490763 Map 13 F1 **B&B**
Stanton Wick Pensford nr Bristol Avon BS18 4BX

The Carpenters Arms is all one would expect of a country inn, complete with roses clambering up the walls and tubs of colourful flowers. It was converted from a row of 17th-century miners' cottages in the tiny hamlet of Stanton Wick, which overlooks the Chew valley. Inside, there are low oak beams, natural stone walls and warming log fires; at one end of the building is a restaurant for formal eating, at the other, the less formal Coopers Parlour. The printed menu here includes grills, home-made soup – gazpacho – devilled lamb's kidneys, filled baguettes and a good choice of vegetarian dishes (pasta shells with olives, tomatoes and fresh herbs). There are also daily specials on the short blackboard menu, for example, beef stir-fry, deep-fried fresh cod and smoked salmon. The restaurant menu has a more elaborate choice of dishes on an à la carte menu. Traditional sweets include bread and butter and summer puddings, and the speciality ice creams are home-made. There are some six wines available by the glass from a good realistically-priced wine list and a handful of real ales to wash down the eats. Immaculate bedrooms are appropriately cottagey in style, with pine furniture and pretty co-ordinating fabrics and wall coverings. Modern conveniences are included and there are smart, modern carpeted bathrooms. Badger Inns. *Open 11-11 (Sun 11.30-3, 6-10.30).* ***Bar Food** 12-2.15, 7-10. Free House.* ***Beer** Bass, Butcombe, Wadworth 6X, guest beer. Terrace, outdoor eating.* ***Accommodation** 12 bedrooms, all en suite, £59.50 (single £45.50). Children over 10 welcome overnight, additional bed (£10) available. No dogs. Access, Amex, Visa.*

STAPLE FITZPAINE — Greyhound Inn — FOOD

Tel 01823 480227 Fax 01823 480773 Map 13 E2
Staple Fitzpaine nr Taunton Somerset TA3 5SP

Built as a hunting lodge by the local lord of the manor in 1640, the creeper-clad Greyhound has since been extended a number of times. The result is a series of rambling, connecting rooms, some with flagstone floors, some with old timbers or natural stone walls and stools made out of old barrels. The gravelled terrace garden has a play area with a splendid rustic climbing frame and slide. The bar menu encompasses char-grills with a choice of sauces, baked jacket potatoes, ploughman's platters, sandwiches, a children's menu, Mexican tacos, home-made burgers, devilled whitebait, deep-fried Brie and vegetarian options (spinach, corn and cheese pancakes); a more exciting, daily-changing à la carte menu (fresh asparagus, mussels with elderberries, pan-fried chicken breast with pear and Stilton sauce, monkfish tails with cockles, mussels and prawns) is also available in the bars from Mon-Thu. Live jazz and blues on Thursdays and a comedian performs once a month on a Saturday. Four en-suite letting bedrooms should come into operation early in 1996. *Open 12-3, 5-11 (Sun 12-3, 7-10.30).* ***Bar Food** 12-2, 7-10. Free House.* ***Beer** Exmoor Ale, Flowers Original, Oakhill Best, Boddingtons, guest beer. Terrace, outdoor eating, children's play area. Access, Visa.*

STARBOTTON — Fox & Hounds — FOOD

Tel 01756 760269 Fax 01756 760862 Map 5 D4 **B&B**
Starbotton North Yorkshire BD23 5HY

A typical 400-year-old stone-built, white-painted Yorkshire pub the inside of which is quite unspoilt, with flagstone floors, a few plates on the wall for decoration and a motley collection of jugs, pots and mugs hanging from the ceiling beams, plus a real fire in the stone fireplace in winter. In summer there are a few tables outside. What is untypical about the Fox & Hounds is Hilary McFadyen's excellent cooking with an ever-changing blackboard menu offering the likes of Moroccan-style lamb with apricots, prunes and

almonds, lamb and mint burger, spinach and mince lasagne, vegetable and chestnut crumble and mixed bean casserole. At lunchtimes there is also a ploughman's lunch (three cheeses) that comes with an apple and Hilary's own home-baked granary bread, Yorkshire pudding with various fillings and crusty French stick sandwiches. Extra more elaborate evening dishes may feature chicken supreme in garlic and green peppercorn sauce and baked salmon steak with herb crust and a white wine sauce. Finish off with fudgy nut and raisin pie or home-made ice cream. Two single, charming bedrooms with en-suite shower rooms offer comfortable overnight accommodation with TV and tea and coffee-making kit. *Open 11.30-3, 6.30-11 (Sun 12-3, 7-10.30). Closed Mon eve, all day Mon Oct-Mar.* ***Bar Food*** *12-2, 7-9 (except Mon). Free House.* ***Beer*** *Theakston Best, Old Peculier & XB, Black Sheep, guest beers. Terrace, outdoor eating.* ***Accommodation*** *2 bedrooms, both en suite, £44 (single £30). Children welcome overnight. Accommodation closed mid Dec-mid Feb. Access, Visa.*

STAVERTON — Sea Trout Inn — FOOD B&B

Tel 01803 762274 Fax 01803 762506 Map 13 D3
Staverton nr Totnes Devon TQ9 6PA

A warm welcome heralds a pleasant stay at the Sea Trout, a country inn that is a particular favourite of fishermen. The fishing theme runs through the pub, some specimens mounted in showcases, others depicted in paintings or on plates. There's a conservatory leading from the restaurant to the patio-style garden complete with pond and fountain. Bedrooms are decorated in cottagey style and have TVs, telephones, tea-makers and en suite facilities (three with shower only). The extensive bar menu features local produce, notably fresh fish, and additional home-made blackboard specials are offered; initial inspections just before this Guide went to press showed serious intent. The pub is not suitable for children under six. *Open 11-3, 6-11 (Sun 12-3, 7-10.30). Free House.* ***Beer*** *Fergusons Dartmoor Best, Wadworth 6X, Bass, guest beer. Garden.* ***Accommodation*** *10 bedrooms, all en suite, £58 (single £39.50) winter reductions. Children welcome overnight (under-3s stay free in parents' room, 3-12s £8.75), additional bed and cot available. Access, Amex, Visa.*

STEDHAM — Hamilton Arms — FOOD

Tel 01730 812555 Map 11 A6
School Lane Stedham nr Midhurst West Sussex GU20 0NZ

Suhail Hussain's and Mudita Karnasuta's little piece of the Orient is hardly what one expects to find in a quiet Sussex village. As they say: "with so little magic left in the world you owe it to yourself to visit us" – be it advertising hyperbole or a genuinely warm invitation, the Hamilton Arms is out of the ordinary and worth dropping by. Bar food encompasses toasted sandwiches and the usual pub favourites (lasagne, fish and chips, steak and kidney pie and so on) but there is a choice of Thai dishes – from 'mixed titbits' to one-dish noodle and rice dishes, red and green curries and roast duck with light sesame sauce and pickled ginger – alongside the real ale (and Singha Thai beer). Waitresses in national costume serve in the Nava Thai Restaurant, adjacent to the bar, where a long list of unpronouncable dishes (but helpfully translated) entices diners further. Special menus on Valentine's Day and Thai New Year in early April. 10% of the net profits of the pub are put towards the Mudita Trust which supports abused, distressed and underprivileged children in Thailand; proceeds from an annual Eastern Cultural Fete held on the village green opposite the pub every Spring Bank Holiday also benefit the Trust. *Open 11-11, Sun 12-3, 7-10.30.* ***Bar Food*** *12-2.30, 6-10.30, Sun 12-2.30, 7-9 (no food Mon).* ***Beer*** *King & Barnes Sussex, Courage Directors, Marston's Pedigree. Access, Visa.*

STEEP — Harrow Inn — FOOD

Tel 01730 262685 Map 15 D3
Steep nr Petersfield Hampshire GU32 2DA

The 400- to 500-year-old Harrow is a modest little pub tucked down a sleepy country lane that dwindles into a footpath by a little stream. The tenancy has been in the same family since 1929 and in 1992 landlord Edward McCutcheon finally managed to buy the inn from the brewery and keeps it very much as it must have been in the last century (earlier, even). Two small rooms have boarded walls, an old brick inglenook fireplace, scrubbed wooden tables and a hatch-like bar, behind which barrels of beer sit on racks, with bundles of drying flowers hanging above. There's a small cottagey garden to one side, and some old sloping rustic benches and tables out at the front. Toilets are in a separate brick building on the other side of the lane. The food is limited to a few wholesome snacks, generously-filled sandwiches, a split-pea- and ham-based soup full of fresh vegetables served with great

chunks of bread; a few salads and ploughman's platters of beef, cheese or home-cooked ham; home-made Scotch eggs and, perhaps, home-made quiche or lasagne. Apart from the beers, there's a good selection of fruit wines. The Petersfield Bypass on the A3 has drastically changed the road layout round these parts, so here we go: heading south or north on the A3, take the A272 turning to Midhurst & Petersfield, follow exit road to roundabout, take first left on to A272 Midhurst road (old A3); at bottom of hill (about 350yds) take first turning on the left (opposite the garage); follow this road to Sheet church (about 350yds), take the road on the left opposite the church signposted Steep ½ mile – this will take you via the level crossing and the motorway bridge to the Harrow Inn. Directions courtesy of the landlord, who will be waiting to serve you a well-deserved ale or two! *Open 11-2.30 (Sat to 3), 6-11 (Sun 12-3, 7-10.30). **Bar Food** 12-2, 6.30-9.30 (Sun 7.30-9.30). Free House. **Beer** Flowers Original, Boddingtons, Strong County Bitter, Fuggles. Garden, outdoor eating. No credit cards.*

STEEPLE ASTON — Red Lion — FOOD

Tel 01869 340225 Map 14a C1

South Street Steeple Aston Oxfordshire OX6 3RY

Colin and Margaret Mead run this pretty 330-year-old village pub, just off the main Oxford-Banbury A4260. A small flower-filled terrace leads into a comfortable beamed bar to the left and a small dining-room to the right. Very well kept beer, a multitude of malt whiskies and an extensive wine list all complement Margaret's cooking. Quality lunchtime snacks include home-made hot-pot in winter, rare roast beef sandwiches and ploughman's lunches made with British cheeses are specialities in the bar, while a more creative and imaginative small menu (3-course meal with coffee is priced according to main dish) is offered in the dining-room at night, making use of game in season and local produce. Home-made puddings include Craigellachie cream (Scottish syllabub made with syrup of marmalade and malt whisky). *Open 11-3, 6-11 (Sun 12-3, 7-10.30). **Bar Food** 12-2 (except Sun). Restaurant 7.30-9.15 (except Sun & Mon). Free House. **Beer** Hook Norton Best, Wadworth 6X, guest beer. Garden, outdoor eating. Access, Visa.*

STIFFKEY — Red Lion — FOOD

Tel & Fax 01328 830552 Map 10 C1

44 Wells Road Stiffkey Wells-next-the-Sea Norfolk NR23 1AJ

Nestling in the Stiffkey valley amid rolling Norfolk countryside, this peaceful village once boasted three pubs, but all became victims of the Watney revolution in the 1960s. After 28 years as a private house the Red Lion, a fine 16th-century white-painted brick and flint cottage on the main coast road, was resurrected in 1990 as a free house and has been thriving ever since, attracting a loyal local clientele. Inside, three charming rooms have bare board or quarry-tiled floors, three warming logs fires – one in a splendid inglenook – and a simple rustic mix of wooden settles, pews and scrubbed tables. Apart from the ambience, it is the good home-cooked food that draws people here. A printed menu lists snacks and starters, such as a choice of ploughman's platters, salads, generously filled sandwiches, a hearty soup – leek and celery – chicken terrine, soft herring roes on toast and smoked trout paté, as well as pub favourites like home-made pies. More imaginative main meals, served with fresh crisp vegetables, may include brill with basil sauce, tenderloin of pork with apples and cider or duck bonne femme, and are listed on a daily-changing blackboard. For pudding try the apple and rhubarb crumble or banana and yoghurt cheesecake. Good range of East Anglian beers and a short list of wines. After a day on the beach or strolling the Peddars Way, this is a good stop for families, who have use of a large and airy rear conservatory with access to the terraced garden. *Open 11-3, 6-11 (winter from 7, Sun 12-3, 7-10.30). **Bar Food** 12-2, 7-9 (summer 6.30-9.30). Free House. **Beer** Greene King Abbot Ale, Adnams Extra, Woodforde's Wherry, Nelson's Revenge & Great Eastern Ale. Garden, outdoor eating. Access, Visa.*

Many **B&B** establishments offer reduced rates for weekend and out-of-season bookings. Always ask about special deals for longer stays. Beware half-board terms in inns where we do not recommend the **FOOD.**

STILTON — Bell Inn — FOOD

Tel 01733 241066 **Fax 01733 245173** Map 7 E4 **B&B**

Great North Road Stilton nr Peterborough Cambridgeshire PE7 3RA

Reputedly the oldest coaching inn on the Great North Road, the Bell boasts a Roman well in its courtyard and an impressive 15th-century stone frontage. Discreetly concealed from the road are two wings of en-suite bedrooms whose 20th-century trappings include telephones, satellite television and whirlpool baths, while tokens of the past are confined to the odd four-poster bed. This is a pity, as the rest of the building is simply splendid. The village bar retains its stone-flagged floor and cosy alcoves huddled round the great log fire; this is where the original Stilton cheese was sold to travellers in the 1720s. Today it's served on its own with plum bread, or in a celery soup, or in a lamb casserole with Stilton dumplings. For the less single-minded, there's zucchini and seafood creole, ham hock served with coarse grain mustard sauce or sweet and sour fried vegetables, followed by home-made traditional desserts like bread-and-butter pudding and summer pudding. More serious food on a weekly-changing table d'hote menu is on offer in the galleried restaurant, where linen-covered tables are widely spaced in two sections under gnarled oak beams and a vaulted ceiling with original exposed rafters. Recommended in our *1996 Hotels and Restaurants Guide. Open 12-2.30, 6-11 (Sun 12-3, 7-10.30).* ***Bar Food*** *12-2, 6.30-9 (Sun 7-9). Free House.* ***Beer*** *Marston's Pedigree, Ruddles County, Tetley, guest beer. Garden, outdoor eating.* ***Accommodation*** *19 bedrooms, all en suite, £64/£74/£84 (single £59/£69). Children welcome overnight (under-5s stay free if sharing parents' room), additional bed (£10) and cot available. No dogs. Access, Amex, Diners, Visa.*

STOCKLAND — Kings Arms Inn — FOOD

Tel 01404 881361 **Fax 01404 881732** Map 13 E2 **B&B**

Stockland nr Honiton Devon Ex14 9BS

Well signposted from the Chard-Honiton stretch of the A30 this cream-faced thatched village pub dates from the 16th century, became a coaching inn in the early 18th century and is now Grade II listed. Although this rambling building has been considerably renovated and extended in recent years it retains a marvellously unspoilt interior, especially in the beamed Cotley Bar dining area. Divided by a medieval oak screen, it has a vast inglenook, padded wall benches, high-back settles and good sturdy refectory tables. The daily-changing blackboard menu is popular with local diners, listing simple starters like Brie in filo, garlic mushrooms and chicken liver paté, followed by Cotley rack of lamb, sirloin of beef roulade, seafood in filo pastry or fillets of dab with crabmeat. Booking is advisable at all times.
A separate snack menu is available at lunchtimes only and features a selection of omelettes, pancakes, curries, steak and kidney pie, steaks and the usual sandwiches and ploughman's platters. As well as local ales there is a good choice of German bottled beers, a tremendous range of Island malt whiskies and an interesting wine list, with at least eight offered by the glass. Live music on Sunday evenings. Three neat and comfortable bedrooms are traditionally furnished and offer TV, phones, beverage-making facilities and clean, older-style bathrooms. No children under ten in the dining-room. *Open 12-3, 6.30-11 (Sun 12-3, 7-10.30).* ***Bar Food*** *12-1.45, 6.30-9 (Sun from 7), no food Sun lunchtime. Free House.* ***Beer*** *Exmoor Ale, John Smith's, Hall and Woodhouse Badger Best, Ruddles County. Garden, outdoor eating. Family room.* ***Accommodation*** *3 bedrooms, all en suite, £30 (single £20). Children welcome overnight, additional bed available £10. Accommodation closed 24 & 25 Dec. Access, Visa.*

STOCKPORT — Red Bull — FOOD

Tel 0161 480 2087 Map 6 B2

14 Middle Hillgate Stockport Cheshire SK3 4YL

Modest little pub with good, unpretentious home-cooking – pea and bacon soup, large open sandwiches, gammon and egg, and fish and chips. You might also find a daily curry, lasagne, a good cheeseboard, a couple of vegetarian options, plaice fillets or chicken Kiev. Homely puddings like treacle sponge and custard, apple and blackberry pancake roll or chocolate fudge cake. Children welcome ar lunchtime only. *Open 11.30-3, 5-11, Fri & Sat 11-11, Sun 12-3, 7-10.30.* ***Bar Food*** *12-2.45.* ***Beer*** *Robinson's Best & Hatters Mild. No credit cards.*

STOKE ST GREGORY — Rose & Crown — FOOD

Tel 01823 490296 **Fax 01823 490996** Map 13 E2 **B&B**
Woodhill Stoke St Gregory Somerset TA3 6EW

In the hamlet of Woodhill, the Rose & Crown is a 17th-century cottage pub with a delightful patio and, indoors, a fairly subtle horsey theme, lots of nooks and crannies, timbers and brasses aplenty. The centrepiece of the bar area is the 60ft well which is decorated with plants. Landlady Irene Browning's wildlife pictures hang on the walls. Diners are still travelling miles for the famous scrumpy chicken and cherry cheesecake, just two of their good home-made dishes. Other popular dishes include grilled skate (fresh fish from Brixham harbour), or on the fixed-price menu: California salad, hot peppered mackerel or grilled trout with almonds, and a choice of home-made ice cream specialities. The granary bread used to make the sandwiches and accompany the ploughman's lunches is home-made. There is a 3-course traditional Sunday roast lunch. Bedrooms are modest with modern fittings and equipped with TVs, radios, beverage-making facilities and hairdryers. Those in the main building have private facilities – two boasting en suite jacussi baths – while the two bedrooms located in the cottage annexe share a sitting room and bathroom (also let as self-catering accommodation). All residents have use of the heated swimming pool in the cottage garden. *Open 11-3, 6.30-11 (Sun 12-3, 7-10.30).* ***Bar Food*** *12-2 (Sun to 2.30), 7-10. Free House.* ***Beer*** *Exmoor Ale, Eldridge Pope Royal Oak & Hardy Country Ale, guest beer. Terrace, outdoor eating.* ***Accommodation*** *5 bedrooms, 2 en suite £36 (single £22.50). Children welcome overnight, additional bed available. No dogs. Access, Visa.*

STOKE-BY-NAYLAND — Angel Inn ★ — FOOD

Tel 01206 263245 **Fax 01206 337324** Map 10 C3 **B&B**
Stoke-by-Nayland nr Colchester Suffolk CO6 4SA

Soft lamplight glows invitingly in the window of this solid, beautifully restored 16th-century inn which can be found beside the B1068 in the village centre. Eight years of careful renovation and conversion by owners Peter Smith and Richard Wright have revealed the true charm of this fine building. Inside, the delightful bar divides into two; a comfortable lounge area with exposed carved beams, tiled, polished brick and carpeted floors, a brick fireplace, log-burning stove and wooden furnishings, and a real relaxing sitting room with deep sofas, wing chairs and a grandfather clock. Tasteful touches like fresh flowers and candles on tables, quality prints and paintings, a few antique pieces and a warming dark green and cream decor enhance the overall ambience. The Angel fills early with discerning diners seeking out the imaginative, twice daily-changing blackboard menus which feature predominantly fresh fish – delivered daily from Billingsgate – as well as well sauced meat dishes, including local game, and unusual vegetarian choices. A typical meal may start with home-made chilled watercress soup or smoked trout fillet with a mango and mint dressing, followed by grilled whole pink snapper, supreme of chicken stuffed with goat's cheese served with a grape coulis or guinea fowl in its own mousseline with a mushroom sauce, with baked brioche pudding, thick orange and lemon tart to finish. Traditional Sunday lunch. Well-priced selection of global wines. The same menu applies in the charming Well Room restaurant – once the old brewhouse – with its high-vaulted ceiling, 52-foot well and green linen covered tablecloths. Tables can be booked here (£1.50 cover charge). Reached via a small gallery above this room are five decent-sized, individually decorated bedrooms, all with stylish co-ordinating wallpaper and fabrics, comfortable easy chairs and spotlessly clean ensuite facilities (all with bath and shower). A further room is housed in an annexe across the rear courtyard. Winner of our Bed & Breakfast Pub of the Year award in 1995. No children in the bar, no under-10s overnight. Wheelchair access. *Open 11-2.30, 6-11 (12-3, 7-10.30).* ***Bar Food*** *12-2, 6.30-9. Free House.* ***Beer*** *Greene King Abbot Ale & IPA, Nethergate Bitter (summer) or Old Growler (winter), Adnams Southwold, guest beer. Patio, outdoor eating.* ***Accommodation*** *6 bedrooms, all en suite £57.50 (single £44). No dogs. Access, Amex, Diners, Visa.*

STOKENHAM — Tradesman's Arms — FOOD

Tel 01548 580313 Map 13 D3
Stokenham nr Kingsbridge Devon

Tucked in the heart of a picturesque old village, this 14th-century cottage takes its name from the tradesmen who once used the coastal bridle path between Kingsbridge and Dartmouth, using the inn as their first night's lodging. With so many pubs catering for the hundreds of visitors that crowd this area in the summer, it is refreshing to find this small, refined village local doing just the opposite, even refusing to let children inside. Inside, you will find few tradesmen in the quaint, beamed and simply-furnished main bar, which has an upmarket ambience with tasteful classical music, 'Harrods' bar towels and a clientele to

match. More rustic than smart, the bar enjoys fine views from the three small windows across the valley to the church. The adjacent dining-room has a collection of modern settles and light oak tables topped with red and green gingham tablecloths, candles and dried flowers. The draw here, other than the genuinely warm welcome, is the honest home-cooked food. There are no frills and pretence to the short printed menu on each table which features main dishes like chicken with tarragon sauce, pork steak with cider and rosemary, rack of lamb with red wine and redcurrant, tagliatelle with courgette and tomato sauce and a selection of freshly prepared patés served with warm toast and salad. A separate lunch menu highlights the range of sandwiches and ploughman's platters on offer and a small blackboard lists a few dishes of the day, notably a fresh fish (delivered daily from Plymouth) option, such as Dart River salmon. Rather than a roast on Sundays, authentic Indian curries make up the menu and are extremely popular – booking advisable. The well-stocked bar dispenses, over 50 malt whiskies and a list of only eight wines, which surprisingly includes a Chateau Latour 1958 at £150. *Open 12-2.30, 7-11 (Sun 12-3, 7-10.30). Closed Sun-Thur evenings Jan-Mar.* ***Bar Food*** *12-2, 7-9.30. Free House.* ***Beer*** *Bass, Adnams Southwold, Greene King IPA, Thompson's Porter, guest beer. Garden, outdoor eating. No credit cards.*

We endeavour to be as up-to-date as possible but inevitably some changes to landlords, chefs and other key staff occur after the Guide has gone to press.

STONY STRATFORD — Cock Hotel — B&B

Tel 01908 567733 Map 15a D1

High Street Stony Stratford nr Milton Keynes Bucks MK11 1AH

In the heart of town, this former coaching inn dates from 1300 and was rebuilt after a fire in 1750. 'Ride a cock horse to Banbury Cross' – the horse was apparently from the Cock Hotel stables and with its neighbour the Bull gave rise to the phrase 'Cock and Bull story'. Investment in the building has seen the comfortable pubby bar and adjacent lounge refurbished with modern wallpaper and deep sofas, the addition of a permanent function marquee to the sheltered walled garden and the upgrading of the 28 en-suite bedrooms. All are well furnished, the superior rooms (housed in a converted ballroom) having lightwood furniture and clean bath/shower rooms, some with bidet. Residents' lounge. Handy for racing at Silverstone, but supplements may apply during busy periods. *Open 11-3, 5.30-11 (Sun 12-3, 7-10.30). Free House.* ***Beer*** *Theakston Best, XB & Old Peculier, Jennings Best, guest beer. Walled garden, outdoor eating.* ***Accommodation*** *28 bedrooms, all en suite, £57.50 (single £47.50), weekend reductions. Children welcome overnight, additional bed (£10) and cot (£5). Access, Amex, Diners, Visa.*

STOURTON — Spread Eagle Inn — B&B

Tel 01747 840587 Map 14 B3

Stourhead Stourton nr Warminster Wiltshire BA12 6QE

Zzz... ☺

Fine 18th-century brick inn owned by the National Trust and peacefully located within a neat complex of buildings – tea room and National Trust shop – close to the tiny parish church and Stourhead House with its magnificent landscaped gardens, enchanting lakes and woodland walks. As one would expect, the interior of the inn has been tastefully refurbished, the bars sporting sturdy wooden furnishings, good prints and paintings and warming open fires. High standards extend to the five charming en-suite bedrooms which retain architectural details, including Georgian and Regency fireplaces, and boast quality co-ordinating fabrics, antique and older-style furniture, easy chairs and various ornaments, clocks and pieces of china adding a homely touch. Each room has a TV, telephone, beverage-making kit and spotless bathroom with both a bath and overhead shower. The inn can get busy in the summer months with Stourhead visitors, but out-of-season this is an idyllic rural retreat. Food was disappointing on our last visit, so half-board accommodation offers in winter look less appealing than they might at first appear. *Open 11-11 (Winter 11-10.30, Sun 12-3, 7-10.30). Free House.* ***Beer*** *Ash Vine, Bass, Eldridge Pope Hardy Ale. Family Room.* ***Accommodation*** *5 bedrooms, all en suite, £69 (single £45). Children welcome overnight, additional bed (£12.50) and cot available (£5). No dogs. Access, Amex, Visa.*

STOW BARDOLPH **Hare Arms** FOOD

Tel 01366 382229 **Fax 01366 385522** Map 10 B2
Stow Bardolph nr Downham Market Norfolk PE34 3HT

A picturesque country pub in a delightful Norfolk village nine miles south of King's Lynn off the A10. Inside is pleasantly refurbished and immaculately run, with a cosy bar, elegant restaurant, popular conservatory extension (also the family room) and an intriguing coach house in the garden for children. The pub gets its name, not from the animal, but from a prominent local family, still found in these parts. Good bar food ranges from a fairly routine printed menu listing sndwiches (lunch only), home-made curries, lasagne and grills alongside standard favourites with chips; daily-changing blackboard specials include excellent pies – steak and kidney or pigeon – or more imaginative dishes like pork steak in peppercorn sauce and plaice fillet rolled and stuffed with spinach, all served with ready-plated vegetables. Puddings include Mississippi mud pie and lemon lush pie. A bi-monthly changing table d'hote dinner menu is offered in the restaurant as well as a seasonally changing à la carte choice. *Open 11-2.30, 6-11 (Sun 12-3, 7-10.30).* ***Bar Food*** *12-2, 7-10.* ***Beer*** *Greene King IPA & Abbot Ale, guest beers. Gardens, outdoor eating. Family room. No credit cards.*

STRATFIELD TURGIS **Wellington Arms** FOOD B&B

Tel 01256 882214 **Fax 01256 882934** Map 15a D4
Stratfield Turgis nr Basingstoke Hampshire RG27 OAS

Zzz... 

Hard by the A33, a charming old inn with a handsome white Georgian facade and a mix of the old and the new inside. The cosy, pubby L-shaped bar features a polished flagstone floor, a characterful mish-mash of wooden tables and chairs laid for bar snacks, stained-glass detail around the bar itself and swagged heavy drapes above the tall windows; it leads directly round into a friendly drawing room in country-house style with open fire, sunken-cushioned sofas, gilt-framed oil portraits and glass-cased stuffed birds. French windows open on to a small lawned area where bench picnic tables are set. Light meals and snacks include sandwiches and ploughman's platters, scrambled eggs with smoked salmon, venison sausages, home-made pies, pasta served with salad and daily blackboard specials (perhaps Cajun chicken or venison stroganoff) complete the picture. Fifteen bedrooms in the original building include two 'luxury doubles' (one a suite with a heavily-carved four-poster and spa bath, the other with a pastel green, highly decorative suite of furniture); 20 further rooms are in a two-storey modern extension to the rear, uniformly decorated with Laura Ashley pastel blues and yellows plus modern light oak furniture suites, and overlook a grassed area; hotel room facilities like a comfortable armchair, remote-controlled TV, powerful showers and tea/coffee making facilities are standard. A couple of modern suites serve as both small meeting rooms and family rooms with pull-down additional beds. Breakfast is served to residents in the traditional restaurant. Next door to the Duke of Wellington's estate (Stratfield Saye House, where river fishing can be arranged) and close to Wellington Country Park (ideal for family outings). Badger Inns. *Open 11-11 (Sun 12-3, 7-10.30).* ***Bar Food*** *12-2.30 & 6.30-10 (Sun 7-9.30).* ***Beer*** *Hall & Woodhouse. Garden, outdoor eating.* ***Accommodation*** *35 bedrooms, all en suite, £65/£75/£85/£100 (single £55/£65), weekend £48/£75 (single £38), family room £100. Children welcome overnight (under-12s £10), additional cot & bed available. Access, Amex, Diners, Visa.*

STRATFORD-ON-AVON **Dirty Duck** A

Tel 01789 297312 Map 14 C1
Waterside Stratford-on-Avon Warwickshire CV35 6BA

This "theatre of the gastronomic arts" once went by the name of the "Black Swan", the traditional "Mucky Duck" of English pub folklore. Today's crowds are drawn more in hopes of meeting a theatre type than a gastronome, the panelled and wood-block Theatre Bar containing a gallery at autographed photographs of RSC stars down the years which will keep many a theatre-goer long a-guessing. Standing above and back from the Waterside with its crazy-paved patio, it's the closest pub to the Royal Shakespeare theatre, with one of the town's most peaceful river views framed by massive horse chestnut trees. Just 50 yards down the road the hand-operated chain-link ferry (20p) conveys foot passengers back across the Avon to the playgrounds, amenities and long-term car parks. Whitbread Wayside Inns. *Open 11-11 (Sun 12-3, 7-10.30).* ***Beer*** *Flowers IPA & Original, Boddingtons. Patio/terrace, outdoor eating. Access, Amex, Diners, Visa.*

STRINESDALE Roebuck Inn FOOD

Tel 0161 624 7819 Map 6 B2
Brighton Road Strinesdale nr Oldham Greater Manchester OL4 3RB

A family welcome from Sue, Mark, Mary and Peter, and a prodigious choice from the menu await those who venture up the moor to the Howarth and Walters families' imposing hillside pub; the pub's not easy to find on a map – it's about a mile off the A672, taking Turfpitt Lane south of Denshaw. While the little ones can choose from fish fingers, beefburgers or sausages, a monthly-changing specials board can help buck the otherwise chips-and-peas mentality. Go, perhaps, for avocado with cottage cheese and crab meat, beef braised until tender in a pint of 'Boddies' and cream-soaked sticky toffee pudding. Sandwiches and ploughman's platters are readily available lunch and evening for those in need of a lighter bite. Value-for-money mid-week 3- and 4-course set menus. From bookable tables by the picture windows, views down the moor's edge end in an urban skyline; in the foreground a paved yard beckons animal-loving youngsters whose parents don't mind them getting mucky. *Open 12-2.30, 6-11 (Sun 12-10.30). **Bar Food** 12-2.30, 6.30-10 (Sun 12-10). Free House. **Beer** Oldham Bitter, Everards/Whitbread Chester's Best Mild, Boddingtons. Garden, outdoor eating, children's play area. Access, Amex, Visa.*

STROUD Old Nelson B&B

Tel 01453 765821 **Fax 01453 765964** Map 14 B2
Stratford Lodge Stratford Road Stroud Gloucestershire GL5 4AF

From the M5 Junction 13 follow the Superstore signs when coming into Stroud on the A419 to find this pub where a block of bedrooms were added a few years ago. All the rooms, except for two specially adapted disabled bedrooms, have en suite baths and showers. Family rooms with sofa beds offer good value with inexpensive breakfasts. There's a spacious non-smoking conservatory and safe garden, but no play area. Part of the Premier Lodge chain. *Open 11-11 (Sun 12-10.30). **Beer** Tetley Best, Greenall Original, Bass. Garden. Family rooms. **Accommodation** 32 bedrooms, all en suite, £39.50 (weekend reductions). Children welcome overnight (accommodated free in parents' room), additional bed and cot available. Access, Amex, Diners, Visa.*

STURMINSTER NEWTON Swan Inn B&B

Tel 01258 472208 **Fax 01258 473767** Map 14 B4
Market Place Sturminster Newton Dorset DT10 1AR

Pride of place in the market place of this busy little town goes to the Swan, a fine, brick 18th-century coaching inn that offers a warm welcome to both locals and visitors alike. Completely refurbished four years ago it has a comfortably furnished open-plan main bar with brick fireplace and open fire, and an adjacent attractively decorated dining-room. Tasteful fabrics and furnishings extend upstairs to the five individually styled en-suite bedrooms. one of which has a four-poster bed. Relaxing pastel shades of colour, quality wallpaper, co-ordinating fabrics, decent prints and good modern pine furniture ensure a comfortable stay. Added comforts include remote-control TVs, clock-radios, telephones and tea-making equipment. Rather compact bathrooms have both baths and overhead showers. All bedrooms overlook the bustling market place and housekeeping is of a high standard. Badger Inns. *Open 10.30-2.30, 6.30-11 (Sun 12-3, 7-10.30. **Beer** Hall & Woodhouse, Badger Best. Garden, outdoor eating. **Accommodation** 5 bedrooms, all en suite, £52.50 (single £39). Access, Amex, Diners, Visa.*

SULGRAVE Star Inn FOOD B&B

Tel 01295 760389 Map 14a C1
Manor Road Sulgrave Oxfordshire OX17 2SA

Zzz...

A cosy, creeper-clad village pub, created out of a 300-year-old former farmhouse, where Andy Willerton provides the bonhomie and partner Caroline Shoebridge the home cooking. Blackboard menus provide something for most tastes and appetites from double-decker sandwiches (perhaps oak-smoked ham or Norwegian prawn) and humus on toast via duck and vegetable broth and filo-wrapped tiger prawns to chicken Madras, fresh salmon fishcakes and a mixed grill. At Sunday lunchtimes the menu includes a traditional roast. For afters try lemon fudgecake, toffee crunch cheesecake or pecan pie. Ploughman's platters and sandwiches are not available weekend evenings. A small patio and lawn to the rear of the car park provides for summer eating and drinking. Three spotless bedrooms, all with en-suite shower rooms, feature old timbers and modern comforts like remote-control TV and tea and coffee kits but no telephone. A fourth en-suite bedroom, a mini-suite with

sitting room, was due to be completed at the end of the year. *Open 11-2.30, 6-11 (Sun 12-3, 7-10.30). **Bar Food** 12-2, 6.30-9.30 (Sun 7-9). **Beer** Hook Norton Best & Old Hooky, guest beer. **Accommodation** 3 bedrooms, all en suite, £40 (single £25). Children welcome overnight (cot age stay free in parents' room). No dogs. Accommodation closed 25 Dec. No credit cards.*

SUTTON — White Horse Inn — B&B

Tel 01798 869221 **Fax 01798 869291** Map 11 A6
Sutton nr Pulborough West Sussex RH20 1PS

In a sleepy village tucked beneath the South Downs and amid a maze of narrow lanes – signposted off the A285 Petworth to Chichester road – the 250-year-old White Horse offers peaceful overnight accommodation in six en-suite bedrooms. All rooms are well fitted out with dark mahogany furniture, pale floral fabrics and spotlessly clean tiled bathrooms (one with shower only). Added comforts include TVs, beverage-making facilities, telephones and hairdryers, with mineral water, a basket of fruit and magazines being welcoming touches. Reached via its own path across the rear garden, the phone-free Gardners Cottage room is ideal for those seeking isolation, although a handy brolly by the door will encourage a trip to the bar on rainy nights. Good standard of housekeeping. If follows that public areas are smart and well looked after with attractive prints, carpets and fabrics, fresh flowers and traditional darkwood furniture. *Open 11.2.30, 6-11 (11-3, 6-11 Sat, 12-3, 7-10.30 Sun). **Beer** Bateman's XB, Young's Bitter, Courage Best & Directors, Arundel Best Bitter. Garden, outdoor eating. **Accommodation** 6 bedrooms, all en suite, £58 (single £48). Children welcome overnight, additional child's bed in parents' room (£10), cot and high-chair provided. Access, Amex, Diners, Visa.*

SUTTON GAULT — Anchor Inn — FOOD

Tel 01353 778537 **Fax 01353 776180** Map 10 B2
Bury Lane Sutton Gault nr Ely Cambridgeshire CB6 2BD

Deep in Fen country, just off the A142 at Sutton village, the Anchor is protected from the 'hundred foot drain' (built by the Dutch in 1650 to drain the Fens and now called the New Bedford River) by a veritable rampart of earthworks. Descend, then pass a new riverside patio into the low, brick-built pub. Beer jugs hang from hooks in the low-beamed bar, racked Burton Ale is served direct from cask and landlord Robin Moore's preference for classical music seems entirely apposite to the setting. A long menu which relies heavily on fresh produce indicates careful shopping. The daily-changing menu starts with local game salami with home-made chutney and grilled dates wrapped in bacon on a mild mustard cream sauce and progresses to fresh seafood bourride, aubergine and ricotta cannelloni and rack of lamb with redcurrants and rosemary sauce, wild rabbit braised in cider with prunes and herbs and pan-fried pigeon breasts with rich Burgundy sauce. Home-made puddings are served with clotted cream, include tarte au citron and pecan nut and maple pie. A medley of unusual British cheeses with warm bread is another option. Those with children or particularly favouring the non-smoking Inglenook Room are well advised to book; it's virtually essential at weekends. In addition to the beer and a 100-plus wine list predominantly from Lay and Wheeler, other beverage choices include freshly squeezed orange juice and cups of cappuccino, chocolate or speciality teas. B&B is now offered in two en-suite bedrooms upstairs (not yet inspected). *Open 12-2.30, 7-11 (Sat from 6.30, Sun 12-3, 7-10.30). **Bar Food** 12-2, 6.30-9.30 (Sun 7-9). Free House. **Beer** Greene King IPA, Ind Coope Burton Ale. Garden, outdoor eating. Family room. Access, Amex, Visa.*

SWANTON MORLEY — Darby's — FOOD

Tel & Fax 01362 637647 Map 10 C1 **B&B**
Swanton Morley nr Dereham Norfolk NR20 4JT

Zzz... 

A "family" free house converted from two brick cottages in 1986 by the licensee – John Carrick – a local farmer, after the local mega-brewery closed the village's last traditional pub. A rustic ambience has been created in the main bar with beams, exposed brick walls and open brick fireplace with log fire. Both here and in the neatly laid out dining area visitors can enjoy reliable, home-cooked meals, as well as filled baguettes and ploughman's platters. Main menu choices include popular favourites, plus a mixed garden salad with smoked cheese, cashew nuts and pesto vinaigrette, beef and oyster pie and vegetarian dishes like tomato, spinach and Brie bake. Daily blackboard specials may feature shellfish chowder,

lamb casserole with red wine and rosemary and braised sausages with an onion and beer gravy. Puddings may include lemon crunch flan and white and dark chocolate mousse. Sunday roasts are a popular attraction. Younger diners have their own menu (Peter Rabbit – small ham salad) which is served in the dining area or in the small children's room, complete with a box of toys for impatient toddlers. Those seeking overnight accommodation will be surprised when directed 3/4 mile along the narrow lane to Park Farm, a fine farmhouse peacefully located in open countryside. Six fresh, airy and spotless en-suite bedrooms (four with showers only) are housed in a splendid cattleyard conversion offering exposed ceiling timbers, freestanding pine furnishings, TVs, clock-radios and beverage-making facilities. One room is geared to accept wheelchair visitors. Overflow accommodation in the farmhouse is more modest; four bedrooms, including two character attic rooms share two bathrooms. Guests wishing to venture to the pub have use of a free taxi service and sleeping children will be well looked after if parents want a night out. The welcome attributed to visiting children extends beyond the menu, children's room and toy box into the garden, where a vast enclosed play area – Darbyland – on a soft wood-chip floor boasts a swing, see-saw, climbing net and frame. Down on the farm there is a connecting family room, provision of a further bed and cot, high-chair at breakfast, a kitchen area for mums to prepare food and numerous animals to keep youngsters amused. 2- to 13-year olds are charged £1 per year old per night. *Open 11-2.30, 6-11 (Sun 12-3, 7-10.30). **Bar Food** 12-2, 7-10 (12-10 Sat, 12-2.30, 7-9.30 Sun). **Beer** Adnams Broadside, Woodforde's Wherry & Mardler's Mild, John Smith's, four guest ales. **Accommodation** 9 bedrooms, 5 en suite £39 (single £24). Dogs and children welcome overnight (cot and high-chair available). Garden, eating outside, children's play area. Access, Visa.*

Many **B&B** establishments offer reduced rates for weekend and out-of-season bookings. Always ask about special deals for longer stays. Beware half-board terms in inns where we do not recommend the **FOOD.**

SWAVESEY — Trinity Foot — FOOD

Tel 01954 230315 Map 15 F1

Huntingdon Road Swavesey Cambridgeshire CB4 5PD

Fairly modern pub next to the A604, named after Trinity College's hunt (Colonel Whitbread was Master of the Trinity Beagles), or rather more specifically, its horse-less followers. Parts of the building go back to 1870. The fish shop on the corner (which is also owned by the pub) supplies the superb fish for the many dishes on the menu – from oysters to baked salmon, grilled Dover sole, fresh lobster and monkfish in Pernod and cream. A more standard menu of pub favourites offers omelettes, ploughman's platters, grills to fillet steak, sandwiches, salads and a small selection of sweets – banana split, apple and blackberry sponge. Airy conservatory. *Open 11-2.30, 6-11 (Sun 12-3). Closed Sun evening. **Bar Food** 12-2 (Sun to 1.30), 6-9.30 (Fri & Sat to 10). **Beer** Flowers Original, Boddingtons. Patio, outdoor eating. Access, Amex, Visa.*

TALKIN VILLAGE — Blacksmiths Arms — FOOD B&B

Tel 01697 73452 Map 4 C2

Talkin Village Brampton Cumbria CA8 1LE

At the heart of this immaculately kept village just 9 miles from Carlisle and only 6 from the M6 at Junction 43, the revitalised Blacksmiths Arms is the pub all and sundry are talkin' about. The Bagshaws, Pat and Tom, run it very much as a family concern with quiet good humour and nothing appears too much trouble for them. Pat's kitchen tries not to overextend itself while offering a wide range of fare from the "Hot and Simple" steak and kidney pie, leg lamb chop and fresh haddock in her own beer batter through to some more adventurous daily specials such as chicken provençal, beef teriyaki and crispy garlic and herb prawns. Sandwiches and ploughman's lunches are also offered at both lunchtime and in the evening. Simplicity has also remained the key to careful conversion of the bedrooms, all of which now boast full en-suite facilities. Decor follows a country theme without being overly cottagey, furniture and fittings are of durable quality and colour TVs and tea- and coffee-making kits ensure an entirely adequate degree of guests' comfort. *Open 11-3.30, 6-11 (to 10.30 Sun). **Bar Food** 12-2, 7-9. **Beer** Boddingtons, Theakston's Best, occasional guest beer. Garden, outdoor eating. Family Room. **Accommodation** 5 bedrooms, all en suite, £38 (single £28). Children welcome overnight (accommodated free in parents' room), additional bed available. Accommodation closed 24 & 25 Dec. Access, Amex, Visa.*

TANGLEY — Fox Inn — FOOD

Tel 01264 730276 Map 14a B4
Tangley nr Andover Hampshire SP11 0RU

Well worth the diversion off the A343 north of Andover, the Fox is a remote white-painted brick and flint cottage pub with a welcoming atmosphere in its tiny, rustic bars and homely restaurant. Reliably good food from the landlady cook (Gwen Troke), her daily-changing blackboard menus listing value-for-money lunchtime snacks – decent vegetable soup served with basket of warm bread, cassoulet, steak and kidney pie, chili bean pot and tagliatelle with blue cheese, celery and bacon. More imaginative evening restaurant fare (also available in the bar) may include tenderloin of pork with calvados, mustard and cream and marinated leg of lamb with a redcurrant and spring onion sauce. Home-made ice cream, summer pudding or chocolate roulade are some of the puddings. The landlord, John Troke, has a comprehensive wine list, eight of which are available by the glass. Accommodation comprises one spacious and comfortable twin-bedded room which is furnished in modern pine and has a spotless en-suite shower room. TV, tea-maker, mini-fridge and help-yourself Continental breakfast with muffins, bread, jam, honey, marmalade, cheese, ham and fruit. *Open 11-3, 6-11 (Sun 12-3, 7-10.30). **Bar Food** 12-2, 6.30-10 (Sun from 7). Free House. **Beer** Bass, Royal Oak, Courage Best. Garden, outdoor eating. **Accommodation** 1 bedroom with shower, £40. Children welcome overnight, additional bed available. Closed 25 & 26 Dec eve. No credit cards.*

TARPORLEY — Rising Sun — FOOD

Tel 01829 732423 Map 6 B2
High Street Tarporley Cheshire CW6 0DX

High-street pub satisfying both diners and drinkers; very popular in the area and with the local cricketers. Forty-plus item bar food blackboard runs the gamut of choices from steak bordelaise down to spaghetti bolognaise; sandwiches and ploughman's at lunchtime only. Evening grills are supplemented by duck with cherries, beef stroganoff and veal cordon bleu. Bookings taken for Sunday lunches. One little bar is available for just drinking. *Open 11.30-3, 5.30-11 (Sun 12-3, 7-10.30). **Bar Food** 11.30-2 (Sun 12-2), 5.30-9.30. **Beer** Robinsons Best Bitter & Mild. Garden. Pub closed Sun eve. No credit cards.*

TARPORLEY — Swan Hotel — B&B

Tel 01829 733838 **Fax 01829 732932** Map 6 B2
50 High Street Tarporley Cheshire CW6 0AG

Formerly a coaching-house of reknown, the Swan was destroyed by fire in 1735 and rebuilt with its unusual Georgian frontage around 1769. Within, however, the flagstoned kitchen bar containing heraldic insignia of the Fettered White Swan, dates back to 1565. More recently, new owners have converted a coach house, where the six newest bedrooms are now housed. Stylish modern designs and patterned, matching fabrics lend the original bedrooms a distinctly classy feel, to which the TV, tea tray and trouser press add suitably up-to-date comfort. En-suite bathrooms offer heated towel rails, smart towels and toiletries. Bar snacks are no longer offered; a brasserie menu has taken their place (but has not yet been inspected). *Open 11-11 (Sun 12-3, 7-10.30). **Beer** Weetwood Ales, Wadworth 6X, Charles Wells Bombardier. Garden. **Accommodation** 20 bedrooms, all en suite, £52.95 (single £46). Children welcome overnight, additional bed (£5) and cot available. Access, Amex, Diners, Visa.*

TARRANT MONKTON — Langton Arms — FOOD B&B

Tel 01258 830225 **Fax 01258 830013** Map 14 B4
Tarrant Monkton nr Blandford Forum Dorset DT11 8RX

Zzz...

Thatched, rose- and creeper-clad, this mellow 17th-century brick pub, picturesquely situated opposite the parish church, is surely everybody's idea of a traditional village inn. Since acquiring the pub, Philip and Lauren Davison (previously at *La Belle Alliance* restaurant in Blandford Forum for ten years) have made positive changes and are successfully attracting a mixed clientele, in particular offering a warm welcome to children; they not only have their own room filled with toys but also a separate menu, food bar and excellent play areas in the spacious and safe rear garden. A splendid 'local' atmosphere pervades the beamed bars where drinkers can sample well-kept small brewery beers and diners can tuck into reliable home-cooked bar meals. Favourite dishes – cottage pie, lasagne, braised lamb's

liver and onions – are listed on a printed menu, while daily specials such as seafood broth, lamb's kidneys in coarse-grain mustard sauce, vegetable and broccoli mornay and apple and strawberry crumble are highlighted on two boards. Evenings bring speciality themes for different nights of the week – fish 'n' chips on Monday, pasta and pizza on Wednesdays, steaks on Thursdays. Extra evening dishes and a Sunday lunch menu are served in the adjacent Langton's Bistro. In general, food prices are exceptionally keen. Summer barbecues are a regular and popular feature. At least 12 wines are offered by the glass from a short list supplied by Christopher Piper wine merchants. Three single-storey blocks built around the rear courtyard house six spacious and well-maintained en-suite bedrooms, all with bath and shower, furnished in pine and sporting pretty duvets and curtains. TV, tea-maker, telephone and hairdryer are standard extras. *Open 11.30-2.30, 6-11 (Sat 11-11, Sun 12-3, 7-10.30).* ***Bar Food*** *11.30-2, 6-10 (Sun 12-2.30, 7-10). Free House.* ***Beer*** *Smiles Best, Ringwood Old Thumper, Shepherd Neame Spitfire, guest beers. Garden, outdoor eating, children's play area.* ***Accommodation*** *6 bedrooms, all en suite, £54 (family room £59, single £39). Children welcome overnight, additional bed and cot (£5) available. Access, Visa.*

TATENHILL Horseshoe Inn A

Tel 01283 564913 Fax 01283 511314 Map 6 C3
Main Street Tatenhill nr Burton-on-Trent Staffordshire DE13 9SD

A splendid summer spot just two miles from the A38 Burton-on-Trent by-pass, in the village once owned by Lady Godiva. So busy does it get that the staff run their little socks off, though generally the fun stops about there as, more restaurant-style than pub, there's waitress service to all interior tables. The garden, though, is pretty special in the summer months with loads of play equipment, a Norman castle and Wendy house. Children's menu lunchtimes only and regular barbecue events. Long hours on Bank Holiday weekends; long games of dominoes to while away the winter evenings. *Open 11.30-3, 5.30-11 (Sat 11.30-11, Sun 12-3, 7-10.30).* ***Beer*** *Marston's Pedigree & Head Brewer's Choice, Owd Roger in winter. Garden, outdoor eating. Children are welcome. Access, Visa.*

TESTCOMBE Mayfly A

Tel 01264 860283 Map 14 C3
Testcombe nr Stockbridge Hampshire SO20 6AZ

Idyllically situated right on the banks of the swiftly flowing River Test, this beamed old farmhouse (dated 1808) has a traditional bar, a bright conservatory and a splendid riverside terrace. Unrivalled tranquil river scenes, complete with ducks and swans, make the Mayfly a popular drinking spot, but on fine sunny days the whole place can be unbearably crowded, so arrive early to appreciate its superb position. The buffet food operation tries hard to cater for the volume of people. Be prepared to queue for the food and then be patient for a seat at peak times, especially in the summer. On the A3057 Stockbridge-Andover road. Whitbread Wayside Inns. *Open 11-11 Mon-Sat (Sun 12-10.30). Free House.* ***Beer*** *Flowers Original, Boddingtons, two guest beers. Riverside garden. Family room. Access, Visa.*

TETBURY Gumstool Inn FOOD

Tel 01666 890391 Fax 01666 890394 Map 14 B2
Calcot Manor Tetbury Gloucestershire GL8 8YJ

A recent addition to Calcot Manor country house hotel with its own driveway and car park. Designed as a traditional pub, complete with an open fireplace and old flagstone floor, it has the diner very much in mind. The kitchen shares the hotel's team and early signs are very encouraging. Home-made soup, toasted bacon and egg sandwich with fruit chutney and filled baguettes are offered among the snacks, along with more substantial dishes like sausage casserole, char-grilled salmon with salad and a butter sauce and chicken and ham pie with mushroom and leeks; daily blackboard specials add further interest. Children are allowed in the bar to eat and are offered their own menu; six high-chairs provided.
A south-facing terrace provides additional tables in fine weather. Booking is already essential for weekend eating. *Open 11.30-2.30, 6-11 (Sun 12-2.30, 7-10.30).* ***Bar Food*** *12-2, 7-9.30.* ***Beer*** *Bass, Duckers (house beer), Wadworth 6X, Worthington, guest beer. Garden, outdoor eating. Access, Amex, Diners, Visa.*

THAME **Abingdon Arms** FOOD

Tel 01844 260116 Map 15a D2
21 Cornmarket Thame Oxfordshire OX9 2BL

Known locally as 'The Abo', this 18th-century, former coaching inn offers a fairly modest face to the main street of town but inside several rooms have been opened up to create a long bar with rug-strewn, bare board floors, some exposed brickwork, magazines and newspapers to read and a lively, friendly atmosphere. To the rear, an old barn, is used for functions in the evening; beyond this a beer garden comes with rustic tables (some with rustic baby seats attached), slide, swing and climbing frame. Features of the menu are hugely thick 'doorstep' sandwiches and bowls of home-made tagliatelle with various toppings. Other items range from ploughman's platters and burgers to steak and kidney pudding, bangers and mash, Exeter stew with parsley dumplings and an all-day breakfast. All main menu items are available in children's portions at half price. *Open 11-11.* ***Bar Food*** *12-3 (to 2.30 Sun), 6-9.30 (to 8.30 Fri & Sat, to 9 Sun). Free House.* ***Beer*** *Hook Norton, Brakspear, Tetley, guest beers. Garden, outdoor eating area. Pub closed 25 Dec. Access, Visa.*

THAXTED **Farmhouse Inn** B&B

Tel 01371 830864 **Fax 01371 831196** Map 10 B3
Monk Street Thaxted Essex CM6 2NR

Surrounded by open fields and farmland, 1 mile south of the village off the B184, this former 16th-century farmhouse has been much extended and modernised in recent years and provides overnight accommodation in eleven rooms with en-suite bath and shower. Located around a courtyard, bedrooms are standard and functional with built-in furniture, TVs, telephones, tea- and coffee-making facilities and adequate bathrooms. Ideal for a peaceful, rural stopover en route to a flight out of Stansted Airport, only 8 miles away. *Open 11-3, 6-11 (Sat 11-11, Sun 12-3, 7-10.30). Free House.* ***Beer*** *Wadworth 6X, Greene King IPA, Adnams Southwold.* ***Accommodation*** *11 bedrooms, all en suite £42.50 (single £32.50). Garden, children's play area. Access, Amex, Visa.*

THELBRIDGE **Thelbridge Cross Inn** B&B

Tel 01884 860316 **Fax 01884 860316** Map 13 D2
Thelbridge nr Witheridge Devon EX17 4SQ

Two miles west of Witheridge on the B3042 this attractive, white-painted inn is isolated high up in a very rural part of Devon with views across to Dartmoor. The much modernised interior is carpeted and open-plan in layout with some comfortable settees, a couple of log fires and is delightfully free of live music, juke box or pool table. The bar offers some good local cider, country wines and some sixty whiskies including twenty malts. The adjacent barns have been well converted to provide a comfortable block of seven bedrooms and a large self-catering apartment. Bedrooms are rather compact with pretty matching fabrics and modern units, but room is found for a telephone, TV, tea-maker and a small fully-tiled private shower room in each. An occasional attraction is the original 'Lorna Doone' stagecoach which brings extra Sunday lunch trade. *Open 11.30-3, 6.30-11 (Sun 12-3, 7-10.30). Free House.* ***Beer*** *Bass, Butcombe Bitter. Garden, children's play area.* ***Accommodation*** *8 bedrooms, all en suite, £50 (family room sleeping four £70, single £35). No dogs. Access, Amex, Diners, Visa.*

THOMPSON **Chequers Inn** A

Tel 01953 483360 Map 10 C2
Griston Road Thompson Thetford Norfolk IP24 1PX

Well off the beaten track, this splendid, long and low, thatched 14th-century inn is worth finding – 1 mile off the A1075 Watton to Thetford road along a tiny lane on the edge of the village – for its peaceful location and unspoilt charm. Beneath the steep-raked thatch of this ancient ale house, once a row of several cottages, lies a series of low-ceilinged inter-connecting rooms served by a long bar. Wonky wall timbers, low doorways, open log fires, a rustic mix of old furniture and collections of farming implements, brass and copper characterise the well-maintained and atmospheric interior. Good rear garden with rural views and children's play area. Handy for excellent local woodland walks. *Open 11-3, 6-11 (Sun 12-3, 7-10.30). Free House.* ***Beer*** *Adnams, Burton, Tetley, Woodforde's, guest beer. Access, Diners, Visa.*

THORNTON Ring O'Bells FOOD

Tel 01274 832296 Fax 01274 831707 Map 6 C1
Hilltop Road Thornton Bradford West Yorkshire BD13 3QL

Up on a windy, woody moor just 3 miles from Bradford, the Ring O'Bells is firmly established as one of the area's top dining venues. Over the last two years the combined talents of Clive and Ann Preston at the helm and daughter Michelle Bone part of the team in the kitchen have gained quite a reputation for their food. Behind some jokey names on the menu there are substantial Yorkshire offerings: for 'Bully Beef' read 'roast topside of beef with rich gravy and Yorkshire pudding', while the 'Ring O'Bells Reviver' produces mountainous steak and kidney pie with vegetables. The daily blackboards, however, eschew such flippancy and much of what is produced is seriously good. Avocado bound in a dill mayonnaise garnished with melon balls and lightly poached prawn and terrine of home-made black pudding and apricots typify the starters. The day's fish special might be smoked cod fillet grilled with a prawn and mussel sauce; no less popular is a daily game dish: perhaps partridge with cherry sauce, or traditional braised rabbit. Similarly inventive sweets include 'Caribbean Carousel', a brandy snap basket filled with a home-made fruit sorbet. Early-evening (5.30-7) table d'hote menus, served in the bar, offer good value. Nonetheless Ring O'Bells remains essentially a pub, with well-spaced tables set away from the bar and a restaurant area (booking advised, no smoking) providing the same food and waitress service with just a little more comfort. Choice of 8 wines by the glass. *Open 11.30-3.30, 5.30-11 (Sun 12-3, 7-10.30). **Bar Food** 12-2, 5.30-9. **Beer** Webster's Yorkshire, Black Sheep Bitter, guest beer. Pub closed 25 Dec. Access, Visa.*

THRESHFIELD Old Hall Inn FOOD

Tel 01756 752441 Map 6 C1
Threshfield Skipton North Yorkshire BD23 5HB

A lovely stone-built Dales inn, based on a Tudor hall from which its name comes, the Taylors' pub gains further character from its idiosyncratic individuality. An eccentric mix of flagstone floors, classical music and chamber pots suspended from the ceiling is accentuated by the "Brat Board" at ankle height by the fireplace: chicken nuggets and chips followed by two scoops of multi-flavoured ice creams seem fairly brat-proof. One daily-changing blackboard menu offers up to 15 starters and main courses; perhaps steak and mushroom pie, jumbo fish and chips, Dales sausage with onion gravy, Wensleydale ploughman's and wild boar and pheasant pie with a Cumberland sauce, with fresh market seafood specials. More elaborate evening dishes might include half a roast duckling with caramelised almonds, boned and rolled lamb with a mint and redcurrant-flavoured gravy, fillet of brill with home-dried tomato and spinach filling on a warm olive oil vinaigrette, a gargantuan mixed grill and vegetarian options. A perennially hectic place; ordering and paying at the bar can be a little chaotic, though for a little peace and quiet the garden is a delightful alternative. *Open 11.30-3, 6-11 (Sun 12-3, 7-10.30). **Bar Food** 12-2, 6.15-9.30 (no food all day Mon and Sun eve). Free House. **Beer** Younger's Scotch, Timothy Taylor's Best & Landlord, Theakston Best, guest beer. Garden, outdoor eating. Family rooms. Inn closed all day Monday end Oct-mid May & Sun eve (except mid May-end Oct). No credit cards.*

THURSLEY Three Horseshoes A

Tel 01252 703268 Map 15a E4
Dye House Road Thursley nr Godalming Surrey GU8 6QD

One minute off the A3 between Milford and Hindhead, a characterful, 300-year-old beamed local with Thursley Common and the Devil's Punchbowl nearby. 1½-acre garden. No juke box or games machines. Children only welcome if over 5 and eating at lunchtime – it's too small a pub! *Open 12-3 (Sat from 11), 6-11 (Sun 12-3, 7-10.30). Free House. **Beer** Gale's Butser Brew Bitter & HSB, Fuller's London Pride. Garden. Access, Visa.*

Many **B&B** establishments offer reduced rates for weekend and out-of-season bookings. Always ask about special deals for longer stays. Beware half-board terms in inns where we do not recommend **FOOD.**

TICHBORNE | Tichborne Arms | FOOD

Tel 01962 733760 Map 15 D3
Tichborne nr Alresford Hampshire SO24 0NA

Heavy thatch predominates throughout this idyllic hamlet nestling in the peaceful Itchen Valley and also cloaks the local pub, making it a popular attractive destination for both lunch and supper. Over the years, a series of fires have destroyed the pub here, but the present structure, built in 1940, survives and is very much the hub of village life, being the venue for the village carol service, harvest supper and the polling station – a good turn out is generally guaranteed! At other times, locals and visitors alike are attracted here to sample the range of real ales dispensed straight from the cask and to taste the reliable home-cooked food that is served in both the small comfortable panelled bar and in the larger and livelier 'locals' bar. Home-made soup, generously filled jacket potatoes and salads are supplemented by a good range of daily specials such as liver, bacon and onion casserole, chicken breast with apricots and brandy, and steak and mushroom pie, with home-made raspberry jam sponge and custard to finish. The well tended and sheltered rear garden is a perfect spot for warm weather imbibing. No children under 14 allowed inside the pub. Six miles from M3 Junction 9. *Open 11.30-2.30, 6-11 (Sun 12-3, 7-10.30). **Bar Food** 12-1.45, 6.30-9.45 (Sun 7-9.30). Free House. **Beer** Wadworth 6X, Ansells, Flowers IPA, Fuggles IPA, Boddingtons, guest beer. Garden, outdoor eating. No credit cards.*

TIDESWELL | George | B&B

Tel 01298 871382 Map 6 C2
Commercial Road Tideswell Derbyshire SK17 8NU

Market town coaching inn dating from 1730. Small snug, traditional locals' noisy tap room, dining lounge and dining-room proper. Shaded courtyard garden with goldfish pond, creeping vines and flowers. Beautiful parish church known as 'Cathedral of the Peak' next door. The four-poster and double rooms have en-suite shower rooms, the other two have their own basins and share one bathroom and toilet. Live music every Friday evening. *Open 11-3, 7-11 (Sun 12-3, 7-10.30). **Beer** Hardys & Hansons Kimberley Classic, Best Bitter & Mild. Courtyard. **Accommodation** 4 bedrooms, 2 with shower en suite, £44 (£58 four-poster, single £20). Children welcome overnight (rate depends on age), additional bed available. Check-in by arrangement. Access, Amex, Visa.*

TILLINGHAM | Cap & Feathers | A

Tel 01621 779212 Map 11 C4
8 South Street Tillingham nr Southminster Essex CM0 7TH

Crouch Vale Brewery's only tied house – a delightfully unspoilt, classic white-painted, weather-boarded Essex village inn dating from 1427. A timeless, old-fashioned atmosphere remains within the warm and woody low-ceilinged interior with its eclectic mix of traditional furnishings, board floors and a real open fire. Several distinct areas ramble about, including a small rear carpeted area with woodburner and dresser, and a section housing time-honoured pub games (table skittles and an ancient bar billiards table that still operates on shillings); no music, one-armed bandits or quiz machines here! Home-cooked blackboard specials feature locally-smoked fish and meats. Modest bed and breakfast accommodation, the three rooms sharing a shower room. *Open 11.30-3, 6-11 (Sun 12-3, 7-10.30). **Beer** Crouch Vale IPA, Best, Millenium Gold, Strong Anglian Special & Winter Warmer, guest beer. Garden. Family room. No credit cards.*

TILLINGTON | Horseguards Inn | FOOD | B&B

Tel 01798 342332 Map 11 A6
Tillington nr Petworth West Sussex GU28 9AF

Charming 300-year-old inn peacefully positioned opposite the parish church just off the A272 Petworth to Midhurst road. Raised up from the village lane it was originally three cottages and enjoys good views towards the South Downs. Inside, a rambling series of relaxing and tastefully refurbished rooms feature exposed stripped beams, original pine panelling, open fires, various antique and pine furnishings and collections of hunting prints, brass blow lamps and polo mallets. Beyond the small bar area each table is neatly laid with fresh flowers and candles, as this is very much a dining pub attracting an upmarket clientele

thought out and Floyd's inimitable style – love it or hate it – is writ large upon the place. Recommended in our *1996 Hotels & Restaurants Guide. Open 10.30-11, Sun 12-3, 7-10.30.* ***Bar Food*** *12-2.30, 6-9.30 (Sun from 7). Restaurant Meals 12-2, 7-9 (No restaurant food D Sun, all Mon, 25 or 26 Dec). Free House.* ***Beer*** *Dartmoor Best Bitter, Bass, Blackawton, guest beer. Garden, summer barbecue.* ***Accommodation*** *4 rooms, all en suite, £125/£175, not suitable for pets or children. Sunbed, sauna, boat, snooker. Access, Amex, Visa.*

TUNBRIDGE WELLS — Sankeys Cellar Wine Bar — FOOD

Tel 01892 511422 Map 11 B5

39 Mount Ephraim Tunbridge Wells Kent TN4 8AA

Reached via a flight of steps from the street, this informal cellar wine bar/bistro has a pubby atmosphere with its York stone paved floor, gas lighting, rustic pine tables, kitchen chairs, church pews, antique mirrors and pub bric a brac. Go for enjoyable seafood dishes, or just for a relaxing glass of wine or pint of real ale, especially sitting out on the very Continental, sun-drenched patio in summer. Excellent daily-changing bar meals range from fishy dishes like Mediterranean crab soup, ever-popular moules marinière with matchstick frites, fresh cod and chips and home-made fishcakes to paté, Caesar salad, a daily pasta dish and duck cassoulet. Puddings may include strawberries with crème brulée, tarte aux pommes and chocolate brandy cake. Imaginatively filled baguettes are also available. Restaurant fare normally available in the four neatly-laid upstairs rooms can also be ordered in the cellar bar. Interesting list of wines with at least 12 available by the glass. Live music on Sunday evenings (but no food). *Open 10-11, Sat 10-3, 6-11, Sun 7-10.30 (closed L Sun).* ***Bar Food*** *12-2.30 (Sat and Sun to 2), 7-10 (no bar food Sun eve, restaurant closed L Sat & all Sun). Free House.* ***Beer*** *one changing real ale. Terrace, outdoor eating. Closed 25 & 26 Dec. Access, Amex, Diners, Visa.*

TURVEY — Three Cranes — B&B

Tel 01234 881305 Map 15 E1

High Street Loop Turvey Bedfordshire MK43 8EP

Enjoying a peaceful village setting adjacent to the parish church and close to an interesting abbey, this predominantly Victorian stone inn offers comfortable and good-value overnight accommodation in five cottagey bedrooms: attractive and welcoming, with modern pine furnishings, tasteful wallpaper and contrasting fabrics and clean en-suite facilities; TV, radio and tea-making kits are standard. The spick and span feeling extends downstairs into the neatly-furnished and well-decorated, open-plan bar which displays plenty of plants, decent framed prints, plates and other pieces of china. The front of the building is a real picture in summer with hanging baskets, flower borders and virginia creeper, while to the rear is a safe, sheltered garden. TV-monitored car parking overnight. *Open 11-3, 6-11 (Sun 12-3, 7-10.30). Free House.* ***Beer*** *Fuller's London Pride & ESB, Bass, Smiles Best, Timothy Taylor's Landlord, guest beer. Garden, children's play area.* ***Accommodation*** *5 bedrooms, all with shower en suite, £40 (single £30). Children over 6 welcome overnight, price by arrangement, additional bed available. Check-in by arrangement. No dogs. Closed 3 days at Christmas. Access, Visa.*

TURVILLE — Bull & Butcher — FOOD

Tel 01491 638283 Map 15a D3

Turville Buckinghamshire RG9 6QU

Back in the early 1600s some workmen on the local church went on strike for want of refreshments, prompting an enterprising cottager to turn his home into one; thus the Bull & Butcher was born. Inside the attractive black-and-white timbered building are two unspoilt, low-ceilinged bars with cushioned wall benches and settles, open fires, a collection of horse brasses and a welcoming atmosphere. A daily-changing blackboard generally lists a choice of patés – garlic or smoked salmon – good pub favourites like cottage pie, moussaka, spinach lasagne and steak and oyster pie, as well as steaks, Dover sole, balti curries, salads and the ever-popular Brakspear pie. Steak sandwiches and ploughman's lunches are also offered. Good puddings include chocolate and cherry roulade and Nancy's treacle tart (prepared by the 83-year-old lady who lives across the lane). Winter Sunday roasts. Excellent local walks, quaint village and an impressive white windmill on the hill opposite. *Open 11-3, 6-11 (Sun 12-3, 7-10.30).* ***Bar Food*** *12-2, 7-9.45.* ***Beer*** *Brakspear. Garden, outdoor eating. Closed 25 & 26 Dec eve. Access, Visa.*

Tushingham — Blue Bell Inn — A

Tel 01948 662172 Map 6 B3
Bell O' Th' Hill Tushingham Whitchurch Cheshire SY13 4QS

"Bell O' Th' Hill" is the sign to look for by a new stretch of the A41, four miles north of Whitchurch. Standing in extensive grounds on a bend in the old road is this remarkable building of 17th-century origins with a black and white, timbered frame, massive oak doors and a wealth of original timbers, oak panelling and memorabilia within. There's a single bar, the pub's focal point, where the ales are real and the welcome's a mite unusual. Landlord Patrick Gage hails from California, while his wife Lydia is from Moscow. This somehow matches the mild eccentricity of an establishment which lists amongst its claims to fame the presence of a ghost duck and the more physical presence of a Great Dane and a miniature poodle. Wooden benches in front for an alfresco drink look suitably ancient, while "paddock" rather than garden would describe the safe outdoor allocated to youngsters who are particularly welcome to play with the Gage children (and the dogs). *Open 12-3, 6-11 (Sun 12-3, 7-10.30). Free House.* ***Beer*** *Hanby Drawwell & Treacleminer, guest beer. No credit cards.*

Tutbury — Ye Olde Dog & Partridge Inn — B&B

Tel 01283 813030 **Fax 01283 813178** Map 6 C3
High Street Tutbury nr Burton-on-Trent Staffordshire DE13 9LS

ZZz...

With parts dating back to the 15th-century, this resplendent half-timbered inn on the high street is as popular today as it was in the 18th century when it was extended to accommodate passengers on the busy Liverpool to London coaching route. Successive extensions and improvements over the centuries can be traced within. Tapestries adorn the main bar with its thatched servery, and residents enjoy use of a restful timber-framed lounge well away from the busy self-service Carvery restaurant. The oldest accommodation, with creaking floors and oak panelling, are the three rooms in the original buildings, while the adjacent Georgian house, built around an impressive central spiral staircase contains the bulk of the bedrooms which are more routinely up-to-date. Accoutrements which run to satellite TV, mini-bars and forceful over-bath pulse showers are all decidedly up-market for a pub, and tend to be priced accordingly, though the weekend rates are something of a bargain. *Open 11-2.30, 6-11 (Sun 12-2.30, 7-10.30). Free House.* ***Beer*** *Marston's Pedigree, guest beer. Garden, outdoor eating.* ***Accommodation*** *17 bedrooms, all en suite, £72.50 (weekend £49.50/£78 four-poster, single £55/£62.50). Children welcome overnight, additional bed available. Access, Amex, Visa.*

Ulcombe — Pepper Box Inn — FOOD

Tel 01622 842558 Map 11 C5
Fairbourne Heath Ulcombe Maidstone Kent ME17 1LP

The Pepper Box is a cottagey pub with low eaves and white-painted stone walls, surrounded by fields of corn and affording views across the expanse of the Kentish Weald. Dating back to the 15th-century, it was once the haunt of smugglers and takes its name (apparently unique) from their favourite weapon, the Pepper Box pistol. A three-piece suite takes pride of place in front of an inglenook fireplace in the beamed bar and old pewter mugs hang above the bar counter along with decorative hopbines. A Shepherd Neame-owned house, the tenancy has been in the same family since 1958 with Sarah and Geoff Pemble currently providing the hospitable welcome. Highlights of a reliable bar menu include steak and kidney pudding, home-made fish pie, and daily dishes such as lamb steak Dijonaise, chicken stuffed with asparagus and roast duck with honey sauce. Good-value roast plus ploughman's platters and sandwiches replace the regular menu at lunch on Sunday. There's a short list of wines, and the Shepherd Neame ales are drawn direct from the barrels behind the bar. No children inside, but they are welcome in the large, pretty garden. *Open 11-3, 6.30-11 (Sun 12-3, 7-10.30).* ***Bar Food*** *12-2 & 7-9.45 (no food D Sun).* ***Beer*** *Shepherd Neame. Garden, outdoor eating area. Closed 25 Dec eve. Access, Visa.*

ULVERSTON **Bay Horse Inn** ★ FOOD

Tel 01229 583972 **Fax 01229 580502** Map 4 C4 **B&B**
Canal Foot Ulverston Cumbria LA12 9EL

1½ miles from Ulverston (from the A590, follow the signs for Canal Foot and continue driving through the Glaxo factory), an old pub in a lovely location on the shore of the Leven Estuary. Sympathetically converted, with an intimate conservatory restaurant that makes the most of the picturesque views over the water. The bar retains a pubby character with its old beams and gleaming brassware and one can enjoy a drink or snack at one of the few tables set out by an old stone breakwater. Chef Robert Lyons gives full rein to his wide-ranging repertoire; he worked with John Tovey at nearby *Miller Howe* for 18 years and the influence is still evident in dishes like home-made cheese and herb paté served with cranberry and ginger purée, tomato and orange salad and a garlic and herb bread; melon with air-dried Cumbrian ham and a damson cheese pastry tartlet; pork and Stilton sausages with an apple sauce and tomato and apricot chutney; a dish described on the menu as 'flakes of smoked haddock, brandied sultanas and water chestnuts cooked in a rich Cheddar cheese cream sauce, baked with a savoury breadcrumb topping' show that Robert's idea of bar food is somewhat different to that of most landlords! Nevertheless, snacks are not overlooked, as starters can be ordered with a baked potato as a more substantial dish and filled home-made baps are also offered. Lunch in the restaurant offers a limited choice of two dishes at each of the four courses (£14.50) plus a few more desserts. In the evening, both an à la carte and a grill menu with well-hung Aberdeen Angus steaks are offered; the carte might start with leek, Gruyère and wild mushroom pastry tartlet served on a bed of caramelised apple and apricot, following with Lunedale guinea fowl stuffed with a cheese and herb paté and roasted with honey, lemon and fresh thyme; finally, fresh raspberry frangelico crème brulée with lemon biscuits or a cheese platter with home-made biscuits and soda bread – serious stuff. There are two wine lists, though customers tend to choose mainly from the outstanding New World list (80+) which features many gems at keen prices. Bedrooms are generally not large, but six of the seven enjoy splendid views across the estuary from picture windows that open on to a balcony. All have the same pale yellow walls, matching bed covers and curtains in a variety of attractive fabrics and the usual amenities of direct-dial phone, remote-control TV, hairdryers and the like. Beds are turned down in the evening. Smart bathrooms, all with showers over the tub, come with quality toiletries and little extras like DIY dry-cleaning kit and a jar of soap flakes. Half-board terms only, with good reductions for two- or three-night weekend stays. "Children under 12 are not catered for." Recommended in our *1996 Hotels & Restaurants Guide. Open 11-11 (Sun 12-3, 7-10.30).* ***Bar Food*** *12-2 (except Mon). Restaurant Meals 12-1.30 (except Sun & Mon), 7.30 for 8. Free House.* ***Beer*** *Mitchell's Lancaster Bomber, Marston's Pedigree, guest beer. Riverside terrace, outdoor eating.* ***Accommodation*** *7 rooms, all en suite, £150 +10% service (half-board only, single £80 +10% service). No children under 12. Access, Visa.*

UPPER BENEFIELD **Wheatsheaf Hotel** FOOD

Tel 01832 205254 **Fax 01832 205245** Map 7 E4 **B&B**
Upper Benefield nr Oundle Northamptonshire PE8 5AN

Situated beside the A427 Corby to Oundle road, this stone inn was originally built as a farmhouse in 1659 and subsequently became a coaching inn with the addition of stables to the rear. These have been neatly converted to house eight functional en-suite bedrooms, featuring modern pine furnishings, built-in wardrobes and good writing space for visiting businessmen. TVs, tea-makers, telephones and radios are standard throughout. Beyond the routine printed bar menu offered in the Game Keepers Room is a list of simple home-made blackboard specials, such as sweetcorn and orange soup, sauté of chicken in mushroom sauce, steak and kidney pie, Hungarian goulash and poached salmon in lemon butter, followed by almond bread-and-butter pudding or baked Alaska, which are served in the homely open-plan bar. Sandwiches and ploughman's platters are served all day. A separate restaurant (where a pianist plays on Saturday nights) has a new Italian theme; we specifically recommend the bar food. Children's facilities include high-chairs, board games and toys and a swing in the garden. *Open 11-11 (Sun usual hours).* ***Bar Food*** *12-2, 6-10 (Sun 7-9). Family room. Free House.* ***Beer*** *Directors, guest beer. Garden, outdoor eating.* ***Accommodation*** *10 bedrooms, all en suite, £55 (single £45); weekend reductions (£48/£38). Children welcome overnight, additional bed (£5) and cot (£2) available. Dogs by arrangement. Access, Amex, Diners, Visa.*

Upper Sheringham Red Lion FOOD

Tel 01263 825408 Map 10 C1
Holt Road Upper Sheringham Norfolk NR26 8AD

Converted from three rather plain, 300-year-old brick and flint cottages, this homely village inn is popular locally for its above-average home-cooked food. Two friendly bars are filled with a rustic mix of sturdy country pine tables and chairs and high-backed settles on quarry-tiled and bare boarded floors, and are delightfully music- and game-free. The smaller snug bar is also a no-smoking room. Reliable bar food is listed on a sensibly short, often twice-daily-changing blackboard menu, which averages a choice of only eight interesting dishes. Begin with a well flavoured soup – parsley and cauliflower – served with a basket of fresh bread or tomato and basil salad and follow it with a decent ham and vegetable pie, beef in black olive sauce, fresh salmon with home-made dill hollandaise and salad or poached chicken breast with bacon, tomato and onion, all accompanied by crisp, fresh vegetables. Puddings include apricot and apple crumble, summer pudding and fresh peaches poached in port and cinnamon. Fresh Sheringham crab is always on the board and special meals include 3-course Wednesday evening suppers in winter (Wednesday barbecues in summer), seafood night on Thursdays and on Saturdays their mustard-glazed ham lunch attracts folk from miles around. Sunday lunchtimes see a choice of traditional roasts, probably rib of beef and leg of pork. No sandwiches (or chips, for that matter), bu ploughman's lunches are offered. Well-kept Adnams Best and a choice of over 60 malt whiskies. *Open 11.30-3, 6-11 (Oct-May from 7), Sun 12-3, 7-10.30. Free House.* ***Bar Food*** *12-2, 7-9.* ***Beer*** *Adnams Best, Woodforde's Wherry Best Bitter, guest beer. Garden, outdoor eating. Children welcomed. No credit cards.*

Upton French Horn FOOD

Tel 01636 812394 Map 7 D3
Main Street Upton nr Southwell Nottinghamshire NG23 5SY

Plenty of good things are to be found within the Carters' almost self-effacing local. A single bar where the majority of tables are pre-laid for diners, dispenses the range of Wards ales, bottled beers and ciders from around the globe and a fair choice of wines by the glass. Behind the bar hangs the polished French horn, albeit little blown, and they don't make a great song and dance about their competently cooked bar food either. Fresh fish predominates on the blackboard, the daily choices including, perhaps, skate wings, trout with prawns and almonds and monkfish kebabs. Meaty alternatives are along the lines of lamb chops and minted gravy and pork in ginger whilst a separate vegetarian menu offers the likes of brie and broccoli crepes in mushroom sauce. Sandwiches and ploughman's platters served all day. Upstairs in a rear, pantiled former barn the restaurant opens on Sunday for lunch; in the evenings, when the accent is on steaks, grills and game, booking is advised. *Open 11-11, (Sun 12-10.30).* ***Bar Food*** *11.30-3 (Sun 12-4.30), 7-10.30 (light snacks 2.30-6).* ***Beer*** *Wards Thorne Best Bitter & Waggledance Honey Beer, Vaux Double Maxim. Garden, outdoor eating. Closed 25 Dec. No credit cards.*

Upton Bishop Moody Cow FOOD

Tel 01989 780470 Map 14 B1
Upton Bishop nr Ross-on-Wye Hereford & Worcester HR9 7TT

South Herefordshire pub-goers will remember this one (just off the M50 from Junction 3 or 4) as the Lord Wellington. Extension of the old stone building to incorporate a formerly derelict barn and a new kitchen in the old living quarters have produced an entirely different animal. Creature comforts have certainly been improved in an ambience enhanced by wall-to-wall carpeting and candle-lit tables. In the hands of a trio of enthusiastic young leaseholders there's a lot of promise in menus which cover a full range from bangers with bubble and squeak to Chateaubriand with béarnaise. This is not all cow pie: interspersed in the daily menus are their unusual soups, warm pigeon salad, pasta carbonara and seafood pancake among the starters or snacks and main courses from aubergine bake or savoury strudel through chargrills of steak or salmon to pork fillet stuffed with spinach and apricots and chicken curry served up in half a pineapple. Sandwiches and ploughman's platters are served all day. The atmosphere of a chummy village local lives on and 10p from the sale of every pint of the cleverly-named Raging Bull (a "dark, bitter" bitter brewed on the premises, ABV 4.2%, £1.20 a pint in August 1995) goes towards the Upton 2000 fund for a new village hall – so why not sink a pint and help contribute towards their sinking-fund? There's also a food take-away service, live jazz on Thursday nights and quarterly cookery

demonstrations; mood swings which are indicative surely of a conscious effort to do more than just fill the old Lord's boots. *Open 12-2.30, 6.30-11 (Sun 12-2.30, 7-10.30).* ***Bar Food*** *12.30-2, 7-9.30. Free House.* ***Beer*** *Herefordshire Wye Valley Best, Boddingtons, West Country Pale Ale, Raging Bull (own brew), Bass. Outdoor eating. Access, Visa.*

VENTNOR — Spyglass Inn — FOOD B&B

Tel 01983 855338 Map 15 D4
The Esplanade Ventnor Isle of Wight PO38 1JX

☺

After totally rebuilding the distinctively pink-painted Spyglass Inn, Stephanie and Neil Gibbs (both native Islanders) reopened it in 1988. Wandering around the several interconnecting rooms, which include two reserved for non-smokers and several where children are welcome, it is difficult to believe that the pub is not hundreds of years old. The bar counter is built of old pews and the whole place is full of old seafaring prints and photographs, as well as numerous nautical antiques ranging from a brass binnacle and ship's wheel to old oars and model ships in glass cases. The setting could not be better, at one end of the seafront with a front terraced area stretching right to the edge of the sea wall. In winter, the waves break right over the wall and more than one customer has been known to get a soaking by mis-timing their exit from the pub. In summer, there's an outside bar and kiosk at the end of the promenade selling shellfish and ice cream. Inside, you might try hot chicken with a peanut dip or home-made cottage pie, but the thing to look out for is the local seafood: crab served out of its shell in generous bowlfuls with salad, and locally-caught lobsters. In winter, there are home-made soups from a blackboard menu, and on Saturday nights a candle-lit dinner, for which booking is advisable, complete with pianist. There is live music nightly (less frequently in winter) from a small group who might play country, folk or jazz; the 'Beaujolais breakfast' is now an annual event in the third week of November. Three neat little flatlets with upholstered rattan furniture and a sea-facing balcony offer accommodation for up to two adults and two children; DIY breakfasts in the kitchenettes. A public car park is just 50 yards away, but check your brakes before venturing down here – the road to the seafront has hairpin bends and a gradient of 1 in 4. *Open 10.30-11 (closed 3-7 mid Sept-May), Sun 12-3, 7-10.30.* ***Bar Food*** *12-2.15, 7-9.30. Free House.* ***Beer*** *Hall & Woodhouse Badger Best, Tanglefoot & Hard Tackle, guest beers. Patio/terrace, outdoor eating. Family room.* ***Accommodation*** *3 en-suite flatlets, sleeps 4, £45 July-Sept. Children welcome overnight. Closed 25 Dec eve. Access, Visa.*

WADDESDON — Five Arrows Hotel — FOOD B&B

Tel 01296 651727 Fax 01296 658596 Map 15a D2
High Street Waddesdon Buckinghamshire HP18 0JE

Zzz... ☺

A delightful Victorian confection built by the Rothschilds to house the architects and artisans working in nearby Waddesdon Manor (NT) – itself worth a visit. The name comes from the family crest with its arrows representing the five sons sent out by the dynasty's founder to set up banking houses in the financial capitals of Europe. Restored in 1993 from top to toe and often bedecked with flowers (there's a fine garden to the rear) the hotel/inn is now run by a new management team: Robert Selby and chef Julian Worster. One enters straight into the bar from which open several rooms with antique tables, colourful upholstered chairs plus the odd settee and armchair with pictures from Lord Rothschild's own collection on the walls along with numerous photos of old Waddesdon – charmingly un-pub-like. A short modern blackboard menu might offer a selection of cold meats, pork, chicken and orange terrine with walnut toast, seared marlin with coconut milk and ginger, Greek chargrilled chicken with yoghurt and cucumber, organic fillet steak with rich wine sauce, and home-made puddings like treacle tart and chocolate liqueur terrine. The good wine list majors on the various Rothschild wine interests that extend to Portugal and Chile as well as the famous Chateau Lafite. Six good-sized bedrooms are individually decorated with matching en-suite bathrooms (two with shower and WC only) and boast extra large beds (with pure Egyptian cotton sheets) and antique Victorian washstands along with modern comforts: remote-control TV, direct-dial phones and tea/coffee-making facilities. No smoking in the bedrooms. *Open 11.30-3 & 6-11, Sun 12-3 & 7-10.30.* ***Bar Food*** *12-2.30, 7-9.30 (Sun to 9). Free House.* ***Beer*** *Fuller's London Pride, Chiltern Brewery Beechwood Bitter, Theakston Old Peculier. Garden.* ***Accommodation*** *6 bedrooms, all en suite, £65 (single £50). Access, Visa.*

WALL | Hadrian Hotel | B&B

Tel 01434 681232 Map 5 D2
Wall nr Hexham Northumberland NE46 4EE

A handsome Jacobean-style 16th century house standing in its own attractive gardens by the A6079, about a mile from Hadrian's Wall and only three from nearby Hexham. The best feature for residents is the welcoming, if small, foyer lounge with deep sofas set around the open fire. Unopposed in this tiny village, the bar is a convivial place for meeting the locals. Four bedrooms boast full en-suite facilities (three with bath). In the remainder are wash-hand basins and free-standing plastic shower cubicles whose practicality, like the water pressure, is limited. Colour TVs and beverage trays are standard. Now under new ownership. *Open 11.30-3, 6-11.* ***Beer*** *Vaux Sampson, Wards Thorne. Family room.* ***Accommodation*** *6 bedrooms, 4 en suite, £49 (single £35). Check-in by arrangement. No dogs. Access, Visa.*

WALLISWOOD | Scarlett Arms | A

Tel 01306 627243 Map 11 A5
Walliswood Surrey RH5 5RD

Originally a pair of 17th-century labourers' cottages, this attractive white-painted and red-tiled roofed village pub preserves a splendid unspoilt interior. Four small rambling rooms have low ceilings, sturdy wooden furnishings on either carpeted or flagstoned floors, various country prints and old photos, and a good open fire to sit in front of on cold winter days. Relaxing chatty atmosphere and the full complement of well-kept King & Barnes real ales. Benches and brollies fill the front lawn for peaceful summer alfresco drinking. No children under 14 indoors. *Open 11-2.30, 5.30-11 (Sun 12-3, 7-10.30).* ***Beer*** *King & Barnes Festive, Broadwood, Sussex & Mild plus Old Ale in winter. Garden. No credit cards.*

WALTHAM-ON-THE-WOLDS | Royal Horseshoes | B&B

Tel 01664 464289 Map 7 D3
Melton Road Waltham-on-the-Wolds nr Melton Mowbray Leicestershire

A compact, thatched and ivy-covered pub with a cottagey interior, on a corner of the busy A607 by the sign to Belvoir Castle. Melton Mowbray is about 5 miles. Stands opposite the old village church built in sandstone with a distinctive spire. The patio and beer garden to the rear is a sun trap in which to enjoy a summer ale. Plenty of parking beyond. Now under new ownership. *Open 12-3, 6-11 (Sun 12-3, 7-10.30). Free House.* ***Beer*** *John Smith's, Bass, Marston's Pedigree, Ruddles County, two guest beers.* ***Accommodation*** *4 bedrooms, all en suite, £40 (single £25). Children welcome overnight. Check-in by arrangement. Access, Visa.*

WANSFORD-IN-ENGLAND | The Haycock ★ | FOOD B&B

Tel 01780 782223 **Fax 01780 783031** Map 7 E4
Wansford-in-England Peterborough Cambridgeshire PE8 6JA

Zzz...

A lovely 17th-century honey-coloured stone coaching inn in 6 acres of grounds next to the junction of A1 and A47. It has been much extended, in sympathetic style, the most recent additions being a large conference/ballroom (a lovely setting for functions with its soaring oak beams, enormous fireplace and private garden, catering for up to 200) and the stone-walled Orchard Room with all-day bar and coffee-shop menu (7am-11pm, with a fine lunchtime buffet). Other day rooms include a pubby bar and two traditional lounges. Bedrooms in the older parts of the building are full of character, but all have been decorated with great style and flair using high-quality fabrics and furnishings; one ground-floor twin room has a wide door and handrails for disabled guests. Bathrooms are equally luxurious. Extensive grounds include lovely gardens that stretch along the banks of the river Nene and the village cricket pitch. The variety of food on offer in both bar (excellent bar snacks – spinach and Gruyère fritters with apple and mango chutney, a choice of fresh pasta dishes, haddock and chips, fritto misto, Cheffy's beef steak and kidney pie, grilled gammon with egg and chips, Montgomery Cheddar or Colston Bassett Stilton, chocolate truffle cake, crème brulée), Orchard Room (one room is non-smoking) and restaurant caters for all tastes and pockets; an outdoor barbecue takes place daily in summer with seating for 100 in a courtyard. Candelabras and highly-polished silver add to the mellow, traditional atmosphere of the twin dining-rooms. The restaurant menu is pretty traditional too, with a daily roast sirloin of prime English beef always featuring on the silver trolley. A wine list doesn't need to be long to be considered outstanding, if, as is the case here, it has been

carefully compiled to complement the style of restaurant and offers both helpful notes and sensible prices! There's also a good selection of wines served by the glass. Now owned by Arcadian Hotels; hotel, inn and pub all rolled into one. Recommended in our *1996 Hotels & Restaurants Guide. Open 7.30am-10pm.* ***Bar Food*** *12-10.30 7 days.* ***Accommodation*** *50, all en suite, from £85 to £98 (single from £68 to £85), four-poster £120, suite £130. Garden, croquet, fishing, pétanque, helipad. Access, Amex, Diners, Visa.*

WARDLOW — Bull's Head — FOOD

Tel 01298 871431 Map 6 C2
Wardlow nr Tideswell Derbyshire SK17 8RP

A friendly village local with a dining emphasis only three miles from Ashford-in-the-Water: the B6465 passes scenic Monsal Head on the way. Illuminated specials boards probably present the best options: mushroom soup, potted shrimps with toast, chicken tikka masala, steak au poivre. Plenty of interesting desserts like fruit crumbles, raspberry torte and Bakewell pudding, and Hartington blue Stilton. Sandwiches at lunchtime only. Family dining in the Loose Box; picnic tables in a small but scenic garden. *Open 12-2.30, 6.30-11.30 (Sun 12-3, 7-10.30). Closed L Tue & L Thu.* ***Bar Food*** *12-2.15 (except Mon & Tue), 6.30-9.30 (Sun 7-9). Free House.* ***Beer*** *Wards Bitter & Vaux Sampson. Garden, outdoor eating. Family room. No credit cards.*

WARENFORD — Warenford Lodge ★ FOOD

Tel 01668 213453 Map 5 D1
Warenford nr Belford Northumberland NE70 7HY

There's a wonderfully eclectic range of good bar food on offer at the rather un-pubby Warenford Lodge, a solid stone building on the village loop road off the A1; there's no sign outside so you'll have to look hard for it. Inside, it's a handsome old place, with exposed thickset stone and a modern air which blends well with the atmosphere of an old-fashioned private house. There are little mullion windows, polished light pine tables and cushioned benches in the split-level bar, a big stone fireplace in the lower part, and a woodburning stove (no longer used) in the upper area, which has armchairs and sofas just made for relaxing; the bar area is probably more attractive an area in which to eat than the restaurant. Menus change here twice yearly, in spring and autumn, reflecting seasonal produce and appetite, but a random selection of favourites might well feature marinated seafood salad with herbs, Lindisfarne oysters, Northumbrian fish soup or baked halibut. Other dishes on last year's Spring/Summer menu included port royal lamb (flavoured with cinnamon and orange), and cold roasted pork stuffed with fruit. Not all puddings are home-made, but those that are, such as a baked lemon pudding, are wonderful. The menu is clever, well presented and most unusual – a shining star in the firmament of pubs! The unifying factor behind it all, exotic or homely, is the instinctive, hearty cooking of the landlady, Marion Matthewman, at work in the kitchen while Ray tends to the bar. Owing to the popularity of the Warenford you need to book for weekend evenings (or any time in summer). *Open Sat & Sun 12-2, Tue-Sun 7-11. Closed all Mon, L Mon-Fri.* ***Bar Food*** *12-2 (Sat & Sun only), 7-9.30 (Tue-Sun). No real ales. Garden. No outdoor eating. Access, Diners, Visa.*

WARHAM ALL SAINTS — Three Horseshoes — FOOD B&B

Tel 01328 710547 Map 10 C1
Warham All Saints Wells-next-the-Sea Norfolk NR23 1NL

Warham is a sleepy rural backwater situated only a mile or so from the North Norfolk coast. At its heart, close to the church, lies the Three Horseshoes, a timeless gem of a village local, comprising a row of 18th-century brick and flint cottages and the Old Post Office which closed 14 years ago. Owned by nearby Holkham hall until 1960 it is a rare survivor, remaining delightfully unchanged internally since the 1930s. An old-fashioned ambience pervades the three unspoilt rooms with numerous gas-lights, nicotine yellow walls, scrubbed deal tables, plain wooden chairs and red leatherette railway waiting room-style benches, a 1930s' one-arm bandit and a pianola which performs occasionally. A good choice of home-cooked food is served, especially traditional Norfolk dishes using fresh local produce, including fish and game. Local ladies prepare the meals that appear on the interesting main menu – smokie hotpot, Ann's soused herring, Warham mushroom bake, Brancaster cream mussels, roast Norfolk duck – and the hearty dishes on the daily specials board, for example curried parsnip soup, Warham baked crab and liver, onion and sausage casserole. Fresh vegetables are the order of the day; definitely no chips. Sandwiches are served all day, and smaller appetites may enjoy a 'ploughboy's' lunch! For dessert try the steamed jam sponge or Bakewell tart. Well-conditioned ales are drawn straight from the cask and home-made

lemonade and orangeade is served in the summer. Four homely bedrooms in the adjacent Old Post Office accommodate overnight guests. Simply furnished with old darkwood furniture – some antique pieces – washbasins and latch-doors and share a clean bathroom (one has an en-suite shower). Added touches include a box of tissues, cotton wool, a range of teas and a dressing gown. Residents have use of a sitting room with TV and easy chairs. No under-14s overnight. *Open 11.30-3, 6-11 (Sun 12-3, 7-10.30) Free House.* ***Bar Food*** *12-2, 7-9.* ***Accommodation*** *4 bedrooms, 1 en suite £40 (single £18).* ***Beer*** *Greene King Abbot Ale & IPA, Woodforde's Wherry Bitter, Woodforde's Mardlers Mild, guest beer in summer. Family room. Garden, outdoor eating. Children welcome. No credit cards.*

WARNHAM — Greets Inn — A

Tel 01403 265047 Map 11 A6
Friday Street Warnham West Sussex RH12 3QY

Tucked along Friday Street on the western edge of the village – off the A24 north of Horsham – this attractive tile-hung and timbered old farmhouse dates from 1320. Preserved inside is the original layout of a series of charming rooms radiating out from a central bar which boasts a stone floor, a vast inglenook with log fire, a fine high-backed settle and sturdy tables. Part stripped pine and oak furnishings and gleaming copper and brass artefacts characterise the unspoilt rooms and traditional local's bar. Good alfresco seating in the sheltered rear garden among the roses, flower beds and apple trees. *Open 11-2.30, 6-11 (Sun 12-3, 7-10.30).* ***Beer*** *Wadworth 6X, Flowers Original, Whitbread (Morrells) Strong Country Bitter, Fuller's London Pride. Garden, lawn, outdoor eating area, tables in garden. Access, Visa.*

WARREN STREET — The Harrow — FOOD

Tel 01622 858727 Map 11 C5 **B&B**
Hubbards Hill Warren Street Lenham nr Maidstone Kent ME17 2ED

☺

Once a resting place for Canterbury pilgrims, now a converted and refurbished downland inn not far from the A20 above Lenham (signposted) and the M20. Simple cushioned chairs and stools around little tables in the open-plan lounge, much used for dining and warmed in winter by a good log fire. Separate, neatly laid-up conservatory restaurant (with a separate menu) but it's the bar food that we recommend, to be enjoyed overlooking the sun-trap courtyard and garden with waterfall and pool – access for residents and restaurant diners only. Standard range of bar snacks supplemented by decent home-made specials such as spicy pan-fried marinated chicken, seafood lasagne with salad and garlic bread, and a generous portion of steak and kidney pie accompanied by six fresh vegetables. Sandwiches and ploughman's platters served all day. Good bed and breakfast too, the fifteen spacious bedrooms being kitted out with neat darkwood furniture, clean bathrooms and added comforts (TV, beverage facilities, direct-dial phones). Five family rooms. *Open 11.30-2.30, 7-11 (Sun 12-3, 7-10.30).* ***Bar Food*** *12-2, 7-10. Free House.* ***Beer*** *Shepherd Neame, guest beers. Water garden, patio, outdoor eating area.* ***Accommodation*** *15 bedrooms, all en suite, £49.50 (single £39.50). Children welcome overnight (under-5s stay free in parents' room, 5-14 years old £5). Access, Amex, Visa.*

WASDALE HEAD — Wasdale Head Inn — B&B

Tel 019467 26229 **Fax 019467 26334** Map 4 C3
Wasdale Head Gosforth Cumbria CA20 1EX

Zzz...

At the head of Wasdale, in a setting of romantic grandeur, with steep fells by way of backdrop, this is a famous traditional mountain pub popular with walkers and climbers. Ritson's Bar, named after its first landlord (the world's biggest liar) has high ceilings, a polished slate floor, wood panelling, and cushioned old settles. Food is largely traditional. There's a residents' bar and a relaxing lounge. Bedrooms are comfortable and unfussy with telephones and beverage trays provided. 9 self-catering cottages right next to the pub are available from £230 to £560 per week. *Open 11-3, 5.30-11 (Sun 12-10.30).* ***Beer*** *Jennings Cumberland, Yates, Theakston Best & Old Peculier, guest beer in summer. Riverside garden, outdoor eating. Family room.* ***Accommodation*** *9 bedrooms, all en suite, £58 (single £29). Children welcome overnight (0-2 free), additional bed & cot available. Dogs £3. Pub and accommodation closed mid Nov-28 Dec. Access, Visa.*

WASS Wombwell Arms ★ FOOD B&B

Tel 01347 868280 Map 5 E4

Wass North Yorkshire YO6 4BE

Zzz...

This whitewashed village inn dates from the 18th century and sits in the shadow of the Hambleton hills, just a couple of miles from the A170, east of Thirsk. The interior consists of four connecting rooms with stylish fabrics and furnishings. The first room to the left of the entrance has lightwood floorboards, stripped pine tables and chairs, and half-panelling. This room is especially good for families. The bar and its adjoining dining area have a mix of flagstone and red-tiled flooring, some exposed stone walls, more panelling and original beams. Some walls have attractive Laura Ashley wallpapers, while farmhouse kitchen-style tables are covered with colourful cloths. The final room is similarly appointed. Throughout the pub, there are splendid fresh and dried flower displays, watercolours of chickens, foxes and other country subjects, magazines and books. Over the bar is an original drawing of TV's Captain Pugwash, drawn for the landlord by its creator John Ryan, an old boy of nearby Ampleforth College. A huge blackboard displays the day's choice of interesting bar food. Rather bistro in style, this is the preserve of Lynda Evans, who is a more than competent cook. Only fresh, mostly local produce is used, and the choice is extensive and varied: perhaps cauliflower and almond soup, local venison and redcurrant, minted lamb and tipsy chicken with red wine. There are good vegetarian dishes too, Wensleydale mushrooms or tomato and basil flan. Wholemeal sandwiches and ploughman's platters at lunchtime only. Desserts are well up to standard, with sticky toffee pudding, chocolate truffle and hot nut sundae. Booking recommended for weekends. The three bedrooms are equally impressive. Two doubles and a twin are kitted out in colourful Laura Ashley wallpapers, with matching curtains and duvet covers, and stripped pine furniture. They're impeccably kept and offer a selection of magazines as well as televisions and radio alarms. Each room is en suite, one with a shower, two with baths. To immaculate housekeeping is added a sense of fun: plastic ducks are provided. Alan Evans looks after the bar and is an extremely jovial host. A quite exceptional country pub, well worth a detour. *Open 12-2.30-7-11 (Sun 12-3, 7-10.30).* ***Bar Food*** *(no food Sun eve or all day Mon in winter except bank holidays and Christmas week) 12-2, 7-9.30. Free House.* ***Beer*** *Timothy Taylor Landlord, Black Sheep, guest beer. Family room.* ***Accommodation*** *2 bedrooms, both en suite, £49 (single £24.50). Children over 8 years welcome overnight (8-10 yrs free if sharing parents' room), additional bed available. Check-in by arrangement. No dogs. Pub closed on Mondays in winter and 1 week January. Access, Visa.*

WATERLEY BOTTOM New Inn B&B

Tel 01453 543659 Map 13 F1

Waterley Bottom North Nibley nr Dursley Gloucestershire GL11 6EF

Ruby Sainty's friendly, idiosyncratic pub takes some driving to down the country lanes from North Nibley on the B4060, yet cyclists and walkers find it unerringly from their maps. The setting is serene, the garden a blaze of colour shaded by beech, silver birch and horse chestnut; for the youngsters, swings, see-saw and a terrestrial tree house are a safe distance away. Overnight guests are assured the tranquillity of this hidden valley quite undisturbed. The two bedrooms have TVs and hot beverage kits (but no phones) and share a single bathroom; breakfast is worth getting up for; book well in advance. *Open 12-2.30, 7-11 (Sun 12-2.30, 7-10.30). Free House.* ***Beer*** *Cotleigh WB (house brew) & Tawny, Smiles Best, Theakston Old Peculier, Greene King Abbot Ale, guest beer.* ***Accommodation*** *2 rooms, £35 (single £20). Garden, outdoor play area. No credit cards.*

WATH-IN-NIDDERDALE Sportsman's Arms FOOD B&B

Tel 01423 711306 Map 6 C1

Wath-in-Nidderdale Pateley Bridge nr Harrogate N Yorkshire HG3 5PP

Zzz...

Nestling in a wooded valley just 2 miles from Pateley Bridge, the Sportsman's is prominently signed across a tiny stone hump-backed bridge over the Nidd. A carpeted lounge bar with its own side entrance suggests at once that this is no pub for the beer-swilling brigade – there may be no real ales but there is a connoisseur's collection of malt whiskies. As one would expect from an inn whose restaurant is recommended in our *1996 Cellnet Hotels & Restaurants Guide* the food, too, has an identity all its own. Rich black pudding with tomatoes and mushrooms and moules marinière can be starters or just a snack;

Scarborough woof with a garlic crust and pork loin with prunes, orange and ginger are decidedly main meals. Further dishes might be chicken stuffed with apricots and a pistachio sauce, Nidderdale trout or spicy Cajun chicken. Sandwiches and ploughman's platters are served all day. Alongside ever-present sticky toffee pudding with fresh cream and summer pudding, there's a scrumptious tarte au citron which is definitely not to be missed. Stripped pine doors are the unifying theme of the single corridor of bedrooms which are of modest size and appointment: returning guests appreciate rather the total peace and quiet and an absence of room telephones (however, there are TVs in the rooms). While all are equipped with wash basins, only two have en-suite facilities; two WCs and two separate bathrooms are shared by the rest. A long, leisurely and very large breakfast is served at 9am.
Open 12-2.30-7-11 (Sun 12-2.30, 7-10.30). No real ale. ***Bar Food*** *12-2, 7-9.30 (Sun 12-2.30, 7-9).* ***Accommodation*** *7 bedrooms, 2 with shower en suite, £58 (single £37). Children welcome overnight (cot and extra bed if sharing parents' room). Dogs welcome in rooms. Garden, outdoor eating. Access, Visa.*

WATLINGTON — Chequers — A

Tel 0149161 2874 Map 15a D3
Love Lane Watlington Oxfordshire OX9 5RA

A useful stop, less than two and a half miles from Junction 6 of the M40. It's a characterful, rambling old pub with a lovely summer garden and conservatory (children are now allowed in here). Unprepossessing exterior, cosy interior with an eclectic mix of paraphernalia - from dried flowers to an unusual collection of bottles and paintings. *Open 11.30-2.30, 6-11 (Sun 12-3, 7-10.30).* ***Beer*** *Brakspear. Garden. Access, Diners, Visa.*

WATTON-AT-STONE — George & Dragon — FOOD

Tel 01920 830285 Map 15 F1
High Street Watton-at-Stone Hertfordshire SG14 3TA

The George & Dragon is popular with a wide range of customers, from OAPs to business men and women, and its well-balanced bar menu attracts a fair number of locals. On any one day, the menu could offer George & Dragon smokie (gratinéed flaked, smoked haddock with tomato concasse), lambs kidneys in cream wine and mustard or matelote normande (whitefish and scallops in cream), white anchovy fillets marinated in olive oil and garlic served with mixed leaf salad, roast breast of duck with rich red wine sauce. Fish is delivered daily and prices never exceed £10 – perhaps grilled hake with garlic butter. In addition, traditional roast lunch is served on Sundays. Sandwiches and ploughman's served all day. Desserts such as summer pudding, sticky toffee pudding and apricot and apple crumble. The bars are usually bustling with diners, some of whom travel some distance to eat here. The public bar is a locals' spot, though, with keen cribbage players, black and white photographs of the pub and village in days gone by, and furnishings similar to the main bar, in the oldest part of the building, which has a wonderfully homely atmosphere enhanced by jovial management and welcome touches like fresh flowers and the day's newspapers. There are also exposed beams, open fireplaces, yellow stained walls hung with a mixture of framed oil and watercolour paintings, and two large bay windows admitting lots of natural light. Furnishings are a mixture of blue upholstered bench seating and simple wood chairs around oak tables topped with candles. There is one modern regulation though, singlet tops are prohibited in the bars. This is a difficult pub to miss, as it dominates the centre of the village, and is of pink-painted pebbledash. There's a flower-filled garden and patio for kinder weather. Children are welcome in the dining-room only.
Open 11-2.30, 6-11 (Sun 12-3, 7-10.30). ***Bar Food*** *12-2, 7.15-10 (no food Sun eve).* ***Beer*** *Greene King. Garden, patio/terrace, outdoor eating. Access, Diners, Visa.*

WELL — Chequers — FOOD

Tel 01256 862605 Map 15a D4
Well nr Odiham Hampshire RG25 1TL

Deep in the heart of the Hampshire countryside, this 17th-century pub provides a retreat from the modern world and an opportunity to enjoy the old-world charm. A flourishing vine covers the patio outside, and inside, the homely rustic bar features low wooden ceilings, panelled walls, bare floorboards, plenty of beams and a mix of old scrubbed tables, chairs and church pews. Shelves of books and old photographs and prints adorn the walls. Bar food is reliably good with the emphasis being on interesting and light home-cooked meals. The daily-changing selection of dishes is chalked up on a blackboard in the bar and the good-value choice ranges from freshly-prepared soup (perhaps celery and apple) to chef's pasta, Cajun chicken with Caesar salad, open steak sandwich and ratatouille au gratin. Samdwcihes and ploughman's platters are served all day. Home-made puddings include lemon torte, banoffi pie and apple strudel. The adjacent pine-panelled restaurant is neatly

arranged with tables laid with linen clothes and fresh flowers; a differnet menu is served here on Fri & Sat evenings only. A peaceful drink or meal can be savoured in the attractive rear garden, which affords rural views across fields. On Friday nights the pub can get a bit 'down from town' – but then again, maybe that's obviously its attraction to the regulars! Five miles from the M3 Junction 5. *Open 11-3, 5.30-11 (Sun 12-3, 7-10.30).* ***Bar Food** 12-2.30, 7-10 (Sun to 9.30). Free House.* ***Beer** Boddingtons, Flowers Original, guest beer. Garden, outdoor eating. Family room. Access, Visa.*

WELLS-NEXT-THE-SEA Crown Hotel FOOD B&B

Tel 01328 710209 Fax 01328 711432 Map 10 C1
The Buttlands Wells-next-the-Sea Norfolk NR23 1EX

Outward appearances are sometimes deceptive, the facade of the Crown being a case in point. It stands at the foot of a tree-lined village green, the Buttlands, where medieval marksmen once practised their archery. Compared to the elegant Georgian terraced houses which surround the green, the Crown's black and white painted exterior has the rather care-worn look of a modest town pub. But what a jewel it is inside! The bar progresses on three levels from front to back, where a family-friendly conservatory of high-backed settles opens on to the rear patio and stableyard. Within, there's an open log fire, high bar stools and low copper-topped, barrel-shaped tables, the walls throughout covered with portraits and memorabilia of Horatio Nelson – born in a nearby village and whose sister reputedly lived on the Buttlands. The beer's good and the bar menu is extensive. Single-course meals of pasta dishes and omelettes come in generous portions and there are also grills, from a mini 'steakwich' through to a full mixed grill. Plenty of salads, sandwiches, ploughman's platters, and sausage/burger/fish finger combinations for the children complete the picture. The adjoining restaurant continues the interior's Victorian theme (but it is the bar food that we recommend here); booking is essential for Sunday lunch. To describe the bedrooms as modest is not to decry them: they are simply but adequately furnished and even the smallest offers a view of the charming old town, across the Lion Yard where the London mail coach once pulled in, and over pantiled roofs to the sturdy Norman church below. The seal is set on a enjoyable stay by a tranquil night's rest in these evocative surroundings, a hearty and enjoyable English breakfast, and the friendly service and warm hospitality of the Foyers family and their youthful staff. *Open 11-2.30, 6-11 (Sun 12-2.30, 7-10.30).* ***Bar Meals** 12-2, 6-9 (to 9.30 in summer). Free House.* ***Beer** Adnams, Marston's Pedigree, Bass. Terrace, outdoor eating.* ***Accommodation** 15 bedrooms, 10 en suite, £68 (£58 not en suite, single £35 not en suite). Children welcome overnight (under-10s £10, 10-15s £15), cot available (£3). Access, Amex, Diners, Visa.*

WEOBLEY Ye Olde Salutation Inn FOOD B&B

Tel 01544 318443 Fax 01544 318216 Map 14 A1
Market Pitch Weobley Hereford & Worcester HR4 8SJ

Zzz...

Chris and Frances Anthony run this wonderfully evocative former 14th-century ale and cider house. It commands the view down picturesque Broad Street to Weobley parish church, and is both the village local and a bespoke country inn. Frances supervises a hard-working kitchen which daily produces both traditional and imaginatively different bar meals: diners may feast on the likes of home-baked ham with leek sauce, seafood and pasta bake, lamb's liver and bacon or steak and Guinness pie. Vegetarian specials might be lentil and apricot terrine or pasta and blue-cheese bake. For a lighter lunchtime-only meal try a ploughman's or hot filled roll (cheese, bacon and mushroom or steak) made with bread baked freshly on the premises. Popular desserts like bread-and-butter pudding with an apricot coulis and clotted creamor banoffee pie. The non-smoking Oak Room restaurant serves a highly popular 3-course Sunday lunch (booking essential), but our specific recommendation is for bar food. Victorian furniture, cast-iron bedsteads and brass-topped bathroom fittings set the tone in the bedrooms. The three larger rooms (one with a four-poster) have en-suite WC/shower rooms, while two smaller doubles have recently been turned into one with a Victorian-style bathroom en suite. To follow the most restful of nights, a splendid country breakfast is served in the recently added conservatory. Due to the building's age, guests are requested not to smoke in their rooms, though smoking is permitted in the residents' lounge. (An adjacent self-contained cottage with lounge, kitchen/diner, bathroom and two double bedrooms accommodates up to 5 people in the first timber-framed building to be put up in Weobley since the 17th century). A fitness room has exercise machines – perhaps rather incongruous given the surroundings. Pub rooms are not unsuitable for children under 14 (except babes in arms), but the cottage is fine for families. *Open 11-3, 7-11 (Sun 12-3, 7-10.30).* ***Bar Food** 12-2, 7-9.30 (Sun & Mon to 9). Free House.* ***Beer** Boddingtons, Hook Norton, guest beer. Garden, outdoor eating.* ***Accommodation** 3 bedrooms, all en suite, £55 (single £32.50). Children over 14 years welcome overnight, also babies by prior arrangement. Accommodation closed 25 Dec. Access, Amex, Diners, Visa.*

West Bexington — Manor Hotel — FOOD — B&B

Tel 01308 897785 **Fax 01308 897035** Map 13 F2
Beach Road West Bexington nr Bridport Dorset DT2 9DF

Richard and Jayne Childs' old manor house is just a short walk from Chesil Bank and has a stone-walled cellar bar, leafy conservatory and residents' lounge. Books, magazines and dried flower arrangements add a homely, welcoming touch to simply furnished but well-equipped bedrooms that come complete with tea and coffee kits, TVs, direct-dial phones, sherry, elderflower water and goodnight chocolates. A couple of larger, family bedrooms will sleep up to four (two additional beds are supplied). Bar food encompasses sandwiches, ploughman's platters, lasagne, good fish dishes (perhaps crab and fish pie or monkfish au poivre), oysters, rabbit pie and children's favourites. Good choice at Sunday lunchtimes. *Open 11-11 (Sun 12-10.30). **Bar Food** 12-2, 6.30-10 (Sun from 7). Free House. **Beer** Ind Coope Dartmoor Bitter, Wadworth 6X, BurtonAle. Garden, outdoor eating, children's play area. Family room. **Accommodation** 13 bedrooms, all en suite, £78 (single £45). Children welcome overnight, additional bed (£7.50) and cot available. No dogs. Accommodation closed 25 Dec. Access, Amex, Diners, Visa.*

West Bromwich — Manor House — A

Tel 0121 588 2035 Map 6 C4
Hall Green Road Stonecross West Bromwich West Midlands B71 2EA

Five minutes' drive from the M6 motorway, a 13th-century, moated manor house run as a pub by Banks's, the Wolverhampton brewery. It's surrounded by well-tended lawns, so it can be a useful spot to break a motorway drive on a sunny day; inside, the main hall has a steeply-pitched roof, kitsch medieval theming, piped music and formulaic food (almost all dishes served with great mounds of chip-shop chips). Nevertheless, it is an interesting, atmospheric oasis for a flagon of ale. Directions from M6 J9: take A461 towards Wednesbury, then first left into Woden Road East; at T-junction turn left into Crankhall Lane; continue some way up to roundabout, pub is just by right turning into Hall Green Road. *Open 12-2.15, 6-9.15 (5.30-9.30 Sat), 12-9.15 Sun; opening hours may vary. **Beer** Banks's. Garden. Access, Visa.*

West Camel — Walnut Tree — FOOD — B&B

Tel 01935 851292 Map 13 F2
West Camel nr Sparkford/Yeovil Somerset BA22 7QW

Smartly modernised and extended 100-year-old village inn located half a mile off the A303 between Sparkford and Ilchester, and named after the magnificent walnut tree that stands in the pretty shrub filled garden. Pristinely kept carpeted bar, lounge and separate restaurant featuring lots of plush chairs and benches, some comfortable easy chairs and sofas and attractive silk flower arrangements. Good relaxing ambience in which to enjoy reliable, above-average bar food. Fresh local produce is used in compiling the value-for-money, twice-daily-changing blackboard menu which may list Crewkerne goat's cheese salad with walnut oil dressing and Dorset crab gateaux among the starters, followed by Mendip lamb casseroled in red wine with herbs and fresh fish from Poole – perhaps cod fillet pan-fried with prawns and beansprouts and skate wing oven-baked with capers and garlic. Excellent accompanying vegetable selection – definitely a chip-free zone! A ploughman's lunch is also offered. Puddings might include lemon tart with fruit syrup and white chocolate cream crunch. All the four current bedrooms have been completely refurbished and individually decorated in the last year; TV, direct-dial phone, radio, hairdryer and trouser press are provided. Three rooms have en-suite bath and shower, one just a shower. Three new bedrooms, one with a four-poster and each with a little patio, were due to be completed by the end of 1995. *Open 11-2.30, 5.30-11 (Sun 12-2.30, 7-10.30). **Bar Food** 12-2, 7-9.30 (Sun to 9). Free House. **Beer** Butcombe Bitter, Flowers. Garden, outdoor eating. **Accommodation** 4 bedrooms, all en suite, £49 (single £32). Dogs by arrangement. Access, Visa.*

See the **County Round-Up** tinted pages for details of all establishments in county order.

WEST HOATHLY Cat Inn FOOD

Tel 01342 810369 Map 11 B6
West Hoathly nr East Grinstead West Sussex

Homely, half tile-hung pub overlooking the parish church in this sleepy, off-the-beaten-track Sussex village. Beams, panelling, a fine inglenook fireplace with ancient carvings and comfortable cushioned bench seating in a cosy alcove characterise the old-fashioned interior, which remains free of intrusive music and games. Reliable bar food – listed on a changing blackboard menu – may be pricey, but portions are generous and the quality of the home-cooked dishes most acceptable. Typical choices include crab paté, fresh anchovies and French bread to start, followed by home-made hamburger with green peppercorn sauce, steak and kidney pie and kidneys in red wine, all served with crisp vegetables. Sanwiches and ploughman's served all day. Banana cheesecake and chocolate mousse may feature on the short list of puddings. Summer seating on the front terrace with village views. *Open 11-2.30, 6-11 (Sun 12-3, 7-10.30).* ***Bar Food*** *12-1.45, 7-9.30 (no food Sun eve).* ***Beer*** *Harveys Best, guest beers. Patio, outdoor eating. No credit cards.*

WEST HUNTSPILL Crossways Inn B&B

Tel 01278 783756 Map 13 E1
West Huntspill nr Highbridge Somerset TA9 3RA

Popular proprietor-run 17th-century inn located beside the A38 and a handy overnight stop for travellers using the M5 (3 miles from Junctions 22 and 23). Simple old-fashioned interior comprising a series of inter-connecting low-ceilinged rooms, featuring exposed beams, winter log fires, a mix of sturdy furniture and a welcoming atmosphere. Clean and comfortable accommodation in three neat, modern pine-furnished upstairs bedrooms. Two boast compact en-suite facilities, the third's bathroom is private but not en-suite, and all have TV's and beverage-making kits for added comfort. Picnic tables among the fruit trees in the rear garden. *Open 11-3, 5.30-11 (Sun 12-3, 7-10.30). Free House.* ***Beer*** *Flowers IPA & Original, Royal Oak, guest beers. Garden. Family room.* ***Accommodation*** *3 bedrooms, 2 en suite (one with bath), £34 (single £24). Children welcome overnight (under-12s stay free in parents' room), additional bed and cot available. Check-in by arrangement. Access, Visa.*

WEST ILSLEY Harrow Inn ★ FOOD

Tel 01635 281260 Map 14a C3
West Ilsley nr Newbury Berkshire RG16 0AR

A mile from the Ridgeway footpath on the edge of the Berkshire Downs, in a lovely village green setting, complete with lazy ducks on the pond, there are many good reasons to visit the ever-popular Harrow Inn. Within, antique furniture and several country settles create a smartly rustic but simple and old-fashioned atmosphere. There's plenty of space in which to relax and enjoy an excellent pint of Morland (who founded their brewery in this village in 1711, but are now based in Abingdon) and some tip-top food, which is as good as always – the consistency of approach and cooking is admirable. The menu changes seasonally and is supplemented by a daily-changing specials board (broccoli and Stilton tart with walnut pastry, beef and king prawn kebabs with risotto rice, macaroni cheese with vegetables, chicken with cider and apples) – a variety wide enough to suit all tastes and pockets. Soups, salads, bread and puddings are reliably good, the home-made puddings (pineapple upside down cake, home-made almond ice cream, treacle tart, sticky toffee pudding, 18th-century creamed apple flan with unpasteurised local Peasemore cream from a Guernsey herd) especially, and a fine selection of constantly varying British cheeses puts the seal on a splendid bill of fare. Portions are generous and vegetarians are thoughtfully catered for (perhaps aubergine and sweet potato africaine); granary rolls, sandwiches and ploughman's platters are also offered all day. All in all, a properly pubby combination of the imaginative and homely, which keeps people coming back. You can even take home one of their particularly good pies. Regular 'pie nights' (last Tuesday in the month). A good garden for children has playthings and animals (ducks, geese, goat, chickens). *Open 11-3, 6-11 (Sun 12-3, 7-10.30).* ***Bar Food*** *12-2.15, 6-9.15 (Sun 7-9).* ***Beer*** *Morland. Garden, outdoor eating, children's play area. Access, Visa.*

WEST PENNARD Lion at Pennard FOOD B&B

Tel 01458 832941 Map 13 F1

Glastonbury Road West Pennard Somerset BA6 8NH

A comfortable informality exudes from the central stone-flagged and low-beamed bar, where easy chairs sit around a huge inglenook that boasts a roaring log fire in winter. Radiating off are the neatly-set dining-room and a cosy parlour which doubles as both family and breakfast room. There's local praise for some well-kept real ale, the skittle alley and the bar food. Menus run from burgers to steaks, with daily specials such as beef and Stilton pie, toad-in-the-hole, and home-made pasties with herb pastry added on the blackboard. Breaded garlic prawns, Somerset pork chop with apple, cream and brandy and lamb steak with cranberry and rosemary sauce might complete the picture. Sandwiches and ploughman's platters served at lunchtime only. Traditional roasts replace the regular menu at Sunday lunchtimes. Bright duvets have smartened up the bedrooms in the adjacent former stable block. Bathrooms are neat, clean and carpeted, while extras include colour TVs, dial-out phones and radio alarm clocks. *Open 12-3, 6.30-11 (Sun 12-3, 7-10.30).* ***Bar Food*** *12.30-2, 6.30-9 (Sat to 9.30, Sun from 7). Free House.* ***Beer*** *Oakhill, Wadworth 6X, guest beer. Garden, outdoor eating. Family room.* ***Accommodation*** *7 bedrooms, all en suite, £45 (£50 high season, single £30). Children welcome overnight (under-10s free if sharing parents' room), additional bed (£12). Check-in by arrangement. No dogs. Access, Amex, Diners, Visa.*

WEST STAFFORD Wise Man Inn FOOD

Tel 01305 263694 Map 13 F2

West Stafford nr Dorchester Dorset DT2 8AG

With Thomas Hardy's birthplace at Bockhampton close by, this homely, thatched village pub is a very popular refreshment spot. Virginia creeper and a variety of colourful hanging baskets and flower-troughs adorn the rendered facade. Also on the front wall is a poem hymning the virtue of ale, attributed to Hardy: 'health lies in the equipoise', apparently. Inside, the traditional two-bar layout and central off-sales remains intact, with the public bar sporting a wood-block floor; a toby jug and antique pipe collection and simple darkwood furniture plus padded wall-bench seating characterise the modest interior throughout. If planning to eat, go for the home-made specialities that are highlighted on the comprehensive printed menu. These may vary from a freshly prepared soup – potato and onion – chicken tikka and chili to steak and mushroom pie and a daily fresh fish dish. Six or seven vegetarian choices are also offered. Sandwiches are served in the public bar and ploughman's platters are offered all day. *Open 1.30-2.30, 6.30-11 (Oct-May from 7), Sun 12-2.30, 7-10.30.* ***Bar Food*** *12-2, 6.30-9.* ***Beer*** *Flowers Original & IPA, Boddingtons Bitter. Garden, patio, outdoor eating. Access, Visa.*

WEST WITTON Wensleydale Heifer FOOD B&B

Tel 01969 22322 Fax 01969 24183 Map 5 D4

West Witton Wensleydale North Yorkshire DL8 4LS

Zzz...

The signs of good breeding which abound at John and Anne Sharp's well-tamed heifer are manifest. At the heart of every good pub is the bar:- here it holds no more than four tables and attracts a healthy mixture of residents and locals and dispenses a hearty pint of Theakstons. To one side a snug room and chintz foyer lounge are available for sitting out, while to the other the bistro daily pushes out the fatted calf with quite serious intent. Goats cheese served in filo pastry with walnut vinaigrette and prawns à la pil pil are typical precursors to lamb's kidneys with Dijon mustard and cream and tagliatelli carbonara. Sandwiches are served in the bar at lunchtimes only along with a Yorkshire Cheese lunch of three varieties of Wensleydale of course. Accommodation comprises traditionally furnished and comfortable en-suite bedrooms not only in the pub itself but also in the Old Reading Room, standing in its own garden over the road. All rooms have radio, TV and beverage trays with telephones providing a baby listening facility. *Open 11-11.* ***Bar Food*** *12-2, 7-9 (7-9.30 Fri/Sat eve). Free House.* ***Beer*** *John Smith's, Theakston Best & Old Peculier.* ***Accommodation*** *15 bedrooms, all en suite £70 (single £49). Dogs welcome in rooms. Garden. Access, Amex, Diners, Visa.*

We do not accept free meals or hospitality – our inspectors pay their own bills and **never** book in the name of Egon Ronay's Guides.

WEST WYCOMBE George & Dragon FOOD

Tel 01494 464414 Fax 01494 462432 Map 15a D3
West Wycombe nr High Wycombe Buckinghamshire HP14 3AB

Set in a National Trust village beside the A40, this imposing Tudor coaching inn was refurbished inside and out last year. Beyond the fine cobbled archway entrance (one of several surviving original features) lies an appealing period bar with large oak beams, settles and Windsor chairs by a roaring fire. Friendly staff offer a promising bar food menu ranging from potted Stilton and cream of broccoli and bacon soup to decent home-made pies filled with chicken and asparagus, sole and grape or rabbit and reliable specials like game pastie with sloe and crab apple sauce. Follow with a rich, gooey treacle tart or fresh fruit crumble. Up the haunted staircase are eight bedrooms (£60 double), all also recently refurbished but not inspected in time for this Guide. Peaceful rear garden with a play area for children. *Open 11-2.30, 5.30-11 (Sat 11-11), Sun 12-2.30, 7-10.30.* ***Bar Food*** *12-2 (Sun to 1.45), 6-9.30 (Sun 7-9).* ***Beer*** *Courage Best & Directors, guest beer. Garden, outdoor eating, children's play area. Family room. Access, Amex, Diners, Visa.*

WESTON Otter Inn FOOD

Tel & Fax 01404 42594 Map 13 E2
Weston nr Honiton Devon EX14 0NZ

☺

Situated 400 yards off the busy A30 and beside the River Otter, this much-extended 14th-century cottage is a popular refreshment stop en route to and from the West Country, and a particular favourite with families. The original old cottage interior is delightfully unspoilt with a vast inglenook fronted by comfortable armchairs and old tables. Plenty of prints, books and various bric-a-brac make this a cosy and relaxing spot in which to sit. The main bar extension is very much in keeping with heavy beams, a real assortment of old sturdy tables and chairs, an unusual chamber pot collection hanging from the beams and the added touch of fresh flowers on each table. Beyond some double doors is a skittle alley and games room. A hand-scripted bar menu highlights many of the usual snacks such as sandwiches, salads, ploughman's lunches, filled jacket potatoes and steaks; main-course specialities include deep-fried cod and haddock platter, breaded scampi, steak and kidney pie, fresh pastas, aromatic chicken, bangers and mash. Daily dishes chalked up on boards offer more variety and greater interest, often with home-made soup and a choice of fish and meat specials and a vegetarian dish of the day. Children who have been cooped up in the car for long periods will relish their own 'ducklings' menu ("ask for crayons and paper to keep you happy") and the space in the splendid riverside garden, which offers youngsters the chance to paddle in a very safe shallow section of the river; they may also be entertained by the resident rabbits, guinea pigs, ducks and chickens. Babes in arms are extremely well catered for, with free baby food offered and changing facilities provided in the Ladies. *Open 11-3, 6-11, Sun 12-3, 7-10.30. Free House.* ***Bar Food*** *12-2, 6.30-10 (Sun 12-2, 7-9.30), children allowed in bar to eat.* ***Beer*** *Eldridge Pope Hardy Country, Boddingtons, Worthingtons, guest beer. Family room. Garden, outdoor eating, indoor and outdoor play area. Access, Visa.*

WHITELEAF Red Lion B&B

Tel 01844 344476 Map 15a D2
Upper Icknield Way Whiteleaf nr Princes Risborough Buckinghamshire HP27 0LL

Cream and red-painted 17th-century village pub, set back from the lane in a quiet, attractive village. Inside, the two homely and cosy interconnecting rooms and adjacent dining-room are neatly arranged with a pleasant mix of polished pine and antique settles, a good log fire and various brasses, sporting prints and dried flower arrangements. Reached via stairs behind the bar are four simply-furnished bedrooms with modern dark-patterned fabrics, TV and tea makers and compact en-suite facilities (only one with bath). Front-facing rooms enjoy good rural views. *Open 11.30-3, 5.30-11 (Sun 12-3 & 7-10.30). Free House.* ***Beer*** *Hook Norton Best, Wadworth 6X, Morland PA, Brakspear. Garden, outdoor eating.* ***Accommodation*** *4 bedrooms, all en suite (one with bath), £39.50 (single £29.50). Children welcome overnight, extra bed supplied. Check-in by arrangement. No credit cards.*

We endeavour to be as up-to-date as possible but inevitably some changes to landlords, chefs and other key staff occur after the Guide has gone to press.

WHITEWELL — Inn at Whitewell — FOOD

Tel 01200 448222 Map 6 B1 **B&B**

Whitewell Forest of Bowland nr Clitheroe Lancashire BB7 3AT

ZZz...

Set amid the wild beauty of North Lancashire, well away from the hurly burly, the Whitewell Inn stands next to the village church, overlooking the River Hodder (on which the inne has eight miles of fishing rights) at the head of the Trough of Bowland, one of the least-known areas of outstanding natural beauty in the country. Back in the 14th century, the inn was home to the keeper of the King's deer, and the Queen still owns the building as part of the Duchy of Lancaster. Inside, it's wonderfully relaxed, laid-back, even mildly eccentric, with a haphazard arrangement of furnishings and bric-a-brac. In the main bar there are wooden tables, old settles, roundback chairs, a stone fireplace, log fire in cold weather, and heavy ceiling beams. An entrance hall has colourful rugs, more settles, even a piano, and a selection of magazines, papers and books for some serious loitering. A wide variety of pictures, dotted about the building, come from the Inn's own art gallery; there's also a small wine merchant business. Food is served in both the bar and restaurant, which overlooks the river; the bar meal selection offers the likes of a daily home-made soup, country terrine with tomato relish, fish pie (with haddock, scallops, scampi and prawns), lamb and leek pie, spicy chicken and almond casserole, Cumberland bangers with champ (Irish mashed potatoes with spring onions), salads, substantial sandwiches, cheeses from London's Neal's Yard Dairy and home-made puddings – all good stuff. The bar supper menu is similar but varies slightly, perhaps offering baked queen scallops, warm salad of lamb's kidneys with mushrooms and pink peppercorns, un-dyed Norfolk kippers and roast breast of duck. Good Arabica coffee is served in cafetière and ground coffee is also packed for taking home – typical of the kind of thought that goes into Richard Bowman's running of the inn. Calorific desserts like sticky toffee pudding and a good wine list complete the picture. There are eleven bedrooms, all furbished with antique furniture, peat fires and Victorian baths. Unusual extras include video recorders and superb stereo systems, as well as books, magazines, and a set of binoculars; the best and largest rooms overlook the river and the country beyond (and attract the higher tariff). Everything is usually immaculately clean. On sunny days the attractive rear lawn furnished with simple benches is an ideal spot to relax and soak in the view. *Open 11-3, 6-11 (Sun 12-3, 7-10.30).* ***Bar Food*** *12-2, 7.30-9.30. Free House.* ***Beer*** *Marston's Pedigree, Boddingtons. Riverside garden, outdoor eating.* ***Accommodation*** *11 bedrooms, all en suite, £65/£72 (suite £93, single £49/£55). Children welcome overnight. Access, Amex, Diners, Visa.*

WHITMORE — Mainwaring Arms — A

Tel 01782 680851 Map 6 B3

Whitmore nr Newcastle-under-Lyme Staffordshire ST5 5HR

Close to the site of the Manor of Whitmore, which was listed in the Domesday Book, the same families, Mainwarings and Whitmores, have run a hostelry here since time immemorial. Today's version, in cream-painted brick and creeper-clad with an ivy-covered porch, plays host to a wide cross-section of locals in congenial surroundings. Timber cross-beams frame the single mahogany bar and access to three large yet cosy rooms, each with its own log fire in winter. For summer evening entertainment, tiered patios to the rear are the setting for regular barbecues. Sundry sandwiches and the likes of deep-fried fish at lunchtimes only. Three miles from Junction 15 of the M6. *Open 12-3, 5.30-11 (Fri & Sat 12-11, Sun 12-3, 7-10.30). Resident ghost. Free House.* ***Beer*** *Bass, Boddingtons, Marston's Pedigree. Patio. No credit cards.*

WHITNEY-ON-WYE — Rhydspence Inn — FOOD

Tel 01497 831262 Map 9 D4 **B&B**

Whitney-on-Wye nr Hay-on-Wye Hereford & Worcester HR3 6EU

Set in the heart of Kilvert country, on the A438 about a mile out of Whitney-on-Wye, this is a well-loved, reliably entertaining inn with a delightful timbered interior, two attractive bars with real fires, old furniture and beams aplenty. Nice touches include magazines and newspapers, creating an atmosphere in keeping with the old library chairs. The charming dining-room and restaurant overlook the garden. Five comfortable bedrooms have beams, sloping floors, plus an armchair at the least; some rooms are more romantic; one has a four-poster; all have TVs and hot beverage facilities but no phones. Bar food suggestions include ploughman's platters, steak and kidney pie, smoked haddock rarebit, pan-fried monkfish with pine nut salad, fresh tagliatelle with home-smoked chicken. Separate restaurant menu

(not recommended here) including popular Sunday lunches. Summer lunchers can enjoy the view over the Wye Valley from the terraced garden. *Open 11.30-2.30, 7-11.30 (Sun 12-2.30, 7-10.30).* ***Bar Food*** *11-2 (Sun from 12), 7-9.45.* ***Beer*** *Bass, Robinson, Felinfoel. Garden, outdoor eating. Family room.* ***Accommodation*** *7 bedrooms, all en suite, £55-£65 according to season (single £27.50-£32.50, 4-poster £75). Children welcome overnight (under-2s stay free in parents' room), additional bed (£12.50). No dogs. Access, Amex, Visa.*

WHITWELL — Noel Arms — B&B

Tel 01780 460334 **Fax 01780 460531** Map 7 E3
Main Street Whitwell Rutland Water Leicestershire LE15 8BW

A modest pub very much of two halves, the thatched original building with a tiny village bar standing sideways on to the road (A606). Hidden behind is landlord Sam Healey's labour of love, a stone extension, tucked into the hillside, containing lounge bar, dining-rooms (one with a fish tank), and, above, the wing of dormer-windowed bedrooms. Neatly appointed with colourful duvets and freestanding furniture, all enjoy the benefit of colour TV, radios, phones and beverage trays, though only four have en-suite bathrooms. The remainder share facilities along the tiny corridor. Barely a long cast from the banks of Rutland Water, the bar's a base for fishing stories late into the night, and the hearty fisherman's breakfast makes a fine start the following morning. *Open 10-11 (Sun 12-10.30). Free House.* ***Beer*** *Tetley Bitter, Ruddles County, guest beer. Patio, outdoor eating. Family Room.* ***Accommodation*** *9 bedrooms, 4 en suite, £49 (£29 & £38 not en suite, single £40). Children welcome overnight (under-12s stay free in parents' room). Access, Visa.*

WIDECOMBE-IN-THE-MOOR — Rugglestone Inn — FOOD

Tel 01364 621327 Map 13 D3
Widecombe-in-the-Moor Devon TQ13 7TF

Unspoilt gem of a rural pub set beside moorland within walking distance of the picturesque village. Named after the Ruggle Stone, a huge mass of granite nearby, this rustic stone inn comprises two tiny rooms, one a delightful, old-fashioned parlour with beams, open fire and simple furnishings; both are devoid of modern-day intrusions. Excellent Bass and Butcombe Bitter are tapped straight from the cask and served with one of the hearty, home-made 'one-pot' meals – chicken pie, steak and kidney pie, cauliflower cheese, cottage pie – that make a satisfying meal. Ploughman's platters are served all day. Puddings include blackcurrant tart and walnut and syrup tart with clotted cream. All the food is cooked and delivered daily by two local girls who have a shop in the village. Across the babbling brook to the front of the pub lies a lawn with benches and peaceful moorland views. No children under 14 inside. Parking used to be difficult but there is now an adjacent field for cars. *Open 11-2.30, 6-11 (opening earlier in high season, later in winter), Sun 12-3, 7-10.30.* ***Bar Food*** *12-2 (to 2.30 Sat & Sun), 6.30-9 (opening later and closing earlier in winter). Free House.* ***Beer*** *Bass, Butcombe Bitter. Garden, outdoor eating. No credit cards.*

WIGGLESWORTH — Plough Inn — FOOD B&B

Tel 01729 840243 Map 6 B1
Wigglesworth nr Skipton North Yorkshire BD23 4RJ

For over fifteen years now the Goodall family have operated, enlarged and improved their 18th-century country inn which was once the farm buildings and ale house of a vast Dales estate. The busy food operation features the output of a wood-burning pit barbecue whose contents can be hot- or cold-smoked over hickory, mesquite or oak chippings. Around the resultant rack of ribs, hickory chicken and smoked halibut steak is a menu full of Yankeeisms, from potato skins with sour cream and hickory dips "thro'" Caesar salad and smoked chicken to "steak and prawn combo". More traditionally, there are still bistro-style bar snacks served in the original village bar and evening meals in a bright conservatory restaurant. Accommodation offered is either Standard (over the original pub) or Superior in a carefully conceived extension which blends in immaculately with the original timbered black-and-white frontage. Within are all the trappings of modern-day comfort from TV and radio to direct-dial phones and tea and coffee trays: all the rooms are of a decent size with well-kept en-suite bathrooms and effective double glazing. While the front rooms look across a village street where practically nothing happens from day to day, those to the rear soak in the ever-changing moods of the twin Dales peaks of Ingleborough and Pen-Y-Ghent. *Open 11-3, 7-11 (Sun 11-3, 7-10.30). Free House.* ***Beer*** *Tetley Best, Boddingtons.* ***Bar Food*** *12-2, 7-10 (restaurant only eve).* ***Accommodation*** *12 bedrooms, all en suite £47 (single £33). Children welcome overnight, cot available. Garden, outdoor eating. Family room. Access, Diners, Visa.*

WILMCOTE — Mason's Arms — FOOD

Tel 01789 297416 Map 14 C1

Wilmcote nr Stratford-upon-Avon Warwickshire CV37 9XX

Just off the A3400 three miles north of Stratford, Wilmcote is the former home of Mary Arden. The home of "pub grub" in the village is to be found at the Mason's, though any journey through its voluminous menus should be trodden with care. Various sandwiches and ploughman's with crusty bread and pickle are served at lunchtime only, but look carefully to (also checking the specials board) to find dishes like poached salmon with prawn sauce, lentil and mushroom cannelloni and boeuf bourguignon, steak and kidney pie and halibut steaks with parsley sauce. Largely unaltered since the gentry's coaches pulled in to water their horses, the Mason's front rooms are evocatively those of a village inn. Twin conservatories to the rear provides refuge from the 52-seater restaurant (one menu is served throughout) and offer views, mainly, of the car park but also of the rambling pub gardens. *Open 11-3, 6-11 (Sun 12-3, 7-10.30). Free House.* ***Bar Food*** *12-2, 6.30-9.30 (7-9 Sun).* ***Beer*** *Hook Norton Best, Boddingtons, Wadworth 6X, guest beers. Garden. Access, Visa.*

WINCHCOMBE — Old White Lion — B&B

Tel 01242 603300 **Fax 01242 221969** Map 14 C1

37 North Street Winchcombe Gloucestershire GL5H 5PS

A reminder that good things come in very small packages, the hitherto unsung, 400-year-old Old White Lion is a rare find. Only the tiny enamelled inn sign and black oak door distinguish it from the other listed buildings in North Street. With a cosy front room, tiny rear parlour easy chairs and varnished tables, the whole place has a relaxed and homely air. Six small bedrooms, restored with great care and good taste, also have a special feeling of closeness to antiquity with many of their original features unaffected by careful and unobtrusive addition of the requisite televisions and clock radios, though phones have not been added. While five rooms (including just one single) have en-suite WCs and showers only, there's a roomier 4-poster bedroom with both a corner bath and separate shower en suite. *Open 11-11. Free House.* ***Beer*** *Marston Best & Pedigree, guest beer. Garden. Family room.* ***Accommodation*** *6 rooms, all en suite, from £50 (single £35). Children welcome overnight, additional bed supplied. Access, Visa.*

WINCHESTER — Wykeham Arms ★ — FOOD — B&B

Tel 01962 853834 **Fax 01962 854411** Map 15 D3

75 Kingsgate Street Winchester Hampshire SO23 9PE

Tucked away in the narrow back streets of Winchester, immediately south of the Cathedral Close (by Kingsgate on the junction between Canon Street and Kingsgate Street), Graeme and Anne Jameson's mellow, redbrick, 250-year-old 'Wyk' is one of the finest hostelries in the land. The main bar, which is mostly for drinkers, has old-fashioned schoolroom desks with integral seats, some authentically carved with the initials of inattentive pupils from years gone by. Collections of hats, mugs and fascinating old prints and cartoons adorn the bar and no less than six other interconnecting rooms, all set up for eating, with a special dining area for non-smokers. The old pine, candle-lit dining tables each have a brass money slot to collect donations for the upkeep of the cathedral. 'The Wyk' is by no means a secret and booking for food is essential. A blackboard menu at lunchtime changes daily, offering unusual but successful combinations of flavours like Stilton and quince paté, 'Wyk' cottage pie served with crusty bread, pork, sage and apple casserole. Main course suggestions on the evening menu are fillets of smoked haddock poached in Dijon mustard and caper sauce, filo parcels of rabbit and celery set on a lentil, bacon and tarragon sauce, chicken breast with caramelised onions and celeriac with a chervil jus. A separate pudding menu offers mouth-watering choices like carrot and ginger pudding with fudge sauce and white chocolate and Drambuie mousse with bananas. The Sunday menu comprises various cold platters (game pie, ham, sausage plait, beef, ploughman's) that are served with salad and a cottage loaf. Twenty names on the well-chosen wine list are also available by the glass, and for summer eating and drinking there is a neat walled garden. Individually decorated bedrooms have stylish matching bedcovers and curtains and mostly honeyed pine furniture. All have mini-bars, hot beverage facilities, TV and telephone, plus homely extras like fresh flowers, books, magazines and pot-pourri. Modern en-suite bathrooms, all with showers over tubs, boast quality Woods of Windsor toiletries. First-rate cooked breakfasts, with freshly squeezed orange juice, are served in a charming period breakfast room on the first floor. No children under 14 overnight or in restaurant, three non-smoking rooms. *Open 11-11.* ***Bar Food*** *12-2.30 (sandwiches served till 6), 6.30-8.45 (Sun 3-8.30).* ***Beer*** *Eldridge Pope. Garden, outdoor eating.* ***Accommodation*** *7 bedrooms, all en suite, £75 (single £65). Children over 14 welcome overnight. Access, Amex, Visa.*

WINEHAM Royal Oak A

Tel 01444 881252 Map 11 B6
Wineham nr Haywards Heath West Sussex BN5 9AY

Part-tiled, black-and-white timbered cottage dating back to the 14th century and located on a country lane between the A272 and B2116 near Henfield. It is a classic ale house, a true rural survivor that has been serving the locals for over 200 years and is delightfully traditional and unspoilt in every way. Head-cracking low beams, huge inglenook with warming winter fire, part wooden and part stone flagged floor topped with sturdy wooden furnishing characterise the charming bar and tiny rear room. Old corkscrews, pottery jugs and mugs, old photographs and other old artefacts adorn the walls. Ale is drawn straight from the cask in a rear room and in keeping with ale house tradition food is limited to good freshly-made sandwiches – smoked salmon, cheese, home-cooked ham and beef – and a thick soup served on cold winter days. The pub has been in the same family since 1945. Extensive summer gardens and adjacent children's/function room with TV and books. *Open 11-2.30, 5.30-10.30 (Fri & Sat to 11), Sun 12-2.30, 7-10.30.* ***Beer*** *Whitbread Pompey Royal, Boddingtons, Wadworth 6X, Harveys Best. Garden, outside eating, tables in garden. Family room. No credit cards.*

WINFORTON Sun Inn ★ FOOD B&B

Tel 01544 327677 Map 9 D4
Winforton Hereford & Worcester HR3 6EA

Just three miles inside England on the A438 Wye Valley Road, the Sun is hospitably run by Wendy and Brian Hibbard. Tireless and enthusiastic, Wendy is dish-crazy. Her seemingly endless stream of inventiveness produces something different and exciting whenever we visit, whatever the season. Her winter regular, the hearty stockpot soup and summer's latest addition, a lettuce and lovage version, are a typical case in point; winter's speciality pigeon pie, made to Brian's "secret recipe", is likely replaced, perhaps, by monkfish medallions with ginger and coriander as the warmer weather approaches. Thai chicken starters might appear in filo pastry with tangy lemon sauce and Singapore steamboat prawns are sensationally hot and spicy. Ever-popular, the braised oxtails in cider sauce with root vegetables are slow-cooking perfected for the traditionalist's palate; those with more adventure enthuse equally over the Kashmiri lamb shoulder in a mildly curried sauce. Carefully cooked and neatly-presented dishes of vegetables (perhaps lightly-honeyed carrots and caraway-seeded cabbage) might be the embellishments – rather than mere accompaniments – which serve to point up the star quality of Wendy Hibbard's cooking. Incidentally, Wendy never uses salt in her cooking. Her ploughman's lunch offers a superb choice of British farmhouse cheeses and wins our Ploughman's Lunch of the Year award for 1996 (see Award pages). Her puddings, conceived both to amuse and satisfy, are equally stellar: tipsy bread-and-butter pudding, a nuts-upon-nuts tart and the figgy ice cream clearly illustrate the point. Overnight accommodation is offered in three en-suite bedrooms; they share a private entrance and unfussy decor of commendable quality, their accoutrements including TV, radio, beverage tray and hairdryer; a pay phone is located in the hall. *Open 11.30-3, 6.30-11 (Sun 12-3, 7-10.30). Pub closed all Tue Nov-May and Tue eve Jun-Oct)* ***Bar Food*** *(not closures) 12-2, 7-9.30 (Sat to 9.45, Sun to 9.15). Children allowed in bar to eat. Free House.* ***Beer*** *Woods Parish, Jennings Cumberland Bitter, guest beer.* ***Accommodation*** *3 bedrooms, all en suite, £42 (single £27). Garden, outdoor eating. Access, Visa.*

WINKTON Fisherman's Haunt Hotel B&B

Tel 01202 484071 **Fax 01202 478883** Map 14 C4
Salisbury Road Winkton Christchurch Dorset BH23 7AS

The river Avon is just across the road from this well-kept, wistaria-clad hotel, which stands on the B3347 Christchurch-Ringwood road about 2 miles from Bournemouth (Hurn) Airport. Stuffed fish and an old well with running spring water are unusual features of the characterful beamed bars, and there is an airy conservatory. The good bedrooms, which are in the main 17th-century building, extended coach house and nearby cottage, blend pretty fabrics with a mixture of modern and traditional furnishings. All offer TVs, telephones and tea-makers and two rooms also boast four-poster bed. *Open 10.30-2.30 (Sat to 3), 6-11 (Sun 12-3, 7-10.30). Free House.* ***Beer*** *Ringwood Best & Fortyniner, Bass, Wadworth 6X. Garden. Family Room.* ***Accommodation*** *20 bedrooms, 16 en suite, £59.50 (single £37.50). Children welcome overnight (under-11s stay free in parents' room, 2-10s £7.50), additional bed, and cot available. Access, Amex, Diners, Visa.*

WINSFORD Royal Oak Inn FOOD B&B

Tel 01643 851455 Fax 01643 851388 Map 13 D2
Winsford Exmoor National Park Somerset TA24 7JE

Zzz... 🍷

Re-building, following a serious fire, was nearing completion as we went to press and, when complete, everything promises to be as good as new – or as good as old, actually, as this lovely old thatched inn dates back to the 12th century. Located in a sleepy, picture-postcard pretty Exmoor village, the inn doubles up as village local as well as attracting the hunting, shooting, and fishing fraternity from abroad. The latter come for the inn's fishing rights to a mile of the river Winn that runs through the village. The intention is to keep the same style of bar menu, with home-made favourites like pasties, game pie and steak and kidney pudding plus sandwiches and ploughman's lunches. Five bedrooms in a modern annexe and the family cottage formed out of an old cowshed were undamaged by the fire. Of the eight rooms in the main building (some nestling under the newly re-thatched eves), five will have four-poster beds; all will now have new high-tech telephones along with the usual amenities. *Open 11-2.30, 6-11 (Sun 12-3, 7-10.30).* ***Bar Food*** *12-2 & 7.30-9.30 (from 6.30 in summer, Sun 7-9 or 9.30).* ***Beer*** *Flowers Original & IPA, guest beer. Patio, outdoor eating.* ***Accommodation*** *14 bedrooms, all en suite, £85 (single £60). Children welcome overnight, additional bed (from £5) and cot supplied. Access, Amex, Diners, Visa.*

WINSLOW Bell Hotel B&B

Tel 01296 714091 Fax 01296 714805 Map 15a D1
Market Square Winslow Buckinghamshire MK18 3AB

Handsome Georgian coaching inn that proudly overlooks the market square in this pleasant small town. After a period of uncertainty new owners have over the past year reversed the fortunes of this welcoming establishment, which features a good pubby bar with heavy beams and inglenook fireplace, and comfortable lounge areas with oak and leather furniture, easy chairs, attractive prints and plates. There are seventeen bedrooms, two designed for the disabled, all spacious with floral fabrics, reproduction darkwood furniture – one with a four-poster – clean, tiled bathrooms and added extras like TVs, telephones, tea-makers, hairdryers and trouser presses. *Free House.* ***Beer*** *Greene King. Garden. Family room.* ***Accommodation*** *17 bedrooms, all en suite, £39.50 (single £34.50). Children welcome overnight. Access, Diners, Visa.*

WINTERTON-ON-SEA Fisherman's Return FOOD B&B

Tel 01493 393305 Map 10 D1
The Lane Winterton-on-Sea Norfolk NR29 4BN

Small it maybe, but this prettily-kept row of former fishermen's cottages is an ideal hang-out for locals and visitors alike, be they fishermen or not. Built in traditional brick and flint, the buildings are probably 16th-century, and unaltered over the last quarter century or more. The public bar is lined in varnished tongue-and-groove panelling and hung with sepia photographs and prints of Lowestoft harbour, the Norfolk Broads and the pub itself. Some of these, movie buffs will note, are not as old as they seem. Centrestage, the cast-iron wood-burner opens up in winter to add a glow of warmth to an already cheery atmosphere. A smaller and possibly older lounge, low-ceilinged, with a copper-hooded fireplace and oak mantel, is carpeted these days and ideal for a quick, if cramped, snack. Families will more likely head to the "Tinho", a timbered rear extension with pool table and games machines which leads mercifully quickly to a lovely enclosed garden with a pets' corner and an adventure playground. The printed menu offers standard pub fare, but look to the blackboard for daily specials like smoked haddock mornay with granary bread and salad, spiced beef with fresh ginger on savoury wild rice or spinach-stuffed cannelloni on a nutty tomato base. Toasted sandwiches and ploughman's platters are served all day. A tiny flint-lined spiral staircase leads up under the eaves to three cosy bedrooms, which share the house television (propped up on a seaman's trunk) and two bathrooms (one with shower only). The largest room, a family room, also has a sitting area with its own television. Modest comforts, maybe, but entirely adequate for a brief stay, a stone's throw from the beach and long walks over the dunes. Visitors are made truly welcome by John and Kate Findlay, and seen on their way with the heartiest of seafarer's breakfasts. *Open 11-2.30, 6.30-11 (from 7 in winter), Sun 12-3, 7-10.30, open all day Sat in summer.* ***Bar Meals*** *11.30-2, 6-9.30 (winter from 7). Free House.* ***Beer*** *Elgood's Cambridge, John Smith's, Adnams, Fuggles Imperial IPA, guest beers. Garden, outdoor eating, children's play area. Family room.* ***Accommodation*** *3 bedrooms, £45 (single £30). Children welcome overnight, additional bed (£5) available. Check-in by arrangement. No credit cards.*

Withypool — Royal Oak Inn — FOOD B&B

Tel 01643 831506 **Fax 01643 831659** Map 13 D1
Withypool Somerset TA24 7QP

Zzz...

A stylish, friendly and thoroughly laid-back country inn, well-beloved of hunting and shooting parties in season. The Royal Oak was a favoured haunt in the 1860s of *'Lorna Doone's'* author, R.D. Blackmore. Despite modern-day bedroom comforts, little enough appears changed today: hunting trophies adorn the Resident's Bar, while the Rod Room Bar is dedicated more to angling memorabilia. Here the daily-changing blackboard menu of scampi and prawn brochettes, lamb casserole with lentils and poached local salmon supplements an all-encompassing bar menu with everything from sandwiches to grilled steaks. At dinner, table d'hote menus in the restaurant start at £19.50 for 3 courses with main courses à la carte (supreme of chicken stuffed with spinach; grilled fillet of haddock with tarragon sauce) priced around £14. The comfortable bedrooms have a comprehensive range of facilities: TV, radio, direct-dial phone, hot beverage facilities and hairdryer. A couple of the bathrooms have shower/WC only. By night, the peace and quiet are total. Withypool is just off the B3223 from Dulverton. Not suitable for children under 10. *Open 11-2.30, 6-11 (Sun 12-3, 7-10.30, to 11 in summer).* ***Bar Food*** *12-2, 6.30-9.30 (Sun from 7). Free House.* ***Beer*** *Castle Eden, Webster's Yorkshire, Flowers.* ***Accommodation*** *8 rooms, 7 en suite, £72 (single £32). Access, Amex, Diners, Visa.*

Wolterton — Saracens Head — FOOD B&B

Tel 01263 768909 Map 10 C1
Wolterton nr Erpingham Norfolk NR11 7LX

Zzz...

To locate this isolated and very individual rural inn follow signs for Erpingham off the A140 Aylsham to Cromer road, then pass through Calthorpe before bearing left on to a narrow lane, signposted Wolterton; your efforts will be well rewarded. Only 250 yards from the main gates to Wolterton Hall, this most unusual red-brick inn was built in 1806 by Lord Walpole as a coaching inn for the main house and was modelled on a Tuscan farmhouse. Inside, the ambience is decidedly civilised and upmarket with high ceilings, soothing terracotta painted walls with friezes, stylish patterned clothed tables, open log fires and an eclectic mix of built-in leather wall settles and wicker chairs. Scatter cushions, magazines, newspapers and evening candlelight enhance the relaxed atmosphere. Landlord/chef Robert Dawson-Smith produces an interesting, short selection of dishes that are listed on a blackboard menu that changes twice daily. No chips, scampi or sandwiches (bread and cheese is available at lunchtime, though) are served here, so expect pub fare that is well above average and book a table! Imaginative choices may begin with Stilton and orange pate, crispy aubergines and red pesto mayonnaise, Morston mussels in cider and cream, followed by braised local pigeon in Marsala, stir-fry white fish with ginger and orange, all accompanied with a dish of well-cooked vegetables. Finish with a traditional pudding, such as sticky brown bread and butter pudding or upside down apple tart. Popular events are the roast Sunday lunch, the special Sunday 2-course supper, a weekday "two choice" lunch and the monthly "feast" nights – French, seafood and Old English for example. Short list of well-chosen wines. Individual charm extends to the top floor of the inn into the four attractive en-suite bedrooms, each furnished with freestanding pine – one with brass bed – wicker chairs and quality fabrics. TV, hairdryer, and beverage-making facilities are standard, but fresh milk and earthenware jars of tea and coffee are a welcome touch, as are the excellent breakfasts. Sheltered courtyard garden and delightful walled garden for sunny days. *Open 11-3, 6-11 (Sun 12-3, 7-10.30). Free House.* ***Bar Food*** *12.15-2.15, 7-9.30.* ***Accommodation*** *2 bedrooms, both en suite £45 (single £35). Children welcome overnight. Check-in by arrangement.* ***Beer*** *Adnams, guest beer. Garden, eating outside. Access, Amex, Visa.*

Wooburn Common — Chequers Inn — FOOD B&B

Tel 01628 529575 **Fax 01628 850124** Map 15a E3
Wooburn Common nr Beaconsfield Buckinghamshire HP10 0JQ

The charming 17th-century Chequers Inn lies midway between the M4 and M40, perched on the rolling Chiltern Hills and has been carefully and lovingly developed over the years by Peter Roehrig. Find him chatting to the locals in the convivial beamed bar, where you'll find simple but stylish snacks. Choose from open sandwiches, ploughman's, celery and Stilton, tossed salad of avocado, smoked salmon and prawns with hazelnut dressing or

mignons of pork fillets with a Dijon mustard and red wine sauce. There is a separate restaurant but our specific recommendation here is for bar food. The cottagey bedrooms all have en-suite facilities and are equipped with TVs (plus Sky), telephones, clock-radios, trouser presses, tea/coffee making facilities. One room has a four-poster. *Open 11-11 (Sun 12-3, 7-10.30).* ***Bar Food*** *12-2.30, 6-9.30. Free House.* ***Beer*** *Fuller's London Pride, Marston's Pedigree, Wadworth 6X. Garden, outdoor eating.* ***Accommodation*** *17 bedrooms, all en suite, £77.50 (single £72.50). Children welcome overnight, additional bed available. No dogs. Access, Amex, Visa.*

WOODBASTWICK — Fur & Feather — A

Tel 01603 720003 Map 10 D1
Woodbastwick Norwich Norfolk NR13 6HQ

Nestling within an unspoilt estate village on the edge of the Norfolk Broads, this picturesque thatched brick building was converted from two farm cottages into a pub only a few years ago. Owned by Woodforde's brewery, who established their brewhouse in the farm buildings behind some eight years ago, the Fur and Feather serves as the 'Brewery Tap' dispensing their full range of award-winning cask ales. Tip-top Wherry Best Bitter, Nelson's Revenge, Great Eastern, Baldric, the 1992 champion beer Norfolk Nog and the deceptively strong Headcracker (ABV 7%) can all be enjoyed in the traditionally refurbished bars or on the peaceful front lawn on fine weather days. *Open 11-3, 6-11 (Sun 12-3, 7-10.30).* ***Beer*** *Woodforde's. No credit cards.*

WOODCHESTER — Ram Inn — A

Tel 01453 873329 Map 14 B2
South Woodchester nr Stroud Gloucestershire GL5 5EL

One of Gloucestershire's more way out pubs both in clientele and location – a splendid spot above the A46 (follow signs uphill to South Woodchester). Visitors are rewarded with fine views back down the valley and across to Minchinhampton Common. Niceties are kept to a minimun with picnic tables on a tarmac patio, assorted pine tables and bentwood chairs in the L-shaped bar and plain floorboards surrounding the single stone-built box counter. Two log fires are a great draw in winter. The Ram's pride and joy, however, is its selection of real ales – (any nine are on tap at any one time) – running through the alphabet from Archers and Boddington to Uley Old Spot. These are devoted drinker's ales, to be savoured somewhat seriously. *Open 11-3, 5.30-11, Sat 11-11, Sun 12-10.30. Free House.* ***Beer*** *Uley Bitter & Old Spot, Archers, Boddingtons, Ruddles Best & County, Fuller's London Pride, guest beer. Garden. Access, Visa.*

WOODNEWTON — White Swan — FOOD

Tel 01780 470381 Map 7 E4
Main Street Woodnewton Northamptonshire PE8 5EB

When the White Swan was closed and bought by a developer in 1988 the villagers thought they had lost their pub, but after a campaign which involved residents lobbying council planning meetings, the White Swan was saved and reopened, after extensive renovations, in 1990. Simple, single oblong room, one end focusing on the bar and a wood-burning stove, with the other end neatly set up as a dining-room. Bar food is pretty straightforward: soup, burgers, steak and kidney pie, all-day breakfast, jumbo sausage, jacket potatoes, cod in batter, sandwiches and ploughman's lunches. The restaurant menu is eclectic in the extreme, but in a similar, straightforward style. Occasional summer barbecues (Bank Holiday Mondays). *Open 12-3, 7-11 (Sun 12-7, 7-10.30).* ***Bar Food*** *12-2, 7-10. Free House.* ***Beer*** *Morland Old Speckled Hen, Fuller's London Pride, Geoffrey Hudson's Bitter (local brew), Shepherd Neame Spitfire. Garden, outdoor eating. Access, Visa.*

We endeavour to be as up-to-date as possible but inevitably some changes to landlords, chefs and other key staff occur after the Guide has gone to press.

Woodstock Feathers Hotel FOOD B&B

Tel 01993 812291 Fax 01993 813158 Map 14a B2
Market Street Woodstock Oxfordshire OX7 1SX

Zzz...

Eight miles north of Oxford, within walking distance of Blenheim Palace. Situated in the heart of a historic village, behind a 17th-century Cotswold-stone frontage, the Feathers hotel offers a comfortable range of superior accommodation with bedrooms differing in price by size (suites are particularly attractive). All have elaborately draped curtains and a useful range of extras that includes mineral water, chocolates, fresh flowers, magazines and tea on arrival. Some rooms have draped awnings over the beds, while the best have four-posters. Bathrooms are luxuriously fitted in marble throughout, with bathrobes and an abundance of toiletries provided. The upstairs drawing room with a library and open fire is the most inviting of the day rooms and a cosy bar has flagstone flooring and an open fireplace. During warm weather the courtyard garden is a delightful spot for light meals (which are also served in the bar). A quiet, sophisticated air pervades the dining-room, where à la carte and fixed-price menus provide a choice of interesting options. Recommended in our *1996 Hotels & Restaurants Guide*. Lighter eating in the Whinchat Bar – from hot courgette soup or pickled quail's eggs with saffron mayonnaise to marinated herring with dill and brandy, baked forest mushrooms and goat's cheese with sweet peppers, honey-baked ham with new potato salad, and toasted marshmallow with berry compote. Afternoon tea is served 3.30-5.30. Service is courteous and efficient. *Bar open 12-2, 6-9.30, Sun 12-2.30, 7-9.30.* ***Bar Food*** *12.30-2.15, 7.30-9.15 (no bar food Sat or Sun eve; open Bank Holidays).* ***Beer*** *Wadworth 6X. Courtyard garden. Family room.* ***Accommodation*** *17 rooms, 16 en suite, £99-£145 (single £75/£98), breakfast charged separately. Children welcome overnight, additional bed (£20) and cot available. Access, Amex, Diners, Visa.*

Woolhope Butcher's Arms FOOD B&B

Tel 01432 860281 Map 14 B1
Woolhope Hereford & Worcester HR1 4RF

Zzz...

The infectious enthusiasm of the Power family and a commendable reliance on local produce bring customers from far and wide to their pub which is not easily found down the narrow country lanes. A black-and-white timber frontage, copiously hung with flower baskets, and the neat, colourful brookside garden and patio induce an anticipation more than adequately fulfilled by the food. Leek and hazelnut terrine, mushroom biryani and Woolhope wild rabbit and cider pie head the bar menu, alongside soup, sandwiches (lunchtime only), garlic mushrooms, chicken curry, a butcher's grill and plenty of home-made puddings (perhaps ginger and coffee meringue cake, banana split or summer pudding). The three bedrooms are small and cosy: decor is in an appropriate cottage style, and they share a bathroom. There's abundant peace and quiet in this hidden valley, and a substantial breakfast, come the morning. *Open 11.30-2.30, 6.30-11, Sun 12-2.30, 6.30-10.30.* ***Bar Food*** *12-2, 7-9.30. Free House.* ***Beer*** *Hook Norton Best & Old Hookey, Marston's Pedigree, guest beer. Garden, outdoor eating.* ***Accommodation*** *3 rooms £39 (not en suite), £25 single. Check-in by arrangement. Children welcome overnight (under-10s stay £10). Accommodation closed 24 & 25 Dec. No credit cards.*

Woolley Moor White Horse FOOD

Tel 01246 590319 Map 6 C3
White Horse Lane Woolley Moor Derbyshire DE5 6FG

Bill and Jill Taylor are the landlords of the smart, friendly and very popular White Horse. Approached from the A61 at Stretton, Woolley Moor is a tiny hilltop hamlet above the river Amber at the point where it flows into Ogston reservoir. The large paddock and garden have a sandpit, swings, and small adventure playground to help keep the youngsters happy and there's both a boules pitch and a football pitch. There are at least two dozen trestle tables outside; bag one for a summer lunch, but remember the number before going inside to order. Within there's restaurant seating for around 60 people, and it fills up quickly, so booking is recommended. This dining area, reached through a stone archway, was originally the pub lounge, a cottagey, carpeted area in two sections, with large picture windows and attractive lace-clothed tables. On the printed menu, dishes such as beef Italienne, game pie, or mushroom stroganoff are offered. Desserts could include treacle and

walnut tart or lemon and ginger crunch. Blackboard specials may include garlic prawns or kidneys provençale. It's substantial stuff, nicely cooked and presented and, above all, tasty. Half a dozen or so New World wines now feature on the short wine list. The Smoke Room still remains the village local, with is quarry-tiled floor, red leather banquettes, Britannia tables and prominent dartboard; Monday night dominoes are played in a seriously competitive spirit. This is where a good drop of ale comes in. In addition to draught Bass, a healthy rotation of guest beers is publicised well in advance, a good proportion of them from independent breweries. Piped music, when playing, is of the classical kind. This is a smart and impressive pub, professionally managed, and it runs like clockwork. *Open 11.30-2.30, 6.30-11 (from 6 in summer), Sat 11.30-3, 6-11, Sun 12-3, 7-10.30.* ***Bar Food*** *11.30-2 (Sun 12-2.30), 6.30-9 (Sat to 9.30, no food Sun eve). Free House.* ***Beer*** *Bass, Bateman's Dark Mild, three guest beers. Garden, outdoor eating, children's play area. Pub closed Sun eve. No credit cards.*

WOOTTON RIVERS Royal Oak FOOD

Tel 01672 810322 Map 14a A4 **B&B**
Wootton Rivers nr Marlborough Wiltshire SN8 4NQ

Situated only 100 yards from the Kennet and Avon Canal in one of Wiltshire's most picturesque villages, this 16th-century, black and white timbered, thatched pub offers visitors an old-world charm in its low heavily beamed and comfortably furnished bars and dining room. Plates and prints adorn the walls and atmosphere in which to enjoy well-kept ale – Wadworth 6X drawn from the wood and Brakspear's – and a wide choice of bar food. The comprehensive printed menu features standard snacks and favourites, including a good range of steaks, while the photocopied handwritten menu advertises the freshly prepared daily specials. Begin with home-made soup or avocado, mozzarella, tomato and basil salad followed by a hearty steak and Guinness pie – full of chunky meat in a rich gravy – fillets of pork in green peppercorn sauce, all of which are served with a selection of fresh vegetables. Popular puddings include treacle and almond tart and Greek yoghurt with honey and kiwi fruit. Six fresh, clean and comfortable bedrooms – four with en-suite or private facilities – are located in a large modern house to the rear of the pub. Guests have the use of communal tea- and coffee-making facilities in the TV lounge and for early risers their own breakfasts, the ingredients of which are supplied, with the washing-up being attended to later. Breakfast can also be taken in the pub. Pub areas are not suitable for children under four. *Open 11-3 (coffee from 10.30), 6-11, Sun 12-10.30.* ***Bar Food*** *12-2.30, 7-9.30 (Sun to 9). Free House.* ***Beer*** *Brakspear Bitter, Wadworth 6X, two guest beers. Patio, outdoor eating. Family room.* ***Accommodation*** *6 bedrooms, 4 en suite showers, £35 (single from £25). Children welcome overnight, (under-2s stay free in parents' room, 2-5s £5, 5-10s £10), additional bed available. Dogs by arrangement. Access, Visa.*

WOOTTON WAWEN Bull's Head FOOD

Tel 01564 792511 Map 14 C1
Stratford Road Wootton Wawen Warwickshire B95 6BD

A smart, black-and-white timber-framed pub just a mile or so from the picturesque village of Henley-in-Arden (A3400) with flagstone floors and low, gnarled oak beams. Determined emphasis on fresh fish attracts an ever-increasing clientele, the iced seafood platter proving a tempting indulgence on a hot summer's evening. Notable equally for size and variety, hearty portions of moules marinière, lemon sole in caper sauce, whole red snapper with orange sauce and sea bream with spinach sauce tempt diners choosing from the daily-updated blackboards. The less fishy, meanwhile, may plump for calf's liver and bacon with celeriac mashed potatoes or escalope of turkey with avocado and mozzarella. Sandwiches at lunchtime only. A fair and generously-priced selection of wines by the glass is supplemented by good-value bin-end bottles. *Open 12-3.30, 6-11 (Sun 12-3, 7-10.30).* ***Bar Food*** *12-2.30, 7-10.30 (Sun to 9.30). Children allowed in bar to eat. Free House.* ***Beer*** *Marston's Best & Pedigree, Morland Old Speckled Hen, Wadworth 6X, Greene King Abbot Ale & Fuller's London Pride, Adnams. Garden, terrace, outdoor eating. Access, Visa.*

Many **B&B** establishments offer reduced rates for weekend and out-of-season bookings. Always ask about special deals for longer stays. Beware half-board terms in inns where we do not recommend **FOOD.**

WORTH St Crispin Inn B&B

Tel 01304 612081 Map 11 D5
The Street Worth nr Sandwich Kent CT14 0DF

Zzz...

Peacefully located along the village street just off the A258 south of Sandwich, this attractive and pleasantly refurbished local has a single, characterful bar, which is full of heavy timbers, brick walls, a big log fire and a collection of rustic pine tables and chairs. Interesting range of eight real ales tapped straight from the cask behind the bar. Spacious rear terrace with an all-weather retractable awning and an excellent summer garden with benches among the flower borders and trees. Four charming upstairs bedrooms – one with a fine half-tester bed – have stripped pine doors, a good mix of older/antique style furniture and clean en suite facilities with showers over tubs. Three further, larger rooms are housed in a converted outbuilding and feature modern built-in furniture and compact bathrooms. All have satellite TV and tea-makers. The pub is a handy base for golfers playing the Royal links courses at the end of the lane. *Open 11-3, 6-11 (Sun 12-3, 7-10.30). Free House.* ***Beer*** *Mansfield Bitter, Shepherd Neame Master Brew, Gale's HSB, Marston's Pedigree, four guest beers. Rear garden and courtyard, summer barbecue (Sun), outdoor eating area.* ***Accommodation*** *7 bedrooms, all en suite, £50 (single £35). Children welcome overnight (under-5s stay free in their parents' room), additional bed available (£5). Check-in by arrangement. Access, Visa.*

WYBUNBURY Swan Inn FOOD

Tel & Fax 01270 841280 Map 6 B3
Main Road Wybunbury Cheshire CW5 7NA

Few signs remain here of the 18th-century farmhouse with an unusual bow-front opposite St Chad's church, where only the 15th-century leaning tower survives today. The Church was abandoned in 1972, and the tower's last vertical correction occurred in 1989. Even more recent straightening-out of the Swan divides the interior into alcoves separated by curtains, brass rails and banquettes, and warmed by real fires in winter. The menu – gammon steak, steak and kidney pie, ham and leek pie, steaks – is equally traditional and unchanging, supplemented by a daily specials boards: filled baguettes of steak and onions, steak and kidney pie and home-made summer fruit pavlova are not untypical. Traditional Sunday lunch. Outside in summer are a 'Pop Shop', and plentiful new children's play equipment and neatly-spaced picnic tables on a lawn by the lychgate. *Open 11-3 (not Mon), 6.30-11 (Sun 12-3, 7-10.30).* ***Bar Food*** *12-2, 6.30-9.30 (except Sun eve).* ***Beer*** *Boddingtons, Jennings, Tetley, guest beers. Garden, children's play area. Family room. Pub closed lunch Monday. No credit cards.*

WYE New Flying Horse Inn B&B

Tel 01233 812297 Map 11 C5
Upper Bridge Street Wye Kent TN25 5AN

Zzz...

With a 400-year-old history, this well maintained village centre inn is characterised by low ceilings, black beams, open brickwork and a large open fireplace. The spick and span main bar has gleaming, copper-topped tables and simple chairs while the neat lounge bar boasts some comfortable armchairs and access to the splendid sun-trap patio and extensive lawned garden. Six main-building bedrooms – including one four-poster and one spacious family room – have been smartly refurbished with attractive pastel colours, quality fabrics and some decent individual pieces of furniture. Good bathrooms with showers over tubs. In addition, there are four uniform, en-suite rooms in a converted stable block. Invicta Country Inns. *Open 11-11.* ***Beer*** *Shepherd Neame. Garden and patio, outdoor eating area, summer barbecue.* ***Accommodation*** *10 bedrooms, all en suite, from £47.50 (single £37.50). Children welcome overnight (under-5s stay free in parents' room). Dogs by arrangement. Access, Visa.*

WYKEHAM Downe Arms Hotel B&B

Tel 01723 862471 **Fax 01723 864329** Map 5 F4
Wykeham Scarborough North Yorkshire YO13 9QB

An imposing stone building at the roadside (A170) just five miles from Scarborough, the hotel has remained part of the Downe family estates since its conversion into a coaching inn some 120 years ago. A century later the Orangery, designed by Sir Martin Beckett on an 18th century theme, was added to provide extensive function facilities. The rather less-than-

pubby bar and lounge nonetheless remain suitably comfortable and intimate for the resident guest, and there's a spacious garden and patio for family use in summertime. En-suite facilities were added to the bedrooms just seven years ago, althugh the listed nature of the original structure limited several to WC and shower rooms only. All are kept, however, in apple-pie order with bright matching fabrics adding a welcome splash of colour. *Open 11.30-3, 6.30-11 (Sun 12-3, 7-10.30). Free House.* ***Beer*** *Tetley Best, Theakston Best & XB. Family room.* ***Accommodation*** *10 bedrooms, all en suite, £35 (single £22.50). Children welcome overnight, additional bed available if sharing (£17.50), cot and high-chair also available. Garden. Access, Visa.*

WYRE PIDDLE Anchor Inn FOOD

Tel 01386 552799 Map 14 B1
Main Street Wyre Piddle nr Pershore Hereford & Worcester WR10 2JB

Standing low and white-painted at the roadside, bedecked with fairy lights and flower baskets, the Anchor reveals its wealth of talents on further investigation. This is one of the region's premier summer pubs with its grassy terraces and rolling lawn graduating down to the Avon river bank where holidaymakers may moor their narrowboats. Views across the river take in the verdant Vale of Evesham whence come the asparagus and strawberries that enrich the summer menus. Menus change daily in any case: popular for snacks are the home-made soup, and home-made chicken, mushroom and brandy paté. Home-made steak and kidney pie, spinach cannelloni and vegetable dauphinoise are substantial bar meals, with spotted dick or chocolate pudding and chocolate sauce to follow. No sandwiches, but ploughman's platters are available all day. An elevated dining-room has possibly the best view (although it's the bar food that we specifically recommend here). Family Sunday lunch. Watch out for the theme nights, live music and ten real fruit wines. *Open 11-2.30, 6-11 (Sun 12-3, 7-10.30).* ***Bar Food*** *12-2.30 (Sun to 2), 7-9.45 (Sun to 9).* ***Beer*** *Marston's Pedigree, Flowers, IPA, Boddingtons and one guest beer. Garden. Family room. Access, Visa.*

WYTHAM White Hart A

Tel 01865 244372 Map 14a C2
Wytham Oxfordshire OX2 8QA

This famous old creeper-clad pub in the centre of the pretty village of Wytham has a part-panelled bar with a flagstone floor, open fire and high back settles. Outside is a very pretty courtyard garden, popular for barbecues in the summer beyond which extra seating has been provided by converting the loose boxes in the old stables into booths. *Open 11-11, Sun 12-10.30.* ***Beer*** *Tetley Bitter, Burton Aylesbury, guest beer. Garden. Family room. Access, Amex, Visa.*

YATTENDON Royal Oak FOOD

Tel 01635 201325 **Fax 01635 201926** Map 14a C4 **B&B**
The Square Yattendon nr Newbury Berkshire RG16 0UF

Zzz...

Wisteria-clad inn formed out of a row of 16th-century cottages in the village square. Cromwell dined here before the Battle of Newbury in 1664. Of the three interconnecting rooms (orange rag-painted walls above dado pine-panelling, inglenook fireplaces), two are laid-up for eating at reservable tables. The up-market offerings might include moules marinière, risotto of squid with a filo tartlet of tomato and mozzarella, and gravad lax with dill and mustard mayonnaise among the starters, followed by main dishes such as confit of rabbit leg with mushroom tagliatelle, calf's liver and bacon with onion gravy and mash or blanquette of veal. A blackboard lists the soup and fish dish of the day. Finish with bread-and-butter pudding, chocolate mousse or home-made ices. Bedrooms all come with remote-control TVs, direct-dial phones, trouser presses and hairdryers. Pretty decor is no longer pristine and some details of maintenance and refurbishment still need attention. The three en-suite rooms (two others have private bathrooms across the corridor) are to be preferred. For summer eating and drinking there are a couple of tables out in an attractive walled garden with vine-covered trellises. Regal Hotels. *Open 11-3, 6-11 (Sun 12-3, 7-10.30).* ***Bar Food*** *12-2.30, 6.30-9.45 (Sat to 10), Sun 12-2.30, 7-9.30)* ***Beer*** *Ruddles, Wadworth 6X, guest beer. Garden, outdoor eating.* ***Accommodation*** *5 rooms, 3 en suite, £85 (single £60). Children welcome overnight. Access, Amex, Diners, Visa.*

YEALAND CONYERS New Inn FOOD

Tel 01524 732938 Map 4 C4

40 Yealand Rd Yealand Conyers Carnforth Lancashire LA5 9SJ

Signed off the A6 north of Carnforth, and just a mile or two short of the Cumbrian border, the village attracts its fair share of visitors both to Leighton Hall and the nearby Leighton Moss Nature Reserve. An added attraction, conveniently located between the two, is Ian and Annette Dutton's ivy-clad listed pub. Cumbrian foodies connect the Dutton name with the *Miller Howe Café* in Windermere and this by association with John Tovey, whose protegés pepper the Lake District. Here the village's only pub bar is quite gentrified, with carpeting and marble-topped tables, regularly doubling as the overflow to a 40-seat dining area, daily filled to capacity. Food-wise the legacy, if not the hand of Tovey remains; the ubiquitous side salad bowls are forcefully flavoured not only with orange, fresh pineapple and grapes but also dried banana and candied walnuts beneath a cream cheese dressing and mustardy vinaigrette. All-day snacks include home-made soup (perhaps carrot and coriander), filled baps, jacket potatoes, quiche and snacks which include the 'Miller Howe cheese and herb paté'. Look to the blackboard for main courses which may include Indian mushrooms, haddock fillet with tomato and cream sauce and lambs' liver with onion marmalade and red wine gravy. Puddings include sticky toffee and tipsy trifle. *Open 11-11.* ***Bar Food*** *11-9.30.* ***Beer*** *Robinson's Hartleys XB, Hatters Mild, Bitter, Frederic's & Old Tom. Garden, outdoor eating. Access, Visa.*

We endeavour to be as up-to-date as possible but inevitably some changes to landlords, chefs and other key staff occur after the Guide has gone to press.

FREQUENT
CALLER PLUS

FOR CUSTOMERS MAKING OVER 30 MINUTES OF CALLS A WEEK.

REGULAR
CALLER PLUS

BETWEEN 8 AND 30 MINUTES PER WEEK.

OCCASIONAL
CALLER

UP TO 7 MINUTES PER WEEK.

A, B or C. Choosing Cellnet, is that easy.

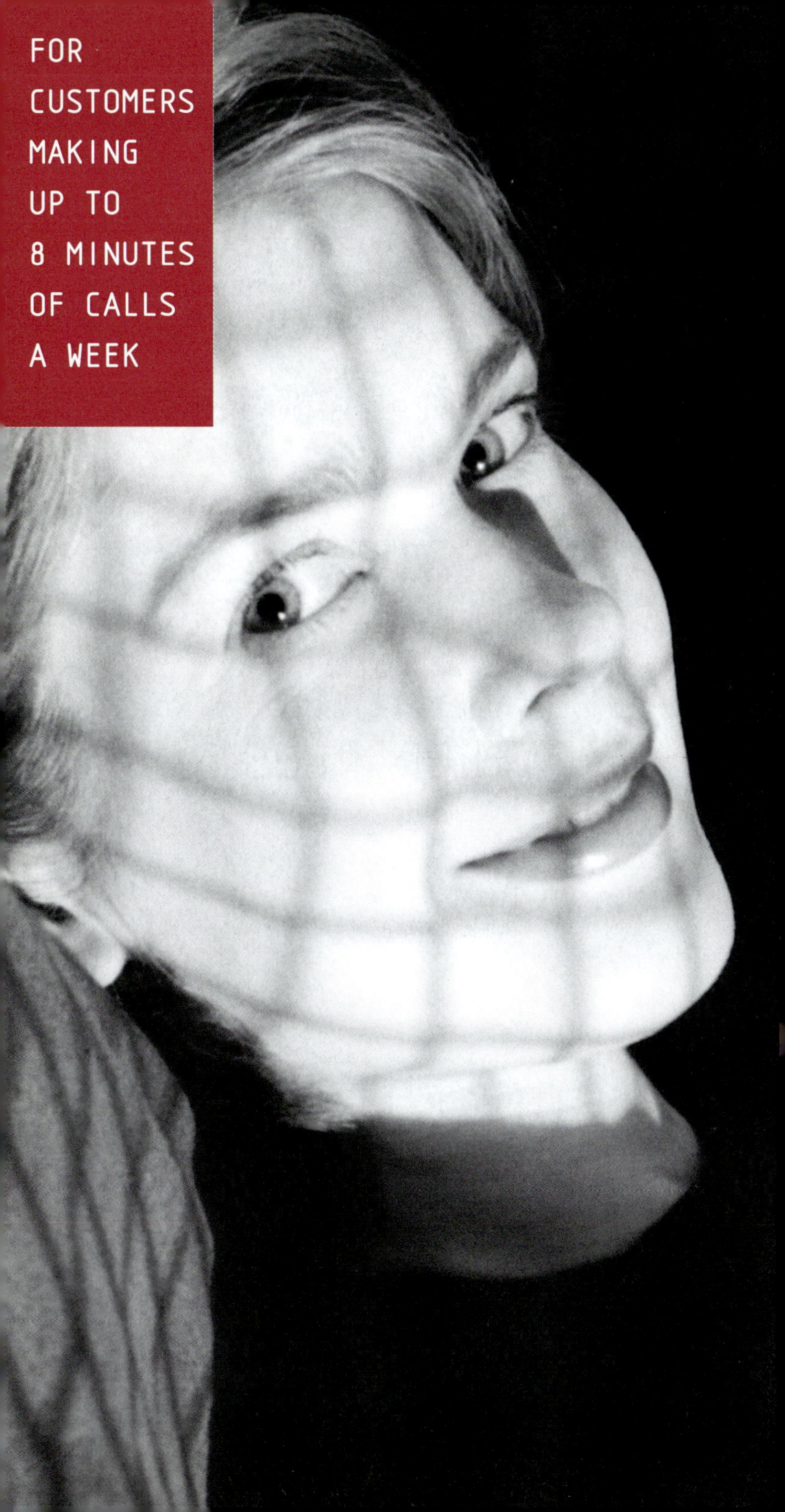
FOR
CUSTOMERS
MAKING
UP TO
8 MINUTES
OF CALLS
A WEEK

FOR
CUSTOMERS
MAKING
OVER 30
MINUTES
OF CALLS
A WEEK

FREQUENT CALLER PLUS

FOR BUSINESS USERS WHO TRAVEL EXTENSIVELY IN THE UK AND ABROAD

If you're likely to make over 30 minutes of calls per week, and must be contactable at all times – in the UK and overseas – you need Cellnet Frequent Caller Plus.

Connected to Cellnet's digital service, you'll enjoy clearer calls and optimum call security. And you'll be able to keep in touch around the world.

What's more with 2-way data flow – including FAX – Cellnet sets the pace for mobile data communications.

For users who need a mobile phone for use in the UK only, and wish to benefit from a wide choice of low cost handsets, Frequent Caller offers connection to Cellnet's analogue service.

KEY BENEFITS

- Digital call quality*
- Optimum security*
- International roaming* – the ability to make and receive calls abroad.
- 2-way data communications*
- National UK coverage

NETWORK FEATURES

- Call Divert
- Call Waiting
- Operator enquiries

OPTIONAL SERVICES

- Callback[†] intelligent messaging
- Short Message Service*

Features and services asterisked above cannot be accessed from an analogue phone.*

THE NET THAT SETS YOU FREE

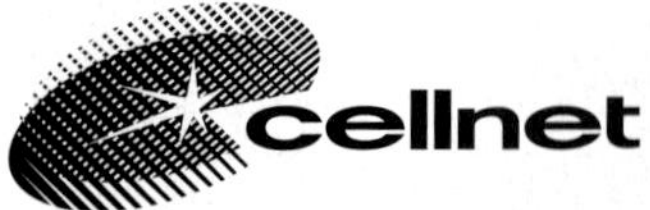

for further information call

0800 214000

[†]Callback is a value added service provided by Cellnet Solutions Ltd, a company in the Cellnet Group. Other messaging services may be available that use the Cellnet Callback advanced network feature. Using these services will incur extra charges.

FOR
CUSTOMERS
MAKING
8 - 30
MINUTES
OF CALLS
A WEEK

Scotland

ABERDEEN — Prince of Wales — FOOD

Tel 01224 640597 Map 3 D4
7 St Nicholas Lane Aberdeen Grampian AB1 1HF

By a modern shopping centre (St Nicholas) in the heart of the city the Prince of Wales dates back to the middle of the last century ('est 1850') and still has a very Victorian feel with bare board floor, old flagstones, panelled walls, some booth seating and the longest bar counter in town. Straighforward cooking is available at lunchtimes only from a self-service counter. On-the-ball new chef Graham Taylor manages well with dishes such as chicken and ham or steak and kidney pies, fried haddock and beef olives. Substitute these with salads, jacket potatoes or a soup for smaller appetites, throw in a pile of filled baps (made and served over the bar until they run out) – and it's a winning combination.
*Open 11am-12pm. **Bar Food** 11.30-2 Mon-Sat only. Free House. **Beer** Bass, Caledonian 80/- Ale, Theakston's Old Peculier, Orkney Dark Island, guest beers. No credit cards.*

ALMONDBANK — Almondbank Inn — FOOD

Tel 01738 583242 Map 3 C5
Main Street Almondbank Tayside PH1 3NJ

Just off the A85 to the west of Perth, on the village main street, the whitewashed Almondbank Inn enjoys fine views over the River Almond from its small well-kept rear garden. It's not a quiet pub: a juke box in the bar regularly pumps out the latest hits, and there's a pool table on the first floor. Food is taken fairly seriously, however, and the Birdcage Bistro, despite some tacky descriptions ("calling all chicken lovers" and "have an ice day") produces generally pleasing food, the majority of it from fresh produce, including some first-rate home-made chips. All the beef used is Aberdeen Angus from the licensee's own family butcher, and even the scampi is fresh and crumbed on the premises. The menu itself is long, running from first courses like deep-fried Camembert with cranberry sauce, to main courses such as steak and onion pie, oriental supreme of chicken, and a whole list of Angus minute steaks with a variety of sauces. All come with fresh vegetables, as well as the aforementioned chips. Puddings are largely ice-cream based and there's good cappuccino and espresso coffee. On Friday and Saturday evenings, a slightly different menu is heavy on steak (Western sizzler Mexicano sirloin) and chicken dishes (Carribean supreme with banana and pineapple), and prices throughout are very reasonable. The uniformed staff are friendly and approachable. *Open 11-2.30, 5-11 (Fri & Sat 11-11.30, Sun 12.30-11).*
***Bar Food** 12-2.15 (Sun from 12.30), 5-8.30 (Fri & Sat 6.30-10). Free House.*
***Beer** Broughton Greenmantle 80/-. Riverside Garden, outdoor eating. Access, Visa.*

ANSTRUTHER — Dreel Tavern — A

Tel 01333 310727 Map 3 D5
16 High Street Anstruther Fife KY10 3DL

Attractive, traditional three-storey 16th-century stone pub with a garden overlooking Dreel Burn. Real fires. *Open 11-midnight (Sun from 12.30). Free House. **Beer** Caledonian 80/- Ale, Alloa Archibald Arrol's 80/-, Orkney Dark Island, guest beer. Garden.*
No credit cards.

APPLECROSS — Applecross Inn — FOOD B&B

Tel 01520 744262 Map 2 A3
Shore Street Applecross Highland IV54 8LR

If you don't fancy going over the highest pass in the British Isles (and it's a bit hairy in parts) take the equally glorious 'shore' route to find this most unpretentious of pubs that looks out across Raasay to the Isle of Skye beyond. Run by expatriate Yorkshirefolk Berni and Judith Fish, with Bernie looking after the bar while Judith makes good use of excellent seafood in the kitchen. The blackboard menu includes the likes of local fresh haddock, steaks and chicken roasted with garlic and herbs, but the things to go for are the queen scallops cooked in wine and cream with mushrooms, squat lobster cocktail, dressed crab salad perhaps, or a half-pint of shell-on prawn tails with a dip. Homely puds like rhubarb crumble and raspberry cranachan and a good cheeseboard follow. Five modest bedrooms are clean and cosy and share a shower room, a pine bathroom and memorable sea views.
A peat fire warms the small lounge that is also used by the owners, and the large garden is right on the shore. No smoking in the bedrooms. Fifty malt whiskies on offer. *Open 11am-12pm (to 11.30 Sat, from 12.30 Sun), closed 2.30-5 Tue-Fri, Sun eve and Mon lunch in*

*winter. **Bar Food** 11-9. **Beer** McEwan's 80/-, Theakston's. Seashore garden. **Accommodation** 5 bedrooms (none en suite), £45 (single £22.50). Children welcome overnight (under-5s stay free in parents' room, 5-14s £10). Accommodation closed 25 Dec and 1 Jan. Access, Visa.*

ARDENTINNY — Ardentinny Hotel — FOOD

Tel 01369 810209 Fax 01369 810345 Map 3 B5 **B&B**
Ardentinny Loch Long nr Dunoon Strathclyde PA23 8TR

Zzz...☺

White-painted hotel on the very edge of Loch Long, 20 minutes' drive from Dunoon and the car ferry to Gourock. Its position within the Argyll Forest Park (where there are 50 miles of traffic-free walks), views over the loch to the submarine base and moody 2000ft Creachan Mor, plus an interesting, rambling garden are the hotel's main attractions. Hearty bar food is served in both pubby Viking and Harry Lauder bars and the Buttery; Clyde yachtsmen, who can tie up at the hotel's own jetty or free moorings, are regular visitors. A good choice of food might include clam chowder with crackers, salmon and broccoli fishcakes with dill mustard sauce, oysters, moules marinière (Fri-Sun only), smoked salmon, deep-fried haddock with chips, seafood, dressed crab salad, plus steaks and Musselburgh pie (big, chunky pieces of braised steak braised with ale and mussels) in the evenings. Sunday brunch is a popular affair, but the restaurant menu was disappointingly executed on our last visit. The best bedrooms (all up a narrow, winding staircase) are designated 'Fyne' and attract a considerable supplement for their fine views, larger bathroom and remote-controlled television; accommodation is generally modest but comfortable, neat and bright; some rooms have showers only and others are large enough for families (further supplements are payable). Tariff reductions mid-Mar to end May and during October. A few steps lead directly down from the hotel to the pebbly shoreline; ask the way to the nearby sandy beach with its lovely, rhododendron-lined setting. The hotel can arrange boat trips for pleasure or fishing, and mountain bikes can also be hired. *Bar open 11-11 (often later on Fri & Sat eve). **Bar Food** 12-2.30, 6-9.30 (Sat 12-3.30, 6-9.30, Sun noon-9). Children's menu, children allowed in bar to eat. No real ale (Belhaven). Lochside garden & shore, outdoor eating. **Accommodation** 11 bedrooms, all en suite, £86 (single from £45), reductions Mar-mid May & Oct. Children welcome overnight, additional beds (£10), cots supplied (£3); dogs £3. Access, Amex, Diners, Visa.*

ARDFERN — Galley of Lorne Inn — A

Tel 01852 500284 Map 3 B5
Ardfern by Lochgilphead Argyll Strathclyde PA31 8QN

Just off A816, north of Lochgilphead and just south of Arduaine, heading down towards Craignish Castle on B8002. David and Susana Garland's inn is as close to a traditional pub as you'll find round these parts of Argyll; inside, there's a cosy, down-to-earth bar, an airy L-shaped dining-room with picture windows and straightforward bedroom accommodation (nine rooms, two with en-suite bath: double £54-£64, single £32 – not yet inspected). On a recent Monday night visit a small, friendly crowd were enjoying live music from two accordionists and the log fire was roaring; sunnier days see the large garden coming into its own with its views over the quiet yacht moorings at the top of Loch Craignish and the surrounding hills. Home-made shortbread is offered with coffee between 9.30 and midday, after which McEwan's or a wee dram might be a more appropriate tipple. Reports of bar food are good and we will report next year on our longer-term findings. *Open 11-2.30, 5-11 (11-12 Fri & Sat, 12-12 Sun); hours may vary, generally longer in winter than in summer. Garden. **Beer** McEwan's 80/-, Theakston's Best (under pressure). No credit cards.*

ARDUAINE — Loch Melfort Hotel, Chartroom Bar — FOOD

Tel 01852 200233 Fax 01852 200214 Map 3 B5
Arduaine by Oban Strathclyde PA34 4XG

Self-styled as "the finest location on the West Coast", Loch Melfort Hotel is indeed in a glorious setting, with a vast panorama of water and mountains unfolding past the field that sweeps down from the hotel to the water's edge. All the public rooms have picture windows to make the most of the wonderful views down the Sound of Jura. The pine-furnished Chartroom is an informal bar room, open to all comers, where the picture windows make the most of the views. A long bar food snack menu encompasses both filled baguettes and steaks; blackboard specials might offer gazpacho or tomato and basil soup, grilled langoustines, meltingly tender calf's liver cooked in sage butter and served with a lime jus, new potatoes and crisp mangetout, or salmon, trout and prawn fishcakes with a creamy asparagus sauce. Desserts are a poor relation. Yachtsmen can tie up at the

hotel's own moorings, row in and walk up to the hotel through the front field (there are even showers provided for non-residents). Lawned gardens lead around the hotel and off to Arduaine Gardens, which are run by the National Trust for Scotland and well worth a visit to see the rhododendrons, azaleas and magnolias. Not a pub at all, but a glorious setting in which to enjoy some good bar food and a pint – the picnic tables outside the bar must be much in demand when the sun comes out. 19 miles south of Oban on A816. *Open 10-11.* ***Bar Food** served until 9pm. No real ales. Garden, moorings.*
Closed Jan 5-Feb 25. Access, Amex, Visa.

ARDVASAR — Ardvasar Hotel — B&B

Tel 01471 844223 Map 3 A4
Ardvasar Sleat Isle of Skye Highland IV45 8RS

Bill and Gretta Fowler's handsome, white-stone coaching inn dates back to the 18th century, and is a mile from the Armadale ferry (from Mallaig), in the wooded Sleat peninsula (often referred to as the Island's Garden). Not far from the shore, it has superb views across the Sound of Sleat to the mountains beyond. This year improvements to the heating system will allow them to open in winter and, to aid this process, there are a cockle-warming two dozen malt whiskies available at the bar! Accommodation in ten rooms, all en suite. Open all day in summer months. Car hire in Broadford (17 miles away, closer to the Kyle of Lochalsh-Kyleakin ferry). ***Beer** regularly-changing guest beer. Patio/terrace. **Accommodation** 10 rooms, all en suite £60. Accommodation closed all Nov, 10 days Christmas. Access, Visa.*

BEAULY — Lovat Arms — B&B

Tel 01463 782313 Fax 01463 782862 Map 2 B3
High Street Beualy Highland IV4 7BS

Substantial red-stone hotel next to the petrol station in the centre of town. Owned by the Fraser family whose clan tartan is much used in the good-quality soft furnishings of the public areas. These include a banquette-seated lounge bar and an entrance hall/reception that, with its real log fire and deep armchairs, also doubles up very well as the lounge. Bespoke carpeting proudly displays the clan crest and motto. A different tartan features in each of the 22 bedrooms, of which the best, often with elaborate bedhead drapes or canopies, are on the first floor; rooms 10, 11 and 12 (above a noisy public bar) are best avoided if you plan an early night. Some room service is available (although not advertised). *Open 11-11 (Fri to 1, Sat to 11.45, Sun from 12.30). Free House. **Beer** regularly-changing guest beer. **Accommodation** 22 rooms, all en suite, £74. Access, Visa.*

BRIG O'TURK — Byre Inn — FOOD

Tel 01877 376292 Map 3 B5
Brig O'Turk by Callander Central FK17 8HT

With a lovely wooded setting deep in the Trossachs, this former, now somewhat extended, cattle byre has a sort of hotchpotch Victorian flavour (inspite the piped music) in both the rough-walled original byre with its iron 'tractor seat' stools at the bar counter and in the carpeted eating room beyond with antique and reproduction dining chairs. During the day, it operates very much as a regular pub with a bar lunch menu including various sandwiches along with steak pie, chicken stuffed with haggis on a mustard sauce, haddock deep-fried in Greenmantle batter and the like. At night, it becomes more of a restaurant (although one can still have just a drink) with a formal à la carte menu only served throughout: main dishes might include venison in red wine, chicken breast served with tarragon and smoked salmon sauce, and quails filled with herbs, ham and pine kernels with rich game sauce. There's also always fresh fish, a vegetarian dish of the day and 6-8 Scottish cheeses including Tobermory and Orkney cheddars. Just 24 wines on the list but 18 of them available by the glass. Tables outside for drinking and lunchtime eating. No children under 8. *Open 12-3, 6-11 (Sat & Sun 12-11). **Bar Food** 12-2.30, 6-9. Free House. **Beer** Broughton Greenmantle Ale & Special Bitter. Garden, outdoor eating. Pub closed 3 weeks Jan. Access, Visa.*

Many **B&B** establishments offer reduced rates for weekend and out-of-season bookings. Always ask about special deals for longer stays. Beware half-board terms in inns where we do not recommend the **FOOD.**

BURRELTON — Burrelton Park Hotel — FOOD B&B

Tel 01828 670206 **Fax 01828 670676** Map 3 C5
High Street Burrelton by Cooper Angus Tayside PH13 9NX

Nine miles north of Perth on the A94 this is a long, low roadside inn in typical Scottish vernacular style. It is as neat outside in its brown and cream livery as it is well-kept within. An extensive all-day menu of home-cooked fare ranges from lentil soup and peach halves stuffed with cheese and herb paté to Lancashire hot pot and steaks to gravad lax and schnitzels of pork with apples, onions and cider plus good home-made fruit pies amongst the puds. The bar has green stained-pine cladding and tile-topped tables, while the smart restaurant features some fine oriental rugs on the walls. Six spotless, low-ceilinged bedrooms have TVs but no phones, and good en-suite bathrooms, each with thermostatically-controlled shower over the tub. Efficient double glazing effectively cuts out the traffic noise. Note that credit cards are not accepted for bills of less than £20.
Open 11-11 (Fri & Sat to 12). ***Bar Food*** *12-10.30 (Restaurant 6.30-10). Free House.* ***Beer*** *Theakston's, guest beer. Family room.* ***Accommodation*** *6 bedrooms, all en suite, £45 (single £30). Children welcome overnight, additional bed and cot available. Dogs by arrangement. Pub closed 1 Jan. Access, Visa.*

BUSTA — Busta House Hotel — FOOD B&B

Tel 01806 522506 **Fax 01806 522588** Map 2 D1
Busta Brae Shetland Islands ZE2 9QN

This 16th-century former laird's home overlooking the sea is a tremendously civilised hotel in a wild place, simply furnished in Scottish rural style. Open to non-residents for good home-cooked bar lunches and suppers – smoked Shetland salmon, pork and pepper terrine, nut roast with tomato sauce, peppered chicken and pork fillet with rice, followed by bramble Cranachan or orange and lemon cheesecake. Alternatively the restaurant offers a 5-course daily-changing fixed-price menu. All fresh vegetables, and Raven Ale from 'nearby' Orkney. 136 malt whiskies on offer! Four acres of walled garden, small private sea harbour, and holidays arranged of the fly/sail and drive kind too. P&O ferries sail to the Shetland Islands from Aberdeen. *Open 12-2.30 (Sun from 12.30), 6-11 (Sun from 6.30).* ***Bar Food*** *12-2 (Sun 12.30-2), 6.30-9.30 (6.30-9 winter, except Fri & Sat).* ***Beer*** *Orkney Raven Ale. Garden, outdoor eating.* ***Accommodation*** *20 bedrooms, all en suite, £84 (single £63). Children welcome overnight (if sharing parents' room £10), additional bed and cot available. Bar and accommodation closed 22 Dec-3 Jan. Access, Amex, Diners, Visa.*

CANONBIE — Riverside Inn — FOOD B&B

Tel 013873 71512 Map 4 C2
Off A7 Canonbie Dumfries & Galloway DG14 0UX

This pristine white-painted Georgian country inn is in a quiet spot overlooking the river Esk, just over the Scottish border, some twelve miles off the top of the M6. Within, it's authentically rural rather than rustic in style, neat, clean and simple with a definite and individual charm which is, however, not the nicotine-stained creaky timbered gloom of the classic English alehouse. The carpeted bar has simple country chairs, some cushioned, some not, around sewing machine tables, and a stone fireplace and bar front; a few discreet decorations line the plain cream walls, framed fishing flies, the odd old cider jar, but there are otherwise few frills. The dining-room is similar, but with proper eating-height tables and chairs, and the small, cosy residents' lounge, which has the air of a private-house sitting room, has a chintzy three-piece suite and a few other chairs arranged around a log-effect fire. Bar food takes particular care with first-rate fresh ingredients – local fish (some of it from the river only yards away), local suppliers, an increasing use of organic and farm produce, vegetables from their own garden, and a fine range of unpasteurised British cheeses. The long-standing hosts share the cooking duties, producing as starters home-made soups (often intriguing combinations like pea and lemon); light, well-flavoured terrines and patés – especially fishy ones like smoked fish cream or haddock roulade. Main courses offer casseroles like venison in red wine with green peppers and wild rabbit in cider or chargrilled steaks, proper fish and chips, and the fish kebab is always worth a try. Bread comes from the renowned Village Bakery at Melmerby. Gorgeous and often unusual puddings too. There's also a daily-changing 5-course table d'hote restaurant menu. Bedrooms are the prettiest feature of the inn, two of them with draped bedheads, another with a four-poster bed, and all individually styled with good-quality fabrics and thoughtful little extras, electric blankets among them. Bathrooms are spotless, with decent toiletries. Satisfying, hearty breakfasts.
Bar Food *12-2 (except Sun), 7-9. Free House.* ***Beer*** *Yates, guest beer. Garden, outdoor*

See over

eating, children's outdoor play area. Accommodation 6 bedrooms, all en suite, £72 (single £55). Children welcome overnight (cot age free if sharing parents' room). Dogs by arrangement. Pub and accommodation closed 2 weeks February and 2 weeks November, 25/26 Dec & 1 Jan. Access, Visa.

CARBOST — Old Inn — B&B

Tel & Fax 01478 640205 Map 2 A3
Carbost Isle of Skye Highland IV47 8SR

On the shores of Loch Harport, and near the Talisker distillery, a charming, chatty little island cottage, popular as a walkers' base. Accommodation is offered in six rooms, all en suite; one family room has a connecting bunk room for children. Occasional entertainment in summer. *Open 11-2.30 (Sun from 12.30), 5-12 (Sat to 11, Sun 6.30-11) & all day in summer. No real ales. Family room. Lochside patio/terrace, children's play area.* ***Accommodation*** *6 rooms, £45 (single £22.50). Children welcome overnight (under-4s stay free in parents' room, 5-9s £6, 10-15s £11). Access, Visa.*

CASTLECARY — Castlecary House Hotel — B&B

Tel 01324 840233 Fax 01324 841608 Map 3 C5
Castlecary Village by Cumbernauld Strathclyde G68 0HD

The original private house has been extended to incorporate a large lively bar with fruit machines, a large selection of draught beers and a more peaceful, partitioned-off 'snug' with plush seating. Good modern bedrooms, popular with the commercial trade, are mostly in a couple of 'cottage' blocks set motel-style around the car park. Comfortable beds have crisp cotton sheets and feather pillows and all rooms have direct-dial phones, remote-control TV, beverage tray, trouser press and fully-tiled bathroom (about half with tub and half with showers). Four single rooms in the main building share a shower room and come at a considerably reduced rate. Two flats have a double and a twin room each (£66 plus £10 per extra adult). Four more rooms have recently been converted from an old building. *Bar open 11-11 (Fri-Sun to 11.30). Free House.* ***Beer*** *Belhaven, Bass, Caledonian Deuchars IPA, three guest beers.* ***Accommodation*** *44 bedrooms, 41 en suite, £45 (Club £55, single £15). Children welcome overnight (0-12yrs free if sharing parents' room), additional bed (£10) and cot available. Access, Amex, Diners, Visa.*

CLACHAN SEIL — Tigh-an-Truish Inn — FOOD B&B

Tel 01852 300242 Map 3 B5
Clachan Seil by Oban Seil Strathclyde PA34 4QZ

Miranda Brunner's fiercely traditional 18th-century inn – right by the single-span 'Bridge over the Atlantic' at the top of Seil Sound – is not signposted from A816, so check your map to find the turning on to B844 (towards Easdale and on to the isle of Luing). Delightfully unchanged (and rather basic) within: boarded nicotine yellow ceiling, old pine bar counter with a wonderful old wooden bar seating arrangement, open fire and twin dartboards. Limited winter menu (perhaps only soup and sandwiches, lunchtime only), but recommended for high-season bar food – home-made soup, venison in Drambuie and cream, beef and mushroom pie, locally-caught prawns, roast lamb and pork, followed by such home-made sweets as chocolate biscuit cake and sticky toffee pudding. Bed and breakfast is available in two good-sized bedrooms, one with bath, the other shower only, with breakfast very much a self-service affair. The inn has its own petrol station "across the way", right nex to the wonderful bridge – well worth a detour, particularly if the delightful, rare purple flowers on it are in bloom (around the end of May or early June). Incidentally, the name means the house of the trousers in Gaelic and refers back to the 1745 Rebellion when soldiers used to change from their trousers to kilts (banned on duty) here.
Open all day in summer, usual hours in winter. ***Bar Food*** *12-2.15, 6-8.30.*
Free House. Beer McEwan's 80/-. Garden, outdoor eating. Family room.
Accommodation *2 bedrooms, both en suite, £40 (single £25). Children welcome overnight, additional beds (£5). Accommodation closed December/January. No credit cards.*

CLACHAN SEIL — Willowburn Hotel — FOOD B&B

Tel 01852 300276 Map 3 B5
Clachan Seil by Oban Isle of Seil Strathclyde PA34 4TJ

A little further down the road from the 'Bridge over the Atlantic' (which dates back to 1792) is this bungalow-style hotel and pubby bar with a lovely garden. In a lovely setting, with lawned gardens leading down to the shore of Seil Sound, the Willowburn is neither

really a pub nor an inn but a small, bungalow-style hotel built in the '60s. There is, however, a pubby bar with pine ceiling, wood-burning stove and bar counter built of local slate (plus picture windows overlooking the water). Good bar snacks feature local seafood like squat lobsters with lemon mayonnaise dip and half-a-pint of prawns, along with spicy bean and vegetable hot pot, Aberdeen Angus steak, gammon steak sautéed in pineapple juice, sandwiches and home-made puds such as hot toffee sponge and chocolate fudge pudding. A few tables outside on the lawn are popular when the weather allows. Both the comfortable residents' lounge and dining-room enjoy fine views across the sound, as do all but one of the neat, well-kept bedrooms with TV, tea-making kit and modern, en-suite bathrooms (four with shower and WC only). *Open 12.30-2, 6-11.* ***Bar Food*** *12.30-2, 6-8.30. Free House.* ***Beer*** *Tartan Special, Younger's 60/-. Garden, outdoor eating.* ***Accommodation*** *6 bedrooms, all en suite, half-board terms only £84 (single £42). Hotel closed Nov-Easter (open for New Year). Access, Visa.*

CRAIL — Golf Hotel — B&B

Tel 01333 450206 Fax 01333 450795 Map 3 D5
4 High Street Crail Fife KY10 3TB

Neat old black and white inn in the centre of town with a choice of bars, one modestly comfortable in red plush, the other more characterful with exposed stone walls and beamed ceiling. Upstairs, five immaculate bedrooms have pretty duvets with matching curtains, pine furniture and neat en-suite shower rooms with WC. All have remote-control TVs and tea/coffee-making facilities but no phones. A further TV with satellite channels is to be found in the comfortable and appealing residents' lounge. *Open 11-12 (Sun 12-12). No real ales.* ***Accommodation*** *5 bedrooms, all en suite, £40. Dogs by arrangement. Access, Visa.*

CROMARTY — Royal Hotel — B&B

Tel & Fax 01381 600217 Map 2 C3
Marine Terrace Cromarty Highland IV11 8YN

Formed out of a row of 18th-century coastguards' cottages facing the Cromarty Firth, the black and white painted 'Royal' is run by welcoming hosts Stewart and Yvonne Morrison and is a hotel of considerable charm. Except in the warmest of weather a real fire burns in the homely lounge off which a Lloyd-Loom-furnished sun lounge looks across the road to the water beyond. The lounge bar features armchairs along with banquettes or you can challenge the locals to a game of pool or darts in the Public Bar. Immaculate, individually decorated bedrooms, each with a sea view, have traditional furniture and crisp pure cotton bedding. Twenty miles from Inverness but only ten yards from the beach and sea!
Bar open 11-12 (Fri to 1am). No real ales (Belhaven Best). Garden, children's play area. Family room. ***Accommodation*** *10 bedrooms, 8 en suite, £55 (single £32). Access, Amex, Visa.*

DUNDEE — Mercantile Bar — A

Tel 01382 225500 Map 3 C5
100 Commercial Street Dundee Tayside DD1 2AG

A large, reconstructed, family-run Victorian bar in an old converted haberdashery shop setting. Over 500 photos and prints with a trading or drinking theme adorn the walls and over 200 malt whiskies and 30 draught beers are on offer. "It's a city centre pub for city centre people". *Open 11-11 (Thu-Sat to midnight, Sun 7-11 only). Free House.* ***Beer*** *McEwan's 80/-, Maclay's 80/-, Burton Ale, Belhaven St Andrew's Ale, Theakston's Best & Bitter, Younger's No.3. Pub closed Sunday lunch, 25 Dec and 1 Jan. Access.*

DYSART — Old Rectory Inn — FOOD

Tel 01592 651211 Map 3 C5
West Quality Street Dysart Fife KY1 2TE

Just a few hundred yards off the main road from Kirkcaldy to Leven, in the pretty village of Dysart, is the imposing single-storey Rectory Inn, resplendent on its corner site perched above the fishing harbour, and with a delightful walled garden. The main bar is beamed, while a second room is served by a large hatch, and there's a third small room through the dining area. Furnishings are a mixture of old solid wood tables and chairs and more modern upholstered bench seating. Dining is very much the thing, and tables are pre-set with mats, fresh flowers and free-range butter. An extensive menu is supplemented by daily specials listed on a blackboard in the main bar. At lunchtime potted beef, haggis Drambuie, smoked ham shank, venison and mushroom casserole: at suppertime vegetable

mulligatawny, boiled leg of ham and asparagus with Stilton sauce. Delicious fresh cream pavlova or bread-and-butter pudding are bar favourites for puddings. Salads are of the help-yourself sort, from around eight different selections at the hatch. Real coffee with accompanying cream is a bonus and of the bottomless sort. Many fellow-lunchers are evidently regulars, on first-name terms with the owner-licensees, who are, however, commendably uncliquey and friendly to strangers. It's also a popular business lunch venue in a small local way. The additional evening dining-room menu is quite different, with lots more meat and fish dishes. A whole Stilton is renewed each week and at least seven wines are served by the glass. Vegetarians are not left out: a choice of four dishes includes rice and vegetable stuffed pancakes with a cheese sauce. *Open 12-3, 6.30-11.* ***Bar Food*** *12-2, (Sun to 2.30), 6.30-9.30. Children over 8 allowed in bar to eat. Free House.* ***Beer*** *McEwan's 80/-. Garden, outdoor eating. Pub closed Sun night and all Mon, 1 week mid-Jan, 2 weeks mid-Oct. Access, Amex, Visa.*

EDINBURGH — Doric Tavern Wine Bar & Bistro — FOOD

Tel 0131-225 1084 Map 3 C6

15-16 Market Street Edinburgh Lothian EH1 1DE

Wine bar style upstairs, particularly as the first encounter is with the little bistro-style eating area; the separate little bar is at the back, often crammed with students and other trendy types. But there's no mistaking it's a pub downstairs, in the spartan public bar, complete with dartboard by the door (watch out when entering). Start with the 'Doric kebab' or mixed seafood chowder, followed by grilled tuna with chili and lime, aubergine and mozzarella grilled with cheese, or haggis, whisky, neeps and tatties. Tremendous atmosphere in the evenings, with deep reds and blues, and candlelight. Eleven wines available by the small or large glass, parking difficult. *Open noon-1am (Fri & Sat to 2am, Sun closed except during Edinburgh festival).* ***Bar Food*** *12-10.30 (limited menu 2.30-6.30).* ***Beer*** *Caledonian Deuchars IPA & Golden Promise (organic). Pub closed 25 & 26 Dec, 1 & 2 Jan. Access, Amex, Visa.*

EDINBURGH — Fishers — FOOD

Tel 0131-554 5666 Map 3 C6

1 The Shore Leith Edinburgh Lothian EH6 6QW

Fishers is a jewel cast up from the sea, an outstanding seafood speciality bar which serves full meals all day, noon to 10.30pm. It's taken root in a renovated corner building at the end of The Shore, at the foot of what looks like an ancient bell-tower or lighthouse. The bar area, in which you can also eat, groups high stools around higher-still tables. Up a short flight of steps, the main eating area features light-wood panelling with night-sky blue tables and chairs, windows half of frosted glass, half giving a view to the harbour and beyond, and all presided over from a great height by a bejewelled mermaid figure. The pricing structure and the variety of food on offer are admirably suited to most appetites and pockets, whether for serious eating or quick snacking. It's worth going the full three rounds from starter to pudding, and make an evening of it, when it's also wise to book. In addition to the photocopied/handwritten menu, a blackboard of daily specials offers a host of starters and main courses which should appeal to more than fish fans alone. Seafood soup competes for attention with seafood gratinée, smoked salmon and smoked halibut on a bed of leeks with caper and red onion dressing, seafood platter or one of the day's specials; goat's cheese salad with sun-dried tomatoes and pine-nut paté with oatcakes. Salads are crunchy, fresh and in plenty – endive, Chinese leaves, tomatoes, radishes, mangetout and spring onions. Choose your dressing from a piquant selection of different vinaigrettes (eg onion, hazelnut or raspberry) thoughtfully provided on each table. If any room remains, there are simple home-made fruit flans, pies and crumbles. Altogether excellent quality and value for money. *Open 11am-1am.* ***Bar Food*** *12-10.30. Free House.* ***Beer*** *three regularly-changing guest beers. Riverside, outdoor eating. Family room. Pub closed 25 Dec, 1 Jan. Access, Amex, Diners, Visa.*

EDINBURGH — Tattler — FOOD

Tel 0131-554 9999 **Fax 0131-226 5936** Map 3 C6

23 Commercial Street Leith Edinburgh Lothian EH6 6JA

To step into the Tattler is to step several decades back into the subdued splendour of Scottish Victoriana – fringed table lamps, some of smoked glass, a bird cage in the window, a chaise longue by the bar and, most charming of all, attentive and old-fashioned courtesy from the bar staff. The bar is popular itself – a gentlemanly local for unhurried chat – but most come to eat. Music is speakeasy 1920s, with live piano some evenings. The walls are

adorned with humorous antique prints and an intricately-carved dark wood fireplace with inset tiles completes the picture. Diners may choose to use the lounge, parlour, snug, restaurant or bar – it's one menu throughout. A very popular starter is cabbage, bacon and Stilton soup – the main course list strikes a good balance between fish and meat dishes: a Dunbar crab salad, grilled swordfish steak, roast beef or lamb on Sundays and the homely 'Leithers prawn and haddie' is an enduring favourite, combining smoked haddock and prawns baked in a cheese sauce. Portions are generous. A plump chicken breast comes stuffed with haggis and served with whisky sauce leaving little room for home-made desserts like banana and toffee cheesecake or the huge coupes of ice cream. Blackboard specials change daily. From 11.30am on Sundays, a full cooked breakfast is served. It's truly first-class value for money: an opportunity to splurge without overspending. *Open 11-1am (Sun from 12.30). **Bar Food** 11-3, 5.30-11. Free House. **Beer** Tetley Bitter, Caledonian 80/- Ale, Maclay's. Family Room. Access, Amex, Diners, Visa.*

EDINBURGH — Waterfront Wine Bar — FOOD

Tel 0131-554 7427 Map 3 C6
1c Dock Place Leith Edinburgh Lothian EH6 6LU

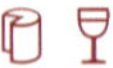

The Waterfront's plain, redbrick exterior gives little indication of what lies within – this is one of Edinburgh's favourite food and drink spots. By the entrance there are about 23 wines served by the glass, as well as unusual beers. Through the first doorway is a low-ceilinged room lit by low lamps, nautical maps and wine-crate panels doubling as wallpaper. Further back, the romantically-sited conservatory ("always fully booked") is attractively overhung by a growing vine, and looks out over the water; beyond this, a narrow pontoon seats a few summer tipplers. Service is casual but friendly; music is kept low and is usually classical or light jazz. Ashtrays are changed with unfailing regularity. There are no fixed or printed menus, and the dishes of the day are all listed on a blackboard: leek and blue cheese soup and grilled sardines persillé make good starters. Dishes with wild mushrooms are regularly featured and they have their own smokehouse. Well above the usual pub grub dishes are, however, surprisingly more basic than they sound – there's brochettes of monkfish and bacon with coriander and crayfish sauce, pink pigeon breast with parmesan risotto and, to finish, créme brulée and chocolate terrine. Coffee is fresh and good (no cappuccino). A very reasonable set-price menu runs along the same lines in winter. Over 150 wines on the list, including some very old Madeiras and pre-war brandies. Book well in advance for a weekend evening. No children under 5 in the pub. *Open 12-11 (Fri & Sat to midnight, Sun from 12.30). **Bar Food** 12-2.30 (Sat & Sun 12-3), 6-9.30 (Fri & Sat to 10). Children over 5 allowed in bar to eat. Free House. **Beer** Caledonian 80/- Ale & Deuchars IPA. Riverside pontoon, outdoor eating. Access, Visa.*

ELIE — Ship Inn — FOOD

Tel 01333 330246 Map 3 C5
The Toft Elie Fife KY9 1DT

Part of a terrace of old cottages down by the harbour with wooden benches around the dark-painted, boarded walls, beamed ceiling and back room with booth seating. There are two restaurant rooms with old dining tables, sturdy kitchen chairs and, on the first floor, a small balcony with coin-operated binoculars for scanning the harbour. The single menu, available throughout, features traditional home-made dishes such as Stilton mushroonms, hot prawn ramekin and green-lipped mussels as starters and scampi thermidor, chicken Rob Roy and steak and Guinness pie for main course. Standard desserts. Blackboard specials, Sunday roast and children's menu and portions available. Cakes and biscuits are served with tea and coffee throughout the day. In July and August, tables on the sea wall opposite the Ship are served by an open-air barbecue. When the tide is out a vast expanse of sand is revealed where the Ship's own cricket team plays regular Sunday fixtures. *Open 11am-midnight, Sun 12.30-11. **Bar Food** 12-2.30 (Sun 12.30-3), 6-9.30 (Sun to 9). Free House. **Beer** Belhaven 80/- Ale, Boddingtons, Theakston's Best. Family room. Pub closed 25 Dec. Access, Visa.*

FOCHABERS — Gordon Arms — B&B

Tel 01343 820508 Fax 01343 820300 Map 2 C3
High Street Fochabers Grampian IV32 7DH

Antlers decorate the exterior of a former coaching inn standing alongside the A96 and a short walk away from the River Spey, while the public bar sports a variety of fishing bric-a-brac – including stuffed prize catches. Simple overnight accommodation is provided by 13 well-equipped bedrooms (TVs, tea-makers, hairdryers and direct-dial telephones), which include both older rooms with large carpeted bathrooms and a number of smaller but quieter ones in the extension. *Open all day 11-11. Free House.* ***Beer*** *Theakston's, guest beer. Garden. Family room.* ***Accommodation*** *13 bedrooms, all en suite, £70 (single £50). Children welcome overnight, additional bed (from £10) and cot available. Access, Amex, Visa.*

GARVE — Inchbae Lodge — FOOD B&B

Tel 01997 455269 Fax 01997 455207 Map 2 B3
Inchbae by Garve Highland IV23 2PH

Zzz...

Now under the new ownership of Patrick and Judy Price, Inchbae Lodge (a few miles north of Garve on the A835 by the Blackwater river on which the hotel has a mile of fishing rights) is a former private hunting lodge with a very pubby bar that is popular with locals. Blue-cushioned banquettes run around the panelled walls, with rustic tables and some exposed stonework. The bar menu, which can cope with most appetites, ranges from a good soup with home-baked bread, Brie and walnut salad and a large platter of West Coast mussels cooked in wine with tomatoes and herbs to omelettes, baked potatoes, pasta dishes, deep-fried scampi with tartare sauce and Scottish steaks with a choice of sauces. There's always a selection of home-made puds and children get their own special menu. Bedrooms, half in the original lodge and half in an adjacent red cedar chalet, have no TVs, radios or telephones to disturb the peace and all but three have shower and WC only. Those in the main building are prettiest with plum and pale green colour scheme, pine and country antique furniture; three rooms have an extra bed. Smokers should choose the chalet rooms. Two lounges, warmed by real fires in winter, are filled with a motley collection of sofas and easy chairs. Children are welcome and a high-tea of children's favourites (leave room for 'no-bit' yogurt or toffee dinosaur biscuits with chocolate dipping sauce) is served at 5pm in the bar before the grown-ups' dinner. The 30-seat, no-smoking dining-room (dinner only, daily-changing four courses, served 7.30-8.30pm) is also recommended in our *1996 Hotels & Restaurants Guide. Open 11-2.30, 5-11 (Sun 12.30-2.30, 6.30-11).* ***Bar Food*** *12-2, 5-8.30, (Sun 12.30-2, 6.30-8.30). No real ales (Belhaven Best).* ***Accommodation*** *12 rooms, all en suite, £60 (single £35). Children welcome overnight (under-18s stay free in parents' room). Garden, children's playground. Pub and accommodation closed 25 & 26 Dec. Access, Visa.*

GIFFORD — Tweeddale Arms — FOOD B&B

Tel 01620 810240 Fax 01620 810488 Map 3 D6
High Street Gifford Lothian EH41 4QU

Probably the oldest building in the village, the black and white Tweeddale Arms lies alongside a peaceful village green. The comfortable, mellow lounge features some old oil paintings while the bar has tapestry-style upholstery and baskets of dried flowers hanging from the old beams. The bar menu, which changes every few weeks, offers a good selection of carefully cooked dishes ranging from some excellent garlic bread, quenelles of paté with oatcakes and cream of cucumber soup to curried lamb Madras and smoked salmon in prawn sauce, with a few home-made puds. Those with a large appetite can try the 'Dutch table rice' – curried chicken shrimps, ham and rice criss-crossed with strips of bacon and crépe plus banana and pineapple fritter and gherkins and tomato salad. Good clean bedrooms have either light or darkwood freestanding furniture and modern en-suite bathrooms. All have TV, direct dial phone, trouser press and a tea/coffee-making kit. Three family rooms. A nice old inn, family run in friendly fashion. *Open 11-11 (Fri & Sat to 12).* ***Bar Food*** *12-2, 7-9. Free House.* ***Beer*** *Burton Ale, Morland Speckled Hen, Greenmantle, two guest beers. Garden, children's play area. Family room.* ***Accommodation*** *17 bedrooms, all en suite, £60 (single £47.50). Children welcome overnight (under-12s stay free in parents' room), additional bed and cot available. Access, Visa.*

GLASGOW **Babbity Bowster** FOOD

Tel 0141-552 5055 **Fax 0141-552 7744** Map 3 C5
16/18 Blackfriars Street Glasgow Strathclyde G1 1PE

A renovated Robert Adam town house in the city's business district is the setting for the splendidly informal and convivial Babbity Bowster (named after a dance), which is not exactly a pub, rather, a light and stylish ground floor café-bar, with a restaurant and hotel attached. There's an outdoor patio with a covered awning that is pulled back when the weather permits. Food of all kinds is served all day – haggis, neeps and tatties, bean hot-pot, spiced chicken stovies, braised oxtail in red wine and onion gravy and a choice of barbecued dishes in the summer. On the first floor, the Schottische Restaurant (also named after a dance) provides lunch, light meals and supper. *Meals from 8am, bar open 11-12 (Sun from 11.30).* ***Bar Food*** *12-11. Free House.* ***Beer*** *Maclay's 70/-, 80/-, Kane's Amber Ale & Oat Malt Stout, guest beer. Patio/Terrace, outdoor eating. Access, Amex, Visa.*

GLASGOW **Upstairs at the Ubiquitous Chip** FOOD

Tel 0141-334 5007 Map 3 C5
26 Ashton Lane Glasgow Strathclyde G12 8SJ

Busy bar above famous the Glasgow restaurant, near to the university and famously trendy and Bohemian. Eating here is largely a vehicle for some serious people-watching and supping from the fine wine list but it's impressive bar food of a resolutely simple kind. Try the filo basket of mixed field mushrooms with cream and nutmeg, flan of peat smoked haddies with rhubarb sauce, vegetarian bridie with red wine and thyme sauce, lamb's kidney suet pudding with rich Madeira gravy and local cheeses including Mull of Kintyre Truckle cheddar and Inverlochy goat's cheese. On Sundays, breakfast is served from 12.30pm. Furstenburg, the heady and delicious unpasteurised German lager served here, is to be treated with respect. *Open 11-11 (Fri & Sat to midnight, Sun from 12.30).* ***Bar Food*** *12-11 (Sun from 12.30).* ***Beer*** *Caledonian 80/- Ale & Deuchars IPA. Closed 25 Dec, 1 Jan. Access, Amex, Diners, Visa.*

GLENDEVON **Tormaukin Hotel** FOOD

Tel 01259 781252 **Fax 01259 781526** Map 3 C5 **B&B**
Glendevon by Dollar Tayside FK14 7JY

Just south of Gleneagles, on the A823, and surrounded by glorious hill country, this ruggedly handsome old white-painted inn is remarkably peaceful, except when it's busy, which is apparently often. The warm and welcoming interior consists of several communicating rooms, all with lots of exposed stone, rough whitewashed walls and ceiling beams. Old settles (one of them beautifully carved), upholstered stools and roundback chairs surround heavy iron-legged tables. Old black and white photographs, colourful plates and pictures adorn the walls, and a splendid open fire makes the Tormaukin an ideal retreat from the chill Scottish winter. Food's a major attraction, to the extent that the bar menu makes a plea for patience at busy times; this printed list is supplemented by a daily specials board. Begin with perhaps deep-fried 'tattie skins', or marinated herring fillets with apple and sour cream salad followed by venison sausages in port and orange sauce, Thai salmon filo parcels baked with ginger, lime coriander and garlic and brown sugar pavlova filled with strawberry and orange compote. Cooking is competent, if unspectacular; fresh local produce makes all the difference. To the other side of the entrance, an exposed stone and beam-laden restaurant features smartly laid polished tables, candle-lit in the evening. A roast is available on Sundays. Scottish cheese is featured on the board and all the puddings are home-made. Bedrooms are extremely comfortable and appropriately styled in keeping with the inn's age. Original features include yet more exposed stone and a generous sprinkling of beams. Floral fabrics match with pretty wallcoverings, furniture is pine and freestanding, beds are comfortable, sheets crisp. Nice local toiletries and plenty of towels compensate for slightly cramped sizes. Four of the rooms, in a converted stable block, are more contemporary in style, and all the bedrooms are named after whiskies (a theme continued in the bar where a fair selection of malts are available). Service is admirably efficient and friendly. *Open 11-11, Sun from 12.* ***Bar Food*** *12-2, 5.30-9.30 (Sun 12-9.30). Free House.* ***Beer*** *Burton Ale, Harviestoun Original 80/-, two guest beers. Patio, outdoor eating.* ***Accommodation*** *10 bedrooms, all en suite (7 with baths, 3 with showers), £60 (single £47). Children welcome overnight (rate depends on age), additional bed & cot available. Hotel closed 2nd and 3rd week January. No dogs. Access, Amex, Diners, Visa.*

GLENELG — Glenelg Inn — FOOD

Tel & Fax 01599 522273 Map 3 B4 **B&B**
Glenelg by Kyle of Lochalsh Highland IV40 8JR

Zzz...

With a fine location on the shore of Glenelg Bay, Christopher Main's sympathetically refurbished inn combines a rustic bar with civilised restaurant and, created out of the old stable block, six spacious bedrooms which have been individually decorated and charmingly furnished with antiques. All have good bathrooms but that with the 'master bedroom' is particularly sybaritic; room number one (£47) is above the bar. The bar menu, for residents only on Sunday, offers main dishes as varied as Oriental chicken stir-fry, seafood chowder and pork stroganoff (only main courses are served in the evening) with the addition of soups, sandwiches and pastries at lunchtime. In the no-smoking, intimate restaurant, the fixed-price dinner menu (served from 7.30 to 9pm, recommended in our *1996 Hotels & Restaurants Guide*) might offer home-made venison liver paté or local prawns grilled in garlic butter followed by Loch Hourn monkfish, pan-fried fillet of Scotch beef or local scallops, then raspberry cranachan or sticky toffee pudding. After dinner, residents repair to the 'morning room' (the first to arrive puts a match to the log fire on cool evenings) where the atmosphere lends itself to conviviality; Victorian paintings and photos, a green leather Chesterfield, stag's head and various antiques and objets d'art make a comfortable setting. Trips can be organised in either the rigid inflatable boat or the inn's trawler yacht Swallow of Glenelg. A large, walled and fenced-in garden overlooks the sea and is safe for children. No dogs in bedrooms. *Open 12-2.30, 5-11.* ***Bar Food*** *(no food Nov-Mar) 12-2.30, 7-9. Garden. No real ales.* ***Accommodation*** *6 bedrooms, all en suite, £77. Children welcome overnight (under-3s stay free in parents' room), additional bed and cot available. Dogs by arrangement. Check-in by arrangement. Pub closed Sun & lunchtimes Nov-Mar, accommodation closed Nov-Mar. No credit cards.*

GLENFARG — Bein Inn — FOOD

Tel 01577 830216 **Fax 01577 830211** Map 3 C5 **B&B**
Glenfarg Tayside PH2 9PY

In front of the river Farg this pebbledash former drovers' inn is five minutes' drive from Junction 9 of the M90 by the A912 south of Perth. Inside has an unfussy and homely feel. There are old, well-worn wing chairs aplenty and a grandfather clock in one corner. The small, uncluttered bar has red plastic upholstered banquettes, wooden chairs and walls littered with clan coat of arms plaques, a large map of Scotland, rugby cartoons, golf prints and a few pieces of horse tack. On the food side, evenings see a concentration on the restaurant and its à la carte menu, whilst in the bar there is a blackboard 'lunch special' (3-courses, eg chilled melon, diced veal and broccoli in white wine sauce, Black Forest Gateau), a lunchtime bar menu including chicken en croute and ham and vegetable ragout, plus a supper menu with similar fare. In addition a new chargrill steakhouse and tapas bar has been opened downstairs. Good overnight accommodation is provided in thirteen bedrooms, 11 of them housed in an extension, the upper floors of which connect with the main building via of a corridor. Ground-floor rooms are the largest, upper rooms very compact. All are furnished in unpretentious fashion with fitted units, matching curtains and duvets, with fully-tiled bathrooms (shower over the bath). The remaining two rooms are in the main house, neither of them en suite, but sharing a well-maintained bathroom. The area is thick with golf courses and hence the Bein is popular with golfers. *Open 11-2.30 (Sun from 12.30), 5-11.* ***Bar Food*** *12-2, 5-9. Free House.* ***Beer*** *Belhaven Sandy Hunter's Traditional Ale. Family Room.* ***Accommodation*** *13 bedrooms, 11 en suite, £56 (single £38). Children welcome overnight, additional bed and cot available. Access, Visa.*

GLENFINNAN — The Prince's House — B&B

Tel 01397 722246 **Fax 01397 722307** Map 3 B4
Glenfinnan by Fort William Highland PH37 4LT

Continue past the Glenfinnan Monument and dramatic railway viaduct on the celebrated A830 Road to the Isles to find this neat little 17th-century former staging inn. Previously called the Stage House, owners Robert and Carole Hawkes are now concentrating on the Bonnie Prince Charlie theme; Glenfinnan is the place where Bonnie Prince Charlie landed from France in 1745 to claim the Scottish throne. Accommodation is offered in eight rooms, all en suite (closed Dec-Mar, no children under 5); some have wonderful views. Head of the clan is the new 'McDonald suite' (£98), closely contested by the 'Chieftains' rooms (£78). Concessions are made to Continental guests at breakfast, when sliced luncheon roll, tomato and cheese are offered (but sliced processed cheese still in its wrapper could be said to lack a certain style in anyone's language). The hotel has fishing rights on

Loch Shiel and several boats are available for hire (£25 per day); mountain bikes are also available for hire. *Open all day 11-11. Free House.* ***Beer*** *Burton Ale in summer.* ***Accommodation*** *9 rooms, all en suite, from £66 (single £43). Accommodation closed Dec-end Jan (exc New Year), weekends only Feb & Mar. Access, Amex, Visa.*

GREENLAW — Castle Inn — FOOD B&B

Tel 01361 810217 **Fax 01361 810500** Map 3 D6
Greenlaw Borders TD10 6UR

Greenlaw is a small town on a major road, not far from Hume Castle and other attractions. The handsome Georgian Castle Inn is the sort of place you could take a variety of people for lunch and feel confident that they would find something to their taste. It is expensive for bar meals, by local standards, and falls into the middle ground of bar meal and restaurant. The Mirror Room, where drinking and dining take place, has a large mirror above a marble fireplace transforming what would otherwise be a hall into a splendid room, with a comfortable sitting area by the fireplace and elegant Georgian windows through which there's a view to well-kept gardens. The octagonal room or the small library make excellent rooms in which to take coffee, and the bar itself is popular with locals on Friday nights and weekend lunchtimes. Family facilities are excellent: high-chairs, baby foods, a Freddy Fox children's menu, books in the library and cheerful, tolerant staff. The printed menu, supplemented by blackboard specials, is certainly very varied, with home-made soups (eg French onion) filled pancakes (curry, turkey, and ham or steak casserole), steak and mushroom pie, lamb chops and a large vegetarian selection. Bread is crusty and fresh (mini-baguettes are used for sandwiches), butter comes in pots, tables are laid with mats rather than cloths, and puddings are displayed in a chill cabinet. A 2-course traditional Sunday lunch is served with a choice of ragout or roast. *Open 12-3, 5.30-11.* ***Bar Food*** *12-2.30 (Sun to 2), 6.30-10 (Sun from 6.30). Free House.* ***Beer*** *Caledonian 80/- Ale, Broughton Greenmantle Ale. Garden. Family room.* ***Accommodation*** *6 bedrooms, 2 en suite (£45, single £22.50). Children welcome overnight (under-2s stay free in parents' room, family room £45/£48), additional bed and cot available. Access, Amex, Diners, Visa.*

INNERLEITHEN — Traquair Arms — FOOD B&B

Tel 01896 830229 **Fax 01896 830260** Map 4 C1
Traquair Road Innerleithen Borders EH44 6PD

Off the main road (well signposted) which runs through Innerleithen and five minutes' walk from the River Tweed is the Traquair Arms Hotel, a handsome stone building on the road leading to St Mary's Loch, which is, incidentally, a delightful journey across country roads to one of the most picturesque parts of the Borders. The bar leads off the hotel reception area; dine (from the à la carte) here, or in the more comfortable dining-room (which also offers a table d'hote in the evenings), or, if weather permits, in the garden. The choice of dining areas and a wide choice of freshly prepared meals is typical of the Traquair Arms' admirable flexibility which also runs to breakfast, morning coffee, afternoon tea and high tea. A well-stocked bar features the Traquair's own Bear Ale on tap, with a teddy bear-clad pump. A variety of omelettes and salads is served in the bar and hot dishes include Finnan Savoury (smoked haddock in cheese, onion and cream sauce), Traquair steak pie (cooked in home-brewed ale), and at least three vegetarian dishes. One benefit of dining in the bar is that the glass doors lead off into the garden, which is enclosed and safe for energetic children. The cheeseboard features Scottish cheeses only. Service is genuine and informal, the atmosphere convivial. Bed and breakfast is recommended – particularly the handsome Scottish morning meal, complete with superb kippers. Children are positively welcomed, even the most boisterous – as they say themselves "we don't turn anyone away here". Traquair House, next door, is well worth a visit – it's a romantic old house with pretty grounds and the old brewhouse; the front gates of Traquair are firmly shut, and will never open again until a Stuart returns to the throne of Scotland. *Open 11-11 (Sun to 12).* ***Bar Food*** *12-9. Free House.* ***Beer*** *Traquair Bear Ale, Theakston's Best, Broughton Greenmantle Ale, occasional guest beer. Garden, outdoor eating.* ***Accommodation*** *10 bedrooms, all en suite, £64 (single £42). Children welcome overnight (0-5yrs free in parents' room, 5-12 yrs 50% adult rate if sharing parents' room), additional bed and cot available. Pub closed 2 days Christmas. Access, Amex, Visa.*

See the **County Round-Up** tinted pages for details of all establishments in county order.

KENMORE — Kenmore Hotel — B&B

Tel 01887 830205 **Fax 01887 830262** Map 3 C5
Kenmore by Aberfeldy Tayside PH15 2NU

Zzz..

The Kenmore claims to be Scotland's oldest inn, dating from 1572, in a lovely Perthshire village overlooking the River Tay; at the east end of Loch Tay on the A827. The Poet's Parlour bar, devoted to Burns, is cosy, with green tartan seats; Archie's Bar is simpler, with glorious views of the river. Bedrooms, 14 in a Victorian gatehouse opposite, vary considerably in decor and furnishings with everything from melamine to antiques. Guests have concessionary use of the swimming pool and leisure facilities at the nearby Kenmore Club. Kenmore attracts both fishermen (they have 3 miles of private beats on the Tay) and golfers. Riverside garden. Family room. ***Accommodation*** *39 bedrooms, all en suite, £117 (half-board only, single £70). Children welcome overnight. Access, Amex, Visa.*

KILBERRY — Kilberry Inn — ★ FOOD B&B

Tel & Fax 01880 770223 Map 3 A6
Kilberry by Tarbert Strathclyde PA29 6YD

An invigorating 16-mile drive down a winding, single-track road with superb views will bring you to this single-storey white cottage located half a mile from the glorious coastline. John and Kath Leadbeater, English chef-proprietors, are vigorously interested in good food, and justifiably proud of their achievements here, in an out of the way spot where the vegetables come via van and taxi, and fresh fish is strangely hard to get. It's very much a dining pub, though locals and others are equally welcome to drop in for a drink. The building was originally a crofting house, and the snugly comfortable little bar, with a peat fire at one end, a wood-burning stove at the other, still has an unpretentious rural style. Leading off at the left, the brighter, plainer dining and family room has good-sized pine dining tables. The daily blackboard-listed short menu (perhaps only four or five main courses at lunchtime) is cheerfully annotated. Typical dishes might include fresh tomatoes stuffed with "locally-caught haggis", a hearty country sausage pie with fresh salad or local salmon fish pie; at night a few fancier dishes are also added: perhaps chunks of rump steak cooked in Theakston's Old Peculier Ale or prime pork fillet cooked in cider with apples. Kath has a famously light hand and the pastry is superb. She also makes the bread as well as a selection of over 25 pickles, jams and chutneys on sale at the bar. Whatever you do, make sure you leave room for one of Kath's delicious fruit pies, which are laid out on the counter as soon as they come out of the oven. Equally scrumptious are the bread-and-butter pudding, fresh lemon cream, grapefruit cheesecake and chocolate fudge. Accommodation is offered in two smart en-suite bedrooms (£55 double, £32.50 single, no smoking, breakfast served 8-9am, no food Sundays apart from breakfast): one double and one twin. Note that the pub is closed in winter and never opens on Sundays. ***Bar Food*** *12.15-2, 6.30-9. Free House.* ***Beer*** *large range of Scottish bottled beers. Family room (no smoking). Inn closed Sun, also mid October-Easter (open at New Year). Access, Visa.*

KILLIECRANKIE — Killiecrankie Hotel — B&B

Tel 01796 473220 **Fax 01796 472451** Map 3 C4
Killiecrankie by Pitlochry Tayside PH16 5LG

Zzz..

Surrounded by glorious central Scotland scenery and in four acres of its own landscaped gardens overlooking the river Garry and the Pass of Killiecrankie this former dower house is a fine, white-painted old property. The reception hall and mahogany-panelled bar (which has a sun-trap extension) of this smart, traditional country hotel have displays of stuffed animals and an upstairs lounge offers various board games plus a variety of books as distractions. Well-equipped pine-furnished bedrooms, all with smart modern bathrooms. Turn off the A9 north of Pitlochry. *Open 11-2.30 (Sun from 12.30), 5.30-11 (Sun from 6.30). Garden. No real ales.* ***Accommodation*** *10 bedrooms, all en suite, £96. Children welcome overnight (under-5s free if sharing parents room), additional bed and cot available. Pub & accommodation closed Jan and Feb. Access, Visa.*

We endeavour to be as up-to-date as possible but inevitably some changes to landlords, chefs and other key staff occur after the Guide has gone to press.

KILLIN — Clachaig Hotel — B&B

Tel 01567 820270 Map 3 B5
Falls of Dochart Killin Central FK21 8SL

18th-century ex-smithy and coaching inn, once closely linked with the McNab clan, and beautifully set overlooking the spectacular Falls of Dochart with the River Tay a five-minute walk down the road. Rather basic inside, with the bar usurped by juke box and pool table. The bedrooms are equipped with TVs, tea/coffee-making facilities and hairdryers on request. The best of them have dramatic views over the Falls. Recent reports, however, are of falling standards. *Open 11-12 (Fri & Sat to 1am). Free House. **Beer** McEwan's 80/-, Theakston's. Garden, outdoor eating. Family room. **Accommodation** 9 bedrooms, 8 en suite, £42 (single £21). Children welcome overnight (under-3s stay free in parents' room). Pub closed 25 Dec. Access, Visa.*

KILMAHOG — Lade Inn — FOOD

Tel 01877 330152 **Fax 01877 331078** Map 3 B5
Kilmahog by Callander Central FK17 8HD

After 60 years of private ownership the Lade Inn is once again part of the surrounding Leny Estate owned by the Roebuck family. One bar to the left of the entrance hall has panelling, pine tables and chairs; there's another bar to the right. The non-smoking dining area has large windows and leads out into the garden. The walls are mainly exposed stone and what looks like mock beams; bars are carpeted throughout, while prints and whisky boxes adorn the walls; the whole effect is clean, fresh and spacious. The new landlords have separated the food operation between a more expensive restaurant à la carte and the 'Wayside Feast' bar menu of which deep-fried haggis with a whisky and grain mustard sauce, fried lamb chop with rosemary gravy and grilled trout with lime butter are typical. Sandwiches at lunchtime only. There are high-chairs for children. ***Bar Food** 12-3.15, 5.30-9.15. Free House. **Beer** Greenmantle, McEwan's 80/-, three guest ales. Garden, outdoor eating. Family Room. Access, Visa.*

See the **County Round-Up** tinted pages for details of all establishments in county order.

KINCARDINE O'NEIL — Gordon Arms Hotel — FOOD B&B

Tel 013398 84236 Map 3 D4
North Deeside Road Kincardine O'Neil Grampian AB34 5AA

An early 19th-century coaching inn of sombre grey stone, the Gordon Arms stands alongside the busy A93, almost opposite the derelict 13th-century village church. Behind a rather anonymous exterior is an inn of warm and informal atmosphere. The main bar area is spacious, sparsely furnished and utterly unpretentious, its high ceiling creating echoes on quiet days, plain-painted walls minimally dotted with pictures, and the part bare-floorboard, part modestly-carpeted floor topped with varying sizes of tables and a motley crew of cushioned chairs. A large rough-stone fireplace is decorated with old cider jars, and the wall above hung with a couple of fishing rods (this is a rich fishing area); there's a piano and splendid antique sideboard. A separate public bar has part panelled walls, old black and white photographs of the area, a television set and electronic games. There are four menus. A short lunch choice carries standard items like steak pie, chicken curry and deep-fried haddock whilst a more interesting and enterprising dinner menu offers the likes of venison and red wine pie, 'black and quack' (roast mallard duck with blackcherries and honey and brandy sauce), salmon and mushroom pie and a choice of steaks being typical: the house special is Highlander steak with haggis and mustard sauce. Those who can't wait can go for the high tea menu whilst a comprehensive and popular vegetarian carte is available at any time. Bread is baked on the premises, and there's a fair selection of organic wines. Puddings are home-made (brandy oyster). They also do a very popular Scottish high tea, in which tea, toast, scones and cakes are included in the price of a main course. The seven bedrooms are comfortable and unfussy. Care has been taken to keep decor and furnishing in keeping with the building's age, and all are of useful size. Some fine pieces of antique furniture are partnered by a worn, but very comfortable armchair. Four of the en-suite rooms have compact shower rooms, and two more have slightly larger bath/shower. *Open 11.30-11 (Thu-Sun to 12). **Bar Food** 12-2.00, 5-9.00 (Summer to 10). Free House. **Beer** Courage, guest beer. Garden/terrace, outdoor eating. **Accommodation** 7 bedrooms, 6 en suite, £45 (single £28). Children welcome overnight, (under-5s stay free in parents' room), additional bed (from £5) and cot available. Access, Amex, Visa.*

KIPPEN — Cross Keys — FOOD

Tel 01786 870293 Map 3 C5 **B&B**

Main Street Kippen Central FK8 3DN

A simple, welcoming Scottish pub with rooms, rather than an inn proper, set in a pleasant rural village not far from Stirling. The locals' public bar is large and basic, with pool table, fruit machine and television; a smaller, long and narrow lounge is where most of the food is served, and a larger family room has high-chairs primed and ready for use. Most of the walls are of exposed stone, colour-washed white, and the furnishings a collection of old, polished tables and chairs. Bar food, chosen from a standard printed menu (perhaps bramble and port liver paté, fresh salmon or steak pie), is enhanced by daily specials, for example breast of chicken with lemon and tarragon or the unique 'humble haddie' pancakes. Soups are thick and warming. Most of the produce is from local suppliers and Kippen's bakery supplies the bread. There's also a small more modern restaurant offering more elaborate fare. If staying the night, ask for one of the rooms under the eaves, which have sloping ceilings and fine views. Bedrooms are simple and homely, with the usual tea and coffee kits, and wash handbasins. Towels of good quality are provided, and there are extra blankets in the wardrobe. Housekeeping in the rooms is usually good. There is no residents' lounge, just the main bars downstairs, busy even midweek with diners and locals. Breakfasts, served on linen-laid tables in the restaurant, are hearty traditional fry-ups (but not too greasy) and service is pleasant and helpful. There's a beer garden, with a children's play area, at the rear with access from both the public and lounge bars. *Open 12-2.30 (Sun from 12.30), 5.30-12.* ***Bar Food*** *12-2 (Sun from 12.30), 5.30-9.30. Free House.* ***Beer*** *Broughton Greenmantle Ale, Younger's No.3. Garden, outdoor eating. Family room.* ***Accommodation*** *3 bedrooms, sharing a bathroom, £39 (single £19.50). Children welcome overnight (under-5s stay free in parents' room). Check-in by arrangement. Pub closed 1 Jan. Access, Visa.*

> Many B&B establishments offer reduced rates for weekend and out-of-season bookings. Always ask about special deals for longer stays. Beware half-board terms in inns where we do not recommend the **FOOD**.

KIRKCALDY — Hoffmans ★ — FOOD

Tel 01592 204584 Map 3 C5

435 High Street Kirkcaldy Fife KY1 2SG

Hoffmans is an extraordinary place. Situated to the east of the town centre (don't be confused by the High Street address), it's an unlikely looking venue for a pub serving imaginative food, but first impressions can deceive. The interior, converted in 1990 by owners Paul and Vince Hoffman, is very smart with subtly toned wall covering, brown upholstered bench seating, polished tables, a large central ceiling fan, angled mirrors, and fake greenery. The attractive seascape and still life oils are courtesy of Hoffman sisters, and rather fine colour photographs from a couple of regulars. But the food is the thing here, and so popular that booking is advised for lunch as well as dinner. And rightly so. Vince Hoffman is so confident in the quality of his raw ingredients that local suppliers are listed at the front of the menu, which is handwritten and changes daily. Often it's not even decided on until just before opening time, when suppliers and fishmongers have been visited and produce assessed. Fish is a particular interest of Vince's, from traditional deep-fried haddock to steak of fresh halibut glazed with a spicy chili and lime dressing. The raw materials are first class (no dye in smoked fish), the handling first rate, and the prices remarkable: at lunchtime, main courses like beef olives, lamb casserole or lemon chicken cost under £5. In the evening, the room is partitioned, half the space reserved for drinkers, the other run as an à la carte bistro, where tables are laid, candles lit, and waitresses serve. Dishes are slightly more expensive, such as breast of duck with rhubarb and onion chutney, loin of lamb with mint and bilberry sauce and steak glazed with creamy whisky and mushroom sauce. Vince's wife Jan makes all the puddings: Dundee Bonnet, ice creams. Capable service is also genuinely friendly, thanks to the Hoffman teamwork. It's not a drinkers' pub and children are encouraged – the idea being to "try to wean them into using pubs for the right reasons". High-chairs and "portions of proper food" are available. *Open 11am-midnight.* ***Bar Food*** *12-2, 7-10. Free House.* ***Beer*** *McEwan's 80/-, guest beer. Pub closed all Sun. No credit cards.*

KIRKCUDBRIGHT Selkirk Arms Hotel FOOD B&B

Tel 01557 330402 **Fax 01557 331639** Map 4 B3
Old High Street Kirkcudbright Dumfries & Galloway DG6 4JG

In 1794 Robert Burns was sufficiently impressed with the food here to compose the Selkirk Grace: "Some have meat and cannot eat; and some would eat that want it; but we have meat and we can eat; and sae the Lord be thanket." If he could see it today he'd find a new lounge-bar/bistro, part of the ambitious plans of owners John and Susan Morris who were also in the business of creating an additional new bar and restaurant as we went to press. However, despite its new setting, the fundamental bar food operation will not be changing. The lunchtime menu will still feature favourites like steak and Guinness pie and fresh haddock alongside baked potatoes and a range of open sandwiches and toasties. The evening à la carte featuring starters like deep-fried breaded Brie with Cranberry sauce, main courses like supreme of chicken stuffed with herb cream, plus fish, salad and grill sections will also remain. The majority of the well-kept bedrooms have light oak fitted furniture; all have TVs, direct-dial phones, hairdryers, beverage trays and modern bathrooms. There's also a particularly attractive, sheltered garden with tables for summer eating. *Open 11-12.* ***Bar Food*** *12-2, 6-9.30.* ***Beer*** *three guest beers. Garden, outdoor eating.* ***Accommodation*** *16 bedrooms, all en suite, £70 (single from £45). Children welcome overnight (under-5s stay free in parents' room), additional bed and cot available. Dogs by arrangement. Access, Amex, Diners, Visa.*

KIRKTON OF GLENISLA Glenisla Hotel FOOD

Tel & Fax 01575 582223 Map 3 C4
Kirkton of Glenisla nr Alyth Tayside PH11 8PH

This old coaching inn is set high up in Glenisla, one of the 'Angus Glens', and dates back over 300 years to the days before the Jacobite rebellion. A warm welcome avails today's travellers in the split-level, beamed bar with its real fire (even in summer on chilly days) and posies of heather and wild flowers on the tables. At lunchtime the daily-changing menu offers favourites like haddock and chips, ploughman's platters, Aberdeen Angus steaks, macaroni cheese and Cumberland sausage. At night, ever-popular main courses such as breast of duck with morello sauce, trio of lamb with mint sauce and grilled Esk salmon may be preceded by King Orkney scallops steamed in white wine with shallots and chicken liver and Cognac paté, and followed by bread-and-butter pudding and fruit compote. Afternoons bring cream teas with scones fresh from the oven and home-made jam. Children have their own games room with a pool table. *Open 11-11 (Fri & Sat 12).* ***Bar Food*** *12.30-2.30, 6.30-8.45.* ***Beer*** *Theakston's Best, McEwan's 80/-, Boddingtons. Garden, outdoor eating. Family room. Pub closed 25 & 26 Dec. Access, Visa.*

KYLESKU Kylesku Hotel FOOD B&B

Tel 01971 502231 **Fax 01971 502313** Map 2 B2
Kylesku Highland IV27 4HW

Zzz...

By-passed by the new bridge over Loch Glencoul in the early 80s, the modest Kylesku Hotel enjoys a glorious location down by the old ferry slipway where today small boats land the local seafood that forms the backbone of the blackboard menu in a rather unprepossessing bar. Mussels baked in garlic, scallops, grilled salmon, fresh Lochinver haddock, langoustines grilled in their shells and served with a spicy mayonnaise dip and locally smoked salmon. Other items include home-made terrines, omelettes, roast chicken and fries and a few home-made puds. The hotel now does boat trips up to the Eas Coul Aulin, Britain's highest waterfall. Five of the bedrooms are en suite, two with private facilities. The bar has 40 malts plus two speciality 'whiskies of the week'. Open all year but ring to check first if you want to stay between November and February. *Open 10.30-11.* ***Bar Food*** *11-2.30, 6-9.45. Free House.* ***Beer*** *(Tennent's 80/-, McEwan's Export). Garden, outdoor eating, barbecues. Family room.* ***Accommodation*** *7 bedrooms, 5 en suite, £48 (single £25). Children welcome overnight (under-6s stay free in parents' room). Access, Visa.*

LOCH ECK Coylet Inn FOOD

Tel & Fax 01369 840426 Map 3 B5 **B&B**

Loch Eck nr Kilmun Strathclyde PA23 8SG

Owner Richard Addis has been here 25 years now and thankfully little has changed in that time, least of all the really special setting – just the west coast road to Dunoon, shrouded in trees, separates the pretty white building from the glorious beauty of Loch Eck and the hills beyond. Not another house can be seen in any direction; be early for a window seat in the bar or dining-room. Inside, it charms in an unaffected way. The public bar is handsome and cosy, and friendly local ghillies and others gather on bar stools to pass the time of day. Through the hall is an attractively simple little dining bar, where families (even tiny babies) are welcome. Through into the dining-room proper are half a dozen tables (one, large group size, in the prize window spot), wheelback chairs and a piano. The food is a mix of standard bar menu stuff, from sandwiches (even in the evening) and ploughman's platters to vast, well-cooked platefuls of haddock and chips, or sizzling steaks; the quality draws both locals and tourists. But it's worth choosing from the specials board – a twice-daily changing short blackboard list. It might typically feature home-made liver paté and Scotch broth, local game in season, steak and kidney pie, salmon fishcakes, grilled local salmon or trout at lunchtime. In the evening, the board may feature mushrooms au gratin, venison collops in port and red wine sauce and langoustine risotto. If the risotto is on, you should order it and enjoy a generous pile of tender, fresh Loch Fyne langoustines in a delicious sauce with garlic, cream, wine and herbs: a true and memorable bargain. Vegetables are also exceptional: crisp mangetout, perfect new potatoes and tender carrots all included in the main-course price. Puddings, all home-made, are also good, and come in hefty portions: chocolate roulade, pineapple cheesecake or a real apple pie are typical of the choice. Upstairs are three tiny little bedrooms which offer simple comfort. All have sash windows with views over the loch, and pretty cottagey print paper and fabrics. The twin is a bit bigger than the two doubles. The shared bathroom, a very attractive, immaculately clean, carpeted and pine-panelled room, is bigger than any of them. Breakfasts are ungreasy and commendably accommodating of personal preferences. Finally, a word about the service, which is genuine and friendly from both the resident owners and their few, able staff. Lochside garden. *Open 11-2.30 (Sun from 12.30), 5-11 (Fri & Sat to 12 Sun from 6.30).* ***Bar Food*** *12-2 (Sun from 12.30), 5.30-9.30 (Sun 7-9). Free House.* ***Beer*** *Younger's No. 3, McEwan's 80/-, Caledonian Deuchars IPA. Garden, outdoor eating. Family room.* ***Accommodation*** *3 bedrooms, sharing facilities, £35 (single £17.50). Children welcome overnight. Check-in by arrangement. No dogs. No credit cards.*

MARKINCH Town House Hotel FOOD

Tel 01592 758459 **Fax 01592 741238** Map 3 C5 **B&B**

High Street Markinch Fife KY7 6DQ

Framed music hall song-sheets and old photographs of the locals and the locality grace the watered silk-effect walls of the plush bar/lounge at this town-centre inn which is now very much designed for eating rather than just drinking. Choose from the à la carte or an imaginative table d'hote menu. Scottish favourites such as haggis and Glayva terrine with mustard and fillet of Tay salmon stand alongside such exotic fare as chicken fillet stuffed with banana topped with peanut crush and beef Madeira plus seafood crepe, prawn fritters, steaks, and macaroni and broccoli bake. Puds are also unusual: bread-and-butter pudding flan and apple and custard crumble tart. Spicing and flavours are less adventurous than the choice of dishes but cooking is careful and sound. Waitress service. Four, bright, well-kept bedrooms offer TV and tea/coffee-making facilities plus little extras like tissues and cotton wool balls but no telephones. Three have en-suite bathrooms, the other a private but not en-suite shower room with WC. *Open 12-11.* ***Bar Food*** *12-2, 6-9. Free House. No real ales.* ***Accommodation*** *4 bedrooms, 3 en suite £50 (Single £40). Check-in by arrangement. Pub closed 25 & 26 Dec, 1 & 2 Jan. Access, Amex, Diners, Visa.*

MELROSE Burts Hotel FOOD

Tel 01896 822285 **Fax 01896 822870** Map 4 C1 **B&B**

Market Square Melrose Borders TD6 9PN

Located 200 yards from the River Tweed – "Scotland's favourite salmon river" – is the imposing 18th-century inn at the heart of still-fairly-sleepy, affluent Melrose. Bar food shows an appetizing balance of the comfortingly traditional and modern aspirational – and this philosophy could be said to sum up the whole hotel. A typical meal is parfait of turkey

with Cumberland sauce followed by pan-fried liver, and, to finish, lime, orange and grapefruit with strawberry charlotte royale. Vegetarian options available. Good Scottish produce is featured on two table d'hote menus in the refurbished restaurant. Sunday lunch is always a roast. The bedrooms are light, contemporary and in pristine order; five have just shower/WC. Over 40 malt whiskies, eight wines by the glass. ***Bar Food*** *12-2, 6-9.30 (Fri & Sat to 9.30). Free House.* ***Beer*** *Belhaven 80/- Ale, Courage Directors, guest beer. Garden, outdoor eating.* ***Accommodation*** *21 bedrooms, all en suite, £74 (single £43). Children welcome overnight (under-6s stay free in parents' room). Pub closed 25 & 26 Dec. Access, Amex, Diners, Visa.*

MOFFAT — Black Bull — B&B

Tel 01683 220206 **Fax 01683 220483** Map 4 C2
Churchgate Moffat Dumfries & Galloway DG10 9EG

Modernised 16th-century street-side local with a beer garden outside and duckpond nearby in a curiously old-fashioned, isolated little spa town, whose life blood is coach party tourism. There is now a total of eight bedrooms – four look on to the courtyard and four on to the churchyard opposite. Each bedroom has a different colour scheme and is fully equipped with TV, telephone (in en-suite rooms), and tea/coffee-making facilities. Games room for children. 100 malt whiskies at the bar "... although it might be 99 after last night!". *Open 11-11 (Fri & Sat to 1 am).* ***Beer*** *Theakston's Best, McEwan's 80/-, two weekly-changing guest beers. Garden. Family Room.* ***Accommodation*** *8 bedrooms, 6 en suite, from £40 (single £25). Children welcome overnight (under-14s stay free in parents' room), additional bed and cot available. No dogs. Access, Visa.*

MONYMUSK — Grant Arms Hotel — FOOD B&B

Tel 01467 651226 **Fax 01467 651494** Map 3 D4
The Square Monymusk Inverurie Grampian AB51 7HJ

With 6,000 acres of rough and driven shooting and 10 miles of salmon and trout fishing on the river Don this is very much a sporting inn as the decor of the panelled bar – antlers, stag's head, stuffed bird and old fishing rods – confirms. A typically solid, unspectacular 18th-century Scottish inn on the village green, the bedrooms are clean and bright if not luxurious. All have radio alarms, telephones and tea/coffee-making facilities but no televisions (there is one in the residents' lounge). The bar menu offers something for most tastes – fresh oysters, fish soup, farmhouse mixed grill and steaks plus some slightly more exotic concoctions. *Open 11-2.30 & 5-11 (Sun 12-11).* ***Bar Food*** *12.30-2, 6.30-9. Free House.* ***Beer*** *Scottish & Newcastle 80/-, two guest beers. Garden, outdoor eating, children's play area. Family room.* ***Accommodation*** *16 bedrooms, 7 en suite £62 (single £43). Children welcome overnight. Access, Amex, Visa.*

NETHERLEY — Lairhillock Inn — FOOD

Tel 01569 730001 **Fax 01569 731175** Map 3 D4
Netherley Stonehaven Grampian AB3 2QS

Standing alone surrounded by fields, the Lairhillock is easily spotted from the B979, thanks to the large white INN daubed on its roof. The closest major village to the inn is Peterculter, some four miles to the north; Netherley's a mile to the south. Formerly a farmhouse, the original building is 17th-century, extensions are in sympathy, and the interior is full of old rustic atmosphere. The large lounge is dominated by a central log-burning fireplace; walls are half-panelled, and exposed floorboards covered with numerous rugs. The public bar, in the oldest part, is by far the most characterful room, with its exposed stone, panelling, open fire, old settles and bench seating, every kind of horse tack, polished brasses and numerous other bits and pieces. Bar food is certainly taken seriously at the Lairhillock, where only fresh produce is used, cooked to order. The menu carries a fair choice, changing daily. Typically there might be wild boar terrine, 'Brewer's grill' (haggis, black pudding and bacon with apple sauce), bratwurst sausage with mushroom and onion sauce. The hugely popular sticky toffee pudding ('without which the place would fall apart') and clootie dumpling form the foundations of the pub's daily-reconstructed dessert menu. It gets extremely busy, especially on Friday and Saturday evenings. Across from the main building, in the old stables, is the evening restaurant, with its high-beamed ceiling, stone walls, red-tiled flooring, candlelight, piano player, solid polished tables and a wide and interesting choice of dishes too. A variety of Scottish cheeses is always available. Service is pleasantly informal but always efficient. A conservatory with panoramic views furnished

with Lloyd Loom tables and chairs provides an ideal room for families to eat. *Open 11-2.30, 5-11 (Fri & Sat to 12, Sun from 6).* ***Bar Food*** *12-2, 6-9.30 (6-10 Fri/Sat). Free House.* ***Beer*** *Courage Directors, Thwaites Craftsman, McEwan's 80/-, Boddingtons, Flowers, three guest ales. Patio/Terrace, outdoor eating. Access, Amex, Diners, Visa.*

NEW ABBEY — Criffel Inn — B&B

Tel 01387 850305 Map 4 B2
New Abbey nr Dumfries Dumfries & Galloway DG2 8BX

☺

After four decades of fine service Jenny McCulloch has finally retired and sold the Criffel. However, it's a solid Victorian place where things don't change much from year to year, and new landlords the McAllisters are aware that they've inherited not just a pub but a philosophy, and, for the moment, plan to change nothing. Upstairs, the residents' lounge has a domestic feel and bedrooms, with wood-effect melamine fitted furniture, go in for a medley of floral patterns. Two bedrooms are en suite, one has a 'tin' shower cubicle in the room and two others share an immaculate bathroom. *Open 11-2.30 & 5-11 (Fri & Sat to midnight, Sun 12.30 11pm). No real ales (Belhaven). Patio.* ***Accommodation*** *5 bedrooms, 2 en suite, £46 (single £20). Children welcome overnight (under-5s stay free in parents' room, 6-12s half-price), additional bed and cot available. Access, Visa.*

NEWTON STEWART — Creebridge House Hotel — FOOD B&B

Tel 01671 402121 **Fax 01671 403258** Map 4 A2
Minnigaff Newton Stewart Dumfries & Galloway DG8 6NP

☺

Formerly home to the Earls of Galloway, the 18th-century, stone-built Creebridge House is set in very pretty gardens. It's a hotel rather than an inn but the bar, with low ceilings, reclaimed pitch pine timber furniture, old oak beams and horse-brasses has a comfortable country pub feel about it. There's a good range of bar meals from a snacky lunchtime only menu (including sandwiches and baked potatoes) to the more substantial pan-fried sirloin of Gollam beef with mushroom and wine sauce, fresh salmon with herb and lemon crust and tomato coulis and "posh fish and chips" (local haddock fillet in real ale batter) served in newspaper on your plate. There's a separate restaurant offering set price menus. Bedrooms which include four family suites are all well kept and equipped with TVs (some remote-controlled), telephones, hairdryers and tea/coffee-making kits – although room service is also available throughout the day and evening. Good, modern en-suite bathrooms, all with shower and tub plus the normal toiletries. Day rooms include an elegantly proportioned Georgian lounge. Visitors are invited to sample 'a taste of Scotland' from a choice of some 40 malt whiskies. *Open 12-2.30, 6-11 (Fri, Sat & Sun to 11.30).* ***Bar Food*** *12-2 (Sun from 12.30), 6-9 (Sat to 10, Sun from 7). Free House.* ***Beer*** *Burton, Boddingtons, Orkney Dark Island, two guest beers. Garden, outdoor eating. Family room.* ***Accommodation*** *20 bedrooms, all en suite, £75 (single £40). Children welcome overnight (under-12s free if sharing in parents' room), additional bed and cot available. Access, Amex, Visa.*

PORT APPIN — The Pierhouse — FOOD B&B

Tel 01631 730302 **Fax 01631 730521** Map 3 B5
Port Appin Pier nr Appin Strathclyde PA38 4DE

Turn off A828 and head on down to the end of the road where you'll find the distinctive twin round-fronted buildings of the low, white Pierhouse; its setting is delightfully tranquil and picturesque, right on the water's edge of Loch Linnhe, where the little Lismore passenger ferry docks. The terrace, the picture-windowed main bar room (open all day) and small, residents' sitting room make the most of the evolving weather scene that plays out over the towering Morvern Hills beyond the Isle of Lismore. In the four small, unpretentious dining areas (one is no-smoking) the best few tables are at the picture windows, although those by the warming fire are an attraction in winter; bright, interesting artwork – from George Devlin and Robin McGregor – adorns the whitewashed walls. Callum Macleod provides energetic, happy service with a smile and a sense of humour, taking obvious pride in his mother Sheila's particularly good cooking. 'Clam chowder' made with scallops and salmon stock (but, seemingly, with no clams) is quite superb, as are cracked clab claws with home-made mayonnaise, Lismore oysters and large langoustines from Loch Linnhe (some way from Dublin Bay – as described on the menu). Seafood dishes may be served with cheese and wine, lemon and butter or garlic butter sauces, but when it's so fresh (dark blue Mull lobsters, oysters and giant crabs are kept in submerged creels off the pier) and the quality so good it seems appropriate to let the natural ingredients' flavours

speak for themselves. Half a dozen Aberdeen Angus beef, venison and chicken dishes complete the main-course picture. Those puddings that are home-made, such as bread-and-butter pudding made with French bread or a light, bitter chocolate roulade, are the ones to choose. Fine bar snacks are served at lunchtime only. If it's really quiet in winter you may need to tell them you're coming. Eleven smart, pine-furnished bedrooms are in a sympathetically designed two-storey building to one side of the former ferry house; the front bedrooms have glorious loch and island views, but the bathrooms are windowless. A large family room has a double and a single bed (plus room for a cot) together with good hanging and shelf space. Generous breakfasts. Owners Alan and Sheila Macleod and family are most hospitable; they clearly enjoy making their living in such a glorious setting and thoroughly deserve our 1996 Pub Hosts of the Year Award. Advance arrangements can be made to see nearby Castle Stalker and basking seals by boat. Yacht moorings available for diners and overnight guests. Disabled facilities. *Open 11-11.* ***Bar Meals*** *12-3, 6.30-9.30.* ***Accommodation*** *11 bedrooms, all en suite, £70 (family room £80). Children welcome overnight, additional cot provided. Bicycle and boat hire, moorings. Accommodation closed 25 Dec. No dogs. Access, Visa.*

PORTPATRICK — Crown Hotel — FOOD B&B

Tel 01776 810261 **Fax 01776 810551** Map 4 A2
North Crescent Portpatrick Stranraer Dumfries & Galloway DG9 8SX

Right down by the harbour, the blue and white-painted Crown is a bustling, friendly place where the several unpretentious rooms that form the bar – with a real fire even in summer on chilly days, and a motley collection of prints above dado panelling – contrast with a stylishly informal restaurant and smart, appealing bedrooms. The latter have loose rugs over polished parquet floors, a variety of good freestanding furniture and attractive floral fabrics along with pristine bathrooms and the standard modern necessities of direct-dial phone and TV; there is one family suite. Restaurant and bar share the same menu (except for the basket meals and sandwiches that are served in the bar only), which majors on seafood. Chef Robert Campbell knows that the lobster and crabs are fresh because he's out in his boat at 6 o'clock each morning to collect them. Much of the other fish is bought direct from the Fleetwood trawlers that call in at Portpatrick to unload their catches. Grilled scallops wrapped in bacon, moules marinière, prawns and sweet pickled herring, whole plaice with almonds and chips, vegetarian pancake and beef and vegetable casserole are a few examples from a longish menu. Service is swift and efficient, no smoking in the 40-seated conservatory/restaurant area. *Open 11-11.30.* ***Bar Food*** *12-2 (Sat & Sun to 2.30), 6-10. Free House.* ***Beer*** *S&N 70/- & 80/-, Theakston's. Garden, outdoor eating.* ***Accommodation*** *12 bedrooms, all en suite, £70 (single £35). Children welcome overnight (under-4s stay free in parents' room, 4-10s £10), additional bed & cot available. Access, Visa.*

RATHO — Bridge Inn — FOOD

Tel 0131-333 1320 Map 3 C6
27 Baird Road Ratho Lothian EH28 8RA

Starting life as a farmhouse and becoming a hostelry when the Union Canal was built alongside, the Bridge Inn fell into decline along with the canal and was almost derelict when taken over by the irrepressible Ronnie Rusack some 23 years ago. Not content with just reviving the Inn, Ronnie has been instrumental in making some seven miles of the canal navigable again and runs two restaurant barges, specially adapted barges to give the disabled trips along the canal (a charity he founded and which has now spread to other Scottish canals), a boat for short pleasure trips and other smaller craft for hourly hire (picnic hampers can be provided); he has even established a duck breeding programme! Inside, the original Inn features boarded walls and a collection of the many old bottles found when clearing the canal; a family-orientated extension (the 'Pop Inn') features wheelback chairs and views over the water. One can choose from the Pop Inn's informal menu throughout the day – Bargees broth, seafood basket, 'roast of the day', home-made burgers, gammon steak with tangy peach sauce and various locally made puds – or from the à la carte menu served lunch and evening in the bar, which becomes fairly restauranty in the evening with cloths on the tables. Steaks are a good bet here with good Scottish meat cooked on an open grill in full view and a good choice of sauces. Children have their own special menu of favourites (with the likes of fish fingers, chicken drumsticks and fruit jelly and ice cream) as do the over 60s (with the 'Golden Years' menu) should they wish it. There's an 'adult-powered' carousel on the patio, a 'pirate boat' play area in the grounds, proper baby-changing and nursing facilities (that come complete with complimentary nappies and baby

powder etc) and plenty of high-chairs and booster seats. There is hardly room to list everything that goes on here, the annual Scottish Open Canal Jump Competition is held each June and before Christmas there are special 'Santa Cruises' to a 'grotto' built each year on an island by the local art college. Five miles from Edinburgh airport. *Open noon-11 (Fri & Sat 11am-12pm, Sun 12.30-11).* ***Bar Food*** *Noon-9.30 (Sun 12.30-8). Free House.* ***Beer*** *Belhaven 80/- Ale, guest beer. Garden, outdoor eating, children's play area. Access, Amex, Diners, Visa.*

St Andrews — Grange Inn — FOOD

Tel 01334 472670 **Fax 01334 478703** Map 3 D5
Grange Road St Andrews Fife KY16 8LJ

Part of a group of pretty little old cottages about a mile out of town (to the south-east) and with fine views over St Andrews and the Tay Estuary to the Angus Hills beyond. The Grange Inn is now almost exclusively a restaurant although there is a tiny atmospheric bar with flagstone floor, ancient fireplace and beamed ceiling. Also recommended in our *1996 Hotels & Restaurants Guide*, three separate dining-rooms are cottagey with bare stone walls and a charming mix of rustic and antique furniture. The menu sticks mainly to fairly straightforward grills and the excellent local seafood, with details of the day's catch appearing on a blackboard menu along with seasonal items like asparagus. Sticky toffee pudding, chocolate roulade and crème brulée exhaust the pudding menu although there is also always some Stilton and a couple of Scottish cheeses to be had along with wheat wafers or oatcakes. Friendly, welcoming atmosphere. *Set L £9.50/£11.95 (Sun £10.50/£12.95).* ***Bar Food*** *12.30-2.15, 6.30-9.15.* ***Beer*** *McEwan's 80/-. Garden. Family room. Pub closed Mon & Tue Nov-Mar. Access, Amex, Diners, Visa.*

> We only recommend food (Bar Food) in those establishments highlighted with the **FOOD** symbol.

St Boswells — Buccleuch Arms Hotel — FOOD

Tel 01835 822243 **Fax 01835 823963** Map 4 C1 **B&B**
The Green St Boswells Borders TD6 0EW

Alongside the main A68, this substantial red stone inn/hotel dates back to the 1700s when this was one of the main coaching routes between Scotland and England. A spacious wood-panelled bar boasts pink draylon upholstery and a nicely varied bar menu available throughout the day: home-made chicken liver paté, fillet of haddock and various home-made puds. For residents there is an elegantly proportioned lounge. Bedrooms are in good order, with traditional darkwood furniture and colourfully matching duvet covers and curtain. All have TV, telephone and tea/coffee-making facilities (although room service is also offered) and all but one have decent en-suite bathrooms. Rooms to the rear are quieter but there is little or no traffic noise at night. Friendly staff create a pleasant atmosphere. *Open 11-11 (Sun from 12).* ***Bar Food*** *12-2, 6-9 (to 10 Fri & Sat). Free House.* ***Beer*** *Broughton Greenmantle Ale. Garden, outdoor eating. Family room.* ***Accommodation*** *18 bedrooms, 17 en-suite, £68 (single £38). Children welcome overnight (under-14s stay free in parents' room). Access, Visa.*

St Mary's Loch — Tibbie Shiels Inn — FOOD

Tel 01750 42231 Map 4 C1
St Mary's Loch Borders TD7 5NE

The Tibbie Shiels Inn itself is a lovely whitewashed single storey cottage with add-ons, on the shore of St Mary's Loch, in the glorious Yarrow valley. Tibbie Shiels started the Inn in 1826 and it's now famous throughout the Borders and elsewhere. It can be recommended for three main things: first, the atmospheric bar, busy with friendly locals and fishing and sailing types, second the quality of the meat dishes (Scottish lamb and Aberdeen Angus beef), and third the situation of the Inn itself: the large dining-room overlooks the beautiful loch and surrounding hills in this utterly remote and enchanting place. Dishes include spicy chicken and rice, holy mole chili, Yarrow trout, 8oz lamb chop, supreme of chicken with apricot, Pernod and walnut sauce, venison in red wine and home-made cloutie dumpling. The Tibbie is an excellent place to stop after a sojourn on the Southern Upland Way. Five en-suite rooms are available for bed and breakfast (£46). *Open 11-11 (Fri & Sat to midnight, Sun from 12.30).* ***Bar Food*** *12.30-2.30, 4-8.30. Free House.* ***Beer*** *Belhaven 80/- Ale, Broughton Greenmantle Ale. Patio/terrace, outdoor eating. Family room. Pub closed on Monday Nov-Easter. Access, Visa.*

SHERIFFMUIR — Sheriffmuir Inn — FOOD

Tel 01786 823285 **Fax 01786 823969** Map 3 C5
Sheriffmuir nr Dunblane Central FK15 0LN

Built just 6 months before the battle of Sheriffmuir was fought almost literally on its doorstep between the Jacobites and the Hanoverians, the Inn has a wild and lovely location high up in the Ochil Hills, yet is easy to reach and well signposted from the main A9. Inside, all is neat and comfortable with pink plush upholstery, a new fireplace and a warm welcome. Go for the home-made items from a menu that ranges from ploughman's platters, filled baked potatoes (lunchtime only), garlic mushrooms and good freshly-made soups to steak and Guinness pie, Mexican nacho chicken, scampi, haddock and steaks.
A daily-changing blackboard menu adds a few more dishes like a hearty game casserole, trout and beef stroganoff. *Open 11.30-2.30, 5.30-11 (Sat 11.30-11 & Sun 12-11).* ***Bar Food*** *11.30-2.30, 5.30-9. Free House.* ***Beer*** *Burton Ale, Alloa, guest beers. Garden, outdoor eating, children's play area. Family room. Access, Visa.*

STONEHAVEN — Marine Hotel — FOOD — B&B

Tel 01569 762155 **Fax 01569 766691** Map 3 D4
9 The Shorehead Stonehaven Grampian AB3 2JY

Down by the harbour, the ground-floor bar of the Marine Hotel is very pubby with boarded walls, copper-topped tables, games machine, juke box, pool table and a changing selection of real ales. The same menu is served here as in the lounge/bar and in the more family-oriented, first-floor dining-room with its blue nautical decor and waitress service. It carries standard pub fare which people come back for – golden fried haddock, chili with garlic bread, steaks and salads – while an exotic blackboard offers baltis, curries and Mexican dishes. For children there are the usual fish finger/pizza offerings and a couple of high-chairs. Six modest but clean bedrooms (the two largest are family rooms with cots available) all have harbour views and are furnished with fitted white melamine units and matching duvets and curtains, have shower cabinets in the rooms but share two loos. All have phones, televisions and beverage kits. *Open 11-11.45 (Sun from 12).* ***Bar Food*** *12-2, 5-9.30 (to 9 in winter). Children welcome overnight (under-3s stay free in parents' room, 3-12s £5). Free House.* ***Beer*** *Bass, Timothy Taylor, five guest beers. Family room.* ***Accommodation*** *6 bedrooms, £37.50 (single £27.50). Access, Amex.*

STRATHBLANE — Kirkhouse Inn — B&B

Tel 01360 770621 **Fax 01360 770896** Map 3 B5
Glasgow Road Strathblane Central G63 9AA

Zzz...

Substantial inn/hotel on the A81 just south of town at the foot of the Campsie Fell (popular with hill walkers). Bedrooms are done out in a variety of pleasant colour schemes, those at the back have 'woodchip' walls, and most have either light or darkwood units. All the usual hotel facilities are here (remote-control TV, trouser press, beverage tray) plus a room service menu that runs to hot meals 24 hours a day. En-suite bathrooms all have tubs. Downstairs, choose between the cocktail bar with brown plush banquette seating or the large public bar that, with its new tartan carpet, is less basic than its designation might suggest but does come with pool table, fruit machine and juke box. Friendly staff. *Bar open 11-11 (Fri & Sat to midnight, Sun from 12.30). Free House.* ***Beer*** *Maclay's 80/-. Garden, beauty salon.* ***Accommodation*** *15 rooms, all en suite, £73 (suite £82, single £55). Children welcome overnight (under-12s free if sharing parents' room), additional bed and cot available. Access, Amex, Diners, Visa.*

Many **B&B** establishments offer reduced rates for weekend and out-of-season bookings. Always ask about special deals for longer stays. Beware half-board terms in inns where we do not recommend the **FOOD.**

SWINTON — Wheatsheaf Hotel — FOOD B&B

Tel & Fax 01890 860257 Map 3 D6
Main Street Swinton Borders TD11 3JJ

The village of Swinton is six miles north of Coldstream, on the way to nowhere, and is easy to miss. The Wheatsheaf, dominating this simple Scots farming hamlet, overlooks the plain little village green and has very limited parking; at busy periods, the main street is full up with cars. This is very much a dining pub (drinking – and smoking – go on in the pool-tabled, fruit-machined public bar at the back, so separate from the food operation that most visitors aren't even aware it exists) with a very well-regarded restaurant, the Four Seasons, and it's wise to book even for bar meals, such is the reputation of the pub in the Borders. The emphasis is on fresh food: a menu reproduced on one blackboard, daily specials listed on another – moules marinière and marinated herrings with dill to start braised oxtails with root vegetables, grilled langoustines in garlic butter and breast of wild wood pigeon forrestière for main course with a choice of home-made puddings (eg fudge and drambuie ice cream) to finish. Tables are laid with cloths and place mats; freshly baked wheaten rolls are presented as a matter of course, and butter comes in a slab on a saucer, with no foil packets or sauce sachets in sight. Salads are imaginative and fresh. Service, from uniformed waitresses, is assured. All bedrooms have modern facilities. No smoking in the sun-lounge/dining-room. ***Bar Food** (except Mon) 12-2, 6-9.30 (Sun 12.30-2.15, 6.30-9). Free House. **Beer** Broughton Greenmantle Ale, guest beer. Garden, outdoor eating, children's play area. **Accommodation** 4 bedrooms, 3 en suite, £60 (single £42). Children welcome overnight (under-5s stay free in parents' room, 5-10s £5), additional bed & cot available. Pub closed all Mon, last two weeks Feb & last week Oct. Access, Visa.*

TALLADALE — Loch Maree Hotel — B&B

Tel 01445 760288 **Fax 01445 760241** Map 2 B3
Talladale by Achnasheen Wester Ross Highland IV22 2HL

Zzz...

A purpose-built fishing hotel beautifully situated on the banks of Loch Maree between Gairloch and Kinlochewe. The glorious outdoors is certainly a major attraction, and inside things have changed dramatically from the former time-warp Victorian cosiness. The hotel owns eight boats (complete with mandatory ghillies) for sea trout and salmon fishing on the loch. Family rooms sleep three. *Bar open 11-11. Garden, fishing, boating. No real ales. **Accommodation** 30 bedrooms, all en suite, £80. Children welcome overnight (under-14s £12 if sharing parents' room), additional bed and cot available. Access, Visa.*

TAYVALLICH — Tayvallich Inn — FOOD

Tel 01546 870282 Map 3 A5
Tayvallich by Lochgilphead Strathclyde PA31 8PR

This simple, white-painted dining pub – though it's fine to pop in for a drink, most people come for the food – is in a marvellously pretty location at the centre of a strung-along-the-road, scattered village stretching around a natural harbour at the top of Loch Sween. Sit outside, on the front terrace, at one of the five parasolled picnic tables, and enjoy the view of a dozen little boats, and low wooded hills fringing the lochside; the word Tayvallich means "the house in the pass". Inside, the Tayvallich is surprisingly modern – smartly pine-clad, with a little bar and larger adjoining dining-room proper. The bar is tile-floored, with raffia back chairs and little wood tables, the dining-room similar, but spacious and relaxing, with a woodburning stove, attractive dresser, and bentwood chairs around scrubbed pine dining tables. The star of the handwritten menu is the freshest local seafood which is so local that oysters come from just yards away in Loch Sween itself, and 'hand-dived' scallops from the Sound of Jura just round the coast. Langoustines are local and beautifully fresh, as is lobster; plump mussels, imaginative and crisp salads. Their seafood platter must surely be among the very best in the whole of the British Isles – well worth the long, seemingly endless descent down the one-track, bluebell-lined road (B8025) from Crinan (B841)! Finger bowls are provided, along with clean napkins, with each course. Portions are generous and the whole atmosphere is very informal and relaxed. Holidaymakers turn up in shorts and babies are commendably tolerantly treated, with clip-on chairs, specially rustled up toddler food and chips, of course! Puddings are all made by landlady Mrs Grafton are of the chocolate nut slab and banoffee pie sort. Non-fish choices could include Cajun chicken or vegetable and cheese bake. *Open 11-midnight Mon-Sun July & August 11-2.30, 5-11 (to 1am Sat, midnight Sun). **Bar Food** 12-2, 6-9. Free House. **Beer** Tetley. Patio/grassy foreshore, outdoor eating. Inn closed all Monday from Nov-end Mar. Access, Visa.*

TURRIFF — Towie Tavern — FOOD

Tel 01888 511201 **Fax 01651 872464** Map 2 D3
Auchterless nr Turriff Grampian AB53 8EP

A favourite for its satisfying, wholesome food, this is a roadside pebbledash pub on the A497, some four miles south of Turriff and a short distance from the National Trust's 13th-century Fyvie Castle. Seafood is featured at the Towie and the menu changes monthly, with daily blackboard specials. The 'Fisherman's choice' offers whatever is available that day: plaice, herring, mackerel or perhaps haddock (poached or deep-fried) or 'skippers macaroni' (with smoked haddock, cheese prawn, tomato and onion). Vegetarians are catered for (filo parcels of vegetables with herb and cream sauce bound inside with Bonchester cheese) and puddings are home-made (Paris-Brest – choux bun filled with fruits – with butterscotch sauce). Smartly rustic decor. More elaborate fare in the restaurant. 50 whiskies. *Open 11-2.30, 6-12 (Sun 12-11). **Bar Food** 12-2, 6-9 (Fri & Sat to 10, Sun 12-8.30). Free House. Beer Theakston's, guest beer. Terrace, outdoor eating. Access, Visa.*

TWEEDSMUIR — Crook Inn — B&B

Tel 01899 880272 **Fax 01899 880294** Map 4 C1
Tweedsmuir nr Biggar Borders ML12 6QN

Famous old drovers' inn standing on the A701 Moffat to Edinburgh road, in glorious Tweed valley countryside. A strange but winning amalgam of old stone-flagged farmers' bar and 1930s' ocean liner-style lounges in the airy modern extension. Burns wrote Willie Wastle's Wife in what is now the bar, and locally-born John Buchan set many of his novels in the area. Neat bedrooms are simple in their appointments, with no TVs or telephones. There are a few Art Deco features in the lounge and some of the bathrooms. A craft centre (glass-making a speciality) has recently been created from the old stable block. Guests can also enjoy free fishing on 30 miles of the River Tweed. *Bar open 11-12 (Sun 11-11). Free House. **Beer** Broughton Greenmantle Ale. Garden. Family room. **Accommodation** 7 rooms, 6 en suite, £52 (single £36). Children welcome overnight (under-12s stay free in parents' room), additional bed and cot available. Access, Amex, Diners, Visa.*

ULLAPOOL — Argyll Hotel — B&B

Tel 0185 461 2422 Map 2 B2
Argyll Street Ullapool Highland IV26 2UB

Well-kept, white-painted inn one street back from the harbourside. The comfortable main bar has ruffled curtains, velour banquettes, wheelback chairs and 60 plus malt whiskies behind the bar. For character, there's a small public bar – the only one in Ullapool and virtually unchanged in 50 years – where the locals gather. Upstairs, 12 bedrooms offer modest comfort with pretty wallpaper, simple modern units, TV and beverage kit but no phone. Six are en suite (three with tubs and three with showers), the others sharing two good bathrooms. A note behind the doors states that breakfast is served from 8 to 9 and checkout by 10am, but in practice things are a bit more flexible. Families are welcome, with two rooms having an extra bed in addition to a cot and a further bed being available. Own parking. No dogs. *Open 11am-11.30pm (Sun from 12.30). Free House. **Beer** Tennent's 80/-, Bass, guest beers. **Accommodation** 12 bedrooms, 6 en suite, £50 (single £25). Children welcome overnight, (under-5s stay free in parents' room), additional bed and cot available. Pub closed 1 Jan. No dogs. Access, Visa.*

ULLAPOOL — Ceilidh Place — FOOD B&B

Tel 01854 612103 **Fax 01854 612886** Map 2 B2
West Argyle Street Ullapool Highland IV26 2TY

One street back from the harbour, this row of whitewashed cottages does not really have the atmosphere of a pub or an inn (indeed Ceilidh Place is impossible to classify being a glorious mixture of bookshop, picture gallery, arts centre, hotel, coffee shop and restaurant), but there is a bar which shares space with the coffee shop where by day there's counter service of a range of home-made goodies like soup, filled rolls and baked potatoes, nut roast, haddock and chips, chicken and ham pie, Bakewell tart, scones and carrot cake. From early evening there's table service and a printed menu from which you can have just a single dish in the coffee shop/bar or create a more formal meal in the conservatory area with its white-clothed tables. Mushroom and walnut paté with oatcakes, falafels with minty yoghurt dip, bouillabaisse, wild salmon poached in white wine lemon and dill, beef stroganoff and casserole of local venison are just a sample of the wide variety of dishes on offer. Upstairs are 13 spotless bedrooms (three not en suite) simply but appealingly

appointed, some with dark-stained fitted units, some with the odd antique and most with beamed ceilings. Dado-boarded bathrooms all have tubs with hand-held shower attachments. Telephones are standard with TVs and beverage trays available on request. The first floor residents' lounge with large windows on two sides is quite delightful. A separate Club House offers budget accommodation with bunk beds and communal showers and it is here that live entertainment – anything from jazz, folk or classical concerts to poetry readings – is to be found several nights a week in summer. Ceilidh Place now has another establishment called John Maclean's General Merchants down by the harbour which is a delicatessen, bakery shop (they have their own bakery on Ullapool's industrial estate) and general store selling everything from books to haberdashery with a small coffee shop on the first floor. *Open all day 11-11, Sun usual hours.* ***Food*** *9.30-9.30. Free House.* ***Beer*** *McEwan's 80/-, Orkney Dark Island, Belhaven Light. Outdoor eating.* ***Accommodation*** *13 bedrooms, 10 en suite, £90 (single £45). Children welcome overnight, additional bed (from £6) and cot (and high-chair) available free. Closed two weeks Jan. Access, Amex, Amex, Diners, Visa.*

ULLAPOOL — Ferry Boat Inn — FOOD / B&B

Tel & Fax 01854 612366 Map 2 B2
Shore Street Ullapool Wester Ross Highland IV26 2UJ

On the quayside, Richard and Valerie Smith's Ferry Boat is formed out of a couple of 18th-century former crofter's cottages. Inside the smallish bar with its real fire, huge collection of neatly-framed foreign bank notes and half-curtained windows, the atmosphere is cosy and friendly and helped along on most Thursday evenings (more often in summer) by local folk musicians who gather here to play together. The bar food menu offers sound home-cooked fayre: vegetable broth, ploughman's platters, local haddock with chips and peas, beef casserole, meat loaf and (lunchtime only) sandwiches. Puds like lemon meringue pie, coffee and ginger mousse and apple and raisin cake are particularly noteworthy. When the small restaurant (summer evenings only) is busy there is no bar food in the evenings, but one can just have a main course from the short set menu. Bedrooms, now all en suite (three with shower and WC only), come in a variety of pleasant colour schemes with simple darkwood fitted units. Three at the front have splendid views, but some of the others have virtually none. There are beverage trays but no phones or TVs, although a small TV lounge is provided for residents. Beer lovers should note that in addition to the six regular keg beers there is a constantly-changing selection of two cask-conditioned beers that can come from as far afield as Penzance and the Orkneys. Open 11-11 (Sun from 12.30). *Bar Food 12-2.30, 6-9 (Sun from 6.30). Free House.* ***Beer*** *Belhaven, McEwan's, two guest beers.* ***Accommodation*** *9 rooms, all en suite, £58 (single £32). Children welcome overnight, additional bed and cot available. Pub closed 1 Jan. Access, Diners, Visa.*

WEEM — Ailean Chraggan Hotel — FOOD / B&B

Tel 01887 820346 Map 3 C4
Weem by Aberfeldy Tayside PH15 2LD

Beautifully set against a steep woodland backdrop and with two acres of gardens overlooking the Tay this is a delightful little cottage inn. The bright, sunny, well-kept bar has a central log-burning stove, with a dining area beside the picture windows. Simple, well-cooked food is highlighted by superb local seafood; try the Loch Etive mussels, served in huge steaming portions with garlic bread, or the Sound of Jura prawn platter. Bedrooms are also recommended: spacious and light with nice pieces of old furniture, armchairs, and, in two rooms, small dressing areas. All are equipped with TVs, hairdryers and tea/coffee-making facilities. Ask for one of the front bedrooms, which have inspiring views to wake up to. Patio and lawned garden to front and side. *Open 11-11.* ***Bar Food*** *12-2, 6.30-9.30. Free House. No real ales. Garden, outdoor eating, children's play area.* ***Accommodation*** *3 bedrooms, all en suite, £56 (single £28). Children welcome overnight (half price), additional bed and cot available. Closed two weeks in January. Access, Visa.*

See the **County Round-Up** tinted pages for details of all establishments in county order.

Wales

ABERDOVEY Penhelig Arms Hotel FOOD

Tel 01654 767215 **Fax 01654 767690** Map 8 C3 **B&B**
Aberdovey Gwynedd LL35 0LT

Zzz...

Built in the early 1700s as Y Dafarn Fach (The Little Inn) and for generations an integral part of the village's history. The black-and-white painted inn stands right on the main road (A493) with unrivalled views across the Dyfi estuary to Ynyslas. In front, now the tiny car park and sun terrace, was a shipbuilder's yard at the turn of the century, while behind the Towyn to Machynlleth train rumbles out of a tunnel to the request stop at Penhelig Halt. For such a narrow site the Penhelig Arms utilises every square inch of available space and packs in a wealth of charm under the ever-present guidance of proprietors Robert and Sally Hughes (winners of our Pub Hosts of the Year award last year). Its popularity at lunchtime ensures a regular overflow from bar to dining-room. Menus are updated daily, offering the likes of fresh Conway crab or bacon and egg sandwiches, cream of pea and fennel soup, broccoli and walnut lasagne, a choice of omelettes and home-baked ham with eggs and chips; plus chicken in a ginger- and cardamom-spiced cream sauce, whole Conway plaice with herb butter, a salad of avocado, salami, mushrooms and croutons, raspberry trifle, treacle tart and lemon soufflé. Quality and price move up a gear at dinner. Sunday lunchtime sees a reduced bar menu as the traditional roast is always popular. In addition to real ales there's a range of house wines from an enthusiast's cellar; champagne at £3 a glass isn't offered everywhere! Care and attention to detail has gone into ensuring residents' every comfort in a relaxed atmosphere that contrives to make one feel immediately at home. What the smaller bedrooms lack in space they make up for in appealing interior design, careful addition of up-to-date comforts (TV, telephone to hairdryers and quality toiletries) and immaculately-kept en-suite bathrooms. All but one have a share of the view, one of the finest of any hotel in Wales, and three superior rooms have a little extra space with easy chairs and super little front-facing balconies. It goes almost without saying that a splendid Welsh breakfast will set you up for the day's touring, sightseeing or just lazing around which lies ahead. *Open 11-3, 6-11 (Sun 12-3, 7-10.30).* ***Bar Food*** *12-2, 7-9. Free House.* ***Beer*** *Tetley Bitter, Burton, guest beer. Outdoor eating.* ***Accommodation*** *10 bedrooms, all en suite, £68-£78 (single £39). Children welcome overnight, additional bed & cot available. Pub closed 25 & 26 Dec. Access, Visa.*

We only recommend food (Bar Food) in those establishments highlighted with the **FOOD** symbol.

ABERGAVENNY Llanwenarth Arms Hotel FOOD

Tel 01873 810550 **Fax 01873 811880** Map 9 D5 **B&B**
Brecon Road Abergavenny Gwent NP8 1EP

A refined roadside inn (on the A40) between Abergavenny and Crickhowell, standing on an escarpment above the Usk valley. Chef/landlord D'Arcy McGregor's creative cooking leaves little to chance, his bar menus making full use of the best local produce available. The seasonally-changed main menu is served throughout the two bars, family conservatory dining area and splendid summer terrace set some 70 feet above the river with views across to Sugar Loaf Mountain. Smoked trout salad, fresh pasta, poached salmon, king prawns in a Chinese-style sauce, goujons of hake, chicken wrapped in Parma ham, steaks and pan-fried venison with a port and redcurrant sauce give the style; home-made puds range from profiteroles to waffles and bread-and-butter pudding (served with brown bread ice cream for the indulgent). Cauliflower and ham soup, omelette with ham, asparagus and Cheddar cheese, mixed grill, baked lamb chops with Madeira sauce might feature as daily specials. Residents enjoy the use of their own lounge, and a Victorian-style conservatory furnished with comfortable cane furniture. Bedrooms, approached by way of a sheltered courtyard, are attractively furnished and immaculately kept, each one enjoying its fair share of the view. TVs, telephones, trouser presses, tea/coffee making facilities and hairdryers are all standard; bathrooms also have over-bath showers and ample supplies of toiletries. Salmon and trout fishing for residents. *Open 11-3, 6-11 (Sun 12-2, 7-10.30).* ***Bar Food*** *12-2 (Sun to 1.15), 6-9.45 (Sun 7-8.15). Free House.* ***Beer*** *Bass, Ruddles County. Patio, outdoor eating. Family room.* ***Accommodation*** *18 bedrooms, all en suite, £59 (single £49). Children welcome overnight (under-16s half price), additional bed & cot available (£5). No dogs. Access, Amex, Diners, Visa.*

ABERGORLECH Black Lion FOOD

Tel 01558 685271 Map 9 B5

Abergorlech nr Carmarthen Dyfed SA32 7SN

At the heart of one of Wales's best-kept villages, the white-painted Black Lion stands between a tiny stone chapel and the Cothi River bridge; private fishing beats are nearby. The single bar with flagstone floors and high settles leads to a flat-roofed dining extension. On the main menu, pink trout, fillet steaks, boeuf bourguignon and generous salads satisfy the heartiest appetites, while blackboard daily specials might feature lasagne, chicken Kiev or vegetable lasagne. Opposite the pub, a scenic riverside garden with picnic tables features regular summer barbecues. Children welcome. *Open 12-3.30, 7-11 (from 6.30 in summer), Sun 12-3, 7-10.30.* ***Bar Food*** *12-2.30 (no food Mon L), 7-9.30. Free House.* ***Beer*** *Worthington, guest beer. Riverside garden, outdoor eating. Access, Visa.*

AFON-WEN Pwll Gwyn Hotel FOOD

Tel 01352 720227 Map 8 C2

Afon-wen nr Mold Clwyd CH7 5UB

Formerly a 17th-century coaching inn of some renown with an unusual remodelled Victorian frontage (on the A541), Pwll Gwyn's fortunes are being revived today by enthusiastic and energetic tenants Andrew and Karen Davies. Andrew provides the brains (and the brawn) behind an intelligently run kitchen whose output is much dictated by his shopping from Liverpool's markets. Best bets for the bar food, therefore, come from the daily blackboard: avocado, chicken and curry mayonnaise, liver and smoked bacon with gravy and potato cake or fillets of brill with mushrooms, wine and cream. Desserts, too, are impressive: cappuccino cake and toffee crunch cheesecake feature on a long list of home-made delights. More substantial cooking with a classical base comes in the form of weeekly changing specials available in the two separate dining-rooms (one for non-smokers); special event evenings (Italian, Chinese, Indian) and summer barbecues are a regular feature. *Open 12-3, 7-11, Sun 12-3, 5-10.30 (from 7 in winter).* ***Bar Food*** *12-2.30, 7-9.30.* ***Beer*** *Greenalls. Garden, outdoor eating. Family room.* ***Accommodation*** *3 bedrooms, £30 (single £15). Children welcome overnight. No dogs. Access, Visa.*

BABELL Black Lion Inn FOOD

Tel 01352 720239 Map 8 D1

Babell nr Holywell Clwyd CH8 8PZ

Eating in the patio dining-room here offers not only impressive views of the Clywdian range without but also tempting value on the menu and blackboard within. For starters, black pudding in mustard sauce or grilled smoked mackerel and to follow, the likes of kidneys Turbigo, beef casserole and grilled plaice with lemon butter sauce. Nightly, except Sunday, in the Liszt Room, a four-course dinner is more formally silver-served and priced according to choice of main course. A classical French-biased wine list includes some carefully selected 'Landlord's Delights', while listed separately are 'Syd's wines of the month' – a Californian Kinderwood Ruby Cabernet, perhaps, or a Mexican Fumé Blanc; 'Syd' is the hospitable Fosters' effervescent daughter. Even after 29 years here, there is undimming enthusiasm for good food and impeccable service. *Open Tue-Fri 12-2, Tue-Sat 7-9.45 (plus late supper licence to 10.30).* ***Bar Food*** *12-2 (except Sat & Sun), 7.15-10.30 (except Sun). Garden. Family room. Free House.* ***Beer*** *Boddingtons. Pub closed all day Mon, lunch Sat & all day Sun (except Easter Sun & Mother's Day). Access, Amex, Visa.*

> Many **B&B** establishments offer reduced rates for weekend and out-of-season bookings. Always ask about special deals for longer stays. Beware half-board terms in inns where we do not recommend the **FOOD.**

BEAUMARIS — Liverpool Arms Hotel — FOOD B&B

Tel 01248 810362 Map 8 B1
Castle Street Beaumaris Anglesey Gwynedd LL58 8BA

A handsome Georgian-fronted inn with a maritime history recalling the days when there was a busy shipping trade between Beaumaris and Liverpool. At its heart the Admiral's Tavern contains a wealth of memorabilia and relics which include timbers both from Nelson's Victory and the 1830s' HMS Conway which was wrecked in the Menai Strait in 1953. A Quarterdeck and non-smoking Port Room are ideally set aside for sampling from Colleen Evans's daily-changing fare. There is no printed menu, instead a blackboard offers home-made pies and casseroles alongside, perhaps, popular lunchtime platters like Coronation chicken, beef stir-fry and assorted smoked fish; evening specials can range from sausage and apple slice to a 20oz rump steak served with Stilton sauce. The White Star Line replicated signs to 'First Class Accommodation', approached by a fine listed oak-panelled staircase, are no exaggeration. Bedrooms are boldly decorated and bathrooms smartly tiled; tea trays, TVs and dial-out telephones are all provided. Honeymooners might enjoy the four-poster suite, and youngsters can double up in the bunk beds of one of the two family rooms. Lower tariff in winter. *Open 11-11 (Sun 12-3, 7-10.30). **Bar Food** 12-2, 6-9. Free House. **Beer** Tetley Best, Bass. Family room. **Accommodation** 10 bedrooms, all en suite, from £50 (four-poster £76, family room from £70, single £30). Access, Visa.*

BEAUMARIS — Ye Olde Bull's Head Inn — FOOD B&B

Tel 01248 810329 **Fax 01248 811294** Map 8 B1
Castle Street Beaumaris Anglesey Gwynedd LL58 8AP

A stone's throw from Beaumaris Castle, the Grade II listed Bull dates back to 1472, though it was largely rebuilt in 1617. The original posting house of the borough, its courtyard arch houses the largest single-hinged gate in Britain. Within its cavernous bars is a valuable array of antique weaponry, an ancient brass water clock and the town's old ducking stool. With its newly-extended family room to the rear, this makes an ideal spot for lunch. Daily menus offer the best local produce splendidly scaled down for pubby enjoyment: alongside a smoked chicken and lentil broth and Welsh cheese ploughman's may be baked fillet of codling with herb crust or strips of roast sirloin of beef with marinated peppers. A grilled hamburger comes with rosemary and onion gravy, amply garnished sandwiches include roast beef, cottage cheese and tuna: sweets may be warm almond tart or bread-and-butter pudding with home-made custard. Toby jugs and tun dishes adorn the hammer beams and roof struts of a first-floor restaurant which overlooks the courtyard. Partner Keith Rothwell was joined by a new head chef last year and their dinner menu now takes over from bar food in the evenings. The smartly-refurbished bedrooms are named after characters from the novels of Charles Dickens, a frequent visitor to the inn. Each room is individually decorated and contains its own special features: exposed rafters and beams, oddly-shaped doors and ingeniously-fitted bathrooms, all remain sympathetic to the Bull's unbroken history, while the phones, TVs and bedside radios satisfy today's requirements. Last summer a further four individually-decorated rooms in converted stables came on stream; the best ('Mr Pickwick') has a four-poster and all feature antique beds and furniture. The 'Artful Dodger' twin room is not en suite and is let to parents with children (£15 each) who are old enough to sleep in their own room. *Open 11-11, Sun 12-10.30. **Bar Food** 12-2.30 only (not Sun). Free House. **Beer** Bass, Worthington Best, guest beer. Family room. **Accommodation** 15 bedrooms, all en suite, £73/£75 (four-poster £87/£89, single £49). Children welcome overnight, additional bed (£15) & cot available (£7.50). No dogs. Pub closed 25 Dec evening. Access, Visa.*

BETTWS NEWYDD — Black Bear — FOOD

Tel & Fax 01873 880701 Map 9 D5
Bettws Newydd Usk Gwent WP5 1JN

Stephen Molyneux has now purchased this rather unfashionable-looking old pub off the B4598 two miles from Usk. It's an unexpected setting to find some really rather good cooking, served all day; nevertheless, the fact that Stephen's £20 three-course, surprise "see what comes out of the kitchen" menu has many takers shows that he has already inspired confidence in his regular customers. Down just three steps from a single, black and red quarry-tiled bar, the half a dozen neatly-set tables with pink cloths and cane chairs seem almost incongruous. Fish is definitely the thing here and a prominently displayed blackboard menu reflects the latest deliveries: perhaps grilled sardines, Cornish cod with crispy beer

batter and home-made chips, panaché of seafood with a warm basil vinaigrette, brill with lobster and brandy sauce or monkfish with spring onion, ginger and oyster sauce; lobsters, mussels and crab are also often available. Frills are minimal and quirky, flavours forceful and highly individual. Steaks and steak and kidney pie might satisfy non-fish eaters. Real ales are drawn direct from the cask – you may find an unusual local brew, Free Miners Bitter or Speculation. Fenced and lawned garden. *Open 11-11 (Sun 12-10.30).* ***Bar Food*** *12-10. Free House.* ***Beer*** *three changing real ales. Garden, outdoor eating. No credit cards.*

BETWS-YN-RHOS Ffarm Hotel FOOD

Tel 01492 680287 Map 8 C1
Betws-yn-Rhos nr Abergele Clwyd LL22 8AR

Eating is the main event at the Lomax family's discreet venue, hiding signless behind an impressive crenellated stone facade. The 18th-century granite manor house set in two acres of garden has been comfortably modernised and guests can choose to eat in either the bar, hall or library (suitable for families). The daily-changing blackboard menu offers specials such as rack of Welsh lamb in a redcurrant sauce, salmon with crab sauce, chicken Creole and rice, leek, cheese and herb risotto bake followed by locally-made ice creams or apple, apricot and sultana steamed pudding. Very young children are not encouraged. Smiling service. *Open 7-11 only.* ***Bar Food*** *7-9.30 only. Free House.* ***Beer*** *Tetley Traditional. Garden, outdoor eating. Closed at lunchtimes all week. Access, Visa.*

BODFARI Dinorben Arms FOOD

Tel 01745 710309 Fax 01745 710580 Map 8 C2
Bodfari nr Denbigh Clwyd LL16 4DA

The 17th-century Dinorben Arms is off the A541 (taking the B5429 and sign to Tremeirchion). New landlord David Rowlands has injected a new lease of life to this well-known old pub since taking over, with much refurbishment undertaken and new menus on offer. The emphasis is still very much on home-cooking and the standard is unlikely to change as long as Irene and Mary are in the kitchen (they've been there for 34 years between them!). Lunchtimes concentrate on the self-served smörgåsbord and in the evenings both cold starters and sweets are mostly served buffet-style in the Well Bar. The 'Chicken Rough', originally presented to be eaten with fingers, lives on since being introduced in 1961; the Farmhouse Buffet (Wed/Thu) and Carverboard (Fri/Sat) are more recent evening additions. Special dishes nightly may include rack of Welsh lamb or grilled trout, however there are plenty more snacky items, children's and vegetarian choices (perhaps aubergine moussaka). Families are well catered for in their own room and on the smart, flower-decked, tiered patios and at the top of the extensive hillside gardens is a children's adventure play area; changing unit in Ladies. For dedicated drinkers there are four real ales, eight wines by the glass, 25 cognacs, and over 120 whiskies. *Open 12-3.30, 6-11 (Sun 12-3.30, 7-10.30).* ***Bar Food*** *12-2.30 (Sun to 3.30), 6-10.30 (Sun from 7). Free House.* ***Beer*** *John Smith's, Webster's Yorkshire, Ruddles, guest beer. Garden, outdoor eating, children's play area. Family room. Access, Visa.*

BURTON GREEN Golden Grove Inn A

Tel 01244 570445 Map 8 D2
Llyndir Lane Burton Green nr Wrexham Clwyd LL12 0AS

Best found by turning off the B5445 at Rossett, by the signs to Llyndyr Hall; at the end of a lane seemingly leading nowhere stands a group of black and white timber-framed buildings which comprise the pub and its many outhouses. Within is a treasure trove of antiquity with some splendid 14th-century oak beams and magical old inglenooks and fireplaces. A modern extension housing a carvery dining-room leads to drinking patios and a large, safe garden replete with swings and wooden play equipment, justifiably popular in the summer months; regular barbecues. Choice of 35 malt whiskies. New joint tenants – Owen Roberts and Christene Morris – of Marston's took over in March 1995; Christene's husband is in the kitchen and producing a good-looking menu (not yet inspected). *Open 12-3, 6-11 (from 7 in winter), Sat 12-11 in summer.* ***Beer*** *Marston's Best & Pedigree. Garden, outdoor eating, children's play area. Access, Visa.*

See the **County Round-Up** tinted pages for details of all establishments in county order.

CARDIGAN — Black Lion Hotel — B&B

Tel 01239 612532 Map 9 B4
High Street Cardigan Dyfed SA43 1HJ

The Black Lion claims to be the oldest coaching inn in Wales, having established itself in 1105 as a 'one-room grog shop'. Much enlarged (but originally medieval) town-centre inn, refurbished two years ago, with a characterful beamed interior, complete with linenfold panelling in one of the bars. Pine-furnished bedrooms, and a comfortable upstairs television lounge, as well as a quaint little writing room. Bedrooms are equipped with tea/coffee-making facilities, TV and telephone. A family suite sleeps up to five; one double room also has a single bed and there's a connecting twin room – both share a bathroom. Function room for up to 100. *Open 11-11 (from 10 for coffee), Sun 12-10.30). Free House.* ***Beer*** *Bass, Hancock's.* ***Accommodation*** *14 bedrooms, all en suite, £40 (family suite price according to age, single £30). Children welcome overnight, additional bed (no charge under 10 years) & cot available. No dogs. Access, Visa.*

CHEPSTOW — Castle View Hotel — FOOD B&B

Tel 01291 620349 **Fax 01291 627397** Map 9 D6
16 Bridge Street Chepstow Gwent NP6 5EZ

Four miles from the M4 Junction 22, this 300-year-old house was constructed mostly using stone from Chepstow Castle which commands the huge riverbank opposite. Ivy-covered and genuinely welcoming, it's immaculately kept by Martin and Vicky Cardale. The original stone walls and timbers enhance the setting for a snack. Through both light and 'bigger bites', the bar menu encompasses omelettes and steak sandwiches, vegetables crepes and hazelnut and mushroom fettuccine, with turkey, ham and sweetcorn or steak, kidney and Tetley pie as carnivorous alternatives. In the dining-room, an evening table d'hote is supplemented by a short à la carte on which the local Wye salmon is a regular feature. Up-to-date bedrooms with mahogany furniture and en-suite bathrooms (two with shower/WC only); radio and TV (with use of videos), mini-bars, direct-dial phones and beverage trays are standard throughout. The cottage suite (sleeping up to four) incorporates a quiet residents' lounge; overlooking the garden – a restful spot – are two spacious family rooms sleeping up to 4. *Open 12-2.30, 6-11 (Sun 12-2.30, 6-10.30).* ***Bar Food*** *12-2, 6.30-9.30 (no food Sun eve). Free House.* ***Beer*** *Tetley, Butcombe. Garden, outdoor eating.* ***Accommodation*** *13 bedrooms, all en suite, £60.40 (single £40.45). Children welcome overnight (under-14s stay free in parents' room, 14-16s half-price) additional bed & cot available. Closed first two weeks in Jan. Access, Amex, Diners, Visa.*

CLARBESTON ROAD — Picton Inn — A

Tel 01437 731615 Map 9 A5
Clarbeston Road nr Haverfordwest Dyfed SA63 4UH

The village lies amid fertile farmland between the Presselli hills and Cardigan Bay. Abutting the railway halt, Clarbeston Road's rebuilt Victorian inn exudes a general air of mock antiquity, assisted by a genuinely smoky fire under its huge oak lintel. A red brick pine-shelved column divides the bar from an open-plan eating area. *Open 11-11, Sun 12-3, 7-10.30.* ***Beer*** *Crown Buckley The Reverend James Original Ale, guest beer. Garden, outdoor eating. No credit cards.*

CLYDACH — Drum & Monkey ★ — FOOD

Tel 01873 831980 Map 9 D5
Clydach Blackrock Abergavenny Gwent NP7 0LW

Perched at the side of the A465 in a spectacular position overlooking Clydach Gorge, the pub was only recently rescued from dereliction. Look carefully for the old road, signed to Clydach North, as the pub is inaccessible from the main highway. 'A restaurant with lounge bar' most aptly describes the interior: half-a-dozen bar tables set round the open fire, its stone walls hung with horsebrasses, and the dining-room with widely-spaced tables a touch more formal. Chef-patron Jon West's sensible policy, however, is that diners may eat in either location; moreover, the choice is impressive and his food is superb. For a snack (in the bar at lunchtime only) try smoked salmon and scrambled eggs, seafood tagliatelle, mackerel and prawn omelette, club sandwich, sweet and sour spare ribs, paté with French bread. Fresh daily specials from the fish-board – their speciality – may be red mullet in shellfish or king scallops in leeks and ginger, while some classy skills are exhibited in the filo pastry basket of chicken tikka with cucumber and mint raita, fillet of beef Wellington with Madeira sauce and Cajun-seasoned pork tenderloin with creamed parsnips and wholegrain mustard sauce; leave room for the superb light and dark chocolate cheesecake. The three-

course (£12.45 including a glass of wine) Early Bird evening menu (6-7.30, Sun 7-7.30) offers excellent value for money. Popular for Sunday lunch (£8.95/£10.95). *Open 12-3, 6-11, Sun 12-3, 7-10.30. Meals 12-2, 6-9.30 (Sun 7-9). Free House.* ***Beer*** *Crown Buckley Buckley's Best. Access, Visa.*

CLYTHA | Clytha Arms | FOOD

Tel & Fax 01873 840206 Map 9 D5
Clytha nr Abergavenny Gwent NP7 9BW

Clytha stands on the old main road (now the B4598) between Abergavenny and Usk. A few years ago it was closed and close to dereliction; today it is decidedly a pub for eating in, and chef-patron Andrew Canning certainly knows how to cook. For starters sample the asparagus with parmesan or lemon butter or plump for the grilled mixed shellfish Italian. Main courses deliver some fine fresh fish (Dover sole with tarragon and prawns) and country-style cooking from supreme of chicken Basque-style to wild mushroom lasagne. In lighter mood, bar snacks are typified by home-made fish soup, laverbread with bacon and cockles, faggots with peas and beer gravy and treacle sponge and custard. The flagstoned public bar with its dartboard and skittles table may present unforeseen hazards – to which the tree-lined garden provides a serene summer alternative. *Open 11.30-3.30 (not Mon), 6-11, Sun 12-3, 7-10.30.* ***Bar Food*** *12-2.15 (not Sun or Mon), 7.30-9.30 (no food Sun eve). Free House.* ***Beer*** *Hook Norton Best Bitter, Theakston Best, Bass, three guest beers. Garden, outdoor eating area, children's play area. Family room. Pub closed Mon lunch. Access, Visa.*

CREIGIAU | Caesar's Arms | FOOD

Tel 01222 890486 **Fax 01222 892176** Map 9 C6
Cardiff Road Creigiau nr Cardiff Mid Glamorgan CF4 8NN

A mostly-dining country pub in a dip of the road just outside the village (8 miles from the centre of Cardiff and 3 miles from the M4 J33) is the latest venture of Champers' restaurant owners, Benigno Martinez, Mark Sharples and Earl Smikle (also the chef). The well-tried formula of chargrilled steaks and fish, cooked in full view, with accompanying self-served salads, garlic bread and chip shop-style chips works equally well here. Whole seabass baked in rock salt and spicy Bajan fishcakes are considered specialities, and dishes with mussels, cockles, laverbread and trout make good use of local ingredients. Typical daily specials might include stir-fried scallops with samphire, Dover sole with prawn and mushroom sauce or rack of lamb with rosemary. The regular menu also encompasses game terrine, pint of prawns, oysters, goujons of hake and salmon, honeyed crispy duck, beef kebab, raspberry pavlova, apple and strawberry crumble with custard and chocolate and orange torte. The outside dining area is now a conservatory with double-glazed walls that dissassemble in summer to provide alfresco dining. popular Sunday lunch destination. Excellent wine list, with several available by the glass. There's a garden and the neighbouring paddock is home to a horse. Children are "tolerated" but not encouraged. *Open 12-3, 6-10.30 (Sun 12-6 only).* ***Bar Food*** *12-2.30 (Sun to 6), 7-10.30 (not Sun eve).* ***Beer*** *Hancock's HB. Garden. Closed Sunday evening. Access, Amex, Diners, Visa.*

CRICKHOWELL | Bear Hotel | FOOD

Tel 01873 810408 **Fax 01873 811696** Map 9 D5 **B&B**
Brecon Road (A40) Crickhowell Powys NP8 1BW

Zzz...

One of the original coaching inns on the London to Aberystwyth route, the Bear today bristles with personality and honest endeavour. Front bars, a hive of activity, are resplendent with oak panelling, ornamental sideboards and welcoming log fires. Recent refurbishment of three of the inn's oldest bedrooms has revealed open stone fireplaces which date it back to 1432. Further top-grade bedroom accommodation is housed in a modern Tudor-style courtyard extension, and in a garden cottage containing two bedrooms and a suite with its own spa bath. Four-poster beds and antique furniture abound. Snacks in the bar encompass deep-fried laverbread, cockle and bacon balls covered in sesame seeds, mussels in garlic butter, prawn and chicken Thai toast appetisers with dips and plaice and salmon goujons with a garlic and lime mayonnaise dip. Bread-and-butter pudding and lemon crunch pie are house speciality puddings. Plenty of standards (paté, filled pancakes and pork pie) in small portions for little people; filo parcels of Brie with cranberry marmalade and sliced beef

tomatoes on a layer of spinach with basil, pesto and mozzarella for vegetarians. *Open 11-3, 6-11.* ***Bar Food*** *12-2, 6-10 (Sun 7.30-9.30). Free House.* ***Beer*** *Bass, Ruddles Best & County, Webster's Yorkshire Bitter. Garden, outdoor eating. Family room.* ***Accommodation*** *29 bedrooms, all en suite, £52-£68 (single £42-£49). Children welcome overnight, additional bed & cot available. Access, Amex, Visa.*

CRICKHOWELL Nantyffin Cider Mill FOOD

Tel 01873 810775 Map 9 D5
Brecon Road Crickhowell Powys NP8 1SG

At the junction of A479 with A40, just over a mile west of Crickhowell, a pink-painted former cider mill (the original cider press is preserved in the recently completed dining-room) standing on the Tretower estates bordering the north-west bank of the Usk. Bar snacks and light meals (one menu throughout) are served in an intimate, carpeted lounge bar, and in summer in the length of a riverside garden. Snacks vary from lunchtime-only ploughman's lunch and open sandwiches (Loch Fyne smoked salmon, peppered sliced beef) to all-day lamb's liver and bacon with mash and onion gravy, lasagne, home-made steak and kidney pie, and grilled black pudding with a mild Welsh whisky sauce, braised red cabbage and mushrooms. More substantial offerings might be an Italian summer salad, slow-cooked 'barbecue belly pork confit' with Oriental spices and a plum sauce or half a roast duck on potato rösti with an orange, ginger and honey sauce. Interesting vegetarian options: slow-roasted aubergine with aromatic couscous and a light Thai curry sauce or a steamed cabbage parcel (filled with rice, nuts, cheese and vegetables) on a mushroom sauce. Daily fresh fish and seafood features on the blackboard (scallops in a mango salsa, baked skate on lemon risotto, sea bream on warm niçoise salad, fillet of cod with buttered spinach and hollandaise); game in season. There's also a good selection of calorific desserts and Welsh cheeses. Fixed-price Sunday lunch menu. Children are offered half portions of most dishes as well as chicken nuggets and fish fingers. *Open 12-3, 6-11 (from 7 in winter), Sun 12-2, 7-10.30.* ***Bar Food*** *12-2 (Sat to 2.30), 6.30-10 (Sun 7-9.45). Free House.* ***Beer*** *three regularly-changing guest beers. Garden, outdoor eating. Pub closed first 2 weeks Jan and all day Mon (all year). Access, Visa.*

DINAS MAWDDWY Dolbrodmaeth Inn B&B

Tel 01650 531333 Map 8 C3
Dinas Mawddwy nr Machynlleth Powys SY20 9LP

A former farmhouse tucked off the A470 with gardens sloping down to the River Dovey, this is a little gem. Engineer Graham Williams, once with the BBC, and wife Jean, a former cookery teacher, run this rebuilt inn (almost destroyed by fire in 1982), which now houses two cosy bars and an airy dining lounge. From the latter there are picturesque views of grounds that include a paddock, river walk and private fishing. The eight bedrooms are floored with carpet tiles and sport bright home-spun curtains and duvets, designed and made by an artistic daughter; direct-dial telephones were installed last year. Though small, the bathrooms are brightly tiled with over-bath showers and multifarious energy-conscious features – even the beer cooling system boasts hot water output. Families are welcome: two rooms interconnect as a suite and one room boasts a double and single bed (plus room for a cot); children's games (and badminton) can be played on the large lawn. The new Celtica Centre and the Centre for Alternative Technology – both in Machynlleth, 10 miles away – are also worthwhile attractions for families. *Open 11-11 (Sun 12-3, 7-10.30). Free House.* ***Beer*** *Tetley Bitter, Burton Ale. Garden, lawn, outdoor eating, tables in garden.* ***Accommodation*** *8 bedrooms, all en suite, £45 (single £35). Children welcome overnight, free in cots if sharing parents' room, £10 for additional bed. Pub closed two weeks Feb. Access, Diners, Visa.*

EAST ABERTHAW Blue Anchor FOOD

Tel 01446 750329 Map 9 C6
East Aberthaw nr Barry South Glamorgan CF6 9DD

The old village of Aberthaw is hidden away between the Vale of Glamorgan and the sea. Long before a vast power station came along to spoil the view there was talk here of smuggling and the creeper-covered Blue Anchor is said to have played its full part in the trade in contraband. The pub's warren of tiny rooms had more than its share of hidey-holes and stone staircases now leading nowhere, giving the whole pub a wonderfully evocative

feel. These days you'll not get robbed for the price of a pint (with six or seven real ales from which to choose) and, in the bar, meals scarcely cost a King's ransom. For starters or a snack there may be traditional Welsh rarebit, home-made lasagne verdi, curry of the day, caulifower cheese, salads, fish pie or lamb stew with herb dumplings; sandwiches, jacket potatoes and children's favourites complete the bar food menu. Only restaurant meals in the evening. *Open 11-11 (Sun 12-10.30).* ***Bar Food*** *Mon-Sat 12-2 only. Free House.* ***Beer*** *Crown Buckley Buckley's Best, Marston's Pedigree, Wadworth 6X, Boddingtons, Flowers IPA, Theakston Old Peculier, guest beer. Outdoor eating. Access, Visa.*

ERBISTOCK — Boat Inn — FOOD

Tel 01978 780143 Map 8 D2

Erbistock nr Ruabon Clwyd LL13 0DL

A dead end lane past the Victorian church leads to the Boat, in an unrivalled position on the banks of the River Dee; there was once a ferry crossing here. Essentially pubby with its cosy flagstoned bar and open fires, it's a fine spot year round for a casual drink, but their is also a fairly serious attitude to food. At lunchtimes sandwiches and Dee salmon are a big draw (plain sliced or crispbreads available on request). On a daily bar menu, carrot and chive soup, Cumberland sausage with raspberry sauce and Barnsley lamb chop are typical choices. Table d'hote menus in the dining-rooms with seasonal alternatives à la carte. Serious attention to raw materials and cooking is without question, though the service at times can be painfully slow. No under-14s in bar. Accommodation is offered in a self-contained flat (not inspected). *Open 11-3 (maybe later in summer), 6.30-11, Sun 12-10.30 (summer), 12-5, 7-10.30 (winter).* ***Bar Food*** *12-2, 7-9.30. Free House.* ***Beer*** *Plassey, Cains Formidable Ale, Shepherd Neame. Riverside garden, outdoor eating. Family room. Access, Amex, Visa.*

FELINDRE FARCHOG — Salutation Inn — B&B

Tel 01239 820564 Map 9 B5

A487 Felindre Farchog nr Crymych Dyfed SA41 3UY

Felindre, a dot on the map where the A487 road bridge crosses the Nyfer, is the Salutation. Well-tended lawns slope down to the river, and there are gardens and terraces for a peaceful drink. The single-storey bedroom wing is neat and well-appointed. Bright duvets set the tone, with satellite TV, radio alarms, tea-makers and hairdryers providing up-to-date refinements. Three family rooms have bunk beds, and cots are also provided free of charge. Bar snacks and restaurant. *Open 11.30-3, 5.30-12 (12-2, 6-10 in winter), Sun 12-2, 7-10.30. Free House.* ***Beer*** *Burton. Riverside garden, outdoor eating. Family room.* ***Accommodation*** *9 bedrooms, all en suite, £48 (single £30). Children welcome overnight, (under-2s stay free in parents' room, 2-14s £5) additional bed & cot available. Access, Visa.*

GLANWYDDEN — Queen's Head — FOOD

Tel 01492 546570 **Fax 01492 546487** Map 8 C1

Llandudno Junction Glanwydden Gwynedd LL31 9JP

One mile from Rhos-on-Sea and three miles from Llandudno, this one-time wheelwright's cottage – now the Queen's Head village pub – is particularly popular for a lunch stop-off. Hidden down a maze of country lanes, Glanwydden is best found by following the Llanrhos road from Penrhyn Bay (B5115). Motivator of the Queen's Head's admirable food operation is chef/landlord Robert Cureton, who sets great store by careful shopping for his daily-updated menus. Start, perhaps, with a home-made soup like mushroom with red wine and haxelnuts or carrot, coriander and ginger, served with a crusty granary roll; alternatives might include smoked trout paté, deep-fried Pencarreg cheese with cranberry preserve or baked black pudding with puréed apple and brandy. Main courses might include a trio of vegetarian options, 'lighter meals' (pizza, lasagne, 'tasty baps', cheese-topped Conwy mussels), good fresh seafood (lemon sole with orange and hazelnut butter, local crab, poached salmon), Jamaican chicken curry, grilled local lamb cutlets with a plum and port wine sauce, and salads. The cold seafood platter is a house speciality and can be enjoyed either as a starter shared by two or as a main course. Finish with a selection from the particularly good nursery puddings displayed on the Welsh dresser – perhaps bread-and-butter pudding, treacle tart or nectarine and elderflower fool. Hand-pulled beers are suitably well kept and the wine list is above average, compiled in association with Rodney Densem Wines of Nantwich; the house champagne is £17.95! Parties of six or more may only book for the early evenings or Sunday lunch. *Open 11-3, 6-11, Sun 12-3, 7-10.30.* ***Bar Food*** *12-2, 6-9 (Sun from 7).* ***Beer*** *Tetley, Burton, Benskins Best. Terrace, outdoor eating. Pub closed 25 Dec. Access, Visa.*

HANMER — Hanmer Arms — B&B

Tel 01948 830532 **Fax 01948 830740** Map 6 A3
Hanmer nr Whitchurch Clwyd SY13 3DE

Standing in the shadow of St Chad's church at the heart of a quiet hamlet now mercifully by-passed by the A539. The mellow brick Hanmer Arms is certainly of 16th-century origin, with a history more firmly linked to the old communities of the Shropshire Lake District than the present-day county of Clwyd. In a newly hollowed-out interior of this self-styled 'village hotel' are contained two bars, reception lounge and restaurant, with further dining and function rooms on the upper level. Bar floors are polished wood and on the walls is gleaming brassware retaining much of the feel of a traditional local but with little authenticity left beyond its brick facade. The strong point here lies in the apartment-style bedrooms laid out in the reconstructed barn and outhouses which stand around a central cobbled courtyard full of old farming artefacts. Decorated in country style with full en-suite bathrooms, they are well equipped with phones, radio alarms and satellite TV. The most spacious have plenty of room to accommodate families overnight, while for the businessman there's also plenty of work space. Boardroom and conferences for up to 90 delegates. *Open 11.30-11 (Sun 12-10.30). Free House.* ***Beer*** *Tetley Best, Burton Ale. Lawned and fenced-in garden.* ***Accommodation*** *26 bedrooms, all en suite, from £52 (suites £58, weekends £38/£45, single £42). Children welcome overnight (under-9s share parents' room free), additional bed and cot supplied. Access, Amex, Diners, Visa.*

See the **County Round-Up** tinted pages for details of all establishments in county order.

HAY-ON-WYE — Kilverts — FOOD B&B

Tel 01497 821042 **Fax 01497 821580** Map 9 D5
Bull Ring Hay-on-Wye Powys HR3 5AG

An inimitable collection of hats and Victorian Spy cartoons imbue the bar of Colin Thomson's hotel/pub/bar with great character; the atmosphere is also enhanced nightly by the playing of an upright piano. Food is a further attraction, with the likes of home-made 6oz beefburgers alongside daily specials ranging from laverbread, bacon and cockles on toast (plus sandwiches and ploughman's platters at lunchtime) to spinach and mushroom roulade; fresh fish (shark steak) is best from Thursdays to Sundays; other dishes might include rack of lamb with redcurrant and thyme sauce, chicken curry. Home-made desserts like tiramisu, crème brulée and summer pudding. Residents' accommodation is both comfortable and stylish with brass bedsteads, smoked-glass tables and attractive floral bed linen. In addition to tea trays, direct-dial phones, TVs and radios (incorporating a baby-listening service), accoutrements include hairdryers and trouser presses. Bathrooms are a little utilitarian, nonetheless incorporating powerful showers and copious amounts of hot water. A marquee is erected for functions in summer – it's also a venue for Hay Jazz at the end of July. *Open 11-11 (Bank Holidays to 11.30), Sun 12-10.30.* ***Bar Food*** *12-2, 7-9.30. Free House.* ***Beer*** *Boddingtons, Whitbread Castle Eden, Bass. Patio, garden, outdoor eating.* ***Accommodation*** *11 bedrooms, all en suite (5 with shower only), £54-£60 (winter from £48, single £27). Children welcome overnight (under-6s stay free in parents' room, 6-12s £6), additional bed & cot available. Accommodation closed 24 Dec, pub & accommoadtion closed 25 Dec. Access, Amex, Visa.*

LANDSHIPPING — Stanley Arms — FOOD

Tel 01834 891227 Map 9 A5
Landshipping nr Narberth Dyfed SA67 8BE

One must cultivate a certain desire to come to the Stanley Arms: it's five miles by road from Canaston Bridge (on the A40), a lengthy walk through the Minwear Forest and 200 yards from the moorings at Landshipping Cove, high up the Cleddau estuary. It is therefore a true pub-lovers' pub with a good mix of locals, yachtsmen, walkers and caravanners. Those with a serious taste for real ale will enjoy a splendid pint while any potential wastage is enthusiastically incorporated in Trish Fursse's beef and Guinness casserole. Alongside pints of shell-on prawns and daily fresh fish in summer are bites of broccoli with cheesy dip, tuna and pasta bake and the ever-popular grilled one-pound Cumberland sausage. Live music on Friday and Saturday nights. *Open 12-3, 6-11 (Sun 12-3, 7-10.30).* ***Bar Food*** *12-2, 7-9.30 (Sun to 9). Free House.* ***Beer*** *Bass, Worthington, guest beers. Garden, outdoor eating. No credit cards.*

LLANARMON DYFFRYN CEIRIOG — West Arms Hotel — FOOD B&B

Tel 01691 600665 **Fax 01691 600622** Map 8 D2
Llanarmon Dyffryn Ceiriog nr Llangollen Clwyd LL20 7LD

Zzz...

In a picturesque hamlet at the head of the Ceiriog valley, this 16th-century former farmhouse stands to the front of well-manicured gardens which run down to the river bridge. Black and white painted outside and bedecked with creeper and summer flowers, it's a haven of cosy comfort within, the tone set by open log fires, flagstone floors, blackened beams and rustic furniture. Tucked round the back, the Wayfarers' Bar serves a modest selection of well-prepared snacks in chintzy surroundings with an adjacent family lounge and patio. Following soup, chicken liver paté and herb mushrooms with garlic butter, local Ceiriog trout heads a list of main meals which might include Cumberland sausages and vegetable lasagne. Jam roly-poly and bread-and-butter pudding are typical of the traditional puddings. Bedrooms retain the period comfort afforded by handsome antique furnishings alongside modern fitted bathrooms: homely extras include pot pourri and quality toiletries. Five rooms are reserved for non-smokers and the two suites have plenty of space for family use (sleeping up to 5). *Open 11-11, Sun 12-3, 7-10.30.* ***Bar Food*** *12-2, 6.30-9 (Sun from 7). Free House.* ***Beer*** *Boddingtons. Garden, outdoor eating. Family room.* ***Accommodation*** *13 bedrooms, all en suite, £100 (single £50). Children welcome overnight, additional bed (£25) & cot (£5) are available. Hotel closed 2 weeks Jan/Feb. Access, Amex, Diners, Visa.*

LLANDDAROG — Butcher's Arms — FOOD

Tel 01267 275330 Map 9 B5
Llanddarog nr Carmarthen Dyfed SA32 8NS

Well into a second decade at the Butcher's, self-taught butcher, proprietor and accomplished chef David James still runs his kitchen with unbridled enthusiasm. There have been changes aplenty over the years, of which the by-passing of Llanddarog by the A40 is not the least significant; hidden up a side road by the church, the Butcher's Arms is now a serene spot. As fads have come and gone, however, the kitchen here has remained constant and the food consistent. Familiar lunch dishes include avocado and bacon salad, cheese, ham and potato pie and seasonal tagliatelle with prawns and asparagus. Home-made potato pies with spinach or ham and cheese are as popular today as a decade ago. In the evenings, generously-priced specials which supplement the menu are even more substantial. Fresh fish may be salmon en croute with lemon sauce or trout with orange and almonds; a home-made lasagne may contain chicken and sweetcorn. There may be Welsh lamb with mint and cider sauce, chicken à la King and perhaps King Henry's feast, a single beef rib roast. All this occurs in a pub which is by any standards tiny. Mavis James looks after the bookings (advised at weekends) and ordering with the same care that she applies to polishing the ubiquitous brass and miners' lamps, tending a roaring winter fire or arranging the floral displays which fill the fireplace in summer. The Butchers remains a village local, with a robust pint of Felinfoel a firm favourite among the loyal band of Welsh-speaking regulars. *Open 11-3 (not Sun), 5.30-11.* ***Bar Food*** *11-2.30 (not Sun), 6-9.45 (Sat 5.30-9.45, Sun 7-9.30). Free House.* ***Beer*** *Felinfoel Bitter, Dark & Double Dragon, guest beers. Front patio, outdoor eating. Pub closed Sun lunchtime. Access, Visa.*

LLANDOVERY — King's Head Inn — B&B

Tel 01550 720393 Map 9 C5
Market Square Llandovery Dyfed SA20 0AB

Medieval stonework and timbers are still in evidence throughout the bars of this black-painted town-centre building. Charles I's insignia, incorporated in the Inn's sign, commemorates the later construction of the upper storeys. Here the bedrooms have been sympathetically added and are kept reasonably up-to-date with neat bathrooms, tea-makers and radio-alarms. There is also a first-floor residents' TV lounge. A flagstoned rear entrance in Stone Street leads into the Old Bank (which once it was) where light meals and bar snacks are served. There are no reductions for children, except where they stay in parents' room in their own cot. *Open 11-3, 5.30-11, Sun 12-3, 7-10.30. Free House.* ***Beer*** *Hancock's. Accommodation 4 bedrooms, all en suite, £44 (single £26). Children by arrangement. No credit cards.*

LLANFAIR WATERDINE Red Lion Inn B&B

Tel 01547 528214 Map 9 D4

Llanfair Waterdine nr Knighton Powys LD7 1TU

You cross the River Teme, just off the B4355, some four miles from Knighton (Powys) and in so doing enter England. The Red Lion is a low, stone, whitewashed pub in a tiny hamlet containing a Post Office and the parish church (opposite); to the side is an attractive walled garden with picnic tables from where the ground slopes away, sharply, down to the river. Within, there's a stone-flagged village bar and a red-carpeted lounge-bar-with-dining with a huge inglenook fire flanked by piles of logs, plus much brass and tack. A small conservatory dining area is to the rear. Two of the three small but neatly kept bedrooms have washbasins and share bathroom facilities, the third has an en-suite bathroom. There's an air of total peace and quiet and there are fine views down the valley. Children are not allowed indoors. No food Sunday nights. *Open 12-3 (not Tue), 7-11 (Sun 12-2, 7-10.30). Free House. **Beer** Marston's Pedigree, Tetley, guest beer. Garden. **Accommodation** 3 bedrooms, 1 en suite, £40 (single £25). No children overnight. No dogs. Check-in by arrangement. Pub closed lunchtime Tuesdays. Accommodation closed over Christmas period. No credit cards.*

LLANFIHANGEL CRUCORNEY Skirrid Inn A

Tel 01873 890258 Map 9 D5

Llanfihangel Crucorney Gwent NP7 8DH

With some justification, the bloody Skirrid claims to be the oldest pub in Wales. It is recorded that one John Crowther was hanged here for sheep stealing in 1116; that the legendary Owain Glyndwr marshalled his troops in this yard before his march upon Pontrilas; and that rope marks on the old oak beams are from sentences handed down by the hanging Judge Jeffries following the papist plot of 1679. Today's high-ceilinged bar retains original Welsh slate, some Tudor oak settles and a collection of beaten copper pans and salvers echoing the inn's long and colourful history. Children are welcomed in the dining-room and garden only; hitching posts for horses in the yard. Two bedrooms are both en suite and one has a four-poster bed; there are rumours of friendly hauntings! 4½ miles north of Abergavenny, signposted off the A465 Hereford road. *Open 11-3, 6-11, Sat 11-11, Sun 12-3, 7-10.30. **Beer** Ushers. Garden. Family room. No dogs. No credit cards.*

LLANFIHANGEL-NANT-MELAN Red Lion Inn FOOD B&B

Tel 01544 350220 Map 9 D4

Llanfihangel-nant-Melan nr New Radnor Powys LD8 2TN

A popular stopping point on the A44 between the Midlands and Aberystwyth, the Johns family's pub goes from strength to strength. Not least among its virtues is chef Gareth's unstinting attention to fresh 'real food' – he produces pub food that is decidedly above average. His fried cod with chips and mushy peas and traditional bangers with mash and gravy as popular at lunchtimes as the more accomplished dishes like seafood with a creamy herb sauce and collops of beef with Madeira and pickled walnuts on the more involved evening menu. A home-made soup like cream of leek and nutmeg is made daily and their own paté is always popular. Family roast lunch on Sundays, home-made homely puddings (gooseberry shortcake, hazelnut mocha meringue, old-fashioned sherry trifle, tiramisu) and a commendable board of British cheeses (seven varieties, perhaps including Welsh Cheddar, Sage Derby and locally-produced farmhouse cheeses) provide further proof that the kitchen here is in good hands. Three spacious chalet bedrooms without TV or telephones offer abundant peace and quiet, well back from the road, with lightweight candy-striped duvets in summer and 'hotties' provided for winter nights. Bathrooms, with shower/WC only, are best described as practical, if a little spartan. Two family rooms sleep three. Conservatory and separate, no-smoking dining-room. *Open 11.30-2.30 (not Tue), 6.30-11 (Sun 12-3, 7-10.30). Bar Food 11.30-2.30, 6.30-9.30 (Sun from 12). Free House. **Beer** Hook Norton. Garden, outdoor eating. Family room. **Accommodation** 3 bedrooms, all en suite, £30 (family room £40, single £17.50). Children welcome overnight (under-2s stay free in parents' room, over-2s £5), additional bed (£10) supplied. Check-in by arrangement. Bar closed Tuesday. Access, Visa.*

LLANFRYNACH White Swan FOOD

Tel 01874 665276 Map 9 C5
Llanfrynach nr Brecon Powys LD3 7BZ

Polished flagstones, open log fire in a vast inglenook, exposed oak beams and cattle byres separating the tables lend the White Swan a general air of antiquity, to which piped classical music adds a surprising footnote. There's plenty of space inside and an attractive rear patio of stone-topped tables under a straggling trellis. Food sticks to well-tried standards, but quantities are generous – Welsh lamb chops, cottage pie, and home-made sweets such as crème caramel, sherry trifle. Llanfrynach is a sleepy village just off the A40 three miles from Brecon. *Open 12-3, 7-11 (not Mon), Sun 12-2.30, 7-10.30.* ***Bar Food*** *12-2 (Sun to 1.30), 7-10 (Sun to 9); no food last three weeks in Jan. Free House.* ***Beer*** *Brains, Flowers IPA. Garden, outdoor eating. Pub closed all Mon, 3 weeks Jan. No credit cards.*

LLANGATTOCK Vine Tree Inn FOOD

Tel 01873 810514 Map 9 D5
The Legar Llangattock nr Crickhowell Powys NP8 1HG

A picturesque row of low, pink-painted cottages just across a meadow from the River Usk, fronted by roadside picnic tables and a fine magnolia. Opposite, the stone packhorse bridge marks the old river crossing into Crickhowell. Exposed original stonework divides Stuart and Cynthia Lennox's pub into a succession of cosy alcoves, devoted almost entirely to eating. A blackboard menu runs the gamut of safe choices (stockpot soup, corn on the cob, prawn cocktail, mackerel paté, lasagne, scampi, fresh fish and steaks) interspersed with a few more adventurous selections (smoked venison, half a pineapple filled with chicken and prawn curry, pork stuffed with apricots in a tangy orange sauce), all generously served. Try, perhaps, baked eggs provençale, ham and asparagus 'Ardenne', pork chop in almond and cheese sauce, or the speciality 'Chicken Cymru' with white wine sauce with mushrooms and tomato. Half a dozen vegetarian options include vegetable chasseur, lasgane, curry and nut roast with tomato and basil sauce. Families are decidedly welcome and small portions readily available: booking though, is well advised. *Open 12-3, 6-11, Sun 12-3, 7-10.30.* ***Bar Food*** *12-2.30, 6.30-10 (Sun from 7). Free House.* ***Beer*** *Flowers Original & West Country Pale Ale, Boddingtons. Family room. No credit cards.*

LLANGOLLEN Britannia Inn B&B

Tel 01978 860144 Map 8 D2
Horseshoe Pass Llangollen Clwyd LL20 8DW

Zzz...

Cut back into the hillside by the A542 below the spectacular Horseshoe Pass, the inn stands two miles above the town: directly below are the ruins of Crucis Abbey. Quite possibly this site started out in the 11th century as a hostel for the abbey and the monks' ale house, waters from the adjacent stream being used for the brew. Today's ales are a little more sophisticated, as is the accommodation, though some original and some later, 15th-century, features can still be seen. Bedrooms are cottage-style with lacy cotton bedspreads and have brass four-poster beds. All rooms are on the small side with compact en-suite facilities (two with WC and showers only), colour TVs and coffee-making kits. There are no telephones in the rooms: guests may simply wake to the dawn chorus and enjoy the memorable valley views. *Open 11.30-3, 6-11, Sun 11-10.30. Free House.* ***Beer*** *Boddingtons, Flowers IPA, Theakston Best & Old Peculier.* ***Accommodation*** *7 bedrooms, all en suite, from £50 (winter £40, single £35/£25). Children welcome overnight, additional bed (£5) & cot available. Check-in by arrangement. Small dogs by arrangement only. Access, Amex, Diners, Visa.*

LLANGORSE Red Lion B&B

Tel 01874 658238 Map 9 D5
Llangorse nr Brecon Powys LD3 7TY

☺

Just a mile from Llangorse Lake, at the heart of the village by St. Paulinus Church, stands the Rosiers' welcoming local. Picnic tables in front by the village stream make it a picturesque spot. Riding, fishing and water-skiing (mid-week only), all available locally, draw many regulars to the Red Lion. Accommodation in neat pastel-shade bedrooms with attractive duvets is practical rather than luxurious, though TV, radio-alarms and tea-makers ensure an acceptable level of comfort. Five have well-kept bathrooms

en suite, the remainder (with showers and washbasins only) share a couple of adjacent toilets. Built into the hillside, all rooms have level access to a rear garden reserved for residents. Good selection of twenty malt whiskies. *Open 11.30-3, 6.30-11, Sun 12-3, 7-10.30. Free House.* ***Beer*** *Flowers Original, Morland Old Speckled Hen, Boddingtons. Streamside terrace/patio, outdoor eating. Family room.* ***Accommodation*** *10 bedrooms, 5 en suite, £40-£50 (family room £60, single £25). Children welcome overnight, additional bed (£10 but no charge for under-12s) & cot available. No dogs. Pub closed lunchtime Mon-Fri, Nov-Mar. No credit cards.*

LLANGRANNOG — Ship Inn — FOOD

Tel 01239 654423 Map 9 B4
Llangrannog Dyfed SA44 6SL

Just 50 yards from the beach, the white-painted Ship Inn is located down a narrow winding road (watch out for a very steep hairpin bend) in a delightful little seaside village. It's run by two couples, the Boxes and the Browns: Lynne and De are responsible for the bar menu which, in addition to standard items like steak and kidney pie, steaks (well hung by the local butcher), ploughman's, jacket potatoes and sandwiches, roams far and wide with pizza, and from the blackboard 'Specials' menu, Dijon kidneys, broccoli and cheese pie and tandoori chicken masala. Local seafood features strongly in summer with dressed crab, baked local herring, skate, or, given 24hrs' notice, a special seafood platter that includes lobster, scallops, cockles, mussels, whelks, crab and prawns. Drinks are served from noon to 11 pm every day and guests can eat in one of the two bars or outside under colourful awnings that keep the showers at bay while you watch the world go by. *Open 12-11, Sun 12-10.30.* ***Bar*** *Food 12-3, 6-10 (Sun from 7 in winter). Free House.* ***Beer*** *Courage Directors, Ruddles County, Courage Dark, Webster's Yorkshire Outdoor eating. Family room. Access, Visa.*

LLANGYNWYD — Olde House Inn — A

Tel & Fax 01656 733310 Map 9 C6
Llangynwyd nr Maesteg Mid Glamorgan CF34 9SB

☺

At the heart of Llangynwyd's original village off the A4063, the Olde House is notable for its antiquity (dating back to 1147), its massive thatched roof, metre-thick Welsh stone walls and ubiquitous memorabilia. Modern-day amenities include a spacious conservatory dining-room, vast graded patios with a barbecue pit and a children's adventure playground complete with an old tractor. Drinkers may appreciate the selection of around 60 malt whiskies but the pub is "95% a food operation". *Open 11-11, Sun 12-10.30. Free House.* ***Beer*** *Morland Old Speckled Hen, Flowers IPA & Original. Garden, children's play area. Access, Amex, Diners, Visa.*

LLANNEFYDD — Hawk & Buckle — B&B

Tel 01745 540249 **Fax 01745 540316** Map 8 C1
Llannefydd nr Denbigh Clwyd LL16 5ED

Zzz...

Stone-built in the 17th century, tiny Llannefydd stands high up in the Denbigh hills. Steady improvements here have produced an inn of high quality, run and personally supervised by Bob and Barbara Pearson. Residents enjoy use of their own lounge bar and may mull over their morning papers without fear of noisy intrusion. En-suite bedrooms with TVs, direct-dial telephones and fully equipped bathrooms are decorated in co-ordinating fabrics and mostly pastel shades; guests may choose between duvets or traditional bedding. The best rooms, one of them with a pine four-poster, are on the upper floor from where guests enjoy the finest views down to Cefn Meiriadog and the North Wales coast. *Open 12-2, 7-11, Sun 12-2, 7-10.30. No real ales.* ***Accommodation*** *10 bedrooms, all en suite, £50 (single £38). No children under 8 years overnight. No dogs. Pub closed lunchtimes Mon, Tue, Thu & Fri in winter (Oct-end Apr). Closed 25 Dec. Access, Visa.*

Many **B&B** establishments offer reduced rates for weekend and out-of-season bookings. Always ask about special deals for longer stays. Beware half-board terms in inns where we do not recommend the **FOOD**.

LLANTRISANT — Greyhound Inn — B&B

Tel 01291 672505 **Fax 01291 673255** Map 9 D6
Llantrisant nr Usk Gwent NP5 1LE

Just 2½ miles from Usk, the Greyhound occupies a hillside, with fine views of the Lowes River valley which flows to the sea at Newport some 9 miles downstream. The low stone 17th-century farm house is much extended now with split-level bar and succession of drinking and eating rooms stepped into the hill. Conversion of the farmer barn has produced a dozen en-suite bedrooms with blackened roof trusses and decorated in a cottage style becoming both the building's nature and its rural location. Up-to-the-minute equipment includes remote-control TV and direct-dial phones; two larger family rooms have an extra bed; all have both bath and showers. French windows in the best, ground-floor rooms open on to private patios in a garden setting with lily pond and ornamented fountain. There is no direct access from the nearby A449 dual carriageway, so be sure to obtain exact directions on booking. Hundreds of trees have been planted and all rooms are double-glazed to prevent any intrusive road noise. *Open 11-3, 6-11, Sun 12-4, 7-10.30. Free House. **Beer** Wadworth 6X, Flowers Original, Marston's Pedigree, Boddingtons, Greene King Abbot Ale, guest beer. Garden, patio. Family Room. **Accommodation** 10 bedrooms, all en suite, £60 (single £50). Children welcome overnight (babies stay free in parents' room), additional bed (£5) & cot available. No dogs. Accommodation closed 24 & 25 Dec. Access, Visa.*

LLANYRE — Bell Country Inn — B&B

Tel 01597 823959 Map 9 C4
Llanyre Llandrindod Wells Powys LD1 6DY

Standing in hills above Llandrindod Wells, just two miles away, Llanyre is handily placed for visitors to mid-Wales with the Elan and upper Wye valleys nearby and multifarious outdoor activity within handy reach. Built originally for drovers headed with their flocks to 'foreign parts' (Gloucester and Hereford), the Bell provided clean straw and stabling throughout the 17th and 18th centuries. Today's version offers high-quality accommodation in recent extensions. Standard equipment includes satellite TV, radio alarms and telephones as well as beverage trays, trouser presses and hair dryers. Bedrooms are brightly decorated in pastel shades with generously-sized duvets and bathrooms sport smart white porcelain fitments with powerful over-bath showers. Two larger rooms are suitable for family use (under-11s stay free and a cot is available), one of these on the ground floor is quite suitable for disabled guests. *Open 11-3, 6-11 (Sun 12-3, 7-10.30), 11-11 in summer. Free House. **Beer** Worthington Best, Theakston XB, guest beer. Small garden. **Accommodation** 9 bedrooms, all en suite, £57.50 (single £32.50/£35). Children welcome overnight, under-11s stay free in parents' room, additional bed (£20) and cot available. Access, Amex, Diners, Visa.*

LLOWES — Radnor Arms — FOOD

Tel 01497 847460 Map 9 D5
Llowes Powys HR3 5JA

Landlord of the Radnor Arms for over ten years, Brian Gorringe offers culinary refinement in this 1000-year-old drinking house. The old stone building with a stone roof is overlooked by the Black Mountains on one side, the Beacons on another and the Beggins on the third. With only a dozen tables and no more than 40-60 seats, it's surprising to encounter six blackboards announcing 99 starters, snacks, main dishes and puddings from which to choose! The Radnor Arms divides by means of heavy oak panels into the bar area proper, popular by day, and a more spacious, lofty-beamed garden side for more leisurely evening enjoyment, and for which you ought to book. Either way, there's good beer on handpump plus a few unusual bottled beers and a modest selection of house wines. The menu on the blackboards might include cod and chips, French onion soup, cottage pie, paella Valenciana, venison in port wine and Guinness, tiger prawns with garlic bread, haddock mornay, or monkfish with princess scallops in lemon and champagne sauce. Sandwiches, filled rolls and ploughman's platters are served all day. Puddings include gateau Véronique and omelette viennoise. Some homely touches help to extend a warm Welsh welcome. Cruets and coffee sets are of hand-made Black Mountain pottery, and there are woolly dolls and framed three-dimensional paper cut-outs for sale. *Open 11-3, 6.30-11 (not Mon), Sun 12-3 only. **Bar Food** 11-2.30, 6.30-11 (except Sun eve and Mon). Free House. **Beer** Felinfoel Traditional. Garden, outdoor eating. Pub closed all Mon and Sun eve (except Bank Holidays). No credit cards.*

LLWYNDAFYDD — Crown Inn — FOOD

Tel 01545 560396 Map 9 B4
Llwyndafydd nr New Quay Dyfed SA44 6FH

A handsome, white-painted 18th-century inn at the head of the hidden romantic valley of Cwm Tudu below which German U-boats may have landed to obtain fresh water during the First World War. This highly popular spot with families in summer has a large patio and play area for the children (who are offered regular favourites on their own menu). In addition to a standard range of adult bar food (the evening restaurant menu is pricier) there are well-made curries and daily specials on a board like local fish (baked cod in cheese and prawn sauce, pan-fried local plaice, Teifi sewin and salmon), wild rabbit casserole, stir-fried pork with sweet and sour sauce) and braised pigeon breast with tomato and mushrooms. Home-made pizzas, from children's size to family size, are made to order. Ice cream features on the dessert choice alongside home-made gateau and cheesecake. Popular for Sunday lunch (half price for children). *Open 12-3, 6-11 (Sun 12-3, 7-10.30).* ***Bar Food*** *12-2, 6-9 (Sun 12-3, 7-9). Free House.* ***Beer*** *Boddingtons, Flowers IPA & Original, Bass, guest beer. Garden, outdoor eating area, tiered patios. Pub closed Sun evenings Oct-Mar (except Christmas period). Access, Visa.*

LLYSWEN — Griffin Inn ★ FOOD

Tel 01874 754241 **Fax 01874 754592** Map 9 D5 **B&B**
Llyswen Brecon Powys LD3 0OU

Zzz...  

Mythically speaking, the griffin is a creature of vast proportions, half lion, half dragon, its whole being considerably less awesome than its constituent parts. No such problems exist for Richard and Di Stockton, for their Griffin is nothing short of splendid in all departments and conspicuously well run. That locally-caught salmon and brook trout feature so regularly on the menu is scarcely surprising as the Griffin employs its own ghillie, and fishing stories abound in the bar, which is the centre of village life. It's hung with framed displays of fishing flies and maps of the upper and lower reaches of the Wye valley, and dominated by a splendid inglenook fire. In the adjacent lounge, low tables, high-backed Windsor chairs and window seats make a comfortable setting in which to sample their new 'Tiffin' menu (dishes for two people); this might offer spicy chicken with noodles or a vegetarian risotto followed by a long choice of home-made sweets (hot choc pud with choc custard, bread-and-butter pudding 'with cream, ice cream or lumpy custard', chocolate profiteroles, rum and banana trifle), ice creams, sorbets and Welsh cheeses. Evening meals provide a wider choice of more substantial fare, either in the no-smoking restaurant or the bars, as space allows. Here you might order cream of mushroom and thyme soup, Stilton, celery and port terrine, lamb's kidneys Turbigo, braised oxtail in Old Ale, grilled Welsh lamb cutlets or ratatouille pasta au gratin. Tip-top Sunday lunch is only served in the dining-room (no bar food) and booking is suggested at least a week ahead. The ten bedrooms, all but one with en-suite facilities, revert to the fishing theme. To say that they are cottagey is not to decry the pretty floral curtains and bed-covers; they are wonderfully tranquil, and though there are telephones, television is considered superfluous. Two new rooms are in an annexe across the road. A family suite has its own lounge, shares a bathroom and sleeps four. The splendid residents' lounge on the upper floor of the inn's oldest part is dramatically set under original rafters dating, it is thought, back to its origins as a 15th-century sporting inn. There is no garden but children may eat in the bar and small portions are served; two high-chairs provided. *Open 12-3, 7-11, Sun 12-3, 7-10.30.* ***Bar Food*** *12-2 (no bar food Sun), 7-9 (Sun cold supper for residents only); Sun lunch at 1pm in dining-room only. Free House.* ***Beer*** *Boddingtons, Flowers IPA, Bass, Brains, Marston's Pedigree. Outdoor eating.* ***Accommodation*** *10 bedrooms, 9 en suite, £50 (family room £80, single £28.50). Children welcome overnight, additional bed & cot available. Access, Amex, Diners, Visa.*

We endeavour to be as up-to-date as possible but inevitably some changes to landlords, chefs and other key staff occur after the Guide has gone to press.

LYDART — Gockett Inn — FOOD

Tel 01600 860486 Map 9 D5
Lydart nr Monmouth Gwent NP5 4AD

This former staging post on the St David's to London route stands atop an escarpment (now the B4293) three miles outside Monmouth; 'Gockett' was the local name for the black grouse which inhabited these heathlands until their extinction a century or so ago. Central to the Inn's modern attractions are Hazel Short's daily selected menus, wherein brevity is made a virtue by careful buying of top-quality foodstuffs, and by her innovative approach to traditional recipes. Home-made soups are thick, flavourful, and popular, along with the likes of prawns with fresh raspberry vinaigrette, paté maison with Cumberland sauce, tagliatelle with smokey bacon, leek and black pudding tart. Though all are officially starters, a light lunch of two of them is equally acceptable, except on Sundays, when bookings should be made for the fixed-price lunch. Alongside the hefty pies other main courses are equally substantial: poussin with mild fresh fruit curry sauce, fillet of beef en croute filled with Stilton cheese and Madeira sauce, plus vegetarian lasagne. The pudding list which follows is simple but commendable in scope, mostly home-made offerings like treacle tart, with home-made custard and bread-and-butter pudding. Leather banquettes, silk flowers and gathered drapes lend a bright, cottagey feel to the original dining-room which is hung with horse brasses and copper bed-warmers. A more recent extension to the bar has increased the space and leads to an enclosed rear patio, and a neat garden for alfresco eating in fine weather. *Open 11-11, Sun 12-10.30.* ***Bar Food*** *12-2, 7-10 (7-9 Sun). Free House.* ***Beer*** *Bass, guest beers. Garden, outdoor eating, disabled WC. Family room. Access, Visa.*

We do not accept free meals or hospitality – our inspectors pay their own bills and never book in the name of Egon Ronay's Guides.

MARFORD — Trevor Arms — B&B

Tel 01244 570436 Map 8 D2
Marford Wrexhall Clwyd LL12 8TA

Quaint 17th-century architecture is a feature of Marford's original buildings, which all incorporate a cross to ward off evil spirits. The Trevor Arms, built later as a coaching inn, echoes these features and also plays its full part in village life centred on a very busy locals' bar which occupies the pub's oldest part. The original and somewhat modest bedrooms are also housed here. Though not lacking in modern appointments such as TV, radio and direct-dial phones most offer only shower/WC en-suite bathrooms. Two newest rooms, one with a four-poster the other a family room sleeping up to three, have en-suite baths; two further rooms are due to come on line in 1996. In addition to its large garden and children's play area, the latest attraction is a covered barbecue patio complete with freestanding gas heaters for use on chillier evenings. *Open 11-11 (Sun 12-10.30).* ***Beer*** *Thomas Greenall's Original, Greenall's Draught, Stones, guest beer. Garden, summer barbecue, lawn. Family room.* ***Accommodation*** *18 bedrooms, all en suite, from £40.50 (single £29.50), cooked breakfast £3.50 pp extra. Children welcome overnight, additional bed (from £5). No dogs. Access, Visa.*

MOLD — We Three Loggerheads — FOOD

Tel 01352 810337 Map 8 D2
Loggerheads nr Mold Clwyd CH7 5PG

Standing alongside the A494, some three miles from Mold, a squarish 16th-century stone pub with somewhat inelegant white-painted brick additions. Public bars and games room are a touch charmless; the extension, a pine-clad pillared room with closely-set tables, captain's chairs and banquette seating is devoted to eating. In addition to the printed menu of standard pub grub (ploughman's platters and so on) is a daily blackboard of unusual, globe-trotting fare. There are roadside picnic tables on the patio, next to the Alun River bridge. Bass Taverns. *Open 12-3.0, 5.30-11, Fri & Sat 11-11, Sun 12-3.30, 7-10.30.* ***Bar Food*** *12-2.30, 6-10. Riverside patio, outdoor eating.* ***Beer*** *Bass, Worthington. Access, Visa.*

NEVERN — Trewern Arms Hotel — B&B

Tel 01239 820395 Map 9 A5
Nevern nr Newport Dyfed SA42 0NB

Zzz... 

This hidden hamlet in a valley on the B4582 is a world all on its own with historic pilgrims' church and Celtic cross, nurseries, cheese dairy and cake shop. Across the stone bridge over the Nyfer (or Nevern), the Trewern Arms is creeper-clad with sparkling fairy lights, exuding a magical air. Bedrooms, carefully added to the original 18th-century stone building, are furnished in cane and pine with floral curtains and matching duvets. The bathrooms are all en suite (7 with shower/WCs only); TVs and tea-makers are standard. There are three spacious family rooms (one sleeping up to four). A foyer lounge upstairs has plenty of literature for walkers and fishermen, and the lounge bar below sports comfortable armchairs and sofas. *Open 11-3, 6-11, Sun 12-3, 7-10.30. Free House.* ***Beer*** *Whitbread Castle Eden, Flowers Original, guest beers. Garden, outdoor eating, children's play area. Family room.* ***Accommodation*** *9 bedrooms, all en suite, £45 double (family room £55, single £30). Children welcome overnight, additional bed (£10 for under-12s) available. No dogs. Access, Visa.*

NOTTAGE — Rose & Crown — B&B

Tel 01656 784850 **Fax 01656 772345** Map 9 C6
Nottage Heol-y-Capel nr Porthcawl Mid Glamorgan CF36 5ST

Just a mile from Royal Porthcawl Golf Club and the town's West Bay stands this white-painted row of stone-built former cottages at the heart of a tiny hamlet. In an area short of good pub accommodation, its friendly, refurbished village bar and neat cottage bedrooms are justly popular. Pastel shaded decor with fitted pine furniture, practical bathrooms and room comforts including phone, TV and trouser press promise a restful and comfortable stay. Scottish Courage. *Open 11.30-11, Sun 12-3, 7-10.30.* ***Beer*** *John Smith's, Ruddles County & Best, Webster's Yorkshire. Garden, children's play area.* ***Accommodation*** *8 bedrooms, all en suite, £39.95 (single £35.95). Children welcome overnight (under-2s stay free in parents' room, 2-11s £2.50), additional bed & cot available. Guide dogs only. Access, Amex, Diners, Visa.*

OLD RADNOR — Harp Inn — FOOD B&B

Tel & Fax 01544 350655 Map 9 D4
Old Radnor Presteigne Powys LO8 2RH

Zzz...

It's worth the drive scarcely a mile uphill from the A44 just to soak in the views of the Radnor Forest and surrounding hills from the common ground which separates the Harp from Old Radnor's Norman church. Flagstone floors and abundant old beams epitomise the character of the three interlinked rooms which form the bar and dining areas. A wonderful mish-mash of antique settles, assorted tables and bric-a-brac imbue it with a comfortably lived-in feel. On a mantelpiece beside the bar the candle of welcome (an expedient accessory when the power fails) burns in perpetuity. The Copes' kitchen adopts a homely approach and Dee makes a virtue of simplicity. Lunchtime snacks range from home-made soup to ploughman's platters, sandwiches garnished with crisps and salad, paté with toast, a pasta dish, sautéed mushrooms on toast and baked potatoes; daily specials might include salade niçoise or home-potted salmon. For dinner (booking advised) one might commence with deep-fried Brie, following with a daily special of poached salmon hollandaise or more regular beef curry, chicken Kiev and a giant Yorkshire pudding filled with steak and kidney; desserts seem less inviting. Four spotless bedrooms, cosy and quiet without phones or TVs, share a brace of bathrooms in a higgledy-piddledy upper floor whose creaking, uneven floors and wood-pegged roof trusses are further evidence of the Harp's antiquity (reputedly 15th-century). Ever-practical, they've even adapted the roof-space for passing walkers to bed down in. A tiny galley kitchen is fully stocked with a wide range of provisions to cook for yourself. For those to whom all this may strike a chord, the Harp should be harmoniously in tune. *Open 11.30-11 (Sun 12-3, 7-10.30).* ***Bar Food*** *12-2, 7-9 (not Mon), Sat & Sun 12-2.30, 7-9.30. Free House.* ***Beer*** *Wood's Special, Wye Valley Hereford Bitter & Pale Ale, guest beer in summer. Garden, outdoor eating, summer barbecue at weekends.* ***Accommodation*** *4 bedrooms, share 2 bathrooms, £35 (single £25/£35). Children welcome, additional bed (£10) & cot supplied. No credit cards.*

PANT MAWR — Glansevern Arms Hotel — B&B

Tel 01686 440240 Map 9 C4
Pant Mawr nr Llangurig Powys SY18 6SY

The art of "old-fashioned innkeeping" is still alive and well at the Glansevern Arms, which has been owned and run by Mr Edwards and family since 1966. On the A44, four miles west of Llangurig towards Aberystwyth (19 miels away), the inn commands a magnificent position amid the Plynlimon range, overlooking the upper reaches of the River Wye. An intimate bar and lounge soak in the glorious hill scenery by day and glow with warmth from log fires at night. Residents equally enjoy the peace and quiet afforded by bedrooms with private sitting areas, uninterrupted by any phones, where the views should provide a greater attraction than television. Also recommended in our *1996 Hotels & Restaurants Guide*. 'Old-fashioned' may often be used in a derogatory sense to describe such an operation, but here it seems entirely apposite. The hotel has one mile of fishing rights on the river and there are three reservoirs within easy reach. *Open 11-2, 6.30-11, Sun 12-3, 7-10.30. **Beer** Bass. **Accommodation** 7 rooms, all en suite, £55 (single £35). Children welcome overnight (under-12s half-price), additional bed available. Closed 1 week Christmas. No credit cards.*

PEMBROKE FERRY — Ferry Inn — FOOD

Tel 01646 682947 Map 9 A5
Pembroke Ferry nr Pembroke Dock Dyfed SA72 6UD

Fresh fish and seafoods rightly predominate at the Ferry, which stands by ripping tidal waters right under the Cleddau Bridge – turn off the A477 by the tolls. Local oysters share the daily blackboard with the likes of popular sea bass, hake florentine in cheese sauce and whole baby turbot. For those of less fishy persuasion are the home-cured ox tongue, sirloin steak, bacon steak with parsley sauce and a vegetable puff pastry parcel. As there is only one small bar, children are welcome inside only at lunchtime (if well behaved) or they can roam the riverside patio and rocks when weather and tide permit. Sunday lunch carvery (and bar snacks). Choice of around 20 malt whiskies. *Open 11.30-2.45, 6.30-11, Sun 12-2.45, 7-10.30. **Bar Food** 12-2 (carvery lunch Sun to 1.30), 7-10 (Sun to 9.30). Free House. **Beer** Bass, Hancock's HB. Waterside patio/terrace, outdoor eating. Pub closed 25 & 26 Dec. Access, Visa.*

PENALLT — Boat Inn — A

Tel 01600 712615 Map 14 A2
Long Lane Penallt nr Monmouth Gwent NP5 4AJ

Despite its Monmouthshire address, this Wye valley pub is commonly known as 'The Boat at Redbrook'; a signpost will direct you to park by the football field on the A466 Monmouth to Chepstow road and cross by a footbridge adjoining the disused railway line. In the pub garden, log tables teeter on the hillside which is by-passed on two sides by streams that cascade into the River Wye. Beer aficionados, attracted in part by Tuesday's folk and Thursday's Blues nights, are offered a fine selection of beers direct from the cask. Pot meals of country-cidered pork and rice, rogan josh, pan haggerty and aubergine Parmesan mostly assume secondary importance. There are rolls most lunchtimes, occasional barbecues in the summer months, and country wines on offer. Open all day Saturday during the football season. *Open 11-3, 6-11 (Sat in winter 11-11), Sun 12-3, 7-10.30. Free House. **Beer** 8-10 regularly-changing real ales: Thwaites, Fuller's London Pride, Theakston XB & Old Peculier, Shepherd Neame Spitfire. Riverside garden. Family room. Pub closed 25 Dec eve. No credit cards.*

PENMAENPOOL — George III Hotel — B&B

Tel 01341 422525 **Fax 01341 423565** Map 8 C3
Penmaenpool nr Dolgellau Gwynedd LL40 1YD

Squeezed in between the A493 (which is at roof level) and the head of the Mawddach Estuary, the 17th-century George III Hotel is run by five members of the Cartwright family. It enjoys magnificent views – shared by all but two of the bedrooms – across the water to wooded hills beyond. The unpretentious Dresser Bar – so named because the bar counter is made out of the bottom half of an old Welsh dresser – is a place where wooden tables are polished, brass ornaments gleam and a welcoming fire burns in the grate. The rrefurbished Cellar Bar (actually at ground level) is open only in the summer when there

are also tables outside, on what was a railway line, next to the water. Residents have there own cosy lounge with beamed ceiling and inglenook fireplace. The bedrooms, half of which are in the adjacent, former Victorian railway station, have all benefited from recent refurbishment and have traditional free-standing furniture and pretty floral fabrics – William Morris in the old station rooms – plus smart modern bathrooms. All have direct-dial phones, TV, trouser press and beverage kit. Families should head for the Cellar Bar; the children's menu offers popular favourites; baby-changing facilities are provided. Free fishing permits for residents. *Open 11-11, Sun 12.30-3, 7-10.30. Free House.* ***Beer*** *Ruddles Best, John Smith's, guest beer. Garden, children's play area.* ***Accommodation*** *11 bedrooms, all en suite, £88 (single £45). Children welcome overnight, additional bed (under-12s £12.50) & cot supplied. Access, Visa.*

PENYBONT — Severn Arms Hotel — B&B

Tel 01597 851224 **Fax 01597 851693** Map 9 C4
Penybont nr Llandrindod Wells Powys LD1 5UA

A white-painted former coaching inn by the junction of the A488 and A44, at the heart of the Ithon Valley. Loved by JB Priestley for its creaky floors, old oak beams and sloping ceiling, it has some of the best family rooms around, tucked under the eaves of the pub's top storey, with pastoral views down the garden to a wooden bridge over the river. Caring management by Geoff and Tessa Lloyd has extended over eleven years and the bedrooms are both immaculately kept and well equipped; all en suite, most have trouser presses and all have TV, radio, direct-dial phones and tea-making facilities. From the flagstoned entrance there's access to the village bar festooned with local football trophies, a more sedate lounge bar and extensive dining-room. Residents enjoy use of their own quiet TV lounge on the first floor. *Open 11-2.30, 6-11, Sun 12-2.30, 7-10.30. Free House.* ***Beer*** *Tetley, Worthington, Bass. Garden, outdoor eating.* ***Accommodation*** *10 bedrooms, all en suite, £50 (single £28). Children welcome overnight, additional bed and cot supplied. Accommodation closed one week Christmas-New Year. Access, Amex, Diners, Visa.*

PISGAH — Halfway Inn — A

Tel 01970 880631 Map 9 C4
Devil's Bridge Road Pisgah nr Aberystwyth Dyfed SY23 4NE

650 feet up, overlooking the Rheidol Valley below, Raywood and Sally Roger's marvellous country pub is in a lovely setting with magnificent views. It's well known as a beer-lovers' favourite, with its choice of up to four real ales. Never modernised or extended, this 250-year-old Inn retains a traditional feel – candle-lit in the evenings and log fire in winter. Families use the Stone Room bar (walls made of stone). The grassy upper car park offers free overnight pitching for campers and pony-trekkers can leave their mounts in a paddock. *Open 11.30-2.30, 6.30-11 (may be open all day in summer), Sun 12-3, 7-10.30. Free House.* ***Beer*** *Felinfoel Double Dragon, Flowers Original, Whitbread Castle Eden, guest beer. Garden. Family room. No credit cards.*

RAGLAN — Beaufort Arms Hotel — B&B

Tel & Fax 01291 690412 Map 9 D5
High Street Raglan Gwent NP5 2DY

Recent alterations uncovered remains of the original Tudor timberwork which are now preserved in the unusual and characterful Country Bar. Rumour has it that there still remains a secret underground passage from here to nearby Raglan Castle. Residents have use of their own lounge and bedrooms are kitted out with white wood furniture, floral fabrics, radios, telephones, TVs and beverage trays. *Open 12-3, 6-11, Sun 12-2, 7-10.30.* ***Beer*** *Courage Directors & Best, two guest beers.* ***Accommodation*** *15 bedrooms, all en suite, £45 (single £35). Children welcome overnight (family room sleeping four £55). Dogs by arrangement. Access, Amex, Diners, Visa.*

Many **B&B** establishments offer reduced rates for weekend and out-of-season bookings. Always ask about special deals for longer stays. Beware half-board terms in inns where we do not recommend the **FOOD.**

RED WHARF BAY — Ship Inn — FOOD

Tel 01248 852568 **Fax 01248 853568** Map 8 B1
Red Wharf Bay nr Benllech Anglesey Gwynedd LL75 4RJ

Landlord Andrew Kenneally has now been at the low, white-painted Ship for 25 years. The inn is fronted by hanging baskets and stands right on the bay shore. Quarry-tiled floors plus genuine exposed beams and stonework make for an interesting interior where the ship's wheels and chiming clocks, Tom Browne cartoons and Toby Jug collection give it great character. With food as the main draw, there's a steady stream of early arrivals and local regulars to sample from a selection of bar food which is sensibly varied daily between cold and hot choices and never overly long. Typical dishes might include deep-fried cockles, cream of celery soup, baked cod with peppers and tomatoes, grilled lemon sole, vegetable goulash, pepperpot beef and ginger, traditional Welsh sausages with a leek sauce, mussels in garlic topped with cheese and Caerphilly, apple and sweet potato bake; finish with sticky toffee pudding or rhubarb and ginger crumble. The new Cellar Room is no-smoking. There's a separate children's menu served in a smaller rear family room or out in the shoreside garden. A no-smoking restaurant opens upstairs for diners at weekends.
*Open 11-3.30, 7-11 (11-11 mid-June to mid-Sept Mon-Sat & Bank Holidays), Sun 12-3, 7-10.30. **Bar Food** 12-2.15, 7-9.15 (from 6 in summer), Sun 12-2, 7-9. Free House. **Beer** Friary Meux, Tetley Best, guest beer. Garden, front patio, outdoor eating area, tables in garden. Family room. Access, Visa.*

SHIRENEWTON — Carpenters Arms — FOOD

Tel 01291 641231 Map 9 D6
Shirenewton nr Chepstow Gwent NP6 6BU

On the B4235 Usk road, 4 miles from Chepstow (turn by the race course) the Carpenters is a row of roadside cottages which once housed the local smithy and carpenter's shop, now quite literally hollowed out into a succession of seven interconnecting rooms served from a single bar. The choice of real ales is a serious draw and a plethora of baguettes and baked potatoes the regular lunchtime accompaniments. Amid a regularly-changing blackboard menu relying in large part on convenience items there's still room to seek out a quality sirloin steak and home-made steak and mushroom pie; daily specials might extend the range to include paella and chicken in leek and Stilton sauce. Home-made puddings include a popular rhubarb crumble. Cars park right up to the door on a bend in the road where some picnic tables front the building amid a blaze of summer flowers in tubs and hanging baskets. There is no garden here, and well-behaved children are just about tolerated within.
*Open 11-2.30, 6-11 (may be open all day in Summer), Sun 12-3, 7-10.30. **Bar Food** 12-2, 7-9.30. Free House. **Beer** Fuller's London Pride, Flowers IPA, Wadworth 6X, Boddingtons, Marston's Pedigree & Owd Rodger, guest beers. Patio, outdoor eating. No credit cards.*

SHIRENEWTON — Tredegar Arms — FOOD — B&B

Tel 01291 641274 Map 9 D6
Shirenewton nr Chepstow Gwent NP6 6RQ

Zzz...

Dominating the crossroads at the heart of this small hillside village of stone cottages (signed both from A48 and B4285 some five miles from Chepstow), the Tredegar Arms is in the sure hands of experienced locals Rob and Val Edwards. Facing a servery ingeniously cut back under a central staircase, the lounge bar is the focal point for food which already shows a refreshing balance between conventional and empirical fare. Tandoori chicken pieces and sesame prawn toasts are among less usual curtain raisers to traditional main courses such as liver, bacon and onions and grilled trout with roasted almonds. Decidedly different specials recently on offer included a honeyed lamb ragout with mint, a 'cock-a-roosting fricassee' in parsley and lemon sauce, 'Bully Hole Bottom Pepperpot' and a fiery 'Welsh Dragon pie', actually made with lamb. Upstairs are two letting bedrooms, each with its own WC and shower room en suite. Equipped with colour TVs and tea- and coffee-making equipment, they are unfussily furnished and spotlessly kept and enjoy super views down the valley to the distant Severn estuary. A truly restful night is followed by gargantuan country breakfasts.
*Open 11-3, 6-11 (may be open all day in summer), Sun 12-3, 7-10.30. **Bar Food** 12-2, 7-9.30 (Sun to 9). Free House. **Beer** Hook Norton Best, Hancock's HB, three guest beers. **Accommodation** 2 rooms, both en suite, £40 (single £25). Check-in by arrangement. No dogs. No credit cards.*

SWANSEA — Langland Court Hotel — B&B

Tel 01792 361545 **Fax 01792 362302** Map 9 C6
31 Langland Court Road Langland Swansea West Glamorgan SA3 4TD

Zzz...

Especially favoured by those less enamoured of Swansea's noisy nightlife, Langland Court has a fine hilltop location on Mumbles Head some four miles from the city. Take the A4067 along the seafront and follow signs to Caswell from Mumbles village. Striking first impressions are created by the grand oak staircase which dominates the foyer. To one side, the former Polly Garter's bar, named in commemoration of local boy Dylan Thomas, is now more a 'pubby' wine bar and bistro, with residents finding relaxation in the lounge and bar whose patio doors open on to the garden. Tudor-style front bedrooms, some with antique four posters, and the stylish attic rooms with third-bed alcoves are the pick of the main house accommodation, enjoying fine views down to the Bristol Channel. Alternative accommodation is in more modestly-sized bedrooms across a quiet road in the Coach House. Bathrooms, bedroom facilities which include TV, radio and direct dial phones and housekeeping generally are of a high standard throughout. Three family rooms sleep up to four. Dogs allowed in the Coach House only. *Open 12-11 (Sun to 10.30). No real ales. Garden.* ***Accommodation*** *21 bedrooms, all en suite, £75-£83 (Sunday £65 double, family rrom £95-£103, single £55-£61). Children welcome overnight, additional bed (under-16s £12) & cot (£3) available. Dogs by arrangement. Access, Amex, Visa.*

TRECASTLE — Castle Coaching Inn — FOOD B&B

Tel 01874 636354 **Fax 01874 636457** Map 9 C5
Brecon Road Trecastle Brecon Powys LO3 84H

A famous inn on the old coaching route through the Brecons. The opened-out bar and dining areas make good use of natural daylight and retain sufficient of the pub's original features such as the flagstone floors and vast open fireplace to preserve the Castle's unique character. A new chef has recently taken over and the blackboard bar menus now offer the likes of sandwiches, ploughman's platters, chili con carne and steak and ale pie – less inviting than before. All the bedrooms are en suite, with smartly-tiled bathrooms and up-to-date amenities that include direct-dial phones, TVs, radio alarm clocks and hairdryers. There are two good-sized family rooms, one with bunk beds (children stay free in their parents' room). To the pub's rear there's a safe, enclosed garden in which to enjoy panoramic views down the Gwyddor valley. *Open 11-3, 6-11, Sun 12-3, 7-10.30.* ***Bar Food*** *12-2, 6.30-9.30 (Sun from 7.30). Free House.* ***Beer*** *Courage Directors, John Smith's. Garden, outdoor eating.* ***Accommodation*** *10 bedrooms, all en suite, £40 (single £35). Children welcome overnight, additional bed & cot available. No dogs. Access, Visa.*

TRELLECH — Village Green — FOOD B&B

Tel 01600 860119 Map 9 D5
Trellech nr Monmouth Gwent NP5 4PA

Bob and Jane Evans's 450-year-old village local combines bistro-style food with the more traditional concept of pub-with-restaurant. Thus we find here a combination of all three with an à la carte restaurant (recommended in our *1996 Hotels and Restaurants Guide*) and a brace of pubby bars that offer traditional pub snacks like ploughman's platters, sandwiches and baked potatoes. Between the two bars a stone-walled bistro, festooned with dried flowers hanging from its rafters, offers an inviting menu: home-made soup, smoked halibut with pickled samphire, bresaola with walnut oil and toasted pine kernels, spicy lamb sausage with mango sauce and breaded king prawns with lime mayonnaise – and these are just starters! Main courses are displayed on daily-changing blackboards and might include Tuscan fish stew, pigeon breast with blueberries, stincotto with pasta and butterbeans, cod with mushy peas and salmon with leek and mushrooms in lattice pastry. It's back to the menu for sweets such as sticky coffee and ginger pudding, pecan and caramel tart, apple and shortbread pie and baked banana calypso with toffee ice cream. This is all inventive stuff and well worth a detour. Alongside the pub two small bedroom suites with kitchenettes are let on a bed-and-breakfast or self-catering basis. There is room for a small family (children accommodated free) and TV is provided, but no phones; the en-suite facilities have WC and showers only. *Open 11-2.30, 6.30-12 (not Mon), Sun 12-3 only.* ***Bar Food*** *12-2, 7-9.45 (not Mon or Sun eve).* ***Beer*** *Bass.* ***Accommodation*** *2 bedrooms, both en suite, from £45 (single £35). Children welcome overnight (under-8s free in parents' room), additional bed available. Check-in by arrangement. Closed Sun eve, all Mon (except Bank Holiday Monday evenings), 1 week Jan. No dogs. Access, Visa.*

TREMEIRCHION Salusbury Arms FOOD

Tel 01745 710262 Map 8 C1
Tremeirchion St Asaph Clwyd LL17 0HN

A former estate coaching house with origins dating back to the 14th-century. The Grade II listed pub takes its name from Tremeirchion's ancestral owners. At the heart of village life, the Salusbury Arms is enjoying a fresh lease of life under Jim and Heulwen O'Boyle. The building has been carefully restored and is spick-and-span within, with a cosy feel to its interlinked village bar, lounges and dining-room. Jim's regularly-changing real ales are a serious attraction, as is Heulwen's bubbling welcome. The Salusbury Grill, home-made steak and kidney pie (or chicken and vegetable) are regular favourites and there's usually a range of specials like chicken curry and salmon with hollandaise sauce alongside regular bar snacks like sandwiches, baked potatoes, vegetarian burgers, scampi and breaded plaice; brunch fry-ups are also offered at lunchtime. A cheery welcome for children (who'll find a lovely garden to play in), a burgeoning trade in family Sunday lunches (booking advised), and a Welsh songstress entertaining on weekend evenings completes the picture. *Open 11-11 (Sun 12-3, 7-10.30). **Bar Food** 12-2.30, 7-9.30 (not Sat eve). No food Sun evening. Free House. **Beer** Boddingtons, Morland Old Speckled Hen, guest beers. Garden, lawn, outdoor eating, tables in garden. Family room. Access, Visa.*

TYN-Y-GROES Groes Inn FOOD

Tel 01492 650545 Map 8 C2
Tyn-y-Groes nr Conwy Gwynedd LL32 8TN

Claiming to be the first licensed house in Wales, 'Taverne-y-Groes' (by the cross) boasts a history unbroken since 1573 and is now family-run by Tony and Dawn Humphreys and their son Justin. The present building (from which are splendid views of the Conwy estuary) contains much 16th- and 17th-century interior timberwork in a succession of low-ceilinged rooms that have been extended these days to include a formal dining-room and non-smoking conservatory that leads to the large rear garden. Daily blackboards proclaim the most promising bar food: Indian haddock, crispy roast duck, lamb with rosemary and apricot casserole, with the likes of sticky toffee pudding to follow. Bookings may be made for a three-course lunch, and there's à la carte dining nightly. This establishment is generally not suitable for children under 10; over-10s are confined to the conservatory and garden. 15 bedrooms are due to be added in 1996. *Open 12-3, 6.30-11.30 (12-2.30, 7-11.30 in winter), Sun 12-4, 6.30-11. **Bar Food** 12-2, 6.30-9 (Sun 12-2.15, 6.30-9). Free House. **Beer** Tetley, Burton. Garden, outdoor eating. Pub closed Sun nights in winter. Access, Visa.*

USK Three Salmons Hotel B&B

Tel 01291 672133 **Fax 01291 673979** Map 9 D5
Usk Gwent NP5 1BQ

Zzz...

For long an inn of renown, the Three Salmons once hosted a civic luncheon to mark the opening of the nearby Chain bridge over the Usk, in 1812. Much of the original listed building has recently undergone a massive restoration including total retiling of the roof in Welsh grey slate. The single bar and public areas at street level are now immaculate and there's a friendly sense of purpose amongst the staff. A separate bar and function room are on the first floor. In the main building little expense has been spared in upgrading the bedrooms to modern-day requirements: nestling under high-pitched eaves and roof timbers they are individual in character and furnished to a high standard with smart new en-suite bathrooms in gleaming, gold-tapped, white porcelain. An annexe across the street was once the 'Livery and Bait Stables'; outside, the Ostler's Bell still hangs. The dozen bedrooms within were completely revamped last year; three more rooms in the Coach House were also brought on stream. Improvements continue. *Open 11-11 (Sun 12-3, 7-10.30). Free House. **Beer** Whitbread Best, Flowers Original. **Accommodation** 24 rooms, all en suite, from £60 (four-poster £73, single from £39.50). Children welcome overnight, additional bed & cot available (£10). No dogs. Access, Amex, Visa.*

> We endeavour to be as up-to-date as possible but inevitably some changes to landlords, chefs and other key staff occur after the Guide has gone to press.

WHITEBROOK — Crown at Whitebrook — FOOD B&B

Tel 01600 860254 **Fax 01600 860607** Map 14 A2
Whitebrook nr Monmouth Gwent NP5 4TX

It is a long mile up tracks and down lanes from the A466 at the Bigswear bridge to Roger and Sandra Bates's 'auberge', hidden away in the wooded Wye valley. Self-styled as a restaurant with rooms, its rather unprepossessing exterior and brown window shutters lend it a Continental air. Within, there is homely overnight comfort, culinary expertise from Sandra, front-of-house hospitality from Roger, low beams and lovely views over the pretty garden. A light lunch menu (king prawn and bacon salad, smoked haddock and cheese tart, tartelette alsacienne, filo-wrapped spicy banana) is offered, but the three-course lunch menu – served in the cottagey, beamed dining-room – is such good value (with four or five choices at each course) that it should not be missed: a recent menu offered broccoli and almond soup, warm mushroom mousse on a bed of sautéed wild mushrooms, black pudding with onions, apples and calvados, and home-smoked sewin with horseradish cream to start; included in the main-course choice was roast Welsh lamb with rosemary and filo-wrapped salmon with a chive and cream sauce (served with a side dish of up to nine fresh vegetables); to finish, lime cheesecake with blackberries and strawberries, thin almond and apple tart with berries and cream, and roasted pear on a crouton with caramel sauce and marbled chocolate ice cream. Very pleasant, family service. Dinner is rather more formal, revealing the true depth of the quality in the cooking; booking is absolutely essential. Good Welsh cheeses. Lightly whispering trees are likely to be the only intrusion to a thoroughly restful night here. The individually decorated bedrooms (six of which were completely refurbished last year) are bright and comfortable, with up-to-date accoutrements including direct-dial phones, tea-makers, TVs and clock radios; spotless bathrooms are neatly carpeted. 'Manor Room' rate, with four-poster and whirlpool bath, is £67. Hearty Welsh breakfasts. Don't come looking for real ales, instead sample the dozen or more malt whiskies, the copious choice of cognacs or delve into the long wine list with plenty of half bottles and helpful notes. Not a pub, but such a lovely, inn-like place in which to stay and eat that we make it a special case for entry in this Guide; also recommended in our *1996 Hotels & Restaurants Guide*. ***Meals*** *12-2, 7-9.30. Garden, outdoor eating.* ***Accommodation*** *12 bedrooms, all en suite, £80 (half-board £120, single £50/£77). Children welcome overnight (under-10s share parents' room free), additional bed (£10) & cot available. Closed Sun eve & Mon lunch to non-residents, 2 weeks Jan, 2 weeks Aug, 25 & 26 Dec. Access, Amex, Diners, Visa.*

Many **B&B** establishments offer reduced rates for weekend and out-of-season bookings. Always ask about special deals for longer stays. Beware half-board terms in inns where we do not recommend the **FOOD.**

Channel Islands & Isle of Man

Alderney

ST ANNE — Georgian House ★ FOOD

Tel & Fax 01481 822471 Map 13 F4
Victoria Street St Anne Alderney

Zzz...

Liz and Stephen Hope's three-storey Alderney house has a Georgian facade and a cosy little bar, two open fireplaces and a strongly traditional dining-room within. The 'Garden Beyond' has an open-air bar and grill and is a strong asset in the summer. Food here is of the highest standard and a far cry from standard pub grub. Locally caught fish and crustaceans feature strongly. The lunch menu is kept simple with the likes of wonderful moules à la crème, whole fresh Alderney crab (price depends on weight), beef stroganoff, choice of omelette or ploughman's lunches. In addition, the chalkboard announces daily specials like home-made chicken and leek soup, bargain Herm oysters, fresh plaice or half a lobster salad (priced according to weight). The dinner menu is more elaborate with a platter of fruits de mer (24hrs' notice recommended in winter) or 12oz sirloin from the bone flambéed in brandy. Home-made desserts are a must – summer pudding in the form of a layered terrine is made with local berries and the raspberry flan with fruit from the owners' garden. Special 3-course Sunday lunch menu. Bedroom accommodation (not yet inspected, but reports are of a high quality, with direct-dial telephones and en-suite bathrooms) is now offered in a suite with its own sitting room and balcony plus two single rooms. A courtesy car to the harbour is available if booked at the time of reservation. *Open 10.30-3, 6.30-12.* ***Bar Food*** *12-2.30, 7-10. Free House.* ***Beer*** *Ringwood Best & Fortyniner. Garden, outdoor eating.* ***Accommodation*** *1 suite (£50-£55 according to season), 2 singles (£25-£27.50), all en suite (ask about package deals including air fare). Pub closed Tue evenings. Access, Amex, Diners, Visa.*

Guernsey

LE BOURG — Deerhound Inn Hotel FOOD B&B

Tel 01481 38585 **Fax 01481 39443** Map 13 E4
Le Bourg Forest Road Forest Guernsey GY8 0AN

A converted old Guernsey farmhouse situated above Petit Bot valley and beach, off the main road and not far from the airport. The Piriou and Bonthelius family proprietors offer a warm welcome and have completely redecorated the restaurant and all the rooms since taking over in 1993. Their chef is Swedish but the bar food menu if fiercely traditional, offering the likes of home-made paté, a choice of dual-priced (starter/main) pasta dishes, large or double-decker sandwiches, salads and the usual favourites for 'little people'. One of the bedrooms is a family room with bunk beds; the TV lounge can act as a children's playroom and there are swings, see-saw and a slide in the garden. Baby-listening devices are provided and baby-sitting can be arranged. *Open 10.30-11.45, Sun 12-2 (to 3.30 with min. £3.50 meal), 6-9.30 (close 11).* ***Bar Food*** *12-1.45, 7-9.30.* ***Beer*** *Tetley, Theakston Best, Guernsey Summer Ale (Dog's Breath Ale). Garden, outdoor eating, children's play area.* ***Accommodation*** *10 bedrooms, 4 with en suite showers, £30-£50 according to season (single £15-£30). Children welcome overnight (under-3s stay free in parents' room, 3-12s half-price), additional beds and cots available. Access, Amex, Visa.*

CASTEL — Hotel Hougue du Pommier B&B

Tel 01481 56531 **Fax 01481 56260** Map 13 E4
Castel Guernsey GY5 7FQ

Zzz...

Adjacent to Guernsey's indoor lawn bowling centre, a lovely inn dating back to 1712. 'Hougue du Pommier' means 'apple-tree hill' and the apples from the ten acres of orchards surrounding this fine old Guernsey farmhouse were once used to make local cider. The Tudor Bar features a traditional atmosphere, with beams and an inglenook fireplace. Quiet bedrooms overlooking the particularly well-kept gardens are comfortable, with remote-control TVs, telephones and beverage trays. The solar-heated swimming pool is in a secluded spot surrounded by trees; nearby is a sauna, sunbed room and games room wih ping-pong table and video games. There's also a 10-hole pitch-and-putt golf course and

a putting green. The sandy beaches of Grandes Rocques and Cobo are ten minutes' walk away. Children's high Tea served from 6pm. *Bar open 11-2, 6-11.30, Sun 12-3.30, 6-11.30 (Sunday open to diners and residents only). **Beer** Guernsey Brewery. Garden. **Accommodation** 43 bedrooms, all en suite, £48-£74 according to season (4-poster £68-£94, de luxe £63-£89, single £24-£48). Children welcome overnight (0-5 yrs £5, 5-12 yrs 50% of tariff), additional beds and cots available. No dogs. Access, Amex, Diners, Visa.*

KINGS MILLS — Fleur du Jardin Hotel — FOOD / B&B

Tel 01481 57996 **Fax 01481 56834** Map 13 E4
Kings Mills nr Castel Guernsey GY5 7JT

Zzz...

Named after a prize-winning herd of Guernsey cattle kept here when it was a working farm, this 16th-century inn is in the centre of Kings Mill village, close to Vazon Bay, and has a tastefully traditional country feel. Several low-ceilinged, beamed dining-rooms interconnect, creating a quiet atmosphere. The cooking is the highlight here; highlights of a recent meal included a particularly good home-made potato and herb soup, mozzarella-topped vegetable and nut risotto (using brown rice), a generous helping of fresh fruit salad and proper espresso coffee. The usual pub fare fills out the extensive menu, but the daily specials – strong on fish and game – are probably the best bet, typically grilled swordfish steak, oven-baked lemon sole lemon, local sea bass or game pie with juniper berries. Also a popular place for a four-course Sunday roast lunch served in both the bar and restaurant. The bedrooms are attractive and amenities include remote-control TVs, telephones and tea/coffee-making facilities; some rooms have trouser presses and small refrigerators. There's a beautiful view of the surrounding countryside from the heated outdoor swimming pool. Eight or nine wines are available by the glass. Two acres of gardens and plenty of parking. *Open 11-11.30. **Bar Food** 12-2, 6.30-9.30 (Sun 7-9). Free House. **Beer** Guernsey Brewery. Garden, outdoor eating, children's play area. **Accommodation** 17 bedrooms, all en suite, from £52.50 to £72 according to season; 2-bedroom suite (sleeping 4): £150 half-board. Children over 4 welcome overnight (4-under 12 50% adult rate if sharing parents' room, high-tea included), additional beds available. No dogs. Access, Amex, Visa.*

PLEINMONT — Imperial Hotel — B&B

Tel 01481 64044 **Fax 01481 66139** Map 13 E4
Pleinmont Torteval Guernsey GY8 0PS

Attractive little hotel ideally located at the south end of sandy Rocquaine Bay, also overlooking the harbour at Portelet. Lounge bar, restaurant (now restored to its all-wood design of 100 year ago) and most of the bedrooms benefit from a beautiful view of the bay; sea view rooms attract a supplement (up to £2.50 per person per day). Four rooms have attractive balconies with patio furniture; all have clean and bright accommodation with tea-coffee facilities, colour TV and direct-dial telephone. Self-catering apartment also available. Children are welcome if well behaved. Safe garden and a short walk from the beach. The hotel leads on to 20 miles of cliff walks. *Open 10.30-11.45 (Mon-Wed to 11 in winter, Sun 11-3). **Beer** Randalls. Garden, outdoor eating. **Accommodation** 17 bedrooms, all en suite, £36-£56 according to season (single £18-£38), £30-£45 room only; special tariff with car hire included (£45-£65); two-bedroomed suite sleeping four £120-£160 half-board. Children welcome overnight (0-2 years free, 2-11 £10 when sharing parents' room). Lounge bar closed Sun eve Nov-Mar. Accommodation closed Nov-Mar. Access, Visa.*

ST PETERS — Longfrie Inn — A

Tel 01481 63107 Map 13 E4
Rue de Longfrie St Peters Guernsey GY7 9RX

Guernsey's most popular family pub, in a rural setting. Formerly a 16th-century farmhouse, there's now an indoor 'fun factory' (supervised indoor bedlam might a more apposite description; 50p entrance charge, open 12.30-2.30, 6-8.30) for children under 10, a large beer garden with swings, ample car parking, and standard pub fare menu (sandwiches are available). Baby changing facilities, high-chairs and friendly staff complete the family-friendly atmosphere; adults without children may find it all too much before 8.30pm! St Pierre du Bois (St Peter in the Wood) is known as St Peters on the island. Under the same ownership as *Fleur du Jardin* (see entry under Kings Mills) since 1994. B&B (not inspected) is offered in five rooms (£36-£50). *Open 11-3, 5.30-11.30, Sun 12-3, 7-10.30. **Beer** Guernsey Brewery. Garden, children's play area. Access, Amex, Diners, Visa.*

St Peter Port **Ship & Crown** **A**

Tel 01481 721368 Map 13 E4
Pier Steps St Peter Port Guernsey GY1 2NB

Usually-buzzing yachting pub opposite the marina. St Peter Port's most traditional pub with lots of maritime pictures and memorabilia in both the simply-furnished, busy main bar and quieter back drinking area. This was the Germans' naval HQ during the World War II island occupation. Thanks to the new Guernsey laws children are now welcome in the bar all day, but Sunday licensing laws still require purchase of a bar meal. *Open 10am-11.45pm, Sun 12-3.30, 6-11.* ***Beer*** *Guernsey Sunbeam Bitter, guest beer. No credit cards.*

Herm

Herm Island **Ship Inn** **FOOD**

Tel 01481 722159 **Fax 01481 710066** Map 13 E4
Herm Island via Guernsey GY1 3HR

"Paradise is just 20 minutes by ferry from St Peter Port, Guernsey. Safe, clean, pollution free. No cars, no crowds, no stress." How many hotels can boast an island as their garden? The harbourside White House Hotel offers comfortable accommodation (recommended in our *Hotels & Restaurants Guide*: 38 rooms, half-board terms only, from £110) for those who want to escape the hurly-burly of mainland life. Self-catering cottages, flats and camping are also available on the island, booking through the hotel. Under the same ownership as the hotel is the Ship Inn – a small, carpeted bar area with roaring log fire, connected to the first-floor Captain's coffee shop, a carvery-style restaurant. 'To pipe you aboard' are the likes of crab cocktail or bargain Herm oysters; continue with 'the daily catch' (perhaps fresh plaice), one of an extensive selection of baguettes, 'midshipman's main courses' (steaks or vegetarian salad) or the lunchtime carvery (daily roast). Children are very welcome and offered their own young sea dogs' menu (king-size sausage, fish fingers, chicken or vegetarian sweetcorn nuggets). Morning coffee with pastries, afternoon teas and Sunday lunch in the restaurant complete the picture. Don't leave the island without trying one of their splendid ice cream sundaes made with the highest buttermilk-content ice cream in the world. No dogs within the pub, but welcome on the island on a lead. *Open from 9am-10.45pm (Sun 12-2.30).* ***Bar Food*** *9am-9.30pm, Sun 9-2.30. Patio, outdoor eating. Pub closed Sun eve & Oct to end Mar. Access, Visa.*

Jersey

Gorey **Dolphin Hotel** **B&B**

Tel 01534 853370 **Fax 01534 857618** Map 13 F4
Gorey Pier Gorey Jersey JE6 3EW

The Dolphin Hotel is right on Gorey Pier, beneath the medieval Mont Orgueil castle, on Jersey's east coast and not far from the wide Grouville Bay which offers safe bathing and beach sports. Fish nets and boating accessories adorn the public Fisherman's Bar & Grill. Adequate bedrooms are equipped with remote-control TVs, telephones, radios, trouser presses, hairdryers and beverage trays. Most rooms have just en-suite showers; only two have en-suite baths. Best rooms are on the top floor overlooking the Pier. *Bar open 9.30am-11.30pm, Sun 11-1, 4.30-11.30. Free House.* ***Beer*** *five beers (not real ales).* ***Accommodation*** *17 bedrooms, all en suite, from £36-£64 according to season (single £18-£32). Children welcome overnight (under-3s stay free in parents' room, 3-12s 50% of tariff), extra bed and cot supplied. Dogs by arrangement. Access, Visa.*

St Aubin **Old Court House Inn** **FOOD**

Tel 01534 46433 **Fax 01534 45103** Map 13 F4 **B&B**
St Aubin The Bulwarks Jersey JE3 9FS

A family-run hotel/restaurant/inn with a 'forever young' outlook and a popular alfresco eating trade (bookings taken). Dating back to 1450, the original 'Courthouse' at the rear of the building was largely restored in 1611. The front portion of the property was a wealthy merchant's homestead with enormous cellars that (from the 17th century) stored privateers' plunder alongside legitimate cargo. The front terrace, now graced with a new conservatory, overlooks the harbour and is a fine place to sample the bar food, as is the rear courtyard. The menu includes moules marinière, grilled prawns, Cumberland sausage and ploughman's lunches, although seafood is the real attraction, with speciality fisherman's platters (for two,

with a whole lobster), good-value oysters, lobster Thermidor and "crab to pick". Children have their own short menu or smaller portions, charged accordingly. The beamed cellar bars are always popular and the upstairs bar has recently been turned into the Mizzen Restaurant (still recognisable by Bergerac fans as the Royal Barge pub). A Sunday lunch menu is served throughout. Charming bedrooms, the best with harbour views, are furnished with old pine; the two-bedroomed penthouse suite offers a large bathroom, a pleasant lounge with a beautiful view of the harbour and a private sun terrace with garden furniture. *Bars open 11-11, Sun 11-1 (to 3.30 if eating), 4.30-11.30.* ***Bar Food** 12.30-2.30, 7.30-9.30, Sun 12.30-3.30 (no bar food Sun eve). Free House.* ***Beer** Marston's Pedigree, Theakston Best, Flowers, up to 5 guest beers. Family room.* ***Accommodation** 9 rooms, all en suite, £60-£89 according to season, single £30-£60; suite £90-£180 sleeps up to 4. Children under 6 free, over-6s half-price if sharing parents' room, additional bed provided. Accommodation closed 25 Dec. Access, Amex, Diners, Visa.*

St Brelade — Old Smugglers Inn — FOOD

Tel 01534 41510

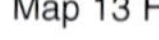

Ouaisné Bay St Brelade Jersey JE3 8AW

Two 13th-century fishermen's cottages were rebuilt from their ruins in 1721 by local fishermen and remained as such until the early 1900s when they were enlarged and developed into a small residential hotel retaining most of the original granitework, beams and fireplaces. After the German occupation the property underwent further changes and the Old Smugglers emerged. Today, it is one of the few 'genuine' free houses on the island. A succession of small dining-rooms (including a newly opened 50-seater family room) serve food from 'The Treasure Chest' menu. Food is taken seriously and there's an extensive selection of tempting dishes – Yankee fried potato skins, local seafood chowder, king prawns won ton with sweet chili sauce, chef's spicy barbecue-style baby back ribs, Smugglers' ocean bake, lasagne or Greek vegetable moussaka. No smoking area. No children under 14 in the bar; children's menu (with lollies) and baby-changing facilities provided. Folk nights on Sunday. *Open 11-11, Sun 11-1, 4.30-11.* ***Bar Food** 12-2, 6-8.45 (all day Sun, but no food Sunday eve in winter). Free House.* ***Beer** Bass, guest beers. Terrace. Family room. No credit cards.*

St Helier — Tipsy Toad Town House — A

Tel 01534 615000 **Fax 01534 615003** Map 13 F4

57-59 New Street St Helier Jersey JE2 3RB

A sister brew pub to the *Star & Tipsy Toad*, opened in July 1994, converted from a warehouse. The sprawling interior has a very big bar that serves an open-plan drinking and dining area; an impressive, two-floor-high brewing area is open to view behind glass screens. Busy, bustling and attracting a youngish crowd. Regular real ale festivals. No food on Sunday except in winter. Good facilities include an in-house ale shop, baby changing unit, disabled loo and function room area upstairs for up to 230 people. *Open 11-11, Sun 11-1, 4.30-11. Free House.* ***Beer** own brews: Jimmy's Bitter, Horny Toad, Crazy Diamond & Cyril's Bitter plus up to 12 guests. Access, Amex, Visa.*

St Lawrence — British Union Hotel — FOOD

Tel 01534 861070 Map 13 F4

Main Road St Lawrence Jersey

A pleasant pub with a good atmosphere and warm welcome, across the road from St Lawrence Parish Church. A central bar divides two lounges with an additional family/games room to the rear. Well-prepared daily specials like steak and ale pie, chicken and mushroom pancake, and fresh Jersey plaice with garlic prawns; ice cream with gateau or apple pie for dessert. Owned by Guernsey's Ann Street Brewery. *Open 9.30am-11.30pm Mon-Sat, 11-1, 4.30-11.30 Sun.* ***Bar Food** 12-2 (except Sun), 6-8.15 (Sun from 6.30 summer only); no food Sunday in winter.* ***Beer** Guernsey Sunbeam, Ann Street Ann's Treat. Patio, outdoor eating. Family room. No credit cards.*

St Ouen — Lobster Pot, Coach House — FOOD

Tel 01534 482888 **Fax 01534 481574** Map 13 F4
L'Etacq St Ouen Jersey JE3 2FB

Ostensibly a modern hotel and restaurant converted from an old granite farm house, but the converted cow byre is now a pubby Coach House Bar. It plays a contrasting role to the busy restaurant (recommended in our *Hotels & Restaurants Guide* for its local seafood specialities mainly in a French style, booking recommended), offering a good mix of lunchtime bar food that ranges from baked potatoes to omelettes, burger, steaks, and salads (crab, fruits de mer, prawns, lobster – some of the seafood is landed just 200 yards away, so it's as fresh as you can get). A large open-air paved terrace with plastic tables and chairs is the main attraction in good weather. Attractive location, overlooking sandy St Ouen's Bay. Thirteen large, en-suite bedrooms (double/twin £71-£107 according to season, single £45-£63) have modern hotel amenities; the best rooms have sea views and attract a higher tariff. Parking for 65 cars. No dogs. *Coach House open 10-6 (earlier closing in winter).* ***Bar Food*** *12-3.30. Access, Amex, Diners, Visa.*

St Peter's Village — Star & Tipsy Toad Brewery — FOOD

Tel 01534 485556 **Fax 01534 485559** Map 13 F4
St Peter's Village Jersey JE3 7AA

Right on the A12, in St Peter's Village, with its own brewery. The attractive decor retains some character with the granite walls, old coal stoves and oak panelling. Young, enthusiastic staff prepare good basic pub food like surf'n'turf, chicken Kiev or grilled tuna steak. The brewery can be visited on arranged tours. Indoor and outdoor play areas in addition to the 'Little Toadies' children's menu (prices include ice cream!) and baby-changing facilities make this a perfect pub for families. There is live music Friday to Sunday nights and the Tipsy Toad folk festival is held during the 3rd week of September.
Open 10am-11pm, Sun 11-1, 4.30-11. Bar Food 12-2.15, 6-8.15, no food Sun (or Mon eve in winter). Free House. ***Beer*** *own brews: Jimmy's Bitter, Horny Toad, Crazy Diamond & Cyril's Bitter plus two guests. Beer garden, children's play area, disabled facilities. Family room, indoor play area. Access, Amex, Visa.*

Sark

Sark — Dixcart Hotel & Bar — FOOD — B&B

Tel 01481 832015 **Fax 01481 832164** Map 13 E4
Sark via Guernsey GY9 0SD

Surrounded by 50 acres of gardens, a charming public bar adjacent to the Dixcart Hotel (recommended in our *Hotels & Restaurants Guide*) and under the same ownership. Oak wall panelling, solid pine furniture and paintings by local artists on the walls give a warm atmosphere. Bar snacks come from the kitchen of the hotel's restaurant (also recommended) and include home-made pies (fish, chicken and mushroom and steak and kidney), breaded plaice or scampi, sandwiches, baked potatoes and other main-courses pub favourites (liver and onions, burger, chicken Kiev) as well as a list of daily dishes. Children have their own no-smoking 'Snug' with toys and TV plus familiar 'children's choices' on the menu.
Open 11-11.30 (to 10 in winter, often later but a snack must be purchased). ***Bar Food*** *12-3, 6-9.30. Garden, outdoor eating. Family room.* ***Accommodation*** *15 rooms, from £30-£70 according to season. Children welcome overnight (0-4 50%, 5-9 60%, 10-14 75% of tariff); dogs £3.50 per day. Access, Amex, Diners, Visa.*

We endeavour to be as up-to-date as possible but inevitably some changes to landlords, chefs and other key staff occur after the Guide has gone to press.

Isle of Man

PEEL Creek Inn FOOD

Tel 01624 842216 **Fax 01624 843359** Map 4 A4
The Quayside Peel Isle of Man IM5 1AT

Slap bang on the harbour front, a bustling pub with a large, bright and unpretentious bar. Robert and Jean McAleer are industrious and friendly and they are always busy serving seafood specialities from the fish yard nearby. Home-made Manx kipper paté, fresh crab salad, Manx scallops ('queenies') served on the shell in a mornay sauce, avocado sunrise (fresh crab, prawns and pineapple) might all feature on the menu or among the blackboard specials. Other offerings range from open sandwiches to curries and steak and kidney pie. Several fruit tarts or home-made gateaux to follow. Junior diners are offered smaller portions. Full selection of Irish spirits – from Bushmills to Dry Cork Gin – and at least 12 wines may be opened to order. Easy parking. A major new heritage centre is currently being built and should open early in 1997. *Open 11-10.45 Mon-Sat & 12-1.30, 8-10 Sun.* ***Bar Food*** *11-10.45 (Sun 12-1.30, 8-10).* ***Beer*** *Okells Bitter & Mild, Tetley, Cains, guest beer. Outdoor eating on the quayside. Children welcome in bar 12-2.30 only if eating. Pub closed 25 Dec. Access, Visa.*

Northern Ireland

BALLYCASTLE House of McDonnell A

Tel 01265 762975 Map 20 D1
71 Castle Street Ballycastle Co Antrim BT64 6AS

Unusually, even for a characterful old pub, McDonnell's is a listed building and as such no changes are allowed inside or out. Not that change is much on the cards anyway, as it has been in the family for 250 years and is clearly much loved – as visitors soon discover from the colourful chatelaine Eileen O'Neill. She enjoys nothing better than sharing the history of the long, narrow, mahogany-countered bar which was once a traditional grocery-bar. Alas, no food is now offered, but The Open Door, a good traditional Northern Ireland bakery across the road, has hot snacks and a wide range of fresh sandwiches to order. Inside the pub is a fine collection of original etched mirrors. Traditional Irish music on Wednesday and Friday nights and folk music on Saturday nights throughout the year. "In every sense, a real, traditional Irish pub." *Open 11.30-11 (Sun 12.30-2.30 & 7-10), 7-11 mide May-mid Oct. No credit cards.*

BELFAST Crown Liquor Salon A

Tel 01232 325368 Map 20 D2
44 Great Victoria Street Belfast Co Antrim BT2 7BA

Belfast's most famous and best-preserved bar, High Victorian and wonderful in its exuberant opulence. "Gaslight glints on painted windows, vivid in amber and carmine, on gilded glass and on highly-patterned tiles which abound everywhere. It reflects from shining brass, from ornate mirrors, and glows against the burnished ceiling embossed with entwining curves. Richly-carved wood, a granite-topped bar, bright panels of plasterwork – and a floor laid in a myriad of mosaics completes the picture of relentless decoration" – we couldn't put it better as it truly is an architectural fantasy. The building belongs to the National Trust and is run by Bass Taverns. Every visitor to Belfast should experience the joy of a pint in one of the delightful 'snugs' – if snugs could talk there would be many a tale to tell from these clandestine retreats! Upstairs, The Britannic Lounge, with an Edwardian feel, is fitted out with original timbers from the *SS Britannic*, sister ship to the Titanic. *Open 11.30-11, Sun 12.30-2.30 & 7-10. Beer Bass. No credit cards.*

BELFAST Kelly's Cellars A

Tel 01232 324835 Map 20 D2
30/32 Bank Street Belfast Co Antrim BT1 1HL

A protected building, this characterful bar boasts the oldest cellars in Ireland, dating back to 1720. Food is served in the upstairs bar at lunchtime. Thursday evenings bring live traditional Irish music, with rock music on Friday and Staurday nights. *Open 11.30-11 (Thu-Sat to 1am). Closed Sun & some Bank Holidays. Access, Visa.*

BUSHMILLS Bushmills Inn B&B

Tel 01265 732339 Fax 01265 732048 Map 20 C1
25 Main Street Bushmills Co Antrim BT57 8QA

After the Giant's Causeway, the world's oldest distillery at Bushmills is the biggest attraction in the area (and well worth a visit; mid-week is most interesting); the Bushmills Inn also attracts year-round local support. The exterior, including a neat garden at the rear main entrance, creates a welcoming impression that extends into the hall, with its open fire and country antiques, and other public areas that encompass several bars and a large dining-room. Bedrooms are quite modest, individually decorated and comfortably furnished; some family rooms are remarkable for their ingenious use of space. A beamed loft provides a splendid setting for private functions (up to 85 people) and the 'secret library' a unique venue for special occasions. *Open 12-11 (Sun 12.30-4.30, 7-10).* ***Accommodation** 11 rooms, all en suite, £78 (single £48). Children welcome overnight (£18 if sharing, cots £8). Garden, fishing. Access, Visa.*

Many **B&B** establishments offer reduced rates for weekend and out-of-season bookings. Always ask about special deals for longer stays. Beware half-board terms in inns where we do not recommend the **FOOD.**

Carnlough — Londonderry Arms — FOOD

Tel 01574 885255 Fax 01574 885263 Map 20 D1
20 Harbour Road Carnlough Glens of Antrim Co Antrim BT44 0EU

In the same family for nearly half a century, this hotel and bar makes a good stop at a most attractive little harbour on the famous scenic coastal route and it's well known for 'good, plain food'. The same snacks are available in both bars (hotel and public): soup with home-baked wheaten bread, scones, open prawn sandwich, paté, chef's lunchtime roast plus daily specials like fried Carnlough salmon and lobster in season. Twenty-one bedrooms furnished in traditional style (but our recommendation is specifically for bar food). *Open 11.30-1 (Sun 12-10.30). Bar Food 11.30-9. Garden. Access, Amex, Diners, Visa.*

Carnlough — The Waterfall — A

No telephone Map 20 D1
High Street Carnlough Co Antrim BT44 0EP

Not as old as it may first appear to be, the little public bar is nevertheless full of charm, with red-tiled floor and low-beamed ceiling. Both the fireplace and bar are made of reclaimed bricks from an old mill across the road and there's a clatter of memorabilia hanging from the ceiling; the walls are used to show off a collection of horse tackle and old posters. Behind, there's a cosy lounge bar with a stained-glass window, decorative plates and another brick fireplace. A welcoming place with a lovely friendly atmosphere.
No credit cards.

Carrickfergus — Wind-Rose Wine Bar — FOOD

Tel 01960 364192 Fax 01960 351164 Map 20 D2
The Marina Carrickfergus Co Antrim BT38 8BE

Overlooking the marina, a well-appointed formal restaurant (booking essential) on the upper floor is approached by an exterior spiral staircase and has clear views across Belfast Lough. A typical meal might be terrine of monkfish followed by cutlets of lamb and spinach soufflé with the house speciality crepes Suzette to finish. The ground-floor wine bar below has a pubby atmosphere with a strongly nautical theme and provides simple bar foood. *Open 12-12. **Bar Food** 12-2.30 (snacks 2.30-5), 7-9. Closed Sun & Mon, 25 & 26 Dec. Access, Amex, Visa.*

Crawfordsburn — Old Inn — B&B

Tel 01247 853255 Fax 01247 852775 Map 20 D2
15 Main Street Crawfordsburn Co Down BT19 1JH

Located off the main Belfast to Bangor road, this 16th-century inn is in a pretty village setting and is supposed to be the oldest in continuous use in all Ireland. Its location is conveniently close to Belfast and its City Airport. Oak beams, antiques and gas lighting emphasise the natural character of the building, an attractive venue for business people (conference facilities for 150, banqueting for 90) and private guests alike. Individually decorated bedrooms vary in size and style; most have antiques, some four-posters and a few have private sitting rooms; all are non-smoking. Romantics and newly-weds should head for the honeymoon cottage. Free private car parking for overnight guests. No dogs. *Open 11.30-11.30 (Sun 12-3, 7-10). **Accommodation** 32 rooms, £85 (single £70). Garden. Closed 25 & 26 Dec. Access, Amex, Diners, Visa.*

Cushendall — P J McCollam — A

No telephone Map 20 D1
23 Mill Street Cushendall Co Antrim BT4 0RR

In the family for 300 years and under the current ownership of Joe McCollam for the last 73 years, this magical place has a tiny front bar complete with a patchwork of photographs of local characters, many of them sheep farmers (and great fiddle players) who come down from the glens at weekends. The range in the old family kitchen behind the bar is lit on cold evenings and a converted 'cottage' barn across the yard makes a perfect setting for the famous traditional music sessions. Hospitable and full of character. *Open 11.30-11 (Sun 7-10pm only). Closed Sunday lunchtime. No credit cards.*

DUNDRUM — Buck's Head Inn — FOOD

Tel 01396 751868 **Fax 01396 751898** Map 20 D2
77 Main Street Dundrum nr Newcastle Co Down BT33 0LU

Situated on the main Belfast-Newcastle road, this attractive, welcoming family-run pub offers fairly traditional bar food from a blackboard menu which changes daily. The decor within the pub is traditional in a comfortably understated way, creating a warm, relaxed atmosphere. The restaurant is in a conservatory area added to the back of the pub, looking out on to a sloping, walled beer garden where tables are set up in summer. Light, bright and pleasantly furnished with cane chairs and well-appointed tables, the menu includes variations on old favourites like deep-fried Brie on a bed of crispy salad with hot garlic butter or roast duckling with orange and ginger sauce, but also less predictable offerings such as grilled sardines with fresh tomato sauce. Three-course Sunday lunch. Local produce is put to good use in both bar and restaurant meals. *Open 11.30-11, Sun 12-2.30, 5.30-10.* ***Bar Food*** *all day (Restaurant Meals 12-2.30, 5.30-9.30 (not Sun eve). Garden, outdoor eating. Closed 25 Dec. Access, Amex, Visa.*

ENNISKILLEN — Blakes of the Hollow — A

Tel 01365 322143 Map 20 C2
6 Church Street Enniskillen Co Fermanagh BT74 7JE

Named after the natural dip at the centre of the town where it is located, Blakes has been in the same family since 1929. Although its age and agelessness (it was restored in 1882) are the main attractions, body and soul can be kept together on the premises by the consumption of sandwiches and soup (the latter at lunchtime only). *Open 11.30-11 (Sun 7-10). Closed lunch Sun. No credit cards.*

HILLSBOROUGH — The Hillside Bar ★ — FOOD

Tel 01846 682765 Map 20 D2
21 Main Street Hillsborough Co Down BT26 6AE

🍷

Our Ireland Pub of the Year in 1995, The Hillside is a delightful, well-run bar dating from 1777 (if not earlier). It's easily found in the centre of this pretty little town and, within, the bar's atmosphere is warm and cosy in both the main bar and a smaller one to the side, warmed by a fire; throughout, the atmosphere is gently rustic – dark green paint and soft country browns and greys in natural materials – and comfortably set up for eating. At lunchtime there's a self-service arrangement, giving way to a bar menu served by charming young staff in uniform T-shirts during the afternoon and evening. Typical fare from the bar menu might include Hillside paté, a really excellent rough liver paté served with Cumberland sauce (or cranberries perhaps in season) and hot, toasted wheaten bread, chicken and mushroom pie – crisp home-made pastry over a creamy chicken and mushroom filling – and a ploughman's lunch or tagliatelle carbonara. Home-made beef burgers are flame-grilled and come with hash browns and a choice of sauces; one can finish with a home-baked fruit pie or a daily dessert special. Proper real ale from local brewers, Hilden, and a wine list that offers good wines by the glass; you can even get a pint of Guinness at either room temperature or chilled. Outside seating for 30. ***Bar Food*** *from 11.30, self-service to 2.30 (Sat to 3); bar menu to 8pm and 12.30-2 Sun (table service).* ***Beer*** *Hilden Ale, McEwan's 80/-, Morland Old Speckled Hen. Closed Good Friday & 25 Dec. Access, Amex, Diners, Visa.*

We do not accept free meals or hospitality – our inspectors pay their own bills and never book in the name of Egon Ronay's Guides.

Republic of Ireland

Egon Ronay's Jameson Guide Ireland replaces the Republic of Ireland section in this Guide. The new edition of the Ireland Guide is published in March 1996.

County Round-ups

London Pubs by Postal District

See **How To Use This Guide**, on Pages 10-11, for an explanation of our categories (FOOD, B&B, Atmosphere) and symbols.

Location	Establishment	Star	Food	Atmosphere	Family	Waterside	Telephone
E14	Grapes			▲		▲	0171-987 4396
EC1	Cock Tavern		▲				0171-248 2918
EC1	The Eagle	★	▲				0171-837 1353
EC1	Fox & Anchor		▲				0171-253 4838
EC1	The Hope & Sir Loin		▲				0171-253 8525
EC1	The Peasant	★	▲				0171-336 7726
EC1	Thomas Wethered		▲				0171-278 9983
EC1	Ye Olde Mitre Tavern			▲			0171-405 4751
EC2	Old Dr Butler's Head			▲			0171-606 3504
EC3	Lamb Tavern		▲				0171-626 2454
EC4	Black Friar			▲			0171-236 5650
EC4	Old Bell Tavern			▲			0171-583 0070
EC4	Witness Box		▲				0171-353 6427
EC4	Ye Olde Cheshire Cheese		▲				0171-353 6170

N1	Albion		▲			0171-607 7450
N1	Eagle Tavern			▲		0171-253 4715
N1	Marquess Tavern		▲			0171-354 2975
NW1	The Engineer	★	▲			0171-722 0950
NW1	The Lansdowne	★	▲			0171-483 0409
NW3	Flask			▲		0171-435 4580
NW3	Jack Straw's Castle			▲		0171-435 8885
NW3	Spaniards Inn			▲		0181-455 3276
NW8	Crockers Folly		▲			0171-286 6608
SE1	Anchor			▲	▲	0171-407 1577
SE1	Founders Arms			▲	▲	0171-928 1899
SE1	George Inn			▲		0171-407 2056
SE1	Horniman's		▲		▲	0171-407 3611
SE5	Phoenix & Firkin		▲			0171-701 8282
SW1	Buckingham Arms		▲			0171-222 3386
SW1	The Grenadier		▲			0171-235 3074
SW1	Morpeth Arms		▲			0171-834 6442
SW1	Nag's Head		▲			0171-235 1135
SW1	Orange Brewery			▲		0171-730 5984
SW1	The Star			▲		0171-235 3019
SW3	The Australian		▲			0171-589 3114
SW3	Coopers Arms		▲			0171-376 3120
SW3	Front Page		▲			0171-352 2908
SW3	Phene Arms		▲			0171-352 3294
SW6	Imperial Arms		▲			0171-736 9179

Location	Establishment	Star	Food	Atmosphere	Family	Waterside	Telephone
SW6	Jim Thompson's		▲				0171-731 7636
SW6	White Horse		▲				0171-736 2115
SW10	Chelsea Ram	★	▲				0171-351 4008
SW10	Sporting Page		▲				0171-352 6465
SW11	The Castle		▲				0171-228 8181
SW18	Alma		▲				0181-870 2537
SW18	The Ship		▲			▲	0181-870 9667
SW19	Fox & Grapes			▲			0181-946 5599
W1	French House		▲				0171-473 2799
W1	The Guinea		▲				0171-499 1210
W1	Newman Arms		▲				0171-636 1127
W1	O'Conor Don		▲				0171-935 9311
W2	The Cow		▲				0171-221 0021
W2	Monkey Puzzle		▲				0171-723 0143
W2	Prince Bonaparte		▲				0171-229 5912
W2	The Westbourne	★	▲				0171-221 1332
W4	Bell & Crown			▲		▲	0181-994 4164
W4	City Barge			▲		▲	0181-994 2148
W6	Dove		▲			▲	0181-748 5405
W8	Britannia			▲			0171-937 1864
W8	Churchill Arms		▲				0171-727 4242

W8	Windsor Castle			▲			0171-727 8491
W11	Ladbroke Arms			▲			0171-727 6648
WC1	Cittie of York			▲			0171-242 7670
WC1	Lamb		▲				0171-405 0713
WC1	Princess Louise			▲			0171-405 8816
WC2	Lamb & Flag		▲				0171-237 4088
WC2	Opera Tavern			▲			0171-836 7321
WC2	Salisbury			▲			0171-836 5863

England Pubs by County

See **How To Use This Guide**, on Pages 10-11, for an explanation of our categories (FOOD, B&B, Atmosphere) and symbols.

Location	Establishment	Star	Food	Bed & Breakfast	Atmosphere	Sleep	Families	Waterside	Telephone.
Avon									
Almondsbury	Bowl Inn			▲		▲			01454 612757
Aust	Boar's Head				▲				01454 632278
Bathampton	George Inn		▲				▲	▲	01225 425079
Bathford	Crown		▲				▲		01225 852297
Bristol	Highbury Vaults				▲				0117 973 3203
Combe Hay	Wheatsheaf		▲						01225 833504
Congresbury	White Hart		▲				▲		01934 833303
Kelston	Old Crown Inn				▲				01225 423032
Oldbury-on-Severn	Anchor Inn		▲					▲	01454 413331
Stanton Wick	Carpenters Arms		▲	▲					01761 490202
Tormarton	Compass Inn			▲					01454 218242

Bedfordshire									
Bedford	Embankment Hotel			▲				▲	01234 261332
Broom	Cock Inn				▲				01767 314411
Houghton Conquest	Knife & Cleaver			▲					01234 740387
Keysoe	Chequers Inn				▲		▲		01234 708678
Little Odell	Mad Dog				▲				01234 720221
Odell	Bell		▲					▲	01234 720254
Radwell	Swan Inn		▲						01234 781351
Turvey	Three Cranes			▲					01234 881305
Berkshire									
Aldworth	Bell Inn				▲				01635 578272
Beenham Village	Six Bells		▲	▲					01734 713368
Cookham Dean	Inn on the Green		▲				▲		01628 482638
Cookham Dean	Jolly Farmer		▲				▲		01628 482905
Crazies Hill	Horns		▲						01734 401416
East Garston	Queens Arms Hotel			▲					01488 648757
East Ilsley	Swan			▲			▲		01635 281238
Frilsham	Pot Kiln				▲				01635 201366
Hampstead Marshall	White Hart Inn		▲	▲					01488 658201
Hare Hatch	Queen Victoria		▲						01734 402477
Highclere	The Yew Tree		▲	▲					01635 253360
Hurley	Dew Drop Inn				▲				01628 824327
Kintbury	Dundas Arms		▲	▲				▲	01488 658263
Knowl Hill	The Bird in Hand			▲		▲			01628 826622

Location	Establishment	Star	Food	Bed & Breakfast	Atmosphere	Sleep	Families	Waterside	Telephone
Shefford Woodlands	Pheasant Inn		▲						01488 648284
Sonning	Bull				▲				01734 693901
Stanford Dingley	Bull Country Inn		▲				▲		01734 744409
West Ilsley	Harrow Inn	★	▲				▲		01635 281260
Yattendon	Royal Oak		▲	▲		▲			01635 201325

Buckinghamshire

Location	Establishment	Star	Food	Bed & Breakfast	Atmosphere	Sleep	Families	Waterside	Telephone
Beaconsfield	Greyhound		▲						01494 673823
Bellingdon	Bull		▲				▲		01494 758163
Bledlow	The Lions of Bledlow				▲				01844 343345
Bolter End	Peacock		▲						01494 881417
Easington	Mole & Chicken		▲						01844 208387
Fingest	Chequers Inn				▲				01491 638335
Ford	Dinton Hermit		▲						01296 748379
Forty Green	Royal Standard of England				▲				01494 673382
Great Kimble	The Bernard Arms		▲	▲					01844 346172
Great Missenden	George				▲				01494 862084
Ibstone	The Fox			▲		▲	▲		01491 638289
Little Hampden	Rising Sun		▲						01494 488393
Long Crendon	The Angel	★	▲	▲		▲			01844 208268
Marsh Gibbon	The Greyhound		▲						01869 277365

Moulsoe	Carrington Arms		▲						01908 218050
Old Amersham	King's Arms				▲				01494 726333
Penn Street	Hit or Miss		▲				▲		01494 713109
Saunderton	Rose & Crown Inn			▲					01844 345299
Skirmett	Old Crown		▲						01491 638435
Stony Stratford	Cock Hotel			▲					01908 567733
Turville	Bull & Butcher		▲						01491 638283
Waddesdon	Five Arrows Hotel		▲	▲		▲	▲		01296 651727
West Wycombe	George & Dragon		▲						01494 464414
Whiteleaf	Red Lion			▲					01844 344476
Winslow	Bell Hotel			▲			▲		01296 714091
Wooburn Common	Chequers Inn		▲	▲					01628 529575

Cambridgeshire

Barrington	Royal Oak		▲						01223 870791
Bythorn	White Hart		▲						01832 710226
Cambridge	Eagle				▲				01223 301286
Cambridge	Free Press		▲						01223 68337
Cambridge	Tram Depot				▲				01223 324553
Duxford	John Barleycorn		▲						01223 832699
Fen Drayton	Three Tuns				▲				01954 230242
Fenstanton	King William IV		▲						01480 462467
Fowlmere	Chequers Inn		▲						01763 208369
Grantchester	The Rupert Brooke				▲				01223 840295
Holywell	Old Ferry Boat Inn			▲			▲	▲	01480 463227
Horningsea	Plough & Fleece		▲						01223 860795

Location	Establishment	Star	Food	Bed & Breakfast	Atmosphere	Sleep	Families	Waterside	Telephone
Keyston	Pheasant Inn	★	▲						01832 710241
Madingley	Three Horseshoes	★	▲						01954 210221
Milton	Jolly Brewers				▲				01223 860585
Molesworth	Cross Keys			▲					01832 710283
Needingworth	Pike & Eel			▲					01480 463336
Newton	Queen's Head		▲						01223 870436
St Neots	Chequers Inn		▲				▲		01480 472116
St Neots	Eaton Oak			▲			▲		01480 219555
Stilton	Bell Inn		▲	▲					01733 241066
Sutton Gault	Anchor Inn		▲					▲	01353 778537
Swavesey	Trinity Foot		▲						01954 230315
Wansford-in-England	The Haycock	★	▲	▲		▲		▲	01780 782223
Cheshire									
Bickley Moss	Cholmondeley Arms		▲	▲			▲		01829 720300
Bollington	Church House Inn		▲	▲					01625 574014
Brereton Green	Bears Head		▲	▲					01477 535251
Broadheath	Old Packet House		▲	▲					0161-929 1331
Chester	Ye Olde Kings Head			▲					01244 324855
Fullers Moor	Copper Mine		▲				▲		01829 782293
Higher Burwardsley	The Pheasant	★	▲	▲		▲	▲		01829 770434
Lower Peover	Bells of Peover				▲				01565 722269

Macclesfield	Sutton Hall		▲	▲		▲			01260 253211
Over Peover	The Dog		▲	▲					01625 861421
Stockport	Red Bull		▲						0161-480 2087
Tarporley	Rising Sun		▲						01829 732423
Tarporley	Swan Hotel			▲					01829 733838
Tushingham	Blue Bell Inn				▲		▲		01948 662172
Wybunbury	Swan		▲				▲		01270 841280

Cleveland

Ellerby	Ellerby Hotel		▲	▲		▲	▲		01947 840342
Sedgefield	Dun Cow Inn			▲		▲			01740 620894

Cornwall

Charlestown	Pier House Hotel			▲				▲	01726 67955
Charlestown	Rashleigh Arms			▲					01726 73635
Constantine	Trengilly Wartha Inn		▲	▲		▲	▲		01326 340332
Egloshayle	Earl of St Vincent				▲				01208 814807
Fowey	King of Prussia			▲		▲	▲	▲	01726 832450
Fowey	Ship Inn			▲					01726 833751
Gunwalloe	Halzephron Inn	★	▲	▲		▲			01326 240406
Helford	Shipwrights Arms				▲			▲	01326 231235
Kingsand	Halfway House Inn		▲	▲			▲	▲	01752 822279
Lostwithiel	Royal Oak		▲	▲					01208 872552
Ludgvan	White Hart				▲				01736 740574
Mithian	Miners Arms		▲				▲		01872 552375
Morwenstow	Bush				▲				01288 331242

Location	Establishment	Star	Food	Bed & Breakfast	Atmosphere	Sleep	Families	Waterside	Telephone
Mousehole	Ship Inn			▲				▲	01736 731234
Mylor Bridge	Pandora Inn		▲					▲	01326 372678
Padstow	Old Custom House Inn			▲			▲	▲	01841 532359
Pelynt	Jubilee Inn			▲			▲		01503 220312
Penelewey	Punch Bowl & Ladle				▲				01872 862237
Perranuthnoe	Victoria Inn			▲					01736 710309
Philleigh	Roseland Inn		▲				▲		01872 580254
Polkerris	Rashleigh Inn				▲			▲	01726 813991
Port Gaverne	Port Gaverne Hotel			▲		▲		▲	01208 880244
Porthleven	Harbour Inn			▲				▲	01326 573876
Porthleven	Ship Inn				▲			▲	01326 572841
Sennen Cove	Old Success Inn			▲		▲		▲	01736 871232
St Agnes	Driftwood Spars Hotel			▲			▲	▲	01872 552428
St Austell	White Hart			▲			▲		01726 72100
St Kew	St Kew Inn				▲			▲	01208 841259
St Mawes	Rising Sun		▲	▲					01326 270233
St Mawgan	Falcon Inn				▲		▲	▲	01637 860225
Tregadillett	Eliot Arms				▲				01566 772051
Cumbria									
Ainstable	New Crown Inn			▲					01768 896273
Appleby-in-Westmorland	Royal Oak Inn			▲					01768 351463

Armathwaite	Duke's Head Hotel			▲		▲		▲	01697 472226
Askham	Punch Bowl		▲						01931 712443
Bassenthwaite Lake	Pheasant Inn			▲					01768 776234
Beetham	Wheatsheaf			▲					01539 562123
Boot	Burnmoor Inn			▲					01946 723224
Bowland Bridge	Hare & Hounds			▲		▲	▲		01539 568333
Buttermere	Bridge Hotel			▲				▲	01768 770252
Cartmel Fell	Masons Arms	★	▲				▲		01539 568486
Casterton	Pheasant Inn			▲					01524 271230
Crosthwaite	Punch Bowl	★	▲						01539 568237
Dent	Sun Inn				▲				01539 625208
Elterwater	Britannia Inn			▲		▲			01539 437210
Eskdale Green	Bower House Inn		▲	▲		▲	▲	▲	01946 723244
Faugh	String of Horses Inn		▲	▲		▲			01228 70297
Gretna	Gretna Chase Hotel			▲					01461 337517
Hawkshead	Drunken Duck Inn		▲	▲		▲			01539 436347
Hawkshead	Queen's Head Hotel		▲	▲			▲		01539 436271
Hesket Newmarket	Old Crown				▲				01697 478288
Kirkby Lonsdale	Snooty Fox Tavern		▲	▲			▲		01524 271308
Langdale	Three Shires Inn			▲		▲		▲	01539 437215
Loweswater	Kirkstile Inn			▲			▲		01900 85219
Melmerby	Shepherds Inn		▲				▲		01768 881217
Metal Bridge	Metal Bridge Inn			▲			▲	▲	01228 74206
Ravenstonedale	Black Swan Inn			▲					01539 623204
Ravenstonedale	The Fat Lamb			▲					01539 623242
Scales	White Horse		▲						01768 779241

Location	Establishment	Star	Food	Bed & Breakfast	Atmosphere	Sleep	Families	Waterside	Telephone
Talkin Village	Blacksmiths Arms		▲	▲					01697 73452
Troutbeck	Mortal Man Inn		▲	▲		▲			01539 433193
Ulverston	Bay Horse Inn	★	▲	▲				▲	01229 583972
Wasdale Head	Wasdale Head Inn			▲		▲		▲	01946 726229
Derbyshire									
Ashford-in-the-Water	Ashford Hotel			▲			▲		01629 812725
Bamford	Yorkshire Bridge Inn		▲	▲		▲	▲		01433 651361
Birch Vale	Sycamore Inn			▲			▲		01663 742715
Birchover	Druid Inn		▲						01629 650302
Brassington	Ye Olde Gate				▲				01629 540448
Calver	Chequers Inn		▲	▲		▲			01433 630231
Castleton	Castle Hotel			▲			▲		01433 620578
Castleton	Ye Olde Nag's Head		▲	▲					01433 620248
Derby	Abbey Inn				▲				01332 558297
Derby	Ye Olde Dolphin Inn				▲				01332 349115
Dronfield	Old Sidings		▲					▲	01246 410023
Eyam	Miners Arms		▲	▲					01433 630853
Grindleford	Maynard Arms		▲	▲		▲	▲		01433 630321
Hathersage	Hathersage Inn			▲					01433 650259
Hope	Poachers Arms			▲					01433 620380
Little Longstone	Packhorse				▲				01629 640471

Litton	Red Lion				▲		▲		01298 871458
Over Haddon	Lathkil Hotel		▲	▲		▲			01629 812501
Tideswell	George			▲					01298 871382
Wardlow	Bull's Head		▲						01298 871431
Woolley Moor	White Horse		▲				▲		01246 590319

Devon

Alphington	Double Locks		▲				▲	▲	01392 56947
Ashprington	Durant Arms		▲						01803 732240
Ashprington	Waterman's Arms		▲	▲		▲	▲	▲	01803 732214
Bantham	Sloop Inn			▲				▲	01548 560215
Beer	Anchor Inn		▲	▲		▲		▲	01297 20386
Blackawton	Normandy Arms			▲					01803 712316
Branscombe	Masons Arms		▲	▲					01297 680300
Brendon	Stag Hunters Hotel		▲	▲				▲	01598 741222
Broadhembury	Drewe Arms		▲						01404 841267
Butterleigh	Butterleigh Inn				▲				01884 855407
Cheriton Bishop	Old Thatch Inn		▲	▲					01647 24204
Chillington	Chillington Inn		▲	▲			▲		01548 580244
Cockwood	Anchor Inn		▲					▲	01626 890203
Cockwood	Ship Inn		▲					▲	01626 890373
Coleford	New Inn		▲	▲		▲		▲	01363 84242
Cornworthy	Hunters Lodge		▲				▲		01803 732204
Cullompton	Manor House Hotel			▲					01884 32281
Dalwood	Tuckers Arms		▲	▲					01404 881342
Dartington	Cott Inn		▲	▲		▲			01803 863777

Location	Establishment	Star	Food	Bed & Breakfast	Atmosphere	Sleep	Families	Waterside	Telephone
Dartmouth	Cherub		▲						01803 832571
Dartmouth	Royal Castle Hotel			▲		▲	▲	▲	01803 833033
Doddiscombleigh	Nobody Inn		▲	▲		▲			01647 252394
Frithelstock	Clinton Arms		▲	▲			▲		01805 623279
Harberton	Church House Inn				▲				01803 863707
Hatherleigh	George Hotel			▲		▲	▲		01837 810454
Hatherleigh	Tally Ho			▲					01837 810306
Haytor Vale	Rock Inn		▲	▲		▲			01364 661305
Holne	Church House Inn			▲					01364 631208
Horndon	Elephant's Nest		▲						01822 810273
Horsebridge	Royal Inn		▲					▲	01822 870214
Kingskerswell	Barn Owl Inn		▲	▲		▲			01803 872130
Kingsteignton	Old Rydon Inn	★	▲				▲		01626 54626
Knowstone	Masons Arms		▲						01398 341231
Lifton	Arundell Arms		▲	▲					01566 784666
Lower Ashton	Manor Inn		▲						01647 252304
Lydford	Castle Inn		▲	▲			▲		01822 820242
Lynmouth	Rising Sun Hotel			▲		▲		▲	01598 753223
Moretonhampstead	White Hart Hotel			▲					01647 440406
Newton St Cyres	Crown & Sceptre		▲				▲	▲	01392 851278
Plymouth	China House				▲			▲	01752 260930
Rockbeare	Jack in the Green	★	▲						01404 822240

Shaldon	Ness House Hotel			▲			▲	▲	01626 873480
South Pool	Millbrook Inn		▲					▲	01548 531581
South Zeal	Oxenham Arms			▲					01837 840244
Spreyton	Tom Cobley Tavern			▲					01647 231314
Staverton	Sea Trout Inn		▲	▲					01803 762274
Stockland	King's Arms Inn		▲	▲					01404 881361
Stokenham	Tradesman's Arms		▲						01548 580313
Thelbridge	Thelbridge Cross Inn			▲			▲		01884 860316
Torcross	Start Bay Inn		▲				▲	▲	01548 580553
Trusham	Cridford Inn	★	▲	▲		▲			01626 853694
Tuckenhay	Floyd's Inn (Sometimes)		▲	▲		▲		▲	01803 732350
Weston	The Otter		▲				▲	▲	01404 42594
Widecombe-in-the-Moor	Rugglestone Inn		▲						01364 621327

Dorset

Abbotsbury	Ilchester Arms			▲		▲			01305 871243
Askerswell	Spyway Inn				▲			▲	01308 485250
Blandford Forum	Crown Hotel			▲					01258 456626
Bridport	Bull Hotel			▲					01308 422878
Bridport	George Hotel		▲	▲		▲	▲		01308 423187
Buckland Newton	Gaggle of Geese				▲			▲	01300 345249
Cerne Abbas	New Inn			▲					01300 341274
Cerne Abbas	Red Lion		▲						01300 341441
Church Knowle	New Inn				▲		▲		01929 480357
Corfe Castle	Fox				▲				01929 480449
Corscombe	Fox Inn	★	▲						01935 891330

Location	Establishment	Star	Food	Bed & Breakfast	Atmosphere	Sleep	Families	Waterside	Telephone
Cranborne	Fleur de Lys			▲					01725 517282
Dorchester	King's Arms			▲					01305 265353
East Chaldon	Sailors Return		▲						01305 853847
Farnham	Museum Hotel		▲	▲					01725 516261
Loders	Loders Arms		▲						01308 422431
Milton Abbas	Hambro Arms		▲	▲					01258 880233
Motcombe	Coppleridge Inn		▲	▲		▲	▲		01747 851980
Nettlecombe	Marquis of Lorne		▲	▲			▲		01308 485236
North Wootton	Three Elms			▲			▲		01935 812881
Piddlehinton	Thimble Inn				▲			▲	01300 348270
Pimperne	Anvil Hotel			▲					01258 453431
Plush	Brace of Pheasants		▲				▲		01300 348357
Powerstock	Three Horseshoes Inn		▲	▲		▲	▲		01308 485328
Semley	Benett Arms		▲						01747 830221
Shave Cross	Shave Cross Inn				▲				01308 868358
Shroton	Cricketers		▲						01258 860421
Sturminster Newton	The Swan Inn			▲					01258 472208
Tarrant Monkton	Langton Arms		▲	▲		▲	▲		01258 830225
Trent	Rose & Crown		▲				▲		01935 850776
West Bexington	Manor Hotel		▲	▲				▲	01308 897616

West Stafford	Wise Man Inn		▲						01305 263694
Winkton	Fisherman's Haunt Hotel			▲				▲	01202 484071

Co Durham

Blanchland	Lord Crewe Arms Hotel		▲	▲		▲	▲		01434 675251
Fir Tree	Duke of York		▲	▲					01388 762848
Greta Bridge	The Morritt Arms Hotel			▲					01833 627232
Middleton-in-Teesdale	Teesdale Hotel		▲	▲					01833 640264
Romaldkirk	Rose and Crown	★	▲	▲		▲			01833 650213
Running Waters	Three Horse Shoes Inn			▲					01913 720286

Essex

Burnham-on-Crouch	Ye Olde White Harte Hotel			▲				▲	01621 782106
Clavering	Cricketers		▲						01799 550442
Colchester	Foresters Arms		▲						01206 42646
Colchester	Rose & Crown Hotel			▲			▲		01206 866677
Dedham	Marlborough Head Hotel		▲	▲					01206 323124
Gosfield	Green Man		▲						01787 472746
Great Chesterford	Plough				▲		▲		01799 530283
Hastingwood Common	Rainbow & Dove				▲				01279 415419
High Roding	Black Lion				▲				01371 872847
Horndon-on-the-Hill	The Bell Restaurant	★	▲	▲		▲			01375 673154
Little Braxted	Green Man		▲						01621 891659
Little Canfield	Lion & Lamb				▲		▲		01279 870257
Littlebury	Queen's Head		▲	▲			▲		01799 522251
Mill Green	Viper				▲				01277 352010

Location	Establishment	Star	Food	Bed & Breakfast	Atmosphere	Sleep	Families	Waterside	Telephone
Rickling Green	Cricketers' Arms			▲			▲		01799 543210
Saffron Walden	Eight Bells		▲						01799 522790
Saffron Walden	Saffron Hotel		▲	▲					01799 522676
Thaxted	Farmhouse Inn			▲					01371 830864
Tillingham	Cap & Feathers				▲				01621 779212
Toot Hill	Green Man		▲						01992 522255
Gloucestershire									
Amberley	Black Horse				▲		▲		01453 872556
Ampney Crucis	Crown of Crucis			▲		▲		▲	01285 851806
Barnsley	The Village Pub			▲					01285 740421
Bibury	Catherine Wheel		▲	▲				▲	01285 740250
Birdlip	The Air Balloon				▲				01452 862541
Blockley	Crown Inn & Hotel		▲	▲		▲			01386 700245
Broad Campden	Bakers Arms		▲						01386 840515
Brockhampton	Craven Arms		▲						01242 820410
Chipping Campden	Eight Bells Inn		▲	▲					01386 840371
Chipping Campden	Noel Arms			▲		▲			01386 840317
Clearwell	Wyndham Arms		▲	▲		▲	▲		01594 833666
Coln St Aldwyns	The New Inn	★	▲	▲		▲			01285 750651
Ewen	Wild Duck Inn			▲		▲			01285 770310
Ford	Plough Inn		▲	▲			▲		01386 584215

Frampton Mansell	Crown Hotel			▲		▲			01285 760601
Great Rissington	The Lamb	★	▲	▲		▲			01451 820388
Gretton	Royal Oak		▲				▲		01242 602477
Guiting Power	Ye Olde Inne		▲						01451 850392
Kingscote	Hunters Hall		▲	▲			▲		01453 860393
Little Compton	Red Lion		▲	▲					01608 674397
Lower Oddington	The Fox		▲						01451 870888
Moreton-in-Marsh	Redesdale Arms			▲					01608 650308
Northleach	Wheatsheaf Hotel		▲	▲		▲			01451 860244
Oddington	Horse & Groom			▲		▲	▲		01451 830584
St Briavels	George			▲					01594 530228
Stroud	Old Nelson			▲					01453 765821
Tetbury	Gumstool Inn		▲						01666 890391
Waterley Bottom	New Inn			▲					01453 543659
Winchcombe	Old White Lion			▲		▲			01242 603300
Woodchester	Ram Inn				▲				01453 873329

Greater Manchester

Diggle	Diggle Hotel			▲					01457 872741
Manchester	Lass O'Gowrie				▲				0161-273 6932
Manchester	Mark Addy		▲					▲	0161-832 4080
Manchester	New Ellesmere			▲			▲		0161-728 2791
Mellor	Devonshire Arms		▲						0161-427 2563
Middleton	Olde Boars Head				▲				0161-643 3520
Saddleworth	Green Ash Hotel			▲		▲			01457 871035
Strinesdale	Roebuck Inn		▲				▲		0161-624 7819

Hampshire

Location	Establishment	Star	Food	Bed & Breakfast	Atmosphere	Sleep	Families	Waterside	Telephone
Alresford	Globe on the Lake		▲				▲	▲	01962 732294
Beauworth	Milbury's				▲		▲		01962 771248
Bentworth	Sun		▲						01420 562338
Boldre	Red Lion				▲				01590 673177
Bramdean	Fox Inn		▲						01962 771363
Buckler's Hard	Master Builder's House Hotel			▲				▲	01590 616253
Buriton	Five Bells		▲						01730 263584
Bursledon	Jolly Sailor				▲			▲	01703 405557
Cadnam	White Hart		▲				▲		01703 812277
Cheriton	Flower Pots		▲	▲					01962 771318
Crawley	Fox & Hounds		▲	▲		▲			01962 776285
Damerham	Compasses Inn		▲	▲		▲	▲		01725 518231
Dummer	The Queen		▲						01256 397367
Dunbridge	Mill Arms Inn		▲						01794 340401
East Meon	Ye Olde George Inn		▲	▲				▲	01730 823481
Ellisfield	Fox		▲						01256 381210
Emery Down	New Forest Inn		▲	▲			▲		01703 282329
Faccombe	Jack Russell Inn			▲		▲	▲	▲	01264 737315
Langstone	Royal Oak				▲		▲	▲	01705 483125
Linwood	High Corner Inn			▲			▲		01425 473973
Longstock	Peat Spade Inn		▲						01264 810612

Lower Froyle	Prince of Wales		▲						01420 23102
Lower Wield	Yew Tree Inn		▲				▲		01256 389224
Micheldever	Dever Arms		▲						01962 774339
Odiham	George Hotel			▲					01256 702081
Ovington	Bush Inn		▲					▲	01962 732764
Pilley	Fleur de Lys		▲						01590 672158
Priors Dean	White Horse		▲				▲		01420 588387
Rockbourne	Rose & Thistle		▲						01725 518236
Sherfield English	Hatchet Inn		▲						01794 322487
Sparsholt	Plough		▲				▲		01962 776353
Steep	Harrow Inn		▲						01730 262685
Stratfield Turgis	Wellington Arms		▲	▲		▲			01256 882214
Tangley	Fox Inn		▲	▲		▲			01264 730276
Testcombe	Mayfly				▲			▲	01264 860283
Tichborne	Tichborne Arms		▲						01962 733760
Titchfield	Fisherman's Rest				▲			▲	01329 842848
Well	Chequers		▲						01256 862605
Winchester	Wykeham Arms	★	▲	▲					01962 853834

Hereford & Worcester

Bretforton	Fleece Inn				▲		▲		01386 831173
Brimfield	The Roebuck & Poppies	★	▲	▲		▲			01584 711230
Carey	Cottage of Content			▲		▲		▲	01432 840242
Dorstone	Pandy Inn		▲						01981 550273
Fownhope	Green Man			▲		▲	▲		01432 860243
Kempsey	Walter de Cantelupe Inn		▲						01905 820572

Location	Establishment	Star	Food	Bed & Breakfast	Atmosphere	Sleep	Families	Waterside	Telephone
Knightwick	Talbot Hotel		▲	▲			▲	▲	01886 821235
Ledbury	The Feathers Hotel		▲	▲					01531 635266
Ledbury	Ye Olde Talbot Hotel			▲			▲		01531 632963
Leominster	Royal Oak			▲			▲		01568 612610
Little Cowarne	The Three Horseshoes		▲	▲		▲	▲		01885 400276
Ombersley	King's Arms		▲						01905 620315
Pembridge	New Inn		▲						01544 388427
Ruckhall	Ancient Camp Inn			▲		▲			01981 250449
Sellack	Loughpool Inn		▲					▲	01989 730236
Shobdon	Bateman Arms		▲						01568 708374
Upton Bishop	The Moody Cow		▲						01989 780470
Weobley	Ye Olde Salutation Inn		▲	▲		▲			01544 318443
Whitney-on-Wye	Rhydspence Inn		▲	▲		▲			01497 831262
Winforton	Sun Inn	★	▲	▲					01544 327677
Woolhope	Butchers Arms		▲	▲		▲		▲	01432 860281
Wyre Piddle	Anchor Inn		▲				▲	▲	01386 552799
Hertfordshire									
Ayot St Lawrence	Brocket Arms			▲		▲	▲		01438 820250
Barley	Fox & Hounds		▲				▲		01763 848459
Chenies	Red Lion		▲						01923 282722
Chorleywood	Sportsman Hotel			▲					01923 285155

Elsenham	Crown		▲				▲		01279 812827
St Albans	Garibaldi		▲						01727 855046
St Albans	Rose & Crown				▲				01727 851903
Watton at Stone	George & Dragon		▲						01920 830285

Humberside

Barnoldby-le-Beck	Ship Inn				▲				01472 822308
Driffield	Bell Hotel			▲					01377 256661
Low Catton	Gold Cup Inn				▲		▲	▲	01759 371354
North Dalton	Star Inn			▲					01377 217688
Skidby	Half Moon Inn		▲				▲		01482 843403

Isle of Wight

Bonchurch	Bonchurch Inn				▲				01983 852611
Chale	Clarendon Hotel & Wight Mouse Inn		▲	▲			▲		01983 730431
Seaview	Seaview Hotel		▲	▲			▲	▲	01983 612711
Ventnor	Spyglass Inn		▲	▲			▲	▲	01983 855338

Kent

Barming	The Bull				▲				01622 726468
Benenden	King William IV		▲						01580 240636
Biddenden	Three Chimneys		▲						01580 291472
Boughton Aluph	Flying Horse Inn		▲	▲					01233 620914
Burham	Golden Eagle		▲						01634 668975
Canterbury	Falstaff Hotel			▲					01227 462138

Location	Establishment	Star	Food	Bed & Breakfast	Atmosphere	Sleep	Families	Waterside	Telephone No.
Charing	Royal Oak Hotel			▲					01233 712307
Chiddingstone	Castle Inn				▲				01892 870247
Chilham	White Horse				▲				01227 730355
Chilham	Woolpack			▲			▲		01227 730208
Cliffe	Black Bull		▲						01634 220893
Eastling	Carpenter's Arms		▲	▲					01795 890234
Fordcombe	Chafford Arms		▲						01892 740267
Goudhurst	Star & Eagle Inn			▲					01580 211512
Ightham Common	Harrow Inn	★	▲						01732 885912
Ivy Hatch	The Plough	★	▲						01732 810268
Lenham	Dog & Bear			▲			▲		01622 858219
Marshside	Gate Inn		▲				▲	▲	01227 860498
Newnham	George Inn		▲						01795 890237
Pluckley	Dering Arms		▲				▲		01233 840371
Ringlestone	Ringlestone Inn		▲				▲		01622 859900
Selling	White Lion		▲						01227 752211
Sevenoaks	Royal Oak		▲	▲					01732 451109
Smarden	Bell		▲				▲		01233 770283
Smarden	Chequers Inn		▲	▲					01233 770217
Smarts Hill	Bottle House Inn		▲						01892 870306
Speldhurst Hill	George & Dragon		▲						01892 863125
Tunbridge Wells	Sankeys Cellar Wine Bar & Bistro		▲						01892 511422

Ulcombe	Pepper Box		▲						01622 842558
Warren Street	Harrow Inn		▲	▲		▲			01622 858727
Worth	St Crispin Inn			▲		▲			01304 612081
Wye	New Flying Horse Inn			▲		▲			01233 812297
Lancashire									
Blacko	Moorcock Inn		▲				▲		01282 614186
Downham	Assheton Arms		▲						01200 441227
Goosnargh	Bushells Arms		▲						01772 865235
Lydgate	White Hart	★	▲				▲		01457 872566
Mellor	Millstone Hotel		▲	▲		▲	▲		01254 813333
Rochdale	Egerton Arms				▲		▲		01706 46183
Whitewell	Inn at Whitewell		▲	▲		▲		▲	01200 448222
Yealand Conyers	New Inn		▲						01524 732938
Leicestershire									
Braunston	Blue Ball Inn		▲						01572 722135
Braunston	Old Plough		▲				▲		01572 722714
Empingham	White Horse		▲	▲		▲	▲		01780 460221
Glooston	Old Barn		▲	▲					01858 545215
Hallaton	Bewicke Arms		▲				▲		01858 555217
Kegworth	Cap & Stocking		▲						01509 674814
Leicester	Welford Place		▲						0116 247 0758
Lyddington	Old White hart		▲						01572 821703
Market Overton	Black Bull		▲						01572 767677
Old Dalby	Crown Inn		▲				▲		01664 823134

Location	Establishment	Star	Food	Bed & Breakfast	Atmosphere	Sleep	Families	Waterside	Telephone
Shardlow	The Old Crown		▲					▲	01332 792392
Somerby	Old Brewery Inn				▲				01664 454866
Waltham-on-the-Wolds	Royal Horseshoes			▲					01664 464289
Whitwell	Noel Arms			▲					01780 460334
Lincolnshire									
Aswarby	Tally Ho		▲	▲					01529 455205
Collyweston	Cavalier Inn			▲					01780 444288
Donington-on-Bain	Black Horse			▲		▲	▲		01507 343640
Duddington	Royal Oak Hotel			▲		▲			01780 444267
Gedney Dyke	The Chequers		▲						01406 362666
Lincoln	Wig & Mitre		▲						01522 535190
Louth	Masons Arms			▲					01507 609525
Newton	Red Lion		▲				▲		01529 497256
Springthorpe	New Inn		▲						01427 838254
Stamford	Bull and Swan			▲					01780 63558
Stamford	The George of Stamford		▲	▲		▲			01780 55171
Merseyside									
Barnston	Fox & Hounds		▲						0151-648 1323
Liverpool	Philharmonic Dining Rooms				▲				0151-709 1163
Raby	Wheatsheaf Inn				▲				0151-336 3416

Middlesex

Shepperton	Anchor Hotel			▲					01932 221618
Shepperton	King's Head				▲				01932 221910
Shepperton	Warren Lodge			▲				▲	01932 242972

Norfolk

Blickling	Buckinghamshire Arms			▲		▲	▲	▲	01263 732133
Brisley	Bell		▲						01362 668686
Burnham Market	Hoste Arms		▲	▲		▲	▲		01328 738257
Burnham Thorpe	Lord Nelson				▲		▲		01328 738241
Cley-next-the-Sea	George & Dragon Hotel			▲			▲		01263 740652
East Dereham	King's Head Hotel			▲			▲		01362 693842
Eastgate	Ratcatchers Inn		▲				▲		01603 871430
Great Ryburgh	Boar Inn			▲		▲			01328 829212
Holkham	Victoria Hotel			▲					01328 710469
King's Lynn	Tudor Rose			▲					01553 762824
Norwich	Adam & Eve				▲				01603 667423
Scole	Scole Inn			▲					01379 740481
Smallburgh	Crown		▲	▲					01692 536314
Snettisham	Rose & Crown			▲			▲		01485 541382
Stiffkey	Red Lion		▲				▲		01328 830552
Stow Bardolph	Hare Arms		▲				▲		01366 382229
Swanton Morley	Darby's		▲	▲		▲	▲		01362 637647
Thompson	Chequers Inn				▲		▲		01953 483360
Tivetshall St Mary	Old Ram			▲		▲	▲		01379 676794
Upper Sheringham	Red Lion		▲				▲		01263 825408

Location	Establishment	Star	Food	Bed & Breakfast	Atmosphere	Sleep	Families	Waterside	Telephone
Warham All Saints	Three Horseshoes		▲	▲					01328 710547
Wells-next-the-Sea	Crown Hotel		▲	▲					01328 710209
Winterton-on-Sea	Fisherman's Return		▲	▲			▲		01493 393305
Wolterton	Saracens Head		▲	▲		▲			01263 768909
Woodbastwick	Fur & Feather				▲				01603 720003
Northamptonshire									
Blakesley	Bartholomew Arms			▲					01327 860292
Castle Ashby	Falcon Hotel		▲	▲		▲			01604 696200
East Haddon	Red Lion Hotel		▲	▲			▲		01604 770223
Easton-on-the-Hill	Exeter Arms		▲						01780 57503
Fotheringhay	Falcon Inn		▲						01832 226254
Nassington	Black Horse Inn		▲						01780 782324
Upper Benefield	Wheatsheaf Hotel		▲	▲			▲		01832 205254
Woodnewton	White Swan		▲						01780 750010
Northumberland									
Bamburgh	Lord Crewe Arms			▲					01668 214243
Belford	Blue Bell Hotel			▲		▲	▲		01668 213543
Carterway Heads	Manor House Inn		▲	▲					01207 255268
Chatton	Percy Arms Hotel			▲			▲		01668 215244
Corbridge	Angel Inn		▲	▲		▲			01434 632119

Craster	Jolly Fisherman				▲			▲	01665 576461
Dunstan	Cottage Inn			▲					01665 576658
Haltwhistle	Milecastle Inn		▲						01434 320682
Haydon Bridge	General Havelock Inn		▲				▲		01434 684376
Hexham	Dipton Mill Inn		▲						01484 606577
Longframlington	Granby Inn		▲	▲					01665 570228
Low Newton by the Sea	The Ship				▲			▲	01665 576262
Newton-on-the-Moor	Cook & Barker Inn		▲	▲					01665 575234
Rennington	Mason's Arms			▲		▲			01665 577275
Seahouses	Olde Ship Hotel		▲	▲		▲		▲	01665 720200
Stannersburn	Pheasant Inn		▲	▲		▲			01434 240382
Wall	Hadrian Hotel			▲					01434 681232
Warenford	Warenford Lodge	★	▲						01668 213453

Nottinghamshire

Arnold	Burnt Stump				▲		▲		0115 963 1508
Colston Bassett	Martins Arms		▲						01949 81361
Drakeholes	Griff Inn		▲	▲				▲	01777 817206
Elkesley	Robin Hood Inn		▲				▲		01777 838259
Nottingham	Lincolnshire Poacher				▲				0115 941 1584
Nottingham	Ye Olde Trip to Jerusalem				▲				0115 947 3171
Redmile	Peacock Inn		▲					▲	01949 842554
Upton	French Horn		▲						01636 812394

Oxfordshire

Aston	Flower Pot		▲	▲		▲			01491 574721

Location	Establishment	Star	Food	Bed & Breakfast	Atmosphere	Sleep	Families	Waterside	Telephone
Banbury	Ye Olde Reine Deer Inn		▲						01295 264031
Barnard Gate	The Boot Inn		▲						01865 881231
Beckley	Abingdon Arms		▲						01865 351311
Bledington	King's Head Inn	★	▲	▲		▲	▲		01608 658365
Blewbury	Blewbury Inn		▲	▲					01235 850496
Brightwell Baldwin	Lord Nelson		▲						01491 612497
Burcot	Chequers		▲						01865 407771
Burford	The Angel		▲	▲					01993 822438
Burford	Inn For All Seasons		▲	▲		▲			01451 844324
Burford	Lamb Inn		▲	▲					01993 823155
Chadlington	Tite Inn		▲				▲		01608 676475
Charlbury	Bell Hotel			▲		▲			01608 810278
Charlbury	The Bull at Charlbury		▲	▲					01608 810689
Chislehampton	Coach & Horses			▲		▲			01865 890255
Church Enstone	Crown Inn			▲					01608 677262
Clanfield	The Plough at Clanfield			▲		▲			01367 810222
Clifton	Duke of Cumberland's Head		▲	▲					01869 338534
Clifton Hampden	Plough Inn		▲	▲		▲	▲		01865 407811
Cumnor	Bear & Ragged Staff	★	▲						01865 862329
Dorchester-on-Thames	George Hotel			▲					01865 340404
Drayton	Roebuck		▲	▲					01295 730542
Eynsham	Newlands Inn		▲				▲		01865 881486

Freeland	Shepherd Hall Inn			▲			▲		01993 881256
Frilford Heath	Dog House Hotel			▲			▲		01865 390830
Fyfield	White Hart				▲				01865 390585
Godstow	Trout				▲			▲	01865 54485
Great Tew	Falkland Arms		▲	▲					01608 683653
Hailey	The Bird In Hand		▲	▲		▲	▲		01993 868321
Henton	Peacock Hotel			▲		▲			01844 353519
Longworth	Blue Boar		▲						01865 820494
Lower Brailes	George Hotel		▲	▲			▲		01608 685223
Maidensgrove	Five Horseshoes		▲						01491 641282
Middleton Stoney	Jersey Arms			▲		▲			01869 343234
Nettlebed	White Hart		▲	▲					01491 641245
Nuffield	Crown		▲						01491 641335
Oxford	The Bear				▲				01865 721783
Remenham	The Little Angel		▲					▲	01491 574165
Roke	Home Sweet Home Inn		▲						01491 838249
Satwell	Lamb Inn				▲		▲		01491 628482
Shenington	Bell		▲						01295 670274
Shipton-under-Wychwood	Lamb Inn		▲	▲					01993 830465
Shipton-under-Wychwood	Shaven Crown Hotel		▲	▲					01993 830330
Sibford Gower	Wykham Arms		▲				▲		01295 780351
South Leigh	Mason Arms				▲		▲		01993 702485
Stanton St John	Star Inn		▲				▲		01865 351277
Steeple Aston	Red Lion		▲						01869 340225

Location	Establishment	Star	Food	Bed & Breakfast	Atmosphere	Sleep	Families	Waterside	Telephone
Winsford	Royal Oak Inn		▲	▲		▲			01643 851455
Withypool	Royal Oak Inn		▲	▲		▲			01643 831506
Staffordshire									
Alstonefield	George Inn				▲				01335 310205
Baldwin's Gate	Slater's			▲		▲	▲		01782 680052
Cauldon	Yew Tree				▲				01538 308348
Cresswell	Izaak Walton Inn		▲						01782 392265
Eccleshall	St George Hotel			▲					01785 850300
Onecote	Jervis Arms		▲				▲	▲	01538 304206
Tatenhill	Horseshoe Inn				▲		▲		01283 564913
Tutbury	Ye Olde Dog & Partridge Inn			▲		▲			01283 813030
Whitmore	Mainwaring Arms				▲				01782 680851
Suffolk									
Bardwell	Six Bells		▲	▲			▲		01359 250820
Bury St Edmunds	The Nutshell				▲				01284 764867
Dunwich	Ship Inn		▲	▲			▲		01728 648219
Glemsford	Black Lion		▲						01787 280684
Horringer	Beehive		▲				▲		01284 735260
Hoxne	Swan		▲						01379 668275

Icklingham	Red Lion		▲						01638 717802
Ixworth	The Pykkerell Inn		▲						01359 230398
Lamarsh	Red Lion				▲		▲		01787 227918
Lavenham	Angel Inn		▲	▲		▲	▲		01787 247388
Long Melford	Bull Hotel			▲					01787 378494
Pin Mill	Butt & Oyster				▲			▲	01473 780764
Snape	Golden Key		▲						01728 688510
Southwold	The Crown	★	▲	▲		▲			01502 722275
Stoke-by-Nayland	Angel Inn	★	▲	▲					01206 263245
Surrey									
Albury Heath	King William IV				▲				01483 202685
Blackbrook	Plough		▲						01306 886603
Chiddingfold	Crown Inn			▲		▲			01428 682255
Elstead	Woolpack		▲				▲		01252 703106
Grayswood	Wheatsheaf Inn	★	▲	▲			▲		01428 644440
Hascombe	White Horse		▲						01483 208258
Hurtmore	The Squirrel				▲		▲		01483 860223
Mickleham	King William IV		▲						01372 372590
Shamley Green	Red Lion		▲	▲					01483 892202
Thursley	Three Horseshoes				▲				01252 703268
Walliswood	Scarlett Arms				▲				01306 627243
East Sussex									
Alciston	Rose Cottage				▲				01323 870377
Berwick	Cricketers				▲				01323 870469

Location	Establishment	Star	Food	Bed & Breakfast	Atmosphere	Sleep	Families	Waterside	Telephone
Blackboys	Blackboys Inn		▲					▲	01825 890283
Brighton	Greys		▲						01273 680734
Firle	Ram Inn		▲	▲					01273 858222
Fletching	Griffin Inn		▲	▲		▲	▲		01825 722890
Forest Row	Brambletye Hotel			▲					01342 824144
Horam	Gun Inn		▲				▲		01825 872361
Kingston	The Juggs		▲				▲		01273 472523
Mayfield	Rose & Crown		▲	▲		▲			01435 872200
West Sussex									
Burpham	George & Dragon Inn		▲					▲	01903 883131
Byworth	Black Horse		▲						01798 342424
Chilgrove	White Horse Inn		▲	▲					01243 535219
Compton	Coach & Horses		▲						01705 631228
Edburton	Tottington Manor		▲	▲		▲			01903 815757
Elsted	Three Horseshoes				▲				01730 825746
Elsted Marsh	Elsted Inn		▲				▲		01730 813662
Fittleworth	Swan Inn			▲			▲		01798 865429
Fulking	Shepherd & Dog		▲						01273 857382
Hermitage	Sussex Brewery				▲				01243 371533
Lodsworth	Halfway Bridge Inn		▲						01798 861281
Lower Beeding	Jeremy's at The Crabtree	★	▲						01403 891257

Lurgashall	Noah's Ark				▲				01428 707346
Midhurst	Angel Hotel	★	▲	▲		▲			01730 812421
Nuthurst	Black Horse				▲			▲	01403 891272
Oving	Gribble Inn				▲				01243 786893
Petworth	Welldiggers Arms		▲						01798 342287
Rusper	Star Inn				▲				01293 871264
South Harting	Ship Inn		▲						01730 825302
South Harting	White Hart		▲				▲		01730 825355
Stedham	Hamilton Arms		▲						01730 812555
Sutton	White Horse			▲					01798 869221
The Haven	The Blue Ship				▲				01403 822709
Tillington	Horseguards Inn		▲	▲		▲			01798 342322
Warnham	Greets Inn				▲				01403 265047
West Hoathly	Cat Inn		▲						01342 810369
Wineham	Royal Oak				▲				01444 881252

Tyne & Wear

New York	Shiremoor House Farm		▲				▲		0191-257 6302
Newcastle-upon-Tyne	Cooperage				▲			▲	0191-232 8286

Warwickshire

Alderminster	Bell		▲						01789 450414
Ashby St Ledgers	Olde Coach House Inn		▲	▲		▲	▲		01788 890349
Broom	Broom Tavern		▲				▲		01789 773656
Ettington	Houndshill			▲					01789 740267
Ilmington	Howard Arms		▲	▲		▲			01608 682226

Location	Establishment	Star	Food	Bed & Breakfast	Atmosphere	Sleep	Families	Waterside	Telephone
Lowsonford	Fleur de Lys				▲		▲	▲	01564 782431
Stratford-upon-Avon	Dirty Duck				▲				01789 297312
Wilmcote	Mason's Arms		▲						01789 297416
Wootton Wawen	The Bull's Head		▲						01564 792511
West Midlands									
Ansty	Ansty Arms			▲			▲		01203 611817
Baginton	Old Mill Inn			▲				▲	01203 303588
Coventry	William IV		▲						01203 686394
Himley	Crooked House				▲		▲		01384 238583
Langley	Brewery Inn				▲			▲	0121-544 6467
West Bromwich	Manor House				▲				0121-588 2035
Wiltshire									
Axford	Red Lion Inn		▲	▲					01672 520271
Bottlesford	Seven Stars		▲				▲		01672 851325
Bowden Hill	Rising Sun				▲				01249 730363
Box	Bayly's		▲	▲					01225 743622
Brinkworth	Three Crowns		▲						01666 510366
Broad Chalke	Queen's Head Inn			▲					01722 780344
Bromham	Greyhound Inn		▲						01380 850241
Burton	Old House at Home		▲						01454 218227

Castle Combe	Castle Inn			▲		▲			01249 783030
Castle Combe	White Hart				▲				01249 782295
Charlton	Horse & Groom		▲	▲		▲			01666 823904
Chicksgrove	Compasses				▲		▲		01722 714318
Corsham	Methuen Arms			▲					01249 714867
Devizes	Bear		▲	▲					01380 722444
Ebbesbourne Wake	Horseshoes Inn		▲	▲		▲	▲		01722 780474
Fonthill Gifford	Beckford Arms			▲					01747 870385
Ford	White Hart at Ford		▲	▲				▲	01249 782213
Hindon	Lamb at Hindon		▲	▲					01747 820573
Holt	Old Ham Tree		▲	▲					01225 782581
Lacock	George Inn		▲				▲		01249 730263
Melksham	King's Arms Hotel			▲					01225 707272
North Newnton	Woodbridge Inn	★	▲	▲			▲	▲	01980 630266
Nunton	Radnor Arms		▲				▲		01722 329722
Pitton	Silver Plough		▲						01722 712266
Ramsbury	Bell		▲						01672 520230
Rowde	George & Dragon	★	▲						01380 723053
Salisbury	Haunch of Venison				▲				01722 322024
Salisbury	King's Arms			▲					01722 327629
Semington	Lamb on the Strand		▲						01380 870263
Sherston	Rattlebone Inn				▲				01666 840871
Stourton	Spread Eagle			▲		▲	▲		01747 840587
Wootton Rivers	Royal Oak		▲	▲					01672 810322

Location	Establishment	Star	Food	Bed & Breakfast	Atmosphere	Sleep	Families	Waterside	Telephone
North Yorkshire									
Asenby	Crab & Lobster		▲						01845 577286
Askrigg	King's Arms Hotel		▲	▲		▲	▲		01969 650258
Bainbridge	Rose & Crown Hotel			▲					01969 650225
Buckden	Buck Inn		▲	▲		▲		▲	01756 760228
Carlton-in-Coverdale	Foresters Arms		▲	▲					01969 640272
Carthorpe	Fox & Hounds		▲						01845 567433
Coxwold	Fauconberg Arms		▲	▲			▲		01347 868214
Cray	White Lion				▲		▲	▲	01756 760262
Danby	Duke of Wellington			▲					01287 660351
East Witton	Blue Lion		▲	▲		▲			01969 624273
Elslack	Tempest Arms			▲		▲	▲	▲	01282 842450
Goathland	Mallyan Spout		▲	▲		▲	▲		01947 896486
Harome	Star Inn		▲				▲		01439 770397
Helmsley	Feathers Hotel			▲			▲		01439 770275
Hetton	Angel Inn	★	▲						01756 730263
Horton-in-Ribblesdale	Crown Hotel		▲	▲			▲	▲	01729 860209
Hovingham	Worsley Arms Hotel			▲		▲			01653 628234
Kirkbymoorside	George & Dragon Hotel		▲	▲		▲			01751 433334
Linton-in-Craven	Fountaine Inn		▲				▲		01756 752210
Middleham	Black Swan			▲					01969 622221
Moulton	Black Bull		▲						01325 377289

Newton-on-Ouse	Dawnay Arms				▲		▲	▲	01347 848345
Nosterfield	Freemason's Arms		▲						01677 470548
Nunnington	Royal Oak		▲						01439 748271
Osmotherley	Three Tuns		▲	▲					01609 883301
Pickering	The White Swan		▲	▲		▲			01751 472288
Pickhill	Nag's Head		▲	▲		▲			01845 567391
Reeth	Buck Hotel			▲			▲		01748 884210
Ripley	Boar's Head Hotel		▲	▲		▲			01423 771888
Rosedale Abbey	Milburn Arms		▲	▲		▲			01751 417312
Rosedale Abbey	White Horse Farm Hotel		▲	▲		▲			01751 417239
Sawley	Sawley Arms		▲						01765 620642
Saxton	Plough Inn	★	▲						01937 557242
Starbotton	Fox & Hounds		▲	▲					01756 760269
Threshfield	Old Hall Inn		▲				▲		01756 752441
Topcliffe	Angel Inn			▲		▲	▲		01845 577237
Wass	Wombwell Arms	★	▲	▲		▲			01347 868280
Wath-in-Nidderdale	Sportsman's Arms		▲	▲		▲			01423 711306
West Witton	Wensleydale Heifer		▲	▲		▲			01969 622322
Wigglesworth	Plough Inn		▲	▲			▲		01729 840243
Wykeham	Downe Arms			▲		▲			01723 862471

South Yorkshire

Cadeby	Cadeby Inn				▲		▲		01709 864009
Cawthorne	Spencer Arms				▲				01226 790228
Penistone	Cubley Hall		▲				▲		01226 766086

Location	Establishment	Star	Food	Bed & Breakfast	Atmosphere	Sleep	Families	Waterside	Telephone
West Yorkshire									
Grange Moor	Kaye Arms		▲						01942 848385
Harewood	Harewood Arms			▲		▲			0113 288 6566
Haworth	Old White Lion Hotel			▲					01535 642313
Heath	King's Arms				▲				01924 377527
Holywell Green	Rock Inn Hotel			▲					01422 379721
Ledsham	Chequers Inn				▲				01977 683135
Leeds	Whitelocks				▲				0113 245 3950
Meltham	Will's O'Nat's		▲						01484 850078
Ripponden	Old Bridge Inn				▲			▲	01422 822595
Shelf	Duke of York			▲					01422 202056
Shelley	Three Acres	★	▲	▲		▲			01484 602606
Sowerby Bridge	The Hobbit			▲			▲		01422 832202
Thornton	Ring O'Bells		▲						01274 832296

Scotland Pubs by County

See **How To Use This Guide**, on Pages 10-11, for an explanation of our categories (FOOD, B&B, Atmosphere) and symbols.

Location	Establishment	Star	Food	Bed & Breakfast	Atmosphere	Sleep	Families	Waterside	Telephone
Borders									
Greenlaw	Castle Inn		▲	▲			▲		01361 810217
Innerleithen	Traquair Arms		▲	▲			▲		01896 830229
Melrose	Burts Hotel		▲	▲		▲			01896 822285
St Boswells	Buccleuch Arms Hotel		▲	▲					01835 822243
St Mary's Loch	Tibbie Shiels Inn		▲					▲	01750 42231
Swinton	Wheatsheaf Hotel		▲	▲			▲		01890 860257
Tweedsmuir	Crook Inn			▲					01899 880272
Central									
Brig o'Turk	Byre Inn		▲						01877 376292
Killin	Clachaig Hotel			▲		▲		▲	01567 820270
Kilmahog	Lade Inn		▲						01877 330152
Kippen	Cross Keys		▲	▲			▲		01786 870293
Sheriffmuir	Sheriffmuir Inn		▲				▲		01786 823285
Strathblane	Kirkhouse Inn			▲		▲			01360 770621

Location	Establishment	Star	Food	Bed & Breakfast	Atmosphere	Sleep	Families	Waterside	Telephone
Dumfries & Galloway									
Canonbie	Riverside Inn		▲	▲		▲		▲	01387 371512
Kirkcudbright	Selkirk Arms Hotel		▲	▲			▲		01557 330402
Moffat	Black Bull			▲			▲		01683 220206
New Abbey	Criffel Inn			▲			▲		01387 850305
Newton Stewart	Creebridge House Hotel		▲	▲		▲	▲		01671 402121
Portpatrick	Crown Hotel		▲	▲			▲	▲	01776 810261
Fife									
Anstruther	Dreel Tavern				▲				01333 310727
Crail	Golf Hotel			▲					01333 450206
Dysart	Old Rectory Inn		▲					▲	01592 651211
Elie	Ship Inn		▲				▲	▲	01333 330246
Kirkcaldy	Hoffmans	★	▲				▲		01592 204584
Markinch	Town House Hotel		▲	▲					01592 758459
St Andrews	Grange Inn		▲						01334 472670
Grampian									
Aberdeen	Prince of Wales		▲						01224 640597
Fochabers	Gordon Arms			▲					01343 820508
Kincardine O'Neil	Gordon Arms Hotel		▲	▲					01339 884236
Monymusk	Grant Arms Hotel		▲	▲					01467 651226

Netherley	Lairhillock Inn & Restaurant		▲				▲		01569 730001
Stonehaven	Marine Hotel		▲	▲				▲	01569 762155
Turriff	Towie Tavern		▲				▲		01888 511201
Highland									
Applecross	Applecross Inn		▲	▲				▲	01520 744262
Ardvasar	Ardvasar Hotel			▲					01471 844223
Beauly	Lovat Arms Hotel			▲					01463 782313
Busta	Shetland Busta House Hotel		▲	▲		▲		▲	01806 522506
Carbost	Old Inn			▲				▲	01478 640205
Cromarty	Royal Hotel			▲		▲		▲	01381 600217
Garve	Inchbae Lodge		▲	▲				▲	01997 455269
Glenelg	Glenelg Inn		▲	▲		▲	▲		01599 522273
Glenfinnan	The Prince's House			▲					01397 722246
Kylesku	Kylesku Hotel		▲	▲				▲	01971 502231
Talladale	Loch Maree Hotel			▲		▲			01445 760288
Ullapool	Argyll Hotel			▲					01854 612422
Ullapool	Ceilidh Place		▲	▲					01854 612103
Ullapool	Ferry Boat Inn		▲	▲				▲	01854 612366
Lothian									
Edinburgh	Doric Tavern Wine Bar & Bistro		▲						0131-225 1084
Edinburgh	Fishers		▲					▲	0131-554 5666
Edinburgh	Tattler		▲						0131-554 9999
Edinburgh	Waterfront Wine Bar		▲					▲	0131-554 7427
Gifford	Tweeddale Arms		▲	▲			▲		01620 810240

Location	Establishment	Star	Food	Bed & Breakfast	Atmosphere	Sleep	Families	Waterside	Telephone
Ratho	Bridge Inn		▲				▲	▲	0131-333 1320
Strathclyde									
Ardentinny	Ardentinny Hotel		▲	▲		▲	▲	▲	01369 810209
Ardfern	Galley of Lorne Inn				▲			▲	01852 500284
Arduaine	Loch Melfort Hotel Chartroom Bar		▲					▲	01852 200233
Castlecary	Castlecary House Hotel			▲					01324 840233
Clachan Seil	Tigh-an-Truish Inn		▲	▲				▲	01852 300242
Clachan Seil	Willowburn Hotel		▲	▲		▲		▲	01852 300276
Glasgow	Babbity Bowster		▲						0141-552 5055
Glasgow	Upstairs at the Ubiquitous Chip		▲						0141-334 5007
Kilberry	Kilberry Inn	★	▲	▲					01880 770223
Loch Eck	Coylet Inn		▲	▲			▲		01369 840426
Port Appin	The Pierhouse & Seafood Restaurant		▲	▲				▲	01631 730302
Tayvallich	Tayvallich Inn		▲				▲	▲	01546 870282
Tayside									
Almondbank	Almondbank Inn		▲					▲	01738 583242
Burrelton	Burrelton Park Inn		▲	▲					01828 670206
Dundee	Mercantile Bar				▲				01382 225500
Glendevon	Tormaukin Hotel		▲	▲					01259 781252
Glenfarg	Bein Inn		▲	▲				▲	01577 830216

Kenmore	Kenmore Hotel			▲		▲		▲	01887 830205
Killiecrankie	Killiecrankie Hotel			▲		▲			01796 473220
Kirkton of Glenisla	Glenisla Hotel		▲				▲		01575 582223
Weem	Ailean Chraggan Hotel		▲	▲					01887 820346

Wales Pubs by County

Location	Establishment	Star	Food	Bed & Breakfast	Atmosphere	Sleep	Families	Waterside	Telephone
Clwyd									
Afonwen	Pwll Gwyn Hotel		▲				▲		01352 720227
Babell	Black Lion Inn		▲						01352 720239
Betws-yn-Rhos	Ffarm Hotel		▲						01492 680287
Bodfari	Dinorben Arms		▲				▲		01745 710309
Burton Green	Golden Grove Inn				▲		▲		01244 570445
Erbistock	Boat Inn		▲					▲	01978 780143
Hanmer	Hanmer Arms Village Hotel			▲					01948 830532
Llanarmon Dyffryn Ceirog	West Arms Hotel		▲	▲		▲	▲	▲	01691 600665

Location	Establishment	Star	Food	Bed & Breakfast	Atmosphere	Sleep	Families	Waterside	Telephone
Llangollen	Britannia Inn			▲		▲			01978 860144
Llannefydd	Hawk & Buckle Inn			▲		▲			01745 540249
Marford	Trevor Arms			▲			▲		01244 570436
Mold	We Three Loggerheads		▲					▲	01352 810337
Tremeirchion	Salusbury Arms		▲				▲		01745 710262
Dyfed									
Abergorlech	Black Lion		▲				▲	▲	01558 685271
Cardigan	Black Lion			▲					01239 612532
Clarbeston Road	Picton Inn				▲				01437 731615
Felindre Farchog	Salutation Inn			▲			▲	▲	01239 820564
Landshipping	Stanley Arms		▲					▲	01834 891227
Llanddarog	Butchers Arms		▲				▲		01267 275330
Llandovery	King's Head Inn			▲					01550 720393
Llangrannog	Ship Inn		▲					▲	01239 654423
Llwyndafydd	Crown Inn		▲				▲		01545 560396
Nevern	Trewern Arms Hotel			▲		▲	▲	▲	01239 820395
Pembroke Ferry	Ferry Inn		▲					▲	01646 682947
Pisgah	Halfway Inn				▲		▲		01970 880631
Mid Glamorgan									
Creigiau	Caesar's Arms		▲						01222 890486

Llangynwyd	Olde House Inn				▲		▲		01656 733310
Nottage	Rose & Crown			▲					01656 784850

South Glamorgan

East Aberthaw	Blue Anchor Inn		▲						01446 750329

West Glamorgan

Swansea	Langland Court Hotel			▲		▲			01792 361545

Gwent

Abergavenny	Llanwenarth Arms Hotel		▲	▲			▲	▲	01873 810550
Bettws Newydd	Black Bear		▲						01873 880701
Chepstow	Castle View Hotel		▲	▲					01291 620349
Clydach	Drum & Monkey	★	▲						01873 831980
Clytha	Clytha Arms		▲				▲		01873 840206
Llanfihangel Crucorney	Skirrid Inn				▲				01873 890258
Llantrisant	Greyhound Inn		▲	▲			▲		01291 672505
Lydart	Gockett Inn		▲						01600 860486
Penallt	Boat Inn				▲			▲	01600 712615
Raglan	Beaufort Arms Hotel			▲					01291 690412
Shirenewton	Carpenters Arms		▲						01291 641231
Shirenewton	Tredegar Arms		▲	▲		▲			01291 641274
Trellech	Village Green		▲	▲			▲		01600 860119
Usk	Three Salmons			▲		▲			01291 672133
Whitebrook	Crown at Whitebrook		▲	▲		▲		▲	01600 860254

Location	Establishment	Star	Food	Bed & Breakfast	Atmosphere	Sleep	Families	Waterside	Telephone
Gwynedd									
Aberdovey	Penhelig Arms Hotel & Restaurant		▲	▲		▲		▲	01654 767215
Beaumaris	Liverpool Arms Hotel		▲	▲					01248 810362
Beaumaris	Ye Olde Bulls Head Inn		▲	▲		▲			01248 810329
Glanwydden	Queen's Head		▲						01492 546570
Penmaenpool	George III Hotel			▲		▲		▲	01341 422525
Red Wharf Bay	Ship Inn		▲				▲	▲	01248 852568
Tyn-y-Groes	Groes Inn		▲						01492 650545
Powys									
Crickhowell	Bear Hotel		▲	▲		▲			01873 810408
Crickhowell	Nantyffin Cider Mill		▲				▲	▲	01873 810775
Dinas Mawddwy	Dolbrodmaeth Inn			▲			▲		01650 531333
Hay-on-Wye	Kilverts		▲	▲		▲	▲		01497 821042
Hay-on-Wye	Old Black Lion		▲	▲					01497 820841
Llanfair Waterdine	Red Lion Inn			▲					01547 528214
Llanfihangel-Nant-Melan	Red Lion Inn		▲	▲		▲			01544 350220
Llanfrynach	White Swan		▲						01874 665276
Llangattock	Vine Tree		▲						01873 810514
Llangorse	Red Lion			▲			▲		01874 658238
Llanyre	Bell Country Inn			▲					01597 823959
Llowes	Radnor Arms		▲						01497 847460

Location	Establishment	Star	Food	Bed & Breakfast	Atmosphere	Sleep	Families	Waterside	Telephone
Llyswen	Griffin Inn	★	▲	▲		▲	▲		01874 754241
Old Radnor	Harp Inn		▲	▲		▲			01544 350655
Pant Mawr	Glansevern Arms			▲					01686 440240
Penybont	Severn Arms Hotel			▲					01597 851224
Trecastle	Castle Coaching Inn		▲	▲			▲		01874 636354

Channel Islands & Isle of Man

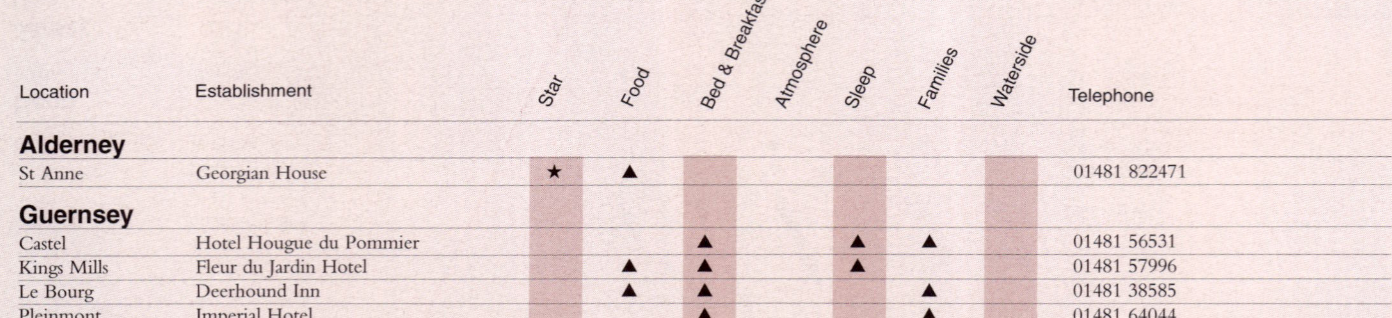

Location	Establishment	Star	Food	Bed & Breakfast	Atmosphere	Sleep	Families	Waterside	Telephone
Alderney									
St Anne	Georgian House	★	▲						01481 822471
Guernsey									
Castel	Hotel Hougue du Pommier			▲		▲	▲		01481 56531
Kings Mills	Fleur du Jardin Hotel		▲	▲		▲			01481 57996
Le Bourg	Deerhound Inn		▲	▲			▲		01481 38585
Pleinmont	Imperial Hotel			▲			▲		01481 64044

Location	Establishment	Star	Food	Bed & Breakfast	Atmosphere	Sleep	Families	Waterside	Telephone
St Peter Port	Ship & Crown				▲				01481 721368
St Peters	Longfrie Inn				▲		▲		01481 63107
Herm									
Herm	Ship Inn		▲						01481 722159
Jersey									
Gorey	Dolphin Hotel			▲					01534 853370
St Aubin	Old Court House Inn		▲	▲				▲	01534 46433
St Brelade	Old Smugglers Inn		▲				▲		01534 41510
St Helier	Tipsy Toad Town House				▲				01534 615000
St Lawrence	British Union Hotel		▲				▲		01534 861070
St Ouen	The Lobster Pot Coach House		▲						01534 482888
St Peter's Village	Star & Tipsy Toad Brewery		▲				▲		01534 485556
Sark									
Sark	Dixcart Hotel		▲	▲			▲		01481 832015
Isle of Man									
Peel	Creek Inn		▲					▲	01624 842216

Northern Ireland Pubs

Location	Establishment	Star	Food	Bed & Breakfast	Atmosphere	Sleep	Families	Waterside	Telephone
Co Antrim									
Ballycastle	House of McDonnell				▲				01265 762975
Belfast	Crown Liquor Saloon				▲				01232 325368
Belfast	Kelly's Cellars				▲				01232 324835
Bushmills	Bushmills Inn			▲			▲		01265 732339
Carnlough	Londonderry Arms		▲						01574 885255
Carnlough	The Waterfall				▲				
Carrickfergus	Wind-Rose Wine Bar & Restaurant		▲						01960 364192
Cushendall	PJ McCollam				▲				
Co Down									
Crawfordsburn	Old Inn			▲					01247 853255
Dundrum	Buck's Head Inn		▲						01396 751868
Hillsborough	Hillside Bar	★	▲						01846 682765
Co Fermanagh									
Enniskillen	Blakes of the Hollow				▲				01365 322143

Maps

2/3
4/5
20
6/7
8/9
10/11
14a/15a
16/19
14/15
12/13

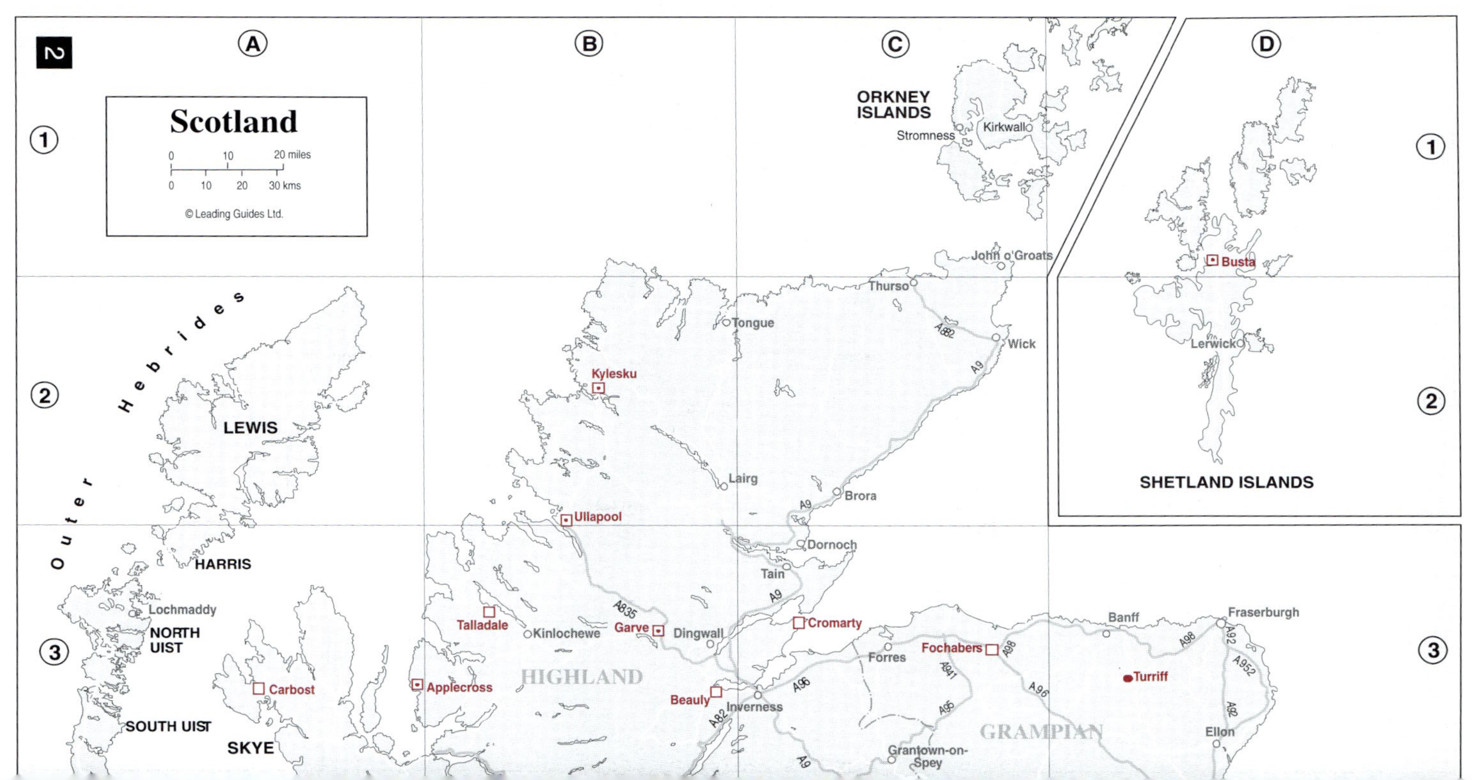
2
A
B
C
D
1
2
3
Scotland
0 10 20 miles
0 10 20 30 kms
© Leading Guides Ltd.
ORKNEY ISLANDS
Stromness
Kirkwall
John o'Groats
Thurso
Wick
A882
A9
Tongue
Kylesku
Lairg
Brora
Ullapool
Dornoch
Tain
Outer Hebrides
LEWIS
HARRIS
Lochmaddy
NORTH UIST
SOUTH UIST
SKYE
Carbost
Applecross
Talladale
Kinlochewe
A835
Garve
Dingwall
Cromarty
HIGHLAND
Beauly
Inverness
A82
A96
Forres
Fochabers
A941
A95
A98
Grantown-on-Spey
GRAMPIAN
Banff
Turriff
Fraserburgh
A92
A952
Ellon
SHETLAND ISLANDS
Busta
Lerwick

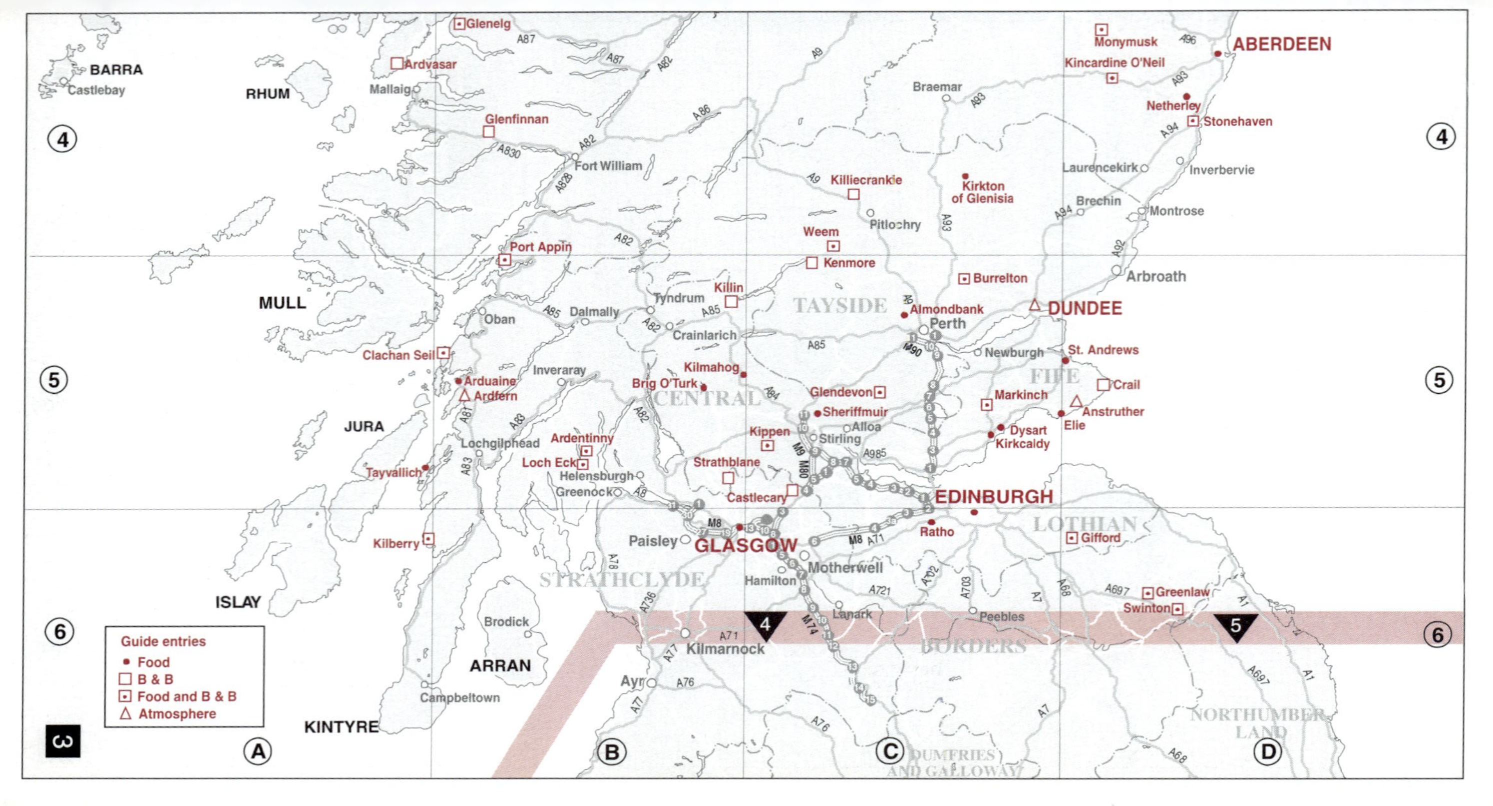
ABERDEEN
Monymusk
Kincardine O'Neil
Netherley
Stonehaven
Braemar
Laurencekirk
Inverbervie
Brechin
Montrose
Arbroath
Kirkton of Glenisia
Killiecrankie
Pitlochry
Weem
Kenmore
Burrelton
DUNDEE
Almondbank
Perth
TAYSIDE
Killin
Tyndrum
Crainlarich
Dalmally
Oban
Port Appin
Fort William
Glenfinnan
Glenelg
Ardvasar
Mallaig
BARRA
Castlebay
RHUM
MULL
JURA
ISLAY
KINTYRE
ARRAN
Brodick
Campbeltown
Clachan Seil
Arduaine
Ardfern
Inveraray
Lochgilphead
Tayvallich
Kilberry
Ardentinny
Loch Eck
Helensburgh
Greenock
Kilmahog
Brig O'Turk
CENTRAL
Glendevon
Sheriffmuir
Alloa
Stirling
Kippen
Strathblane
Castlecary
Newburgh
St. Andrews
FIFE
Crail
Markinch
Anstruther
Elie
Dysart
Kirkcaldy
EDINBURGH
Ratho
LOTHIAN
Gifford
GLASGOW
Paisley
Motherwell
Hamilton
STRATHCLYDE
Lanark
Peebles
Greenlaw
Swinton
Kilmarnock
Ayr
BORDERS
NORTHUMBERLAND
DUMFRIES AND GALLOWAY
Guide entries
Food
B & B
Food and B & B
Atmosphere
A
B
C
D
4
5
6
3

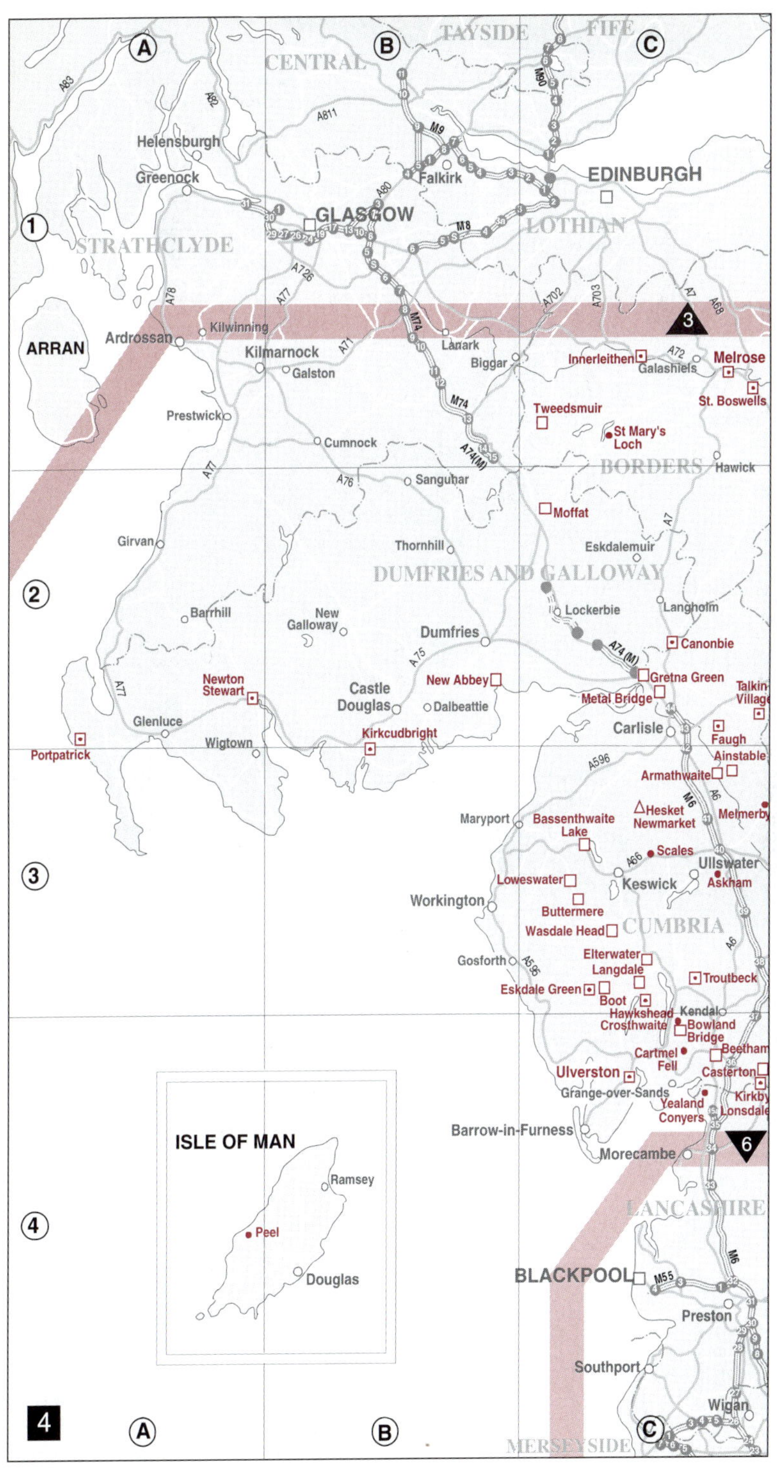

TAYSIDE
FIFE
CENTRAL
Helensburgh
Greenock
Falkirk
EDINBURGH
GLASGOW
LOTHIAN
STRATHCLYDE
ARRAN
Ardrossan
Kilwinning
Kilmarnock
Galston
Lanark
Biggar
Innerleithen
Galashiels
Melrose
St. Boswells
Prestwick
Tweedsmuir
St Mary's Loch
Cumnock
BORDERS
Hawick
Sanquhar
Moffat
Girvan
Thornhill
Eskdalemuir
DUMFRIES AND GALLOWAY
Barrhill
New Galloway
Lockerbie
Langholm
Dumfries
Canonbie
Newton Stewart
Castle Douglas
New Abbey
Gretna Green
Talkin Village
Metal Bridge
Glenluce
Dalbeattie
Carlisle
Faugh
Portpatrick
Wigtown
Kirkcudbright
Ainstable
Armathwaite
Maryport
Bassenthwaite Lake
Hesket Newmarket
Melmerby
Scales
Ullswater
Loweswater
Keswick
Askham
Workington
Buttermere
CUMBRIA
Wasdale Head
Gosforth
Elterwater
Langdale
Troutbeck
Eskdale Green
Boot
Kendal
Hawkshead
Crosthwaite
Bowland Bridge
Cartmel Fell
Beetham
Ulverston
Casterton
Grange-over-Sands
Kirkby Lonsdale
Yealand Conyers
Barrow-in-Furness
Morecambe
ISLE OF MAN
Ramsey
Peel
Douglas
LANCASHIRE
BLACKPOOL
Preston
Southport
Wigan
MERSEYSIDE
A
B
C
1
2
3
4
3
6

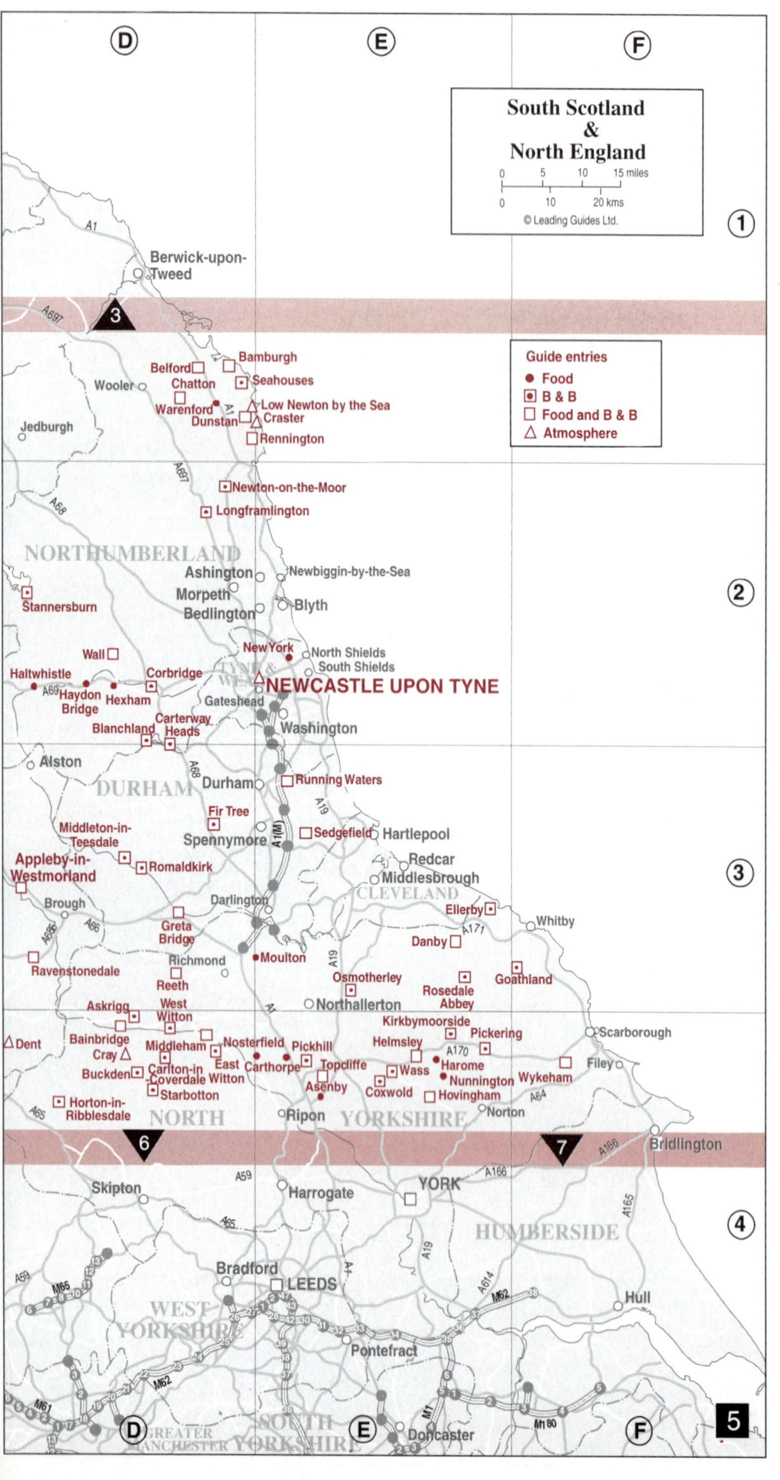

South Scotland
&
North England
0 5 10 15 miles
0 10 20 kms
© Leading Guides Ltd.
Guide entries
Food
B & B
Food and B & B
Atmosphere
Berwick-upon-Tweed
Bamburgh
Belford
Seahouses
Wooler
Chatton
Warenford
Low Newton by the Sea
Dunstan
Craster
Jedburgh
Rennington
Newton-on-the-Moor
Longframlington
NORTHUMBERLAND
Ashington
Newbiggin-by-the-Sea
Morpeth
Stannersburn
Blyth
Bedlington
New York
North Shields
South Shields
Wall
Haltwhistle
Corbridge
NEWCASTLE UPON TYNE
Haydon Bridge
Hexham
Gateshead
Carterway Heads
Washington
Blanchland
Alston
Durham
Running Waters
DURHAM
Fir Tree
Middleton-in-Teesdale
Spennymoor
Sedgefield
Hartlepool
Appleby-in-Westmorland
Romaldkirk
Redcar
Middlesbrough
CLEVELAND
Brough
Darlington
Ellerby
Whitby
Greta Bridge
Danby
Moulton
Richmond
Ravenstonedale
Osmotherley
Goathland
Reeth
Rosedale Abbey
Northallerton
Askrigg
West Witton
Kirkbymoorside
Pickering
Scarborough
Dent
Bainbridge
Middleham
Nosterfield
Pickhill
Helmsley
Cray
East Witton
Carthorpe
Topcliffe
Harome
Filey
Buckden
Carlton-in-Coverdale
Wass
Nunnington
Wykeham
Asenby
Coxwold
Hovingham
Starbotton
Horton-in-Ribblesdale
NORTH
Ripon
YORKSHIRE
Norton
Bridlington
Skipton
Harrogate
YORK
HUMBERSIDE
Bradford
LEEDS
Hull
WEST YORKSHIRE
Pontefract
GREATER MANCHESTER
SOUTH YORKSHIRE
Doncaster
5

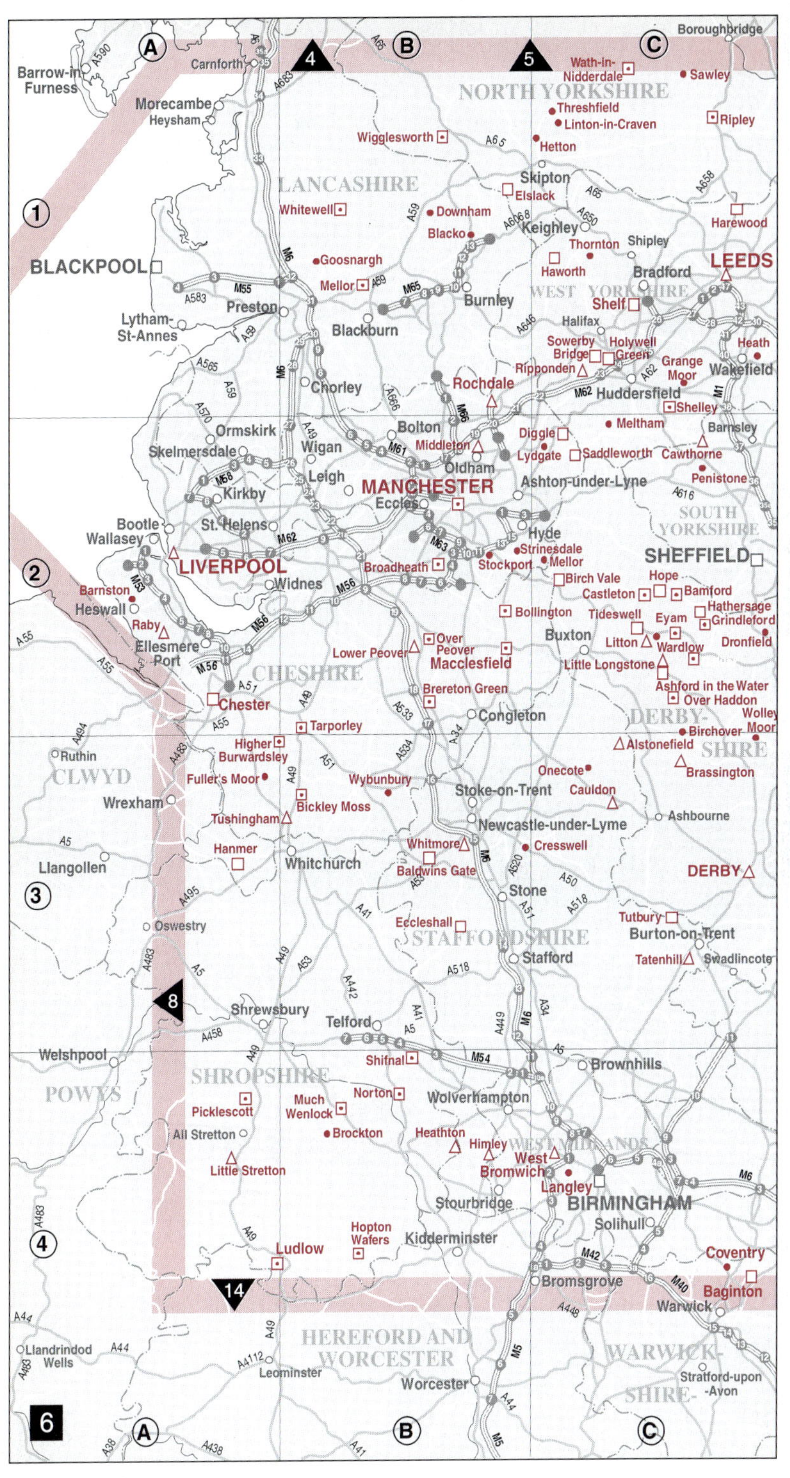

A
B
C
4
5
Boroughbridge
Barrow-in-Furness
Carnforth
Wath-in-Nidderdale
Sawley
NORTH YORKSHIRE
Morecambe
Heysham
Threshfield
Linton-in-Craven
Ripley
Wigglesworth
Hetton
Skipton
LANCASHIRE
Elslack
Harewood
1
Whitewell
Downham
Blacko
Keighley
Thornton
Shipley
BLACKPOOL
Goosnargh
Haworth
Bradford
LEEDS
Mellor
Burnley
WEST YORKSHIRE
Shelf
Preston
Lytham-St-Annes
Blackburn
Halifax
Sowerby Bridge
Holywell Green
Heath
Grange Moor
Wakefield
Ripponden
Rochdale
Chorley
Huddersfield
Shelley
Meltham
Barnsley
Ormskirk
Bolton
Diggle
Middleton
Skelmersdale
Wigan
Lydgate
Saddleworth
Cawthorne
Oldham
Leigh
Penistone
MANCHESTER
Ashton-under-Lyne
Kirkby
Eccles
SOUTH YORKSHIRE
Bootle
St. Helens
Hyde
Wallasey
Strinesdale
Mellor
SHEFFIELD
LIVERPOOL
Broadheath
Stockport
2
Widnes
Birch Vale
Hope
Barnston
Castleton
Bamford
Heswall
Bollington
Tideswell
Hathersage
Grindleford
Raby
Eyam
Ellesmere Port
Over Peover
Lower Peover
Buxton
Litton
Wardlow
Dronfield
Macclesfield
Little Longstone
CHESHIRE
Ashford in the Water
Brereton Green
Over Haddon
Chester
Congleton
DERBYSHIRE
Wolley Moor
Tarporley
Birchover
Higher Burwardsley
Alstonefield
Ruthin
CLWYD
Onecote
Brassington
Fuller's Moor
Wybunbury
Wrexham
Stoke-on-Trent
Cauldon
Bickley Moss
Ashbourne
Tushingham
Newcastle-under-Lyme
Whitmore
Cresswell
Hanmer
Whitchurch
DERBY
Llangollen
Baldwins Gate
3
Stone
Tutbury
Eccleshall
Oswestry
STAFFORDSHIRE
Burton-on-Trent
Stafford
Tatenhill
Swadlincote
8
Shrewsbury
Telford
Welshpool
Shifnal
Brownhills
SHROPSHIRE
POWYS
Norton
Much Wenlock
Wolverhampton
Pickle scott
All Stretton
Brockton
Heathton
Himley
WEST MIDLANDS
West Bromwich
Little Stretton
Langley
Stourbridge
BIRMINGHAM
Solihull
4
Hopton Wafers
Kidderminster
Ludlow
Coventry
14
Bromsgrove
Baginton
Warwick
HEREFORD AND WORCESTER
WARWICKSHIRE
Llandrindod Wells
Leominster
Worcester
Stratford-upon-Avon

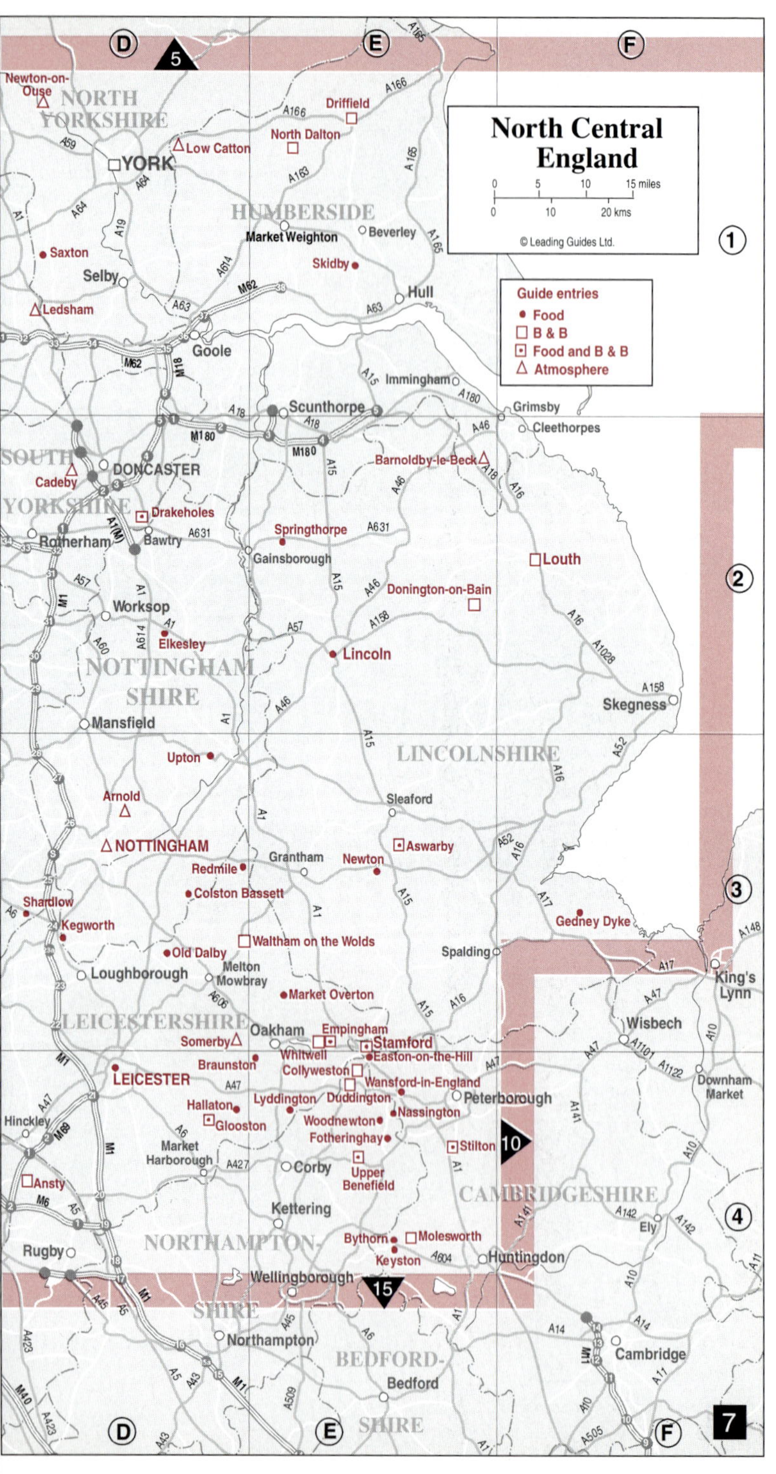
North Central England
0 5 10 15 miles
0 10 20 kms
© Leading Guides Ltd.
Guide entries
Food
B & B
Food and B & B
Atmosphere
Newton-on-Ouse
NORTH YORKSHIRE
YORK
Low Catton
Driffield
North Dalton
HUMBERSIDE
Market Weighton
Beverley
Skidby
Saxton
Selby
Ledsham
Hull
Goole
Immingham
Scunthorpe
Grimsby
Cleethorpes
SOUTH YORKSHIRE
Cadeby
DONCASTER
Drakeholes
Barnoldby-le-Beck
Springthorpe
Rotherham
Bawtry
Gainsborough
Louth
Donington-on-Bain
Worksop
Elkesley
Lincoln
NOTTINGHAMSHIRE
Skegness
Mansfield
Upton
LINCOLNSHIRE
Arnold
Sleaford
NOTTINGHAM
Aswarby
Redmile
Grantham
Newton
Colston Bassett
Shardlow
Kegworth
Gedney Dyke
Waltham on the Wolds
Old Dalby
Spalding
Loughborough
Melton Mowbray
King's Lynn
Market Overton
LEICESTERSHIRE
Wisbech
Oakham
Empingham
Somerby
Stamford
Whitwell
Easton-on-the-Hill
Braunston
Collyweston
LEICESTER
Wansford-in-England
Downham Market
Lyddington
Duddington
Peterborough
Hallaton
Nassington
Hinckley
Glooston
Woodnewton
Fotheringhay
Stilton
Market Harborough
Corby
Upper Benefield
Ansty
CAMBRIDGESHIRE
Kettering
Ely
Rugby
NORTHAMPTONSHIRE
Bythorn
Molesworth
Keyston
Huntingdon
Wellingborough
Northampton
Cambridge
BEDFORDSHIRE
Bedford
D
E
F
1
2
3
4
5
10
15
7

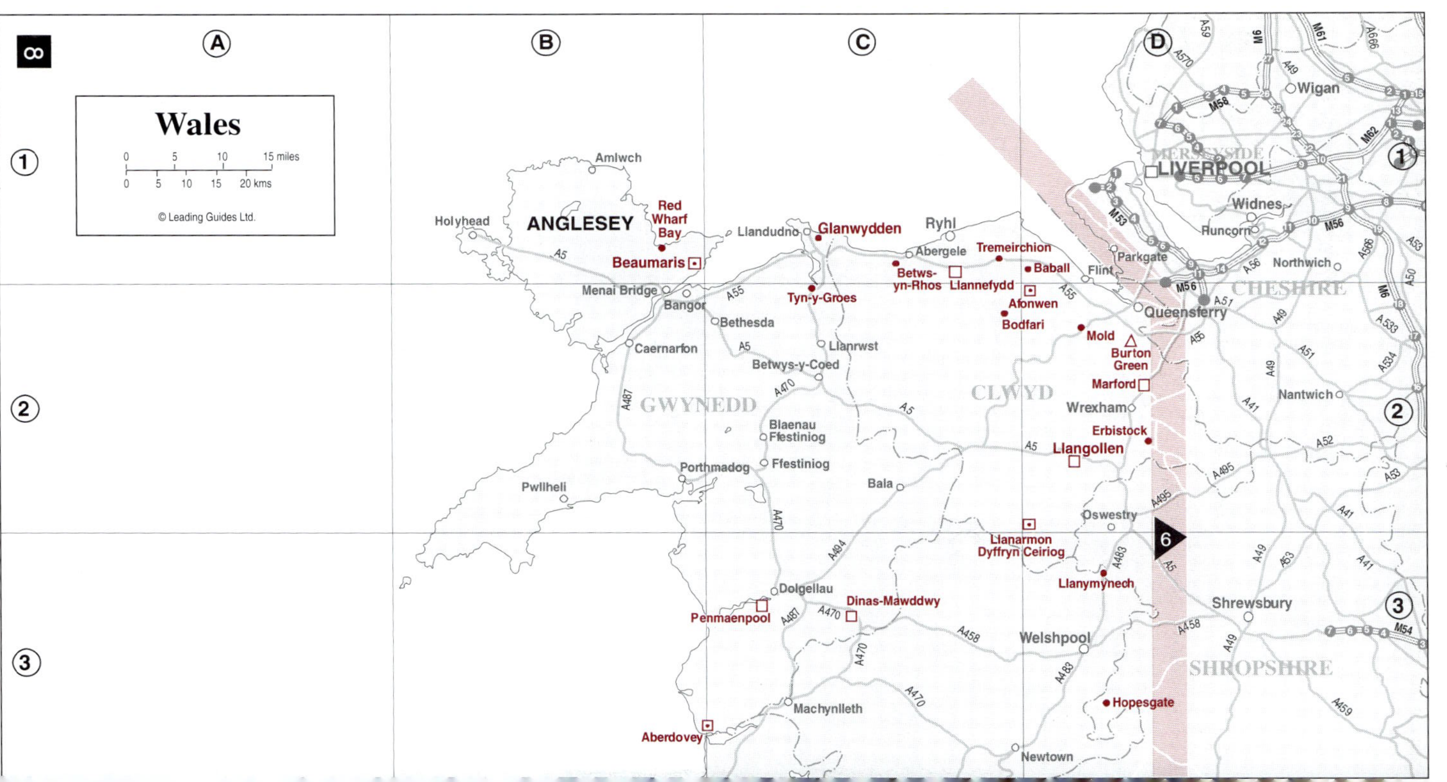
Wales
0 5 10 15 miles
0 5 10 15 20 kms
© Leading Guides Ltd.
A
B
C
D
1
2
3
ANGLESEY
Holyhead
Amlwch
Red Wharf Bay
Beaumaris
Menai Bridge
Bangor
Caernarfon
Llandudno
Glanwydden
Ryhl
Abergele
Tremeirchion
Betws-yn-Rhos
Llannefydd
Baball
Afonwen
Bodfari
Tyn-y-Groes
Bethesda
Llanrwst
Betwys-y-Coed
Flint
Parkgate
Queensferry
Mold
Burton Green
Marford
Wrexham
Erbistock
Llangollen
GWYNEDD
CLWYD
Blaenau Ffestiniog
Ffestiniog
Porthmadog
Pwllheli
Bala
Oswestry
Llanarmon Dyffryn Ceiriog
Llanymynech
Dolgellau
Dinas-Mawddwy
Penmaenpool
Welshpool
Machynlleth
Aberdovey
Newtown
Hopesgate
Shrewsbury
SHROPSHIRE
CHESHIRE
MERSEYSIDE
LIVERPOOL
Widnes
Runcorn
Northwich
Nantwich
Wigan
6
A5
A55
A470
A487
A494
A458
A483
A495
A49
A41
A51
A52
A53
A56
A57
A59
A570
A533
A534
A566
A666
A50
A459
M53
M56
M58
M6
M61
M62
M54

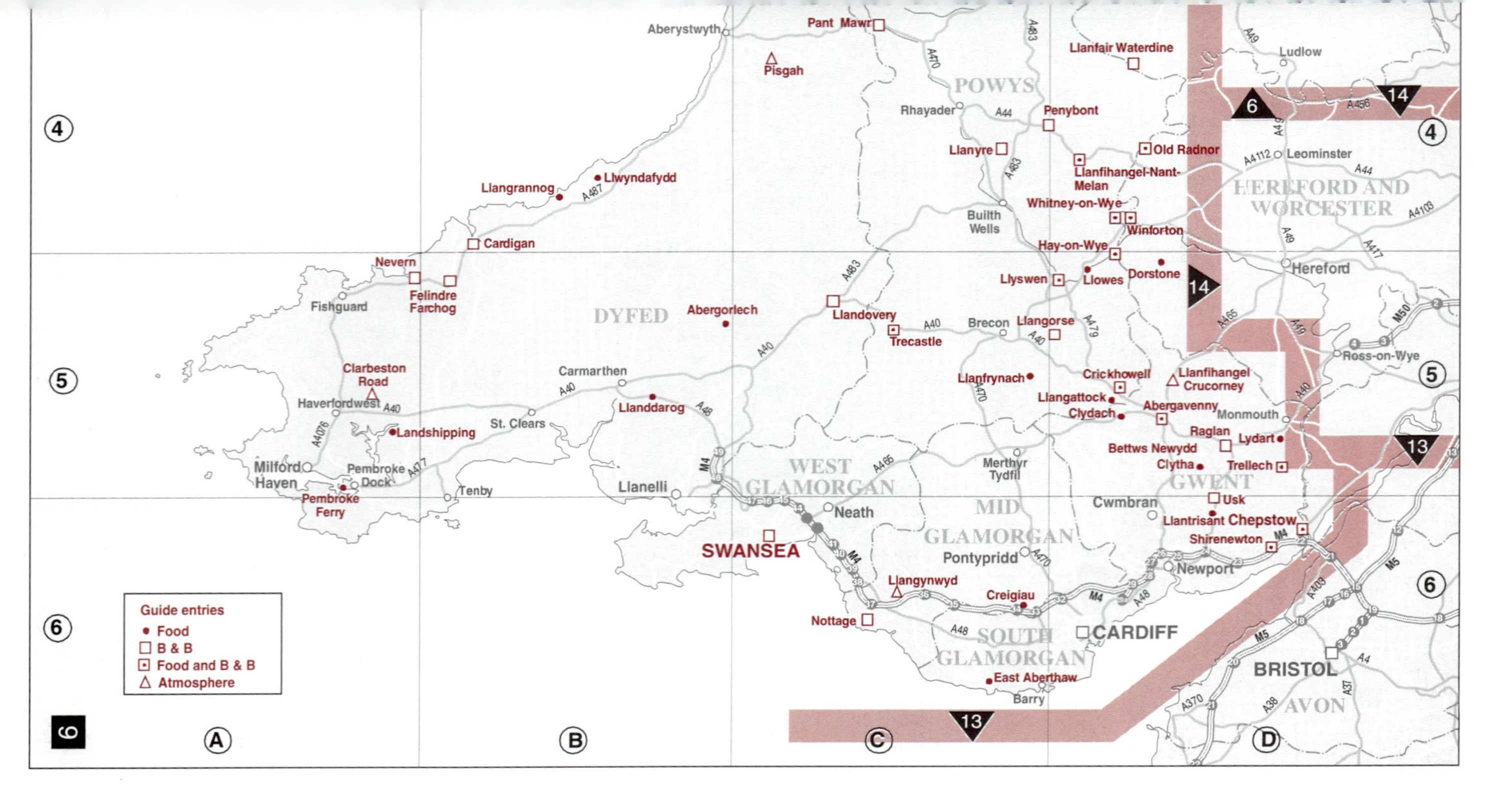
Guide entries
• Food
□ B & B
⊡ Food and B & B
△ Atmosphere
9
A
B
C
D
4
5
6
13
14
6
POWYS
DYFED
WEST GLAMORGAN
MID GLAMORGAN
SOUTH GLAMORGAN
GWENT
HEREFORD AND WORCESTER
AVON
Aberystwyth
Pant Mawr
Pisgah
Llanfair Waterdine
Ludlow
Rhayader
Penybont
Llanyre
Old Radnor
Llanfihangel-Nant-Melan
Leominster
Llangrannog
Llwyndafydd
Builth Wells
Whitney-on-Wye
Winforton
Cardigan
Hay-on-Wye
Hereford
Nevern
Felindre Farchog
Llyswen
Llowes
Dorstone
Fishguard
Abergorlech
Llandovery
Trecastle
Brecon
Llangorse
Ross-on-Wye
Clarbeston Road
Carmarthen
Llanfrynach
Crickhowell
Llanfihangel Crucorney
Haverfordwest
Llanddarog
Llangattock
Clydach
Abergavenny
Monmouth
Landshipping
St. Clears
Raglan
Lydart
Bettws Newydd
Clytha
Trellech
Milford Haven
Pembroke Dock
Merthyr Tydfil
Tenby
Llanelli
Pembroke Ferry
Usk
Neath
Cwmbran
Llantrisant
Chepstow
Shirenewton
SWANSEA
Pontypridd
Newport
Llangynwyd
Creigiau
Nottage
CARDIFF
BRISTOL
East Aberthaw
Barry
A49
A456
A44
A4112
A4103
A417
A465
A470
A483
A487
A40
A479
A4076
A477
A48
M4
M50
M5
A403
A4
A37
A38
A370

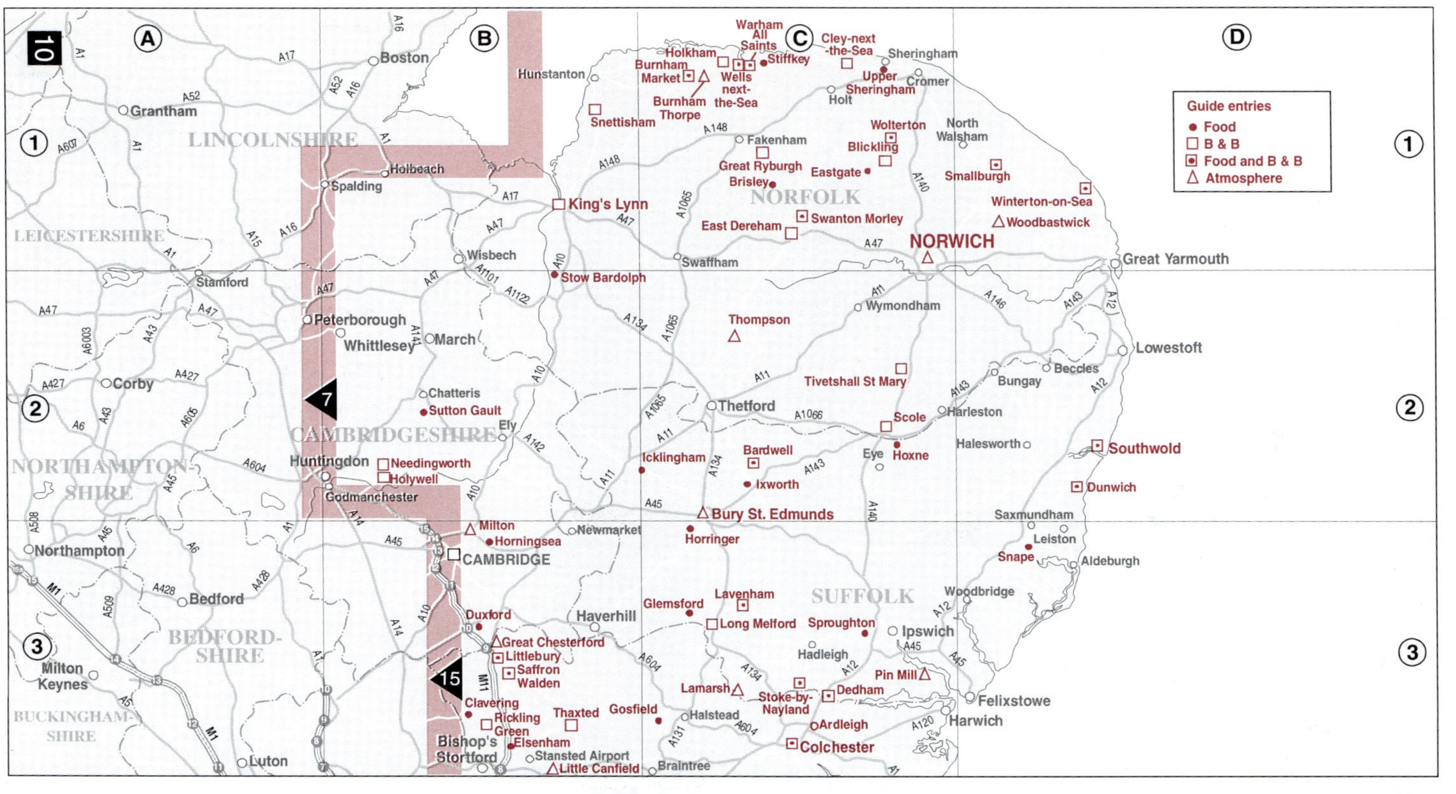
10
Guide entries
Food
B & B
Food and B & B
Atmosphere
A
B
C
D
1
2
3
7
15
LINCOLNSHIRE
LEICESTERSHIRE
NORTHAMPTON-SHIRE
CAMBRIDGESHIRE
BEDFORD-SHIRE
BUCKINGHAM-SHIRE
NORFOLK
SUFFOLK
Grantham
Boston
Hunstanton
Holbeach
Spalding
Stamford
Peterborough
Whittlesey
March
Wisbech
Corby
Chatteris
Sutton Gault
Ely
Huntingdon
Needingworth
Holywell
Godmanchester
Northampton
Bedford
Milton Keynes
Luton
Milton
Horningsea
CAMBRIDGE
Newmarket
Duxford
Great Chesterford
Littlebury
Saffron Walden
Clavering
Rickling Green
Elsenham
Bishop's Stortford
Stansted Airport
Little Canfield
Thaxted
Gosfield
Braintree
Halstead
Haverhill
Glemsford
Lavenham
Long Melford
Lamarsh
Stoke-by-Nayland
Colchester
Ardleigh
Dedham
Pin Mill
Hadleigh
Sproughton
Ipswich
Felixstowe
Harwich
Woodbridge
Snape
Leiston
Aldeburgh
Saxmundham
Dunwich
Southwold
Halesworth
Eye
Hoxne
Scole
Harleston
Bungay
Beccles
Lowestoft
Great Yarmouth
Bury St. Edmunds
Horringer
Ixworth
Bardwell
Icklingham
Thetford
Thompson
Tivetshall St Mary
Wymondham
NORWICH
Woodbastwick
Winterton-on-Sea
Smallburgh
North Walsham
Cromer
Sheringham
Upper Sheringham
Cley-next-the-Sea
Holt
Wolterton
Blickling
Eastgate
Swanton Morley
East Dereham
Brisley
Great Ryburgh
Fakenham
Swaffham
Stow Bardolph
King's Lynn
Snettisham
Burnham Market
Burnham Thorpe
Holkham
Wells-next-the-Sea
Warham All Saints
Stiffkey

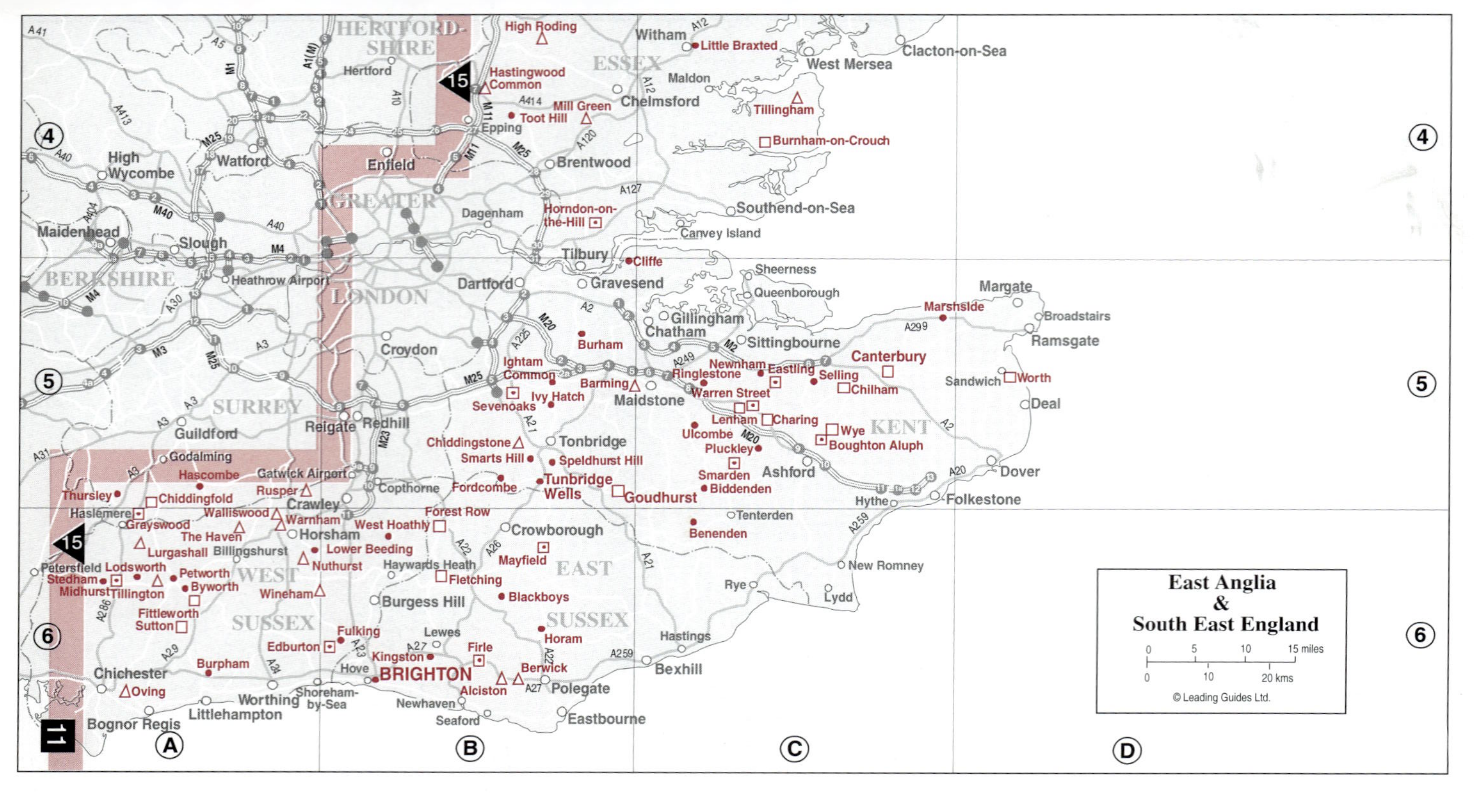
East Anglia
&
South East England
0 5 10 15 miles
0 10 20 kms
© Leading Guides Ltd.
11
15
A B C D
4 5 6
HERTFORDSHIRE
ESSEX
GREATER LONDON
BERKSHIRE
SURREY
KENT
WEST SUSSEX
EAST SUSSEX
High Roding
Witham
Little Braxted
West Mersea
Clacton-on-Sea
Hertford
Hastingwood Common
Maldon
Chelmsford
Tillingham
Toot Hill
Mill Green
Epping
Burnham-on-Crouch
High Wycombe
Watford
Enfield
Brentwood
Horndon-on-the-Hill
Dagenham
Southend-on-Sea
Canvey Island
Maidenhead
Slough
Tilbury
Cliffe
Heathrow Airport
Dartford
Gravesend
Sheerness
Queenborough
Margate
Broadstairs
Ramsgate
Gillingham
Chatham
Marshside
Burham
Sittingbourne
Croydon
Canterbury
Ightam Common
Newnham
Eastling
Selling
Ringlestone
Barming
Warren Street
Chilham
Sandwich
Worth
Deal
Sevenoaks
Ivy Hatch
Maidstone
Guildford
Reigate
Redhill
Lenham
Charing
Wye
Ulcombe
Boughton Aluph
Chiddingstone
Tonbridge
Smarts Hill
Speldhurst Hill
Pluckley
Godalming
Hascombe
Gatwick Airport
Smarden
Ashford
Dover
Tunbridge Wells
Thursley
Chiddingfold
Rusper
Copthorne
Fordcombe
Goudhurst
Biddenden
Hythe
Folkestone
Haslemere
Walliswood
Crawley
Forest Row
Tenterden
Grayswood
Warnham
West Hoathly
Horsham
Crowborough
Benenden
The Haven
Lurgashall
Billingshurst
Lower Beeding
Mayfield
Petersfield
Lodsworth
Nuthurst
Haywards Heath
New Romney
Stedham
Petworth
Byworth
Fletching
Midhurst
Tillington
Wineham
Blackboys
Rye
Lydd
Fittleworth
Burgess Hill
Sutton
Fulking
Lewes
Horam
Hastings
Edburton
Firle
Kingston
Berwick
Bexhill
Chichester
Burpham
Hove
BRIGHTON
Polegate
Oving
Alciston
Worthing
Shoreham-by-Sea
Newhaven
Littlehampton
Seaford
Eastbourne
Bognor Regis
A41
A5
M1
A1(M)
A10
A12
A414
M11
A120
M25
A413
A40
A404
M40
M4
A127
A30
A3
M3
A2
M20
A225
A249
M2
A299
A21
M23
A20
A31
A286
A22
A26
A259
A29
A24
A23
A27

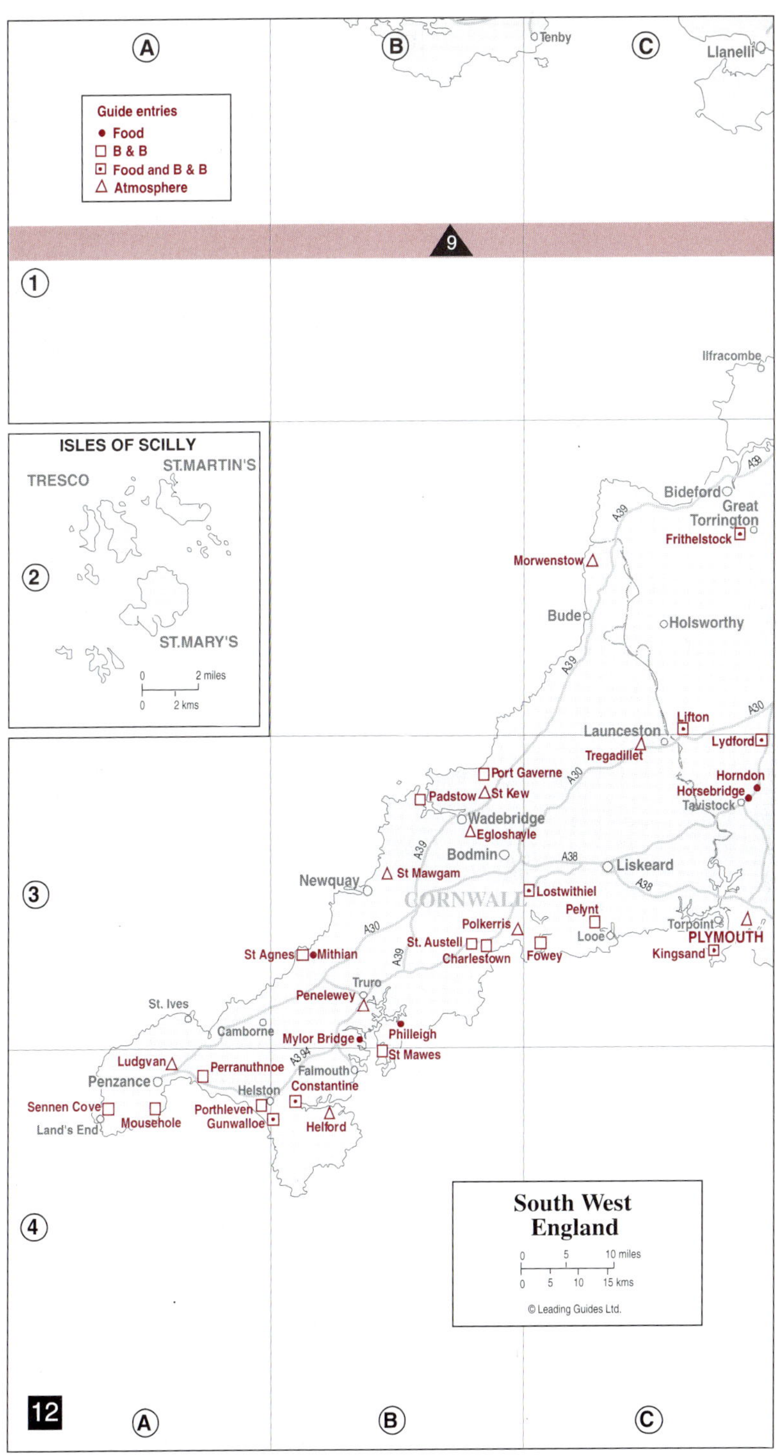
A
B
C
Tenby
Llanelli
Guide entries
Food
B & B
Food and B & B
Atmosphere
9
1
Ilfracombe
ISLES OF SCILLY
ST.MARTIN'S
TRESCO
ST.MARY'S
0 2 miles
0 2 kms
2
A39
Bideford
Great Torrington
Frithelstock
A39
Morwenstow
Bude
Holsworthy
A39
Lifton
A30
Launceston
Lydford
Tregadillet
Port Gaverne
A30
Horndon
Padstow
St Kew
Horsebridge
Tavistock
Wadebridge
Egloshayle
A39
Bodmin
A38
Liskeard
Newquay
St Mawgam
A38
3
CORNWALL
Lostwithiel
Pelynt
Polkerris
Torpoint
A30
PLYMOUTH
St. Austell
Looe
St Agnes
Mithian
A39
Charlestown
Fowey
Kingsand
Truro
Penelewey
St. Ives
Camborne
Mylor Bridge
Philleigh
A394
St Mawes
Ludgvan
Perranuthnoe
Falmouth
Penzance
Helston
Constantine
Sennen Cove
Porthleven
Mousehole
Gunwalloe
Helford
Land's End
4
South West England
0 5 10 miles
0 5 10 15 kms
© Leading Guides Ltd.
A
B
C

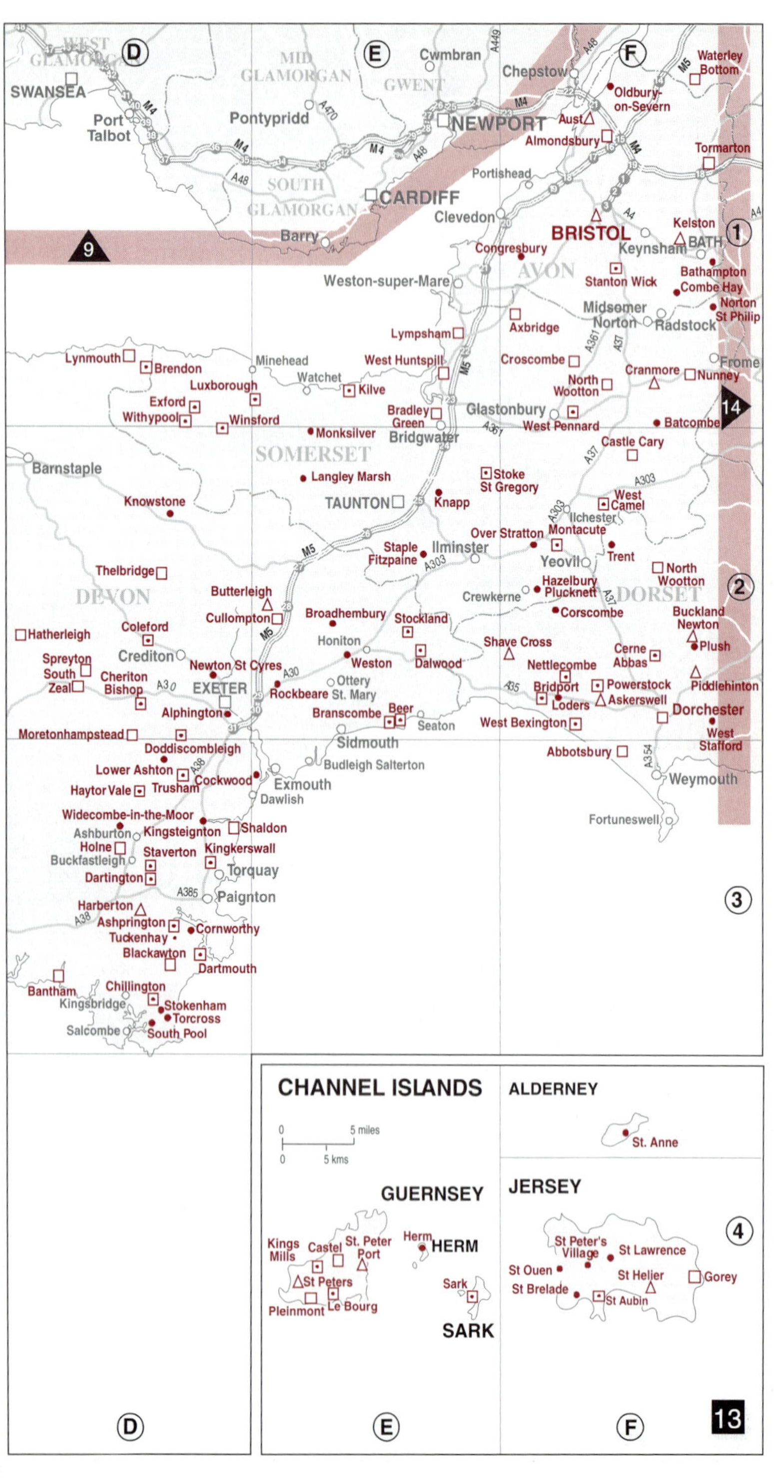

D
E
F
WEST GLAMORGAN
MID GLAMORGAN
GWENT
SOUTH GLAMORGAN
SWANSEA
Port Talbot
Pontypridd
Cwmbran
Chepstow
NEWPORT
CARDIFF
Barry
9
Waterley Bottom
Oldbury-on-Severn
Aust
Almondsbury
Tormarton
Portishead
Clevedon
BRISTOL
Keynsham
Kelston
BATH
1
Congresbury
AVON
Stanton Wick
Bathampton
Combe Hay
Norton St Philip
Weston-super-Mare
Midsomer Norton
Radstock
Axbridge
Lympsham
Frome
Lynmouth
Brendon
Minehead
Watchet
West Huntspill
Croscombe
Cranmore
Nunney
Luxborough
Kilve
North Wootton
14
Exford
Withypool
Winsford
Bradley Green
Glastonbury
Bridgwater
West Pennard
Batcombe
Monksilver
SOMERSET
Castle Cary
Barnstaple
Langley Marsh
Stoke St Gregory
Knowstone
TAUNTON
Knapp
West Camel
Ilchester
Over Stratton
Montacute
Staple Fitzpaine
Ilminster
Trent
Yeovil
Thelbridge
North Wootton
2
DEVON
Butterleigh
Crewkerne
Hazelbury Plucknett
DORSET
Cullompton
Broadhembury
Stockland
Corscombe
Buckland Newton
Hatherleigh
Coleford
Honiton
Shave Cross
Plush
Spreyton
Crediton
Weston
Dalwood
Cerne Abbas
South Zeal
Cheriton Bishop
Newton St Cyres
Nettlecombe
EXETER
Ottery St. Mary
Rockbeare
Bridport
Powerstock
Piddlehinton
Loders
Askerswell
Alphington
Branscombe
Beer
Seaton
Dorchester
West Bexington
Moretonhampstead
Sidmouth
West Stafford
Doddiscombleigh
Abbotsbury
Budleigh Salterton
Lower Ashton
Cockwood
Weymouth
Haytor Vale
Trusham
Exmouth
Dawlish
Widecombe-in-the-Moor
Fortuneswell
Ashburton
Kingsteignton
Shaldon
Holne
Buckfastleigh
Staverton
Kingkerswell
Torquay
Dartington
Paignton
3
Harberton
Ashprington
Cornworthy
Tuckenhay
Blackawton
Dartmouth
Bantham
Chillington
Kingsbridge
Stokenham
Torcross
Salcombe
South Pool
M4
M5
M48
A4
A48
A470
A449
A361
A37
A303
A30
A35
A38
A385
A354
CHANNEL ISLANDS
0 5 miles
0 5 kms
ALDERNEY
St. Anne
GUERNSEY
Kings Mills
Castel
St. Peter Port
Herm
HERM
St Peters
Sark
Pleinmont
Le Bourg
SARK
JERSEY
St Peter's Village
St Lawrence
St Ouen
St Helier
Gorey
St Brelade
St Aubin
4
D
E
F
13

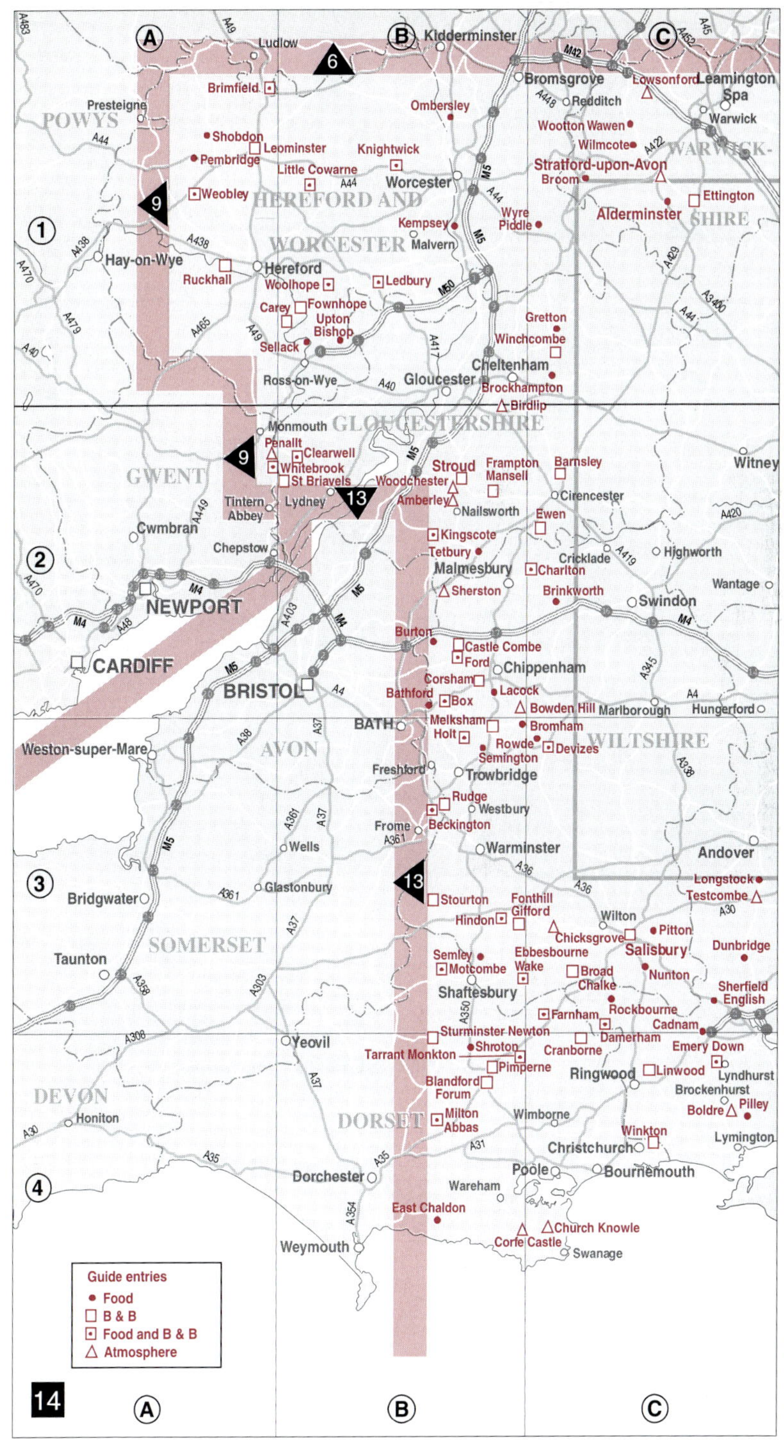
Ludlow
Kidderminster
Brimfield
Bromsgrove
Lowsonford
Leamington Spa
Presteigne
POWYS
Ombersley
Redditch
Warwick
Shobdon
Leominster
Knightwick
Wootton Wawen
Wilmcote
Pembridge
Little Cowarne
Worcester
Stratford-upon-Avon
Broom
Weobley
HEREFORD AND WORCESTER
Kempsey
Malvern
Wyre Piddle
Ettington
Alderminster
WARWICKSHIRE
Hay-on-Wye
Hereford
Ruckhall
Woolhope
Ledbury
Carey
Fownhope
Upton Bishop
Sellack
Gretton
Winchcombe
Cheltenham
Ross-on-Wye
Gloucester
Brockhampton
Birdlip
Monmouth
GLOUCESTERSHIRE
Penallt
Clearwell
Whitebrook
St Briavels
Stroud
Frampton Mansell
Barnsley
Witney
GWENT
Woodchester
Amberley
Tintern Abbey
Lydney
Nailsworth
Cirencester
Ewen
Cwmbran
Kingscote
Chepstow
Tetbury
Cricklade
Highworth
Malmesbury
Charlton
NEWPORT
Wantage
Sherston
Brinkworth
Swindon
Burton
Castle Combe
CARDIFF
Ford
Chippenham
BRISTOL
Corsham
Bathford
Box
Lacock
Bowden Hill
Marlborough
Hungerford
BATH
Melksham
Bromham
Holt
Rowde
Devizes
WILTSHIRE
Weston-super-Mare
AVON
Semington
Freshford
Trowbridge
Rudge
Westbury
Frome
Beckington
Wells
Warminster
Andover
Longstock
Bridgwater
Glastonbury
Testcombe
Stourton
Fonthill Gifford
Hindon
Wilton
Chicksgrove
Pitton
SOMERSET
Salisbury
Dunbridge
Semley
Ebbesbourne Wake
Motcombe
Broad Chalke
Nunton
Taunton
Shaftesbury
Sherfield English
Farnham
Rockbourne
Cadnam
Sturminster Newton
Damerham
Emery Down
Yeovil
Shroton
Tarrant Monkton
Cranborne
Pimperne
Ringwood
Linwood
Lyndhurst
Blandford Forum
Brockenhurst
DEVON
Boldre
Pilley
Honiton
Milton Abbas
DORSET
Wimborne
Winkton
Lymington
Christchurch
Dorchester
Poole
Bournemouth
Wareham
East Chaldon
Church Knowle
Corfe Castle
Swanage
Weymouth
Guide entries
● Food
□ B & B
⊡ Food and B & B
△ Atmosphere

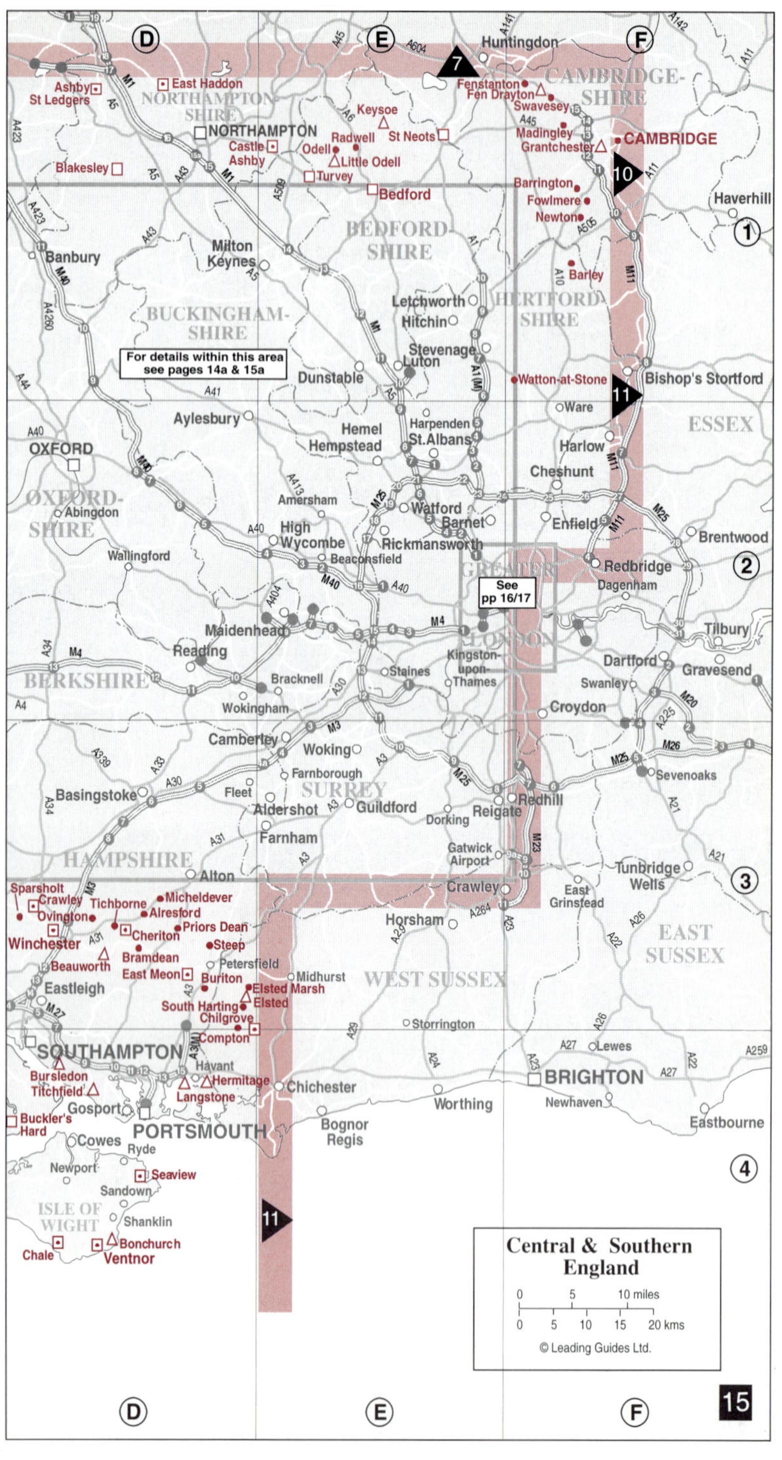

D
E
F
Huntingdon
7
CAMBRIDGE-SHIRE
Ashby St Ledgers
East Haddon
NORTHAMPTON-SHIRE
NORTHAMPTON
Keysoe
Fenstanton
Fen Drayton
Swavesey
Madingley
Grantchester
CAMBRIDGE
Radwell
St Neots
Castle Ashby
Odell
Little Odell
Turvey
Blakesley
Bedford
10
Barrington
Fowlmere
Newton
Haverhill
1
BEDFORD-SHIRE
Banbury
Milton Keynes
Barley
BUCKINGHAM-SHIRE
Letchworth
Hitchin
HERTFORD-SHIRE
For details within this area see pages 14a & 15a
Stevenage
Luton
Dunstable
Watton-at-Stone
Bishop's Stortford
11
Aylesbury
Harpenden
Ware
Hemel Hempstead
St.Albans
ESSEX
OXFORD
Harlow
Cheshunt
OXFORD-SHIRE
Abingdon
Amersham
Watford
Barnet
Enfield
Brentwood
High Wycombe
Rickmansworth
Wallingford
Beaconsfield
Redbridge
2
GREATER LONDON
See pp 16/17
Dagenham
Maidenhead
Tilbury
Reading
Kingston-upon-Thames
BERKSHIRE
Staines
Dartford
Gravesend
Bracknell
Swanley
Wokingham
Croydon
Camberley
Woking
Farnborough
Sevenoaks
Basingstoke
Fleet
SURREY
Redhill
Aldershot
Guildford
Dorking
Reigate
Farnham
Gatwick Airport
Tunbridge Wells
HAMPSHIRE
Alton
3
Crawley
East Grinstead
Sparsholt
Crawley
Tichborne
Micheldever
Ovington
Alresford
Horsham
Cheriton
Priors Dean
Winchester
Steep
EAST SUSSEX
Bramdean
Beauworth
East Meon
Petersfield
Eastleigh
Buriton
Midhurst
WEST SUSSEX
Elsted Marsh
Elsted
South Harting
Chilgrove
Storrington
Compton
SOUTHAMPTON
Lewes
Havant
Bursledon
Hermitage
Chichester
BRIGHTON
Titchfield
Langstone
Worthing
Gosport
Newhaven
Eastbourne
Buckler's Hard
PORTSMOUTH
Bognor Regis
Cowes
Ryde
Newport
Seaview
4
Sandown
ISLE OF WIGHT
Shanklin
11
Chale
Bonchurch
Ventnor
Central & Southern England
0 5 10 miles
0 5 10 15 20 kms
© Leading Guides Ltd.
D
E
F

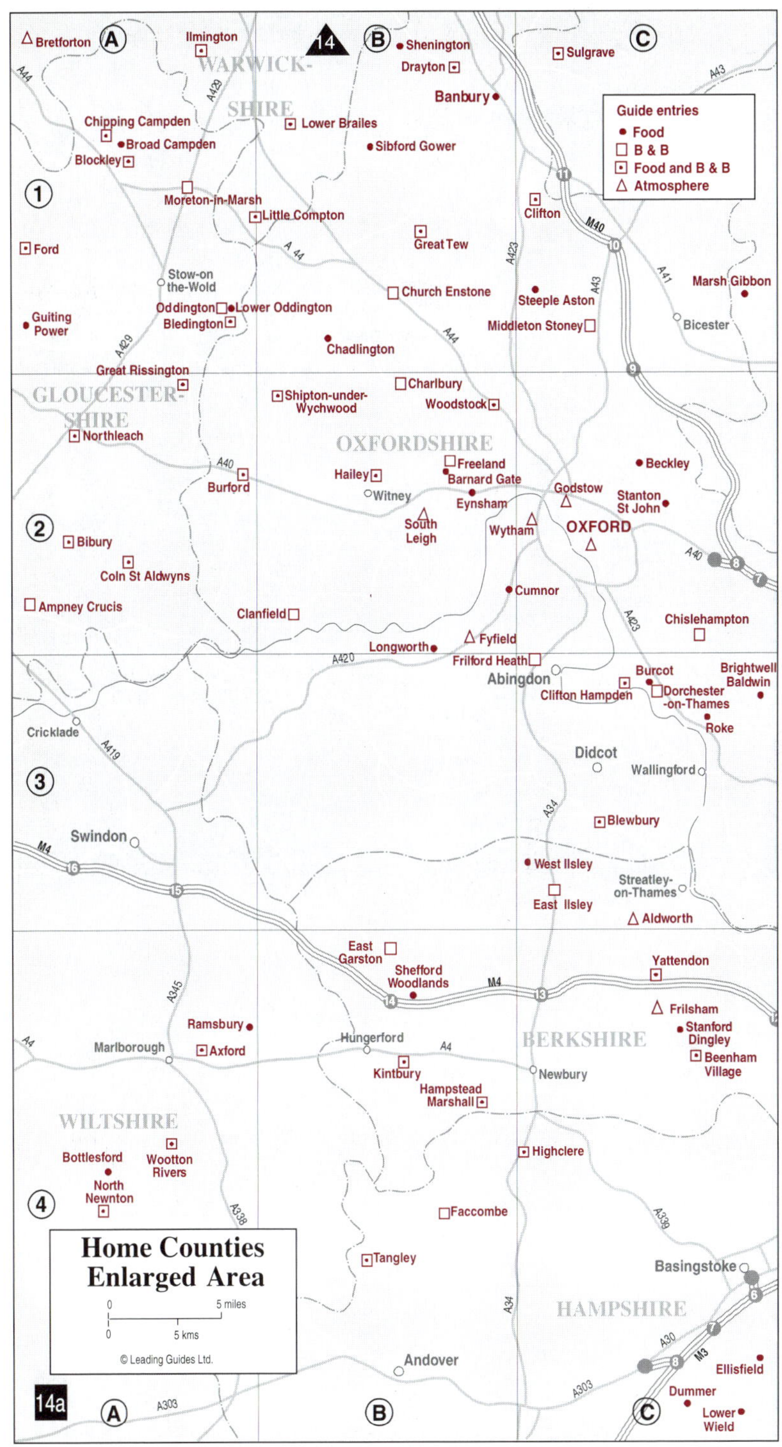
14
Guide entries
Food
B & B
Food and B & B
Atmosphere
WARWICK-SHIRE
GLOUCESTER-SHIRE
OXFORDSHIRE
BERKSHIRE
WILTSHIRE
HAMPSHIRE
Bretforton
Ilmington
Shenington
Drayton
Sulgrave
Banbury
Chipping Campden
Broad Campden
Blockley
Lower Brailes
Sibford Gower
Moreton-in-Marsh
Little Compton
Clifton
Great Tew
Ford
Stow-on the-Wold
Church Enstone
Steeple Aston
Marsh Gibbon
Oddington
Lower Oddington
Bledington
Middleton Stoney
Bicester
Guiting Power
Chadlington
Great Rissington
Charlbury
Shipton-under-Wychwood
Woodstock
Northleach
Freeland
Barnard Gate
Beckley
Burford
Hailey
Witney
Eynsham
Godstow
Stanton St John
South Leigh
Wytham
OXFORD
Bibury
Coln St Aldwyns
Cumnor
Ampney Crucis
Clanfield
Chislehampton
Fyfield
Longworth
Frilford Heath
Abingdon
Burcot
Brightwell Baldwin
Clifton Hampden
Dorchester -on-Thames
Roke
Cricklade
Didcot
Wallingford
Blewbury
Swindon
West Ilsley
Streatley-on-Thames
East Ilsley
Aldworth
East Garston
Shefford Woodlands
Yattendon
Frilsham
Ramsbury
Stanford Dingley
Hungerford
Marlborough
Axford
Beenham Village
Kintbury
Newbury
Hampstead Marshall
Bottlesford
Wootton Rivers
Highclere
North Newnton
Faccombe
Tangley
Basingstoke
Andover
Ellisfield
Dummer
Lower Wield
Home Counties Enlarged Area
0
5 miles
0
5 kms
© Leading Guides Ltd.
14a

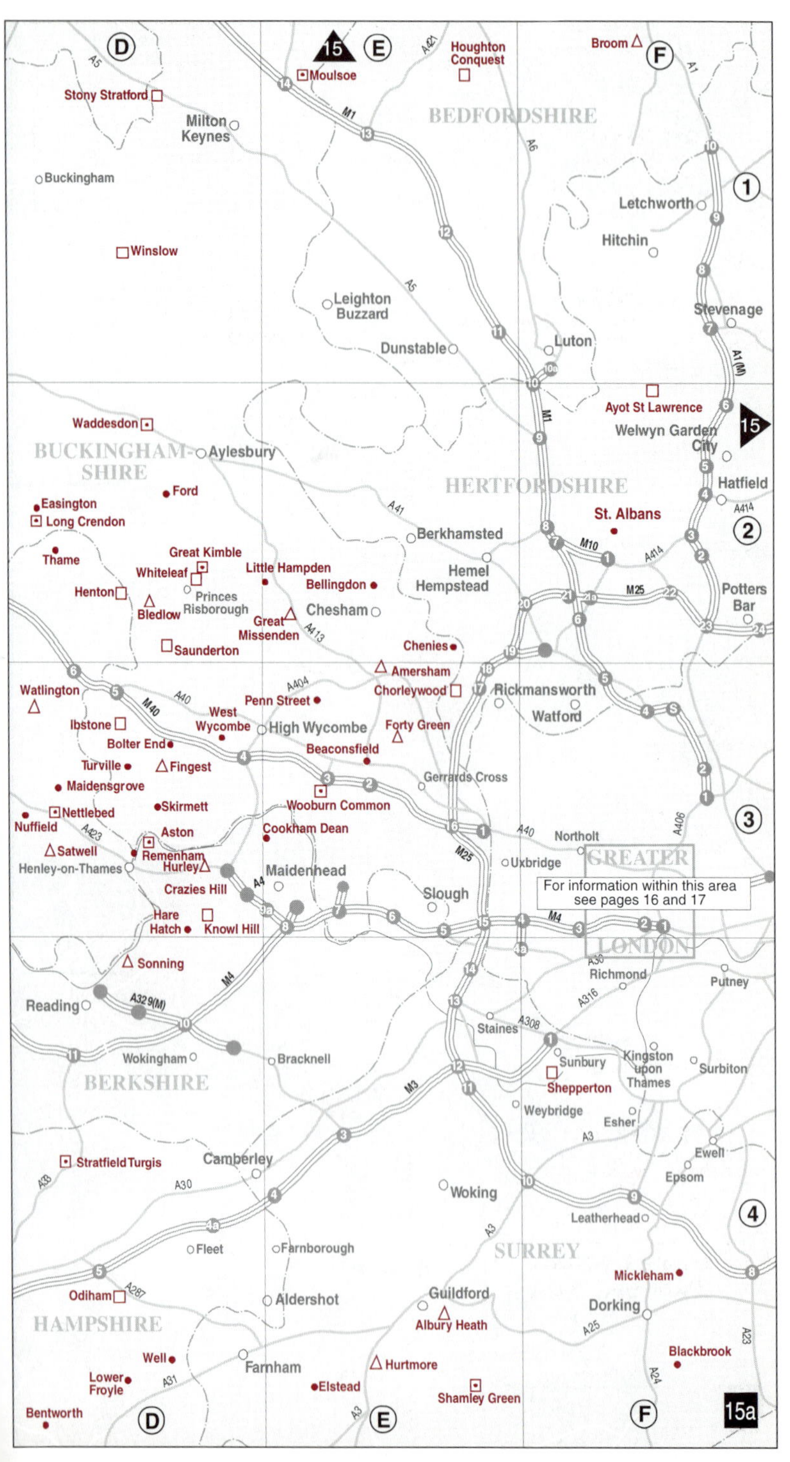

D
E
F
15
Moulsoe
Houghton Conquest
Broom
Stony Stratford
Milton Keynes
BEDFORDSHIRE
Buckingham
Letchworth
Hitchin
Winslow
Leighton Buzzard
Stevenage
Dunstable
Luton
Ayot St Lawrence
Waddesdon
Welwyn Garden City
BUCKINGHAMSHIRE
Aylesbury
HERTFORDSHIRE
Hatfield
Ford
Easington
Long Crendon
St. Albans
Berkhamsted
Thame
Great Kimble
Whiteleaf
Little Hampden
Hemel Hempstead
Henton
Bellingdon
Princes Risborough
Potters Bar
Bledlow
Chesham
Great Missenden
Saunderton
Chenies
Amersham
Watlington
Chorleywood
Rickmansworth
Penn Street
West Wycombe
Watford
Ibstone
High Wycombe
Forty Green
Bolter End
Beaconsfield
Turville
Fingest
Gerrards Cross
Maidensgrove
Skirmett
Nettlebed
Wooburn Common
Nuffield
Aston
Cookham Dean
Northolt
Satwell
Remenham
Uxbridge
GREATER LONDON
Henley-on-Thames
Hurley
Maidenhead
For information within this area see pages 16 and 17
Crazies Hill
Slough
Hare Hatch
Knowl Hill
Sonning
Richmond
Putney
Reading
Staines
Wokingham
Bracknell
Kingston upon Thames
Sunbury
Surbiton
BERKSHIRE
Shepperton
Weybridge
Esher
Ewell
Epsom
Stratfield Turgis
Camberley
Woking
Leatherhead
Fleet
Farnborough
SURREY
Odiham
Mickleham
Aldershot
Guildford
Dorking
HAMPSHIRE
Albury Heath
Blackbrook
Well
Farnham
Hurtmore
Lower Froyle
Elstead
Shamley Green
Bentworth
M1
M10
M25
M40
M4
M3
A329(M)
A1(M)
1
2
3
4

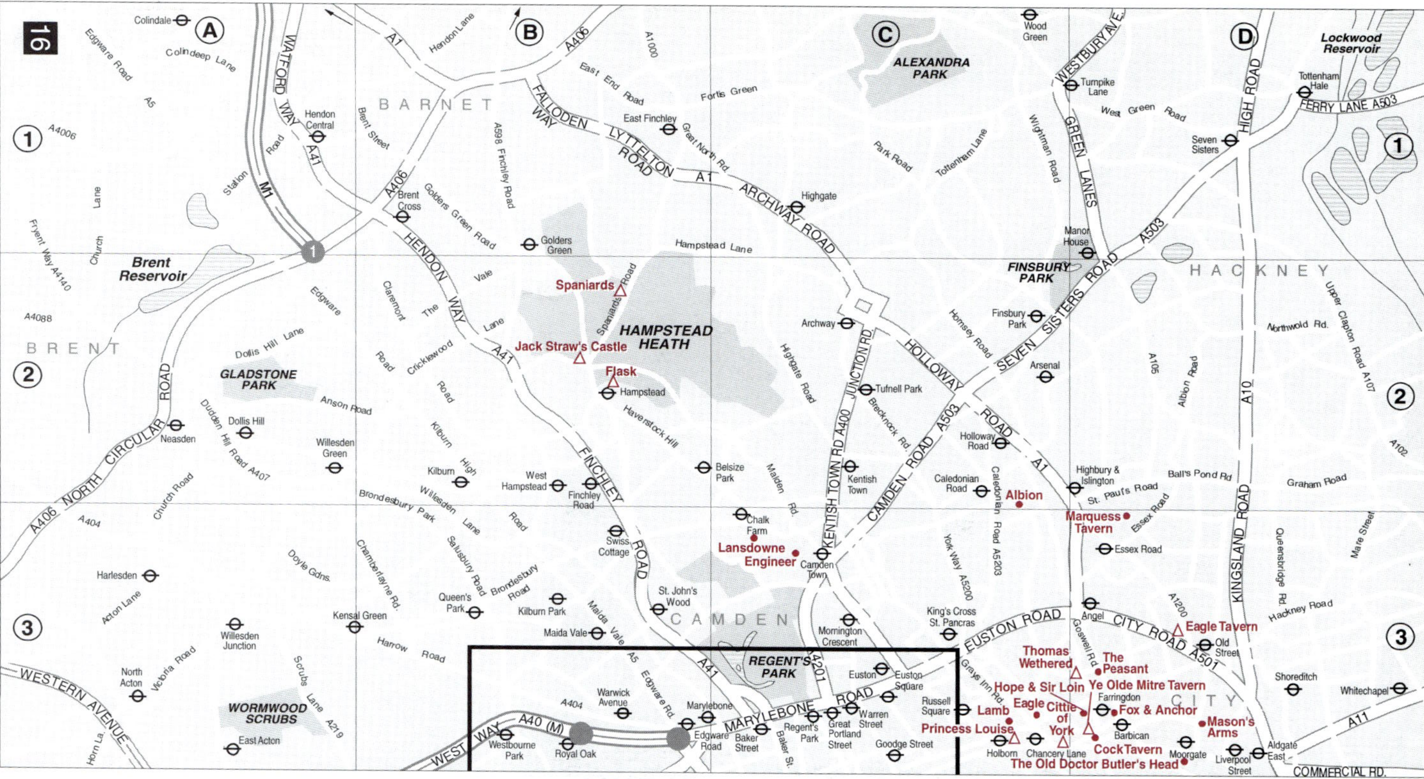

A
B
C
D
1
2
3
BARNET
BRENT
CAMDEN
HACKNEY
CITY
Brent Reservoir
Lockwood Reservoir
GLADSTONE PARK
WORMWOOD SCRUBS
HAMPSTEAD HEATH
ALEXANDRA PARK
FINSBURY PARK
REGENT'S PARK
Spaniards
Jack Straw's Castle
Flask
Lansdowne Engineer
Albion
Marquess Tavern
Eagle Tavern
Thomas Wethered
The Peasant
Hope & Sir Loin
Ye Olde Mitre Tavern
Lamb
Eagle
Cittie of York
Fox & Anchor
Mason's Arms
Princess Louise
Cock Tavern
The Old Doctor Butler's Head
Colindale
Hendon Central
Brent Cross
Golders Green
East Finchley
Highgate
Archway
Hampstead
Tufnell Park
Kentish Town
Camden Town
Chalk Farm
Belsize Park
Finchley Road
West Hampstead
Swiss Cottage
St. John's Wood
Kilburn
Willesden Green
Dollis Hill
Neasden
Harlesden
Willesden Junction
Kensal Green
Queen's Park
Kilburn Park
Maida Vale
Warwick Avenue
Royal Oak
Westbourne Park
Edgware Road
Marylebone
Baker Street
Regent's Park
Great Portland Street
Warren Street
Euston
Euston Square
Goodge Street
Russell Square
King's Cross St. Pancras
Mornington Crescent
Holborn
Chancery Lane
Farringdon
Barbican
Moorgate
Liverpool Street
Aldgate East
Old Street
Angel
Shoreditch
Whitechapel
Essex Road
Highbury & Islington
Caledonian Road
Holloway Road
Arsenal
Finsbury Park
Manor House
Turnpike Lane
Wood Green
Seven Sisters
Tottenham Hale
North Acton
East Acton
WATFORD WAY
M1
A41
A1
A406
NORTH CIRCULAR ROAD
HENDON WAY
FINCHLEY ROAD
FALLODEN WAY
LYTTELTON ROAD
ARCHWAY ROAD
HOLLOWAY ROAD
SEVEN SISTERS ROAD
GREEN LANES
WESTBURY AVE.
HIGH ROAD
FERRY LANE A503
KINGSLAND ROAD
CITY ROAD A501
EUSTON ROAD
MARYLEBONE ROAD
CAMDEN ROAD A503
KENTISH TOWN RD A400
JUNCTION RD
WESTWAY
A40 (M)
WESTERN AVENUE
COMMERCIAL RD.
A11

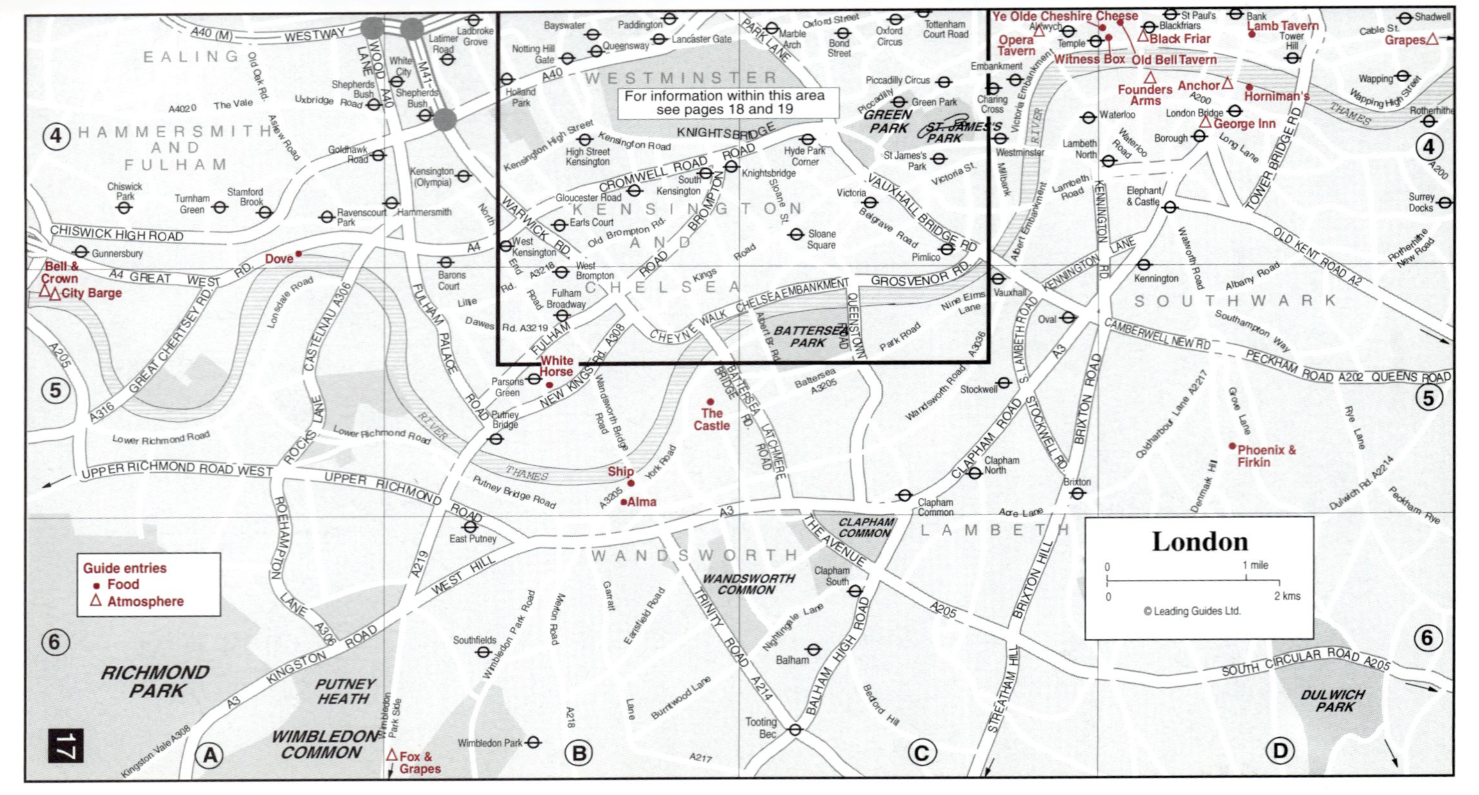
London
0 1 mile
0 2 kms
© Leading Guides Ltd.
Guide entries
● Food
△ Atmosphere
For information within this area see pages 18 and 19
Ye Olde Cheshire Cheese
Lamb Tavern
Grapes
Opera Tavern
Black Friar
Witness Box
Old Bell Tavern
Founders Arms
Anchor
Horniman's
George Inn
Bell & Crown
City Barge
Dove
White Horse
The Castle
Ship
Alma
Phoenix & Firkin
Fox & Grapes
EALING
HAMMERSMITH AND FULHAM
WESTMINSTER
KENSINGTON AND CHELSEA
SOUTHWARK
LAMBETH
WANDSWORTH
GREEN PARK
ST. JAMES'S PARK
BATTERSEA PARK
CLAPHAM COMMON
WANDSWORTH COMMON
RICHMOND PARK
PUTNEY HEATH
WIMBLEDON COMMON
DULWICH PARK
RIVER THAMES
A
B
C
D
4
5
6
17

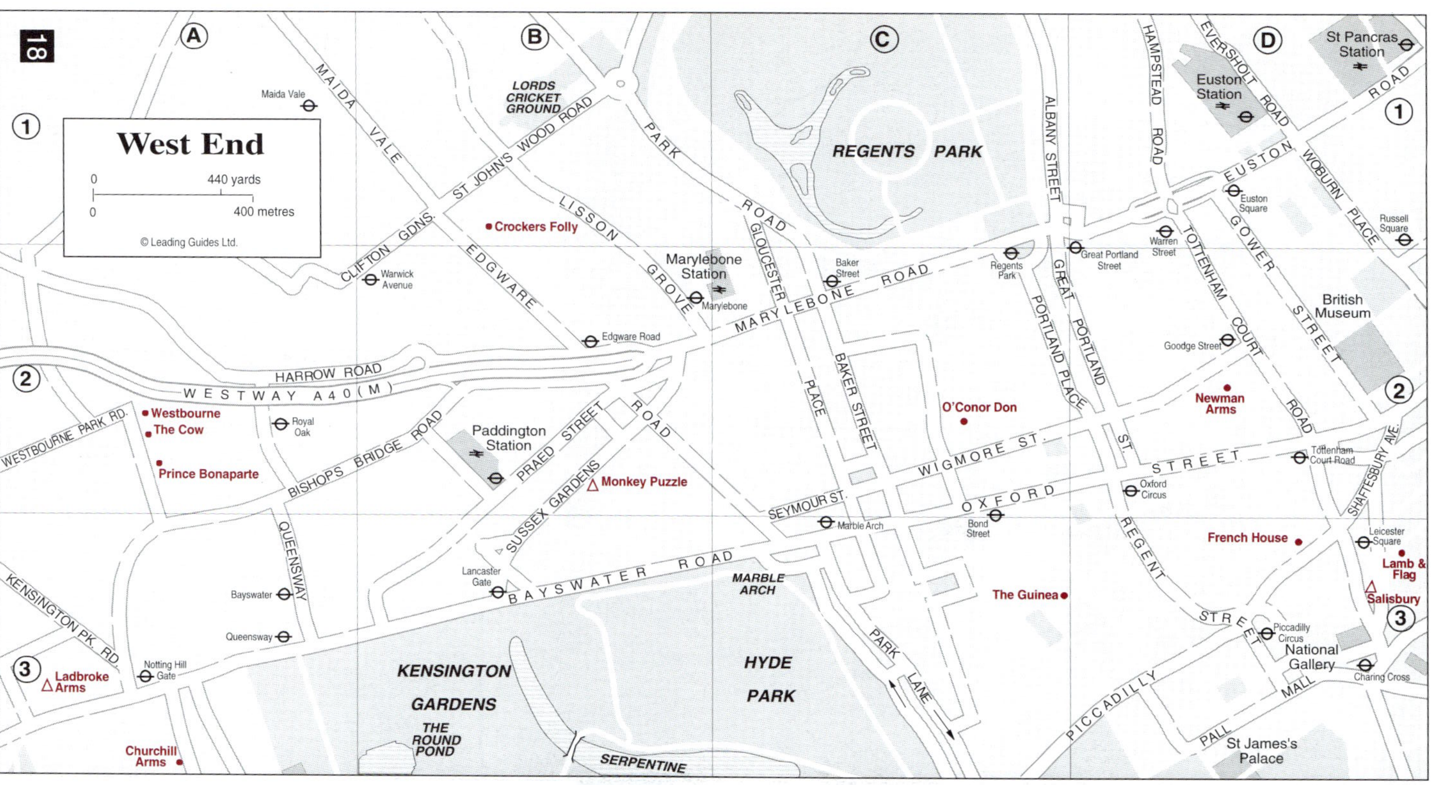
West End
0 440 yards
0 400 metres
© Leading Guides Ltd.
A
B
C
D
1
2
3
Maida Vale
MAIDA VALE
LORDS CRICKET GROUND
ST JOHN'S WOOD ROAD
PARK ROAD
REGENTS PARK
ALBANY STREET
HAMPSTEAD ROAD
EVERSHOLT ROAD
Euston Station
St Pancras Station
EUSTON ROAD
WOBURN PLACE
Euston Square
Russell Square
Crockers Folly
LISSON GROVE
CLIFTON GDNS.
Warwick Avenue
EDGWARE ROAD
Edgware Road
Marylebone Station
Marylebone
GLOUCESTER PLACE
Baker Street
MARYLEBONE ROAD
Regents Park
Great Portland Street
Warren Street
TOTTENHAM COURT ROAD
GOWER STREET
British Museum
Goodge Street
HARROW ROAD
WESTWAY A40(M)
WESTBOURNE PARK RD.
Westbourne
The Cow
Royal Oak
Prince Bonaparte
BISHOPS BRIDGE ROAD
Paddington Station
PRAED STREET
SUSSEX GARDENS
Monkey Puzzle
BAKER STREET
PORTLAND PLACE
GREAT PORTLAND ST.
O'Conor Don
Newman Arms
WIGMORE ST.
OXFORD STREET
Tottenham Court Road
SHAFTESBURY AVE.
Oxford Circus
Bond Street
SEYMOUR ST.
Marble Arch
QUEENSWAY
Bayswater
Queensway
Lancaster Gate
BAYSWATER ROAD
MARBLE ARCH
French House
Leicester Square
Lamb & Flag
Salisbury
REGENT STREET
The Guinea
Piccadilly Circus
National Gallery
Charing Cross
KENSINGTON PK. RD.
Ladbroke Arms
Notting Hill Gate
Churchill Arms
KENSINGTON GARDENS
THE ROUND POND
SERPENTINE
HYDE PARK
PARK LANE
PICCADILLY
PALL MALL
St James's Palace

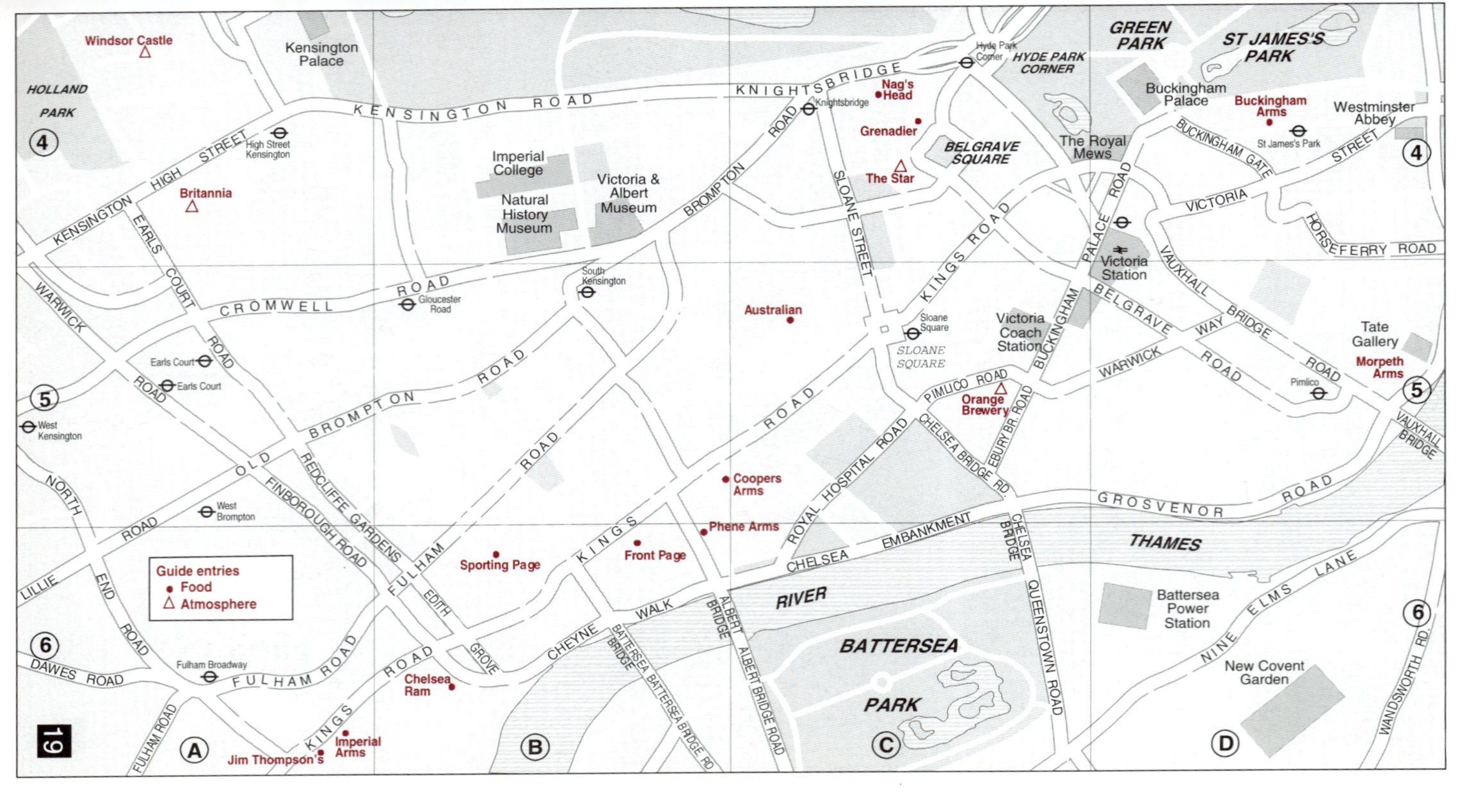

Windsor Castle
Kensington Palace
HOLLAND PARK
KENSINGTON ROAD
KNIGHTSBRIDGE
Nag's Head
Hyde Park Corner
HYDE PARK CORNER
GREEN PARK
ST JAMES'S PARK
Buckingham Palace
Buckingham Arms
Westminster Abbey
High Street Kensington
Knightsbridge
Grenadier
BELGRAVE SQUARE
The Royal Mews
BUCKINGHAM GATE
St James's Park
STREET
KENSINGTON HIGH STREET
Britannia
Imperial College
Natural History Museum
Victoria & Albert Museum
BROMPTON ROAD
The Star
SLOANE STREET
VICTORIA
HORSEFERRY ROAD
PALACE ROAD
Victoria Station
EARLS COURT ROAD
South Kensington
CROMWELL ROAD
Gloucester Road
Australian
KINGS ROAD
VAUXHALL BRIDGE ROAD
WARWICK ROAD
Sloane Square
SLOANE SQUARE
Victoria Coach Station
BUCKINGHAM
BELGRAVE WAY
Tate Gallery
Morpeth Arms
Earls Court
WARWICK
PIMLICO ROAD
Orange Brewery
Pimlico
West Kensington
BROMPTON ROAD
CHELSEA BRIDGE RD
EBURY BR. ROAD
VAUXHALL BRIDGE
OLD
ROYAL HOSPITAL ROAD
Coopers Arms
NORTH
West Brompton
FINBOROUGH ROAD
REDCLIFFE GARDENS
GROSVENOR ROAD
Phene Arms
CHELSEA EMBANKMENT
CHELSEA BRIDGE
THAMES
Sporting Page
Front Page
Guide entries
● Food
△ Atmosphere
FULHAM
RIVER
LILLIE
END
ROAD
EDITH
WALK
ALBERT BRIDGE
Battersea Power Station
NINE ELMS LANE
CHEYNE
BATTERSEA BRIDGE
BATTERSEA
DAWES ROAD
Fulham Broadway
FULHAM ROAD
Chelsea Ram
GROVE
BATTERSEA BRIDGE RD
ALBERT BRIDGE ROAD
PARK
QUEENSTOWN ROAD
New Covent Garden
WANDSWORTH RD.
FULHAM ROAD
KINGS
Imperial Arms
Jim Thompson's
A
B
C
D
4
5
6

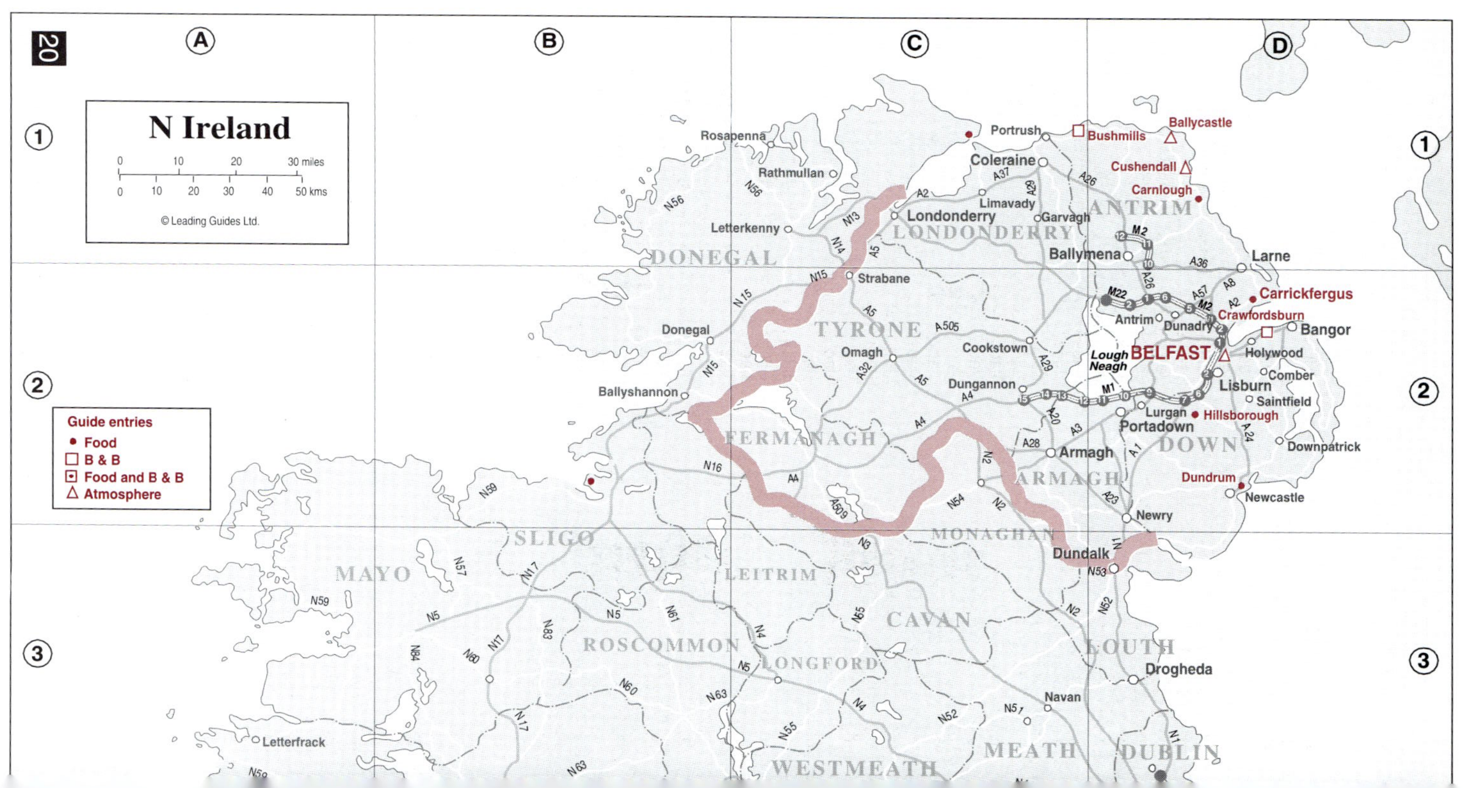
N Ireland
0 10 20 30 miles
0 10 20 30 40 50 kms
© Leading Guides Ltd.
Guide entries
Food
B & B
Food and B & B
Atmosphere
A
B
C
D
1
2
3
Portrush
Bushmills
Ballycastle
Cushendall
Carnlough
Coleraine
Limavady
Garvagh
Londonderry
Rosapenna
Rathmullan
Letterkenny
Strabane
Donegal
Ballyshannon
Omagh
Cookstown
Dungannon
Ballymena
Larne
Carrickfergus
Crawfordsburn
Bangor
Antrim
Dunadry
Lough Neagh
BELFAST
Holywood
Comber
Lisburn
Saintfield
Lurgan
Hillsborough
Portadown
Armagh
Downpatrick
Dundrum
Newcastle
Newry
Dundalk
Drogheda
Navan
Letterfrack
ANTRIM
LONDONDERRY
DONEGAL
TYRONE
FERMANAGH
ARMAGH
DOWN
MONAGHAN
SLIGO
LEITRIM
CAVAN
MAYO
ROSCOMMON
LONGFORD
LOUTH
MEATH
WESTMEATH
DUBLIN

Index

Readers' Comments

Egon Ronay's Old Speckled Hen Guide 1996 Pubs & Inns

Please let us know of any establishments you think should be in the next edition and let us have your comments (both good and bad) on those which are included in this year's Guide. *(Pubs & Inns 1996).*

Name and address of establishment	**Your recommendation or complaint**

Name and address of establishment	**Your recommendation or complaint**

Your name and address *(BLOCK CAPITALS PLEASE)*

Readers' Comments

Egon Ronay's Old Speckled Hen Guide 1996 Pubs & Inns

Please let us know of any establishments you think should be in the next edition and let us have your comments (both good and bad) on those which are included in this year's Guide. *(Pubs & Inns 1996).*

Name and address of establishment	**Your recommendation or complaint**

Name and address of establishment	Your recommendation or complaint

Your name and address *(BLOCK CAPITALS PLEASE)*

Readers' Comments

Egon Ronay's Old Speckled Hen Guide 1996 Pubs & Inns

Please let us know of any establishments you think should be in the next edition and let us have your comments (both good and bad) on those which are included in this year's Guide. *(Pubs & Inns 1996).*

Name and address of establishment | **Your recommendation or complaint**

Name and address of establishment | **Your recommendation or complaint**

Your name and address *(BLOCK CAPITALS PLEASE)*

READERS' COMMENTS

Egon Ronay's Old Speckled Hen Guide 1996 Pubs & Inns

Please let us know of any establishments you think should be in the next edition and let us have your comments (both good and bad) on those which are included in this year's Guide. *(Pubs & Inns 1996).*

Name and address of establishment	**Your recommendation or complaint**

Name and address of establishment	**Your recommendation or complaint**

Your name and address *(BLOCK CAPITALS PLEASE)*

Readers' Comments

Egon Ronay's Old Speckled Hen Guide 1996 Pubs & Inns

Please let us know of any establishments you think should be in the next edition and let us have your comments (both good and bad) on those which are included in this year's Guide. *(Pubs & Inns 1996).*

Name and address of establishment	**Your recommendation or complaint**

Name and address of establishment	Your recommendation or complaint

Your name and address *(BLOCK CAPITALS PLEASE)*

Readers' Comments

Egon Ronay's Old Speckled Hen Guide 1996 Pubs & Inns

Please let us know of any establishments you think should be in the next edition and let us have your comments (both good and bad) on those which are included in this year's Guide. *(Pubs & Inns 1996).*

Name and address of establishment	**Your recommendation or complaint**

Name and address of establishment	**Your recommendation or complaint**

Your name and address *(BLOCK CAPITALS PLEASE)*

Readers' Comments

Egon Ronay's Old Speckled Hen Guide 1996 Pubs & Inns

Please let us know of any establishments you think should be in the next edition and let us have your comments (both good and bad) on those which are included in this year's Guide. *(Pubs & Inns 1996).*

Name and address of establishment	Your recommendation or complaint

Name and address of establishment	**Your recommendation or complaint**

Your name and address *(BLOCK CAPITALS PLEASE)*

Readers' Comments

Egon Ronay's Old Speckled Hen Guide 1996 Pubs & Inns

Please let us know of any establishments you think should be in the next edition and let us have your comments (both good and bad) on those which are included in this year's Guide. *(Pubs & Inns 1996).*

Name and address of establishment	**Your recommendation or complaint**

Name and address of establishment	**Your recommendation or complaint**

Your name and address *(BLOCK CAPITALS PLEASE)*

Readers' Comments

Egon Ronay's Old Speckled Hen Guide 1996 Pubs & Inns

Please let us know of any establishments you think should be in the next edition and let us have your comments (both good and bad) on those which are included in this year's Guide. *(Pubs & Inns 1996).*

Name and address of establishment	**Your recommendation or complaint**

Name and address of establishment	**Your recommendation or complaint**

Your name and address *(BLOCK CAPITALS PLEASE)*

Readers' Comments

Egon Ronay's Old Speckled Hen Guide 1996 Pubs & Inns

Please let us know of any establishments you think should be in the next edition and let us have your comments (both good and bad) on those which are included in this year's Guide. *(Pubs & Inns 1996).*

Name and address of establishment	**Your recommendation or complaint**

Name and address of establishment

Your recommendation or complaint

Your name and address *(BLOCK CAPITALS PLEASE)*

Readers' Comments

Egon Ronay's Old Speckled Hen Guide 1996 Pubs & Inns

Please let us know of any establishments you think should be in the next edition and let us have your comments (both good and bad) on those which are included in this year's Guide. *(Pubs & Inns 1996).*

Name and address of establishment	**Your recommendation or complaint**

Name and address of establishment	Your recommendation or complaint

Your name and address *(BLOCK CAPITALS PLEASE)*

In good health and.......

The Britannia Food Safety & Hygiene Award

Valid for one year, the Britannia Food Safety & Hygiene Award demonstrates and acknowledges high standards of food safety and hygiene (the award certificate may be removed should standards fall below the level required).

1995 Britannia Food Safety & Hygiene Award holders include:-

Alexandra Hotel, Pound Street, Lyme Regis
The Ancient Raj, 9 The Parade, Frimley
Cafe Rouge, Canary Wharf, London, E14
Claygate Tandoori, The Parade, Claygate, Surrey
Cliveden, Taplow, Berkshire
Corkers Restaurant & Cafe Bar, 1 High Street, Poole, Dorset
Cornish Arms, Pendoggett, Port Isaac, Cornwall
Derwentwater Hotel, Portinscale, Keswick, Cumbria
The Dorchester Hotel, Park Lane, London, W1A
Dumbleton Hall, Evesham, Worcestershire
Brighton Hydro Hotel, 465 South Promenade, Blackpool
Ednam House Hotel, Bridge Street, Kelso, Roxburghshire
Fairwater Head Hotel, Hawkeschurch, Axminster, Devon
Farleyer House Hotel, Aberfeldy, Perthshire
Friars Carse, Auldgirth, Dumfries
The Gonville Hotel, Gonville Place, Cambridge
Hook Tandoori, 1 Fairholme Parade, Hook, Basingstoke
The Knife & Cleaver, The Grove, Houghton Conquest, Bedford
Mr Kuet Chinese Takeaway, 3 Fairmead Road, Saltash, Cornwall
La Capannina, 24 Romilly Street, London, W1
Lloyds of London, 1 Lime Street, London, EC3M
Langstone Cliff Hotel, Dawlish Warren, Devon
Lucullus Seafood Restaurant, 48 Knightsbridge, London, SW1
MEPC (UK) Ltd, 12 St James's Square, London, SW1Y
Oatlands Park Hotel, Oatlands Drive, Weybridge
Old Watch Restaurant, 14 The Square, St Mawes, Cornwall
Nobody Inn, Doddiscombsleigh, Exeter, Devon
Poissonnerie De L'Avenue, 52 Sloane Avenue, London, SW3
Saqui Tandoori, 317 Richmond Road, Kingston-upon-Thames
Serena Restaurant, 12 St Peters Street, Huddersfield
Splinters, 12 Church Street, Christchurch, Dorset
Tontine Hotel, 6 Ardgowan Square, Greenock
Whatley Manor Hotel, Easton Grey, Malmesbury, Wiltshire
Waterhead Hotel, Coniston, Cumbria

Savouring the Subtle Blend of Flavours.

Happy thought.~ "Such a richness of flavours! Complex, but not cluttered. A hint of nuttiness perhaps… a suggestion of plump, ripe autumn fruit? Beautifully seasoned, too… so mellow and mature. Excellent body, superbly smooth and, I daresay, wickedly more-ish.

"As I've always said, my friend, why settle for sponge when one can have fruitcake!"

BREWED BY MORLAND OF ABINGDON. EST'D. 1711.

MORLAND
"OLD SPECKLED HEN"
Strong Pale Ale

Hunting for Perfection~
Ahhh...

FOUND! THE ALE THAT MAKETH THE MEAL.